Preventing Currency Crises in Emerging Markets

**A National Bureau
of Economic Research
Conference Report**

Preventing Currency Crises in Emerging Markets

Edited by **Sebastian Edwards and Jeffrey A. Frankel**

The University of Chicago Press

Chicago and London

SEBASTIAN EDWARDS is the Henry Ford II Professor of International Business Economics at the Anderson Graduate School of Management at the University of California, Los Angeles (UCLA) and a research associate of the National Bureau of Economic Research. JEFFREY A. FRANKEL is the James W. Harpel Professor of Capital Formation and Growth at the Kennedy School of Government and director of the International Finance and Macroeconomics program at the National Bureau of Economic Research.

To Rudiger Dornbusch, from whom
we have learned so much.

The University of Chicago Press, Chicago 60637
The University of Chicago Press, Ltd., London
© 2002 by the National Bureau of Economic Research
All rights reserved. Published 2002
Printed in the United States of America
11 10 09 08 07 06 05 04 03 02   1 2 3 4 5
ISBN: 0-226-18494-3 (cloth)

Library of Congress Cataloging-in-Publication Data

Preventing currency crises in emerging markets / edited by Sebastian
    Edwards and Jeffrey A. Frankel.
        p.   cm. — (A National Bureau of Economic Research
    conference report)
    Papers presented at a conference held in Islamorada, Fla., in Jan.
2001.
    Includes bibliographical references and index.
    ISBN 0-226-18494-3 (cloth : alk. paper)
    1. Currency question—Developing countries—Congresses.
2. Financial crises—Developing countries—Congresses.
I. Edwards, Sebastian, 1953– II. Frankel, Jeffrey A. III. National
Bureau of Economic Research. IV. Series.

HG1496 .P74 2002
332.4'91724—dc21
                                                                    2002018128

⊚ The paper used in this publication meets the minimum requirements of the American National Standard for Information Sciences—Permanence of Paper for Printed Library Materials, ANSI Z39.48-1992.

Contents

Acknowledgments

This volume consists primarily of papers that were presented at a National Bureau of Economic Research Conference held in Islamorada, Florida, in January 2001, together with comments and discussion. A preconference held in Cambridge, Massachusetts, in July 2000 kept everyone on track. The main purpose of the conference was to bring together a group of academics, officials in the multilateral organizations, and public- and private-sector economists to discuss issues related to the prevention of financial crises in the emerging market countries.

A companion conference was held two months later to discuss the management of crises in emerging market countries, once they occur. The corresponding volume is *Managing Currency Crises in Emerging Markets,* edited by Michael Dooley and Jeffrey A. Frankel.

These two conferences were part of a larger NBER project on Exchange Rate Crises in Emerging Markets, directed by Frankel together with Martin Feldstein. The editors would like to thank the Ford Foundation for support and Feldstein for originating the entire project.

Introduction

Sebastian Edwards and Jeffrey A. Frankel

Financial crises have become recurrent, profound, and diverse. When Richard Cooper gave the Graham Memorial Lecture at Princeton in 1971, currency crises followed a regular pattern across countries. Most financial crises in emerging markets could be traced to large fiscal imbalances financed by the local central bank, and this remained true until the mid-1990s. In a world with fixed nominal exchange rates and limited capital mobility, excessive domestic credit creation leads to a trade deficit, the depletion of international reserves, and, eventually, a devaluation crisis.[1] Theoretically, this prototypical crisis is neatly explained by Krugman's (1979) "first-generation" speculative attack model. Kamin (1988), Edwards (1989), and Edwards and Santaella (1993) studied in detail more than sixty currency crises in the 1950–85 period and concluded that most of them were indeed rooted in inconsistent fiscal policies. In this world of "first-generation" crises, crisis prevention policies are rather straightforward: By running a balanced public sector budget, the country in question can avoid a drop in international reserves and, thus, will be spared from a currency crash.

In 1995 Michel Camdessus, then the International Monetary Fund's managing director, said that the 1994 devaluation of the Mexican peso was

Sebastian Edwards is the Henry Ford II Professor of International Business Economics at the Anderson Graduate School of Management at the University of California, Los Angeles (UCLA) and a research associate of the National Bureau of Economic Research. Jeffrey A. Frankel is James W. Harpel Professor of Capital Formation and Growth at the Kennedy School of Government and director of the International Finance and Macroeconomics program at the National Bureau of Economic Research.

1. Chile's currency crisis of 1982 is an important exception to this pattern. The collapse of the peso took place in a context of fiscal surplus and was largely the result of capital inflows reversals and a weak domestic banking sector.

the first financial crisis of the twenty-first century. By this he meant that the Mexican crisis did not fit the old pattern of fiscally driven currency collapses. Although in 1994—and partially due to a contested presidential election—Mexico had in fact relaxed its fiscal stance somewhat, the macroeconomic picture was far from fiscally inconsistent. The country had made enormous strides toward fiscal discipline in the years since the crisis of 1982. At the heart of the 1994 Mexican crisis were investors' souring expectations, a rapid reversal of capital flows, and mounting dollar-denominated short-term debt (the infamous *tesobonos*). These, in turn, were attributable to an overvalued peso, some domestic political shocks, increases in U.S. interest rates, and a weak banking sector. The rapid decline of international reserves during 1994 and the eventual collapse of the peso in December of that year were the result of the combination of these factors, and not of an overly expansive fiscal policy.[2] Even more clearly than in the case of Mexico, the currency crises in East Asia in 1997 represented an important departure from the first-generation explanation. In virtually every one of the East Asian crisis countries, the fiscal accounts were largely under control. Also, as in Mexico, short-term foreign debt—and in particular debt to international banks—was high in all of these countries. In East Asia the domestic banking sectors were weak and poorly supervised. Once the currency came under attack, an already volatile situation became explosive.

After the collapse of the Thai baht in July of 1994, the crisis was rapidly propagated across East Asia. Even the currencies and financial markets of some economies that were thought to have among the strongest fundamentals in the world—Taiwan, Hong Kong, and Singapore—were intermittently attacked during 1997 and 1998. The extent to which currency crises are transmitted across countries—what sometimes is referred to as "contagion"—became particularly important in 1998 when, as a result of the Russian currency collapse, the currencies, bonds, and stock markets of virtually all emerging-market countries around the world came under severe pressure. A statement by Mexico's Secretary of the Treasury José Angel Gurría vividly captures policy makers' concerns and frustrations with financial contagion: "Ninety percent of Mexicans have never heard of the Duma, and yet the exchange rate and interest rates that they live with every day were being driven by people with names like Kiriyenko and Chernomydrin and Primakov" (Gurría 1999).

The situation eased toward the end of 1998. When Brazil finally succumbed to the speculative pressure by devaluing in January 1999, the adverse effects on the real economy that the East Asia crisis had led us to expect did not materialize. Nevertheless, the end of the decade offered little hope that we had seen the end of crises in emerging markets. Argentina and

---

2. To be sure, these factors in addition to mounting political instability resulted in a decline in the demand for money in Mexico. The fact that the Bank of Mexico sterilized the decline in reserves during most of 1994 made things worse.

Turkey were both placed under intense speculative pressure in the fall of 2000. In the face of doubts regarding its political ability to address internal problems, particularly regarding banking, Turkey was ultimately forced in February 2001 to abandon the exchange rate policy that had been the foundation of its still-new stabilization program. By the end of 2001, Argentina's decade long experiment with a fixed exchange rate and a currency board had collapsed.

In the last few years, and in an effort to explain the crises of the 1990s, scholars have developed new, "second- and third-generation" models of speculative attacks and currency crises. The second-generation models feature "multiple equilibria" that are consistent with a given set of fundamentals; they emphasize that even a country with relatively strong monetary discipline can be hit by a crisis. The third-generation models return to fundamentals, but they locate the problem in moral hazard and the structure of the countries' financial system, rather than in macroeconomic policies. Some truth lies in each of these sets of factors, and each is represented in our volume.

The papers collected in this volume were presented at a conference in January 2001.[3] The main purpose of the conference was to bring together a group of academics, officials in the multilateral organizations, and public- and private-sector economists to discuss issues related to the prevention of financial crisis in the emerging-market countries. (A companion conference was held two months later to discuss the management of crises in emerging-market countries once they occur. The corresponding volume is *Managing Crises in Emerging Markets,* edited by Michael Dooley and Jeffrey Frankel.)

In organizing this conference, our point of departure was the idea that, because of the changing nature of financial crises in the emerging economies, it was necessary to seriously rethink prevention policies. We were particularly interested in examining the most important characteristics of recent crises in light of new and rapidly evolving theories. To this end, we called on both theoretical and applied economists, and we made an effort to include specific case studies as well as broad cross-country comparisons. The topics covered in the conference included exchange rate regimes, contagion, the current account of the balance of payments, the role of private-sector investors and of speculators, the reaction of the official (including the multilateral) sector, capital controls, bank supervision and weaknesses, the role of large players (including hedge funds), and the role of cronyism and corruption.

We have divided the rest of the volume into five parts. In part I we deal with the role of the current account and trade flows in financial crises. Part II concentrates on international financial players—including banks, large hedge funds, private investors, and speculators—and on the channels

---

3. The paper by Reinhart and Reinhart, however, was presented at the accompanying conference held in Monterey, California, in March 2001.

through which crises are transmitted across countries. In part III we include two papers that analyze the effectiveness of capital controls as a way of preventing a crisis from becoming massive and costly. Because Malaysia is the one major country to have responded to the crisis in 1998 by imposing capital controls, both papers in this section focus on that experiment. Part IV is devoted to the role of balance sheets, crony capitalism, and corruption. Finally, part V serves to highlight an essay that surveys the main characteristics of the "new" financial crises.

Part I: The Current Account and Vulnerability to Crisis

In "Does the Current Account Matter?" Sebastian Edwards investigates in detail the behavior of the current account in emerging nations, and in particular its role—if any—in financial crises. Edwards reviews alternative models of current account behavior and develops a dynamic model of current account sustainability. The empirical analysis is based on a massive data set that covers over 120 countries during more than twenty-five years. A main goal of this paper is to analyze whether there is evidence supporting the idea that there are costs involved in running very large deficits.

Edwards argues that equilibrium models of frictionless economies are of little help in understanding actual current account behavior or assessing a country's degree of vulnerability. He shows that, although current models of current account sustainability provide useful information about the long run, they are of limited use in determining if a country's current account deficit is too large at a particular moment in time.

Edwards's empirical analysis shows that large current account deficits are not persistent. Very few countries run large deficits for as much as five years in a row, and only a handful have run large deficits for ten years. The data suggest that the typical mechanics of current account deficits is that countries that experience large imbalances do so for a limited time; after a while these imbalances are reduced, and a current account reversal is observed. An analysis of current account reversals using a large (unbalanced) panel of countries for 1970–97 indicates that, contrary to what has been recently suggested, reversals do have a negative effect on economic performance. They negatively affect aggregate investment; moreover, even after controlling for investment, the regression analysis suggests that reversals have a negative impact on gross domestic product (GDP) growth. The Edwards chapter also addresses the narrower question of whether larger deficits increase the probability of a country's experiencing a currency crisis. The analysis suggests that the answer to this question depends on the definition of *crisis,* as well as on the sample used in the analysis. When Africa is excluded from the sample, an increase in the current account deficit raises the probability of a crisis, independently of how *crisis* is defined.

In "Are Trade Linkages Important Determinants of Country Vulnerability to Crises?" Kristin J. Forbes uses a comparative data set with forty-eight countries to investigate the importance of trade channels in the international propagation of financial crises. After surveying the literature on trade effects, Forbes develops an analytical framework that considers three possible channels through which international trade can affect the propagation of crises: a competitive effect, an income effect, and a bargain effect. The competitive effect is related to the way in which a major devaluation affects relative prices in the world economy. If the crisis country is large enough, a devaluation of its currency will result in cross price effects, negatively affecting prices of other countries' exports. The income effect is a more traditional transmission channel and is related to the decline in real income in the crisis country and the consequent decline in its demand for imports. Countries that export heavily to the crisis country will, thus, be affected by a reduction in their own exports. The final effect—the so-called bargain effect—allows a noncrisis country to import selected goods at a bargain price.

In the empirical application of this framework, Forbes uses a vast comparative data set, covering forty-eight countries during the period 1994–99. The countries in her data set experienced sixteen crises during this time period.[4] A particularly important contribution of this paper is the construction of a new competitiveness indicator, which uses micro-level data to calculate the way in which a crisis affects bilateral exports. Using data on stock market returns for each of the forty-eight countries, Forbes investigates the relative importance of the effects described above on the international propagation of crises. Her findings suggest that countries that compete with exports from a crisis country experience significant reductions in stock returns in the period following a crisis. Likewise, countries that export heavily to crisis countries are affected by financial turmoil. Interestingly, Forbes's results suggest that trade channels are indeed more important than standard macroeconomic channels in explaining the international propagation of financial crises. According to Forbes, her analysis has important implications for adjustment and assistant packages by the multilateral organizations. In particular, she argues that crisis-related adjustment packages that ignore these trade linkages will tend to be somewhat ineffective in reducing the negative effects of financial crises on other nations.

Part II: International Financial Players and Contagion

In "What Hurts Emerging Markets Most? G3 Exchange Rate or Interest Rate Volatility," Carmen M. Reinhart and Vincent Raymond Reinhart analyze the way in which advanced countries' exchange rate policies affect

---

4. As do many of the authors in this volume, Forbes uses the Eichengreen, Rose, and Wyplosz (1996) definition of *crisis*. For an alternative definition of *crisis,* see Frankel and Rose (1996).

emerging countries.[5] In particular, the Reinharts ask whether reducing Group of Three (G3) exchange rate volatility—through the adoption of a target zones exchange rate system, for instance—would reduce emerging markets' macroeconomic vulnerability. Since most emerging markets' debt is expressed in U.S. dollars, a more stable dollar exchange rate could, in principle, help the poorer nations. The authors point out that reducing G3 exchange rate volatility implies an important trade-off. In particular, since sterilized intervention is largely ineffective, reducing exchange rate instability would require an active use of monetary policy. Monetary intervention, in turn, will have an effect on G3 interest rates. The trade-off, then, is that lower G3 exchange rate instability will be translated into higher G3 interest rate volatility.

Based on the North-South links literature, Reinhart and Reinhart develop a framework with which to analyze the way in which exchange rate and interest rate policies in the advanced countries affect capital flows to the emerging countries. In their empirical analysis they look in detail at the behavior of capital flows to a large number of developing countries. They consider the period 1970–99 and concentrate on six groups of countries. An important finding in their analysis is that, historically, G3 exchange rate volatility appears to have no effect on (net) capital flows to the emerging nations. This is the case when all poorer countries are considered as a group, as well as when the individual regional groups are analyzed. They do find, however, that higher G3 exchange rate volatility has been associated with lower portfolio flows to the emerging nations. An increase in direct foreign investment compensates for this drop in private portfolio capital. Reinhart and Reinhart's detailed empirical investigation leads them to conclude that "from the perspective of the emerging-market economies, the case for limiting G3 exchange rate volatility is not proven."

In "When is U.S. Bank Lending to Emerging Markets Volatile?" Linda S. Goldberg uses new data to analyze U.S. banks' lending practices toward emerging nations. In particular, she investigates the extent to which U.S. banks that lend to the emerging markets respond to changing macroeconomic conditions, both in the United States and in the borrowing countries. An important feature of this analysis is that the author makes formal comparisons between U.S. lending to emerging and industrialized nations. Goldberg uses an extensive data set drawn from the Country Exposure Reports filed by individual U.S. banks with the Federal Financial Institutions Examinations Council (FFIEC). This unique data set contains over 20,000 observations and provides detailed information on individual U.S. banks' claims on foreign countries. Goldberg estimates a series of panel regressions

5. This paper was not discussed at the conference at Cheeca Lodge, Islamorada. Instead, it was presented and discussed at the accompanying conference on "Managing Currency Crises in Emerging Markets," which was held in March 2001. Because the paper deals with "crisis prevention" issues, we decided to include it in this volume.

to analyze the way in which U.S. banking responds to cyclical conditions abroad and in the United States.

Goldberg finds that during the last twenty years a larger number of banks have become engaged in international lending to emerging nations. She also finds that smaller U.S. banks tend to concentrate their lending to Latin America. Smaller banks' international lending to the emerging nations is more volatile than lending by larger banks. Large banks, on the other hand, tend to concentrate on lending to the industrialized nations. A particularly important finding of this study is that foreign countries' macroeconomic developments—either their rate of GDP growth or the behavior of their domestic interest rates—do not appear to affect U.S. banks' international lending decisions. On the other hand, macroeconomic conditions in the United States are an important determinant of U.S. banks' international lending. When the U.S. economy expands, U.S. banks' lending to other industrialized countries tends to expand. However, U.S. economic expansions are associated with a contraction of U.S. banks' lending to Latin America and Asia. Perhaps the most important conclusion of Goldberg's analysis is that, overall, U.S. bank lending to emerging nations has not been particularly volatile. On the whole, there is no evidence of lending retrenchment during times of crisis.

The role of large market participants—including hedge funds and other highly leveraged institutions—is the subject of the chapter by Giancarlo Corsetti, Paolo Pesenti, and Nouriel Roubini, "The Role of Large Players in Currency Crises." Most models assume that speculators are numerous and atomistic in their behavior: each player acts in self-interest and considers himself too small to have an effect on the market price. Indeed, financial markets are usually thought to meet this ideal of neoclassical economic theory better than markets in almost any other good or service. If there are speculative bubbles or attacks that take the market price away from fundamentals, it is not due to any deliberate market manipulation by individual speculators.

Given the interest in "George Soroses" and other players who are large enough to affect the market—for example, allegations of market manipulation in Hong Kong in 1998—some attention to the possible role of larger players is overdue. In this chapter, the authors present a model in which the presence of a large trader can increase the chance of a crisis. Size is defined in terms of market power, which is in turn determined by access to information that others lack, and not by the magnitude of financial resources alone. The setting is the sort of second-generation model developed originally by Obstfeld (1994): A speculative attack is the outcome of a prisoner's dilemma game, in which each speculator sells the currency for fear that he will be left "holding the bag" if he is the only one *not* to sell. A large trader matters because, for any given set of fundamentals, he affects the probability that the others will undertake a speculative attack. Specifically, his presence makes others more aggressive in their behavior.

Some case studies offer evidence suggestive of the role of large players.

Examples include the attack on the Thai baht in 1997, the crisis in Malaysia in 1997–98 that prompted the prime minister to point the finger at foreign speculators, the "double play" on the Hong Kong stock and foreign exchange markets in 1998, and pressure on the Australian dollar in the summer of 1998.

In "Contagion: How to Measure It?" Roberto Rigobon discusses the mechanisms through which currency crises are propagated across countries. He uses high-frequency data to investigate the way in which financial disturbances—including those that are associated with a financial crisis—are transmitted from country to country. He asks whether particular channels, such as trade links or common creditors, affect the international transmission of disturbances. In addition, Rigobon analyzes whether the parameters that capture the main features of the transmission mechanism experience structural breaks at the time of a crisis.

Rigobon argues that empirical models traditionally used to address "contagion" issues are subject to serious limitations. In particular, he points out that in the presence of heteroskedasticity, omitted variables, or simultaneous equation problems, traditional tests—including standard tests that look for structural breaks—are subject to serious biases. In light of these limitations of traditional methods, Rigobon suggests a new approach to testing for parameter stability under very general conditions. This new approach is valid if two assumptions are met: the analysts know in which country the crisis was initiated, and changes in the other countries' covariance matrixes are generated by disturbances emanating from the crisis country. Rigobon uses his new procedure on high-frequency data for emerging-market bond and stock market returns. His results suggest that trade linkages and regional proximity affect the extent to which disturbances are transmitted internationally in the bond market. Interestingly enough, his results indicate that these variables play no significant role in the transmission of disturbances across different national stock markets.

In "Credit, Prices, and Crashes: Business Cycles with a Sudden Stop," Enrique G. Mendoza discusses the role played by "sudden stops" of capital inflows in triggering a financial crisis. Mendoza begins his discussion by arguing that sudden stop (SS) episodes are qualitatively different from standard balance-of-payments crises. Although in the latter case the economy experiences a deep collapse, followed by a rather sharp recovery, in a run-of-the-mill balance-of-payments crisis the economy suffers a prolonged recession. Mendoza develops a model of an economy subject to *excess volatility,* which is able to capture the main features of SSs. In this model, under most states of nature the economy functions in a frictionless fashion. There are some states of nature, however, in which the economy becomes subject to a binding credit constraint. More interestingly, the economic frictions and distortions set in motion by this credit constraint can be triggered either by investors' expectations or by foreign or domestic shocks.

Mendoza's analysis has important implications for crisis prevention policies: First, regulatory policies that increase the probability of the credit-constraint state of nature can be highly counterproductive. These policies would include liquidity requirements, value-at-risk collateralization, and margin requirements. Second, programs aimed at avoiding SSs—contingent credit facilities, for instance—need credibly to commit very large amounts of funds. Third, in the longer term, SS crises can only be avoided (or minimized) through the implementation of micropolicies aimed at eliminating the credit-market imperfections that are at the root of this phenomenon.

Mendoza uses his model to investigate the dynamics of the 1994 Mexican peso crisis. After calibrating the model with Mexican data, Mendoza addresses three key questions: how frequent, how large, and how costly SSs are. The main conclusions from this exercise are that the possibility of SSs has a very small effect on the long-run characteristics of the business cycle. However, SSs can be large and can potentially have very large negative welfare effects. For instance, in one of the exercises, an SS can generate a decline in output of nontradable goods on the order of 10–20 percent of GDP. Mendoza argues that an important implication of this type of analysis is that increased policy credibility, of the type achieved by dollarizing the monetary system, can go a long way toward reducing the importance and costs associated with SSs.

Part III: Capital Controls: The Malaysian Experience

In the aftermath of the East Asian crisis, a number of analysts argued that unrestricted capital mobility was at the center of global financial instability. People as different as former World Bank Chief Economist Joe Stiglitz and financier George Soros have endorsed the view that speculators focus exclusively on the short run and tend to flee countries at the first signs of trouble. Worse yet, speculators are often affected by rumors, stampeding toward the exit and leaving behind them a wrecked financial sector.

Supporters of this view have argued that restricting capital mobility would reduce the frequency and depth of financial crises in emerging nations. Much of the recent debate on capital controls has centered on the benefits of controls on capital inflows, similar to those implemented by Chile between 1991 and 1998. This type of capital control is aimed at limiting the volume of short-term flows, tilting the composition of capital flows toward the longer run.

While many economists believe that price-based controls on inflows may be a useful tool for mitigating financial instability, most are quite negative about controls on capital *outflows*. Malaysia's decision to impose controls on capital outflows in September of 1998 was received with skepticism and alarm by the international financial community. The vast majority of analysts argued that these controls would create serious distortions, scare off investors, and retard growth. Until now, there has been no systematic evaluation of Malaysia's experience with controls on outflows during 1998–99. The two chapters in this part of this volume address the Malaysian episode in detail.

Ethan Kaplan and Dani Rodrik's "Did the Malaysian Capital Controls Work?" provides a detailed empirical evaluation of Malaysia's unorthodox reaction to the currency upheaval of 1997–98. The authors note that officials at the International Monetary Fund (IMF) and the major investment banks argued that these controls, and the accompanying decisions to peg the exchange rate and lower domestic interest rates, would result in a slower recovery and a significant reduction in foreign direct investment (FDI) into Malaysia. This latter (potential) effect of capital controls was considered to be particularly devastating, as Malaysia has traditionally relied very heavily on FDI. In light of developments in the region since September 1998 (Malaysia did recover, but so did Korea and Thailand, which did not rely on controls) the majority of analysts believe that the imposition of controls on capital outflows did not work in Malaysia. According to the authors, however, this reasoning is flawed because it ignores a key difference in the timing of the adjustment programs: Korea and Thailand started their respective adjustment programs in mid- and late 1997, whereas Malaysia did not seriously launch its (heterodox) adjustment program until September 1998.

In order to take this timing issue into account in an evaluation of Malaysia's program, the authors implement a "time-shifted differences-in-differences" technique. This methodology allows them to compare these countries' performance relative to the launching of their respective programs. Better yet, this technique permits the authors to evaluate directly the effects of the Malaysian capital controls on the country's macroeconomic performance, relative to the counterfactual of an IMF program. Their analysis concentrates on a number of key macroeconomic variables, including real GDP, industrial production, inflation, interest rates, and a series of financial sector indicators. The results from this analysis suggest that, when measured relative to the launching of the respective programs, Malaysia's heterodox-cum-capital-controls program fared better than Korea's IMF-sponsored adjustment programs. As the authors show, however, if a standard difference-in-difference estimation is performed, Malaysia's program does not look so effective. In concluding their analysis, Kaplan and Rodrik "invite the reader to make up his or her mind on which of these counterfactuals makes more sense."

In "Malaysia's Crisis: Was it Different?" Rudi Dornbusch approaches Malaysia's experience with capital controls from another angle. Dornbusch asks whether Malaysia's rather solid performance in 1999–2000 can be attributed to its heterodox program, or whether it was the result of other factors, including a friendly international economic environment. In this chapter Dornbusch argues that Malaysia's main difference arose from the forceful reaction of the political leadership to the crisis. He chronicles how

Prime Minister Dr. Mahathir bin Mohamad took an attitude that was strongly anti-IMF and anti–capital markets in the period following the crisis, blaming speculators for his country's troubles. This anti–international financial markets rhetoric intensified in late 1998 when Deputy Prime Minister Anwar was ousted. According to Dornbusch—and in this he agrees with Kaplan and Rodrik—the main difficulty in evaluating Malaysia's performance is that its economic recovery coincided with a general improvement in world economic conditions, including major interest rates cuts by the Federal Reserve.

Dornbusch argues that a serious comparative evaluation of Malaysia's capital controls program requires an understanding of the initial conditions, and in particular of whether at the outset of the crisis Malaysia was more "vulnerable" than the rest of the East Asian economies. In his view, the most important vulnerability factors include misaligned exchange rates, nonperforming loans in the banking sector, and risk in the national balance sheet due to excess short-term debt. Dornbusch's analysis of vulnerability factors suggests that Malaysia's initial conditions were not worse than those of the other East Asian countries. In fact, he argues that, for a number of the key indicators, Malaysia appears to have been on a better footing than the rest of the region. This was the case, for instance, for the debt-equity ratio and for the ratio of short-term external debt to international reserves. The second question addressed by Dornbusch is whether Malaysia's recovery in 1999–2000 can be attributed to the capital controls adjustment program of September 1998. He argues that, although it is indeed tempting to think that the controls were behind the recovery, it is also possible to argue that improving conditions were solely the result of better external conditions. According to Dornbusch, when Malaysia's indicators began to improve, "markets had already settled in Asia and interest rates had started to decline—and would soon do so everywhere under the impact of Federal Reserve rate cuts and a reduction in jitters."

Part IV: Balance Sheet and "Crony Capitalism"

Early studies on currency crises focused almost exclusively on the role of flows, including the way in which imports and exports react to a real exchange rate devaluation. In the 1980s, however, it became increasingly apparent that in a world with increased capital mobility, currency crises have very important balance sheet effects. In particular, if the corporate sector has significant liabilities expressed in foreign currency, a devaluation can generate massive bankruptcies. As the corporate sector has difficulties paying its debts, local banks' nonperforming loans will mount. This process is usually compounded by the fact that during the expansive phase of the cycle many banks engage in questionable practices. They lend to friends and "cronies" and tend to inflate the value of collateral. Once the tide changes and the economy slows down, banks are slow to write off bad loans and reluctant to make provisions. As the experiences of Mexico, Indonesia, and other crisis countries have shown, banks' difficulties can grow quickly and become very costly to clean up. Ultimately, both the corporate and the banking sectors must be restructured. In many cases—Mexico is probably the best known—a number of banks go under and must be bailed out by the authorities. Taxpayers, unavoidably, end up footing the bill. The cost of these currency-cum-banking crises can be enormous, surpassing in some cases 20 percent of the country's GDP. The six papers collected in this part of this volume address different aspects of balance sheet effects, including the role they played in the Korean crisis, the way they interact with corruption, and their implications in designing optimal exchange rate policies.

In "Negative Alchemy? Corruption, Composition of Capital Inflows, and Currency Crises," Shang-Jin Wei and Yi Wu analyze the effects of corruption and lack of transparency on capital flows composition. Their point of departure is the finding by Frankel and Rose (1996) that the composition of capital flows is an important determinant of the probability of a country's facing a crisis. According to these results, countries whose capital inflows are tilted toward FDI have a lower probability of a currency crisis. Wei and Wu develop a model in which the composition of capital inflows may be affected by the degree of corruption in the host country. In their setup, a higher degree of corruption results in a lower percentage of FDI relative to overall capital inflows, because the need to pay bribes tends to increase with the frequency with which foreign investors interact with local officials. The fact that portfolio and bank creditors are more likely to be bailed out in cases of crisis also affects the composition of capital flows: Banks and portfolio creditors will be more willing to do business with corrupt countries.

In their empirical analysis, Wei and Wu use a large data set on bilateral capital flows and a series of alternative indexes on corruption. They estimate a number of panel regressions using information for 1994–96. Their results indicate that corruption and lack of transparency indeed affect the composition of capital flows. Countries that are perceived as being more corrupt tend to receive relatively less FDI and a relatively higher proportion of bank loans. These findings hold for different specifications of the capital flows equations and are robust to the estimation technique as well as to the controls included in the regressions. Wei and Wu argue that to the extent that a lower reliability in FDI increases the probability of a crisis, reducing corruption represents an important crisis prevention mechanism.

The chapter by Robert Dekle and Kenneth Kletzer, "Domestic Bank Regulation and Financial Crises: Theory and Empirical Evidence from East Asia," as do the other chapters in this part of the book, deals with the banking relationships that have been implicated in the Asian financial system due to the problems of moral hazard.

If crises of the 1970s and 1980s were represented by the first-generation approach, and if the 1992–93 exchange rate mechanism (ERM) crises inspired the second-generation models, then the East Asian crises of 1997–98 provided motivation for the third-generation models. As previously noted, in the latter third of the twentieth century East Asia earned a relatively good reputation for fiscal discipline and monetary stability. It was difficult to attribute crises here to the traditional culprit of excessive macroeconomic expansion. The third-generation approach instead interprets recent crises as illustrations of the perils of moral hazard. Borrowers and lenders are less likely to be careful in evaluating the true profitability of investment opportunities if they believe they will be bailed out in the event that the project goes awry.

The third-generation model starts from the assumption that government officials have a pool of resources that can potentially be used to bail out political cronies if they get into financial difficulty.[6] This pool is mainly identified with the central banks' holdings of foreign exchange reserves. Well-connected banks are able to borrow from abroad to finance risky projects, such as real estate development or a new factory in the already glutted steel industry. They are aware of the risk, but they believe that they will be bailed out by the government if things go badly. In the worst countries, loan guarantees have been explicitly promised. In other cases, the government may have tried to declare in advance that it will not be responsible for private debts, but this disclaimer is not believed.[7]

Why does the crisis occur when it does? Asian countries did not suddenly develop critical structural flaws in their financial systems for the first time in 1997. The timing of the attack again arises from the calculations of speculators who fear that if they wait too long there will not be enough foreign exchange reserves to go around. However, there is a key difference from the first-generation models, which watched reserves decline steadily over time and identified the timing of the attack as the point at which reserves sank to a particular critical level. The third-generation models watch liabilities rise steadily over time, artificially encouraged by moral hazard. They identify the timing of the attack with the point at which the liabilities have climbed to the critical level, given by the level of reserves. At that point, speculators suddenly cash in their investments. If they waited any longer, they might not be able to get their money out. The speculative attack, as usual, then forces the central bank to abandon the exchange rate.

Dekle and Kletzer develop a variant of this approach. The banking system becomes progressively more fragile in the presence of public loan guarantees and poor regulation, until the inevitable crisis occurs in which capi-

---

6. Two key references are Michael Dooley (2000) and Paul Krugman (1998).

7. Carlos Diaz-Alejandro (1985). A "no bailout" declaration lacks credibility particularly in the case of domestic banks. When the crisis comes, the pressure for the government to rescue insolvent banks will be irresistible for two reasons. First, most depositors are small savers, not sophisticated investors; and second, bank failures can have a devastating effect on the rest of the economy, particularly because banks constitute the payments system.

tal flows reverse. The model generates a rise in capital flows and bank debt relative to GDP an accompanying fall in the value of banks relative to corporations before the crisis, and a recession when the crisis hits. A consideration of five individual East Asian cases produces the conclusion that the model's assumptions fit the circumstances fairly well in Korea and Thailand, where crises occurred, but less so in Malaysia, and not at all in Singapore and Taiwan, where a crisis did not occur.

The chapter by Luis Felipe Céspedes, Roberto Chang, and Andrés Velasco, "Dollarization of Liabilities, Net Worth Effects, and Optimal Monetary Policy," analyzes optimal exchange rate and monetary policies in emerging countries. More specifically, the authors investigate whether domestic monetary authorities should actively defend their currencies against speculative attacks. They argue that the answer to this question depends, in principle, on whether the corporate sector in the country in question has foreign exchange rate liabilities. Indeed, recent suggestions that emerging countries should give up their national currencies and adopt a major currency as legal tender—the so called dollarization proposal—have been based on the idea that in the presence of dollarized liabilities, currency depreciation can be very costly. In order to confront this issue, the authors develop a formal model with balance sheet effects and staggered labor contracts, and they make formal welfare comparisons regarding the effects of exogenous shocks under alternative exchange rate and monetary policy regimes. The comparison is centered on two possible regimes: a credible fixed exchange rate and a discretionary flexible exchange rate. In this model, domestic output is produced by heterogeneous workers, investment is partially financed with foreign loans, and foreign borrowing is subject to information asymmetries and agency costs. This, in turn, means that the economy may be subject to balance sheet effects.

The authors calibrate their model and use a standard government loss function to compare the effects of alternative policy responses to an external disturbance. They formally analyze several discretionary policies and a fixed exchange rate policy. Their results indicate that, under discretion, the optimal policy response implies a complex combination of interest rate management and exchange rate adjustments. This policy is similar to a flexible inflation-targeting rule with an exchange rate feedback. More importantly for the current debate on appropriate exchange rate regimes, they find that, in terms of social welfare, any of the discretionary policies dominates the fixed exchange rate option. According to the authors, the superiority of flexible (discretionary) exchange rate policy holds independently of the existence of balance sheet effects.

In "*Chaebol* Capitalism and the Currency-Financial Crisis in Korea," Anne O. Krueger and Jungho Yoo investigate the causes behind the Korean currency-financial crisis of 1997–98. They argue that although the crisis was the result of the interaction of a number of factors, it is important to determine which were the dominant ones. This exercise is particularly relevant for the design of future prevention policies. Krueger and Yoo begin their analysis by reviewing the evolution of the Korean development policies since the 1960s. They discuss the country's export promotion policies of the early years, the "competitive" real exchange rate policy, and the directed-credit policies. The authors analyze the capital account liberalization policies of the 1990s and argue that there is little prima facie evidence that the relaxation of controls on capital mobility was the main cause of the collapse of the won in 1997 and the massive financial crisis that followed.

Krueger and Yoo carefully investigate of the evolution of *chaebol* financial and economic performance during the last decade and a half. They are particularly interested in understanding whether excessive and reckless lending to these conglomerates was a major cause of the crisis. Their main conclusion is that the *chaebol* were in a very weak financial position long before the crisis erupted. Moreover, questionable loans and even outright bad loans were kept in the banks' books, creating a very weak banking structure. Although good overall economic conditions and, in particular, a strong demand for Korea's exports allowed the banks to continue to operate, their vulnerability was constantly growing. During the very good years of 1994 and 1995, the *chaebol* continued to borrow, and the banks continued to lend. Project profitability was low, however, and *chaebol* dangerously increased their level of indebtedness. When the good times came to an end in 1997, the *chaebol* needed even more funds, but at that time banks were unable to provide them. The increase in interest rates in 1997 could not be tolerated by the *chaebol,* and their financial weakness became increasingly apparent. According to Krueger and Yoo, the exchange rate crisis did not generate the financial and banking crisis; rather, higher interest rates did. They further argue that the depreciation of the won had a relatively small effect on banks' balance sheets. In fact, since *chaebol* are major exporters, a (real) depreciation would tend to improve their financial prospects and thus would have an indirect effect on their creditor banks.

In "Living with the Fear of Floating: An Optimal Policy Perspective," Amartya Lahiri and Carlos A. Végh discuss policies aimed at defending a currency under attack. During the East Asian crisis, the IMF standard policy of raising interest rates was severely criticized by a number of analysts. A number of economists, including some World Bank senior officials, argued that this interest rate policy was inadequate; according to the critics, higher interest rates introduce overly recessionary forces, without being particularly effective in fending off the attack on the currency. In this paper, Lahiri and Vegh build a model to formally analyze the optimal central bank response to a speculative attack. The model considers a small country that produces two tradable goods; nominal wages are subject to rigidities, and some firms are subject to a "credit in advance" constraint—that is, they require bank loans in order to have positive output. In this model, interest rate shocks, which are associated with money demand shocks, have two effects. On the one hand, they increase the cost of credit and result in lower output, and on the other hand, they result in higher bank deposits.

Lahiri and Vegh use their model to compute the monetary authorities' optimal reaction to a demand for money shock. The menu of options is limited to either a one-shot intervention in the foreign exchange market or a change in government bonds' interest rates. The authors show that in their model the existence of nominal wage rigidities implies that it is optimal to maintain the exchange rate unchanged. That is, in this setting, fixed nominal exchange rates will be preferred even in the face of large shifts in the demand for money. They show that the optimal response implies combining an interest rate change with intervention in the foreign exchange market by selling (or buying) international reserves. The authors argue that if there are (social) costs of altering the existing stock of international reserves, the optimal response to a shock may include the adoption of a dirty floating exchange rate regime.

Aaron Tornell's chapter, "Policy in an Economy with Balance Sheet Effects," investigates policy responses to crisis in the presence of enforceability problems, bailout problems, and balance sheet effects. Tornell argues that many recent crises have taken place in countries that were particularly vulnerable to external shocks. According to him, these vulnerable economic national structures were the result of neither bad policies nor corruption; rather, they were deliberate, second-best policies aimed at achieving very fast economic growth. Many recent crises, Tornell argues, were the result of bad luck, rather than of bad policies. In order to illustrate this point he discusses in some detail the most important features of the Mexican peso crisis of December 1994.

Tornell's model assumes an economy that produces tradable and nontradable goods and is subject to two main distortions. First, enforceability problems limit the amount of debt that producers can issue. This reduces borrowing, investment, and growth. Second, there are (implicit) bailout guarantees, which help relax the borrowing constraint. In this setting the country can follow either a risky or a safe equilibrium path. The interaction of the enforceability and bailouts distortions results in a fragile economy that may be subject to self-fulfilling crises.

Tornell argues that within this particular framework, many of the traditional crisis prevention policies are misguided. For example, he argues that outlawing bailouts would reduce borrowing, investment, and growth under every state of nature. Likewise, he argues that forbidding dollar-denominated debt would also reduce a country's (expected) growth. Tornell is careful to point out that his analysis does not imply that bailouts should be generalized and very large, nor that banks should be encouraged to hold huge dollar-denominated portfolios. It does mean, however, that the outright prohibition of these policies is likely to be, ex ante, welfare reducing.

An important implication of Tornell's model is that prudential regulation should be improved. In terms of postcrisis policies, Tornell makes two points: First, in order to reduce the output cost of crises, bailouts should not be restricted to lenders; some bailouts should be granted to borrowers. Second, bailouts should be granted at once and not in a piecemeal fashion. He also argues that appropriate exchange rate and interest rate response after a crisis is country-specific, and no generalizations can be made.

Part V: Conclusion

In the closing chapter, "A Primer on Emerging-Market Crises," Rudi Dornbusch provides an overview of the most important features of recent financial and currency crises in emerging countries. He begins with the distinction between the old-style crises with macroeconomic origins—overexpansion and overvaluation—and the new-style crises, in which capital flows exhibit "sudden stops" (Calvo 1998).

A key question for the models is why the attacks occur when they do. The answer from the first-generation models is that attacks occur when reserves decline to a level at which investors realize that if they wait any longer to trade in their domestic currency for foreign, there won't be enough to go around. The answer from the third-generation models is that attacks occur when the level of liabilities that have a claim on bailout protection rises to the level of reserves available for the bailing-out. The second-generation models intentionally leave the timing somewhat indeterminate.

The other key questions on which the Dornbusch review focuses include the following: What makes countries vulnerable? Why are the economic costs so large once a crisis does occur? And what are the appropriate remedies? Balance sheet effects are central in answering these questions. A country is vulnerable when its liabilities are shorter term than its assets and are dollar denominated rather than domestic denominated. In the event of a currency crisis, banks and firms will have trouble servicing their debts out of their domestic revenues and may go bankrupt. Investors are aware of this problem, which means that countries with bad balance sheets are vulnerable to speculative attacks precipitated even by small events. Consequently, Dornbusch offers the aphorism "good balance sheets, no crisis."

References

Calvo, Guillermo. 1998. Capital flows and capital market Crises: The simple economics of sudden stops. *Journal of Applied Economics* 1 (1): 35–54.

Cooper, Richard. 1971. Currency devaluation in developing countries. *Princeton Essays in International Finance* no. 86. Princeton University, Department of Economic, International Finance Section.

Diaz-Alejandro, Carlos. 1985. Good-bye financial repression; hello financial crash. *Journal of Development Economics* 19 (September): 324–61.

Dooley, Michael. A model of crises in emerging markets. *Economic Journal* 110 (460): 256–72.

Edwards, Sebastian. 1989. *Real exchange rates, devaluation and adjustment.* Cambridge: MIT Press.

Edwards, Sebastian, and Julio Santaella. 1993. Devaluation controversies in the developing countries: Lessons from the bretton woods era. In *A retrospective on the Bretton Woods system: Lessons for international monetary reform,* ed. Michael Bordo and Barry Eichengreen, 405–60. Chicago: University of Chicago Press.

Eichengreen, Barry, Andrew Rose, and Charles Wyplosz. 1996. Contagious currency crises. NBER Working Paper no. 5681. Cambridge, Mass.: National Bureau of Economic Research, April.

Frankel, Jeffrey, and Andrew Rose. 1996. Currency crashes in emerging markets. *Journal of International Economics* 41 (3/4): 351–66.

Gurria, J. Angel. 1999. Identifying the pending agenda for stability. *Global Emerging Markets* 2 (2): 22–25.

Kamin, Steven. 1988. Devaluation, external balance, and macroeconomic performance: A look at the numbers. *Princeton Studies in International Finance* no. 62. Princeton University, Department of Economics, International Finance Section.

Krugman, Paul. 1979. A model of balance of payments crises. *Journal of Money, Credit and Banking* 11:311–25.

———. 1998. What happened to Asia? January. Available at [http://web.mit.edu/krugman/www/DISINTER.html].

Obstfeld, Maurice. 1994. The logic of currency crises. *Cahiers Economiques et Monetaires* 43:189–213.

I

The Current Account and Vulnerability to Crisis

1

Does the Current Account Matter?

Sebastian Edwards

1.1 Introduction

The currency crises of the 1990s shocked investors, academics, international civil servants, and policy makers alike. Most analysts had missed the financial weaknesses in Mexico and East Asia, and when the crises erupted almost every observer was surprised by their intensity.[1] This inability to predict major financial collapses is viewed as an embarrassment of sorts by the economics profession. As a result, during the last few years macroeconomists in academia, in the multilateral institutions, and in investment banks have been frantically developing crisis "early warning" models. These models have focused on a number of variables, including the level and currency composition of foreign debt, debt maturity, the weakness of the domestic financial sector, the country's fiscal position, its level of international reserves, political instability, and real exchange rate overvaluation, among others. Interestingly, different authors do not seem to agree on the role played by current account deficits in recent financial collapses. While some analysts have argued that large current account deficits have been behind major currency crashes, according to others the current account has not been overly important in many of these

Sebastian Edwards is the Henry Ford II Professor of International Business Economics at the Anderson Graduate School of Management at the University of California, Los Angeles (UCLA) and a research associate of the National Bureau of Economic Research.

The author thanks Alejandro Jara and Igal Magendzo for excellent assistance and benefited from discussions with Ed Leamer and James Boughton. The author is also grateful to Alejandro M. Werner and Jeffrey A. Frankel for helpful comments.

1. It should be noted that the crises in Russia (August 1998) and Brazil (January 1999) were widely anticipated.

episodes.[2] The view that current account deficits have played a limited role in recent financial debacles in the emerging nations is clearly presented by U.S. Treasury Secretary Larry Summers, who argued in his Richard T. Ely lecture that "[t]raditional macroeconomic variables, in the form of overly inflationary monetary policies, large fiscal deficits, *or even large current account deficits,* were present in several cases, but are not necessary antecedents to crisis in all episodes" (Summers 2000, 7, emphasis added).

The purpose of this paper is to investigate in detail the behavior of the current account in emerging economies, and in particular its role—if any—in financial crises. Models of current account behavior are reviewed, and a dynamic model of current account sustainability is developed. The empirical analysis is based on a massive data set that covers over 120 countries during more than twenty-five years. Important controversies related to the current account—including the extent to which current account deficits crowd out domestic saving—are also analyzed. Throughout the paper I am interested in whether there is evidence to support the idea that there are costs involved in running "very large" deficits. Moreover, I investigate the nature of these potential costs, including whether they are particularly high in the presence of other types of imbalances.

The rest of the paper is organized as follows: In section 1.2 I review the way in which economists' *views* on the current account have evolved in the last twenty-five years or so. The discussion deals with academic as well as policy perspectives and includes a review of evolving theoretical models of current account behavior. The analysis presented in this section shows that there have been important changes in economists' views on the subject, from "deficits matter" to "deficits are irrelevant if the public sector is in equilibrium," back to "deficits matter," to the current dominant view that "current deficits *may* matter." In this section I argue that "equilibrium" models of frictionless economies are of little help in understanding actual current account behavior or assessing a country's degree of vulnerability. In section 1.3 I focus on models of the current account sustainability that have recently become popular in financial institutions, both private and official. More specifically, I argue that although these models provide some useful information about the long-run sustainability of the external sector accounts, they are of limited use in determining if, at a particular moment in time, a country's current account deficit is "too large." In order to illustrate this point, I develop a simple model of current account behavior that emphasizes the role of stock adjustments. In section 1.4 I use a massive data set to analyze some of the most important aspects of current account behavior

---

2. For discussions on the causes behind the crises see, for example, Corsetti, Pesenti, and Roubini (1998), Sachs, Tornell, and Velasco (1996), the essays in Dornbusch (2000), and Edwards (1999).

in the world economy during the last quarter century. The discussion deals with the following issues: (a) the distribution of current account deficits across countries and regions; (b) the relationship between current account deficits, domestic saving, and investment; (c) the effects of capital account liberalization on capital controls on the current account; and (d) the circumstances surrounding major current account reversals. I investigate, in particular, how frequent and how costly these reversals have been. In section 1.5 I deal with the relationship between current account deficits and financial crises. I review the existing evidence and present some new results. Finally, section 1.6 contains some concluding remarks.

1.2 Evolving Views on the Current Account: Models and Policy Implications

In this section I analyze the evolving view on current account deficits, focusing on theoretical models as well as policy analyses. I show that economists' views have changed in important ways during the last twenty-five years, and I argue that many of these changes have been the result of important crisis situations in both the advanced and the emerging nations.

1.2.1 The Early Emphasis on Flows

In the immediate post–World War II period, most discussions on a country's external balance were based on the elasticities approach and focused on flows behavior. Even authors who fully understood that the current account is equal to income minus expenditure—including Meade (1951), Harberger (1950), Laursen and Metzler (1950), Machlup (1943), and Johnson (1955)—tended to emphasize the relation between relative price changes and trade flows.[3]

This emphasis on elasticities and the balance of trade also affected policy discussions in the developing nations. Indeed, until the mid-1970s, policy debates in the less developed countries were dominated by the so-called "elasticities pessimism" view, and most authors focused on whether a devaluation would result in an improvement in the country's external position, including its trade and current account balances. Cooper's (1971a, b) influential work on devaluation crisis in the developing nations is a good example of this emphasis. In these papers Cooper analyzed the consequences of twenty-one major devaluations in the developing world in the 1958–69 period, focusing on the effect of these exchange rate adjustments on the real exchange rate and on the balance of trade. Cooper (1971a) argued that although the relevant elasticities were indeed small, devaluations had, overall, been successful in helping to improve the trade and current account balances in the countries in his sample. In an extension of Cooper's work,

---

3. See, for example, Meade's (1951) discussion on pages 35–36.

Kamin (1988) confirmed the results that, historically, (large) devaluations tended to improve developing countries' trade balance.

Authors in the structuralist tradition argued that in the developing nations trade and current account imbalances were "structural" in nature and severely constrained poorer countries' ability to grow. According to this view, however, the solution was not to adjust the country's peg, but to encourage industrialization through import substitution policies. In Latin America this view was persuasively articulated by Raul Prebisch, the charismatic executive secretary of the U.N. Economic Commission for Latin America; in Asia it found its most respected defender in Professor Mahalanobis, the father of planning and the architect of India's Second Five Year Plan; and in Africa it was made the official policy stance with the Lagos Plan of Action of 1980.

1.2.2 The Current Account as an Intertemporal Phenomenon: The Lawson Doctrine and the 1980s Debt Crisis

During the second part of the 1970s, and partially as a result of the oil price shocks, most countries in the world experienced large swings in their current account balances. These developments generated significant concern among policy makers and analysts and prompted a number of experts to analyze carefully the determinants of the current account. Perhaps the most important analytical development during this period was a move away from trade flows and a renewed and formal emphasis on the intertemporal dimensions of the current account. The departing point was, of course, very simple and was based on the recognition of two interrelated facts. First, from a basic national accounting perspective, the current account is equal to saving minus investment. Second, since both saving and investment decisions are based on intertemporal factors—such as life cycle considerations and expected returns on investment projects—the current account is necessarily an intertemporal phenomenon. Sachs (1981) forcefully emphasized the intertemporal nature of the current account, arguing that, to the extent that higher current account deficits reflected new investment opportunities, there was no reason to be concerned about them.

Theoretical Issues

Obstfeld and Rogoff (1996) have provided a comprehensive review of modern models of the current account that assume intertemporal optimization on behalf of consumers and firms. In this type of model, consumption smoothing across periods is one of the fundamental drivers of the current account. The most powerful insight of the modern approach to the current account can be expressed in a remarkably simple equation. Assuming a constant world interest rate, equality between the world discount factor $[1/(1 + r)]$ and the representative consumer's subjective discount factor β, and no borrowing constraints, the current account deficit (CAD) can be written as[4]

(1) $$CAD_t = (Y_t^* - Y_t) - (I_t^* - I_t) - (G_t - Gt^*),$$

where Y_t, I_t, and G_t are current output, consumption, and government spending, respectively. Y_t^*, I_t^*, and G_t^*, on the other hand, are the "permanent" levels of these variables. The permanent value of Y (Y_t^*) is defined as

(2) $$Y_t^* = \frac{r}{1+r} \sum_{j=t} \left(\frac{r}{1+r}\right)^{j-t} Y_j.$$

The sum runs from $j = t$ to infinity. That is, equation (2) defines the permanent value of Y as the annuity value computed at the constant interest rate r. The definitions of I_t^* and G_t^* are exactly equivalent to that of Y_t^* in equation (2).

According to equation (1), if output falls below its permanent value, ($Y_t^* - Y_t$) > 0, there will be a higher current account deficit. Similarly, if investment increases above its permanent value, there will be a higher current account deficit. The reason for this is that new investment projects will be partially financed with an increase in foreign borrowing, thus generating a higher current account deficit. Likewise, an increase in government consumption above Gt^* will result in a higher current account deficit. Although equation (1) is very simple, it captures the fundamental insights of modern current account analysis. Moreover, extensions of the model, including the relaxation of the assumption that the subjective discount factor is equal to the world discount factor, do not alter its most important implications. If, however, the constant world interest rate assumption is relaxed, the analysis becomes somewhat more complicated. In this case, the current account deficit will be fundamentally affected by the country's net foreign assets position and by the relationship between the world interest rate and its "permanent" value, r_t^*. With a variable world interest rate, equation (1) becomes

(3) $$CAD_t = (Y_t^* - Y_t) - (I_t^* - I_t) - (G_t - G_t^*) - (r_t^* \quad r_t)B_t - \xi_t,$$

where B_t is the country's net foreign asset position. If the residents of this country are net holders of foreign assets, $B_t > 0$ (see Obstfeld and Rogoff 1996). The consumption adjustment factor, ξ_t, arises from the fact that the world discount factor is not any longer equal to the consumers' subjective discount factor. Notice that under most plausible parameter values ξ_t is rather small (Obstfeld and Rogoff 1996). An important implication of equation (3) says that if the country is a net foreign debtor ($B_t < 0$) and the world interest rate exceeds its permanent level, the current account deficit will be higher.

---

4. Obstfeld and Rogoff (1996, 74). For models that generate similar expressions see, for example, Razin and Svensson (1983), Frenkel and Razin (1987), and Edwards (1989).

A number of versions of optimizing models of the current account have appeared in the literature published since 1980. Razin and Svensson (1983), for example, built an optimizing framework to explore the validity of the Laursen-Metzler-Harberger condition developed in the 1950s and concluded that the insights from these early models were largely valid in a fully optimizing, two period, general equilibrium model. Edwards and van Wijnbergen (1986) explored the current account implications of alternative speeds of trade liberalization. They found out that in a framework in which the country in question faced a borrowing constraint, a gradual liberalization of trade was preferred to a cold-turkey approach. Frenkel and Razin (1987) analyzed the way in which alternative fiscal policies affected the current account balance through time. Edwards (1989) introduced nontradable goods in an effort to understand the connection between the real exchange rate and the current account through time. Sheffrin and Woo (1990) used an annuity framework to develop a number of specific testable hypotheses from the intertemporal framework. Ghosh and Ostry (1995) tested the intertemporal model using data for a group of developing countries. They argue that, overall, their results adequately capture the most important features of modern optimizing models of the current account.

Numerical simulations based on the intertemporal approach sketched above suggest that a country's optimal response to negative exogenous shocks is to run *very high* current account deficits. These large deficits are, of course, the mechanism through which the country nationals smooth consumption. An important consequence of this models' result is that a small country can accumulate a very large external debt and will have to run a sizeable trade *surplus* in the steady state in order to repay it. The problem, however, is that the external accounts and the external debt ratios implied by these models are *not* observed in reality. Obstfeld and Rogoff (1996), for example, develop a model of a small open economy with Ak technology and a constant rate of productivity growth that exceeds world productivity growth.[5] This economy faces a constant world interest rate r and no borrowing constraint. Under a set of plausible parameters, the steady-state trade surplus is equal to 45 percent of gross domestic product (GDP), and the steady-state ratio of debt to GDP is equal to 15.[6] Needless to say, neither of these figures has been observed in modern economies (on actual distributions of the current account see the discussion in section 1.4 of this paper). Fernandez de Cordoba and Kehoe (2000) developed an intertemporal model of a small economy to analyze the effects of lifting capital controls on the dynamics of the current account. The basic version of their model assumes both tradable and nontradable goods, physical capital, and interna-

---

5. "Small" means that the cost of borrowing does not rise with the quantity.
6. Obstfeld and Rogoff (1996) do not claim that this model is particularly realistic. In fact, they present its implications to highlight some of the shortcomings of simple intertemporal models of the current account.

tionally traded bonds, and no borrowing constraint. An important feature of the model—and one that sets it apart from that of Obstfeld and Rogoff (1996) discussed above—is that the rate of technological progress is equal to that of the rest of the world. The authors calibrate the model for the case of Spain and find that the optimal response to a financial reform is to run a current account deficit that peaks at 60 percent of GDP.[7] As the authors themselves acknowledge, this figure tends to contradict strongly what is observed in reality. Following the financial liberalization reform, Spain's current account deficit peaked at 3.4 percent of GDP.

The fact that these models predict *optimal* levels of the current account deficit that are an order of magnitude higher than those observed in the real world poses an important challenge for economists. A number of authors have tried to deal with these disturbing results by introducing adjustment costs and other type of rigidities into the analysis. Blanchard (1983), for example, developed a current account model with investment installation costs to investigate the dynamics of debt and the current account in a small developing economy, such as that of Brazil. A simulation of this model for feasible parameter values indicated that a country with Brazil's characteristics should accumulate foreign debt in excess of 300 percent of its gross national product (GNP). Moreover, according to this model, in the steady state the country in question should run a trade surplus equal to 10 percent of GDP. Although these numbers are not as extreme as those obtained from simple models without rigidities, they are quite implausible and are not usually observed in the real world. Fernandez de Cordoba and Kehoe (2000) introduced a series of extensions to their basic model in an effort to generate more plausible simulation results. They showed that it was not possible to improve the results by simply imposing a greater degree of curvature into the production possibility frontier. They also show that by assuming costly and slow factor mobility across sectors they could generate current account deficits in their simulation exercises that were more modest, although still very high from a historical perspective. More recently, a number of authors have developed models with borrowing constraints in an effort to generate current account paths that are closer to reality.

Policy Interpretations of the Intertemporal Approach

An important policy implication of the intertemporal perspective is that policy actions that result in higher investment opportunities will necessarily generate a deterioration in the country's current account. According to this view, however, this type of worsening of the current account balance should *not* be a cause for concern or for policy action. This reasoning led Sachs (1981, 243) to argue that the rapid increase in the developing coun-

---

7. Their analysis is carried out in terms of the trade account balance. In this model there are no differences between the trade and current account balances.

tries' foreign debt in the 1978–81 period was not a sign of increased vulnerability. It is interesting to quote Sachs extensively:

> The manageability of the LDC debt has been the subject of a large literature in recent years. If my analysis is correct, much of the growth in LDC debt reflects increased in investment and should not pose a problem of repayment. *The major borrowers have accumulated debt in the context of rising or stable, but not falling, saving rates.* This is particularly true for Brazil and Mexico. . . . (Sachs 1981, 243, emphasis added)

This view was also endorsed by Robischek (1981), one of the most senior and influential International Monetary Fund (IMF) officials during the 1970s and 1980s. Commenting on Chile's situation in 1981—a time when the country's current account deficit surpassed 14 percent of GDP—he argued that, to the extent that the public sector accounts were under control and that domestic saving was increasing, there was absolutely no reason to worry about major current account deficits. As it turned out, however, shortly after Robischek expressed his views, Chile entered into a deep financial crisis that ended with a major devaluation, the bankruptcy of the banking sector, and a GDP decline of 14 percent (see Edwards and Edwards 1991). The argument that a large current account deficit is not a cause of concern if the fiscal accounts are balanced has been associated with former Chancellor of the Exchequer Nigel Lawson and has come to be known as Lawson's Doctrine.

The respected Australian economist Max Corden has possibly been the most articulate exponent of the intertemporal policy view of the current account. In the important article "Does the Current Account Matter?" Corden (1994) makes a distinction between the "old" and "new" views on the current account. According to the former, "a country can run a current account deficit for a limited period. But no positive deficit is sustainable indefinitely" (Corden 1994, 88). The "new" view, on the other hand, makes a distinction between deficits that are the result of fiscal imbalances and those that respond to private sector decisions. According to the new view, "an increase in the current account deficit that results from a shift in private sector behavior—a rise in investment or a fall in savings—*should not be a matter of concern at all*" (Corden 1994, 92, emphasis added).

The eruption of the debt crisis in 1982 suggested that some of the more important policy implications of the new (intertemporal) view of the current account were subject to important flaws. Indeed, some of the countries affected by this crisis had run very large current account deficits in the presence of increasing investment rates or balanced fiscal accounts. In that regard, the case of Latin America is quite interesting. With the exception of oil producer Venezuela, current account deficits skyrocketed in 1981. This was the case in countries with increasing investment, such as Brazil and Mexico, as well as in countries with a balanced fiscal sector *and* rising investment, such as Chile.

1.2.3   Views on the Current Account in the Post-1982 Debt Crisis Period

In light of the debt crisis of 1982, a number of authors explicitly moved away from the implications of the Lawson Doctrine and argued that large current account deficits were often a sign of trouble to come, even if domestic savings were high and increasing. Fischer (1988) made this point forcefully in an article on real exchange rate overvaluation and currency crises: "The primary indicator [of a looming crisis] is the current account deficit. Large actual or projected current account deficits—or, for countries that have to make heavy debt repayments, insufficiently large surpluses— are a call for devaluation" (115). An important point raised by Fischer was that what matters is not whether there is a large deficit, but whether the country in question is running an "unsustainable" deficit. In his words, "if the current account deficit is 'unsustainable' . . . or if reasonable forecasts show that it will be unsustainable in the future, devaluation will be necessary sooner or later" (115). In the aftermath of the 1990s crises, (as will be discussed in section 1.3 of this paper) the issue of current account sustainability moved decisively to the center of the policy debate. In the years immediately following the 1982 debt crisis, Cline (1988) also emphasized the importance of current account deficits, as did Kamin (1988), whose extensive empirical work suggested that the trade and current accounts "deteriorated steadily through the year immediately prior to devaluation" (14). In their analysis of the Chilean crisis of 1982, Edwards and Edwards (1991) argued that Chile's experience—in which a 14 percent current account deficit was generated by private-sector–induced capital inflows—showed that the Lawson Doctrine was seriously flawed.

1.2.4   The Surge of Capital Inflows in the 1990s, the Current Account, and the Mexican Crisis

During much of the 1980s the majority of the developing countries were cut off from the international capital markets, and either ran current account surpluses or small deficits. This was even the case for the so-called East Asian Tigers, which had not been affected by the debt crisis. Indeed, between 1982 and 1990 Hong Kong, Korea, and Singapore posted current account surpluses, while Indonesia, Malaysia, the Philippines, and Thailand ran moderate deficits. Indonesia's and Thailand's deficits were the highest in the group, averaging 3.2 percent of GDP.

Starting in 1990, however, a large number of emerging countries were able once again to attract private capital. This was particularly the case in Latin America, where by 1992 the net volume of funds had become so large—exceeding 35 percent of the region's exports—that a number of analysts began to talk about Latin America's "capital inflows problem" (Calvo, Leiderman, and Reinhart 1993; Edwards 1993). Naturally, the counterpart of these large capital inflows was a significant widening in capital account deficits as well as a rapid accumulation of international reserves. During the first half of the 1990s, and in the midst of international capital abundance, there was a resurgence of Lawson's Doctrine in some policy circles. This was particularly the case in analyses of the evolution of the Mexican economy during the years preceding the peso crisis of 1994–95. In 1990 the international financial markets rediscovered Mexico, and large amounts of capital began flowing into the country. As a result, Mexico could finance significant current account deficits—in 1992–94 they averaged almost 7 percent of GDP. When some analysts pointed out that these deficits were very large, the Mexican authorities responded by arguing that, since the fiscal accounts were under control, there was no reason to worry. In 1993 the Bank of Mexico maintained that "the current account deficit has been determined exclusively by the private sector's decisions. . . . Because of the above and the solid position of public finances, *the current account deficit should clearly not be a cause for undue concern*" (179–80, emphasis added). In his recently published memoirs, former President Carlos Salinas de Gortari (2000) argues that the very large current account deficit was not a cause of the December 1994 crisis. According to him, two of the most influential cabinet members—Secretary of Commerce Jaime Serra and Secretary of Programming, and future president, Ernesto Zedillo—pointed out in the early 1990s that, since the public sector was in equilibrium, Mexico's large current account deficit was harmless.[8]

Not everyone, however, agreed with this position. In the 1994 Brookings Panel session on Mexico, Stanley Fischer argued that

[t]he Mexican current account deficit is huge, and it is being financed largely by portfolio investment. Those investments can turn around very quickly and leave Mexico with no choice but to devalue . . . [a]nd as the European and especially the Swedish experiences show, there may be no interest rate high enough to prevent an outflow and a forced devaluation. (1994, 306)

The World Bank staff expressed concern about the widening current account deficit. In *Trends in Developing Economies 1993,* the Bank staff wrote: "In 1992 about two-thirds of the widening of the current account deficit can be ascribed to lower private savings. . . . If this trend continues, it could renew fears about Mexico's inability to generate enough foreign exchange to service debt" (World Bank 1993, 330).

1.2.5   Views on the Current Account in the Post-1990s Currency Crashes

In the aftermath of the Mexican crisis of 1994, a large number of analysts maintained, once again, that Lawson's Doctrine was seriously flawed. In an address to the Board of Governors of the Interamerican Development

---

8. See Salinas de Gortari (2000), pages 1091–94.

Bank, Lawrence Summers (1996), then the U.S. deputy secretary of the treasury, was extremely explicit when he said, "current account deficits cannot be assumed to be benign because the private sector generated them" (46). This position was also taken by the IMF in postmortems of the Mexican debacle. In evaluating the role of the fund during the Mexican crisis, the director of the Western Hemisphere department and the chief of the Mexico division wrote: "[L]arge current account deficits, regardless of the factors underlying them[,] are likely to be unsustainable (Loser and Williams 1997, 268). According to Secretary Summers, "close attention should be paid to any current account deficit in excess of 5 percent of GDP, particularly if it is financed in a way that could lead to rapid reversals."

Whether "large" current account deficits were in fact a central cause of the East Asian debacle continues to be a somewhat controversial issue. Using the available evidence, in a recent comprehensive study Corsetti, Pesenti, and Roubini (1998) analyze the period leading to the East Asian crisis and argue that there is some support for the position that large current account deficits were one of the principal factors behind the crisis. According to them, *"as a group, the countries that came under attack in 1997 appear to have been those with large current account deficits throughout the 1990s"* (7, emphasis in the original). They then add in a rather guarded way, "prima facie evidence suggests that current account problems may have played a role in the dynamics of the Asian meltdown" (8). Radelet and Sachs (2000) have also argued that large current account deficits were an important factor leading to the crisis. Additionally, commenting on the eruption of the crisis in Thailand, the Chase Manhattan Bank (1997) argued that large current account deficits had been a basic cause of the crises. A close analysis of the data shows, however, that with the exceptions of Malaysia and Thailand the current account deficits were not very large. Take, for instance, the 1990–96 period: for the five East Asia crisis countries, the deficit exceeded the arbitrary 5 percent threshold only twelve out of thirty-five possible times. The frequency of occurrence is even lower for the two years preceding the crisis, at three out of ten possible times (Edwards 1999).

In view of the (perceived) limited importance of the current account, many authors have developed crisis models in which the current account deficit is not central. In Calvo (2000), for example, a currency crisis responds to financial fragilities in the country in question and is independent of the current account. A particularly important fragility is the mismatch between the maturity of banks' assets and obligations. Chang and Velasco (2000) have developed a series of models in which a crisis is the result of self-fulfilling expectations. A somewhat different line of research has emphasized the role of borrowing constraints. In this setting, the nationals of the country in question cannot borrow as much as they wish from the international financial market; an upward-sloping supply for foreign funds limits their ability to smooth consumption. An appealing feature of this type of model is that the optimal current account deficit does not take the implausible values generated by the small country models discussed above. Moreover, in borrowing constraints models, changes in the level of the borrowing constraint—generated by changes in the lender's expectations, for example—can indeed result in currency crises. A good example is Atkeson and Rios-Rull's (1996) model of a credit-constrained country. In this setting, current account problems may arise even if fiscal and monetary policies are consistent; a change in investors' perceptions is all that is necessary.

An important consequence of the 1990s currency crashes was that market participants, and in particular private investors, became concerned with the evolution of emerging nations' current account balances. This concern has been translated into formal efforts to develop models of current account "sustainability." The issue at hand has been succinctly put by Milesi-Ferretti and Razin (1996): "What persistent level of current account deficits should be considered sustainable? Conventional wisdom is that current account deficits above 5% of GDP flash a red light, in particular if the deficit is financed with short-term debt."

1.3   How Useful are Models of Current Account Sustainability?

As mentioned in the preceding section, in the aftermath of the Mexican crisis many analysts argued that the so-called "new" view of the current account, based on Lawson's Doctrine, was seriously flawed. While some, such as Bruno (1995), argued that large deficits stemming from higher investment (as in East Asia) were not particularly dangerous, others maintained that any deficit in excess of a certain threshold—say, 4 percent of GDP—was a cause for concern. Partially motivated by this debate, Milesi-Ferretti and Razin (1996) developed a framework to analyze current account sustainability. Their main point was that the "sustainable" level of the current account was that level consistent with solvency. This, in turn, means the level at which "the ratio of external debt to GDP is stabilized" (Milesi-Ferretti and Razin 1998). Analyses of current account sustainability have become particularly popular among investment banks. For instance, Goldman Sachs's GS-SCAD model developed in 1997 has become popular among analysts interested in assessing emerging nations' vulnerability. More recently, Deutsche Bank (2000) has developed a model of current account sustainability both to analyze whether a particular country's current account is "out of line" and to evaluate the appropriateness of its real exchange rate.

The basic idea behind sustainability exercises is captured by the following simple analysis. As pointed out, solvency requires that the ratio of the (net) international demand for the country's liabilities (both debt and nondebt liabilities) stabilize at a level compatible with foreigners' net demand for these claims on future income flows. Under standard portfolio theory, the net international demand for country j's liabilities can be written as

$$(4) \qquad \delta_j = \alpha_j(W - W_j) - (1 - \alpha_{jj})W_j,$$

where α_j is the percentage of world's wealth (W) that international investors are willing to hold in the form of country j's assets; W_j is country j's wealth (broadly defined), and α_{jj} is country j's asset allocation on its own assets. The asset allocation shares α_j and α_{jj} depend, as in standard portfolio analyses, on expected returns and perceived risk. Assuming that country's j wealth is a multiple λ of its (potential or full employment) GDP, and that country's j wealth is a fraction β_j of world's wealth W, it is possible to write the (international) net demand for country's j assets as[9]

$$(5) \qquad \delta_j = [\alpha_j \theta_j - (1 - \alpha_{jj})]\lambda_{jj} Y_j,$$

where Y_j is (potential) GDP, and $\theta_j = (1 - \beta_j)/\beta_j$. Denoting $\{[\alpha_j \theta_j - (1 - \alpha_{jj})]\lambda_{jj}\} = \gamma_j^*$, then,

$$(6) \qquad \delta_j = \gamma_j^* Y_j.$$

Equation (6) simply states that, in long-run equilibrium, the net international demand for country j's assets can be expressed as a proportion γ_j^* of the country's (potential or sustainable) GDP. The determinants of the factor of proportionality are given by equation (3) and, as expressed, include relative returns and perceived risk of country j and other countries.[10]

In this framework, and under the simplifying assumption that international reserves don't change, the "sustainable" current account ratio is given by[11]

$$(7) \qquad (C/Y)_j = (g_j + \pi_j^*) \{[\alpha_j \theta_j - (1 - \alpha_{jj})] \lambda_{jj}\},$$

where g_j is the country's sustainable rate of growth, and π_j^* is a valuation factor (approximately) equal to international inflation.[12] Notice that if $[\alpha_j \theta_j - (1 - \alpha_{jj})] < 0$, domestic residents' demand for foreign liabilities exceeds foreigners' demand for the country's liabilities. Under these circumstances, the country will have to run a current account surplus in order to maintain a stable (net external) liabilities-to-GDP ratio. Notice that according to equation (4) there is no reason for the "sustainable" current account deficit to be the same across countries. In fact, that would only happen by sheer coincidence. The main message of equation (4) is that "sustainable" current

9. This expression will hold for every period t; I have omitted the subscript t in order to economize on notation.

10. The assumptions of constant λ and θ are, of course, highly simplifying.

11. As a result of this assumption, equation (6) overstates (slightly) the "sustainable" current account ratio.

12. Under the restrictive assumption that international inflation is equal to zero, this expression corresponds exactly to Goldman Sachs's equation (8). See Ades and Kaune (1997, 6).

Table 1.1   External World's Desired Holdings of a Country's Liabilities
                   (% of GDP)

Country	Desired Holding
Argentina	48.4
Brazil	38.3
Bulgaria	42.8
Chile	48.4
China	129.2
Colombia	38.3
Czech Republic	31.3
Ecuador	31.3
Hungary	31.3
India	47.2
Indonesia	53.9
Korea	55.4
Malaysia	53.9
Mexico	38.3
Morocco	31.9
Panama	38.3
Peru	48.4
The Philippines	57.1
Poland	55.4
Romania	38.3
Russia	38.3
South Africa	38.3
Thailand	64.6
Turkey	38.3
Venezuela	38.3

Source: Goldman Sachs.

account balances vary across countries and depend on whatever variables affect portfolio decisions and economic growth. In other words, the notion that no country can run a sustainable deficit in excess of 4 or 5 percent of GDP, or any other arbitrary number, is nonsense.

Using a very similar framework to the one developed above, Goldman Sachs has made a serious effort to actually estimate long-run sustainable current account deficits for a number of countries (Ades and Kaune 1997). Using a twenty-five-country data set, Goldman Sachs estimated the ratio of external liabilities foreigners are willing to hold—γ_j^* in the model sketched above—as well as each country's potential rate of growth. Table 1.1 contains Goldman Sachs's estimates of γ_j^*, while table 1.2 presents their estimates of long-run sustainable current account deficits. In addition to estimating these steady-state imbalances, Goldman Sachs calculated asymptotic convergence paths toward those long-run current accounts. These are presented in table 1.2 under short-run sustainable balances. Several interesting features emerge from these tables. First, there is a wide vari-

Table 1.2   **Sustainable Current Account Deficit (SCAD) (% of GDP)**

Country	1997 CAD	SCAD	Steady-State SCAD
Argentina	2.7	3.9	2.9
Brazil	4.5	2.9	1.9
Bulgaria	−2.6	0.4	2.4
Chile	3.7	4.2	2.9
China	−1.4	12.9	11.1
Colombia	4.8	2.6	1.9
Czech Republic	8.6	2.1	1.3
Ecuador	2.0	−0.5	1.3
Hungary	4.0	0.8	1.3
India	1.8	3.8	2.8
Indonesia	3.0	4.0	3.4
Korea	3.8	4.9	3.6
Malaysia	4.1	4.9	3.4
Mexico	1.7	2.1	1.9
Morocco	1.8	0.3	1.3
Panama	6.1	0.8	1.9
Peru	5.1	3.3	2.9
The Philippines	4.2	4.5	3.8
Poland	3.8	4.7	3.6
Romania	0.5	2.3	1.9
Russia	−2.8	2.5	1.9
South Africa	1.8	3.0	1.9
Thailand	5.4	6.0	4.5
Turkey	1.2	2.1	1.9
Venezuela	−4.6	2.2	1.9

Source: Goldman Sachs.

ety of estimated long-run "sustainable" deficits. Second, with the notable exception of China—whose estimated "sustainable" deficit is an improbable 11 percent of GDP—the estimated levels are very modest, ranging from 1.9 to 4.5 percent of GDP. Third, although the range for the short-run sustainable level is broader, in very few countries does it exceed 4 percent of GDP. Fourth, the estimates of the ratio of the external liabilities foreigners are willing to hold for each country—γ_j^* in the model sketched above—exhibit more variability. Here the range (excluding China) goes from 31.5 to 64.6 percent of GDP.

Although this type of analysis represents an improvement with respect to arbitrary current account thresholds, it is subject to a number of serious limitations, including the fact that it is exceedingly difficult to obtain reliable estimates for the key variables. In particular, there is very little evidence on equilibrium portfolio shares. Also, the underlying models used for calculating the long-run growth tend to be very simplistic.

The most serious limitation of this framework, however, is that it does not take into account, in a satisfactory way, transitional issues arising from changes in portfolio allocations. These can have a fundamental effect on the way in which the economy adjusts to changes in the external environment. For example, the speed at which a country absorbs surges in foreigners' demand for its liabilities will have an effect on the sustainable path of the current account (Bacchetta and van Wincoop 2000).

The key point is that even small changes in foreigners' net demand for the country's liabilities may generate complex equilibrium adjustment paths for the current account. These current account movements will be necessary for the new portfolio allocation to materialize and will not generate a disequilibrium, or unsustainable balance. However, when this equilibrium path of the current account is contrasted with threshold levels obtained from models, such as the one sketched above, analysts could (incorrectly) conclude that the country is facing a serious disequilibrium.

In order to illustrate this point, assume that equation (8) captures the way in which the current account responds to change in portfolio allocations. In this equation, γ_t^* is the new desired level (relative to GDP) of foreigners' (net) desired holdings of the country's liabilities; γ_{t-1}^*, on the other hand, is the old desired level.

$$(8) \quad (C/Y)_t = (g + \pi^*)\,\gamma_t^* + \beta(\gamma_t^* - \gamma_{t-1}^*) - \eta[(C/Y)_{t-1} - (g + \pi^*)\,\gamma_t^*],$$

where, as before, $\gamma^* = \{[\alpha_j\,\theta_j - (1 - \alpha_{jj})]\lambda_{jj}\}$. According to this equation, short-term deviations of the current account from its long-run level can result from two forces. The first is a traditional stock adjustment term, $(\gamma_t^* - \gamma_{t-1}^*)$, that captures deviations between the demanded and the actual stock of assets. If $\gamma_t^* > \gamma_{t-1}^*$, then the current account deficit will exceed its long-run value. The speed of adjustment, β, will depend on a number of factors, including the degree of capital mobility in the country in question and the maturity of its foreign debt. The second force, which is captured by $-\eta\,[(C/Y)_{t-1} - (g + \pi^*)\,\gamma_t^*]$ in equation (7), is a self-correcting term. This term plays the role of making sure that in this economy there is some form of "consumption smoothing." The importance of this self-correcting term will depend on the value of η. If $\eta = 0$, the self-correcting term will play no role, and the dynamics of the current account will be given by a more traditional stock adjustment equation. In the more general case, however, when both β and η are different from zero, the dynamics of the current account will be richer, and discrepancies between γ_t^* and γ_{t-1}^* will be resolved gradually through time.

As may be seen from equation (8), in the long-run steady state, when ($\gamma_t^* = \gamma_{t-1}^*$) and $(CY)_{t-1} = C/Y$, the current account will be at its sustainable level, $(g + \pi^*)\,\{[\alpha_j\,\theta_j - (1 - \alpha_{jj})]\,\lambda_{jj}\}$. The dynamic behavior for the net stock of the country's assets in the hands of foreigners, as a percentage of GDP, will be given by equation (9).

$$(9) \qquad \gamma_t = \frac{\gamma_{t-1} + (C/Y)_t}{1 + g + \pi^*}.$$

The implications of incorporating the adjustment process can be illustrated with a simple example based on the Goldman Sachs computations presented above. Notice that according to the figures in table 1.1, by the end of 1996 there was a significant gap between Goldman Sachs's estimates of foreigners' desired holdings of Mexican and Argentine liabilities: Although the Mexican ratio stood at 38.3 percent of the country's GDP, the corresponding figure for Argentina was 48.4 percent. Assume that for some reason—a reduction in perceived Mexican country risk, for example—this gap is closed to one-half of its initial level and that the demand for Mexican liabilities increases to 43 percent of Mexican GDP. Figure 1.1 presents the estimated evolution of the sustainable current account path under the assumptions that Mexican growth remains at 5 percent and that world inflation is zero—both assumptions made by Goldman Sachs. In addition, it is assumed that $\beta = 0.65$, $\eta = 0.45$, and that the increase in γ^* is spread over three years.

The results from this simple exercise are quite interesting: First, as may be seen, the initial level of the sustainable current account level is equal to 1.9 percent of GDP, exactly the level estimated by Goldman Sachs (see table 1.2). Second, the current account converges to 2.15 percent of GDP, as suggested by equation (7). Third, and more important for the analysis in this section, the dynamic of the current account is characterized by a sizable overshooting, with the "equilibrium path" deficit peaking at 3.5 percent of GDP. If, on the other hand, it is assumed that the increase in γ^* takes place in one period, the equilibrium deficit would peak at a level in excess of 5 percent, a figure twice as large as the new long-term sustainable level. What makes this exercise particularly interesting is that these rather large overshootings are the result of very small changes in portfolio preferences. This strongly suggests that in a world where desired portfolio shares are constantly changing, the concept of a sustainable equilibrium current account path is very difficult to estimate. Moreover, this simple exercise indicates that relying on current account ratios—even ratios calculated using current "sustainability" frameworks—can be highly misleading. These dynamic features of current account adjustment may explain why so many authors have failed to find a direct connection between current account deficits and crises.

The analysis presented above suggests two important dimensions of adjustment and crisis prevention. First, current account dynamics will affect real exchange rate behavior. More specifically, current account overshooting will be associated with a temporary real exchange rate appreciation. The actual magnitude of this appreciation will depend on a number of variables, including the income demand elasticity for nontradables and the labor intensity of the nontradable sector. In order for this dynamic adjustment to be smooth, the country should have the ability to implement the required real exchange rate depreciation in the second phase of the process. This is

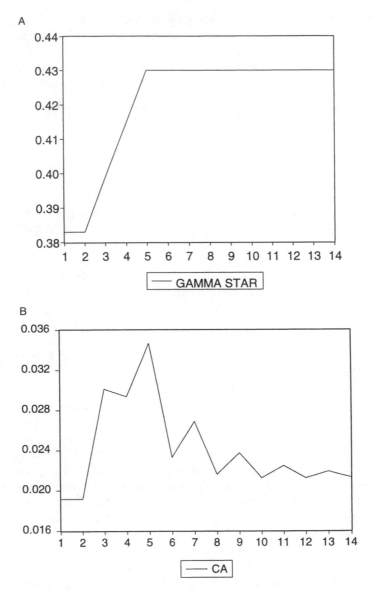

Fig. 1.1   On the equilibrium path of the current account deficit: A simulation exercise;
A, **Assumed evolution of foreigners' net demand for Mexico's liabilities;** ***B,*** **Simulated equilibrium path of Mexico's current account deficit**

likely to be easier under a flexible exchange rate regime than under a rigid one. Second, if foreigners' (net) demand for the country's liabilities declines—as is likely to be the case if there is some degree of contagion, for example—the required current account compression will also overshoot. In the immediate future the country will have to go through a very severe adjustment. This can be illustrated by the following simple example. Assume that as a result of external events—a crisis in Brazil, say—the demand for Argentine liabilities declines from the level estimated by Goldman Sachs, 48.4 percent of GDP, to 40 percent of GDP. While the long-run equilibrium current account, as calculated by Goldman Sachs, would experience a very modest decline from 2.9 percent to 2.4 percent of GDP, in the short run the adjustment would be drastic. In fact, the simple model developed above suggests that after two years the deficit would have to be compressed to approximately 0.5 percent of GDP.[13]

1.4   Current Account Behavior Since the 1970s

In this section I provide a broad analysis of current account behavior in both emerging and advanced countries. The section deals with three specific issues: (1) the distribution of the current account across regions, (2) the persistence of high current account deficits, and (3), a detailed analysis of current account reversals and their costs. The discussion of the relationship, if any, between current account deficits and financial crises is the subject of section 1.5.

1.4.1   The Distribution of Current Account Deficits in the World Economy

In this subsection I use data for 149 countries during 1970–97 to analyze some basic aspects of current account behavior. I am particularly interested in understanding the magnitudes of deficits through time. This first look at the data should help answer questions such as "From a historical point of view, is 4 percent of GDP a large current account deficit?" and "Historically, for how long have countries been able to run 'large' current account deficits?" The data are from the World Bank comparative data set. However, when data taken from the IMF's *International Financial Statistics* are used, the results obtained are very similar. Throughout the analysis I have concentrated on the current account *deficit* as a percentage of GDP; that is, in what follows, a positive number means that the country in question, for that particular year, has run a current account deficit. In order to organize the discussion I have divided the data into six regions: (1) industrialized countries, (2) Latin America and the Caribbean, (3) Asia, (4) Africa, (5) the Middle

---

13. This assumes that growth is not affected. If, as is likely, it declines, the required compression would be even larger.

Table 1.3   Number of Observations per Region Used in Current Account Analysis

Year	Industrialized	Latin America	Asia	Africa	Middle East	Eastern Europe	Total
1970	8	5	5	2	2	0	22
1971	9	6	5	2	3	0	25
1972	10	6	6	2	3	0	27
1973	10	6	6	2	3	0	27
1974	11	7	7	10	4	1	40
1975	18	10	9	18	5	1	61
1976	20	17	10	23	8	1	79
1977	22	25	11	32	9	1	100
1978	22	27	11	36	9	1	106
1979	21	29	12	37	9	1	109
1980	21	32	13	40	10	3	119
1981	22	32	15	41	10	3	123
1982	22	32	15	42	10	4	125
1983	22	32	15	42	10	4	125
1984	22	33	17	42	10	5	129
1985	22	33	17	44	10	5	131
1986	22	31	17	45	10	5	130
1987	22	32	17	47	10	6	134
1988	22	32	17	47	10	6	134
1989	22	32	17	47	10	6	134
1990	22	32	17	46	11	6	134
1991	23	32	17	45	10	7	134
1992	23	33	18	44	10	13	141
1993	23	33	18	44	10	18	146
1994	23	33	18	44	11	20	149
1995	23	31	18	36	11	20	139
1996	23	26	18	28	7	21	123
1997	20	17	18	22	7	19	103
Total	550	696	384	910	232	177	2,949

Source: Author's calculations.

East and Northern Africa, and (6) Eastern Europe. In table 1.3 I present the number of countries in each region and year for which data are available. This table summarizes the largest data set that can be used in empirical work. As will be specified later, in some of the empirical exercises I have restricted the data set to countries with populations above half a million people and income per capita above US$500 in 1985 purchasing power parity (PPP) terms. For a list of the countries included in the analysis, see the appendix.

Tables 1.4, 1.5, and 1.6 contain basic data on current account deficits by region for the period 1970–97. In table 1.4 I present averages by region and year. Table 1.5 contains medians, and in table 1.6 I present the 3rd quartile by year and region. I have used the data on the 3rd quartile presented in this table as cutoff points to define "high deficit" countries. Later in this section I analyze the persistence of high deficits in each of the six regions.

Table 1.4   Average Current Account to GDP Deficit Ratios, by Region, 1970–97

Year	Industrialized	Latin America	Asia	Africa	Middle East	Eastern Europe	Total
1970	−0.02	7.59	−0.52	0.92	7.86	n.a.	2.40
1971	−0.28	5.59	0.08	5.25	−0.13	n.a.	1.66
1972	−1.54	3.86	1.80	6.16	−4.39	n.a.	0.66
1973	−1.18	3.40	0.53	7.18	0.61	n.a.	1.04
1974	3.00	3.30	3.55	−3.22	−10.14	1.50	0.24
1975	1.49	2.44	2.02	4.72	−9.52	3.52	1.81
1976	2.20	1.42	0.81	5.70	−10.59	3.81	1.60
1977	1.86	4.09	0.90	3.77	−5.88	5.15	2.26
1978	0.52	3.39	2.82	8.62	0.77	1.88	4.28
1979	1.43	4.28	3.54	6.51	−8.18	1.54	3.35
1980	2.22	7.13	9.40	7.12	−9.02	2.06	5.02
1981	2.47	10.15	10.15	10.68	−8.00	3.17	7.30
1982	2.41	9.09	9.94	12.38	−1.67	1.46	8.02
1983	1.24	6.39	9.52	8.76	1.61	1.47	6.11
1984	0.99	4.16	5.83	6.19	1.32	0.40	4.14
1985	1.17	2.72	4.67	6.44	1.45	1.54	3.82
1986	0.98	5.44	3.60	6.60	1.30	2.80	4.43
1987	1.04	5.37	2.24	4.75	1.25	0.17	3.51
1988	0.91	4.28	1.65	5.80	0.54	−1.05	3.41
1989	1.20	5.28	2.85	4.64	−2.99	0.33	3.24
1990	1.18	4.59	2.31	4.51	−4.73	2.96	2.88
1991	0.68	7.19	2.56	4.79	n.a.	1.78	6.26
1992	0.44	5.47	2.33	6.31	7.90	−0.14	4.17
1993	−0.45	5.89	5.10	6.75	5.64	1.26	4.46
1994	−0.35	4.65	3.38	6.47	−0.31	0.91	3.39
1995	−0.32	4.43	5.07	8.00	−1.63	2.59	3.91
1996	−0.44	5.29	4.33	8.51	−2.60	6.45	4.56
1997	−0.66	3.87	3.79	4.57	−3.89	6.51	3.09
Total	0.87	5.28	4.12	6.56	−0.40	2.52	4.09

Source: Computed by the author using raw data obtained from the World Bank.
Note: A positive number denotes a current account deficit. A negative number represents a surplus.
n.a. = not available.

A number of interesting features of current account behavior emerge from these tables. First, after the 1973 oil shock, there were important changes in current account balances in the industrial nations, the Middle East, and Africa. Interestingly, no discernible change can be detected in Latin America or Asia. Second, and in contrast to the previous point, the 1979 oil shock seems to have affected current account balances in every region in the world. The impact of this shock was particularly severe in Latin America, where the deficit jumped from an average of 3.4 percent of GDP in 1978 to over 10 percent of GDP in 1981. Third, these tables capture vividly the magnitude of the external adjustment undertaken by the emerging economies in the 1980s. What is particularly interesting is that, contrary

Table 1.5   Median Current Account to GDP Deficit Ratios, by Region, 1970–97

Year	Industrialized	Latin America	Asia	Africa	Middle East	Eastern Europe	Total
1970	−0.41	4.06	0.94	0.92	7.86	n.a.	0.86
1971	−0.51	4.83	1.10	5.25	5.74	n.a.	1.08
1972	−1.06	1.70	1.57	6.16	2.88	n.a.	0.44
1973	0.18	1.24	0.77	7.18	5.42	n.a.	0.95
1974	2.94	4.10	3.02	2.39	0.14	1.50	2.97
1975	1.34	4.52	3.23	6.56	−2.73	3.52	3.40
1976	2.71	1.41	0.62	5.00	−6.65	3.81	3.27
1977	2.11	3.80	−0.03	4.24	−3.71	5.15	2.84
1978	0.68	3.48	2.74	9.95	3.01	1.88	3.60
1979	0.66	4.68	3.73	6.52	−8.89	1.54	3.32
1980	2.35	5.59	5.03	8.36	−3.96	4.95	4.66
1981	2.73	9.06	5.92	10.09	1.46	2.72	6.58
1982	2.02	7.60	5.10	9.85	−1.53	1.88	6.41
1983	0.88	4.70	7.18	6.59	5.10	1.48	4.33
1984	0.22	3.66	2.12	3.76	4.89	1.43	2.51
1985	0.98	2.07	3.13	4.42	2.61	1.51	2.91
1986	−0.12	2.99	2.42	3.76	2.30	1.93	2.68
1987	0.42	4.15	1.34	5.22	3.04	0.76	2.61
1988	1.15	2.25	2.68	5.50	2.00	0.72	2.66
1989	1.54	4.41	3.35	3.76	−0.39	1.70	2.85
1990	1.60	3.00	3.41	3.78	−0.58	3.69	2.83
1991	0.91	4.83	3.17	3.64	9.74	0.70	3.02
1992	0.86	4.34	1.94	5.65	7.29	0.40	3.01
1993	0.55	4.60	4.18	6.81	4.20	1.58	3.18
1994	−0.37	3.19	4.63	5.65	−0.38	1.39	2.49
1995	−0.71	3.90	4.91	4.81	−2.14	1.99	2.70
1996	−0.56	3.97	4.76	4.15	−0.99	4.50	3.28
1997	−0.57	4.12	3.61	3.71	−2.39	6.29	2.94
Total	0.77	4.12	3.14	5.33	1.95	1.93	3.17

Source: Computed by the author using raw data obtained from the World Bank.
Note: n.a. = not available

to popular folklore, this adjustment was not confined to the Latin American region. Indeed, the nations of Asia and Africa also experienced severe reductions in their deficits during this period. Fourth, the industrialized countries regained sustained surpluses only after 1993. Finally, during the most recent period, current account deficits have been rather modest from a historical perspective. This has been the case in every region, with the important exception of Eastern Europe.

The data on 3rd quartiles presented in table 1.6 show that 25 percent of the countries in our sample had, at one point or another, a current account deficit in excess of 7.22 percent of GDP. Naturally, as the table shows, the 3rd quartile differs for each region and year, with the largest values corresponding to Africa and Latin America. I use the 3rd-quartile data in table

Table 1.6   **Third Quartile of Current Account to GDP Deficit Ratios, by Region, 1970–97**

Year	Industrialized	Latin America	Asia	Africa	Middle East	Eastern Europe	Total
1970	0.64	6.86	1.28	1.93	9.85	n.a.	4.06
1971	0.43	7.77	1.74	8.28	9.31	n.a.	4.55
1972	0.30	2.37	3.63	11.96	5.30	n.a.	2.59
1973	1.33	4.12	1.30	9.99	5.81	n.a.	4.12
1974	4.41	10.05	5.61	4.64	14.44	1.50	5.52
1975	4.46	6.78	5.06	8.44	13.98	3.52	7.75
1976	4.38	4.23	6.19	8.80	4.36	3.81	5.47
1977	3.62	7.37	4.49	7.86	2.47	5.15	6.35
1978	2.50	7.07	4.80	12.85	9.17	1.88	9.17
1979	2.76	6.60	6.57	12.30	5.17	1.54	7.62
1980	3.70	12.92	8.46	13.11	2.63	5.99	10.60
1981	4.32	15.06	10.04	12.85	5.85	7.38	11.76
1982	4.05	11.74	11.49	14.48	8.26	2.63	10.57
1983	2.41	8.33	9.01	12.39	7.73	2.61	8.33
1984	3.08	6.56	4.88	8.78	8.17	1.46	5.69
1985	3.75	6.05	4.82	9.68	7.45	1.85	6.42
1986	3.51	7.75	5.16	8.19	9.36	4.69	6.44
1987	3.24	8.79	4.07	9.69	6.35	2.53	6.35
1988	3.03	7.67	4.30	9.49	4.65	1.75	6.51
1989	3.60	7.61	5.91	7.02	5.43	2.02	5.69
1990	3.37	7.64	6.08	8.93	2.77	8.25	6.13
1991	2.78	11.57	6.61	9.05	17.96	3.51	7.57
1992	2.67	8.04	4.70	9.01	15.72	3.68	6.86
1993	1.65	8.81	6.42	8.80	11.45	4.45	7.86
1994	1.83	7.27	6.46	8.88	6.62	3.57	6.50
1995	1.64	5.42	8.06	10.42	4.24	5.54	6.61
1996	1.83	7.02	8.10	9.25	3.32	9.16	7.60
1997	1.91	5.93	6.89	7.05	2.94	11.07	6.29
1998							
Total	3.06	8.16	6.37	10.09	7.14	4.84	7.22

Source: Computed by the author using raw data obtained from the World Bank.
Note: n.a. = not available

1.6 to define "large current account deficit" countries. In particular, if during a given year a particular country's deficit exceeds its region's 3rd quartile, I classify it as being a "high-deficit country."[14] An important policy question is how persistent high deficits are. I deal with this issue in table 1.7, where I have listed those countries that have had a "high current account deficit" for at least *five years in a row*. The results are quite interesting and indicate that a rather small number of countries experienced very long periods of high deficits. In fact, I could detect only eleven countries with high

14. Notice, however, that the actual cutoff points correspond to fairly large deficits even for the Middle Eastern countries.

Table 1.7   Countries with Persistently High Current Account Deficits, by Region, 1975–97

Region	Period
Industrialized Countries	
Australia	1981–97
Canada	1989–94
Greece	1979–85
Ireland	1976–85
Malta	1993–97
New Zealand	1975–88, 1993–97
Latin America and the Caribbean	
Grenada	1986–96
Guyana	1979–85
Honduras	1975–79
Nicaragua	1980–90
Asia	
Bhutan	1981–97
Laos	1980–90
Maldives	1980–85
Nepal	1985–97
Vietnam	1993–97
Africa	
Congo	1990–97
Côte D'Ivoire	1980–92
Equatorial Guinea	1987–91
Guinea-Bissau	1982–94
Mali	1984–89
Mauritania	1975–88
Mozambique	1986–96
São Tomé	1981–90
Somalia	1982–87
Sudan	1990–97
Swaziland	1978–85
Tanzania	1990–97
Middle East	
Cyprus	1977–81
Eastern Europe	
None	

Source: Computed by the author.

Note: The countries in this list have had a "high current account deficit" for at least five years in a row. See the text for the exact definition of "high current account deficit."

deficits for ten or more years. Of these, five are in Africa, three are in Asia, and, perhaps surprisingly, only two are in Latin America and the Caribbean. Interestingly enough, Australia and New Zealand are among the very small group of countries with a streak of high current account deficits in excess of ten years. In the subsection that follows I will analyze some of the most important characteristics of deficits reversals.

1.4.2   Current Account Reversals: How Common, How Costly?

In this section I provide an analysis of current account reversals. In particular I ask three questions: First, how common are large current account deficit reversals? Second, from a historical point of view, have these reversals been associated with currency or financial crashes? Third, how costly, in terms of economic performance indicators, have these reversals been? With respect to this third point, I argue that the most severe effect of current account reversals on economic performance takes place indirectly, through their impact on investment. The analysis presented in this subsection complements the results in a recent important paper by Milesi-Ferretti and Razin (2000).[15]

I use two alternative definitions of current account reversals: *Reversal1* is defined as a reduction in the deficit of at least three percent of GDP in one year, and *Reversal2* is defined as a reduction of the deficit of at least 3 percent of GDP in a *three-year* period. Due to space considerations, the results reported here correspond to those obtained when the *Reversal1* definition was used. However, the results obtained under the alternative—and less strict—definition, *Reversal2,* were very similar to those discussed in this subsection.[16]

The first question I ask is how common reversals are. This issue is addressed in table 1.8, where I present tabulations by region, as well as for the complete sample, for the *Reversal1* variable. As may be seen, for the sample as a whole the incidence of "reversals" was equal to 16.7 percent of the yearly episodes. This reversal occurrence varied across regions; not surprisingly, given the definition of reversals, the lowest incidence is in the industrialized countries (6 percent). The two highest regions are Africa and the Middle East, with 27 and 26 percent of reversals respectively. Both from a theoretical and from a policy perspective, it is important to determine whether these reversals are short lived or sustained. Short-term reversals may be the result of consumption smoothing, while more permanent ones are likely to be the consequence of policy-related external adjustments. I address this issue by asking in how many "reversal" cases the current account deficit was still lower three years after the reversal was detected. The answer lies in the two-way tabulation tables presented in table 1.9.[17] These results indicate that, for the sample as a whole, 45 percent of the "reversals" were translated into a medium-term (three-year) improvement in the current account balance. The degree of permanency of these reversals varied by re-

---

15. My data set, however, is larger than that of Milesi-Ferretti and Razin (2000).

16. These definitions of reversal are somewhat different from those used by Milesi-Ferretti and Razin (2000).

17. This table includes only countries whose population is greater than half a million people and whose GDP per capita is above $500. It also excludes countries whose current account was in surplus.

Table 1.8   **Current Account Reversals: Tabulations by Region, 1970–97**

	Frequency	Percent	Cumulative
Industrialized			
0	451	93.96	93.96
1	29	6.04	100.00
Total	480	100.00	
Latin America			
0	359	81.04	81.04
1	84	18.96	100.00
Total	443	100.00	
Asia			
0	250	85.91	85.91
1	41	14.09	100.00
Total	291	100.00	
Africa			
0	230	72.56	72.56
1	87	27.44	100.00
Total	317	100.00	
Middle East			
0	156	74.29	74.29
1	54	25.71	100.00
Total	210	100.00	
Eastern Europe			
0	134	85.90	85.90
1	22	14.10	100.00
Total	156	100.00	
All countries			
0	1580	83.29	83.29
1	317	16.71	100.00
Total	1897	100.00	

Source: Author's calculations.

Note: Reversals are defined as a reduction in the deficit of at least 3 percent of GDP in one year. A number 1 captures reversals. The data set has been restricted to countries with populations in excess of half a million people and GDP per capita over $500 at PPP value.

gion, however. In the advanced countries, 75 percent of the reversals were sustained after three years; the smallest percentage corresponds to the Latin American nations, where only 37 percent of the reversals were sustained after three years.

In their influential paper, Milesi-Ferretti and Razin (2000) analyzed the effects of current account reversals on economic performance and in particular on GDP growth. They relied on two methods to address this issue. They first used a "before and after" approach and tentatively concluded that "reversals in current account deficits are not necessarily associated with domestic output compression" (302). Since "before and after" analyses are subject to a number of serious shortcomings, Milesi-Ferretti and Razin also address the issue by estimating a number of multiple regressions

Table 1.9   **Current Account Reversals and Medium-Term Improvement**

CAD Improvement	Reversal in 1 year (Greater than 3%)		
	0	1	Total
Industrial			
0	128	5	133
1	156	12	168
Total	284	17	301
Latin America			
0	156	33	189
1	174	19	193
Total	330	52	382
Asia			
0	137	18	155
1	116	13	129
Total	253	31	284
Africa			
0	211	72	283
1	231	61	292
Total	442	133	575
Middle East			
0	45	11	56
1	62	8	70
Total	107	19	126
Eastern Europe			
0	67	6	73
1	36	6	42
Total	103	12	115

Source: Author's calculations.
Note: CAD improvement is in a three-year period, forward.

on different samples. Their dependent variable is the rate of per capita output growth, and the independent variables include a measure of exchange rate overvaluation, an index of openness, the level of indebtedness, initial GDP, and the investment-to-GDP ratio, among others. After analyzing the results obtained from this regression analysis, the authors argue that "reversals . . . are not systematically associated with a growth slowdown" (303).

Milesi-Ferretti and Razin (2000) reach this conclusion after estimating growth equations that control for investment (among other variables). It is highly probable, however, that current account reversals affect *investment itself,* and that through this channel they affect real GDP growth. The reason for this potential effect of reversals is rather simple: investment is financed by the sum of national and foreign saving. The latter, of course, is exactly equal to the current account deficit. Thus, any current account reversal will imply a reduction in foreign saving. What will happen to aggregate saving, and thus to investment, will depend on the relationship between foreign and national saving. The existing empirical evidence on this matter strongly suggests that foreign saving partially, and only partially, crowds out domestic saving. Edwards (1996), for example, estimated a number of private saving equations for developing countries and found that the coefficient of the current account deficit was significant and in the neighborhood of –0.4. Loayza, Schmidt-Hebbel, and Servén (2000) used a new data set on private savings in emerging economies and estimated that the coefficient of the current account deficit was –0.33 and highly significant. These results, then, suggest that a decline in foreign saving—that is, a lower current account deficit—will reduce aggregate saving and, thus, aggregate investment. Since there is ample evidence supporting the idea that investment has a positive effect on growth, the previous argument would suggest that, in contrast with Milesi-Ferretti and Razin's (2000) claim, current account reversals will have a negative, albeit indirect, effect on growth.

In order to investigate whether indeed current account reversals have affected aggregate investment negatively, I estimated a number of investment equations using panel data for a large number of countries for the period 1970–97. The recent empirical literature on investment, including Attanasio, Picci, and Scorcu (2000), indicates that investment exhibits a strong degree of persistence through time. This suggests estimating equations of the following type:[18]

$$(10)\quad \text{INVGDP}_{tj} = \beta\,\text{INVGDP}_{t-1,j} + \delta\,\text{GOVCONS}_{tj}$$
$$+\ \phi\,\text{TRADE\_OPENNESS}_{tj} + \gamma\,\text{REVERSAL}_{tj} + \omega_{tj},$$

where INVGDP is the investment-to-GDP ratio, GOVCONS is the ratio of government expenditure to GDP, and TRADE_OPENNESS is an index that captures the degree of openness of the economy. REVERSAL is a variable that takes the value of 1 if the country in question has been subject to a current account reversal, and 0 otherwise.[19] Finally, ω is an error term, which takes the following form:

$$\omega_{tj} = \varepsilon_j + \mu_{tj},$$

where ε_j is a country-specific error term and μ_{tj} is an independently and identically distributed (i.i.d.) disturbance with the standard characteristics.

The estimation of equation (10) presents two problems. First, it is well known from early work on dynamic panel estimation by Nerlove (1971) that if the error contains a country-specific term, the coefficient of the lagged de-

---

18. On recent attempts to estimate investment equations using a cross section of countries see, for example, Barro and Sala-i-Martin (1995) and Attanasio, Picci, and Scorcu (2000).

19. In principle, the log of initial GDP may also be included. However, because of the panel nature of the data, and given the estimation procedures used, this is not possible.

pendent variable will be biased upward. There are several ways of handling this potential problem. Possibly the most basic approach is using a fixed effect model, in which a country dummy (one hopes) picks up the effect of the country-specific disturbance. A second way is to estimate the instrumental variables procedure recently proposed by Arellano and Bond (1991) for dynamic panel data. This method consists of differentiating the equation in question, equation (10) in our case, in order to eliminate the country-specific disturbance ε_j. The differenced equation is then estimated using instrumental variables, where the lagged dependent variable (in levels), the predetermined variables (also in levels), and the first differences of the exogenous variables are used as instruments. In this paper I report results from the estimation of equation (10) using both a fixed effect procedure and the Arellano and Bond method.

A second problem in estimating equation (10) is that, since current account reversals are not drawn from a random experiment, the REVERSAL$_{jt}$ dummy is possibly correlated with the error term. Under these circumstances, the estimated coefficients in equation (10) will be biased and misleading. In order to deal with this problem I follow the procedure recently suggested by Heckman, Ichimura, and Todd (1997, 1998) for estimating "treatment interventions" models. This procedure consists of estimating the equation in question using observations that have a common support for both the treated and the nontreated. In the case at hand, countries that experience a reversal are considered to be subject to the "treatment intervention." From a practical point of view, a two-step procedure is used. First, the conditional probability of countries facing a reversal, called the *propensity score,* is first estimated using a probit regression. Second, the equation of interest is estimated using only observations whose estimated probability of reversal falls within the interval of estimated probabilities for countries with actual reversals. I follow the Heckman, Ichimura, and Todd (1997, 1998) sample correction both for the fixed effect and the Arellano and Bond procedures. In estimating the propensity scores I used a panel data probit procedure and included as regressors the level of the current account deficit in the previous period, the level of the fiscal deficit, domestic credit creation, and time-specific dummies. The results obtained from this first step are not presented here due to space consideration but are available on request. Table 1.10 contains the results of estimating investment equation (10) on an unbalanced panel of 128 countries for the period 1971–97. In part A of table 1.10 I present the results obtained from the estimation of the Arellano-Bond instrumental variables procedure. In part B of table 1.10 I present the results from the fixed effect estimation. In both cases I have introduced the REVERSALS indicator both contemporaneously and with a one-period lag. In the Arellano-Bond estimates, the standard errors have been computed using White's robust procedure that corrects for

Table 1.10   **Investment and Current Account Reversals**

INVGDP	Coeff.	Robust Std. Err.	z	$P > |z|$	95% Conf. Interval	
A. Arellano-Bond Instrumental Variables[a]						
INVGDP LD	0.6212481	0.0835012	7.44	0.000	0.4575887	0.7849075
GOVCON D1	0.0819257	0.0106311	0.77	0.441	−0.1264401	0.2902916
REV D1	−2.021207	0.2545002	−7.94	0.000	−2.520018	−1.522396
REVLAG	−0.8834781	0.2235849	−3.95	0.000	−1.321696	−0.4452596
TRADE D1	0.0436178	0.0127593	3.42	0.001	0.0186101	0.0686255
_CONS D1	−0.0480371	0.0169209	−2.84	0.005	−0.0812014	−0.0148727

Number of obs.	1,800					
Number of groups	127					
Wald χ^2	181.56					
Minimum number of obs.	1					
Maximum number of obs.	25					
Mean number of obs.	14.17323					

	Coeff.	Std. Err.	t	$P > |t|$	95% Conf. Interval	
B. Fixed Effects Method[b]						
INVGDP1	0.7655012	0.0139967	54.69	0.000	0.7380497	0.7929527
GOVCON	0.0326171	0.0186247	1.75	0.080	−0.0039113	0.0691455
REV	−2.05903	0.1622943	−12.69	0.000	−2.377336	−1.740724
REVLAG	−0.8404217	0.1585791	−5.30	0.000	−1.151441	−0.5294026
TRADE	0.0324689	0.0051885	6.26	0.000	0.0222927	0.042645
_CONS	3.266194	0.4745214	6.88	0.000	2.335521	4.196867

sigma_u	1.6838827	
sigma_e	2.4746612	
ρ[c]	0.31647855	
R^2		
within	0.6523	
between	0.9301	
overall	0.8357	
Number of obs.	1,927	
Number of groups	128	
Obs. per group		
minimum	1	
average	15.1	
maximum	26	
$F(5,1794)$	672.98	
Prob $> F$	0.0000	

[a]Arellano-Bond dynamic panel data. Group variable (*i*): imfcode; time variable (*t*): year. Arellano-Bond test that average autocovariance in residuals of order 1 is 0: H0, no autocorrelation; $z = -4.46$; Prob $> z$ = 0.0000. Arellano-Bond test that average autocovariance in residuals of order 2 is 0: H0, no autocorrelation; $z = -1.08$; Prob $> z = 0.2809$.

[b]Fixed-effects (within) regression. Group variable (*i*): imfcode. F test that all u_i = 0: $F(127, 1794) = 2.61$; Prob $> F = 0.0000$.

[c]Fraction of variance due to u_i.

heteroskedasticity. The results obtained are quite interesting. In both panels the coefficient of the lagged dependent variable is relatively high, capturing the presence of persistence. Notice, however, that the coefficient is significantly smaller when the Arellano-Bond procedure is used. The coefficient of GOVCON is positive and nonsignificant. The estimated coefficient of trade openness is significant and positive, indicating that, after controlling for other factors, countries with a more open trade sector will tend to a higher investment-to-GDP ratio. More importantly for this paper, the coefficients of the contemporaneous and lagged reversal indicator are significantly negative, with very similar point estimates. Interestingly, when the REVERSAL variable was added with a two-year lag, its estimated coefficient was not significant at conventional levels.

In order to check for the robustness of these results, I also estimated equation (10) using alternative samples and definitions of current account reversals. The results obtained provide a strong support to those shown here and indicate that, indeed, current account reversals have affected economic performance negatively through the investment channel. An important question is whether the compression in investment is a result of private or public sector behavior. An analysis undertaken on a smaller sample (forty-four countries) suggests that, although both private- and public-sector investment are negatively affected by current account reversals, the impact is significantly higher on private investment. According to these estimates, available from the author, a current account reversal results in a decline in private investment equal to 1.8 percent of GDP; the long-term reduction of public-sector investment is estimated to be, on average, 0.5 percent of GDP.

An important question is whether current account reversals have affected economic growth through other channels. I investigated this issue by using the large data set to estimate a number of basic growth equations of the following type.

$$(11) \quad \text{GROWTH}_{tj} = \beta \, \text{INVGDP}_{tj} + \delta \, \text{GOVCONS}_{tj}$$
$$+ \, \phi \, \text{TRADE\_OPENNESS}_{tj} + \theta \, \text{LOGGDPO}_{j}$$
$$+ \, \gamma \, \text{REVERSAL}_{tj} + \xi_{tj},$$

where GROWTH_{tj} is growth of GDP per capita in country j during year t, and LOGGDPO_{j} is the initial level of GDP (1970) for country j. As Barro and Sala-i-Martin (1995) have pointed out, the coefficient of GOVCONS is expected to be negative, while that of openness is expected to be positive. If there is a catching-up in growth, we would expect that the estimated coefficient of the logarithm of 1970 GDP per capita will be negative. The main interest of this analysis is the coefficient of REVERSAL. If sharp and large reductions in the current account deficit have a negative effect on investment, we would expect the estimated γ to be significantly negative. The error ξ_{tj} is assumed to be heteroskedastic, with a different variance for each country (panel). Thus, assuming k panels (countries):

$$(12) \qquad E(\xi\xi') = \begin{pmatrix} \sigma_1^2 I & 0 & \cdots & 0 \\ 0 & \sigma_2^2 I & \cdots & 0 \\ \cdot & \cdot & \cdot & \cdot \\ \cdot & \cdot & \cdot & \cdot \\ \cdot & \cdot & \cdot & \cdot \\ 0 & 0 & \cdots & \sigma_k^2 I \end{pmatrix}$$

Equation (12) was estimated using the feasible generalized least squares procedure (FGLS) suggested by Beck and Katz (1995) for unbalanced panels. The samples in the different estimations were determined by the availability of data on the different regressors. The data were obtained from the World Bank and from the Summer and Hestons data set. In the base estimates I used the definition of current account reversals given by *Reversal1* above. The basic results obtained from the estimation of equation (11) are presented in table 1.11. In addition to the regressors in equation (11), I introduced time-specific dummy variables. As may be seen from the table, the results obtained support the hypothesis that current account reversals have had a negative effect on GDP per capita growth, even after controlling by investment. Moreover, the coefficients for the other variables in the regression have the expected signs and are significant at conventional levels. When alternative estimation techniques were used, including fixed effects, the results obtained were very similar.[20]

1.5   Current Account Deficits and Financial Crises: How Strong Is the Link?

As we pointed out in section 1.2 of this paper, a large number of recent empirical studies have been unable to find a strong and significant connection between large current account deficits and financial crises (Frankel and Rose 1996). However, much of the policy literature—both from investment banks and from the multilateral institutions—insists that large deficits have been at the center of recent crises. In this section, I address this issue by analyzing in some detail the evidence on financial crises in a large cross section of countries. The section is organized as follows: In section 1.5.1, I deal with the definition of *crisis*. In section 1.5.2, I provide some preliminary evidence on the connection between current account reversals and crises, as well as between high current account deficits and crises. In this analysis I use

---

20. Naturally, when fixed effects are used it is not possible to include (the log of) initial GDP as a regressor.

Table 1.11   **GDP Growth and Current Account Reversals: Feasible Least Squares with Heteroskedastic Panels**

GDP Growth	Coeff.	Std. Err.	z	$P > \|z\|$	95% Conf. Interval	
INVGDP	0.1732786	0.0129535	13.38	0.000	0.1478901	0.198667
GOVCON	−0.044147	0.0129061	−3.42	0.001	−0.0694425	−0.0188514
TRADE	0.0066118	0.0021185	3.12	0.002	0.0024595	0.010764
LOGGPP0	−0.7458834	0.0754805	−9.88	0.000	−0.8938225	−0.5979443
REV	−0.8387433	0.2063497	−4.06	0.000	−1.243181	−0.4343053
REVLAG	−0.3106008	0.2014468	−1.54	0.123	−0.7054293	0.0842277
D73	1.270318	0.759329	1.67	0.094	−0.2179398	2.758575
D74	−1.342419	0.7482716	−1.79	0.073	−2.809004	0.1241666
D75	−3.115973	0.7482444	−4.16	0.000	−4.582505	−1.649441
D76	0.6267746	0.7248618	0.86	0.387	−0.7939283	2.047478
D77	−0.9757318	0.6522791	−1.50	0.135	−2.254175	0.3027116
D78	0.1379759	0.5050662	0.27	0.785	−0.8519357	1.127887
D79	−1.096983	0.6317958	−1.74	0.083	−2.33528	0.1413142
D80	−2.360201	0.6280218	−3.76	0.000	−3.591101	−1.129301
D81	−2.826354	0.6242467	−4.53	0.000	−4.049855	−1.602853
D82	−4.194326	0.6217559	−6.75	0.000	−5.412945	−2.975707
D83	−2.990355	0.6199746	−4.82	0.000	−4.205483	−1.775227
D84	−1.221758	0.6185186	−1.98	0.048	−2.434032	−0.0094836
D85	−1.784731	0.6187208	−2.88	0.004	−2.997401	−0.5720605
D86	−1.75282	0.617261	−2.84	0.005	−2.962629	−0.5430107
D87	−1.596635	0.6173792	−2.59	0.010	−2.806676	−0.3865935
D88	−0.7132081	0.6150168	−1.16	0.246	−1.918619	0.4922027
D89	−1.492796	0.6147887	−2.43	0.015	−2.69776	−0.2878324
D90	−2.005303	0.6140373	−3.27	0.001	−3.208794	−0.8018121
D91	−2.686583	0.6082038	−4.42	0.000	−3.878641	−1.494526
D92	−2.38132	0.6155925	−3.87	0.000	−3.587859	−1.17478
D93	−2.23038	0.6150288	−3.63	0.000	−3.435814	−1.024945
D94	−0.8790476	0.6164939	−1.43	0.154	−2.087353	0.3292582
D95	−0.9938183	0.5940141	−1.67	0.094	−2.158065	0.170428
D96	−1.480438	0.6129868	−2.42	0.016	−2.68187	−0.2790063
D97	−1.263988	0.6449348	−1.96	0.050	−2.528037	0.0000611
_Cons	7.826786	0.8179467	9.57	0.000	6.22364	9.429932

Number of obs.	1,856
Number of groups	111
Obs. per group	
Minimum	1
Average	19.28987
Maximum	26
Wald χ^2 (31)	708.80
Prob $> \chi^2$	0.0000
Estimated covariances	111
Estimated autocorrelations	0
Estimated coefficients	32
Log-likelihood	−4.913.651

Notes: Cross-sectional time-series FGLS regression. Coefficients: generalized least squares; panels: heteroskedastic; correlation: no autocorrelation.

statistical methods borrowed from the epidemiology literature. Finally, in section 1.5.3, I provide some empirical results, obtained using econometric techniques, on the relationship between large current account deficits and financial crises. I argue that whether one finds a connection depends largely on three factors: (1) the definition of *crisis,* (2) the sample considered, and (3) the lag structure used in the analysis.

1.5.1 Defining a Crisis

Paul Krugman has recently said that "there is no generally accepted formal definition of a currency crisis, but we know them when we see them" (Krugman 2000, 1). While some authors, including myself in Edwards (1989) and Edwards and Santaella (1993), have defined a currency crisis as a very significant depreciation of the currency (see also Frankel and Rose 1996 and Milesi-Ferretti and Razin 2000) others have defined a crisis as a situation in which a country's currency is depreciated or its international reserves are seriously depleted (Eichengreen, Rose, and Wyplosz 1996; Goldstein, Kaminsky, and Reinhart 2000). In this paper, and in order to cast a very wide net in the empirical analysis, I have used two alternative criteria for defining crises.

The first definition follows Frankel and Rose (1996) and defines a currency crisis as a situation in which there is a currency depreciation of at least 25 percent as well as a 10 percent increase in the rate of depreciation. I call this variable *aevent.*[21] The second definition is broader, and includes as crises situations in which the country in question has experienced a large depreciation or a significant loss in reserves. In constructing this variable, which I call *acrisis,* I followed a three-step procedure:

1. I created a weighted average index of monthly rate of change of the exchange rate ($\Delta e/e$) and of reserves ($\Delta R/R$), such that both components of the index have equal sample volatility: $I_t = \Delta e/e - (\sigma_e/\sigma_R) \cdot (\Delta R/R)$.

2. I define a crisis (C_t) to have taken place when the index exceeds the mean of the index plus three standard deviations:

$$C_t = \begin{cases} 1 \ if \ I_t \geq mean \ (I_t) + 3\sigma_I \\ 0 \qquad otherwise \end{cases}$$

3. I annualized the crisis index by considering each year as a June-June period. In other words, a year t is assigned a crisis ($=1$) if any month between June of year t and June of year $t + 1$ is a crisis.

As Milesi-Ferretti and Razin (2000) have pointed out, results from crisis analyses may be affected by the treatment of currency upheaval in consecutive years. In order to address this issue, I defined two additional crisis

---

21. The index was constructed on monthly data. In order to annualize it, I consider June-to-June years.

Table 1.12 **Frequency of Crises: Alternative Indicators**

	Frequency	Percent	Cumulative
aevent: (mean) event			
0	2818	94.09	94.09
1	177	5.91	100.00
Total	2995	100.00	
aevent2			
0	2318	95.79	95.79
1	102	4.21	100.00
Total	2420	100.00	
acrisis: (mean) crisis			
0	2548	90.26	90.26
1	275	9.74	100.00
Total	2823	100.00	
acrisis2			
0	1564	88.91	88.91
1	195	11.09	100.00
Total	1759	100.00	

Source: Author's calculations.
Note: See the text for the exact definition of these indicators.

indicators that exclude adjacent "crises." These indicators consider a three-year window after each crisis: *aevent2* is the three-year window corresponding to *aevent,* and *acrisis2* is the corresponding indicator for *acrisis.*

How frequent have currency crises taken place, according to these indicators? This question is addressed in table 1.12, where I present tabulations for the four indexes for the complete sample. As may be seen, the frequency of "crises" goes from 4 percent to 11 percent of the country-year observations. In terms of the distribution across regions (the results are not presented in detail due to space considerations) according to both *aevent* indicators, crises have had a higher frequency in Eastern Europe; the lowest frequency is in the industrialized nations, with no crises recorded. The *acrisis* index records a frequency at approximately 10 percent in Latin America, Asia, and Africa; the *acrisis2* index shows that the highest frequency of crises has been in Africa, with a 13.7 percent frequency of occurrence.

1.5.2 Current Account Reversals and Crises: A Preliminary Analysis

An important finding from the preceding analysis is that current account reversals are common and quite frequent. Countries in every region tend to run deficits that occasionally exceed their long-run sustainable level. This means that, as documented above, at some point the country must go through an adjustment process in which the current account deficit is reversed and moves closer to its long-run equilibrium. From a policy perspective, it is important to understand whether current account reversals are related to currency crises. In order to address this issue, I followed a case-control methodology.[22] This approach consists of using a χ^2 statistic to formally test whether there is a significant relationship between a particular outcome (the case) and another variable to which both case and control variables have been exposed. The first step in applying this approach, then, is to separate observations into a case group and a control group. A country that for a given year experienced a "crisis" is considered to be a case, and noncrisis observations constitute the control group. The second step consists of calculating how many observations in both the case and control groups have been subject to a current account reversal. From this information an odds ratio is computed, and a χ^2 test is computed in order to determine whether the odds ratio is significantly different from 1. If the null hypothesis cannot be rejected, then there is evidence supporting the hypothesis that countries that are subject to a reversal have a significant probability of experiencing a crisis.

The computation of the χ^2 test statistic using contemporaneous values of crisis and reversals results in the *rejection* of the null hypothesis that reversal countries are associated with a crisis. This result holds for all four definitions of a crisis. The *p*-values of the χ^2 tests are on the order of 0.6, or higher. This result is consistent with the conclusions reached through a less formal analysis, and using a smaller data set, by Milesi-Ferretti and Razin (2000).

A possible limitation of a simple application of this χ^2 test, however, is that from a theoretical point of view the relationship between reversals and crises implies complex timing and causality issues. In fact, there are reasons to believe that reversals may occur at the same time as a crisis, before a crisis, or even after a crisis. For instance, the reversal may be so pronounced that the country in question has no alternative but to devalue its currency or deplete its international reserves. There is no reason, however, why these phenomena would take place at exactly the same time. Also, the reversal may be the result, rather than the cause, of a devaluation. For this reason, I also asked whether there is statistical evidence that there is a current account reversal in the "neighborhood" of a crisis. In order to do this, I define a new variable, *reversaln,* that takes a value of one on the year a reversal was detected, as well as in the previous and next years. The results from this second test suggest that it is not possible to reject the null hypothesis that currency crises occur "in the neighborhood of" current account reversals. This is the case for any of the four crisis definitions used in this study. In table 1.13 I present the results obtained from the computation of these χ^2 statistics when the *aevent* definition of crisis was considered as the "case." In order to illustrate the nature of the results I have presented the χ^2 corresponding to two definitions of reversals. In part A I used the narrow one-year definition of reversal, while in part B I use the broader three-year neighborhood definition of reversal. As may be seen, although in part A the χ^2 test is not sig-

---

22. This approach is used frequently by epidemiologists. I became interested in the statistical techniques used by epidemiologists while doing research on financial crisis contagion across countries (see Edwards 2000). See Fleiss (1981) for details on the actual case-control method.

Table 1.13   **Case-Control χ^2 Test: Analysis of Crisis and Current Account Reversals (for *Aevent* definition of crisis)**

	Exposed	Unexposed	Total	Proportion Exposed
A. Exposed: Reversal1 *definition of current account reversal*[a]				
Cases	28	124	152	0.1842
Controls	410	1,793	2,203	0.1861
Total	438	1,917	2,355	1.1860

	Point Estimate		95% Conf. Interval	
Odds ratio (Cornfield)	0.9874902		0.6481554	1.504718
Prev. frac. ex. (Cornfield)	0.0125098		−0.504718	0.3518446
Prev. frac. pop	0.0023282			

	Exposed	Unexposed	Total	Proportion Exposed
B. Exposed: Reversaln1 *definition of current account reversal*[b]				
Cases	52	35	87	0.5977
Controls	563	679	1,242	0.4533
Total	615	714	1,329	0.4628

	Point Estimate		95% Conf. Interval	
Odds ratio (Cornfield)	1.791829		1.15408	2.718784
Attr. frac. ex. (Cornfield)	0.4419112		0.1335086	0.6405185
Attr. frac. pop.	0.2641308			

Source: Computed by the author.
Note: Prev. = previous; frac. = fraction; ex. = explained; pop. = population; attr. = attributed.
[a]$\chi^2 (1) = 0.00$; Prob. $> \chi^2 = 0.9536$.
[b]$\chi^2 (1) = 6.82$; Prob. $> \chi^2 = 0.0090$.

nificant, in part B it is highly significant—the *p*-value is 0.009.[23] Results obtained for the other three definitions of a crisis are very similar and are available from the author on request.

1.5.3   Current Account Deficits and Currency Crises: A Formal Analysis

In a recent and influential paper, Frankel and Rose (1996) empirically analyzed the determinants of currency crashes. Their data set included 105 countries for the period 1970–91, and their definition of a crisis was confined to devaluations in excess of 25 percent.[24] The results from their probit

23. These results, however, should be interpreted with caution, as they are subject to all the limitations of this type of case-control analysis, including the fact that no causality can be established. In this case, however, I am not particularly interested in causation.
24. See section 1.5.1 for a discussion of their definition.

regression analysis indicated that a number of variables were good predictors of a currency crash. These included the fraction of the debt obtained in concessional terms, the ratio of foreign direct investment (FDI) to GDP, the reserves-to-imports ratio, the rate of growth of domestic credit, the country's rate of growth, and international interest rates. In terms of the present paper, what is particularly interesting is that in Frankel and Rose (1996) the current account deficit was not significant, and in many of the regressions it even had the *wrong* sign. This led the authors to conclude that, "curiously, neither current account nor government budget deficits appear to play an important role in a typical crash" (365).[25]

My own initial analysis of the determinants of crises, using an almost identical data set, supports the results reported by Frankel and Rose (1996). When a broad sample and their regressors are used, the current account seems to play no role in major currency crashes.[26] This is the case independently of the estimation technique used, and of whether the actual value of the current account deficit or a dummy for high deficits is included as a regressor. To my surprise, the incorporation of an independent variable that interacted the fiscal and current account deficits (the "twin" deficits) did not change the result.

In order to investigate this issue further, and in an effort to determine the robustness of these results, I followed four avenues of analysis: First, I inquired whether the results would hold under alternative data sets. In particular, I investigated whether the exclusion of particular regions would alter the finding of current account "irrelevance." Second, I considered alternative sets of independent variables in the estimation of probit equations for crises. In particular I considered alternative lag structures, and I included some variables that capture the economic structure of the countries in the sample. Third, I considered alternative definitions of *crisis.* More specifically, I estimated a number of probit equations for all four definitions of crisis described in subsection 1.5.1 of this paper: *aevent, aevent2, acrisis,* and *acrisis2.* Fourth, I used different estimation techniques and considered assumptions regarding the nature of the error term, including the assumption that it takes a random effect form. Generally speaking, the results obtained were not affected by the technique used, and for this reason I only report the basic results.

In the estimation of crisis models I used the following regressors:[27] (1) percentage of debt in commercial terms; (2) percentage of debt in concessional terms; (3) percentage of debt at variable rate; (4) percentage of short-term debt; (5) FDI; (6) public-sector debt as percentage of GDP; (7) debt to the multilateral institutions; (8) the ratio of (gross) international reserves to imports; (9) the ratio of foreign debt to GDP; (10) the rate of

25. This finding is not affected by any of the sensitivity tests undertaken by the authors.
26. By "broad sample" I mean one that includes all regions in the world.
27. Most, but not all, of these regressors were used by Frankel and Rose (1996). The results reported here are not directly comparable to those of Frankel and Rose (1996), since the data sets are somewhat different.

growth of domestic credit; (11) deviations of the real exchange rate from PPP (a measure of "overvaluation"); (12) the rate of growth of GDP; (13) the degree of openness of the economy, measured as imports plus exports divided by GDP; (14) the ratio of government expenditure to GDP; (15) interest rates in the advanced countries; and (16) the current account deficit. All the variables are from the World Bank and, as in the Frankel and Rose (1996) paper, cover the 1971–92 period. With the exception of the crisis indexes, trade openness, and government consumption, these variables correspond to those used by Frankel and Rose (1996).

In reporting the regressions, I follow the tradition of presenting the effects of a unitary change in the independent variables on the probability of a crisis. In all of the regressions I report White's robust standard errors that correct for heteroskedasticity.

The results obtained when all variables are entered contemporaneously and all regions are included are presented in table 1.14. The results are quite interesting and, to a large extent, in agreement with expectations. In terms of the current account—the variable of greatest interest in this paper—the results show significant differences, depending on the definition of *crisis* used. For both the *acrisis* and *acrisis2* indicators, the estimated coefficient of the current account deficit to GDP is positive and significant at the 10 percent level. On the other hand, when the *aevent* and *aevent2* currency crash indicators are used as the dependent variable, the estimated coefficients of the current account deficits are not significant, and in the case of *aevent2,* the sign is incorrect (although it is not significantly different from zero). Of course, the results for the *events* correspond to the Frankel and Rose (1996) findings discussed above. In terms of the other regressors, the results in table 1.14 suggest that higher reserves and higher growth reduce the probability of both types of crisis. Large FDI plays a particularly important role in reducing the probability of an *event* type of crisis. A high percentage of debt in commercial terms increases the probability of both types of crisis. A greater degree of openness reduces the probability under all crisis definitions. Notice that in contrast with the Frankel and Rose (1996) results, a higher public deficit ratio significantly increases the probability of *aevent*-type crises.

The results presented in table 1.14 were obtained using a data set that covers every region. There are, however, important reasons to believe that (most) African countries have behaved differently during the period under study. This is the case for two reasons: First, during the complete period under analysis a large number of African nations belonged to the CFA currency zone and were institutionally shielded from devaluations. Second, it is well known that during most of this period even non-CFA African nations had a great reluctance to adjust their parity. This was the case even when the external imbalance was very large (World Bank 1994). An important question, then, is how these results will be affected if the African nations are excluded from the sample. This is done in table 1.15, where probit

Table 1.14   **Crisis Probit Model: All Regions, 1971–92 (Probit Estimates)**

Definition	dF/dx	Robust Std. Err.	z	$P > \|z\|$	x-bar	95% Conf. Interval	
A. acrisis *Definition*							
COMRAT	0.0033323	0.0017217	1.90	0.057	21.0027	−0.000042	0.006707
CONRAT	−0.0010057	0.0007642	−1.30	0.193	32.5979	−0.002504	0.000492
VARRAT	−0.0025776	0.0016872	−1.51	0.131	21.9735	−0.005884	0.000729
FDISTOCK	0.0052372	0.0022728	−2.27	0.023	2.62669	−0.009692	0.000783
SHORTTOT	0.0019636	0.0015704	1.27	0.203	14.6745	−0.001114	0.005041
PUBRAT	0.0009573	0.0010942	0.88	0.381	72.419	−0.001187	0.003102
MULTIRAT	0.0020735	0.0008301	2.44	0.015	21.4711	0.000447	0.0037
DEBTY	0.0002462	0.0002104	1.16	0.247	59.5954	−0.000166	0.000659
RESERVEM	−0.0000357	0.0000375	−0.94	0.345	324.331	−0.000109	0.000038
DEFRAT	0.0011096	0.0016363	0.68	0.497	5.15325	−0.002097	0.004317
DLCRED	0.0010474	0.0003367	3.23	0.001	21.875	0.000387	0.001707
DLY	−0.0027143	0.0013687	−2.00	0.046	3.51322	−0.005397	0.000032
ISTAR	0.0020625	0.0030204	0.68	0.497	8.64066	−0.003857	0.007982
OVERVALN	0.0001934	0.0004058	0.48	0.634	−7.88634	−0.000602	0.000989
TRADE	−0.0009073	0.0005028	−1.74	0.082	46.3937	−0.001893	0.000078
GOVCON	−0.0001539	0.0017092	−0.09	0.928	14.0511	−0.003504	0.003196
CAD	0.0031167	0.0016689	1.83	0.067	4.36866	−0.000154	0.006388

obs. *P*	0.1031149		
pred. *P*	0.0773022	(at x-bar)	
Number of obs.	931		
Wald χ^2 (17)	56.70		
Prob > χ^2	0.0000		
Pseudo R^2	0.1103		
Log-likelihood	−274.9083		

Definition	dF/dx	Robust Std. Err.	z	$P > \|z\|$	x-bar	95% Conf. Interval	
B. acrisis2 *Definition*							
COMRAT	0.0046036	0.0026754	1.65	0.100	19.9146	−0.00064	0.009847
CONRAT	−0.0012766	0.0010286	−1.24	0.213	34.1878	−0.003293	0.000739
VARRAT	−0.0044843	0.0025206	−1.71	0.086	21.1016	−0.009425	0.000456
FDISTOCK	−0.0046245	0.0028175	−1.65	0.099	3.12262	−0.010147	0.000898
SHORTTOT	0.0014552	0.0020551	0.71	0.479	14.7062	−0.002573	0.005483
PUBRAT	−0.0001517	0.0014676	−0.10	0.918	72.5714	−0.003028	0.002725
MULTIRAT	0.003031	0.0010866	2.66	0.008	21.5175	0.000901	0.005161
DEBTY	0.0002802	0.0003342	0.83	0.404	54.2499	−0.000375	0.000935
RESERVEM	−0.0000196	0.0000514	−0.38	0.703	328.907	−0.00012	0.000081
DEFRAT	0.0020843	0.002524	0.82	0.410	4.60205	−0.002863	0.007031
DLCRED	0.0020764	0.0005264	4.02	0.000	18.7089	0.001045	0.003108
DLY	−0.002937	0.0019957	−1.48	0.140	3.97093	−0.006849	0.000975
ISTAR	0.0052748	0.0038629	1.36	0.173	8.50495	−0.002296	0.012846
OVERVALN	0.0005167	0.000559	0.91	0.361	−8.22226	−0.000579	0.001612
TRADE	−0.0008263	0.0006416	−1.28	0.201	47.0451	−0.002084	0.000431
GOVCON	0.0016096	0.002514	0.65	0.518	13.8002	−0.003318	0.006537
CAD	0.0039213	0.0023943	1.61	0.107	3.95843	−0.000771	0.008614

obs. *P*	0.1209964		
pred. *P*	0.0854189	(at *x*-bar)	
Number of obs.	562		
Wald χ^2 (17)	56.69		
Prob > χ^2	0.0000		
Pseudo R^2	0.1387		
Log-likelihood	−178.57014		

Table 1.14   (continued)

Definition	dF/dx	Robust Std. Err.	z	$P > \|z\|$	x-bar	95% Conf. Interval	
			C. aevent *Definition*				
COMRAT	0.0003686	0.0008709	0.42	0.671	20.962	−0.001338	0.002075
CONRAT	−0.000823	0.0004234	−1.82	0.069	32.6715	−0.001653	6.9e−06
VARRAT	−0.0007301	0.0008421	−0.86	0.388	21.9302	−0.002381	0.000921
FDISTOCK	−0.0033417	0.0012196	−2.69	0.007	2.62084	−0.005732	−0.000951
SHORTTOT	−0.0000499	0.0008731	−0.06	0.955	14.6571	−0.001761	0.001661
PUBRAT	−0.0001298	0.0006229	−0.21	0.836	72.4703	−0.001351	0.001091
MULTIRAT	−0.0002948	0.0005312	−0.56	0.578	21.4961	−0.001336	0.000746
DEBTY	0.0002863	0.0001209	2.49	0.013	59.7336	0.000049	0.000523
RESERVEM	−0.0000194	0.0000197	−1.01	0.315	325.061	−0.000058	0.000019
DEFRAT	0.0016828	0.0009088	1.85	0.065	5.21531	−0.000098	0.003464
DLCRED	0.0004128	0.0002005	2.53	0.012	21.8889	0.000026	0.000812
DLY	−0.001096	0.0008227	−1.34	0.179	3.51907	−0.002708	0.000516
ISTAR	−0.0000236	0.0017433	−0.01	0.989	8.63804	−0.00344	0.003393
OVERVALN	−0.0003881	0.0002363	−1.64	0.102	−7.82043	−0.000851	0.000075
TRADE	−0.001114	0.0003071	−3.06	0.002	46.3682	−0.001716	−0.000512
GOVCON	−0.0037107	0.0012011	−2.97	0.003	14.071	−0.006065	−0.001357
CAD	0.0003098	0.0010221	0.30	0.764	4.37692	−0.001693	0.002313

obs. *P*	0.0706638						
pred. *P*	0.0296255	(at *x*-bar)					

Number of obs.	934	
Wald χ^2 (17)	70.66	
Prob $> \chi^2$	0.0000	
Pseudo R^2	0.2072	
Log-likelihood	−189.0942	

Definition	dF/dx	Robust Std. Err.	z	$P > \|z\|$	x-bar	95% Conf. Interval	
			D. aevent2 *Definition*				
COMRAT	−0.000135	0.0009079	−0.15	0.883	19.8866	−0.001914	0.001644
CONRAT	−0.0003336	0.000392	−0.85	0.395	35.0182	−0.001102	0.000435
VARRAT	7.77e−06	0.0008146	0.01	0.992	20.4507	−0.001589	0.001604
FDISTOCK	−0.0015405	0.0009866	−1.62	0.104	3.08108	−0.003474	0.000393
SHORTTOT	0.0005935	0.0007601	0.81	0.416	14.3259	−0.000896	0.002083
PUBRAT	0.000125	0.0005304	0.24	0.810	72.7421	−0.000914	0.001164
MULTIRAT	−0.0004797	0.0005018	−0.94	0.349	22.8628	−0.001463	0.000504
DEBTY	0.0002004	0.0001292	1.62	0.105	54.0278	−0.000053	0.000454
RESERVEM	−0.0000252	0.0000191	−1.38	0.166	328.073	−0.000063	0.000012
DEFRAT	0.0022043	0.0010298	2.11	0.035	4.93033	0.000186	0.004223
DLCRED	0.0005069	0.000229	2.74	0.006	18.4827	0.000058	0.000956
DLY	−0.0015771	0.0008004	−1.90	0.057	4.18559	−0.003146	−8.3e−06
ISTAR	0.0000685	0.0014788	0.05	0.963	8.62569	−0.00283	0.002967
OVERVALN	−0.0001668	0.0002045	−0.84	0.402	−7.73555	−0.000568	0.000234
TRADE	−0.0007145	0.0002938	−2.41	0.016	48.7758	−0.00129	−0.000139
GOVCON	−0.0028422	0.001161	−2.20	0.028	14.5617	−0.005118	−0.000567
CAD	−0.0007552	0.0009831	−0.79	0.432	4.27947	−0.002682	0.001172

obs. *P*	0.0555556		
pred. *P*	0.0206342	(at *x*-bar)	

Number of obs.	702	
Wald χ^2 (17)	48.97	
Prob $> \chi^2$	0.0001	
Pseudo R^2	0.2208	
Log-likelihood	−117.36778	

Notes: Probit estimates. The tests that the underlying coefficient is 0 are z and $P > \|z\|$.

Table 1.15   **Probit Model of Currency Crises, Africa Excluded, 1971–92 (Probit Estimates)**

Definition	dF/dx	Robust Std. Err.	z	$P > \lvert z \rvert$	x-bar	95% Conf. Interval	
A. acrisis Definition							
COMRAT	0.0029271	0.0020359	1.42	0.157	26.3123	−0.001063	0.006917
CONRAT	−0.0012155	0.0008973	−1.32	0.186	28.4099	−0.002974	0.000543
VARRAT	−0.0020405	0.0019753	−1.02	0.306	27.1534	−0.005912	0.001831
FDISTOCK	−0.005784	0.0024845	−2.24	0.025	3.17666	−0.010653	0.000915
SHORTTOT	0.0016729	0.002148	0.81	0.418	15.9367	−0.002537	0.005883
PUBRAT	0.0014678	0.0013265	1.13	0.258	69.9099	−0.001132	0.004068
MULTIRAT	0.0026282	0.000894	2.77	0.006	19.8038	0.000876	0.00438
DEBTY	3.91e–06	0.0003489	0.01	0.991	53.1143	−0.00068	0.000688
RESERVEM	−7.38e–06	0.0000403	−0.18	0.855	412.658	−0.000086	0.000072
DEFRAT	0.0010166	0.0019793	0.52	0.606	4.5621	−0.002863	0.004896
DLCRED	0.0008556	0.0003243	2.85	0.004	25.8435	0.00022	0.001491
DLY	−0.0021348	0.0017565	−1.24	0.215	3.8471	−0.005577	0.001308
ISTAR	0.0026776	0.0036062	0.73	0.466	8.48895	−0.00439	0.009746
OVERVALN	−0.0000309	0.0005285	−0.06	0.953	−5.23607	−0.001067	0.001005
TRADE	−0.0010877	0.0006823	−1.48	0.140	47.171	−0.002425	0.00025
GOVCON	0.0017909	0.0023691	0.76	0.448	13.3222	−0.002852	0.006434
CAD	0.0048408	0.0021958	2.08	0.037	3.62618	0.000537	0.009145

obs. *P*	0.1075085
pred. *P*	0.0718758 (at *x*-bar)

Number of obs.	586
Wald χ^2 (17)	47.59
Prob $> \chi^2$	0.0001
Pseudo R^2	0.1381
Log-likelihood	−172.36345

Definition	dF/dx	Robust Std. Err.	z	$P > \lvert z \rvert$	x-bar	95% Conf. Interval	
B. acrisis2 Definition							
COMRAT	0.004239	0.0031281	1.27	0.203	25.0805	−0.001892	0.01037
CONRAT	−0.0013723	0.0013069	−1.08	0.279	30.3854	−0.003934	0.001189
VARRAT	−0.0049427	0.0028411	−1.67	0.095	26.3258	−0.010511	0.000626
FDISTOCK	−0.0015863	0.0024665	−0.65	0.515	3.68785	−0.006421	0.003248
SHORTTOT	0.001403	0.0024508	0.57	0.569	16.3144	−0.003401	0.006207
PUBRAT	−0.0001419	0.001806	−0.08	0.937	69.3619	−0.003682	0.003398
MULTIRAT	0.003184	0.0011121	2.54	0.011	19.659	0.001004	0.005364
DEBTY	0.0001755	0.0006922	0.25	0.800	47.3123	−0.001181	0.001532
RESERVEM	0.0000193	0.0000523	0.37	0.709	418.177	−0.000083	0.000122
DEFRAT	0.0015161	0.0030651	0.49	0.625	3.85896	−0.004491	0.007524
DLCRED	0.0016191	0.0005431	3.02	0.003	22.0399	0.000555	0.002684
DLY	−0.0028787	0.0026685	−1.12	0.261	4.74403	−0.008109	0.002352
ISTAR	0.0047575	0.0043004	1.12	0.264	8.25318	−0.003671	0.013186
OVERVALN	0.004106	0.0006962	0.59	0.555	−3.96003	−0.000954	0.001775
TRADE	−0.0019974	0.0007404	−2.51	0.012	48.4653	−0.003448	−0.000546
GOVCON	0.0074273	0.0029808	2.69	0.007	12.9495	0.001585	0.01327
CAD	0.0066269	0.0030252	2.15	0.032	2.94552	0.000698	0.012556

obs. *P*	0.1232092
pred. *P*	0.0684454 (at *x*-bar)

Number of obs.	349
Wald χ^2 (17)	56.33
Prob $> \chi^2$	0.0000
Pseudo R^2	0.2104
Log-likelihood	−102.86684

Table 1.15 (continued)

Definition	dF/dx	Robust Std. Err.	z	$P > \|z\|$	x-bar	95% Conf. Interval	
			C. aevent *Definition*				
COMRAT	0.0005594	0.0009588	0.58	0.561	26.2654	−0.00132	0.002439
CONRAT	−0.0004993	0.0005171	−0.89	0.373	28.4811	−0.001513	0.000514
VARRAT	−0.0002586	0.000949	−0.27	0.787	27.1044	−0.002119	0.001601
FDISTOCK	−0.0029753	0.0012766	−2.27	0.023	3.16641	−0.005477	0.000473
SHORTTOT	0.0009613	0.0011325	0.91	0.363	15.9162	−0.001258	0.003181
PUBRAT	0.0012306	0.0008209	1.71	0.086	69.9671	−0.000378	0.00284
MULTIRAT	−0.0006806	0.0006162	−1.21	0.227	19.7912	−0.001888	0.000527
DEBTY	0.0000792	0.0001567	0.51	0.613	53.3316	−0.000228	0.000386
RESERVEM	−0.0000334	0.0000222	−1.57	0.115	412.677	−0.000077	0.00001
DEFRAT	0.0011607	0.0009477	1.19	0.233	4.61603	−0.000697	0.003018
DLCRED	0.0002325	0.0001554	1.85	0.064	25.8675	−0.000072	0.000537
DLY	−0.0015439	0.0009927	−1.73	0.084	3.85051	−0.003489	0.000402
ISTAR	0.0001112	0.0019632	0.06	0.955	8.4883	−0.003737	0.003959
OVERVALN	−0.0003815	0.0002373	−1.49	0.137	−5.18871	−0.000847	0.000084
TRADE	−0.0010118	0.0003537	−2.52	0.012	47.1363	−0.001705	0.000318
GOVCON	−0.0021182	0.0012636	−1.57	0.116	13.35	−0.004595	0.000358
CAD	0.0018845	0.0011319	1.62	0.105	3.64741	−0.000334	0.004103

obs. *P*   0.0748299
pred. *P*   0.0253162 (at x-bar)

Number of obs.   588
Wald χ^2 (17)   64.52
Prob $> \chi^2$ 0.0000
Pseudo R^2 0.2262
Log-likelihood   −121.01338

Definition	dF/dx	Robust Std. Err.	z	$P > \|z\|$	x-bar	95% Conf. Interval	
			D. aevent2 *Definition*				
COMRAT	−0.000477	0.0006752	−0.72	0.472	24.5388	−0.0018	0.000846
CONRAT	−0.0001558	0.0003666	−0.41	0.680	31.8778	−0.000874	0.000563
VARRAT	0.0003588	0.0006383	0.57	0.569	24.764	−0.000892	0.00161
FDISTOCK	−0.0011275	0.0007419	1.46	0.145	3.82585	−0.002582	0.000327
SHORTTOT	0.0000871	0.0007133	0.12	0.901	15.8634	−0.001311	0.001485
PUBRAT	0.0002927	0.0005123	0.63	0.529	69.6303	−0.000711	0.001297
MULTIRAT	−0.0011583	0.0005954	−2.48	0.013	21.8597	−0.002325	8.6e–06
DEBTY	0.0001485	0.000146	1.05	0.295	45.5271	−0.000138	0.000435
RESERVEM	−0.000016	0.0000162	−1.10	0.271	427.66	−0.000048	0.000016
DEFRAT	0.000573	0.0007951	0.71	0.476	4.27868	−0.000985	0.002131
DLCRED	0.0000761	0.000141	0.61	0.541	21.1944	−0.0002	0.000353
DLY	−0.0013861	0.0008992	−1.99	0.046	4.62599	−0.003148	0.000376
ISTAR	−0.0002626	0.0011823	−0.22	0.823	8.3681	−0.00258	0.002055
OVERVALN	−0.0003454	0.0001643	−2.03	0.042	−4.5647	−0.000667	−0.000023
TRADE	−0.0008508	0.0003236	−3.50	0.000	50.8592	−0.001485	−0.000217
GOVCON	−0.0004142	0.0008319	−0.48	0.630	13.843	−0.002045	0.001216
CAD	0.001496	0.0009603	1.62	0.105	3.12759	−0.000386	0.003378

obs. *P*   0.0636792
pred. *P*   0.01217 (at x-bar)

Number of obs.   424
Wald χ^2 (17)   44.63
Prob $> \chi^2$ 0.0003
Pseudo R^2 0.2642
Log-likelihood   −73.926915

Notes: Probit estimates. The tests that the underlying coefficient is 0 are z and $P > \|z\|$.

regressions for our four crisis definitions are presented for a non-Africa sample. As may be seen, when this is done, the estimated coefficient of the current account deficit is positive and significant either at the 5 or 10 percent level. It is important to notice that what makes a difference here is whether Africa is included in the sample. If instead of focusing on Africa I use GDP per capita as the key variable to split the sample, as Milesi-Ferretti and Razin (2000) do, and I include only middle-income countries, the results are not as distinct as those reported in table 1.15.

The results presented above follow Frankel and Rose (1996) and control for a number of variables, including the external debt ratio, capital flows in the form of FDI, and international reserves. A problem with including this group of controls, however, is that it becomes difficult to interpret the current account coefficient in the probit regressions. The reason for this is that we are not allowing the current account deficit to be financed through the traditional channels: an increase in indebtness or a reduction in international reserves. In fact, in the results reported above, as well as in Frankel and Rose (1996), higher account deficits are being financed exclusively by an increase in non–debt-generating capital inflows. It is interesting to understand, however, if an increase in the current account deficit that is financed by running up the debt or depleting international reserves increases the probability of a crisis. The results in table 1.16, which were obtained when both reserves and debt are not included as controls, show that an increase in the current account deficit financed by traditional means indeed increases the probability of an *aevent* type of crisis.[28]

As a final exercise, and in order to analyze the robustness of these results, I investigated whether they held under different lag structures for the regressors. In particular I considered the following structure: all debt variables were entered contemporaneously, as were the structural variables, and the country performance and policy variables were entered with a one-period lag. The results obtained indicate that when this alternative lag structure is used, the coefficient of the current account deficit remains positive and significant at conventional levels. When every regressor is entered with one lag, the coefficient of the current account deficit remains positive and significant. In that case, however, some of the debt variables became nonsignificant.

To sum up, the results presented in this section suggest that the effects of larger current account deficits on crisis depend on both the definition of a crisis and on the regions of the world being covered. More specifically, the results indicate that when the broader definitions *acrisis* and *acrisis2* are used, a higher current account deficit increases the probability of crisis in the larger sample. Higher current account deficits also increase the proba-

28. The results for an *acrisis* type of crisis are similar and are not reported here due to space considerations.

Table 1.16   **Crisis and the Current Account: Probit Estimates, Alternative Set of Controls (Africa Excluded, 1970–92)**

Aevent	dF/dx	Robust Std. Err.	z	$P > \|z\|$	x-bar	95% Conf. Interval	
COMRAT	−0.0000411	0.0008099	−0.05	0.960	26.3022	−0.001629	0.001546
CONRAT	−0.0005226	0.000528	−0.93	0.354	28.4596	−0.001557	0.000512
VARRAT	0.000294	0.000864	0.34	0.731	27.1331	−0.001399	0.001988
FDISTOCK	−0.0034274	0.0013471	−2.52	0.012	3.15382	−0.006068	−0.000787
SHORTTOT	0.0009178	0.0011867	0.81	0.417	15.9153	−0.001408	0.003244
PUBRAT	0.0012746	0.0008641	1.65	0.099	70.0393	−0.000419	0.002968
MULTIRAT	−0.0007383	0.0006296	−1.27	0.202	19.7436	−0.001972	0.000496
DEFRAT	0.017021	0.000881	1.85	0.064	4.68826	−0.000025	0.003429
DLCRED	0.0002103	0.0001511	1.66	0.096	26.0009	−0.000086	0.000506
DLY	−0.0018491	0.0010946	−1.87	0.062	3.83729	−0.003995	0.000296
ISTAR	0.0003013	0.0020829	0.14	0.885	8.48095	−0.003781	0.004384
OVERVALN	−0.000391	0.0002352	−1.52	0.128	−5.48445	−0.000852	0.00007
TRADE	−0.0010849	0.0003564	−2.56	0.011	47.1491	−0.001783	−0.000386
GOVCON	−0.0019375	0.0012981	−1.43	0.153	13.455	−0.004482	0.000607
CAD	0.0024955	0.001186	2.09	0.037	3.71074	0.000171	0.00482

obs. P	0.0761421	
pred. P	0.0279486	(at x-bar)

Number of obs.	591
Wald χ^2 (17)	65.13
Prob $> \chi^2$	0.0000
Pseudo R^2	0.2198
Log-likelihood	−124.15434

Notes: Excludes reserves and debt. Probit estimates. The tests that the underlying coefficient is 0 are z and $P > \|z\|$.

bility of *aevent* crises significantly when the African nations are excluded from the sample.

1.6   Concluding Remarks

The main question addressed in this paper is whether the current account "matters." If this question is interpreted very narrowly, in the sense that countries with an arbitrarily defined large current account deficit almost inevitably face a crisis, then the answer is no. If, however, it is interpreted more broadly, as suggesting that there are costs involved in running very large deficits, the research reported in this paper suggests that the answer is a qualified yes.[29]

29. Naturally, a major challenge in this work is defining what a "large" deficit means. In theory, "large" should mean "significantly larger than the sustainable level." In practice, however, and as is shown in section 1.3 of this paper, existing sustainability models are not very useful, especially in a dynamic environment. For this reason, in this paper I have defined a "high deficit" arbitrarily, as a deficit that for that year exceeds the 3rd quartile of the deficit distribution for the region to which the country belongs.

The analysis presented in this paper has shown that large current account deficits tend not to be persistent. Very few countries run large deficits for five years in a row, and only a handful have run large deficits for ten years in a row. As the analysis in section 1.4 of this paper suggests, the typical pattern of current account deficits is that countries that experience large imbalances do so for a limited time; after a while, these imbalances are reduced, and a current account reversal is observed. In section 1.4 I analyzed in detail the consequences, in terms of economic performance, of current account reversals using a large (unbalanced) panel of countries for 1970–97. Using recently developed econometric techniques, I found that, contrary to what has been recently suggested, reversals do have a negative effect on economic performance. They negatively affect aggregate investment; moreover, even when I control for investment, the regression analysis suggests that reversals have a negative impact on GDP growth per capita.

In section 1.5 I addressed the narrower question of whether larger deficits increase the probability of a country experiencing a currency crisis. My results suggest that the answer to this question depends on the definition of a crisis as well as on the sample used in the analysis. As the detailed explanation in that section indicates, my results show that when Africa is excluded—and I argue that there are good reasons for doing so—an increase in the deficit raises the probability of a crisis, independently of how this term is defined. When the complete sample is used, higher deficits increase the probability of broadly defined crises. They have no statistical effect on narrowly defined crashes, however.

In sum, my conclusion is that, in spite of recent claims of the irrelevance of current account deficits, the evidence provides rather strong support for the view that, from a policy perspective, large deficits should be a cause for concern. This does not mean, of course, that every large deficit leads to a crisis; nor does it mean that only when there is a large current account deficit can a crisis take place.

References

Ades, Alberto, and Federico Kaune. 1997. A new measure of current account sustainability for developing countries. New York: Goldman Sachs Emerging Markets Economic Research.

Arellano, Manuel, and Stephen Bond. 1991. Estimation of dynamic models with error components. *Journal of the American Statistical Association* 76:245–67.

Atkeson, Andrew, and Jose-Victor Rios-Rull. 1996. The balance of payments and borrowing constraints: An alternative view of the Mexican crisis. Federal Reserve Bank of Minneapolis Staff Report no. 212.

Attanasio, Orazio P., Lucio Picci, and Antonello E. Scorcu. 2000. Saving, growth, and investment: A macroeconomic analysis using a panel of countries. *Review of Economics and Statistics* 82 (2): 182–211.

Bacchetta, Philippe, and Eric van Wincoop. 2000. Trade in nominal assets and net international capital flows. *Journal of International Money and Finance* 19 (1): 66–91.

Bank of Mexico. *The Mexican Economy,* various issues. Mexico City: Bank of Mexico.

Barro, Robert J., and Xavier Sala-i-Martin. 1995. *Economic Growth.* Cambridge: MIT Press.

Beck, Nathaniel, and Jonathan N. Katz. 1995. What to do (and not to do) with time-series cross-section data. *American Political Science Review* 89 (3): 124–47.

Blanchard, Olivier. 1983. Debt and the current account deficit in Brazil. In *Financial policies and the world capital market: The problem of Latin American countries,* ed. Pedro Aspe-Armella, Rudiger Dornbusch, and Maurice Obstfeld, 95–109. Chicago: University of Chicago Press.

Bruno, Michael. 1995. Currency crises and collapses: Comment. *Brookings Papers on Economic Activity,* Issue no. 2:278–85.

Calvo, Guillermo A. 2000. Balance of payments crises in emerging markets: Large capital inflows and sovereign governments. In *Currency crises,* ed. Paul Krugman, 3–28. Chicago: University of Chicago Press.

Calvo, Guillermo A., Leonardo Leiderman, and Carmen Reinhart. 1993. Capital inflows and real exchange rate appreciation in Latin America: The role of external factors. *IMF Staff Papers* 40 (March): 868–907.

Chang, Roberto, and Andres Velasco. 2000. Exchange-rate policy for developing countries. *American Economic Review* 90 (2): 71–75.

Chase Manhattan Bank. 1997. Emerging markets after Thailand: Guilt by association or flattered by comparison? Unpublished report, October 1.

Cline, William R. 1988. International debt: Progress and strategy. *Finance and Development* 25 (2): 9–11.

Cooper, Richard N. 1971a. Currency devaluation in developing countries. *Princeton Studies in International Finance* no. 86. Princeton University, Department of Economics, International Economics Section.

———. 1971b. *Issues for trade policy in the seventies.* Tübingen, Germany: Mohr.

Corden, W. Max. 1994. *Economic policy, exchange rates, and the international system.* Oxford: Oxford University Press.

Corsetti, Giancarlo, Paolo Pesenti, and Nouriel Roubini. 1998. Paper tigers? A model of the Asian crisis. Paper presented at the NBER-Bank of Portugal International Seminar on Macroeconomics. 14–15 June, Lisbon, Portugal.

Deutsche Bank. 2000. *Global market research.* New York: Deutsche Bank. March.

Dornbusch, Rudiger. 2000. *Keys to prosperity: Free markets, sound money, and a bit of luck.* Cambridge: MIT Press.

Edwards, Sebastian. 1989. Structural adjustment policies in highly indebted countries. In *Developing country debt and economic performance* vol. 2, ed. Jeffrey D. Sachs, 234–67. Chicago: University of Chicago Press.

———. 1993. Exchange rates as nominal anchors. *Weltwirtschaftliches Archiv* 129: 1–33.

———. 1996. Why are Latin America's savings rates so low? An international comparative analysis. *Journal of Development Economics* 51 (1): 5–44.

———. 1999. On crisis prevention: Lessons from Mexico and East Asia. In *Financial markets and development,* ed. Alison Harwood, Robert E. Litan, and Michael Pomerleano, 269–334. Washington, D.C.: Brookings Institution.

———. 2000. Contagion. *The World Economy* 23 (7): 873–900.

Edwards, Sebastian, and Alejandra Edwards. 1991. *Monetarism and liberalization: The Chilean experience.* Chicago: University of Chicago Press.

Edwards, Sebastian, and Julio Santaella. 1993. Devaluation controversies in the developing countries: Lessons from the Bretton Woods era. In *A retrospective on the*

Bretton Woods System: Lessons for international monetary reform, ed. Michael D. Bordo and Barry J. Eichengreen, 405–60. Chicago: University of Chicago Press.

Edwards, Sebastian, and Sweder van-Wijnbergen. 1986. The welfare effects of trade and capital market liberalization. *International Economic Review* 27 (1): 325–41.

Eichengreen, Barry, Andrew K. Rose, and Charles Wyplosz. 1996. Contagious currency crises. NBER Working Paper no. 5681. Cambridge, Mass.: National Bureau of Economic Research, April.

Fernandez de Cordoba, Gonzalo, and Timothy J. Kehoe. 2000. Capital flows and real exchange rate fluctuations following Spain's entry into the European Community. *Journal of International Economics* 51 (1): 128–51.

Fischer, Stanley. 1988. Real balances, the exchange rate, and indexation: Real variables in disinflation. *Quarterly Journal of Economics* 103 (1): 27–49.

———. 1994. Comments on Dornbusch and Werner. *Brookings Papers on Economic Activity,* Issue no. 1:304–09.

Fleiss, J. L. 1981. *Statistical methods for rates and proportions.* New York: John Wiley and Sons.

Frankel, Jeffrey A., and Andrew Rose. 1996. Currency crashes in emerging markets: An empirical treatment. *Journal of International Economics* 41 (November): 351–66.

Frenkel, Jacob A., and Assaf Razin. 1987. *Fiscal policies and the world economy: An intertemporal approach.* Cambridge: MIT Press.

Ghosh, Atish R., and Jonathan D. Ostry. 1995. The current account in developing countries: A perspective from the consumption-smoothing approach. *World Bank Economic Review* 9: 45–67.

Goldstein, Morris, Graciela L. Kaminsky, and Carmen R. Reinhart. 2000. *Assessing financial vulnerability: An early warning system for emerging markets.* Washington, D.C.: Institute for International Economics.

Harberger, Arnold. 1950. Currency depreciation, income and the balance of trade. *Journal of Political Economy* 2 (February): 341–57.

Heckman, James J., Hidehiko Ichirmua, and Petra Todd. 1998. Matching as an econometric evaluation estimator. *Review of Economic Studies* 65 (2).

Johnson, Harry G. 1955. Economic expansion and international trade. *Manchester School of Economic and Social Studies* 23.

Kamin, Steven B. 1988. Devaluation, exchange controls, and black markets for foreign exchange in developing countries. Board of Governors of the Federal Reserve System, International Finance Discussion Paper no. 334. Washington, D.C.: Board of Governors of the Federal Reserve System.

Krugman, Paul. 2000. *Currency crises.* Chicago: University of Chicago Press.

Laursen, Svend, and Lloyd Metzler. 1950. Flexible exchange rates and the theory of employment. *Review of Economics and Statistics* 32.

Loayza, Norman, Klaus Schmidt-Hebbel, and Luis Servén. 2000. What drives private saving around the world? World Bank Development Research Group Working Paper no. 2309. Washington, D.C.: World Bank.

Loser, Claudio M., and Ewart S. Williams. 1997. The Mexican crisis and its aftermath: An IMF perspective. In *Mexico 1994,* ed. Sebastian Edwards and Moises Naim, 259–73. Washington, D.C.: Carnegie Endowment.

Machlup, Fritz. 1943. *International trade and international income multiplier.* Philadelphia: Blakiston.

Meade, James E. 1951. *The balance of payments.* London: Oxford University Press.

Milesi-Ferretti, Gian Maria, and Assaf Razin. 1996. Sustainability of persistent current account deficits. NBER Working Paper no. 5467. Cambridge, Mass.: National Bureau of Economic Research, September.

———. 1998. Sharp reduction in current account deficits: An empirical analysis. *European Economic Review* 42:127–45.

————. 2000. Current account reversals and currency crises: Empirical regularities. In *Currency crises,* ed. Paul Krugman, 285–326. Chicago: University of Chicago Press.

Nerlove, Marc. 1971. Further evidence on the estimation of dynamic economic relations from a time series of cross-sections. *Econometrica* 39:359–82.

Obstfeld, Maurice, and Kenneth Rogoff. 1996. *Foundations of international macroeconomics.* Cambridge: MIT Press.

Radelet, Steven, and Jeffrey Sachs. 2000. The onset of the East Asian financial crisis. In *Currency crises,* ed. Paul Krugman, 105–58. Chicago: University of Chicago Press.

Razin, Assaf, and Lars E. O. Svensson. 1983. The current account and the optimal government debt. *Journal of International Money and Finance* 2 (2): 459–501.

Robichek, E. Walter. 1981. Some reflections about external public debt management. *Estudios Monetarios VII:* 139–49. Santiago, Chile: Banco Central de Chile.

Sachs, Jeffrey. 1981. The current account and macroeconomic adjustment in the 1970s. *Brookings Papers on Economic Activity,* Issue no. 1:201–68. Washington, D.C.: Brookings Institution.

Sachs, Jeffrey, Aaron Tornell, and Andrés Velasco. 1996. Financial crises in emerging markets: The lessons of 1995. *Brookings Papers on Economic Activity,* Issue no. 1:147–217. Washington, D.C.: Brookings Institution.

Salinas de Gortari, Carlos. 2000. *Memorias.* Madrid: Editorial Plaza y Janes.

Sheffrin, Steven M., and Wing Thye Woo. 1990. Testing an optimizing model of the current account via the consumption function. *Journal of International Money and Finance* 9 (2).

Summers, Lawrence H. 1996. Commentary. In *Volatile capital flows,* ed. Ricardo Hausmann and Liliana Rojas-Suarez, 17–25. Washington, D.C.: Inter-American Development Bank.

————. 2000. International financial crises: Causes, prevention, and cures. *American Economic Review* 90 (2): 3–21.

World Bank. 1993. *Trends in developing economies.* World Bank.

————. 1994. *Trends in developing economies.* World Bank.

Comment   Alejandro M. Werner

This paper touches upon three issues. First, it comprehensively reviews the evolution of the academic and policy makers' views on the role of the current account during the last twenty-five years. Second, it goes over models of current account sustainability used in financial institutions to argue that, although these models provide certain information regarding sustainability, they are useless to determine whether, at a particular point in time, a country is running large current account deficits. Finally, the paper presents the results from a huge data set on

1. The distribution of current account deficits across time and across regions.
2. The channels though which sudden stops affect growth.
3. The relationship between current account deficits and financial crises.

Alejandro M. Werner is director of economic studies at Bank of Mexico.

Let me say that I am sympathetic to the idea that current accounts matter, and that I think the evidence presented in this paper shows this to be the case and goes deeper into the channels through which this takes place. In my comments, I will concentrate on two issues: first, the empirical relevance of the sustainability model presented in the paper, and second, the relationship between current account reversals and crises.

Models of Current Account Sustainability

Given that the sustainable level of the current account should be determined by the willingness of the rest of the world to finance it, Edwards begins from standard portfolio theory and derives the net demand for a country's liabilities. This is a perfectly reasonable way to explain the determinants of the sustainable level for the current account deficit. However, to judge whether this model provides a sensible order of magnitude for the sustainable current account deficit in different countries, Edwards uses the results of a model developed by Goldman Sachs. He claims that,

> Using a very similar framework to the one developed above, Goldman Sachs has made a serious effort to actually estimate long-run sustainable current account deficits for a number of countries (Ades and Kaune 1997). . . . [T]he estimated levels . . . [range] from 1.9 to 4.5 percent of GDP. . . . [A]lthough the range for the "Short-Run Sustainable Level" is broader, in very few countries does it exceed 4 percent of GDP.

Although the Ades and Kaune model was also developed to calculate sustainable current account deficits, it is conceptually different from the model presented in Edwards's paper. In the Ades and Kaune model, the net international demand for a country's liabilities is not derived from a portfolio model. When calculating this net demand, Ades and Kaune take into account a country's incentives for defaulting on its debt. Therefore, the international net demand for a country's liabilities is determined by the maximum amount international capital markets can safely lend without triggering a default. Thus, the stock of a country's liabilities held by foreigners and the sustainable current account deficit will be determined by the equality between the benefit of defaulting (and suffering the penalty of losing access to the international capital market) and the benefit of maintaining access to the international capital market.

The literature that is closest to Edwards' derivation of the sustainable current account deficit and that should be used to test the relevance of this model is the one that tries to explain the equity home bias puzzle (see French and Poterba 1991; Tesar and Werner 1998; Lewis 1999). In this literature, the international investor chooses the proportion of his or her wealth that he or she wants to hold in domestic equity, and finds a demand for domestic stocks equivalent to equation (4) in Edwards's paper. When these models are confronted with the evidence, the degree of diversification implied by them is much larger than that observed in the real world. According to Lewis (1999, 578), "Clearly no degree of risk intolerance can justify such a low level of foreign portfolio allocation. Thus, these numbers suggest the presence of home bias."

These results imply that the portfolio diversification model predicts a much larger demand for a country's liabilities than the one observed in practice. Thus, they also predict current account deficits larger than those observed in the real world. Therefore, in addition to the problems associated with the transitions related to changes in portfolio allocations, it seems that these models also have important shortcomings in their implications for the long-run sustainable level for the current account deficit.

Empirical Issues

With respect to the empirical section, I will like to complement the paper's results on the relationship between current account reversals and currency crises with the Mexican experience. In particular, the Mexican crisis of December 1994 clearly shows that the current account reversal took place after the collapse of the currency. This supports the results of the paper that show that the relationship between the current account and crises implies complex timing issues.

As is clear from figure 1C.1, in 1994 Mexico suffered a capital account

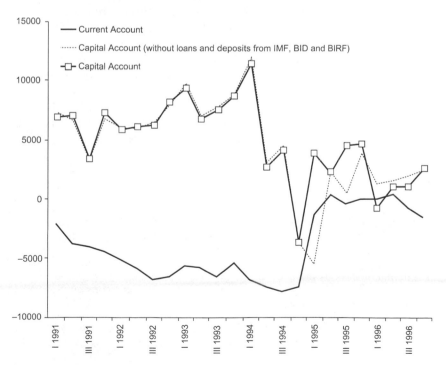

Fig. 1C.1   Current and capital account balance

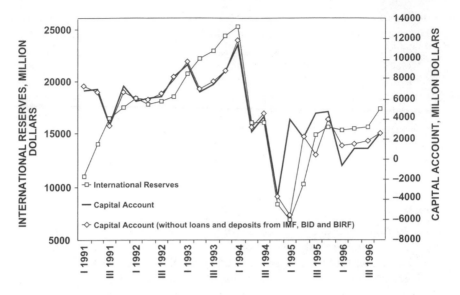

Fig. 1C.2   Capital account and international reserves

surplus reversal. In that year, the capital account balance went from a surplus of 11.4 billion dollars in the first quarter to –3.7 billion dollars in the fourth quarter. As shown in figure 1C.1, the current account deficit continued its downward trend during 1994. Obviously, domestic absorption was cushioned from the correction in the capital account surplus by the foreign reserve loses incurred by the central bank (see fig. 1C.2). Once reserves were depleted, the currency crisis ensued and the correction in the current account took place.

In conclusion, I think the paper is an important contribution to the literature and provides new and important evidence of the role that current account deficits play in currency crises, and the channels through which large current account reversals affect growth.

References

Ades, Alberto, and Federico Kaune. 1997. A new measure of current account sustainability for developing countries. Goldman Sachs Emerging Markets Economic Research. 29 September.

French, Kenneth R., and James M. Poterba. 1991. International diversification and international equity markets. *American Economic Review* 81 (2): 526–66.

Lewis, Karen. 1999. Trying to explain home bias in equities and consumption. *Journal of Economic Literature* 37:571–608.

Tesar, Linda, and Ingrid Werner. 1998. The internationalization of securities markets since the 1987 crash. In *Brookings-Wharton papers on financial services,* ed. Robert E. Litan and Anthony M. Santomero. Washington, D.C.: Brookings Institution.

Discussion Summary

A few people made remarks on whether and why current accounts matter for predicting crises. According to *Jeffrey A. Frankel,* it is important to distinguish whether the current account deficit matters for causing currency crises or for other things, such as long-term growth. As far as crises are concerned, it is important to determine whether a current account deficit is a necessary or a sufficient condition, or, as the economic profession views it, whether there is a statistically significant relationship between current account deficits and crises. Frankel commended the author for emphasizing the difference between the isolated effect of the current account on crises (in a multivariate setting) and the effect in a univariate regression.

Frankel made a couple of additional comments, offering an insight on the history of thought regarding the Lawson fallacy. The statement attributed to Nigel Lawson is that the current account deficit is not a cause for concern if foreign borrowing goes to the private sector. Lawson later qualified this statement, pointing out that this is not to say that high current account deficits will never lead to a crisis. According to Frankel, this qualification is a weak "straw man." Frankel went on to comment on the paper's approach to identifying the impact of a sudden reversal of the current account on the output growth rate. He said that a sudden reversal is most likely to take the form of a reduction in investment. The author showed that, indeed, the sudden reversal of the current account affects the growth rate through this channel.

Anne O. Krueger discussed why and how the composition of a current account deficit matters. She emphasized that the correct distinction is not between public and private uses of foreign capital, but rather of how efficiently the money is spent. The former distinction is useless for a category as fungible as the current account. She brought up the example of Brazil: When Brazil increased its interest rates, the private sector responded by borrowing from abroad while the public sector borrowed domestically. Krueger questioned whether this made any difference. As for the matter of sustainability, she stressed that the important difference is between rapidly growing countries excess demand for investment, and countries that have very high investment rates in order to sustain some degree of growth without an increase of productivity. For example, Korea had 10 percent of current account deficit during its ten years of most rapid growth. She suggested that the author find variables to capture productivity in the study of current account. Later in the discussion, *Jungho Yoo* echoed Krueger's comment on how foreign savings (current account) are utilized.

Liliana Rojas-Suarez supported Krueger's point. She said that a current account should be understood as being on a sustainable path if the economy is generating trade balances that enable it to avoid an ever-increasing accumulation of net foreign liabilities without the need either to devalue or to adjust economic activity severely. In this regard, the quality of investment is extremely relevant. A current account deficit that is basically the result of highly productive investment is likely to be more sustainable than a current account deficit resulting from low saving. The reason is that highly productive investment increases the economy's production capacity. Higher future output, in turn, enables the economy to pay back its foreign liabilities. She said that, in general, funding the current account deficit with foreign direct investment tends to help sustainability because FDI tends to go to productive investment projects, especially on the tradable goods sector.

Relating to the discussion of how the quality of investments affects the sustainable debt level, *Michael P. Dooley* agreed that, historically, what countries do with the money seems to have been important. However, he added, the conclusion might be the opposite of that implicit in the previous paragraph: If defaulting on the external debt is a strategic decision, then the better a debtor uses the capital inflow, the more independent the debtor becomes, and the more likely it will default.

That for which the current account deficit matters was also discussed. *Jorge Braga de Macedo* suggested that the paper could broaden the scope, rather than limiting the discussion to emerging markets or adjustable pegs. For example, he said that current accounts still matter within the euro zone. Even if there will no longer be currency crises, there could still be debt or banking crises in the euro zone. *Jaume Ventura* pointed out that the question of how well current account deficits predict crises is different from the conventional approach to its welfare consequences. In (intertemporal) models of the current account, a large deficit has no welfare costs and does not ask for government intervention. *Eduardo Borensztein* commented on whether current account deficits could predict crises. He said that an IMF study focusing on emerging markets (twenty-seven countries) found that current account deficits are very significant predictors of crises. The somewhat weak result of the paper in this regard may suggest that the effects of current accounts differ across different groups of countries.

On the paper's treatment (exclusion) of African countries, Braga de Macedo disagreed with the author. He said that the devaluation in some African countries in 1994 showed that Africa is just like any other region, and that excluding these countries from the sample seemed unjustified. Frankel said that, in his paper with Andrew Rose, he and Rose found no significant relationship between current accounts and crises in univariate regressions. Edwards' finding of a significant correlation could be the result of excluding African countries from the sample. Dooley supported this point by citing his 1987 paper with Frankel and Don Mathieson, which found that non-market borrowers (those who depend primarily on official financing) have much larger and more persistent current account imbalances. This, he said, could explain why the Edwards paper found different results when dropping African countries. Krueger suggested the author could include African countries but exclude the official aid flows to the region.

Martin Feldstein commended the paper's emphasis on the transition between different optimal stock levels of foreign capital. He said that this emphasis was very important because countries easily confuse the temporary increase of capital flows as a result of a shift in the desired *stock* level with a sustainable higher level of current account *flow,* as in the case of Mexico.

Ventura commented on the idea of sustainability, saying that transversality conditions were introduced in the early models where the current account was assumed to equal domestic saving. In these models, checking sustainability simply means to confirm empirically, the transversality condition, which is a theoretical artifact. The approach of this paper, however, is different from that of the earlier literature in that the current accounts are a result of portfolio choices. Ventura questioned the meaning of sustainability in this new context.

Rudi Dornbusch said that the sudden-stop view would predict crises first and large current account reversals second. He suggested that the author look into this relationship.

Krueger also expressed concerns about the data on different forms of capital flows, such as equity and foreign direct investment. She said that the use of derivatives is most likely to blur the distinction among such categories.

Kristin J. Forbes asked what the author's view was on the (high) U.S. current account deficit.

Regarding that for which the current account matters, Edwards said that in the newer version of the paper, he had made it explicit. That is, large current account deficits do not unavoidably lead to catastrophic crises, but they do, with high degree of likelihood, result in large welfare losses. He said that the policy implication of the paper is very important. For example, there is a heated discussion on whether the Mexican current account deficit (about 4 percent) is too large. Should Mexico allow the exchange rate to depreciate to handle that deficit, or should it be left to float and possibly lead to a crisis? The concern of the paper is whether a large current account warrants a policy intervention.

A related question is when to "apply the break," as some countries (such as Chile) use large account deficits as targets for their monetary policies.

On the questions of the crowding out of foreign saving by domestic saving and on the use of saving, he said that the quality of investment could possibly be proxied by interacting the deficit and the competitiveness index from the World Economic Index.

Finally, on the current high level of the U.S. current account, Edwards said that no industrial country has had so high a level of current deficit in his data set, and that he believes this level is unsustainable.

Are Trade Linkages Important Determinants of Country Vulnerability to Crises?

Kristin J. Forbes

2.1 Introduction

The latter half of the 1990s was punctuated by a series of financial and currency crises: the Mexican peso collapse in 1994; the East Asian crisis in 1997–98; the Russian collapse in 1998; and the devaluations in Brazil and Ecuador in 1999. One striking characteristic of many of these crises was how an initial country-specific event was rapidly transmitted to markets of very different sizes and structures around the globe. These events have prompted a surge of interest in "contagion" and in the determinants of a country's vulnerability to crises that originate elsewhere in the world. Despite this interest, however, there continues to be little agreement on why many of these crises that began in relatively small economies had such large global repercussions.

One channel through which a country-specific crisis could have global repercussions is trade. If two countries trade directly, export to the same country, or simply compete in the same industry, then a crisis in one of the countries could change the relative prices or quantities of goods traded by that country and have spillover effects in the other economy. Theoretical models have shown exactly how these trade linkages could transmit a crisis in one country to another country. There is an ongoing debate, however, on

Kristin J. Forbes currently is deputy assistant secretary of quantitative policy analysis at the U.S. Department of the Treasury. She is on leave from the Sloan School of Management at the Massachusetts Institute of Technology, where she is the Mitsubishi Career Development Professor of International Management. She is also a faculty research fellow of the National Bureau of Economic Research.

The author wishes to thank Sebastian Edwards, Jeffrey A. Frankel, Federico Sturzenegger, and conference participants for useful suggestions and comments.

whether these trade linkages have been large or significant determinants of how different countries were affected by recent financial crises.

Informal evidence suggests why this debate is unresolved. There is little direct trade between Brazil and Russia, and even minimal competition in third markets between these two countries. Brazil, however, was severely impacted by the Russian crisis in 1998, suggesting that trade linkages may not have been important in the transmission of this crisis. On the other hand, Argentina is one of Brazil's major trading partners. Argentina is also one of the countries most affected by Brazil's devaluation in 1999, suggesting that trade may have been important in the transmission of the Brazilian crisis. Numerous other examples from the series of currency crises in the 1990s could support either of these arguments.

This paper addresses the debate on whether trade linkages were important determinants of countries' vulnerability to recent currency crises. It decomposes trade linkages into three channels by which a country could be affected by a crisis elsewhere in the world: a competitiveness effect (in which changes in relative prices affect a country's ability to compete abroad); an income effect (in which a crisis affects incomes and the demand for imports); and a cheap-import effect (in which a crisis reduces import prices for a trading partner and acts as a positive supply shock). Then the paper uses data on aggregate trade flows and four-digit industry trade flows to measure the strength of these three channels between every country experiencing a crisis from 1994 through 1999 and a sample of developed and developing countries around the world.

Using these statistics, the paper estimates how trade linkages affected a country's stock market returns during recent crises. It finds that the competitiveness and income effects are both negative, significant, and economically important. In other words, if a country competes in the same industries as a crisis country, or exports directly to the crisis country, then the country will have significantly lower stock returns during the crisis. There is also weak evidence of a positive cheap-import effect. The combined impact of these three trade linkages appears to be much greater than that of other macroeconomic variables. These trade linkages, however, explain only about one-fourth of the variation in stock market returns during recent crises, suggesting that other cross-country linkages, such as financial channels, may also be important.

A final result from this empirical analysis is that the way a country responds to a currency crisis is an important determinant of how the crisis impacts other economies. For example, countries respond to pressure on their exchange rates by devaluing their own currencies (or allowing them to depreciate). Other countries attempt to maintain stable currency values and instead increase interest rates significantly. Other countries pay out international reserves, or use some combination of these three defenses. Empirical results suggest that the competitiveness effect is large and significant only when a crisis country allows its currency to be devalued (or to depreciate) substantially. Results also suggest that the income effect is large and significant only when a crisis country raises interest rates substantially. Therefore, the importance of trade linkages depends on how a country responds to the initial crisis. This has important implications for preventing and predicting how future crises spread internationally.

This paper makes a number of contributions to the literature. First, it emphasizes that the term *trade* actually captures several different (and possibly counteracting) channels that can be divided into three distinct effects: competitiveness, income, and cheap-import effects. Second, it creates a number of new and more accurate statistics to measure these trade linkages. For example, most papers attempting to measure trade competition in third markets analyze aggregate trade flows to common markets. The fact that two countries are highly dependent on a common market, however, does not mean the two countries compete directly. For example, if a high proportion of Saudi Arabia's oil and of Brazil's coffee goes to the same third market, Saudi Arabia and Brazil are not direct competitors. By focusing on trade in specific industries, instead of aggregate trade flows, this paper's statistics provide more accurate measures of trade competition.

Fourth, and finally, by utilizing this industry-level trade data, the paper can reduce any omitted-variables bias. More specifically, several papers finding that trade linkages help transmit crises admit that trade flows are highly correlated with financial flows. It is extremely difficult to disentangle these linkages (and even to measure financial linkages), so estimates of the importance of trade linkages may actually be capturing the impact of financial linkages.[1] Financial flows are generally country specific and similar across industries, however, whereas many trade flows vary across industries. Therefore, by using industry-level data, this paper can more accurately identify the impact of trade linkages and reduce any omitted-variables bias.

The remainder of this paper is as follows. Section 2.2 reviews previous empirical work assessing the importance of trade in the international transmission of crises. Section 2.3 surveys the related theoretical work, and then uses this work to decompose trade into three different (and possibly opposing) linkages. Section 2.4 uses an index of exchange rates, interest rates, and reserve levels to identify the crisis events used in the rest of the paper. Section 2.5 introduces the model and data set and calculates a number of statistics measuring trade linkages across countries. It discusses these statistics, especially the industry-based competitiveness measure, in some detail. Section 2.6 presents regression estimates, including an extensive series of sensitivity tests. It finds that competitiveness and income effects are

---

1. Glick and Rose (1999), Kaminsky and Reinhart (2000), and Van Rijckeghem and Weder (2001) all raise this point.

significant and economically important determinants of country vulnerability to crises. Section 2.7 examines different types of crises and shows that the way a country responds to exchange-market pressure determines which trade linkages are important transmission mechanisms. Finally, section 2.8 summarizes the key results of the paper and concludes with an important policy implication.

2.2   The Empirical Literature: Is Trade Important?

A number of empirical papers have attempted to measure the importance of trade in the international transmission of crises. This section discusses the basic methodology and results of each of these papers. It begins with three empirical papers arguing that trade linkages are important determinants of how crises spread. Then it discusses three papers that claim that trade linkages were not important during recent crises. The section concludes by summarizing three recent papers arguing that trade linkages are important, but overshadowed by other transmission mechanisms.

One of the first empirical papers to assess the importance of trade and find strong support for this propagation mechanism was Eichengreen and Rose (1999). This paper uses a binary-probit model to test whether the probability of a crisis occurring in twenty industrial countries between 1959 and 1993 is correlated with the occurrence of a speculative attack in other countries at the same time. In one series of tests, the authors weight the occurrence of crises in other countries by a trade matrix (which is based on bilateral trade flows in manufacturing[2]) and by a matrix of macroeconomic variables. They find that this trade-weighted matrix is highly significant and robust, while the macro-weighted matrix is insignificant. They conclude that their results lend "some support to our favored interpretation that it is trade links rather than macroeconomic similarities that have been the dominant channel for the contagious transmission in the sample period" (1999, 50).[3]

Glick and Rose (1999) build on this framework in the most complete and thorough analysis, to date, of the role of trade in the international transmission of crises. They focus on five major currency crises between 1971 and 1997 and test whether the probability of a country being attacked during a crisis is affected by trade linkages between that country and the crisis country. Glick and Rose include a much larger sample of countries than do Eichengreen and Rose (1999) and use a number of different statistics to measure trade linkages. They focus on a trade statistic measuring exports to

2. More specifically, this weighting matrix is based on the MERM weights constructed by the International Monetary Fund and used to compute its real effective multilateral exchange rates. The weights, created in October 1994, are based on unit labor costs, use a convex combination of import and export trade flows, and are time-invariant.

3. The working paper version was Eichengreen, Rose, and Wyplosz (1996).

common third markets, although they also run sensitivity tests using bilateral trade flows, a combination of these two statistics, and exports to common markets weighted by country size. These trade measures are consistently large and significant, indicating that "a stronger trade linkage is associated with a higher incidence of currency crises" (1999, 613). Once again, macroeconomic controls are generally insignificant.

Instead of using aggregate trade flow data, Forbes (2000) uses firm-level information to measure the importance of trade in the international transmission of crises. The paper's sample includes information on more than 10,000 companies from around the world during the Asian and Russian crises. It focuses on the variation in different companies' stock market performance to test not only which types of companies were most affected by these crises, but also how these crises spread internationally. Results show that companies that had sales exposure to the crisis country or that competed in the same industry as the crisis country had significantly lower stock returns during these two crises. The paper concludes that direct trade effects (called *income effects*) as well as competition in export industries (called *product-competitiveness effects*) "were both important transmission mechanisms during the later part of the Asian crisis and the Russian crisis" (Forbes 2000, 1 [abstract]).

Although these three papers find strong evidence for the role of trade, a number of other empirical papers argue that trade was not important in the propagation of recent crises. In one of the earliest papers classifying specific channels through which crises spread internationally, Masson (1998) categorizes trade as a spillover and argues that spillovers were not important during the 1994 Mexican crisis or the 1997 Asian crisis. He argues that since exports to Mexico and Thailand constituted a small proportion of total exports from their neighbors, regional spillover effects through trade would have been modest. Masson also calculates the loss in competitiveness of five Asian countries (as measured by changes in their real effective exchange rates) during the Asian crisis. Since this competitiveness effect was small (at least before the November depreciation of the won), he argues that these spillovers cannot explain the spread of the crisis from Thailand throughout Asia. Masson concludes that spillover effects "cannot explain the coincidence of speculative pressures felt by a number of emerging market economies at the time of the Mexican and Thai crises" (Masson 1998, 3).

Baig and Goldfajn (1998) also argue that trade was not important in the spread of the Asian crisis. They calculate direct trade flows between each of the East Asian economies, and assert that "they are not adequate to account for what happened in East Asia. The trade linkages among the five countries in discussion are not very striking. . . . The export share to Thailand constituted less than 4 percent of total exports for each of the four countries in discussion, making intra-country trade an unlikely source of pressure on financial markets." Baig and Goldfajn also consider indirect trade linkages, such as export competition in the United States and Japan, but "don't find much evidence in support of this argument either. The Asia 5 countries do not share very similar third-country export profiles that would amount to severe competitiveness pressures" (Baig and Goldfajn 1998, 7).

Another paper that argues that trade was not significant has a more limited focus. Harrigan examines how the Asian crisis affected prices and volumes in different U.S. manufacturing sectors. He concludes that "[t]he impact of the Asia[n] crisis on U.S. industries was small and localized. Only one sector, the steel industry, experienced falling prices and output in the wake of the crisis" (2000, 79). Harrigan admits that there was a decreased demand for U.S. manufactured goods in Asia during the crisis, but claims that this was offset by increased demand elsewhere in the world (including within the United States). He also reports that U.S. import volumes from Asia increased only moderately during this period, despite the large fall in import prices, because U.S. demand for Asian imports is relatively inelastic.

These three papers argue that trade was not important in the international transmission of recent crises, and the first three papers discussed in this section argue that trade was important. Most recent empirical work, however, takes an intermediate stance and claims that trade linkages can have some role, but that they are generally overshadowed by other factors.[4] In one such paper, Kaminsky and Reinhart (2000) examine the spread of the Mexican and Asian crises. They use both bilateral and third-country trade linkages (measured by export shares in similar industries) to construct "trade cluster" statistics. They then use these statistics to estimate how trade affects the conditional probability that an initial crisis will spread to other countries. They find that the bilateral-trade cluster for Latin America is more important than for other regions, but emphasize that all of these trade measures are less influential than financial linkages. They conclude that trade may have played some role in the transmission of the Thai crisis to Malaysia, Korea, and the Philippines, but that it "can certainly not help explain Argentina and Brazil following the Mexican devaluation nor Indonesia following the Thai crisis" (2000, 167).

Van Rijckeghem and Weder (2001) also argue that financial linkages may be more important than trade linkages in explaining country vulnerability to crises. They use data from the Bank for International Settlements (BIS) to construct several measures of competition for bank funds during the Mexican, Thai, and Russian crises. Then they use these statistics, as well as a series of trade and macroeconomic variables, to estimate the conditional probability that an initial crisis will affect other countries. They find that if

4. More recently, a number of papers have tested for the relative importance of trade flows, financial linkages, and macroeconomic variables in the transmission of recent crises. These papers build on one or more of the approaches outlined in this section. They generally find that trade linkages are important but overshadowed by other transmission channels. For example, see Caramazza, Ricci, and Salgado (2000), De Gregorio and Valdés (2001), or Gelos and Sahay (2001).

either trade linkages *or* financial linkage are included in the model, the variables are usually highly significant. When both trade and financial linkages are included simultaneously, however, one of the two often becomes insignificant. They conclude that "spillovers through common bank lenders were important in transmitting" these three crises, and emphasize that "trade and financial linkages appear to be highly correlated," thereby making it difficult to differentiate empirically between these two effects (Van Rijckeghem and Weder 2001, 12–13).

Wincoop and Yi (2000) also find mixed support for trade linkages in their examination of the impact of the Asian crisis on short-run U.S. gross domestic product (GDP) growth. They argue that the Asian crisis spread to the United States through three channels: decreased demand for U.S. exports due to the recession in Asia; exchange-rate movements that reduced the U.S. price of imports from Asia; and capital outflows from Asia that lowered the cost of capital and therefore increased demand in the United States. They estimate that the significant negative impact on U.S. growth from the first effect was entirely counteracted by the positive impact on U.S. growth from the third effect. (The estimated impact of second effect was minor.) Therefore, Wincoop and Yi suggest that even though the Asian crisis directly affected the United States through trade, this effect was entirely offset by other transmission channels.

To summarize, a number of empirical papers have tested for the role of trade in the international transmission of currency crises. The results are as varied as the approaches and techniques used. Some papers argue that trade linkages were large and significant; others argue that they were not important, especially in the spread of the Mexican, Asian, and Russian crises. Some of the most recent papers find a small role for trade—although one generally overshadowed by other propagation channels. Therefore, this debate on the importance of trade in the international transmission of recent crises can be resolved only through further careful empirical work.

2.3   The Theory: Why Might Trade Be Important?

The theoretical literature modeling exactly how trade can transmit crises is much more limited than the empirical literature testing for its importance. This section begins by briefly summarizing the key theoretical papers on the subject. Then it develops a framework for the empirical analysis in the remainder of the paper. It emphasizes that trade incorporates three distinct channels: a competitiveness effect, an income effect, and a cheap-import effect. Since any two of these channels could work in opposite directions, it is necessary to control simultaneously for each of them when analyzing the importance of trade in a country's vulnerability to financial crises.

Gerlach and Smets (1995) is the first paper to model formally how a devaluation in one country can affect trade flows and thereby cause a crisis in another country. In their model, two countries are linked through trade in merchandise and financial assets. A successful attack on one country's exchange rate causes a devaluation and improves the competitiveness of that country's merchandise exports. This produces a trade deficit in the second country and a gradual decline in its central bank's international reserves. This ultimately leads to a speculative attack on the second country's currency. Gerlach and Smets also model a secondary effect of the initial devaluation. This devaluation lowers import prices in the second country, which reduces the aggregate price level and domestic demand. Residents of the country swap domestic currency for foreign exchange, which further depletes the central bank's holdings of international reserves. As a result, the second country could shift to an equilibrium in which the central bank does not hold enough reserves to withstand a speculative attack.

Corsetti et al. (2000) use microfoundations to develop a more detailed and rigorous model of how trade can transmit crises internationally. They model two channels through which a devaluation in one country can affect other countries. In the first channel, the devaluation lowers the relative price of a country's exports and therefore shifts demand away from countries that produce similar goods. In the second channel, the cheaper exports improve the terms of trade for other countries, allowing them to finance higher levels of consumption for any given levels of nominal income. Either of these two effects could dominate, so that a devaluation in one country does not necessarily lead to a welfare loss in other countries. In fact, under certain situations the second channel could dominate, and the country that devalues could "beggar thyself" while simultaneously generating a welfare improvement for other countries.

These theoretical papers explain how trade can transmit crises internationally.[5] A key point from this literature, especially when combined with the empirical review in section 2.2, is that trade incorporates a number of distinct channels. As clearly shown in Corsetti et al. (2000) and Wincoop and Yi (2000), the various channels that constitute trade could counteract each other. As a result, the aggregate impact of trade linkages could be small, even though individual trade channels are large and significant. Therefore, any empirical work on how trade linkages transmit crises should control for each of these channels simultaneously.

5. One additional theoretical paper that deserves note is Paasche (2000). This paper does not focus on trade per se but shows how a small shock to a country's terms of trade (which could be caused by a devaluation elsewhere in the world or by a reduction in demand for a country's exports) can be magnified by credit constraints and thereby have large domestic consequences. This type of model could be combined with any of the other theoretical models to amplify these trade effects. Also see Harrigan (2000) and Pesenti and Tille (2000). Harrigan provides a nontechnical discussion of the effect of the Asian devaluations on prices and quantities in the United States and Asia. Pesenti and Tille discuss the direct impact of bilateral trade flows between countries, as well as the indirect impact of competition in third markets. They provide several numerical examples to show how a devaluation in one country could affect other countries through competition in third markets.

The empirical analysis in the remainder of this paper follows this approach. It attempts to measure simultaneously whether these three trade linkages were important determinants of how recent crises impacted other countries. More specifically, it focuses on three trade channels: a competitiveness effect, an income effect, and a cheap-import effect. The competitiveness effect is the first channel modeled in Corsetti et al. (2000). This trade effect occurs when one country devalues its currency, reducing the relative price of that country's exports and shifting demand away from goods that compete with those exports. If exports from the crisis country constitute a large enough share of global production in a given industry, prices in that industry could fall worldwide. Therefore, even if a country does not directly compete with exports from the crisis country in any specific markets, its export competitiveness could be damaged through these global industry effects.[6]

The second trade channel is what this paper calls an income effect.[7] This occurs when a crisis affects a country's income level (or even its income distribution) and growth rate, which in turn affects that country's demand for imports. Other countries that export directly to the crisis country will experience shifts in demand for their goods. Most of the empirical work discussed in section 2.2 assumes that any income effect is negative, since recent crises have generated a sharp contraction in economic growth and reduction in aggregate demand (within the crisis country). The historical evidence on the impact of currency crises on growth and demand, however, is mixed.[8] In many cases a currency crisis leads to a devaluation, which improves growth performance and aggregate demand in the crisis country. Therefore, the sign of any income effect is a priori indeterminate.

The final trade channel that this paper examines is a cheap-import effect.[9] This occurs when a country devalues its currency, reducing the relative price of its exports and improving the terms of trade in other countries. Imports into noncrisis countries are now available at cheaper prices, potentially allowing them to finance higher levels of consumption for any given levels of nominal income. This trade linkage could have a positive impact on a country's welfare when a crisis occurs elsewhere in the world.

To summarize, this paper tests whether three trade channels (competitiveness, income, and cheap-import effects) are important determinants of

6. There could also be secondary competitiveness effects if exports from the country that devalued are used as inputs for the production of goods in other countries. In this case, the currency crisis could improve, rather than reduce, the competitiveness of these products.

7. Wincoop and Yi (2000) call this a domestic demand effect.

8. For example, Gupta, Mishra, and Sahay (2000) examine the response of output during crises. They find that about 40 percent of crises have been expansionary. Also see Goldstein, Kaminsky, and Reinhart (2000, chap. 7), for a survey of the literature examining how currency crises affect a variety of economic indicators.

9. This is also called the bilateral trade effect in Corsetti et al. (2000) and the supply effect in Wincoop and Yi (2000).

a country's vulnerability to recent financial crises. This paper does not test for the importance of other transmission channels, such as common bank lenders, capital flows' responding to changes in interest rates, or changes in investor sentiment. Although these other channels are undoubtedly important and may even interact with trade flows, this paper maintains its narrow focus in order to assess the significance and magnitude of these trade linkages carefully.

2.4 The Crisis Events

In order to test for the role of trade linkages during recent crises, it is necessary to begin by defining exactly when these crises occurred. In many cases, such as the Mexican peso devaluation in December 1994, it is not only clear that a crisis occurred, but also fairly straightforward to date when the crisis began. Other cases, however, are much more difficult to define. For example, in the aftermath of the Mexican devaluation, Argentina raised short-term interest rates to 44 percent (versus about 7 percent immediately before the Mexican crisis) and still suffered a large outflow of reserves.[10] Does this qualify as a crisis? Or, even though Brazil did not devalue its currency until January 1999 (an event that most people would agree is a crisis), how should we classify periods such as the week in early September 1998, when Brazil raised interest rates from about 20 to 40 percent to forestall a devaluation?

These situations suggest that focusing only on exchange rate movements may miss important periods of pressure on a country's currency. Therefore, I follow a convention frequently used in the currency crisis literature and construct an "exchange-market pressure index," which accounts for movements in a country's exchange rate, interest rate, and reserve levels. Although this index is somewhat ad hoc, it does capture the three main defenses (devaluing its currency, raising interest rates, or paying out reserves) that a country has against a speculative attack. More specifically, I construct a weighted index of exchange-market pressure (EMP) similar to that introduced in Eichengreen, Rose, and Wyplosz (1996):

$$(1) \qquad \text{EMP}_{nt} = \alpha\%\Delta e_{nt} + \beta[(i_{nt} - i_{Ut}) - (i_{ny} - i_{Uy})] - \gamma(\%\Delta r_{nt} - \%\Delta r_{Ut}),$$

where e_{nt} is the nominal exchange rate for country n's currency in U.S. dollars at time t; i_{nt} is the short-term interest rate for country n at time t; i_{Ut} is the short-term interest rate for the United States at time t; i_{ny} and i_{Uy} are the same two interest rates calculated as rolling averages for the previous year (starting at date $t - 1$)[11]; and r_{nt} and r_{Ut} are the ratios of international reserves

10. Data sources are discussed below.
11. This component of the index is generally calculated as a period-to-period change instead of a period-to-year change. I depart from this convention to adjust for the fact that a country may raise interest rates to defend its currency for longer than one period. This is particularly important for this paper's analysis because the time periods (t) are weeks instead of months or quarters.

to the money supply for country n and the United States, respectively. Each component of the index is entered so that higher values of the index indicate greater levels of EMP. Each component of the index is also weighted by the inverse of the standard deviation for each series (the α, β, and γ) in order to equalize conditional volatilities and ensure that no single series dominates the index.

In order to focus on recent currency crises (and to correspond with the trade data used in section 2.5), I calculate this EMP index for five years—from 1 July 1994 through 31 June 1999. The data for U.S. dollar exchange rates and short-term interest rates are compiled on a weekly basis from Datastream. The data on reserves and the money supply (M1) are collected from the International Financial Statistics CD-ROM published by the International Monetary Fund (IMF; 2000). This information is available on a monthly basis only, so I interpolate to estimate weekly statistics. Also, I exclude countries with an annual rate of consumer price inflation greater than 100 percent.[12] Further information on data sources and definitions is available at the beginning of the appendix. The resulting sample used to calculate the EMP index consists of the forty-five countries listed in the note to table 2.1.[13]

The final step is to specify the critical value for the EMP index such that index values above this level qualify as a crisis. I use the criteria

(2) $$Crisis_{nt} = 1 \quad \text{if } EMP_{nt} > \mu_{EMP} + 5\sigma_{EMP}$$

$$= 0 \quad \text{otherwise}$$

where $Crisis_{nt}$ is an indicator variable equal to 1 if a crisis occurs in country n at time t; μ_{EMP} is the mean of the EMP index; and σ_{EMP} is the standard deviation of the index. These criteria generate forty-one country-week crisis periods.[14] Many of these one-week crisis periods, however, are clearly part of a single crisis event (e.g., Mexico has 5 one-week "crises" between 19 December 1994 and 19 March 1995). Therefore, I include any crisis-week that occurs within one year of a country's initial crisis as part of a single crisis

---

12. Adjusting this cutoff to either 50 or 150 percent has minimal impact on the results. I also exclude Kenya, Luxembourg, Pakistan, Russia (before 1997), and Sri Lanka because none of these countries has the trade data during this period that are necessary for the analysis in the remainder of the paper.

13. Since this paper uses weekly data and includes interest rates as one component of the EMP index, the sample of countries is smaller than in other papers that calculate a similar crisis index. The shorter time periods are critical, however, to identifying the crisis windows accurately, as well as to capture short periods of intense EMP. Moreover, the focus of this paper is to measure country vulnerability to these crises, and the sample of countries used for this analysis is larger.

14. The sensitivity analysis examines the impact of using lower critical values to define the crisis events. As shown in section 2.6, this has no significant impact on results. I focus on the stricter definition of a crisis for two reasons. First, a less stringent definition includes many events that are not intuitively crises. Second, and most important, a less stringent definition identifies a number of weeks as crises that occur simultaneously in different countries. This complicates any empirical analysis of how each crisis affects other countries.

Table 2.1   The Crisis Events

Country	Crisis Event Dates
Mexico	12/19/94–12/25/94; 01/16/95–01/29/95; 02/27/95–03/05/95; 03/13/95–03/19/95
Ecuador (1)	01/23/95–02/12/95; 10/30/95–11/05/95
Argentina	03/06/95–03/12/95
Venezuela (1)	12/11/95–12/17/95; 04/15/96–04/21/96
Venezuela (2)	05/12/97–05/18/97
Czech Republic	05/19/97–05/25/97
Thailand	06/30/97–07/06/97
The Philippines	07/07/97–07/13/97; 09/29/97–10/05/97
Indonesia	08/11/97–08/17/97; 08/25/97–08/31/97; 09/29/97–10/05/97; 12/08/97–12/14/97; 01/19/98–01/25/98; 03/02/98–03/08/98; 05/18/98–05/24/98
Korea	12/29/97–01/04/98
India	01/19/98–01/25/98
Russia	05/18/98–05/31/98; 07/06/98–07/12/98; 08/10/98–09/06/98; 09/14/98–09/20/98
Venezuela (3)	06/15/98–06/21/98; 09/14/98–09/20/98
Slovak Republic	09/28/98–10/04/98
Ecuador (2)	10/19/98–10/25/98; 01/11/99–01/17/99; 03/01/99–03/07/99
Brazil	01/11/99–01/17/99

Notes: Crises are defined as weeks when $EMP_{nt} > \mu_{EMP} + 5\sigma_{EMP}$. Countries included in the sample to test whether they experienced a crisis between 1 July 1994 and 31 June 1999 are Argentina, Australia, Austria, Belgium, Brazil, Canada, Chile, Colombia, Czech Republic, Denmark, Ecuador, Finland, France, Germany, Greece, Hong Kong, Hungary, India, Indonesia, Ireland, Israel, Italy, Japan, Korea, Malaysia, Mexico, Morocco, the Netherlands, New Zealand, Norway, Peru, the Philippines, Poland, Portugal, Russia (after 1996), Singapore, Slovak Republic, South Africa, Spain, Sweden, Switzerland, Thailand, United Kingdom, and Venezuela. The United States is included in the sample but cannot experience a crisis due to the way the index is defined.

event. In other words, a country can have, at most, one crisis per year. This generates a sample of sixteen recent crises, listed chronologically in table 2.1. The weeks included in each crisis event are listed in the second column of the table. The average length of a crisis is 2.6 weeks.

This list captures most of the recent events that gained attention as major currency crises, as well as a number of less publicized events. For example, the list includes the most obvious crises since mid-1994: the Mexican devaluation in December 1994; the Thai crisis in July 1997; the Korean devaluation in December 1997; the Russian crisis in August 1998; and the Brazilian devaluation in January 1999. It also includes some less obvious crises, such as the pressure on Argentina's peso in March 1995 and on India's rupee in January 1998. Many of these events do not include a major currency devaluation, but instead reflect a significant rise in interest rates or a loss in reserves to counter the pressure on the exchange rate.[15] One interesting pattern in table 2.1 is that crises tend to be bunched in time as well as by region. For example, there were several crises in Latin America at the end of 1994 and throughout 1995. This was followed by a relatively calm period, until the Thai devaluation in 1997 was quickly followed by a series of crises across Asia.

2.5   The Model, Data, and Trade Statistics

Now that the crisis events have been identified, it is possible to estimate whether the three trade channels are important determinants of a country's vulnerability to recent crises. For simplicity, I refer to the country experiencing the initial crisis as the ground-zero country.[16] The base model, which is estimated for the sample of sixteen crises, is

$$(3) \qquad Return_{n,e} = \theta_1 Compete_{n,e} + \theta_2 Income_{n,e} + \theta_3 Cheap\ Import_{n,e}$$
$$+ \theta_4 X_{n,e} + \theta_5 P_e + \varepsilon_{n,e},$$

where $Return_{n,e}$ is the stock market return for country n over the crisis event e; $Compete_{n,e}$ is a measure of any competitiveness-effect linkages between country n and the ground-zero country; $Income_{n,e}$ is a measure of any income-effect linkages between country n and the ground-zero country; $Cheap\ Import_{n,e}$ is a measure of any cheap-import effect linkages between country n and the ground-zero country; $X_{n,e}$ is a set of macroeconomic control variables for country n; and P_e is a set of period dummies (for each crisis event e). These period dummies are included to control for any global events or aggregate shocks that affect all countries during the crisis. Each of the independent variables is measured during the year prior to the starting date of the crisis; for example, the trade and macroeconomic variables for the Thai crisis (which began in June 1997) are measured in 1996.[17] This timing convention is used so that the independent variables do not incorporate any impact of the crisis.

This model focuses on stock returns (the dependent variable) to measure a country's vulnerability to a crisis for several reasons. First, stock returns are available for a large sample of countries (an even larger sample than that used to calculate the crisis index). Second, since stock returns are measured

---

15. Section 2.7 analyzes how these different types of crises (i.e., largely driven by currency devaluations versus interest rate increases) determine how a crisis affects other countries.

16. This terminology is borrowed from Glick and Rose (1999).

17. The one exception is the Mexican crisis (which occurred during various weeks between 19 December 1994 and 19 March 1995. Due to data limitations for the trade variables, the independent variables are measured in 1994. Since the crisis occurred near year-end, however, there should be minimal feedback on the annualized trade and macroeconomic variables.

at a much higher frequency than most macroeconomic and trade variables, stock returns can more accurately pinpoint the effects of a specific crisis. This is particularly important when a series of crises (such as those in Thailand, the Philippines, and Indonesia) are bunched together in time. Third, since stock returns incorporate the immediate impact of a crisis as well as the expected longer-term effects, stock returns should capture the total impact of a crisis on a particular country. Granted, stock returns also have a number of shortcomings. Any sort of investor behavior that drives markets from their long-term equilibria could reduce the ability of stock returns to capture the long-term impact of a crisis accurately.[18] Despite these shortcomings, stock returns are the most accurate indicator available for a large sample of countries at the high frequency necessary to isolate the impact of different crises that occur close together in time.

The data used to measure each of the variables in equation (3) come from a variety of sources. For the base analysis, stock returns ($Return_{n,e}$) are measured as abnormal weekly stock returns (written as percentages) for the market index in country n expressed in U.S. dollars.[19] The stock index data are from Datastream. For crisis events that last longer than one week, $Return_{n,e}$ is calculated as the average abnormal stock return over each week that qualifies as a crisis (as specified in table 2.1). Therefore, for the Mexican crisis (which is defined as including the five weeks between 19 December 1994 and 19 March 1995), $Return_{n,e}$ is calculated as the average, abnormal, weekly stock return over the five weeks identified as crisis events in table 2.1. The macroeconomic variables are taken from the International Financial Statistics CD-ROM (IMF 2000) and the World Development Indicators CD-ROM (World Bank 2000). The appendix provides further information on each of these data sources and definitions, including a table of summary statistics.

The three trade linkage variables are calculated using data from the International Trade Center, UN Statistics Division (1999), which reports bilateral trade flows between most countries in the world by four-digit Standard Industrial Trade Classification (SITC) codes between 1994 and 1998. The competitiveness variable ($Compete_{n,e}$) is calculated as a weighted product of two terms. The first term is exports from the ground-zero country in a given industry as a share of global exports in that industry. This term captures how important exports from the crisis country are to the industry, and therefore the potential impact of the crisis on the industry as a whole. The

18. For example, Barberis, Shleifer, and Vishny (1998) show that markets tend to underreact to individual news and overreact to a long series of related news.

19. Abnormal stock returns are calculated as stock returns during the crisis period minus average returns (i.e., normal returns) for the year preceding the start of the crisis. One week preceding the start of the crisis is excluded from the calculation of normal returns in case there were any unusual market movements directly before the crisis.

second term is total exports from country n in the same industry, as a share of country n's GDP. This term captures the importance of each industry to country n, and therefore country n's potential vulnerability to the crisis. Finally, these products are calculated and summed across all four-digit industries for each country-crisis pair and weighted by the maximum calculated value (and multiplied by 100). This creates an index whose values can range from 0 to 100.[20] In other words, the competitiveness variable for country n during crisis event e can be written

$$(4) \qquad Compete_{n,e} = \frac{100}{Max_{Compete}} \sum_{k} \left(\frac{Exp_{0,k,W}}{Exp_{W,k,W}} \cdot \frac{Exp_{n,k,W}}{GDP_n} \right)$$

where $Exp_{0,k,W}$ is exports from the ground-zero country in industry k to every other country in the world (W); $Exp_{W,k,W}$ is exports from every country in the world in industry k to every other country in the world; $Exp_{n,k,W}$ is exports from country n in industry k to every other country in the world; GDP_n is gross domestic product for country n; and $Max_{Compete}$ is the maximum value of the product in parentheses for every country-crisis pair in the sample. All variables are measured in U.S. dollars for the one-year period ending before the start of the crisis event e. The k industries are 1,075 four-digit SITC groups.

Since *Compete* is a key variable for this paper's analysis, tables 2.2 and 2.3 provide further information on this index. Table 2.2 presents a sample of values for the first ratio in the product in parentheses in equation (4). It lists the ten largest four-digit export industries for each ground-zero country (when measured as a share of world exports in each industry). Not surprisingly, smaller countries tend to have smaller shares of global exports in most industries. For example, the most important export industry for the Slovak Republic is flat, cold-rolled producers' iron (SITC group 6734), which comprises only 3.5 percent of global exports in this industry. Larger countries, on average, have larger shares of export industries. Korea, for example, accounts for 41 percent of the world's exports of fabric made of synthetic-filament yarn (SITC group 6531). Several small and medium-sized economies dominate specific export markets, however, especially for certain agricultural products and natural resources. For example, India accounts for 82 percent of world exports in castor oil seeds (SITC group 2235); the Philippines account for 58 percent of global exports in coconut oil fractions (SITC group 4223); the Czech Republic accounts for 51 percent of global exports in lignite (SITC group 3222); and Russia accounts for 48 percent of global exports in gaseous natural gas (SITC group 3432). Any other

---

20. Ideally, this competitiveness indicator would also incorporate the elasticities of substitution between goods from different countries. To the best of my knowledge, however, these statistics do not currently exist.

Table 2.2   **Major Exports from the Crisis Countries**

SITC Code	SITC Definition	Share of World Exports (%)
Mexico: 1994		
7511	Typewriters, word-processing machines	24.9
2667	Synthetic staple fiber, spinning	20.0
2832	Copper mattes, etc.	19.6
2313	Other natural gums	19.6
0544	Tomatoes, fresh, chilled	16.4
7474	Safety, relief valves	15.7
7731	Insulated wire, etc. conductors	14.9
7611	Color television receivers	14.7
2483	Wood, coniferous, worked, shaped	14.3
6973	Domestic cooking, heating appliance, non-electric	11.3
Ecuador: 1995		
2655	Abaca, manila hemp, waste	34.1
0573	Bananas, fresh or dried	22.5
6576	Hat-shapes, forms, bodies	12.8
0721	Cocoa beans	9.8
0361	Crustaceans, frozen	6.3
0593	Juice, other citrus fruit	5.0
0723	Cocoa paste	4.7
0711	Coffee, not roasted	4.3
0713	Extracts, etc. of coffee	2.6
0371	Fish, prepared, preserved, N.E.S.	2.4
Argentina: 1995		
4215	Sunflower seed oil, etc.	35.5
4211	Soya bean oil, fractions	27.6
2224	Sunflower seeds	24.9
0176	Bovine meat, prepared, preserved, N.E.S.	23.3
4213	Groundnut oil, fractions	22.4
0124	Meat of horses, mules, etc.	18.6
0813	Oil-cake, oilseed residue	18.4
0616	Natural honey	17.1
0171	Extract, juice meat, fish	17.1
4212	Cottonseed oil, fraction	16.8
Venezuela: 1995		
6724	Ingots of iron or steel	17.0
6713	Pellets, etc. of pig iron, etc.	12.8
2239	Flour, meal, from oilseeds	11.8
6932	Barbed wire, etc. of iron, steel	9.4
3330	Crude petroleum	8.1
5984	Mixed alkyl benzenes, etc., N.E.S.	5.3
6841	Aluminum, aluminum alloy, unwrought	4.8
4218	Sesame oil, fractions	4.7
0471	Other cereal flours	4.4
6733	Flat, cold-rolled, production iron	3.7

Table 2.2   (continued)

SITC Code	SITC Definition	Share of World Exports (%)
Czech Republic: 1997		
3222	Lignite	50.6
6576	Hat-shapes, forms, bodies	13.1
2784	Asbestos	9.5
6999	Articles tungsten, etc., N.E.S.	8.4
2516	Chemical wood pulp, sulphite	8.3
2237	Oil seeds, etc., N.E.S.	7.7
6659	Glass articles, N.E.S.	7.6
5811	Artificial sausage casings	7.1
3250	Coke, semi-coke, ret. carbon	6.9
8913	Non-military arms	6.5
Thailand: 1997		
2311	Natural rubber latex	47.2
0548	Vegetable products, roots, tubers	38.2
0423	Rice, milled, semi-milled	37.8
2312	Natural rubber, excl. latex	36.5
6129	Other leather articles, N.E.S.	27.5
0372	Crustacea, mollusk, prepared, N.E.S.	27.4
6673	Precious, semiprecious stones	23.6
0471	Other cereal flours	22.4
0621	Fruit, etc. preserved by sugar	20.7
2732	Gypsum, limestone, etc.	20.1
The Philippines: 1997		
2655	Abaca, manila hemp, waste	58.4
4223	Coconut oil fractions	58.3
2231	Copra	15.9
2657	Coconut fiber and waste	14.9
2841	Nickel ores, concentrates	12.9
2891	Precious metal ore, concentrates	12.8
8451	Babies' garments, clothes, accessories	8.9
8437	Shirts, mens', boys', knit	8.3
8944	Festive articles, etc., N.E.S.	7.3
3442	Gas hydrocarbon, liquid, N.E.S.	6.7
Indonesia: 1997		
6343	Plywood, solely of wood	44.8
3431	Natural gas, liquified	44.8
4224	Palm kernel oil, fractions	44.3
0721	Cocoa beans	35.4
2831	Copper ores, concentrates	32.0
2312	Natural rubber, excl. latex	31.6
4223	Coconut oil, fractions	27.2
8512	Sports footwear	26.9
6344	Other plywood, veneered panels	24.4
6871	Tin, tin alloys, unwrought	20.2

(continued)

Table 2.2 (continued)

SITC Code	SITC Definition	Share of World Exports (%)
	Korea: 1997	
6531	Fabric, synthetic-filament yarn	40.8
6118	Leather, special finish	32.1
6562	Labels, badges, etc., not embroidered	29.3
7917	Rail, tram, coach, etc., N.E.S.	27.1
8831	Cine film, 35mm+, developed	26.6
6132	Heads, tails, paws, etc.	25.6
7932	Ships, boats, other vessels	23.8
7863	Transport containers	23.0
6551	Pile fabric, knit, crochet	23.0
6965	Other articles of cutlery	22.7
	India: 1998	
2235	Castor oil seeds	81.9
4225	Castor oil, fractions	80.3
6121	Leather belting, etc.	56.6
6116	Goat or kid skin leather	36.5
6545	Fabric, woven jute, other textile	34.1
0741	Tea	31.0
2922	Natural gums, resins, etc.	29.9
2225	Sesame (sesamum) seeds	27.4
6585	Curtains, other furnishings	26.9
6513	Cotton yarn, excl. thread	25.6
	Russia: 1998	
3432	Natural gas, gaseous	47.9
6727	Semi-finished iron, etc., 25%+c	40.0
6831	Nickel, nickel alloy, unwrought	36.4
7187	Nuclear reactors, parts, N.E.S.	29.8
2723	Natural calcium phosphates	23.2
2224	Sunflower seeds	22.5
6726	Semi-finished iron, steel	21.8
2481	Railway, tramway sleepers	20.7
2474	Wood, coniferous, rough, untreated	20.1
6841	Aluminum, aluminum alloy, unwrought	19.9
	Slovak Republic: 1998	
6734	Flat, cold-rolled, producers' iron	3.5
6714	Ferro-manganese	3.3
2112	Whole bovine hide < 8kg dry	3.1
7468	Other ball, roller bearing	2.9
7918	Rail, tram freight cars, etc.	2.9
6611	Quicklime etc., excluding 522.6	2.8
8731	Gas, liquid, electric meters	2.3
6715	Other ferro-alloys	2.1
7912	Other locomotives, tenders	2.1
6732	Flat, hot-rolled, producers' iron	1.9

Table 2.2   (continued)

SITC Code	SITC Definition	Share of World Exports (%)
	Brazil: 1999	
2654	Sisal, agave fibers, waste	78.2
2851	Aluminum ore, concentrate	55.8
4314	Waxes, animal, vegetable origin	48.3
0611	Sugars, beet or cane, raw	39.6
0591	Orange juice	39.5
2815	Iron ore, concentrate, not agglomerates	39.1
4225	Castor oil, fractions	38.0
2816	Iron ore agglomerates	33.5
0176	Bovine meat, prepared, preserved, N.E.S.	29.5
6712	Pig iron, etc., primary form	28.4

Source: Calculations based on International Trade Center, U.N. Statistics Division.
Notes: N.E.S. = not elsewhere specified.

country that was highly dependent on export revenues in any of these industries could have been extremely vulnerable to competitiveness effects from crises in these ground-zero countries.

Table 2.3 lists the calculated values of *Compete*. The first part of the table reports values for each of the fifty-eight countries in the sample for each crisis event. The bottom part of the table lists a number of summary statistics for the entire sample. The values of *Compete* range from almost 0 to 100, with a mean of 5.0 and standard deviation of 9.3. Larger values of *Compete* indicate that a country's economy was more dependent on industries that were most affected by the crisis. The highest value of *Compete* occurs for Singapore during the Korean crisis. Some of the four-digit industries generating this large competitiveness effect are electronic microcircuits; input or output units; storage units for data processing; color television receivers; sound and video recording; parts for telecommunications equipment; and ships, boats, and other vessels. Many of the other large values of *Compete* occur between countries dependent on natural resources and ground-zero countries that export a large quantity of these resources. For example, some of the larger values of *Compete* occur for oil-dependent Oman and Norway during the crises in Russia and Venezuela.

It is also worth noting several trends in *Compete* across crisis events. The average value of *Compete* fluctuates significantly across episodes and is much lower for crises that occur in small countries. For example, the mean value of *Compete* is less than 1 for crises that originate in Ecuador and the Slovak Republic, but more than 12 for the crisis in Korea. *Compete* is also smaller for countries that are less integrated with the rest of the world, even after adjusting for country size. For example, the Indian economy is more than four times larger than the Indonesian economy (as measured by

Table 2.3 Competitiveness-Effect Statistics

								Crisis Events							Slovak		
	Mexico	Ecuador	Argentina	Venezuela	Venezuela	Czech Republic	Thailand	The Philippines	Indonesia	Korea	India	Russia	Venezuela	Republic	Ecuador	Brazil
Country n	1994	1995	1995	1995	1997	1997	1997	1997	1997	1997	1998	1998	1998	1998	1998	1999
Argentina	1.69	0.21	—	0.84	1.49	0.52	1.61	0.34	1.48	2.35	2.63	3.25	1.77	0.27	0.35	7.67
Australia	2.43	0.31	2.44	2.06	1.52	1.30	2.88	0.72	6.29	6.28	2.67	7.41	2.03	0.39	0.35	8.34
Austria	8.23	0.11	1.14	0.45	0.41	3.56	4.29	1.41	3.47	11.20	2.63	8.11	0.46	1.25	0.13	4.80
Bangladesh	1.71	0.89	0.98	0.08	0.11	0.93	6.26	1.90	5.97	5.14	9.18	0.95	0.14	0.46	1.28	1.31
Belgium	15.26	0.79	3.39	1.41	1.37	5.99	11.19	2.39	7.32	28.50	19.46	17.85	1.66	3.10	2.14	13.88
Brazil	2.06	0.50	3.46	0.63	0.45	0.55	1.37	0.36	1.47	2.17	1.96	2.65	0.40	0.28	0.13	—
Canada	9.11	0.47	2.14	2.73	3.04	3.30	3.88	1.92	5.89	12.76	1.87	26.29	3.87	1.37	0.65	8.75
Chile	7.48	0.34	2.29	0.53	0.31	0.99	3.68	4.79	19.37	6.34	1.78	15.54	0.37	0.41	0.44	4.72
China	7.46	0.33	2.03	0.87	0.82	2.14	8.24	2.59	6.29	11.80	5.49	3.97	0.99	0.69	0.31	3.16
Colombia	5.38	5.44	0.66	2.45	4.39	0.82	3.34	1.11	6.36	2.86	2.73	6.97	5.02	0.25	4.04	13.13
Croatia	7.24	0.33	2.17	0.66	0.67	2.79	5.36	2.11	5.01	17.71	3.68	4.15	1.06	1.32	0.40	4.44
Cyprus	1.36	0.04	1.55	0.17	0.18	0.53	1.45	0.50	1.09	1.02	1.34	0.46	0.25	0.25	0.05	0.85
Czech Republic	9.05	0.18	2.04	1.35	1.18	—	6.96	1.79	6.10	16.55	4.99	10.80	1.32	2.41	0.20	9.25
Denmark	5.40	0.52	1.72	0.67	0.90	2.33	5.93	1.28	3.78	8.90	3.17	7.11	1.49	0.89	0.75	3.98
Ecuador	17.01	—	3.33	12.52	13.73	0.57	18.10	9.45	21.30	5.29	10.11	20.17	16.99	0.24	—	5.41
Egypt	2.88	0.56	1.06	2.62	2.14	0.42	2.01	0.23	2.94	0.91	3.38	3.44	2.12	0.15	0.29	0.62
Estonia	—	—	—	—	0.99	7.67	14.60	4.33	18.19	17.36	9.21	20.89	1.88	2.94	4.68	—
Finland	6.78	0.35	0.76	0.45	0.42	3.02	3.62	1.67	8.12	17.95	1.56	7.79	0.52	1.59	0.10	6.37
France	4.71	0.12	1.89	0.35	0.32	1.84	3.05	1.04	1.76	8.29	1.79	3.81	0.36	0.74	0.17	3.56
Germany	5.79	0.09	0.99	0.38	0.37	2.27	3.02	0.98	1.70	10.15	2.09	4.47	0.45	0.94	0.12	3.92
Greece	2.14	0.26	1.10	0.39	0.46	0.78	2.55	0.88	2.23	3.46	3.39	1.66	0.50	0.39	0.16	2.00
Hong Kong	5.95	0.07	0.70	0.17	0.15	1.36	7.24	4.28	4.24	-12.88	4.58	1.40	0.13	0.38	0.10	0.79
Hungary	7.89	0.13	4.45	0.62	0.66	3.77	6.98	2.08	4.48	11.73	4.33	7.64	0.77	1.87	0.21	8.65
Iceland	2.07	2.12	12.95	2.93	2.08	0.57	24.05	1.39	10.44	12.89	4.91	15.04	2.21	1.02	2.99	5.42
India	1.54	0.42	1.23	0.26	0.25	0.68	5.04	0.83	2.93	3.65	—	1.23	0.29	0.23	0.47	—
Indonesia	7.79	2.18	1.65	5.01	4.35	1.55	14.31	3.47	—	9.58	5.21	16.66	5.96	0.66	2.07	12.65
Ireland	13.00	0.36	4.17	0.64	0.51	4.80	15.15	6.23	4.26	21.60	6.45	12.25	0.57	1.30	0.32	8.64
Israel	3.86	0.13	0.80	0.44	0.21	1.01	7.29	1.39	1.86	6.69	18.89	2.03	0.22	0.38	0.15	1.74
Italy	4.91	0.09	1.16	0.29	0.25	2.43	4.69	1.29	3.17	10.82	3.29	1.81	0.28	0.82	0.16	3.59

Japan	2.87	0.02	0.26	0.11	0.10	0.72	1.81	0.90	0.62	6.95	0.53	1.47	0.13	0.31	0.02	1.28
Korea	7.54	0.10	1.13	0.36	0.38	1.84	6.66	4.08	4.19	—	3.07	2.73	0.49	1.04	0.18	5.57
Malaysia	32.64	1.94	3.36	6.40	5.72	3.71	40.40	17.17	71.43	59.60	5.16	15.30	7.07	1.48	1.67	10.61
Mauritius	6.41	0.70	3.39	1.13	0.46	1.99	45.86	10.77	11.45	14.93	18.29	1.34	0.39	1.08	0.91	70.29
Mexico	—	0.67	1.03	2.65	5.26	2.46	6.70	2.48	5.47	14.49	2.92	10.73	6.71	0.97	1.24	5.82
Morocco	4.45	0.47	1.81	0.19	0.19	0.71	6.04	1.74	3.70	5.81	3.33	7.89	0.26	0.32	0.63	—
The Netherlands	10.54	0.64	3.84	0.98	1.00	3.41	8.94	3.42	5.30	17.60	5.38	17.24	1.20	1.52	1.03	8.70
New Zealand	3.52	0.30	5.17	1.54	1.32	2.30	3.60	0.63	3.10	5.73	2.23	9.44	1.58	0.83	0.35	4.78
Norway	16.18	2.79	3.87	18.16	21.86	1.14	2.92	0.72	13.08	6.92	1.75	69.73	28.16	0.83	3.51	4.09
Oman	50.53	8.59	8.69	57.49	59.71	0.87	1.69	0.76	28.24	4.69	1.53	97.31	78.46	0.39	9.16	—
Peru	3.16	0.67	0.82	0.35	0.78	0.24	1.96	1.57	3.59	5.69	2.27	4.36	0.96	0.09	0.82	4.89
The Philippines	6.15	2.37	0.95	0.35	0.17	1.25	12.69	—	9.53	25.59	4.07	2.13	0.20	0.45	2.23	3.81
Poland	5.82	0.14	1.05	0.67	0.49	3.17	3.80	1.34	4.26	9.64	2.59	5.15	0.53	0.97	0.23	3.79
Portugal	7.64	0.20	0.97	0.25	0.28	2.62	5.27	2.55	5.35	10.76	4.55	1.98	0.34	1.02	0.35	6.42
Romania	5.12	0.09	2.38	1.66	1.02	4.10	5.93	2.35	8.98	12.96	5.37	10.09	1.10	2.18	0.11	5.30
Russia	—	—	—	—	6.82	1.48	1.25	0.48	5.42	4.11	1.19	—	8.39	0.96	0.91	6.79
Singapore	46.04	1.39	3.68	1.18	1.02	6.24	60.04	27.60	23.22	100.00	9.21	15.44	1.06	1.94	0.55	10.93
Slovak Republic	12.08	0.21	3.11	1.96	1.83	6.01	6.72	1.69	6.50	18.81	5.00	21.46	2.56	—	0.24	12.43
Slovenia	14.80	0.21	1.99	1.47	1.09	6.61	9.16	2.49	9.16	21.10	5.48	7.83	1.28	2.69	0.22	8.24
South Africa	2.29	0.07	1.39	0.61	0.94	1.64	3.34	0.92	3.62	4.74	7.29	8.25	0.47	0.56	0.12	6.77
Spain	5.70	0.18	1.20	0.34	0.35	1.76	3.12	0.89	2.01	8.76	2.35	2.92	0.43	0.76	0.32	3.94
Sweden	8.64	0.08	1.16	0.80	0.45	3.35	4.21	1.63	3.29	11.52	2.27	10.20	0.55	1.43	0.16	7.98
Switzerland	4.62	0.07	0.94	0.28	0.26	2.53	4.51	1.20	2.21	8.92	5.35	2.01	0.32	0.79	0.08	3.13
Thailand	10.74	2.14	2.44	0.56	0.48	2.22	—	5.80	17.93	19.09	12.81	4.45	0.93	0.88	2.82	—
Tunisia	14.02	0.86	1.75	3.97	4.21	2.60	9.28	5.20	10.15	9.78	8.59	9.61	4.92	1.19	0.96	2.78
Turkey	4.21	0.11	1.32	0.40	0.35	1.83	3.82	1.59	3.67	7.39	6.47	3.19	0.40	0.61	0.14	2.93
United Kingdom	6.22	0.29	1.02	1.71	1.90	1.79	3.94	1.52	2.69	9.33	2.81	4.66	2.06	0.59	0.29	2.56
United States	1.89	0.04	0.72	0.14	0.13	0.63	1.39	0.64	0.73	3.40	0.66	1.46	0.15	0.23	0.04	1.64
Venezuela	19.27	3.56	3.69	—	—	0.97	1.24	0.20	14.06	2.79	1.37	41.34	—	0.56	3.80	3.73
Summary statistics																
Mean	8.79	0.84	2.28	2.69	2.85	2.26	8.15	2.90	7.90	12.59	4.85	10.97	3.60	0.94	0.99	6.86
Standard Deviation	9.52	1.47	2.08	8.10	8.43	1.72	10.82	4.39	10.45	14.83	4.21	16.12	11.03	0.70	1.57	9.58
Minimum	1.36	0.02	0.26	0.08	0.10	0.24	1.24	0.20	0.62	0.91	0.53	0.46	0.13	0.09	0.02	0.62
Maximum	50.53	8.59	12.95	57.49	59.71	7.67	60.04	27.60	71.43	100.00	19.46	97.31	78.46	3.10	9.16	70.29

Notes: Sample statistics as follows: mean = 4.97; standard deviation = 9.33; minimum = 0.02; maximum = 100.00. Dash indicates data not available.

GDP), but the mean value of *Compete* for the Indian crisis was less than half that for the Indonesian crisis. Both of these characteristics of *Compete* suggest that this variable captures the intuitive prediction that crises in larger and more export-oriented economies would have greater competitiveness effects on other countries.

The other two trade variables used to estimate equation (3) are more straightforward. The income-effect variable (*Income*) is measured as total exports from each country n to the ground-zero country as a percent of country n's GDP. In other words, the income-effect variable for country n during crisis event e can be written

$$(5) \qquad Income_{n,e} = \frac{\sum_k Exp_{n,k,0}}{GDP_n},$$

where $Exp_{n,k,0}$ is exports from country n in industry k to the ground-zero country; and GDP_n is gross domestic product for country n. All variables are measured in U.S. dollars for the one-year period ending before the start of the crisis event e.

Income captures the impact of the crisis on the demand for exports from other countries. Table 2.4 presents the calculated values of *Income*. The first part of the table lists the values for each of the countries in the sample, and the bottom part lists a number of summary statistics. The values of *Income* range from 0 to 15 percent, with a mean of 0.2 and a standard deviation of 0.8. Not surprisingly, countries located in the same geographic region as the ground-zero country tend to be more reliant on exports to the crisis country and therefore to be more vulnerable to any income effect. For example, the largest value of *Income* (15 percent) measures the reliance of the Slovak Republic on exports going to the Czech Republic. The second largest value of *Income* (12 percent) measures exports from Estonia (as a share of GDP) going to Russia.

The final trade variable, the cheap-import effect (*Cheap Import*) is measured as total imports from the ground-zero country into country n as a percentage of consumption and investment in country n.[21] In other words, the cheap-import effect variable for country n during crisis event e can be written

$$(6) \qquad Cheap\ Import_{n,e} = \frac{\sum_k Imp_{n,k,0}}{Consumption_n + Investment_n},$$

where $Imp_{n,k,0}$ is imports into country n in industry k from the ground-zero country; and *Consumption$_n$* and *Investment$_n$* are total private consumption

---

21. The denominator of this ratio includes private consumption and gross domestic investment in order to focus on the portion of GDP which is most affected by lower import prices. Other components of GDP, such as government consumption and net exports, are less affected by changes in import prices.

Table 2.4   Income-Effect Statistics

<table>
<thead>
<tr><th rowspan="3">Country n</th><th colspan="16">Crisis Events</th></tr>
<tr><th>Mexico
1994</th><th>Ecuador
1995</th><th>Argentina
1995</th><th>Venezuela
1995</th><th>Venezuela
1997</th><th>Czech
Republic
1997</th><th>Thailand
1997</th><th>The
Philippines
1997</th><th>Indonesia
1997</th><th>Korea
1997</th><th>India
1998</th><th>Russia
1998</th><th>Venezuela
1998</th><th>Slovak
Republic
1998</th><th>Ecuador
1998</th><th>Brazil
1999</th></tr>
</thead>
<tbody>
<tr><td>Argentina</td><td>0.11</td><td>0.03</td><td>—</td><td>0.08</td><td>013</td><td>0.00</td><td>0.05</td><td>0.02</td><td>0.08</td><td>0.07</td><td>0.07</td><td>0.08</td><td>0.11</td><td>0.00</td><td>0.03</td><td>2.57</td></tr>
<tr><td>Australia</td><td>0.04</td><td>0.00</td><td>0.01</td><td>0.00</td><td>0.00</td><td>0.01</td><td>0.29</td><td>0.20</td><td>0.45</td><td>1.30</td><td>0.23</td><td>0.02</td><td>0.00</td><td>0.00</td><td>0.00</td><td>0.07</td></tr>
<tr><td>Austria</td><td>0.05</td><td>0.00</td><td>0.04</td><td>0.01</td><td>0.02</td><td>0.74</td><td>0.08</td><td>0.02</td><td>0.12</td><td>0.13</td><td>0.05</td><td>0.39</td><td>0.02</td><td>0.38</td><td>0.00</td><td>0.12</td></tr>
<tr><td>Bangladesh</td><td>0.01</td><td>0.00</td><td>0.01</td><td>0.00</td><td>0.00</td><td>0.00</td><td>0.04</td><td>0.03</td><td>0.01</td><td>0.03</td><td>0.06</td><td>0.04</td><td>0.00</td><td>—</td><td>0.00</td><td>0.03</td></tr>
<tr><td>Belgium</td><td>0.16</td><td>0.02</td><td>0.08</td><td>0.03</td><td>0.03</td><td>0.24</td><td>0.31</td><td>0.06</td><td>0.11</td><td>0.19</td><td>1.17</td><td>0.64</td><td>0.04</td><td>0.06</td><td>0.01</td><td>0.34</td></tr>
<tr><td>Brazil</td><td>0.19</td><td>0.05</td><td>0.76</td><td>0.05</td><td>0.06</td><td>0.00</td><td>0.05</td><td>0.04</td><td>0.04</td><td>0.11</td><td>0.02</td><td>0.09</td><td>0.09</td><td>0.01</td><td>0.02</td><td>—</td></tr>
<tr><td>Canada</td><td>0.14</td><td>0.01</td><td>0.03</td><td>0.08</td><td>0.07</td><td>0.01</td><td>0.05</td><td>0.03</td><td>0.11</td><td>0.34</td><td>0.05</td><td>0.04</td><td>0.11</td><td>0.00</td><td>0.01</td><td>0.16</td></tr>
<tr><td>Chile</td><td>0.41</td><td>0.17</td><td>1.28</td><td>0.15</td><td>0.21</td><td>0.00</td><td>0.17</td><td>0.15</td><td>0.22</td><td>1.30</td><td>0.10</td><td>0.06</td><td>0.21</td><td>—</td><td>0.21</td><td>1.05</td></tr>
<tr><td>China</td><td>0.04</td><td>0.01</td><td>0.05</td><td>0.01</td><td>0.01</td><td>0.02</td><td>0.15</td><td>0.12</td><td>0.17</td><td>0.92</td><td>0.10</td><td>0.23</td><td>0.01</td><td>0.00</td><td>0.01</td><td>0.11</td></tr>
<tr><td>Colombia</td><td>0.13</td><td>0.40</td><td>0.08</td><td>0.67</td><td>0.78</td><td>0.00</td><td>0.01</td><td>0.00</td><td>0.00</td><td>0.03</td><td>0.00</td><td>0.06</td><td>0.91</td><td>0.00</td><td>0.50</td><td>0.10</td></tr>
<tr><td>Croatia</td><td>0.00</td><td>0.07</td><td>0.00</td><td>0.00</td><td>0.03</td><td>0.20</td><td>0.01</td><td>0.00</td><td>0.00</td><td>0.00</td><td>0.00</td><td>0.81</td><td>0.00</td><td>0.11</td><td>0.02</td><td>0.00</td></tr>
<tr><td>Cyprus</td><td>—</td><td>0.00</td><td>—</td><td>—</td><td>—</td><td>0.02</td><td>0.02</td><td>0.00</td><td>0.00</td><td>0.01</td><td>0.01</td><td>0.14</td><td>—</td><td>0.03</td><td>0.00</td><td>—</td></tr>
<tr><td>Czech Republic</td><td>0.04</td><td>0.02</td><td>0.04</td><td>0.01</td><td>0.01</td><td>—</td><td>0.08</td><td>0.01</td><td>0.03</td><td>0.08</td><td>0.12</td><td>1.46</td><td>0.01</td><td>5.54</td><td>0.02</td><td>0.07</td></tr>
<tr><td>Denmark</td><td>0.09</td><td>0.00</td><td>0.05</td><td>0.03</td><td>0.02</td><td>0.10</td><td>0.10</td><td>0.03</td><td>0.08</td><td>0.25</td><td>0.06</td><td>0.50</td><td>0.02</td><td>0.02</td><td>0.01</td><td>0.09</td></tr>
<tr><td>Ecuador</td><td>0.46</td><td>—</td><td>0.43</td><td>0.05</td><td>0.38</td><td>0.00</td><td>0.00</td><td>0.01</td><td>0.00</td><td>1.65</td><td>0.01</td><td>0.71</td><td>0.25</td><td>0.00</td><td>—</td><td>0.18</td></tr>
<tr><td>Egypt</td><td>0.00</td><td>—</td><td>0.00</td><td>0.00</td><td>0.00</td><td>0.00</td><td>0.00</td><td>0.00</td><td>0.00</td><td>0.05</td><td>0.06</td><td>0.03</td><td>0.00</td><td>0.00</td><td>—</td><td>0.02</td></tr>
<tr><td>Estonia</td><td>0.00</td><td>—</td><td>0.00</td><td>0.00</td><td>0.00</td><td>0.06</td><td>0.00</td><td>0.07</td><td>0.01</td><td>0.24</td><td>0.06</td><td>0.01</td><td>0.01</td><td>0.02</td><td>—</td><td>0.00</td></tr>
<tr><td>Finland</td><td>0.06</td><td>0.01</td><td>0.08</td><td>0.03</td><td>0.03</td><td>0.20</td><td>0.30</td><td>0.12</td><td>0.24</td><td>0.47</td><td>0.20</td><td>2.46</td><td>0.03</td><td>0.05</td><td>0.00</td><td>0.24</td></tr>
<tr><td>France</td><td>0.10</td><td>0.00</td><td>0.08</td><td>0.02</td><td>0.02</td><td>0.08</td><td>0.06</td><td>0.03</td><td>0.08</td><td>0.13</td><td>0.06</td><td>0.18</td><td>0.02</td><td>0.03</td><td>0.01</td><td>0.14</td></tr>
<tr><td>Germany</td><td>0.14</td><td>0.01</td><td>0.06</td><td>0.02</td><td>0.02</td><td>0.39</td><td>0.15</td><td>0.06</td><td>0.11</td><td>0.28</td><td>0.12</td><td>0.45</td><td>0.03</td><td>0.13</td><td>0.01</td><td>0.26</td></tr>
<tr><td>Greece</td><td>0.02</td><td>0.00</td><td>0.01</td><td>0.00</td><td>0.00</td><td>0.04</td><td>0.04</td><td>0.01</td><td>0.06</td><td>0.04</td><td>0.02</td><td>0.35</td><td>0.00</td><td>0.01</td><td>0.00</td><td>0.06</td></tr>
<tr><td>Hong Kong</td><td>0.11</td><td>0.00</td><td>0.03</td><td>0.00</td><td>0.00</td><td>0.00</td><td>0.22</td><td>0.21</td><td>0.13</td><td>0.22</td><td>0.03</td><td>0.01</td><td>0.00</td><td>—</td><td>0.00</td><td>0.04</td></tr>
<tr><td>Hungary</td><td>0.01</td><td>0.00</td><td>0.02</td><td>0.01</td><td>0.00</td><td>0.64</td><td>0.03</td><td>0.01</td><td>0.02</td><td>0.03</td><td>0.05</td><td>2.07</td><td>0.00</td><td>0.53</td><td>0.00</td><td>0.18</td></tr>
<tr><td>Iceland</td><td>0.00</td><td>0.00</td><td>0.00</td><td>0.00</td><td>0.00</td><td>0.02</td><td>0.01</td><td>0.00</td><td>0.00</td><td>0.10</td><td>0.01</td><td>0.45</td><td>0.00</td><td>0.00</td><td>0.00</td><td>0.11</td></tr>
<tr><td>India</td><td>0.02</td><td>—</td><td>0.00</td><td>0.00</td><td>0.00</td><td>0.01</td><td>0.11</td><td>0.05</td><td>0.15</td><td>0.13</td><td>—</td><td>0.23</td><td>0.01</td><td>0.00</td><td>—</td><td>0.00</td></tr>
<tr><td>Indonesia</td><td>0.08</td><td>0.00</td><td>0.01</td><td>0.00</td><td>0.00</td><td>0.01</td><td>0.36</td><td>0.30</td><td>—</td><td>1.44</td><td>0.32</td><td>0.04</td><td>0.01</td><td>0.00</td><td>0.00</td><td>0.18</td></tr>
<tr><td>Ireland</td><td>0.17</td><td>0.01</td><td>0.03</td><td>0.01</td><td>0.03</td><td>0.18</td><td>0.15</td><td>0.32</td><td>0.04</td><td>0.46</td><td>0.07</td><td>0.44</td><td>0.02</td><td>0.03</td><td>0.01</td><td>0.20</td></tr>
<tr><td>Israel</td><td>0.10</td><td>0.02</td><td>0.06</td><td>0.02</td><td>0.01</td><td>0.05</td><td>0.35</td><td>0.21</td><td>0.01</td><td>0.38</td><td>0.37</td><td>0.26</td><td>0.02</td><td>0.02</td><td>0.01</td><td>0.30</td></tr>
<tr><td>Italy</td><td>0.09</td><td>0.01</td><td>0.10</td><td>0.03</td><td>0.04</td><td>0.14</td><td>0.11</td><td>0.03</td><td>0.09</td><td>0.23</td><td>0.05</td><td>0.34</td><td>0.05</td><td>0.06</td><td>0.03</td><td>0.28</td></tr>
<tr><td>Japan</td><td>0.09</td><td>0.01</td><td>0.14</td><td>0.04</td><td>0.01</td><td>0.00</td><td>0.40</td><td>0.18</td><td>0.20</td><td>0.64</td><td>0.05</td><td>0.02</td><td>0.02</td><td>0.00</td><td>0.01</td><td>0.07</td></tr>
<tr><td>Korea</td><td>0.32</td><td>0.03</td><td>0.12</td><td>0.02</td><td>0.02</td><td>0.04</td><td>0.51</td><td>0.37</td><td>0.61</td><td>—</td><td>0.24</td><td>0.37</td><td>0.05</td><td>0.01</td><td>0.02</td><td>0.56</td></tr>
<tr><td>Malaysia</td><td>0.54</td><td>0.01</td><td>0.08</td><td>0.02</td><td>0.02</td><td>0.02</td><td>3.18</td><td>0.93</td><td>1.21</td><td>2.39</td><td>1.18</td><td>0.09</td><td>0.05</td><td>0.00</td><td>0.00</td><td>0.37</td></tr>
</tbody>
</table>

(continued)

Table 2.4 (continued)

	Crisis Events													Slovak		
Country n	Mexico 1994	Ecuador 1995	Argentina 1995	Venezuela 1995	Venezuela 1997	Czech Republic 1997	Thailand 1997	The Philippines 1997	Indonesia 1997	Korea 1997	India 1998	Russia 1998	Venezuela 1998	Republic 1998	Ecuador 1998	Brazil 1999
Malaysia	0.54	0.01	0.08	0.02	0.02	0.02	3.18	0.93	1.21	2.39	1.18	0.09	0.05	0.00	0.00	0.37
Mauritius	0.00	—	0.01	—	—	0.00	0.05	0.01	0.00	0.01	0.33	0.00	—	—	—	0.03
Mexico	—	0.03	0.07	0.05	0.15	0.00	0.03	0.02	0.02	0.10	0.02	0.01	0.23	—	0.05	0.19
Morocco	0.11	0.00	0.00	0.01	0.01	0.01	0.00	0.00	0.05	0.03	1.16	0.12	0.02	0.00	0.00	0.00
The Netherlands	0.07	0.01	0.05	0.03	0.02	0.16	0.13	0.07	0.10	0.23	0.13	0.53	0.03	0.07	0.02	0.13
New Zealand	0.22	0.00	0.04	0.10	0.09	0.00	0.28	0.26	0.35	1.03	0.14	0.32	0.11	0.00	0.00	0.14
Norway	0.02	0.00	0.01	0.01	0.01	0.04	0.10	0.06	0.03	0.15	0.05	0.22	0.03	0.01	0.00	0.16
Oman	—	—	0.00	0.00	0.00	—	0.05	0.02	0.00	0.11	0.52	0.15	0.00	—	—	—
Peru	0.33	0.12	0.05	0.17	0.21	0.00	0.06	0.05	0.05	0.24	0.03	0.01	0.22	0.00	0.17	0.29
The Philippines	0.06	0.00	0.01	0.00	0.00	0.00	0.94	—	0.17	0.45	0.04	0.01	0.00	0.00	0.00	0.04
Poland	0.03	0.00	0.02	0.01	0.01	0.58	0.10	0.03	0.03	0.08	0.04	0.01	0.02	0.21	0.00	0.07
Portugal	0.02	0.00	0.07	0.01	0.01	0.02	0.02	0.01	0.00	0.03	0.02	0.07	0.01	0.01	0.00	0.21
Romania	0.02	0.02	0.14	0.01	0.06	0.06	0.13	0.05	0.03	0.14	0.18	0.72	0.07	0.07	0.01	0.02
Russia	0.00	0.00	0.00	0.00	0.00	0.42	0.05	0.03	0.01	0.24	0.21	—	0.00	0.40	0.01	0.06
Singapore	0.29	0.01	0.27	0.04	0.01	0.02	7.76	2.51	—	4.15	2.33	0.78	0.02	0.00	0.00	0.35
Slovak Republic	0.21	0.03	0.08	0.00	0.00	14.58	0.11	0.01	0.12	0.04	0.19	1.69	0.01	—	0.01	0.02
Slovenia	0.01	0.02	0.04	0.01	0.01	0.78	0.04	0.01	0.02	0.05	0.06	1.79	0.02	0.31	0.01	0.08
South Africa	0.03	0.01	0.06	0.02	0.03	0.00	0.10	0.04	0.12	0.47	0.13	0.03	0.05	0.00	0.01	0.13
Spain	0.28	0.01	0.19	0.03	0.04	0.06	0.05	0.02	0.06	0.11	0.04	0.16	0.06	0.02	0.03	0.24
Sweden	0.11	0.01	0.10	0.03	0.03	0.14	0.26	0.10	0.21	0.26	0.13	0.40	0.05	0.04	0.01	0.40
Switzerland	0.15	0.02	0.09	0.03	0.03	0.15	0.25	0.07	0.12	0.32	0.16	0.16	0.04	0.06	0.02	0.32
Thailand	0.08	0.00	0.03	0.00	0.00	0.02	—	0.35	0.53	0.56	0.20	0.08	0.01	0.00	0.00	0.00
Tunisia	0.00	0.00	0.02	0.03	0.00	0.00	—	—	0.08	0.01	0.81	0.02	0.00	0.00	0.00	0.12
Turkey	0.01	0.01	0.02	0.01	0.01	0.05	0.04	0.03	0.03	0.06	0.03	1.08	0.00	0.01	0.00	0.02
United Kingdom	0.06	0.01	0.03	0.03	0.02	0.10	0.13	0.05	0.11	0.18	0.20	0.16	0.03	0.02	0.01	0.11
United States	0.73	0.02	0.06	0.06	0.06	0.01	0.09	0.08	0.05	0.34	0.04	0.04	0.08	0.00	0.02	0.17
Venezuela	0.43	0.25	0.06	—	—	—	0.00	—	0.00	0.02	0.01	0.03	—	—	0.34	0.70
Summary statistics																
Mean	0.13	0.03	0.09	0.04	0.05	0.037	0.033	0.13	0.12	0.40	0.21	0.61	0.06	0.17	0.03	0.23
Standard Deviation	0.15	0.07	0.20	0.09	0.12	1.96	1.10	0.36	0.20	0.69	0.40	1.57	0.13	0.78	0.09	0.38
Minimum	0.00	0.00	0.00	0.00	0.00	0.00	0.00	0.00	0.00	0.00	0.00	0.00	0.00	0.00	0.00	0.00
Maximum	0.73	0.40	1.28	0.67	0.78	14.58	7.76	2.51	1.21	4.15	2.33	11.53	0.91	5.54	0.50	2.57

Notes: Sample statistics as follows: mean = 0.19; standard deviation = 0.78; minimum = 0.00; maximum = 14.58. Dash indicates data not available.

and gross domestic investment, respectively, for country n. All variables are measured in U.S. dollars for the one-year period ending before the start of the crisis event e.

Cheap Import captures the potential effect of lower import prices in the ground-zero country on the other countries in the sample. Table 2.5 lists the calculated values and summary statistics. Many of the values, including the summary statistics, are similar to those for *Income*.[22] Countries located in the same geographic region as the ground-zero country tend to have higher shares of imports from that country and therefore to be more vulnerable to any cheap-import effects.

2.6 Estimation Results and Sensitivity Tests

Table 2.6 reports results when these measures of *Compete, Income,* and *Cheap Import* are used to estimate the model specified in equation (3).[23] Column (1) reports results when only the trade variables (and no macroeconomic controls) are included in the model. Columns (2) through (7) add a variety of macroeconomic controls that are frequently used in this literature. Column (6) uses the same control variables as the base specification in Glick and Rose (1999), and column (7) includes all of the control variables simultaneously. Each of the trade variables has the predicted sign in table 2.6, although each is not consistently significant across columns. More specifically, the coefficient for the competitiveness effect is always negative and significant at the 1 percent level. The coefficient for the income effect is always negative and significant at the 5 percent level, as long as some macroeconomic controls are included in the specification. The coefficient for the cheap-import effect is always positive, although usually insignificant.

These estimates suggest that not only are the trade effects significant, but their magnitude can be large. Since the point estimates fluctuate across columns, I focus on the estimates in column (2). This specification includes the control variables most frequently cited in the literature, as well as the greatest number of observations (for any specification that includes macroeconomic controls). The point estimate for the competitiveness effect in column (2) is −0.05. This indicates that if a country's competitiveness index was 10 points higher, its abnormal weekly stock return is predicted to be 0.5 percentage points lower, on average, during each week of the crisis. Moreover, since the average length of a crisis in table 2.1 is 2.6 weeks, and the Russian crisis is defined as lasting for 8.0 weeks, the cumulative impact on a country's stock market index could be much greater. A concrete example can help clarify the magnitude of this competitiveness effect. During the Thai crisis, the competitiveness index for Korea was 6.7 and for Malaysia was

---

22. The correlation between *Income* and *Cheap Import* is 87 percent.
23. The period dummy variables are not reported but are always jointly significant.

Table 2.5   **Cheap-Import Effect Statistics**

Country n	Mexico 1994	Ecuador 1995	Argentina 1995	Venezuela 1995	Venezuela 1997	Czech Republic 1997	Thailand 1997	The Philippines 1997	Indonesia 1997	Korea 1997	India 1998	Russia 1998	Venezuela 1998	Slovak Republic 1998	Ecuador 1998	Brazil 1999
								Crisis Events								
Argentina	0.11	0.04	—	0.02	0.05	0.01	0.03	0.01	0.03	0.18	0.05	0.05	0.02	0.01	0.04	2.59
Australia	0.03	0.00	0.02	0.00	0.00	0.01	0.25	0.07	0.40	0.53	0.14	0.00	0.00	0.00	0.00	0.06
Austria	0.04	0.02	0.01	0.00	0.00	0.74	0.07	0.03	0.08	0.13	0.10	0.23	0.00	0.39	0.02	0.10
Bangladesh	0.00	0.00	0.00	—	—	0.00	0.18	0.00	0.17	1.14	3.20	0.24	—	—	0.00	0.13
Belgium	0.14	0.02	0.15	0.06	0.05	0.17	0.33	0.05	0.25	0.17	0.65	0.75	0.07	0.07	0.08	0.76
Brazil	0.08	0.00	0.86	0.13	0.16	0.01	0.03	0.00	0.04	0.19	0.04	0.05	0.16	0.01	0.00	—
Canada	0.78	0.02	0.02	0.09	0.12	0.02	0.17	0.09	0.10	0.45	0.11	0.09	0.15	0.01	0.02	0.19
Chile	0.60	0.42	2.17	0.32	0.50	0.00	0.08	0.03	0.15	0.88	0.10	0.02	0.40	—	0.38	1.52
China	0.02	0.00	0.06	0.01	0.00	0.01	0.27	0.05	0.32	1.77	0.12	0.54	0.00	0.00	0.01	0.14
Colombia	0.45	0.35	0.27	1.53	1.47	0.02	0.02	0.01	0.04	0.21	0.06	0.09	1.66	0.01	0.40	0.57
Croatia	0.02	0.14	0.08	0.00	0.00	1.26	0.03	0.00	0.04	0.20	0.13	2.49	0.02	0.44	0.13	0.39
Cyprus	0.02	0.00	0.41	0.00	0.00	0.10	0.35	0.04	0.27	0.68	0.34	2.13	0.05	0.04	0.00	0.15
Czech Republic	0.02	0.06	0.06	0.00	0.00	—	0.09	0.02	0.09	0.36	0.14	4.03	0.01	4.98	0.03	0.22
Denmark	0.01	0.01	0.20	0.01	0.04	0.10	0.16	0.03	0.14	0.18	0.16	0.22	0.04	0.02	0.00	0.20
Ecuador	1.04	—	0.34	1.10	1.12	0.02	0.01	0.00	0.07	0.39	0.02	0.21	1.75	0.01	—	1.13
Egypt	0.01	0.00	0.19	0.00	0.00	0.07	0.06	0.02	0.16	0.30	0.31	0.53	0.01	0.01	0.00	0.42
Estonia	—	—	—	—	—	-0.51	0.08	0.00	0.14	1.38	0.24	15.01	—	0.28	0.07	—
Finland	0.03	0.03	0.03	0.02	0.01	0.13	0.14	0.06	0.13	0.20	0.09	2.69	0.02	0.05	0.01	0.21
France	0.05	0.01	0.03	0.01	0.02	0.05	0.13	0.03	0.09	0.14	0.10	0.33	0.02	0.02	0.01	0.18
Germany	0.03	0.02	0.06	0.03	0.02	0.41	0.12	0.07	0.12	0.23	0.15	0.60	0.02	0.15	0.02	0.23
Greece	0.01	0.01	0.08	0.01	0.00	0.09	0.07	0.01	0.10	0.55	0.10	0.56	0.00	0.03	0.01	0.09
Hong Kong	0.08	0.00	0.16	0.00	0.01	0.06	2.15	0.67	1.14	7.60	1.29	0.47	0.01	—	0.00	0.37
Hungary	0.01	0.02	0.02	0.00	0.00	1.19	0.06	0.01	0.09	0.36	0.11	4.46	0.00	0.97	0.01	0.44
Iceland	0.01	0.00	0.00	0.00	0.00	0.13	0.09	0.01	0.05	0.40	0.09	0.86	0.00	0.02	0.00	0.04
India	0.01	0.00	0.02	0.00	0.01	0.02	0.05	0.00	0.16	0.24	—	0.17	0.00	0.01	0.00	0.00
Indonesia	0.03	0.00	0.07	0.00	0.01	0.02	0.52	0.04	—	1.14	0.35	0.14	0.00	0.00	0.00	0.26
Ireland	0.03	0.02	0.03	0.00	0.01	0.08	0.50	0.12	0.12	0.77	0.16	0.02	0.01	0.02	0.00	0.09
Israel	0.01	0.01	0.07	0.01	0.00	0.03	0.21	0.01	0.00	0.43	0.35	0.19	0.00	0.00	0.01	0.08
Italy	0.01	0.02	0.09	0.02	0.03	0.08	0.07	0.02	0.10	0.11	0.15	0.47	0.03	0.07	0.02	0.24

	1	2	3	4	5	6	7	8	9	10	11	12	13	14	15	16
Japan	0.08	0.01	0.00	0.01	0.11	0.07	0.39	0.37	0.11	0.25	0.00	0.01	0.01	0.01	0.01	0.03
Korea	0.28	0.05	0.00	0.01	0.35	0.22	—	0.82	0.12	0.25	0.01	0.01	0.02	0.02	0.02	0.06
Malaysia	0.30	0.00	0.00	0.00	0.42	0.87	4.60	1.61	0.90	2.93	0.01	0.00	0.00	0.12	0.00	0.02
Mauritius	0.15	—	—	—	0.06	5.70	0.72	0.65	0.08	0.39	0.01	—	—	0.53	—	0.00
Mexico	0.28	0.02	0.01	0.14	0.06	0.07	0.34	0.08	0.04	0.08	0.01	0.08	0.08	0.08	0.01	—
Morocco	0.00	0.00	0.05	0.01	0.62	0.13	0.18	0.08	0.01	0.04	0.04	0.01	0.01	0.27	0.00	0.02
The Netherlands	0.57	0.02	0.00	0.06	0.63	0.26	0.29	0.38	0.12	0.40	0.01	0.10	0.10	0.30	0.00	0.05
New Zealand	0.06	0.05	0.00	0.01	0.01	0.16	0.49	0.26	0.06	0.21	0.08	0.00	0.00	0.04	0.02	0.03
Norway	0.20	0.01	0.01	0.05	0.63	0.11	0.18	0.06	0.02	0.09	0.00	0.02	0.02	0.03	0.00	0.03
Oman	—	—	—	—	—	—	—	—	—	—	—	—	0.00	0.12	—	0.01
Peru	0.63	0.39	0.00	0.93	0.04	0.04	0.41	0.03	0.00	0.06	0.01	1.01	0.32	0.62	0.32	0.34
The Philippines	0.22	0.00	0.00	0.00	0.59	0.33	2.23	0.88	—	0.82	0.01	0.00	0.02	0.02	0.02	0.04
Poland	0.19	0.07	0.38	0.00	2.11	0.10	0.54	0.13	0.02	0.08	0.93	0.00	0.00	0.04	0.07	0.01
Portugal	0.57	0.02	0.01	0.07	0.31	0.16	0.34	0.05	0.02	0.12	0.03	0.05	0.02	0.09	0.02	0.09
Romania	0.40	0.06	0.21	0.22	4.02	0.08	1.39	0.06	0.00	0.06	0.27	0.20	0.04	0.13	0.06	0.00
Russia	0.29	0.03	0.08	0.01	—	0.22	0.22	0.03	0.00	0.02	0.15	0.01	0.00	0.00	0.03	0.00
Singapore	0.32	0.00	0.00	0.04	0.20	1.41	6.42	—	1.98	10.20	0.07	0.08	0.06	0.12	0.00	0.11
Slovak Republic	0.11	0.06	—	0.00	8.91	0.12	1.14	0.10	0.01	0.08	16.03	0.00	0.00	0.06	0.06	0.03
Slovenia	0.30	0.09	0.70	0.00	1.70	0.12	0.60	0.20	0.01	0.12	1.55	0.00	0.00	0.07	0.09	0.01
South Africa	0.19	0.01	0.00	0.00	0.03	0.29	0.48	0.10	0.02	0.15	0.02	0.05	0.03	0.15	0.01	0.01
Spain	0.29	0.04	0.02	0.06	0.29	0.13	0.20	0.21	0.03	0.13	0.04	0.08	0.08	0.17	0.04	0.24
Sweden	0.14	0.00	0.03	0.06	0.27	0.13	0.16	0.10	0.02	0.09	0.11	0.08	0.08	0.03	0.00	0.03
Switzerland	0.13	0.01	0.04	0.01	0.35	0.15	0.13	0.04	0.02	0.19	0.09	0.00	0.00	0.03	0.01	0.03
Thailand	0.00	0.01	0.00	0.02	0.44	0.44	1.55	0.54	0.33	—	0.04	0.01	0.01	0.03	0.00	0.06
Tunisia	0.27	0.04	0.01	0.00	0.69	0.21	0.21	0.07	0.01	0.06	0.11	0.00	0.00	0.33	0.04	0.00
Turkey	0.23	0.02	0.01	0.01	1.22	0.17	0.42	0.09	0.01	0.05	0.06	0.00	0.00	0.04	0.02	0.02
United Kingdom	0.15	0.01	0.01	0.03	0.24	0.26	0.35	0.17	0.15	0.20	0.06	0.03	0.03	0.03	0.01	0.05
United States	0.16	0.03	0.00	0.21	0.07	0.11	0.37	0.14	0.13	0.19	0.01	0.22	0.16	0.03	0.03	0.88
Venezuela	0.71	0.06	0.00	—	0.00	0.03	0.11	0.01	0.00	0.01	0.00	—	—	0.39	0.02	0.37
Summary statistics																
Mean	0.35	0.04	0.18	0.12	1.11	0.37	0.82	0.22	0.10	0.42	0.45	0.11	0.08	0.17	0.04	0.11
Standard Deviation	0.42	0.09	0.71	0.35	2.42	0.87	1.40	0.30	0.30	1.41	2.15	0.29	0.26	0.32	0.09	0.22
Minimum	0.00	0.00	0.00	0.00	0.00	0.02	0.11	0.00	0.00	0.01	0.00	0.00	0.00	0.00	0.00	0.00
Maximum	2.59	0.40	4.98	1.75	15.01	5.70	7.60	1.61	1.98	10.20	16.03	1.47	1.53	2.17	0.42	1.04

Notes: Sample statistics as follows: mean = 0.30; standard deviation = 1.05; minimum = 0.00; maximum = 16.03. Dash indicates data not available.

Table 2.6 Regression Results

	Only Trade Variables (1)	Base Specification (2)	Alternate Macroeconomic Controls (3)	(4)	(5)	Glick and Rose (1999) Macroeconomic Controls (6)	Full Set of Macroeconomic Controls (7)
Competitiveness effect	-0.042***	-0.052***	-0.065***	-0.049***	-0.066***	-0.056***	-0.067***
	(0.016)	(0.018)	(0.020)	(0.018)	(0.020)	(0.019)	(0.020)
Income effect	-0.514	-1.021***	-1.136**	-0.964***	-1.256**	-1.095**	-1.243**
	(0.332)	(0.360)	(0.557)	(0.365)	(0.548)	(0.536)	(0.571)
Cheap-import effect	0.083	0.588**	0.446	0.525**	0.566	0.470	0.553
	(0.235)	(0.262)	(0.387)	(0.268)	(0.379)	(0.383)	(0.409)
Private credit growth		-1.536***			-1.779***		-2.373
		(0.535)			(0.535)		(1.788)
Government consumption/GDP		2.718		2.658			6.428
		(2.910)		(3.005)			(4.063)
Current account surplus/GDP		2.754			-0.304	5.133	3.469
		(3.382)			(4.923)	(3.424)	(5.076)
Bank reserves/assets		-1.069		-1.299			0.650
		(1.591)		(1.637)			(2.163)

	(1)	(2)	(3)	(4)	(5)	(6)	(7)
Private capital inflows/GDP	-0.100 (0.690)	0.564 (0.580)			0.937 (1.307)		0.362 (1.429)
Domestic credit growth			-1.455** (0.687)	0.280 (1.106)		0.328 (1.275)	2.142 (1.728)
Government surplus/GDP			-5.002 (4.661)		-3.375 (4.682)	0.161 (4.218)	1.289 (5.153)
Money supply (M2)/reserves			1.647 (1.568)		0.759 (1.539)	1.169 (1.557)	0.214 (2.015)
Openness (total trade/GDP)			1.080** (0.440)		0.786 (0.512)		0.524 (0.516)
Growth in GNP per capita				-9.090 (6.175)	-6.823 (7.421)		-6.199 (7.566)
Inflation (in CPI)				-0.275** (0.130)		-0.284** (0.143)	-0.181 (0.195)
N	796	727	469	727	467	468	460
R^2	0.25	0.27	0.20	0.27	0.22	0.20	0.23

Notes: Standard errors (in parentheses) are White-adjusted for heteroskedasticity. All specifications also include period dummy variables (with the Brazilian crisis as the excluded variable). Variables are defined in the appendix.

***Significant at the 1 percent level.

**Significant at the 5 percent level.

40.4. Therefore, during the one week of the Thai crisis, the competitiveness effect is correlated with a 0.3 percent decline in the Korean stock market and a 2.1 percent decline in the Malaysian market (holding everything else constant).

The point estimate for the second trade variable, the income effect, is −1.02. This implies that if a country's ratio of exports to the crisis country (as a share of GDP) was 1 percentage point higher, its abnormal stock return is predicted to be about 1 percentage point lower, on average, during each week of the crisis. To put these numbers in a more meaningful context, Poland's ratio of exports to Russia during the Russian crisis was 1.5 percent and Finland's ratio was 2.5 percent. Assume that both stock market indices were equal to 100 at the beginning of the Russian crisis, and that these two countries were otherwise identical. By the end of the eight-week Russian crisis, the income effect predicts a decline in the Polish market of about 12 percent and in the Finnish market of about 20 percent. This suggests that small differences in export exposure to a crisis country (such as the 1 percentage point difference between Finland and Poland) can significantly affect a country's vulnerability to a crisis when accumulated over time (an 8 percentage point difference between the two markets).

Potentially counteracting this income effect, however, is the cheap-import effect. The point estimate for the cheap-import effect is 0.59. This implies that if a country's import penetration ratio was 1 percentage point higher, the country's abnormal stock return is predicted to be 0.59 percentage points higher, on average, during each week of the crisis. To put this in context, during the Brazilian crisis the import penetration ratio was 1.5 for Chile and 2.6 for Argentina. According to the regression results, after the one-week Brazilian crisis the cheap-import effect is correlated with an increase in the Chilean and Argentine stock market indexes of 0.9 and 1.5 percentage points, respectively (again holding everything else constant).

Since these trade variables are highly correlated (especially the income and cheap-import effects), it is more meaningful to examine the combined impact of all three variables rather than focus on one effect in isolation. Table 2.7 performs this analysis for the countries and crises discussed above. It estimates the model specified in column (2) of table 2.6 (excluding the country-crisis pairs used for the relevant out-of-sample predictions) and assumes that the stock market index for each country is 100 directly before the crisis.[24] Columns (1) through (3) report the predicted weekly impact on each country's stock market index from each of the trade effects. Column (4) combines these into the total aggregate predicted weekly impact from the trade variables, and column (5) reports the total predicted impact of all the macroeconomic control variables. Column (6) lists the

24. To simplify this comparison, it also assumes that normal returns for each market are zero.

Table 2.7 Country Examples: Predicted Trade and Macroeconomic Effects

	Predicted Weekly Trade Effects				Total Predicted Weekly Return			Actual Average Weekly Return (7)
	Competitiveness (1)	Income (2)	Cheap-Import (3)	Trade (4)	Macro Controls (5)	Full Model[a] (6)	
Thai crisis							
Korea	−0.35	−0.52	0.15	−0.72	−0.17	4.53	4.67
Malaysia	−2.11	−3.24	1.72	−3.63	−0.29	1.50	−1.53
Russian crisis							
Finland	−0.41	−2.52	1.58	−1.34	0.70	0.83	−4.43
Poland	−0.27	−1.52	1.24	−0.55	−0.27	0.65	−5.87
Brazilian crisis							
Argentina	−0.40	−2.63	1.53	−1.50	−0.02	−4.61	−5.56
Chile	−0.25	−1.07	0.89	−0.43	−0.07	−3.59	−3.26

Notes: Predicted impact on weekly stock market indices based on out-of-sample coefficient estimates using the model in column (2) of table 2.6.

[a] Full model includes trade and macroeconomic variables, as well as the crisis-specific dummy variables.

model's predicted abnormal weekly returns (the sum of the predicted trade and macroeconomic effects, as well as the crisis-event dummies), and column (7) reports the actual, abnormal weekly stock market return for each country during the given crisis.

The statistics in this table make a number of key points. First, the magnitude of the trade effects can be large. For example, trade linkages during the Thai crisis were predicted to reduce Malaysia's weekly stock return by 3.6 percentage points. Moreover, for longer crises (such as the eight-week Russian crisis) the cumulative impact of these trade effects can be much larger. Second, the predicted impact of the trade variables tends to be larger than the predicted impact of the macroeconomic variables. For example, during the Brazilian crisis the macroeconomic variables predicted virtually no impact on Argentina's stock market index, while the trade variables predicted a decrease of 1.5 percentage points (about one-third of the actual decrease). Third, the simple regression model in equation (3) has only partial success in predicting stock market movements during recent crises. In most of the examples in the table, predicted stock market returns are much lower (in absolute value) than actual returns. This is not surprising, given the fairly low R^2s in table 2.6. On the other hand, the model does fairly well in explaining stock market returns during crises that have more regional than global effects (such as the Thai and Brazilian crises), but does not have as much explanatory power for crises that have greater global effects (such as the Russian crisis).

These central results could be influenced by a number of factors, such as sample selection, variable definitions, and model specification. Therefore, this section closes by describing a number of sensitivity tests. Results are highly robust, so table 2.8 reports only a selection of these estimates.[25] First, I test for the impact of sample selection. I drop one country at a time, one crisis at a time, and the five extreme observations for each variable. Next, since the distribution of *Compete* is skewed to the right, I drop the five largest values for *Compete*. Results are reported in column (2) of table 2.8. Then, since Venezuela and Ecuador have more than one crisis each (which could place too much weight on events in these countries), I include only the first crisis event for each country in the sample. Finally, since many of the extreme values for the competitiveness effect occur in oil-exporting countries during crises in oil-producing regions, I exclude the major oil exporters from the sample. These results are reported in column (3) of table 2.8. In each of these tests, the coefficients on the competitiveness and income effects are negative and significant. The cheap-import effect is always positive, but its significance fluctuates.

As a second series of sensitivity tests, I examine the effect of using alternate variable definitions. I begin by redefining the income effect as exports

25. Full results are available from the author.

Table 2.8   Sensitivity Tests

	Base Results (1)	Exclude Outliers for Compete[a] (2)	Exclude Major Oil Exporters[b] (3)	Redefine Income Effect[c] (4)	Add OECD Dummy (5)	Weight Trade Variables[d] (6)	Add Regional Dummies[e] (7)
Competitiveness effect	-0.052***	-0.054**	-0.054***	-0.062***	-0.049**	-0.228**	-0.049***
	(0.018)	(0.022)	(0.021)	(0.018)	(0.018)	(0.104)	(0.017)
Income effect	-1.021***	-1.012***	-1.022***	-0.251***	-1.027***	-0.006**	-1.041***
	(0.360)	(0.356)	(0.376)	(0.097)	(0.359)	(0.003)	(0.358)
Cheap-import effect	0.588**	0.590**	0.597**	0.219	0.607**	-0.468	0.616**
	(0.262)	(0.260)	(0.275)	(0.160)	(0.263)	(1.066)	(0.261)
Private credit growth	-1.536***	-1.546***	-1.633***	-1.383***	-1.407**	-1.491***	-1.783***
	(0.535)	(0.535)	(0.552)	(0.497)	(0.560)	(0.548)	(0.539)
Government consumption/GDP	2.718	2.681	2.955	2.317	2.166	2.957	-2.275
	(2.910)	(2.913)	(3.012)	(2.898)	(2.941)	(2.953)	(4.411)
Current account surplus/GDP	2.754	2.519	2.138	1.710	2.321	1.641	4.012
	(3.382)	(3.398)	(3.924)	(3.351)	(3.440)	(3.350)	(3.627)
Bank reserves/assets	-1.069	-1.008	-0.808	-1.265	-0.769	-0.929	-2.676
	(1.591)	(1.589)	(1.639)	(1.590)	(1.581)	(1.616)	(1.679)
Private capital inflows/GDP	-0.100	-0.078	0.074	-0.256	-0.286	-0.174	-0.052
	(0.690)	(0.690)	(0.727)	(0.688)	(0.698)	(0.694)	(0.756)
OECD dummy					0.371		
					(0.303)		
N	727	722	691	727	727	727	727
R^2	0.27	0.26	0.26	0.27	0.27	0.26	0.28

Notes: Standard errors (in parentheses) are White-adjusted for heteroskedasticity. All specifications also include period dummy variables (with the Brazilian crisis as the excluded variable). Variables are defined in the appendix.

***Significant at the 1 percent level.

**Significant at the 5 percent level.

[a]The five largest values for Compete are excluded.

[b]Major oil exporters defined as countries for which the ratio of oil and gas exports to GDP is greater than 5 percent. Countries in the sample that qualify as major oil exporters are Ecuador, Norway, Oman, and Venezuela.

[c]Income effect redefined as exports from country n to the crisis country as a percentage of total exports from country n.

[d]Trade variables weighted by currency and interest rate movements in the ground-zero country; see text for details.

[e]Regional dummy variables are Africa, Australasia, Central and South America, East Asia, former communist Europe (including Russia), Central and South America, North America, and Western Europe. The excluded region is the Middle East.

from country n to the crisis country as a share of total exports from country n (instead of as a share of country n's GDP). Then I recalculate the cheap-import effect as imports into country n from the crisis country as a share of total imports into country n (instead of the sum of consumption and investment in country n). Finally, I use normal returns instead of abnormal returns for the dependent variable. (In other words, I no longer subtract each country's average stock market return for the year preceding the crisis.) The first set of results is reported in column (4) of table 2.8. The coefficients for the competitiveness and income effects remain negative and significant in each of these tests.

As a third set of robustness tests, I estimate a number of variations to the base specification. Since there is no reason to believe that the relationship between the trade variables and the stock returns is linear, I include logarithmic, squared, and/or cubed terms for each of the trade variables. In most cases, the linear model outperforms the extended models, although there is weak evidence that the income effect may decrease at higher values. Next, I add a number of additional control variables, such as GDP, GDP per capita, an OECD dummy, and an oil-exporter dummy. Then, since different crises are driven by different combinations of currency and interest rate movements (a question investigated in more depth in the next section), I weight each of the trade variables by the change in the relevant variable in the ground-zero country.[26] Finally, since the trade variables (especially the income and cheap-import effects) may be capturing regional effects, I add a series of detailed regional-dummy variables to the base specification. A sample of these results is reported in columns (5) through (7) of table 2.8. In each case, the coefficients for the competitiveness and income effects remain negative and significant. Moreover, it is worth emphasizing the results in the last column that include the regional dummy variables. These regional dummy variables are jointly significant and several are individually significant. Even after controlling for these regional effects, however, the competitiveness and income effects are still negative and highly significant. This suggests that the trade variables are not simply capturing regional effects, such as financial linkages or regional learning.

As a final series of sensitivity tests, I change the definition of a crisis used in equation (2); more specifically, I use two less-stringent criteria for an event to qualify as a crisis. First, I define a crisis as any week for any country in the sample in which

$$(7) \qquad\qquad EMP_{nt} > \mu_{EMP} + 3\sigma_{EMP}.$$

The resulting sample of crisis events is listed in table 2.9. There are now twenty-seven crises (versus sixteen in the base analysis), lasting an average

26. More specifically, I weight *Compete* and *Cheap Import* by the percent change in the ground-zero country's exchange rate, and I multiply *Income* by the percent change in the ground-zero country's interest rate spread. Data sources and variable definitions are described in section 2.4.

Table 2.9   **Alternate Crisis Events: Crises Defined as $EMP_{nt} > \mu_{EMP} + 3\sigma_{EMP}$**

Country	Crisis Event Dates
Mexico	11/28/94–01/08/95, 01/16/95, 02/27/95–04/02/95, 10/30/95–11/12/95
Ecuador (1)	01/23/95–02/12/95, 10/30/95–11/05/95, 11/27/95–12/03/95, 12/18/95–12/24/95
The Philippines (1)	02/20/95–02/26/95
Argentina	02/27/95–03/12/95
South Africa (1)	04/17/95–04/23/95, 02/12/96–02/18/96, 04/01/96–04/14/96
Colombia	12/04/95–12/10/95
Venezuela (1)	12/11/95–12/17/95, 12/25/95–12/31/95, 04/15/96–04/21/96
South Africa (2)	04/15/96–04/28/96
Ecuador (2)	07/01/96–07/07/96
Venezuela (2)	03/10/97–03/16/97, 05/12/97–05/18/97, 05/26/97–06/02/97, 11/10/97–11/16/97, 02/16/98–02/22/98
Czech Republic	05/19/97–06/01/97
Slovak Republic (1)	05/19/97–06/08/97
Thailand	06/30/97–07/06/97, 12/08/97–12/14/97, 12/29/97–01/04/97
The Philippines (2)	07/07/97–07/13/97, 09/29/97–10/05/97, 12/08/97–12/14/97
Indonesia	08/11/97–08/31/97, 09/29/97–10/05/97, 12/08/97–12/14/97, 01/05/98–01/11/98, 01/19/98–01/25/98, 02/09/98–02/22/98, 03/02/98–03/08/98, 03/30/98–04/05/98, 04/13/98–04/19/98, 05/04/98–05/10/98, 05/18/98–05/24/98, 06/08/98–06/14/98
Brazil (1)	10/27/97–11/30/97, 12/15/97–12/21/97, 09/07/98–09/27/98
Russia (1)	11/17/97–11/23/97, 05/18/98–05/23/98, 07/06/98–07/13/98, 08/10/98–09/20/98
Korea	12/01/97–12/14/97, 12/29/97–01/04/97
India	01/19/98–01/25/98
Malaysia	03/02/98–03/08/98
Venezuela (3)	04/20/98–04/26/98, 06/15/98–06/21/98, 09/14/98–09/20/98
South Africa (3)	06/22/98–06/28/98
Slovak Republic (2)	09/14/98–10/04/98, 05/17/99–05/23/99
Ecuador (3)	09/21/98–09/27/98, 10/19/98–10/25/98, 11/02/98–11/08/98, 01/11/99–01/17/99, 01/25/99–02/07/99, 02/22/99–03/07/99
Norway	12/07/98–12/13/98
Russia (2)	12/28/98–01/03/99
Brazil (2)	01/11/99–01/24/99, 02/22/99–02/28/99

Note: See notes to table 2.1 for a full list of countries included in the sample.

of 4.0 weeks (versus an average of 2.6 weeks in the base analysis). Second, I redefine a crisis as any week in which

$$(8) \qquad\qquad EMP_{nt} > \mu_{EMP} + 1.5\sigma_{EMP}.$$

The resulting fifty-seven crisis events are listed in table 2.10, with the average crisis lasting 5.3 weeks. Finally, I reestimate the model in equation (3) using these larger samples of crisis events. Results for three different specifications are reported in table 2.11. The competitiveness and income effects remain negative and significant in each specification, and the bargain effect remains positive (with fluctuating significance).

To conclude, this series of sensitivity tests suggests that the competitiveness and income effects are negative, significant, and robust. The cheap-import effect is generally positive, although its significance varies across specifications. These trade effects can be large and economically important determinants of a country's vulnerability to a crisis that originates elsewhere in the world. It is worth emphasizing, however, that this simple model does not explain most of the variation in countries' stock market returns. The R^2s range from about 0.20 to 0.28 for the various specifications in tables 2.6 and 2.8, and the trade and macroeconomic variables often underpredict stock market movements in the comparisons in table 2.7. Therefore, although trade linkages (and macroeconomic variables) are important, they are clearly not the only factors affecting a country's stock market returns. Other factors, such as financial linkages or changes in investor sentiment, may also be important determinants of country's vulnerability to financial crises.

2.7   Do Different Types of Crises Generate Different Trade Effects?

The previous analysis used an exchange-market pressure index, which incorporated changes in exchange rates, interest rates, and reserve levels, to define a series of crises from 1994 through 1999. There are, however, significant differences across these crises, especially in the relative importance of each component of the EMP index. Many of these crises, such as those in Mexico and Thailand, involved substantial currency devaluations. During other crises, such as in Argentina, the currency's value remained fairly stable and the government responded by raising interest rates and paying international reserves.

Moreover, the way a country responds to increased pressure on its exchange rate could determine how the crisis is transmitted to other countries. For example, if a crisis includes a large currency devaluation, then exports from the crisis country will become relatively cheaper on international markets and the crisis could spread through competitiveness and cheap-import effects. On the other hand, if the currency's value remains fixed, there should not be significant competitiveness or cheap-

Table 2.10 Alternate Crisis Events: Crises Defined as $EMP_{nt} > \mu_{EMP} + 1.5\sigma_{EMP}$

Country	Crisis Event Dates
Slovak Republic (1)	07/18/94–07/24/94
Poland	09/12/94–09/18/94
India (1)	09/19/94–09/25/94, 10/03/94–10/30/94, 12/05/94–12/25/94
Mexico (1)	11/07/94–01/08/95, 01/16/95–01/29/95, 02/20/95–04/02/95, 04/10/95–04/16/95, 10/30/95–11/12/95
Argentina	12/19/94–12/25/94, 02/27/95–03/26/95
Thailand (1)	01/09/95–01/15/95
Ecuador (1)	01/23/95–02/19/95, 09/18/95–09/24/95, 10/23/95–11/05/95, 11/13/95–12/03/95, 12/18/95–12/31/95
Venezuela (1)	01/30/95–02/05/95, 12/11/95–12/17/95, 12/25/95–12/31/95
The Philippines (1)	02/20/95–03/12/95, 03/20/95–04/09/95
South Africa (1)	03/27/95–04/23/95, 01/29/96–03/03/96
Austria	05/08/95–05/14/95
Belgium	05/08/95–05/14/95
Norway (1)	05/08/95–05/14/95
Switzerland	05/08/95–05/14/95
India (2)	10/16/95–10/22/95, 10/30/95–11/05/95, 12/25/95–12/31/95, 01/29/95–02/04/96, 02/19/96–02/25/96, 03/04/96–03/10/96
Colombia (1)	11/27/95–12/24/95, 02/05/96–02/11/96, 02/26/96–03/03/96
South Africa (2)	03/25/96–04/28/96, 07/08/96–07/14/96, 07/22/96–07/28/96
Venezuela (2)	04/15/96–04/21/96, 03/10/97–03/16/97
Greece (1)	05/20/96–05/26/96, 11/25/96–12/01/96, 12/16/96–12/22/96
Ecuador (2)	07/10/96–07/07/96
New Zealand	01/20/97–01/26/97
Thailand (2)	02/03/97–02/09/97, 06/30/97–07/06/97, 07/28/97–08/03/97, 08/11/97–08/24/97, 11/10/97–11/16/97, 12/08/97–12/14/97, 12/29/9701/11/97
Colombia (2)	02/24/97–03/02/97, 12/22/97–12/28/97
Slovak Republic (2)	03/24/97–04/20/97, 05/19/97–06/08/97
Russia (1)	04/07/97–04/13/97, 10/13/97–10/19/97, 10/27/97–11/02/97, 11/10/97–11/17/97, 12/01/97–12/14/97
Czech Republic	05/12/97–06/10/97, 11/24/97–11/30/97
Venezuela (3)	05/12/97–06/01/97, 11/10/97–11/16/97, 01/19/98–01/25/98, 02/16/98–02/22/98, 04/20/98–04/26/98
The Philippines (2)	06/30/97–07/13/97, 07/21/97–07/27/97, 08/25/97–08/31/97, 09/29/97–10/05/97, 12/08/97–12/14/97, 12/22/97–12/28/97, 06/08/98–06/14/98
Malaysia	07/07/97–07/20/97, 12/08/97–12/14/97, 12/29/97–01/11/98, 01/19/98–01/25/98, 03/02/98–03/08/98

(*continued*)

Table 2.10   (continued)

Country	Crisis Event Dates
Indonesia (1)	07/14/97–07/20/97, 08/11/97–09/21/97, 09/29/97–10/05/97, 10/13/97–10/19/97, 11/03/97–11/23/97, 12/01/97–12/14/97, 12/29/97–01/11/98, 01/19/98–01/25/98, 02/09/98–02/22/98, 03/02/98–03/08/98, 03/30/98–04/05/98, 04/13/98–04/19/98, 05/04/98–05/10/98, 05/18/98–05/31/98, 06/08/98–06/14/98, 06/22/98–06/28/98
Greece (2)	09/15/97–09/21/97, 10/27/97–11/02/97, 08/10/98–08/16/98
Australia (1)	10/20/97–10/26/97, 07/20/98–07/26/98
Mexico (2)	10/20/97–10/26/97, 08/17/98–09/13/98, 09/28/98–10/04/98
Brazil (1)	10/27/97–12/28/97, 08/31/98–10/25/98
Korea (1)	11/17/97–12/21/97, 12/29/97–01/04/97, 03/30/98–04/05/98
Chile (1)	11/24/97–12/07/97, 12/15/97–12/28/97
Norway (2)	11/24/97–12/28/97
Ecuador (3)	12/01/97–12/14/97, 12/22/97–12/28/97, 03/30/98–04/05/98, 05/11/98–05/17/98, 08/03/98–08/23/98, 08/31/98–09/13/98, 09/21/98–09/27/98, 10/19/98–11/22/98
Singapore	12/08/97–12/14/97, 01/05/98–01/11/98
India (3)	01/12/98–01/25/98
Colombia (3)	03/30/98–04/12/98, 06/01/98–06/07/98, 08/31/98–09/13/98, 10/05/98–10/11/98
Russia (2)	04/27/98–05/04/98, 05/18/98–05/31/98, 07/06/98–07/12/98, 08/10/98–09/20/98, 10/12/98–10/18/98, 12/28/98–01/03/99
South Africa (3)	05/25/98–05/31/98, 06/08/98–07/05/98, 08/03/98–08/09/98, 08/24/98–08/30/98, 09/28/98–10/04/98
Venezuela (4)	06/15/98–06/21/98, 09/14/98–09/20/98, 11/30/98–12/06/98
Indonesia (2)	07/20/98–07/26/98, 08/03/98–08/16/98, 11/02/98–11/08/98
The Philippines (3)	08/03/98–08/09/98
Canada	08/17/98–08/30/98
Slovak Republic (3)	08/17/98–08/23/98, 09/14/98–10/04/98, 05/10/99–05/23/99
Israel	10/05/98–10/11/98
Australia (2)	10/19/98–10/25/98
Japan	10/19/98–10/25/98, 11/02/98–11/08/98
Brazil (2)	10/26/98–11/08/98, 01/11/99–01/24/99, 02/22/99–02/28/99
Ecuador (4)	11/30/98–12/13/98, 01/11/99–02/14/99, 02/22/99–03/07/99, 03/15/99–03/21/99, 03/29/99–04/04/99
Norway (3)	11/30/98–12/13/98, 12/21/98–12/27/98, 06/21/99–06/27/99
Chile (2)	12/07/98–12/13/98, 12/21/97–12/27/97, 06/14/99–06/20/99
Korea (2)	12/21/98–12/27/98
Peru	01/04/99–01/10/99

Table 2.11   Regression Results: Alternate Crisis Definitions

	Crises Defined As $EMP_{nt} > \mu_{EMP} + 3\sigma_{EMP}$			Crises Defined As $EMP_{nt} > \mu_{EMP} + 1.5\sigma_{EMP}$		
	Base Specification	Alternate Macroeconomic Controls	Full Set of Macroeconomic Controls	Base Specification	Alternate Macroeconomic Controls	Full Set of Macroeconomic Controls
Competitiveness effect	-0.056***	-0.053**	-0.054**	-0.065**	-0.089**	-0.091**
	(0.020)	(0.024)	(0.023)	(0.033)	(0.039)	(0.040)
Income effect	-0.927***	-1.067**	-1.216**	-0.671***	-0.724***	-0.744***
	(0.334)	(0.489)	(0.511)	(0.203)	(0.214)	(0.215)
Cheap-import effect	0.582**	0.698	0.816	0.353**	0.344**	0.359**
	(0.276)	(0.406)	(0.423)	(0.145)	(0.163)	(0.165)
Private credit growth	-0.092		-1.641	-0.110		0.191
	(0.604)		(1.314)	(0.330)		(0.945)
Government consumption/GDP	3.642		7.693**	-2.476		0.102
	(2.218)		(3.358)	(1.393)		(2.100)
Current account surplus/GDP	3.969		5.481	-0.716		-0.372
	(2.493)		(3.419)	(1.703)		(2.278)
Bank reserves/assets	1.185		2.360	-1.859**		-0.236
	(1.185)		(1.614)	(0.837)		(1.105)
Private capital inflows/GDP	0.137		0.409	0.161		-0.379
	(0.437)		(0.859)	(0.315)		(0.623)
Domestic credit growth		-0.459	1.438		0.087	-0.131
		(0.938)	(1.295)		(0.757)	(0.781)
Government surplus/GDP		-2.163	2.552		6.354**	6.792**
		(2.895)	(3.283)		(2.868)	(3.424)

(continued)

Table 2.11 (continued)

	Crises Defined As $EMP_{nt} > \mu_{EMP} + 3\sigma_{EMP}$			Crises Defined As $EMP_{nt} > \mu_{EMP} + 1.5\sigma_{EMP}$		
	Base Specification	Alternate Macroeconomic Controls	Full Set of Macroeconomic Controls	Base Specification	Alternate Macroeconomic Controls	Full Set of Macroeconomic Controls
Money supply (M2)/reserves		0.450	−0.169		2.169**	2.209**
		(1.399)	(1.618)		(0.886)	(1.081)
Openness (total trade/GDP)		0.256	−0.314		0.436**	0.520**
		(0.305)	(0.369)		(0.216)	(0.249)
Growth in GNP per capita		−0.674	1.417		1.605	1.477
		(5.699)	(6.212)		(3.394)	(3.604)
Inflation (in CPI)		0.023	0.007		−0.038	−0.036
		(0.146)	(0.175)		(0.087)	(0.131)
N	1,245	809	797	2,657	1,726	1,707
R^2	0.12	0.13	0.14	0.24	0.25	0.26

Notes: Standard errors (in parentheses) are White-adjusted for heteroskedasticity. All specifications also include period dummy variables (with the Brazilian crisis as the excluded variable). Variables are defined in the appendix.

***Significant at the 1 percent level.

**Significant at the 5 percent level.

Table 2.12   **Crisis Subgroups**

With Weekly Currency Devaluation[a] ≥ 10%	With Weekly Interest Rate Increase[b] ≥ 30%
Mexico	Mexico
Venezuela (1)	Ecuador (1)
Thailand	Argentina
The Philippines	Venezuela (2)
Indonesia	Czech Republic
Korea	The Philippines
Russia	Indonesia
Ecuador (2)	India
Brazil	Russia
	Venezuela (3)
	Slovak Republic
	Ecuador (2)

Notes: Based on the crisis events listed in table 2.1.

[a]Devaluation/depreciation measured as the nominal exchange rate based on U.S. dollars. See section 2.4 for further information.

[b]Interest rates are short-term and based on the difference between the spread with the short-term U.S. interest rate versus the same spread averaged over the previous year. See section 2.4 for further information.

import effects. Similarly, if the crisis includes a large increase in interest rates, this is likely to slow investment and growth in the crisis region. This could lead to a larger income effect than if interest rates were left unchanged or decreased.

To test whether differences across crises determine how they impact other countries, I divide the sample of crises identified in table 2.1 into two subgroups. The first subgroup is any crisis that includes a currency devaluation of 10 percent or more during at least one week of the crisis. The second subgroup is any crisis that includes an increase in the interest rate spread of 30 percent or more during at least one week of the crisis.[27] The crises that qualify in these subgroups are listed in table 2.12. As shown in the table, slightly more than half of the crises include a major currency devaluation, and three-fourths of the crises include a major increase in interest rates.

Next, I reestimate equation (3) for each of these crisis subgroups, using the same methodology, definitions, and specification as the base results reported in section 2.6. Table 2.13 reports results. Column (1) repeats estimates for the entire sample of sixteen crises. Columns (2) and (3) report results for crises that include and do not include, respectively, a major currency devaluation. Columns (4) and (5) report results for crises that in-

27. Both statistics are calculated as described in section 2.4. More specifically, the exchange rate is calculated as the nominal U.S. dollar exchange rate. The interest rate is calculated as the short-term interest rate spread (versus the U.S. rate) less the same spread averaged over the previous year.

Table 2.13   Regression Results Based on Crisis Subgroups

		Crisis Events			
	Full Sample (1)	With a Major Devaluation[a] (2)	With No Major Devaluation[a] (3)	With a Major Interest Rate Increase[b] (4)	With No Major Interest Rate Increase[b] (5)
Competitiveness effect	−0.052*** (0.018)	−0.047*** (0.018)	−0.050 (0.078)	−0.049** (0.024)	−0.047 (0.032)
Income effect	−1.021*** (0.360)	−0.845 (0.449)	−1.344** (0.638)	−1.030*** (0.342)	−0.578 (1.137)
Cheap-import effect	0.588** (0.262)	0.310 (0.293)	1.015 (0.573)	0.633** (0.248)	0.065 (0.913)
Private credit growth	−1.536*** (0.535)	−0.978 (0.787)	−2.165*** (0.839)	−1.967*** (0.599)	−0.041 (1.138)
Government consumption/GDP	2.718 (2.910)	7.137** (3.105)	−2.548 (5.404)	0.242 (3.289)	9.168 (6.188)
Current account surplus/GDP	2.754 (3.382)	5.667 (3.738)	−2.733 (6.421)	2.627 (3.838)	0.375 (7.005)
Bank reserves/assets	−1.069 (1.591)	2.096 (1.762)	−5.507 (3.068)	−2.640 (1.778)	4.003 (3.219)
Private capital inflows/GDP	−0.100 (0.690)	0.598 (0.680)	−0.589 (1.281)	−0.675 (0.746)	3.666** (1.770)
N	727	406	321	556	171
R^2	0.27	0.26	0.28	0.27	0.25

Notes: Standard errors (in parentheses) are White-adjusted for heteroskedasticity. All specifications also include period dummy variables (with the Brazilian crisis as the excluded variable). Variables are defined in the appendix.

***Significant at the 1 percent level.
**Significant at the 5 percent level.
[a]Major devaluation defined as an increase in the nominal U.S. dollar exchange rate of at least 10 percent within at least one week of the crisis. See table 2.12 for the crisis list.
[b]Major interest rate increase defined as an increase of at least 30 percent within at least one week of the crisis in the short-term interest rate spread (compared to the U.S. rate) less the average spread over the past year. See table 2.12 for the crisis list.

clude and do not include, respectively, a major increase in interest rates. Most of the estimates in table 2.13 support the predictions discussed above. The competitiveness effect is negative and highly significant during crises that include a major devaluation, but highly insignificant during crises that do not include a major devaluation. The income effect is negative and highly significant during crises that include a major increase in interest rates, but is highly insignificant during crises that do not include a major increase in interest rates. Estimates for the cheap-import effect are generally insignificant and are the only coefficients that do not follow the above predictions. This is not surprising, however, given the general lack of robustness for this coefficient.

These results have an important implication. When a country's exchange rate is under pressure during a crisis, the country's response is a critical determinant of how the local crisis affects the rest of the world. If the country responds by devaluing its currency (or allowing its currency to depreciate), then other countries that compete with the crisis country's exports will be affected by the change in relative export prices. On the other hand, if the country responds by raising interest rates, this will directly affect countries that export to the crisis country, probably through a contraction in income and investment. Therefore, the way a country responds to a crisis is an important determinant of how that crisis affects other economies.

2.8 Summary and Conclusions

This paper analyzed whether trade linkages were important determinants of a country's vulnerability to currency crises. It began by discussing previous empirical work on this subject in some detail. Most of these papers use aggregate data on bilateral trade flows between countries. Results are mixed. Some papers argue that trade linkages are important determinants of a country's vulnerability to a crisis, whereas others argue that trade is not important, especially in the transmission of recent currency crises. A serious limitation of this macro-level work is that the trade data are not disaggregated by industry, and therefore do not accurately measure competition in third markets. Moreover, many of these papers could suffer from omitted-variables bias since trade flows are highly correlated with other cross-country linkages, such as financial flows, that are extremely difficult to measure.

Next, this paper surveyed several theoretical papers that explain how trade could transmit crises internationally. More specifically, it explained that "trade" incorporates three distinct channels: a competitiveness effect, an income effect, and a cheap-import effect. A competitiveness effect occurs when one country devalues its currency, increasing the relative competitiveness of its exports and hurting the competitiveness of exports from other countries. An income effect occurs when a crisis affects income and growth within the crisis country, thereby affecting (and probably reducing) purchases of imports from abroad. A cheap-import effect occurs when a country devalues its currency, reducing the relative price of its exports and thereby reducing prices in countries that import these goods. Although each of these three trade linkages could transmit a crisis internationally, these various effects may not all work in the same direction. For example, the income effect could partially counteract the cheap-import effect. Therefore, when measuring the importance of trade linkages, it is necessary to isolate each of these effects and measure them independently.

This was the paper's main goal. It attempted to measure the significance and magnitude of each of these three trade linkages in countries' vulnerability to recent crises. To do this, it used trade flow data between most countries in the world, disaggregated at the four-digit industry level. By using industry-level data, the paper was able to measure competition in third markets more accurately than past work on this subject. In order to perform this analysis, the paper constructed a number of statistics measuring the importance of trade linkages during the sixteen most severe crises between 1994 and 1999. The most interesting statistic was the competitiveness variable, which measured the importance of the crisis country to each export industry as well as how dependent other countries were on those industries.

Estimation results suggested that trade linkages were highly significant determinants of a country's vulnerability to recent crises. Countries that competed in the same industries as major exports from the crisis country had significantly lower stock market returns during these crises. Countries that had a larger share of exports going to the crisis countries also had significantly lower stock returns. These competitiveness and income effects remained both highly significant and economically important across an extensive series of sensitivity tests, including less stringent definitions of what constitutes a crisis. Although estimates of the third trade effect (the cheap-import effect) usually had the expected sign, its significance fluctuated across these sensitivity tests. Countries that had a larger share of imports from the crisis country had slightly higher stock returns during these events. Taken as a whole, these results suggest that trade linkages were highly significant determinants of a country's abnormal stock returns during recent currency crises.

Another series of results from this empirical analysis concerned the magnitude and relative importance of trade and other macroeconomic variables in explaining different countries' vulnerability to financial crises. Although trade and macroeconomic variables were significant and economically important, these variables explain only a portion of stock market movements. For example, in the base regression results, trade and macroeconomic variables explained about one-fourth of the variation in countries' abnormal stock returns during recent crises. Three-fourths of the variation is therefore not explained in this simple model. This suggests that other factors, such as financial linkages and investor behavior, may also be important. Estimates also suggested that the impact of trade linkages was greater in magnitude than that of a country's macroeconomic characteristics.

A final empirical result is that the importance of these trade linkages depends on the way the crisis country responded to pressure on its exchange rate. When a country responded by devaluing its currency (or allowing it to depreciate), the competitiveness effect was negative and highly significant. When the country maintained a relatively stable exchange rate, there was no significant competitiveness effect. On the other hand, when a country responded to exchange-market pressure by raising interest rates substantially, the income effect was negative and highly significant. If the country kept interest rates fairly steady (or raised them by only a small amount), there was no significant income effect. Therefore, the way a country responded to pressure on its exchange rate was a significant determinant of how the crisis affected other countries and, in particular, which trade linkages were important.

This series of results has important implications for the role of international institutions in responding to future financial crises. Real linkages between countries, such as trade, are important determinants of how a crisis spreads internationally. Multilateral assistance or bailout packages will have limited success in reducing these cross-country linkages. On a more positive note, however, multilateral institutions could provide a crisis country with a wider variety of options (with respect to exchange rate and interest rate policy) than would otherwise be available. Therefore, even though multilateral institutions could not prevent the inevitable transmission of a crisis through these trade linkages, they might influence how the country responds to any exchange-market pressure and therefore influence which countries are most affected by the crisis.

Appendix
Data Sources and Definitions

Data to Calculate the Exchange-Market Pressure Index

1. *Nominal exchange rates.* Exchange rates expressed as the local currency per U.S. dollar as reported by Datastream.

2. *Short-term interest rates.* As reported by Datastream. The short-term rate is measured by the interbank rate (preferred) or the call rate. If neither of these is available, then the shortest-term rate available is used. The U.S. interest rate is the Federal Fund's rate.

3. *International reserves to the money supply.* The ratio of total international reserves less gold divided by narrow money (M1). Reserve data are from line 1L.dzf, and M1 data are from 34..zf from the International Financial Statistics (IMF 2000). Weekly data are interpolated from the monthly data.

4. *Inflation.* Annual percentage change in consumer prices. Data are from line 64.xzf from IMF (2000).

Data to Calculate the Trade-Effect Regressions

1. *Stock market returns.* Based on stock market indices in U.S. dollars as reported by Datastream. Abnormal returns are calculated as the weekly stock return during the given time period minus the average weekly return (i.e., normal return) for the previous year. Calculation of the normal return excludes one week prior to the start date for the calculation of the abnormal return, in order to exclude any unusual market movements directly before a crisis.

2. *Competitiveness effect.* The weighted product of two terms: exports from the ground-zero country in a given industry as a share of global exports in that industry; and total exports from country n in the same industry, as a share of country n's GDP. These products are summed across industries for each country-crisis pair and weighted by the maximum calculated value (and multiplied by 100). This creates an index that can take values from 0 to 100. All trade data are in U.S. dollars and are reported by the International Trade Center, UN Statistics Division (1999).

3. *Income effect.* Calculated as the ratio of total exports to the ground-zero country as a share of GDP. Export data are from the International Trade Center, UN Statistics Division (1999). GDP is reported in the World Development Indicators (World Bank 2000).

4. *Cheap-import effect.* Calculated as the ratio of total imports from the ground-zero country to the sum of private consumption and gross domestic investment. Private consumption is the market value of all goods and services, including durable products purchased or received as income in kind by households, but excluding purchases of dwellings. Gross domestic investment consists of outlays on additions to the fixed assets of the economy, plus net changes in the level of inventories. Import data are from the International Trade Center, UN Statistics Division (1999). Statistics in the denominator are reported in World Bank (2000).

5. *Private credit growth.* Average annual growth in credit to the private sector. This excludes credit to governments and public enterprises. Data are from line 32d..zf of IMF (2000).

6. *Government consumption/GDP.* The ratio of general government consumption to GDP as reported in the World Bank (2000). General government consumption includes all current spending for purchases of goods and services (including wages and salaries). It also includes most expenditures on national defense and security, but excludes government military expenditures that are part of government capital formation.

7. *Current account surplus/GDP.* The current account balance as a percentage of GDP, where a positive value indicates a surplus. Data are from World Bank (2000).

8. *Bank reserves/assets.* The ratio of domestic currency holdings and deposits with the monetary authorities to claims on other governments, nonfinancial public enterprises, the private sector, and other banking institutions. Reported in World Bank (2000).

9. *Private capital inflows/GDP.* The ratio of gross private capital flows to GDP as reported in World Bank (2000). Gross private capital flows are the sum of the absolute values of direct, portfolio, and other investment inflows and outflows recorded in the balance of payments financial account, excluding changes in the assets and liabilities of monetary authorities and general government. The indicator is calculated as a ratio to GDP converted to international dollars using purchasing power parities.

10. *Domestic credit growth.* Average annual growth in domestic credit. Data are from line 32..zf of IMF (2000).

11. *Government surplus/GDP.* The government budget surplus as a percentage of GDP, where a positive value indicates a surplus. The government budget surplus is from line 80 of IMF (2000), and GDP data are from World Bank (2000).

12. *Money supply/reserves.* The ratio of money and quasi money (M2) to gross international reserves as reported the World Bank (2000). Money and quasi money is the sum of currency outside banks, demand deposits other than those of the central government, and the time, savings, and foreign currency deposits of resident sectors other than the central government (which corresponds to the sum of lines 34 and 35 of IMF 2000). Gross international reserves are holdings of monetary gold, special drawing rights, reserves of IMF members held by the IMF, and holdings of foreign exchange under the control of the monetary authorities.

13. *Openness.* The ratio of total trade to GDP. Total trade is calculated as the sum of all imports and exports as reported by the International Trade Center, UN Statistics Division (1999). GDP is reported in World Bank (2000).

14. *Growth in GNP per capita.* Average annual growth in gross national product (GNP) per capita. Data taken from World Bank (2000).

15. *Inflation.* Domestic consumer price index (CPI) inflation as reported in line 64 of IMF (2000).

References

Baig, Taimur, and Ilan Goldfajn. 1998. Financial market contagion in the Asian crisis. IMF Working Paper no. WP/98/155. Washington, D.C.: International Monetary Fund.

Barberis, Nicholas, Andrei Shleifer, and Robert Vishny. 1998. A model of investor sentiment. *Journal of Financial Economics* 49:307–43.

Caramazza, Francesco, Luca Ricci, and Ranil Salgado. 2000. Trade and financial contagion in currency crises. IMF Working Paper no. WP/00/55. Washington, D.C.: International Monetary Fund.

Corsetti, Giancarlo, Paolo Pesenti, Nouriel Roubini, and Cédric Tille. 2000. Competitive devaluations: Toward a welfare-based approach. *Journal of International Economics* 51:217–41.

De Gregorio, José, and Rodrigo Valdés. 2001. Crisis transmission: Evidence from the debt, tequila, and Asian Flu crises." In *International financial contagion,* ed. Stijn Claessens and Kristin Forbes, 99–127. Boston, Mass.: Kluwer Academic.

Eichengreen, Barry, and Andrew K. Rose. 1999. Contagious currency crises: Channels of conveyance. In *Changes in exchange rates in rapidly developing countries: Theory, practice, and policy issues,* ed. Takatoshi Ito and Anne O. Krueger, 29–50. Chicago: University of Chicago Press.

Eichengreen, Barry, Andrew K. Rose, and Charles Wyplosz. 1996. Contagious currency crises. NBER Working Paper no. 5681. Cambridge, Mass.: National Bureau of Economic Research.

Forbes, Kristin. 2000. The Asian flu and Russian virus: Firm-level evidence on how crises are transmitted internationally. NBER Working Paper no. 7807. Cambridge, Mass.: National Bureau of Economic Research, July.

Gelos, Gaston, and Ratna Sahay. 2001. Financial market spillovers: How different are the transition economies? In *International financial contagion,* ed. Stijn Claessens and Kristin Forbes, 329–66. Boston, Mass.: Kluwer Academic.

Gerlach, Stefan, and Frank Smets. 1995. Contagious speculative attacks. *European Journal of Political Economy* 11:45–63.

Glick, Reuven, and Andrew K. Rose. 1999. Contagion and trade: Why are currency crises regional? *Journal of International Money and Finance* 18:603–17.

Goldstein, Morris, Graciela Kaminsky, and Carmen Reinhart. 2000. *Assessing financial vulnerability: An early warning system for emerging markets.* Washington, D.C.: Institute for International Economics.

Gupta, Poonam, Deepak Mishra, and Ratna Sahay. 2000. Output response during currency crises. International Monetary Fund. Mimeograph.

Harrigan, James. 2000. The impact of the Asia Crisis on U.S. industry: An almost-free lunch? *Federal Reserve Bank of New York Economic Policy Review* 6 (3): 71–79.

International Monetary Fund (IMF). 2000. International Financial Statistics [database on CD-ROM]. June.

International Trade Center, UN Statistics Division. 1999. Trade Analysis System for Personal Computers [database on CD-ROM].

Kaminsky, Graciela, and Carmen Reinhart. 2000. On crises, contagion, and confusion. *Journal of International Economics* 51:145–68.

Masson, Paul. 1998. Contagion: Monsoonal effects, spillovers, and jumps between multiple equilibria. IMF Working Paper no. WP/98/142. Washington, D.C.: International Monetary Fund.

Paasche, Bernhard. 2000. Credit constraints and international financial crises. Carnegie-Mellon University, Department of Economics. Mimeograph.

Pesenti, Paolo, and Cédric Tille. 2000. The economics of currency crises and contagion: An introduction. *Federal Reserve Bank of New York Economic Policy Review* 6 (3): 3–16.

Van Rijckeghem, Caroline, and Beatrice Weder. 2001. Sources of contagion: Is it finance or trade? *Journal of International Economics* 54 (2): 293–308.

Wincoop, Eric van, and Kei-Mu Yi. 2000. Asia Crisis post-mortem: Where did the money go and did the United States benefit? *Federal Reserve Bank of New York Economic Policy Review* 6 (3): 51–70.

World Bank. 2000. World development indicators [database on CD-ROM].

Comment   Federico Sturzenegger

This paper combines a number of attractive features, each one of which is an important contribution in its own right. First, the paper constructs a new database that distinguishes different trade links among countries. This useful database is reproduced completely in the paper, making it

Federico Sturzenegger is dean of the business school at Universidad Torcuato Di Tella.

available for everyone to use in future research. Second, the paper designs new tests with this database and, as a result, delivers some new findings. The results have relevant implications for policy design and crisis prevention.

Briefly, the main contribution of the paper is that it decomposes three types of mechanisms by which trade may determine the vulnerability of a country to crises in other countries: a *competitiveness effect,* which measures how a country may be affected as an exporter in a common third market; an *income effect,* which captures the way a crisis may affect the exports to the crisis country; and finally, a *cheap-import effect,* which works in the opposite direction, capturing the increased income as result of the country's ability to obtain imports at lower prices for the crisis country.

The results indicate that these channels are relevant for predicting the stock market performance response to a crisis. Furthermore, and perhaps most important from a policy perspective, it is shown that the propagation characteristics differ depending on the kind of crisis the ground-zero country experiences. For example, if the ground-zero country responds to the crisis by increasing interest rates rather than by depreciating the exchange rate, it is shown that the effects on other countries are not the same. This is obviously useful information for the design of policy prescriptions aimed at reducing the international spread of crises.

However, two questions come to mind when evaluating the empirical results. First, we need to ask to what extent these trade variables may be capturing something other than trade—perhaps, for example, the role of financial factors. This is the point made by Van Rijckeghem and Weder (1999), among others. My assessment of the debate is that to some extent this is probably so, but also that two factors tend to dilute the relevance of this criticism of the paper. First, even if we think of the trade variable as a composite of trade and finance effects, the links unveiled still provide information useful in assessing the vulnerability of other economies to a crisis. Second, and more important, the breaking up of the trade effects into the different channels, together with the fact that they work as expected, means that something beyond finance is going on here.

A more serious concern in the estimation refers to the way overlapping effects are taken into account. When the Tequila crisis hits Mexico, all countries in the region suffer. This, in turn, sets off a second round of income effects, and potentially competitiveness and cheap-import effects among the countries involved. However, the specification in equation (3) relates only to the ground-zero country and thus ignores these second-round effects. Consider, for example, a country like Peru. As a result of the Tequila crisis Peru was affected not only through its trade links with Mexico, but also through its trade links with Chile, Brazil, and other Latin American countries that were also affected by the Mexican crisis. All these other effects are left out of the estimation. In the end, this may imply that the coefficients may overestimate the impact of the ground-zero country while probably underestimating the overall trade effect.

One way to deal with this may be to define some very distinct and separate crises (my suggestions would be Tequila, Venezuela, Czech, Asia [beginning in Thailand], India, Russia, and Brazil) and let the whole effects play out. This could be done by introducing the relationship with all countries affected in the second round in equation (3), or by computing a matrix of relationships among countries and making these the independent variables in the estimation. In the current specification, a country may show a strong trade effect from its relation with the ground-zero country even when not trading with it, as a result of its trading with a third country that has a strong relation with both. In any case, these are interesting lines for future research.

This potential misspecification problem is further confirmed by looking at a particular country and checking how well the model predicts the impact of crises on the chosen measure, the stock market. Table 2C.1 computes the effect of each crisis on Argentina, thus expanding the examples presented in table 2.7. As can be seen, with the exception of the Brazilian crisis (which explains about 20 percent of the change in the stock market), all others appear to have had a very small impact. On the one hand, this can be considered supportive of the model. The crisis with Brazil was the only one affecting an important trade partner (the other important trade partners of Argentina are the European Union and the United States). On the other hand, the results cast some doubt on the specification of the model. As can

Table 2C.1   **The Effects on Argentina**

	Competitiveness Effect	Income Effect	Bargain Effect	Total Effect	Stock Market Change	Total Effect/Stock Market Change
Mexico	−0.09	−0.11	0.06	−0.14	−4.39	3.1
Ecuador (1)	−0.02	−0.06	0.05	−0.04	−2.24	1.6
Venezuela (1)	−0.04	−0.08	0.01	−0.11	4.78	wrong sign
Venezuela (2)	−0.08	−0.13	0.03	−0.18	2.21	wrong sign
Czech Republic	−0.03	0.00	0.01	−0.02	1.81	wrong sign
Thailand	−0.08	−0.05	0.02	−0.12	2.72	wrong sign
The Philippines	−0.02	−0.02	0.01	−0.03	1.07	wrong sign
Indonesia	−0.08	−0.08	0.02	−0.14	−2.12	6.6
Korea	−0.12	−0.07	0.11	−0.09	3.76	wrong sign
India	−0.14	−0.07	0.03	−0.18	−2.89	6.2
Russia	−0.34	−0.16	0.06	−0.44	−6.73	6.6
Venezuela (3)	−0.09	−0.11	0.01	−0.19	5.05	wrong sign
Slovak Republic	−0.01	0.00	0.01	−0.01	−6.41	0.1
Ecuador (2)	−0.02	−0.03	0.02	−0.03	0.57	wrong sign
Brazil	−0.40	−2.62	1.52	−1.50	−6.99	21.5

Note: All numbers are percentages.

be seen from the table, the Venezuelan crisis of 1998 is estimated to have had a larger impact on Argentina than did the Tequila crisis—such was not the case, however. In fact, the Tequila crisis had such a large effect on Argentina that it even triggered a crisis there by March 1995. Furthermore, many crises that did not affect Argentina (Thailand, the Philippines, etc.) are predicted by the model to have had an effect. Two interpretations in line with the discussion above can thus explain why the table gives an interpretation of the links that does not match our prior beliefs. The first is that, except for some very obvious cases, trade effects are certainly overshadowed by financial effects (and even in the geographically proximate cases, the trade effect may be picking up some financial link effects). The second is that the cross-effects are not properly taken into account, so that the model has difficulties distinguishing between crises with stronger regional effects and those that do not.

Another concern that can be raised is the use of stock market data, rather than a contagion or crisis dummy, as dependent variable. The latter has been the standard practice in the literature (see, e.g., Eichengreen, Rose, and Wyplosz 1996; Glick and Rose 1999; and Edwards, chap. 1 in this volume). Yet the choice of the stock market data has also received support in the literature. Kaminsky, Lizondo, and Reinhardt (1998) identify sharp declines in equity markets as being among the best indicators of forthcoming currency crises. Work at investment banks, such as Ades, Masih, and Tenengauzer (1998), also uses the stock market (together with other variables) as a predictor of financial crises in emerging markets.

The use of the stock market data has the appeal of capturing the whole market-value effect of the propagation (and its predicted future effect), but has the disadvantage that it is likely to mix real, financial, and contagion effects. Stocks measure the present discounted value of future dividends, and thus can change through changes in the numerator (dividends) or the denominator (discount factor). The changes in the numerator are the direct links one would like to associate with trade. However, the price of stocks may be affected by changes in the discount factor, which I like to associate with pure contagion or with a financial channel. In this regard, the use of this dependent variable is particularly susceptible to mixing financial and trade effects.

The paper fits in a tradition of papers that try to unveil the propagation mechanisms of crises among countries. It probably will not settle the debate as to whether the effects are financial or trade related. It is likely that the debate will never be settled, in fact, because it is not one or the other but both, which surely play an important role. Furthermore, if trade effects are important, shouldn't one expect an effect on country risk and financing costs?

In spite of leaving this issue unsettled, the paper makes an important contribution: By unveiling the different channels by which trade works and by making the point that the way the crisis is handled has implications for how it propagates, it gives us a better understanding of crises than the one we had before reading the paper.

References

Ades, Alberto, Rumi Masih, and Daniel Tenengauzer. 1998. GS watch: A new framework for predicting financial crises in emerging markets. Goldman Sachs, Economic Research. Unpublished paper.
Eichengreen, Barry, Andrew Rose, and Charles Wyplosz. 1996. Contagious currency crises. NBER Working Paper no. 5681. Cambridge, Mass.: National Bureau of Economic Research.
Glick, Reuven, and Andrew Rose. 1999. Contagion and trade: Why are currency crises regional? *Journal of International Money and Finance* 18:603–17.
Kaminsky, Graciela, Saul Lizondo, and Carmen Reinhardt. 1998. Leading indicators of currency crises. *IMF Staff Papers* 45 (March): 1–48.
Van Rijckeghem, Caroline, and Beatrice Weder. 1999. Sources of contagion: Finance or trade? IMF Working Paper no. WP/99/146. Washington, D.C.: International Monetary Fund.

Discussion Summary

Anne O. Krueger commented that the paper controlled only for whether there was a change of real exchange rate, but that it did not take into account the magnitude of the change. She suggested that the author include the real exchange rate changes weighted by shares of bilateral trade as a control variable. Krueger cited her study on the impact of real exchange rate change on India's trade, in which she found a large effect of real exchange rate.

Amartya Lahiri commended the paper for isolating each margin on which that trade can affect the international transmission of crises. He also said, however, that the overall effects of trade on crisis transmission seemed to be quite small. Moreover, since the sample contained a group of heterogeneous countries, the assumption that the trade effects are the same across countries is not likely to hold.

Linda S. Goldberg made two remarks. First, regarding the paper's conclusion that trade matters more than macrovariables, she posed the question whether trade per se matters or is just a conduit for real effects of exchange rate changes. Second, she remarked on the related literature. She found the equation used in the paper for computing the competitive effect reminiscent of the exchange rate pass-through literature and she suggested the author to relate the two. She also noted the literature on the link among exchange rates, investment, and stock prices. The paper's discussion on industry structure and the pricing for different countries and industries fits well into that literature.

Eduardo Borensztein wondered whether the aggregate stock market index really measured countries' vulnerability to crises. He said that in some countries the stock market is not comprehensive and is dominated by a few companies that are unrelated to international trade. Borensztein also commented on the definition of crises, and he suggested using three standard deviations as the cutoff level between tranquil and crisis periods. Recognizing that some countries have experienced increases in exchange rate volatility over time, he said that one could take a rolling sample in those cases.

Roberto Rigobon commented that the prediction exercise of the paper is performed within the sample, and that it should be performed out of sample.

Giancarlo Corsetti commended the paper for putting together a trade data set that is finally close to our theories.

Shang-Jin Wei commented that trade effects might not be stable across different crisis periods because the magnitudes of the crises were very different, and that this might have contributed to the seemingly abnormal results of the paper. Wei suggested solving this problem through redefining trade effect variables by including the actual decline in the crisis countries' income levels. Second, Wei noted that the paper focused on the direct trade effects in the international transmission of crises and said that there can be subsequent rounds of indirect trade effects. For example, Korea suffered directly from the Thai devaluation as well as from the Indonesian devaluation resulting from the Thai crisis. He said that one way to capture these indirect effects is to use a longer window of stock returns.

Nouriel Roubini suggested that the paper should control for channels of financial contagion for the following two reasons. First, controlling for such channels could shed some light on the source of contagion (i.e., whether it is trade or common creditors in financial markets). Second, the paper used stock market returns to measure a country's vulnerability to crises, but reasons other than trade could potentially explain the findings of the paper. For example, if there is a crisis in a country, it usually crashes its stock market and leads to contagion through financial channels. That is, crises could be transmitted from one financial market to another through financial channels as opposed to trade channels. Therefore, one has to control for the financial contagion when studying trade effects in transmitting crises in order not to overstate the results.

On using stock market returns to measure countries' vulnerability to crises, *Kristin J. Forbes* replied that the paper uses this measure to capture how the country as a whole is affected by crises. Stock market returns capture not only the immediate impacts, but also the expected longer-term impacts, and therefore are a preferred measure. Some of the trade effects, such as the competitiveness effect, will take a long time to work their way into other variables. Other advantages of using stock market returns are that they are widely available for a range of countries, and they are high frequency, especially important when crises occur one after the other. Stock return data are among the few variables that are available at a sufficiently high frequency to isolate the impacts of different crises that are bunched together in time.

On the definition of crises (exchange-market pressure index), Forbes said that the paper used a high cutoff level—five standard deviations—because of the higher volatility in the weekly data (versus monthly or quarterly data used elsewhere). She promised to redefine the crisis index with a lower cutoff level, which may imply a larger sample.

Finally, on the importance of trade effects, Forbes agreed with others that trade is important, but maintained that it is not the whole story: It explains only a quarter of the variation in stock market returns. She also emphasized, however, that the overall trade effects should be multiplied by the number of weeks that a crisis lasts.

II

International Financial Players and Contagion

What Hurts Emerging Markets Most?
G3 Exchange Rate or Interest Rate Volatility?

Carmen M. Reinhart and Vincent Raymond Reinhart

3.1 Introduction

Although fashions concerning appropriate exchange rate arrangements have shifted over the years, advocacy for establishing a target zone surrounding the world's three major currencies has remained a hardy perennial. Work on target zones (pioneered by McKinnon 1984, 1997, and Williamson 1986, and recently summarized by Clarida 2000) has mostly emphasized the benefits of exchange rate stability for industrial countries. More recently, though, analysts have apportioned some of the blame for financial crises in emerging markets back to the volatile bilateral exchange rates of industrial countries (as in the dissenting opinions registered in Goldstein 1999, for instance). With many emerging-market currencies tied to the U.S. dollar either implicitly or explicitly, movement in the exchange values of the currencies of major countries—in particular the prolonged appreciation of the U.S. dollar in relation to the yen and the deutsche Mark in advance of Asia's troubles—is argued to have worsened the competitive position of many emerging market economies. One method for reducing destabilizing shocks emanating from abroad, the argument runs, would be to reduce the variability of the Group of Three (G3) currencies by estab-

Carmen M. Reinhart, currently on leave from the University of Maryland, is senior policy adviser at the International Monetary Fund and a research associate of the National Bureau of Economic Research. Vincent Raymond Reinhart is director of the Division of Monetary Affairs in the Board of Governors of the Federal Reserve System.

The authors have benefitted from helpful comments from Joshua Aizenman, Olivier Blanchard, Guillermo Calvo, Michael P. Dooley, Eduardo Fernandez-Arias, Jeffrey A. Frankel, and Ernesto Talvi. Jane Cooley provided excellent research assistance. The views expressed are the authors' own and not necessarily those of their respective institutions.

lishing target bands.[1] This paper examines the argument for such a target zone strictly from an emerging-market perspective and will be silent on the costs and benefits for industrial countries.[2]

Given the reality that sterilized intervention by industrial economies tends to be ineffective and that policy makers show no inclination to return to the kinds of controls on international capital flows that helped keep exchange rates stable over the Bretton Woods era, a commitment to damping G3 exchange rate fluctuations requires a willingness on the part of G3 authorities to use domestic monetary policy to that end. This, in turn, may require tolerating more variability in interest rates and, potentially, spending. Under a system of target zones, then, relative prices for emerging-market economies may become more stable in an environment of predictable G3 exchange rates, but greater interest rate volatility may make debt-servicing costs less predictable, and greater G3 income volatility may render demands for the products of emerging-market economies more uncertain. The welfare consequences to an emerging-market economy, therefore, are ambiguous, depending on initial conditions, the specification of behavior, and the dynamic nature of the trade-off between lower G3 exchange rate volatility and higher G3 interest rate variability.

The consequences for the developing South of interest rate, exchange rate, and income volatility in the North comprise only one part of myriad North-South links. Consequently, issues related to G3 exchange rate variability should be viewed within the much larger context (and related literature) of the influence of economic outcomes in developed countries on those in less developed economies. In this paper, we review and revisit the "traditional" North-South links via trade, commodity markets, and capital flows, and add transmission channels in the form of interest rate and exchange rate volatilities.

In section 3.2, we discuss the various channels of North-South transmission and use the example of a simple trade model to establish that, for a small open economy with outstanding debt, the welfare effect of damping variations in the exchange rate by making international interest rates more volatile is ambiguous. Section 3.3 presents stylized evidence on how the monetary policy and economic cycle in the United States influence capital flows to emerging markets as well as growth. In section 3.4, we first examine the contribution of G3 exchange rate volatility to fluctuations in the exchange rates of emerging markets and proceed to analyze the link between

---

1. Of course, since European monetary union, the G3 currencies cover at least fourteen industrial countries—the United States, Japan, and the twelve nations that have adopted the euro. In what follows, we splice together the pre–single currency data on the deutsche Mark with the post-1999 data on the exchange value of the euro.

2..For a cost-benefit analysis from a developed country's perspective on the effects of limiting G3 exchange rate volatility or adopting a common currency, see Rogoff (2001). Of particular relevance here is Rogoff's argument that the strongest case for stabilizing major currency exchange rates may well rest in the way that their volatility influences developing countries.

G3 interest rate and exchange rate volatility and capital flows and economic growth in developing countries. The final section summarizes our main findings and discusses some of the policy implications of our analysis.

3.2 North-South Links

In this section, we discuss the various channels through which economic developments in the major developed economies can potentially affect developing countries. On the developed side, we examine how the exchange rate arrangements among industrial countries influence the mix of interest rate and exchange rate volatility on world financial markets. On the emerging markets side, our focus is on capital flows—their level and composition—and on economic performance, as measured by gross domestic product (GDP) growth.

3.2.1 The Winds from the North: The Role of G3 Exchange Rate Arrangements in Determining the Mix of Interest Rate and Exchange Rate Volatilities

In principle, G3 exchange rates could be induced to stay within a target band through some combination of three tools. First, national authorities could rely on sterilized intervention to enforce some corridor on bilateral exchange rates. However, except to the extent that such intervention tends to signal future changes in domestic monetary policy, researchers have found little empirical support that sterilized intervention in industrial countries is effective.[3] Second, national authorities could impose some form of exchange or capital control, presumably in the form of a transactions tax or prudential reserve requirements. Opponents of such efforts generally argue that capital controls generate financial innovation that undercuts them over time, implying that the controls become either increasingly complicated or irrelevant. Third, monetary policy makers in the major countries could alter domestic market conditions to keep the foreign exchange value of their currencies in a desired range. This could take the form of allowing intervention in the currency market to affect domestic reserves—that is, not sterilizing intervention—or more directly keying the domestic policy interest rate to the exchange value of the currency (as discussed in McKinnon 1997 and Williamson 1986).

Given the lack of evidence of any independent effect of sterilized intervention (over and beyond what subsequently happens to domestic monetary policy), and given the consensus supporting the free international mobility of capital, it would seem that the only instrument available to enforce a target zone would be the domestic monetary policy of the G3 central

---

3. The signaling channel is addressed by Kaminsky and Lewis (1996); Dominguez and Frankel (1993) examine whether there are any portfolio effects of sterilized intervention.

banks. However, this implies some trade-off, in that G3 domestic short-term interest rates would have to become more variable to make G3 exchange rates smoother.

The nature of this trade-off, of course, depends on many factors, particularly the width of the target zone. Wider bands would presumably reduce the need of G3 central banks to move their interest rates in response to exchange rate changes. At the same time, however, wider bands would imply a smaller reduction in the volatility of G3 exchange rates.[4] In addition, G3 interest rates might not be all that is affected by the exchange rate policy. Central bank actions taken to damp G3 exchange rate volatility might also leave their imprint on income in the G3 countries. Wider swings in industrial country interest rates would presumably make spending in those countries more variable, even as the split of that spending on domestic versus foreign goods and services becomes more predictable under more stable G3 exchange rates.

To understand the effects of these trade-offs from an emerging-markets perspective, it is important to remember that most developing countries are net debtors to the industrial world and that typically that debt is short-term and denominated in one of the G3 currencies. As a result, the welfare consequences for an emerging-market economy of G3 target zones depend on exactly how those zones are enforced and the particulars of the small country's mix of output, trading partners, and debt structure.

3.2.2   A Stylized Model of an Emerging Market Economy

The effects of trading interest rate for exchange rate volatility can be seen in a basic single-period, two-good model of trade for a small open economy, as in figure 3.1. This figure represents a country that takes as given the relative price of the two traded goods and receives an endowment in terms of good A. For the sake of simplicity, we assume that its external debt is also denominated in terms of good A and its currency is pegged to that of country A.[5] Volatility of the relative price of the traded goods—which might stem solely from nominal changes in exchange rates between the industrial countries if the small country fixes its exchange rate or if it prices to the industrial country market—pivots the budget line and thus alters the desired consumption combination in the small country. Suppose, for instance, that the currency of country A depreciates relative to that of country B, rotating

4. Some might argue that if G3 target zones anchor inflation expectations in developed countries, both exchange rates *and* interest rates could become more stable. However, many industrial countries in the past decade have adopted some form of inflation targeting, either explicitly or implicitly, which has worked to stabilize inflation expectations and which would make achieving a credibility bonus from adopting a G3 target zone less likely.

5. Behind the scenes of this model in the larger industrial world, it is simplest to think of two large countries, A and B, specialized in the production of their namesake good. The net effect of our assumption about the small economy's endowment and debt structure is that the intercept of the budget line depends on the interest rate in country A.

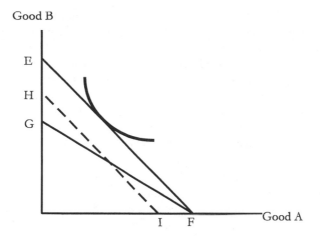

Fig. 3.1   Welfare in a small open economy

the budget line from EF to GF. All else being equal, welfare would decline, representing a cost associated with developments on the foreign exchange market for this small country.

Target zones for the large countries, if effective, would be able to prevent the budget line from rotating as the result of influences emanating from the developed world. However, this reduced major-country exchange rate volatility will only be accomplished if the major central banks change short-term interest rates in response to incipient changes in cross rates. For most emerging-market economies, which are debtors, such coordination of G3 monetary policy could deliver more stable terms of trade at the expense of a more variable interest service. In this particular case, the central bank of country A would presumably have to raise its domestic short-term interest rate in defense of the currency. Thus, while the slope of the budget line would be unchanged, its location would shift inward, as labeled HI. Regardless of whether the effects of the initial shock were felt through the exchange rate of the interest rate, welfare in this small country would decline. The degree to which it declines if the large countries allow the cross-exchange rate or their interest rates to adjust will depend on many factors.

3.2.3   Going Beyond the Stylized Model

In reality, many developing countries send primary commodities onto the world market, there is some substitutability in world demand for those countries that produce manufactured products, and capital markets are far from perfect. In this section, we review the literature on North-South linkages to broaden our understanding of the issues related to G3 exchange rate arrangements.

As opposed to the simple example, most emerging-market economies face some slope to the demand curve for their exports. As a result, any changes in G3 income induced by changes in their interest rates will be reflected in the demand for the exports of their trading partners to the extent that imports in the developed economy have a positive income elasticity.[6] The higher the share of exports that are destined for the developed country, the more sizable the consequences for the emerging-market economy. On the basis of this channel, for example, Mexico and Canada would be affected far more than Argentina by an economic downturn in the United States. We see evidence of this in the fact that in 1999 about 88 percent of all Canadian and Mexican exports were shipped to the U.S. market, whereas only about 11 percent of Argentina's exports were destined for the United States.[7] Other things being equal, the higher the income elasticity of imports in the developed country, the more pronounced will be the contraction in the country's exports when the developed country slows. In this regard, developing countries that export predominantly manufactured goods (which typically are more sensitive to income) may fare worse than their counterparts exporting primary commodities, which tend to be relatively income-inelastic.[8] The heterogeneity in export structure across developing countries is sufficiently significant to expect, a priori, highly differentiated outcomes. For instance, the contrast between the export structure of East Asian countries (which are heavily skewed to manufactured goods) to that of most African countries (which are predominantly skewed to primary commodities) is particularly striking.[9]

As opposed to the simple example, emerging-market economies generally produce a different mix of goods from those of industrial countries. In that case, the business cycle in the world's largest economies may itself exert a significant influence on the terms of trade of their smaller, developing trading partners. Perhaps the clearest example of such a North-South link comes from international commodity markets, as argued in Dornbusch (1985). Beginning with that work, the literature on commodity price determination has consistently accorded a significant role to the growth performance of the major industrial countries.[10] In particular, recessions in industrial economies, especially the United States, have historically been associated with weakness in real commodity prices. In our simple example,

6. Note that this channel, as it relies on the behavior of the large partner, is present irrespective of the level of development of the smaller trading partners.

7. The stylized evidence on patterns of trade is discussed in the next session.

8. See, for example, Reinhart (1995), who estimates industrial countries' import demand function for various regions and countries with varying degrees of export diversification and primary commodity content.

9. For example, manufactures account for only 10 percent in the Côte D'Ivoire (the Ivory Coast) but account for more than 65 percent of Thai exports.

10. Dornbusch (1985) stresses the role of the demand side in commodity price determination. Borensztein and Reinhart (1994), who incorporate supply-side developments in their analysis, also find a significant and positive relationship between growth in the major economies and world commodity prices.

if the small country's endowment was made up of a commodity, the effects of G3 monetary policy actions on overall demand for those primary goods could induce a sizable shift in the position *and* rotation of the budget line.

Yet the impact of fluctuations in the business cycle on developing economies is probably not limited merely to income and relative price effects. There is a well-established, endogenous, and countercyclical "monetary policy cycle" in the major developed economies. To damp the amplitude of the business cycle, central banks ease monetary conditions and reduce interest rates during economic downturns and hike interest rates when signs of overheating develop. Calvo, Leiderman, and Reinhart (1993) stress the importance of U.S. interest rates in driving the international capital flow cycle. They present evidence that, in periods of low interest rates in the United States, central banks in developing countries in Latin America systematically accumulate foreign exchange reserves and the real exchange rate appreciates. Subsequent studies that examined net capital flows, extending the analysis to a variety of their components over various sample periods and to developing countries in other regions, found similar evidence.

This link between the interest rate and capital flow cycle may arise for a variety of reasons. Investors in the developed economies faced with lower interest rates may be inclined to seek higher returns elsewhere (i.e., the demand for developing country assets increases). It also may be the case that the decline in international interest rates makes borrowing less costly for emerging markets and increases the supply of emerging-market debt. In that case, the decline in the cost of borrowing for emerging-market countries may be even greater than the decline in international interest rates if the country risk premium is itself a positive function of international interest rates. The evidence presented in Fernandez-Arias (1996), Frankel, Schmukler, and Servén (2001), and Kaminsky and Schmukler (2001) support the notion that country-risk premiums in many emerging markets indeed move with international interest rates in a manner that amplifies the interest rate cycle of industrial countries. Thus, a change in G3 interest rates shifts the budget line by more than is shown in our simple example, as procyclical capital flows imply that the change in the industrial country interest rate changes the developing country's interest rate risk premium in the same direction. Moreover, one could posit nonlinearities in the response if large increases in borrowing costs—from balance-sheet strains and credit rationing—have more substantial effects on income prospects than do similar size reductions in borrowing costs.

Table 3.1 provides a summary of the channels of transmission of how developments in the major industrial countries may influence growth in emerging markets. Taken together, the various cells of the table would suggest that the trade and finance effects that arise in developed economies from the growth and interest rate cycles, respectively, tend to at least par-

Table 3.1   Developed and Developing Country Links

Type of Shock	Transmission Channel	Amplifiers	Expected Growth Consequences
	The Growth Cycle: Recessions in the G3		
Income effects	Trade: Lower exports to G3; negative	High trade exposure; high G3 income elasticities	Negative
Relative price effects	Trade: Decline in the terms of trade for developing countries	High primary commodity content in exports; high exposure to cyclical industries in exports	Negative
International capital flows	Finance: Higher capital flows (primarily bank lending) to emerging markets	Large declines in the domestic demand for bank loans	Positive
	The Interest Rate Cycle: Monetary Easings		
International capital flows	Finance: Higher portfolio capital flows to emerging markets	Developed bond and equity markets; high interest rate sensitivity of flows	Positive
Debt servicing	Finance: Lower cost	High levels of debt; sensitive risk premiums to international interest rates	Positive
Interest earnings	Finance: Declining interest income	High level of reserves relative to debt	Not obvious
	High Volatility in G3		
Interest rates	Finance: Complicates debt management	High levels of short-term debt; large new financing needs; an	Not obvious
	Investment: Uncertainty tends to reduce investment consequences	initially high level of FDI	Negative
Bilateral exchange rate	Trade: Reduces trade	Pegging to a G3 currency	Negative?

tially offset one another. However, G3 exchange rate and interest rate volatility would seem a priori to have a negative effect on economic growth in the developing world. Higher interest rate volatility may hamper investment, while higher G3 exchange rate volatility may retard emerging market trade.[11] While the literature on the impacts on trade of exchange rate volatility for developed economies is inconclusive, the comparable analysis of this issue for emerging markets seems much more convincing in concluding that exchange rate volatility tends to reduce trade.

11. Of course, G3 interest rate volatility may also complicate significantly emerging market debt management strategies or make systemic strains more likely.

3.3   The Role of the North's Business and Monetary Policy Cycles: The Stylized Facts

In this section, we present stylized evidence on the North-South links that were discussed in the preceding section. For emerging markets, we examine international capital flows and growth around various measures of the U.S. growth and interest rate cycle and contrast periods of high interest rate and exchange rate volatility to those in which volatility was relatively subdued. We present evidence of the direction of North-South trade and on the impact of G3 developments on international commodity markets.

Our data are annual and span the years 1970 to 1999, and the country groupings are those reported in the International Monetary Fund's *World Economic Outlook* (WEO).[12] For capital flows, these groupings include all emerging markets, Africa, Asia crisis countries, other Asian emerging markets, the Middle East and Europe, and the Western Hemisphere. In reporting aggregate real GDP, the WEO groups the Asian countries somewhat differently. The two reported subgroupings are Asia and newly industrialized Asia, but all other categories remain the same. We examine the cyclical behavior of net private capital flow and its components: net private direct investment (i.e., foreign direct investment [FDI]), private portfolio investment (PI), other net private capital flow (OCF)—which is heavily weighted toward bank lending—and net official flow (OFF).

3.3.1   The Growth Cycle, Capital Flows, and Emerging Market Growth

Given its prominent position in the world economy, the U.S. business cycle (not surprisingly) has important repercussions for the rest of the world. Economic developments in the United States echo loudly in many developed economies, most notably that of Canada; the same holds true for developing economies, especially those in the Western Hemisphere and newly industrialized Asia. To examine the behavior of growth and various types of capital flows to emerging markets, we first split the sample into two states of nature according to two criteria. The first parsing separates the sample into recessions and expansions according to the National Bureau of Economic Research's dating of U.S. business cycle turning points. The second cut of the data divides the sample into periods in which U.S. real GDP growth is above the median growth rate for the sample and periods in which growth is below the median.

Figure 3.2 depicts capital flows to emerging markets (in billions of 1970 U.S. dollars) in recession years versus recovery years for the 1970–99 period. As is evident, net flows to emerging markets are considerably larger in

---

12. The developing country classification in the WEO is comprised of 128 countries. See the WEO for details on the regional breakdown.

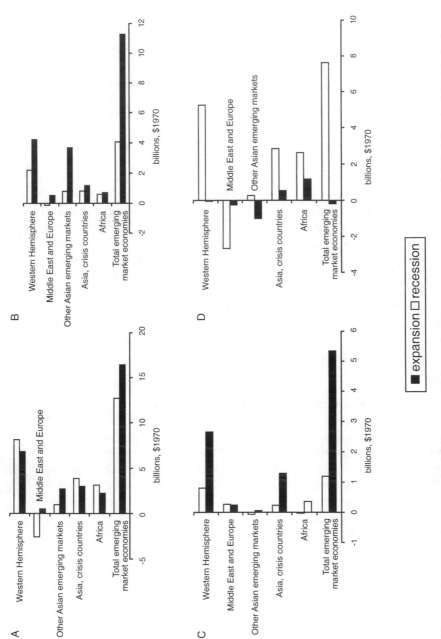

Fig. 3.2 U.S. business cycle and capital flows to emerging market economies (billions of 1970 U.S. dollars): *A,* **Net real private capital flows;** *B,* **Net real private direct investment;** *C,* **Net real private portfolio investment;** *D,* **Other Net real private capital flows**
Source: Authors' calculations using International Monetary Fund *World Economic Outlook* (October 2000).

real terms when the United States is in expansion than when the United States is in recession. Furthermore, this gap between recession and expansion owes itself primarily to a surge in FDI flows (which increase almost threefold from recession to expansion) and to portfolio flows (which increase almost fivefold from recession to expansion). The key offsetting category is other net inflows to emerging markets, which evaporate when the United States is in an expansion rather than recession. This disparate behavior between FDI and portfolio flows is primarily due to bank lending, which accounts for a significant part of other flows. Apparently, banks tend to seek lending opportunities abroad when the domestic demand for loans weakens and interest rates fall, as usually occur during recessions. The U.S. bank lending boom to Latin America in the late 1970s and early 1980s and the surge in Japanese bank lending to emerging Asia in the mid-1990s are two clear examples of this phenomenon.

However, the surge in FDI flows from the mid-1990s to the present is a significant departure from FDI's historical behavior, which is, no doubt, heavily influenced by the wave of privatization and mergers and acquisitions that took place in many emerging markets during recent years. It is possible that because this period of privatizations and surging FDI coincides with the longest economic expansion in U.S. history, the results may imply an exaggerated role for U.S. growth in driving FDI and total net flows. When we ended our sample in 1992, capital flows to emerging markets still diminished during economic downturns in the United States (this exercise is not reproduced here). While FDI flows and portfolio flows continue to be higher in expansions than in recessions, the drop in other flows during expansions more than offsets this tendency.

In sum, from the vantage point of the volume of capital flows to emerging markets, U.S. recessions are not a bad thing. From a compositional standpoint, however, the more stable component of capital flows, FDI, does seem to contract during downturns, suggesting that emerging markets may wind up during these periods relying more heavily on less stable sources of financing—short-term flows.[13]

The analogous exercise was performed for emerging-market average annual GDP growth. As shown in table 3.2, for all developing countries, growth is somewhat slower during U.S. recessions, averaging 4.8 percent per annum versus 5.2 percent average growth during expansion years. However, the pattern is uneven across regions. For the countries in transition, Asia (including the newly industrialized economies), and the Middle East and Europe, growth tends to slow during U.S. recessions, while the opposite is true for Africa and the Western Hemisphere. However, in most instances the differences across regions are not markedly different—an issue we will explore further later.

13. Other flows are mostly short term.

Table 3.2   The Condition of the U.S. Economy and Foreign Real GDP Growth:
                   Annual Rate (%) 1970–99

Region/Country	Condition of U.S. Economy:		Condition of U.S. Monetary Policy:	
	Expansion	Recession	Tightening	Easing
Newly industrialized Asian economies	7.92	7.11	8.79	6.93
Developing countries	5.19	4.82	5.17	5.02
Africa	2.75	3.29	2.63	3.10
Asia	6.70	6.25	6.72	6.46
Middle East and Europe	4.47	4.31	3.87	4.80
Western Hemisphere	3.63	3.81	4.21	3.34

Source: Authors' calculations using International Monetary Fund, *World Economic Outlook* (October 2000).

3.3.2   The Growth Cycle and Trade

If economic downturns in the United States are not necessarily bad for the availability of international lending to emerging markets, slowdowns are likely to have adverse consequences for countries that rely heavily on exports to the United States. Table 3.3 reports the percentage of total exports (as of 1999) of various emerging markets in Africa, Asia, and the Western Hemisphere that are destined for the U.S. market. It is evident that bilateral trade links between the United States and the developing world are strongest for Latin America, although there is considerable variation within the region, with Mexico and Argentina sitting at the opposite ends of the spectrum. However, trade between the United States and the Asian countries shown in this table is by no means trivial, especially if one considers that (as shown in table 3.4) the income elasticity in developed economies for Asian exports is typically estimated to be more than twice as large as the income elasticity for African exports; more generally, the income elasticity of the exports of developing countries that are major exporters of manufactured goods is well above that of those countries whose exports have a higher primary commodity content.

As noted earlier, swings in the economic cycle in the United States and other major industrialized economies typically influence the terms of trade of primary-commodity exporters. According to the various studies reviewed in table 3.5, a 1 percentage point drop in industrial production growth in the developed economies results in a drop in real commodity prices of roughly 0.77 to about 2.00 percent, depending on the study.

3.3.3   The Interest Rate–Monetary Policy cycle

In a world of countercyclical monetary policy in industrial countries, an economic cycle goes hand in hand with an interest rate cycle. As with the

Table 3.3   **North-South Trade Patterns, 1999**

Region/Country	Exports to the U.S. (% of Total Exports)	Imports from the U.S. (% of Total Imports)
Latin America		
Argentina	11.3	19.6
Brazil	22.5	23.8
Chile	19.4	22.9
Colombia	50.3	32.1
Peru	29.3	31.6
Mexico	88.3	74.1
Venezuela	55.4	42.0
Asia		
China Mainland	21.5	11.8
Indonesia	16.1	7.3
Korea	20.6	20.8
Malaysia	21.9	17.4
Philippines	29.6	20.3
Singapore	19.2	17.1
Thailand	21.5	11.5
Africa		
Chad	7.2	2.1
Congo, Republic of	19.0	3.5
Ethiopia	8.4	4.9
Kenya	4.6	6.7
Mozambique	4.8	3.7
South Africa	8.2	13.3
Uganda	5.4	3.3
Zimbabwe	5.8	4.8

Source: International Monetary Fund, *Direction of Trade Statistics* (2000).

Table 3.4   **Industrial Country Demand for Developing Country Exports**

Study and Sample	Importing Country	Exporting Country	Income Elasticity
Dornbusch (1985), 1960 to 1983	Major exporters of manufactures	All non–oil-developing	1.74
Marquez (1990)	Canada	Non–OPEC-developing	2.83
	Germany	Non–OPEC-developing	2.29
	Japan	Non–OPEC-developing	1.22
	United Kingdom	Non–OPEC-developing	1.45
	United States	Non–OPEC-developing	3.04
	Rest of OECD	Non–OPEC-developing	2.61
Reinhart (1995), 1970 to 1991	All developed	All developing	2.05
		Africa	1.28
		Asia	2.49
		Latin America	2.07

Table 3.5   Commodity Prices and Economic Cycles: A Review

Study	Dependent Variable/Sample Period	Measure of Developed-Country Growth Rate Used	Coefficient
Borensztein and Reinhart (1994)	All commodity index/ 1971:1–1992:3, quarterly	Industrial production for developed economies	1.40
	All commodity index/ 1971:1–1992:3, quarterly	Industrial production for developed economies plus GDP for the former Soviet Union	1.54
Chu and Morrison (1984)	All commodity index/ 1958–82, quarterly	GDP weighted industrial production-G7 countries	1.66
Dornbusch (1985)	All commodity index/ 1970:2–1985:1, quarterly	OECD industrial production	2.07
Holtham (1988)	All commodity index/ 1967:2–1982:2, semiannual	GDP growth for the G7 economies	0.51
		Industrial production for the G7 economies	0.77

growth cycle, we proceed to describe the stylized evidence by breaking up the sample in two ways. First, we subdivide the 1970–99 sample into two subsamples, periods in which monetary policy was easing—that is, the monetary policy interest rate in the United States, the federal funds rate, was declining—and periods of tightening, when the federal funds rate was rising.[14]

Figure 3.3 reports the results of this exercise. In years when U.S. monetary policy was easing, emerging markets in all regions (with the exception of Africa, which is almost entirely shut out of international capital markets) receive a markedly higher volume of capital inflows. While FDI and portfolio flows do not change much, other (short-term) flows respond markedly to the interest rate cycle. As shown in the third and fourth columns of table 3.2, average annual GDP growth rates are generally lower during easings of U.S. monetary policy than during tightening episodes—which may simply attest to the fact that Federal Reserve easings most often coincide with a U.S. economic slowdown. This tendency may also suggest that, to the extent that capital inflows have positive consequences for economic activity (an important issue that has not received much attention in the literature), these effects may not be contemporaneous.

14. More specifically, a year was denoted as one of tightening (easing) if the average level of the federal funds rate in December was higher (lower) than that of twelve months earlier. Recognize that this cut of the data does not discriminate between modest and marked policy changes: A 50 basis point drop in the federal funds rate during a given year would be lumped together with a 400 basis point drop. To get at this issue, we also broke the sample into periods when real interest rates are above the sample median and periods in which rates are below the median. (Real ex post interest rates are calculated as the nominal yield on a three-month treasury bill less the annual consumer price inflation rate.) Those results, which are not reported here due to consideration of space, approximate those in the main text.

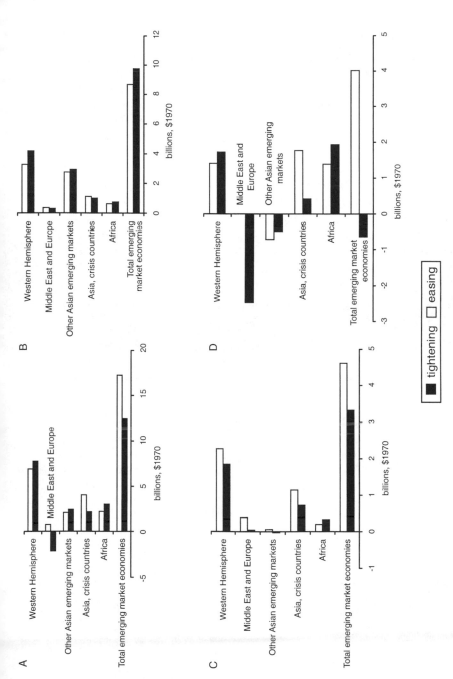

Fig. 3.3   U.S. monetary policy and capital flows to emerging market economies (billions of 1970 U.S. dollars): *A,* **Net real private capital flows;** *B,* **Net real private portfolio investment;** *C,* **Net real private direct investment;** *D,* **Other net real private capital flows**
Source: Authors' calculations using International Monetary Fund *World Economic Outlook* (October 2000).

3.3.4   Stylized Evidence on the Twin Cycles

Given the synchronization of the economic growth and policy cycles, a finer reading of the data is probably warranted. Table 3.6 divides the sample into four states of nature for the United States: recession accompanied by monetary policy tightening; recession accompanied by easing; expansion and tightening; and expansion and monetary policy easing. The role of the business cycle is quite evident in the results. The worst outcome for emerging markets occurs when the United States is in a deep enough recession that monetary policy is being systematically eased (the upper left cell in each regional entry). In general, entries along the minor diagonal—representing either an expansion facilitated by policy easing or a U.S. economy weak enough to be in recession but not so weak as to preclude Federal Reserve tightening—contain fast rates of growth in economic activity. The fastest rates of growth are invariably recorded in the lower right cell, which

Table 3.6   **Emerging Market Economies and U.S. Economic and Policy Cycles**

	Condition of U.S. Economy	Condition of U.S. Monetary Policy	
		Easing	Tightening
Real GDP Growth[a]			
Region/country			
Newly industrialized Asian economies	Recession	6.81	8.16
	Expansion	7.01	8.92
Asia	Recession	6.02	7.07
	Expansion	6.75	6.65
Developing countries	Recession	4.44	6.13
	Expansion	5.39	4.98
Western Hemisphere	Recession	2.78	7.41
	Expansion	3.69	3.57
Net Private Capital Flows[b]			
Source of capital			
Net private capital flows	Recession	13.86	8.58
	Expansion	19.35	13.21
Net private portfolio investment	Recession	1.48	0.19
	Expansion	6.61	3.95
Net private direct investment	Recession	4.24	3.42
	Expansion	11.50	11.03
Other net private capital flows	Recession	8.38	4.98
	Expansion	1.24	−1.78

Source: Authors' calculations using International Monetary Fund, *World Economic Outlook* (October 2000).

[a]Average annual real GDP growth, percent.

[b]Average, billions $1970.

includes those years in which the U.S. economy is expanding and monetary policy tightening. That is, foreign economies historically grow the fastest in the latter stages of the U.S. business cycle when fast U.S. growth is creating pressures on resources that trigger Federal Reserve tightening.

As to capital flows, the priors are less well defined. On the one hand, the Calvo, Leiderman, and Reinhart (1993) hypothesis would suggest that, other things being equal, tighter monetary policy (i.e., rising interest rates) would lead to lower capital flows to emerging markets. On the other hand, while recessions in the North may dampen FDI flows (as these are often linked to trade), economic slowdowns tend to be accompanied by a weakening in the domestic demand for loans—which, in the past, has often led banks to seek lending opportunities abroad (see Kaminsky and Reinhart 2001).

The lower panel of table 3.6 presents net capital flows and its components to all emerging markets during these four states of nature. For net private flows, the largest entry falls in the lower left cell, suggesting that both lower interest rates and faster growth in the United States are potential catalysts for capital flows into emerging markets. However, this feature is not consistent across categories: FDI and portfolio flows thrive when expansions are coupled with falling interest rates, but other flows, which are largely composed of bank lending, do not. Like other flows, these tend to increase in periods of falling interest rates but contract during expansions; other flows are highest when the United States is in recession and interest rates are falling.

3.3.5   The Repercussions of the Twin Cycles: Basic Tests

The preceding discussion does not shed light on the relative statistical significance of the twin cycles. To address that issue, we next run a variety of simple regressions that attempt to explain capital flows and growth in emerging markets through developments in the developed economies, particularly the United States. Our sample spans the period 1970–99 for all regions.

In examining real private flows to all emerging-market economies, we use four different measures of real private capital flows: net capital flows, net direct investment, net portfolio flows, and other capital flows. The regressors in the first set of equations are real U.S. GDP growth and the U.S. short-term nominal interest rate (the yield on the three-month treasury bill). Because neither of these variables poses a potential endogeneity problem, our estimation method is simple ordinary least squares. Table 3.7 reports the results of this regression for all emerging market economies; the appendix reports results for particular regions.

When we examine the results for the emerging market aggregate, as well as for most of the regional subgroups, U.S. nominal interest rates seem to play a more dominant and systematic role in explaining capital flows to emerging markets than does U.S. economic growth. As a general rule, rising U.S. interest rates are associated with falling capital flows to emerging markets. In effect, in many of the regressions, the coefficient on growth is

Table 3.7   Determinants of Real Private Capital Flows to Emerging
                   Market Economies

| | | United States | | |
| | | Nominal | Real GDP | |
Type of Capital Flow	Constant	Interest Rate	Growth	R^2
Net private capital flows	34.21	−2.32	−1.09	0.18
	(8.38)	(0.96)	(1.11)	
Net private direct investment	18.80	−1.57	0.26	0.16
	(6.61)	(0.76)	(0.88)	
Net private portfolio investment	13.55	−1.26	−0.33	0.19
	(4.33)	(0.50)	(0.57)	
Other net private capital flows	2.11	0.50	−1.06	0.09
	(6.16)	(0.71)	(0.82)	

Source: Authors' calculations using International Monetary Fund, *World Economic Outlook* (October 2000) and Council of Economic Advisers, *Economic Report to the President* (2001). *Notes:* Estimated using annual data from 1970 to 1999. Standard errors are in parentheses.

negative, suggesting that when the United States is enjoying rapid growth, capital stays at home. This effect is most pronounced in the category of other net flows, consisting largely of bank lending. Both FDI flows and portfolio flows are consistently interest rate–sensitive.[15]

There are, however, various regional differences worth highlighting. First, U.S. nominal interest rates are significant in explaining portfolio and FDI flows in all regions—but the impacts are greatest in the Western Hemisphere and lowest in Africa. This result may simply emphasize that, among the emerging markets with some access to international capital markets (Asia and Latin America), the latter are more heavily indebted and interconnected with the United States. Second, growth in the United States has a significant and positive influence in explaining FDI to the Western Hemisphere, which is not the case for other regions. Third, as the descriptive analysis anticipated, the other capital flow category behaves very differently from FDI and portfolio flows.

We next perform a comparable exercise for growth similar to that of Dornbusch (1985), who focused on the links between developing debtor countries and their developed counterparts. Dornbusch regressed developing country GDP growth on a measure of Organization for Economic Co-operation and Development (OECD) growth and found the coefficient on the OECD growth measure to be statistically significant, in the 0.28–0.76 range.[16] More recently, Frankel and Roubini (2000) regressed developing

15. Similar results obtain when developed-country real GDP growth rates are used in lieu of the U.S. growth rate, but these results are not reported here due to considerations of space.

16. Dornbusch used industrial production, real GDP growth, and import volume; the sample was taken from 1961 to 1984.

Table 3.8   **Determinants of Real GDP Growth in Emerging Market Economies**

Region/Country	Constant	United States Short Real Interest Rate	United States Real GDP Growth	R^2
Newly industrialized Asian economies	6.25	−0.21	0.56	0.16
	(0.94)	(0.23)	(0.25)	
Developing countries	4.83	−0.24	0.20	0.23
	(0.40)	(0.10)	(0.11)	
Africa	2.95	−0.14	0.05	0.03
	(0.60)	(0.15)	(0.16)	
Asia	6.30	0.16	0.01	0.04
	(0.67)	(0.16)	(0.18)	
Middle East and Europe	3.84	−0.52	0.43	0.17
	(1.04)	(0.26)	(0.28)	
Western Hemisphere	3.73	−0.71	0.32	0.43
	(0.66)	(0.16)	(0.17)	

Source: Authors' calculations using International Monetary Fund, *World Economic Outlook* (October 2000) and Council of Economic Advisers, *Economic Report to the President* (2001).
Notes: Estimated using annual data from 1970 to 1999. Standard errors are in parentheses.

country growth for various regional groupings against the G7 real interest rate; they found that the coefficients on real interest rates were negative and in most cases statistically significant, with the greatest interest sensitivity in the Western Hemisphere.[17]

Our exercise here combines these two approaches. As shown in table 3.8, when GDP growth for the various country groupings is regressed against U.S. growth and the short-term real interest rate, the results tend to be quite intuitive. The sensitivity of growth to U.S. growth is highest (and statistically significant) for the newly industrialized Asian economies, which depend greatly on trade with the United States, and lowest for the remainder of Asia. For all developing countries, both of the regressors have the anticipated signs and are statistically significant. A 1 percentage point decline in U.S. growth rates reduces GDP growth for the developing countries by 0.2 percent, while a 1 percent increase in U.S. real interest rates reduces it by 0.24 percent. Despite strong trade links with the United States for most countries in the region, U.S. growth is only marginally statistically significant for the Western Hemisphere, although the coefficient is positively signed. U.S. growth is also significant for the Middle East and European developing countries. Given its history of relatively high levels of indebtedness and periodic debt-servicing difficulties, it is not surprising that the U.S. real interest rate is significant and that growth is most sensitive to interest rate fluctuations in the Western

17. The coefficient for the Western Hemisphere was −0.77, compared to −0.39 for all market borrowers.

Hemisphere; the coefficient (–0.71) is almost four times as large, in absolute terms, as for all developing countries. Indeed, one cannot reject the hypothesis that a 1 percent increase in U.S. real interest rates leads to a 1 percent decline in growth in the region. Real U.S. interest rates are also statistically significant for the Middle East and Europe. For countries at the other end of the spectrum—the newly industrialized Asian economies, with low levels of external debt and considerable access to private capital markets—U.S. interest rates are not significant, although the coefficient has the expected negative sign. As far as these regressions are concerned, U.S. developments have no systematic relationship with the rest of developing Asia.[18]

3.4 The Consequences of Exchange Rate and Interest Rate Volatility in the North

To examine the issue of whether the volatility of interest rates and G3 exchange rates has adverse consequences for cross-border capital flows to emerging markets and growth, we split our sample into high- and low-volatility periods and conduct a set of exercises comparable to those discussed in the preceeding section.

3.4.1 Background on Exchange Rate Variability in Emerging Markets

The argument that excessive volatility of G3 exchange rates imposes significant costs on emerging markets seems to rely mostly on a spending channel. A large swing in the dollar's value on the foreign exchange market in terms of the yen and the euro translates directly into changes in the competitiveness of countries that link their currencies to the dollar—either through a hard peg or a highly managed float. The evidence in Calvo and Reinhart (2002) suggests that many developing countries fall into that group. They report a widespread "fear of floating," in that many emerging market currencies tend to track the dollar or the euro closely, even in cases that are officially classified as floating.

Some sense of the stakes for emerging-market economies can be had from figures 3.4 through 3.6 and table 3.9. We calculated simple annual averages of the absolute value of the monthly changes in the logarithms of the real deutsche Mark/dollar and real yen/dollar exchange rates from 1970 to 1999, of the percentage point change in the real U.S. treasury bill rate (on the rationale that most developing country borrowing is denominated in U.S. dollars) from 1973 to 1999, and of the monthly changes in the logarithm of U.S. real personal consumption expenditure from 1970 to 1999.

18. An elegant model that broadly supports this pattern of coefficients is provided by Gertler and Rogoff (1990). They offer a framework in which a country's level of wealth influences the extent of agency problems in lending and, therefore, the degree of integration with the world capital market. As a general rule in table 3.8, regions with greater per capita wealth tend to be more tightly linked to U.S. interest rates.

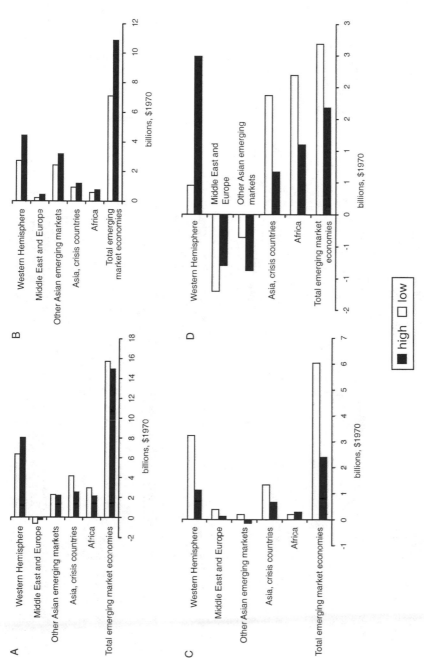

Fig. 3.4 G3 real exchange rate volatility and capital flows to emerging market economies (billions of 1970 U.S. dollars, 1970– 99): *A,* Net real private capital flows; *B,* Net real private direct investment; *C,* Net real private portfolio investment; *D,* Other net real private capital flows

Source: Authors' calculations using International Monetary Fund *World Economic Outlook* (October 2000).

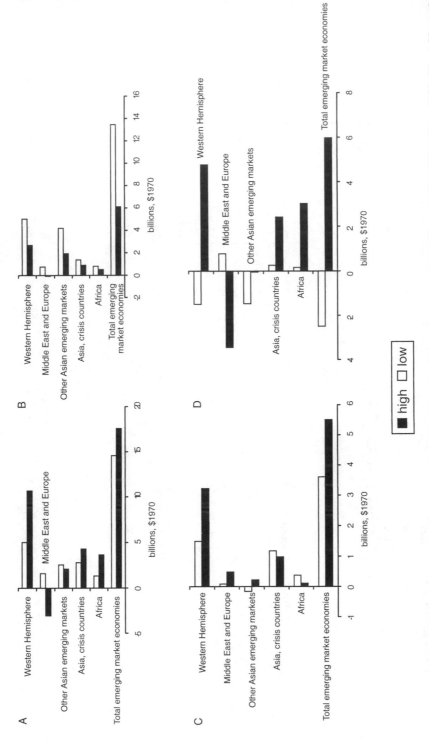

Fig. 3.5 U.S. real short-term interest volatility and capital flows to emerging market economies (billions of 1970 U.S. dollars, 1973–99): *A,* Net real private capital flows; *B,* Net real private direct investment; *C,* Net real private portfolio investment; *D,* Other net real private capital flows
Source: Authors' calculations using International Monetary Fund *World Economic Outlook* (October 2000).

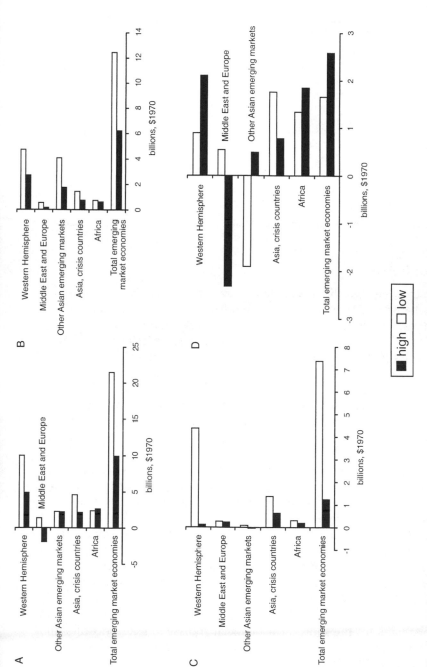

Fig. 3.6   U.S. real consumption volatility and capital flows to emerging market economies (billions of 1970 U.S. dollars, 1970– 99): *A,* Net real private capital flows; *B,* Net real private direct investment; *C,* Net real private portfolio investment; *D,* Other net real private capital flows

Source: Authors' calculations using International Monetary Fund *World Economic Outlook* (October 2000).

Table 3.9   Volatility and Foreign Real GDP Growth: Annual Rate (%), 1970–99

Region/Country	Degree of G3 Currency Volatility		Degree of U.S. Rate Volatility		Degree of U.S. Consumption Volatility	
	High	Low	High	Low	High	Low
Newly industrialized Asian economies	7.95	7.02	6.96	8.49	8.94	6.23
Developing countries	5.33	4.56	4.68	5.54	5.25	4.88
Africa	2.42	2.75	2.73	3.12	3.44	2.30
Asia	6.53	6.89	6.30	6.87	6.64	6.48
Middle East and Europe	4.33	3.37	3.55	5.42	4.90	3.89
Western Hemisphere	4.90	1.98	3.33	4.09	3.87	3.47

Source: Authors' calculations using International Monetary Fund, *World Economic Outlook* (October 2000).

Note: Sample period for U.S. rate volatility is 1973 to 1999.

The three figures split the sample into two states of nature: those in which G3 exchange rate volatility is above and below the sample median (in fig. 3.4), those in which U.S. interest rate volatility is above and below the sample median (in fig. 3.5), and those in which the average annual volatility of U.S. personal consumption expenditure is above and below the median (in figure 3.6). As before, we report the volume of real capital flows by country grouping and type across the sample split. As is evident from figure 3.4, the volatility of G3 exchange rates has little discernible effect on net real private capital flows to emerging-market economies or on any of the major regions reported. Beneath that total, though, there are important compositional effects, in that both portfolio and other net capital flows step lower when G3 exchange rate volatility is higher. The unchanged total is due to the fact that private direct investment moves in the opposite direction: From 1970 to 1999, FDI tended to be higher in those years when G3 exchange rate volatility was on the high side of the median.

Similar offsetting movements of FDI and portfolio and other capital flows are evident when the sample is split according to the volatility of the U.S. short-term real interest rates, as in figure 3.5. In this case, on net, real private capital flows are somewhat higher when U.S. rates move more from month to This follows because the expansion of portfolio and other flows when interest rates are volatile more than makes up for a contraction in FDI. Apparently, the short-term financial transactions in portfolio and other flows are energized by interest rate volatility, even as the longer-term transactions in FDI flag.

The total and major components of private capital flows respond more similarly when the sample is split according to the volatility of U.S. consumption spending, as seen in figure 3.6. Relatively stable personal consumption expenditure (PCE) growth in the United States is associated with larger capital flows, on net, to emerging market economies, especially those taking the form of foreign direct and portfolio investment. To an important extent, this may be due to the combination of a secular decline in U.S. consumption volatility and a secular increase in the volume of capital flows. Simply, low–consumption volatility years predominate later in the sample, when capital flows are also larger.[19]

Table 3.9 reports the average annual growth rates of real GDP in developing countries for different splits of the data determined by the volatilities, in turn, of G3 exchange rates, U.S. interest rates, and U.S. consumption. As a general rule, neither G3 exchange rate volatility nor U.S. consumption volatility appears harmful to growth prospects in emerging market economies. In both cuts of the data, high volatility is associated with about 1/2 to 3/4 percentage point faster growth in developing countries, as we see when comparing columns (1) and (2) for G3 exchange rates or columns (5) and (6) for U.S. consumption. For some regions, particularly newly industrialized Asian economies, the difference is quite large. What is also apparent is that U.S. short-term interest rates, on average, are linked to slower economic growth in the developing world, with differences in growth across the two regimes ranging from 3/8 to nearly 2 percentage points.

The insight that emerges from the simple model is that enforcing target zones in the G3 currencies involves choosing a point along the trade-off between lower exchange rate volatility and higher interest rate volatility. Moreover, to the extent that G3 spending is sensitive to interest rates, there will be a corresponding trade-off between lower exchange rate volatility and higher consumption volatility. We parsed our sample along the dimensions of that trade-off, examining capital flows and GDP growth according to the joint behavior of the relevant volatilities. Table 3.10 records those results. From an emerging-market perspective, G3 target zones imply moving from the upper right cell of each panel, where G3 currency volatility is high but U.S. interest rate of PCE volatility is low, to the lower left cell, where G3 currency volatility is low but U.S. interest rate or PCE volatility is high.

With regard to the upper four panels of the table looking at the comovement of G3 exchange rate and U.S. interest rate volatility, net private capital flows were almost $5 billion higher, on average, in those years in which G3 exchange rates were not volatile and U.S. interest rates were. However, by considering the minor diagonals on the other three panels, it become clear that this is the case because a sizable decline in FDI across the two periods was offset by increases in hotter-money flows—portfolio investment and other private flows. Moreover, it would have been unwise in emerging-market economies over the past twenty-seven years to trade times when G3 exchange rates were volatile but U.S. PCE growth was stable for times when G3 exchange rates were stable but U.S. PCE growth was volatile. Across the

---

19. Two-thirds of the observations on PCE variability in the first half of the sample lie above the median calculated over the entire sample.

Table 3.10   Net Private Capital Flows to Emerging Market Economies and G3 Volatilities

		Condition of G3 Currency Volatility	
		---	---
Source of Capital	U.S. Volatility[a]	Low	High
U.S. Interest Rate and G3 Exchange Rate Volatilities			
Net private capital flows	Low	13.44	15.01
	High	19.91	14.85
Net private portfolio investment	Low	5.09	3.01
	High	9.03	1.39
Net private direct investment	Low	10.01	14.83
	High	7.68	4.25
Other net private capital flows	Low	−1.65	−2.83
	High	3.19	9.21
U.S. PCE and G3 Exchange Rate Volatilities			
Net private capital flows	Low	28.46	16.20
	High	4.47	13.70
Net private portfolio investment	Low	13.50	2.76
	High	0.51	2.04
Net private direct investment	Low	13.02	12.00
	High	3.14	9.74
Other net private capital flows	Low	1.94	1.44
	High	0.82	1.93

Source: Authors' calculations using International Monetary Fund, *World Economic Outlook* (October 2000).
Note: Average, billions $1970, 1973 to 1999.
[a]Column refers to U.S. rate volatility in first half of table and to PCE volatility in second half of table.

bottom four panels of table 3.10, real private flows uniformly fall as they move from the upper right cell to the bottom right cell. Taken together, the results given in table 3.10 provide no evidence that the flow of private capital to emerging market economies would benefit from a G3 target zone.

However, attracting financial capital is only an intermediate goal relative to the ultimate responsibility of national authorities to foster economic growth. Table 3.11 presents averages of real GDP growth from 1973 to 1999 for major country groups split according to the joint behavior of G3 exchange rates and either U.S. interest rates or PCE. Here, the evidence does suggest that trading higher for lower G3 exchange rate volatility, even at the cost of more volatility in either U.S. interest rates or consumption, would benefit growth.

Table 3.12 addresses the possibility of nonlinearities in the responses of developing countries by using an indicator approach. In the two left panels, data on the number of currency crises in developing countries by year (out of the total number of years) are sorted according to G3 exchange rate, U.S.

Table 3.11 **Real GDP Growth in Emerging Market Economies and G3 Volatilities**

Region	U.S. Volatility[a]	Condition of G3 Currency Volatility	
		Low	High
U.S. Interest Rate and G3 Exchange Rate Volatilities			
Newly industrialized Asian economies	Low	8.46	6.44
	High	8.06	7.83
Asia	Low	8.10	6.41
	High	6.89	6.12
Developing countries	Low	4.93	4.42
	High	5.51	5.11
Western Hemisphere	Low	9.04	9.93
	High	7.37	6.20
U.S. PCE and G3 Exchange Rate Volatilities			
Newly industrialized Asian economies	Low	7.44	5.32
	High	9.13	8.60
Asia	Low	7.91	5.41
	High	6.63	7.19
Developing countries	Low	5.92	4.10
	High	4.56	5.25
Western Hemisphere	Low	6.08	6.04
	High	4.51	5.44

Source: Authors' calculations using International Monetary Fund, *World Economic Outlook* (October 2000).

Note: Average annual rate, percent, 1973 to 1999.

[a]Column refers to U.S. rate volatility in first half of table and to U.S. PCE volatility in second half of table.

Table 3.12 **Likelihood of the Twin Crises and G3 Volatilities**

Type of Crises	U.S. Volatility	Condition of G3 Currency Volatility	
		Low	High
Currency crises	Low[a]	0.10	0.25
	High[a]	0.10	0.10
Banking crises	Low[a]	0.05	0.20
	High[a]	0.10	0.15
Currency crises	Low[b]	0.10	0.25
	High[b]	0.10	0.10
Banking crises	Low[b]	0.10	0.20
	High[b]	0.05	0.15

Source: Authors' calculations using International Monetary Fund, *World Economic Outlook* (October 2000).

Note: Percent of the sample of above-the-median crises, 1980 to 1998.

[a]Column refers to U.S. rate volatility.

[b]Column refers to U.S. PCE volatility.

interest rate, and PCE volatility (with the crisis indicator defined according to the methodology in Frankel and Rose 1996, as recently updated and extended to a larger country set by Reinhart 2000).[20] The right panels report similar calculations using the number of banking crises from the same source. As can be seen along the minor diagonals of the four panels, years in which G3 exchange rate volatility was above its median and interest rate volatility in the United States was below its median over the past eighteen years were associated with relatively more crises in developing countries, especially compared to those years when G3 currency volatility was low but U.S. interest rate volatility was high. In that sense, advocates of target zones are correct in noting that crises are more frequent when G3 exchange rates are more volatile. Moreover, that historical record suggests that the situation can be improved upon by reducing that volatility by incurring more interest rate of PCE volatility in the United States.

3.4.2 Basic Tests

The difficulty in interpreting these data, whether on capital flows or GDP growth, is that some of the regularities observed in moving between the cells of these contingency tables may result from systematic macroeconomic changes rather than unique effects from the various volatilities. However, in an earlier section, we offered a simple regression that helped to explain emerging-market economies' capital flows and GDP growth using variables that could be treated as exogenous to the South–U.S. interest rates and economic growth. We now ask whether G3 indicator variables have any ability to explain the residuals to those "fundamental" regressions, and thereby put confidence bands about the estimates of the effects of interest rate and exchange rate volatility on capital flows and GDP growth.

Each block of table 3.13 corresponds to a specification in which the residual from the equation explaining the capital flow concept in the column head is regressed against two G3 dummies (with no constant terms, as the dummies are exhaustive). Those dummies are the same we have used to split the data in the various exercises already reported and capture the U.S. business cycle; U.S. monetary policy; the volatilities of U.S. real short-term rates, G3 exchange rates, and U.S. consumption growth; currency crises; and banking crises.[21] In general, a statistically significant coefficient would indicate that a G3 factor exerted an additional influence beyond that contained in U.S. interest rates and income. As to G3 target zones in particular, there appears to be no significant effect on average of episodes of higher volatilities by either measure for topline net capital flows. Taken literally— no doubt too literally—this would indicate there is no particular *cost* to

20. The results are similar when one employs the methodology of Kaminsky and Reinhart (1999).
21. Thus, there are twenty-eight regressions reported in the table corresponding to four measures of capital flows and seven different sets of states of nature.

Table 3.13   Can "Excess" Real Capital Flows Be Explained by G3 Factors?

Type of Factor	Net Private Capital Flows			
	Total	Direct Investment	Portfolio	Other
U.S. business cycle				
Expansion	0.44	0.69	0.61	−0.88
	(2.72)	(2.14)	(1.39)	(1.98)
Recession	−1.03	−1.61	−1.41	2.06
	(4.16)	(2.14)	(2.13)	(1.98)
U.S. monetary policy				
Tightening	−1.78	0.42	−0.44	−1.78
	(3.58)	(2.85)	(1.86)	(2.62)
Easing	1.19	−0.28	0.29	1.18
	(2.92)	(2.32)	(1.52)	(2.14)
Volatility of U.S. real short-term rates[a]				
High	2.40	−2.53	1.58	3.28
	(3.49)	(2.51)	(1.77)	(2.37)
Low	0.02	4.47	−0.18	−4.30
	(3.36)	(2.42)	(1.71)	(2.29)
Volatility of G3 exchange rates				
High	0.85	3.04	−0.92	−1.34
	(3.11)	(2.32)	(1.59)	(2.27)
Low	−0.97	−3.47	1.05	1.53
	(3.33)	(2.48)	(1.70)	(2.42)
Volatility of U.S. consumption				
High	−4.93	−3.15	−2.76	1.06
	(2.81)	(2.31)	(1.42)	(2.28)
Low	5.63	3.61	3.16	−1.21
	(3.00)	(2.47)	(1.52)	(2.44)
Currency crises[b]				
High	1.44	1.66	3.34	−3.61
	(4.37)	(2.76)	(2.04)	(2.55)
Low	5.25	4.22	1.38	−3.61
	(5.12)	(3.23)	(2.39)	(2.99)
Banking crises[c]				
High	2.34	1.99	3.82	−3.55
	(4.62)	(2.91)	(2.11)	(2.69)
Low	3.83	3.57	1.07	−0.84
	(4.87)	(3.07)	(2.22)	(2.83)

Source: Authors' calculations using International Monetary Fund, *World Economic Outlook* (October 2000) and Council of Economic Advisers, *Economic Report to the President* (2001).

Notes: Relationship of the residual from the capital flow fundamentals equations to G3 dummy variables from 1970 to 1999. Standard errors are in parentheses.

[a]Estimated from 1973 to 1999.

[b]Estimated from 1980 to 1998.

[c]Estimated from 1980 to 1998.

making real interest rates more volatile, but there is also no particular *bene-fit* in damping G3 exchange rate volatility. This statistical evidence ultimately differs little from the theoretical analysis; from the perspective of emerging-market economies, the case for limiting G3 exchange rate volatility is not proven. A similar analysis across regional aggregates, not included here due to considerations of space, provides no reason to question that judgment.

We performed a similar exercise to see if episodes of either volatile G3 ex-change rates or U.S. real interest rates exerted a systematic influence on the growth of output in major emerging-market areas. Those results, reported in table 3.14, tell a similar story. Across the six areas examined, none of the dummy variables related to the various volatilities differed significantly from zero. Taken together, the evidence suggests that advocates of G3 tar-get zones have to identify another mechanism by which financial market volatility in the industrial countries impinges on their neighbors to the South beyond that expected through the flows of trade (with their associ-ated effects on income) or capital.

3.5   Concluding Remarks

In this paper, we have attempted to analyze and quantify how develop-ments in the exchange rate arrangements of the G3 countries influence emerging market economies. The debate on G3 target zones should be placed in the broader context of the ongoing debate on exchange rate arrangements in emerging-market economies, which often hinge on credibility. The advo-cates for dollarization, for instance, argue that a nation with an uneven his-tory of commitment to low inflation can import the reputation of the central bank of the anchor currency. For the issue at hand, however, there are no ob-vious bonuses to smaller countries should G3 central banks damp the fluc-tuations of their currencies—and, as discussed in Rogoff (2001), the benefits to developed countries are limited at best. This also implies that the direct benefits to emerging-market economies should stem only from the lessened volatility of their trade-weighted currencies. However, as Rose (2000) points out, the benefits of reduced exchange rate variability on trade flows, at least, are small compared to those of adopting a common currency.

This is also the place to discuss the limitations to our analysis. In partic-ular, our use of linear, or nearly linear, models may understate the conse-quences of variability in interest rates and exchange rates. To the extent that high world interest rates trigger balance sheet problems in emerging mar-kets, the consequences of the trade-off implied by a target zone may be con-siderable. Indeed, one repeated message of this paper is that emerging-mar-ket economies are different from their industrial brethren, having already surrendered a high degree of autonomy in their monetary policies, often pricing their goods in foreign—not local—currencies, and being vulnerable to sudden exclusion from world financial markets.

Table 3.14   **Can "Excess" Real GDP Growth Be Explained by G3 Factors?**

Type of Factor	Newly Industrialized Asia	Developing Countries	Africa	Asia	Middle East and Europe	Western Hemisphere
U.S. business cycle						
Expansion	8.24	6.07	2.42	−6.82	−0.23	0.69
	(3.02)	(2.26)	(1.53)	(1.97)	(0.68)	(0.69)
Recession	6.54	−0.17	−0.86	1.46	0.54	0.87
	(4.62)	(3.45)	(2.34)	(3.01)	(1.04)	(1.06)
U.S. monetary policy						
Tightening	4.12	4.37	0.29	−7.14	−1.23	−0.47
	(3.91)	(3.11)	(2.06)	(2.76)	(0.85)	(0.87)
Easing	10.14	4.08	2.20	−2.47	0.82	1.55
	(3.19)	(2.54)	(1.68)	(2.25)	(0.70)	(0.71)
Volatility of U.S. real short-term rates[a]						
High	9.74	0.66	2.36	−0.30	−0.85	−0.50
	(4.01)	(2.86)	(2.07)	(2.51)	(0.77)	(0.77)
Low	7.06	8.76	0.93	−9.37	−0.26	0.88
	(3.87)	(2.76)	(1.99)	(2.42)	(0.74)	(0.74)
Volatility of G3 exchange rates						
High	7.67	6.03	−0.40	−4.98	−0.34	0.46
	(3.47)	(2.64)	(1.73)	(2.46)	(0.78)	(0.79)
Low	7.80	2.10	3.54	−3.60	0.39	1.05
	(3.71)	(2.82)	(1.84)	(2.63)	(0.83)	(0.85)
Volatility of U.S. consumption						
High	2.12	1.31	−1.24	−3.83	0.19	0.98
	(3.10)	(2.57)	(1.64)	(2.46)	(0.78)	(0.79)
Low	14.15	7.50	4.50	−4.92	−0.22	0.46
	(3.32)	(2.75)	(1.75)	(2.63)	(0.84)	(0.85)
Currency crises[b]						
High	6.44	3.83	3.03	−7.35	−0.89	0.09
	(4.93)	(3.10)	(2.49)	(2.95)	(0.76)	(0.83)
Low	15.99	10.33	4.23	−5.47	−0.48	0.40
	(5.78)	(3.64)	(2.92)	(3.46)	(0.89)	(0.97)
Banking crises[c]						
High	9.30	4.70	4.24	−6.76	−0.71	0.12
	(5.39)	(3.36)	(2.61)	(3.11)	(0.80)	(0.87)
Low	11.75	8.64	2.76	−6.33	−0.73	0.34
	(5.68)	(3.55)	(2.75)	(3.28)	(0.84)	(0.92)

Source: Authors' calculations using International Monetary Fund, *World Economic Outlook* (October 2000) and Council of Economic Advisers, *Economic Report to the President* (2001).

Notes: Relationship of the residual from the real GDP growth fundamentals equations to G3 dummy variables from 1970 to 1999. Standard errors are in parentheses.

[a]Estimated from 1973 to 1999.

[b]Estimated from 1980 to 1998.

[c]Estimated from 1980 to 1998.

Appendix

Determinants of Real Private Capital Flows to Emerging Market Economies

| Region/Country | United States | | R^2 |
	Nominal Interest Rate	Real GDP	
Africa			
Net private capital flows	0.21	0.04	0.06
	(0.17)	(0.19)	
Net private direct investment	−0.07	0.00	0.15
	(0.03)	(0.04)	
Net private portfolio investment	−0.09	0.04	0.21
	(0.04)	(0.05)	
Other net private capital flows	0.37	0.00	0.15
	(0.18)	(0.20)	
Asia and crisis countries			
Net private capital flows	0.05	−0.42	0.05
	(0.34)	(0.39)	
Net private direct investment	−0.12	−0.02	0.15
	(0.06)	(0.06)	
Net private portfolio investment	−0.25	−0.05	0.13
	(0.13)	(0.15)	
Other net private capital flows	0.43	−0.35	0.18
	(0.25)	(0.29)	
Other Asian emerging markets			
Net private capital flows	−0.26	−0.06	0.03
	(0.27)	(0.31)	
Net private direct investment	−0.64	0.07	0.19
	(0.27)	(0.31)	
Net private portfolio investment	−0.04	−0.04	0.03
	(0.05)	(0.06)	
Other net private capital flows	0.42	−0.09	0.11
	(0.25)	(0.28)	
Middle East and Europe			
Net private capital flows	−1.68	−0.25	0.33
	(0.46)	(0.54)	
Net private direct investment	−0.08	0.08	0.11
	(0.07)	(0.08)	
Net private portfolio investment	0.02	−0.06	0.01
	(0.12)	(0.14)	
Other net private capital flows	−1.63	−0.27	0.39
	(0.40)	(0.46)	
Western Hemisphere			
Net private capital flows	0.04	−0.29	0.01
	(0.47)	(0.54)	
Net private direct investment	−0.41	0.10	0.09
	(0.27)	(0.32)	
Net private portfolio investment	−0.73	−0.21	0.20
	(0.28)	(0.32)	
Other net private capital flows	1.18	−0.21	0.27
	(0.40)	(0.46)	

Source: Authors' calculations using International Monetary Fund, *World Economic Outlook* (October 2000) and Council of Economic Advisers, *Economic Report to the President* (2001).

Note: Estimated using annual data from 1970 to 1999. Standard errors are in parentheses.

References

Borensztein, Eduardo, and Carmen M. Reinhart. 1994. The macroeconomic determinants of commodity prices. *IMF Staff Papers* 41 (2): 236–60.

Calvo, Guillermo, Leonardo Leiderman, and Carmen M. Reinhart. 1993. Capital inflows and the real exchange rate in Latin America: The role of external factors. *IMF Staff Papers* 40 (1): 108–50.

Calvo, Guillermo A., and Carmen M. Reinhart. 2002. Fear of floating. *Quarterly Journal of Economics* CXVII (2): 379–408.

Chu, Ke-Young, and Thomas K. Morrison. 1984. The 1981–82 recession and non-oil primary commodity prices. *IMF Staff Papers* 31 (1): 93–140.

Clarida, Richard H. 2000. G3 exchange rate relationships: A recap of the record and a review of proposals for change. *Princeton Essays in International Economics* no. 219. Princeton University, Department of Economics, International Economics Section.

Dominguez, Kathryn M., and Jeffrey A. Frankel. 1993. Does foreign exchange intervention matter? The portfolio effect. *American Economic Review* 83:1356–59.

Dornbusch, Rudiger. 1985. Policy and performance links between LDC debtors and industrial nations. *Brookings Papers on Economic Activity,* Issue no. 2:303–56.

Fernandez-Arias, Eduardo. 1996. The new wave of private capital inflows: Push or pull? *Journal of Development Economics* 48:389–418.

Frankel, Jeffrey A., and Andrew Rose. 1996. Currency crashes in emerging markets: An empirical treatment. *Journal of International Economics* 41:351–66.

Frankel, Jeffrey A., Sergio Schmukler, and Luis Servén. 2001. Verifiability and the vanishing intermediate exchange rate regime. In *Policy challenges in the next millennium,* ed. Susan Collins and Dani Rodrik, 59–108. Washington, D.C.: Brookings Institution.

Frankel, Jeffrey A., and Nouriel Roubini. 2000. The role of industrial country policies in emerging market crises. paper prepared for the NBER conference on Economic and Financial Crises in Emerging Market Economies, 19–21 October, Woodstock, Vt.

Gertler, Mark, and Kenneth Rogoff. 1990. North-south lending and endogenous domestic capital market inefficiencies. *Journal of Monetary Economics* 26:245–66.

Goldstein, Morris. 1999. *Safeguarding prosperity in a global financial system: Report of an independent task force of the Council on Foreign Relations.* New York: Council on Foreign Relations.

Holtham, Gerald H. 1988. Modeling commodity prices in a world macroeconomic model. In *International Commodity Market Models and Policy Analysis,* ed. Orhan Güvenen, 221–58. Boston: Kluwer Academic Publishers.

International Monetary Fund. 1999. *Direction of trade statistics.* Washington, D.C.: International Monetary Fund.

———. 2000a. *International financial statistics.* Washington, D.C.: International Monetary Fund.

———. 2000b. *World Economic Outlook* database. Available at [http://www.imf.org].

Kaminsky, Graciela L., and Karen K. Lewis. 1996. Does foreign exchange intervention signal future monetary policy? *Journal of Monetary Economics* 37:285–312.

Kaminsky, Graciela L., and Carmen M. Reinhart. 1999. The twin crises: The causes of banking and balance-of-payments problems. *American Economic Review* 89: 473–500.

———. 2001. Bank lending and contagion: Evidence from the Asian crisis. In *Regional and global capital flows: Macroeconomic causes and consequences,* ed. T. Ito and A. Krueger, 73–116. Chicago: University of Chicago Press.

Kaminsky, Graciela L., and Sergio Schmukler. 2001. Emerging market instability:

Do sovereign ratings affect country risk and stock returns? World Bank. Mimeograph.

Marquez, Jaime. 1990. Bilateral trade elasticities. *The Review of Economics and Statistics* 72 (1): 70–77.

McKinnon, Ronald. 1984. *An international standard for monetary stabilization.* Washington, D.C.: Institute for International Economics.

———. 1997. *The rules of the game.* Cambridge: MIT Press.

Reinhart, Carmen M. 1995. Devaluation, relative prices, and trade. *IMF Staff Papers* 42 (2): 290–310.

———. 2000. Sovereign credit ratings before and after financial crises. *World Bank Economic Review,* forthcoming.

Rogoff, Kenneth. 2001. On why not a global currency. *American Economic Review* 91 (2): 243–47.

Rose, Andrew K. 2000. One money, one market: Estimating the effect of common currencies on trade. *Economic Journal* 15.

Williamson, John. 1986. Target zones and the management of the dollar. *Brookings Papers on Economic Activity,* Issue no. 1:165–74.

Comment   Joshua Aizenman

This interesting paper investigates an issue of great importance to emerging markets—the welfare effect of attempts to reduce the exchange rate volatility among the G3 currencies. My discussion will start with an overview of the main message of the paper and will conclude with several remarks regarding the robustness of the arguments advanced in it.

Overview

The Goal

The purpose of the paper is to examine the welfare effect, from an emerging-market perspective, of reducing the G3 currencies' variability. It explores the various channels of North-South transmission and analyzes the link between the G3 exchange rate and interest rate volatility, and economic growth in developing countries.

The Background

Using target zones as a mechanism for reducing the volatility of the G3 currencies has been advocated by various economists, including McKinnon, Williamson, Clarida, and others. These proposals focused mostly on the Organization for Economic Cooperation and Development (OECD). Little attention was given to the implications of adopting the target zone

Joshua Aizenman is professor of economics at the University of California, Santa Cruz, and a research associate of the National Bureau of Economic Research.

regime on the welfare of the emerging markets. This issue may be of special relevance as many developing countries tie their currency to that of one of the G3 countries, frequently to the U.S. dollar, as a manifestation of the "fear of floating" (see Calvo and Reinhart 2000).

The Main Argument

The authors are skeptical regarding the ultimate welfare gains from stabilizing the G3 currencies. They assert that lower volatility of the G3 currencies would ultimately lead to *higher* interest rate volatility. They observe that sterilized intervention does not work and that restricting capital mobility is against the consensus. Hence, the authors conclude that the interest rate adjustment will replace exchange rate adjustment. The welfare consequences of these changes are ambiguous—higher interest rate volatility would be costly to emerging markets (EMs), and these costs may exceed the benefits from more stable G3 currencies.

This argument is illustrated in figure 3C.1. The authors presume the presence of a concave association between the exchange rate and the emerging markets' output. Similarly, the association between the G3 interest rate and the emerging markets' output is concave. This in turn would imply that stabilizing the G3 currencies would increase the emerging markets' expected GDP and welfare, as is illustrated in panel A. However, the resultant greater volatility of the interest rate would reduce the emerging markets' expected GDP and welfare (see panel B). The net balance would be determined by the relative strength of these two conflicting effects.

In section 3.4 the authors review in detail the linkages between the G3 and EM. Among their interesting findings, they report that economic growth in developing countries tends to be faster against the backdrop of a more stable U.S. short-term interest rate. Specifically, EMGrowth (volatile G3 E. rates + stable $i_{U.S.}$) – EMGrowth (volatile $i_{U.S.}$ + stable G3 E. rates) = %1.25. This observation induces them to conclude that there is no natural presumption that the emerging markets would benefit from stabilizing the G3 currencies.

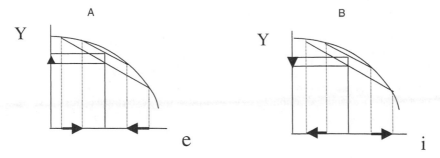

Fig. 3C.1   *A,* **Expected output and exchange rate volatility;** *B,* **Expected output and interest rate volatility**

Response

Is There a Trade-Off Between Interest Rate Volatility
and Exchange Rate Volatility for the G3?

The logic of the paper presumes the existence of a trade-off between interest rate and exchange rate volatility for the G3. With such a trade-off, figure 3C.1 illustrates the ambiguity of the welfare effects attributed to greater exchange rate stability. However, no evidence is presented to support this presumption. The existing literature provides us with little guidance regarding this issue. In fact, several contributions are skeptical about this trade-off. For example, Flood and Rose (1995) failed to find such a trade-off, reporting, "The graphs indicate that there is no substantial tradeoff between exchange rate volatility and the volatility of (domestic) interest rate" (Flood and Rose 1995, 17). A recent update of this study is summarized by Jeanne and Rose (1999), who found that macroeconomic fundamentals do not exhibit regime-varying volatility. These authors advance a possible interpretation for these findings, focusing on the impact of the entry of noise traders to the market. Accordingly, a pure float with an endogenous number of noise traders may give rise to multiple equilibria. The same macrofundamentals are consistent with low exchange rate volatility and a low number of noise traders, or high exchange rate volatility and a high number of noise traders. The multiplicity follows from the observation that noise traders affect the allocation of risk in two ways—they create risk, and they allow for deeper risk sharing. The ultimate impact of the entry of noise traders on the risk premium is ambiguous. Jeanne and Rose illustrate that for certain configurations in which two equilibria exist, the inefficient one is associated with high exchange rate volatility. In that equilibrium, all noise traders are active. Their model provides a nice setup for the multiple equilibrium hypothesis (Eichengreen and Wyplosz 1993). In such an economy, a target zone may eliminate the inefficient equilibrium by restricting the feasible range of exchange rate volatility. In this case there is a "free lunch," in the sense that there is no trade-off between exchange rate volatility and interest rate volatility—the good equilibrium is associated with lower exchange rate volatility as well as with a lower risk premium and lower interest rate volatility.

This argument may be restated in terms of the earlier literature dealing with exchange rate regimes. If most of the shocks are nominal (as will be the case, for example, with an unstable demand for money), greater fixity of the exchange rate may be associated with lower interest rate volatility, if the supply of money was allowed to adjust to the shocks affecting the demand for money.

Interpreting the Empirical Facts

The empirical discussion dealing with the interest rate–monetary policy cycle is very interesting and illuminating. The results dealing with the association between the North volatility and regional GDP and capital flows leave one in doubt. The methodology of comparing the flows of capital and the GDP between periods of relatively stable and unstable interest and exchange rates is useful in motivating the welfare questions, yet it does not allow one to fully assess the impact of policies. Specifically, there are no controls for "level" variables that may explain the capital flows and the GDP. Without controlling for all the level variables that may account for capital flows and the GDP, little can be inferred about the pure effect of volatility.

On the Association between Exchange Rate Volatility
and the Gross Domestic Product

The presumption of the paper about the negative effect of exchange rate volatility on the gross domestic product (GDP) has been subject to recent debate. The earlier Flood and Rose (1995) contribution found a weak trade-off between exchange rate and output volatility. Recently, however, Levy-Yeyati and Sturzenegger (2001) report that for developing countries, less flexible exchange rate regimes are strongly associated with both slower growth and greater output volatility. For industrial countries, different exchange rate regimes do not appear to have any significant impact on growth.

To sum up, this paper is an interesting contribution. It raises several important questions, cautioning us that the welfare effects of attempts to stabilize the G3 on the emerging markets are ambiguous. Resolving these ambiguities requires further investigation.

References

Calvo, Guillermo A., and Carmen M. Reinhart. 2000. Fear of floating. *Quarterly Journal of Economics,* forthcoming.

Eichengreen, Barry, and Charles Wyplosz. 1993. The unstable EMS. *Brookings Papers on Economic Activity,* Issue no. 1:51–124.

Flood, Robert, and Andrew Rose. 1995. Fixing exchange rates: A virtual quest for fundamentals. *Journal of Monetary Economics* 36 (1): 3–37.

Jeanne, Olivier, and Andrew K. Rose. 1999. Noise trading and exchange rate regimes. *Quarterly Journal of Economics,* forthcoming.

Levy-Yeyati, Eduardo, and Federico Sturzenegger. 2001. To float or to trail: Evidence on the impact of exchange rate regimes. Universidad Torcuato Di Tella, Department of Economics. Unpublished Manuscript.

Discussion Summary

Michael P. Dooley remarked that there is no convincing empirical evidence for the existence of a trade-off between interest rate and exchange rate volatility and gave support to the authors' view that monetary policy would be the only tool for supporting a G3 target zone.

Richard Portes made reference to "the balloon analogy" for describing the volatility trade-off. He questioned the paper's dismissal of sterilized intervention as a way of enforcing a target zone and pointed to empirical evidence suggesting that foreign exchange intervention may be effective, at least over certain periods of time.

Robert Flood pointed to the asymmetries of crisis models data and emphasized the importance of unconstrained estimation in order to take account of skewness in the data.

Jeffrey Shafer made a reference to the European economies during the 1980s and argued that there is no observed trade-off between exchange rate and interest rate volatility. He questioned, however, whether soft target zones as opposed to fixed rates would be sufficient to meet the goals of a G3 target zone.

Morris Goldstein made a reference to earlier literature and noted that better bottom-line growth and inflation performance is not a likely outcome of target zones. Thus, the G3 countries would be unwilling to enter such an exchange rate arrangement, and even if they did, weaker G3 economic performance would not be of any help to emerging market economies.

Andrew Rose remarked that no exchange rate model seems to work well, at least not in the short run, and, therefore, even though a trade-off between exchange rates and interest rates seems to exist, this trade-off is hard to quantify. *Martin Eichenbaum* pointed out that as long as there is no clear understanding of what drives exchange rates, the idea of using monetary policy as a tool for steering exchange rates seems problematic. Dooley noted that doing nothing because of the lack of consensus regarding the "right" exchange rate model seems problematic as well.

Jeffrey A. Frankel noted that exchange rates are not always tightly linked to fundamentals and that sterilized intervention has been effective in the past. However, he added, it would be impossible to commit persistent intervention to maintain a target zone goal since a key element for effective sterilized intervention is sparing use of the intervention tool.

Vincent Raymond Reinhart remarked that he was sympathetic to the point made by Dooley regarding the lack of empirical evidence for a trade-off between exchange rates and interest rates and agreed that the assertion of such a trade-off is the weak part of the paper. He noted, in response to Goldstein, that the authors had avoided references to earlier literature, given that the focus of the paper is on emerging market economies. He remarked that even though it is indeed possible to achieve an anchoring of exchange rate expectations under various regimes, the necessary element is credibility; that is, the imposition of a target zone itself is not sufficient. With respect to the issue of the effectiveness of sterilized foreign exchange intervention, Reinhart noted that it is important to distinguish between effectiveness during regimes and effectiveness during episodes.

4

When Is U.S. Bank Lending to Emerging Markets Volatile?

Linda S. Goldberg

4.1 Introduction

Little solid evidence exists on the practices of industrialized country banks operating in emerging markets. Critics of the industrialized countries' banks argue that these agents are unstable lenders who undermine local financial markets. Supporters see the foreign banks as key sources of otherwise scarce capital, with broader positive spillovers on the stability and efficiency of local financial markets. Clearly, there is a need for careful analysis of the lending practices of industrialized country banks to foreign clients. Our goal in this paper is to make progress in this direction by examining the activities of individual U.S. banks with foreign exposures. This microdata approach facilitates a comparison of the lending behavior of these banks in the complete set of countries in which the banks have positions. By working with bank-level data, we can consider which types of U.S. banks (with size as a defining characteristic) are the more volatile lenders, in which regions the lending by these banks is most volatile, and whether lending to certain regions is volatile mainly because of higher volatility of the economic fundamentals of these regions.

The main data we use are from quarterly foreign exposure data filed by each U.S. bank (or bank holding company) and collected as a component

Linda S. Goldberg is a vice president of the Federal Reserve Bank of New York and a research associate of the National Bureau of Economic Research.

Comments by participants at the preconference held at the 2000 NBER Summer Institute, at the January 2001 conference held in Islamorada, Florida, and especially by Simon Johnson are gratefully acknowledged, as well as comments from Leon Taub. The views expressed in this paper are those of the author and do not necessarily reflect the position of the Federal Reserve Bank of New York or the Federal Reserve System. Glenda Oskar provided excellent research assistance.

of the bank supervisory process. The Country Exposure Reports provide a by-country distribution of the foreign claims held by individual U.S. banks,[1] revealing the extent of geographic concentration (and, to a lesser extent, the maturity and type of concentration) of the bank's international holdings. We match these data with bank call report information to achieve corresponding series on the quarterly assets of the same set of banks. Taken together, these data enable us to discuss the international portfolio allocations of individual U.S. banks and consider the evolution of U.S. bank claims abroad.

We pose a number of questions relevant for understanding the scope of U.S. bank activity in international markets. First, what are the characteristics of those U.S. banks that are international players? We describe the number of reporting banks, the average size of these banks, the scope of their international exposures, and the geographical diversification of their portfolios. Second, what drives changes in U.S. bank claims on particular countries or regions? We conduct an econometric analysis of the sensitivity of various international positions to a set of key macroeconomic fundamentals. In the same way that Peek and Rosengren (1997, 2000) showed that Japanese banks transmit shocks from Japan to the United States, we consider whether U.S. banks transmit U.S. business cycle fluctuations to their foreign borrowers. We also posit that U.S. bank international exposures may be closely tied to the performance of particular countries or regions. We examine these relationships, considering throughout whether there are observable differences in these sensitivities across U.S. banks differentiated by their size or across the industrialized or emerging-market partners of the U.S. banks.

Our main findings are the following:

- Over the past two decades, the U.S. banks engaged in international lending have become more diverse: There are now fewer banks overall, and these banks are more polarized in terms of their size and portfolio allocations.
- An increasing portion of reporting U.S. banks, particularly smaller banks, maintains an exclusive focus on Latin American markets. The lending by smaller banks, especially with respect to Latin American and Asian markets, has been more volatile than the lending by larger banks.
- Compared with smaller U.S. banks, larger banks maintain claims on a larger number of countries. About 60 percent of large bank exposure is in industrialized countries, with most of the remaining exposure evenly split between the emerging markets of Latin America and Asia.
- Looking across U.S. banks, their foreign claims are highly correlated

---

1. The use of the term "U.S. banks" in this paper generally includes U.S.-owned banks and U.S. subsidiaries of foreign banks.

with U.S. gross domestic product (GDP) growth, but not with foreign demand conditions. The negative correlation between U.S. bank claims and U.S. GDP growth for industrialized country partners suggests that net claims on these areas contract when the U.S. economy is expanding. A similar result arises for claims on emerging Asia. By contrast, the positive correlation observed for claims on Latin American countries suggests that lending to Latin America expands as the U.S. economy grows.

- Foreign claims of U.S. banks are correlated with real U.S. interest rates but generally uncorrelated with foreign real interest rates. Tighter real lending conditions in the United States are associated with lower real claims on industrialized countries and higher claims on Latin American countries.

- Overall, U.S. banks have not been volatile lenders internationally. Even in periods of international financial crisis, we do not observe statistically significant or extensive retrenchments of the international claims of U.S. banks.

These findings have direct relevance for currency crisis prevention in emerging markets. First, although U.S. banks are active participants in international markets, relatively few of these banks have high shares of their assets located abroad. A large portion of U.S. international claims remains within industrialized countries, but certain regions—most particularly Latin America—are important lending destinations of U.S. banks. In recent years, some small U.S. banks have heavily concentrated claims on Latin American countries and high ratios of foreign claims to overall bank assets.

The sensitivity of foreign claims to the U.S. business cycle parallels the type of observations that have been made by Peek and Rosengren, wherein Japanese banks were conduits for transmission of Japanese shocks to U.S. markets. In our sample, these spillovers are statistically significant for Latin America but not consistently so for other emerging market regions.[2] The positive correlation implies that lending to Latin American countries rises when the United States grows faster, even after controlling for the local GDP growth. Some of this expansion may be related to trade credit provision or investments in Latin America's exporting sectors.

Small countries often express the concern that the international lender— by conducting lending activities directly through foreign-owned branches or indirectly through cross-border exposures—will make the emerging-market economies more sensitive to external fluctuations through the lending channels. Although we concur that there is evidence of international

---

2. In some specifications there is a significantly negative correlation between U.S. GDP growth and U.S. bank claims on Asian emerging markets. Goldberg and Klein (1998) reached similar conclusions for foreign direct investment patterns.

transmission of cycles, some of this correlation would likely be evident even in the absence of a U.S. bank presence. More important is the observation that generally the U.S. lenders are relatively stable providers of credit. Especially important is the lack of correlation between U.S. bank claims on emerging markets and the real demand cycles of those markets. These findings reinforce the conclusions by Dages, Goldberg, and Kinney (2000) that foreign banks operating in emerging markets may play an important role in stabilizing overall lending. Since local banks are highly sensitive to local conditions, stable credit supplies from external lenders may reduce the lending and investment instability in emerging-market economies in times of emerging market financial and balance-of-payments crises. As argued by Palmer (2000), U.S. banks appear to take a long view of their positions in many industrialized and emerging market regions, and local claims are relatively stable as a result.

The remainder of this paper is divided into three sections. Section 4.2 discusses the data, the U.S. banks that are lending abroad, and their international exposures. Section 4.3 econometrically explores the volatility of the international claims of the U.S. banks. Section 4.4 provides concluding remarks related to currency crisis prevention and presents suggestions for further analysis of this rich data source.

4.2   Reporting Banks and Their International Exposures

The main data for our analysis are from Country Exposure Reports filed quarterly by individual banks. The Federal Financial Institutions Examinations Council (FFIEC) report no. 009[3] must be filed by every U.S. chartered insured commercial bank in the fifty states of the United States, the District of Columbia, Puerto Rico, and U.S. territories and possessions, that meets *both* of the following criteria:

(1) It has at least one of the following: a branch in a foreign country; a majority-owned subsidiary in a foreign country; an Edge for Agreement subsidiary; a branch in Puerto Rico or in any U.S. territory or possession (except that a bank with its head office in Puerto Rico or any U.S. territory or possession need not report if it meets only this criterion); or an International Banking Facility (IBF); and

(2) It has, on a fully consolidated bank basis, total outstanding claims on residents of foreign countries exceeding $30 million in aggregate.

---

3. The FFIEC is an umbrella organization that collects and warehouses data for the Federal Reserve, Office of the Comptroller of the Currency, and Federal Deposit Insurance Corporation. Much of the information collected via the FFIEC 009 is made public, aggregated over all reporting banks, via the Country Exposure Lending Survey (FFIEC Statistical Release E.16). Palmer (2000) provides a useful discussion of trends in the aggregated data, with specific emphasis on emerging markets.

Table 4.1   Average Number of Reporting Banks, Over Time and by Region

	1984–89	1990–95	1996–2000
Industrialized countries	182	137	72
Developing Europe	77	37	30
Latin America	183	133	78
Asia	122	85	50
Africa	71	40	27
Middle East	97	78	44
Total reporting banks	192	152	90

The reported data provide considerable detail on the U.S. bank claims on foreign countries, with itemization by individual country. Bank claims are fairly broadly defined, encompassing credit extended to foreign country banks, public entities, and other recipients including individuals and businesses. In addition to direct international flows, bank claims also include revaluation gains on interest rate, foreign exchange, equity, commodity, and other off–balance sheet contracts. The reporting institution is asked to break down the cross-border claims outstanding by type of borrower (banks, public sector entities, other) and by time remaining to maturity (one year and under, one to five years, and over five years). In other quarterly reports, banks also provide information on their total assets located both in the United States and abroad.

There are 200 possible foreign "countries" in which a bank can report an exposure each quarter. These include industrialized countries; countries within emerging Europe (encompassing a number of small countries and countries that were formerly part of the Soviet Union); thirty-five countries under the heading of Latin America; forty under the heading of Asia/Pacific and the Middle East; and fifty-four countries within Africa. Each bank is required to provide detailed information on exposure to a country only when that exposure exceeds 1 percent of the reporting institution's total assets or 20 percent of its total capital, whichever is less.

For the time period spanned by our data, 1984 through 2000:Q2, the number of U.S. reporting banks with foreign exposures changes dramatically (table 4.1). In the second half of the 1980s, an average of 192 banks reported foreign exposures.[4] Almost all reporting banks maintained positions in Latin America and in (non-U.S.) industrialized countries. A smaller pro-

4. Our unbalance panel originally began with 317 banks. Thirty-five banks had only one year or less of nonzero total exposure data and were deleted from our data set. Those observations with zero total exposure at any date were deleted from our sample. There were some foreign banks in our sample whose asset information was not representative of their entire conglomerate. Because this created an inconsistency between the scope of exposure information and the scope of asset information, these banks, classified as Edge Acts Banks and New York State Article 12 corporations, and two other banks with unusual situations were eliminated from the sample.

Table 4.2   Size of Reporting Banks: Total Assets (US$ millions)

	1984–89	1990–95	1996–2000
Total reporting banks	178.8	235.1	446.2
	(261.1)	(309.1)	(677.7)
Quartile 1	15.3	12.2	7.5
	(9.3)	(11.3)	(7.3)
Quartile 2	46.5	67.2	101.9
	(10.0)	(20.1)	(48.9)
Quartile 3	112.4	182.0	321.1
	(40.5)	(49.0)	(79.6)
Quartile 4	541.0	680.1	1,353.2
	(301.7)	(317.9)	(823.4)

Note: Means, with standard deviations in parentheses. Banks are sorted into quartiles by asset size.

portion of banks is involved in developing Asia, with banks less frequently involved in Africa and developing Europe.

The average number of reporting banks declined sharply over the course of the 1990s, down to 152 in the first half and to 90 in the latter half of the 1990s. Much of this reduction is associated with the general tendency toward banking sector consolidation in the United States over this period. Additionally, in the late 1990s some banks opted to report exposures consolidated at a bank holding company level, further reducing the number of distinct reporting institutions.

The data also reveal large changes in the relative popularity of regions among the reporting banks; over time, a smaller share of reporting banks was present in each region of the world. For example, whereas 182 banks had positions in (non-U.S.) industrialized countries in the late 1980s, this number declined to 72 by the late 1990s.[5] The number of U.S. banks active in Latin America declined to 78.

Alongside the sharp decline in the number of banks over the past two decades, we observe important changes over time in the size distribution of the reporting banks (table 4.2). Although the mean and median bank size basically doubled over the period from 1984 through mid-2000, the actual change in the size distribution of these banks was much greater. Sorting banks by quartiles based on their total assets, the average bank in the lowest quartile became considerably smaller, down from $15 million to $7.5 million in assets. In the next quartile of banks, the average size doubled since the mid-1980s, with the representative bank growing from $46 million to $102 million. The size variation within these quartiles of banks also grew considerably. The banks classified in the 3rd and especially the 4th quartile

5. Throughout the paper, when we refer to "industrialized countries" this means industrialized countries other than the United States. The list of countries is provided in table 4A.3.

Table 4.3   **Foreign Portfolio Shares of Reporting Banks**

	1984–89	1990–95	1996–2000
Unweighted average across banks	1.6	1.7	1.9
	(4.8)	(5.8)	(6.9)
Quartile 1	2.8	4.1	5.4
	(6.8)	(9.5)	(12.1)
Quartile 2	1.3	0.8	0.7
	(3.8)	(2.3)	(2.3)
Quartile 3	1.0	0.9	0.7
	(3.4)	(3.5)	(2.7)
Quartile 4	1.1	1.1	0.8
	(4.4)	(4.4)	(3.7)
Weighted average across banks[a]	1.2	1.1	0.8
Reporting Banks with Exposure >1%			
Unweighted average across banks	5.7	6.8	8.2
	(8.6)	(10.6)	(13.0)
Quartile 1	7.6	10.3	13.1
	(11.5)	(14.5)	(17.8)
Quartile 2	4.7	6.7	8.7
	(6.5)	(10.0)	(14.0)
Quartile 3	4.7	4.1	5.3
	(5.7)	(5.5)	(7.4)
Quartile 4	5.8	6.1	5.6
	(9.1)	(9.4)	(8.3)
Weighted average across banks[a]	5.9	6.0	5.7

Note: Means, with standard deviations in parentheses. Foreign exposures as a percent of total bank assets. Banks are divided into quartiles based on parent assets.
[a]Using total asset weights.

more clearly reflect the phenomenon of banking sector consolidation. The average 4th quartile reporting bank tripled in asset size, to more than $1 billion in assets by the late 1990s, with numerous banks considerably larger. From both tables 4.1 and 4.2 we conclude that although the number of reporting banks has declined, the remaining banks have become considerably more diverse.

Beyond differences in size, there are also huge differences across individual banks in their foreign exposure, measured as the sum of cross-border exposure and local country claims, and expressed relative to total bank assets (table 4.3).[6] The first five rows of table 4.3 provide the unweighted averages of foreign exposure shares across all bank observations and within every period. For all banks taken together (and unweighted by bank size) there has been a tendency toward increasing shares of foreign exposure in average U.S. bank portfolios. However, this result is driven by tendencies

6. Observations are included for every period in which a bank reports nonzero foreign exposure.

among the smaller banks actively participating in international markets. These banks have increased their average foreign portfolio share from 2.8 to 5.4 percent of bank assets. By contrast, the larger banks maintain smaller foreign portfolio shares (at approximately 1 percent of bank assets) with the overall shares slightly declining over time. Even when portfolio shares of all banks are weighted by their respective asset positions at each date, the overall foreign portfolio share of U.S. banks reporting foreign exposures has declined over time, to under 1 percent of U.S. bank assets.

The low foreign exposure shares in the first section of table 4.3 make it tempting to conclude that international exposures pose very low degrees of foreign risk to the reporting banks. This conclusion is inappropriate. Risk analysis is more often conducted in relation to parent bank capital or equity and is generally not relative to the bank's overall asset position.[7] If a bank's capital is 10 percent of assets, a foreign portfolio share of 5 percent would suggest that the ratio of foreign exposure to capital is 50 percent for that bank—suggesting that bank equity can be substantially threatened by adverse external conditions. Additionally, the low numbers of the first section of table 4.3 are the result of having many banks with low exposures—at less than 1 percent of assets—reported together with a lesser (but still substantial) number of banks with much higher foreign exposures.

The second section of table 4.3 provides average exposures for only those banks that have foreign exposures greater than 1 percent of assets, a restriction that reduces our sample to only 15 percent of those observations reported in the first section of the table. Observe that these banks can have quite large exposures, rising to 8.2 (5.7) as unweighted (weighted) averages for the late 1990s. The tendency toward increasing exposure over time for the average bank is especially due to the large increases in foreign exposure shares by the smaller and medium-sized banks in the sample. This sample of larger banks has maintained foreign portfolio shares on the order of 5–6 percent of assets for the full period covered by our data.

The form of these exposures has changed over time in terms of regional concentration and in terms of clientele (e.g., banks, public sector borrowers, or other private borrowers). The diversification structure across location and clientele is important for ultimately interpreting our analysis of lending volatility later in the paper. One hypothesis is that when U.S. bank positions are highly dispersed regionally, their lending may be more insulated from region-specific disturbances and less volatile, even to regions experiencing shocks.[8]

Table 4.4 considers the share of all reporting banks, regardless of size,

7. See Palmer (2000) and Bomfim and Nelson (1999) for related discussions of the appropriate measurement of risk.
8. Dages, Goldberg, and Kinney (2000) show that within Argentina and Mexico, loans by domestic privately owned banks are more volatile with respect to local conditions than are loans by foreign-owned banks.

Table 4.4 **Percent of All Reporting Banks Maintaining a Position Exclusively in One Region**

	Exclusive Position in Any Region	Exclusive Position in a Single Region					
		Industrialized Countries	Europe	Latin America	Asia	Africa	Middle East
1984–89	9.1	3.0	0.0	5.8	0.1	0.0	0.1
1990–95	13.6	4.9	0.0	6.7	0.8	0.4	0.5
1996–2000	21.5	4.0	0.0	12.7	2.8	0.5	1.7

Note: Last five columns represent developing country regions.

that maintain claims exclusively in one foreign region.[9] Only 4 percent of all bank observations correspond to an exclusive position in industrialized countries. In stark contrast, by the second half of the 1990s more than 12 percent of banks had foreign exposures exclusively concentrated in developing countries of the Western Hemisphere (e.g., Latin America). These Latin American markets are the main foreign focus of some small, specialized banks operating out of the United States.

Given that a bank maintains an exposure to a particular region, we also examined the likelihood that the same bank is diversified to other regions. Claims on Latin American countries are always likely to be part of a bank's portfolio, regardless of other regions in which a bank maintains positions (see appendix table 4A.1). Moreover, if a bank has a position in Latin America, with the rise in Latin American specialization we observe a parallel decline over time in the likelihood of that bank's also having positions in industrialized economies, Asia, and Africa. If any bank has a position in industrialized countries, there is a greater than 80 percent probability that the bank will also have positions in Latin America and a 60 percent probability that it will also have positions in Asia.

The recipients of U.S. banks' foreign exposure have also evolved over time and across regions (table 4.5). The last sixteen years are characterized by a declining (but still substantial) role of bank-to-bank lending, by a general decline in lending to public entities, and by the rise in lending to a broader group of nonbank private clientele.

Distinguishing across regions, we further observe that

- In industrialized countries, the substantial shift away from bank-to-bank lending matches the rise in nonbank private lending. Public-sector borrowers have played relatively small roles, hovering at about 10 percent of the U.S. bank claims on these regions.
- The importance of public-sector borrowers declined substantially as a fraction of activity in Latin American exposures. The decline was from

9. The regions used by the IMF are industrialized countries, developing Europe, developing Western Hemisphere (mainly Latin America), developing Asia, Africa, and the Middle East.

Table 4.5   Recipient Shares in U.S. Bank Exposure, by Period and Region

	Banks	Public	Other Private
1984–89	47.6	29.1	19.3
Industrialized countries	62.4	12.8	18.7
Developing Europe	36.1	52.1	10.2
Latin America	36.3	40.6	20.8
Asia	47.5	24.4	21.2
Africa	21.2	52.1	23.9
Middle East	45.6	29.3	22.9
1990–95	46.6	21.4	26.6
Industrialized countries	57.9	9.9	24.1
Developing Europe	30.7	41.3	25.9
Latin America	37.5	24.1	35.3
Asia	54.2	11.8	23.3
Africa	22.6	45.3	27.3
Middle East	39.5	40.4	18.1
1996–2000	44.2	15.0	34.7
Industrialized countries	49.0	10.8	32.6
Developing Europe	37.0	28.7	30.6
Latin America	42.4	10.1	43.9
Asia	53.0	4.6	27.7
Africa	29.7	32.0	29.8
Middle East	43.3	35.1	18.9

Note: Percent of total exposure by bank.

about 40 percent of individual bank claims in the mid- to late 1980s to just above 10 percent by the late 1990s. In absolute terms, there has been a huge increase in U.S. bank private lending to Latin American companies, with a smaller decline in public borrowing.

• For developing Asia, although the role of public borrowers has decreased since the late 1980s, the shift toward direct lending to nonbank private clients has not been as pronounced as is observed in other regions.

Also of interest is the source of these claims, which may be generated by cross-border operations or by lending by U.S. branch or subsidiary operations already located in foreign markets (table 4.6). The ratio of cross-border claims to total bank claims is near 100 percent for almost all regions and almost all banks in the lower three quartiles of banks. Local lending activities are prevalent mainly among the larger banks. Averaging over banks in the 4th quartile (again, without weighting by bank size), the share of U.S. bank claims that are generated by local lending is 16 percent for industrialized countries, 24 percent for developing Asia, and 10 percent for Latin American countries.

As a final descriptive exercise before turning to the volatility of claims of section 4.3, in table 4.7 we show the average importance of particular regions to the foreign exposures of the reporting banks. First, U.S. banks hold

Table 4.6 **The Relative Importance of Cross-Border versus Local Lending, by Region and by Quartile: % of Cross-Border Exposure**

	Industrialized Countries	Developing Country Regions				
		Europe	Latin America	Asia	Africa	Middle East
1984–89						
All reporting banks	94.1	99.2	98.5	93.5	97.5	98.1
Quartile 1	99.9	99.9	100.0	99.7	100.0	100.0
Quartile 2	99.0	100.0	100.0	99.1	99.9	100.0
Quartile 3	95.9	100.0	99.0	97.5	99.5	100.0
Quartile 4	78.3	98.1	94.1	83.5	95.7	95.5
1990–95						
All reporting banks	91.9	98.0	97.0	89.3	95.2	98.0
Quartile 1	99.7	100.0	99.9	99.1	100.0	100.0
Quartile 2	98.1	100.0	99.8	97.8	99.7	100.0
Quartile 3	92.5	99.9	96.4	95.1	100.0	100.0
Quartile 4	74.8	96.3	90.1	74.6	92.2	95.2
1996–2000						
All reporting banks	92.2	96.3	96.4	85.3	91.5	97.4
Quartile 1	100.0	100.0	99.8	96.7	100.0	100.0
Quartile 2	96.3	99.9	97.8	89.8	100.0	100.0
Quartile 3	91.6	98.8	96.6	91.5	100.0	100.0
Quartile 4	84.2	96.3	90.5	76.0	92.2	96.0

Table 4.7 **Regional Total Exposure Shares, Over Time and by Bank Type**

	Industrialized Countries	Developing Country Regions				
		Europe	Latin America	Asia	Africa	Middle East
1984–89						
All banks	55.5	1.0	26.0	13.3	2.4	1.8
Quartile 1	51.5	0.9	37.5	5.5	1.7	3.1
Quartile 2	52.6	1.2	34.0	10.2	1.1	0.9
Quartile 3	53.5	0.9	29.4	12.7	1.9	1.6
Quartile 4	56.3	1.0	24.2	14.0	2.7	1.9
1990–95						
All banks	58.4	0.9	21.7	16.5	1.3	1.3
Quartile 1	57.1	1.1	34.7	3.0	1.8	2.4
Quartile 2	53.5	0.3	29.0	16.0	0.4	0.8
Quartile 3	56.4	0.7	30.1	11.1	0.7	1.0
Quartile 4	59.2	1.0	19.1	18.0	1.4	1.4
1996–2000						
All banks	57.5	1.9	22.6	15.6	1.2	1.2
Quartile 1	20.9	1.6	70.9	2.1	1.0	3.6
Quartile 2	48.4	0.3	32.1	17.8	0.4	1.0
Quartile 3	50.1	1.1	33.9	12.7	0.9	1.4
Quartile 4	60.3	2.2	18.7	16.4	1.4	1.0

Note: Unweighted by bank size: share of region in a bank's total foreign exposure.

very small portions of their foreign portfolios in the regions of developing Europe, Africa, and the Middle East. On average, each of these regions is on the order of 1–2 percent of the foreign portfolio, regardless of the size of the banks. Among the largest banks, developing Europe gained popularity (to 2.2 percent of portfolios) in the second half of the 1990s. Among the smallest banks, the Middle East is in some cases a higher portion of bank portfolio (at 3–4 percent).

Reinforcing our earlier observations, table 4.7 shows the importance of claims on the Latin American countries to the portfolios of both large and small banks. While small banks have had disproportionately large emphasis on Latin American claims (at 37 percent in 1984–89, compared with 24 percent for the banks in the largest quartile), the role of Latin American investments soared for the smaller banks over the second half of the 1990s. For 1st quartile banks, Latin American claims reached over 70 percent of overall foreign exposures by the end of the 1990s. Claims on industrialized countries have generally been 50–60 percent of the foreign exposures of U.S. banks and remain at these levels for those banks without a more exclusive Latin American focus.

4.3   The Volatility of International Exposures of U.S. Banks

Although the previous section has demonstrated that significant differences exist across banks and over time in the size and composition of U.S. bank foreign claims, it did not address the reasons for and timing of changes in these claims. We now turn to this more dynamic issue, asking whether fluctuations in claims are econometrically explained by changes in the fundamentals of the countries in which these banks have claims and by changes in the fundamentals of the United States.

To examine the fluctuations of bank claims on specific groups of countries, we divide banks by asset size categories and into the three time intervals (1984–89, 1990–95, 1996–2000). We consider three arbitrary size divisions. First, we define as smaller banks those with less than $50 million in overall assets (all in real terms). Medium banks have assets of $50 million to $250 million, and larger banks have assets in excess of $250 million. Banks are assigned to these categories for each period in which they are in operation. Thus, if a bank grows from $100 million in assets in 1987 to $500 million in 1997, that bank will first be considered a medium-sized entity, and later, after crossing the arbitrary size threshold, will be a larger bank for the purpose of our specification.

The econometric unraveling of this volatility is easily motivated by basic portfolio theory. In that spirit, we model a bank's exposure to a country as dependent on the real rate of returns on investments in that country c, which are assumed to be functions of local interest rates, i_t^c and on real GDP growth rates, $GGDP_t^c$. These foreign country fundamentals are assessed relative to home market conditions, captured by U.S. real interest rates and U.S. real GDP growth. Thus, we express the (log) claims of bank i into country c at time t, Exp_t^{ic}, as[10]

(1) $\qquad \text{Exp}_t^{ic} = a_0^i + a_1^i t + a_2^r + a_2^r t + b \cdot i_t^c + c \cdot i_t^{us} + d \cdot \text{GGDP}_t^c$

$\qquad\qquad + e \cdot \text{GGDP}_t^{us}.$

The terms $a^i + a_1^i t$ allow for the possibility that some banks have higher average changes and higher trend changes in the foreign exposure of their claims, independent of the time series variables in our specification. The terms $a^r + a_2^r t$ allow for the possibility that, regardless of observable fundamentals, some regions are more popular destinations for investment across banks. This popularity is modeled as having mean and trend components.

In order to avoid estimation problems potentially arising from the unit root properties of GDP growth, real interest rate, and claim series, we first difference equation (1). With this differencing, the bank and regional constant terms drop out, and the bank and regional trend terms enter the resulting first-difference specification in levels.

(2) $\qquad \Delta\text{Exp}_t^{ic} = a_1^i + a_2^r + b \cdot \Delta i_t^c + c \cdot \Delta i_t^{us} + d \cdot \Delta\text{GGDP}_t^c$

$\qquad\qquad + e \cdot \Delta\text{GGDP}_t^{us}$

Equation (2) is our basic testing specification, stating that the *change* in a U.S. bank claims on any country has the following: a bank-specific component common across all regions (which can represent a trend toward or against further internationalization of a bank's overall exposure level); a region-specific component (which can represent a trend change in the popularity of claims of particular regions); components correlated with changes in foreign country and in U.S. real interest rates; and components correlated with changes in GDP growth rates for the foreign country and for the United States.

Using this specification, we pose the following questions to the bank data on country exposures:

- Do banks adjust exposure to different regions in similar ways in response to fluctuations in the macroeconomic fundamentals of those regions? Empirically, this translates into tests for common b and d across regions.
- Is U.S. bank exposure to some regions relatively more sensitive to changes in U.S. interest rates and U.S. output performance? Empirically, this translates into tests for common c and e across countries.

---

10. We performed a parallel analysis using the share of country c claims in the bank's portfolio (i.e., claims relative to bank assets), instead of merely examining the changes in the actual bank claims on country c. The few substantive differences in results are noted later in this section.

- Are smaller banks generally more volatile lenders? Empirically, this would translate into systematic differences in estimated coefficients b, c, d, and e across banks, divided by size.

To estimate the elasticities of country claims with respect to fundamentals, we gather country-specific data on real GDP and real interest rates. Although our country sample initially contains 200 countries in which U.S. banks may have claims, we trim the sample in a number of reasonable dimensions. First, most banks have held positions in a much smaller set of countries. Looking across all banks together, on average banks maintain exposures with respect to twenty to twenty-five countries. Again, the aggregates mask big differences across larger and smaller banks (appendix table 4A.2). The larger banks in our sample (in the 4th quartile) tend to be invested in many more countries, with the average across these banks at eighty-six countries in the late 1980s, declining to sixty-six countries in the late 1990s. Overall, compared with smaller and mid-sized banks, larger banks have a greater number of countries in which they maintain relatively smaller foreign exposures.

Moreover, there are some countries in which U.S. banks have little or no exposure. By deleting these countries, we eliminate 51 of the 180 countries for which banks individually could provide foreign exposure data.[11] Additional countries are dropped from our sample due to the absence of adequate data on interest rates or GDP.[12] Because more data are generally available on GDP than on interest rates by country, we run the regression specification in a number of ways to generate appropriate insights on GDP and interest rate elasticities, while maximizing the number of countries and interval of observations explored. We find that the regression results are robust to the slightly narrower data sample that includes country real interest rates as well as real GDP growth. Consequently we report only the fully specified regressions.

We also want to limit the downward bias on significance that could potentially arise from keeping in the sample the large number of banks with very small foreign portfolio shares. The large quantity of bank observations with foreign exposure shares well below 1 percent of bank assets indicates that a relatively small number of U.S. banks account for a large share of the

11. Among the 200 initial "country" choices for reporting are about 20 international organizations and regional aggregates. We delete these "country" observations immediately. For our econometrics, we reduce the sample of countries examined by eliminating countries where U.S. banks, *in aggregate,* have less than $10 million of total exposure. With other data-related exclusions, we are left with 105 countries for the regression analysis.

12. We generally use lending rates (IFS 60P), "the lending rate to meet the short and medium term financing needs of the private sector, differentiated by credit worthiness of borrowers and objectives of financing" (IMF 2001). If this rate is unavailable for a country, we use deposit rates (IFS 60L) or treasury bill rates (IFS 60C). Appendix table 4A.3 details which countries are ultimately included in our empirical specifications, along with a categorization of which countries fall under the heading of Europe, Latin America, Asia, Africa, and other regions.

Table 4.8   Regression Analysis Using Full Panel of Banks and Branches, Unweighted

	Industrialized Countries	Developing Countries				
		Europe	Latin America	Asia	Africa	Middle East
Δi_t^c	0.026	0.000	0.000	0.043	−0.019	−0.001
	(0.044)	(0.001)	(0.000)	(0.031)	(0.045)	(0.003)
Δi_t^{us}	−0.074***	−0.020	0.042*	−0.098**	0.017	−0.102
	(0.015)	(0.623)	(0.021)	(0.041)	(0.155)	(0.116)
$\Delta GGDP_t^c$	−0.001	0.000	−0.001	−0.001**	0.001	0.005
	(0.003)	(0.000)	(0.005)	(0.001)	(0.050)	(0.024)
$\Delta GGDP_t^{us}$	−0.106***	−0.134	0.063**	−0.142**	0.011	−0.135
	(0.021)	(0.312)	(0.029)	(0.056)	(0.215)	(0.158)
Adjusted R^2	0.485					
N	21,700					

Note: Standard errors in parentheses. All regressions include regional fixed effects and bank fixed effects. Includes only bank observations with foreign exposure exceeding 1 percent of bank assets.

***Statistical significance at the 1 percent level.

**Statistical significance at the 5 percent level.

*Statistical significance at the 10 percent level.

overall bank foreign exposure. We trim the data sample to that used in the first section of table 4.3 by eliminating from the reported regressions all observations for which bank total foreign exposure is less than 1 percent of total bank assets.

4.3.1   Results

Regressions based on equation (2) demonstrate significant differences in the effects of fundamentals on bank claims on countries in different regions. In table 4.8 we include all bank observations. In table 4.9 we report the results of regressions that differentiate across banks on the basis of size. In the reported specifications, the results are unweighted. The interpretation is that the results describe what—on average—influences the claims of individual banks, irrespective of differences across banks in the relative size of their claims on countries. The results should not, therefore, be viewed as describing the evolution of total credit to specific countries or regions.

The first row of table 4.8 shows that, across all U.S. banks reporting foreign exposures, the claims on specific countries are on average relatively insensitive to fluctuations in the real interest rates of those countries. Moreover, the GDP growth rates of both industrialized and emerging-market economies do not generally influence the claims on these countries by the average reporting bank.[13] The lack of significance of own-country GDP

13. This result also appears in regressions using portfolio shares of country claims (exposure to a country relative to U.S. bank total assets) as the dependent variable.

Table 4.9　　　　　**Regression Results, by Region and by Bank Size (unweighted specification)**

	Industrialized Countries	Developing Countries				
		Europe	Latin America	Asia	Africa	Middle East
A. Banks with Assets below $50 Million						
Δi_t^c	0.157**	0.000	0.000	0.021	−0.010	−0.001
	(0.078)	(0.001)	(0.000)	(0.035)	(0.046)	(0.003)
Δi_t^{us}	−0.086***	−0.052	0.025	0.011	0.263	−0.089
	(0.023)	(0.624)	(0.027)	(0.092)	(0.183)	(0.117)
$\Delta GGDP_t^c$	0.000	0.000	−0.001	−0.001	0.010	0.003
	(0.003)	(0.000)	(0.007)	(0.001)	(0.050)	(0.024)
$\Delta GGDP_t^{us}$	−0.126***	−0.293	0.041	0.029	0.313	−0.114
	(0.032)	(0.333)	(0.037)	(0.127)	(0.251)	(0.160)
Adjusted R^2	0.2585					
N	10,912					
B. Banks with Assets between $50 Million and $250 Million						
Δi_t^c	0.043		−0.003	0.153*	−0.843*	
	(0.054)		(0.003)	(0.085)	(0.465)	
Δi_t^{us}	−0.025		−0.055	−0.197***	−0.747**	0.096
	(0.026)		(0.046)	(0.062)	(0.355)	(1.205)
$\Delta GGDP_t^c$	−0.027***		−0.017	−0.056		
	(0.011)		(0.049)	(0.070)		
$\Delta GGDP_t^{us}$	−0.041		−0.077	−0.278***	−1.051**	−0.015
	(0.036)		(0.064)	(0.086)	(0.497)	(0.941)
Adjusted R^2	0.3649					
N	4,250					
C. Banks with Assets Greater Than $250 Million						
Δi_t^c	−0.178*	0.270	0.000	0.175	−0.255	10.212
	(0.101)	(0.244)	(0.000)	(0.109)	(0.232)	(7.215)
Δi_t^{us}	0.109***	5.571	0.121**	−0.069	−0.904	
	(0.027)	(8.520)	(0.052)	(0.063)	(0.981)	
Δi_t^c	0.006	−0.030	−0.002	−0.082	1.035*	
	(0.014)	(0.042)	(0.009)	(0.059)	(0.534)	
Δi_t^{us}	−0.148***	0.643	0.169**	−0.112	0.423	
	(0.038)	(1.003)	(0.072)	(0.087)	(0.985)	
Adjusted R^2	0.2028					
N	6,538					

Notes: Standard errors in parentheses. All regressions include regional fixed effects and bank fixed effects. Table includes only bank observations with foreign exposure exceeding 1 percent of bank assets.

***Significant at the 1 percent level.

**Significant at the 5 percent level.

*Significant at the 10 percent level.

growth and own-country interest rates for U.S. banks' claims on emerging markets is a consistent pattern observed across regression specifications.

More important determinants of U.S. bank claims abroad are the patterns in U.S. macroeconomic variables. Industrialized and Latin American country regions are the two regions in which these U.S. variables often have statistically significant effects. All else being equal, when interest rates rise in the United States, U.S. banks consistently reduce their claims on other industrialized countries, suggesting the possibility of substitution across markets. Likewise, higher U.S. GDP growth is consistently associated with reduced claims on other industrialized countries.

Higher U.S. GDP growth and interest rates have mixed effects on emerging markets, with some sensitivity to the regression specifications. For example, higher U.S. interest rates are associated with higher claims on Latin American countries in the unweighted regressions of table 4.8. Similar results arise in a claims-weighted version of this regression. For Asia, the sign of this relationship is negative for the average bank reported in table 4.8 but becomes positive in claims-weighted specifications. The direction of U.S. GDP growth on emerging-market claims is consistent across the unweighted and weighted regression specifications but differs across Latin America and Asia. Claims on Latin America expanded for a reporting U.S. bank when the United States grew faster, but on average claims on Asian countries contracted.

Next, we consider whether the broad description arising from table 4.8 is also pertinent when we divide banks according to their size but again compute regressions for the "average bank," that is, regressions unweighted by bank size or total claims.[14] We find that there are in fact observable differences across smaller and larger banks in the determinants of their claims on foreign countries. These differences are apparent through comparisons of parts A, B, and C of table 4.9.

First, for the banks in the smallest asset class category (part A), we observe differences in the role of fundamentals for claims on the (non-U.S.) industrialized countries versus those on emerging markets. While increases in industrialized country real interest rates are associated with larger claims on industrialized countries, claims on emerging markets are uncorrelated with real local lending rates. Claims on the (non-U.S.) industrialized countries fall when U.S. interest rates rise, consistent with some substitution between claims on the United States and other industrialized country borrowers. For the average small bank, none of the emerging-market macroeconomic fundamentals included in the regressions were statistically significant and qualitatively important determinants of changes in their claims

---

14. Bank size has been shown to be a relevant consideration in the U.S. lending markets: For example, as Hancock and Wilcox (1998) show, in response to declines in their own capital small banks shrank their loan portfolios considerably more than did large banks.

on specific emerging markets. These patterns of results were robust to the inclusion of crisis period dummy variables in the regression specifications.[15]

For the larger banks shown in part C, we again see the pattern of local country macroeconomic fundamentals being important mainly in the context of U.S. bank claims on industrialized countries. Within the emerging-market groupings, U.S. bank claims on Latin American countries expand when the United States grows faster and when U.S. interest rates rise.[16] For the other emerging-markets regions, claims on specific countries are not as tightly correlated with the macroeconomic fundamentals.

Finally, we generally observe larger point estimates on the coefficients in the regression specifications using observations for the larger U.S. banks. The differences in these point estimates are statistically significant in the context of claims on Latin American countries. Especially with respect to positions in emerging-market economies, the regressions suggest that trends in claims may be very significant for the smaller banks, as opposed to emerging market macroeconomic fundamentals. By contrast, larger bank positions have less important regional trends and appear to be more responsive to fundamentals. These patterns of results are robust to inclusion of crisis period dummy variables.

4.4   Concluding Remarks

Foreign credit to emerging markets is viewed as one means for deepening emerging capital markets and potentially reducing the severity of crises when they occur. One relevant issue is the stability of foreign bank claims on these markets and the source of volatility in these claims. U.S. banks generally seem to have been steady providers of credit to these markets in the face of fluctuations in emerging-market growth rates and interest rates. Because lending by banks within emerging markets is likely to be more sensitive to conditions in their home markets, these results suggest that the U.S. banks may contribute to more stable overall credit supplies in emerging markets.

On the other hand, the bank claims on emerging markets by large U.S. banks are sensitive to U.S. cyclical conditions. The countries end up with a more diversified supply of credit, but claims on emerging markets could fluctuate with conditions in foreign markets. The patterns of exposure of

15. We considered five distinct crisis dates: Latin American debt crisis (1984:1–1985:1); ERM crisis (1992:3–1993:1); Tequila crisis (1994:4–1995:1); Asia crisis (1997:3–1997:4); and Russian default (1998:3–1998:4). We entered these five period dummies into the regression specification of equation (2), permitting the effects to differ across the countries of the six regions in which U.S. banks have positions.

16. For claims on Latin America, there are qualitative differences between these results and those generated using U.S. bank portfolio allocations. The alternative approach shows that claims on Latin American countries, when measured relative to the overall assets of the specific banks, fall—not rise—significantly as U.S. GDP growth and real interest rates increase.

small U.S. banks may be driven more by trends, while the exposures of larger U.S. banks may be driven more by changes in market fundamentals. There is little evidence of systematic differences in the behavior of U.S. bank claims across periods associated with international financial crises.

Appendix

Table 4A.1   **U.S. Bank Conditional Exposures by Region**

	Industrialized Countries	Developing Europe	Latin America	Asia	Africa	Middle East
1984–89						
Industrialized countries	1.00	0.40	0.94	0.64	0.38	0.38
Developing Europe	0.98	1.00	0.99	0.86	0.74	0.78
Latin America	0.92	0.39	1.00	0.61	0.37	0.49
Asia	0.99	0.54	0.98	1.00	0.54	0.61
Africa	1.00	0.78	0.99	0.91	1.00	0.73
Middle East	0.97	0.62	0.98	0.78	0.55	1.00
1990–95						
Industrialized countries	1.00	0.25	0.85	0.57	0.27	0.27
Developing Europe	0.98	1.00	0.98	0.80	0.68	0.83
Latin America	0.86	0.25	1.00	0.53	0.27	0.51
Asia	0.96	0.34	0.89	1.00	0.36	0.58
Africa	0.97	0.61	0.96	0.77	1.00	0.79
Middle East	0.90	0.38	0.91	0.62	0.40	1.00
1996–2000						
Industrialized countries	1.00	0.36	0.89	0.62	0.34	0.34
Developing Europe	0.96	1.00	0.96	0.81	0.63	0.82
Latin America	0.78	0.32	1.00	0.53	0.31	0.52
Asia	0.92	0.45	0.89	1.00	0.46	0.60
Africa	0.95	0.66	0.98	0.86	1.00	0.86
Middle East	0.87	0.50	0.94	0.66	0.49	1.00

Note: Conditional on activity in a region in the stub column, the row entries provide the probability of also having a position in the other regions.

Table 4A.2   **Average Number of Countries in Which Banks Have Foreign Exposures**

	Exposures		
	1984–89	1990–95	1996–2000
All reporting banks	27	20	21
Quartile 1	14	12	13
Quartile 2	24	14	15
Quartile 3	35	33	35
Quartile 4	86	76	66

Note: Banks are divided into quartiles according to their asset size.

Table 4A.3   Countries Included in Regression Analysis, Using IFS Classification

	Developing Countries				
Industrialized Countries	Developing Europe	Western Hemisphere (Latin America)	Asia and Pacific	Africa	Middle East
Australia	Bulgaria	Argentina	Bangladesh	Chad	Bahrain
Austria	Croatia	Bahamas	China	Congo	Egypt
Belgium	Cyprus	Barbados	Fiji	Côte d'Ivoire	Israel
Canada	Czech	Belize	Hong Kong	Equatorial	Jordan
Denmark	Republic	Bolivia	India	Guinea	Kuwait
Finland	Estonia	Brazil	Indonesia	Gabon	Oman
France	Hungary	Chile	Malaysia	Ghana	Saudi Arabia
Germany	Kazakhstan	Colombia	Mongolia	Guinea-	
Greece	Latvia	Costa Rica	Pakistan	Bissau	
Iceland	Lithuania	Dominican	Papua New	Kenya	
Ireland	Macedonia	Republic	Guinea	Mauritius	
Italy	Poland	Ecuador	The	Morocco	
Japan	Romania	El Salvador	Philippines	Niger	
Luxembourg	Russia	Guatemala	Singapore	Nigeria	
The	Slovakia	Guyana	South Korea	Senegal	
Netherlands	Slovenia	Haiti	Sri Lanka	South Africa	
New Zealand	Turkey	Honduras	Thailand	Tunisia	
Norway	Ukraine	Jamaica	Vanuatu	Zambia	
Portugal		Mexico			
Spain		Nicaragua			
Sweden		Panama			
Switzerland		Paraguay			
United		Peru			
Kingdom		Suriname			
		Trinidad and Tobago			
		Uruguay			
		Venezuela			

References

Bomfim, Antulio and William Nelson. 1999. Profits and balance sheet developments at U.S. commercial banks in 1998. *Federal Reserve Bulletin* 85 (June): 369–95.

Dages, B. Gerard, Linda Goldberg, and Daniel Kinney. 2000. Foreign and domestic bank participation in emerging markets: Lessons from Mexico and Argentina. *Economic Policy Review* 6 (3): 17–36.

Goldberg, Linda, and Michael Klein. 1998. Foreign direct investment, trade and real exchange rate linkages in developing countries. In *Managing capital flows and exchange rates: Lessons from the Pacific Basin,* ed. Reuven Glick, 73–100. Cambridge: Cambridge University Press.

Hancock, Diana, and James Wilcox. 1998. The credit crunch and the availability of credit to small business. *Journal of Banking and Finance* 22 (August): 983–1014.

International Monetary Fund (IMF). 2001. *International Financial Statistics* 54 (12): 20.

Palmer, David. 2000. U.S. bank exposure to emerging-market countries during recent financial crises. *Federal Reserve Bulletin* 86 (2): 81–96.

Peek, Joe, and Eric Rosengren. 1997. The international transmission of financial shocks: The case of Japan. *American Economic Review* 87 (4): 495–505.

———. 2000. Collateral damage: Effects of the Japanese bank crisis on real activity in the United States. *American Economic Review* 90 (1): 30–45.

Comment   Simon Johnson

Linda S. Goldberg has provided us with fascinating information on three important questions. First, which U.S. banks lend outside the United States? Second, what is the pattern of this international lending, and how has this changed over time? Third, which parts of this bank lending are relatively volatile, and what drives this volatility? On all three issues, Goldberg both provides us with valuable new facts and points the way to further empirical and theoretical research.

Goldberg establishes that a great deal of cross-border lending is accounted for by relatively small banks, particularly those focused on Latin America. Very large banks also lend internationally but do so more through their own subsidiaries. Over time, fewer banks have been engaged in international lending, presumably as a result of bank consolidation. However, some of the smaller banks have increased their foreign exposure shares over time. There has also been an interesting increase in lending to the nonbank private sector.

Goldberg also shows that the portfolio share of foreign lending for U.S. banks is moved by U.S. gross domestic product (GDP) growth, not by U.S. interest rates (with interesting differences between the coefficients on lending to developed and emerging markets). This lending also does not appear to be sensitive to local GDP fluctuations or to movements in local real interest rates.

Goldberg has created a fascinating new data set that allows fresh insight into important questions. She has also covered a great deal of ground in terms of the preliminary analysis presented here. My suggestions are intended to indicate possible areas for further research (probably in the form of several separate papers).

My first question concerns exactly why U.S. banks lend overseas. Does this help them generate a superior return on equity, or does it represent

Simon Johnson is an associate professor of entrepreneurship at the Sloan School of Management, Massachusetts Institute of Technology, and a faculty research fellow of the National Bureau of Economic Research.

some form of agency problem—or, perhaps, even a way to circumvent regulatory controls (e.g., perhaps it is easier to engage in connected lending to overseas affiliates)? Why is there so much more lending to Latin America by smaller banks than to Europe or Asia or anywhere else? Why does lending to Latin America have different characteristics, for example in terms of its sensitivity to U.S. GDP growth?

The volatility of U.S. bank lending could be usefully compared in more detail to that of local lending in various markets. Goldberg has already looked at this question in other work, but this new data set should allow further insight. Does it help or hurt stability when there is a large amount of lending by U.S. banks in a particular economy? Do U.S. banks pull out at the first sign of trouble, or are they able to take a longer view? Is there evidence that their presence is at all stabilizing, compared with the behavior of local banks? (See, e.g., the recent work of Rafael La Porta and Florencio Lopez-de-Silanes on Mexican banks after 1994.) The preliminary results presented here suggest that U.S. banks are not volatile lenders, but it would be helpful to look at this issue in more detail (and possibly to write the conclusive paper on this topic).

It would be useful to know more about the nature of overseas borrowers from U.S. banks. Some more work may be needed to combine this data with information on the reported exposure of publicly traded banks (and when they take loan loss provisions), but it will probably repay the effort. Are U.S. banks lending to exporters? Does this practice skim the cream off local banking relationships? Does this address the concerns about the constraints on financing development in weak legal systems measured by Rajan and Zingales (1998)? Does it help to keep the economy going even if local banks collapse? Quantifying these various effects would be very useful.

Looking at particular countries where there has been severe disruption of the banking system would be helpful (e.g., Indonesia from 1998.) To get at these issues, it might be worth starting the data set a little earlier (e.g., in the late 1970s or 1980) to compare the effect of several crises, for example those in 1982 and 1994–95. These data could also be related to controversies about the timing and causes of crises.

Does the nature of U.S. lending differ according to the institutional characteristics of the countries involved? For example, is lending to European Organization for Economic Cooperation and Development (OECD) countries different in a measurable way compared with lending to emerging markets or just poorer countries? Using the La Porta et al. (1998) classification of institutional systems would be useful here (e.g., as an alternative to the geographic classification in table 4.1).

Overall, Goldberg has written an extremely useful paper that provides important facts for researchers and regulators. It is my strong hope that Goldberg will use this information to write several more important papers.

References

La Porta, Rafael, Florencio Lopez-de-Silanes, Andrei Shleifer, and Robert W. Vishny. 1998. Law and finance. *Journal of Political Economy* 106:1113–55.
Rajan, Raghuram, and Luigi Zingales. 1998. Financial dependence and growth. *American Economic Review* 88:559–86.

Discussion Summary

Charles W. Calomiris made three suggestions. He first offered the following explanation for the cyclicality of domestic and foreign bank lending in emerging markets. During a boom, domestic banks have access to cheap capital (from retained earnings) and thus can expand lending, which they sustain even in the initial contraction phase because they have a comparative advantage in identifying the quality of loans. During the period of deep recession, however, domestic banks cannot lend (because they have lost most of their capital), while foreign banks enter the market as a result of relaxed regulation on entry barriers. Thus, foreign lending is countercyclical. He suggested taking into account the business cycle of the recipient country when studying the bank-lending behavior.

His second suggestion was to isolate the relative capital cost effect from the portfolio opportunity effect by controlling for the cost of raising equity, as for example by using variables like underwriting costs. He also suggested to control for Spanish GDP cycle when studying Latin American countries.

Sebastian Edwards commented on the specific breakdown points of the period. The first subperiod of 1984–89 coincided with the Brady plan, at which time many banks exited the market; the end of the second subperiod of 1990–95 was around the time of Mexican crises, which also led many banks to go bankrupt.

He raised questions on the time series results of the paper because the sample period is very heterogeneous. For example, Argentina and Peru had hyperinflation, and Mexico underwent a series of crises; moreover, the banking sector in Latin America was very much regulated until 1989, and therefore the interest rates were not meaningful before that. He said that these structural changes during the sample period could be the reason for some of the strange findings in the paper (the dramatically different results for lending to Latin American and Europe). Lastly, Edwards suggested that one could do some more advanced studies on events such as financial integration by combining this data set and information on emerging markets' financial integration.

Rudi Dornbusch raised the question of whether the lending by small banks to Latin America is trade credit (which is safer and has extra tax benefits). He said that if this was the case, then one could run a gravity regression (before Andrew Rose does it) on lending of this particular sector. (Later in the discussion *Nouriel Roubini* conjectured that a large part of the lending of small U.S. banks in Latin America may reflect the money-laundering activities of small Miami banks instead of the provision of trade credits.)

Robert Dekle suggested that when looking at the transmission of shocks, one could include the nonperforming loan ratio and the Bank for International Settlements (BIS) capital ratio to capture the weakness of the banking sector.

Michael P. Dooley made the remark that a piece of the folklore is that European banks behave differently from the U.S. banks, so it would be interesting to include European banks as a control group and see whether U.S. banks are indeed different. He also suggested including variables such as the Federal Reserve Bank's ratings on emerging countries and the individual bank's loan loss experience in these countries in the regressions.

Joshua Aizenman suggested using exchange rates and measures of the probability of crises and country risk in the regressions.

Carlos A. Végh commented on the issue of volatility and cyclicality. First, what is the explanation for the fact that small foreign banks are more procyclical than big foreign banks? Second, he raised a question on the relative procyclicality of foreign banks compared to domestic banks. This is important for understanding whether foreign banks make cycles in these countries more or less pronounced. Third, he talked about the finding that U.S. banks' lending to emerging countries is highly correlated with the U.S. GDP. He said that when the United States is in a boom, interest rates go up, which typically implies that the GDP growth in emerging economies goes down, so U.S. lending is countercyclical to the cycles of emerging countries.

Jeffrey A. Frankel, in support of Vegh's last argument, cited a paper by Calvo, Leiderman, and Reinhart in which the authors argue that a reason for the large capital inflow to emerging countries in the early 1990s was the slow growth of Japan and United States.

John McHale commented on the weak sensitivity of U.S. lending to economic conditions in emerging countries. He asked how consistent this was with the turnaround of capital inflows to emerging markets during crises, and whether the behavior of U.S. banks was different from that of non-U.S. banks. Second, he commented on the finding that foreign lending is insensitive to local interest rates. As he pointed out, high interest rates can be attractive to foreign investors but may also signal bad economic conditions (a crisis). The finding of the weak effects might be the result of using pooled data, which suggests that one should control for crisis periods versus regular periods.

Roubini suggested that this rich data set could be used to test hypotheses related to theories about capital flight, and in particular to test whether capital flights occur because of common creditor effects or contagion. This can be done by looking at what motivates banks' behavior during crises.

Linda S. Goldberg agreed that cycles are very important in studying foreign banks' lending behavior and indicated that she intended to incorporate that angle in subsequent work. This, she said, would contribute to a better understanding of the role of interest rates. She also said that it would be worthwhile to rethink the way regions were defined. An alternative could be to define country groups by their income levels. She agreed that the event study that Roubini suggested would be interesting and noted that one could also compare the U.S. banks' and Spanish banks' lending in Latin American countries. On the volatility of U.S. (or overall foreign) banks' lending relative to domestic bank lending, she cited one of her earlier studies. In that paper she showed that lending from both foreign and domestic private banks was procyclical (with respect to the local economy), but that the local lending was more procyclical because one of the sources of local banks' funding—local deposits—is more procyclical.

The Role of Large Players in Currency Crises

Giancarlo Corsetti, Paolo Pesenti, and Nouriel Roubini

5.1 Introduction

What role, if any, do large traders and other highly leveraged institutions (HLIs) such as hedge funds (HFs) and proprietary desks of commercial and investment banks play in determining and propagating market volatility during crisis episodes? Some policy makers and analysts have expressed concern that the activity of large players in small markets ("big elephants in small ponds") may trigger crises that are not justified by fundamentals, destabilizing foreign exchange and other asset markets, creating systemic risk, and threatening the stability of the international financial system.

A typical argument is that the presence of large agents increases a country's vulnerability to a crisis because their short-term portfolio strategies provide a focal point for speculative behavior and induce small investors, other things being equal, to be more aggressive in their position-taking. True, phenomena such as herding (buying or selling an asset because other

Giancarlo Corsetti is professor of economics at the University of Rome III and a research fellow of the Center for Economic Policy Research. Paolo Pesenti is research officer at the Federal Reserve Bank of New York and a faculty research fellow of the National Bureau of Economic Research. Nouriel Roubini is associate professor of economics at the Stern School of Business, New York University, and a research associate of the National Bureau of Economic Research.

Special thanks go to Amil Dasgupta, Steve Morris, and Hyun Song Shin, with whom the authors had many useful discussions on the topic of this paper. The authors are also grateful to their discussant, Jaume Ventura, whose comments were very helpful in redrafting section 5.2. Sebastian Edwards, Jeffrey Frankel, Thad Russell, Dorothy Sobol, and seminar participants at the NBER conference offered many valuable suggestions. The authors thank Raymond Guiteras and Scott Nicholson for excellent research assistance and Rojit Vanjani for data support. The views expressed herein are those of the authors and not necessarily those of the NBER, the Federal Reserve Bank of New York, the Federal Reserve System, or any other institution with which the authors are affiliated.

participants buy or sell at the same time), momentum trading (buying an asset when its price rises and selling when its price falls), noise trading, bandwagon effects, short-termism, and the like can occur in financial markets even if all agents are small and atomistic. However, market power stemming from size, reputation, and ability to leverage may give large players a significant role in affecting market dynamics with destabilizing consequences.

Specifically, concerns about the aggressive, possibly manipulative, practices of large traders were expressed in 1998 by the authorities of a number of small and medium-sized economies. To assess these allegations, the HLI working group of the Financial Stability Forum (FSF) established in 1999 a study group on market dynamics in small and medium-sized economies, which conducted a study of the 1998 market turmoil and the role played by HLIs in six countries (Hong Kong, Australia, New Zealand, South Africa, Singapore, and Malaysia).

Although the group could not reach consensus on the allegations of destabilization and distortion of market integrity, the report found circumstantial evidence of aggressive trading practices, pointing out the material role played by large players in some crises. Notably, the conclusions of the Market Dynamics Study Group, published in April 2000 (Financial Stability Forum 2000), were somewhat different from a previous study on HFs by the International Monetary Fund (IMF 1998). The IMF study, which was limited to the events in Asia up to late 1997, had concluded that HFs had not played a significant role in the early market turbulence.

In light of the results of these reports and, more generally, in light of the policy and academic debate on the 1997–98 events, our contribution aims to reconsider in detail, at both theoretical and empirical levels, the role that large players can play in currency crises and market dynamics.

This paper is organized as follows. In section 5.2 we present a stylized model of speculative attacks, analyzing the effect of large investors on the vulnerability of a country to currency crises. We first focus on a model in which speculative attacks are the outcome of self-fulfilling shifts in expectations from "good" to "bad" equilibria, in situations in which the economic fundamentals are neither too strong (ruling out crises altogether) nor too weak (so that a crisis is unavoidable).

Next, we consider a model with asymmetric and private information, building on the "global-games" literature (Morris and Shin 2000, Corsetti et al. 2000). In this model, the impact of a large trader on the market depends on the interaction of three elements: size, reputation for quality of information, and the ability to signal its portfolio position to the rest of the market. The key result is that, in general, the presence of large investors makes all other investors more aggressive, in the sense that the latter choose to liquidate their currency positions for stronger economic fundamentals relative to the case in which there are no large investors.

We conclude the theoretical section by discussing extensions of the model and several open issues: Do large traders destabilize markets? How large must a trader be to have a significant impact on market behavior? Do large players always benefit from signalling their trading? Or do they benefit from trading quietly to avoid adverse movement of prices while building their positions? Do they inhibit contrarian trade? Can large players manipulate markets (through cornering, "talking one's book," spreading rumors, etc.)?

On the basis of the results of section 5.2, section 5.3 provides an overview and an extension of the empirical literature on the behavior of large investors in currency markets. We first look at the evidence on the correlation between exchange rate movements and major market participants' net currency positions. We next consider a few recent case studies. A number of sources, ranging from press articles to academic case studies, have suggested that large HFs and HLIs played a role in numerous episodes of market distress in the 1990s, including the following: the exchange rate mechanism crisis in 1992–93; the 1994 U.S. bond market turbulence; the 1994–95 Mexican peso crisis; the speculative attack on the Thai baht in 1997; the fall of the Korean won in 1997; the crisis of the Malaysian ringgit in 1997–98; the "double play" on the Hong Kong stock and foreign exchange markets in 1998; the pressures on the Australian dollar in June and August 1998; the unraveling of the "carry trade" in the summer of 1998 and the rally of the Japanese yen; and the Russia to Brazil contagion episode in the summer and fall of 1998. We focus on a sample of these events and conclude by highlighting the links between our analysis and the findings of the FSF (2000) study.

There are two important premises to our assessment of the role of large players in crisis episodes. First, in the context of our study, a *large player* is defined as an agent with market power. The influence of a large player on the market outcome is not, however, mechanically related to its size, as measured by the value of asset holdings or market share. Clearly, players with equal size can differ in their ability to influence the portfolio strategies of other agents in the market, owing to, for instance, access to superior information or special forecasting ability. There are a number of reasons to expect a positive association between a trader's size and its reputation for quality of information. For instance, traders controlling a large portfolio of assets are able to devote more resources to data collection and analysis and thus are more likely to obtain superior information. However, large traders need not be better informed in all circumstances. If smaller market participants can better exploit information asymmetries and other market inefficiencies, the actions of large traders may have only limited influence. To shed light on this issue, our analysis is carried out under different assumptions about the precision of the large trader's information relative to the rest of the market.

Second, while herding may have exacerbated swings in capital flows and the ensuing changes in asset prices, it was a large set of investors—domestic and foreign, small and large, highly leveraged and not—who jointly contributed to market volatility in the turmoil episodes of the 1990s. Thus, although it is important to study the specific role that large HLIs might have played in these episodes, it is crucial to understand their role in the broader macroeconomic context in which these events occurred. In fact, most of the crisis episodes considered in this study unfolded against the backdrop of deteriorating macroeconomic fundamentals, policy uncertainties, and structural weaknesses.

5.2   Modeling the Role of Large Traders in Speculative Attacks

In this section we analyze leading theories of currency and financial crises, with the goal of understanding the role of large traders in generating and sustaining speculative attacks. We consider two classes of models of coordination games. The first allows for multiple instantaneous equilibria and sunspots, therefore interpreting the crisis as a switch from one rational-expectations equilibrium to another. The second focuses on games in which agents rely on private information in forming their beliefs about the fundamentals of the economy, as well as about other agents' beliefs and strategies. In these latter games, known as global games, the nature of crises is rooted not in the multiplicity of equilibria but in a stochastic flow of unobservable private information.

Our analysis focuses on static games, analyzing the decision process of agents who have to decide, independently and simultaneously, whether or not to attack a currency. A subsection deals with an example of a dynamic game with Bayesian learning (as discussed in Dasgupta 2001), in which agents may choose to take a position before the rest of the market or to wait so as to gain information by observing trading activity. We conclude with a discussion of open issues, pointing at a new generation of models that synthesize desirable features from different approaches.

5.2.1   A Unified Analytical Framework

To begin, consider a small open economy where the central bank pegs the exchange rate at some parity. The economy is populated by a continuum of risk-neutral traders, each of whom can take an infinitesimal position against the currency. In addition, there may be a single trader who can take a "large"—that is, discrete—position against the currency.

Let ℓ denote the mass of financial resources that are mobilized by (small and large) speculators when attacking the currency. The variable ℓ varies between zero (nobody attacks the currency) and 1 (the whole market attacks the currency).[1] As a stylized way to model heterogeneity in agents' size, we allow for a single large player that can mobilize resources up to $\lambda \le 1$. The combined mass of resources available to small traders then amounts to $1 - \lambda$.

Because the focus of the analysis is on speculative attacks, we abstract

---

1. To motivate the boundaries on ℓ, one can think of factors such as credit constraints, short-sale restrictions, or prudential guidelines limiting the size of speculative open positions in a currency market.

from welfare-related considerations (a devaluation can be either good or bad for the economy), so the reasons that monetary authorities decide to relinquish the peg are not explicitly analyzed. It may be helpful to keep in mind the textbook example of an economy endowed with a stock of international reserves, where the central bank is willing to defend the exchange rate only as long as reserves are above some predetermined critical level. The central bank sets this level based on its assessment of the economic fundamentals of the country, indexed by θ in our model. The critical level is low when fundamentals are strong (θ is high): the central bank is willing to use a large amount of reserves to defend the exchange rate. Conversely, the critical level is high when fundamentals are weak (θ is low): even a mild speculative attack can force the central bank to abandon the peg.

The condition for a currency collapse is therefore

$$(1) \qquad\qquad\qquad \ell \geq \theta.$$

Since $0 \leq \ell \leq 1$, a collapse always occurs if θ is negative (the economic outlook is so bad that the central bank has no incentive to maintain the peg even if no attack materializes) and never occurs if $\theta > 1$. A collapse may or may not occur for $0 \leq \theta \leq 1$, depending on whether the currency is attacked by a sufficient mass of speculators.

For simplicity, we assume that the ex post payoffs to individual agents are independent of the state of fundamentals.[2] From the viewpoint of each agent, taking a speculative position in the currency market entails a cost $t \leq 1$, including both transaction costs and the differential between the domestic and the foreign interest rate. Thus, if an agent attacks the currency but the currency docs not collapse, its ex post payoff is $-t$, that is, the loss due to transaction costs incurred when speculating. If, instead, the currency collapses, the ex post payoff is assumed to be $1 - t$. If the agent does not attack, the payoff is identically equal to 0. All of these payoffs are measured per unit of domestic currency.

Agents take their speculative positions independently and simultaneously.[3] The timing is as follows: (1) Agents have a uniform ignorance prior about θ—that is, θ is uniformly distributed over the real line.[4] At the beginning of the period, they receive a signal about the state of fundamentals.

---

2. As will be apparent in what follows, the extension to the general case would confirm and strengthen our results.

3. In most of our study, we abstract from intertemporal considerations and focus on one-period models. Below we discuss a model that allows for a sequential-move game among speculators.

4. As pointed out by Morris and Shin (2000), improper priors make it possible to concentrate on the updated beliefs of the traders conditional on their signals without taking into account the information contained in the prior distribution. In any case, results with the improper prior can be seen as the limiting case as the information in the prior density goes to zero. See Hartigan (1983) for a discussion of improper priors and Morris and Shin (section 2) for a discussion of the latter point.

(2) Agents take their speculative positions in the foreign exchange market at given prices; ℓ is determined. (3) The state of the economy θ is revealed. (4) The central bank either defends or devalues the exchange rate according to equation (1).

5.2.2   Models with Symmetric Information

Common Knowledge and Multiple Equilibria

We now discuss models of currency and financial crises that stress the role of multiple equilibria, focusing first on the baseline case in which all agents are atomistic. Consider the following specification of the information structure: previous to trading, *all* agents receive the same public signal y about the fundamentals θ:

$$(2) \qquad\qquad y = \theta + \tau\eta \qquad \tau > 0$$

where $E(\eta) = 0$ and the probability distribution function of η is symmetric and smooth (we write H for the cumulative distribution function).[5] Note that agents do not know the exact state of the fundamentals. Given the uniform prior about θ, their posterior distribution of the fundamentals is H, with mean y and standard deviation τ.

To calculate the expected payoff for an individual agent i, one needs to specify its conjecture about the positions taken by the rest of the market. Consider the two extreme conjectures, which will be the relevant ones in equilibrium. The first is that all agents other than i attack the currency. Conditional on $\ell = 1$, the expected payoff from attacking for i can be written as

$$(3) \qquad (1 - t)\Pr(\theta \leq 1 \mid y) - t\Pr(\theta > 1 \mid y) = H\left(\frac{1 - y}{\tau}\right) - t.$$

If the public signal is such that this expected payoff is nonnegative, it is optimal for i to speculate against the currency. Since all agents are identical, this must be true for everyone in the economy: when the above expression is nonnegative, $\ell = 1$ is an equilibrium.

The second conjecture is that no one attacks. Conditional on $\ell = 0$, the expected payoff from attacking is:

$$(4) \qquad (1 - t)\Pr(\theta \leq 1 \mid y) - t\Pr(\theta > 1 \mid y) = H\left(\frac{0 - y}{\tau}\right) - t.$$

As before, if the public signal is such that the individual expected payoff is negative, it is optimal for i not to attack the currency. As all agents are identical, $\ell = 0$ is an equilibrium. Note that equation (3) is larger than equation (4): Individual payoffs are strategic complements. That is, given the signal y, they are increasing in the action taken by other agents in the economy.

For the sake of comparison with the global-game model discussed below,

5. This implies $\Pr(\eta \leq x) = \Pr(\eta \geq -x) = H(x)$.

we now rearrange equations (3) and (4) to describe the optimal behavior by individual speculators in terms of "trigger strategies." Note that, conditional on everyone else attacking, the maximum value of the public signal at which an agent optimally chooses to attack is

(5) $$y^* \equiv 1 - \tau H^{-1}(t).$$

Conditional on $\ell = 1$, the optimal strategy pursued by any individual agent is to attack if and only if $y \leq y^*$. By the same token, if everyone else refrains from attacking ($\ell = 0$), the threshold value for an agent to choose not to attack is

(6) $$\underline{y}^* \equiv 0 - \tau H^{-1}(t).$$

Thus, conditional on $\ell = 0$, an agent refrains from speculation if and only if $y > \underline{y}^*$.

Now, either threshold is a rational-expectations equilibrium. However, what determines the choice of one threshold over the other is not explained by the model. Simply, it is assumed that exogenous uncertainty—the same for all individuals—drives the threshold selection. Note that, because $y^* > \underline{y}^*$, the model predicts that an attack will occur for certain (irrespective of which equilibrium threshold is selected) if $y \leq \underline{y}^*$, but it will never occur if $y > y^*$. In the first case, the signal about fundamentals is so bad that each individual's expected payoff from attacking is nonnegative regardless of the action taken by the rest of the market: everyone attacks the currency. In the second case, the expected payoff is negative even if everyone else attacks the currency: no one speculates.

When the public signal is in the range $\underline{y}^* < y \leq y^*$, the economy may or may not be hit by a speculative run on the currency, depending on which threshold is chosen by the speculators.[6] Note that for it is rational for each individual to participate in the attack only if everyone else attacks the currency. As all agents choose the same threshold, this model assumes common knowledge not only of the public signal on the fundamentals but also of the actions undertaken by every individual in the market. This means that, in equilibrium, each individual must somehow know that all the other agents have simultaneously chosen to attack.

Large Traders in Models with Symmetric Information

We now recast the model to allow for a large trader. The presence of a large trader does not affect the upper threshold, y^*, corresponding to an equilibrium in which all agents attack the currency. What *does* change is the lower threshold, $\underline{y}^*$. When the signal on the fundamentals is positive but

---

6. We should note here that a speculative attack by the entire market does not necessarily coincide ex post with a collapse of the currency, as this only occurs if the ex post value of the fundamentals θ is smaller than 1.

weak, the speculative firepower of a large investor may be sufficient to force a devaluation, even if no small agent participates in the attack. The expression for the lower threshold equation (6) is therefore replaced by

$$(7) \qquad\qquad \underline{y}^*(\lambda) \equiv \lambda - \tau H^{-1}(t).$$

Thus, the larger the trader's size λ, the larger the range of public signals that trigger an attack and the lower the range of signals over which an attack may or may not occur. The conclusion from this model is straightforward. The presence of a large trader increases the vulnerability of a peg, as this trader trivially solves the "coordination problem" in a speculative attack for signals in the interval between 0 and λ.

Although in this benchmark model we cannot analyze the effects of varying the relative precision of the large trader's information (the signal is the same for every agent), we can nonetheless derive an important result by varying the precision of the public signal. From equations (5) and (7), it is apparent that (if t is relatively small, i.e., $t < 1/2$) both thresholds $\underline{y}^*(\lambda)$ and y^* are increasing in τ. Higher uncertainty—say, a mean-preserving spread of the distribution of the public signal—leads all agents to raise the trigger for an attack, regardless of the equilibrium on which agents coordinate.

In equilibrium, small traders always take the same side of the market as the large one. To avoid misunderstandings of this model, we stress that this does not imply that the large trader has signalling ability or represents a focal point. For $y < \underline{y}^*(\lambda)$, the currency is expected to collapse even if no small trader attacks the currency. For $\underline{y}^*(\lambda) < y \le y^*$, the presence of a large trader makes no difference; in this region, an attack by a large trader does not represent a focal point, at least no more so than any other event relevant to the coordination of agents' expectations on a particular equilibrium. This is not to deny that signalling and focal points may be relevant in equilibrium selection. However, these elements require a different approach, possibly loosening the assumption of common knowledge about the fundamentals.

5.2.3   Models with Asymmetric Information

We now turn to a class of coordination games according to which incomplete information is the key element of a theory of speculative behavior. The approach in this section is based on the mechanism of equilibrium selection first analyzed by Carlsson and van Damme (1993) for the case of two agents, then in a series of papers by Morris and Shin for a continuum of agents, including a contribution to the theory of currency crises (Morris and Shin 1998). Building on this approach, Corsetti et al. (2000) have provided a comprehensive theory of the role of large traders in a currency crisis. The analysis in this subsection discusses this contribution in detail.

The main feature of the global-games approach to speculative crises is that agents do not share information about the fundamentals of the economy, but observe informative *private* signals about it. Even if the noise of the private signals becomes very small, individual information about the fundamentals never becomes common knowledge among traders. In other words, upon receiving its own signal, the representative trader can only *guess* the signals reaching the other traders, as well as their conjectures about each other's information and guesses. It cannot, however, count on the other traders to *know* its information and conjectures—each agent forms its beliefs based exclusively on its own information. This departure from the assumption of common knowledge of the signal is crucial for the results that follow.

The Global-Games Approach to Currency Speculation

Once again, we start by abstracting from the presence of a large trader (i.e., $\lambda = 0$). As in the previous section, agents have a uniform ignorance prior over θ; however, here there is no public signal to all agents. Rather, each small trader in the continuum receives a private signal,

$$(8) \qquad x_i = \theta + \sigma\varepsilon_i \qquad \sigma > 0,$$

where the distribution of ε_i is smooth and symmetric (we let F denote the cumulative distribution function). Although there is no public information about θ, the distribution of the fundamentals θ as well as of signals x_i is common knowledge.[7]

Conjecture that, as before, all agents (optimally) follow a trigger strategy: they attack if and only if their signal is below some optimally selected threshold x^*; otherwise, they refrain from attacking. As noise is independent of the fundamentals, the expected mass of agents attacking the currency is equal to the probability that any particular agent receives a signal below x^*. Thus, for a given x^*, the population of agents attacking the currency at θ will be

$$(9) \qquad \ell(x^*, \theta) = \Pr(x_i \le x^* \mid \theta) = F\left(\frac{x^* - \theta}{\sigma}\right).$$

---

7. To understand the logic of the model in the absence of common knowledge of the signal, it is useful to look at an example in which the noise in the private signal is distributed uniformly with a bounded support of size $\pm\beta$ around the realization of θ. Agent i knows that the fundamentals are distributed in an interval of size β on each side of x_i, that is, $\theta \in [x_i - \beta, x_i + \beta]$. As the realization of θ may fall on an extreme of this interval, agent i cannot exclude that the signal of agent j is equal to $x_i = x_i + 2\beta$. However, if agent j receives a signal as far as 2β from x_i, j concludes that θ is in an interval of size 2β around $x_i + 2\beta$ and, most importantly, cannot exclude that agent i's signal x_i is 4β distant from its actual position. Iterating once more the argument above, we see that agent i cannot exclude that agent j believes that agent i's own beliefs about agent j's signal are as far as 6β from x_i, and so on. Note the paradox in this result. Agent i is 100 percent sure that θ is β-close to i's own signal. Agent i also knows that all other agents get a signal within an interval of 2β. However, the fact that agents do not have common information useful to locate the position of the fundamentals makes them worry about the possibility that their opponents' beliefs about fundamentals and signals wander quite far away from where the fundamentals and the signals actually are.

Now, we know that a crisis occurs when ℓ is at least as large as θ, that is, when

$$(10) \qquad \ell(x^*, \theta) = F\left(\frac{x^* - \theta}{\sigma}\right) \geq \theta.$$

Thus, the maximum value of the fundamentals at which a crisis materializes must satisfy

$$(11) \qquad \ell(x^*, \theta^*) = F\left(\frac{x^* - \theta^*}{\sigma}\right) = \theta^*.$$

This means that, given x^*, the peg collapses for any realization of the fundamentals below θ^* and survives otherwise.

Next, if agents expect the currency to collapse for any $\theta \leq \theta^*$, the expected profit from an attack—conditional on receiving the signal x_i—is

$$(12) \qquad (1 - t)\Pr(\theta \leq \theta^* \mid x_i) - t\Pr(\theta > \theta^* \mid x_i) = F\left(\frac{\theta^* - x_i}{\sigma}\right) - t.$$

Because agents attack if and only if their expected profit is nonnegative, the minimum value of the signal x_i at which they attack, x^*, satisfies

$$(13) \qquad F\left(\frac{\theta^* - x^*}{\sigma}\right) - t = 0.$$

Thus, given θ^*, agents optimally choose to attack upon receiving a private signal smaller or equal to x^* as defined above.

The equations (11) and (13) represent a system of two equations in two unknowns (x^* and θ^*) that completely characterize the equilibrium of the model.[8] Solving this system, it is easy to see that the equilibrium in trigger strategies is unique. From equation (13) above, accounting for the symmetry of the signal, it follows that

$$(14) \qquad 1 - F\left(\frac{x^* - \theta^*}{\sigma}\right) = t.$$

Comparing equations (13) and (14), the threshold value for the fundamental is

$$(15) \qquad \theta^* = 1 - t.$$

Note that $1 - t$ is also the proportion of agents attacking the currency at $\theta = \theta^*$. Using this result in equation (11) yields a closed-form solution for the individual threshold:

---

8. The system above is a Bayes-Nash equilibrium. According to the standard definitions, a strategy for an agent is a rule that prescribes an action for each realization of the agent's private signal. A profile of strategies (one for each agent) is an equilibrium if, conditional on the information available to each agent i, and given the strategies followed by other agents, the action prescribed by the strategy followed by agent i maximizes the conditional expected payoff (utility).

(16) $x^* = \theta^* - \sigma F^{-1}(t) = 1 - t - \sigma F^{-1}(t).$

Note that, if we let the noise in the private signal go to zero, the trigger point tends to the threshold value for the fundamental: $x^* \to \theta^*$. As agents become more confident about the information content of their signal, the level of the optimal trigger tends to coincide with the threshold value θ^*. A well-known feature of this model is that not only is its trigger-strategies equilibrium unique, but agents also optimally select the trigger strategy characterized above over any other possible strategy. The proof of uniqueness can be found in Morris and Shin (2000).[9]

Large Traders in Models with Asymmetric Information

A large trader of size λ is now introduced in the economy. The small traders keep receiving private signals x_i with the properties stated above, and the large trader receives a private signal denoted by x_l:

(17) $x_l = \theta + \sigma_l \varepsilon_l \qquad \sigma_l > 0$

where the distribution of ε_l is smooth and symmetric (we write L for the cumulative distribution). Notably, σ_l can and will differ from σ. In other words, the precision of the signal of the large trader (which is the inverse of the variance of the signal σ_l^2) can differ from the precision of the signal of a typical small trader.

This is a realistic feature of the model. On the one hand, as argued in the introduction, it is widely believed that large traders tend to have access to superior information. On the other hand, even if large traders are better informed on average, under some circumstances the ranking of information may favor small traders. It is therefore useful to analyze both cases. In the model, it is assumed that all agents in the market are aware of their relative information precision; that is, the distribution of the signals, including the relative size of σ and σ_l, is common knowledge.

To derive the equilibrium, conjecture again that all players play trigger strategies.[10] From the previous subsection, we know that the mass of small traders attacking the currency is equal to the probability that any particular agent receives a signal below some optimal trigger x^*, as in equation (9).

---

9. Two points are worth noticing. First, the equilibrium is unique in the sense that agents choose a unique threshold for their signal. With a continuum of agents there is no aggregate uncertainty, so there is also a unique level of the fundamentals that triggers a crisis. In equilibrium, however, agents may and will choose different actions depending on the specific realizations of their signals. In other words, there will be heterogeneity in the behavior of investors— to be contrasted with the strong result in common-knowledge, multiple-equilibrium models in which everybody takes the same action in equilibrium. Second, the structure of information is crucial to uniqueness. As shown by Morris and Shin (2000), were agents to receive both a private and a public signal, there would be some threshold for the relative precision of these two signals beyond which the equilibrium in trigger strategies is no longer unique—despite the presence of private information, we are back to the case discussed in the previous section.

10. We refer to Corsetti et al. (2000) for proof that trigger strategies would be optimally selected even if agents were allowed to choose other types of strategies.

Now, the small traders amount to a percentage $1 - \lambda$ of the market. Thus, the condition for a crisis to occur as a result of an attack exclusively by the small traders is equivalent to equation (10) rescaled by $1 - \lambda$:

$$(18) \qquad (1-\lambda)F\left(\frac{x^* - \theta}{\sigma}\right) \geq \theta,$$

and the value of the fundamentals below which the currency collapses satisfies

$$(19) \qquad (1-\lambda)F\left(\frac{x^* - \theta}{\sigma}\right) = \underline{\theta}.$$

If the large trader attacks the currency as well, the financial resources mobilized by speculators on the left-hand side of equation (18) are increased by λ. Following the same steps as above, consider the level of fundamentals $\overline{\theta}$ that solves

$$(20) \qquad \lambda + (1-\lambda)F\left(\frac{x^* - \overline{\theta}}{\sigma}\right) = \overline{\theta}.$$

Obviously it is $\underline{\theta} < \overline{\theta}$. When the fundamentals are below $\underline{\theta}$, the currency collapses whether or not the large trader attacks. When the fundamentals are between $\underline{\theta}$ and $\overline{\theta}$, the peg collapses if and only if all traders, small and large, speculate against the currency. To sum up, with a large trader we have two thresholds for the fundamentals ($\underline{\theta}$ and $\overline{\theta}$) instead of a single one (θ^*). Note that the distance between the two is not equal to λ.

Next, consider the expected payoff of the large trader. This agent knows that, if it attacks, the currency will collapse for any $\theta \leq \overline{\theta}$. Clearly, it chooses to attack as long as the expected profit conditional on its signal is nonnegative, that is, as long as

$$(21) \qquad (1-t)\Pr(\theta \leq \overline{\theta} \mid x_l) - t\Pr(\theta > \overline{\theta} \mid x_l) = L\left(\frac{\overline{\theta} - x_l}{\sigma_l}\right) - t \geq 0.$$

The highest value of the signal at which it attacks—that is, its trigger, x_l^*—thus solves

$$(22) \qquad L\left(\frac{\overline{\theta} - x_l^*}{\sigma_l}\right) = t.$$

To evaluate the expected payoff of the typical small trader is not as easy. Small traders know that the currency will certainly collapse for any realization of the fundamentals worse than $\underline{\theta}$. When θ is between $\underline{\theta}$ and $\overline{\theta}$, a collapse will only occur if the large player participates in the attack—that is, if and only if the large trader receives a signal worse than x_l^*. The expected profit from an attack conditional on the signal x_i must therefore be written in such a way as to keep these different regions of the fundamentals separated from each other.

Conditional on the signal x_i, we write the posterior density over θ for a small trader as

(23) $$\frac{1}{\sigma} f\left(\frac{\theta - x_i}{\sigma}\right).$$

The expected payoff to attack conditional on signal x_i is therefore[11]

(24) $\quad \Pr(\theta \leq \underline{\theta} \mid x_i) + \Pr(\underline{\theta} \leq \theta \leq \overline{\theta}, x_l \leq x_l^* \mid x_i) - t$

$$= F\left(\frac{\underline{\theta} - x_i}{\sigma}\right) + \frac{1}{\sigma} \int_{\underline{\theta}}^{\overline{\theta}} f\left(\frac{\theta - x_i}{\sigma}\right) L\left(\frac{x_l^* - \theta}{\sigma_l}\right) d\theta - t.$$

The analysis of the model can be considerably simplified with a change of variables, using the following definitions:

(25) $$z \equiv \frac{\theta - x^*}{\sigma}, \, \underline{\delta} \equiv \left(\frac{\underline{\theta} - x^*}{\sigma}\right), \text{ and } \overline{\delta} \equiv \frac{\overline{\theta} - x^*}{\sigma}.$$

It can be shown that both $\underline{\delta}$ and $\overline{\delta}$ are monotonically decreasing in x^*. The threshold for the large player (x_l^* in equation [22]) can now be written as

(26) $$x_l^* = x^* + \sigma\overline{\delta} - \sigma_l L^{-1}(t)$$

while the optimal threshold for the small players, x^*, is the unique solution to the following equation:

(27) $$F(\underline{\delta}) + \int_{\underline{\delta}}^{\overline{\delta}} f(z) L\left(\frac{\sigma}{\sigma_l}(\overline{\delta} - z) - L^{-1}(t)\right) dz - t = 0.$$

Once x^* is determined,[12] the large trader's switching point, x_l^*, and the two thresholds for the fundamentals are also uniquely determined.

Does a Large Trader Increase Financial Fragility?
The Role of Size and Information Precision

In contrast to the model with small traders only, the model with a large player has no closed-form solution. However, the key results can be analyzed by focusing on its limiting properties—that is, by letting agents become arbitrarily well informed about the fundamentals.

Consider the case in which the information of the large trader is arbitrarily more precise than the information of the rest of the market, that is, $\lim \sigma/\sigma_l = \infty$. Evaluating equation (27) under this maintained assumption, we observe that for any $\theta \leq \overline{\theta}$ (that is, for any $z \leq \overline{\delta}$) the probability that a

---

11. Note that this expression requires the signal of the large trader to be independent from the signal of a typical small trader.

12. Observe that the function on the left-hand side of equation (27) is continuous and strictly increasing in both $\underline{\delta}$ and $\overline{\delta}$, variables that are in turn continuous and strictly decreasing functions of x^*. Also note that the left-hand side of equation (27) is positive for sufficiently small x^*, while it becomes negative for sufficiently large x^*. Thus, there is a unique x^* solving equation (27).

precisely informed large trader chooses to attack is equal to 1. We can thus write:

$$(28) \qquad F(\underline{\delta}) + \int_{\underline{\delta}}^{\overline{\delta}} f(z)dz = F(\overline{\delta}) = t.$$

This expression has a simple interpretation. If in the limit the noise in the large trader's signal is zero, small traders need simply guess the position of the fundamentals, thereby forming their best estimate of the signal to the large trader. Intuitively, a large trader with extremely precise information does not add any noise to the estimation problem of small traders: they need not worry about the large trader's errors.

To solution of the model is then

$$(29) \qquad \overline{\theta} = \lambda + (1 - \lambda)F(-\overline{\delta}) \rightarrow \lambda + (1 - \lambda)(1 - t)$$

$$x^* \rightarrow \overline{\theta} - \sigma F^{-1}(t)$$

$$x_I^* = \overline{\theta} - \sigma_I L^{-1}(t).$$

These expressions establish a first important result. In equilibrium, $\overline{\theta}$, x_I^* and x^* are increasing in the size of the large player, λ. A larger λ makes the large and the small traders more aggressive, in the sense that they optimally choose to attack for higher values of their signals. In particular, since $\overline{\theta} > 1 - t = \theta^*$, relative to the benchmark with small traders only, the presence of a large, well-informed trader increases the fragility of the market by making small traders willing to attack the currency for stronger fundamentals.[13]

What if the information of the large trader is *less* precise than that of the small players? Will the size of the large trader still affect the fragility of the market (despite inferior information)? Interestingly, the answer is a qualified yes. Referring to Corsetti et al. (2000) for details, when lim $\sigma/\sigma_I = 0$ the influence of an uninformed large trader on the small traders' strategies is either null or moderate, depending on the size of λ. If λ is small enough, varying λ does not affect the equilibrium strategy of small traders: Intuitively, the noisy behavior of the large trader is offset, in equilibrium, by the net positions taken by the bulk of the market. If λ is large enough, the "erratic" be-

---

13. A heuristic argument can help to clarify the latter point. As we observed in the first part of section 5.2.3, without a large trader ($\lambda = 0$) the threshold for an attack by small traders only is equal to $1 - t$. This means that, at $\theta = 1 - t$, a proportion of $1 - t$ of traders attacks the currency. Now, suppose that each small trader has a share λ of resources taken away, and that this share is given to a single large trader with arbitrarily precise information. At $\theta = 1 - t$, the amount of resources thrown into the market by small traders falls from $1 - t$ to $(1 - t)(1 - \lambda)$. However, at $\theta = 1 - t$, because of her arbitrarily precise information, the large trader will always attack the currency, using the full amount of the resources given to it. Thus, the overall amount of resources in the market increases from $1 - t$ to $\lambda + (1 - t)(1 - \lambda)$, so that $1 - t$ can no longer be the threshold of the fundamentals at which the currency collapses. However, this means that, in the presence of a large trader, the region of the fundamentals where the currency is expected to collapse becomes wider, and small agents are willing to follow a more aggressive trading strategy.

havior of the large trader cannot be offset by the rest of the market. Its presence still makes all traders more aggressive, but to a lesser extent than in the case discussed above.

We can now draw our main conclusions from this model by stressing two key elements for a theory of speculative attacks with large traders. The first element is size. In the model, λ is positively related to the small traders' expected payoff, through its influence on the region of fundamentals in which a collapse of the currency is possible. As the upper bound of this region, $\bar{\theta}$, is increasing in λ, speculative attacks can be successful for stronger fundamentals. Consistently, the threshold x^*—that is, the maximum estimated value of the fundamentals at which small traders are willing to attack the currency—is also increasing (in some limit cases nondecreasing) in λ.

The second element is the relative precision of information, as indexed by the ratio σ/σ_l. For a given λ, a high degree of large trader's information accuracy (i.e., an arbitrarily small σ_l) reduces the uncertainty about the behavior of the large player itself and increases the expected payoff of the small agents for any given signal. Small traders thus become more aggressive in the market (i.e., they attack at a higher threshold x^*). Interestingly, a large player with relatively low precision of information can still exert some influence on market participants' behavior, but the extent of its influence is much lower.

Note the difference between the prediction of this model and the main conclusion of the model with multiple equilibria. In the latter model, a large trader increases the vulnerability of a peg independently of the behavior of small traders—recall that the presence of a large trader only affects the lower threshold $\underline{y}^*$ of the signal, increasing it by an amount equal to the trader's size. However, for signals in the upper end of the region of multiple equilibria, the large trader makes no difference. In the global-games model, however, the impact of a large player on the market outcome depends crucially on her influence on the behavior of small traders. Moreover, the large player makes a difference for strong fundamentals: It is the upper threshold $\bar{\theta}$ that is increasing in λ as, for a bigger λ, both the large and the small traders bet against the currency for stronger values of their signals x_l^* and x^*.

Thus, although multiple equilibrium models shed light on the effects of a large trader when fundamentals are relatively weak, the global-games model shows that the presence of a large trader may make a difference in economies with relatively strong fundamentals. Together, these two classes of models show that, in some circumstances, pegs that may not (or would not) collapse in the absence of a large trader may well be expected to crumble if one big elephant steps into a small pond.

Signalling and Herding

An important lesson from the above model is that a large trader can increase the fragility of a peg even when the market can at best guess the large trader's actual portfolio position and information. Her mere presence influences the equilibrium portfolio strategies in the market as a whole, especially when the large trader has more precise information. We may reasonably expect this influence to increase further if the large trader is given the opportunity to let the market learn its positions or information.

Consider the following problem of dynamic coordination with learning—an example that can be framed in a modified version of the above model.[14] After receiving their signals about the state of the fundamentals, both the large and the small traders can now choose between moving first or waiting one period before taking a speculative position in the foreign exchange market. The state of the economy θ is revealed after all agents have built up their positions, and the payoffs are independent of the timing of the move, so that there are no costs to waiting. Late movers can observe the trading flow generated by early movers, raising the possibility of signalling (by assumption, there is no other form of communication).

Should small traders move first? To the extent that their size is infinitesimal, small traders' individual positions do not influence trading flows in any appreciable way. As each small trader ignores the impact of its own action on the market, it cannot hope to affect the market by moving first. However, small traders may obtain some informational benefit by waiting. Thus, it can be concluded that small traders will weakly prefer to be late movers. It is plausible to assume that, if indifferent whether to be early or late movers, small traders will move late.

Now, since the large trader knows that small traders have no reason to move early, it will never learn anything by waiting. Still, its portfolio position cannot be ignored by the market. Instead, by letting people know its portfolio position, it may increase the probability that its strategy will be successful. Thus, a large trader weakly prefers to move early. Once again, it is plausible to assume that, if indifferent about the timing of the move, the large trader will move early.[15]

From here on, the analysis follows the same steps outlined in the previous subsection, but with an important qualification: Now the decision taken by small traders is conditional on the action taken by the large trader. Conjecture that the large trader chooses to attack only if its signal is lower than x_l^*, where, as in equation (22), this threshold is defined by

(30) $$\Pr(\theta \leq \bar{\theta} \mid x_l = x_l^*) = t$$

14. We draw once again on Corsetti et al. (2000). The example comes from a class of models discussed in Dasgupta (2001).

15. A large trader's incentive to move first is strong when its estimate of the fundamentals is not too good or too bad, leading it to believe that an attack will be successful only if many small traders join. Conversely, if the private signal x_l is bad enough, the large trader may expect a currency collapse regardless of speculation by small traders. In this case, as there is no cost in waiting, the large trader will be indifferent whether to attack early or late (the same consideration applies for signals x_l that are sufficiently good).

If the large trader does not attack, its inaction signals that, based on its own information, it finds the economy to be strong (that is, $x_l > x_l^*$). However, those small traders that receive a bad signal about the fundamentals may nonetheless choose to attack the currency, thinking that enough small traders will join the attack and cause a collapse. Consequently, there will be an optimal threshold $\underline{x}^*$, below which small traders attack the currency even when the large trader has not taken a speculative position against it. This optimal threshold is defined by

$$(31) \qquad \Pr(\theta \leq \underline{\theta} \mid x_l > x_l^*, x_i = \underline{x}^*) = t$$

if a finite solution to this equation exists. Otherwise, if the left-hand side of the above equation is strictly larger (smaller) than the right-hand side, $\underline{x}^*$ is set equal to $+\infty$ $(-\infty)$.

Of course, when the large trader attacks the currency, it signals to the small traders a quite different assessment of the strength of the economic fundamentals (as $x_l \leq x_l^*$). Relative to the previous case, small traders are willing to attack for a wider range of signals they receive. The optimal trigger conditional on an attack by the large trader, denoted $\overline{x}^*$, is defined by

$$(32) \qquad \Pr(\theta \leq \overline{\theta} \mid x_l \leq x_l^*, x_i = \overline{x}^*) = t$$

if a finite solution to this equation exists. Otherwise, $\overline{x}^*$ is set equal to $+\infty$ or $-\infty$, depending on whether the left-hand side of the above equation is larger or small than the right-hand side.

Through its influence on the trigger strategies of small traders, the large investor induces some herding in the market; for a given distribution of private signals, its position affects the number of agents taking the same side of the market. The extent of herding will depend on the equilibrium value of the two thresholds above. If these are not finite, there will be a stronger form of herding: the position of the large trader will determine the position of all other agents in the market.[16]

To illustrate this point, suppose the signal of the large trader is arbitrarily precise relative to the signals received by the rest of the market. In this case there are no finite solutions for the triggers of small traders, but $\underline{x}^* = -\infty$ and $\overline{x}^* = +\infty$, while $\underline{\theta}$ and $\overline{\theta}$ converge to 0 and 1, respectively. In equilibrium, a large trader with superior information effectively leads the pack of the small traders with no defection: each small agent ignores its own private signal and always takes the same side of the market as the large trader (we return to this in the next section).[17]

In the limiting case $\sigma/\sigma_l \to \infty$, herding does not depend on the size λ of the

---

16. The thresholds of the fundamentals below which the currency collapses solve $(1 - \lambda)\Pr[x_i \leq x^* \mid \theta = \underline{\theta}] = \underline{\theta}$ if the large trader has not attacked the currency, and $\lambda + (1 - \lambda)\Pr[x_i \leq \overline{x}^* \mid \theta = \overline{\theta}] = \overline{\theta}$ otherwise.

17. See Dasgupta (1999) for a theoretical discussion of herding in coordination games.

large investor. As long as $\lambda > 0$, even a relatively small player can have the strongest impact as long as the market regards its information as arbitrarily precise. That is to say, the only dimension in which size is important is the signalling ability associated with it, that is, the fact that the market does not ignore the influence of its actions on the equilibrium outcome.

Size makes a difference, however, when the large trader's information is less than arbitrarily precise, and becomes very important if the ranking of information precision tilts in favor of small players. To see this, suppose that a large player without precise information gets a relatively bad signal on the fundamentals. By moving first and attacking the currency, it cannot hope to affect significantly the beliefs of the other agents, which know that its information is relatively inaccurate. Yet, by moving first, the large trader can reduce the small traders' uncertainty about its action in equilibrium. Small agents will decide their optimal behavior knowing it has (or has not) thrown its resources on the market. If it attacks, for a larger λ, a smaller resource gap remains to be filled for a speculative attack to be successful.

To summarize, the dynamic effects of a large trader are related *both* to information about the fundamentals and to the size of resources already devoted to an attack. In the limiting case (the information of the large trader is extremely accurate), the first factor overshadows the second. However, for some lower degree of precision of information, we may expect the second factor to dominate.

5.2.4   Open Issues

Do Large Players Destabilize Markets?

In the long-standing academic and policy debate on whether speculation is destabilizing, the role of large players is a particularly hot item. One view is that large traders and arbitrageurs able to collect and process superior information improve the efficiency of the price mechanism. Also, because of their ability and willingness to take leveraged positions, HLIs can be an important source of market liquidity. The alternative view emphasizes their role as catalysts of market panic and short-termism. The literature provides many example in which market efficiency is jeopardized by the behavior of noisy traders even when they are atomistic, let alone when the size of their speculative positions make them primary suspects as market "agitators."

Indeed, an oft-voiced concern is that the presence of large players may not lead only to short-term, high-frequency excess volatility of exchange rates and other asset prices, but also to persistent and destabilizing deviations of asset prices from their equilibrium values, with negative effects on real economic activity. This is the case, for instance, if the actions of large players can trigger currency crises that would not have otherwise occurred, or force monetary authorities to prevent a currency collapse at the cost of hiking interest rates and halting growth.

In fact, it is rather difficult to prove that any specific economy fits this description. Some have argued, however, that Hong Kong in 1998 was the nearest case of an economy whose fundamentals were generally sound, in spite of some macro weaknesses, but that came close to the collapse of its currency board regime as a result of aggressive speculation against its forex and stock markets. In this example, only a controversial direct intervention of the authorities in the equity market prevented a break of the peg and further sharp falls in its equity market (see section 5.3.3). However, the effects of defending the peg with high interest rates, likely exacerbating the recessionary effects of the Asian crisis on the domestic economy, were quite costly. While it remains controversial to assess whether the actions of large players have a destabilizing impact (and counterfactuals are hard to assess when fundamentals interact with complex market dynamics), the welfare costs of *potential* destabilization have been a matter of concern for policy makers in small and medium-sized economies.

In the models discussed above, the mere presence of a large trader makes all other agents more aggressive and ready to bail out for stronger values of the fundamentals. Although the analysis does not explicitly address welfare issues, it is compatible with models in which the economy ends up being worse off after a currency collapse. We should note that the above analysis rests on the key assumption that the large trader *profits* in the event of a devaluation. This may not always be the case. As large traders take speculative positions in many different markets, it is plausible that, under some circumstances, they may actually lose because of currency instability. To mention but one example, in 1998 several large financial institutions were reportedly long in Russian assets. Given the size of their portfolios and the relative thinness of the market for such assets, a precipitous unwinding of long positions would have exposed these institutions to heavy losses. Attempts to hedge these positions through forward purchases were thwarted when the fall of the ruble led counterparts to default on their contracts.

This example suggests that, in some situations, large traders may well prefer exchange rate stability to a devaluation. To analyze this case in the theoretical model presented in this section, one needs to allow for a more general payoff function, reflecting the initial portfolio positions of large players. In this case the presence of a large trader may end up making small players less (instead of more) aggressive in the currency market, thus reducing the likelihood of speculative attacks and sharp currency devaluations.

Do Large Players Have Substantial Market Impact?

One may claim that the estimated total size of large players' activity (say, HFs' net currency positions) is too small, relative to the depth of the forex market and the amount of international reserves available to the governments, to be a determining factor in a currency crisis.[18] But if markets think that large players have access to superior information, the model presented above suggests that even modest short positions by HFs may lead a large number of other investors to herd. As many investors mirror the behavior of large funds, the overall buildup of short positions against a currency is a multiple of the cumulative positions of these funds—indeed, large enough to trigger a currency crisis.

In this respect, the FSF (2000) study suggests that, in the 1990s, some macro HFs had built a very strong reputation in terms of information precision and ability to forecast macro developments. In addition, anecdotal evidence suggests that many financial institutions stood ready to provide credit to HFs as well as services in executing forex trade, at least in part as a way to track the investment strategy of these funds. Information about what HFs were doing was indeed considered a valuable asset by a wide range of investors.

We should note here that small agents may try to infer the action by informed large traders even when they do not have information about order volumes. Under the plausible assumption that large trades tend to affect prices, small agents without knowledge of order volumes can exploit the information implicit in price movements by buying when prices are rising and selling when prices are falling. In other words, price changes are interpreted as signals that large players are buying or selling. This case for *positive feedback* strategies, however, crucially depends on the degree of asymmetric information in the market. One may think that strong asymmetries are not likely in foreign exchange markets, because the information about macroeconomic variables is mostly public. However, in the case of emerging markets, certain players with privileged access to policy makers are usually believed to have better information than average market participants, as well as superior skills in analyzing public data.

Two factors play a key role here: leverage capacity and overall market liquidity. As regards the first factor, some players, such as HFs, are less restricted than others (such as institutional investors) in taking large leveraged positions. In a speculative attack, these agents could mobilize massive resources up to a multiple of their capital base.

As regards market liquidity, the evidence suggests that forex liquidity drops significantly in periods of turmoil (see FSF 2000). Thus, while the overall cumulative short position by HFs may be small relative to the depth and liquidity of the market in normal times, its relative size may increase significantly when market liquidity shrinks during crisis periods. This effect is particularly strong under institutionalized fixed exchange rate regimes

---

18. Note that another large player in any forex market dynamics is the monetary authority, which may affect currency values through its intervention in the forex market. What usually distinguishes monetary authorities from other large players is the objective function: maximization of the country's welfare function for the former, and profit maximization for the latter. However, in some episodes, even monetary authorities in emerging economies have allegedly engaged in currency trading for balance-sheet purposes.

such as currency boards, because these regimes limit the overall degree of liquidity in the financial system. Even medium-sized sales of domestic currency to purchase foreign currency can dry up liquidity very quickly, leading to interest rate spikes such as the ones in Hong Kong in 1998 and in Turkey and Argentina in late 2000. It should be stressed that a drying-up of liquidity is an endogenous feature of an equilibrium with speculative attacks. In the model above, for instance, it is an implication of the herding result, as the speculative position by a large informed agent makes all agents take the same side of the market.

Do Large Players Intentionally Foster Herding?

The above theoretical analysis vindicates the view that large players can effectively behave like market leaders by signaling their investment strategies ("talking one's book"), driving a large number of traders toward shorting a particular currency or asset market. Nonetheless, this result by no means implies that herding is *always* in the interest of large players, nor that we should expect them to engage systematically in signalling games, revealing their positions and information to the rest of the market. In fact, major market participants may well try to prevent herding while they build (or unwind) their short positions. It is only when positions have been built that herding by other agents (taking short positions or selling the currency outright) may become advantageous, as a way to increase the pressure on the exchange rate and push a currency peg to break.

Suppose a large player is planning to short a currency or an equity index in expectation of a future fall in prices warranted by weakening fundamentals. In order to minimize any effect from its trading on current prices, its preference would be to build its positions secretly. The same consideration applies to the case of a large player that is trying to unwind its short positions, because herding would generate adverse upward pressures on prices. Actually, if anything, a large player that is shorting an asset or unwinding a short position may prefer the other agents to take a contrarian trading position, so as to minimize price movements.

In other words, when building a position, a large player has a clear interest in trading at prices that do not reflect its private information. Only *after* it has built up its position does its benefit if its information becomes public, as prices would then move in the desired direction. At that point, there is a clear incentive to engage in signaling, as analyzed in the period model presented above.[19]

---

19. This issue is in part debated in the literature on optimal trading strategy. In the model by Easley and O'Hara (1987), for instance, large trading size signals that some informed agent is trading on the basis of superior information. These authors argue that an investor trading on superior information will nonetheless prefer to take large positions at any given prices. The alternative view, presented by Barclay and Warner (1993), is that informed traders do not want to let the market learn their information by observing their position. Thus they engage in "stealth trading," for instance, by placing multiple medium-size orders). Of course, the reaction by small players will crucially depend on which trades (large or small) they perceive to be more informative; see Lee, Lin, and Liu (1999) for a discussion of this issue.

We note here that the goal of building a speculative position without moving prices is helped by the presence of public authorities committed to stabilizing prices—as is the case in a fixed exchange rate regime. It is still true that early herding may be bad news for speculators: Early speculative pressure on the currency may translate into higher interest rates and forward prices, raising the costs of shorting positions in that currency. Thus, there are still advantages to keeping early moves secret. However, price stabilizing schemes, such as fixed rate regimes, usually lead domestic authorities to provide a large amount of liquidity at current prices. Under a flexible exchange rate regime, instead, attempts to build large short positions without affecting prices require other investors to take the other side of the market (playing contrarian and being long) as monetary authorities are not committed to providing foreign currency at a fixed price. Again, only once such positions have been taken does noisy signalling become profitable by pushing exchange rates down.

Do Large Players Inhibit Contrarian Trade?

In the model discussed under "Signalling and Herding" in section 5.2.3, strong herding only occurs in the limiting case when the large trader is arbitrarily better informed than the rest of the market. Otherwise, there will always be some agents who are willing to take contrarian trading positions based on their own beliefs about the sustainability of the existing regime. It is worth stressing that small agents do not necessarily lose when taking long positions in the currency against the large one. Even when the large trader has superior information, its private information may not reflect the true state of the economy.

Indeed, there is circumstantial evidence that, on a number of occasions during the 1997–99 period, some HFs experienced heavy losses as the majority of market investors traded against them. In some episodes, the losses followed HFs' attempts to bet on exchange rate stability or appreciation by taking long positions on currencies under speculative pressure (such as the alleged long positions by some large funds on the Indonesian rupiah in the winter of 1997). Clearly, it is possible that large investors engage in strategic games against each other. If so, differences in information and beliefs about the evolution of fundamentals in a market would play a much larger role than a stylized theoretical model with only one large trader and a mass of small traders may suggest.

Still, one cannot rule out the possibility that, despite differences in information and opinions, the size and reputation of large players taking aggressive positions in the market may, at times, drive out contrarian investors. As compared with the usually high leverage capacity of hedge and investment funds, for instance, risk aversion and credit constraints may effectively limit the amount of stabilizing speculation that individuals and other institutions can provide. In other words, in a speculative attack against a currency, small investors who are risk averse and credit constrained may refrain from contrarian trading, even if they believe that fundamentals do not warrant a devaluation. Paradoxically, these investors may end up taking the same short positions as the large institutions initiating the attack.

While plausible and realistic, these conjectures should nonetheless be analyzed systematically in models of speculative attacks explicitly allowing for credit constraint and risk aversion. Differences in leverage and attitude toward risk need not mechanically imply that small investors stay on the sideline or follow a large player in a lemminglike fashion.

The theory of speculative attacks with large traders should also be developed so as to explain, rather than assume, differences in the size of the speculative positions taken by economic agents. When trading size is endogenous, individual agents know that choosing a large position helps solve the coordination problem inherent in a speculative attack—for the reasons discussed above, the chances of success are increasing in the magnitude of speculation. However, agents choosing a large speculative position also have more at stake. A risk-averse agent's marginal willingness to speculate can decrease rapidly as its open position grows. There are therefore two contrasting forces shaping the optimal speculative behavior of investors, one suggesting larger, the other smaller portfolio positions.

In general, herding phenomena result from the complex and, at times, unpredictable interaction of decisions of a large number of players, both small and large. Whether domestic and foreign investors herd, whether domestic investors herd more or less than foreign ones, whether offshore (and highly leveraged) foreign investors herd more or less than onshore foreign investors, and whether larger investors are leaders of the pack are all empirical questions that must be addressed in case studies.

Can Large Players Manipulate Markets?

The basic question addressed by the literature on market manipulation is whether it is possible for a trader to buy an asset, drive the price up, and then sell the asset at this inflated price, thereby earning a profit (see, e.g., Kyle 1984; Vila 1987, 1989; Jarrow 1989; Bagnoli and Lipman 1998; Benabou and Laroque 1990; Kumar and Seppi 1992). Although most of this literature does not directly address large players, these studies highlight potentially important issues to complement our analysis above.

Conceptually, one can distinguish between three types of market manipulation (see Allen and Gale 1992):

1. Action-based manipulation, based on actions that change the actual or perceived value of the assets. This includes actions by insiders (such as owners and or managers) as well as insider trading.

2. Information-based manipulation, based on the release of false information or the spread of false rumors.

3. Trade-based manipulation, which occurs when a trader attempts to manipulate a stock simply by buying and then selling, without taking any publicly observable action to alter the value of the firm or releasing false information to change the price. This form of manipulation includes attempts to corner the market for a good or an asset.

Because investors do not control national policy making, action-based manipulation seems unlikely in international currency markets. Information-based manipulation (rumor spreading) is a somewhat more interesting possibility. Information-based manipulation models, however, require that the manipulators have a real or perceived information advantage. The presence of inside information pertaining to the value of corporate securities makes this assumption highly plausible in stock markets, but it is harder to envision in foreign exchange markets. Still, even in these markets, there could be particular conditions in which rumors and leaks, say, about the actions of reputable players, may have strong effects that do not occur in normal times.

While trade-based manipulation is in principle the most relevant issue for the purpose of this paper, it is not clear that such manipulation can be profitable. Buying a stock tends to push its price up, while selling it tends to push the price down. Consequently, if a large trader who attempts to manipulate a market through trade ends up buying high and selling low, how can she make a profit?[20] For a large trader with market power to profit from trade manipulation it is necessary that other (small) agents trade on the opposite side of the market. However, if the manipulator makes net relative profits, these agents will lose. Who would take a position that implies net expected losses or negative risk-adjusted returns?

Market manipulation appears to be profitable only in particular circumstances, when there are agents with an informational disadvantage or agents who have to sell or buy for some exogenous reason, perhaps receiving benefits that compensate them for the losses in the trade.[21] In the contribution by Allen and Gorton (1992), for instance, traders with superior information can inflict losses on a specialist, thanks to exogenous trades by agents who face binding liquidity constraints. The authors of this study correctly observe that the welfare implications of this example of trade manipulation are ambiguous: why should policy makers care if some investors make money at the expense of less informed specialists?

Market corners are another form of trade-based manipulation. For instance, a trader may obtain control of a sufficiently large share of the supply of an asset that must be delivered in the futures or forward market.[22] This

20. Indeed, Jarrow (1992) shows formally that profitable manipulation is impossible in an efficient market.
21. Theoretical examples are given by Kyle (1985), Jarrow (1992), Allen and Gorton (1992), Allen and Gale (1992), and Kumar and Seppi (1992).
22. As in the cases of the Salomon Brothers' Treasury market corner and the Hunt Brothers' corner of the silver market.

type of manipulation may not be feasible in markets, such as the forex, where the relevant assets are not in fixed supply. Finally, we should note that the issue of collusion, alleged to be a factor in recent market dynamics episodes, has not been systematically studied by the literature on manipulation.

Based on this overview of the literature, we can only attempt a preliminary assessment of the theoretical case for market manipulation by large players in the forex market. The key observation is that successful manipulation requires relatively strict informational and behavioral conditions. For example, an individual fund should be large enough or leveraged enough to be able to corner the market for a particular currency. Alternatively, if no player was large enough to affect markets by itself, manipulation would require collusion among investors. In the absence of outright collusion, some HFs would have to lead the trading strategies of a sufficient number of traders—perhaps by verbal manipulation, "talking down" a currency to encourage other market players to sell short. Although such convergence of strategies is possible, there is currently no evidence that it occurred in any of the turbulence episodes of the 1990s.

Manipulation is hard to prove even when it is clear that a large agent talked down a currency or market. Suppose that a major market participant, believing that a currency is overvalued, places global macro bets shorting that currency and publicly announces its views to this effect. Because there is a broad range of uncertainty on whether a currency is overvalued, how can one prove that the large agent's public statement is a form of market manipulation?

We conclude this section by noting that, although the social impact of manipulation of individual equities may be ambiguous (because it leads to a redistribution of wealth from less informed specialists to more informed investors), successful manipulation of currency markets may have serious welfare implications. Price movements away from fundamentals could be associated with large and undesirable real effects such as employment losses and fiscal and monetary imbalances. Moreover, wealth would be redistributed from vulnerable emerging-market economies to powerful international investors.

5.3   Large Players and Currency Markets: Empirical Studies

A key lesson of the 1997–99 episodes is that no single factor can entirely explain the volatility in cross-border capital flows, nor the large swings in asset prices that capital volatility sometimes causes. Corporate, financial, and policy weaknesses in emerging markets are often exacerbated by adverse monetary and macroeconomic developments in advanced economies; countries with different domestic fundamentals have been equally vulnerable to shifts in market sentiment among international investors. As a result, small countries that have been the recipients of international capital have also been increasingly worried by forces beyond their control in international capital markets.[23] No wonder the role of HFs and other HLIs in global financial crises has been closely scrutinized and often criticized, especially during the second half of the last decade.

The evidence on the portfolio strategies of HFs and HLIs and their impact in currency turbulence episodes is mixed. IMF (1998) finds some evidence that HFs, acting as market leaders, helped precipitate the ERM crisis in 1992, although they appear to have done so in response to economic fundamentals. Regarding the same episode, Fung and Hsieh (1999b) show that the 25 percent net asset value (NAV) gain of the Quantum Fund in September 1992 can be explained by its position against the British pound.[24] However, this episode hardly proves that a single large player can cause the collapse of an otherwise sound currency. It is generally agreed that the pound was overvalued in 1992 and that a devaluation was necessary to restore the competitiveness of the U.K. economy.[25] Although specific HFs might have contributed to triggering the fall of the pound, this episode hardly fits the view that speculators successfully forced a devaluation not justified by fundamentals.[26]

More recently, the authorities of a number of countries—such as Malaysia, Hong Kong, and Australia—have claimed that the HFs' role was significant in several recent crises: Such funds have been accused of leading market dynamics, intentionally causing herding, and manipulating currencies and other asset markets. However, some studies, especially IMF (1998) and other research (see Brown, Goetzmann, and Park 2000; Fung, Hsieh, and Tsatsaronis 2000), have expressed skepticism. A typical argument made in these studies is that HFs were "at the rear of the herd of investors rather than in the lead." This view is partly at odds with the conclusions of the more recent FSF official study (FSF 2000) of the 1998 turmoil, which focused on a sample of small and medium-sized economies such as Hong Kong, Australia, New Zealand, South Africa, Singapore, and Malaysia. Whereas the IMF study concluded that HFs had played only a minor role in 1997, FSF found a more significant impact of HFs and prop desks in the episodes of turmoil in 1998.

23. See Schadler et al. (1993) and Mussa et al. (1999) for emerging-market experience with volatile capital flows and some possible policy responses.

24. The authors infer the directional exposure of the Quantum Fund to several currencies from data on its weekly or daily net asset values.

25. The debate on the 1992–93 crisis of the European Monetary System is assessed in Eichengreen and Wyplosz (1993), Buiter, Corsetti, and Pesenti (1998a, b), and Eichengreen (2000).

26. In other episodes, notably the 1994 bond market turbulence, IMF (1998) shows that HFs as a group bet on a decline in interest rates, realizing substantial losses when they instead rose. Fung and Hsieh (1999a) and Fung, Hsieh, and Tsatsaronis (2000) show that the Quantum Fund took positions in anticipation of a strengthening of the U.S. dollar against the yen in February 1994, then suffered sharp losses as the yen appreciated. They also consider the performance of several large macro HFs in the episodes of market turmoil in 1997–98. We return to these case studies below.

Some preliminary evidence about the performance of HFs for the period 1997–98 is presented in figures 5.1–5.4, where we plot the time series of the NAVs of four large macro HFs,[27] in parallel with the Standard & Poor's 500 index and the yen/dollar exchange rate.[28] Over this period, large macro HFs were reported to be taking substantial long positions in the U.S. equity market; they may also have been involved in the "yen carry trade" (borrowing in yen to finance positions in other currencies or assets), as argued by Fung and Hsieh (1999b).

For the Quantum fund, figure 5.1 suggests a strong correlation between the NAV and the Standard & Poor's 500 index in the first eleven months of 1997. The comovement is loose afterwards. Parallel movements between the yen/dollar exchange rate and the NAVs of the four HFs are apparent in the fall of 1998, in coincidence with the rally of the yen. Over the same period, the NAVs of these funds also seem to be affected by the fall in the U.S. equity markets following the turmoil generated by the Russian crisis and the near-collapse of Long-Term Capital Management (LTCM).

A striking feature of the performances of these four funds during the 1997–98 period is the size of fluctuations. The Jaguar Fund's NAV rose by 100 percent between the beginning of 1997 and August 1998 but lost 25 percent of its value between August 1998 and the end of 1998. The Emerging Growth Fund rose by 40 percent between January and May 1997, then fell sharply, remaining on a downward trend until the end of 1998, when its NAV was about 40 percent below its level at the beginning of 1997. The Quasar Fund was volatile but on average rose by about 50 percent between the beginning of 1997 and August 1998; after that, it plunged by 50 percent. By the end of 1998, its NAV was at the same level as at the beginning of 1997. The Quantum Fund rose by about 30 percent between the beginning of 1997 and November 1997, but then it was mostly on a downward trend, approaching, at the end of the sample, a level close to the one at the beginning of 1998. Overall, the performance of three of these four funds in the 1997–98 period was far from exceptional: Two funds had on average zero returns over the period, while one lost almost 40 percent of its value. The fourth fund gained over 40 percent over the same period.

In what follows we provide a reassessment of the foreign exchange strategies of large players in light of our theoretical analysis. A few selected case studies on turbulence episodes in emerging markets are preceded by an analysis of the evidence on the aggregate foreign currency positions of large market participants in advanced economies.

---

27. These are the Quantum Fund, the Quasar International Fund, the Emerging Growth Fund of the Quantum Group, and the Jaguar Fund. They were among the largest macro HFs in the industry over the period considered. Data on their weekly (Wednesday) NAVs have been collected from the *Financial Times*.

28. Similar charts appear in Fung, Hsieh, and Tsatsaronis (2000), who consider the performance of the HFs only up to 1997.

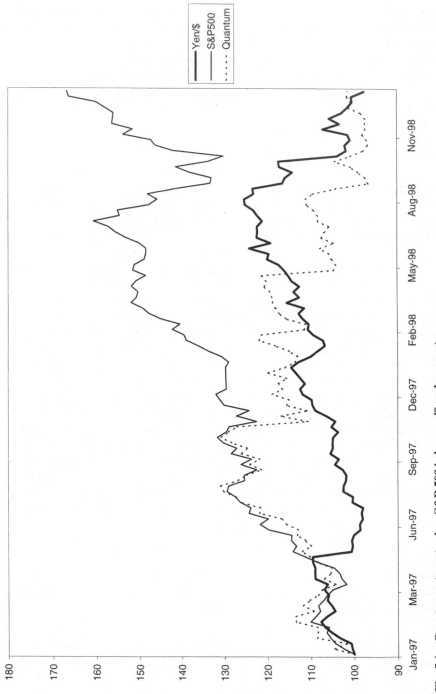

Fig. 5.1   Quantum net asset value, S&P 500 index, yen/$ exchange rate
Source: Financial Times and DRI

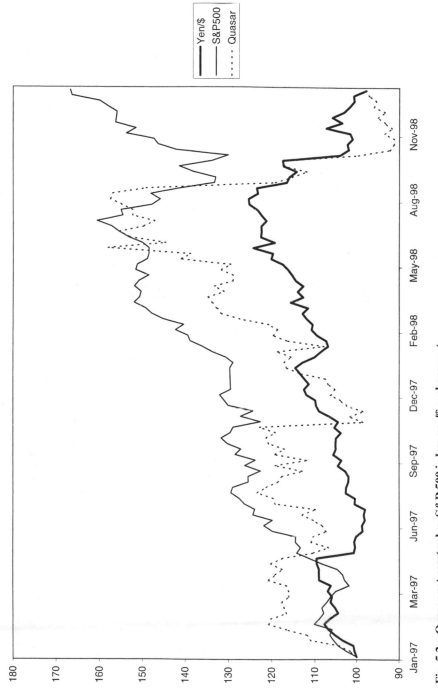

Fig. 5.2 Quasar net asset value, S&P 500 index, yen/$ exchange rate
Source: Financial Times and DRI

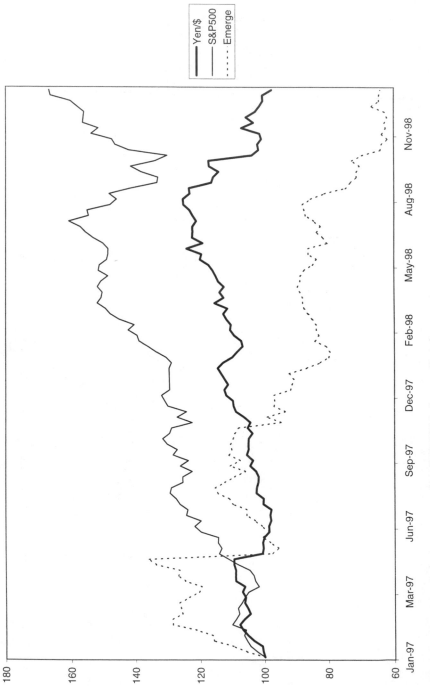

Fig. 5.3   Emerging growth net asset value, S&P 500 index, yen/$ exchange rate
Source: Financial Times and DRI

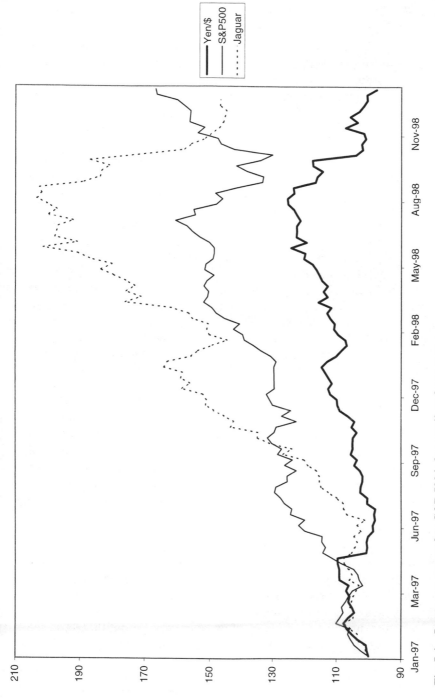

Fig. 5.4   Jaguar net asset value, S&P 500 index, yen/$ exchange rate
Source: Financial Times and DRI

Legend:
Yen/$
S&P500
Jaguar

5.3.1 The Treasury Foreign Currency Reports
of Major Market Participants

We have argued before that a number of elements may contribute to a financial institution's market power—asset size and leverage ability, visibility and reputation for superior information. In this section we investigate the links among these elements, focusing on the currency market. Do large players affect the price of foreign currency? Can they have access to better information than average market participants? Can they count on superior forecasts of future exchange rate developments? Do they consistently take long (short) positions in currencies whose value tends to appreciate (depreciate) over time? To address these questions, at least on a preliminary basis, we analyze the evidence on the foreign currency positions of the largest participants in the U.S. forex market.

Major foreign exchange market participants are required by law to file weekly and monthly reports on their holdings of foreign currency.[29] An institution qualifies as a major participant if, on the last business day of either March, June, September, or December during the previous year, it had more than the equivalent of $50 billion in foreign exchange contracts on its books. Contracts include sales and purchases in the spot, forward, futures, and options markets. Actual currency holdings (deposits) and any other foreign currency–denominated securities are not included in the reports. U.S.-based institutions file a consolidated report for their domestic and foreign subsidiaries, branches, and agencies. Subsidiaries of foreign entities operating in the United States file only for themselves, not for their foreign parents. Market participants with foreign currency holdings of less than $50 billion but greater than $1 billion need only file a quarterly report.

In their weekly Treasury Foreign Currency (TFC) reports, major participants indicate the amounts of foreign currency outstanding at the close of business each Wednesday.[30] The currencies included in the reports are the Canadian dollar, German mark, Japanese yen, Swiss franc, pound sterling, and, since 1999, the euro. Also since 1999, reporting institutions approximate all other currency positions under the aggregate entry "U.S. dollar." Data are organized into four categories: foreign exchange spot, forward, and futures purchased; foreign exchange spot, forward, and futures sold; net options position delta equivalent value long or [short]; net reported dealing position long or [short]. The first two categories represent the outstanding amounts of foreign exchange that the reporter has contracted to receive or deliver. Contracts are reported on a gross basis, and when the contracts provide for the exchange of one currency for another, both the purchase and the sale are reported. Options (third category) are reported if

---

29. 31 United States code 5315; 31 Code of Federal Regulation 128, Subpart C.
30. The reports are filed no later than noon on the Friday following the Wednesday to which the report applies.

the aggregate notional principal amount of contracts purchased and sold exceeds $500 million equivalent. Options are reported in terms of net "delta equivalent," an estimate of the relationship between an option's value and an equivalent currency hedge, that is, the amount of currency with the same gain or loss characteristics as the option for small movements in the exchange rate.[31] The fourth category is defined as the actively managed net dealing position monitored and used by each reporter for internal risk management purposes. Estimates of net dealing position typically come from internally generated reports.

Based on the TFC reports, since 1994 the Treasury Bulletin publishes information on the weekly, monthly, and quarterly foreign currency position taken by all large players collectively. No information is released on single participants' positions, and data on their net dealing positions are unavailable even at the aggregate level. A previous study (Wei and Kim 1999) has used this data set, covering the sample period 1994–96. Our paper covers the entire sample available at the time of writing, January 1994 through June 2000. In 1996 thirty-six reporters qualified as major participants; of these, twenty-nine were commercial banks and the remaining seven were other forms of financial institutions, including HFs. By 2000, the number of reporters was down to twenty-five, of which eighteen were banking institutions.

Table 5.1 provides summary statistics on major participants' weekly positions, all expressed in millions of U.S. dollars.[32] Gross sales and purchases of foreign currency are rather large (for instance, sales of Japanese yen average $1,459 billion, and purchases of marks average $1,252 billion) but net positions are relatively small across currencies (net positions in yen are about $20 billion in absolute value, and net positions in marks are on average $7.5 billion). The limited size of net relative to gross positions is partly due to large market participants' role as intermediaries: Reported foreign currency transactions typically involve two offsetting operations, such as a purchase of foreign currency from the market on behalf of a client and the sale of foreign currency to the client itself. However, limited net positions also indicate unwillingness by major participants to maintain large speculative positions at high (weekly) frequency. It is worth noting, however, that large players' net positions have increased over time, on average, across all currencies in the sample except the Canadian dollar.

Figures 5.5–5.11 plot the weekly time series of aggregate net foreign currency positions, defined as purchases minus sales of foreign exchange spot,

---

31. Technically, the "delta equivalent" value represents the product of the first partial derivative of an option valuation formula with respect to the price or rate of the underlying contract, multiplied by the notional principal of the contract.

32. We consider data on positions in German marks only until the end of 1998. After 1999, positions in marks are reported only if the institution separately manages the exchange rate risk of the euro and the legacy currencies; otherwise, all legacy currency amounts are reported as euro-denominated contracts.

Table 5.1 **Summary Statistics on the Treasury Foreign Currency Position Data**

		1994–2000			
	Observations	Mean	Standard Deviation	Minimum	Maximum
U.K. pound					
Purchased	337	622,847	165,994	339,847	917,309
Sold	337	611,583	159,274	339,060	906,447
Net options position	337	1,208	1,563	−5,473	6,243
Net foreign currency position	337	12,472	8,551	−2,576	40,193
Swiss franc					
Purchased	337	334,790	62,349	216,129	519,961
Sold	337	339,857	65,951	215,423	531,052
Net options position	337	3,191	3,073	−4,473	10,394
Net foreign currency position	337	−1,876	3,823	−15,385	14,936
Japanese yen					
Purchased	337	1,429,063	219,094	870,624	2,100,231
Sold	337	1,459,080	225,300	882,762	2,121,832
Net options position	337	10,142	3,625	2,824	23,085
Net foreign currency position	337	−19,876	11,933	−57,232	−704
Canadian dollar					
Purchased	337	173,793	40,995	87,799	246,798
Sold	337	171,609	42,452	86,141	248,266
Net options position	337	−1,929	1,092	−4,410	995
Net foreign currency position	337	256	2,716	−11,423	7,179
		1997–2000			
U.K. pound					
Purchased	182	755,470	96,081	568,827	917,309
Sold	182	737,607	95,455	550,143	906,447
Net options position	182	1,330	1,924	−5,473	6,243
Net foreign currency position	182	19,193	5,561	4,284	40,193
Swiss franc					
Purchased	182	361,052	65,812	216,129	519,961
Sold	182	365,670	71,133	215,423	531,052
Net options position	182	2,054	3,246	−4,473	8,340
Net foreign currency position	182	−2,564	4,771	−15,385	14,936
Japanese yen					
Purchased	182	1,573,070	186,778	1,175,914	2,100,231
Sold	182	1,611,159	184,751	1,202,603	2,121,832
Net options position	182	11,602	3,580	4,868	23,085
Net foreign currency position	182	−26,487	12,141	−57,232	−870
Canadian dollar					
Purchased	182	205,602	18,538	159,173	246,798
Sold	182	204,945	20,030	154,471	248,266
Net options position	182	−1,936	1,394	−4,410	995
Net foreign currency position	182	−1,279	2,424	−11,423	4,719
		1994–96			
U.K. pound					
Purchased	155	467,122	63,818	339,847	631,167
Sold	155	463,606	61,889	339,060	622,839
Net options position	155	1,065	971	−1,640	3,209
Net foreign currency position	155	4,580	2,672	−2,576	12,291

Table 5.1 (continued)

	Observations	Mean	Standard Deviation	Minimum	Maximum
			1994–2000		
Swiss franc					
Purchased	155	303,952	40,233	247,431	449,426
Sold	155	309,547	42,788	250,865	458,367
Net options position	155	4,527	2,213	803	10,394
Net foreign currency position	155	−1,068	1,980	−7,897	3,942
Japanese yen					
Purchased	155	1,259,971	102,189	870,624	1,477,491
Sold	155	1,280,511	105,852	882,762	1,500,136
Net options position	155	8,427	2,852	2,824	13,996
Net foreign currency position	155	−12,113	5,013	−25,856	−704
Canadian dollar					
Purchased	155	136,443	25,747	87,799	204,644
Sold	155	132,465	24,595	86,141	198,807
Net options position	155	−1,920	564	−3,215	−526
Net foreign currency position	155	2,058	1,770	−1,015	7,179
			1994–98		
German mark					
Purchased	259	1,252,768	126,035	1,025,474	1,694,490
Sold	259	1,248,805	116,520	1,026,360	1,643,567
Net options position	259	3,519	5,386	−12,705	11,892
Net foreign currency position	259	7,481	12,606	−10,647	50,989
			1994–96		
German mark					
Purchased	155	1,214,599	103,602	1,025,474	1,557,578
Sold	155	1,215,384	101,510	1,026,360	1,547,771
Net options position	155	6,529	2,644	−1,728	11,892
Net foreign currency position	155	5,744	9,237	−7,616	25,603
			1997–98		
German mark					
Purchased	104	1,309,654	135,209	1,102,822	1,694,490
Sold	104	1,298,617	120,066	1,109,383	1,643,567
Net options position	104	−968	5,315	−12,705	7,834
Net foreign currency position	104	10,069	16,099	−10,647	50,989
			1999–2000		
Euro					
Purchased	78	1,707,470	126,408	1,470,427	1,994,301
Sold	78	1,714,560	124,464	1,478,126	1,996,041
Net options position	78	−3,919	2,879	−9,953	2,451
Net foreign currency position	78	−11,009	10,916	−33,426	23,001
			1999–2000		
U.S. dollar					
Purchased	78	5,198,645	188,140	4,549,910	5,665,935
Sold	78	5,228,695	177,475	4,598,793	5,657,587
Net options position	78	3,175	6,119	−9,481	17,290
Net foreign currency position	78	−26,875	17,362	−70,953	20,912

Notes: Data are reported in millions of U.S. dollars. Purchased (sold) refers to spot, forward, and futures contracts purchased (sold) in that currency. Net options position is the net delta-equivalent value of the total options position. Net foreign currency position is calculated as net contracts purchased plus net options position.

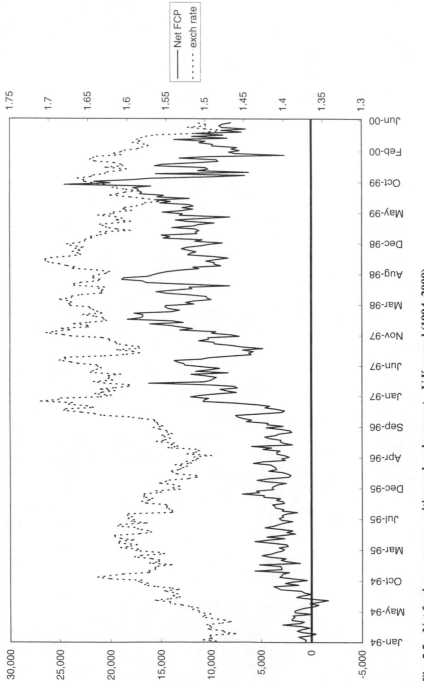

Fig. 5.5 Net foreign currency position and exchange rate, U.K. pound (1994–2000)

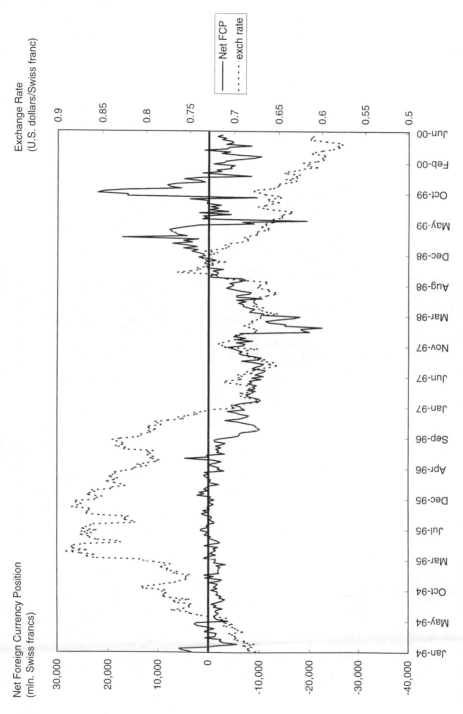

Net Foreign Currency Position
(mln. Swiss francs)

Exchange Rate
(U.S. dollars/Swiss franc)

Net FCP
----- exch rate

Fig. 5.6   Net foreign currency position and exchange rate, Swiss franc (1994-2000)

Net Foreign Currency Position
(bln. yen)

Exchange Rate
(U.S. Dollars/Japanese yen)

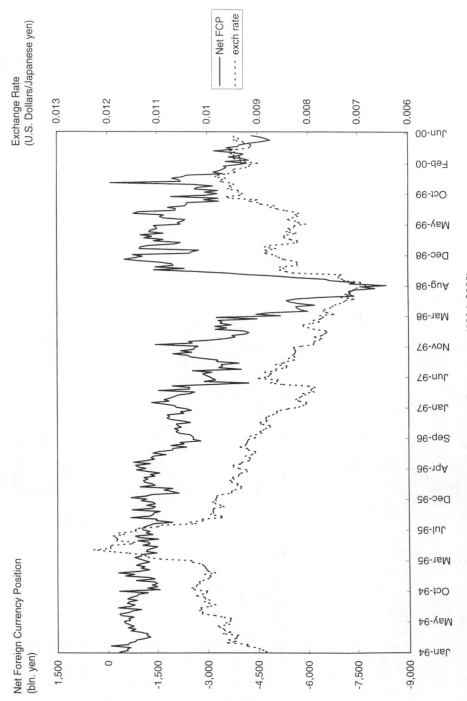

Fig. 5.7 Net foreign currency position and exchange rate, Japanese yen (1994–2000)

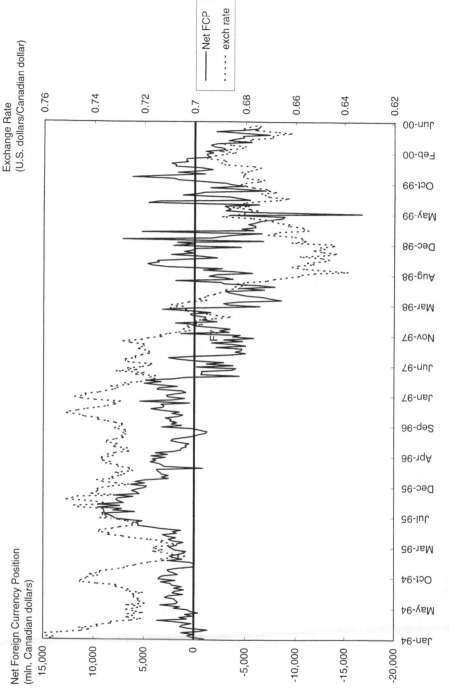

Fig. 5.8 Net foreign currency position and exchange rate, Canadian dollar (1994–2000)

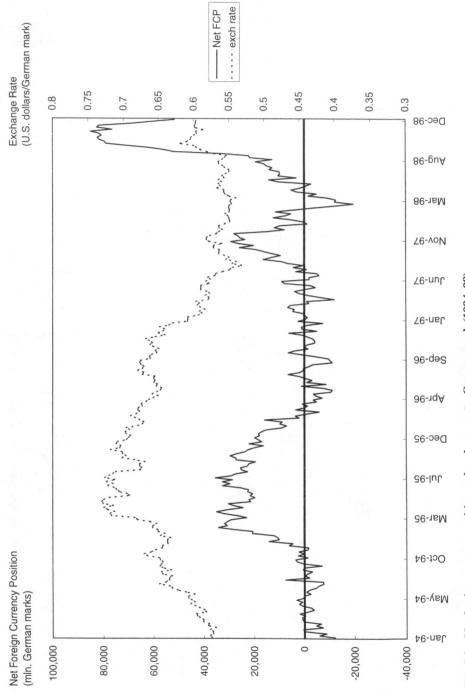

Fig. 5.9 Net foreign currency position and exchange rate, German mark (1994–98)

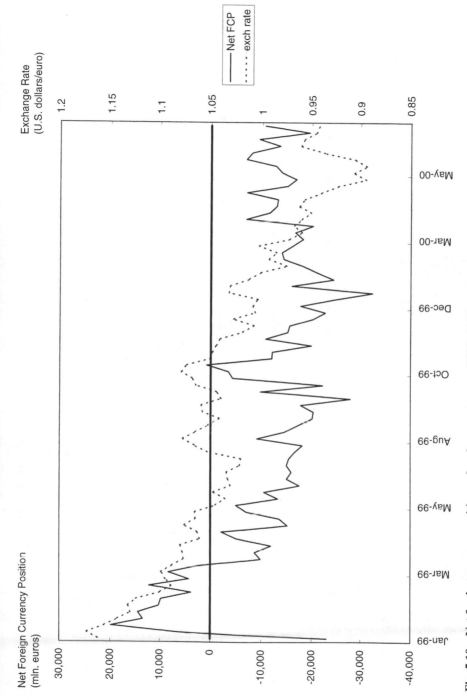

Fig. 5.10   Net foreign currency position and exchange rate, euro (1999–2000)

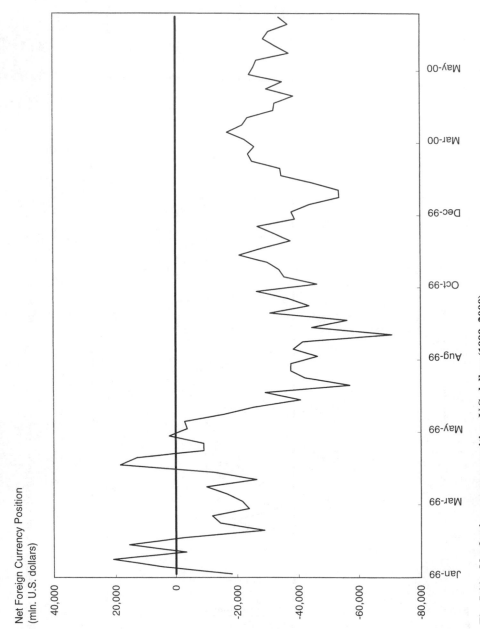

Net Foreign Currency Position
(mln. U.S. dollars)

Fig. 5.11 Net foreign currency position, U.S. dollars (1999–2000)

forward, and futures, plus net options positions, all expressed in millions of local currency (except for the contracts in yen, expressed in billions). The figures also plot the relevant exchange rates, expressed as U.S. dollars per unit of local currency. Visual inspection of these figures leaves the impression that the two series tend to move in parallel: When a currency strengthens against the dollar, large players systematically increase their purchases and reduce their sales of that currency, unwinding their net positions in dollars.

For example, in figure 5.7, the weakening of the yen relative to the U.S. dollar from the fall of 1997 through the summer of 1998 is strongly correlated with increasing net short positions on the yen, rising from about ¥2 trillion (about $16 billion at the prevailing exchange rate) to over ¥8 trillion (about $56 billion). The rally of the yen between August and October 1998 is also associated with a sharp and rapid unwinding of major participants' short positions. In the case of the German mark (fig. 5.9), the cycle of appreciation against the U.S. dollar in the first half of 1995 and depreciation in the second half of that year appears to be correlated with an initial buildup of long positions in marks and their subsequent reversal. Similar episodes are noticeable for the pound, the euro, the Canadian dollar, and the Swiss franc. There are, however, exceptions: Notably, the weakening of the euro in 1999 (fig. 5.10) seems to be associated with larger short positions on this currency until the summer of 1999 but not afterwards.

Obviously, the direction of causality is not clear. On the one hand, large players may affect the price of the currency simply because of the size of their net positions. On the other hand, large players observe current exchange rates and take into account the perceived strength or weakness of the currency in determining their net position at the close of business, substantially extrapolating some persistence in the behavior of the exchange rate over the very short term. Superior information by large players may also explain why current positions appear at times to be associated with contemporaneous and future exchange rate levels.

To provide formal statistical evidence on these correlations, we regress the current (Wednesday) exchange rate on the foreign currency position denominated in local currency.[33] For sensitivity analysis we exclude from the sample outliers[34] and consider two subsamples, 1994–96 (as in the Wei and Kim 1999 study) and 1997–2000. The first column of table 5.2 reports the results. In general, the regressions provide evidence in support of a strong positive link between exchange rates and simultaneous net positions. The results are particularly striking in the case of the pound, the Canadian dollar, the yen, the Swiss franc, and the euro. The link is weaker in the case of the German mark, as the coefficient is statistically significant only at the 10

33. For sensitivity analysis, we also regress the exchange rate on currency positions converted into U.S. dollars. The results are substantially similar.
34. The outliers are identified visually as 5/19/1999 (Canadian dollar), 9/15/1999 (Swiss franc), and 1/6/1999 (euro). Outliers play little role in our results.

Table 5.2   **Regressions of Level Exchange Rate on Net Foreign Currency Position**

	Net FCP		
	Current	One-Week Lag	Net FCP lag
U.K. pound			
1994–2000	69.0**	33.5**	37.8**
	(4.46)	(11.50)	(11.50)
1994–96	109.0**	71.5**	47.6*
	(18.9)	(28.0)	(28.0)
1997–2000	22.4**	9.3	18.3
	(9.06)	(13.00)	(13.10)
Canadian dollar			
1994–2000	40.1**	23.7**	21.7**
	(3.60)	(5.47)	(5.49)
1994–96	9.39**	6.90	4.40
	(3.53)	(6.95)	(6.89)
1997–2000	9.83*	6.20	6.70
	(5.44)	(6.49)	(6.44)
Excluding outliers			
1994–2000	41.6**	25.4**	20.5**
	(3.70)	(5.76)	(5.62)
1994–96	9.39**	6.90	4.40
	(3.53)	(6.95)	(6.89)
1997–2000	10.4*	6.6	6.5
	(5.74)	(6.95)	(6.56)
Swiss franc			
1994–2000	28.8**	18.9	12.6
	(7.58)	(13.30)	(13.30)
1994–96	25.2	35.9	−5.4
	(18.3)	(29.9)	(30.2)
1997–2000	1.8	4.2	−3.0
	(3.93)	(6.76)	(6.76)
Japanese yen			
1994–2000	4.17**	1.90**	2.42**
	(0.3)	(0.9)	(0.9)
1994–96	3.99**	2.30	2.50
	(1.2)	(2.0)	(2.0)
1997–2000	1.98**	0.70	1.34*
	(0.294)	(0.785)	(0.785)
German mark			
1994–98	3.19*	−6.7	10.2
	(1.68)	(6.65)	(6.69)
1994–96	19.9**	2.6	17.9**
	(1.84)	(5.38)	(5.36)
1997–98	3.83**	−0.1	4.0
	(0.703)	(3.13)	(3.15)

Table 5.2   (continued)

| | Net FCP | | |
	Current	One-Week Lag	Net FCP lag
Euro			
1999–2000	30.7**	26.5**	9.4
	(6.2)	(8.6)	(8.5)
Excluding outliers			
1999–2000	33.4**	26.5**	9.4
	(5.9)	(8.6)	(8.5)

Notes: The first column reports results of the regression of the level exchange rate (US$ per unit of foreign currency) on the current net foreign currency position (in millions of local currency, except for billions of Japanese yen). The second column reports results including the one-week lag of the net foreign currency position (Net FCP_lag). Coefficient estimates and standard errors (reported in parentheses) are multiplied by 10^7. Constants are not reported.

**Significant at the 5 percent level.

*Significant at the 10 percent level.

percent level; it is significant at the 5 percent level if we regress the exchange rate on net positions expressed in U.S. dollars. Breaking the sample into two periods does not significantly alter the results; in general, the *t*-statistics fall in the most recent subsample, with the notable exception of the yen.

The relation between the exchange rate and net position is also significant when we introduce lagged values of the latter variable. In the second column of table 5.2 we report results based on regressing the Wednesday exchange rate on current and one-week lagged net positions. The coefficients of both regressors are significantly positive in the cases of the pound, the Canadian dollar, and the yen. In other words, past net positions help to predict current exchange rates:[35] Large players tend to take long positions in currencies that are strong and remain so for a while—a result reflecting some degree of persistence in exchange rates.[36]

Are net positions associated with changes (rather than levels) of exchange rates over time? If a significant relation were found between net positions and movements of the exchange rate, two interpretations would be possible. On the one hand, if large players had superior information, they should be able to anticipate currency movements, selling short before depreciation. On the other hand, large players could affect the movement of the exchange rate simply because of the size of their trading.

Table 5.3 reports the results of regressing the ex post exchange rate de-

35. Separate regressions, not reported here, show that the correlation between current positions and future levels of the exchange rate holds significantly for horizons up to two months for most currencies.

36. Also, this result is not inconsistent with an interpretation according to which large players' positions today influence other market participants' behavior, leading them to take similar net positions over time (a form of momentum trading).

Table 5.3   **Regression of Log Difference Exchange Rate on Net Foreign Currency Position**

Currency	Horizon (Days)						
	1	2	3	5	10	20	60
U.K. pound							
1994–2000	0.40	–0.10	–0.50	–0.60	–1.10	–2.10	–9.49**
	(0.498)	(0.748)	(0.897)	(1.030)	(1.47)	(1.99)	(2.89)
1994–96	–2.0	–0.2	–2.0	–2.3	–2.7	4.8	–30.6**
	(2.08)	(3.20)	(3.94)	(4.69)	(6.49)	(8.53)	(12.70)
1997–2000	2.00*	2.77*	3.00	3.00	5.00	8.01*	12.80**
	(1.11)	(1.64)	(1.89)	(2.18)	(3.14)	(4.31)	(6.08)
Canadian dollar							
1994–2000	–0.80	–1.20*	–0.90	–0.20	–0.20	1.00	8.43**
	(0.471)	(0.656)	(0.849)	(0.958)	(1.320)	(1.780)	(2.910)
1994–96	–0.8	–0.3	0.4	1.3	1.6	5.8	–0.3
	(0.857)	(1.200)	(1.790)	(2.030)	(2.790)	(3.960)	(6.590)
1997–2000	–0.3	–1.4	–1.4	–1.5	–2.3	–2.6	10.4**
	(0.817)	(1.140)	(1.360)	(1.540)	(2.110)	(2.750)	(4.460)
Excluding outliers							
1994–2000	–0.827*	–1.150*	–0.700	–0.400	–0.500	1.200	8.440**
	(0.486)	(0.677)	(0.878)	(0.988)	(1.360)	(1.840)	(3.000)
1994–96	–0.8	–0.3	0.4	1.3	1.6	5.8	–0.3
	(0.857)	(1.200)	(1.790)	(2.030)	(2.790)	(3.960)	(6.590)
1997–2000	–0.3	–1.3	–1.0	–2.0	–3.1	–2.5	10.6**
	(0.862)	(1.210)	(1.440)	(1.620)	(2.220)	(2.910)	(4.710)
Swiss franc							
1994–2000	–1.38**	–2.17**	–1.70	–1.30	–2.70	–5.110*	–10.70**
	(0.646)	(0.993)	(1.170)	(1.420)	(2.020)	(2.870)	(5.080)
1994–96	0.9	2.0	1.8	0.5	0.6	7.6	81.5**
	(2.3)	(3.28)	(4.05)	(4.84)	(7.07)	(10.1)	(18.6)
1997–2000	–1.41**	–2.86**	–2.69**	–2.00	–3.99*	–8.20*	–24.00**
	(0.647)	(1.050)	(1.170)	(1.490)	(2.100)	(2.870)	(4.340)
Japanese yen							
1994–2000	–2.30	1.00	9.73**	2.50	1.80	–2.50	–54.10**
	(2.6)	(4.1)	(5.0)	(5.8)	(8.4)	(12.5)	(23.1)
1994–96	–2.8	7.7	24.8	44.6**	81.4**	169.0**	487.0**
	(10.0)	(15.8)	(18.6)	(21.8)	(31.5)	(49.1)	(96.0)
1997–2000	–1.8	1.2	10.5	1.9	–1.2	–10.4	–85.2**
	(3.77)	(5.83)	(7.16)	(8.34)	(12.20)	(17.70)	(29.60)
German mark							
1994–98	0.388**	0.400	0.400	0.500	0.800	0.900	–2.200
	(0.174)	(0.274)	(0.331)	(0.389)	(0.545)	(0.799)	(1.430)
1994–96	0.5	0.6	0.8	0.5	1.1	1.6	0.9
	(0.371)	(0.551)	(0.683)	(0.785)	(1.110)	(1.600)	(2.940)
1997–98	0.30	0.30	0.40	0.60	0.90	1.00	–2.77*
	(0.182)	(0.314)	(0.371)	(0.453)	(0.625)	(0.934)	(1.590)
Euro							
1999–2000	–0.80	–0.70	–1.00	–2.00	–3.20	–6.49**	–5.60
	(0.7)	(1.0)	(1.1)	(1.5)	(2.2)	(2.9)	(4.1)
Excluding outliers							
1999–2000	–0.80	–0.90	–1.20	–2.00	–3.40	–6.94**	–6.40
	(0.7)	(1.0)	(1.1)	(1.6)	(2.2)	(2.9)	(4.1)

Notes: The table reports the coefficient of the regression of the log-difference exchange rate (US$ per unit of foreign currency) on the net foreign currency position. Coefficient estimates and standard errors (reported in parentheses) are multiplied by 10^7. Constants are not reported.

**Significant at the 5 percent level.

*Significant at the 10 percent level.

preciation rate on lagged net positions. As above, for sensitivity analysis we report estimates for the two subsamples and excluding outliers. We consider different time horizons for the rate of depreciation: one day (Thursday on Wednesday), two days, three days (Monday on Wednesday), five days (Wednesday on Wednesday), two weeks, four weeks, and twelve weeks. The results are, to say the least, mixed.

There is some indication that large players take positions against currencies that tend to depreciate. At very short horizons (from one to three days) there is at least one statistically significant, positive coefficient for the mark and the yen (three days). In the case of the pound, the coefficient is significant only at the 10 percent level and only in the 1997–2000 subsample. There is a statistically significant relation, but with the wrong sign, in the case of the Swiss franc. In many cases the coefficients are not significant, and some have the wrong sign. The picture does not change if we lengthen the horizon of the depreciation.[37] When we compare our results with previous studies, the evidence that exchange rate changes are correlated with the net positions of large players is only marginally stronger.[38]

To sum up, although high-frequency noise in exchange rate changes may explain the weak correlation between net positions and short-term changes in exchange rates, the level regressions point to persistent low-frequency movements ("long cycles" of exchange rates) associated with aggregate net positions. Overall, the evidence suggests that the net positions of large players are significantly correlated with exchange rates; this can be attributed to either size or informational advantages.

5.3.2 The Pressures on the Thai Baht in the Spring and Summer of 1997

We now turn to case studies of currency crises in which HFs and other large traders were alleged to have played a key role. The first episode we consider is the attack on the Thai baht, whose fall in the summer of 1997 started the Asian currency and financial crisis.[39]

An assessment of Thai economic fundamentals suggests that the currency was overvalued. The country had run large current account deficits for almost a decade, and the currency had appreciated in real terms. Exter-

37. When twelve weeks are considered, there is a strongly significant relation for the pound, the Canadian dollar, the Swiss franc, the euro, and the yen. The problem is that, with the only exception being the Canadian dollar, the sign is always negative—that is, large players systematically take long positions in currencies that, on average, tend to depreciate over the next quarter. One could interpret this result as implying some mean reversion in exchange rate returns.

38. Wei and Kim (1997) do not find any significant positive association between large participants' position in a foreign currency and the latter's subsequent appreciation. A nonparametric approach finds some weak support for a positive association, but not on a systematic basis. Recall that this study is limited to the 1994–96 period, whereas we extend the sample up to the year 2000.

39. For a reconstruction of the Asian crisis and the debate surrounding these events see Corsetti, Pesenti, and Roubini (1999).

nal imbalances had been financed through short-term unhedged liabilities, making the country vulnerable to a liquidity run. Also, there were severe weaknesses in the financial system that eventually led to a banking crisis. On the other hand, high growth, high investment and savings rates, and a prudent fiscal policy suggest that the country was not seriously mismanaged.

The analytical models discussed in the first part of this paper suggest that a country with weak fundamentals may be vulnerable to the market dynamics either generated or fed by short positions taken by large players. Smaller players react to the actions taken by the large player by becoming more aggressive in their speculative behavior. Thus, one question is whether large HFs were "leaders of the pack" in this particular currency crisis episode. On this issue, the IMF (1998) study is skeptical, arguing that the HFs were at the rear rather than at the head of the pack (see also Eichengreen and Mathieson 1999).

This conclusion appears to be somewhat at odds with the very information available in the IMF study, let alone other sources of evidence. For instance, IMF (1998) shows that some large HFs had already taken significant short positions against the Thai baht in the spring of 1997, presumably based on a negative economic assessment of Thai fundamentals (stressing the size and persistence of the current account deficit and the overvaluation of the exchange rate). The estimated net short position of the HFs in Thailand was about $7 billion.[40] Fung, Hsieh, and Tsatsaronis (2000) estimate that twelve HFs had about $5 billion in short positions against the Thai baht at the end of June 1997.[41]

The evidence on HFs' taking short positions before the eruption of the crisis is indirectly confirmed by the econometric results presented in table 5.4, part A. Using weekly data, we regress the NAV of four large macro HFs[42] against the Standard & Poor's 500 index, the yen/dollar exchange rate, and the value of the Thai baht in the period from February through July 1997—when the baht was under pressure.[43] As argued before, the first two regressors control for the hypothesis that these funds had significant in-

40. This is an estimate of direct forward transactions with the Bank of Thailand. Short positions may have been larger as "hedge funds may also have sold baht forward through offshore intermediaries, onshore foreign banks, and onshore domestic banks, which then off-loaded their positions (commitments to purchase) to the central bank. Hence, there is no way of accurately estimating their total transactions" (Eichengreen and Mathieson 1999).

41. Estimated short positions are lower after July 1997 as such funds took profits on their shorts and partially closed these positions. Thus, while HFs may have played a role in triggering the initial collapse of the baht, they played a lesser role in the continued fall of the currency throughout the summer and fall of 1997. For example, according to Fung and Hsieh (1999a) there is no evidence that the Quantum Fund had shorted the baht during September 1997, when this currency fell sharply.

42. These are the same considered in figures 5.1–5.4 and section 5.3.1.

43. For the Jaguar Fund the sample period is the full 1997–98 period, as we found significant effects of all regressors throughout the sample.

Table 5.4   **Hedge Fund Net Asset Value Regressions**

	S&P	Yen	Baht
	A. February 1997–July 1997		
Quantum	0.65**	0.08	0.25**
	(0.1)	(0.16)	(0.06)
Quasar	0.10	0.98**	0.29**
	(0.12)	(0.18)	(0.07)
Emerging growth	N/A	2.62**	0.31**
		(0.22)	(0.12)
Jaguar (1997–98)	0.72**	1.61**	0.29**
	(0.06)	(0.10)	(0.04)

	S&P	Yen	HIBOR
	B. May 1998–September 1998		
Quantum	0.51	0.32	0.00
	(0.38)	(0.74)	(0.12)
Quasar	1.08**	2.30**	0.14*
	(0.26)	(0.50)	(0.08)
Emerging growth	N/A	2.21**	−0.32**
		(0.51)	(0.09)
Jaguar (1997–98)	0.99**	1.64**	0.12**
	(0.05)	(0.10)	(0.02)

	S&P	Yen	Hang Seng
	C. May 1998–September 1998		
Quantum	0.22	0.79	0.16
	(0.35)	(0.57)	(0.15)
Quasar	0.28	3.75**	0.23**
	(0.23)	(0.37)	(0.10)
Emerging growth	N/A	1.87**	0.47**
		(0.42)	(0.11)
Jaguar (1997–98)	0.83**	1.20**	−0.28**
	(0.05)	(0.12)	(0.03)

	S&P	Yen	Ringgit
	D. February 1997–July 1997		
Quantum	0.90**	0.40**	0.27
	(0.14)	(0.19)	(0.38)
Quasar	0.22	1.20**	0.83**
	(0.15)	(0.20)	(0.40)
Emerging growth	N/A	2.60**	0.42
		(0.26)	(0.60)
Jaguar (1997–98)	0.49**	1.37**	0.50**
	(0.07)	(0.09)	(0.05)

Notes: Standard errors in parentheses. Constants are not reported.
**Significant at the 5 percent level.
*Significant at the 10 percent level.

vestments in the U.S. equity markets and may have shorted the Japanese yen to fund positions in other markets (Fung and Hsieh 1999b). The results show significant effects of the Thai baht on the NAV of the four funds: The NAVs increase when the baht weakens. The Standard & Poor's index and the yen/dollar rate also enter significantly in these regressions with the expected sign.[44]

The overall short positions by large traders ($7 billion in the estimate by IMF 1998) represent only a quarter of the Bank of Thailand's $28 billion forward book at the end of July 1997. This suggests that many other investors besides HFs had built short positions in baht before the currency's fall in July. According to the IMF study, although "HFs apparently sold some long-dated forward contracts on the baht in February 1997, the bulk of their forward sales to the Bank of Thailand seems to have occurred in May" when significant speculative pressure on the currency started to build up and Thailand introduced some capital controls to limit the speculation against its currency.[45]

On balance, the conclusion in the IMF study that HFs were at the rear of the pack is not strongly supported by the data. Although lack of information prevents a full assessment of the sequence of events and movements by players of different sizes, a plausible interpretation is that large macro HFs detected rather early the fundamental weaknesses of the baht and the likelihood of a devaluation. Since the buildup of short positions started in February and continued through May, one could argue that HFs actually moved first and were followed by a wide range of domestic and international investors.

On the basis of our analysis in the second part of section 5.2.4, the argument that the HFs were "small" in the baht market (short positions for $7 billion against $25 billion at the central bank) needs to be qualified. If the HFs' short positions had been built by the time of the May attack (after the capital controls of 15 May and the spikes in offshore rates, it became much more expensive to short the currency), they would have accounted for a large fraction of the forward book of the central bank by the end of May. Although the eventual fall of the baht was certainly triggered by fundamental weaknesses in the economy, the evidence is not inconsistent with the view that HFs moved first and their presence made other investors more aggressive in their trading strategies.

44. The Standard & Poor's index is not included in the Emerging Growth Fund because this fund invests mostly in emerging markets. Indeed, the Standard & Poor's regressor is not significant when included in the regressions.

45. In one week in May, the central bank intervened by selling about $15 billion. Since this intervention was in the forward market, this information did not become public until August 1997. Smaller speculative attacks had occurred in January, February, and March (see Ito 1999).

5.3.3   The "Double Play" Hypothesis in Hong Kong

In 1998, the currency and other asset markets in Hong Kong felt significant speculative pressures as the Asian crisis worsened. Local authorities argued that large macro HFs were attempting to influence Hong Kong's forex and equity markets (Hong Kong Monetary Authority [HKMA] 1999; HKMA and Reserve Bank of Australia 1999; Tsang 1998). Allegedly, large traders were implementing a "double play": shorting the equity market, then shorting the currency, so as to lead monetary authorities either to abandon the fixed exchange rate or to increase interest rates sharply, or both, and profit from falling stock prices.

In the view of the Hong Kong authorities, the double play proceeded as follows. First, HFs shorted the Hong Kong (spot) stock market as well as the Hang Seng Index futures. HFs allegedly prefunded their Hong Kong dollar needs via swaps with multilateral financial institutions that had heavily borrowed in 1997 and 1998. Next, by using forward purchases of U.S. dollars and spot sales of Hong Kong dollars, they tried to induce a devaluation. Apparently, the size of the short positions of these HFs in the forex and stock markets were very large.

Suppose that, to defend the currency board arrangement, the Hong Kong Monetary Authority (HKMA) had intervened in the foreign exchange market only, drying up market liquidity and causing a correspondingly large increase in interest rates. The monetary tightening would have caused a sharp drop in equity prices, to the benefit of the HFs and other investors who had taken short positions in the stock market.

Suppose instead that, to avoid this stock market collapse, the HKMA had kept interest rates low, while allowing the exchange rate to devalue. Again, the HFs would have reaped large gains, this time through their positions in the currency markets. In either scenario, speculators would have gained from their positions in the stock market or in the forex market, or both.[46]

The HKMA, however, chose a different and unconventional option, consisting of monetary tightening to prevent devaluation and, in August 1998, sizable interventions in the stock markets to support stock prices.[47] In the

---

46. Chakravorti and Lall (2000) develop an analytical model of simultaneous speculative attack on currency and equity markets that is designed to explain the double play hypothesis for Hong Kong. They identify the conditions under which a simultaneous shorting of equity and currency/money markets is a potentially profitable strategy. The model suggests that a simultaneous shorting of the two markets could result from poor economic fundamentals and an increase in the probability that a devaluation may occur. They also explicitly model the effects of central bank intervention in the stock market (as occurred in Hong Kong).

47. In the two weeks between August 14 and 28, 1998, the HKMA purchased approximately US$15 billion of stocks and futures. This represented about 7 percent of the Hong Kong market capitalization and about 30 percent of the free float in the market.

view of the Hong Kong authorities, this radical action was necessary to inflict losses on speculators and give them sufficient cause to be wary of future attempts to corner the market. In the words of Financial Secretary Donald Tsang, the speculative attack "was a contrived game with clearly destructive goals in mind [to] drive up interest rates, drive down share prices, make the local population panic and exert enough pressure on the linked exchange rate until it breaks" (Tsang 1998).

The FSF (2000) study supports the double play hypothesis. Large macro HFs appear to have detected fundamental weaknesses early and started to build large short positions against the currency. According to available estimates, HLIs' short positions in the HK$ market were close to U.S.$ 10 billion (6 percent of GDP), but some observers believe that the correct figure was much higher. Several large macro HFs that had shorted the currency also took very large short positions in the equity markets, and these positions were correlated over time.[48] When the news spread that large HFs were building short positions, other investors followed.

Indirect evidence on the positions of HFs in the Hong Kong currency and equity markets can be provided by regressing the NAV of the four large macro HFs in our sample against the Standard & Poor's 500 index, the yen/dollar rate, the Hang Seng equity index, and a short-term interest rate measure in Hong Kong (the three-month Hong Kong Interbank Offered Rate [HIBOR]) for the period May to September 1998. A negative relation between NAV and the equity index is consistent with short positions of the fund in the Hong Kong equity market. Also, because Hong Kong kept the exchange rate fixed throughout the sample period, profitable short positions in the currency markets would show up as a positive coefficient on the short-term interest rate—interest rate hikes lead to an increase in the forward exchange rate, raising the NAV of a portfolio including short positions in the currency. Results are presented in parts B and C of table 5.4, where we find strong and significant effects of the expected sign (negative on the Hang Seng index and positive on the HIBOR) for one of the funds, and a significant effect of the HIBOR for another fund.[49]

According to the local authorities (Tsang 1998), unsubstantiated rumors and false information about the health of the financial sector and the pos-

48. "Among those taking short positions in the equity market were four large HFs, whose futures and options positions were equivalent to around 40 percent of all outstanding equity futures contracts as of early August prior to the HKMA intervention. Position data suggest a correlation, albeit far from perfect, in the timing of the establishment of the short positions. Two HFs substantially increased their positions during the period of the HKMA intervention. At the end of August, four hedge funds accounted for 50,500 contracts or 49 percent of the total open interest/net delta position; one fund accounted for one-third. The group's meetings suggested that some large HLIs had large short positions in both the equity and currency markets" (FSF 2000, 131).

49. The coefficients of the Hang Seng index on two other funds are significant but with the wrong sign. It is possible that losses inflicted on short equity positions by the Hong Kong intervention may account for this result.

sibility of a devaluation were being spread in the local press and in financial markets, apparently to push down the stock market, spike interest rates, and put pressure on the currency. The FSF (2000) study mentions circumstantial evidence of aggressive trading behavior in the forex market: "Aggressive trading practices by HLIs reportedly included concentrated selling intended to move market prices, large sales in illiquid offshore trading hours, and 'spoofing' of the electronic brokering services to give the impression that the exchange rate had moved beyond the HKMA's intervention level. There were frequent market rumors, often in offshore Friday trading, that a devaluation of the Hong Kong dollar or Chinese renminbi would occur over the weekend" (FSF 2000, 130–31).

However, the empirical findings do not provide, per se, evidence of market manipulation. Macroeconomic conditions in Hong Kong and East Asia in the summer of 1998 (a sharp recession in Hong Kong and a worsening financial and economic crisis in the entire East Asian region, with a falling yen and a threat of currency devaluation in China) were causing concern among investors about the Hong Kong stock market while raising doubts about the survival of the Hong Kong currency peg, in spite of the commitment by the authorities to maintain the currency board. Shorting both the Hong Kong stock market and its currency at that time could have been interpreted as a rational strategy for all investors, domestic and foreign, highly leveraged and not, behaving according to normal market rules and conventions. In other words, the hypothesis of rational investors' taking short positions in two markets (based on an assessment of economic fundamentals) and the hypothesis of a double play (suggesting market manipulation) are observationally equivalent

5.3.4   The Malaysian Ringgit

The role played by macro HFs in the fall of the Malaysian ringgit remains controversial. Local authorities have forcefully argued that their presence made a significant difference. However, several studies (IMF 1998 and Brown, Goetzmann, and Park 2000) suggest that their role was minor.

As in the case of many other currencies in the region, the pressure on the ringgit was undoubtedly driven by fundamental weaknesses in the economy, namely a large current account deficit and a structurally weak financial system, as well as financial and trade contagion from the fall of other Association of Southeast Asian Nations currencies. Nonetheless, it is unresolved whether HFs were leaders of the pack in the circumstances that triggered the fall of the ringgit and the continued pressures on the currency throughout 1997 and 1998.

How large were HFs' short positions against the ringgit? The aforementioned IMF study suggests that their positions were relatively small at the time of the devaluation of the baht, July 1997, when pressures on the Malaysian currency started to rise. Fung, Hsieh, and Tsatsaronis (2000)

reach similar conclusions, estimating that the combined short positions in the ringgit market by twelve HFs amounted to less than $1 billion in June and July 1997.

A study by Brown, Goetzmann, and Park (2000) reaches analogous conclusions. Using returns data, these authors derive estimates of the positions in the Malaysian ringgit over time by the largest ten currency funds. They find that positions in the ringgit did fluctuate dramatically in the second half of the 1990s but were not correlated with movements in the exchange rate. More generally, they identify periods when the HFs had very large exposures to Asian currencies, both positive and negative, but find no relation between these positions and current, past, or future movements in exchange rates.

Some aspects of this study, however, are problematic. Specifically, these authors did not have access to data on net positions but inferred them from observed returns, so serious measurement errors are possible. For example, some of their estimates imply that the gross foreign currency positions on the ringgit were at times close to 200 percent of Malaysian GDP. For instance, in February 1996 the estimated short position by HFs was greater than $200 billion. At the end of June 1997, when the pressure on the currency started to mount, the estimated HFs short positions reached a new peak of $100 billion. Now, either these estimates are subject to significant measurement error or, if correct, their size makes it difficult to argue that HFs' portfolios had no impact on the value of the Malaysian currency. Statistical tests suggest that, for two of the four funds in our sample, NAVs were significantly correlated with movements of the ringgit after controlling for the Standard & Poor's and the yen/dollar rate.[50]

Ultimately, even when one accounts for the apparent gross mismeasurement, the study leaves open the possibility that large traders built sizable positions at the start of the speculative pressure against the ringgit (late June and early July 1997). This is consistent with the view that HFs took large positions before other domestic and foreign investors began to short the currency. In this regard, and based mostly on circumstantial evidence, the FSF (2000) study came to the conclusion that "the ringgit came under heavy selling pressure around May 1997 during the pressures on the Thai baht. Leveraged institutions reportedly had substantial short positions at this time. Pressures continued after the authorities floated the ringgit in July" (FSF 2000, 133).

5.3.5 The Pressures on the Australian Dollar in the Summer of 1998

The view that HFs played a significant role in the pressures on the Australian dollar in the summer of 1998 has been presented in Reserve Bank of

---

50. See part D of table 5.4. In the regressions, the sample period for the Jaguar Fund is 1997–98, but it is February–July 1997 for the other three funds.

Australia (1999). The Australian view is nuanced. The Australian authorities accept that a moderate depreciation of the Australian dollar might have been justified by fundamentals in June and August of 1998. In June, the Australian currency was negatively affected by a weakening Japanese yen and by concerns about the spread and deepening of the Asian crisis. In August, the pressure on the Australian currency was triggered by the Russian collapse and expectations of falling commodity prices in a global slowdown.

Although acknowledging the rationale for a depreciation in light of these fundamental weaknesses, the Australian view was that large macro HFs manipulated foreign currency markets to force a depreciation well in excess of what was justified by fundamentals. The Australian authorities argued that, even though the Australian dollar exchange rate market was very liquid and had one of the highest turnover rates among Organization for Economic Cooperation and Development countries, HFs were nonetheless trying to manipulate it in different ways. First, HFs were supposedly able to borrow Australian dollar funds from Australian banks in large amounts in order to build speculative positions in the foreign exchange market. Second, a few large HFs were allegedly signalling their short positions in the Australian dollar market, effectively becoming leaders for a wide set of funds and financial institutions. As a result, by taking very large short positions against the Australian dollar while inducing other investors to follow a similar strategy, the HFs were effectively able to corner the market.

Reportedly, the overall short positions against the Australian dollar were sizable in the summer of 1998. Only a very aggressive intervention by the Reserve Bank of Australia in June and August (and eventually the unraveling of the yen carry trade) could stop what looked like a large speculative attempt to cause an unwarranted collapse of the currency.

An interesting feature of the Australian case is that the speculative attack hit a flexible, rather than a fixed, exchange rate regime. FSF (2000) provides a systematic study of the Australian episode, suggesting that HLIs built up speculative short positions against the Australian dollar from late 1997 onward. The speculative activity intensified in April and May 1998: By the end of May, the currency had fallen 24 percent below its peak in late 1996. In June 1998, the pressures on the currency increased, with short positions by HFs and other HLIs estimated at roughly $10 billion, about 2 percent of Australian GDP.

The study found evidence of aggressive trading, shrinkage of liquidity, the spread of rumors, the moving of contrarians to the sidelines, and herding along the HLI positions. In particular, "having already accumulated large short positions, a few HLIs—primarily large macro HFs—according to some market participants took actions in late May and early June to attempt to push the exchange rate lower. These actions reportedly included spreading rumors about an upcoming attack in the currency to deter buyers, and aggressive trading. A key feature of this latter was to concentrate large amounts of sales into periods of thin trading. These actions were reported by market participants to be designed in part to cause those who might have taken contrarian positions to withdraw from the market. One consequence was that exporters, who had been consistent buyers of Australian dollars at higher levels, not only stood aside and stopped buying at this time but some even began selling as the currency looked to fall to record lows" (FSF 2000, 128).

5.3.6   Financial and Currency Turmoil in South Africa in 1998

The case study of South Africa in 1998 is interesting for a number of reasons. First, the country had a semiflexible exchange rate regime, yet the authorities heavily intervened in the forward market to defend the currency when strong speculative pressures emerged in the spring of 1998. Second, as in Hong Kong, investors may have attempted a double play. In this case, however, the double play was staged in the bond and forex markets rather than in the equity and forex markets. Third, according to FSF (2000), the main role in the financial market was played by proprietary desks of large international financial firms, rather than large macro HFs.

As in previous episodes, macro policy was generally sound, but the economy was hit by a number of shocks at the time of the turmoil. In the spring of 1998, the economy was suffering from political uncertainty, a fall in the price of gold and other export commodities, and a confidence deterioration, all of which led to a downgrade of GDP growth forecasts. Until April 1998, many nonresident investors—including HLIs—had built long positions in South African assets (especially government bonds). A major reversal of capital flows occurred in May and June 1998, with outflows by nonresidents estimated at about 24 billion rand.

These speculative pressures led between April and August to a 25 percent fall of the rand, a 40 percent plunge of the equity market, and sharp increases in the yields on medium-term bonds from 12.9 percent to 21.6 percent. The central bank initially responded to the pressure on the currency by aggressively intervening in the forward market (selling about $8 billion of reserves forward in May and June). Total short foreign exchange positions were estimated to be about US$8–9 billion (approximately 7 percent of GDP), thus equivalent to total forward interventions. At the same time, investors could easily build short fixed-income positions in the government bond market by borrowing in the large and liquid repo market. As reported in FSF (2000), some suggested that a double play took the form of aggressive sales of the currency to spike short-term interest rates and profit from short positions in the bond market.

The fall in the rand accelerated in June after the reserve bank stopped intervening. The publication of the forward book showed that the reserve bank was then vulnerable to large losses from previous forward intervention. Attempts to influence the course of market prices to the HLIs' own advantage were once again reported to have taken place: "[A]t times trading was reported as very aggressive, including the sale of large parcels to the market at any price and greater than normal trading in periods of illiquidity, sometimes apparently with sustained price impact" (FSF 2000, 141).

5.3.7   The Conclusions of the FSF Study on Market Dynamics in Turmoil Episodes

In our analysis above we have often built upon the FSF (2000) study, an extensive study whose overall results are consistent with the key implications of our theoretical analysis. The ambivalent conclusions of this study provide an excellent summary of the complex and multifaceted debate on the role of HLIs in currency crises:

- "Under normal market conditions, HLIs do not threaten the stability of medium-sized markets. Together with other market participants, HLIs can play an important role translating views about the fundamentals into prices and face the same incentives as other market participants to avoid outsized positions. Because of their ability and willingness to take leveraged positions, HLIs can be an important source of market liquidity and can, over time, contribute positively to market development."
- "From time to time, HLIs may establish large and concentrated positions in small and medium-sized markets. When this is the case, HLIs have the potential to materially influence market dynamics. The size and duration of the effects can be amplified through herding or through other market participants moving to the sidelines and depend critically on the strength of the fundamentals and the behavior of 'ongoing' transactors in the domestic currency."
- "The judgment as to whether HLI positions are destabilizing has to be made on a case-by-case basis. Several members of the study group believe that large HLI positions exacerbated the situations in several of the case-study economies in 1998, contributing to unstable market dynamics and significant spillovers. These members of the group are of the view that HLI positions and tactics can at times represent a significant independent source of pressure. Some other group members do not think that there is sufficient evidence to advance such judgments on the basis of the 1998 experience, given the uncertainty prevailing in the markets at that time. They believe that the impact of HLIs on markets is likely to be very short-lived and that, provided fundamentals are strong, HLI positions and strategies are unlikely to present a major independent driving force in market dynamics."
- "The group is concerned about the possible impact on market dynamics of some of the aggressive practices cited in the case-study economies

during 1998; it is not, however, able to reach a conclusion on the scale of these practices, whether manipulation was involved and their impact on market integrity. Some group members believe that the threshold for assessing manipulation can be set too high and that some of the aggressive practices raise important issues for market integrity. They are of the view that there is sufficient evidence to suggest that attempted manipulation can and does occur in foreign exchange markets and should be a serious source of concern for policy makers (FSF 2000, 125–26).

As a conclusion to the assessment of the 1990s crisis episodes, it is worth recalling that foreign exchange market pressures rapidly diminished in the late summer and early fall of 1998, when large HFs and other HLIs reduced their activity following a number of events: the Russian devaluation and default; the collapse of LTCM and the ensuing liquidity and credit squeeze in the financial markets of advanced economies; the sharp appreciation of the yen in September and October of 1998, which brought losses to those HLIs that had heavily shorted the yen and played the aforementioned carry trade. Also, "unorthodox" policy actions such as the massive Hong Kong intervention in its equity market, capital controls in Malaysia, and intervention against bond-shorters in South Africa contributed to a squeeze on the speculative short positions of HLIs.[51]

5.4 Conclusion

This paper has presented a theoretical and empirical analysis of the role of large players in currency crises. Our study contributes to an analytical literature that, while still in its infancy, is making significant progress in understanding how the existence of large players may affect foreign exchange market dynamics. On the empirical side, results are constrained by the fact that detailed data on major market participants' positions and strategies are limited. However, the evidence presented in our paper and in a number of recent studies sheds some light on the role played by large players in recent episodes of currency turmoil.

In sum, our analysis does not contradict the conventional wisdom that large players possess the following traits: they are better informed or perceived to be better informed, they are able to build sizable short positions via leverage; they tend to move first based on an assessment of fundamental weaknesses; they contribute to currency pressures in the presence of weak or uncertain fundamentals; they are closely monitored by smaller investors prone to herd on their observed or guessed positions, even when the small traders would act as contrarians based on the private information

51. See the 1999 IMF International Capital Market Report (IMF 1999) for a detailed discussion of these and other "unorthodox" interventions in financial markets.

available to them; and they may recur to aggressive trading practices. Undoubtedly, future theoretical and empirical research will shed further light on many of the aspects discussed here.

We conclude with three observations. First, the role of large players in financial markets may have recently changed. Some large macro hedge funds and other HLIs have closed down or retrenched their operations.[52] Perhaps in part as a consequence of this retrenchment, there is now some concern that liquidity in the forex market may have been reduced and greater asset price volatility may have emerged. However, it is still too early to assess whether such liquidity shrinkage has occurred and what its causes and consequences are.

Second, the disappearance of several large macro HFs after 1998 may in part be the result of the ongoing phase-out of fixed exchange rate regimes; one after another, most noninstitutionalized exchange rate pegs have been abandoned (Mexico, Asia, Russia, Brazil). Large macro bets against a peg are easier to make, since large short positions can be built at low cost when the monetary authority provides foreign currency at a fixed price. With flexible rates, instead, there is always a two-sided currency risk, and the costs of building short positions depend on whether, and to what extent, other agents (other than the central bank) are willing to take the opposite side of these transactions. Attempts to build speculative positions lead to continuous time movements in the exchange rate, reducing not only the incentive to speculate but also the scope for sharp (thus profitable) adjustment. Indeed, large macro directional bets on the flexible exchange rates of the G3 economies allegedly led to losses in 1999 and 2000, contributing to the eventual demise of some large macro HFs.

Third, the policy implications of the role of large players in market dynamics are complex and multifaceted. The official sector began to address these issues within the HLI working group of the FSF. This group considered both the implications of HLIs for systemic risk in global financial markets and the role of HLIs in market dynamics in small and medium-sized economies.

Regarding systemic risk, the recommendations of this working group's report mirrored many of the recommendations of the report of the U.S. President's Working Group on Capital Markets (1999). The recommendations included measures aimed at better risk management by HLIs and their counterparties (better credit assessments, better exposure measurement, establishment of credit limits, and collateral management techniques), better creditor oversight (greater intensity of scrutiny of firms that are falling short

---

52. LTCM was closed down following its near collapse in 1998; the Tiger Group funds were closed down in 2000 following a period of poor investment returns; the operations of the Quantum Group funds have been scaled down; the Moore Capital Group decided to return $2 billion of capital to its investors; and several forex prop desks of large financial firms have been either closed or scaled down in their operations.

and periodic reaffirmation of compliance with sound practices), and enhanced practices of public disclosure and reporting to authorities.

Regarding the issue of market dynamics in small and medium-sized economies, the HLI report also made a number of recommendations. First, the report noted that enhanced risk management practices could address some of the concerns raised by emerging markets by constraining excessive leverage. Second, it noted that trading on organized exchanges, requiring market participants to report to regulators, and possibly requiring position limits as well could alleviate some of the pressures caused by large and concentrated positions. Third, the FSF recommended that market participants themselves articulate guidelines for market conduct in the area of foreign exchange trading. These market guidelines would address the concerns of smaller and medium-sized economies about the trading practices that might have contributed to exacerbating market pressures in period of market turmoil.

References

Allen, Franklin, and Douglas Gale. 1992. Stock-price manipulation. *Review of Financial Studies* 5:503–29.

Allen, Franklin, and Gary Gorton. 1992. Stock price manipulation, market microstructure and asymmetric information. *European Economic Review* 36:624–30.

Bagnoli, Mark, and Barton L. Lipman. 1996. Stock price manipulation through takeover bids. *RAND Journal of Economics* 27 (1): 124–47.

Barclay, Michael J., and Jerold B. Warner. 1993. Stealth trading and volatility: Which trades move prices? *Journal of Financial Economics* 34:281–305.

Benabou, Roland, and Guy Laroque. 1992. Using privileged information to manipulate markets: Insiders, gurus, and credibility. *Quarterly Journal of Economics* 107 (3): 921–58.

Brown, Stephen, William Goetzmann, and James Park. 2000. Hedge funds and the Asian currency crisis. *Journal of Portfolio Management* 26 (4): 95–101.

Buiter, Willem, Giancarlo Corsetti, and Paolo Pesenti. 1998a. *Financial markets and European monetary cooperation: The lessons of the 1992–93 exchange rate mechanism crisis.* Cambridge, U.K.: Cambridge University Press.

———. 1998b. Interpreting the ERM crisis: Country-specific and systemic issues. Princeton Studies in International Finance no. 84. Princeton University, Department of Economics, International Finance Section.

Carlsson, H., and E. van Damme. 1993. Global games and equilibrium selection. *Econometrica* 61:989–1018.

Chakravorti, Sujit, and Subir Lall. 2000. The double play: Simultaneous speculative attacks on currency and equity markets. Federal Reserve Bank of Chicago, Working Paper.

Corsetti, Giancarlo, Amil Dasgupta, Stephen Morris, and Hyun Song Shin. 2000. Does one Soros make a difference? The role of a large trader in currency crises. Cowles Foundation Discussion Paper no. 1273. New Haven, Conn.: Yale University.

Corsetti, Giancarlo, Paolo Pesenti, and Nouriel Roubini. 1999. What caused the Asian currency and financial crisis? *Japan and the World Economy* 11 (3): 305–73.

Dasgupta, Amil. 1999. Social learning with payoff complementarities. Yale University, Department of Economics, Working Paper.

———. 2001. Coordination, learning, and delay. Yale University, Department of Economics, Working Paper.

Easley, David, and Maureen O'Hara. 1987. Price, trade size, and information in securities markets. *Journal of Financial Economics* 19:69–90.

Eichengreen, Barry. 2000. The EMS crisis in retrospect. NBER Working Paper no. 8035. Cambridge, Mass.: National Bureau of Economic Research, December.

Eichengreen, Barry, and Donald Mathieson. 1999. Hedge funds: What do we really know? Washington, D.C.: *Economic Issues* no. 19 (September) Washington, D.C.: International Monetary Fund.

Eichengreen, Barry, and Charles Wyplosz. 1993. The unstable EMS. *Brookings Papers on Economic Activity,* Issue no. 1:51–143. Washington, D.C.: Brookings Institution.

Financial Stability Forum (FSF). 2000. Report of the Market Dynamics Study Group of the FSF Working Group on Highly Leveraged Institutions. 5 April 2000. [http://www.fsforum.org/Reports/RepHLI.html].

Fung, William, and David A. Hsieh. 1999a. Hedge fund risk management. Duke University, Fuqua School of Business. Mimeograph.

———. 1999b. A primer on hedge funds. *Journal of Empirical Finance* 6 (September): 309–31.

Fung, William, David A. Hsieh, and Konstantinos Tsatsaronis. 2000. Do hedge funds disrupt emerging markets? In *Brookings-Wharton Papers on Financial Services 2000,* ed. Robert E. Litan and Anthony M. Santomero, 377–421. Washington, D.C.: Brookings Institution.

Hartigan, J. A. 1983. *Bayes theory.* Berlin: Springer-Verlag.

International Monetary Fund (IMF). 1998. Hedge funds and financial market dynamics. IMF Occasional Paper no. 166. Washington, D.C.: International Monetary Fund, May.

———. 1999. *International capital markets,* September. Washington, D.C.: International Monetary Fund.

Ito, Takatoshi. 1999. The development of the Thailand currency crisis: A chronological review. Hitotsubashi University, Institute of Economic Research, Working Paper.

Jarrow, Robert A. 1992. Market manipulation, bubbles, corners and short squeezes. *Journal of Financial and Quantitative Analysis* 27 (3): 311–36.

Kumar, Praveen, and Duane J. Seppi. 1992. Future manipulation with "Cash Settlement." *Journal of Finance* 47:1485–1502.

Kyle, Albert S. 1984. A theory of futures market manipulations. In *The industrial organization of futures markets,* ed. Ronald Anderson, 141–74. Lexington, Mass.: Lexington Books.

———. 1985. Continuous auctions with insider trading. *Econometrics* 46:1429–45.

Lee, Yi-Tsung, Ji-Chai Lin, and Yu-Jane Liu. 1999. Trading patterns of big versus small players in an emerging market: An empirical analysis. *Journal of Banking and Finance* 23:701–25.

Morris, Stephen, and Hyung Shin. 1998. Unique equilibrium in a model of self-fulfilling currency attacks. *American Economic Review* 88:587–97.

———. 2000. Global games: Theory and applications. Cowles Foundation Discussion Paper no. 1275R. Yale University.

Mussa, Michael, Alexander Swoboda, Jeromin Zettelmeyer, and Olivier Jeanne.

1999. Moderating fluctuations in capital flows to emerging market economies. *Finance and Development* 36 (3): 9–12.

President's Working Group on Financial Markets. 1999. Hedge funds, leverage, and the lessons of long-term capital management. [http://www.ustreas.gov/press/releases/docs/hedgfund.pdf]. Transmitted to Congress 28 April 1999.

Reserve Bank of Australia. 1999. Hedge funds, financial stability, and market integrity. Paper presented at the EMEAP Deputies Meeting. 25 March, Melbourne, Australia.

Schadler, Susan, Maria Carkovic, Adam Bennett, and Robert Kahn. 1993. Recent experiences with surges in capital inflows. IMF Occasional Paper no. 108. Washington, D.C.: International Monetary Fund.

Tsang, Donald. 1998. Speech, delivered at the Hong Kong Trade Development Council, Frankfurt, Germany, 29 September 1999.

Vila, Jean-Luc. 1987. The role of information in the manipulation of futures markets. CARESS Working Paper no. 87-26. Philadelphia, Penn.: University of Pennsylvania.

———. 1989. Simple games of market manipulation. *Economics Letters* 29:21–26.

Wei, Shang-Jin, and Jungshik Kim. 1999. The big players in the foreign exchange market: Do they trade on information or noise? Harvard University, Center for International Development, Working Paper.

Comment   Jaume Ventura

The paper by Corsetti, Pesenti, and Roubini studies how the presence of large investors affects the nature of currency crises. Its motivation is the alleged prominent role that some hedge funds and investment banks have played in recent episodes of this sort. Regardless of whether this is factually correct or not, I am convinced that the topic is of great interest. In this comment, I raise a few issues that the paper either overlooks or does not treat with sufficient clarity. To illustrate them, I use a bare-bones version of the model that removes all uncertainty (public and private) about fundamentals.

The simplest model is the "speculators" game. In this game, one or more investors command resources of mass 1. Let θ be the state of the country or fundamentals, and assume everybody observes it. Define $\ell \in (0,1)$ as the fraction of resources that are used to attack the currency. The currency collapses if and only if fundamentals are weak relative to the size of the attack, that is, if $\theta \leq \ell$. Investors have no intrinsic interest in the country. If they abstain from attacking the currency, their payoff is zero independently of whether the currency collapses. Investors see the country merely as an opportunity to make profits from inconsistent policy making. They can commit their resources to the attack by paying a per-unit cost of $t < 1$. If the currency collapses, they gain a per-unit profit equal to one. Otherwise their profit is zero. With these assumptions, we can write the payoff matrix of investors in table 5C.1:

Jaume Ventura is associate professor of economics at the Massachusetts Institute of Technology and a faculty research fellow of the National Bureau of Economic Research.

Table 5C.1   **"Speculators" Game**

	Collapse	No Collapse
ATTACK	$1-t$	$-t$
NO ATTACK	0	0

Assume first that the unit mass of resources is uniformly distributed among a continuum of atomistic investors. If $\theta > 1$, the currency does not collapse regardless of the investors' actions. Knowing this, nobody attacks, and $\ell = 0$. If $\theta \le 0$, the currency collapses regardless of the investors' actions. Knowing this, all investors attack and $\ell = 1$. In the range $0 < \theta \le 1$, there are two possible equilibria. If investors believe nobody else will attack, then $\ell = 0$ and the currency does not collapse. If investors believe everybody else will attack, then $\ell = 1$ and the currency collapses. How do investors select the equilibrium when this happens? Simply assume there is a sunspot variable that coordinates them and takes one of two values, ATTACK and NO ATTACK, with probabilities π and $1 - \pi$, respectively. Under this assumption, if $0 < \theta \le 1$ the currency collapses with probability π.

Assume next a fraction $\lambda < 1$ of the unit mass of resources is owned by a single large investor and the rest is uniformly distributed among the continuum of atomistic investors. How does this change in market structure affect the likelihood of a currency crisis? To develop some intuition, consider three alternative (and arbitrary) rules of behavior for the large investor:

1. *The large investor is a hawk.* Assume the large investor always attacks. If $\theta \le \lambda$, the currency collapses. If $\theta > 1$, the currency does not collapse. If $\lambda < \theta \le 1$, there are two equilibria. If atomistic investors believe that only the large investor will attack, then $\ell = \lambda$, and the currency does not collapse. If atomistic investors believe everybody else will attack, then $\ell = 1$, and the currency collapses. The presence of a hawkish large investor raises the lower threshold of the range of multiple equilibria. As $\lambda \to 1$, this range disappears as this threshold converges to 1.

2. *The large investor is a dove.* Assume the large investor never attacks. If $\theta \le 0$, the currency collapses. If $\theta > 1 - \lambda$, the currency does not collapse. If $0 < \theta \le 1 - \lambda$, there are two equilibria. If atomistic investors believe nobody else will attack, then $\ell = 0$, and the currency does not collapse. If atomistic investors believe other atomistic investors will attack, then $1 = 1 - \lambda$, and the currency collapses. The presence of a dovish large investor lowers the upper threshold of the range of multiple equilibria. As $\lambda \to 1$, this range disappears as this threshold converges to zero.

3. *The large investor follows the crowd.* Assume the large investor attacks only if it expects other investors to attack. If $\theta \le 0$, the currency collapses. If $\theta > 1$, the currency does not collapse. If $0 < \theta \le 1$, there are two equilibria. If investors believe nobody else will attack, then $\ell = 0$, and the currency

does not collapse. If investors believe everybody else will attack, then $\ell = 1$, and the currency collapses. The presence of a follow-the-crowd large investor has no effect on the equilibrium of the game.

What are these examples telling us? As λ grows, the large investor gradually replaces atomistic investors in the task of allocating resources.[1] If its investment strategy is more aggressive than those of the atomistic investors it replaces, more resources will be used to attack the currency in some range of the fundamentals. An obvious reason for this is that the resources transferred are now invested more aggressively. However, because the actions of investors are strategic complements, the presence of a more aggressive investor also leads other investors to be more aggressive. This brings me to the first point: *The effects of a large investor on the likelihood of a currency crisis depend on how aggressive its strategy is relative to those of the atomistic investors it replaces.*

None of the examples above describe the solution to the "speculators" game. They instead describe the solutions to three alternative games in which atomistic investors are rational speculators, but large investors are irrational in some specific ways. The only purpose of the examples was to develop intuition on how the behavior of a large investor affects the likelihood of a crisis and the behavior of other investors. Assume from now on that the large investor is rational and chooses its investment strategy optimally. Is this enough to tell us whether the large investor behaves more or less aggressively than the atomistic investors it is replacing?

Let's start by describing the actual solution to the "speculators" game. If $\theta > 1$, the currency does not collapse. If $\theta \le \lambda$, the currency collapses because the large investor always attacks. If we assume that it does not, then its payoff is zero rather than $\lambda \cdot (1 - t) > 0$. If $\lambda < \theta \le 1$, there are two equilibria. If investors believe nobody else will attack, then $\ell = 0$, and the currency does not collapse. If investors believe everybody else will attack, then $\ell = 1$, and the currency collapses. In this range the currency collapses with probability π. Note that the large investor chooses a more aggressive investment strategy than that of the atomistic investors it is replacing. In the range $0 < \theta \le \lambda$ it chooses to attack with probability 1, whereas the (replaced) atomistic investors attack with probability π. For all other values of the fundamentals, the strategy of the large investor is identical to those of the (replaced) atomistic ones. Therefore, the presence of a large investor raises the likelihood of a currency crisis.

Is this a robust result? A simple modification of the game dispels any hope in this direction. In the "speculators" game, investors have no intrinsic interest in the country and only see in the latter an opportunity to profit

---

1. Naturally, this is in a figurative sense. I am analyzing a class of games indexed by λ. Within each game there is no transfer of resources among investors.

Table 5C.2   **"Creditors" Game**

	Collapse	No Collapse
ATTACK	0	0
NO ATTACK	$r - d$	r

from inconsistent policies. From their perspective, the best possible scenario is a currency collapse. Consider instead a "creditors" game, in which investors have already invested in the country a unit mass of resources. Perhaps they have lent to domestic banks or the government at an interest rate r higher than the world interest rate of zero. The risk, of course, is that the currency devalues by an amount $d > r$. In the "creditors" game, the best possible scenario for investors is that the currency does not collapse. If investors attack (i.e., sell their investments and leave the country), their payoff is the world interest rate regardless of whether the currency collapses or not. If they do not attack (i.e., keep their investments and stay in the country), their payoff is r if the currency does not collapse and $r - d < 0$ if it does. This is shown in the payoff matrix in table 5C.2.

As a description of recent currency crises, the "creditors" game seems at least as realistic as the "speculators" game. Moreover, in the absence of a large investor, both games exhibit the same equilibria.[2] However, the presence of a large investor leads to opposite results in both games. To see this, let's describe the solution to the "creditors" game: If $\theta \leq 0$, the currency collapses regardless of the actions of investors. If $\theta > 1 - \lambda$, the currency does not collapse because the large investor never attacks. If we assume that it does not, then its payoff is zero rather than $\lambda \cdot r > 0$. If $0 < \theta \leq 1 - \lambda$, there are two equilibria. If investors believe nobody else will attack, then $\ell = 0$, and the currency does not collapse. If investors believe everybody else will attack, then $\ell = 1$, and the currency collapses. Assuming that the same sunspot variable selects the equilibrium in both games, the currency collapses with probability π in the range of multiple equilibria. In the "creditors" game, the large investor chooses a less aggressive strategy than that of the atomistic investors it is replacing, and as a result the likelihood of a currency crisis decreases.

The common thread in these two games is that atomistic investors are nervous about the behavior of other investors. There is always a preferred outcome, but achieving it requires coordination. In the "speculators" game, the preferred outcome was to profit from policy inconsistencies. In the "creditors" game, the preferred outcome was to preserve good investment opportunities in the country. For some range of fundamentals, the large investor can decide market outcomes and effectively choose its preferred equilibrium. Because the incentives of small and large investors are aligned,

2. They even exhibit the same payoffs if $r = 1 - t$ and $d = 1$.

this equilibrium will also be preferred by atomistic investors. This leads us to the second point: *With atomistic investors, a coordination failure is possible in that the equilibrium chosen is "bad" from the investors' perspective. The presence of a large investor partially solves this coordination failure and raises the likelihood of achieving the equilibrium considered "good" from the investors' perspective.*

A natural generalization of this intuition applies in games in which there is conflict among investors. The simplest illustration of this point is a "mixed" game, in which a fraction ϕ of the unit mass of resources is owned by "speculators" (i.e., investors with the payoff matrix of the "speculators" game) and the rest by "creditors" (i.e., investors with the payoff matrix of the "creditors" game). If all investors are atomistic, the "mixed" game delivers the same equilibrium as the previous two games. However, the effects of a large investor depend on its type in an intuitive fashion. It is easy to check that the presence of a large investor lowers the range of multiple equilibria and raises the likelihood of achieving the equilibrium that is preferred by investors of its own type.[3]

The last issue I want to take on here is that of the interaction between the large investor and the government. In the games analyzed so far, governments can take no action that affects the likelihood of a currency crisis. In real episodes, governments do not passively wait until investors have made up their minds. On the contrary, they actively try to affect their decisions through announcements and promises of various sorts. Does the presence of a large investor affect the government's options to affect the resolution of a crisis?

Consider the "speculators" game again, but assume now that the government can bribe investors. More precisely, before investors choose their strategies, the government can credibly commit to pay them b if the currency does not collapse. Clearly, this bribe has no effect at all on the outcome of the game if the fundamentals are too strong or too weak, that is, if $\theta > 1$ or $\theta \leq 0$. Therefore, there is no point in the government's offering it in this case. The question I address here is whether the government can use a bribe to affect the outcome of the game when fundamentals are in the intermediate region, that is, $0 < \theta \leq \lambda$.[4] In this region, the bribe transforms the payoff matrix of investors as shown in table 5C.3.

3. More fun is possible if we allow for two large investors with different types in the "mixed" game. Assume that each of them commands a fraction λ of the resources of her type. Then the range of multiple equilibria is $\lambda \cdot \phi < \theta < 1 - \lambda \cdot (1 - \phi)$. As $\lambda \to 1$, the range of multiple equilibria disappears as both thresholds converge to ϕ.

4. It is crucial here that this bribe be contingent on the outcome of the game (or the collective actions of the investors) and not on each individual investor's action. If the latter type of conditioning were feasible, an intriguing possibility arises. Assume that, in the range $0 < \theta \leq 1$, the government promises a very large payment if the currency collapses to all those investors (large and small) that did not attack. If this promise is credible, the government has found a free lunch. Now the dominant strategy for all investors is never to attack when $0 < \theta \leq 1$, so the government has coordinated investors toward the desired equilibrium. Because the currency never collapses, this has been achieved at zero cost.

Table 5C.3   **"Speculators" Game with a Bribe**

	Collapse	No Collapse
ATTACK	$1 - t$	$b - t$
NO ATTACK	0	b

Assume first that all investors are atomistic and, within the range of multiple equilibria, they select the equilibrium with the now-familiar sunspot variable that leads them to attack with probability π and not to attack with probability $1 - \pi$.[5] Then the presence of a bribe does not influence the equilibrium of the game or the likelihood of a currency crisis. Why? Altering the incentives of investors makes no difference if the latter cannot coordinate their actions to reach their preferred outcome. Because the bribe would be ineffective, the government will never offer it in the first place.

Things can be quite different, however, if there is a large investor and the bribe is sufficiently attractive. Assume $b \geq 1 - t$. In this case, the solution of game is as follows: If $\theta \leq 0$, the currency collapses, whereas if $\theta > 1 - \lambda$, the currency does not collapse. If $0 < \theta \leq 1 - \lambda$, the currency collapses with probability π. If $b < 1 - t$, the solution of the game is the same as if there were no bribe. Therefore, a large enough bribe succeeds in reducing the likelihood of a currency collapse. If the government attaches enough value to sustaining the currency, the equilibrium bribe is $1 - t$. Otherwise, the equilibrium bribe is zero. What is going on? If the bribe is attractive enough, investors no longer prefer a currency collapse. They would rather take the bribe instead. If investors can coordinate their efforts even partially to reach their preferred outcome, the government has an incentive to use a bribe to align this preference with its own. When this happens, the large investor changes its strategy, and this reduces the likelihood of a currency collapse.[6]

In the presence of a large investor, the outcome of the "speculators" game is not robust to giving the government the option to offer a bribe, since the latter will be used to affect the incentives of the large investor and the outcome of the game. The same is not true for the "creditors" game, because the incentives of the government and the large investor are already aligned. Any government bribe would simply be a waste of resources and, recogniz-

5. This assumption now has some bite. The presence of the bribe has converted the "speculators" game into a Stackelberg game with the government as the leader. This game has a much larger set of equilibria, which includes strategies that condition the attack on the bribe, such as "if $b < b^*$, attack; otherwise, don't." In fact, there is an infinite number of equilibria! The sunspot variable effectively rules out all of these additional equilibria, so that we keep only the two familiar ones.

6. The bribe might be too expensive in this game. After all, it must be at least as high as the benefits that all investors receive if the currency collapses. There might be situations in which the government can target the bribe to reach the large investor without much of a giveaway to the atomistic ones. If this type of targeting is feasible, then the lowest bribe that would change the outcome of the game is $\lambda \cdot (1 - t)$ instead of $1 - t$.

ing that, the government does not offer one. This leads me to the third and final point: *The presence of a large investor tends to reduce the likelihood of a currency crisis, because the government can manipulate its incentives and use it to partially solve the coordination failure in such a way as to avoid a currency collapse.*

When we attempt to map the concept of a bribe to reality, two ideas come to mind. The first and obvious one is reforms. The government might have the ability to credibly commit to some costly policy changes that raise the profitability of foreign investments in the country. Notice, though, that these reforms must be made contingent on the currency's not collapsing. This seems somewhat to contradict actual events, because many countries wait to implement costly reforms until a crisis has already occurred.

A second possibility is to think of the bribe as a high interest rate. Because the value of loans falls after a currency collapse, a high interest rate can be seen as a bribe that is conditional on the currency's not collapsing. In this case, the simple model here gives us some insights regarding the effectiveness of raising the interest rate as a defense against a currency attack. If there is a large investor of the "speculator" type, this defense will succeed for some values of the fundamentals. If the large investor is of the "creditor" type or all investors are atomistic, this defense will never succeed.

Where do we go from here? In this comment, I have used a standard model of coordination failures to raise some questions and submit some conjectures on the role of large investors in currency crises. My hope is that more researchers will devote their time to this problem. Our knowledge of how market structure affects international capital flows is, to say the least, rudimentary, yet I suspect the payoff to research in this area might be quite large. Models of perfect competition have been unable so far to explain basic observations such as why long-term capital flows are so small, or why short-term capital flows are so volatile. Perhaps models of imperfect competition will have more success at this task. However, as the examples here show, sorting out the arguments and the facts is likely to prove a long and treacherous journey.

Discussion Summary

The discussion centered on two themes: the theoretical treatment of large players in the model and the empirical part of the paper.

Aaron Tornell raised the issue of there being more than one large player. There are usually several large actors in a given market, and the industrial organization literature suggests that the ways that a monopoly and an oligopoly work are markedly different. When there is more than one big player, the players interact strategically with each other, and the logic in the paper—which focuses on the interaction between the single large player and many small players—may not carry over in such a situation. He argued that we need a theory that is robust to the number of large players in the market.

Michael P. Dooley made the remark that the largest, highly leveraged, and nonfundamental speculator in these markets is the central bank. In the model's setting, one big player (a hedge fund) is followed by many small players, but in reality, the central bank fulfills the role of large player. As he playfully put it, the central bank sits there with a big hammer and threatens to crush the little players should they bet against it. He agreed with Tornell that the behavior of several large players needs to be modelled instead of the interaction of small players with a single large one.

Roberto Chang agreed with both and commented that the governments in most crisis countries did (or tried to) punish speculators severely. However, this behavior is not represented in the model; instead, the government is assumed to carry out a mechanical role.

Martin Feldstein commented on the role of large players. He said that we tend to think that large players play a negative role because they are effective in increasing the probability of crises, as suggested in the paper. But perhaps the large players are performing a useful role as potential discipliners. For example, they force some countries to move toward flexible exchange rates, and they make countries adopt more sensible domestic fiscal policies. *Federico Sturzenegger* disagreed with the role of large players; he said that the fact that the large players had moved out of the market suggests they could not do anything. *Rudi Dornbusch* gave a different explanation for the exit of hedge funds (large players) from the market: the big players are now old and rich enough!

Sebastian Edwards raised a related question regarding the exchange rate regime and large players. This paper argues that many large players have stopped operating partly due to the fact that a large number of emerging nations abandoned the pegged exchange rate system. The current view on exchange rate regimes is increasingly in favor of the two corner solutions. He asked whether countries that chose to have a fixed regime (in the form of dollarization or currency boards) are more likely to be affected by large players and are more subject to crises.

On the empirical part of the paper, Feldstein asked what the U.S. hedge fund data cover. What is "U.S." for this purpose? Moreover, if a hedge fund is offshore, how offshore can it be to evade being part of the data set?

Linda S. Goldberg suggested that the paper could do more hypothesis tests in the empirical part. For example, on the relationship between the net foreign borrowing position and exchange rates, what part of the change of net foreign position of large players is due to exchange rate movements, and what part is associated with their position? When looking at the dynamics of players and action, what incremental dynamics are expected for exchange rate movements based on the change of position? What are the timing and nature of the dynamics predicted by the theory? Can one do something over time by looking at different dynamics related to the change of composition of the players, or the change of relative sizes of players as predicted by the theory?

Tornell said that the paper only shows that large asset price changes are correlated with the position of some large firms. In order to say this is supportive to the theory of the paper, one should also show that there is no correlation between asset price changes and the position of small firms (as pointed out by *Min Shi*).

Sturzenegger raised a question on endogeneity in the relationship between the change of net foreign position and exchange rate, namely, how does exchange rate change affect the change of net foreign position? He also suggested that one could conduct some case studies, for example, on how large players make announcements and try to influence the market. These events could also be used to do hypothesis tests.

Kristin J. Forbes said that the paper focuses on the role of hedge funds in exchange rate markets only. One extension could be to look at the role of large hedge funds in equity markets. There are some assumptions in the model that do not apply to equity markets. For example, when one compares hedge funds and mutual funds in this market, it seems that mutual funds have superior information, greater transparency, and less leverage; more importantly, hedge funds can short, while other investors cannot. Therefore, it could be interesting to study the broader implications of the model regarding hedge funds in other markets.

Shang-Jin Wei mentioned the only three academic papers on the role of large players and argued that they do not provide supportive evidence for the role of large players. In the Korean case that Kim and Wei looked at, the offshore funds, which are mostly hedge funds, do not seem to be aggressive in the sense of pursuing momentum trading relative to non-offshore funds. The study by Brown, Goetzman, and Park (1998) of hedge funds based on payoff data does not suggest that hedge funds were playing a special role in the Asian crises. Moreover, the fact that Quantum and Tiger groups got off the market is consistent with the view that they are not doing particularly well on an ex post profit basis, which is also confirmed in the Korean case. Thus, his question was whether we are in the stage of identifying supportive evidence for the large player models.

Giancarlo Corsetti talked briefly on the theory. This is a very exciting field of research, and this paper is the first step toward understanding the role of large players. He said that there is a group of students and faculty working on various aspects of the topic—such as oligopoly, game-theoretical approach, risk aversion, credit constraint, and welfare—at Yale right now.

Paolo Pesenti agreed with Martin Feldstein on the positive role of large players. Major market participants can indeed help translate views about fundamentals into prices and can represent sources of market liquidity. Problems arise, however, when aggressive trading has a destabilizing impact, to the extent that highly leveraged institutions attempt to influence market dynamics to their own advantage.

On the "disappearance" of large players, Pesenti cited thirty-six reporters qualified as major market participants in 1996 (twenty-nine of which were commercial banks), but the number was down to twenty-five in 2000, with eighteen banking institutions.

Reference

Brown, Stephen J., William N. Goetzman, and James Park. 1998. Hedge funds and the Asian currency crisis of 1997. NBER Working Paper no. 6427. Cambridge, Mass.: National Bureau of Economic Research, February.

Contagion
How to Measure it?

Roberto Rigobon

6.1 Introduction

The issue of contagion has been one of the most debated topics in international finance since the Asian crises. One interesting aspect of this discussion is the strong agreement among economists about which events have constituted instances of contagion: the debt crises in 1982, the Mexican Tequila effect in December 1994, the Asian "flu" in the last half of 1997, the Russian "cold" in August 1998 (including the long-term capital management [LTCM] crisis), the Brazilian "sneeze" in January 1999, and the Nasdaq "rash" in April 2000. Paradoxically, however, there is no consensus on what contagion means.

This paper deals with the question of how to measure contagion. Therefore, instead of providing a list of all its possible definitions and the procedures to measure it, this paper concentrates on the two most frequently asked questions raised by applied papers in this area: First, what are the channels through which shocks are propagated from one country to the other? In other words, is it trade, macrosimilarities, common lenders, learning, or market psychology that determines the degree of contagion? Second, is the transmission mechanism stable through time? Or more specifically, does it change during a crisis?

Answering either of the previous two questions encounters important

Roberto Rigobon is assistant professor of management, economics, finance, and accounting at the Sloan School of Management, Massachusetts Institute of Technology, and a faculty research fellow of the National Bureau of Economic Research.

The author thanks Giancarlo Corsetti, Sebastian Edwards, Jeffrey A. Frankel, and Enrique G. Mendoza for helpful comments, and conference participants for all their suggestions. Financial support from the NBER is gratefully acknowledge. All remaining errors are the author's.

econometric limitations. Contagion has been associated with high-frequency events; hence, it has been measured on stock market returns, interest rates, exchange rates, or linear combinations of these. These data are plagued by simultaneous equations, omitted variables, conditional and unconditional heteroskedasticity, serial correlation, nonlinearity, and non-normality problems. Unfortunately, no procedure can handle all these problems at the same time; therefore, the literature has been forced to take short cuts.

This paper evaluates the performance of some of those techniques. Obviously, there is not enough space to study all the possible empirical procedures nor all the problems. Thus, the paper discusses the most widely used methodologies in the contagion literature (linear regressions, logit-probit regressions, and tests based on principal components and correlation coefficients[1]) and concentrates on the three main problems exhibited by the data: simultaneous equations, omitted variables, and heteroskedasticity. Issues related to serial correlation, nonnormality, and nonlinearity are left out of the analysis.

The paper briefly examines two new procedures that are robust to the problems studied here: one designed to test for the stability of parameters, and the second one designed to solve the problem of identification. In each case, the assumptions underlying the methodologies and the circumstances in which they can be used are reviewed.

The paper is organized as follows: Section 6.2 introduces the statistical models used in the discussions. Section 6.3 investigates the problems surrounding the second question concerning contagion: how to test for changes in the propagation mechanism. The paper analyzes this question first because the limitations of the standard techniques become evident in simple models. Section 6.3 studies alternative corrections for the standard tests and the conditions under which they can be used. Finally, the section summarizes a new procedure to test for parameter stability under simultaneous equations, omitted variables, and heteroskedasticity, and points out the assumptions required for its use.

Section 6.4 considers the more complicated issue: the measurement of the transmission channels. Several Monte Carlo simulations are presented to illustrate the problems in the interpretation of the results when the propagation channel is measured by probit, ordinary least squares, or principal components methods. At the end of the section, a new procedure to esti-

---

1. I am leaving important aspects of the measurement of contagion out of this analysis, mainly measures based on autoregressive conditional heteroskedasticity (ARCH) models (see Edwards and Susmel 2000), cointegration (see Cashin, Kumar, and McDermott 1995 and Longuin and Slonick 1995), switching regimes (again, see Longuin and Slonick 1995). There are two other techniques that have not yet been used: factor regression models (see Sentana and Fiorentini 1999 for problems of estimation in these models when the factors are heteroskedastic) and limited dependent models under heteroskedasticity (see Chen and Kahn 1999 and Klein and Vella 2000 for estimation problems in these models).

mate the contemporaneous interrelationship across countries is reviewed. This procedure is robust to the data problems emphasized here.

Section 6.5 applies the two new techniques to measure contagion in Latin American and Southeast Asian countries. First, the test on stability of parameters across time is implemented; second, the transmission mechanism is estimated. Section 6.6 explores avenues for future research. Section 6.7 concludes.

6.2   The Models

Several simple models are used to discuss the problems involved in the measurement of contagion. Even though true description of the world is probably the union of these particular pieces, the paper uses minimal statistical frameworks to highlight the problems there more easily.

The country variables of interest are denoted by x_t and y_t. They reflect either stock market returns, exchange rates, interest rates, or combinations of these. Without loss of generality, assume that x_t and y_t have been demeaned and are serially uncorrelated. Common unobservable shocks are denoted by z_t. These should be interpreted as liquidity shocks, risk preferences, investor's sentiments, etc. All the idiosyncratic innovations are denoted by ε_t and η_t. It is assumed that they are independent, with mean zero, and independent from the common shocks as well. The models concentrate on the bivariate case, although most of the results can be easily extended to larger setups.

When the paper focuses on the problems of simultaneous equations, the following model (model 1) to describe the interrelationship between the countries is used.

$$y_t = \beta x_t + \varepsilon_t$$

$$x_t = \alpha y_t + \eta_t$$

where $E(\varepsilon_t) = 0$, $E(\eta_t) = 0$, and $E(\varepsilon_t \eta_t) = 0$, and their variances are denoted by σ_ε and σ_η. When the problem of omitted variables is contemplated, model 2 is used:

$$y_t = \beta x_t + \gamma z_t + \varepsilon_t$$

$$x_t = z_t + \eta_t$$

where, in addition to the previous moment restrictions, it is assumed that $E(\varepsilon_t z_t) = 0$, and $E(\eta_t z_t) = 0$. The variance of the common shock is σ_z.

In all these models, the parameter of interest is β (or whether it has shifted). It is assumed that the equation to be fitted is the following:

(1) $$y_t = \beta x_t + v_t$$

Due to the problems of simultaneous equations and omitted variables, it is well known that this equation cannot be consistently estimated without further information. Formally, $E(x_t v_t)$ is different from zero (the "identification condition") for both model 1 and model 2, which implies inconsistent estimates.

One solution is to find valid instruments. However, for the purpose of the paper, it is assumed that those instruments do not exist. Nevertheless, there are circumstances in which it could be claimed otherwise. For example, it is possible to assume, on the basis of large-economy arguments, that Organization for Economic Cooperation and Development (OECD) countries are unaffected by emerging markets. This would motivate an exclusion restriction, $\alpha = 0$. Even though this assumption might be appealing, it raises important questions of why, during both the Hong Kong and Russian crises, the U.S. and European stock markets were so heavily influenced. In fact, part of the FED's motivation to lower interest rates at the end of 1998 was based on the stability of world markets. Similarly, it is possible to argue that proxies for the common shocks exists. However, most of these measures are, at best, derived from the same prices and volumes the model is explaining. In this paper, it is assumed that the instruments are weak (whenever they exist), and that the problems persist.

To tackle the question on the measurement of the channels of contagion, the statistical framework must be slightly more general. Most of the theories of contagion imply that the transmission of shocks across countries is a function of the strength of the contagion channel. Therefore, a reduced form of the return of country $x_{i,t}$ would be described by a latent factor model as follows:

$$x_{i,t} = \alpha_1 X_{\sim i,t} + \alpha_2 \textbf{TRADE}_{i,\sim i} X_{\sim i,t} + \alpha_3 \text{MACRO}_{i,\sim i} X_{\sim i,t} + \alpha_4 \text{REGION}_{i,\sim i} X_{\sim i,t}$$
$$+ \ldots + \beta_{1,i} \text{LIQUIDITY}_t + \beta_{2,i} \text{RISK}_t + \ldots + \varepsilon_{i,t}$$

where $x_{i,t}$ is the ith country return; $\varepsilon_{i,t}$ is the idiosyncratic shock to country i's fundamentals; $X_{\sim i,t}$ are the returns of the rest of the countries; $\textbf{TRADE}_{i,\sim i}$ is the vector that measures trade between country i and other countries; $\text{MACRO}_{i,\sim i}$ is the degree of macrosimilarities across the countries; and $\text{REGION}_{i,\sim i}$ captures regional characteristics (similarly for other channels of contagion not included in the specification). Common unobservable shocks also affect country returns, and in this example, liquidity shocks and shifts in risk preferences have been modeled. Other shocks could be incorporated.

Each country satisfies an analogous equation, which conforms a system of equations

$$A_1 X_t + A_2 (\text{TRADE}) X_t + A_3 (\text{MACRO}) X_t + A_4 (\text{REGION}) X_t + \ldots$$
$$= B_1 \text{LIQUIDITY}_t + B_2 \text{RISK}_t + \ldots + \varepsilon_t,$$

which can be rewritten as

(2) $AX_t = BZ_t + \varepsilon_t$

$A = A_1 + A_2(\text{TRADE}) + A_3(\text{MACRO}) + A_4(\text{REGION}) + \dots$

$B = (B_1, B_2, \dots)$

$Z_t = (\text{LIQUIDITY}_t, \text{RISK}_t, \dots)'$.

This model is too complex to analyze. Therefore, it is simplified it in two directions. First, model 3 concentrates on the omitted variable problems with multiple regressors. Therefore, A is assumed to be triangular, and B is assumed to be different from zero and nontriangular. In particular, the model with three countries (model 3) is

$$y_t = \beta x_{1,t} + z_t + \varepsilon_t,$$

$$x_{1,t} = \gamma_1 z_t + \eta_{1,t},$$

$$x_{2,t} = \gamma_2 z_t + \eta_{2,t},$$

where y_t and z_t are as before and $x_{i,t}$ are two other countries. The idiosyncratic shocks are assumed to be independent.

In this model, $x_{2,t}$ does not enter the structural equations of y_t. The only relationship between these variables arises from the omitted common shock. The main question is how well the standard procedures capture the true underlying structure of the model.

Second, model 3a focuses on simultaneous equations problems. The common shocks are shut down ($B = 0$), and the three country returns are determined by

$$A \begin{bmatrix} y_t \\ x_{1,t} \\ x_{2,t} \end{bmatrix} = \begin{bmatrix} \varepsilon_t \\ \eta_{1,t} \\ \eta_{2,t} \end{bmatrix},$$

where A is non-block diagonal. Again, the question in this model is related to the identification of matrix A.

These models are (in general) estimated using three procedures: OLS, probit, and principal components. When OLS is used, it is assumed that the research fits the following equation:

(3) $y_t = \beta_1 x_{1,t} + \beta_2 x_{2,t} + v_t$

It is well known that β_1 and β_2 will be biased, but the question is the size and direction of it.

There is another important strand of the contagion literature that estimates models 3 and 3a using probit (logit or multinomial) setups. The equation fitted is

(4) $y_t^* = 1(c + \beta_1 x_{1,t} + \beta_2 x_{2,t} > \bar{y})$.

Again, where c is the constant, the question is the bias of β_1 and β_2.

Finally, the last technique used to determine the importance of the contagion channels is based on principal components estimation on the multivariate system.

6.3 Testing for Changes in the Propagation Mechanism

A large applied literature defines *contagion* as a shift in the transmission channel. Hence, testing for the existence of contagion is implemented as a test for parameter stability.

The most widely used procedures are based on OLS estimates (including generalized least squares [GLS] and feasible generalized least squares [FGLS]), principal components, and correlation coefficients. The objective of the tests is to determine whether there is a change in the coefficients across two different samples, usually crisis and tranquil periods.

As will become clear below, if the data suffer from heteroskedasticity and either of the other two problems (simultaneous equations or omitted variables), then most of the standard techniques are inappropriate to test for the stability of the parameters.

It is important to note that the standard techniques are inappropriate only if all problems are present. For example, if the data are homoskedastic, then the tests for parameter stability are consistent even in the presence of simultaneous equations and omitted variables. In other words, if the structural change test is rejected, then it must be explained by parameter instability. The test result does not indicate which one has changed, nor in which equation, but at least it indicates that a shift has occurred. On the other hand, if there is only heteroskedasticity, then procedures exist to correct all the traditional tests and achieve consistency. It is the interaction between the heteroskedasticity and the other problems what creates the inconsistency in the tests.

The intuition explaining this case is simple: both the endogenous and the omitted variable biases depend on the relative variances. If the data exhibit heteroskedasticity, then the biases shift across the sample. Therefore, it is possible to reject the hypothesis that the estimates are stable because of the change in the biases, and not because of a shift in the underlying parameters.

The objective of this section is to show these results formally. It is organized as follows: First, it analyzes each of the procedures and their problems. Second, it summarizes some of the adjustments that can be introduced to (partially) solve them. In certain cases, exact corrections exist; however, these adjustments are not general and often only approximations can be used. Finally, this section reviews a new test that is robust to the presence of all three problems, indicating the situations in which the test can be used and what assumptions are needed.

6.3.1   Testing Using OLS

The OLS estimates of the first equation in model 1 and model 2 are

$$(5) \qquad \hat{\beta}_{\text{Mod1}} - \beta = \alpha(1 - \alpha\beta)\frac{\sigma_{\varepsilon}}{\alpha^{2}\sigma_{\varepsilon} + \sigma_{\eta}},$$

$$(6) \qquad \hat{\beta}_{\text{Mod2}} - \beta = \gamma\frac{\sigma_{z}}{\sigma_{z} + \sigma_{\eta}},$$

respectively. Note that the bias (in both cases) depends on the relative variances of disturbances.

Assume that the question of interest is whether the parameters are stable along the sample. In general, the structural change test takes two forms; either it estimates a β in the two subsamples and performs a comparison, or it introduces a dummy in one of the subsamples and tests for its significance. Independently of the setup, however, the results indicated below are the same. For simplicity in the exposition, it is assumed that the sample is split and two separate regressions are run.

RESULT 1. *When there is no heteroskedasticity, then regardless of the simultaneous equations or omitted variables problems, the test for structural change is consistent.*

This results comes from the fact that the biases under the null hypothesis are the same in both subsamples. Formally, the difference in the estimates is

$$(\hat{\beta}_{\text{Mod1},s1} - \beta_{s1}) - (\hat{\beta}_{\text{Mod1},s2} - \beta_{s2}) = -\frac{\alpha^{2}}{\alpha^{2} + \dfrac{\sigma_{\eta}}{\sigma_{\varepsilon}}}(\beta_{s1} - \beta_{s2})$$

in model 1 and

$$(\hat{\beta}_{\text{Mod2},s1} - \beta_{s1}) - (\hat{\beta}_{\text{Mod2},s2} - \beta_{s2}) = \frac{1}{1 + \dfrac{\sigma_{\eta}}{\sigma_{z}}}(\gamma_{s1} - \gamma_{s2})$$

in model 2, where $s1$ and $s2$ stand for each subsample.

Under the null hypothesis that α, β, and γ are constant across samples, the difference in the estimates is zero; it is proportional to the change in the parameters. Thus, the rejection occurs only if the parameters have shifted.

RESULT 2. *When the data have heteroskedasticity along with either simultaneous equations or omitted variables problems, the test for stability is inconsistent.*

If there is heteroskedasticity in the sample, the test for stability can be rejected under two cases: (1) if the parameters have changed, or (2) if the variances (and hence the biases) have shifted. To exemplify this point, assume there is heteroskedasticity and that the parameters are constant. The difference in the estimates is

$$\hat{\beta}_{\text{Mod1},s1} - \hat{\beta}_{\text{Mod1},s2} = \alpha(1 - \alpha\beta) \left[\frac{1}{\alpha^2 + \left(\dfrac{\sigma_\eta}{\sigma_\varepsilon}\right)_{s1}} - \frac{1}{\alpha^2 + \left(\dfrac{\sigma_\eta}{\sigma_\varepsilon}\right)_{s2}} \right]$$

in model 1 and

$$\hat{\beta}_{\text{Mod2},s1} - \hat{\beta}_{\text{Mod2},s2} = \gamma \left[\frac{1}{1 + \left(\dfrac{\sigma_\eta}{\sigma_z}\right)_{s1}} - \frac{1}{1 + \left(\dfrac{\sigma_\eta}{\sigma_z}\right)_{s2}} \right]$$

in model 2.

The biases across the samples cancel each other out if there is homoskedasticity or if the heteroskedasticity implies a proportional increase in the variance of all shocks ($\sigma_\eta/\sigma_\varepsilon$ or σ_η/σ_z are invariant). Otherwise, the estimates are different even though the underlying parameters are constant.[2] Moreover, this problem cannot be solved by estimating the parameters using GLS or FGLS.

In conclusion, when there are problems of specification, the test for stability (based on a version of the Chow test) is implicitly testing against the joint alternative hypothesis: the stability of parameters and the homoskedasticity of the residuals. In the particular case of contagion, it is important to remember that the data are characterized by large shifts in second moments. Thus, making any inference about the stability of parameters in the linear regression context is complicated; the test does not provide the reason for the rejection.

6.3.2   Testing Using Principal Components

Principal components is a technique designed to find common factors for a set of time series. The objective of the methodology is well summarized by Kaminsky and Reinhart (2000), who state that "in the case where the original series are identical, the first Principal Component explains 100 percent of the variation in the original series. Alternatively, if the series are orthogonal to one another, it would take as many Principal Components as there are series to explain all the variance in the original series. In that case, no advantage would be gained by looking at common factors, as none exist."[3]

Formally, assume there are K variables each with n observations. Denote the sample data as X and their covariance matrix as Ω. The first component explains the K series as well as possible. Thus, it minimizes the discrepancies of

---

2. Obviously, the changes in parameters and heteroskedasticity exactly cancel each other out and make the test equal to zero. This means that the test has no power against such a set of parameters.

3. See Theil (1971) for a formal derivation.

$$X - a'p$$

where p is the principal components and a' is a matrix of scalars. The variable p is identified only up to a constant, and therefore some normalization is imposed (usually $p'p = 1$ or the diagonal of the p matrix is equated to 1). It can be shown that the first component corresponds to the eigenvector of the largest eigenvalue of Ω. The components of p are known as the loading and reflect the importance of a particular variable in explaining the rest.

Principal components have been widely used to test for the stability of the propagation mechanism because their estimates are consistent even if the data have simultaneous equations and omitted variables problems.[4] This aspect of the measurement is perhaps the greatest advantage of using principal components.

RESULT 3. *When there is no heteroskedasticity, tests of stability based on principal components are consistent.*

The intuition of the structural change test based on principal components is that if the loadings in the first component change, then the parameters underlying the statistical model have shifted as well. Model 1 implies a covariance matrix equal to[5]

$$\Omega = \frac{1}{(1 - \alpha\beta)^2} \begin{bmatrix} \beta^2 \sigma_\eta + \sigma_\varepsilon & \beta\sigma_\eta + \alpha\sigma_\varepsilon \\ \beta\sigma_\eta + \alpha\sigma_\varepsilon & \sigma_\eta + \alpha^2\sigma_\varepsilon \end{bmatrix}.$$

The eigenvalues are given by

$$\frac{1}{2}\sigma_\varepsilon\left(\Theta_1 \pm \sqrt{\Theta_2}\right),$$

where

$$\Theta_1 = 1 + \alpha^2 + (1 + \beta^2)\theta,$$

$$\Theta_2 = (1 + \beta^2)^2\theta^2 - 2[(1 - \beta^2)(1 - \alpha^2) - 4\alpha\beta]\theta + (1 + \alpha^2)^2,$$

$$\theta = \frac{\sigma_\eta}{\sigma_\varepsilon}.$$

The eigenvector of the first eigenvalue (the largest one) is

(7)
$$\begin{bmatrix} \dfrac{1}{2}\dfrac{\sigma_\varepsilon}{\alpha + \beta\theta}(\Theta_3 + \sqrt{\Theta_2}) \\ 1 \end{bmatrix},$$

---

4. See Calvo and Reinhart (1995), Kaminsky and Reinhart (2000), and Masson (1997) for applications in the contagion literature.

5. In this section only the case under endogenous variables is studied; the results are qualitatively the same under omitted variables.

where

$$\Theta_3 = 1 - \alpha^2 - (1 - \beta^2)\theta.$$

Note that the eigenvalues and eigenvectors depend only on the parameters (α and β) and the relative variance of the idiosyncratic shocks (θ).

Therefore, under the assumption of homoskedasticity, a change in the loadings of the principal component indeed implies a shift in the parameters (α and β). This property of the principal components is what grants its usefulness in testing for parameter stability. However, as before, this result holds only in the lack of heteroskedasticity.

RESULT 4. *Tests of parameter stability based on principal components are inconsistent in the presence of heteroskedasticity.*

This result is stronger than the one stated for the OLS case. It says that even in the absence of simultaneous-equation and omitted-variable problems, the tests of structural change based on principal components are inconsistent if the residuals are heteroskedastic. Hence, as oppose to the OLS or the correlation case (see below), there is no procedure that can deal with the existence of heteroskedasticity alone. A shift in the relative variances (θ) alters the loadings, even if α or β is equal to zero.[6]

Again, the fact that contagion is accompanied by large shifts in second moments implies that comparisons of principal components across samples are inadequate as an indication of parameter stability.

6.3.3 Testing Using the Correlation

The first paper (to my knowledge) to test for changes in the propagation mechanism using correlation measures was the influential contribution by King and Wadhwani (1990). The intuition of their test is that changes in the underlying coefficients imply a shift in the correlation coefficients as well. This test has been widely used in the literature because of its simplicity and intuitive implications.

However, the conditions under which a change in correlations implies a shift in the underlying parameters are restrictive. Ronn (1998) shows that increases in variance implies a rise in the correlation.[7]

For instance, assume that the problem of endogenous variables does not exist (make $\alpha = 0$ in model 1). The correlation between x_t and y_t is

$$\rho = \frac{\beta\sigma_\eta}{\sqrt{\sigma_\eta(\sigma_\varepsilon + \beta^2\sigma_\eta)}} = \frac{\beta}{\sqrt{\dfrac{1}{\theta} + \beta^2}},$$

which is a function of θ.

6. This result should be intuitive. By the definition of principal components, movements in the relative variances, in the end, must reflect changes in the loadings because the common component is shifting. This should be true in almost any model.

7. See Boyer, Gibson, and Loretan (1999), Forbes and Rigobon (1999), and Loretan and English (2000) for generalizations of Ronn's result.

Shocks to the variance of x_t imply an increase in θ, which causes the absolute value of the correlation to rise as well. In the limit, when shocks to country x_t are infinitely large, the idiosyncratic shocks to y_t are negligible and the correlation between the two variables is 1. On the other hand, when the variance of η_t goes to 0, the correlation is 0. Note that the correlation moves from 0 to 1 and that the parameter β remains the same.[8]

RESULT 5. *Tests of parameter stability based on (unadjusted) correlation coefficients are inconsistent if the data are heteroskedastic.*

The result is stated on *unadjusted* correlation because there are some cases in which the bias can be corrected. This adjustment was first proposed by Ronn (1998) in the bivariate setting.[9] The main assumptions required are that there are no problems of simultaneous equations or omitted variables and that the heteroskedasticity is fully explained by shifts in η_t and not in ε_t. In this case, the data provide a measure of the change in θ (which is given by the increase in the variance of x_t), and the "unconditional" correlation can be computed where it can be compared across samples, and its stability is consequential for tests of structural change.

The procedure is as follows. Assume the variance of x_t increases in δ; then the correlation in that subsample is given by

$$\rho_c = \frac{\beta}{\sqrt{\dfrac{1}{\theta(1+\delta)} + \beta^2}}.$$

The implied unconditional correlation is the one that would have prevailed if the errors were homoskedastic. Hence, it is given by

$$\rho_u = \frac{\beta}{\sqrt{\dfrac{1}{\theta} + \beta^2}};$$

Solving for the implied unconditional correlation (ρ_u) as a function of the conditional correlations and the shift in the volatility, the following adjustment is found:

$$\rho_c = \rho_u \sqrt{\frac{1+\delta}{1+\delta\rho_u^2}}$$

The ρ_u's can be compared across samples. Under the assumptions stated in this derivation, if they change it is the case that the β's have also shifted. The two main advantages of this procedure are: First, δ can be estimated directly

---

8. See Rigobon (1999) and Forbes and Rigobon (2000) for a simple example highlighting the biases induced by using correlation coefficients.

9. For applications of these corrections, see also Baig and Goldfjan (2000), Gelos and Sahay (2000), and Favero and Giavazzi (2000).

from the sample by looking at the shift in the variance of x_t. This makes the adjustment very simple. Second, there is no need to estimate β to perform a test of its stability.

However, as was mentioned before, this adjustment can be used only if there are no simultaneous equations and omitted variables issues.[10] In fact, in this situation there is no problem using OLS, and thus no need to estimate the correlation coefficient in the first place. This is the main weakness of using correlation coefficients to indicate the stability of a model; the setting under which the change in the correlation coefficient (or its adjustment) is meaningful generally justifies the implementation of other methodologies.

6.3.4   New Procedure

The previous discussion clearly indicates that the empirical question of the stability of parameters across countries faces tremendous econometric difficulties. The properties of the data make procedures designed to cope with one of the empirical issues inappropriate when all the problems are present.

This section describes a new methodology to test for structural change under simultaneous equations, omitted variables, and heteroskedasticity problems. It is a simplified version of Rigobon (2000b). This procedure is based on the assumptions that (1) the country generating the crisis is known, and (2) the changes in the variance of the rest of the countries is explained, at least in the short run, by the country under crisis and not by other idiosyncratic shocks.

The first assumption is relatively uncontroversial. However, it is important to highlight that in several events, this information is unavailable. For example, during the European Monetary System (EMS) crises, which country is to be blamed for the increase in volatility? The second assumption is perhaps the most difficult one to acknowledge. It is a crucial assumption but one that in the contagion literature is reasonable; and, indeed, it is testable. In the discussion below, this property of the test is explored more carefully.

---

10. However, as is claimed in Forbes and Rigobon (1999), if the adjustment is practiced using only the country generating the crisis, then it is still possible to get a good approximation of the unconditional correlation based on "near identification" arguments (see Fisher 1976) where "near-identification" refers to the condition that exists when the variance of the shock in one of the equations is significantly larger than the variance of the shocks in the other equations. In this case, as can be seen in equation (5), the biases tend toward zero in both the simultaneous equations and the omitted variable cases. The estimates get closer to the one in which $\alpha = 0$ or $\gamma = 0$. The periods of crisis closely follow this description. For example, during the Mexican crisis in 1994, the variance of the Mexican stock market increased by fifteen times following the devaluation in December. One limitation of this approach is that the adjustment can be performed only in pair-wise comparisons in which the variable x_t always corresponds to the country under crisis. Hence, the stability of parameters between two countries that are not the originators of the crisis cannot be tested. The procedure proposed by Boyer, Gibson, and Loretan (1999) has the same characteristics as the one indicated in Forbes and Rigobon and therefore can be applied in the same conditions.

Assume the variables are described by model 1.[11] Additionally, assume that it is known that in a subsample the variances of x_t and γ_t rise because the variance of η_t increases, while the variance of ε_t remains constant. In this case, two covariance matrices can be computed, one for the low-volatility period (L) and one for the high-volatility period (H):

$$\Omega^L = \frac{1}{(1-\alpha\beta)^2} \begin{bmatrix} \beta^2\sigma_\eta^L + \sigma_\varepsilon & \beta\sigma_\eta^L + \alpha\sigma_\varepsilon \\ \beta\sigma_\eta^L + \alpha\sigma_\varepsilon & \sigma_\eta^L + \alpha^2\sigma_\varepsilon \end{bmatrix}$$

$$\Omega^H = \frac{1}{(1-\alpha\beta)^2} \begin{bmatrix} \beta^2\sigma_\eta^H + \sigma_\varepsilon & \beta\sigma_\eta^H + \alpha\sigma_\varepsilon \\ \beta\sigma_\eta^H + \alpha\sigma_\varepsilon & \sigma_\eta^H + \alpha^2\sigma_\varepsilon \end{bmatrix}$$

Note that the change in the covariance matrix is given by

$$\Delta\Omega = \frac{\Delta\sigma_\eta}{1-\alpha\beta} \begin{bmatrix} \beta^2 & \beta \\ \beta & 1 \end{bmatrix},$$

which has a determinant equal to zero. In fact, proposition 1 in Rigobon (2000b), applied to the case studied here, states that:

RESULT 6. *The determinant of the change in the covariance (DCC) matrices is zero if the parameters are stable and if the heteroskedasticity is explained by the shift in the variance of only one of the shocks.*

In other words, if the parameters shift or if the two variances change, then the determinant of the difference of the covariance matrices is not zero. The model can have both common shocks and simultaneous equations and this result will still hold.[12]

Two remarks about the test are worth highlighting. First, the test is rejected in two situations: when the parameters shift (which is the interesting case) and when there is heteroskedasticity in more than two idiosyncratic shocks (which is uninteresting for the purposes of studying contagion). Second, the test requires the knowledge of the country generating the increase in volatility, as well as the timing of the volatility. Even though the country producing the crisis can be pointed out in some cases, the tranquil and crisis periods might not be as easy to determine.

These two weaknesses deserve further discussion.

Two Alternative Hypotheses

First, there is no procedure to disentangle the two alternative hypotheses thus far. However, an advantage of the test is that if there is no rejection,

---

11. The omitted variables case produces identical results.

12. Conversations with Giancarlo Corsetti helped me generalize that the test can be applied to models as complicated as the following: $A\binom{xt}{yt} = \Gamma z_t + B\binom{\varepsilon_t^1}{\eta_t^1} + \binom{\varepsilon_t^2}{\eta_t^2}$, where A, Γ, and B are nondiagonal matrices and where the vectors of idiosyncratic shocks ε_t^1 and η_t^1 is transmitted across countries with higher intensity than the other vectors of idiosyncratic shocks, ε_t^2 and η_t^2. In this model, it is still the case that if the heteroskedasticity in a subsample is explained by the shift in the variance of one of the shocks, then the change in the covariance matrix is not full rank. I thank Giancarlo Corsetti for all his comments.

then the assumption of stability (and on the particular form of the heteroskedasticity) are accepted. It is only when the test is rejected that the assumption about the form of the heteroskedasticity becomes crucial for the interpretation of the results.

The question, then, is one of the power of the test. Rigobon (2000c) studies the power against two possible alternative hypotheses: (1) a change in β, and (2) shifts in the two variances. The main conclusions of that exercise is that, with sample sizes around sixty observations, if the parameters are not too large (α and β should be smaller than 0.8) and if the observed heteroskedasticity of x_t and y_t is relatively large (the variances increase by at least five times), then the power of the test against both alternative hypotheses is better than 10 percent.

In applications of contagion, both conditions are generally satisfied. First, concerning the shift in variance, finding changes of the order of ten times are common in stock markets, domestic interest rates, exchange rates, and Brady bond returns. Second, estimates larger than 0.8 imply extremely high interrelationships not found even in Brady bond markets. Moreover, straight OLS regression estimates are generally smaller than 0.8. Due to the endogenous biases it should be expected that these estimates are upwardly biased, suggesting that the true parameters are smaller than 0.8.

Definition of the Periods

The second question is related to the definition of the periods of high and low volatility. One important result of this test is that the determinant of the change in the covariance is consistent even if the windows are misspecified. This implies that the test is robust to badly stipulated periods. This is a major advantage of the test because, in most of the contagion events, the beginnings of the crises are relatively clear but their ends are not. On the other hand, the cost of the misspecification is that the test loses power; thus it is more likely not to find a rejection.

The intuition of the consistency of the test is the following: If the periods are misspecified, the estimated covariance matrices are linear combinations of the true underlying matrices. The difference between the misspecified ones is also a linear combination of the difference of the true ones. If the original change in matrices is less than full rank, the linear combination would be so too. Hence, consistency is assured. The loss in power is also understood from this intuition because the linear combination reduces the difference across the samples by averaging the underlying matrices.

It is impossible, in practice, to define the crisis period precisely. Hence, robustness of the results when the window is modified should be studied.[13]

---

13. See Rigobon (2000b) for an application to test the stability of the international propagation of shocks across stock markets.

When To Use the Test

The traditional techniques testing for structural change, in general, are not appropriate as tests for contagion because the data have simultaneous equations, omitted variables, and heteroskedasticity problems. Some adjustments might reduce the biases, but in fact, there is no guarantee that those corrections improve the test. More important, the conditions under which principal components and correlations estimates can be adjusted are those under which OLS could (and should) be estimated.

The test summarized in this section deals with some of the problems of the data. Obviously, it depends on another important assumption: namely, that the heteroskedasticity must be explained by a subset of the idiosyncratic shocks. This is the major assumption (and therefore a weakness) of the procedure and should be made cautiously.

For example, the application of this methodology during the Mexican crisis satisfies the premises in the test. It is difficult to claim that the increase in the volatility of the other Latin American stock markets (following two weeks after the 19 December 1994 devaluation) is explained by shocks to those particular countries, and was not a direct consequence of Mexican problems. In fact, as is shown in the empirical section, the stability is not rejected for this crisis.

However, using the same procedure to test for stability of parameters during the EMS or Korean crises is more difficult. Which country should be blamed for the increase in volatility during the collapse of the EMS? One, two, or all of them? Indeed, if the test is applied to the EMS and Korean crises, it would be easy to reject that the determinant is zero. For the EMS it is clear that no single country can be pointed out as the source of the heteroskedasticity. For the Korean crisis, there does not exist a period of ten consecutive days without a crisis in another Southeast Asian country. By the characteristics of these two crises, a rejection should be expected. However, claiming that the crisis is due to parameter instability is impossible. Again, this is a case in which the rejections are uninteresting.

In the implementation of this methodology, the two main questions should be: first, whether the data are heteroskedastic, and whether they are large enough. This is the precondition for the second question: can the data be described by shifts in the variances of a subset of the idiosyncratic shocks? If so, then the procedure described here is a valid test of parameter stability. Most of the contagion events, however, can answer both questions affirmatively.

6.4   Measuring the Channels of Contagion

The second question tackled by most empirical applications of contagion is the measurement of the different channels through which shocks are propagate across countries.[14] Regardless of the channels, from the empirical point of view there exist essentially three approaches to measure them: probit, OLS, and principal components.

6.4.1   Measuring Using Probit-Logit

One of the first empirical papers in the contagion literature was Eichengreen, Rose, and Wyplosz (1996). They considered the probability that country y will face a speculative attack, given that country x is suffering one. Their interpretation of contagion is natural and appealing.

To implement their test, they take three steps. First, they define an index (capturing the strength of an speculative attack); second, they characterize a crisis as large movements in such indexes; and third, they compute the interrelationship across countries estimating a probit.[15] In order to test for the importance of the different channels of contagion, they interacted the right-hand side crisis indexes with measures of trade, country similarities, etc. The interpretation of their results are undoubtedly engaging. However, this model encounters two problems, one that occurs when the residuals are heteroskedastic, and one that occurs when there are omitted variables and simultaneous equations problems.

Heteroskedasticity in y_t's Residuals

One of the most difficult problems to solve in limited dependent variable regressions is the consistency of the estimates when the residuals of the selection equation are heteroskedastic. Several procedures have been developed to deal with this issue: maximum score (see Manski 1985; Horowitz 1992, 1993) and symmetric trimming (see Powell 1986; Honore 1992; and Honore, Kyriazidou, and Udry 1997). These methodologies are able to handle the estimation biases. Nevertheless, they have not yet been used in contagion applications. On the other hand, the lack of control for heteroskedasticity significantly affects the estimates. This is the discussion highlighted in this section.

A Monte Carlo simulation is run to quantify the bias. Assume that the returns are described by model 3a, in which the matrix A is given by

$$A = \begin{bmatrix} 1 & -\alpha & -\alpha \\ -\alpha & 1 & -\alpha \\ -\alpha & -\alpha & 1 \end{bmatrix}.$$

---

14. These channels are based on a large theoretical literature and they usually include trade, country similarities, common lender, learning, liquidity, distance, and so forth. See Goldstein, Kaminsky, and Reinhart (2000) and the references therein for a survey of the models.

15. Other papers have also used probit regressions to measure contagion. See Eichengreen et al. (1996) in the context of measuring the probability of issuing foreign debt. See also Bae, Karolyi, and Stulz (2000) for an application using multinomial regressions.

Table 6.1 **Probit Estimates of Both Coefficients for Different Values of α and Different Degrees of Heteroskedasticity**

	First Coefficient: $\hat{\beta}_1$				Second Coefficient: $\hat{\beta}_2$			
	Point Estimate	Diff.	Std. Dev. Diff.	*t*-stat.	Point Estimate	Diff.	Std. Dev Diff.	*t*-stat.
True α = 0.1								
Homoskedasticity	0.1897				0.1887			
Increase in variance								
2	0.1927	−0.0030	0.0071	0.42	0.1567	0.0145	0.0319	2.20
5	0.1965	−0.0067	0.0124	0.55	0.1241	0.0259	0.0646	2.50
10	0.1977	−0.0080	0.0160	0.50	0.1093	0.0311	0.0794	2.55
True α = 0.2								
Homoskedasticity	0.3465				0.3493			
Increase in variance								
2	0.3624	−0.0159	0.0123	1.28	0.2875	0.0199	0.0617	3.11
5	0.3762	−0.0297	0.0205	1.45	0.2292	0.0323	0.1200	3.72
10	0.3825	−0.0360	0.0252	1.43	0.2042	0.0374	0.1450	3.88
True α = 0.3								
Homoskedasticity	0.4728				0.4711			
Increase in variance								
2	0.5037	−0.0310	0.0225	1.38	0.3918	0.0329	0.0793	2.41
5	0.5320	−0.0592	0.351	1.69	0.3188	0.0444	0.1523	3.43
10	0.5429	−0.0702	0.0408	1.72	0.2956	0.0511	0.1755	3.43

Notes: For each simulation 500 draws are computed. The tranquil sample and the high-volatility sample contain 500 observations each.

Assume that the third shock ($\eta_{2,t}$) is the only one that suffers from heteroskedasticity.

The Monte Carlo simulation consists of 500 random-independent draws of the three shocks, with sample size of 1,000 observations each. The sample of $\eta_{2,t}$ is split in two and the second half is assumed to have higher variance. Three different degrees of heteroskedasticity—increases by two, five, and ten times—are studied, as well as three different values of α (0.1, 0.2, and 0.3).

The variables y_t, $x_{1,t}$, and $x_{2,t}$ are computed for each realization. The variable $y_t^* = 1(y_t > 0)$ is calculated afterward, and the probit regression (equation [4]) is estimated: $y_t^* = 1(c + \beta_1 x_{1,t} + \beta_2 x_{2,t})$. The objective of the exercise is to compare the estimates of the coefficients (β_1 and β_2) with and without heteroskedasticity. The results are shown in table 6.1; here, the results for the first coefficient ($\hat{\beta}_1$) are summarized in the first four columns and for the second coefficient ($\hat{\beta}_2$) in the next four columns. The first four rows are the estimates when α = 0.1, the next four rows are the estimates when α = 0.2, and the last four are the results for α = 0.3. For the four rows present for each value of α, the first row holds the results under homoskedasticity, which is the benchmark for comparison; the next three rows are the three heteroskedasticities studied.

For each coefficient, the first column shows the point estimates.[16] The second column is the difference between the estimates with heteroskedasticity and the respective ones under homoskedasticity. The third column shows the computed standard deviation of the difference, which was obtained from the bootstrapping. The fourth column calculates the t-statistic.

Regarding the first coefficient, three remarks can be extracted from the table. First, an increase in the heteroskedasticity of $\eta_{2,t}$ biases the estimates of $x_{1,t}$ upward. Second, the larger the heteroskedasticity, the larger its bias. Third, the larger the true coefficient (α), the higher the relative impact of the heteroskedasticity. Nevertheless, even though these patterns are quite strong, statistically it is impossible to reject the hypothesis that all coefficients are the same as those under homoskedasticity.

The results on the second coefficient are different from those of $\hat{\beta}_1$. First, the bias is downward, as oppose to upward. Second, the patterns of the heteroskedasticity effects and α size on the bias are the same as before. Third, changes in volatility on the order of ten times imply coefficients that are almost half the size of those under homoskedasticity. Fourth, and more important, the differences are statistically significant.

The last exercise performed is the comparison of the $\hat{\beta}_1$ and $\hat{\beta}_2$ estimates for the same set of parameters. By construction (of matrix A), they should be the same; in fact, under homoskedasticity the estimates are almost identical. However, (in this simulation) when one of the variables suffers from heteroskedasticity, its estimate goes down, while the estimate of the other goes up, and their differences are statistically significant.

This latter property is conceivably the most important regarding the interpretation of the results from the contagion literature: If the heteroskedasticity is correlated with some channel, then we could be finding spurious relationships. For example, assume all contemporaneous coefficients are the same and the heteroskedasticity is correlated with the exchange rate regime; in this case the estimates might erroneously indicate that countries sharing the same regime have stronger interrelationships, and thus are more likely to suffer from contagion.

Identification of Parameters

A second difficulty in the estimation of equation (4) arises when the data have either simultaneous equations or omitted variables problems alone. To illustrate this issue, a Monte Carlo simulation, estimating model 4 where the

16. Their standard deviations are not shown because the objective of the simulation is to concentrate on the difference between the estimates. However, it is important to highlight that all of the estimates were statistically different from zero.

underlying returns are given by model 3, is run.[17] The bootstrap performed follows the same procedure as the one described before.

In the simulations, the parameters chosen were as follows: $\beta = 0.2$; $\gamma_1 = 0.1$; γ_2 was varied from 0.1 to 0.5; the variances of ε_t, $\eta_{1,t}$; and $\eta_{2,t}$ are each equal to 1; and the variance of z_t was changed as follows $\{0.1, 1, 5, 10\}$. For the sake of clarity, there is no heteroskedasticity in this exercise. For each choice of parameters, the variance of the shocks is constant across time. The different volatilities of z_t are studied to understand the implications on the estimates when the (relative) importance of the omitted variable changes.

By construction, if the estimates are consistent, $\hat{\beta}_1$ should be equal to β, and $\hat{\beta}_2$ should be equal to zero. In the omitted variable case, when the variance of z_t is small relative to the other shocks, it is expected that the bias is small. The converse should occur when the variance of z_t is large. The results shown in table 6.2 confirm this intuition.

The first set of three columns shows the point estimate, standard deviation, and t-statistic of the $x_{1,t}$ coefficient. The second set of three columns shows the results for the coefficient on $x_{2,t}$. The simulation is run for all five values of γ_2 and four possible variances of z_t. The results from each of the parameters are reported in their respective rows.

As can be seen in table 6.2, it is possible (depending on the variances) to obtain almost any relationship between $\hat{\beta}_1$ and $\hat{\beta}_2$. This result should cast some doubt on contagion tests that have not controlled for simultaneous equations and omitted variables. Indeed, in the theoretical literature of contagion, unobservable shocks, such as liquidity shocks and shifts in risk preferences, have constituted an integral part of the propagation mechanisms.[18] As this section has shown, the existence of these shocks could change the assessment of the size and importance of contagion.

6.4.2   Measuring Using OLS

A second strand of the literature measures the propagation mechanism using OLS regressions.[19] The problems are similar to the ones described in the previous subsection. Thus, the paper does not present the results of the simulations but concentrates mainly on the conclusions.

---

17. The omitted variables problem is simpler to analyze, but similar conclusions are found in simultaneous equation setups.

18. See Calvo (1999), Calvo and Mendoza (2000), and Kodres and Pritsker (1999) for theoretical models of contagion based on common unobservable shocks. The first model examines liquidity shocks; the second, market sentiment shocks; and the third, all these shocks plus other transmission mechanisms.

19. See Baig and Goldfjan (1998, 2000), De Gregorio and Valdés (2000), Favero and Giavazzi (2000), Forbes (1999), Gelos and Sahay (2000), Glick and Rose (1998), and Van Rijckeghem and Weder (2000), to name a few.

Table 6.2   Probit Estimates of Both Coefficients

Relative Variance	$\hat{\beta}_1$: $x_{1,t}$ Coefficient			$\hat{\beta}_2$: $x_{2,t}$ Coefficient		
	Point Estimate	Standard Deviation	t-statistic	Point Estimate	Standard Deviation	t-statistic
			True $\gamma_2 = 0.1$			
0.1	0.2008	0.0411	4.89	−0.0006	0.0400	0.01
1	0.2112	0.0407	5.18	0.0672	0.0404	1.66
5	0.4469	0.0417	10.71	0.3969	0.0414	9.59
10	0.6079	0.0459	13.25	0.5731	0.0478	11.99
			True $\gamma_2 = 0.2$			
0.1	0.2013	0.0425	4.74	0.0036	0.0403	0.09
1	0.2148	0.0411	5.23	0.1357	0.0373	3.63
5	0.3808	0.0451	8.44	0.6422	0.0423	15.16
10	0.4487	0.0584	7.68	0.8011	0.0546	14.68
			True $\gamma_2 = 0.3$			
0.1	0.1999	0.0424	4.72	0.0038	0.0428	0.09
1	0.2109	0.0420	5.02	0.1971	0.0426	4.62
5	0.3230	0.0533	6.06	0.7527	0.0481	15.65
10	0.3544	0.0687	5.16	0.8649	0.0635	13.62
			True $\gamma_2 = 0.4$			
0.1	0.2000	0.0393	5.09	0.0036	0.0415	0.09
1	0.2081	0.0404	5.15	0.2507	0.0398	6.29
5	0.2801	0.0556	5.03	0.8009	0.0503	15.94
10	0.2946	0.0775	3.80	0.8804	0.0658	13.39
			True $\gamma_2 = 0.5$			
0.1	0.1991	0.0401	4.96	0.0033	0.0415	0.08
1	0.2059	0.0406	5.07	0.2970	0.0394	7.54
5	0.2574	0.0619	4.16	0.8058	0.0508	15.85
10	0.2672	0.0877	3.05	0.8686	0.0734	11.83

Notes: Standard deviations computed using bootstrap method. Simulations for different variances of z_t (relative variance). Variances of the other shocks have been normalized to 1. For each simulation, 500 draws are computed. The sample contains 1,000 observations.

Assume the data are described by model 3. The OLS estimates are given (after some algebra) by

$$\hat{\beta}_1 = \beta_1 + \frac{\sigma_z}{\phi}\gamma_1\sigma_{\eta,2}$$

$$\hat{\beta}_2 = \beta_2 + \frac{\sigma_z}{\phi}\gamma_2\sigma_{\eta,1}$$

$$\phi = \sigma_z(\gamma_2^2\sigma_{\eta,1} + \gamma_1^2\sigma_{\eta,2}) + \sigma_{\eta,1}\sigma_{\eta,2}$$

Note that if the true values are $\beta_2 = 0$ and $\beta_1 = \beta$, still the biases can produce any outcome on the estimates. Similar conclusions can be drawn if model 3a is used; see appendix A for the derivation. One advantage of OLS over probit is that OLS is robust to heteroskedasticity, whereas probit is not. In the OLS case, the larger inconvenience that introduces the existence of heteroskedasticity is to underestimate the standard deviations, but there are several procedures that can handle this concern.

6.4.3   Measuring Using Principal Components

As was indicated in section 6.3.2, tests for changes in parameters based on principal components are biased in the presence of heteroskedasticity. In this section, a stronger claim is made: that the estimates, by themselves, are also inconsistent.

Using the same example as in section 6.3.2, equation (7) is the first principal component (reproduced here for convenience):

$$\left[\begin{array}{c} \dfrac{1}{2} \dfrac{\alpha_\varepsilon}{\alpha + \beta\theta} \left(\Theta_3 + \sqrt{\Theta_2} \right) \\ 1 \end{array} \right]$$

Note that the first component is not a linear function of θ. Therefore, the heteroskedasticity (volatility in θ) biases the loadings. For example, assume the countries are positively correlated (which is almost always the case in contagion: α and β are positive). Those countries in which idiosyncratic variance changes more (larger volatility in θ_t) have higher loadings (all other things equal). It is possible, therefore, that strong linkages are found because the heteroskedasticity is high for those countries.

A Monte Carlo simulation was run in this case, but for the sake of brevity the results are not presented; only the conclusions from that exercise are discussed here. First, the heteroskedasticity in the second shock implies that the loading of the first country in the first component is biased downward. This should be expected because when α and β are positive, equation (7) is a convex function of θ. An increase in the heteroskedasticity implies that the second country becomes relatively more important in explaining their common component. Second, when the loadings are compared across different degrees of heteroskedasticity, their estimates are statistically different. Finally, it is easy to show that if the structural errors are properly normalized, the bias disappears. However, this normalization is possible only if the data do not suffer from simultaneous equations or omitted variable problems. In these cases, it is worth asking why one would use principal components when OLS (or FGLS) is consistent. This is conceivably the highest weakness of principal components as a procedure to test and measure contagion. If the heteroskedasticity is not taken into consideration, then the estimates and conclusions might be biased. On the other hand, the only circumstances in which heteroskedasticity can be corrected are those in which OLS should be used.

6.4.4   New Procedure

In the contagion literature, the issues of heteroskedasticity, simultaneous equations, and omitted variables are unavoidable, especially because there are no good instruments to correct for them.[20] Moreover, the fact that most papers use "indexes" instead of exchange rates or interest rates directly exacerbates the problem even more.

In general, the index is constructed as a linear combination of the high-frequency macrovariables. The advantage is, for example, that a speculative attack might have different implications, depending on how central banks decide to cope with it. The index captures the aggregate strength of the response by looking at all its possible consequences. The disadvantage, on the other hand, is that using prices and exchange rates jointly in an index aggravates the endogeneity problems, making the inference about the transmission mechanism more complicated. The use of an index to measure the propagation of shocks has strong theoretical justification, and intuitive appeal, but it is important to remember that it encounters equally strong econometric problems.

In this section, a review of a new procedure developed by Rigobon (2000a) is presented. The objective of the methodology is to provide a consistent estimate of the contemporaneous relationship across variables even if the data suffer from heteroskedasticity, simultaneous equations, and omitted variables. Here, only the case of simultaneous equations is illustrated; for the general treatment see the original reference.

Assume there are K variables jointly determined satisfying the following relationship:

$$AX_t = \varepsilon_t$$

where A is a $K \times K$ nontriangular matrix, X_t is the matrix of country variables, and ε_t is the vector of idiosyncratic shocks. The diagonal of A is set to 1, which is the normalization assumption. Additionally, it is commonly as-

---

20. For example, the use of lag returns is not a valid instrument for simultaneous equations. It is instrumenting for other problems, such as errors in variables, but not for endogeneity.

Arguing that lag-dependent variables are instruments is making the implicit assumption that home stock market returns depend on own past returns and current foreign returns but not on lag foreign returns, and that, conversely, foreign current returns depend on own lag and current home returns, but not on lag home returns. The theoretical foundations for this assumption are extremely weak. If foreign returns are informative about domestic returns at any time and past home returns are informative about current home returns, then why are past foreign returns not informative about current home returns? In fact, I have not (yet) seen a theoretical model that has the three implications. Either all lag values explain contemporaneous returns or not. In practice, the lag-dependent variables are instrumenting for other issues such as errors in variables and the like, but they are not instrumenting for endogeneity. Moreover, causality tests in this environment are biased. It is well known that simultaneous equations with lag endogenous variables can have any implication on the Granger-causality tests.

sumed in macro-applications that the idiosyncratic shocks are uncorrelated: $E(\varepsilon_{i,t}\varepsilon_{j,t}) = 0$ for all $i \neq j$. This is the covariance restriction used in most macro-applications. Even with all these assumptions, however, A cannot be estimated. The reason is that from the reduced form, only the covariance matrix from X_t can be obtained, which constitutes an underidentified system of equations.

Formally, the reduced form is

$$X_t = A^{-1}\varepsilon_t = \eta_t,$$

which implies a covariance matrix

$$\Omega = A'^{-1}\Omega^\varepsilon A^{-1},$$

where Ω^ε is diagonal due to the covariance restriction.

The value of Ω is estimated from the sample and provides $K(K + 1)/2$ independent equations. The unknowns are K from the variances of the idiosyncratic shocks, and $K(K - 1)$ from matrix A. Note that for any $K > 1$ the number of unknowns is strictly larger than the number of knowns. This is the standard identification problem raised by simultaneous equations.

The key feature of Rigobon's identification is the realization that under the exact same restrictions the existence of heteroskedasticity adds additional constraints. The simplest case is one in which the heteroskedasticity can be described by two regimes, high and low variance. In this instance, there are two covariance matrices providing $K(K + 1)$ equations, whereas the number of unknowns is $2K$ from the variances of the idiosyncratic shocks (K for each regime), but *the same* $K(K - 1)$ from matrix A. Thus, the system is just identified: $K(K + 1) = 2K + K(K - 1)$. Moreover, it should be clear that it is overidentified when there are more than two regimes. Therefore, for richer descriptions of the heteroskedasticity, an overidentification test can be used and the parameter stability examined.

The assumptions needed to achieve identification are the following: first, heteroskedasticity of the structural shocks; second, stability of the parameters; and third, uncorrelation of the structural shocks. This is exactly the case in most macro-applications in which vector autoregression (VAR) models have been used, and financial applications in which ARCH (autoregressive conditional heteroskedasticity) or GARCH (generalized ARCH) models have been computed. In the derivation developed here, only unconditional heteroskedasticity has been studied. Similar arguments can be extended to include the case in which only conditional changes in the volatility occur.

Using this methodology, a consistent estimate of A can be obtained regardless of the problem of endogenous and omitted variable biases. Afterward, A can be explained as a function of the different channels of contagion. This is the objective of the next section.

6.5   An Application to Emerging Markets

This section examines the questions of stability in the propagation of shocks across Latin American and Southeast Asian countries around the recent crises, the importance of those linkages, and what determines them. The first question is implemented as the test for parameter stability introduced in section 6.3.4, while the other two questions are answered using the methodology described in section 6.4.4.

Two data sets are used: sovereign bonds and stock markets. The data for stock markets were collected from Datastream and consist of daily stock market returns (in U.S. dollars) for fourteen countries, covering the period from January 1993 to December 1998. The countries studied are Argentina, Brazil, Chile, Hong Kong, Malaysia, Mexico, Peru, the Philippines, Singapore, Korea, Taiwan, Thailand, the United States, and Venezuela.

The sovereign bond data contain the daily country bond returns from January 1994 to December 1998, obtained from the Emerging Markets Bond Index Plus (EMBI+) constructed by JPMorgan. The EMBI+ country indexes track total returns for traded external debt instruments in emerging markets. Most of the bonds covered are Brady bonds, but other foreign-denominated bonds are also taken into consideration. The indexes are computed by simulating a portfolio with the weights determined by risk, market capitalization, liquidity, and collateral considerations. The countries included in the bond data are Argentina, Brazil, Ecuador, Mexico, Panama, Peru, and Venezuela. The only two Southeast Asian countries in the JPMorgan data are Korea and the Philippines, but the number of their observations is small in comparison to the other countries. Thus, they were dropped from the analysis.

Information on U.S. interest rates is obtained from Datastream. For all the results presented in this paper, the ten-year U.S. government bond was used. This bond has the closest maturity to the average sovereign bond in the data. However, robustness checks were performed by using shorter horizons (one-year and three-month), and the results were qualitatively the same.

The objectives of looking at these two markets are to compare the transmission mechanisms, to determine how much trade explains about the propagation mechanism in each of them, and to compute the importance of liquidity shocks in both.

6.5.1   Test for Stability

The stability of parameters for both the stock and the bond markets is studied by performing the determinant of the change in covariance (DCC) test described in section 6.3.4. This test is based on the assumption that, in a subsample, the heteroskedasticity is explained by the heteroskedasticity in only a subset of the shocks. Moreover, it must be a subset of either the idiosyncratic shocks or the common shocks. The easiest way to satisfy this condition is to concentrate the analysis around the crises. During these periods, the assumption that the increase in the variance of all emerging markets is caused by the country producing the crisis is a reasonable one.

As will become clear, a considerable amount of time is devoted to the definition of these windows. The main reason is that, if a rejection is found in a poorly designed test, its interpretation becomes cumbersome.

The Model

It is assumed that returns in stock and bond markets are described by a latent factor model

$$AX_t = \phi(L)X_t + \Gamma z_t + \varepsilon_t,$$

where X_t represent the country returns, A is the contemporaneous linkages (the coefficients of interest), $\phi(L)$ is a matrix of lags, z_t is a one-dimensional unobservable shock, all Γ are the parameters of how common shocks affect country returns (or vulnerabilities), and all ε_t are the idiosyncratic shocks assumed to be uncorrelated among themselves and with respect to the common shock.

For normalization purposes, the diagonal of A is assumed to be equal to 1, and the coefficient on the United States in Γ is set to 0.1. The imposition of this normalization means that studying the relative importance of common shocks versus idiosyncratic shocks cannot be performed by looking at the standard deviation of the shocks. Rather, a variance decomposition exercise must be conducted.

The reduced form of this model is the following:

$$(8) \qquad X_t = A^{-1} \phi(L)X_t + A^{-1}(\Gamma z_t + \varepsilon_t)$$
$$= \Phi(L)X_t + v_t$$

where the reduced-form residuals satisfy

$$(9) \qquad Av_t = \Gamma z_t + \varepsilon_t.$$

Note that the procedure developed in section 6.3.4 deals with the stability and identification of parameters in equation (9). Because the reduced-form residuals share the same contemporaneous properties as the returns, in the estimation, a VAR is first run in the whole sample to eliminate the serial correlation (equation [8]). After the residuals, v_t, are recovered from the estimation, the regimes are defined, and the test for stability is performed on the residuals. This procedure is testing for the stability of A, Γ, and $\phi(L)$. At first glance, the inclusion of $\phi(L)$ in this list this might be surprising, but see appendix B for a formal derivation.

For the sake of brevity, the results from the VARs are not presented.

Definition of the Windows

To implement the DCC test, one must define a high- and a low-volatility regime. Moreover, for the alternative hypothesis to be informative, the periods must be determined in such a way that the assumption about the heteroskedasticity is likely to be satisfied. In practice, concentrating around the crises should increase the likelihood of satisfying such assumptions.

From 1994 to 1998, international markets faced three major crises; these are used to define the regimes. In table 6.3 the low- and high-volatility dates are shown.

For the Mexican crisis, the low-volatility regime is defined as the period from June to December of 1994 right before the devaluation. The high-volatility regime begins with the devaluation on 19 December 1994; the end of this period, however, is unclear. After the Mexican devaluation several other shocks occurred (e.g., the discussion of the rescue package in January). These shocks maintained the high volatility for several months. Therefore, two possible crisis regimes are studied: one ending on 8 January, and the other lasting until 31 March. The choice of 8 January is based on the fact that on 9 January the nonrollover of the short-term debt was announced, producing a large shock in bond markets around the world. Indeed, the EMBI+ dropped by almost 6 percent that day. This shock could be interpreted as a liquidity shock, and thus, in the model estimated here, as a common shock. The DCC would reject if there is heteroskedasticity in both an idiosyncratic and a common shock. Therefore, these samples should be considered separately. In fact, three cases are studied, one beginning with

Table 6.3   Windows for the DCC Test

	Tranquil Window		High-Volatility Window	
	Begins	Ends	Begins	Ends
Mexican crisis				
Currency devaluation	06/01/1994	12/16/1994	12/19/1994	01/08/1995
No rollover	06/01/1994	12/19/1994	01/09/1995	03/31/1995
Currency devaluation + no rollover	06/01/1994	12/16/1994	12/19/1994	03/31/1995
Asian crises				
Hong Kong	01/02/1997	06/02/1997	10/27/1997	11/14/1997
Korea	01/02/1997	06/02/1997	12/01/1997	01/09/1997
Hong Kong + Korea	01/02/1997	06/02/1997	10/27/1997	01/10/1997
Thailand	01/02/1997	06/02/1997	06/10/1997	08/29/1997
All	01/02/1997	06/02/1997	06/10/1997	01/10/1997
Russian crisis				
Russia	03/02/1998	06/01/1998	08/03/1998	08/21/1998
LTCM	03/02/1998	06/01/1998	08/21/1998	09/30/1998
Russia + LTCM	03/02/1998	06/01/1998	08/03/1998	09/30/1998
Brazilian speculative attack	03/02/1998	06/01/1998	10/01/1998	10/30/1998
All	03/02/1998	06/01/1998	08/03/1998	10/30/1998

the devaluation and ending before 9 January, another one beginning on 9 January and lasting until the end of March, and another that includes both periods.

Looking at these two samples together has the following advantages. It should be expected that the DCC test will produce a rejection in the bond market data for the two periods together; this implicitly indicates how powerful the test is with these data. However, if indeed there is a shift in the parameters after 9 January but not before, then the test is rejected when that period is under consideration, as well. In other words, if the rejection occurs only when the two high-volatility samples are put together, one may argue that the rejection is due to the failure to satisfy the heteroskedasticity assumption. On the other hand, if there is a rejection in one of the subsamples, it must be the case that together the two subsamples are also rejected. This will allow us to identify the period in which the parameters have shifted. Similar exercises are implemented in the next two crises.

The Asian crises began in June 1996 with Thailand's devaluation, and lasted into 1998 until the end of the Korean crisis. For the particular case of the Asian crises, the tranquil period is always defined as the six months prior to Thailand's devaluation. Several high-volatility periods are defined. The Thailand crisis began at the start of June 1997; the Hong Kong crisis began on 27 October 1997; and the Korean crisis began around 15 December 1997. The Hong Kong crisis is the only one that has a clear initial date, which is the day on which short-term interest rates increased dramatically. For the other two crises, however, the initial day is unclear because important action took place on the bond and stock markets prior to the exchange rate devaluation.

During the Asian crises several combination of windows are studied. However, it is important to highlight that even though some of these windows include several crises, they should not become a violation of the heteroskedasticity assumption. In the bond market data, all Southeast Asian countries are excluded from the regression; thus, these crises are summarized by the common unobservable shock. Therefore, the common shock is a subset of the shocks and no rejection should be obtained because the heteroskedasticity assumption was not satisfied. On the other hand, for the stock market data, all the countries are included in the regression. Therefore, the Southeast Asian crises can be modeled as changes in the volatility of a subset of the idiosyncratic shocks. Again, the DCC should not be rejected because of ill-specified heteroskedasticity.

Finally, the third crisis studied is the combination of the Russian and LTCM collapses. The tranquil period extends from March to July of 1998, and several high-volatility periods are studied. First, the pure Russian collapse started at the beginning of August. Second, the LTCM problems appeared at the end of August and lasted until the end of September. Finally, in October, another shocks (a speculative attack on the Brazilian currency) occurred. Hence, as in the Mexican case, the LTCM collapse has been associated with an aggregate liquidity shock.

Several sensitivity analyses were performed to evaluate the robustness of the results to (minor) changes in the definition of the windows. The results are robust to those, but robustness to a random definition of regimes should not be expected. It is crucial, and I hope this discussion has made it clear, that in order to implement the test one must first impose a comprehensive view of the changes in second moments. Otherwise, rejections are meaningless.

Stock Markets

Given the regimes and windows, the next step is to estimate the covariance matrix of the residuals from the reduced form and perform the DCC test.

In table 6.4, the change in covariance matrices is shown for all the choices of windows. This table shows how large the heteroskedasticity (on average) is. In order to compute the change in the covariance matrix, two different norms were used. The first column represents the average change in the variances. The relative change for all countries is computed from the covariance matrices and the average is reported. The second column shows the increase in the maximum singular value, which is perhaps the most informative measure.

As can be seen, the volatile regimes represent important changes in variance. For example, during the Mexican crisis an average increase in variance of eight times was observed. Similarly, during the Hong Kong specu-

Table 6.4   Changes in Variances Measured as Several Matrix Norms

	Average Increase in Variances	Increase in Maximum Singular Value
Mexican crisis		
Currency devaluation	3.36	9.23
No rollover	3.61	7.93
Currency devaluation + no rollover	3.59	7.90
Asian crises		
Hong Kong	6.96	12.80
Korea	5.99	20.08
Hong Kong + Korea	1.84	2.05
Thailand	2.15	3.41
All	0.99	0.97
Russian crisis		
Russia	2.70	2.77
LTCM	5.29	4.78
Russia + LTCM	4.34	3.62
Brazilian speculative attack	3.44	3.07
All	4.04	3.17

Table 6.5   **DCC Test for Stock Markets**

	DCC in Stock Market			
	Point Estimate	Standard Deviation	Mass Zero	Rejection
Mexican crisis				
Currency devaluation	−1.4632877	49.559015	0.357	0
No rollover	34.918946	182.90394	0.762	0
Currency devaluation + no rollover	16.135432	63.385381	0.778	0
Asian crises				
Hong Kong	−8,131.1469	5,140.3177	0.381	0
Korea	8.022301	192.47444	0.675	0
Hong Kong + Korea	2.808E-06	0.00078	0.566	0
Thailand	−0.0023061	0.3208153	0.465	0
All	−7.162E-21	2.011E-07	0.408	0
Russian crisis				
Russia	−28.163079	5,145.213	0.668	0
LTCM	2,926.3835	73,705.659	0.418	0
Russia + LTCM	3,171.8639	16,813.048	0.358	0
Brazilian speculative attack	7.6768399	27,581.466	0.676	0
All	−2,091.3015	19,540.064	0.615	0

lative attack the increase in stock markets was almost twelve times. These increases in volatility represent a significant rise in volatility in emerging markets. Remember that the data include countries such as the United States, Singapore, Chile, etc., where the increases in volatility during this sample were smaller than two times.

After the covariance matrices are estimated, the determinant on their change is computed. The results for the stock market test are shown in table 6.5. The first column indicates the point estimate, the second column is the computed standard deviation, the third is the mass below zero, and the fourth is an indicator for which a value of 1 means that the test of stability was rejected. The standard deviation and the mass below zero are computed using a bootstrap. The procedure uses the changes in conditional variance across the windows to produce several covariance matrices, then computes the determinant on the change and estimates both the standard deviation and the mass below zero. Standard deviations are large because the small sample distribution of the determinant is not normal; thus, to give the test some chance of rejection, the mass below zero is used. The dummy is set to 1 if the proportion of the simulations with determinants smaller than 0 (mass below zero) is either 10 or 90 percent.

Observe that in table 6.5, there is no single case in which the test is rejected. The immediate question is whether the test has power. Two remarks should be made in this respect. In Rigobon (2000b) it is shown that for the size of these windows and the observed changes in variance, the test is quite powerful (type II errors were smaller than 10 percent for a test with size 5 percent). Second, as will be seen below, there are some rejections when bond data are used. Therefore, the lack of rejection could not be blamed entirely on the power of the test. This evidence suggests that the propagation of shocks across stock markets is (relatively) stable during the recent crises.

Bond Markets

This section turns its attention to the bond market. The same windows used before were used to test for the stability of parameters among EMBI+ indexes.

In table 6.6, the change in covariance matrices is shown again to highlight the changes in variances experienced in the sample. The interpretation of the columns is the same as before. Note that in this case, however, the shifts in the variances are larger than the ones found in stock markets.

In particular, observe that during the Mexican crisis after the non-rollover announcement the variances doubled. Likewise, the LTCM collapse implied an increase in volatility above the one already experienced by the Russian crash. Take into consideration that this pattern was absent in the stock market data (see table 6.4); this confirms the common wisdom among market participants that the aftermath of the Mexican crisis and the LTCM shocks consisted mainly of shocks to the bond markets.

On the other hand, an interesting aspect of this table is that, excluding the Hong Kong speculative attack, the Asian crises had almost no impact on the variance of Latin American bond markets, at least in their volatilities.

Table 6.6   DCC Test for Bond Markets

	Average Increase in Variances	Increase in Maximum Singular Value
Mexican crisis		
Currency devaluation	12.71	10.14
No rollover	19.96	22.92
Currency devaluation + no rollover	18.56	20.21
Asian crises		
Hong Kong	13.69	15.73
Korea	2.39	3.11
Hong Kong + Korea	1.14	1.28
Thailand	0.82	1.04
All	1.00	1.01
Russian crisis		
Russia	49.15	47.72
LTCM	58.89	56.75
Russia + LTCM	51.54	50.69
Brazilian speculative attack	13.31	11.88
All	38.79	37.53

Notes: Changes in variances measured as several matrix norms.

Table 6.7   **DCC Test for Bond Markets**

	DCC in Bond Market			
	Point Estimate	Standard Deviation	Mass below Zero	Rejection
Mexican crisis				
Currency devaluation	1.3062012	2.1833245	0.76	0
No rollover	14.264603	18.034845	0.94	1
Currency devaluation + no rollover	16.541713	15.496773	0.981	1
Asian crises				
Hong Kong	−0.0002571	0.0008754	0.24	0
Korea	6.841E-10	5.164E-08	0.345	0
Hong Kong + Korea	−1.306E-12	7.95E-11	0.549	0
Thailand	−2.812E-10	5.66E-09	0.325	0
All	1.028E-19	2.00E-11	0.616	0
Russian crisis				
Russia	−0.0005737	0.0011142	0.549	0
LTCM	−6.8381042	5.7270025	0.04	1
Russia + LTCM	−6.3514527	4.5857572	0.021	1
Brazilian speculative attack	0.0029295	0.0009354	0.264	0
All	8.307991	3.1489852	0.993	1

Remember that if the heteroskedasticity is small the DCC test has little power. Thus, a lack of rejection should be expected during the Southeast Asian crisis for the bond data.

The results for the bond market DCC test are shown in table 6.7. The interpretation of the table is the same as for the stock market. In this case, there are two instances in which the parameters are unstable: the 9 January shock and the LTCM collapse. Note that the DCC test is rejected when these crises are analyzed separately or jointly with other events, suggesting that the test is rejected because of a shift in the parameters during those times, and not because of misspecification of the alternative hypothesis.

In the Mexican case the test is rejected if the sample covers the period from January to March, or from 19 December to March. Similarly, the test is rejected for the LTCM crisis alone (end of August plus September) or if it is included with the Russian crisis, or with the Russian and Brazilian attacks. However, no instability was found after October 1998, indicating that the changes in the transmission mechanism across bond markets occurred shortly after the LTCM collapse.

In summary, the events for which the test is rejected reflect incidents of important common shocks occurring in the bond market. Market participants have identified these two particular events with liquidity shocks. In the setup estimated here, there is more to these shocks than a pure liquidity shock. In equation (9) the presence of a liquidity shock has already been taken into consideration by the inclusion of z_t. The fact that the DCC is rejected implies, then, that either the relationship is nonlinear or there is a change in the intensity with which the liquidity shocks are propagated. With the techniques available, unfortunately, there is no procedure that can disentangle these two explanations.

6.5.2   Estimation of the Propagation Mechanism

In this subsection, the contemporaneous relationship between stock markets and bond returns is estimated. The questions of interest are threefold: What is the estimate of A? How much do trade and regional variables explain A? Finally, what is the relative importance of the common shocks (z_t) across crises and regimes?

Model and Identification

As before, it is assumed that returns are described by the same latent-factor model

(10) $AX_t = \phi(L)X_t + \Gamma z_t + \varepsilon_t.$

Assume that there are C common shocks and K endogenous variable. Again, a VAR is estimated first and the tests are performed on the reduced-form residuals equation (9).

Identification. The procedure described in section 6.4.4 shows that under orthogonality of the structural shocks and the existence of heteroskedasticity, it is possible to identify an equation such as equation (10) if the heteroskedasticity is high enough.

Given the number of endogenous and omitted variables, the unknowns in the system of equations are as follows: $K(K-1)$ unknowns are the parameters from matrix A; $C(K-1)$ unknowns are the parameters from Γ after normalization; K times S variances are from the idiosyncratic shocks (there are K variances of idiosyncratic shocks for each regime in heteroskedasticity [S]); and C times S variances are from the common shocks (there are C variances of common shocks for each regime). Therefore, the total number of unknowns is

(11) $\underbrace{K(K-1)}_{\text{from } A} + \underbrace{C(K-1)}_{\text{from } \Gamma} + \underbrace{KS}_{\text{idiosyncratic shocks}} + \underbrace{CS}_{\text{common shocks}}.$

The first condition for identification is that each regime in the heteroskedasticity should add more equations than unknowns. This is required for the order condition to be satisfied. Each new covariance matrix adds $K(K+1)/2$ equations (which is the covariance matrix estimated on the residuals), while it adds K new idiosyncratic variances and C new common shock variances. Therefore, each regime adds more equations than unknowns if and only if

(12)
$$\frac{K(K+1)}{2} > K + C$$

$$K(K-1) > 2C$$

This is the "catch-up" constraint.

After the condition of equation (12) is satisfied, there must be a minimum number of regimes that imply that there are at least as many equations as unknowns. The number of knowns is provided by the covariance matrix in each regime and is equal to

(13)
$$\frac{K(K+1)}{2}S.$$

Therefore, imposing that equation (13) is larger than or equal to equation (11), and solving for S, the minimum number of regimes required for identification is

(14)
$$S \geq 2\frac{(K+C)(K-1)}{K^2 - K - 2C}.$$

In the two examples studied here, one common shock is allowed. Therefore, the number of regimes required for identification in each case is as follows:

1. There are eight countries (endogenous variables) in the bond markets. The catch-up constraint (equation [12]) is easily satisfied and the minimum number of regimes is $S \geq 14/6$.

2. There are fourteen countries in the stock markets. Thus, the inequality in equation (12) is satisfied and the number of regimes required is $S \geq 13/6$.

In summary, three regimes are enough to achieve identification in both examples.

Estimation. From the reduced form, equation (9), the covariance matrix of residuals is given by

(15)
$$\Omega_t^v = A^{-1}\Gamma\Omega_t^z\Gamma'A'^{-1} + A^{-1}\Omega_t^\varepsilon A'^{-1},$$

where the left-hand side is the estimate of the covariance matrix in regime $t \in (1, \ldots, S)$, and the right-hand side expresses the coefficients of interest. This is a nonlinear system of equations that is estimated by generalized method of moments (GMM), in which equation (15) is the set of moment restrictions.[21]

---

21. Actually, instead of computing inverses of A, the moment restriction estimated is $A\Omega_t^v A' - \Gamma\Omega_t^z\Gamma' - \Omega_t^\varepsilon = 0$, which is simpler and more stable. However, the invertibility of A must always be checked.

After the VAR has been estimated and the residuals (which in fact are the same residuals as those used in the previous section); have been recovered, the regimes are defined, the covariance matrices are calculated, and the system of equations is estimated. An important aspect of the identification through heteroskedasticity is that the estimates are consistent even if the regimes are misspecified. Thus, the windows are defined by the periods of medium and high volatility derived from the conditional volatility. Furthermore, the identification is obtained regardless of whether the changes in variance are conditional; thus, the use of the sample covariance matrices to determine the regimes is easily justified.[22]

For stock markets the sample studied runs from July 1994 to the end of 1998. For bond markets, we exclude the Mexican and Russian crises; thus the sample runs from 1 April 1995 until 31 July 1998. The assumption of parameter stability is crucial for the identification, and the previous subsections have already shown that bond markets had unstable parameters during the first quarter of 1995 and after 21 August 1998.

Again, the results from the VAR are not shown.

Stock Markets

Definition of the Regimes. First, taking the residuals from the VAR, a twenty-day rolling window covariance matrix was computed. A norm on the covariance matrix was defined (in this paper, the maximum singular value was used; however, other measures produced very similar splits in the regimes). Second, using the conditional covariance matrices, the regimes were defined as follows: the low-volatility regimes are those dates on which the matrix norm is smaller than the average; the high-volatility regimes are the dates on which the norm is larger than 2 standard deviations of the mean; and the medium-volatility regime is the rest of the sample.

In figure 6.1 the three regimes are shown, with 1 corresponding to the low-volatility, 2 to the medium-volatility, and 3 to the high-volatility periods. There are 848 observations in the low, 329 in the medium, and 95 in the high-volatility regimes. It is important to note that the regimes coincide with most of the crises and events in which contagion is suspected to have existed.

Finally, after the windows are defined, the covariance matrix in each regime is computed and the GMM is implemented to estimate equation (15).

---

22. In a separate paper, I have already solved the problem of identification when only conditional heteroskedasticity exists. The proof is very similar to the one shown here. Deriving the reduced form from a structural model where the residuals have GARCH effects and the structural shocks are uncorrelated produces a restricted GARCH equation that fully identifies the simultaneous coefficients in the level equation. The estimation in this case is simpler because the maximum likelihood estimator (MLE) can be used directly. The intuition of the identification, however, is exactly the same as the one derived here (see Rigobon 2001).

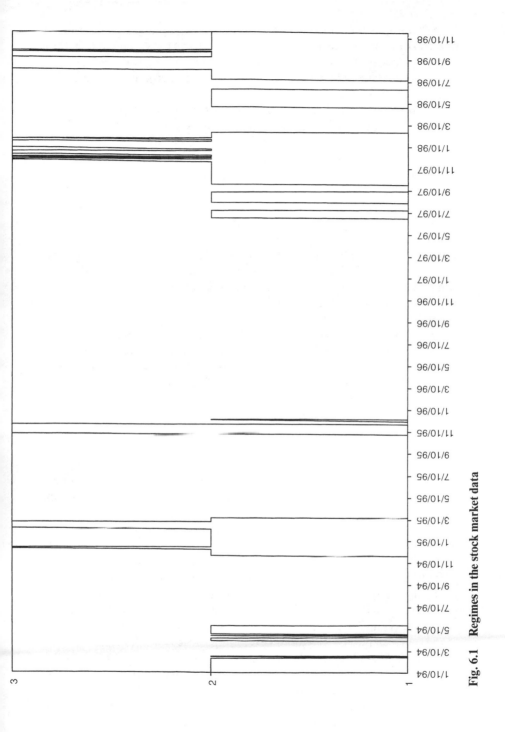

Fig. 6.1   Regimes in the stock market data

Distributions and standard deviations were computed by bootstrap in order to draw several covariance matrices and solve the system of equations for each realization. However, the assumption that the covariance matrices across regimes are independent is unsatisfactory; thus, in order to take into consideration the serial correlation in the covariance matrices, it was assumed that only the change in the covariances was independent across regimes. Therefore, conditional on the point estimates of the covariance matrices of the reduced form, random draws of covariance matrices were obtained consistent with the sample size in each regime and its covariance structure. For each set of covariance matrices the system of equations is solved (using GMM) and the process repeated 100 times. The distribution of the coefficients is the solution to each of the realizations of the system of equations.

Contemporaneous Transmission Mechanism. The results of estimating A are shown in table 6.8. The diagonal is omitted because it is known that it is equal to 1, and the signs of the coefficients have been changed so they can be understood as the elasticities in the right-hand side (its natural interpretation).

The rows represent the equations of each country, and the columns are the regressors. Therefore, the reading of the coefficients is as follows: The row country (Argentina) is contemporaneously affected by the column country (Mexico) by a coefficient of 0.234. The coefficients that are statistically significant different from zero at the 90 percent confidence interval are in boldface type, where the confidence interval is computed using the bootstrapped distribution.

Several remarks on table 6.8 are worth making. First, the coefficients in the U.S. equation are all nonstatistically significant. Note that this was not imposed on the estimation procedure, even though our prior would have suggested so. On the other hand, the United States importantly affects some of the emerging markets.

Second, the coefficients are relatively large, explaining the high comovement that exists among international stock markets. In fact, these coefficients explain correlations of an average of 22 percent among all countries.

Third, in the table, 32 of 182 coefficients are statistically different from zero. Among the Latin American countries, there are 13 significant estimates out of 30 possible coefficients. Similarly, among the Southeast Asian countries, 12 of 42 are significantly different from zero. Interestingly, only 3 (of 84) coefficients across regions (excluding those from the United States) are statistically different from zero; these are the propagations from Chile to Korea, from Chile to Thailand, and from Korea to Mexico. This confirms, quite strongly, the common wisdom that the propagation of shocks across countries was concentrated within geographical regions.

Table 6.9 shows the standard deviations of the coefficients, which are ob-

Table 6.8 Point Estimates of A

								Regressor						
Country	Argentina	Brazil	Chile	Hong Kong	Malaysia	Mexico	Peru	The Philippines	Singapore	Korea	Taiwan	Thailand	United States	Venezuela
Argentina		0.26	0.51	0.09	0.17	0.23	0.55	0.35	0.24	0.04	0.20	0.22	0.76	0.00
Brazil	0.51		0.60	0.33	0.00	0.29	0.69	0.09	0.44	0.08	0.00	0.12	0.61	0.04
Chile	0.24	0.08		0.26	0.13	0.01	0.28	0.23	0.00	0.05	0.36	0.20	0.64	0.00
Hong Kong	0.13	0.00	0.00		0.00	0.00	0.37	0.04	0.63	0.10	0.00	0.21	0.00	0.06
Malaysia	0.22	0.09	0.23	0.72		0.05	0.32	0.27	0.13	0.23	0.37	0.35	0.06	0.05
Mexico	0.35	0.17	0.72	0.31	0.23		0.14	0.22	0.53	0.16	0.08	0.24	0.55	0.00
Peru	0.06	0.00	0.58	0.33	0.27	0.47		0.34	0.02	0.16	0.03	0.23	0.44	0.12
The Philippines	0.00	0.06	0.17	0.02	0.03	0.17	0.02		0.41	0.14	0.47	0.32	0.31	0.00
Singapore	0.14	0.00	0.69	0.38	0.20	0.01	0.25	0.37		0.04	0.17	0.41	0.39	0.01
Korea	0.25	0.14	0.57	0.07	0.16	0.10	0.11	0.39	0.32		0.09	0.39	0.53	0.04
Taiwan	0.23	0.00	0.01	0.43	0.22	0.16	0.48	0.43	0.34	0.18		0.37	0.21	0.04
Thailand	0.06	0.09	0.70	0.15	0.26	0.00	0.49	0.35	0.51	0.31	0.15		0.36	0.00
United States	0.19	0.09	0.09	0.37	0.18	0.24	0.22	0.47	0.30	0.17	0.12	0.30		0.07
Venezuela	0.21	0.00	0.71	0.00	0.11	0.10	0.25	0.59	0.56	0.19	0.39	0.31	0.06	

Table 6.9   Standard Deviation of *A* Estimates

Country	Argentina	Brazil	Chile	Hong Kong	Malaysia	Mexico	Peru	The Philippines	Singapore	Korea	Taiwan	Thailand	United States	Venezuela
Argentina		0.082	0.153	0.080	0.046	0.079	0.115	0.121	0.124	0.025	0.071	0.069	0.170	0.019
Brazil	0.138		0.178	0.106	0.014	0.122	0.169	0.073	0.160	0.069	0.084	0.093	0.182	0.057
Chile	0.060	0.041		0.056	0.024	0.032	0.060	0.062	0.069	0.028	0.071	0.042	0.141	0.014
Hong Kong	0.053	0.031	0.065		0.009	0.041	0.082	0.071	0.119	0.043	0.077	0.068	0.050	0.025
Malaysia	0.076	0.037	0.119	0.111		0.079	0.090	0.082	0.130	0.062	0.091	0.098	0.041	0.031
Mexico	0.106	0.073	0.203	0.118	0.042		0.120	0.109	0.150	0.081	0.079	0.074	0.149	0.026
Peru	0.032	0.032	0.167	0.110	0.041	0.095		0.102	0.052	0.052	0.064	0.078	0.172	0.045
The Philippines	0.074	0.068	0.126	0.071	0.050	0.086	0.049		0.108	0.069	0.087	0.074	0.144	0.011
Singapore	0.047	0.036	0.117	0.085	0.047	0.040	0.053	0.084		0.016	0.048	0.065	0.122	0.018
Korea	0.080	0.078	0.181	0.090	0.062	0.092	0.106	0.143	0.145		0.101	0.111	0.173	0.068
Taiwan	0.040	0.047	0.089	0.140	0.042	0.056	0.123	0.119	0.110	0.064		0.074	0.146	0.025
Thailand	0.044	0.039	0.188	0.124	0.066	0.031	0.108	0.116	0.146	0.072	0.060		0.148	0.035
United States	0.060	0.045	0.105	0.070	0.022	0.049	0.080	0.087	0.085	0.036	0.065	0.045		0.023
Venezuela	0.085	0.039	0.170	0.033	0.020	0.054	0.140	0.164	0.168	0.064	0.157	0.081	0.139	

tained from the bootstrap. One appealing fact from table 6.9 is that the precision of the estimates depends on how severe the country was affected by the crises.

For example, Argentina, Brazil, Hong Kong, Malaysia, Mexico, Korea, and Thailand were either the originators of the crises or the main countries affected. The standard deviations for these estimates is 0.063. On the other hand, U.S. estimates are less precisely estimated; the average standard deviation is 0.1366. The reason for this outcome is the way the identification problem is solved: the heteroskedasticity is the identifying device. The quality of the estimation, and thus its precision, depends on how large the heteroskedasticity is. The larger the shift in the variance of that country, the better-estimated the coefficients of the propagations from that country are. The increases in volatility in emerging markets are almost an order of magnitude larger than those from the United States (or Singapore), which is why those standard deviations are smaller.

Finally, in table 6.10, the quasi–z-statistic was computed. Even though the test of significance was implemented by looking at the distribution, it is informative to calculate the ratio of the average bootstrapped distribution to the standard deviation because the conclusions of both procedures are similar, and this one is much easier to implement. The inconvenience is that the z-statistic tends to overestimate the significance of the coefficients.

For example, if a 90 percent confidence interval is used (as was the case with the bootstrapped distribution) then more coefficients are significant under use of the z-statistic than use of the bootstrapped distribution. In table 6.8, there are 32 out of 182 significant coefficients; using the z-statistic, 47 would have been significant. It is important to mention that all the coefficients that are significant under the bootstrapped distribution are also significant using the z-statistic. On the other hand, if a 95 percent confidence interval is used as the criterion on the z-statistics, then 31 coefficients pass the test. The coefficient that loses significance is the transmission between the United States and Peru.

At first glance, Chile has as many significant coefficients as the United States. Does this mean that Chile is more important than the United States in these data? Certainly not. What this does mean is simply that those coefficients are estimated with more efficiency. To answer the question of importance of countries, however, a different exercise must be performed. The interpretation of the coefficients requires a variance decomposition (performed below). This is the correct measure to evaluate the relative impacts of countries and shocks in this model.

Finally, the patterns shown by the coefficients estimated in matrix A imply unconditional correlations that are relatively large. What are the explanations underlying them? In this interpretation, it is important to remember that these coefficients are the combination of several possible channels of contagion. The question, then, is what are the possible explanations

Table 6.10 z-statistics of A Estimates

Country	Argentina	Brazil	Chile	Hong Kong	Malaysia	Mexico	Peru	The Philippines	Singapore	Korea	Taiwan	Thailand	United States	Venezuela
Argentina		2.98	3.91	0.85	1.47	2.79	1.20	1.38	1.75	0.56	0.71	1.37	3.91	0.47
Brazil	3.42		3.59	1.11	0.25	2.06	2.46	0.67	1.67	0.88	0.87	1.15	2.78	1.35
Chile	1.78	1.94		1.38	0.99	0.64	0.97	1.39	1.46	0.59	1.01	1.18	3.32	0.70
Hong Kong	1.06	0.43	0.71		0.33	1.05	2.18	1.62	4.52	1.95	1.29	1.61	0.57	0.90
Malaysia	0.94	0.52	0.78	3.65		1.29	1.74	0.94	1.58	2.16	0.91	1.73	0.32	1.20
Mexico	2.67	1.83	2.85	1.33	0.63		2.06	1.14	1.93	2.11	1.02	0.88	2.89	0.52
Peru	0.61	0.72	2.50	0.99	0.89	2.05		1.16	0.45	1.00	0.80	0.84	1.93	1.17
The Philippines	1.32	0.94	1.04	1.39	0.94	1.47	0.75		3.53	2.66	1.38	2.40	1.23	0.48
Singapore	0.87	0.95	4.47	2.89	2.72	0.83	0.84	1.82		0.26	0.82	1.89	1.71	0.99
Korea	0.87	1.03	2.49	0.98	0.83	1.04	1.50	1.13	1.53		1.63	2.29	2.68	1.15
Taiwan	0.46	0.64	0.75	1.15	1.09	0.82	1.27	1.09	0.97	0.98		0.84	1.31	0.90
Thailand	0.49	0.67	2.66	1.08	1.54	0.55	1.81	1.90	2.53	1.65	0.84		1.19	0.74
United States	1.40	1.49	1.70	1.14	0.33	1.46	1.32	1.47	1.35	1.50	1.27	0.57		1.47
Venezuela	0.95	0.53	4.04	0.46	0.35	0.62	1.59	1.44	1.73	0.92	1.57	0.86	1.40	

Table 6.11   Vulnerabilities (estimates of γ)

Country	Point Estimate	Standard Deviation	z-statistic
Argentina	0.39	0.26	0.84
Brazil	0.41	0.35	1.05
Chile	0.34	0.14	0.97
Hong Kong	0.09	0.10	0.60
Mayalsia	0.27	0.22	0.87
Mexico	0.44	0.28	0.88
Peru	0.52	0.25	1.01
The Philippines	0.35	0.14	1.02
Singapore	0.38	0.34	0.90
Korea	0.68	0.32	1.02
Taiwan	0.30	0.22	0.71
Thailand	0.64	0.19	0.94
United States	0.10		
Venezuela	0.55	0.28	1.06

behind them? Later in this section, a partial structural model is provided using the analysis of the importance of trade and regional variables.

Vulnerabilities. The GMM procedure also provides an estimate of the sensitivity of countries' stock markets to common shocks. These coefficients are identified only up to a normalization, and in this particular case, the U.S. elasticity was chosen to be equal to 0.1. The results are shown in table 6.11. The first column corresponds to the point estimate. The second column shows the standard deviation computed from the bootstrapped distribution. The third column is the z-statistic, calculated as before.

As was claimed in the introduction, the common shocks represent changes in risk preferences, liquidity shocks, etc. Note that all coefficients (except the one from Hong Kong) are larger than 0.1, suggesting that emerging economies are more vulnerable to common shocks than the United States. For example, Argentina, Brazil, and Mexico are close to four times more vulnerable than the United States to the same common liquidity shock. Even though this pattern is quite informative, it is impossible to reject the hypothesis that the estimates are all equal to zero.

Because the coefficients estimated are difficult to interpret, the next subsection—rather than studying their aspects—analyzes a variance decomposition. First, the proportion of the variance explained by the common shocks versus idiosyncratic shocks is analyzed, and later, the proportion of the variance explained by each country within the idiosyncratic shocks.

Variance Decomposition: Common versus Country-Specific Shocks. The variance decomposition indicates the relative importance of the common shock in each of the regimes and countries. Thus, the analysis of vulnera-

Table 6.12   Variance Decomposition (percentage explained by idiosyncratic shocks)

Country	Variance Decomposition		
	Low	Medium	High
Argentina	89.4	78.8	75.0
Brazil	94.0	88.6	85.5
Chile	92.0	83.7	80.8
Hong Kong	73.4	65.4	57.6
Malaysia	71.5	72.4	64.4
Mexico	86.8	77.5	75.1
Peru	92.6	83.9	81.2
The Philippines	77.4	67.1	49.4
Singapore	72.6	56.8	51.1
Korea	89.2	84.1	89.6
Taiwan	98.1	95.3	87.3
Thailand	72.1	60.8	53.2
United States	95.8	92.7	89.0
Venezuela	97.8	93.3	97.1

bility can also be studied in this context. Moreover, given the interpretation of the common shock as liquidity or risk preferences, this disaggregation can be useful to understand the relevance of those shocks in the explanation of the recent crises.

The variance decomposition was estimated by calculating the total unconditional variance per regime and comparing it with the implied unconditional variance, assuming that the common shocks do not exist. The procedure is as follows: Using the estimated coefficients and variances in each regime, the unconditional covariance matrix is estimated using equation (15). Then the same equation is estimated, but $\Omega z\backslash t$ is set to zero. This is the unconditional covariance with only idiosyncratic shocks (in other words, without common shocks). In table 6.12, the ratio between the variance of each country explained by idiosyncratic shocks alone to the variance when common shocks are included. This procedure is repeated for each regime.

Three remarks can be extracted from the table. First, notice that the United States is almost unaffected by common shocks (surprisingly, Venezuela is also equally unaffected by common shocks). In all three regimes, close to 90 percent of the variation in U.S. stock returns is explained by idiosyncratic shocks. This does not mean that liquidity shocks or risk preferences are unimportant in the United States. What it does mean is that the common component of these shocks can be described mainly as idiosyncratic shocks to the United States. Therefore, in this exercise, the common liquidity shock not affecting the United States is the one that is being evaluated.

Second, the high-volatility regime includes a larger proportion of common shocks: the average decomposition during the high-volatility regime implies that 74 percent of the variation is explained by idiosyncratic shocks.

This should be compared with 86 percent, which is the average of the idiosyncratic-shock explanation during the low-volatility regime. This pattern suggests that during the recent crises a component common to emerging markets contributed to the comovement across stock markets. As will be seen below, this stylized fact is even stronger in bond markets.

Third, during the high-volatility regimes, the countries having the largest component of common shock were the Asian countries. Surprisingly, for the Latin American countries the change in the common component is small from the low- to high-volatility regimes.

Variance Decomposition: Country Idiosyncratic-Shock Contribution. The interpretation of the matrix A coefficients is more easily understood in a variance decomposition exercise. Table 6.13 computes the proportion of the idiosyncratic variance of each row country explained by the country shock column. The total idiosyncratic variance is calculated as $A^{-1}\Omega^\varepsilon A'^{-1}$. To compute the contribution of country j shocks on the other countries, all elements of Ω^ε (except $\omega_{\varepsilon,jj}$) are set equal to zero. Table 6.13 presents the ratio between the diagonals of these two matrices for each country.

The table does not include standard errors on the variance decomposition, and its interpretation must be taken cautiously. However, it has interesting patterns. The reading of the table is as follows: The row country is the variance to be explained, while the columns indicate the shock that is analyzed. For example, Argentinean shocks explain 68 percent of the idiosyncratic variance of Argentina, 18 percent of the Brazilean variance, and 19 percent of the Mexican variance.

Two remarks are worth mentioning. First, note that in more developed markets (the United States and Hong Kong) the majority of the variance is explained by each country's own shocks.

Second, most of the variation per regions is explained by regional idiosyncratic shocks. For example, 73.6 percent of the variation of the Latin American countries is explained by their own regional shocks, 23.0 percent is due to shocks to Asian countries, and 3.4 percent is due to U.S. shocks. On the other hand, 71.0 percent of the volatility in Asia is due to Asian shocks, 18.1 percent is due to Latin American shocks, and 10.9 percent is due to U.S. shocks. In the particular case of the United States, 80.5 percent is accounted for by U.S. idiosyncratic shocks, while 12.5 percent and 7.0 percent are explained by Latin American and Asian shocks, respectively.

Estimating the Importance of Trade. The final exercise is to explain the coefficients from the A matrix by trade and regional variables. Thus, an evaluation of the strength of these channels of contagion is performed in this section.

The additional data collected are the following: Information on trade is obtained from Feenstra's World Data Flows. The trade share is computed as the

Table 6.13   Variance Decomposition (percentage explained by each country shock in the total idiosyncratic shock variance)

Country	Argentina	Brazil	Chile	Hong Kong	Malaysia	Mexico	Peru	The Philippines	Singapore	Korea	Taiwan	Thailand	United States	Venezuela
Argentina	68.1	0.8	2.8	13.1	0.4	0.2	0.1	1.8	8.8	0.7	0.9	1.6	0.1	0.6
Brazil	18.1	24.6	8.3	2.8	0.2	2.4	3.0	0.3	22.1	5.0	0.7	3.3	8.1	1.1
Chile	9.1	0.1	54.0	0.1	1.0	0.9	12.2	1.3	0.1	2.6	0.1	1.9	12.3	4.4
Hong Kong	4.7	0.8	1.8	78.0	0.4	3.2	0.3	0.6	0.8	0.4	0.3	0.5	7.7	0.6
Malaysia	18.9	2.7	7.0	1.6	24.6	1.8	0.1	2.8	0.0	0.0	8.3	1.7	24.5	5.9
Mexico	7.7	0.0	8.2	0.1	0.2	62.4	0.4	0.0	6.7	0.8	1.3	4.2	0.1	8.0
Peru	9.0	1.5	0.0	19.3	0.4	0.1	54.5	3.0	3.1	0.0	2.8	0.1	4.3	1.8
The Philippines	7.0	1.1	0.5	10.4	0.0	9.0	1.8	39.6	4.3	3.6	0.7	2.1	19.0	0.9
Singapore	1.2	0.3	6.5	0.8	0.5	10.1	4.3	0.1	62.5	0.1	0.0	0.0	11.5	2.0
Korea	3.3	0.2	2.1	24.3	0.3	0.0	0.1	5.0	0.0	43.0	9.9	3.8	6.0	2.1
Taiwan	0.0	0.0	11.1	22.4	0.7	19.6	8.6	1.4	0.4	0.1	28.4	0.1	6.4	0.7
Thailand	3.3	1.4	2.5	14.0	0.4	0.1	1.8	2.4	2.3	0.1	5.7	58.5	6.9	0.7
United States	5.3	1.4	1.3	0.6	0.1	0.4	0.3	0.0	0.9	0.0	3.8	1.6	80.5	3.9
Venezuela	1.4	0.0	0.2	5.4	0.2	0.2	10.5	0.1	5.6	2.3	0.3	1.7	0.1	72.0

Table 6.14   **Explaining A-coefficients**

Variable	Coefficient	Standard Error	t-statistic	Prob.
C	0.504718	0.162908	3.098	0.002267
TRADE	0.333628	0.169129	1.972	0.050104
log (DISTANCE)	−0.032304	0.01664	−1.941	0.05382
BORDER	−0.018185	0.058949	−0.308	0.758069
LA	0.36155	0.057056	0.633	0.527122
SEA	−0.020357	0.056898	−0.357	0.720934
R^2	0.06632			
Prob (F-statistic)	0.03241			

Notes: See text for explanation of variables.

average trade share of the countries in the 1990s. Information on distance, border sharing, and belonging to the Latin America (LA) or Southeast Asia (SEA) dummy is also included in the regression. The left-hand side represents the point estimates from matrix A, and the regression run is the following:

$$\beta_{i,j} = c_0 + c_1 LA + c_2 SEA + c_3 TRADE_{i,j} + c_4 BORDER$$
$$+ c_5 \log(DISTANCE) + \varepsilon_t$$

It is likely that this regression has heteroskedasticity because the A coefficients were estimated with different degrees of precision. Therefore, a GLS was estimated in which the covariance matrix of the coefficients obtained in the bootstrapping was used to weight the regression. In table 6.14, the results are shown.

Note that TRADE is almost significant and with the correct sign: high trade share tends to imply a larger contemporaneous coefficient. The point estimate is 0.33 with a standard deviation of 0.17. This estimated will be compared with the one obtained in the bond regression.

The estimates on distance are also (almost) significant and with the correct sign. Surprisingly (at least to the author) is the fact that the regional dummies are not statistically significant. The R^2 is quite low even though the F-test shows that the regression is significant as a whole. Therefore, trade, although it has some explanatory power on the coefficients, has only a limited role in explaining most of the contemporaneous relationship across countries. Future studies should extend the present analysis to provide a better understanding about the transmission mechanism across stock markets. These results, however, contrast with the findings from the bond market; this is the topic that follows.

Bond Markets

The data on bond markets are restricted to the period between April 1995 and July 1998. However, the estimation methodology is the same as in stock markets. In figure 6.2, the volatile regimes are shown (determined with the

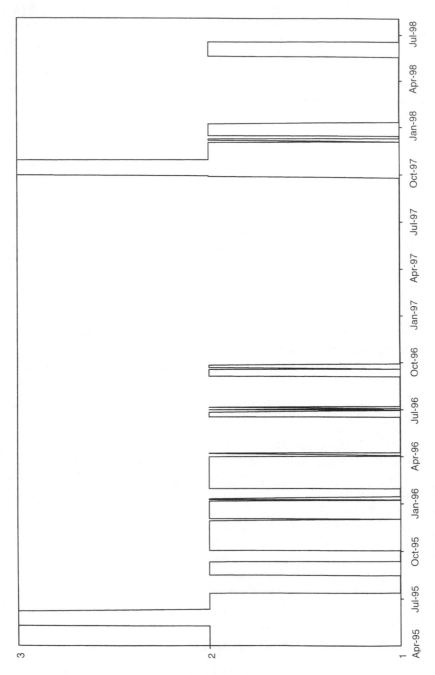

Fig. 6.2   Regimes in the bond market

Table 6.15   *A* **Estimates**

Country	Argentina	Brazil	Ecuador	Mexico	Panama	Peru	Venezuela	United States
Argentina		**0.33**	**0.18**	**0.37**	0.04	0.02	0.19	0.11
Brazil	**0.20**		0.14	**0.51**	0.06	0.12	0.18	**0.47**
Ecuador	**0.36**	0.28		0.20	0.12	**0.35**	**0.44**	**0.62**
Mexico	**0.21**	0.22	0.10		0.07	0.11	**0.29**	0.19
Panama	**0.26**	0.25	0.02	**0.46**		0.29	**0.44**	**0.73**
Peru	0.38	0.13	0.23	**0.43**	0.15		0.09	**0.61**
Venezuela	0.40	0.07	0.06	**0.35**	**0.26**	0.10		0.32
United States	0.03	0.07	0.01	0.04	0.04	0.01	0.02	

procedure highlighted earlier). In this case, there are 526 observations in the low- to medium-volatility regime, 268 in the medium-volatility regime, and 41 in the high-volatility regime. (Notice that the high volatilities occur during the Hong Kong crisis and in June 1995.[23])

Contemporaneous Transmission Mechanism. In table 6.15, the results from estimating matrix *A* are shown. The diagonal is omitted and the sign of the coefficients have been changed so they can be interpreted directly as the right-hand-side elasticities. The table should be read as before: the row country (Argentina) is contemporaneously affected by the column country (Mexico) by the coefficient 0.37.

Those coefficients that are statistically significant at the 90 percent confidence interval are in boldface type. As before, the distributions and the mass below zero are obtained by bootstrapping, using the same procedure as the one described above.

Several lessons can be extracted from the table. First, notice again that the United States is unaffected by any Latin American country. Observe that not only are the coefficients not significant, but the point estimates are very small. This was not imposed in the estimation procedure, but our priors would have indicated that indeed this should be the case.

Second, bond market participants agree that the two most important countries in the sovereign bond market are Argentina and Mexico. The bonds from these two countries are generally used as benchmarks to define prices for other countries. The results from table 6.15 confirm this common wisdom. Mexico affects all Latin American countries in the sample except for Ecuador, while Argentina significantly influences all countries in the region except for Peru and Venezuela.

Third, the United States has an important impact on Latin American

---

23. In June 1995, the rescue package was under way, and good news about Mexico was released; its access to international financial markets was renewed. Thus, laughter is also contagious.

countries. These data were constructed to reflect the country risk premium (in the first stage, the indexes were regressed on U.S. ten-year bond rates). Hence, the fact that the U.S. coefficients are positive and significant indicates that the country risk premium in these countries increases with U.S. interest rates. In other words, the pass-through on international interest rates is greater than 1 (see Frankel 2000).

Finally, notice that the coefficients are similar to those obtained from the stock markets. Even though a direct comparison cannot be made because the samples are very different, it is informative to concentrate on a couple of countries:

1. The Mexican coefficient in the Argentinean equation, for example, is 0.37 here and 0.23 before. Both estimates are statistically different from zero, but their difference is not. The Brazilian coefficient in the same equation is 0.33 here and 0.26 before.

2. Before, Mexico significantly affected Argentina, Brazil, and Peru; here, the same three countries (and two others) are affected. The regularities across the two exercises is worth further exploration.

In table 6.16, the standard deviation of the coefficients is shown. Note that even though the standard deviations of the U.S. equation are quite small, the estimates are not statistically significant from zero. Therefore, the reason for the lack of significance is not the need for precision. As opposed to the stock market case, there is no further pattern among the precision of the estimates.

In table 6.17 the quasi–z-statistic was computed. As before, the statistic tends to overestimate the significance of the estimates. For example, if a single-sided 90 percent confidence interval is used (as was the case with the bootstrapped distribution), then more coefficients are significant. In table 6.15, twenty out of fifty-six coefficients are significant; using the z-statistic, twenty-six would be significant. Again, all the estimates that are significant using the bootstrapped distribution are also significant with the z-statistic.

Table 6.16   Standard Deviations of A Estimates

Country	Argentina	Brazil	Ecuador	Mexico	Panama	Peru	Venezuela	United States
Argentina		0.11	0.09	0.13	0.06	0.04	0.11	0.11
Brazil	0.13		0.09	0.15	0.07	0.08	0.12	0.16
Ecuador	0.18	0.15		0.15	0.14	0.13	0.21	0.25
Mexico	0.12	0.13	0.10		0.08	0.09	0.13	0.16
Panama	0.17	0.19	0.05	0.21		0.18	0.19	0.20
Peru	0.21	0.12	0.13	0.18	0.14		0.10	0.22
Venezuela	0.14	0.08	0.06	0.15	0.09	0.09		0.18
United States	0.04	0.08	0.03	0.06	0.05	0.03	0.03	

Table 6.17   *Z*-statistics of *A* Estimates

Country	Argentina	Brazil	Ecuador	Mexico	Panama	Peru	Venezuela	United States
Argentina		2.95	2.09	2.84	0.74	0.59	1.72	0.98
Brazil	1.50		1.53	3.43	0.92	1.53	1.54	2.95
Ecuador	1.98	1.88		1.32	0.84	2.74	2.14	2.51
Mexico	1.78	1.66	1.03		0.86	1.17	2.27	1.17
Panama	1.54	1.33	0.41	2.23		1.67	2.36	3.63
Peru	1.85	1.16	1.85	2.38	1.09		0.87	2.79
Venezuela	2.94	0.85	1.06	2.35	2.86	1.16		1.77
United States	0.59	0.83	0.50	0.68	0.87	0.32	0.65	

Table 6.18   Vulnerabilities (estimates of γ)

		Vulnerability	
Country	Point Estimate	Standard Deviation	*z*-statistic
Argentina	0.15	0.11	1.32
Brazil	0.29	0.17	1.72
Ecuador	0.17	0.26	0.65
Mexico	0.36	0.17	2.14
Panama	0.60	0.29	2.08
Peru	0.57	0.26	2.17
Venezuela	0.31	0.17	1.86
United States	0.10		

The size of the test is incorrect, but if a coefficient is not significant assuming normality then it will not be so using the small sample distribution.

Before explaining the coefficients with trade and regional variables, the next subsections examine the vulnerability coefficients and the variance decomposition.

Vulnerabilities. The second set of coefficients estimated from the structural equation (10) are the elasticities to aggregate shocks. The coefficients are identified only up to a normalization; thus the United States was equated to 0.1. In table 6.18 the results are shown. The first column corresponds to the point estimate, in which the coefficients with mass above zero larger than 90 percent are highlighted in bold. The second column shows the standard deviation computed from the bootstrapped distribution. The third column is the *z*-statistic, calculated as the ratio between the point estimate and the standard deviation.

Before discussing the coefficients is important to clarify what is, in this case, the interpretation of the shock z_t. In these data, the unobservable common shocks are (as before) changes in risk preferences, liquidity shocks, etc. However, these shocks also include shocks to other countries that are not

Table 6.19   Variance Decomposition (percentage explained by the
                    idiosyncratic shocks)

	Variance Decomposition		
Country	Low	Medium	High
Argentina	50.13	43.48	17.28
Brazil	67.18	53.41	30.36
Ecuador	57.34	40.66	24.30
Mexico	66.30	52.42	31.47
Panama	78.94	65.48	46.27
Peru	79.07	69.67	41.49
Venezuela	66.46	51.65	28.93
United States	99.98	99.94	99.90

included in the sample, in particular, all the Southeast Asian countries. Therefore, the common shock aggregates all these disturbances, and the coefficient is the average response of the countries in the sample to those shocks. This implies that, unfortunately, these estimates cannot be directly compared with those obtained for the stock markets.

An interesting aspect of table 6.18, however, is that the estimates of all countries are larger than the U.S. coefficient. Again, it is impossible to reject the hypothesis that the coefficients are the same as the U.S. one,[24] but they share a pattern similar to the ones obtained from the stock market data.

Variance Decomposition: Common versus Idiosyncratic Shocks. Instead of concentrating on the vulnerability coefficients, it is better to compute the common-shock contribution to the variance. The variance decomposition is estimated as before: The predicted unconditional variance in each regime is computed by using the estimated coefficients and variances; then the predicted variance assuming only idiosyncratic shocks is calculated; and finally, the ratio between these two variances is calculated for each country. The results are reported in table 6.19.

The objective of this exercise is to evaluate the relative importance of common shocks across regimes. Given the range of the data (mainly covering the Southeast Asian crises) and the interpretation of the common shocks in the bond market (mainly SEA as well as liquidity and risk-preference shocks), it should be expected that the contribution of these shocks increases during the high-volatility regimes more than in the stock market case. This intuition is confirmed by the results: In the low-volatility regime (excluding the United States), idiosyncratic shocks explain an aver-

24. Remember that the test performed in the table is to determine whether the coefficient is different from 0, not from 0.10.

age of 66.49 percent of that variation. During the medium-volatility regime, they explain 53.82 percent, which reflects a small drop in the importance of idiosyncratic shocks. In the high-volatility regime, the contribution of idiosyncratic shocks falls to 31.44 percent—less than half of their importance during the low-volatility regime.

Additionally, observe that the United States is almost unaffected by common shocks. In all three regimes, more than 99 percent of the variation in U.S. interest rates is explained by idiosyncratic shocks. This is in sharp contrast with the emerging-market countries, where the common shocks always explain at least 20 percent of the variation.

An interesting comparison between the variance decompositions of bond and stock markets is that the relative importance of the common shocks in this data is significantly larger than in stock markets. However, this comparison should be made with caution.

Variance Decomposition: Country-Idiosyncratic Shock Contribution. We repeat the other variance decomposition for stock markets. Again, we are interested in improving the interpretation of the coefficients in matrix A by looking at the contribution of each shock to the total idiosyncratic shock volatility. This is important, because by looking at the coefficients directly one could draw some misleading conclusions. For example, in table 6.15, the coefficient from the United States to Mexico is nonstatistically significant. Does this means that U.S. interest rates have no explanatory power on Mexican interest rates? The answer is no.

In table 6.20, the results from the variance decomposition are reproduced for the bond market. Note that U.S. interest rates explain a sizeable proportion of the idiosyncratic shocks in each of the Latin American countries in the sample. Indeed, the United States explains as much variance in Argentina as in Mexico, even though one of the coefficients is statistically significant and the other is not.

From the table can be extracted the conjecture that countries whose ex-

Table 6.20   **Variance Decomposition (percentage explained by each country shock in the total idiosyncratic shock variance)**

Country	Argentina	Brazil	Ecuador	Mexico	Panama	Peru	Venezuela	United States
Argentina	24.2	10.4	11.0	10.2	7.5	10.4	4.8	21.4
Brazil	3.9	8.8	6.8	0.1	2.5	29.6	23.2	25.1
Ecuador	0.8	6.0	12.1	8.8	9.6	15.8	15.9	31.1
Mexico	2.9	17.4	8.7	15.7	15.1	11.6	7.4	21.1
Panama	3.9	6.2	13.7	0.3	38.5	12.9	5.5	19.1
Peru	2.4	4.4	19.4	9.0	2.9	12.8	17.8	31.3
Venezuela	1.6	7.2	11.9	13.3	8.7	15.0	7.0	35.4
United States	0.7	3.7	0.5	5.9	3.9	8.4	0.0	76.9¡

Table 6.21   Explaining A-coefficients

Variable	Coefficient	Standard Error	t-statistic	Prob.
C	1.098510242	0.24084432	4.561	5.99E-05
TRADE	0.448457005	0.19432761	2.307	0.027045
log (DISTANCE)	−0.091464254	0.02850499	−3.208	0.002852
BORDER	−0.262485462	0.06064281	−4.328	−0.00012
R^2	0.749			
Prob (F-statistic)	0.000246			

Note: See text for explanation of variables.

change rates are fixed to the dollar (Argentina and Panama) tend to have larger proportions of their own variance explained by their own idiosyncratic shocks. This does not seem to be the case for the other countries in the sample. Additionally, if the variance decomposition is used as a measure of the pass-through of interest rates, these results suggest that countries with strong fixed regimes have a smaller pass-throughs. Another interpretation is that the pass-through is the same across all countries but that the volatility of the fixed exchange rate countries is greater.

Further research should look at the patterns arising from this estimation and should offer not only theoretical explanations, but more conclusive evidence.

Estimating the Importance of Trade. The last examination of the data is a consideration of how much trade can explain the coefficients of matrix A. The procedure is to run a simple linear regression in which the coefficients are explained by trade between the two countries, their distance from one another, and a dummy representing whether they share a border. The information about trade is the same as before.

Again, the coefficients on the left-hand side are estimated with varying degrees of efficiency; in this regression there exists heteroskedasticity that could produce the wrong standard deviations. Therefore, from the first step, the covariance matrix of the estimates is used to estimate a GLS.[25]

In table 6.21 the results from the estimation are reported. First, note that the coefficient on TRADE is significant and with the correct sign. Moreover, notice that the coefficient is 0.449, which is close to the one reported for the stock markets (0.333). The coefficient on the distance is equally significant and with the correct sign. One difference between this regression and table 6.14 is that here the border dummy is very significant. However, the coefficient seems to suggest that it goes in the wrong direction.

25. If the covariance matrix is not used and a straight OLS is estimated, the point estimates are close to the ones reported, but the standard deviations are larger. In that regression, only the constant is statistically significant.

More important is the fact that these three variables explain almost 75 percent of the variation of the coefficients. This is in sharp contrast to the results obtained from the stock market exercise.

6.6   Future Research

The question of how to measure contagion is far from answered. Nevertheless, there has been plenty of research in exchange rates, interest rates, and stock markets. The results are not conclusive, but suggestive: propagations are relatively stable trough time, and trade and regional variables produce a sizeable explanation of the observed comovement. The results in this paper confirm these two views, but more must be done.

There are, however, other aspects of contagion that have not been explored with the same intensity. Indeed, these are areas in which there is hope that some of the inconveniences of the price data can be overcome. The following is a set of questions that, in my opinion, the contagion literature must address; (they are arranged according to my own opinion of their importance and are of uncertain feasibility, but clearly this is almost a random order).

6.6.1   Pattern of Correlations

One unstudied aspect of contagion is the pattern of correlations across different instruments. In particular, the correlation among bond markets returns is twice as large (on average) as the one on stock markets, which is double the one that exists among exchange rates.

As far as I know, this fact has been reported in only two papers: First, Kaminsky and Reinhart (2000) compute the principal components and show that the proportion explained by the first component is larger in bonds than in stock markets. Second, in an earlier paper with Eduardo Fernandez Arias (Arias, Haussman, and Rigobon 1998) we reported this finding by simply looking at the correlations. As was mentioned in the previous sections, if the variances of bond and stock market returns are different, then both the correlation and the principal components estimates are biased. However, the results in this paper confirm this finding. It is the case that the coefficients and unconditional correlations across bond markets is larger than in stock markets. In order to provide some evidence I concentrate on Argentina, Brazil, Mexico, Peru, and Venezuela, which are in both data sets. The correlations among these countries, implied by the unconditional variance regime, are documented in table 6.22.

First, note that the correlations increase with the regimes, as should be expected by the increase in variance implied by the crises. Nevertheless, the correlations obtained in bond markets are an order of magnitude larger than those from stock markets. Remember, this is the predicted correlation given the A and Γ coefficients.

Table 6.22   Unconditional Correlation per Regime

	Stock Market Correlations			Bond Market Correlations		
	Low	Medium	High	Low	Medium	High
Argentina-Brazil	0.61	0.71	0.73	0.78	0.70	0.91
Argentina-Mexico	0.52	0.63	0.64	0.72	0.64	0.85
Argentina-Peru	0.25	0.46	0.44	0.46	0.40	0.82
Argentina-Venezuela	−0.01	0.17	0.08	0.76	0.71	0.92
Brazil-Mexico	0.51	0.59	0.58	0.36	0.60	0.68
Brazil-Peru	0.30	0.44	0.41	0.33	0.43	0.74
Brazil-Venezuela	−0.04	0.08	0.07	0.52	0.62	0.81
Mexico-Peru	0.33	0.51	0.46	0.36	0.42	0.70
Mexico-Venezuela	−0.07	0.05	−0.02	0.57	0.61	0.79
Peru-Venezuela	0.02	0.13	0.15	0.31	0.30	0.76
Average	0.24	0.38	0.35	0.52	0.54	0.80

The previous discussion indicated that common shocks explain a sizeable proportion of the changes in the pattern of correlations across time. It is possible that this is also the explanation for bond prices. That question could not be answered here because the two data sets are not comparable, and the question is beyond the scope of this paper. However, with the techniques illustrated here it is possible that an answered could be provided.

Future research should concentrate on developing the theories and empirical tests to report and explain the stylized facts.

6.6.2   Measurement of Contagion, Revisited

Most of the discussion of contagion has concentrated on the simultaneous reaction across countries; thus, this has been the emphasis in this paper. However, the propagation mechanism could take important lags not fully captured in the A matrix, but in the $\phi(L)$ coefficients.

Regarding the question of stability, the test highlighted in subsection 6.3.4 can detect changes in parameters of the lag variables. However, the measurement of the propagation mechanism was estimated entirely by the contemporaneous relationship (most papers look at weekly, two-day, or daily effects).

In the model estimated in the previous section, all the dynamics from $\phi(L)$ have been disregarded. There are at least two reasons that the previous literature (and this paper) did so: First, the pattern of contemporaneous correlations is puzzling enough. Second, without estimating the simultaneous coefficients, there is no way of estimating economically meaningful lag coefficients. With the methodologies highlighted above it is now possible to estimate the contemporaneous relationship properly, and a closer look at the dynamics of the propagation of shocks could be fruitful.

In this process, reporting the facts and understanding the dynamics become aspects of the discussion of the propagation of shocks. Not only does the estimation of impulse responses play a crucial role, but the definition of sensible statistics over those responses will represent an important part of the discussion of what should (or should not) be considered contagion.

6.6.3   Prices versus Volumes

A third important point is that most of the papers in the area examine prices rather than volumes, mainly due to the easy availability of high-frequency data on the former, and the almost complete unavailability of the latter.

There have been some papers, however, that have studied the behavior of quantities around the recent crises. The three most influential papers in this are Eichengreen and Mody (2000); Froot, O'Connell, and Seasholes (2000); Karolyi and Stulz (1996); and Stulz (1999).

Further research in this area is promising. Most of the theories of contagion have strong implications about trading volumes and investor positions. In fact, the implications on prices are derived from those volume decisions. Looking only at prices misses this rich set of implications. The main limitation is data availability, but it should be clear that if prices encounter important econometric problems, volumes will, as well.

6.6.4   Is the Propagation through the Means or the Variances?

Fourth, the question of whether the shocks are transmitted directly through prices or the fall in prices reflects higher volatilities has not been raised with the emphasis it deserves. The only paper (to my knowledge) looking at these issues is Edwards and Susmel (2000). Unfortunately, they have to make the necessary assumption to avoid the identification problem. The models studied here have highlighted the direct propagation of prices, but they could perfectly represent a reduced form of a volatility transmission model. So far, the procedures emphasized are unable to disentangle the exact channel.

From the theoretical point of view, this is an important question. How the propagation occurs has portfolio (as well as policy) implications. Formally, an extension of model 1, including lags and ARCH effects, is as follows:

$$A\begin{bmatrix} y_t \\ x_t \end{bmatrix} = \Phi(L)\begin{bmatrix} y_t \\ x_t \end{bmatrix} + \begin{bmatrix} \varepsilon_t \\ \eta_t \end{bmatrix},$$

where

$$A = \begin{bmatrix} 1 & -\beta \\ -\alpha & 1 \end{bmatrix},$$

and where σ_ε, σ_η follow a bivariate ARCH:

$$B \begin{bmatrix} \sigma_\varepsilon \\ \sigma_\eta \end{bmatrix}_t = \phi_\sigma(L) \begin{bmatrix} \sigma_\varepsilon \\ \sigma_\eta \end{bmatrix}_t + \phi_\varepsilon(L) \begin{bmatrix} \varepsilon_t \\ \eta_t \end{bmatrix} + \begin{bmatrix} v_{\varepsilon,t} \\ v_{\eta,t} \end{bmatrix},$$

where $v_{\varepsilon,t}$ and $v_{\eta,t}$ are uncorrelated, and the matrices A and B are not diagonal.[26] A reflects the propagation through prices, whereas B explains the propagation through variances. Because in the reduced form only conditional covariance matrices are computed, there is in general no procedure to separate A from B. Future research should develop techniques that could deal with this question.

6.6.5   Nonlinearity and Distribution-Free Techniques

Finally, even though some of the procedures highlighted here are not dependent on a particular distribution of the residuals, most of the papers assume linear models and normal distributions.

A casual look at the data clearly indicates that either the distributions are not normal, or the models are nonlinear (or both). There have been some attempts to look at extreme realizations as a way to compare the behavior of the statistical model in this situation with the model under normal circumstances; see Bae, Karolyi, and Stulz (2000) and Longuin and Slonik (1995) for evidence. Further research in the area is clearly warranted.

6.7   Conclusions

The empirical question of contagion is one of the most difficult to arise in international macroeconomics in recent years. The data suffer from the worst of (what I call) macroproblems: simultaneous equations and omitted variable biases. Moreover, the data also exhibit the worst problems of finance: conditional and unconditional heteroskedasticity, nonlinearity, nonnormality, and serial correlation.

This paper has several objectives. First, it provides a critical view of the techniques used most frequently in applied papers of contagion. The first two sections discuss the biases and inconsistencies that arise in OLS, probit, and (especially) principal components and correlation estimates. In those sections, I propose the use of two new techniques to deal with some of the problems, but certainly further research should continue to improve the procedures.

The second objective of the paper is to use these new techniques in a broad application of contagion (the original papers concentrated on very special cases, or only on simulations). Section 6.5 tested for parameter stability and the importance of trade in bond and stock markets. Two surprising results in this section are as follows: (1) The parameters are stable in

---

26. I have already solved the problem of identification in GARCH models if B is a triangular matrix. This extends Rigobon (2000a) to the case in which only conditional heteroskedasticity exists (see Rigobon 2001).

stock markets across very different crises and periods of time. However, the propagation of shocks across bond markets was not stable during the first quarter of 1995 and during the LTCM crisis. Both instances represented important liquidity shocks to bond markets. The parameter instability could be either a change in the coefficient or a nonlinearity. With the current techniques, unfortunately, no answer can be provided. (2) Regarding the importance of trade in explaining the contemporaneous coefficients, it was found that trade and regional variables are (almost) significant and with the correct sign in explaining contemporaneous coefficients on the bond and stock market returns. In the stock market, these variables explain only 6 percent of the variation, but for bond coefficients they explain almost 75 percent.

Finally, this paper has discussed extensively a list of further areas of research in which new stylized facts, new data, and probably new techniques will have to be developed to gain a better understanding of how shocks are propagated internationally.

Appendix A

Measuring the Channels under Simultaneous Equations using OLS

Assume a simple setup in which

$$A\begin{bmatrix} y_t \\ x_{1,t} \\ x_{2,t} \end{bmatrix} = \begin{bmatrix} \varepsilon_t \\ \eta_{1,t} \\ \eta_{2,t} \end{bmatrix}$$

where

$$A = \begin{bmatrix} 1 & -\alpha & -\alpha \\ -\alpha & 1 & -\alpha \\ -\alpha & -\alpha & 1 \end{bmatrix}.$$

Note that in this case the interrelationships among all variables are the same. Assume we estimate $y_t = \beta_1 x_{1,t} + \beta_2 x_{2,t}$. The OLS estimates of each of the coefficients are (after a great deal of algebra):

$$\hat{\beta}_1 = \alpha + \alpha(1 + \alpha)\sigma_\varepsilon \frac{\alpha\sigma_{\eta 1} - (1 - \alpha)\sigma_{\eta 2}}{\alpha^2 \sigma_{\eta 1}\sigma_\varepsilon + \alpha^2 \sigma_{\eta 2}\sigma_\varepsilon + \sigma_{\eta 1}\sigma_{\eta\varepsilon}}$$

$$\hat{\beta}_2 = \alpha + \alpha(1 + \alpha)\sigma_\varepsilon \frac{\alpha\sigma_{\eta 2} - (1 - \alpha)\sigma_{\eta 1}}{\alpha^2 \sigma_{\eta 1}\sigma_\varepsilon + \alpha^2 \sigma_{\eta 2}\sigma_\varepsilon + \sigma_{\eta 1}\sigma_{\eta\varepsilon}}$$

where the difference in the estimates is

$$\hat{\beta}_1 - \hat{\beta}_2 = (\alpha_{\eta 1} - \sigma_{\eta \varepsilon}) \frac{\alpha \, (1 + \alpha)\sigma_\varepsilon}{\alpha^2 \sigma_{\eta 1} \sigma_\varepsilon + \alpha^2 \sigma_{\eta 2} \sigma_\varepsilon + \sigma_{\eta 1} \sigma_{\eta \varepsilon}}.$$

Note that if the variances of countries $x_{1,t}$ and $x_{2,t}$ are different, then the estimates are also different. Moreover, the country with the higher variance has the larger coefficient. In the limit, assume that the variance of $x_{1,t}$ goes to infinity; then the estimates are

$$\hat{\beta}_1 = \alpha + \alpha(1 + \alpha)\sigma_\varepsilon \frac{\alpha}{\alpha^2 \sigma_\varepsilon + \sigma_{\eta 2}}$$

$$\hat{\beta}_2 = \alpha + \alpha(1 + \alpha)\sigma_\varepsilon \frac{-(1 - \alpha)}{\alpha^2 \sigma_\varepsilon + \sigma_{\eta 2}}.$$

As can be seen, one of the coefficients is biased downward while the other one is biased upward.

Appendix B
Stability Test on the Reduced Form

The structural model is

$$AX_t = \phi(L)X_t + \Gamma z_t + \varepsilon_t,$$

but the stability test is performed on the reduced-form residuals:

$$X_t = A^{-1}\phi(L)X_t + A^{-1}[\Gamma z_t + \varepsilon_t]$$
$$= \Phi(L)X_t + v_t$$
$$Av_t = \Gamma z_t + \varepsilon_t.$$

The question is whether testing on the reduced form also is testing for the parameter stability of the structural equation.

It should be obvious that if there is a change in A or Γ the test on the reduced form is detecting them. The question is whether changes in $\phi()$ can be found, as well. Assume there is a shift in the structural coefficients

$$A_1 X_t = \phi_1(L)X_t + \Gamma_1 z_t + \varepsilon_t \quad \text{for } t < T$$
$$A_2 X_t = \phi_2(L)X_t + \Gamma_2 z_t + \varepsilon_t \quad \text{for } t > T,$$

which implies the following reduced forms:

$$X_t = A_1^{-1}\phi_1(L)X_t + A_1^{-1}\Gamma_1 z_t + A_1^{-1}\varepsilon_t \quad \text{for } t < T$$
$$X_t = A_2^{-1}\phi_2(L)X_t + A_2^{-1}\Gamma_2 z_t + A_2^{-1}\varepsilon_t \quad \text{for } t > T$$

Because in the VAR we are requiring the lag coefficients to be the same in both samples, the actual estimate is an average of $A_1^{-1}\phi_1$ and $A_2^{-1}\phi_2$. Denote this estimate as $\hat{\Phi}$. The residuals from the reduced form, then, will be described by

$$v_t = \begin{array}{l} [A_1^{-1}\phi_1(L) - \hat{\Phi}(L)]\, X_t + A_1^{-1}\Gamma_1 z_t + A_1^{-1}\varepsilon_t \quad \text{for } t < T \\ [A_2^{-1}\phi_2(L) - \hat{\Phi}(L)]\, X_t + A_2^{-1}\Gamma_2 z_t + A_2^{-1}\varepsilon_t \quad \text{for } t > T. \end{array}$$

As can be seen, the residuals of the reduced form are a function of ϕ_i. For simplicity, assume that $A_1 = A_2$, and $\Gamma_1 = \Gamma_2$. Then the covariance matrix of the reduced form in each regime would be

$$\Omega_1 = \Psi_1 X_t X_t' \Psi_1' + A^{-1}\Gamma\Omega_1^z \Gamma' A'^{-1} + A^{-1}\Omega_1^\varepsilon A'^{-1}$$

$$\Omega_2 = \Psi_2 X_t X_t' \Psi_2' + A^{-1}\Gamma\Omega_2^z \Gamma' A'^{-1} + A^{-1}\Omega_2^\varepsilon A'^{-1}$$

$$\Psi_1 \triangleq A_1^{-1}\phi_1(L) - \hat{\Phi}(L)$$

$$\Psi_2 \triangleq A_2^{-1}\phi_2(L) - \hat{\Phi}(L).$$

Note that if the change in the covariance matrix is explained by the shift in ϕ (for example), then the change in the covariance matrix is

$$\Delta\Omega = \Psi_2 X_t X_t' \Psi_2' - \Psi_1 X_t X_t' \Psi_1'.$$

It is unlikely that this transformation of coefficients would be less than full rank, in the same way that the determinant is not necessarily less than full rank when the coefficient A or Γ changes.

References

Arias, Eduardo Fernandez, Ricardo Hausmann, and Roberto Rigobon. 1998. Contagion in bond markets. IDB Working Paper. Washington, D.C.: Inter-American Development Bank.

Bae, Kee-Hong, G. Andrew Karolyi, and René M. Stulz. 2000. A new approach to measuring financial contagion. NBER Working Paper no. 7913. Cambridge, Mass.: National Bureau of Economic Research.

Baig, Taimur, and Ilan Goldfajn. 1998. Financial markets contagion in the Asian crises. IMF Working Paper no. WP/98/155. Washington, D.C.: International Monetary Fund.

————. 2000. The Russian default and the contagion to Brazil. International Monetary Fund and Brazilian Central Bank. Mimeograph.

Boyer, Brian H., Michael S. Gibson, and Mico Loretan. 1999. Pitfalls in tests for changes in correlations. Federal Reserve Board, IFS Discussion Paper no. 597R.

Calvo, Guillermo A. 1999. Contagion in emerging markets: When Wall Street is a carrier. University of Maryland. Mimeograph.

Calvo, Guillermo A., and Enrique Mendoza. 2000. Rational contagion and the globalization of security markets. *Journal of International Economics* 51:79–113.

Calvo, Guillermo A., and Carmen Reinhart. 1995. Capital inflows to Latin America: Is there evidence of contagion effects? World Bank and International Monetary Fund. Mimeograph.

Cashin, Paul, C., Manmohan Kumar, and John McDermott. 1995. International integration of equity markets and contagion effects. IMF Working Paper no. WP/95/110. Washington, D.C.: International Monetary Fund.

Chen, Songnian, and Shakeeb Khan. 1999. $\sqrt{n}$-consistent estimation of heteroskedastic sample selection models. University of Rochester. Mimeograph.

Edwards, Sebastian, and Raúl Susmel. 2000. Interest rate volatility and contagion in emerging markets: Evidence from the 1990s. Anderson School, University of California, Los Angeles, and University of Houston. Mimeograph.

Eichengreen, Barry, and Ashoka Mody. 2000. Contagion from the Russian crisis: Who was infected and why? University of California, Berkeley, and International Monetary Fund. Mimeograph.

Eichengreen, Barry, Andrew K. Rose, and Charles Wyplosz. 1996. Contagious currency crises. NBER Working Paper no. 5681. Cambridge, Mass.: National Bureau of Economic Research.

Favero, Carlo, and Francesco Giavazzi. 2000. Looking for contagion: Evidence from the 1992 ERM crisis. Bocconi University, Milan, Italy. Mimeograph.

Fisher, Franklin M. 1976. The identification problem in econometrics, 2nd ed. New York: Robert E. Krieger.

Forbes, Kristin. 1999. How are shocks propagated internationally? Firm-level evidence from the Russian and Asian crises. MIT. Mimeograph.

Forbes, Kristin, and Ricardo Rigobon. 1999. No contagion, only interdependence: Measuring stock market co-movements. NBER Working Paper no. 7267. Cambridge, Mass.: National Bureau of Economic Research.

———. 2000. Measuring contagion: Conceptual and empirical issues. MIT. Mimeograph.

Frankel, Jeffrey A. 2000. Harvard. Mimeograph.

Froot, Ken, Paul O'Connell, and Mark Seasholes. 2000. The portfolio flows of international investors. Harvard Business School, Harvard University. Mimeograph.

Gelos, Gaston, and Ratna Sahay. 2000. Financial markets spillovers: How different are the transition economies? In *International financial contagion,* ed. Stijn Claessens and Kristin Forbes, 329–66. Boston: Kluwer Academic Publishers.

Glick, Reuven, and Andrew K. Rose. 1999. Contagion and trade: Why are currency crises regional? *Journal of International Money and Finance* 18:603–17.

Goldstein, Morris, Graciela Kaminsky, and Carmen Reinhart. 2000. *Assessing financial vulnerability: An early warning system for emerging markets.* Washington, D.C.: Institute for International Economics.

Gregorio, José de, and Rodrigo Valdés. 2000. Crisis transmission: Evidence from the Debt, Tequila, and Asian Flu crises. Universidad Catolica de Chile, Santiago, Chile. Mimeograph.

Honore, Bo E. 1992. Simple estimation of a duration model with unobserved heterogeneity. *Econometrica* 58 (2): 453–73.

Honore, Bo E., Ekaterini Kyriazidou, and Christopher Udry. 1997. Estimation of type 3 tobit models using symmetric trimming and pairwise comparisons. *Journal of Econometrics* 76 (1–2): 107–28.

Horowitz, Joel L. 1992. A smoothed maximum score estimator for the binary response model. *Econometrica* 60:505–31.

———. 1993. Semiparametric estimation of a work-trip mode choice model. *Journal of Econometrics* 58:49–70.

Kaminsky, Graciela, and Carmen Reinhart. 2000. The center and the periphery: Tales of financial turmoil. George Washington University and University of Maryland. Mimeograph.

Karolyi, G. Andrew, and René M. Stulz. 1996. Why do markets move together? An investigation of U.S.-Japan stock return comovements. *Journal of Finance* 51 (3): 958–86.

King, Mervyn, and Sushil Wadhwani. 1990. Transmission of volatility between stock markets. *Review of Financial Studies* 3 (1): 5–33.

Klein, Rogers, and Frank Vella. 2000. Identification and estimation of the binary treatment model under heteroskedasticity. Rutgers University. Mimeograph.

Kodres, Laura E., and Matthew Pritsker. 1999. A rational expectations model of financial contagion. Board of Governors of the Federal Reserve System Working Paper. Washington, D.C.: Federal Reserve.

Longin, François, and Bruno Solnik. 1995. Is the correlation in internation equity returns constant? 1960–1990. *Journal of International Money and Finance* 14 (1): 3–26.

Loretan, Mico, and William B. English. 2000. Evaluating "correlation breakdowns" during periods of market volatility. Board of Governors of the Federal Reserve System Working Paper. Washington, D.C.: Federal Reserve.

Manski, Charles F. 1985. Semiparametric analysis of discrete response: Asymptotic properties of the maximum score estimator. *Journal of Econometrics* 27:313–34.

Masson, Paul. 1997. Monsoonal effects, spillovers, and contagion. International Monetary Fund. Mimeograph.

Powell, James L. 1986. Symmetrically trimmed least squares estimation for tobit models. *Econometrica* 54:1435–60.

Rigobon, Roberto. 1999. Does contagion exist? The Investment Strategy Pack. Bank for International Settlements, Banking Department

———. 2000a. Identification through heteroskedasticity: The bivariate case. MIT. Mimeograph. Available at [http://www.mit.edu/rigobon/www/].

———. 2000b. On the measurement of the international propagation of shocks: Is the transmission stable? MIT. Mimeograph. Available at [http://web.mit.edu/rigobon/www/].

———. 2000c. A simple test for stability of linear models under heteroskedasticity, omitted variable, and endogenous variable problems. MIT. Mimeograph. Available at [http://web.mit.edu/rigobon/www/].

———. 2001. The curse of non-investment grade countries. NBER Working Paper no. 8636. Cambridge, Mass.: National Bureau of Economic Research.

Ronn, Ehud I. 1998. The impact of large changes in asset prices on intra-market correlations in the stock and bond markets. University of Houston. Mimeograph.

Sentana, Enrique, and Gabriele Fiorentini. 1999. Identification, estimation, and testing of conditional heteroskedastic factor models. CEMFI. Mimeograph.

Stulz, René M. 1999. International portfolio flows and security markets. Charles A. Dice Center for Research in Financial Economics Working Paper no. 99-3. Columbus, Oh.

Theil, Henri. 1971. *Principles of econometrics.* New York: Wiley.

Van Rijckeghem, Caroline, and Beatrice Weder. 2000. Financial contagion: Spillover effects through banking centers. University of Basel, Basel, Switzerland. Mimeograph.

Comment   Enrique G. Mendoza

One of the most widely discussed issues in the context of the research and policy debates that emerged from the emerging-market crises of the 1990s is that of contagion. Yet, as the opening paragraphs of Roberto Rigobon's paper note, there is no consensus on the definition of contagion and even less consensus on how to model it or how to think of its policy implications. This analytical vacuum has not deterred empiricists from torturing financial markets data until results in support of or against one form of contagion or another can be obtained. In this context, Rigobon's article is one of the most thoughtful that the recent empirical literature on the subject has produced.

Rigobon begins with a true scientist's approach and sets aside the ideological controversy on the definition of contagion so as to focus on two key measurement questions at the core of empirical tests of contagion: First, what are the international propagation channels by which shocks from asset markets in one country spill over into those of other countries? Second, is the international transmission mechanism of shocks unstable during periods of crisis? These two questions are critical because the existing literature tends to evaluate whether there is contagion depending on whether the propagation channels feature a certain set of fundamental variables, and on whether during periods of crisis there is a sudden increase in the tendency of markets to move together.

Rigobon's paper evaluates whether the three econometric methods most commonly used in the literature to address the above questions (linear regression, logit-probit regressions, and tests of principal components and correlation coefficients) are useful tools, given the serious statistical problems posed by the data used to conduct the tests. In particular, he explores whether they are well-suited to handle the problems of simultaneous-equation bias, omitted variables, and heteroskedasticity (conditional and unconditional) that are pervasive in the data with which the methods need to work. The paper shows clearly that none of the three methods can handle these problems simultaneously, thus casting serious doubt on the results reported in many existing empirical studies on contagion. Rigobon moves on to propose his own robust estimation method and to develop its statistical foundation.

The objective of my comments is not to take issue with the method, but to highlight the message of its results and to raise some issues that seem very critical and yet are still unresolved by the development of a more accurate method to test for something that remains undefined (i.e., contagion). My interest in focusing on these controversial issues, however, does not under-

Enrique G. Mendoza is professor of economics at the University of Maryland and a faculty research fellow of the National Bureau of Economic Research.

mine either the significance of the flaws that Rigobon's work has identified
in existing tests of contagion or the merits of the method he developed.

The paper uses daily returns data from equity and sovereign bond markets for several countries in Asia and Latin America and for the United
States, and produces four key results:

1. Volatility in equity and bond markets increases sharply during periods
of crisis.

2. Propagation parameters are stable during crises in equity markets but
not during those in bond markets (in the cases of the Mexican crisis and the
Russia/long-term capital markets [LTCM] crisis).

3. Unconditional correlations of returns across emerging markets are
generally high.

4. Trade and regional variables are important for explaining contemporaneous comovements in the returns of equity and bond markets, although
much more for the latter than for the former.

The flaws in the application of the three widely-used econometric methods that Rigobon identified in the empirical literature on contagion are not
disputable, and the robustness of the method proposed in the paper to deal
with the statistical problems posed by the data is also not subject to debate.
What is more controversial is the author's interpretation of the scope of the
method and the message of the results. Rigobon's paper stated as one of its
goals to try to measure contagion without defining it, but it is unclear that
he succeeded. The definition of contagion is difficult, if not impossible, to
separate from assessments of the econometric methods used to study it and
their ability to cope with the problems present in the data. Still, for the def
initions and measures of contagion that have been adopted in several existing studies of the subject, this paper, and Rigobon's previous work with
Kristin Forbes, raise serious issues with the validity of econometric tests
and propose effective ways to address them.

If the author's position that one can proceed without defining contagion
is taken at full value, the interpretation one can give to the results is that
they shed light on important properties of the variance-covariance structure of asset returns across emerging markets, on the variables that determine it, and on its stability during crisis periods. Yet it is difficult to argue
that they help us understand or test contagion, unless a definition of contagion is, after all, adopted. For instance, if contagion is defined as the crisis
instability of propagation parameters, then one can say that Rigobon's
method is a statistically correct approach that measures, tests, and largely
rejects the existence of contagion.

The complex issues raised by the aim to study contagion without defining it explicitly emerge again when one tries to draw lessons from the results
on the significance of trade and regional variables in driving comovements
of returns. Does this mean that contagion is irrelevant? Or that contagion

"unrelated to fundamentals" is irrelevant? Clearly, the answers to these questions depend on how we define contagion. If it is understood to be co-movement in returns driven by "nonfundamental" variables, and the only fundamentals considered of relevance are trade and regional variables, then once again the results reject contagion. However, this requires a very model-specific notion of contagion.

The above issues also plague the rest of the empirical literature on contagion, and Rigobon is right in that the definition itself varies widely from one paper to the next. Some authors confuse contagion with correlation. For example, the notion that, in the presence of nominal rigidities, a large devaluation in one country could spark crises in neighboring countries that happen to be competitors in export markets provides a reasonable channel of co-movement, but it is one that it is very well understood and hardly worth being surprised about. The surprise, rather, was how little of this we observed. Korea experienced several weeks of declining export volumes in the aftermath of the crises in Southeast Asia (despite its very competitive exchange rate), mainly on account of a total loss of access to international credit markets, including the market of trade credits. Observations such as this favor other commonly used notion of contagion as comovements driven by some form of speculation driven by "animal spirits" or market psychology.

This notion of contagion originated in Keynes's view of speculation as resulting from assessing asset values, and economic prospects in general, through "the activity of forecasting the psychology of the market," rather than through attempts to forecast "the prospective yield of assets over their whole life" (Keynes 1936, 158–59). The problem with this Keynesian notion is that, to make it operational, one needs an explicit economic model to identify precisely what is speculation or contagion, and what is enterprise. Once this separation is made, contagion can be measured with familiar concepts such as the excess volatility of asset returns or macroeconomic flows across countries that is not explained by the fundamentals listed under "enterprise." Under this definition of contagion, it follows that contagion need not be correlation. High correlation of returns does not necessarily indicate contagion and contagion does not necessarily imply high correlation. Contagion is model-specific. For instance, a theory of asset prices determines which variables are fundamental variables and how they enter into the determination of equilibrium asset prices; and if the theory features contagion vehicles, it can also determine what is to be measured as excess volatility. Economic models with features like these do exist and typically require different forms of asymmetric information and frictions in financial markets.

One example of a macroeconomic model of contagion was proposed recently by Paasche (2001). He proposes a two-country extension of the Fisherian-deflation model developed by Kiyotaki and Moore (1997). In his setting, a small productivity shock in one country translates into an adverse terms-of-trade shock for a neighboring export-competing country. The neighboring country suffers a sharp adjustment in the current account and output, not as a result of the competition for the export market, but as a result of financial frictions in the form of tightening collateral constraints. For an analyst looking casually at the data, trade and terms-of-trade changes will be associated with these adverse developments, but the channel of transmission is one of "excess volatility" inasmuch as it results from effects of the terms-of-trade shock that are largely magnified by financial frictions.

An example more related to equity markets follows from the work of Mendoza and Smith (2001). They examine an open economy variation of the model of margin requirements and asset-trading costs proposed by Aiyagari and Gertler (1999). Here, households in a small open economy trade equity with specialized foreign securities firms. Due to credit market frictions, households face a margin requirement that limits their ability to leverage their foreign debt on the value of their current equity holdings. Foreign traders face portfolio adjustment costs, intended to capture the notion that foreigners are at a disadvantage relative to domestic agents when trading emerging-markets equity. This disadvantage may result from informational frictions or from explicit institutional arrangements. In this setting, an adverse shock such as a productivity slowdown or a sudden increase in the world's real interest rate may switch the economy into a state in which the margin constraint becomes binding. Households must then fire-sell equity to meet their margin calls, but when they fire-sell equity they meet in world markets with foreign traders that adjusts their portfolios slowly. As a result, there is a sudden reversal in the current account and a collapse in equity prices below fundamental levels in the small open economy. The model dictates exactly how much of the change in net foreign assets, equity holdings, and equity prices is driven by these excess-volatility features, relative to the amount accounted for by fluctuations in the "fundamentals" (which is also pinned down exactly within the model).

The point of these examples is not to argue that they provide the models of contagion we need to focus on. Instead, the idea is simply to show how the Keynesian notion of contagion can be put to work in practice in particular economic models, and to note that the measure of contagion, the list of variables that are included in the fundamentals, and the magnitude of observed asset return comovements that fundamentals account for are all model-dependent concepts. It seems, therefore, that studying the statistical properties of the data with the adequate econometric techniques that Rigobon proposes—but in the light of the predictions of a specific analytical framework that sets a definition of contagion and its appropriate measure—would be a very interesting project for further research.

References

Aiyagari, S. Rao, and Mark Gertler. 1999. "Overreaction" of asset prices in general equilibrium. *Review of Economic Dynamics* 2:3–35.

Keynes, John Maynard. 1936. *The general theory of employment, interest, and money.* New York: Harcourt, Brace, and Co.

Kiyotaki, Nobuhiro, and John Moore. 1997. Credit cycles. *Journal of Political Economy* 105:211–48.

Mendoza, Enrique G., and Katherine A. Smith. 2001. Margin calls, trading costs, and the sudden stops of capital inflows into emerging markets. Duke University, Department of Economics. Mimeograph.

Paasche, Bernhard. 2001. Credit constraints and international financial crises. *Journal of Monetary Economics,* forthcoming.

Discussion Summary

Sebastian Edwards raised a few questions on the estimates in matrix A, namely, how the stock market (or bond market) returns in one country are affected by returns in all other countries in the sample. In particular, he pointed out two counterintuitive findings: First, the bond market returns in Mexico were unaffected by the returns in the United States; and second, the stock market returns in Chile did have a big effect on returns in most other Latin American countries. This is surprising because, in practice, Chile had capital controls during the sample period and a relatively small capital market.

Linda S. Goldberg commented that the estimation of the importance of trade in explaining the coefficients of matrix A through a simple gravity equation–like regression is not as aggressive as other parts of the paper. She suggested putting more structure in the regressions.

Aaron Tornell suggested using H-infinite robust estimation to get around problems caused by nonlinearity of the specification or by nonnormal distribution. *Nouriel Roubini* suggested that the author investigate the relative importance of trade and region in explaining the propagation mechanism. *Amartya Lahiri* raised questions on geographical explanation for unstable propagation parameters. *Giancarlo Corsetti* asked why the paper does not use factor model directly.

Roberto Rigobon recognizes that the two empirical findings pointed out by Edwards (namely, the nil effect of the U.S. bond market returns on the Mexican stock market returns and the large effect of the Chilean stock market on other countries) are different from our prior, and he promises to investigate it. In response to Tornell's question, Rigobon said that linear tests reject nonlinear specification.

Regarding Corsetti's question, Rigobon said that the factor model is a better specification in the case of heteroskedasticity, but not when the disturbance is nonnormal.

Credit, Prices, and Crashes
Business Cycles with a
Sudden Stop

Enrique G. Mendoza

7.1 Introduction

The epidemic of capital-markets crises that hit emerging economies in the 1990s displayed the empirical regularities of a phenomenon that Calvo (1998) labeled a "sudden stop."[1] Sudden stops featured a sharp reversal in private capital inflows, or a shift to large outflows, and a corresponding sharp reversal from large current account deficits into much smaller deficits or small surpluses. These abrupt reversals in foreign financing in turn forced sharp contractions of domestic production and private expenditures; collapses in the real exchange rate, asset prices, and the relative price of nontradable goods in terms of tradable goods; and sharp declines in credit to the private sector. In several cases, sudden stops followed from periods during which external deficits widened gradually, the relative price of nontradables and the real exchange rate appreciated sharply, and economic activity and asset prices boomed, often in tandem with explicit or implicit managed exchange rate regimes.

Enrique G. Mendoza is professor of economics at the University of Maryland and a faculty research fellow of the National Bureau of Economic Research.

Comments by participants at the NBER conference held in Islamorada, Florida, in January 2001 (particularly those of the discussant Joshua Aizenman) at the 2000 meeting of the Society for Economic Dynamics, and at seminars at the Federal Reserve Banks of New York and San Francisco, the International Monetary Fund, Johns Hopkins University, the University of Michigan, Stanford University, and University of California, Santa Cruz are gratefully acknowledged. The author is also grateful to Katherine Smith (this paper benefited from discussions on their joint work) and to Fernando Alvarez, Christopher Carroll, Michael P. Dooley, Rudi Dornbusch, Jonathan Heatcote, Urban Jermann, Kent Kimbrough, and Carlos Végh for helpful comments.

1. Rudi Dornbusch noted that the expression originated in comments from an international banker on the paper on Mexico by Dornbusch and Werner (1994), joking that when financing of large current account deficits is compromised, "it is not the speed that kills, it is the sudden stop."

The features of sudden stops resemble those of the balance-of-payments (BOP) crises that developing countries chronically suffer. The literature on contractionary devaluations, for instance, is built on the observation that in developing countries devaluation is generally followed by recession (see Edwards 1986). However, behind this resemblance hide important differences that pose serious challenges both for research and for policy analysis. In particular, as the empirical analysis of Calvo and Reinhart (1999) showed, the changes in real and financial indicators observed in sudden stops largely exceeded those of typical BOP crises. Moreover, the economic collapses of sudden stops were deep, but the subsequent recoveries were also generally quick and sharp—a tendency labeled "the Mexican Wave" in a *Financial Times* editorial by Martin Wolf (8 August 1999).

The unusual depth of the recessions and price corrections that define sudden stops, as well as their short duration, suggests that it may be useful to study this phenomenon within a framework of *excess volatility*—that is, a framework that can account for sudden stops as a short-lived feature of the cyclical dynamics of a small open economy that coexists with the less dramatic stylized facts of the economy's regular business cycle. The aim of this paper is to develop a basic model with these features and to derive its implications for the design of policies to prevent capital-markets crises in emerging economies.

Sudden stops represent in essence a sudden loss of access to international capital markets; hence, it seems clear that in order to explain sudden stops, researchers must abandon the standard assumption of perfect financial markets typical of equilibrium models of the current account and business cycles in open economies. This paper proposes, in particular, a model in which sudden stops are the result of financial frictions at work in an otherwise frictionless, flexible-price competitive environment. Financial frictions drive endogenous credit constraints that are binding or nonbinding on a particular date depending on the state of nature—although forward-looking behavior on the part of economic agents implies that the distortions induced by these constraints are set in motion simply by the expectation that the constraints might bind in the future. Sudden stops occur in states of nature in which the constraints become endogenously binding, yet the long-run business cycle features of the economy are largely independent of sudden stops. In contrast, social welfare can be drastically reduced.

The switch into a sudden-stop state can be triggered by large policy shocks (or policy-credibility shocks) or by large shocks to domestic productivity or international liquidity (i.e., to the world's real interest rate). Thus, "policy uncertainty" and "involuntary contagion," two widely cited culprits of the recent crises (albeit with different emphasis depending on the country in question), fit the model as explanatory variables of sudden stops.

This analysis provides three important policy lessons for crisis prevention strategies. First, regulatory policies implemented with the intent of containing large capital outflows, such as liquidity requirements, margin requirements, or value-at-risk collateralization, can be counterproductive because they can increase the likelihood or severity of sudden stops. Second, because the paper shows that the resources needed to resolve or prevent a sudden stop vary widely depending on the state of the economy at the time credit constraints become binding, financial arrangements that can effectively preempt sudden stops need to either feature complex state-contingent clauses or *credibly* commit a large amount of funds. Third, a long-term strategy for dealing with sudden stops should emphasize policies aimed at directly addressing the informational and institutional frictions that are the ultimate determinants of credit-market imperfections. These include microeconomic policies (such as the development of credit bureaus undertaken recently in Mexico) as well as macroeconomic policies (such as dollarization, the formation of currency unions anchored on strong currencies, or the internationalization of financial systems).

From the standpoint of the growing research program on emerging-markets crises, this paper aims to add to the literature exploring the use of models of credit frictions to study sudden stops initiated by Calvo (1998). This literature includes the works of, among others, Aghion, Bacchetta, and Banerjee (2000); Caballero and Krishnamurthy (1999); Céspedes, Chang, and Velasco (chap. 12 in this volume); Christiano, Gust, and Roldos (2000); Schneider and Tornell (2000); and Paasche (2001). To date, most of this literature has built extensively on modern adaptations of two classic approaches to model "great depressions" driven by financial frictions in macroeconomics: the Keynesian setup of price or wage stickiness with an external financing premium, examined by Bernanke, Gertler, and Gilchrist (1998), and the Fisherian analysis of debt deflations driven by collateral constraints, introduced by Kiyotaki and Moore (1997).

The analysis conducted here differs from existing studies in its approach to model sudden stops as an excess volatility phenomenon. Most of the models studied so far in the literature feature credit constraints that are always binding along an equilibrium path. Hence, in this class of models it is difficult to account for the abrupt economic collapses of sudden stops as an atypical phenomenon nested within the smoother comovements of regular business cycles. The model proposed here also differs from the existing literature in that it emphasizes the interaction of uncertainty, risk aversion, and incomplete contingent-claims markets in forming the transmission mechanism that links financial frictions to the real economy. In this setting, which is in line with the models studied by Aiyagari (1993), Aiyagari and Gertler (1999), and Eaton and Gersovitz (1981), precautionary saving and state-contingent risk premiums play a key role in driving business cycle dynamics.[2]

---

2. The model proposed here is also consistent with the predictions of models of the consumption function based on buffer-stock saving and liquidity constraints (see Carroll 2000).

In contrast, existing models of sudden stops based on the Kiyotaki-Moore or Bernanke-Gertler-Girlchrist frameworks assume that borrowers and lenders are risk neutral and are often examined under perfect foresight. These assumptions facilitate the study of the effects of credit frictions by producing models that yield closed-form analytical results and that can be easily solved with linear approximation algorithms but leave behind the features of choice under uncertainty, risk aversion, and precautionary saving that are often viewed as critical for the analysis of economies with imperfect credit markets. The trade-off in emphasizing these features is that closed-form solutions are no longer feasible and numerical solutions based on linear approximations are inapplicable. Thus, the predictions of the model must be derived with the aid of nonlinear numerical solution methods.

The credit constraint examined in this paper is designed with the intent of capturing some of the key elements of the credit frictions identified in the recent literature on emerging-markets crises (see Calvo and Mendoza 2000a). The proposed credit constraint follows the Fisherian line in that it emphasizes the credit-market effects of price shocks in an otherwise neoclassical flexible-price environment. In particular, it is shown that sudden stops can be consistent with the optimal adjustment of a flexible-price economy in response to a suddenly binding credit constraint. The constraint takes the form of a *liquidity constraint* that requires borrowers to finance a fraction of their current obligations out of current income, a criterion widely used to screen borrowers in credit markets.

Liability dollarization (i.e., the fact that the debt of emerging economies is mostly denominated in U.S. dollars and a few other strong currencies) is an essential feature of the transmission mechanism by which the liquidity constraint affects the real economy. Because foreign debt is denominated in the international unit of account (i.e., tradable goods) but is leveraged on income valued at a different relative price, sharp fluctuations in the production and relative price of nontradable goods can induce sharp and sudden adjustments in access to foreign financing. These sharp fluctuations in output and prices of nontradables are themselves endogenous outcomes of the model. They represent the equilibrium adjustment of the economy in response to real foreign or domestic shocks or to policy uncertainty. Sudden stops are possible in this environment even though the model is stripped from the powerful debt-deflation intertemporal channel, and without recurring to the Keynesian assumption that prices or wages are inflexible or to the existence of multiple equilibria emphasized in some recent studies (see Calvo 1998; Aghion, Bacchetta, and Banerjee 2000; and chap. 12, this vol.).

The paper is organized as follows. Section 7.2 summarizes empirical evidence on sudden stops and the notion of sudden stops as excess macroeconomic volatility. Section 7.3 sketches the model. Section 7.4 explores the quantitative implications of the model, including its welfare effects. Section

7.5 describes a variation of the model aimed to account for the asset-pricing features of sudden stops. Section 7.6 concludes.

7.2   The Sudden Stops Phenomenon

Calvo and Reinhart (1999) conducted a comprehensive cross-country analysis of sudden stops. They documented fifteen recent episodes of large reversals in net private capital inflows into emerging countries. These reversals exceeded 10 percent of gross domestic product (GDP) in seven of the fifteen cases, and the smallest reversal was equivalent to 4 percent of GDP (Argentina, 1994–95). The adjustments in real GDP that accompanied these sudden stops were also large. Sudden stops (labeled "recent experiences" in tables 8 and 9 of Calvo and Reinhart's paper) produced impact effects on output equivalent to an average decline of 13.3 percent for countries that experienced banking crises, and 12.3 percent for countries that experienced currency crises. These impact effects were much larger than those corresponding to average crisis data for the period 1970–94, which showed declines of 3.2 and 2.7 percent for banking-crisis countries and currency-crisis countries, respectively. Calvo and Reinhart also showed that sudden stops produced larger adjustments in reserves and real exchange rates, and higher bills for bailing out bankrupt banking systems, than those produced by previous BOP crises. This is particularly the case for the East Asian crisis compared to other regions and to East Asia's recent historical record.

The effects of sudden stops on equity prices are well documented in several recent reviews of emerging-markets crises by international organizations (see, in particular, International Monetary Fund [IMF] 1999). Although the extent of true contagion across equity markets is subject to debate (see Kaminsky and Reinhart 2000 and Forbes and Rigobon 1999), stock market indexes fell sharply in countries that suffered sudden stops. By the end of January 1995, nearly a month after the devaluation of the peso, Mexico's stock market index had fallen by more than 50 percent in dollar terms relative to 1 November 1994. The indexes in Brazil and Argentina fell about 20 percent in the same period. In the East Asian crisis, the collapses of equity prices between 1 September and 31 December 1997 ranged from about 20 percent in Hong Kong to almost 70 percent in South Korea. Equity markets rose from these crash levels but continued to perform poorly compared to industrial-country markets (see chap. 3 in IMF 1999). Sudden stops were also associated with higher asset price volatility. The volatility of weekly emerging-market dollar returns doubled from 2 to 4 percent during the East Asian crisis in 1997 and the Russian collapse in 1998.[3]

---

3. These figures are means of rolling thirteen-week standard deviations of equity price indexes in U.S. dollars for sixteen emerging markets (see fig. 3.8 in International Monetary Fund [IMF] 1999).

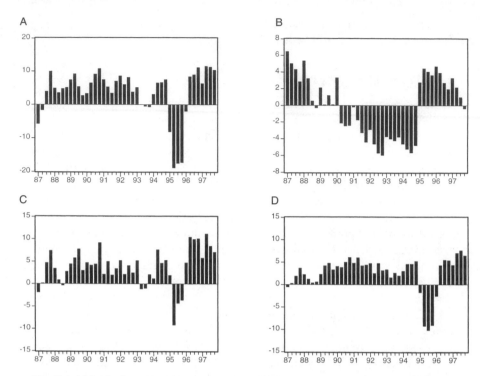

Fig. 7.1   Mexico's sudden stop (percent changes with respect to the same quarter of the previous year): *A,* **Domestic demand;** *B,* **Net exports/GDP ratio;** *C,* **GDP of tradable goods;** *D,* **GDP of nontradable goods**

The cross-country evidence on the macroeconomic features of sudden stops provided by Calvo and Reinhart (1999) is complemented here with time-series evidence that is useful for formalizing the notion of sudden stops as an excess volatility phenomenon. The time-series evidence applies to the sudden stop experienced in Mexico in the aftermath of the collapse of the peso of December 1994.

The time-series analysis uses quarterly data for the period 1980:1 to 1997:4 (except for the world real interest rate, which covers 1983:1 to 1996:3). Figure 7.1 plots growth rates of quarterly national accounts data to illustrate the magnitudes of the sudden stop in private domestic absorption, the trade deficit as a share of GDP, and the output of tradables and nontradables. This figure also shows the period of gradual but sustained expansion and widening trade deficit that preceded the crash, and the relatively rapid recovery after 1995. Note in addition that, from the perspective of this "raw data," without isolating the business-cycle component, the sudden stop in production was larger in the nontradables sector, and the recovery in this sector was also more modest than in the tradables sector.

Figure 7.2 shows the movements in relative prices and exchange rates us-

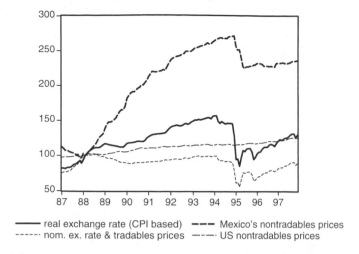

Fig. 7.2   Mexico exchange rates and relative prices (indexes based 1988:2 = 100)

ing monthly data. The picture shows that the severe drop in the real exchange rate at the time of the December 1994 devaluation reflected, in addition to the nominal devaluation, a collapse in the price of nontradables relative to tradables within Mexico. This occurred after the gradual but substantial increase in that relative price and in the real exchange rate that took place for the duration of the exchange rate–based stabilization that started in 1988. Mendoza (2001) documents that the sharp real appreciation and increase in the price of nontradables resulted mainly from a major rise in the cost of use of housing. Guerra de Luna (1997, 1998) show in turn that the high inflation in housing resulted from a large increase in real estate and land prices fueled by the surge in inflows of foreign capital and the expansion in domestic bank credit that preceded the sudden stop. Moreover, the sudden stop featured important corrections in house and land prices in 1995, coinciding with the large reversal of capital inflows and the collapse of domestic credit.

The stylized facts of the Mexican business cycle are computed using the Hodrick-Prescott (H-P) filter to isolate cyclical components of the data. These stylized facts are listed in table 7.1. Mexico's stylized facts display the standard business-cycle pattern for large developing economies (see Mendoza 1995; Agenor, McDermott, and Prasad 2000). The excess volatility implicit in the sudden stop of 1995 can be measured by comparing the depth of the observed recession of that year with regular Mexican business cycles in the sample period—defining the latter as deviations from H-P trends within 2–standard deviation bands. As figure 7.3 shows, the collapses of aggregate GDP, tradables output, nontradables output, consumption, and fixed investment associated with the sudden stop in the second quarter of

Table 7.1   Stylized Facts of Mexican Business Cycles

	Minimum	Standard Deviation	Ratios Relative to Nontradables GDP		First-Order Autocorrelation	Correlation with:		
			Minimum	Standard Deviation		GDP	Tradables GDP	Nontradables GDP
GDP	-7.936	2.734	1.196	0.997	0.647	1.000	0.885	0.946
Tradables GDP	-10.145	3.368	1.529	1.229	0.553	0.885	1.000	0.685
Nontradables GDP	-6.633	2.741	1.000	1.000	0.657	0.946	0.685	1.000
Price of nontradables	-24.409	8.088	3.680	2.951	0.899	0.626	0.534	0.607
Consumption	-8.567	3.347	1.292	1.221	0.664	0.922	0.853	0.846
Government expenditures	-9.126	4.544	1.376	1.658	-0.076	0.419	0.442	0.344
Investment	-28.007	11.083	4.222	4.043	0.783	0.892	0.834	0.815
Net exports	-48.193	19.216	7.265	7.010	0.794	-0.608	-0.713	-0.456
World real interest rate	-1.458	0.881	0.220	0.321	0.771	-0.235	-0.116	-0.279

Notes: These statistics were computed using quarterly, seasonally adjusted data for the period 1980:1–1997:4, except for the real interest rate, which is for the period 1983:1–1996:3. The data were logged and detrended using the Hodrick-Prescott filter with the smoothing parameter set at 1,600. The real interest rate is the London dollar quote of the Eurodollar nominal interest rate minus the consumer price inflation of industrial countries, both reported in the IMF's *International Financial Statistics* as series 60d, code 112 and series 64, code 110, respectively. This is the same measure of the real interest rate proposed by Agenor, McDermott, and Prasad (2000). Net exports are defined as detrended exports minus detrended imports. "Minimum" corresponds to the smallest deviations from the Hodrick-Prescott trends, which are all dated 1995:2 (except for the world real interest rate).

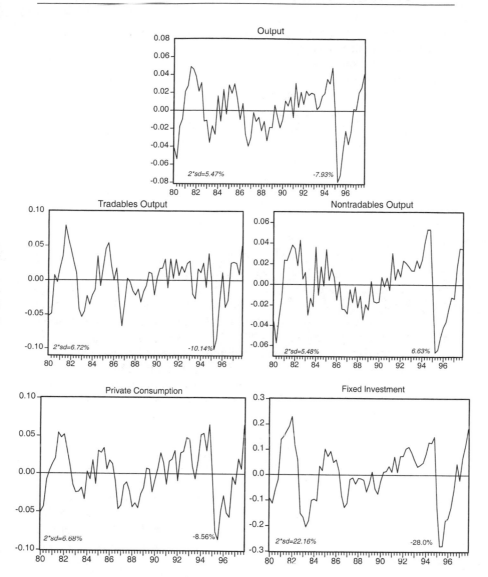

Fig. 7.3   Deviations from trend in output and demand (2*sd indicates the two-standard-deviation bound)

1995 exceeded the 2–standard deviation limits by margins ranging from 1.5 to 6.0 percentage points. They are also the only deviations from trend that exceeded those limits during the entire sample period.

7.3   Sudden Stops in a Flexible-Price Economy with Liquidity Constraints

This section of the paper proposes a modification of the conventional flexible-price intertemporal approach to current-account determination and business cycles in small open economies that allows for sudden stops. The need to modify the conventional approach is obvious in light of its serious empirical shortcomings; models that follow this approach predict smooth movements in foreign debt driven by consumption-smoothing and investment-augmenting effects that are grossly inconsistent with the sudden reversals of capital inflows and collapses of private consumption observed during a sudden stop (see Edwards' chap. 1, this vol., and Mendoza 1991b, 1995). A key element behind these counterfactual results is the assumption of perfect credit markets. In standard intertemporal models of the current account, agents can borrow or lend at the world-determined real interest rate limited only by the reach of their wealth (as implied by the no-Ponzi-game condition). This assumption is relaxed here by considering a credit friction that links the agents' ability to borrow to the endogenous dynamics of prices and income.

Credit frictions are modeled in an exchange economy that abstracts from the existence of money. This leaves behind important real-world features that link credit frictions to the money market and sets aside an explicit analysis of the role of monetary and exchange rate policies (which has been undertaken in other studies, like those of Cespedes, Chang, and Velasco (chap. 12, this vol.) or Mendoza (2001).[4] However, it is important to note that the central elements of the credit channel transmission mechanism envisaged by Fisher (1933) are features of the real credit flows of a nonmonetary economy. This is shown by Calvo's (1998) analysis illustrating how sudden stops can be the outcome of the real-sector features of frictions in credit markets.

7.3.1   Structure of the Model

Consider a small open economy with an exogenous, stochastic endowment of tradable goods $\exp(\varepsilon_t^T) Y^T$, where ε_t^T is a Markovian shock to the mean endowment Y^T or to its world value (i.e., the terms of trade). The economy produces nontradable goods using a Cobb-Douglas technology: $Y_t^N = \exp(\varepsilon_t^N) A K^{1-\alpha} L_t^\alpha$. K is a time-variant capital stock with zero depreciation rate, ε_t^N is a Markovian productivity shock, and L is labor input. Details on the specification of the Markov processes driving all the shocks present in the model are provided in section 7.4.

Firms choose labor demand so as to maximize profits π_t in units of tradable goods (which are the model's numeraire):

$$(1) \qquad \pi_t = \exp(\varepsilon_t^T) Y^T + p_t^N \exp(\varepsilon_t^N) A K^{1-\alpha} L_t^\alpha - w_t L_t$$

The price of nontradables in units of tradables is p_t^N, and the real wage in units of tradables is w_t. At equilibrium, firms demand labor up to the point at which the value of the marginal product of labor equals the real wage:

4. Mendoza (2001) studies the effects of dollarization in a monetary economy with a liquidity requirement similar to the one examined here.

(2) $$p_t^N \alpha \exp(\varepsilon_t^N) A K^{1-\alpha} L_t^{\alpha\,1} = w_t$$

Note that because the value of the marginal product of labor depends on p_t^N, a collapse in the relative price of nontradables (i.e., a collapse in the real exchange rate, since purchasing power parity [PPP] in tradables is assumed to hold) induces a negative shock to labor demand.

Households consume tradable goods C_t^T, nontradable goods C_t^N, and supply labor to firms. They maximize a form of expected utility that incorporates an endogenous rate of time preference (see Epstein 1983). A standard motivation for preferences of this class in models of the small open economy is that they allow the models to produce well-behaved dynamics and deterministic stationary equilibria in which the rate of time preference equals the world real interest rate. In addition, in the model with credit frictions proposed here, endogenous discounting allows the model to support equilibria in which credit frictions may remain binding in the long run (this point is illustrated later in this section). The utility function is

(3) $$U = E_0 \left[\sum_{t=0}^{\infty} \exp\left\{ -\sum_{\tau=0}^{t-1} v[C(C_\tau^T, C_\tau^N) - H(L_\tau)] \right\} u[C(C_t^T, C_t^N) - H(L_t)] \right].$$

In this expression, $U(\cdot)$ is lifetime utility, $C(\cdot)$ is a constant elasticity of substitution (CES) aggregator of consumption of tradables and nontradables, $H(\cdot)$ is a positive, continuously differentiable, and concave function that measures the disutility of labor, $u(\cdot)$ is an isoelastic period utility function, and $v(\cdot)$ is the time preference function.

The specification of the arguments of the u and v functions in terms of the composite good $C - H$ is borrowed from Greenwood, Hercowitz, and Huffman (1988; henceforth GHH). In their one-good model, this assumption eliminates the interaction between consumption (or wealth) and labor supply by making the marginal rate of substitution between consumption and labor supply depend only on the latter. This is not the case in the two-sector model of this paper because the relevant real wage for labor supply decisions is measured in units of aggregate consumption, and hence changes in the relative price of nontradables and in the sectoral allocation of consumption affect labor supply. Still, the GHH specification simplifies the analysis significantly as illustrated below.

The four functions that characterize lifetime utility adopt the following functional forms:

(4) $$C(C_t^T, C_t^N) = [\omega(C_t^T)^{-\eta} + (1 - \omega)(C_t^N)^{-\eta}]^{-1/\eta}$$

(5) $$H(L_t) = \frac{L_t^\delta}{\delta}, \quad \delta > 1$$

(6) $$u[C(C_t^T, C_t^N) - H(L_t)] = \frac{[C(C_t^T, C_t^N) - H(L_t)]^{1-\sigma} - 1}{1 - \sigma}$$

(7) $v[C(C_t^T, C_t^N) - H(L_t)] = \beta\{\ln[1 + C(C_t^T, C_t^N) - H(L_t)]\}$

These functional forms are standard in real business-cycle models of the small open economy (see Mendoza 1991b, 1995). The parameter η determines the elasticity of substitution between consumption of tradable goods and consumption of nontradable goods, which is given by $1/(1 + \eta)$; ω is the standard CES weighing factor; δ determines the elasticity of the supply of labor with respect to the real wage, which is given by $1/(\delta - 1)$, σ is the coefficient of constant relative risk aversion (CRRA); and β determines the sensitivity of the rate-of-time preference with respect to changes in the date-t arguments of the period utility function.

Households maximize utility subject to a standard budget constraint:

(8) $(1 + \tau_t^T)C_t^T + (1 + \tau_t^N)p_t^N C_t^N$

$$= \pi_t + w_t L_t - b_{t+1} + \exp(\varepsilon_t^R)Rb_t - T_t^T - p_t^N T_t^T.$$

Here, τ_t^T and τ_t^N are consumption taxes that apply to purchases of tradables and nontradables and T_t^T and T_t^N are lump-sum taxes levied in units of tradables and nontradables respectively. The variable b represents the economy's net foreign asset position in terms of the only internationally traded asset present in the model: one-period bonds that pay the world-determined gross real interest rate $\exp(\varepsilon_t^R)R$ in units of tradable goods (ε_t^R is a Markovian world interest rate shock, a reasonable proxy for shocks to "international liquidity").

Since the one-period bond is the only asset households exchange with the rest of the world, markets of contingent claims are incomplete, and the small open economy's wealth varies with the state of nature. Given the CRRA form of $u(\cdot)$, insurance-market incompleteness implies in turn that consumption responds to fluctuations in the marginal utility of wealth induced by the exogenous shocks, and that households undertake precautionary saving. The latter leads households to effectively impose on themselves an endogenous borrowing constraint even in the absence of explicit credit constraints driven by credit-market imperfections (as in the buffer-stock saving models of Aiyagari 1993 and Carroll 2000).

The credit-market imperfection present in this model takes the form of a liquidity constraint by which lenders require households to finance a fraction φ, for $0 \leq \varphi \leq 1$, of their current expenses (i.e., consumption, taxes, and debt payments) out of current income:

(9) $w_t L_t + \pi_t \geq$

$$\varphi\{[(1 + \tau_t^T)C_t^T + (1 + \tau_t^N)p_t^N C_t^N] - \exp(\varepsilon_t^R)Rb_t + T_t^T + p_t^N T_t^N\}$$

Given the budget constraint, this liquidity requirement is equivalent to a borrowing constraint that limits debt as a share of current income not to exceed $(1 - \varphi)/\varphi$:

(10)
$$b_{t+1} \geq -\frac{1-\varphi}{\varphi}[w_t L_t + \pi_t]$$

Note that $\varphi = 1$ implies a no-borrowing constraint (i.e., $b_{t+1} \geq 0$ for all t), and as φ converges to 0 the economy approaches the case in which the liquidity constraint is never binding.

Because insurance markets are incomplete, the liquidity constraint gives households an extra incentive to engage in precautionary saving, storing away extra assets in the "good" states of nature for the "bad" states in which the constraint may bind and they may not be able to borrow as much as they would desire in world markets. This contrasts sharply with the outcome that would be obtained under perfect foresight. Under perfect foresight (and a constant discount factor) households would hold the largest amount of debt allowed as long as the marginal utility of current consumption exceeded that of future consumption (see also Aiyagari 1993).

The liquidity requirement is not formally derived as a feature of an optimal credit contract. However, the motivation for it is that it could result from traditional financial-market frictions (such as monitoring costs or bankruptcy risk) or institutional features of credit markets. For instance, Eaton and Gersovitz (1981) show that the probability of default by a risk-averse borrower interacting with a risk-neutral lender in an optimal-contracting framework is increasing in the stock of debt and higher for negative income shocks than for positive income shocks. The liquidity constraint can thus be thought of as a mechanism to (imperfectly) manage default risk by limiting the ability of borrowers to acquire debt and by linking this ability to income realizations. The optimal contract of Eaton and Gersovitz features states of nature in which lending is rationed and an endogenous, equilibrium interest rate premium that increases with the stock of debt. The liquidity constraint will be shown to yield analogous results in that it produces an endogenous risk premium on the use of foreign debt relative to the use of domestic saving to smooth business-cycle volatility and states of nature in which debt is rationed.

Even if the microfoundations of the liquidity requirement are incomplete, the fact is that the borrowing constraint in equation (10) is consistent with standard lending criteria widely used in mortgage and consumer loans. This is the case even in the financial markets of the industrial world (see the evidence reported by Ludvigson 1996). In the United States, for instance, the large financial companies that anchor the mortgage market (*Fannie Mae* and *Freddie Mac*) provide lenders with "scoring" guidelines that effectively require borrowers to keep expected total debt service of prospective borrowers around 1/3 of gross income.[5] Mortgage debt in the United States

---

5. For example, as of October 2000, Fannie Mae guidelines for conventional mortgages with 20 percent down payment required that total housing expenses be kept below 33 percent of gross monthly income and that total debt payments, including mortgage service, be kept below 38 percent of gross monthly income. Assuming a mortgage rate of 7.5 percent, these guidelines required debt to remain below 35 percent of gross monthly income.

as of the second quarter of 2000 was of roughly the same size as the total outstanding corporate debt (about \$4.2 trillion), and total household debt was 42 percent larger than the total corporate debt. These figures suggest that credit constraints of the form postulated above may be as relevant to consider as the constraints on firm financing emphasized more often in studies of the credit channel.

The liquidity requirement has the additional advantage that it captures in a tractable manner the potentially crippling effects of "liability dollarization" in a flexible-price setting. This is because debt contracts are written in units of tradables, but part of the income on which the debt is leveraged originates in the nontradables sector. As a result, a sharp fall in the output of nontradables or in the nontradables relative price can trigger a sudden stop.

The optimality conditions of the household's problem (listed in appendix A) have a straightforward interpretation. The optimal allocation of consumption across tradable and nontradable goods is determined by equating the atemporal marginal rate of substitution between C_t^T and C_t^N with the relative price of nontradables. The optimal supply of labor is set by equating the marginal disutility of labor with the posttax real wage relevant for household decisions, $w_t/[p_t^C(1 + \tau_t^N)]$. Because households care for consumption in terms of the CES aggregator C, the relevant real wage for them is deflated by p_t^C, which is the relative price of aggregate consumption in units of tradables. Optimal saving is determined by equating the lifetime marginal utility cost of sacrificing a unit of current consumption with the corresponding expected marginal benefit. Marginal lifetime utilities include the impatience effect, by which changes to the arguments of period utility at any date t alter the rate at which all future period utilities are discounted. It is also critical to note that, since households desire to consume both tradables and nontradables, the effective return on saving is not just the world real interest rate but the "consumption-based" real interest rate $\exp(\varepsilon_t^R)R[p_t^C(1 + \tau_t^T)/p_{t+1}^C(1 + \tau_{t+1}^T)]$. Thus, the intertemporal relative price of consumption in this two-good economy is endogenous despite the assumption of a small open economy and depends on the dynamics of the relative price of nontradables (which is the key determinant of p^C).[6]

The specification of the model is completed with the description of the government sector. To enable the model to reflect the observed sectoral distribution of government expenditures across tradables and nontradables, it is assumed that the government maintains a constant level of purchases of nontradable goods financed by a constant lump-sum tax. This ensures that

6. Given the CES form of C, p^C corresponds to the CES price index obtained from the standard duality problem of minimizing expenditure for a given level of period utility. This implies that p^C is an increasing, continuously differentiable function of p^N.

the dynamics of the relative price of nontradables reflect only changes in demand and supply by the private sector and not changes in government purchases of nontradables induced by fluctuations in tax revenue. Fluctuations in tax revenue result in fluctuations of government purchases of tradable goods around a given initial amount financed by lump-sum taxes in units of tradables to be calibrated to the data. This assumption introduces the Calvo-Drazen fiscal-induced wealth effect that Calvo and Drazen (1998) and Mendoza and Uribe (2000) found critical for explaining key features of economic fluctuations in developing countries exposed to the risk of uncertain duration of government policy. Under these assumptions, the government budget constraint is given by

(11) $G_t^T + p_t^N G^N = \tau_t^T C_t^T + \tau_t^N C_t^N + T^T + p_t^N T^N$ with $G^N = T^N$.

Tax rates are assumed to be stochastic so as to explore the role of policy uncertainty, or the lack of credibility of existing policies, in triggering sudden stops. The model can accommodate differentiated tax rates and degrees of policy uncertainty with regard to tradable and nontradable goods, but for simplicity the analysis that follows considers the case of a uniform tax $\tau_t^T = \tau_t^N = \tau_t$. This case is interesting to examine because it yields price and wealth distortions on the labor-consumption and saving margins that are nearly equivalent to those produced by the rate of depreciation of the currency in conventional models of exchange rate management in small open economies (see Mendoza and Uribe 2000 and Mendoza 2001 for details). Thus, a reversal from the low-tax regime to the high-tax regime can be interpreted as a shift from a currency peg to a floating exchange rate regime.

The government announces at date 0 the implementation of a policy reform by which taxes are to be reduced from a high level τ^H to a low level τ^L. The policy lacks credibility in the sense that agents assign an exogenous, time-invariant conditional probability to the reversal of the reform $z = \text{pr}[\tau_{t+1} = \tau^H \mid \tau_t = \tau^L]$. The probabilistic process driving the tax rate follows a basic regime-switching specification for discrete-valued random variables governed by an irreducible, ergodic Markov chain. The transition matrix Π and the vector autoregression representation of the Markov process are

$$\Pi = \begin{bmatrix} s & z \\ 1-s & 1-z \end{bmatrix}, \quad \zeta_{t+1} = \Pi\zeta_t + i_{t+1},$$

where $s = \text{pr}[\tau_{t+1} = \tau^H \mid \tau_t = \tau^H]$, ζ is a 2×1 random vector such that $\zeta_t = (1,0)'$ when $\tau_t = \tau^H$ and $\zeta_t = (0,1)'$ when $\tau_t = \tau^L$, and $i_{t+1} \equiv \zeta_{t+1} - E(\zeta_{t+1} \mid \zeta_p, \zeta_{t-1}, \ldots)$. The limiting probabilities of the tax regimes are $P(\tau_t = \tau^H) = z/(1 + z - s)$ and $P(\tau_t = \tau^L) = 1 - [z/(1 + z - s)]$, and the autoregressive representation of the process is $\zeta_{j,t+1} = z + (s - z)\zeta_{j,t} + i_{j,t+1}$ for $j = 1,2$. The average duration of the high-tax regime is $1/(1 - s)$ and that of the low-tax regime is $1/z$.

7.3.2 Competitive Equilibrium and the
Business Cycle Transmission Mechanism

Given an initial foreign asset position b_0 and the probabilistic processes driving the shocks to productivity, the world's real interest rate, and taxes, a competitive equilibrium for this model economy is defined by state-contingent intertemporal sequences for the allocations (C_t^T, C_t^N, C_t, L_t, b_{t+1}, G_t^T, Y_t^N) and prices (p_t^N, p_t^C, w_t) for $t = 0, \ldots, \infty$ such that (a) firms maximize profits subject to their technological constraints, taking p_t^N and w_t as given; (b) households maximize lifetime utility subject to the budget constraint and the liquidity requirement, taking p_t^N, p_t^C, and w_t as given; (c) the government budget constraint holds; and (d) the market-clearing conditions for the markets of tradable and nontradable goods and for the labor market hold.

The competitive equilibrium can be represented by the solution of a modified social planner's problem, which in turn can be solved numerically using dynamic programming methods (see appendix B for details). This simplification is very useful because of the potentially high degree of non-linearity introduced by the borrowing constraint (see Aiyagari and Gertler 1999). The model's numerical solution is summarized by two objects: first, a set of state-contingent optimal decision rules for the controls (C_t^T, C_t^N, C_t, L_t, G_t^T, Y_t^N) and endogenous state (b_{t+1}) that depend on the current realizations of the states (b_t, ε_t^T, ε_t^N, ε_t^R, τ_t^T, τ_t^N); and second, the joint transition and limiting probability distribution functions of these state variables, which jointly with the decision rules also determine the transition and limiting distributions of all of the model's endogenous variables. The equilibrium prices and their corresponding transition and limiting distributions can then be solved for recursively using the optimality conditions of the maximization problems solved by households and firms.

If the liquidity requirement never binds, the model features cyclical dynamics driven by well-known transmission mechanisms. In particular, shocks to productivity and to the world interest rate drive business cycles through the familiar channels examined in real business cycle models of the small open economy (see Mendoza 1991b, 1995). Tax shocks induce fluctuations through the wealth and substitution effects highlighted in the studies on the macroeconomic effects of policy uncertainty by Calvo and Drazen (1998) and Mendoza and Uribe (2000). Given a low-tax state at any date t, the conditional expected tax rate for $t + 1$ is higher than the tax observed at t. This triggers an intertemporal substitution effect similar to the one driving perfect-foresight models of noncredible policies based on Calvo (1986); prices are relatively low at t, and hence agents substitute consumption intertemporally in favor of current consumption. Under uncertainty and in the presence of noninsurable income effects due to the incompleteness of financial markets, Calvo and Drazen (1998) showed that there is also a state-contingent wealth effect. In each period that low taxes prevail, households benefit from the implicit lower level of government absorption, and this gain is added to their permanent income. This effect favors an increasing consumption path for the duration of the low-tax regime, followed by a collapse when a reversal of the tax cut takes place.

The above intuition for the real effects of policy uncertainty reflects results that apply fully in partial equilibrium. In general equilibrium, a reversal of a tax cut is likely to induce a decline in the output of nontradables, labor allocation, and relative price of nontradables. For the price of nontradables to fall, the reduction in demand for nontradable goods induced by the above-mentioned wealth and intertemporal substitution effects must exceed the reduction in supply. In turn, for the supply of nontradables to fall in equilibrium, it must be the case that the combined effect of the reduction in the demand for labor (resulting from the reduced value of the marginal product of labor in the nontradables sector as p^N falls) and the negative effect of the tax hike on labor supply dominates the positive effect on labor supply that results from the decline in p^C (which is caused by the fall in the relative price of nontradables).

The specification of policy uncertainty proposed here differs from that in the Calvo-Drazen model in that the high-tax regime is not an absorbent state (i.e., even when the high tax is observed there is still some probability that the low tax can be reinstated), but the basic intuition of the wealth effects that result from market incompleteness remains valid.[7] The model also differs from the Calvo-Drazen setup in that a reversal to the high-tax state features a "supply side" effect that reduces the supply of labor, as the posttax real wage falls when the tax rate rises.

The presence of the "occasionally binding" borrowing constraint adds important new elements into the model's business-cycle transmission mechanism. In particular, in states of nature in which the credit constraint binds, the following effects occur:

1. The effective real interest rate faced by households increases because the binding borrowing constraint forces them to reduce consumption relative to the case with perfect credit markets. Hence, the collapse in aggregate consumption and in the demand for tradables and nontradables associated with adverse real or policy shocks is magnified if such a reversal makes the economy run into its borrowing limit.

2. The effective marginal reward to labor supply rises because the extra unit of labor enhances the household's ability to borrow. This moderates the negative effect of adverse shocks on labor supply.

3. Consumption, saving, and net foreign asset accumulation (and hence the current account, because b is the model's single means of saving) expe-

7. The Calvo-Drazen case is the limiting case of the model in which $\varsigma = 1$.

rience intertemporal distortions that depend on the combined *dynamic* effects of items 1 and 2 in general equilibrium. This is because the effective intertemporal relative price of aggregate consumption is determined by the consumption-based real interest rate, which depends on the inverse of the rate of change of the relative price of consumption (p_t^C/p_{t+1}^C), which in turn depends on the inverse of the rate of change of the relative price of non-tradables (p_t^N/p_{t+1}^N).

As a result of the above effects, households face an implicit risk premium in the use of foreign debt vis-à-vis their own saving in their efforts to smooth consumption that is analogous to the external financing premium faced by firms in models of sudden stops based on the Bernanke-Gertler financial accelerator. The differences are that in the model proposed here the equilibrium risk premium is determined endogenously and is influenced by the risk-averse nature of the households' preferences (which is more in line with the default risk premium in Eaton and Gersovitz 1981). In contrast, existing open-economy extensions of the Bernanke-Gertler framework assume that the functional form representing the external financing premium in general equilibrium is identical to the partial-equilibrium solution of a costly-monitoring contracting problem under risk neutrality.

The potential for the liquidity requirement to enlarge output collapses as a result of the effects identified in items 1–3 above can be illustrated more clearly by combining the labor demand and supply conditions to derive the following expression for the percent impact effect on the equilibrium allocation of labor that can result from a switch from τ_t^L to τ_t^H:

(13) $\ln(L_t^H) - \ln(L_t^L) \approx$

$$\frac{1}{\delta - \alpha} \times \left\{ -[\tau_t^H - \tau_t^L] + \left[\ln\left(\frac{p_t^{N^H}}{p_t^{C^H}}\right) - \ln\left(\frac{p_t^{N^L}}{p_t^{C^L}}\right) \right] + \left[\frac{1 - \varphi}{\varphi} \left(\frac{\mu_t^H}{\lambda_t^H} - \frac{\mu_t^L}{\lambda_t^L} \right) \right] \right\},$$

where μ_t and λ_t are the nonnegative Lagrange multipliers on the borrowing constraint and the budget constraint respectively and $1/(\delta - \alpha)$ is always positive because of the parameter restrictions $\delta > 1 \geq \alpha \geq 0$. This expression is not a closed-form solution because the relative prices and multipliers in the right-hand side of the expression are endogenous in general equilibrium.

Equation (13) breaks down the impact effect of a tax hike on the equilibrium labor allocation into three effects identified by the three terms in square brackets in the right-hand side. The first effect is the negative effect of the higher tax on labor supply. The second effect is the effect of the change in the price of C^N relative to C (i.e., the ratio p^N/p^C). This price effect is the combined effect of the change in the price of nontradables on labor demand with that of the change in the price of aggregate consumption on labor supply. Given that p^C is the CES price index for the consumption aggregator, it can be shown that p^N/p^C is increasing in p^N. Hence, if the price of nontradables falls with the tax hike, p^C also falls, but the adverse effect of the fall in p^N on labor demand always dominates the positive effect of the fall in p^C on labor supply.[8] Thus, the decline in the equilibrium allocation of labor in response to a tax hike (and hence in output of nontradables) is magnified due to this price effect.

The third effect operating on the equilibrium allocation of labor is the direct effect of the liquidity constraint, and it is only present when the constraint binds. Consider for the sake of simplicity a case in which the constraint switches from nonbinding to binding with the tax hike (i.e., $\mu_t^L = 0$, $\mu_t^H > 0$). In this case, the constraint makes the fall in equilibrium labor *smaller* because of the labor-supply incentive provided by the higher effective marginal reward on the extra unit of labor.[9] However, the binding liquidity constraint also has an indirect effect on equilibrium labor because it distorts relative prices and thus alters the price effect. As shown in section 7.4, when a tax hike triggers a sudden stop (i.e., when it makes the liquidity constraint suddenly binding), the resulting adjustment in consumption can induce a larger collapse in the price of nontradables than in the case without a sudden stop. This indirect effect can dominate the direct effect so that a binding liquidity constraint may enlarge the collapses in labor and nontradables output. Whether p^N falls will depend on how tight the credit constraint is and how much it reduces tradables consumption relative to nontradables consumption.

The discussion above focuses on the case of tax shocks, but similar effects apply to the cases of productivity shocks and shocks to the world interest rate. Hence, sudden stops in the model can be driven by policy uncertainty, by domestic productivity shocks, by foreign shocks affecting the real interest rate, or by a mixture of all three. This variety of causes is important because of differences attributed to the role of each of these shocks in the particular experiences of countries that suffered sudden stops during the 1990s. Policy uncertainty is widely regarded as an important determinant in the sudden stops observed in Latin America, whereas "exogenous shocks" of

---

8. Since p^N is an increasing function of C^T/C^N, it is possible for p^N to increase instead of falling with the tax hike if the collapse in C^T is smaller than the collapse in C^N. The collapse in C^T will tend to be larger because the supply of tradables is more elastic than that of nontradables and because the Calvo-Drazen fiscal-induced wealth effect increases government absorption of tradables when the tax increases.

9. This higher reward is given by $[(1 - \varphi)/\varphi](\mu_t^H/\lambda_t^H)$, which depends on the ratio of the two Lagrange multipliers. The latter in turn is determined by intertemporal effects, since the same ratio determines the interest rate distortion induced by the debt constraint (see appendix A) and is likely to be nonlinear: If the constraint is marginally binding, it may not affect consumption much and will thus have a small effect on λ_t^H, so μ_t^H/λ_t^H increases as the constraint is tightened, but if the constraint is "very tight" it could force a large adjustment in consumption and a large increase in λ_t^H so that μ_t^H/λ_t^H may fall as the constraint is tightened.

foreign or domestic origin are often cited (albeit not without controversy) in accounts of the crises in Southeast Asia.

The binding credit constraint also has an important connection with the choice to model preferences with an endogenous rate of time preference. In particular, it allows the model to determine endogenously whether a given value of φ results in a binding borrowing constraint in the long run for given values of the rest of the model's parameters.

Consider a perfect-foresight variant of the model. In this case, the steady-state consumption Euler equation is

$$(14) \qquad [1 + C(C^T, C^N) - H(L)]^\beta = R\left(1 - \frac{\mu}{\lambda}\right)^{-1},$$

where variables without time subscripts correspond to steady-state values. The term in the left-hand side of this expression is the gross rate of time preference. Equation (14), combined with the rest of the steady-state equilibrium conditions, implies that for given parameter values the model features a critical value φ^{crit} below which the borrowing constraint is not binding. Any such $\varphi \leq \varphi^{crit}$ yields the same steady state, since $\mu = 0$ and R is exogenous. The borrowing constraint binds for $\varphi > \varphi^{crit}$, and the steady-state equilibrium then varies with μ/λ, because the latter depends on the tightness of the borrowing constraint relative to the marginal utility of wealth. In this case, the rate-of-time preference rises to match the higher effective real interest rate in the right-hand side of equation (14), thereby supporting the steady state with the binding borrowing limit. Clearly, a standard time-separable utility function with a constant rate-of-time preference cannot deliver this outcome. For any value of φ, the liquidity constraint is binding or not depending on the exogenous values assigned to the interest rate and the rate-of-time preference. If they are equal, for example, the constraint never binds at steady state.

7.4 A Quantitative Exploration of Business Cycles with a Sudden Stop

7.4.1 Calibration

The numerical analysis starts from a baseline scenario in which the model's parameters are calibrated so that the deterministic stationary equilibrium of the model mimics several average ratios of macroeconomic aggregates taken from Mexican data. Parameters that cannot be directly related to the data are taken from existing econometric studies or set to values typically used in other studies. The calibration is set to a quarterly frequency, although some ratios of national accounts data are derived from annual figures.

One key part of the calibration is setting the values of the parameters that reflect Mexico's ability to access world financial markets. These include both the value of the liquidity coefficient φ and the mean net foreign asset position. The deterministic steady-state ratio b/Y is set to –35 percent following the estimates of Mexico's net foreign asset position for the period 1970–97 provided by Lane and Milesi-Ferretti (1999). This implies that the critical value of the liquidity coefficient is $\varphi^{crit} = 0.741$. Thus, for the borrowing constraint to bind in the deterministic steady state, φ needs to exceed 0.741, although lower values of φ may still yield a binding borrowing limit in the deterministic transition to steady state or in the stochastic dynamics. The calibration assumes that the borrowing constraint does not bind at steady state (i.e., φ < 0.741). The stochastic simulations explore the effects of varying φ from a low value such that the constraint is never binding within the state space over which the model is solved (which the simulations show to be φ = 0.445) to a value φ = 0.714, which limits debt to no more than 40 percent of income valued at tradable goods prices.

The model is calibrated to match several average ratios of macroeconomic time series calculated using aggregate and sectoral national accounts data. A consistent data set of Mexico's sectoral national accounts with sufficient detail to compute these ratios is available only for the period 1988–96 or –98, depending on the variable. The nontradables (tradables) sector is defined by the industries for which the average ratio of total trade to gross production is less (more) than 0.05. The industries that belong to the nontradables sector according to this definition are construction; utilities; retailing and commercial services; financial services; and personal, social, and community services.

The model is calibrated to match the average *aggregate* and *sectoral* GDP, Y, shares of consumption, C, investment, I, and government expenditures, G, measured at current prices. Because investment expenditures are not included in the model, they enter in the calibration as constant lump-sum expenditures in each sector so that the calibration can match the observed GDP shares of consumption (otherwise, consumption shares would be too large). Data for the period 1970–95 yield these average expenditure shares: $C/Y = 0.684$, $I/Y = 0.217$, $G/Y = 0.092$. The sectoral data are available for a shorter sample period, and the information they provide yields only the average shares of aggregate investment and aggregate government expenditures allocated to tradables (I^T/I and G^T/G) and the ratio of tradables GDP to nontradables GDP (Y^T/Y^N). The 1988–98 average of Y^T/Y^N is 0.648. The 1988–96 averages of the other expenditure shares are $I^T/I = 0.576$ and $G^T/G = 0.072$.

The above aggregate and sectoral ratios are combined to obtain the following estimates of the shares of sectoral investment and government purchases in each sector's GDP: $I^T/Y^T = 0.32$, $G^T/Y^T = 0.017$, $I^N/Y^N = 0.151$, and $G^N/Y^N = 0.141$.[10] Estimates of sectoral consumption-output ratios are

---

10. For example, given I/Y, I^T/I, and Y^T/Y^N, I^T/Y^T is given by $(I/Y)(I^T/I)[1 + (Y^T/Y^N)]$.

then derived using the expenditures definition of GDP and the average net exports-GDP ratio for 1970–95, $NX/Y = -0.001$. The consumption-GDP ratios are $C^T/Y^T = 0.665$ and $C^N/Y^N = 0.708$.

The calibration is normalized by setting $Y^T = 1$, $K = 1$, and $p^N = 1$. The average sectoral share of labor income in the nontradables sector for the 1988–96 period yields $\alpha N = 0.364$. The elasticity of substitution between C^T and C^N, $1/(1 + \eta)$, is set to the value estimated by Ostry and Reinhart (1992). Their estimate of η for developing countries is $\eta = 0.316$. Estimates of the wage elasticity of labor supply in Mexico's nontradables sector are not available, so the calibration assumes unitary elasticity as a benchmark, which implies $\delta = 2$. The uniform consumption tax rate is set to $\tau = 0.079$, which is the mean tax rate that results from the regime-switching Markov process specified below. The variable R is set to the quarterly equivalent of a gross real interest rate of 1.065 per year, and σ is set to 2, both standard values in real business-cycle theory.

The calibration values for A, ω, β, T^T, and T^N and the corresponding steady-state levels of C^T, C^N, L, Y^N, and b are jointly determined by solving the nonlinear simultaneous equation system conformed by the steady-state equilibrium conditions of the model, imposing the calibration ratios and parameters described in the previous paragraphs and summarized in table 7.2. The solution implies $A = 1.958$, $\omega = 0.342$, $\beta = 0.027$, $T^T = -0.139$, and $T^N = 0.119$. Note that the value of β implies a small semi-elasticity of the rate of time preference to changes in consumption and labor supply, which makes impatience effects of second order importance.

The remaining parameters that must be set pertain to the stochastic processes of tax-rate, productivity, and interest rate shocks. The process for the uniform tax rate is set to mimic the price distortions on saving and labor supply induced by sudden devaluations of the currency in a monetary variant of the model calibrated to Mexico (see Mendoza 2001 for details). The low-tax state (set to match a permanently fixed exchange rate) is 2.1 percent, and the high-tax state (set to match an annual rate of depreciation of the currency of 50 percent) is 11.8 percent. The mean duration of the low-tax regime is twenty-four quarters (six years), which matches the observed durations of Mexico's managed exchange rate regimes of 1970–76, 1976–82, and 1988–94. The mean duration of the high-tax regime is set to thirty-six quarters (nine years) so as to yield a probability of staying in the high-tax regime higher than that of staying in the low-tax regime (which approximates the standard assumption of the literature on policy temporariness that treats the "bad policy" state as absorbent). The mean durations of the tax regimes imply that the probability of switching from the low tax to the high tax (z) is 4.2 percent per quarter, and the probability of continuation of the high tax state (ς) is 97.2 percent. The mean tax is 7.93 percent, with a standard deviation of 0.047 and a coefficient of first-order autocorrelation equal to 0.93.

Table 7.2   **Parameter Values for the Calibrated Deterministic Stationary State**

	Values
Technology	
α	0.364
A	1.958
YT	1.000
Fiscal policy	
T	0.079
T traded	−0.139
T nontraded	0.119
Credit market	
R	1.016
φ	0.740
b/Y	−0.350
Preferences	
β	0.027
δ	2.000
η	0.316
ω	0.342
σ	2.000
National accounts ratios	
C/Y	0.684
I/Y	0.217
G/Y	0.092
NX/Y	−0.001
YT/YN	0.648
CT/YT	0.665
GT/YT	0.017
IT/YT	0.323
CN/YN	0.708
GN/YN	0.141
IN/YN	0.151

The stochastic processes driving productivity shocks and world interest rate shocks are represented by standard two-state, symmetric Markov processes that satisfy the "simple persistence" rule following the same method applied in Mendoza (1995). These processes are statistically independent of the one driving the tax rates. For simplicity, the simulations assume common productivity shocks across sectors (i.e., $\varepsilon_t^N = \varepsilon_t^T = \varepsilon_t$). Because tradables output is an endowment equal to one unit of tradable goods, the standard deviation of productivity shocks is set to mimic the standard deviation of tradables GDP in Mexico (3.36 percent). The standard deviation of shocks to the world real interest rate is set to 0.881 percent, which is the standard deviation of the H-P filtered measure of the gross world real interest rate proposed by Agenor, McDermott, and Prasad (2000). The correlation coefficient between the two shocks matches the sample correlation of Mexico's tradables GDP with the world's real interest rate (−0.116). Symmetry and simple persistence imply that the shocks share a common first-order serial autocorrelation coefficient, which is set to match the first-order serial autocorrelation of Mexican tradables GDP, 0.553—the autocorrelation of the world real interest rate is slightly higher at 0.771.

7.4.2   Numerical Solutions: How Large and Costly Are Business Cycles with Sudden Stops?

The model is solved by value-function iteration over a discretized state space. The state space consists of the combinations of the two possible realizations of each of the three shocks, $\varepsilon = \{0.0336, -0.0336\}$, $\varepsilon^R = \{0.0088, -0.0088\}$, $\tau = \{0.118, 0.021\}$, and the 1,200 values in an evenly spaced grid of net foreign asset positions spanning the interval $[-2.788, 2.608]$. Thus, there are eight combinations of the triple $(\varepsilon, \varepsilon^R, \tau)$ that describe the possible realizations of exogenous shocks at each date, and a total of $1,200 \times 8 = 9,600$ coordinates in the state space.

Figure 7.4 plots the limiting probability distribution functions (PDFs) of net foreign assets in the economies with perfect credit markets and with the liquidity constraint. The mean net foreign asset position of the economy with perfect credit markets is -0.097, which implies an average b/Y ratio of -4.5 percent. This amount of foreign debt is only 10.9 percent of that held in the deterministic steady state, which illustrates the large amount of precautionary saving that households undertake given the economy's uncertainty and the incompleteness of financial markets (even when the credit market functions perfectly).

Adding the extra incentive for precautionary saving due to the liquidity constraint shifts the economy to a positive value for mean holdings of foreign assets of 0.258 (an average b/Y ratio of 9.3 percent). The economy with the liquidity constraint also differs in that there is a mass of probability (equal to 0.38 percent) concentrated at a threshold net foreign asset position, or maximum debt position, in which the constraint switches from binding in at least some states to nonbinding in all states of nature.[11] Thus, even though the credit constraint is modeled in terms of the *ratio* of debt to current income, optimal "debt management" by liquidity-constrained agents yields a stochastic steady state in which the *level* of the stock of foreign debt never exceeds an endogenous maximum. This level corresponds to the maximum stationary debt position that can be supported with the credit constraint marginally nonbinding under the worst-case-scenario, in which productivity is low, the world real interest is high, and the consumption tax is high. Hence, the liquidity constraint is an effective means to induce credit-market outcomes in which debt is "rationed" and as a result in-

---

11. These features of the limiting distributions of assets in economies with precautionary saving with and without liquidity constraints are qualitatively identical to those obtained in the recent literature on the consumption function in partial equilibrium (see Carroll 2000).

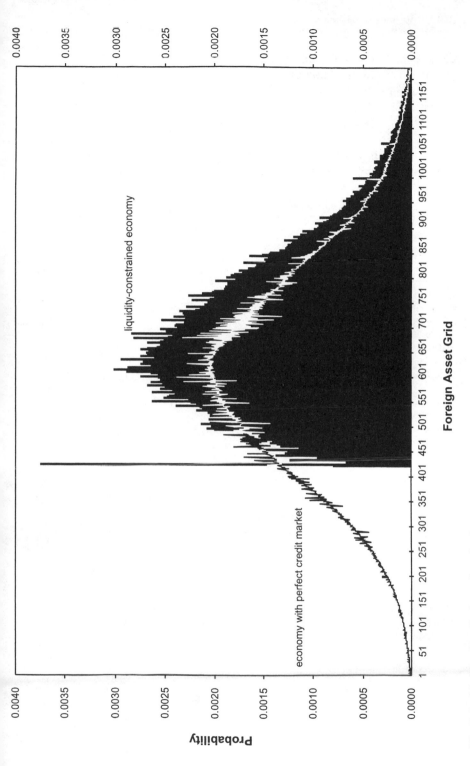

Fig. 7.4 Limiting distributions of net foreign assets

centives to default are weakened, albeit only in the long run. In the short run, the distribution of foreign assets adjusts gradually to reach the limiting distribution, and there are positive-probability states of nature in which debt is high and the economy is exposed to sudden stops depending on the realizations of real and policy-induced shocks.

Table 7.3 lists the business-cycle comovements that correspond to the limiting distributions of the economies with and without liquidity constraints. Both model economies yield standard deviations (relative to the

Table 7.3   Business Cycle Comovements in the Limiting Distribution of Model Economies

	Mean	Standard Deviation	Standard Deviation Relative to GDP of Nontradables	First-Order Autocorrelation	Correlation with GDP
Economy with perfect credit markets					
Net foreign assets	−0.097	0.883	14.274	0.999	0.321
GDP in units of tradables	2.598	7.307	1.829	0.931	1.000
Tradables GDP	1.000	3.368	0.843	0.553	0.387
Nontradables GDP	1.548	3.995	1.000	0.633	0.387
Labor	0.524	5.003	1.252	0.928	0.976
Consumption	0.924	6.254	1.565	0.839	0.823
Consumption of tradables	0.683	10.162	2.544	0.934	0.996
Consumption of nontradables	1.097	5.635	1.411	0.633	0.387
Net exports	0.002	25.987	6.504	0.623	−0.025
Price of nontradables	1.033	11.925	2.985	0.815	0.874
World real interest rate	1.016	0.880	0.220	0.553	−0.071
Economy with liquidity constraint					
Net foreign assets	0.258	0.679	10.957	0.999	0.313
GDP in units of tradables	2.612	7.323	1.830	0.931	1.000
Tradables GDP	1.000	3.368	0.842	0.553	0.391
Nontradables GDP	1.549	4.002	1.000	0.633	0.391
Labor	0.525	5.008	1.252	0.928	0.978
Consumption	0.927	6.266	1.566	0.838	0.823
Consumption of tradables	0.688	10.158	2.538	0.934	0.996
Consumption of nontradables	1.098	5.643	1.410	0.633	0.391
Net exports	−0.004	9.150	2.287	0.599	−0.003
Price of nontradables	1.041	11.880	2.969	0.815	0.874
World real interest rate	1.016	0.880	0.220	0.553	−0.069

Note: All standard deviations are in percent of the corresponding mean, except for that corresponding to the net foreign asset position.

standard deviation of nontradables GDP) and first-order autocorrelations for aggregate consumption and the relative price of nontradables that mimic closely those observed in the data (see table 5.1). The variability of total output and sectoral outputs is somewhat smaller in the models than in the data.

The liquidity constraint has a clear effect on the first and second moments of net foreign assets and net exports, but the rest of the moments listed in table 5.3 vary slightly. The mean of net foreign assets increases and their variability diminishes when the liquidity constraint is present. Clearly, except for these changes in the moments of external variables, the possibility of sudden stops that results from the liquidity constraint has a negligible effect on the long-run business-cycle comovements of the economy.

Figure 7.5 plots the impact effects of a switch from the "best" state with regard to exogenous shocks (i.e., $\varepsilon = 0.0336$, $\varepsilon^R = -0.0088$, $\tau = 0.021$) to the "worst" state (i.e., $\varepsilon = -0.0336$, $\varepsilon^R = 0.0088$, $\tau = 0.118$) as a function of the first 600 coordinates in the foreign-asset grid. Impact effects are reported again for the cases with and without liquidity constraint. These impact effects can be classified into three distinct ranges. First, for a range of sufficiently high foreign asset positions (i.e., low debt) the constraint does not bind, and the impact effects are the same in the two economies. A switch to the "worst" state increases the debt-GDP ratio and widens the current account deficit as a share of GDP. GDP at tradable goods prices, consumption, consumption of tradables, labor, the price of nontradables, and output of nontradables all fall sharply (the declines range from 10 to 20 percent relative to the level in the "best" state). These effects are in line with the wealth and substitution effects described in section 7.3 for the economy without credit constraints. Note also that in the economy without liquidity constraints the magnitude of the effects is roughly the same for *any* foreign asset position (except that the decline in b_{t+1}/Y_t is larger the lower is b_t). Thus, the economy without liquidity constraints *cannot* explain sudden stops, even though it features precautionary saving and its long-run business-cycle moments are similar to those of the economy with liquidity constraints.

The second relevant range of impact effects corresponds to values of b_t lower than the 364th coordinate in the foreign asset grid. In this range, the liquidity constraint is binding regardless of the realizations of the shocks, and hence b_{t+1}/Y_t cannot change across states of nature. Still, the constraint is not equally binding in each state so the other impact effects in figure 7.5 vary. In particular, for this range of foreign asset positions, the declines in Y_t, C_t, C_t^T, L_t, p_t^N, and Y_t^N are smaller the higher the stock of initial debt (i.e., the lower b_t). For foreign asset positions lower than coordinate 100 in the grid, it is even possible to obtain declines in labor supply and nontradables GDP *smaller* than those obtained in the absence of the credit constraint, because the effect of the higher marginal reward on labor supply outweighs all of the other supply and demand effects described earlier. However, this

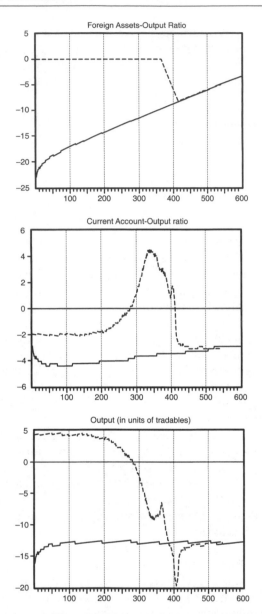

Fig. 7.5 Percent impact effects of a shift from "best" to "worst" state as a function of net foreign assets.

range of foreign asset positions is of little interest because it has a negligible steady-state probability of being observed (see fig. 7.4), and in the economy with credit constraints they represent states from which the economy departs very quickly and has zero probability of returning to. The latter can be observed in figure 7.6, which plots the transitional dynamics of the PDF of foreign assets in the liquidity-constrained economy starting from the lowest

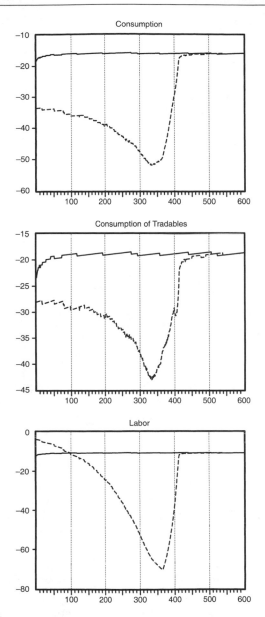

Fig. 7.5   (cont.)

value of b. There is zero probability of observing values of b lower than the 200th coordinate after only two quarters.

The third range of impact effects is particularly important because it corresponds to cases in which the credit constraint is not binding in some states of nature but shifts to become binding in others. In figure 7.5, the constraint shifts from nonbinding to binding as the economy switches from the "best"

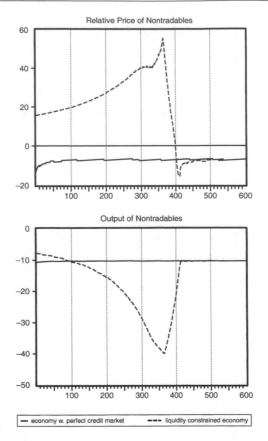

Fig. 7.5   (cont.)

to the "worst" state for values of b_t between the 364th and 417th coordinates in the foreign asset grid. There is still room for adjustment in the b/Y ratio because the constraint is not binding in the "best" state, but the adjustment is smaller than in the economy with perfect credit markets. At the high end of this range, the model yields sudden stop dynamics with a large reversal in the current account deficit and collapses in Y_t, C_t, C_t^T, L_t, p_t^N, and Y_t^N larger than those of the economy with perfect credit markets. These larger collapses follow from the intuition developed to explain the impact effect of a tax hike on labor supply in section 7.3 using equation (13). However, note that in the figure the shift is not only from low to high tax but also from high productivity and low world real interest rate to the opposite condition. This explains why in part of the sudden stop range it is possible for labor and nontradables output to fall sharply even in states in which the price of nontradables is actually rising sharply.

Sudden stops are dramatic events but they are also relatively rare. The range of foreign asset positions that support sudden stops is nearly ruled out of the limiting PDF of foreign assets in the credit-constrained economy by

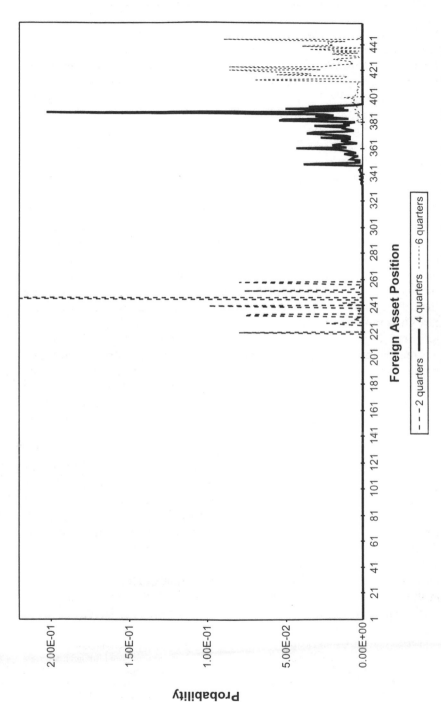

Fig. 7.6   Transition distributions of net foreign assets in a liquidity-constrained economy (from largest initial debt position and random shocks in state 1)

the households' precautionary saving. The only relevant coordinate is the maximum debt point identified earlier, in which the economy is on the threshold of moving into states in which the constraint is not binding regardless of the realizations of the shocks. However, in contrast with the high-debt states from which the economy moves away nearly instantaneously, figure 7.6 shows that even after four to six quarters of transitional dynamics (starting from a high-debt state) the economy is still in a range in which sudden stops are very likely. Thus, due to both the skewness of the steady-state distribution of foreign assets around the sudden stop threshold and the high probability of transiting through states in which sudden stops are very likely off the steady state, one can conjecture that small *unexpected* real shocks or disturbances to market access can be a powerful trigger of sudden stops.

What is the welfare cost of the credit constraint that drives sudden stops? Figure 7.7 plots welfare costs measured as percent compensating variations in consumption across time and states of nature that equalize the lifetime utilities of the economies with and without the constraint. The chart plots the costs at the "best" and "worst" realizations of the exogenous shocks and the conditional mean cost across shocks for given values of b_t. These welfare costs follow a similar pattern as the impact effects of figure 7.5. In the low-debt (high b_t) range in which the liquidity constraint is not binding for any realization of the shocks, there is virtually no welfare loss. Welfare costs rise as the initial foreign asset position falls into the sudden stop range. The largest loss in this range reaches about 0.6 percent. Finally, in the high-debt (low b_t) range in which the constraint binds regardless of the state of nature, welfare costs rise rapidly as b_t falls. The cost reaches 16 percent at the lowest b_t and the "worst" state of nature.

The information contained in the state-contingent welfare losses of figure 7.7 can be aggregated by computing the unconditional mean of welfare costs using the limiting PDF of the economy with perfect credit markets. The mean welfare cost equals 0.3 percent. A comparison of figures 7.4 and 7.7 shows that this estimate reflects mainly welfare losses in the sudden stop range. A cost of 0.3 percent is large when compared to existing results that show that the cost of giving up foreign asset trading to offset business-cycle risk is negligible (see Mendoza 1991a and Cole and Obstfeld 1991). Mendoza estimated the cost at 0.02 percent using a small open economy model with incomplete insurance markets but perfect credit markets calibrated to Canada.[12] The mean welfare cost of the liquidity constraint is fifteen times larger.[13]

12. The model in Mendoza (1991a) includes investment, which gives households a vehicle for precautionary saving even when the economy moves into international financial autarky. The two exercises would not be comparable otherwise because, in the absence of investment, households in that model would have to consume their random endowments each period.

13. A key determinant of the mean welfare cost is the position of the "maximum debt" in the PDF of foreign assets of the credit-constrained economy relative to the mean foreign asset position with perfect credit markets. In the simulations conducted here, that maximum debt is lower than the mean b of the unconstrained economy. Mendoza (2001) finds a much larger expected welfare cost of 4.6 percent when the opposite occurs.

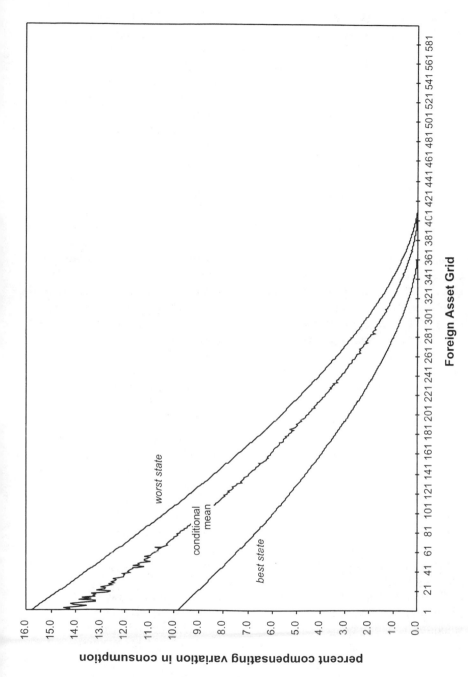

Fig. 7.7 State-contingent welfare losses induced by liquidity constraints

The welfare costs of sudden stops plotted in figure 7.7 have an interesting policy interpretation as measures of the welfare costs associated with an unexpected structural shock that permanently increases φ from φ ≤ 0.445 to φ = 0.714 (the values that support the unconstrained and constrained limiting PDFs in fig. 7.4). This shock can be interpreted as a permanent exogenous shock to world credit-market access or as a domestic policy action aimed at avoiding BOP crises by limiting the ability of the private sector to contract foreign debt (i.e., by introducing capital controls). The intuition under both interpretations is that before the permanent, unanticipated shock to φ, the long-run probability of observing a particular debt position was determined by the PDF of the economy with perfect credit markets. From each of these possible initial conditions, the economy suffers the welfare losses plotted in figure 7.7 as a result of the permanent shock to the ability to borrow. These losses capture the entire transitional dynamics to the new stochastic steady state of the credit-constrained economy. The average loss at 0.3 percent is not excessive, but the losses associated with high-debt scenarios that reach up to 16 percent with positive probability are staggering. The permanent shock to the ability to borrow sets these vulnerable high-debt economies on an adjustment path in which sudden stops are very likely to occur, as the transitional distributions in figure 7.6 show, even though sudden stops are very rare in the long run.

The above results suggest two important lessons. First, well-intentioned policies aimed at preventing sudden stops by introducing capital controls are counterproductive. They increase the probability of sudden stops in the short run and can entail substantial welfare costs. Second, persistent changes on the creditworthiness of emerging economies have the perverse effect of also leading to an increased short-run probability of sudden stops. Foreign creditors may try to manage default risk by increasing φ, but in doing so they also increase the probability of sudden stop–like crises that might have first motivated the increase in φ.

The liquidity constraint also has interesting implications for the welfare cost of business cycles. The cost of business cycles is measured by the compensating variation in consumption across time and states of nature that equalizes the expected lifetime utility of the stochastic model and the deterministic lifetime utility of the same model under perfect foresight (with the shocks set at their mean values). It is well known from the analysis in Lucas (1987) that the cost of business cycles is very small in models with CRRA utility and trend-stationary consumption for any reasonable values of the standard deviation of consumption and the coefficient of relative risk aversion—Lucas's estimates for the U.S. economy range between 0.008 and 0.040 percent for risk aversion coefficients between 1 and 5.

In the model examined here, the mean welfare cost of business cycles is also very small with or without the liquidity constraint. However, business cycles can be significantly more costly for the liquidity-constrained economy. Mean welfare costs of business cycles conditional on the foreign asset position are plotted in figure 7.8. The cost of business cycles is uniformly higher for the liquidity-constrained economy, by as much as 0.5 percent, than for the economy with perfect credit markets in the range of foreign asset positions near the maximum allowable debt (between coordinates 413 and 595 in the foreign asset grid). The costs are approximately the same for higher foreign asset positions.[14] Relative to the mean welfare cost of business cycles in the economy with perfect credit markets *conditional* on values of b higher than the maximum debt of the debt-constrained economy, the mean cost of business cycles under a liquidity constraint exceeds the cost under perfect credit markets by 0.03 percentage points.

The mean cost of business cycles remains small inasmuch as the model retains features similar to those behind Lucas's calculations. It is well known that deviations from his setup can result in much larger estimates of welfare costs of business cycles. For example, if business-cycle risk affects long-run growth (see Aizenman and Marion 1993; Ramey and Ramey 1995; Mendoza 1997), the cost of business cycles can be very large. The aim of the comparison of costs of business cycles conducted here, however, is simply to show that the cost is higher with credit frictions than without them within a standard business-cycle framework.[15]

7.4.3   Sensitivity Analysis: Risk Aversion and Sources of Shocks

The analysis of the dynamics of the model under a liquidity constraint suggests that the quantitative results should depend critically on the coefficient of relative risk aversion, which drives the desire to undertake precautionary saving. The sensitivity of the results to changes in this parameter is examined next. In addition, because some emerging economies that suffered sudden stops are believed to have been less susceptible to policy uncertainty than Mexico, it is worth examining whether the model can generate sudden stops only as a result of exogenous shocks to productivity or the world real interest rate.

An increase in the coefficient of relative risk aversion σ from 2 to 5 significantly increases the incentive to undertake precautionary saving for both the economy with perfect credit markets and the economy with liq-

---

14. Note that for high values of b, in figure 7.8 the welfare cost can be negative (i.e., eliminating all shocks to productivity, the interest rate and taxes can *reduce* welfare). This deviates from the standard result in models like Lucas's because in the incomplete-markets, precautionary-saving model examined here, the elimination of uncertainty has implications for wealth and relative prices. In particular, eliminating tax policy uncertainty eliminates the Calvo-Drazen fiscal-induced wealth effect. If the exercise is repeated without considering tax shocks, the cost of business cycles is small but always positive.

15. Because precautionary saving is one of the mechanisms that drive the linkage between volatility and growth, and the same mechanism drives the dynamics of the credit-constrained economy, it is likely that welfare costs of business cycles will remain higher with credit constraints than without them even in the presence of a linkage between volatility and growth.

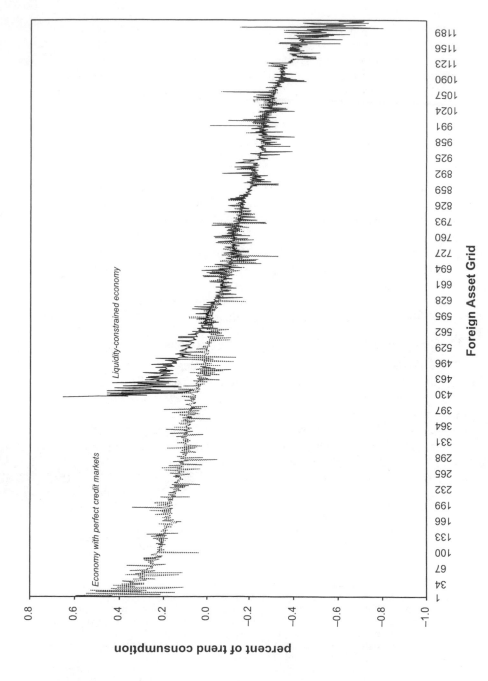

Fig. 7.8   Welfare cost of business cycles (conditional mean across exogenous shock given the net foreign asset position)

uidity constraints. In the economy with perfect credit markets, the mean net foreign asset position increases to 1.35, compared to –0.097 when $\sigma = 2$ (the mean debt-output ratio rises to 0.43, compared to –0.045). The features of business cycles across economies with $\sigma = 2$ and $\sigma = 5$ differ. In particular, the standard deviations of C^T and P^N increase by 0.75 and 3 percentage points respectively, and those of L, Y^N, C^N, and C fall by 0.5 to 0.75 percentage points. However, it is still the case that with $\sigma = 5$ business cycles do not differ much across economies with and without liquidity constraints. When we examine the impact effects of a switch from the "best" to the "worst" state, it also remains the case that the economy with perfect credit markets does not display sudden stops, whereas the economy with the liquidity constraint features a region of foreign asset positions in which sudden stops occur. The features of these sudden stops are qualitatively similar to the ones obtained with $\sigma = 2$, except that with the higher value of σ the impact effect on the price of nontradables is always positive (both with and without the liquidity constraint). In general, the result that the model with the liquidity constraint displays sudden stops while showing similar long-run business-cycle comovements to the economy with perfect credit markets is robust to the increase in σ.

The higher value of σ has important implications for the transitional dynamics of the probability distribution of the model's state variables. In particular, as a comparison of figures 7.6 and 7.9 shows, the distribution (starting from the largest debt position in the state space) converges to the limiting distribution at a much slower pace. Although with $\sigma = 2$ the distribution is out of the sudden stop range after six quarters, in the case with $\sigma = 5$ the distribution assigns a significant probability mass to debt positions in which sudden stops can occur even after fifty quarters. Similarly, the increased degree of risk aversion results in higher welfare costs induced by the liquidity constraint and in relatively higher welfare costs of business cycles with liquidity constraints than with perfect credit markets. The expected welfare cost of the credit constraint increases sharply, to 22.8 percent. The mean cost of business cycles is 3.8 times larger with the liquidity constraint than with perfect credit markets, although the costs of business cycles are still small in both cases (the costs are 0.074 percent with liquidity constraints and 0.019 percent with perfect credit markets).

The sensitivity analysis for the case in which the economy does not face tax policy uncertainty shows important differences in business-cycle properties relative to the baseline economy with tax shocks. In particular, there is a marked fall in the cyclical variability of all macroeconomic aggregates and in their correlations with output. However, when we compare across economies without tax shocks, business cycle regularities continue to be roughly the same with and without liquidity constraints.

Sudden stops also continue to be a feature of the impact effects of the liquidity-constrained economy in response to a switch from a high-

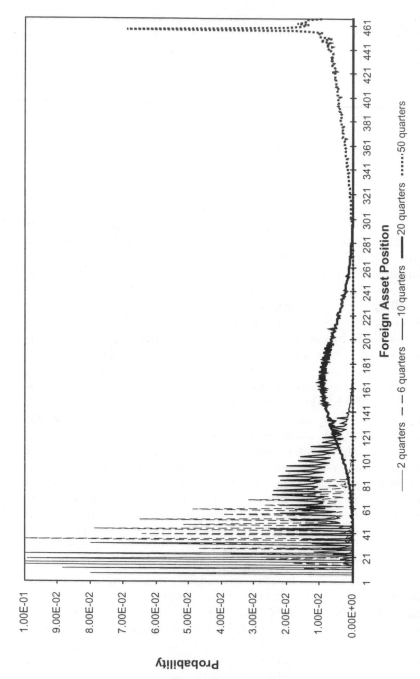

Fig. 7.9 Transition distributions of net foreign assets in a liquidity-constrained economy with risk aversion coefficient set at 5 (from largest initial debt position and random shocks in state 1)

productivity, low–interest rate state to a low-productivity, high–interest rate state when initial debt is sufficiently large. The collapses in labor and aggregate consumption are smaller than in the presence of tax shocks. Without tax shocks, the largest collapses are equal to 35 and 23 percent for labor and consumption respectively, compared to 70 and 45 percent in the economy with tax shocks. Declines in the price of nontradables are harder to account for without tax shocks, but this is true with or without the liquidity constraint—in both cases, the impact effect of a switch from the best to worst states is an increase in the price of nontradables. It is still the case, however, that for the region of the largest sudden stops in output and consumption, the level of the price of nontradables rises by less than in the economy with perfect credit markets. Thus, the key finding that liquidity constraints can result in short-lived sudden stops that are hard to notice in long-run business-cycle comovements is robust to the elimination of tax shocks. Sudden stops can be a feature of the dynamics of economies in which policy uncertainty is not an issue.

The absence of policy uncertainty does significantly alter the welfare implications of the model. Welfare costs of the liquidity constraint are smaller in the economy without tax shocks, as would be expected given the smaller magnitude of the sudden stops in this case. The expected welfare cost of the liquidity constraint falls from 0.3 percent with tax shocks to 0.1 percent without tax shocks. With regard to the effect of the liquidity constraint on the cost of business cycles, the cost of business cycles without tax shocks is roughly the same in the economy with perfect credit markets and in the economy with liquidity constraints (at about 0.14 percent).[16] Hence, in the absence of tax shocks the liquidity constraint has smaller welfare costs and does not increase the cost of business cycles. These results are more in line with Mendoza's (1991a) findings that showed small costs of forcing small open economies facing productivity shocks into international financial autarky.

7.5   Equity Prices, Margin Requirements, and Excess Volatility of Portfolio Flows

The framework developed in section 7.3 is modified here to propose a model in which a credit-market imperfection may induce large shifts in portfolio flows and equity prices. The model is based on a variation of a closed-economy model proposed by Aiyagari and Gertler (1999). The model considers agents in the domestic small open economy that trade

16. Interestingly, the mean cost of business cycles in these cases is *higher* than in the economy with tax shocks, in which the mean cost was less than 0.01 percent. This is because of the Calvo-Drazen fiscal-induced wealth effect triggered by tax shocks. Low-tax states increase wealth because of the implied reduction in unproductive government expenditures. Mendoza and Uribe (2001) showed that policy uncertainty can be welfare-improving in this case.

shares of their capital stock with foreign securities firms while being subject to margin requirements. Foreign firms specialize in holding equity of the small open economy and face portfolio adjustment costs that result from their disadvantaged position in trading equity relative to residents of that economy in terms of information or institutional features. Frankel and Schmukler (1996) provide empirical evidence suggesting that indeed foreign traders are at a disadvantage relative to traders in domestic equity markets of emerging economies.

The model is simplified to consider only a single, homogeneous tradable good. This offers two important advantages in setting up the asset pricing model. First, it implies that the GHH specification of the argument of utility eliminates the wealth effect on labor supply and completely isolates the labor supply decision from the dynamics of consumption, saving, and portfolio choices. Second, since the optimal labor demand and profits of firms are unaffected by credit frictions, the model features a supply side that corresponds exactly to that of a frictionless economy. As a result of these two features, equilibrium dividend streams and labor-market allocations are independent of saving decisions and credit frictions. The trade-off is that in this setting a sudden stop does not induce an unusually large output collapse, even though it still causes excessive current account reversals and collapses of private consumption.

Production is undertaken with the same Cobb-Douglas technology as before: $Y_t = \exp(\varepsilon_t)AK^{1-\alpha}L_t^{\alpha}$. Profit-maximizing firms choose labor demand so that at each date t, labor demand is given by the standard productivity condition

$$(15) \qquad \exp(\varepsilon_t)A\alpha K^{1-\alpha}L_t^{\alpha-1} = w_t.$$

Dividend payments are given by

$$(16) \qquad d_t = \exp(\varepsilon_t)A(1 - \alpha)K^{-\alpha}L_t^{\alpha}.$$

Expected lifetime utility is the same as before (except that C is now made of a single consumption good). Households maximize utility subject to the following budget constraint:

$$(17) \quad (1 + \tau_t)C_t = a_t Kd_t + w_t L_t + q_t(a_t - a_{t+1})K - b_{t+1} + b_t \exp(\varepsilon_t^R)R,$$

where τ_t is a random consumption tax (which can also be interpreted as an import tariff), a_t and a_{t+1} are beginning- and end-of-period shares of the domestic capital stock owned by domestic households, d_t are dividends paid by domestic firms, and q_t is the price of equity. Households also face a *margin requirement* according to which they must finance a fraction κ of their equity holdings out of current saving:

$$(18) \qquad a_t Kd_t + w_t L_t + q_t a_t K + b_t \exp(\varepsilon_t^R)R - (1 + \tau_t)C_t \geq \kappa q_t a_{t+1}K$$

Given the budget constraint, the margin requirement imposes a "collateral" constraint on foreign borrowing of the form

(19) $$b_{t+1} \geq -(1 - \kappa)q_t a_{t+1} K.$$

This constraint differs sharply from the liquidity requirement because it depends on the price of equity, which is a forward-looking variable. Note that the constraint can also be interpreted as restricting the stock of savings (i.e., $q_t a_{t+1} K + b_{t+1}$) to be larger than $\kappa q_t a_{t+1} K$.

The optimality conditions of the households' problem have similar features as before, except that a binding borrowing constraint does not distort labor supply and cannot induce distortions via the dynamics of relative goods prices. A binding borrowing constraint still increases the expected effective real interest rate of the small open economy relative to the world real interest rate. Furthermore, if the expected return on equity is defined as $E_t[R_{t+1}^q] \equiv E_t(d_{t+1} + q_{t+1})/q_t$, the optimality conditions on debt and equity yield the following expression for the equity premium:

(20) $$E_t[R_{t+1}^q] - E_t[\exp(\varepsilon_{t+1}^R)]R$$

$$= \frac{\eta_t - \text{cov}(\lambda_{t+1}, R_{t+1}^q) + \text{cov}(\lambda_{t+1}, \exp[\varepsilon_{t+1}^R]R)}{E_t(\lambda_{t+1})},$$

where λ and η are the nonnegative Lagrange multipliers on the budget constraint and the margin constraint, respectively.

If the world real interest rate is deterministic, the last covariance term in the numerator of the right-hand side of equation (20) vanishes. In this case, and if the margin requirement never binds (i.e., $\eta_t = 0$ for all t), the formula yields the standard equity-premium formula under perfect credit markets. In contrast, a binding margin requirement at date t (i.e., $\eta_t > 0$) causes an excess equity premium because the pressure that the margin call exerts on households to fire-sell equity depresses the current equity price. The effect of the binding margin constraint at t is likely to be persistent because, as shown below, foreign traders adjust their portfolios slowly.

When we use the standard forward-solution method, it follows that optimal portfolio decisions by agents in the small open economy require the equity price to satisfy

(21) $$q_t = E_t\left(\sum_{i=0}^{\infty} \left[\prod_{j=0}^{i} \frac{\lambda_{t+1+j}}{\lambda_{t+j} - \eta_{t+1}(1 - \kappa)} \right] d_{t+1+i} \right).$$

If the margin requirement never binds, this expression reduces to a standard asset-pricing formula. In the case that margin calls are possible, the effects on the price of equity are easier to interpret if the definition $E_t[R_{t+1}^q] \equiv E_t[(R_{t+1}^d + q_{t+1})/q_t]$ is used to rewrite equation (21) as follows:

(22)
$$q_t = E_t\left(\sum_{i=0}^{\infty}\left[\prod_{j=0}^{i}E_t[R_{t+1+j}^q]\right]^{-1}d_{t+1+i}\right),$$

where the sequence of $E_t[R_{t+1+j}^q]$ is given by equation (20). If margin requirements are binding at present or expected to bind in the future, some or all of the expected returns on equity used to discount the future stream of dividends in the above formula increase, and thus the current price of equity falls. Moreover, the date-t equity price falls whenever the margin requirement is expected to bind in the future, *even if it were not binding at date* t (i.e., all that is required for q_t to fall is that $\eta_{t+j} > 0$ for some $j > t$).

As in section 7.3, the government sets the value of the tax or tariff rate τ_t and uses the revenue to finance unproductive expenditures G_t, maintaining a balanced-budget policy:

(23)
$$G_t = \tau_t C_t$$

Thus, sudden changes in taxes or tariffs introduce the Calvo-Drazen fiscal-induced wealth effect present in the model with liquidity constraints.

Foreign securities firms maximize the present discounted value of dividends D to their global shareholders, facing a quadratic adjustment cost in adjusting equity positions in the small open economy. These firms choose their equity position a_{t+1}^* for $t = 0, \ldots, \infty$ so as to maximize

(24) $$D = E_0\left[\sum_{t=0}^{\infty}M_t\{a_t^*K(d_t + q_t) - q_t a_{t+1}^*K - q_t\left(\frac{s}{2}\right)[(a_{t+1}^* - a_t^*)K + \theta]^2\}\right]$$

where $M_0 \equiv 1$ and M_t for $t = 1, \ldots, \infty$ are the *exogenous* discount rates that apply to date-t dividends. The parameter s is a "speed-of-adjustment" coefficient, and θ is a long-run cost of holding a time-invariant equity position in the small open economy. This cost is assumed to be zero if the long-run equity price is to be equal to its "fundamentals" level, as defined below; otherwise the cost is positive and time invariant.

The first-order condition for the optimization problem of securities firms implies a partial-adjustment rule for their portfolio of the form

(25)
$$(a_{t+1}^* - a_t^*)K = s^{-1}\left(\frac{q_t^f}{q_t} - 1\right) - \theta,$$

where q_t^f is the "fundamentals" price of equity defined as

(26)
$$q_t^f = E_t\left(\sum_{i=1}^{\infty}\frac{M_{t+i}}{M_t}d_{t+1}\right).$$

According to equation (25), foreign firms increase their demand for equity by a fraction of the percent deviation of the date-t equity price below the corresponding fundamentals level. This adjustment in demand is inversely related to the value of s. Thus, the informational friction behind the portfolio adjustment cost is key to supporting *equilibrium* equity prices below the fundamentals levels. If securities firms could adjust their portfolios at no cost, households could liquidate the shares they need to meet margin calls at an infinitesimal price discount.

If the margin requirement never binds, the small open economy is one of many identical economies conforming the world economy, so the discount rates in equations (21) and (26) are the same. Thus, if the margin requirement never binds, the equilibrium price is the fundamentals price, and neither domestic residents or foreign traders alter their equity positions. If the constraint binds, however, q_t^f remains the same (because the discount rates of foreign traders are exogenous and the stream of dividends is independent of portfolio decisions), but the equilibrium equity price will fall below it depending on how much pressure the margin call puts on domestic residents to fire-sell equity relative to how quickly the foreign traders are able to adjust their portfolios.

The effects of exogenous shocks to global capital markets (such as shocks to the world real interest rate) on asset prices and equity flows can be examined using this model in an analogous manner to the "liquidity shocks" examined by Aiyagari and Gertler (1999). The effects of productivity shocks, policy shocks, and shocks to the margin coefficient κ can also be studied. These experiments would capture some of the features of the episode of waves of margin calls observed in the aftermath of the Russian default in 1998. During this episode, margin calls were triggered by increasing estimates of potential portfolio losses produced by the value-at-risk models of investment banks that leveraged the operations of hedge funds like Long Term Capital Management. As market volatility increased and asset prices plummeted, value-at-risk estimates worsened, thereby mandating even larger margin calls. Similarly, in the model, shocks that make equity prices fall below fundamentals trigger an endogenous increase in the level of the margin requirement (even if κ remains unchanged). The sharper the decline in equity prices, the larger the size of the margin call.

The model cannot be solved in closed form analytically, so the extent to which it can account for observed equity-price corrections and reversals of portfolio flows during sudden stops is left for further research (see Mendoza and Smith 2001). Nevertheless, the model's deterministic steady state offers interesting insights on the long-run implications of the margin constraint for asset prices. If the margin constraint is not binding at steady state (and hence the long-run portfolio adjustment cost vanishes), the steady-state equity price equals the fundamentals price: $\bar{q} = \bar{q}^f = \bar{d} / (R - 1)$. Implicit in this equality is the fact that the return on equity, $(\bar{q} + \bar{d}) / \bar{q}$, equals the gross rate of return on foreign assets (i.e., there is no equity premium).

If the margin requirement is binding at steady state (and hence $\theta > 0$), the partial-adjustment portfolio rule of securities firms implies that the steady-state equity price satisfies $\bar{q} = \bar{q}^f / (1 + s\theta) < \bar{q}^f$. This price is supported as an equilibrium price from the household's side because the margin requirement and the endogenous rate-of-time preference result in a long-run equity premium: the steady-state rate of return on equity exceeds the world risk-free rate of return by the amount $\kappa(\eta/\lambda)$. Thus, under the assumed specification of preferences, the financial and informational frictions implied by the margin constraint and the portfolio adjustment cost combine to yield a stationary equilibrium in which equity prices can deviate permanently from their fundamentals value and the margin constraint always binds.

7.6   Conclusions and Policy Implications

This paper provides an account of the sudden stops phenomenon of the 1990s emerging markets as an "excess volatility" phenomenon: that is, as unusually large recessions that go unnoticed in long-run business cycle comovements. Sudden stops occur when borrowing constraints become endogenously binding as a result of shocks to productivity, to the world real interest rate, or to domestic policy variables. This is possible because debt contracts are written in units of tradable goods, whereas part of the debt is leveraged on the income of the nontradables sector. Adverse real or policy shocks induce sharp collapses in the production or relative price of nontradables and thus contribute to the tightening of credit constraints. Sudden stops and large fluctuations in the real exchange rate occur in this economy even though goods and factor markets are competitive, prices are completely flexible, and the equilibrium is unique. In addition, welfare analysis shows that the social costs of these sudden stops can be large.

The findings of this study suggest that policy intervention is worth considering but also that the type of policies that can be effective for managing sudden stops need to be carefully chosen. Alternatives considered so far in the literature can be classified as siding with two approaches: an *isolationist* approach, which seeks to avoid sudden stops by imposing capital controls and limiting currency trading, and an *internationalist* approach, which aims to minimize sudden stops by promoting the global integration of domestic financial institutions and by abandoning weak domestic currencies with the adoption of hard currencies (i.e., dollarization).

Policies advocated by internationalists counter two important determinants of sudden stops identified in this paper: the lack of credibility of economic policies in emerging-markets countries and the perverse combination of heavy need but weak incentives for gathering costly information about these countries by global investors and lenders that drives credit-market imperfections (see Calvo and Mendoza 2000b). Dollarization, for example, does away with the need to keep track of country-specific monetary and exchange rate policies, which have proven extremely volatile and hard to predict in periods of capital-markets turbulence. A similar principle applies to fiscal and trade policies that follow regimes with uncertain duration, but which are harder to make credible. Mendoza (2001) finds that the benefits of increased policy credibility in the case of dollarization can be very large. The results of this paper show in addition that the potential gains of structural policies that permanently improve a country's ability to access global capital markets can be substantial.

The analysis of the paper sheds light on some of the drawbacks of policies advocated by isolationists. The dynamic general-equilibrium nature of the model fleshes out the tension between the short-term aim of using capital controls or regulatory practices to target the debt-output ratio of an economy to prevent a sudden stop and the dynamic implications of this policy. For the policy to effectively remove the risk of sudden stops, it must ensure that exposure to large capital outflows is fully avoided, but this can only be guaranteed in the long run and if the stock of foreign liabilities is severely restricted. However, the dynamic welfare cost of this policy can be potentially large because the situation can be viewed as a worst-case scenario equivalent to one in which the model's borrowing constraints are very tight. Sudden stops are avoided, domestic saving is high, and long-run private consumption is high, but this is the result of very costly distortions on short-run dynamics. Moreover, for economies starting from a position of high debt, the implementation of policies to target the debt-output ratio increases the short-run probability and magnitude of sudden stops.

Policies less drastic than capital controls but with a similar aim of stabilizing capital flows—such as short-selling constraints, margin requirements, and collateral constraints linked to value-at-risk estimates—have other negative features. Short-selling constraints exacerbate the loss of incentives to gather costly information, as Calvo and Mendoza (2000b) showed, whereas margin requirements and collateral constraints strengthen the mechanisms that drive excess volatility of asset prices and international capital flows examined in this paper.

The model proposed here is only a first approximation to study sudden stops as an excess volatility phenomenon within a dynamic general equilibrium framework. Three obvious directions for further research are to study the asset-pricing implications of models similar to the one sketched in section 7.5, to introduce capital accumulation and monetary transmission mechanisms, and to endogenize the microfoundations of the credit frictions within the macroeconomic model.

Appendix A

Given the assumptions made in section 7.3 about the lifetime utility function and its components u, v, C, and H, it is easy, although lengthy, to show that the first-order conditions for the households' optimization problem can be reduced to the following expressions:

(A1) $\quad U_C(t)\left(1 - \dfrac{\mu_t}{\lambda_t}\right) = \exp[-v(t)]E_t\left[\dfrac{Rp_t^C(1 + \tau_t^C)}{p_{t+1}^C(1 + \tau_{t+1}^C)}U_C(t + 1)\right]$

(A2) $\quad \dfrac{C_{C^N}(t)(1 + \tau_t^T)}{C_{C^T}(t)(1 + \tau_t^N)} = p_t^N$

(A3) $\quad H'(L_t) = \left[\dfrac{w_t}{p_t^C(1 + \tau_t^N)}\right]\left(1 + \dfrac{\mu_t}{\lambda_t}\dfrac{1 - \varphi}{\varphi}\right)$

The nonnegative multipliers on the liquidity constraint and the budget constraint are μ and λ, respectively. The terms in U_C are derivatives of *lifetime* utility with respect to C. These include "impatience effects," by which changes in consumption or labor supply at any date t alter the rate at which all period utilities after t are discounted.

Appendix B

The competitive equilibrium of the small open economy described in section 7.3 can be characterized as the solution to the following social planner's problem. The state variables of the system at any date t include $b = b_t$ and the observed realizations of the exogenous shocks $\psi \equiv (\varepsilon_t^T, \varepsilon_t^N, \varepsilon_t^R, \tau_t)$. Conditional on these state variables and the Markov processes driving the shocks, the planner chooses an optimal value for $b' \equiv b_{t+1}$ so as to solve the following Bellman equation:

(B1) $\quad V(b, \psi) = \max\{u[\hat{C} - H(\hat{L})]$

$\qquad\qquad + \exp[-v[\hat{C} - H(\hat{L})]]E[V(b', \psi')]\}$

subject to

(B2) $\quad (1 + \tau)\hat{C}^T + \tau\hat{p}^N\hat{C}^N = \exp(\varepsilon^T)Y^T - b' + b\exp(\varepsilon^R)R - T^T$

(B3) $\qquad\qquad\quad \hat{C}^N = \exp(\varepsilon^N)F(K, \hat{L}) - G^N$

(B4) $\quad b' \geq -\left(\dfrac{1 - \varphi}{\varphi}\right)[\exp(\varepsilon^T)Y^T + \hat{p}^N\exp(\varepsilon^N)F(K, \hat{L})]$.

The variables in "hats" represent solutions of a system of four nonlinear simultaneous equations in four unknowns for each coordinate (b, b', ψ) in the state space. If the liquidity constraint in equation (B4) is not binding, the system includes the equilibrium conditions that equate the marginal rate of substitution of C^T and C^N with p^N (eq. [A2]) and the marginal rate of substitution between labor and C^T with the effective real wage (eq. [A3]), and the market-clearing conditions in equations (B2) and (B3). If the liquidity constraint is binding, equation (B4) holds with equality and replaces the labor-consumption optimality condition in equation (A3). The solutions to this system are not the equilibrium of the model, but represent allocations of the "hat" variables that satisfy a subset of the equilibrium conditions given any arbitrary set (b, b', ψ) in the state space.

The above dynamic programming problem is solved by iterations on the Bellman equation in a "discrete" state space. This method accurately captures the nonlinearities induced by the liquidity constraint, although it is slow and memory-intensive.

References

Agenor, Pierre-Richard, C. John McDermott, and Eswar S. Prasad. 2000. Macroeconomic fluctuations in developing countries: Some stylized facts. *World Bank Economic Review*, forthcoming.

Aghion, Philippe, Philippe Bacchetta, and Abhijit Banerjee. 2000. Currency crises and monetary policy with credit constraints. Harvard University, Department of Economics. Mimeograph.

Aiyagari, S. Rao. 1993. Explaining financial market facts: The importance of incomplete markets and transaction costs. *Federal Reserve Bank of Minneapolis Quarterly Review* 17:17–31.

Aiyagari, S. Rao, and Mark Gertler. 1999. "Overreaction" of asset prices in general equilibrium. *Review of Economic Dynamics* 2:3–35.

Aizenman, Joshua, and Nancy Marion. 1993. Policy uncertainty, persistence, and growth. *Review of International Economics* 1 (2): 145–63.

Bernanke, Ben, Mark Gertler, and Simon Gilchrist. 1998. The financial accelerator in a quantitative business cycle framework. NBER Working Paper no. 6455. Cambridge, Mass.: National Bureau of Economic Research.

Cabellero, Ricardo J., and Arvind Krishnamurthy. 1999. Emerging markets crises: An asset markets perspective. MIT, Sloan School of Business. Mimeograph.

Calvo, Guillermo A. 1986. Temporary stabilization: Predetermined exchange rates. *Journal of Political Economy* 94:1319–29.

———. 1998. Capital flows and capital-market crises: The simple economics of sudden stops. *Journal of Applied Economics* 1:35–54.

Calvo, Guillermo A., and Allan Drazen. 1998. Uncertain duration of reform: Dynamic implications. *Macroeconomic Dynamics* 2:443–55.

Calvo, Guillermo A., and Enrique G. Mendoza. 2000a. Capital-markets crises and economic collapse in emerging markets: An informational-frictions approach. *American Economic Review: Papers and Proceedings* 90 (2): 59–64.

———. 2000b. Rational contagion and the globalization of securities markets. *Journal of International Economics* 51:79–113.

Calvo, Guillermo A., and Carmen M. Reinhart. 1999. When capital inflows come to a sudden stop: Consequences and policy options. University of Maryland, Department of Economics, Center for International Economics. Mimeograph.

Carroll, Christopher D. 2000. A theory of the consumption function, with and without liquidity constraints. Johns Hopkins University, Department of Economics. Mimeograph.

Christiano, Lawrence J., Christopher Gust, and Jorge Roldos. 2000. Monetary policy in an international financial crisis. International Monetary Fund, Research Department. Mimeograph.

Cole, Harold L., and Maurice Obstfeld. 1991. Commodity trade and international risk sharing: How much do financial markets matter? *Journal of Monetary Economics* 28:3–24.

Dornbusch, Rudiger, and Alejandro Werner. 1994. Mexico: Stabilization, reform, and no growth. Brookings Papers on Economic Activity, Issue no. 1:253–316. Washington, D.C.: Brookings Institute.

Eaton, Jonathan, and Mark Gersovitz. 1981. Debt with potential repudiation: Theoretical and empirical analysis. *Review of Economic Studies* 48:289–309.

Edwards, Sebastian. 1986. Are devaluations contradictory? *Review of Economics and Statistics* 68:501–08.

Epstein, Larry G. 1983. Stationary cardinal utility and optimal growth under uncertainty. *Journal of Economic Theory* 31:133–52.

Fisher, Irving. 1933. The debt-deflation theory of great depressions. *Econometrica* 1:337–57.

Forbes, Kristin, and Roberto Rigobon. 1999. No contagion, only interdependence: Measuring stock market co-movements. NBER Working Paper no. 7267. Cambridge, Mass.: National Bureau of Economic Research, July.

Frankel, Jeffrey A., and Sergio Schmukler. 1996. Country fund discounts and the Mexican crisis of December 1994. Open Economies Review 7 (1, Suppl.): 551–84.

Greenwood, Jeremy, Zvi Hercowitz, and Gregory W. Huffman. 1988. Investment, capacity utilization, and the real business cycle. *American Economic Review* 87: 402–17.

Guerra de Luna, Alfonso. 1997. La relevancia macroeconómica de los bienes raíces en México [The macroeconomic significance of real estate in Mexico]. Serie Documentos de Investigación, Documento no. 9707, Dirección General de Investigación Económica. Mexico City: Banco de México.

———. 1998. Capital inflows and mortgage crisis: The case of Mexico. Mexico City: Banco de México, Economic Studies Division. Mimeograph.

International Monetary Fund (IMF). 1999. International capital markets, September. Washington, D.C.: IMF.

Kaminsky, Graciela L., and Carmen M. Reinhart. 2000. On crises, contagion, and confusion. *Journal of International Economics* 51:145–68.

Kiyotaki, Nobuhiro, and John Moore. 1997. Credit cycles. *Journal of Political Economy* 105:211–48.

Lane, Philip, and Gian Maria Milesi-Ferretti. 1999. The external wealth of nations: Measures of foreign assets and liabilities for industrial and developing countries. IMF Working Paper no. WP/99/115. Washington, D.C.: International Monetary Fund.

Lucas, Robert E., Jr. 1987. *Models of business cycles.* New York: Basil Blackwell.

Ludvigson, Sydney. 1996. Consumption and credit: A model of time-varying liquidity constraints. Ph.D. diss. Department of Economics, Princeton University.

Mendoza, Enrique, G. 1991a. Capital controls and the gains from trade in a business cycle model of a small open economy. *IMF Staff Papers* 38 (September): 480–505.

———. 1991b. Real business cycles in a small open economy. *American Economic Review* 81 (September): 797–818.

———. 1995. The terms of trade, the real exchange rate, and economic fluctuations. *International Economic Review* 36 (February): 101–37.

———. 1997. Terms-of-trade uncertainty and economic growth. *Journal of Development Economics* 54:323–56.

———. 2001. The benefits of dollarization when stabilization policy lacks credibility and financial markets are imperfect. *Journal of Money, Credit, and Banking* 33 (2): 440–74.

Mendoza, Enrique G., and Katherine A. Smith. 2001. Margin calls, trading costs, and the sudden stops of capital inflows into emerging markets. Duke University, Department of Economics. Mimeograph.

Mendoza, Enrique G., and Martin Uribe. 2000. Devaluation risk and the business cycle implications of exchange rate management. *Carnegie-Rochester Conference Series on Public Policy* 53:239–96.

Ostry, Jonathan D., and Carmen M. Reinhart. 1992. Private saving and terms of trade shocks. *IMF Staff Papers* 39:495–517.

Paasche, Bernhard. 2001. Credit constraints and international financial crises. Journal of Monetary Economics, forthcoming.

Ramey, Garey, and Valerie A. Ramey. 1995. Cross-country evidence on the link between volatility and growth. *American Economic Review* 85:1138–51.

Schneider, Martin, and Aaron Tornell. 2000. Balance sheet effects, bailout guarantees, and financial crises. NBER Working Paper no. 8060. Cambridge, Mass.: National Bureau of Economic Research, December.

Comment   Joshua Aizenman

This very interesting paper addresses a question of great importance to emerging markets—the welfare cost of sudden stops and policy uncertainty. My comments begin with an overview of the paper and close with a discussion of the robustness of the analysis and the policy conclusions.

The purpose of this paper is to interpret sudden stops in the context of a real business cycle (RBC) model with exogenous liquidity constraints. Mendoza uses the proposed model to find the welfare cost of sudden stops and to identify the welfare effects of several policies.

The model focuses on a flexible-price economy with an exogenous stock of capital and a flexible labor market. The financial friction is an exogenous stock/flow borrowing constraint—the present debt can not exceed a constant fraction of current income. The economy is composed of two sectors: a traded and a nontraded sector. All borrowing is done in terms of the traded good. Endogenous discounting allows the model to support an equilibrium in which the credit friction may remain binding in the long run.

Joshua Aizenman is professor of economics at the University of California, Santa Cruz, and a research associate of the National Bureau of Economic Research.

The policy uncertainty is due to exogenous switches between a high and a low tax rate regime. The two sectors are taxed at the same rate. Government expenditure is "wasteful"—it does not affect private utility. The tax shocks are calibrated to mimic the price distortions on saving and labor supply induced by the sudden devaluation in Mexico.

The shocks imply that the liquidity constraint would bind in "bad" states. The liability dollarization magnifies the ultimate welfare effects of negative shocks. The model interprets sudden stops as unusually large recessions that may go unnoticed in long-run business-cycle co-movements. The social costs of sudden stops can be large relative to previous RBC results—0.3 percent in the paper's benchmark calibration (recall that in RBC models with perfect credit markets, the welfare cost of business cycles is very small: 0.01 percent in Lucas 1987).

The main policy lessons are these:

- Regulations that intend to reduce large capital inflows (e.g., liquidity requirements, margin requirements, etc.) can increase the likelihood and severity of sudden stop events.
- Financial arrangements that can effectively preempt sudden stops need to feature complex state-contingent clauses or credibly commit a large amount of funds.
- Beneficial long-term policies include micropolicies (credit bureaus) and macropolicies (dollarization, currency unions, internationalization of financial systems).

The questions addressed are very important. The model and the analysis are competently executed, yet the modeling strategy leaves one skeptical about the conclusions. My main concerns are these:

- The model does not fit a "Korean-type" sudden stop.
- The model may understate the cost of sudden stops, due to the reliance on the RBC approach augmented to allow for an exogenous stock/flow borrowing constraint.
- "Lucas critic" issues limit the ability of the present model to guide us regarding policies.

Sources of Volatility: Domestic Policies Versus "Erratic Access" to International Borrowing

The paper models the outcome of domestic tax policy uncertainty in the presence of exogenous liquidity constraints. These assumptions may fit Mexico, yet the model is a poor description of some countries in the Far East, such as Korea. Before the crisis, the global market viewed Korea as having a stable and responsible fiscal policy. Koreans dubbed the 1997 crisis the "IMF crisis," reflecting the view that the crisis was the outcome of Korea's growing exposure to external exogenous uncertainty. An interesting result that may support this interpretation is the finding (reported in section 7.4.2) that an unanticipated tightening of the liquidity constraint would be associated with a very large welfare cost. In order to address Korea's crisis, one should model an economy characterized by erratic access to the international capital market, stable domestic fiscal policies, and a high saving rate, in which moral hazard provides the impetus for excessive borrowing (Dooley 2000). Such a model would address the hazards of quick and under-regulated financial integration.

On the Welfare Cost of Volatility

The premise of the RBC literature is that there is a meaningful separation between short-run volatility and long-run growth. This separation may explain the finding that the welfare cost of business cycles is negligible. Ramey and Ramey (1995) questioned this outcome by showing that gross national product (GNP) volatility and long-run growth are negatively associated. Aizenman and Marion (1993, 1999) showed that in emerging markets, macroeconomic volatility and private investment (and long-run growth) are negatively associated. These results can be interpreted by focusing on the investment channel in the presence of nonconvexities (for a further discussion on related issues, see Aizenman & Marion 1993; Hopenhayn and Muniagurria 1996; Mendoza 1997; and the overview in Barlevy 2000). The benchmark model used in the present paper does not model the investment channel or allow for an endogenous long-run effect of uncertainty on growth. Hence, the paper's finding that sudden stops are not reflected in long-run business-cycle statistics is the outcome of the modeling strategy and may not hold in models in which long-run growth is systematically affected by policy uncertainty and economic volatility. Addressing these issues remains a challenge for the future literature.

"Lucas Critic" Issues

The liquidity constraint and the policy uncertainty are not modeled, although sudden stop episodes and financial policies should affect both. Little can be inferred about policies without modeling the sources of policy uncertainty and the micro impact of policies and shocks on the liquidity constraint, ρ.

Examples of Possible Structural Effects

The paper focuses on the "representative agent." With distributional conflicts, relatively small welfare costs to the aggregate economy are consistent with large costs to some agents and large benefits to others. This may intensify policy conflicts and policy uncertainty. For example, if a sudden stop caused the distribution of income to deteriorate, it would increase the volatility of the political process, reducing growth (Persson and Tabellini 1994; Alesina and Rodrik 1994).

More generally, one may expect sudden stops to affect the political process and institutions, which in turn may affect the stochastic process that characterizes policies and the adjustment to shocks. For example, the Great Depression led to the creation of new institutions and changed the priorities and the design of policies in the United States. A careful assessment of the welfare effect of sudden stops should address these changes.

The policy uncertainty in emerging markets may have several routes. Among the possible interpretations we find populism (Dornbush and Edwards 1990), labor-capital conflict (Alesina and Tabellini 1989), and outsiders-insiders conflict (Tornell 1998). All of these cases are characterized by a "political distortion," wherein the policy maker does not maximize the expected utility of the representative agent. In these circumstances, the policy maker will not have the incentive to adopt optimal policies, which are designed to maximize the expected utility of the representative agent, as is done in the present paper. In the presence of such a political distortion, there are potential benefits from a crisis (see Alesina and Drazen 1991). Furthermore, adopting the optimal policies may require external enforcement (e.g., IMF conditionality, etc.).

Modeling the micro impact of policies and shocks on the liquidity constraint may be a pre-condition for a full assessment of policies. The assumptions of an exogenous stock/flow borrowing constraint and a representative agent do not allow one to capture the impact of changes in the distribution of income on investment and growth. As an illustration, recall the important contribution by Bernanke and Gertler (1989), which focused on the RBC model with endogenous agency costs. They concluded that

> A redistribution from borrowers to lenders that does not affect total income will lower investment not only in the current period, but for a number of subsequent periods as well. Thus balance sheet considerations may initiate, as well as propagate, cyclical fluctuations . . . The dynamic effects of productivity disturbances may be asymmetric in this set up (sharp investment downturns are more likely than sharp upturns).

A more recent paper by Aghion, Bacchetta, and Banerjee (1999) focused on a model with agency costs, wherein a nontraded input is used as capital and as a collateral. These authors concluded that

> If a major slump is likely to be costly even in the long-run [sic] (because, for example, it sets in process political forces which are destabilizing—as in Indonesia 1998–9), fully liberalizing foreign capital flows and fully opening the economy to foreign lending may not be a good idea at least until the domestic financial sector is sufficiently well-developed (that is, until the credit-multiplier becomes sufficiency large). . . . What brings about financial crises is precisely the rise in the price of non-tradables. If one of these factors (say, real estate) could be identified as playing a key

role in the emergence of a financial crisis, there could be an argument for controlling its price, either directly or through controlling the speculative demand for that good using suitable fiscal deterrents.

Although one may argue about the generalities of these statements, they illustrate that modeling investment in the presence of heterogeneous agents and endogenous agency costs may provide a richer interpretation for the welfare effects of sudden stops and volatility.

To conclude, Mendoza's paper is a very useful step in the quest for a better welfare analysis of sudden stop episodes. Mendoza's comprehensive analysis carefully outlined the implications of sudden stop episodes in the RBC model with an exogenous stock/flow borrowing constraint. It provides a useful base model, which may be enriched further by modeling the investment channel and the political process.

References

Aghion, P., P. Bacchetta, and A. Banerjee. 1999. Capital markets and instability of open economics. In *The Asian financial crisis: Causes, contagion, and consequences,* ed. P. R. Agenor, M. Miller, A. Weber, and D. Vines, 167–94. Cambridge: Cambridge University Press.

Aizenman, J., and N. Marion. 1993. Policy uncertainty, persistence and growth. *Review of International Economics* 1 (2): 145–63.

———. 1999. Volatility and investment: Interpreting evidence from developing countries. *Economica* 66 (262): 157–79.

Alesina, A., and A. Drazen. 1991. Why are stabilizations delayed? *American Economic Review* 81 (5): 1170–88.

Alesina, A., and D. Rodrik. 1994. Distributive politics and economic growth. *Quarterly Journal of Economics* 109 (2): 465–90.

Alesina, A., and G. Tabellini. 1989. External debt, capital flight and political risk. *Journal of International Economics* 27 (3–4): 199–220.

Barlevy, Gadi. 2000. Evaluating the costs of business cycles in models of endogenous growth. Northwestern University, Department of Economics. Mimeograph.

Bernanke, B., and M. Gertler. 1989. Agency costs, net worth, and business fluctuations. *American Economic Review* 79 (1): 14–31.

Dooley, P. M. 2000. A model of crisis in emerging markets. *Economic Journal* 110 (1): 256–72.

Dornbusch, R., and S. Edwards. 1990. Macroeconomic populism. *Journal of Development Economics* 32 (2): 247–77.

Hopenhayn, H. A., and M. E. Muniagurria. 1996. Policy variability and economic growth. *Review of Economic Studies* 63 (4): 611–25.

Lucas, R. E., Jr. 1987. *Models of business cycles.* New York: Basil-Blackwell.

Mendoza, E. G. 1997. Terms of trade uncertainty and economic growth. *Journal of Development Economics* 54:323–56.

Persson, T., and G. Tabellini. 1994. Is inequality harmful for growth? *American Economic Review* 84 (3): 600–21.

Ramey, G., and V. A. Ramey. 1995. Cross-country evidence on the link between volatility and growth. *American Economic Review* 85 (5): 1138–51.

Tornell, A. 1998. Reform from within. NBER Working Paper no. W6497. Cambridge, Mass.: National Bureau of Economic Research.

Discussion Summary

A few people asked questions about the welfare implications of the paper. *Carlos A. Végh* commented that in order to calculate the welfare costs of crises, it is important that the model correctly predict the frequency of crises in which a sudden stop takes place. A first check of the model would be to compare the predicted frequency of crises in Mexico with the actual frequency. *Amartya Lahiri* was concerned with the ability of the model to account for the actual movements of macroeconomic variables. Without this ability, he doubted that it is meaningful to discuss the welfare effects of the model.

Roberto Rigobon proposed that an alternative approach might be to focus on time series implications of the model. We know that real business-cycle models do not imply welfare costs close to the levels we think are reasonable, so we might benefit from directly looking at how crises lead to output falls, unemployment changes, and interest rate changes. *Rudi Dornbusch* also emphasized studying the output effects of crises. He suggested bringing in ideas from the literature on transitional economies—in particular, what Blanchard and Kremer called disorganization effects—where the breakdown of credit closes down the firms in a supply chain and therefore affects the whole economy. This could be fit into the general equilibrium model and would be a much more powerful mechanism than labor supply.

Another common concern was whether the model can explain the 1994 Mexican crisis, as the paper suggests. For example, Végh asked whether the forces of the crisis identified in the model are indeed the ones that had led to the Mexican crisis. *Aaron Tornell* commented that there is no investment in the model. In his interpretation, the model works as follows. Over time, some exogenous shocks make the borrowing constraint binding, which has two effects: Interest rates are higher, which reduces consumption and leads to real depreciation, and labor supply also increases, which offsets the first effect. The welfare effects are amplified in the model through the consumption channel. However, without the investment channel, it seems hard to talk about interest rate movements and labor supply response. Are these indeed what happened in the 1994 Mexican crisis? Dornbusch pointed out that the Mexican crisis was mainly a debt issue, and future research should incorporate how consumers view tax burdens. *Roberto Chang* was also interested in how the specification of the model reflects what happened in the Mexican crisis: For example, he asked what the big policy change was in Mexico before the 1994 crisis. He also wondered how the interpretation of policy in this model would differ from assuming a random process for tax rates (which is the standard in the literature). If this interpretation is correct, then it is not appropriate to discuss policy implications such as the credibility of the regime.

There were some technical remarks. Tornell talked about the issue of multiple equilibria. There are no multiple equilibria in the model, an absence that seems to be at odds with our understanding of the 1994 Mexican crisis. Lahiri talked about the role of the endogenous discount rate. The question was what the model would predict without this feature.

Finally, on the history of thought, Dornbusch related the recent literature on sudden stops to one of his decade-old papers.

Enrique Mendoza agreed with most of the comments. He said that the investment channel that Tornell talked about and the labor market Dornbusch mentioned are both very important, but it would have been very complicated to incorporate them into the model. He also promised to calculate the frequency of crises implied by the model, as suggested by Végh. However, on the issue of multiple equilibria, he said that the purpose of the model is to show that a sudden stop may occur even without multiple equilibria or nominal rigidity (the model assumes flexible price setting).

III

Capital Controls
The Malaysian Experience

8   Did the Malaysian Capital
Controls Work?

Ethan Kaplan and Dani Rodrik

8.1   Introduction

The Asian financial crisis of 1997–98 wrought havoc with the economies of some of the world's most successful performers. Three of the worst-affected countries (Thailand, South Korea, and Indonesia) were forced to call in the International Monetary Fund (IMF) and to embark on IMF-supported—and IMF-designed—programs in order to cope with the financial crisis. In return for financial assistance from the IMF (and other multilateral and bilateral donors), these countries committed to float their exchange rates, raise interest rates, tighten fiscal policy (at least initially), open up their financial markets to foreigners, close troubled banks and financial institutions, and undertake a range of other structural reforms.

Malaysia took a different path. Instead of going to the IMF, the Malaysian authorities imposed sweeping controls on capital account transactions, fixed the exchange rate at MYR3.80 per U.S. dollar (a rate that represented a 10 percent appreciation relative to the level at which the ringgit had been trading immediately before the controls), cut interest rates, and embarked on a policy of reflation.

Did the Malaysian gamble pay off? Malaysia has recovered nicely since the crisis, but so have Korea and Thailand, two countries that took the orthodox path. It is clear that some of the more pessimistic prognostications

Ethan Kaplan is a Ph.D. candidate in economics at the University of California, Berkeley. Dani Rodrik is Rafiq Hariri Professor of International Political Economy at the John F. Kennedy School of Government, Harvard University, and a research associate of the National Bureau of Economic Research.

The authors thank Marcos Chamon, Arin Dube, Jeffrey A. Frankel, K. S. Jomo, Aziz Ali Mohammed, Liliana Rojas-Suarez, and conference participants for useful comments. Dani Rodrik gratefully acknowledges financial support from the Ford Foundation.

about the consequences of capital controls have not been borne out, but can we say something more concrete about the relative merits of the capital controls option as a crisis resolution strategy, at least in this particular case?

There has been increasing acceptance in recent years of capital controls on inflows as a *prudential* measure aimed at preventing a buildup of short-term foreign liabilities, particularly in lower-income countries that do not have the capacity to put in place sophisticated financial supervisory regimes. In the words of Michael Mussa (2000), "[h]igh openness to international capital flows, especially short-term credit flows, can be dangerous for countries with weak or inconsistent macro-economic policies or inadequately capitalized and regulated financial systems.[1] However, the use of capital controls on outflows as a *crisis resolution* measure remains highly controversial, despite a clear-cut economic rationale. As emphasized in "second-generation" models of currency crises, a country can be faced with creditor panic and a run on reserves even when it has strong fundamentals. In these situations, a temporary suspension of capital account convertibility can halt the rush to the exits and provide time for policy makers to take corrective action—it can "rule out the bad equilibrium by *force majeure,*" in Krugman's (1999a) words. However, the risk is that capital controls can prove ineffective, undercut market confidence even further, and be used to delay needed adjustments.

In trying to determine the relative success of the Malaysian response to the Asian crisis, we must evaluate the Malaysian controls from four different yet complementary perspectives.

The first issue is narrowly *financial:* Were the controls effective in segmenting Malaysian financial markets from offshore and international capital markets? The increased sophistication of financial markets, and in particular the spread of derivatives (enabling speculators, for example, to disguise short-term flows as direct foreign investment), has led many observers to be skeptical of governments' ability to target specific types of balance-of-payments flows for restriction.[2] Indeed, one might have been doubtful ex ante that the Malaysian government's controls would have been effective in this sense.

Such doubts seem to have been misplaced. The government had no difficulty in sharply lowering domestic interest rates and making the fixed exchange rate stick without the appearance of a black-market premium for foreign currency. As an IMF report states, "there [were] only a few reports of efforts to evade controls, and no indications of circumvention through underinvoicing or overinvoicing of imports" (Kochhar et al. 1999, 8). Another IMF staff report concludes that the controls were effective in eliminating the

---

1. Mussa precedes this statement by writing: "[T]he experience in recent financial crises could cause reasonable people to question whether liberal policies toward international capital flows are wise for all countries in all circumstances. The answer, I believe, is probably not."
2. See Garber (1998) for a useful discussion of the issues.

offshore ringgit market and choking off speculative activity against the ringgit despite the easing of monetary and fiscal policies (Ariyoshi et al. 1999, 2:50–51). More systematic, comparative evidence is presented by Kaminsky and Schmukler (2000) and Edison and Reinhart (2001). These papers find that the September 1998 controls were successful in lowering interest rates, stabilizing the exchange rate, and reducing the comovement of Malaysian overnight interest rates with regional interest rates.[3]

The second perspective is medium-term *economic.* Did the controls (combined with fiscal and monetary reflation and a fixed exchange rate) allow a faster recovery from the economic crisis and a better economic performance than would have been possible in their absence? In other words, was the financial segmentation put to good use? This is where considerable controversy remains. The question is essentially whether Malaysia would have been better off in the immediate aftermath of the crisis following the orthodox, IMF-prescribed route that the other countries in the region followed. This is the question on which our paper focuses.

Third, we have to contend with a broader *political* question, having to do with the interaction of capital controls with political developments in Malaysia. Opponents of capital controls often argue that controls enlarge the scope for domestic political mischief. The possibility of corruption is mentioned frequently. In Malaysia's case, there is no indication of an increase in petty corruption—the controls were implemented transparently and with remarkable efficiency—but many knowledgeable observers have complained about the intensification of the regime's cronyism. Jomo, for example, argues that the controls served (in part) to bail out the regime's cronies:

> The window of opportunity offered by capital controls has been abused by certain powerfully-connected business interests, not only to secure publicly funded bail-outs at public expense, but even to consolidate and extend their corporate domination, especially in the crucial financial sector. Capital controls have been part of a package focused on saving friends of the regime, usually at the public's expense. (Jomo 2001, 215)[4]

It is also clear that the controls made it easier for Mahathir to get away with firing and humiliating his political rival Deputy Prime Minister Anwar Ibrahim. In fact, Anwar was fired just hours after the ringgit was pegged on 2 September. We shall not have much to say about this angle of the capital controls, but we recognize that a broader evaluation has to take into account their potentially quite negative implications for political governance.

---

3. Malaysia's controls were the only ones that had this result among all the cases that these authors studied. This may be attributed to the more comprehensive nature of the Malaysian capital controls.

4. See also Johnson and Mitton (2001), which provides some evidence that firms connected to Mahathir experienced a more significant rebound in their stock prices subsequent to the imposition of capital controls.

Finally, one needs also to maintain a *long-term* perspective. Even if controls are successful in the short run, it is possible that their long-term economic consequences will prove damaging. If this were to prove the case, Malaysia's medium-term benefits would have to be juxtaposed against longer-term costs before one could determine whether the policies were ultimately worthwhile. In Malaysia's case, one has to worry especially about the impact on foreign direct investment (FDI). Such investment has played an important role in the country's successful economic development to date, and a substantial drop in FDI would be likely to be bad news.[5] The Malaysian authorities were quite careful to target short-term speculative capital flows, insulating FDI, but there nevertheless remains the possibility that the controls will have a long-term deterrent effect on long-term investors. We will not have much to say on this issue, either. The controls are too recent to ascertain with any degree of certainty their long-term consequences.

With regard to the question that is our focus—did the controls help Malaysia recover faster?—the prevailing view is that the answer remains unclear (see, e.g., Dornbusch, chap. 9 in this volume). The imposition of capital controls in Malaysia coincided with a general improvement in the business climate in the region.[6] Most economic indicators for Thailand and, especially, South Korea sharply turned upward just as Malaysia was beginning its own recovery. By many measures, South Korea's rebound since late 1998 has been more impressive than Malaysia's.[7]

We shall argue that this type of comparison misses an important point. In early September 1998, neither Korea nor Thailand faced another imminent financial crisis. Both had gone through an IMF program (or series of programs), which, with some delay, had begun to restore market confidence in these economies. There was no reason to believe that their policy configurations on 1 September 1998 were fundamentally unsustainable. In fact, sizable improvements in key indicators of market sentiment had already taken place in the months preceding September. In both countries, interest rates had come down sharply, the currency had appreciated significantly, and—at least in Korea's case—there had been a large increase in foreign currency reserves.

Contrast that with Malaysia's situation. When the Malaysian authorities instituted capital controls on 1 September 1998, they did so under the belief

5. According to Athukorala (1998, 20), FDI contributed 73 percent of net capital inflows to Malaysia between 1990 and 1994.

6. However, in many ways, the environment in the world was not as good as it had been a year previously, when Thailand and Korea were implementing their IMF programs. Shortly after the imposition of controls in Malaysia, both Brazil and Russia experienced severe crises. Also, whereas Japanese imports had been rising in late 1997, they were in decline again by late 1998.

7. Malaysia suffered lower declines in real wages and manufacturing employment than Korea, however.

that their existing policies were unsustainable because of intense and continued speculative pressure against the ringgit. Indeed, a simple indicator of financial market pressure that we will discuss later in the paper shows that pressure on the ringgit reached its peak just before the Malaysian authorities decided to implement capital controls. The most concrete form that the speculation took was a large differential between onshore and offshore interest rates for ringgit deposits. Unlike in Korea and Thailand, where interest rates had fallen to single-digit levels by the end of the summer, offshore ringgit deposits were paying rates in the range of 20–40 percent. Although domestic interest rates remained stable due to an interest rate ceiling of 2.5 percentage points over the government-determined base lending rate (Kochar et al. 1999, 62), the large onshore/offshore interest rate differential initiated massive capital flight and a subsequent credit crunch. There was widespread speculation in the market that Malaysia would be the next country to go to the IMF.

Thus, when Malaysia altered its policies on 1 September, it did so because its existing policies were unsustainable and ineffectual. It is hard to believe that Malaysia would have experienced Thailand's or Korea's economic performance in subsequent months while *maintaining* its existing policy configuration. We shall suggest a different counterfactual, namely that the alternative to the capital control strategy was to go to the IMF for assistance—that is, to do what the other countries had done earlier. From this perspective, the appropriate counterfactual for Malaysia is the performance exhibited by the other countries subsequent to their resort to IMF assistance. Formally, this calls for a *time-shifted* difference-in-differences methodology to discern the economic consequences of the controls. In other words, we shall treat the timing of the before and after comparisons as country-specific, centering it on the date that each country called in the IMF or, as in Malaysia's case, imposed capital controls.

Later we discuss at length the identifying assumptions needed to make the time shifting valid and the efforts we have made to reduce possible biases. In particular, we try to control for the external environment (including the decline in U.S. interest rates and the resumption of flows to the region) to ensure that our results are not biased by differences in the overall business climate in the region at the time that each of the countries resorted to its crisis resolution policy. If one accepts the identifying assumptions and is persuaded by the robustness checks, the results are quite strong. We find that the Malaysian controls produced better results than the alternative in almost all dimensions. On the real side, the economic recovery was faster, and employment and real wages did not suffer as much. On the financial side, the stock market performed better, interest rates fell more, and inflation was lower. However, we will also present conventional difference-in-differences estimates for the skeptic, which take 1 September 1998 as the turning point for all the countries. These results are more mixed, but

Table 8.1   Financial and Debt Indicators, 1996

	Malaysia	South Korea	Thailand
External debt/GDP	0.39	0.32	0.55
External debt/exports of goods and services	0.41	0.98	1.32
Short-term debt/GDP	0.11	0.20	0.21
Short-term debt/reserves	0.42	2.84	1.03
M2/GDP	1.00	0.46	0.79
M2/reserves	3.64	6.21	3.86
Claims on private sector/GDP	1.45	0.66	1.42
Current account balance (% of GDP)	−4.9	−4.7	−7.9
Stock market capitalization (% of GDP)	310	29	54

Source: Institute of International Finance ([IIF] 1998), except for stock market capitalization, which comes from the World Bank's "Stock Market Capitalization as a Percent of GDP," at [http://wbln0018.worldbank.org/psd/compete.nsf/e376d12c87889e86852564900006610ce?Open/View].

generally less favorable to Malaysia's policies than to policies pursued by Korea and Thailand.

The outline of the paper is as follows. In the next section we briefly review the nature of the Malaysian controls and summarize existing evaluations of their effectiveness. Section 8.3 is devoted to methodological issues and discusses the appropriateness of time-shifted versus conventional difference-in-differences. In section 8.4 we present evidence that the timing of the Malaysian financial crisis differed in significant details from the Korean and Thai crises. Section 8.5 presents the main empirical results. Section 8.6 discusses some alternative interpretations of the evidence. Finally, we offer concluding remarks in section 8.7.

8.2   Malaysia's Capital Controls and Previous Evaluations

Malaysia entered the Asian financial crisis with relatively strong fundamentals and (thanks to an earlier bout with restrictions on capital inflows in 1994) a much smaller share of short-term external debt in total.[8] Table 8.1 shows some key financial data. Malaysia's short-term debt stood well below its foreign exchange reserves, which made it less prone to a run by foreign creditors. At the same time, as a country with a very high level of indebtedness overall, Malaysia was quite vulnerable to turnarounds in general market sentiment that would be reflected in an increase in interest rates or reduction in credit availability.

Malaysia had the world's highest stock market capitalization ratio (310

---

8. In response to a surge of speculative inflows in late 1993 betting on an appreciation of the ringgit, the Malaysian government imposed restrictions on the sale of short-term securities to foreigners in January and February 1994. These restrictions resulted in a sharp reduction in short-term liabilities. See Rodrik and Velasco (forthcoming).

percent of gross domestic product [GDP], compared to 116 percent in the United States and 29 percent in Korea). The rise in equity prices had in turn contributed to a domestic lending boom, leaving Malaysia in mid-1997 with a domestic debt-GDP ratio (170 percent) that was among the highest in the world (Perkins and Woo 2000, 237). Private-sector indebtedness was higher than in Thailand and more than double the ratio in Korea. The stock of M2 was equal to GDP (much higher than corresponding ratios for Korea and Thailand). During periods of financial panic, *all* short-term liabilities, whether domestic or foreign, become potential claims against the government's liquid foreign assets. These high levels of debt suggest that Malaysia was not as well protected against financial turbulence as its external liquidity indicators would suggest.

In response to the Thai crisis and the reversal of capital flows to the region, Malaysian authorities at first implemented an orthodox adjustment policy.[9] Interest rates were raised to stem the decline of the ringgit, and in December 1997 a drastic cut (18 percent) in government spending was announced. This policy package mimicked IMF programs elsewhere and was pushed through by Deputy Prime Minister Anwar Ibrahim. Anwar also made clear that he was committed to exchange rate flexibility and that capital controls would not be implemented. Meanwhile, Prime Minister Dr. Mahathir bin Mohamad was blowing off steam against financial market "speculators" and sending very different signals.

The Malaysian economy failed to respond to the orthodox policies. Consumption and investment demand plunged as a result of capital outflows, high interest rates, and a pessimistic outlook. This gave the opponents of Anwar's policies the upper hand, and at the end of June 1998, Mahathir appointed Daim Zainuddin, a former finance minister, to be minister in charge of "tasks relating to economic development." Daim was told to formulate an alternative to Anwar's policies. Daim and Mahathir were intent on reflating the economy through cuts in interest rates and credit expansion, but there was little effective change in monetary policies over the ensuing months. The attempt to reduce domestic interest rates was undercut by growing speculation against the ringgit in offshore markets. Offshore institutions (mainly in Singapore) borrowed ringgit at premium rates (double or triple the prevailing interest rates in Malaysia) to purchase dollars and bet in favor of the ringgit's collapse. The economy's decline continued. This was the background against which the controls were instituted on 1 September.

The primary objective behind the capital controls was to end speculation against the ringgit. Most of that speculation was coming from short-selling of the ringgit in offshore (mainly Singaporean) markets. These markets were offering high interest rates to attract ringgit deposits, which in turn

---

9. This paragraph and the next are based on Haggard and Low (2000) and Perkins and Woo (2000).

served to fund the shorting of the currency. To shut down offshore trading, the government mandated that all sale of ringgit assets had to go through authorized domestic intermediaries, effectively making offshore trading illegal. All ringgit assets held abroad had to be repatriated. Worried that these measures would lead to an outflow of capital and further depreciation of the currency, the Malaysian government also banned for a period of one year all repatriation of investment held by foreigners. Simultaneously, in an attempt to revive aggregate demand, Malaysia lowered the three-month Bank Negara intervention rate from 9.5 percent to 8 percent, and on 16 September, the liquid asset ratio was reduced from 17 percent to 15 percent of total liabilities. On 15 February 1999, the Central Bank of Malaysia changed the regulations on capital restrictions, shifting from an outright ban to a graduated levy and replacing the levy on capital with a profits levy on future inflows. The controls are described more fully in the appendix.

The government was concerned about the impact of the controls on future capital inflows, particularly of FDI, on which the Malaysian economy is highly dependent. The authorities therefore took pains to ensure that the controls would not affect FDI or current account transactions. Repatriation of profits and dividends from (documented) FDI activities were freely allowed. Foreign currency transactions for current account purposes (including the provision of up to six months of trade credit for foreigners buying Malaysian goods) were also not restricted.

Early reactions to the controls ranged from cautious to hostile. The IMF did not openly condemn Malaysian policies, but it did not hide its views about their inappropriateness either. An IMF spokesman was quoted as saying, "the IMF believes that any restrictions imposed on the movement of capital [are] not conducive to building investor confidence" (quoted in "IMF suggests Malaysian move is a disincentive," *Asian Wall Street Journal,* 2 September 1998, 2). Other observers were less circumspect. Oxford Analytica's *Daily Brief* headline declared, "Exchange controls will undermine Malaysian growth" (15 September 1998). An article in *Forbes International* predicted, "Foreign investors in Malaysia have been expropriated, and the Malaysians will bear the cost of their distrust for years" (Roche 1998). Moody's downgraded Malaysian securities. Morgan Stanley dropped Malaysia from its international index, stating that Malaysia would permanently be excluded from it and that its previous inclusion had been a mistake in the first place.[10] Spreads rose more than 200 basis points for Malaysian bonds in September, while they declined for other East Asian countries (with the exception of Indonesia).

Early prognostications of impending doom were gradually replaced by

---

10. This is reported in Kochhar et al. (1999, 11). A year later, Morgan Stanley announced that it would reinstate Malaysia in its index, explaining that many investors had remained in the Malaysian market.

more upbeat projections, as it became clear that Malaysia was recovering rather than sinking deeper into crisis. It is instructive to follow the transformation in the pages of successive *World Economic Outlooks* of the IMF:

> [T]he introduction by Malaysia in early September of exchange and capital controls may also turn out to be an important setback not only to that country's recovery and potentially to its future development, but also to other emerging market economies that have suffered from heightened investor fears of similar actions elsewhere. (October 1998, 4)

> Despite stimulative monetary and fiscal policies introduced last year, however, domestic demand is expected to strengthen only gradually. (May 1999, 19)

> [A] strong economic recovery is also now underway in response to fiscal and monetary stimulus and the pegging of the exchange rate at a competitive level. (October 1999, 19)

In May 1999, Malaysia went back to the international market with a $1 billion bond issue, paying a premium of 330 points above the U.S. treasury rate. By June 1999, the *Wall Street Journal* would editorialize that "there never was any doubt that preventing money from fleeing Malaysia could provide short-lived relief" (25 June 1999, A18).

The *Wall Street Journal* notwithstanding, whether (and the extent to which) Malaysian controls contributed to economic recovery remains a highly debated matter. Some scholars, such as Merton Miller, continue to view the controls as an unmitigated disaster.[11] The mainstream view is that it is hard to attribute much success to the capital controls because Korea and Thailand also recovered around the same time without using capital controls. Lim's (1999) account is worth quoting at length, as it is representative:

> Following the imposition of capital controls, economic indicators in Malaysia did indeed start improving. But they also improved at the same time in the other crisis-hit countries which did not impose such controls but maintained open capital accounts. All the crisis-hit countries' currencies stabilized and strengthened, their inflation and interest rates fell, their current accounts moved from deficit into substantial surplus and private capital inflows increased, contributing to the replenishment of previously depleted foreign exchange reserves. Their stockmarkets started climbing, and the decline in their GDP growth rates moderated sharply and have now reversed with positive growth predicted for 1999 as a whole everywhere except Indonesia. Until very recently, the recovery in Malaysia actually lagged behind that of its neighbors who were IMF patients, particularly in inflows of foreign direct investment which fell in

11. Miller was quoted in the *Asian Wall Street Journal* as saying that "the experiment with controls was at best useless. . . . The bad news is that the episode was actually harmful to Malaysia and its citizens" (9 July 1999.)

1998 whereas they increased in the other countries (except Indonesia). My own opinion is that capital controls in Malaysia were neither necessary nor sufficient for economic recovery, just as they have obviously not been necessary in the equally if not more impressive recovery of the other crisis-hit Asian countries which followed the more conventional IMF policy prescriptions. Indeed, given Malaysia's much stronger macroeconomic fundamentals and financial institutions before the crisis, one would have expected its recovery to be faster and stronger than that of the other countries. That this has not happened suggests that capital controls—or the heightened political risk which accompanied their imposition—may be exerting a drag on recovery through the discouragement of some foreign capital inflow.

Even sympathizers of capital controls have taken a cool attitude toward the success of Malaysian policies (Krugman 1999b; Jomo 2001), on essentially the same grounds: There was a recovery even in the countries that did not impose controls. Krugman (1999b) writes, "the market panic of 1997–98 was, it turns out, coming to an end just about the time that Malaysia decided to make its big break with orthodoxy."

We shall challenge the view that the financial crisis in Malaysia was about to abate in September 1998 and that an economic recovery was around the corner. Financial market indicators suggest that pressure on the Malaysian currency remained high in Malaysia months after the Korean and Thai currencies had begun to appreciate. It is clear that the Malaysian authorities acted because they believed a sharp change in policies was "needed to avert an imminent financial panic" (Liu 2000, 284). The situation in which Malaysia found itself on 1 September 1998 was akin to that which had forced Thailand and Korea to call in the IMF quite a while back (in July and October 1997, respectively). Moreover, if it is the case that the timing of the financial crisis was different in Malaysia, the fact that Korea and Thailand began to recover at the same time that Malaysia did is not very informative about the relative effectiveness of the Malaysian controls.

8.3   Methodological Considerations

In evaluating the consequences of the Malaysian capital controls, it is natural to use as a counterfactual the experience of the other Asian countries affected by the crisis. This is in fact the strategy adopted by the authors cited above, albeit informally and often implicitly. A difference-in-differences specification is the appropriate framework for thinking about this question.[12] Let y_{it} denote some measure of economic performance of interest, where t stands for time and i stands for one of our four countries ($i =$

12. See Meyer (1995) for a good discussion of the methodological issues in difference-in-differences estimation.

Malaysia, Korea, Thailand, Indonesia). Consider the following representation:

(1)
$$y_{it} = \sum_i \alpha_i d_i + \beta d_{t>\tau} + \gamma d_M d_{t>\tau} + u_{it},$$

where d_t is a country-specific dummy variable ($d_M = 1$ when i = Malaysia and 0 otherwise, and so on); $d_{t>\tau}$ is a time-varying dummy variable that takes the value 1 during the twelve months (or four quarters) that follow $\tau = 1$ September 1998 (i.e., during the one-year period subsequent to the imposition of capital controls in Malaysia), and is 0 otherwise; and u_{it} is the error term. This specification allows y_{it} to have a country-specific, time-invariant intercept (captured by α_i). It also allows y_{it} to be influenced by a common underlying factor during the period that the capital controls were in use in Malaysia (i.e., while the "treatment" is in effect). This time-varying but common effect is captured by the coefficient β. The coefficient of greatest interest is the one on the interaction term $d_M d_{t>\tau}$, γ, which captures the differential effect of the capital controls in Malaysia. With this specification, the average post–September 1998 performance of the comparators (relative to their earlier performance) becomes the counterfactual used in estimating the effectiveness of the Malaysian policies.

Equation (1) represents the conventional application of the difference-in-differences approach to this case. It has the merit that it controls for ("differences out") the effects of both country-specific and time-varying influences that might otherwise be attributed to the use of capital controls. In particular, a common improvement across countries in fundamentals that coincides with the use of capital controls in Malaysia gets washed out by the term $\beta d_{t>\tau}$. We shall present empirical estimates using this approach later on.

However, there is a serious problem with conventional difference-in-differences. For γ to be an unbiased estimate of the effect of the capital controls, an essential identifying condition must hold—we must assume that Malaysia would have experienced the same economic recovery as the other countries in the months following September 1998 had capital controls *not* been imposed. This is implausible for three reasons that we shall elaborate at greater length later in the paper: (1) The timing of the financial crisis was somewhat different in Malaysia. During the summer of 1998, market pressure on Malaysia's currency remained very high, whereas the crisis had already abated in Korea and Thailand. Malaysia's policy configuration during the summer of 1998 looked fundamentally unsustainable. (2) Korea and Thailand had, by September 1998, already undergone nine and fifteen months of "treatment," respectively. In addition, they had both received large loans. It is difficult to believe that Malaysia would have been able to recover immediately to the level of these other countries. (3) Assuming that

Mahathir was intent on firing Anwar, his chief political rival, sometime toward the end of 1998, there were further financial repercussions ahead. Anwar was viewed as the guardian of economic orthodoxy in Malaysia, so his dismissal would likely have aggravated the financial panic.

We will discuss these issues further in the next section. For now, let us simply assume that the Malaysian crisis was deepening in late summer 1998 and that the prevailing policies were unsustainable. Consider the implications for our empirical methodology of the difference in the timing of the crisis and policy response. We would like to know what Malaysia's performance would have been in the absence of capital controls. The answer requires specifying a counterfactual policy response. Luckily, we have a natural counterfactual: going to the IMF for help. This is the course of action that the other countries took once they reached a point in the crisis that required emergency measures. This way of specifying the counterfactual provides us with an alternative identifying assumption: In the absence of capital controls, Malaysia would have had to request IMF assistance to shore up confidence, and its post–September 1998 economic performance would have exhibited the same change that the other economies experienced subsequent to *their* requests for IMF assistance.

This calls for a *time-shifted* difference-in-differences specification, of the following form:

$$(2) \qquad y_{it} = \sum_i \alpha_i d_i + \beta d_{t>\tau_i} + \gamma d_M d_{t>\tau_i} + u_{it}$$

The main difference from before is that the time-varying post-treatment dummy is now country-specific (i.e., $d_{t>\tau_i}$ instead of $d_{t>\tau}$), which reflects the argument that the treatment was applied in different countries at different times. The dummy $d_{t>\tau_i}$ equals 1 during the twelve-month period following country i's first appeal for IMF assistance (and, in the case of Malaysia, during the twelve-month period following the imposition of capital controls), and is 0 otherwise.

With this change, the parameters β and γ acquire somewhat different interpretations from those in the conventional difference-in-differences: β captures the effect of undergoing IMF treatment during an economic crisis (relative to outcomes in more normal times), whereas γ captures the differential effect of capital controls in Malaysia (compared to an IMF program). The specification does not allow us to gauge the effects of an IMF program per se, because we observe an IMF program only during a crisis. Thus, β picks up a mix of IMF and crisis effects. This is not a major concern because our main interest, once again, is in the parameter γ. Under the assumption that Malaysia implemented its capital controls at a stage in the financial crisis that is comparable to that at which the other countries called in the IMF, γ is an unbiased estimate of the effect of the Malaysian controls *relative* to the counterfactual of an IMF program. Note moreover that γ picks up the effects not just of the capital controls, but of the entire post–September 1998 Malaysian package—including the fixed exchange rate, reflation via interest rate cuts, and so on.[13] In particular, it includes the impact of receiving many billions of dollars in loans from the IMF.

A simple analogy helps provide the basic intuition behind the time-shifted difference-in-differences approach we have just outlined. Suppose that two twin sisters, Corinne and May, both catch a virus that, left untreated, will simply continue. Assume that Corinne receives a standard treatment on Sunday. Assume further that May receives no treatment until Wednesday but then receives a special treatment. If we do a standard difference-in-difference analysis, ignoring the fact that the two sisters fell ill on different days, we might look at the difference in the fevers of the two sisters on, say, Friday versus Wednesday. We would then attribute the change in the difference between the sisters' fevers to the medicine that May received. However, such a calculation would be almost certain to lead to the conclusion that the special medicine made the patient worse off. By Wednesday, Corinne has started to recover, while the medicine that May took may not have worked fully.

In this particular case, the disease is the same across individuals, and the individuals are assumed to react to both the disease and any potential medication in an identical manner. Therefore, it is obvious that a more fruitful approach is to compare the time path of the disease after application of the conventional medicine with the time path of the disease following the application of the special treatment. In other words, we would want to time shift across sisters to match the application of the medicine. Replace Corinne with Korea, and May with Malaysia, and the logic of our approach becomes identical.

While time shifting corrects the type of bias just discussed, it creates the potential of another bias. The main risk that we run by using a time-shifted difference-in-differences approach is that there might be a correlation between the external economic environment and $d_{t>\tau_i}$. More concretely, Malaysia may have imposed its controls in a much more favorable environment than prevailed at the time that Korea (or Thailand or Indonesia) implemented its IMF program, and this in turn may account for a substantial part of the speedier recovery in the former country. We cannot entirely rule out this possibility, but we make the following points in our defense.

First, as we shall show below, it is not at all obvious that the external environment was improving for Malaysia during the second half of 1998 in the way that it had been for Thailand and Korea. Pressure on the ringgit remained very strong, even though the Korean won and Thai baht had already started to appreciate. Interest rates in both Korea and Thailand had

13. This is not cause for worry, because these additional policies were enabled in large part by the imposition of capital controls.

declined significantly, whereas offshore interest rates on ringgit deposits remained in double digits. The recession in Korea and Thailand had already bottomed out by September 1998, with Korea in particular exhibiting a healthy rebound, but there were no indications of a similar easing-up in Malaysia. Second, it is not obvious that an improvement in the external environment, to the extent that it did take place, would have produced much benefit for a country that actually cut itself off from international financial markets by implementing capital controls.[14] To the extent that the controls were effective, they would have insulated Malaysia from an improvement in market sentiment (which is in fact an argument that the opponents of capital controls have made). Finally, we try to reduce the scope for spurious correlation by introducing in our time-shifted difference-in-differences regressions several time-varying indicators related to the external context—namely, U.S. interest rates, U.S. inflation rates, U.S. economic activity, and (in the quarterly regressions) a measure of net financial flows to the region.

8.4   Timing and Magnitude of the Malaysian Financial Crisis

Financial indicators for the period suggest that the Malaysian economy was not as hard hit as Thailand, Korea, and Indonesia at the outset of the Asian financial crisis, but that things grew progressively worse for Malaysia even as the pressure eased in Korea and Thailand. We show this using a simple indicator of financial market "pressure" for the three countries.

The financial market pressure index is calculated as a weighted average of the (log) exchange rate, (log) foreign currency reserves (with declines in reserves contributing positively to the index), and the interest rate. This index is similar to the speculative pressure index constructed by Eichengreen, Rose, and Wyplosz (1995). The idea is that financial market pressure must be reflected in a decline in the value of the home currency, a decline in reserves, or an increase in interest rates. As weights, we use the inverse of the monthly standard deviations of each of the indicators, pooling the data for the three countries over the 1989–2000 period. This serves to underweight the more volatile components of the index. In Malaysia's case, we use the offshore interest rate rather than the onshore rate, as the former is the more relevant indicator of speculative pressure. Interest rate caps within Malaysia had made the domestic interest rate largely irrelevant.[15]

Figure 8.1 shows our financial market pressure index for the 1996–2000 period. It is clear from the figure that the speculative attacks differed in their timing. Thailand was hit first, with the peak of the crisis occurring in September 1997. Korea followed with a few months' lag, reaching a peak in

14. Indonesia, for one, did not benefit very much from the return of investor confidence to the region, for reasons that are specific to its own circumstances.
15. Offshore markets did not play as significant a role in the other two countries.

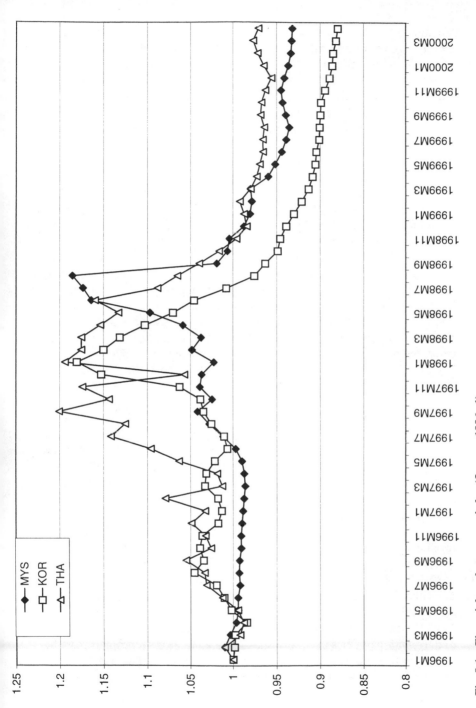

Fig. 8.1   Financial market pressure index (January 1996=1)

January 1998. Malaysia was behind both countries, and it began to experience a sustained increase in the index only during the early months of 1998. The peak value of the index for Malaysia was reached in August 1998, just before the imposition of the capital controls. (The sharp decline in the Malaysian index in September 1998 was due to the closing off of the offshore market and the fixing of the ringgit at an appreciated rate). Note that throughout 1998 the financial pressure index for Malaysia moves in the opposite direction from that for Thailand and Korea. This is a rather clear indication that speculative pressure continued to build up in Malaysia at a time when the other two countries were beginning to breathe more easily.

We can achieve some insight into the reason the indices that the three countries behave so differently by observing the trends in the components of the index. Figure 8.2 shows interest rates, with both onshore and offshore rates displayed for Malaysia. Note the very rapid rise in offshore rates for ringgit after May 1998, at a time when Korean and Thai interest rates were receding from the heights reached in late 1997 and early 1998. Just prior to September 1998, the offshore market was offering ringgit rates of between 20 and 40 percent to attract domestic ringgit (compared to the 11 percent offered by banks in Malaysia). These ringgit deposits were used to fund the short ringgit positions that offshore banks, hedge funds, and portfolio institutions held in expectation of a sharp depreciation.[16] The consequent leakage of ringgit abroad was a major reason that the desired credit expansion within Malaysia failed to take place and that the investment rate plummeted.

Figure 8.3 displays foreign currency reserves. Here the difference between Malaysia and South Korea is especially striking. Korean reserves sharply rebounded in early 1998, while Malaysia's reserves continued to fall. There is no increase in Malaysian reserves until after September 1998. This is also reflected in currency values, as the ringgit continued to depreciate from the end of March (after a rebound in the first quarter of the year) while the won steadily appreciated (fig. 8.4).

By the summer of 1998, Malaysia was viewed from the outside as a country in deep trouble. The media and financial markets were rife with speculation that Malaysia was next in line for an IMF program. The headline of an article in *Barron's* is representative: "Malaise-ia: While Kuala Lumpur Is in Denial, It May Be Next for IMF Aid" (6 July 1998, 28). The trouble was attributed variously to the sidelining of Anwar, the intemperate remarks of Mahathir about the international financial system, and the unsustainability of the reflation policies in view of the pressure on the currency. Far from being out of the woods, the Malaysian economy in late August 1998 was still mired in a financial quagmire. Whether this was partly its own doing is

---

16. See the description of the foreign exchange markets in Bank Negara Malaysia ([BNM] 1999, 572–77).

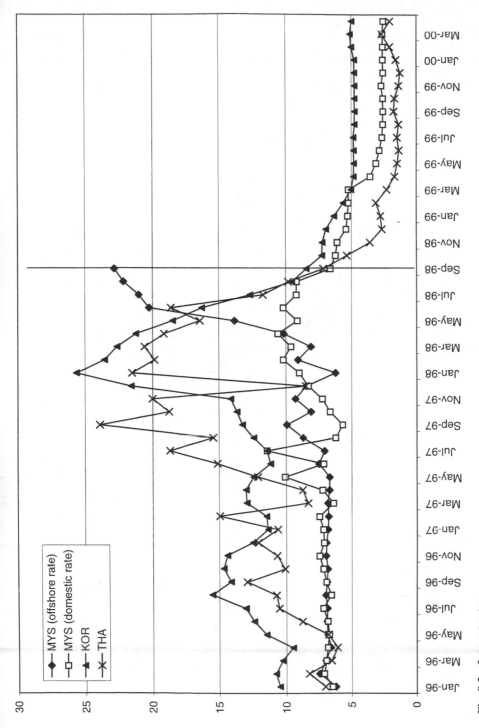

Fig. 8.2 Interest rates

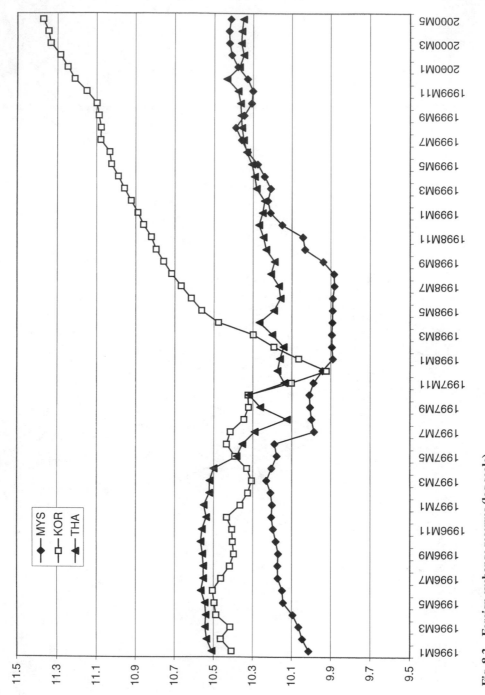

Fig. 8.3 Foreign exchange reserves (log scale)

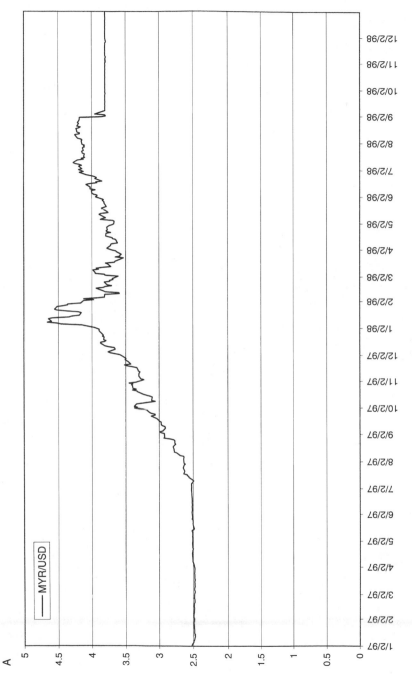

Fig. 8.4 Exchange rates: *A*, Malaysian ringgit; *B*, Korean won; *C*, Thai baht

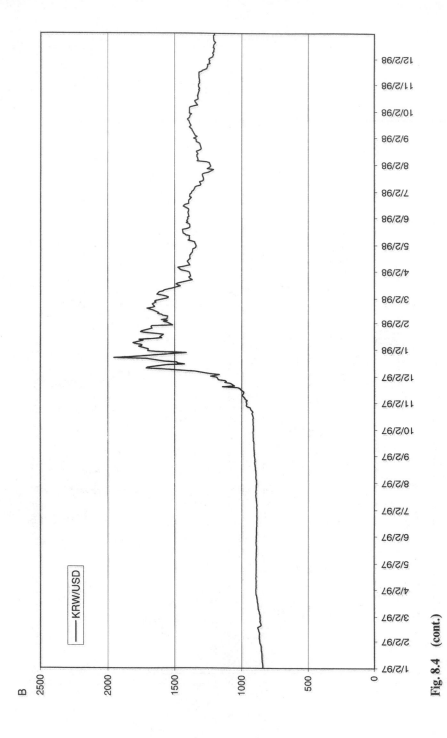

Fig. 8.4 (cont.)

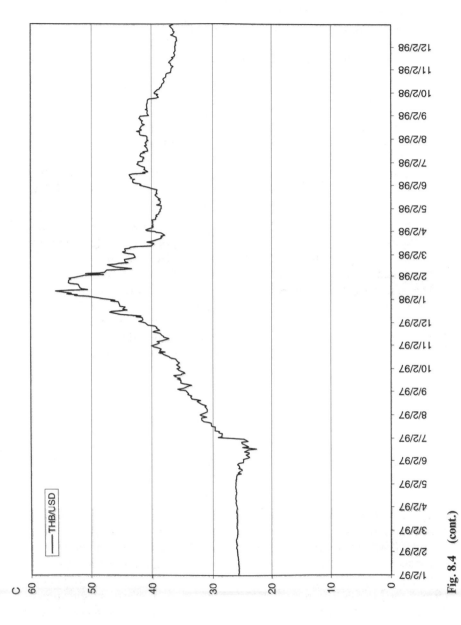

Fig. 8.4 (cont.)

irrelevant from our current perspective.[17] The crucial point is that Malaysia's policy framework in September 1998 looked as fragile as Thailand's had been in July 1997 or Korea's in November 1997.

Moreover, the impending dismissal and jailing of Anwar—assuming Mahathir was intent on getting rid of his onetime ally regardless of economics—would surely have made the financial crisis significantly worse. As Perkins and Woo (2000, 230) note:

> Mahathir had foreseen that Anwar's expulsion would lead to violent street demonstrations that, in turn, would induce large capital outflow, given the extreme nervousness among investors in the midst of the financial crisis. . . . If the capital controls had not been in place when the street demonstrations began, the Malaysian ringgit (MR) and the Kuala Lumpur stock market would most likely have gone into a free fall in the manner that the Indonesian rupiah and the Jakarta stock market did in May 1998, just before Soeharto stepped down from the presidency.

As we pointed out above, financial markets viewed Anwar as the guardian of economic orthodoxy in Malaysia and an important counterweight to Mahathir. His removal—whether accompanied by riots or not—would have been an occasion for a run on the ringgit.

This is important insofar as it suggests that the relevant counterfactual for how the Malaysian economy would have evolved *absent* capital controls must include the consequences of Anwar's firing. Therefore, not only was Malaysia in dire financial straits on the eve of the imposition of capital controls, but there is also good reason to believe that the worst was yet to come.

8.5   Empirical Results

The basic regression we estimate is an augmented version of equation (2), discussed previously:

$$(3) \qquad y_{it} = \sum_i \alpha_i d_i + \beta d_{t > \tau_i} + \gamma d_M d_{t > \tau_i} + \sum_j \delta_j X_{it}^j + \sum_k \phi_k Z_t^k + u_{it},$$

where y_{it} is a measure of economic performance that is of interest (for example, growth); d_i is a set of country dummies; $d_{t > \tau_i}$ is the "treatment-period" dummy, which equals 1 during the twelve-month (or four-quarter) period following country i's first appeal for IMF assistance or, in the case of Malaysia, during the twelve-month (four-quarter) period following the imposition of capital controls, and is 0 otherwise; $d_M d_{t > \tau_i}$ is the interaction term of the Malaysia dummy with $d_{t > \tau_i}$; X_{it}^j is a set of country-specific time-varying variables (country-specific monthly or quarterly dummies): Z_t^k is a

17. One ought to remember also that neither Thailand, with its explosive current account deficit and off-balance sheet sales of its reserves, nor Korea, with its huge and partly disguised short-term foreign liabilities, had been paragons of financial virtue.

set of time-varying variables capturing the external economic environment (U.S. interest rates, U.S. inflation, a measure of U.S. economic activity [monthly industrial production index or quarterly real GDP], a measure of net private financial flows to the region [in the quarterly regressions], and a time trend); and u_{it} is the error term. Note that the specification includes a time trend as well as country-specific monthly or quarterly dummies (to guard against possible spurious correlation arising from seasonality in the timing of treatment in different countries). The external economic environment is controlled for by the inclusion of Z_t^k. The parameter β establishes the baseline post-treatment response, while γ is our estimate of the difference that is attributable to capital controls in Malaysia.[18]

The data come mostly from the *International Financial Statistics* of the IMF. Stock market data are from the Emerging Markets Database, and Malaysian employment and wage data are from the *Monthly Manufacturing Statistics* of Malaysia. Where possible, we use monthly data, but because many indicators of real economic activity are available only on a quarterly basis, we supplement the monthly regressions with quarterly regressions as well. The regressions cover the period 1992–96 ("before") and the one year of treatment ("after"). In a few cases, data availability dictates a shorter time span for the "before" period.[19]

Table 8.2 shows the timing of the treatment windows for each country. Our focus is on the one-year period following the seeking of IMF assistance or the imposition of capital controls. This seems to us to be the relevant time span for answering our central question about the speed and vigor of the recovery. In the case of Malaysia, this corresponds to the September 1998–August 1999 period (1998:4–1999:3 in the quarterly regressions). For the other countries, we pick a starting point that follows as closely as possible the date at which the country first requested IMF assistance. We pick that date rather than the date of program announcement or IMF board approval (also shown in table 8.2) because the time lag between these dates, reflecting the bargaining and negotiation with the IMF, seems to us to be a relevant part of the counterfactual.[20] Note that the timing is somewhat more precise with the use of monthly data.

We shall focus on comparisons with Korea, in the first instance due to the more complete data availability in Korea (in comparison with Thailand and

---

18. Note that with the inclusion of other covariates on the left-hand side of our regression, the difference-in-differences coefficient is a difference that is *conditional* on the covariates.

19. When we include 1997 data in the regressions, the time-shifted results are even more favorable to the Malaysian controls.

20. Had Malaysia gone to the IMF, the implementation of policies would have been delayed, because a certain amount of time would have been lost in negotiations with the IMF on the design of the program. With capital controls, Malaysia was free to implement its policies instantaneously. However, as a robustness check we have also run the regressions taking as the starting point of treatment the date of signing of the letter of intent. This change makes no difference to the results.

Table 8.2   Timing of Treatment Windows

| | Date of First Official Announcement That Country Will Seek IMF Assistance | Date of IMF Executive Board Approval of Program | Treatment Windows | |
| | | | Monthly Regressions | Quarterly Regressions |
Country				
Thailand	28 July 1997	20 August 1997	August 1997–July 1998	1997:3–1998:2
Indonesia	8 October 1997	5 November 1997	October 1997–September 1998	1997:4–1998:3
South Korea	21 November 1997	4 December 1997	December 1997–November 1998	1998:1–1998:4
Malaysia	n.a.	n.a.	September 1998–August 1999	1998:4–1999:3

Sources: Dates are from "Chronology of the Asian Currency Crisis and its Global Contagion," on Nouriel Roubini's web site [http://www.stern.nyu.edu/~nroubini/asia/AsiaHomepage.html] and the IMF web site [http://www.imf.org].

Note: n.a. = not applicable.

Indonesia) on real indicators. However, Korea also has the advantage that it is considered to be the IMF's most successful patient in the region. Since our results indicate that Malaysian controls were also quite successful, it is useful to subject them to a particularly demanding test. Showing that Malaysia did better with its policies than Indonesia did with an IMF program would be hardly convincing, as one might credibly argue that Indonesia's failure arose from idiosyncratic reasons.

Table 8.3 shows the core results, using both time-shifted and conventional difference-in-differences approaches. We present only the coefficient estimates for β and γ and their standard errors for each version of the regression, suppressing other regression output for ease of readability. The way to read the table is as follows. Consider the first row, which shows the results for industrial production. The numbers indicate that in the twelve-month period subsequent to calling in the IMF, Korea witnessed a reduction in its industrial output growth relative to trend of 15.1 percentage points ($\beta = -0.151$). In Malaysia, the reduction in growth following the imposition of capital controls was 5.2 percentage points lower than in Korea ($\gamma = 0.052$), or 9.9 percentage points ($= 15.1 - 5.2$). Both numbers are estimated precisely and are statistically significant at conventional levels. Note that these estimates are conditional on the other controls in the regressions, namely country-specific monthly dummies and the time-varying external variables listed previously.

The last two columns show the corresponding estimates for the conventional difference-in-differences approach. These results are quite different and are less favorable to Malaysia. They suggest that Malaysia's post–September 1998 growth lagged significantly behind Korea's during the same period—a difference in fact of 16.7 percentage points.

The remaining rows repeat the exercise for other variables of interest. The time-shifted difference-in-differences yield consistently strong (and in all cases statistically significant) results in favor of capital controls. Compared to Korea, Malaysia suffered a smaller reduction in manufacturing employment (a difference of 19.1 percent), a smaller drop in real wages (a difference of 10.8 percent), a smaller drop in the stock market (a difference of 22.3 percent), a larger reduction in interest rates (a difference of 3.9 percentage points), less currency depreciation (a difference of 18.5 percent), and a smaller increase in inflation (a difference of 1.8 percent). All of these estimates are statistically significant.

Once again, the conventional difference-in-differences paint a different picture, although the general pattern is less uniform than in the time-shifted case. In some cases these agree with the previous estimates (in particular with regard to employment and real wages). The most striking discrepancies arise, aside from industrial output, for interest rates (a relative increase in Malaysia of 4.9 percent) and inflation (a relative increase in Malaysia of 2.4 percent).

Table 8.3   Estimates of the Effects of Malaysian Capital Controls (monthly data)

Variable	Comparators	Time-Shifted Difference-in-Differences Method		Conventional Difference-in-Differences Method	
		Baseline Effect (β)	Difference in Malaysia (γ)	Baseline Effect (β)	Difference in Malaysia (γ)
Industrial production index (log difference, annual)	Korea	−0.151*** (0.030)	0.052** (0.022)	0.078** (0.037)	−0.167*** (0.025)
Manufacturing employment (log)	Korea	−0.151*** (0.017)	0.191*** (0.012)	−0.138*** (0.011)	0.184*** (0.008)
Real wages (log)	Korea	−0.279*** (0.035)	0.108*** (0.025)	−0.228*** (0.042)	0.067** (0.028)
Stock market index (logs, deflated by CPI)	Korea	−1.018*** (0.108)	0.223*** (0.079)	−0.633*** (0.118)	−0.110 (0.079)
Interest rates (money market, %)	Korea	3.247** (1.511)	−3.944*** (1.106)	−5.986*** (0.879)	4.896*** (0.590)
Exchange rate (HC/$) (logs)	Korea	0.534*** (0.021)	−0.185*** (0.015)	0.391*** (0.015)	−0.040*** (0.010)
Foreign reserves (logs)	Korea	−0.195* (0.117)	−0.446*** (0.086)	0.066 (0.112)	−0.696*** (0.075)
Inflation rate (CPI, annual%)	Korea	0.027*** (0.005)	−0.018*** (0.004)	−0.016** (0.007)	0.024*** (0.005)
Industrial production index (log difference, annual)	Korea, Thailand	−0.184*** (0.030)	0.093*** (0.024)	0.218*** (0.030)	−0.164*** (0.031)
Stock market index (logs, deflated by CPI)	Korea, Thailand, Indonesia	−0.999*** (0.098)	0.201** (0.087)	−0.054 (0.102)	−0.060 (0.116)

(*continued*)

Table 8.3 (continued)

Variable	Comparators	Time-Shifted Difference-in-Differences Method		Conventional Difference-in-Differences Method	
		Baseline Effect (β)	Difference in Malaysia (γ)	Baseline Effect (β)	Difference in Malaysia (γ)
Interest rates (money market, %)	Korea, Thailand, Indonesia	18.133***	−21.063***	−22.055***	0.066
		(3.467)	(3.107)	(3.132)	(3.564)
Exchange rate (HC/$) (logs)	Korea, Thailand, Indonesia	0.741***	−0.435**	−0.068	−0.202
		(0.242)	(0.217)	(0.219)	(0.249)
Foreign reserves (logs)	Korea, Thailand, Indonesia	−0.314***	−0.264***	0.426***	−0.691***
		(0.077)	(0.069)	(0.069)	(0.078)
Inflation rate (CPI, annual%)	Korea, Thailand, Indonesia	0.122***	−0.110***	−0.072***	−0.017
		(0.023)	(0.021)	(0.022)	(0.025)

Source: See text.

Note: Standard errors in parentheses. CPI = Consumer Price Index. HC = home currency.

***Significant at the 1 percent level.

**Significant at the 5 percent level.

*Significant at the 10 percent level.

The bottom panel of table 8.3 recalculates the regressions using as comparators all three countries (Korea, Thailand, and Indonesia) wherever data are available. The coefficients β and γ now have to be interpreted as pertaining to averages for the comparators as a group. The general pattern of results is quite similar to those just reported. Malaysia comes out looking very good in the time-shifted regressions and not so good in the conventional ones. The presence of Indonesia in the comparator sample has a large influence on some of the outcomes—note, for example, the whopping interest rate and inflation results in the time-shifted regressions.[21]

In table 8.4, we present similar estimates with respect to performance measures that are available only on a quarterly basis. For comparison purposes, we also repeat the exercise using quarterly versions of some of the monthly series we discussed above (industrial production, manufacturing employment, real wages, and the stock market index). The time-shifted results are essentially unchanged. With regard to the new variables, we find very strong effects for real GDP growth (a difference in favor of Malaysia of 5.7 percentage points) and private consumption growth (a difference of 8.6 percentage points). We also find a larger reduction in the government surplus, although this is not statistically significant at conventional levels.

How do we interpret these results? Critics of the IMF have argued that the IMF programs in the region aggravated the crisis and exacerbated financial panic (at least during the initial months) by calling for excessively contractionary monetary and fiscal policies, by mandating bank closures, by overreaching in structural reforms, and by not putting enough pressure on creditors for an early standstill on debt repayment.[22] Our findings are consistent with this critique. Taken together, the time-shifted difference-in-differences estimates suggest that the Malaysian policy was more successful in immediately reducing interest rates, stabilizing the currency, and stemming financial panic. This success eased, for the short term at least, worries that the banking system would go under and that there would be a devaluation spiral. The turnaround in market confidence was correspondingly more rapid. In addition, fiscal policy was on balance more expansionary. All these in turn spurred consumption and economic activity.

We would therefore hypothesize that there were two channels through which the capital controls worked. One was the standard Keynesian policy of demand reflation, implemented through expansionary monetary and fiscal policies. The other, and perhaps more operative, channel was the

21. An alternative approach would be to add country-specific interaction terms for Thailand and Indonesia, in which case the same difference-in-differences coefficients can be recovered by subtracting the γs across countries. Because we are interested mainly in the outcomes for Malaysia vis-à-vis the rest of the countries, we do not report those results.

22. Critics differ in their weighting of these different factors. For a variety of critical views, see Krugman (1999a), Radelet and Sachs (2000), Feldstein (1998), Furman and Stiglitz (1998), and United Nations Conference on Trade and Development ([UNCTAD] 2000), among others.

Table 8.4   Estimates of the Effects of Malaysian Capital Controls (Quarterly Data)

Variable	Comparators	Time-Shifted Difference-in-Differences		Conventional Difference-in-Differences	
		Baseline Effect (β)	Difference in Malaysia (γ)	Baseline Effect (β)	Difference in Malaysia (γ)
Real GDP (log increase, annual)	Korea	-0.166***	0.057**	-0.047	-0.075***
		(0.048)	(0.024)	(0.062)	(0.025)
Industrial production index (log increase, annual)	Korea	-0.243***	0.080**	-0.022	-0.166***
		(0.074)	(0.037)	(0.089)	(0.036)
Manufacturing employment (log)	Korea	-0.180***	0.203***	-0.142***	0.184***
		(0.043)	(0.018)	(0.040)	(0.049)
Real wages (log)	Korea	-0.229***	0.092***	-0.164***	0.050***
		(0.049)	(0.021)	(0.045)	(0.008)
Stock market index (logs, deflated by CPI)	Korea	-1.656***	0.320**	-1.180***	-0.147
		(0.307)	(0.152)	(0.339)	(0.135)
Government surplus (% of GDP)	Korea	-0.092***	-0.022	-0.105***	-0.020
		(0.032)	(0.016)	(0.035)	(0.014)

Financial inflows (% of GDP)	Korea	0.097	−0.054	0.090	−0.068
		(0.113)	(0.054)	(0.120)	(0.046)
Real private consumption (log increase, annual)	Korea	−0.245***	0.086**	−0.130	−0.048
		(0.084)	(0.042)	(0.090)	(0.039)
Real investment (log increase, annual)	Korea	−0.479**	−0.032	−0.253	−0.317***
		(0.204)	(0.101)	(0.219)	(0.088)
Real government consumption (log increase, annual)	Korea	0.058	0.082	0.077	0.069
		(0.208)	(0.103)	(0.219)	(0.088)
Real imports (log increase, annual)	Korea	−0.400**	0.140	−0.332	−0.001
		(0.183)	(0.090)	(0.206)	(0.083)
Real exports (log increase, annual)	Korea	0.101	−0.134**	−0.144	0.110*
		(0.135)	(0.067)	(0.138)	(0.056)

Source: See text.

Note: Standard errors in parentheses.

***Significant at the 1 percent level.

**Significant at the 5 percent level.

*Significant at the 10 percent level.

removal of the substantial uncertainty about the financial system and the exchange rate, uncertainty that had previously depressed confidence and business activity. In other words, capital controls worked to revive demand not only because they allowed the government greater monetary and fiscal autonomy, but probably also because they enabled the return of a modicum of stability to financial markets.[23] However, we need further research before we can make a strong case for either of these channels.

Finally, we note that by choosing capital controls over the IMF, Malaysia missed out on the large capital injections that Thailand and Korea received. This makes it even more surprising, if the time-shifted estimates are to be believed, that Malaysian policy outperformed Korean and Thai policy. It would be interesting to know how Malaysian capital controls would have worked had they been accompanied by billions of dollars in loans. We have nothing to say about this counterfactual except to suggest that it would certainly have improved the performance of Malaysia relative to Korea and Thailand.

8.6 Some Alternative Interpretations

We have argued that the time-shifted difference-in-differences provide a more accurate estimate of the effects of Malaysia's capital controls because the most likely alternative to them was not to wait passively for recovery to take hold but to undergo an orthodox program similar to that implemented in the other countries some months earlier. We shall now review some alternative readings of the evidence that are less favorable to the controls.

Malaysia was not confronted with a serious economic crisis of the type faced by the other countries. This view essentially argues that the time-shifted difference-in-differences estimation is not valid because the crisis was much worse in Thailand and Korea than in Malaysia, so that the difference in average performance reflects a difference in the level of the crisis rather than a difference in the policy response. This argument usually takes one of two forms. The first version asserts that Malaysia's economic problems were largely due to the verbal antics of its prime minister. A second version is that the Malaysian crisis was mostly due to the political uncertainty surrounding the internal battle for power between Mahathir and Anwar. Both sources of uncertainty were reduced dramatically with the imposition of the controls and the firing of Anwar on 2 September 1998.

We do not take a position on whether Malaysian policy prior to September 1998, in combination with Prime Minister Mahathir's behavior, led to an unnecessarily large economic downturn. Nevertheless, it is clear that Malaysia was in the midst of a very severe real economic crisis, one compa-

---

23. With a precautionary motive for saving, reduced uncertainty should lead to increased consumption.

Table 8.5   Measures of Economic Activity in Korea and Malaysia Before and After Policy Implementation: Growth Rates (%)

	GDP		Exports		Consumption		Investment	
	Korea	Malaysia	Korea	Malaysia	Korea	Malaysia	Korea	Malaysia
−4Q	6.45	7.44	6.83	11.30	9.76	8.16	8.55	17.16
−3Q	4.83	5.49	7.18	17.45	8.12	−3.44	2.55	−3.43
−2Q	6.04	−3.19	20.04	21.42	7.38	−14.69	4.70	−26.40
−1Q	5.31	−5.36	21.40	17.92	7.32	−16.74	−1.23	−58.17
Policy	3.53	−11.54	32.15	8.94	0.36	−23.67	−4.48	−80.18
1Q	−4.75	−10.83	54.62	4.45	−11.43	−11.44	−21.50	−57.60
2Q	−8.29	−0.75	33.35	0.19	−9.15	1.50	−25.25	−34.42
3Q	−8.45	3.93	24.38	10.62	−7.29	5.28	−25.65	−19.18
4Q	−6.13	8.59	3.45	15.79	−0.22	10.40	−21.05	1.89
5Q	5.27	9.56	−26.97	18.40	10.99	6.65	−2.51	1.65

Source: IMF (various issues).

rable with the crises experienced by Thailand and Korea, by the time the controls were implemented. The crisis went considerably beyond the financial market pressure on the ringgit. Looking at table 8.5, we can see that Malaysia had a larger contraction in economic activity prior to the controls than Korea did at any time during its crisis. Also, in the quarter during which Malaysia implemented controls, the country experienced a larger reduction in output than Korea ever sustained.[24] Given the evidence on output contraction, we believe that it is not tenable to discount the Malaysian crisis as somehow a fiction and due mostly to capital controls.

Malaysia simply benefited from the improvement in the external environment. This represents the standard view of the Malaysian recovery, and we have already given some reasons to be skeptical of it. First, it is not at all clear that Malaysia was benefiting much from the return of investor confidence to the region, which was already under way in September. As we have seen, financial indicators in Malaysia were moving in the direction opposite to those in Korea and Thailand. Even setting aside Anwar's forthcoming political demise, there is no reason to presume that conditions would have improved for Malaysia any time soon. They certainly did not for Indonesia. Nor did they for Russia or Brazil, which were hit by financial panic some months later.

Second, even if one thinks that the pressure against the ringgit was about to ease up, it is not clear why Malaysia would have benefited from the improvement in investor sentiment after having imposed capital controls to insulate itself from financial market conditions. This is a problem, espe-

24. Malaysia implemented capital controls in the last month of the third quarter, so that most of the decline in third-quarter output occurred before the implementation of the controls.

cially if one is predisposed toward open capital accounts as a general rule. It is difficult to argue that capital controls isolate an economy from the benefits of financial markets while maintaining that one receives the same benefits regardless of whether one has capital controls or not.

Finally, as we have already pointed out, we do include in our regressions the salient features of the external environment. In particular, we include a measure of total net financial flows to four countries in the region (South Korea, the Philippines, Indonesia, and Thailand) in the quarterly regressions (table 8.4).[25] This measure is displayed in figure 8.5. The net outflow from these countries averaged $8.0 billion in the first four quarters after Korea went to the IMF, but only $1.7 billion in the first four quarters of the Malaysian controls.[26] We also control (in both our monthly and quarterly regressions) for U.S. interest rates, which fell significantly in October 1998. Since we control for these differences, our results must be interpreted as the effect of capital controls after netting out the impact of the external environment.

Malaysia's recovery was essentially due to the IMF-style policies it had put in place in 1997. A related argument is that the IMF-type policies that Malaysia followed while Anwar was still in charge of economic policy were bearing fruit and that the recovery is attributable to the delayed effect of these policies rather than the controls. As we mentioned above, there is in fact scarce evidence that the real economy was about to turn around in Malaysia. If anything, the economy was sinking deeper as time went on.

While it is impossible to be definitive on this score, it is instructive to compare Malaysia's performance prior to September 1998 with Korea's. Figure 8.6 shows a measure of the "output gap" in industry for the two economies, calculated as the residual from a regression of the industrial output index on a time trend and monthly dummies. The first thing that is clear from the picture is that the recessions in the two economies were not perfectly synchronized: Malaysia's recession lagged behind Korea's, which supports our argument that the timing of the crisis was different in these countries. More to the point in the current context, it is clear that Korea's turning point came in July of 1998, while Malaysia continued to deteriorate. (Malaysia was not the only country in the region for which this was true: Indonesia continued to experience severe decline throughout 1998 and into 1999.) The Malaysian economy bottomed out months later, in January

25. Since financial flows are available only on a quarterly basis, we could not include a similar measure in the monthly regressions. The latter do include other proxies for the external environment, however—namely, U.S. interest rates, inflation, and industrial production.

26. Flows to the region are obviously endogenous, but introducing this variable in the regressions biases the results *against* the Malaysian policies: If the large outflow while countries were under IMF programs is the result in part of the poor performance of those economies, "controlling" for these outflows makes the IMF programs look more successful. Removing flows from the quarterly regressions generally works to the advantage of the Malaysian controls.

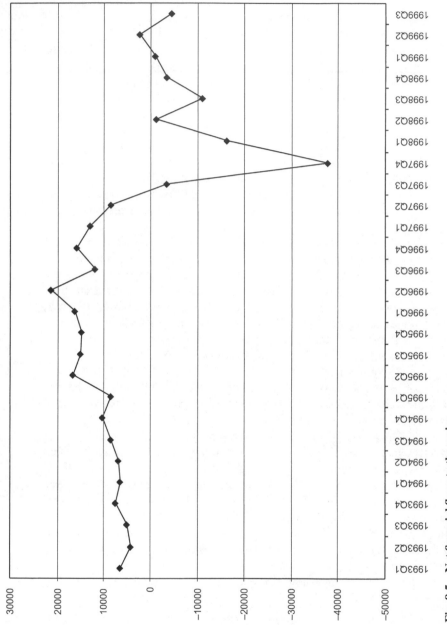

Fig. 8.5   Net financial flows to the region

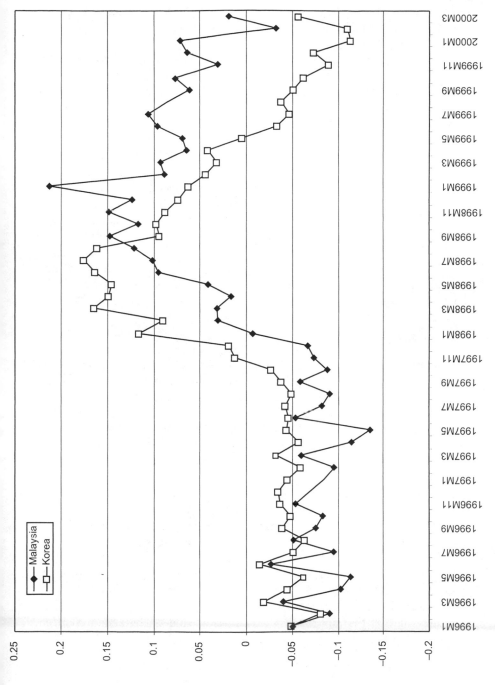

Fig. 8.6 Industrial "output gap"

1999. In other words, by September 1998 one could have been reasonably confident that the Korean recovery had begun. There were no such signs in Malaysia.

Malaysia made things worse for itself by delaying decisive policy action. We have little disagreement with the view that Malaysia would have been better off had it been able to resolve its difficulties before September 1998. However, this is largely irrelevant to the question at hand, and not simply because all the countries in the region experienced their share of self-inflicted harm.

Would Malaysia have been wiser to go to the IMF in late 1997 instead of waiting for another year and reacting as it did in late 1998? Perhaps. However, on the basis of the evidence presented here, one might also argue that Malaysia would have fared even better if it had imposed capital controls sooner—better than with an earlier IMF remedy, and better than it did subsequently. There is presumably less of a downside to capital controls when capital is leaving the region (as in 1998) than when it is coming back (as in 1999). Furthermore, to the extent that delay makes the eventual policy adjustments more costly, our results must underestimate the relative advantage of capital controls.

8.7   Concluding Remarks

We posed three questions at the outset about the near-term consequences of the Malaysian capital controls. Were the controls effective in segmenting financial markets and providing breathing room for monetary and financial policies? Did they allow a speedier recovery than would have been possible via the orthodox IMF route? Did they allow the leadership to do politically nasty things? We have given affirmative answers to all three questions. The longer-term question about the country's access to FDI and other forms of external finance is harder to answer with the available evidence, and we have not said much about it.[27]

This paper's main contribution has been to recast the comparison between Malaysia and the other countries in the region in a manner that, to our mind, makes more sense. Previous comparisons have asked how Malaysia performed relative to Korea or Thailand after September 1998. We have asked instead how Malaysia performed compared to Korea or Thailand when the latter were undergoing their IMF programs (although we made allowance for changes in the external environment). We have shown that the first approach yields answers that on balance make the

---

27. There are indications that FDI into Malaysia may have slowed down and that bond spreads have remained a bit higher in relation to other countries in the region (Liu 2000). On the other hand, Korea and Thailand are left with large debts to the IMF and other international lending institutions; Malaysia did not accumulate such debts.

capital controls look bad. The second approach yields answers that make the controls look very good.

Our preferred counterfactual is based on the view that Malaysian policies in the summer of 1998 were unsustainable, that the pressure against the ringgit was building up, that the economic decline was not about to be reversed on its own, and that the realistic alternative to the capital controls was an IMF program of the type that the other countries undertook. For our results to be credible, it must also be the case that we have adequately controlled for the external environment. On the other hand, the conventional counterfactual requires us to believe that the intense offshore speculation against the ringgit was about to stop of its own accord, that the Malaysian economy was about to turn the corner even without any fundamental change in policies, or that an IMF-style program would have produced an immediate recovery for Malaysia (even though Korea's and Thailand's IMF programs did not do so).

In closing, we simply invite the reader make up his or her mind about which of these counterfactuals makes more sense, and to form conclusions accordingly.

Appendix

Malaysian Controls on Capital and Exchange Controls, 1–2 September 1998

1. Malaysia fixed the exchange rate at MYR3.80 per U.S. dollar.
2. Prior approval was required for nonresidents to be able to buy or sell ringgit forward.
3. All sale of ringgit assets was required to be transacted through approved domestic intermediaries. This effectively shut down the operation of the offshore ringgit market.
4. Nonresidents were required to obtain BNM approval to convert ringgit held in external accounts into foreign currency, except for the purchase of ringgit assets in Malaysia or for the purposes of conversion and repatriation of sale proceeds of investment made by foreign direct investors.
5. Settlements of imports and exports were required to be settled in foreign currency. However, free exchange was maintained for all current account transactions in addition to supply of trade credit to nonresident exporters of Malaysian goods.
6. Credits to external accounts were limited to salaries, wages, rentals, commissions, interest, profits, dividends, or sale of foreign currency, ringgit instruments, securities, or other assets in Malaysia.
7. Debits to external accounts were restricted to settlement for purchase

of ringgit assets and placement of deposits; payment of administrative and statutory expenses in Malaysia; payment of goods and services for use in Malaysia; and granting of loans and advances to staff in Malaysia.

8. Domestic nationals were forbidden to export more than MYR10,000 during any travels abroad. Foreign nationals were forbidden to export more than MYR1,000 upon leaving Malaysia.

9. After 1 September 1998, nonresident sellers of Malaysian securities were required to hold on to their ringgit proceeds for at least twelve months before repatriation was to be allowed.

10. A ban was placed on the provision of domestic credit to nonresident correspondent banks and stockbroking companies.

1999 Changes in Controls

1. As of 15 February 1999, the year-long moratorium on repatriation of investments was replaced with a graduated tax. All capital having entered Malaysia before this date were subject to the following levies on the capital being removed: (a) 30 percent if repatriated within the first seven months after entering Malaysia, (b) 20 percent if repatriated between seven and nine months after entry, (c) 10 percent if repatriated between nine and twelve months of entering, and (d) no levy if repatriated after one year of entry.

2. For funds entering Malaysia after 15 February 1999, capital was free to enter and leave without taxation; however, profits were taxed at the rate of 30 percent if repatriated within one year of entry and 10 percent if repatriated after one year of entry.

References

Ariyoshi, Akira, Karl Habermeier, Bernard Laurens, Inci tker-Robe, Jorge Iván Canales-Kriljenko, and Andrei Kirilenko. 1999. *Country experiences with the use and liberalization of capital controls.* IMF Occasional Paper. Washington, D.C.: International Monetary Fund.

Athukorala, Prema-chandra. 1998. Malaysia. In *East Asia in crisis: From being a miracle to needing one?* ed. Ross H. Mcleod and Ross Garnaut. London: Routledge.

Bank Negara Malaysia (BNM). 1999. *The central bank and the financial system in Malaysia: A decade of change.* Kuala Lumpur: BNM.

Edison, Hali, and Carmen M. Reinhart. 2001. Stopping hot money: On the use of capital controls during financial crises. *Journal of Development Economics,* forthcoming.

Eichengreen, Barry, Andrew K. Rose, and Charles Wyplosz. 1995. Exchange market mayhem: The antecedents and aftermath of speculative attacks. *Economic Policy* 21 (October): 251–312.

Feldstein, Martin. 1998. Refocusing the IMF. *Foreign Affairs* 77 (2): 20–33.

Furman, Jason, and Joseph Stiglitz. 1998. Economic crises: Evidence and insights from East Asia. *Brookings Papers on Economic Activity,* Issue no. 2:1–135. Washington, D.C.: Brookings Institution.

Garber, Peter M. 1998. Derivatives in international capital flow. NBER Working Paper no. 6623. Cambridge, Mass.: National Bureau of Economic Research, June.

Haggard, Stephan, and Linda Low. 2000. The political economy of Malaysian capital controls. In *The political economy of the Asian financial crisis,* ed. Stephan Haggard, 73–86. Washington, D.C.: Institute for International Economics.

Institute of International Finance (IIF). 1998. Comparative statistics for emerging market economies. Washington, D.C.: IIF. December.

International Monetary Fund (IMF). Various issues. *International Financial Statistics.* Washington, D.C.: IMF.

Johnson, Simon, and Todd Mitton. 2001. Who gains from capital controls? Evidence from Malaysia. MIT, Sloan School of Management. Department of Economics. Manuscript, February.

Jomo, K. S. 2001. Capital controls. Chap. 7 in *Malaysian eclipse: Economic crisis and recovery,* ed. K. S. Jomo. London: Zed Books.

Kaminsky, Graciela, and Sergio Schmukler. 2000. Short-lived or long-lasting? A new look at the effects of capital controls. In *Brookings Trade Forum 2000,* ed. S. Collins and D. Rodrik, 125–66. Washington, D.C.: Brookings Institution. Forthcoming.

Kochhar, Kalpana, Barry Johnston, Michael Moore, Inci Otker-Rober, Scott Roger, and Dmitri Tzanninis. 1999. *Malaysia: Selected issues.* IMF Staff Country Report no. 99/86. Washington, D.C.: International Monetary Fund.

Krugman, Paul. 1999a. Analytical afterthoughts on the Asian crisis. MIT, Department of Economics. Unpublished manuscript, September.

———. 1999b. Capital control freaks: How Malaysia got away with economic heresy. *Slate.* Posted 27 September 1999. Available at [http://slate.msn.com/Dismal/99-09-27/Dismal.asp].

Lim, Linda. 1999. *Malaysia's response to the Asian financial crisis.* Statement before the Subcommittee on Asia and the Pacific of the House Committee on International Relations, 16 June.

Liu, Olin. 2000. Malaysia fashions own path to recovery, looks to strengthen growth. *IMF Survey* 29 (17): 282–84.

Meyer, Bruce D. 1995. Natural and quasi-experiments in economics. *Journal of Business and Economic Statistics* 13 (April): 151–62.

Mussa, Michael. 2000. Factors driving global economic integration. Paper presented at Federal Reserve Bank of Kansas City symposium, Global Opportunities and Challenges. 25 August, Jackson Hole, Wyo.

Perkins, Dwight, and Wing T. Woo. 2000. Malaysia: Adjusting to deep integration. In *The Asian financial crisis: Lessons for a resilient Asia,* ed. W. T. Woo, J. D. Sachs, and K. Schwab, 227–55. Cambridge: MIT Press.

Radelet, Steve, and Jeffrey Sachs. 2000. The onset of the East Asian financial crisis. In *Currency crises,* ed. In P. Krugman, 105–61. Chicago: University of Chicago Press.

Roche, David. 1998. The view from the ivory tower. *Forbes Global,* 5 October 1998. Available at [http://www.forbes.com/global/1998/1005/0113046a.html].

Rodrik, Dani, and Andres Velasco. Forthcoming. Short-term capital flows. In *Proceedings of the annual World Bank conference on development economics 1999.* 59–90. Washington, D.C.: World Bank.

UNCTAD. *Trade and development report, 2000.* New York: United Nations Publications.

Comment   Liliana Rojas-Suarez

The paper by Kaplan and Rodrik is an important contribution to the well-known debate on capital controls. Views on the desirability and effectiveness of capital controls have changed quite significantly over the last three decades. As is often the case, consensuses are questioned and revised after a major international financial crisis, and those on capital controls have not been the exception. For example, although in the 1970s there were large numbers of supporters of capital controls, the debt crisis of the 1980s brought about a renewed emphasis on the benefits of capital account liberalization. Many perceived capital controls, especially to the outflows, as an incentive to perpetuate "bad" domestic policies and, therefore, to generate capital flight. To a large extent, multilateral organizations praised the benefits of capital account liberalization, while recognizing that appropriate stabilization policies and structural reforms were needed as preconditions for establishing capital account convertibility on a sustainable basis.[1] Albeit to very different degrees, a large number of emerging markets embarked on a process of freeing international capital transactions as part of their overall reform efforts.

This consensus was revised again after the severe banking crisis that accompanied the exchange rate crisis in Mexico in mid-1994. The crisis led a number of analysts to identify the benefits of capital controls to the inflows as a "prudential" device to avoid intermediation of large amounts of short-term capital inflows through weak banking systems. These controls have taken a variety of forms including taxes, quantitative restrictions, and reserve requirements discriminating against short-term deposits denominated in foreign currency. A policy response to large capital inflows that has gained increased acceptance with International Monetary Fund (IMF) officials is a combination of controls on short-term inflows and liberalization on all other kinds of flows (outflows and long-term inflows).

The East Asian crisis of the late 1990s brought about a renewed interest in the discussion of capital controls. This time around, the motivation was provided by the drastic controls to the *outflows* imposed by Malaysia on 1 September 1998. If capital controls to the *outflows* were assessed to be a malaise of such long-term consequences, why did Malaysia, which imposed controls in the midst of the crisis against the advice of markets and multilateral organizations, seem not to have paid a higher price in terms of economic recovery than the rest of the Asian countries, which abstained from impos-

Liliana Rojas-Suarez is a visiting fellow at the Institute for International Economics.

1. As is well known, important contributions to the literature by Frenkel (1982) and Edwards (1989) concluded that the opening of the capital account should occur late in the sequencing of stabilization and structural reform programs in emerging markets in order to avoid capital flows that would make the reforms unsustainable.

ing controls? Moreover, could it have been the case that the imposition of controls actually benefited Malaysia by accelerating the recovery process?

Kaplan and Rodrik deal with this issue by posing two fundamental questions: (a) were capital controls in Malaysia effective in segmenting Malaysian financial markets from offshore and international capital markets, and (b) did the capital controls allow a faster economic recovery than what could have been achieved under an IMF program? In both cases, their answer is yes. The evidence presented in response to the first question is that the controls resulted in the death of the offshore ringgit market and allowed domestic interest rates to decrease. To respond to the second question, the authors used a time-shifted difference-in-differences methodology (rather than the conventional difference-in-differences) to identify the economic outcomes resulting from the controls. Although the authors are very careful in pointing out the limitations of the chosen methodology as well as the issues that require further research, the clear policy conclusion that readers of this paper derive is that capital controls to the outflows can be a desirable policy tool with which to confront severe external pressures against the exchange rate.

In commenting on this paper, one can follow different paths. It is tempting to stress the limitations of the methodology and the restrictive assumptions needed and, in general, to question the real value of a counterfactual approach in an environment where so many other things are changing. I will, however, resist the temptation to follow that route and instead offer a quite different interpretation of the events.

Let me start by pointing out that I strongly believe that a serious analysis on capital controls in Malaysia needs to go beyond the sole focus on the controls to the *outflows* in September 1998 to incorporate the effects that the history of temporary capital controls on *inflows* had on the economy. Throughout the 1990s Malaysia imposed a series of temporary capital controls. Starting with limits on non–trade-related swap transactions on commercial banks in June 1992 and following with a long list of controls to inflows that lasted for most of 1994 (combined with the outspoken "antispeculators" statements of Prime Minister Dr. Mahathir bin Mohamad), agents dealing with Malaysian securities became aware that sudden changes in the rules governing transactions of cross-border financial flows were not only possible but likely.[2] This, together with limits on interest rates set by the central bank (Bank Negara Malaysia), gave a strong impetus to the growth of the offshore ringgit market, which was free of regulations and controls.[3]

2. For a summary of controls imposed in Malaysia during the 1990s, see Reinhart and Smith (1997).

3. The Central Bank sets the base lending rate (BLR). In addition, it enforces a ceiling over the BLR as the maximum that banks can charge borrowers for most type of loans. See Kochhar et al. (1999).

The motivation for imposing controls during the mid-1990s was to prevent speculative inflows that could lead to an excessive appreciation of the real exchange rate. As is usually the case, the policy intention of containing the inflows was twofold: to maintain monetary policy independence and to avoid a possible sudden reversal of the inflows and the concomitant adverse effects to economic and financial stability. While the controls were successful in the short run in containing the real appreciation of the ringgit, my overall assessment of the experience is that the long-run outcome was negative, as the controls contributed to the exacerbation rather than the amelioration, of the large outflows of 1997–98. I explain this contention in the following paragraphs.

Subsequent to the imposition of controls on inflows, a typical pattern emerged: In the face of profitable opportunities, controlling a market creates incentives to "shift" the market somewhere else, either abroad or to the informal sector (as with Latin America in the 1980s). This is exactly what happened in Malaysia, as evidenced by the growth and deepening of the offshore ringgit market. As often happens, during good times (1995–96) developments in the offshore market did not conflict with the conduct of domestic monetary policy, because the behavior of offshore interest rates was consistent with domestic monetary policy. However, as experience also shows, attempts to segment markets prove extremely difficult in bad times (1997–98). Aware that Mahathir would resist sharp increases in domestic interest rates in the presence of the overall economic slowdown that followed the Thai crisis and weaknesses in domestic financial markets, speculators perceived an opportunity to short the currency.[4] They did so in the "efficient" offshore market, raising interest rates to more than 40 percent when domestic rates were kept at only 10 percent. The resulting massive capital outflows to finance the speculation were inevitable. In other words, by creating the market conditions to allow for large and quick building of positions against the currency, the temporary capital controls imposed *before* September 1998 had long-run adverse consequences. Indeed, contrary to the argument that the temporary controls to the inflows in the mid-1990s limited the extent of the outflows in 1997–98, I would argue that the mechanisms and instruments developed in the offshore market after the inflow controls allowed for a very rapid transfer of large amounts of resources abroad.

It is in this context that Malaysia imposed drastic capital controls on *outflows* on 1 September 1998. How one interprets their effectiveness largely depends on what side of the debate one is on. If one is a defender of capital controls, one will argue, like Kaplan and Rodrik, that the controls worked

4. The extremely high ratio of stock market capitalization to GDP reflected the large amounts of bank credit dedicated to the purchase of stock (see Dornbusch, chap. 9 in this volume). In this environment, it was easily perceived by speculators that sharp increases in domestic interest rates would have severe adverse consequences to domestic financial markets.

because they killed the offshore ringgit market and, therefore, stopped the speculation. However, even assuming that the authors are right and that the speculation was not dying at the time controls were imposed (as argued by International Monetary Fund [IMF] reports; see, e.g., IMF 1999), the critical issue to me is that the attack did not have to start in the first place—at least, not with the severity it did. The combination of a "relative" low domestic interest rate policy, domestic financial fragilities, and a free offshore market that had grown enormously because of the history of controls in Malaysia was deadly. The offshore ringgit market attracted large amounts of capital outflows, and that capital was gone at the time the controls were imposed on 1 September 1998. True, the controls killed the ringgit market, but to call that "effective" is, from my point of view, a somewhat near-sighted account of events. My view is that although temporary drastic capital controls can work in the short run, they also have permanent adverse effects in the long run and tend to reduce the effectiveness of intended policies.

However, Malaysia recovered after the imposition of capital controls to the outflows, and if this recovery can be attributed even partly to the imposition of drastic controls to the outflows, many would find the controls justifiable. Once again, however, there is no consensus about the causes of the recovery. While Kaplan and Rodrik find evidence that Malaysia's output performance was better off with the controls than with the counterfactual of an IMF program, others argue that external events such as the sharp cut in U.S. Federal Reserve rates were at the core of the recovery of the Asian economies, including Malaysia. Given the multiplicity of fast-moving events taking place in the international capital markets, I think the relationship between economic recovery and outflow controls in Malaysia will remain an unresolved issue.

Kaplan and Rodrik support their empirical exercise by arguing that the relevant and realistic alternative to the capital controls in Malaysia was an IMF program, similar to the ones in Korea and Thailand, rather than the continuation of existing policies. Although I can see the merits of analyzing the alternative "counterfactuals," the truly interesting question from my point of view is why capital controls to the outflows were indeed an option open to the Malaysian authorities. Isn't the fear of a potential lack of access to international capital markets a powerful deterrent for countries to follow this policy? We did not see other countries in the Asian region or elsewhere reacting to the crisis with the imposition of drastic controls. Why was Malaysia different? I believe that the best answer to this question can be found in Haggard and Low's (2000) interpretation of events. Mahathir did not fear exclusion from international capital markets because Malaysia had secured funds from Japan through his outspoken support to Japanese foreign policy initiatives, the most prominent one being a Japanese-centered Asian Monetary Fund. Indeed, as shown by Haggard and Low, Japan became a major source of external finance to Malaysia during the period 1998–2000, including funds from the Miyazawa Initiative.

Thus, to me, the lessons are quite different from those than can be derived from Kaplan and Rodrik's paper. First, examining the entire recent history of capital controls in Malaysia leads me to conclude that controls were part of the problem and not part of the solution. It was because of the problems generated by temporary controls on *inflows* in the mid-1990s that radical measures against the *outflows* became a policy choice.

Second, an emerging market does not have to fear loss of access to international capital markets if it can negotiate financial resources on a political basis. Will we see the emergence of a Japan-dominated Asian Monetary Fund as the result of political agreements between countries in the region? Could such an institution be effective in helping to prevent crises, or would the political arrangements exacerbate the moral hazard problem and, instead, contribute to unsustainable policies? Of course, it is now too early to attempt to provide answers to these questions.

Understanding the Malaysian events fully also allows us to explain why other regions of the emerging-market world, such as Latin America, could not be in a position to deal with the international financial crisis and avoid contagion through capital controls. The straightforward reason is that Latin America was not in a position to secure access to international sources of funds beyond those available in the international capital markets or through multilateral organizations.

In 1993, I wrote a paper with Don Mathieson on the issue of capital controls ("Liberalization of the Capital Account"). Our conclusion was that the effectiveness of capital controls could at best be only temporary and that it depended on initial conditions (the degree of economic and financial imbalances). I believe that our basic conclusion remains as valid now as it was then, but the Malaysian experience has added an interesting new dimension to the analysis. Among initial conditions, the off-market political capacity to arrange for external (or internal) sources of funds needs to be taken into account.

References

Edwards, Sebastian. 1989. On the sequencing of structural reforms. NBER Working Paper no. 3138. Cambridge, Mass.: National Bureau of Economic Research, October.

Frenkel, Jacob. 1982. Comment on "The order of economic liberalization: Lessons from Chile and Argentina." *Carnegie-Rochester Conference Series on Public Policy* 17:199–202.

Haggard, Stephan, and Linda Low. 2000. The political economy of Malaysia's capital controls. In *The political economy of the Asian financial crisis,* ed. Stephan Haggard, 73–85. Washington, D.C.: Institute for International Economics.

International Monetary Fund. (IMF). 1999. *International capital markets: Developments, prospects, and key policy issues.* Washington, D.C.: IMF.

Kochhar, Kalpana, Scott Roger, Dimitri Tzanninis, Barry Johnston, Michael Moore, and Inci Otker-Robe. 1999. *Malaysia: Selected issues.* IMF Staff Country Report no. 99/86. Washington, D.C.: International Monetary Fund, August.

Mathieson, Don, and Liliana Rojas-Suarez. 1993. Liberalization of the capital account: Experiences and issues. IMF Occasional Paper no. 103. Washington, D.C.: International Monetary Fund, March.

Reinhart, Carmen, and Todd Smith. 1997. Too much of a good thing: The macroeconomic effects of taxing capital inflows. University of Maryland and International Monetary Fund. Mimeograph.

Discussion Summary

Nouriel Roubini disputed the view that the Malaysian capital controls were effective. According to him, in the summer of 1998 when the controls were imposed, the speculative pressure from the hedge funds was already relieved as a result of the hedge funds' huge losses following the Russian default, the intervention in Hong Kong, and the reversal of the yen. He said that hedge funds had already begun to reduce their positions in these countries at that time, which led to a major appreciation of the currencies of Australia, New Zealand, Singapore, and South Africa.

Roubini also noted that the overall market conditions in Malaysia before the crisis were better than in other crisis countries: The current account deficit was mostly financed by foreign direct investment, and the real depreciation of the ringgit was not as large as in other countries. Despite this, he said, the recession in Malaysia during the crisis was as deep as in other countries, and this implied that there was a lot of political rhetoric against speculators in Malaysia.

Finally, Roubini said the data suggested that Malaysia had similar experiences as other countries. It was growing at a speed similar to that of other countries until 1997, was struck by as big a recession as the others in 1998, and recovered similarly afterward. For example, the fall of nominal interest rates in Korea and Thailand (where no capital control was imposed) between September and December 1998 was as sharp as in Malaysia. In addition, Malaysia was effectively following an IMF program during the crisis period. He concluded that all the evidence suggests that there is no difference effectively across crisis countries and no evidence to support the claim of the effectiveness of capital control policies in Malaysia (relative to the IMF programs followed by other countries).

Shang-Jin Wei pointed out that some of the largest negative effects of capital controls are potentially the loss of confidence and foreign investment and the difficulty for the country to access foreign capital markets. Therefore, it is striking that the paper found that foreign direct investments in Malaysia were not affected. Wei also suggested studying the possible differential effects of capital controls on different forms of capital flows in addition to those on the total amount of capital flows.

Martin Feldstein commented that the wealthy Chinese minority in Indonesia, which used to be protected by the Suharto regime, pulled out its capital at the fall of Suharto. He asked if the Chinese minority played a comparable role in Malaysia and if this posed a considerable risk for the Mahathir regime. Feldstein also asked how the authorities in other Asian countries think of the Malaysian capital control policies as a way to deal with currency crises.

Eduardo Borensztein emphasized international trade as an important part of the external environment. He said that the reason Korea and Thailand did not experience much export expansion after their large devaluation was regional; that is, exports to Asia dropped dramatically. He said that the recovery of the region was very important and explained why the recovery of Malaysia was synchronized with other countries in the region.

On whether the controls were effective, Borensztein added that foreign direct investors could circumvent the control policies through big loopholes, as their remittance and dividend payments were not constrained. Had there been a large differential in interest rates, multinational companies could easily have circumvented the controls. He said that the fact that we did not see these evasive actions on the part of multinationals suggests that the controls were probably not binding.

Robert Dekle noted that the capital controls of Malaysia imposed in 1994 reduced its capital inflow relative to the GDP dramatically (from 2.00 percent to 0.02 percent). He said that this was why Malaysia had much less capital inflow than other countries in 1997 and that it also played a key role in saving Malaysia from the contagion of the crises.

Roberto Rigobon made the remark that the results of the paper were partly driven by the data on interest rates, which were affected by the offshore interest rates. He pointed out that the financial indices constructed with overnight interest rates on stock markets or exchange rates would date the Malaysian crisis much before December 1998 because the devaluation of the ringgit was much greater and overnight interest rates were much higher in 1997. He asked if the finding on the effectiveness of capital controls would be robust to these indices. Rigobon also commented that the finding that capital controls were not, at least, damaging, is a point worth emphasizing, given that most priors about the capital control policies are that they are costly.

Charles W. Calomiris noted that the external environment controls mainly had to do with the United States, which is a major source of the import demand for Malaysia. He suggested including trade-weighted real exchange rate changes of Malaysia's export rivals in the regression.

John McHale asked why Malaysia was under such a great financial pressure in the middle of 1998. He suggested that one possible explanation could be that Malaysia was perceived as a country that would contemplate imposing capital controls and the investors had an incentive to get their money out of the country. The option of imposing capital controls in difficult circumstances can therefore create a situation in which it is actually needed, remarked McHale.

Sebastian Edwards emphasized that when evaluating the control policies, it is important to note that Malaysian capital controls were temporary. He said this is a different situation from the earlier controls reported in his book on exchange rate crises (1999), in which he looked at forty major crises in the 1960s and 1970s and found that capital controls were imposed mostly after the crises and were not lifted after a long period (three years).

Ethan Kaplan first said that he agreed with the comments that the long-run consequences of the capital control policies are not clear. He said that the paper addressed a more modest question, namely, whether capital controls were effective in terms of increasing various measures of real and financial performance, such as growth rates, consumption, investments, and trade.

To the criticism that one cannot compare the experience of Malaysia to that of Korea and Thailand to identify the effects of capital controls because the controls were imposed during a big political change, Kaplan answered the following. He said that this is a general problem with cross-sectional analysis, especially when there are so few observations (countries) and so many characteristics that vary. One has to make a judgement regarding which variables to include, which cannot be done without a prior on what matters and what does not. In the paper, he and *Dani Rodrik* looked for the main difference between the effect of the imposition of control policies in Malaysia versus the effect of the IMF program in other countries, and the results were in favor of Malaysia. He said that one can offer several alternative explanations that are consistent with the findings, such as political changes in Malaysia or external regional effects. Nevertheless, Kaplan said that he believed that capital controls had a decent impact.

On the nature of the different experiences of Malaysia and other crisis countries, Kaplan said that their preliminary study suggested that, among the components of GDP, the differences on the impact for GDP lie in consumption and imports.

Rodrik said that although one could argue about the exact reason for Malaysia's recovery after September 1998, it was not obvious that this recovery would have automatically occurred at that time. Although Korea had clearly begun to recover in September 1998, there was nothing similar going on in Malaysia at that point.

One concern of the Malaysian authorities was social stability and the interethnic balance between the Chinese and Malay communities, which was extremely important for the political leadership. After seeing the experience of Indonesia after the IMF program, which intensified tension and led to interethnic strike, Malaysian authorities were determined to avoid such an outcome. Rodrik said that capital control policies had social benefits if one thought of their role in maintaining the interethnic balance in the face of the potentially explosive situation in Malaysia.

Finally, Rodrik emphasized that the capital control policies were not the same as the IMF programs implemented in other crisis countries. For example, when the IMF came the interest rates went up and banks were closed, whereas with capital controls the interest rates were reduced and there were no bank closures. The fiscal policy proposed by the capital controls was expansionary from the outset as opposed to starting from a contraction and changes over time in the IMF program. Moreover, the exchange rate was fixed under capital controls rather than being allowed to float and therefore suffering a much greater depreciation subsequent to having an IMF program. Finally, the issue of the resolution of the uncertainty was also very different. Once it was clear that the controls were going to be effective, they resolved the uncertainty in the system effectively, which played an important role in the recovery. On the other hand, Rodrik recognized that capital control policies did have distributional consequence; some of the benefits of the stability were reaped by the cronies of Mahathir.

Rodrik concluded by saying that even though it was true that Malaysia looked no different from an average crisis country in terms of real performance, this does not necessarily mean much. Malaysia could have gone the Indonesian way and done much worse, or imposed capital controls sooner and—on the evidence in the paper—done better.

9

Malaysia's Crisis
Was It Different?

Rudi Dornbusch

> Then the unexpected happened. The Asian miracle was shat-
> tered almost overnight and suddenly once fawning economists
> argued that all it really had been was a bubble, over-inflated by
> corruption, cronyism and bad loans. Asians were not only im-
> poverished but were blamed for impoverishing themselves.
> —Mahathir bin Mohamad (1999, 47)

The Asian crisis came as a big surprise to all: investors, credit rating agencies, international institutions, and, not least, officials in the crisis countries.
There is no question that the long-run performance, hard work, high saving
rates, and seemingly competent officials all added up to create a powerful
presumption that all was well.[1] They gave assurance that problems, if any,
would be isolated and manageable, and because everyone held that belief,
everyone reinforced everyone else's unquestioned beliefs. There was equally
no question that, once the weakness in balance sheets revealed itself, everyone's skepticism was profound, and their willingness to remain invested was
undermined. In preceding crises there had been little surprise; after all,
crises tended to occur in the usual suspects of Latin America, which never
came as a surprise. This time, the crisis struck the Asian miracle, but the
mechanisms differ little.

What differs in the case of Malaysia, however, is the forceful reaction of
the leadership and the departure from traditional postcrash responses.
Prime Minister Dr. Mahathir bin Mohamad staged a dramatic rejection not
only of speculators and the international capital market but also of international officialdom. He took recourse to financial restrictions with quite a
bit of grandstanding and, indeed, claimed that the country was successful
in averting worse consequences and recovering precisely because of these
measures. He obviously and righteously delighted in sticking a finger in the

Rudi Dornbusch is Ford Professor of Economics and International Management at the
Massachusetts Institute of Technology and a research associate of the National Bureau of
Economic Research.

1. Of course, there was a discussion about the productivity of Asian economies, but that
concerned the sacrifice in achieving growth, not the vulnerability that made for the imminent
crisis.

eye of the International Monetary Fund (IMF) and Group of Six (G6) treasuries.[2] It remains to be explored whether his claim is indeed appropriate or whether it is primarily the domestic grand-standing of a weakened and challenged leadership that uses international issues to deflect attention from severe domestic political problems.[3]

The Malaysian case deserves attention not only on its own terms but also because the presumption of capital controls in response to crises—failing an early and gracious arrival of the IMF—has become far more of a concern. After all, how can a finance minister assert that it is good policy for the country to experience a meltdown, as a matter of principle, to accommodate departing investors? Moreover, if it could be demonstrated that this policy had an appreciably positive effect in a crisis, policy makers would have to change their views and welcome such a development. Of course, a presumption of capital controls would create a very trigger-happy international environment. It might be argued, with some merit, that the environment is already explosive and that what is missing is a good response. Hence, it is no surprise that countries incline toward the *national solution,* and it does make for good rhetoric.

In evaluating the Malaysian experience, it must be understood that two crises were unfolding simultaneously for this country. One was the Asian financial crisis, which brought down countries with vulnerable financial structures. The other was the domestic political crisis that arose from the challenge to Mahathir by the deputy prime minister and finance minister, Anwar Ibrahim. In the eyes of the leadership, the political crisis must have seemed at least as critical as the financial crisis; indeed, the financial crisis offered a means to sustain and reinforce political control by creating an economic state of siege and policy response. It surely is not a coincidence that Anwar was deposed literally the day after capital controls were imposed.

If capital controls have not delivered economic results clearly superior to those of IMF assistance, that does not mean they failed on the political side. The attacks on speculators who were alleged to have undermined the Asian dream and the Malaysian model were central to the effort to ward off challenges to Mahathir's leadership. These attacks were intended to convince their audience that the economic development model (including the 2020 vision and the ambitious public investment programs) was right and that the rest of the world was wrong. For the time being, they have been effective in this effort.[4]

---

2. I cite G6 because Japan is not on record as questioning Malaysian policy responses. On the contrary, it participated with them and led the call for an Asian IMF and new and different policy responses to regional financial crises.

3. See Haggard (2000), Haggard and Low (2000), and Terence Gomez and Jomo (1999) for the political setting and its link to capital controls.

4. See Mohamad (1999), where Mahathir presents the case.

9.1   Capital Controls

In the 1930s, Nazi Germany invented capital controls, and soon, in an environment of capital flight and competitive depreciation, much of Europe adopted controls as well. The system become pervasive and accepted. Indeed, in the move toward rules paralleling the establishment of the IMF and the rebuilding of a more open world economy, capital account convertibility was not part of the picture. It came to the fore much later, after 1958, when Europe gradually and unevenly shifted to full convertibility. The usual suspects, France and Italy, took until the late 1980s to make the transition. Britain did not abolish exchange control until the Thatcher government, and in Japan or on the periphery the transition took even longer. Opening the capital account became the focus of U.S. financial policy in the late 1980s and particularly of the Rubin-Summers treasury, whose agenda was opening financial services trade and domestic financial deregulation. Repressed finance gave way to an opening of domestic finance and to more substantial freedom for cross-border flows.

The case for integrated international capital markets is just like that for open trade: a more efficient allocation of resources achieved by competition, diversification opportunities, and equalization of risk-adjusted returns. In addition, just as in the case of open trade, an overwhelming case can be made that restrictions to capital flows create a hotbed of privilege and corruption around exceptions and loopholes. Finally, the expectation is that an open capital market—and the accompanying international standards, regulation, and supervision—will do a better job at allocating capital than politicized and corrupt local arrangements.

Although a tremendous amount of work reports on the costs of trade distortions, little is available on the issue of restricted capital accounts.[5] For example, no evidence that countries with open capital accounts (other things being equal) grow faster has been reported, nor has the converse been the case. There is, however, work showing that countries with high black-market premiums (meaning that capital controls are binding) do perform more poorly. However, these premiums reflect not only controls but also macroeconomic instability, and hence may not be conclusive.

We might approach the question of the effects of controls somewhat differently by asking what we would expect from a country imposing controls on capital flows. In the long run, in the absence of regulatory and tax distortions, we would expect controls to imply a less effective allocation of resources and hence less growth or diversification. In the short term, controls play quite a different role. If they are imposed in the midst of a crisis, unan-

---

5. Even the evidence on trade is not unambiguous. See Brock and Durlauf (2000), Rodriguez and Rodrik (1999), and Doppelhofer, Miller, and Sala-i-Martin (2000).

ticipated and temporary, they will work in the sense that they stop outflows, reduce pressure on the exchange and interest rates, and hence avoid a state-of-siege situation that results in excess bankruptcy and disruption. They are analogous to a suspension of trading on the New York Stock Exchange or the Nasdaq or to a bank moratorium—they stop the run and offer time to set things straight.[6] Economists' concern with ad hoc capital controls is less with the description offered here than with the feared implication that they will become a substitute for setting things straight. Malaysia is, of course, a case in point. The major question, obviously, is whether the issue is to gain time or to make lasting changes in freedom of resource allocation. The former endeavor deserves much attention, whereas the latter is politically attractive but lacks economic support.

Moving now to the question of Malaysian controls, what might be argued? Supporters would no doubt claim that in the absence of controls the collapse would have been far deeper, the recovery much more difficult, the lasting damage far more profound. If this is the case, a capital-control country—other things being equal—will look much better than the other countries that are exposed to the same initial shocks but respond with orthodoxy rather than controls. Specifically, to make some progress on these issues, we should answer these three questions:

- On the eve of the crisis, was Malaysia appreciably different in its vulnerability from other crisis countries? If so, is that the possible explanation for its purported success in dealing with the problem?
- Did the policy measures—banking, stock market, and capital controls; business subsidies—perform significantly better than in other economies? Better performance means higher growth, less volatility, and less-pervasive bankruptcy without any offsetting large increases in public debt.
- Is there an indication of lasting costs, or benefits, to the policy choices?

It is as well to anticipate our conclusion. The costs or benefits of capital controls remain ambiguous, despite their ostensible success in Malaysia. In actual fact, Malaysia had more favorable preconditions, it did not perform appreciably better than other crisis countries, and the timing of controls coincided with the reversal of the appreciation of the yen, the end of the crisis elsewhere, and Federal Reserve rate cuts that put an end to the crisis atmosphere in world markets. Nevertheless, the reverse case equally holds.

6. In the aftermath of the 1987 stock market decline, the Brady Commission reviewed the question of suspending trading and came out in support of circuit breakers as a means to restore markets. On the Nasdaq, trading is suspended for companies for whom information is unavailable. These cases seem to present an interesting analogy for defensible limited-time capital flow suspensions. If a circuit breaker lasts half an hour on the New York Stock Exchange, the equivalent for an emerging-market capital flow suspension might be a month.

There is no evidence that capital controls or the failure to apply an explicit IMF program so far had obviously detrimental effects.

9.2 The Background

It is helpful to examine the context of the Malaysian events. The relevant time frame extends from the Thai problems that began in spring of 1997 to the interest rate cuts administered by the Federal Reserve in the aftermath of the Long-Term Capital Management (LTCM) problem and the Russian crisis. Various Asian economies joined the crisis progressively.

May–July 1997	Pressure on Thailand, exchange control, two-tier market, and devaluation occur.
July	The Philippines go to a float; Malaysia abandons support for the ringgit; Thailand goes to the IMF.
August	Thailand suspends forty-two banks; Indonesia abandons rupiah support; Malaysia restricts short selling; Indonesia restricts credit for rupiah trading.
October	Indonesia goes to the IMF; Malaysia announces austerity budget; Hong Kong dollar comes under attack.
November	Korea abandons won support and goes to the IMF.
December	Rescue package is designated for Korea.
January 1998	Malaysia announces full deposit guarantees.
January–August	Asian IMF packages are revised; financial restructuring and downgrading take place.
May	Indonesia's Suharto steps down.
August	Russian crisis occurs; yen peaks.
September	LTCM crisis occurs; Malaysia imposes capital controls; Deputy Prime Minister Anwar Ibrahim is deposed.
September–November	Federal Reserve cuts rates by 75 basis points.

The background of the Asian crisis includes the large buildup of capital inflows in the first half of the 1990s—not foreign direct investment (FDI) but bank loans and portfolio capital (see IMF 1999b). The crisis involves the sudden drying up and reversal of these flows in 1997 and the resulting macroeconomic pressures of currency depreciation, high interest rates, output decline, and financial stress. This reversal in capital flows is shown in the accompanying figure for the Asian crisis economies as a group. The coun-

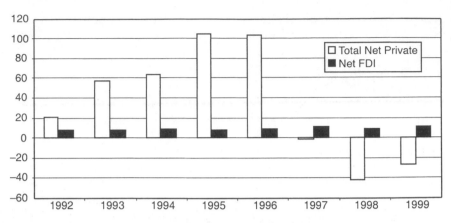

Fig. 9.1   External capital flows for crisis-Asia (US$ billions)

terpart of the reversed capital flows is a reserve loss and current account surpluses in the crisis economies.

The pressure for outflows soon reached all economies. Within six months following the Thai debacle, Indonesia, Malaysia, the Philippines, and Korea had been hit, and Hong Kong had come under attack.

One summary measure of events is the path of real gross domestic product (GDP). After performing well up to 1996, growth declined in 1997 as the economies shifted toward crisis. In the following year, 1998, output declined everywhere; by 1999, recovery was under way. By 2000 even per capita GDP is above precrisis levels. Judged by these standards, the crisis was as short as it was deep. However, other measures show more lasting damage, including an impaired banking system, a significantly higher public debt everywhere, and a loss of growth momentum, accompanied by the resulting temptation for governments to step in. Another measure that might indicate differential performance is the real exchange rate. One might argue that in a capital outflow crisis, other things being equal, countries with controls suffer a less extreme real depreciation. That argument is not borne out by the accompanying figure.

9.3   A Closer Look at Malaysia

This paper does not address the immediate reason for the crisis. Chapter 16 in this volume offers a summary of the vulnerability factors—misaligned real exchange rates, nonperforming loans in the banking sector, and the funding risk of the national balance sheet due to excess debt or mismatches of maturity and currency denomination.

With the pressure of capital outflows and increases in interest rates—already under way since early 1995—and poorer export performance, growth did give way. Ultimately, industrial production declined, only resuming

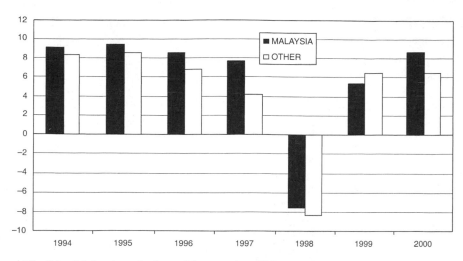

Fig. 9.2   Malaysia and other crisis countries: GDP growth

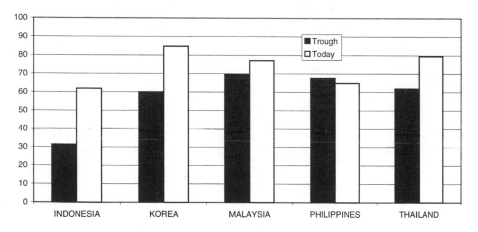

Fig. 9.3   Real exchange rate (January 1970=100)

growth in early 1999; investment as a share of GDP fell sharply, to only half its previous level; the stock market fell sharply; and the real exchange rate depreciated substantially.

Much of the macroeconomic scene involves the problems of banks and firms whose balance sheets are unprepared for exchange rate movements, slowdowns, or recessions. The responses of restructuring, bailing out, and subsidizing are certainly part of the controversial legacy. However, this part of the recovery process does not differ importantly from that of other economies, in which none of these responses took place promptly, decisively, or successfully.

Table 9.1   **Malaysia: Economic Indicators**

	1990–95	1995	1996	1997	1998	1999	2000
Growth	8.9	9.8	10.0	7.5	−7.5	5.4	8.5
Inflation	3.7	3.2	3.3	2.9	5.3	2.8	1.5
Investment[a]	37.5	43.6	41.5	42.9	26.7	22.3	24.1
Budget deficits[a]	−0.4	3.2	3.9	6.1	−0.9	0.2	−2.6
Current account[a]	−5.8	−9.7	−4.4	−5.6	12.9	16.0	12.1
External debt ($Bill)		34.3	39.7	47.2	42.6	43.6	45.0
% of GDP		38.7	39.3	47.1	58.8	55.2	50.4
% short term		19.1	27.9	25.3	17.8		
Reserves ($billions)		23.8	27.0	21.7	26.2	30.9	33.2

Source: Goldman Sachs, except % short term (IMF 1999c).
[a]Percent of GDP

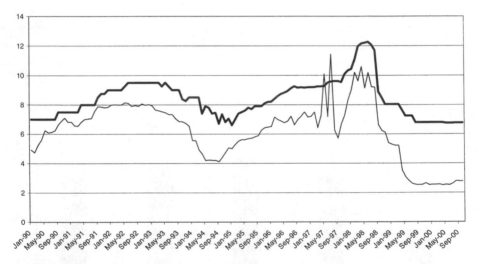

Fig. 9.4   Malaysia: Money market and lending rates

Fig. 9.5   Malaysia: Stock market (index January 94=100)
Source: Datastream.

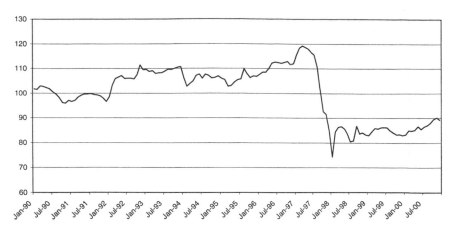

Fig. 9.6   Malaysia: Real effective exchange rate (JPMorgan Index 1990=100)

9.4   Capital Controls and Their Effectiveness

One possibly critical difference between Malaysia and other crisis economies in the region was its imposition of stringent capital controls on 1 September 1998. This went further than the Thai measures, which had already been suspended by then, and the credit measures that had been used elsewhere to avoid financing capital flight. The details of the capital controls essentially involved the mandatory repatriation and one-year holding of offshore ringgit funds as well as restrictions on outflow.[7] These controls were partially relaxed in February 1999 to become a system of graduated exit taxes. FDI flows throughout were exempt, and the exchange rate was fixed. The drastic attack on capital flows had the effect of stopping capital flows in both directions, as shown in figure 9.8, which uses portfolio flow data (made available by State Street Associates).

According to the canons of IMF policy and commitments, the imposition of capital controls was, of course, a radical measure. Whatever the reason it was imposed, Mahathir justified it with a quotation from Paul Krugman: "[E]xtreme measures might be needed for extreme times" (see Mohamed 1999, 106). In his justification for dispensing with classical financial rules, he might equally well have quoted Keynes: "[I]t is better for reputation to fail conventionally than to succeed unconventionally."

Where controls decisive in producing this turn of events, or was it taking place anyway? It is readily seen from the graph above that the stock market recovery turns in September, as does the recovery of industrial production. The same is true for short-term interest rates. It is tempting, therefore, to see the imposition of capital controls as the turning point. However, as the IMF

---

7. See IMF (1999a, 54–56; 1999c). For further references to Malaysian capital controls, see Ariyoshi et al. (2000), Edison and Reinhart (2000), Kaplan and Rodrik (chap. 8 in this volume), and Koay (2000).

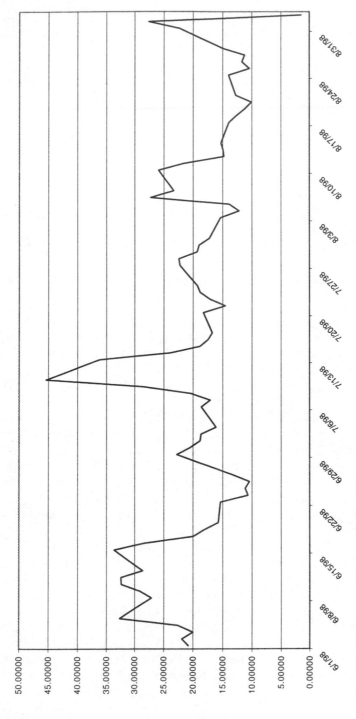

Fig. 9.7   Malaysian offshore daily rates (% per annum)

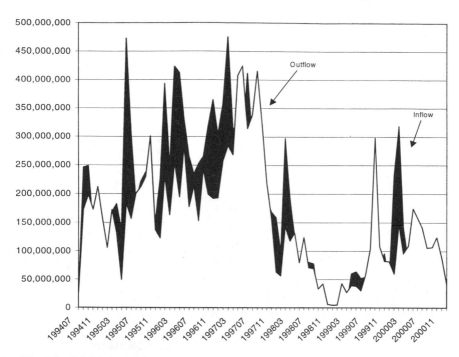

Fig. 9.8   Malaysia: Portfolio flows

has rightly argued, at the time that capital controls were imposed, markets had already settled in Asia and interest rates had started to decline—and would soon do so everywhere under the impact of Federal Reserve rate cuts and a reduction in jitters. In fact, rates in Korea and Thailand had fallen by August to half their June levels, and the same was true in Malaysia.

In fact, as we see from the *offshore* rates for Malaysia and thus the interest rates faced in the open market, which reflect depreciation expectations, much of the pressure had subsided before the 1 September imposition of capital controls. By August, the offshore rates had, in fact, declined to around 10 percent, far below the crisis level. Interestingly, the spike in the graph at the end represents the time the controls were put in place and reaches 28 percent on 1 September! Thus, the claim that the pressure continued unabated is simply not borne out by offshore interest rates. On the contrary, the advent of controls raised rates. The political interpretation of the controls thus deserves more attention.

9.5   Should Malaysia Have Done Better?

Another way of approaching the question of non-IMF policies and the claim that Malaysia performed well with such policies is to ask how the country compared to others in vulnerability. Two issues influence perfor-

Table 9.2   Vulnerability Indicators in 1996

	Stock Market Cap/GDP	Debt/Equity Ratio	Private Bank Credit/GDP	Short-Term External Debt/Reserves
Indonesia	40.0	310.0	55.4	177.0
Korea	28.6	518.0	57.6	193.0
Malaysia	310.0	150.0	89.8	41.0
The Philippines	97.3	160.0	49.0	80.0
Thailand	55	250	100	100

Source: World Bank (2000, 70).

Table 9.3   Nonperforming Loans and Increased Public Debt in 1999

	NPL/Total	NPL/GDP	Increase in Public Debt/GDP (%)
Indonesia	55	22	68.6
Korea	16	23	20.7
Malaysia	24	35	16.0
Thailand	52	53	34.6

Source: IMF (1999a), World Bank (2000).

mance: initial conditions and policy responses. If performance was not substantially different across different countries, one might argue whether it should have been simply because initial conditions were significantly more favorable or unfavorable to start with. In particular, very bad balance sheets would imply more difficulty in dealing with the crisis and hence poorer performance. On the other hand, better vulnerability indicators would mean less stress and hence better performance.

Tables 9.2 and 9.3 show a series of vulnerability indicators. In table 9.3, Malaysia looks relatively good in the debt-equity ratio of the corporate sector and, importantly, the ratio of short-term external debt to reserves. Both the stock market GDP ratio and the private credit GDP ratio are high. These were, indeed, vulnerable areas because the high valuation reflected the vast amount of bank credit lent to stock purchases (7 percent of GDP).

In table 9.3 we look at the status of the banking system by 1999. Malaysia looks relatively favorable in nonperforming loans as a share of total loans. As a ratio of GDP, however, these numbers are high, reflecting the large share of private credit relative to GDP. In Malaysia compares favorably in cleanup cost, all the more so because the Korean numbers almost certainly understate the cost of restructuring the banking system and the corporate sector.

Table 9.4 looks at some numbers for debt and debt structure in the corporate sector. Again, in no way does Malaysia stand out unfavorably. Public debt in 1996 is higher than in Korea or Indonesia, but certainly not alarmingly so; the banking system and private investment (with or without crony-

Table 9.4   **Public Debt, Bank Strength, and Corporate Debt Structure in 1996**

	Public Debt/GDP	Bank Strength Rating	Debt/Equity Ratio (%)	Short-Term Debt/ Total Debt
Indonesia	22.9	D	188	54
Korea	8.8	D	355	57
Malaysia	36.0	C+	118	64
The Philippines	105.1	D+	129	48
Thailand	15.7	D+	236	63

Source: IMF (1998, 36), Asian Development Bank (1999, 27), World Bank (2000, 70).

ism) were financing the development strategy, unlike in Latin America. However, Malaysia initially shows a better-rated banking system, lower debt and equity in corporations, and a maturity of debt that is not substantially shorter than elsewhere.

In sum, Malaysia was in no way more exposed than other crisis countries and, for that reason, should not have been doing worse. Accordingly, it cannot be argued that the effects of capital controls is contained a situation that otherwise would have been much worse than those of other countries. Once again, then, there is no evidence one way or the other.

One more question is whether Malaysia enjoys lasting benefits from the continuing capital control regime (see Bank Negara Malaysia's website for the bureaucratic aspects of ongoing circulars modifying the regime). The answer here is surely that it is far too early to judge the impact, if any. In the Exchange Rate Mechanism experience in Europe, the Netherlands paid a small but lasting price for a one-time devaluation that broke with the tradition of fixed rates on the deutsche Mark. In emerging markets, differentials reflect ongoing control regimes, macroeconomic instability, and, importantly, political uncertainties. To identify the capital control "misconduct" premium is overly ambitious.

References

Ariyoshi, A., K. Habermeier, B. Laurens, I. Otker-Robe, J. Canales-Kriljenko, and A. Kirilenko. 2000. *Capital controls: Country experiences with their utilization.* IMF Occasional Paper no. 190. Washington, D.C.: International Monetary Fund.

Asian Development Bank. 1999. *Asian Development Outlook.* Manila, The Philippines: Asian Development Bank.

Brock, W., and S. Durlauf. 2000. Growth economics and reality. NBER Working Paper no. 8041. Cambridge, Mass.: National Bureau of Economic Research, December.

Doppelhofer, G., R. Miller, and X. Sala-i-Martin. 2000. Determinants of longterm growth: A Bayesian averaging of classical estimates (BACE) approach. NBER Working Paper no. 7750. Cambridge, Mass.: National Bureau of Economic Research, June.

Edison, H., and C. Reinhart. 2000. Capital controls during financial crises: The case of Malaysia and Thailand. Board of Governors of the Federal Reserve. International Finance Discussion Paper no. 662.

Haggard, S. 2000. *The political economy of the Asian financial crisis.* Washington, D.C.: Institute for International Economics.

Haggard, S., and L. Low. 2000. The political economy of Malaysian capital controls. University of California, San Diego. Unpublished manuscript.

International Monetary Fund (IMF). 1998. *International capital markets, September.* Washington, D.C.: IMF.

———. 1999a. *World economic outlook (WEO), October 1999.* Washington, D.C.: IMF.

———. 1999b. Malaysia: Recent economic developments. IMF Staff Country Report no. 99/85. Washington, D.C.: IMF.

———. 1999c. Malaysia: Selected issues. IMF Staff Country Report no. 99/86. Washington, D.C.: IMF.

Koay, S. 2000. Effectiveness of capital controls in Malaysia. Unpublished manuscript, December.

Mohamad, M. 1999. *A new deal for Asia.* Malaysia: Pelanduk.

Rodriguez, F., and D. Rodrik. 1999. Trade policy and economic growth: A skeptic's guide to the cross-national evidence. NBER Working Paper no. 7081. Cambridge, Mass.: National Bureau of Economic Research, April.

Terence Gomez, E., and K. S. Jomo. 1999. *Malaysia's political economy.* Cambridge: Cambridge University Press.

World Bank. 2000. *East Asia: Recovery and beyond.* Washington, D.C.: World Bank.

Comment   Michael P. Dooley

I would like to underline two of the many interesting points Rudi Dornbusch makes in this paper. First, it seems to me that he is correct in arguing that politics had more to do with the imposition of controls in Malaysia than did welfare economics. Controls imposed after nonresidents have committed their funds are an excellent way to deflect blame for a financial crisis away from the authorities and onto foreign speculators. They also distance the chief executive from those who encouraged opening in the first place. This is not just an emerging-market phenomenon. President Nixon condemned the gnomes of Zurich as the Bretton Woods system of fixed exchange rates unraveled in the early 1970s.

In reviewing work on capital controls a few years ago (Dooley 1996) I

Michael P. Dooley is a research associate of the National Bureau of Economic Research and is a managing editor of the *International Journal of Finance and Economics.* He joined the faculty at the University of California, Santa Cruz in 1992 following more than twenty years service at the Board of Governors of the Federal Reserve System and the International Monetary Fund.

found this to be a recurring theme. Economic analysis provides a variety of rationales for capital controls. However, economists are usually embarrassed when politicians invoke their arguments to undertake control programs that are unrelated to the theory. Moreover, once in place, control programs take on a life of their own and outlive the original rationale. This is not a new idea: Cairncross (1973) and Dornbusch (1986) argue convincingly that control programs that might once have been sensible involve substantial long-run costs. Dornbusch's warning in this paper that we will have to see if the Malaysian controls are costly is based on solid historical evidence.

Is there a sensible economic rational for the Malaysian response to the financial crisis? The answer is clearly yes. As Dornbusch points out, a suspension of payments is the classic response to a bank run. If the Asian meltdown was a liquidity crisis, an efficient way to help investors select the good equilibrium is temporarily to stop the run until they come to their senses. In the end, investors will thank authorities for doing so. Moreover, the expectation that the authorities will use controls to stop runs and the unnecessary real costs associated with them will encourage capital inflows.

I do not believe this is a useful model for the Asian crisis, but the International Monetary Fund and many others do. Thus, the question remains: If there are conditions under which capital controls can be an effective policy instrument, why do we have so little evidence that they have been utilized effectively? As Dornbusch points out, one reason is the difficulty in setting out the counterfactual. The other, I suspect, is that political economy makes the sensible use of controls an exceedingly rare event.

References

Cairncross, Alec. 1973. *Control of long-term capital movements.* Washington, D.C.: Brookings Institution.

Dooley, Michael P. 1996. A survey of literature on controls over international capital transactions. *IMF Staff Papers* 43 (4): 639–87.

Dornbusch, Rudiger. 1986. Special exchange rates for capital account transactions. *World Bank Economic Review* 1 (12): 3–33.

Discussion Summary

Nouriel Roubini remarked that the issue of contagion was not discussed in the paper. He said that around the time that Malaysia imposed capital controls, Russia had already imposed similar measures after it devalued and defaulted. *Paul Krugman* also argued that capital controls were a good idea and urged crisis countries to impose them. Given that we know that capital controls can be effective only when they are not anticipated, and that they can actually cause capital flight and even crises when anticipated, Roubini said that it is important to study how contagion affects the effectiveness of the Malaysian capital control policies. This is especially the case because there seems to be a risk of many emerging markets' imposing capital controls.

Roubini also said that it was important to distinguish between radical controls—such as killing offshore markets—and partial controls. One major difference between these two control policies is that partial controls "leak." For example, Thailand imposed controls in May 1997 on nonresidents' ability to borrow in the local currency, which led to a large interest rate spread between the domestic and foreign markets. These controls were effective for a short time, but the substantial difference in interest rates created a huge incentive for investors to take the money abroad for a higher rate of return, which eventually led to the collapse of the Thai baht. Similar partial control policies were in practice in Malaysia in 1998, which may have worsened the situation there by increasing the speculative capital outflow rather than reducing it.

Anne O. Krueger noted that Malaysia had a big problem in 1995, which triggered a large cut in the fiscal deficit and other policies. This brought a partial restabilization to Malaysia's economy and was the reason that Malaysia was in better shape than other countries before the crisis. Krueger suggested referring to the 1995 event in the discussion. Krueger also said that the failure of the return of foreign direct investors to Malaysia might reflect that they lost confidence in forward contracts in Malaysia after the imposition of capital controls.

Martin Feldstein raised a few questions. First, he asked whether Malaysia carried out the kinds of structural reforms that the IMF required in other countries even though it did not officially adopt the IMF program. His second question was related to a point made by *Michael P. Dooley,* namely, that Malaysia actually imposed capital controls before the official announcement of the controls. He asked if the difference between the earlier controls and the official ones merely consisted of the treatment of foreigners, as Malaysian residents could not take money out of Malaysia (while foreigners could) before the official controls were imposed in September 1998. Third, he asked what happened to the foreign creditors whose capital was frozen in Malaysia due to the controls after the controls were lifted.

In response to Feldstein's first question, *Robert Dekle* cited an IMF Selected Issues paper on Malaysia, which described the financial reforms taking place in Malaysia. These reforms were similar to those in other program countries.

Kristin J. Forbes suggested including a discussion of the inefficiencies in the corporate sector before the Asian crisis, such as overleveraging and low profits, in evaluating the capital control policies. She said that one potential beneficial effect of the crisis is that it forces restructuring in the corporate sector and induces the companies to use capital more efficiently, focusing on profitability instead of growth. She asked if there was evidence showing that capital controls prolonged this cleansing process and whether Malaysia would suffer in the long run.

Simon Johnson supported Dornbusch's critique of the methodology used in the paper by Ethan and Rodrick, in particular the timing comparison. He pointed out that there was tremendous political uncertainty in Malaysia in the summer of 1998, due to the fact that Anwar was trying to pursue IMF-type policies that were squeezing the Mahathir-connected firms. The political instability manifested itself in a fight at the party congress, and there was a serious probability of social disorders and even isolated riots. When the capital control policies were imposed and Anwar was deposed, the stock market went up, especially the Mahathir-connected firms, while the Anwar-connected firms suffered. Johnson said that this political struggle dominated everything else. *Linda S. Goldberg* supported this point by saying that it is very difficult to do any type of event study in a complex environment like this one.

Goldberg also noted that Malaysia imposed the capital inflow restriction in 1994. According to her, the theoretical literature predicts that the effects of capital controls on inflows and outflows are equivalent regardless of where the controls were imposed. She asked if one could determine the incremental effects of imposing outflow controls.

Giancarlo Corsetti suggested conducting a survey of large Japanese corporations to figure out whether the reduction of FDI to Malaysia was due to a change of strategy as a result of Malaysia's capital control policies.

Jorge Braga de Macedo drew attention to the broad social costs of the imposition of capital controls. The imposed capital controls dramatically reduced the benefits of financial globalization (in a country that was very much capitalized), sacrificing financial freedom and reducing transparency, which is socially costly on its own. He also reiterated questions regarding the political economy of capital controls, such as who administers them, and the temporary nature of these policies.

Amartya Lahiri suggested taking a different direction in the discussion. Given that we know that capital controls cannot be good in a nondistorted world, an interesting approach would ask what distortion capital controls were meant to correct and whether there was evidence of that distortion.

Rudi Dornbusch responded that Holland once devalued during the time of the Exchange Rate Mechanism, but otherwise it faithfully followed Germany. This kept their interest rate 11 basis points above that of Germany almost to the day when the European Monetary Union was introduced. Dornbusch said that in an entirely quiet world it is possible to identify an effect like this. However, if an emerging-market country sometimes defaulted and now we find a statistically significant impact, we cannot draw a causal relationship from that.

Malaysia did the "unspeakable thing," so its effect must inevitably show, most economists with an orthodox training would say. However, the imposition of capital controls happened in the midst of the greatest crisis of the region, which makes it difficult to find the premium that is associated with it. Moreover, in Malaysia, FDI is substantial and receives special treatment, and the controls are explicitly not targeted to the long-term investors but to the three-month maturity speculators. Therefore, it is hard to find a substantial impact of capital controls unless they had a devastatingly negative effect.

Because capital controls did not really hurt, the populist demand to fight capital flight (rather than saving the economy) was enormously reinforced by Malaysia's experience. Moreover, the situation in Malaysia before the crisis was much more favorable than in other crisis countries, and Malaysia had actually followed a "shadow IMF program" the year before under intense consultation with the IMF.

Dornbusch concluded that the issue of the effectiveness of capital controls is not resolved except for the unfortunate presumption that they help politically. Malaysia's experience is historically important only because it will nourish capital controls as a politically attractive thing to do. He also said that the politics after Indonesia were formidably important in this case. The fall of Suharto meant a potential for instability and a huge redistribution from his beneficiaries to God knows whom. This is going to happen in Malaysia, but after the imposition of capital controls and the deposition of Anwar the problem was solved (or postponed) until further notice. The resolution of the uncertainty was the reason that the asset markets recovered.

Regarding the question raised by Goldberg regarding the effect of the controls on capital outflows given that there were inflow controls in place already, Dornbusch said that the difference between the two controls was that the inflow controls were anticipated whereas the outflow controls were not.

Regarding Feldstein's question as to whether capital controls were anticipated, he said that he did not believe they were. It is true, he said, that after seeing what Indonesia did to its Chinese minority, it seemed possible that the same could happen in Malaysia. In the past twenty-five years there was a systematic redistribution from Chinese to Malays, and those going bust were Malays. Dornbusch agreed that the ethnic issue was very startling in Malaysia.

Finally, Dornbusch reacted to a comment by Corsetti regarding the link between Malaysia and Japan. He pointed out that Malaysia and Japan promoted together the idea of an "Asian IMF" and the need to have extra instruments.

Dornbusch concluded that although there was no evidence one way or the other regarding the effectiveness of capital control policies, the debate will continue. It would be interesting if we found out one day whether the capital controls actually worked in some way or they were totally political, he said.

IV

Balance Sheets and "Crony Capitalism"

Negative Alchemy?
Corruption, Composition of Capital Flows, and Currency Crises

Shang-Jin Wei and Yi Wu

10.1 Motivation

This paper studies the impact of corruption on a country's composition of capital inflows. The importance of this composition was recently highlighted by the currency crises in East Asia, Russia, and Latin America. Several studies (starting with Frankel and Rose 1996 and followed by Radelet and Sachs 1998 and Rodrik and Velasco 1999) have shown that the composition of international capital inflows correlates to the incidence of currency crises. In particular, three types of composition measures have been highlighted in the literature as being particularly relevant to the discussion of currency crises: (a) the lower the share of foreign direct investment in total capital inflows, (b) the higher the short-term debt-reserves ratio, or (c) the higher the share of foreign currency–denominated borrowing in a country's total borrowing, the more likely a currency crisis becomes.

In this paper, we will discuss all three dimensions of the composition of capital flows, but with a greater emphasis on the foreign direct investment (FDI) share in total capital inflows, as we have a larger set of observations and more reliable measure in this area. We will explain this later. One possible reason that a low FDI share in total capital flow is associated with a higher probability of crises is that bank lending or other portfolio invest-

Shang-Jin Wei is an advisor at the International Monetary Fund; a research fellow at Harvard University's Center for International Development, a faculty research fellow of the National Bureau of Economic Research, and a senior fellow at the Brooking Institution, where he holds the New Century Chair in International Economics. Yi Wu is a Ph.D. student at Georgetown University.

This research project is supported in part by a grant from the OECD Development Center. We thank Martin Feldstein, Jeffrey A. Frankel, Helmut Reisen, Dani Rodrik, and Andrei Shleifer for offering very helpful comments; Rafael di Tella, Ernesto Stein, and Ugo Panizza for sharing their data; and Rachel Rubinfeld and Mike Prosser for superb research and editorial assistance.

ment may be more sentiment-driven than is direct investment. Hence, a small (unfavorable) change in the recipient countries' fundamentals may cause a large swing in the portfolio capital flows (e.g., from massive inflows to massive outflows). This can strain the recipient country's currency or financial system sufficiently to cause or exacerbate its collapse (Radelet and Sachs 1998; Rodrik and Velasco 1999; Reisen 1999).

There are at least two views on the causes of crises. On the one hand, it is increasingly common to hear the assertion that so-called crony capitalism may be partly responsible for the onset or the depth of a crisis. Direct statistical evidence for this hypothesis is still sparse, with the notable exception of Johnson et al. (2000).[1] On the other hand, many researchers argue that (fragile) self-fulfilling expectations by international creditors are the real reason for the currency crisis. Crony capitalism and self-fulfilling expectations are typically presented as *rival* explanations.

In fact, the two hypotheses may be linked. The extent of corruption in a country may affect that country's composition of capital inflows in a way that makes it more vulnerable to international creditors' shifts in expectations.

In a narrow sense of the word, *corruption* refers to the extent to which firms (or private citizens) must bribe government officials in their interactions (for permits, licenses, loans, and so forth).[2] However, we prefer to think of corruption more broadly as shorthand for poor public governance, which can include not only bureaucratic corruption, but also deviations from rule of law or excessive and arbitrary government regulations. All the existing empirical indicators of the different dimensions of public governance are so highly correlated that we do not think that we can separately identify their effects at this stage.

A small number of previous papers have looked at the effect of corruption on FDI. Mixing corruption with twelve other variables to form a composite indicator, Wheeler and Mody (1992) failed to find a significant relation between corruption and foreign investment. However, the insignificant result may be due to a high noise-to-signal ratio in the composite indicator. Using U.S. outward investment to individual countries, Hines (1995) did find that foreign investment is negatively related to host country corruption, which he interpreted as evidence of the effect of the U.S. Foreign Corrupt Practices Act. Using a matrix of bilateral international direct investment from twelve source countries to forty-five host countries, Wei (2000a) found

1. For surveys of the literature on corruption and economic development, see Bardhan (1997), Kaufmann (1997), and Wei (1999). More recent papers on corruption include Wei (2000d) and Bai and Wei (2000). None of the surveys covers any empirical study that links crony capitalism with currency crises.

2. We use the term *crony capitalism* interchangeably with *corruption*. Strictly speaking, crony capitalism refers to an economic environment in which relatives and friends of government officials are placed in positions of power and government decisions on allocation of resources are distorted to favor friends and relatives. In reality, crony capitalism almost always implies a widespread corruption, because private firms and citizens in such an environment find it necessary to pay bribes to government officials in order to get anything done.

that the behavior of the FDI flows from the United States and those from other source countries, with respect to host country corruption, is not statistically different. More importantly, however, corruption not only has a negative and statistically significant coefficient, but it also has an economically large effect on inward FDI. For example, in a benchmark estimation, an increase in corruption from the level of Singapore to that of Mexico would have the same negative effect on inward foreign investment as raising the marginal corporate tax by 50 percentage points. Using firm-level data, Smarzynska and Wei (2000) found that host country corruption induces foreign investors to favor joint ventures (over wholly owned firms).

None of the above papers has a measure of government policies toward FDI. Such data are not readily available. The current paper employs two new indexes of government policies toward FDI that are compiled from investment guides for individual countries produced by Pricewaterhouse-Coopers (2000). Although FDI is an important element of this study, the main focus is the effect of corruption on the composition of capital inflows (FDI versus borrowing from foreign banks, in particular). We are not aware of any studies that have examined this question except for Wei (2000b). This paper extends the previous paper in several ways. While Wei focuses on the connection between the ratio of bank loan to FDI and corruption, and bases the analysis on bilateral data, this paper also checks the relative share of portfolio flows versus FDI as well as using more aggregate data from the balance of payments reported by the countries to the International Monetary Fund (IMF). In addition, we report results on a possible relationship between corruption and the maturity structure of foreign borrowing, and between corruption and a country's ability to borrow internationally in its own currency.

Before we proceed to a more formal analysis, it may be useful to have a quick glance at the data. The argument that capital flow composition matters requires that different capital flows have a different level of volatility. For every member country of the IMF for which relevant data are available for 1980–96, we compute the standard deviations of three ratios (portfolio capital inflow to GDP, borrowing from banks to GDP, and inward FDI to GDP).[3] The results are summarized in the upper half of table 10.1 and visually pre-

---

3. Hausmann and Fernandez-Arias (2000) argue that the classification of capital inflows into FDI and other forms may not be accurate and that it is possible for a reversal of an inflow of FDI to take the form of an outflow of bank loans or portfolio flows. As a result, calculations of relative volatility of the different forms of capital flows are not meaningful. We hold a different view. The misclassification can come from two sources: random measurement errors and intentional misreporting by international investors. In the first instance, if capital flows are misclassified at the margin due to random errors, the labels on FDI and other forms of capital flows are still useful. In the second instance, foreign investors may intentionally misreport types of capital flows. Because there is a cost associated with misreporting, there is a limit on the magnitude of the error of this type as well. In the empirical work to be presented later in the paper, the bilateral FDI data are based on FDI source country governments' survey of their firms. The bilateral bank lending data are based on international lending banks' reporting to their governments (which then forward them to the Bank for International Settlements). There are no obvious incentives for multinational firms or international banks to misreport their true FDI or loan positions to their governments.

Table 10.1

Table 10.1   Volatility of FDI/GDP, Bank Loan/GDP, and Portfolio Flow/GDP (1980–96)

	FDI-GDP	Loan-GDP	Portfolio-GDP
A. As Measured by Standard Deviation			
Whole sample[a]			
Mean	0.012	0.041	0.014
Median	0.008	0.033	0.009
Emerging markets[b]			
Mean	0.012	0.046	0.012
Median	0.008	0.035	0.004
OECD[c]			
Mean	0.008	0.020	0.021
Median	0.007	0.014	0.020
Selected countries			
Indonesia	0.007	0.017	0.009
Korea	0.002	0.037	0.014
Malaysia	0.023	0.034	0.023
Mexico	0.007	0.033	0.026
The Philippines	0.009	0.026	0.017
Thailand	0.007	0.028	0.012
B. As Measured by Coefficient of Variation			
Whole sample[a]			
Mean	1.176	1.567	2.764
Median	0.947	1.204	1.702
Emerging markets[b]			
Mean	1.269	2.192	0.813
Median	1.163	1.177	2.042
OECD[c,d]			
Mean	0.737	–1.353	8.508
Median	0.595	1.530	1.004
Selected countries			
Indonesia	0.820	0.717	1.722
Korea	0.591	2.039	1.338
Malaysia	0.490	4.397	3.544
Mexico	0.452	2.048	2.088
The Philippines	0.921	0.956	1.979
Thailand	0.571	0.629	1.137

Sources: Total inward FDI flows, total bank loans, and total inward portfolio investments are from the IMF's *Balance of Payments Statistics* CD-ROM; GDP data are from the World Bank's *GDF* and *WDI* central database.

Notes: Only countries having at least eight nonmissing observations during 1980–96 for all three variables, and having populations greater than or equal to one million in 1995, are kept in the sample. OECD countries (with membership up to 1980) include the following: Australia, Austria, Canada, Denmark, Finland, France, Ireland, Italy, Japan, the Netherlands, New Zealand, Norway, Portugal, Spain, Sweden, Switzerland, the United Kingdom, and the United States. "Emerging markets" are all countries not on the previous list and having a GDP per capital in 1995 less than or equal to US$15,000 (in 1995 US$).

[a] 103 countries

[b] 85 countries

[c] 18 countries

[d] In the case of the volatility of the loan-GDP ratio for the OECD countries, the large difference between the mean and median (–1.353 vs. 1.530) is driven by one outlier (Japan, with a value of –49).

A

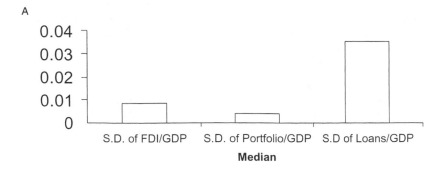

B

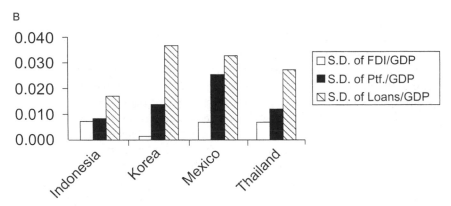

Fig. 10.1   Relative volatility of different capital flows: *A,* **Standard deviations over 1980–96 emerging markets: 85 countries;** *B,* **Standard deviations over 1980–96.**
Source: Authors' calculations.

sented in figure 10.1. For all countries in the sample (103 countries in total), the volatility of FDI-GDP ratio is substantially smaller than the loan-GDP ratio and somewhat smaller than the ratio of portfolio flows to GDP. For the non–Organization for Economic Cooperation and Development (OECD) countries as a group, the FDI-GDP ratio is also much less volatile than the loan-GDP ratio, although its median is higher than the portfolio flow to GDP ratio. The lower part of the same half of the table presents the volatility of the three ratios for a number of individual countries that featured prominently in the recent currency crises. Each country shows a loan-GDP ratio that is at least twice and as much as fifteen times as volatile as the FDI-GDP ratio. For each of these countries, the portfolio capital to GDP ratio is also more volatile than the FDI-GDP ratio. If the sample period is extended to include 1997–98, the differences in volatility would be even more pronounced (not reported). Alternatively, we may look at the coefficient of variation (standard deviation divided by the mean) of these three ratios. These results are presented in the lower half of table 10.1. Again, for the group of emerging-market economies, FDI-GDP is less volatile than the loan-FDI ratio according to this measure. On the other hand, FDI-GDP is less volatile than the portfolio-GDP ratio according to the median, but not the mean, of the group. Therefore, the data are consistent with the hypothesis that FDI is less sentiment-driven and hence more stable as a source of foreign capital.[4]

Corruption is bad for both international direct investors and creditors. Corrupt borrowing countries are more likely to default on bank loans or to nationalize (or otherwise diminish the value of) the assets of foreign direct investors. When this happens, there is a limit on how much international arbitration or court proceedings can help to recover the assets, as there is a limit on how much collateral the foreign creditors or direct investors can seize as compensation.[5]

One may argue that domestic investors have an informational advantage over international investors. Among international investors, international direct investors may have an informational advantage over international portfolio investors (and presumably banks). International direct investors could obtain more information about the local market by having managers from the headquarters stationed in the country that they invest in. As a consequence, the existence of cross-border informational asymmetry may lead to a bias in favor of international direct investment. This is the logic underlying Razin, Sadka, and Yuen's (1998) theory of a "pecking order of international capital flows." However, the existence of corruption could temper this effect. The need for international investors to pay bribery and deal with extortion by corrupt bureaucrats tends to increase with the frequency and the extent of their interactions with local bureaucrats. Given that international direct investors are more likely to have repeated interactions with local officials (for permits, taxes, health inspections, and so forth) than international banks or portfolio investors, local corruption would be more detrimental to FDI than other forms of capital flows. Likewise, direct investment involves greater sunk cost than bank loans or portfolio investment. Once an investment is made, when corrupt local officials begin to demand bribes not to set up obstacles, direct investors would be in a weaker bargaining position than international banks or portfolio investors. This ex post disadvantage of FDI would make international direct investors more cautious ex ante in a corrupt host country than international portfolio investors.[6]

---

4. The pattern reported here is the opposite of that in Dooley, Claessens, and Warner (1995).

5. In the old days, major international creditors and direct investors might rely on their navies to invade defaulting countries to seize more collateral. Such is no longer a (ready) option today.

6. Tornell (1990) presented a model in which a combination of uncertainty and sunk cost in real investment leads to underinvestment in real projects even when the inflow of financial capital is abundant.

There is a second reason that international direct investment is deterred more by local corruption than international bank credit or portfolio investment. The current international financial architecture is such that international creditors are more likely to be bailed out than international direct investors. For example, during the Mexican and subsequent Tequila crises and the more recent Asian currency crisis, the IMF, the World Bank, and the Group of Seven (G7) countries mobilized a large amount of funds for these countries to prevent or minimize the potentially massive defaults on bank loans. Thus, an international bailout of the bank loans in an event of a massive crisis has by now been firmly implanted in market expectations. (In addition, many developing country governments implicitly or explicitly guarantee the loans borrowed by the private sector in the country.[7]) In contrast, there have been no comparable examples of international assistance packages for the recovery of nationalized or extorted assets of foreign direct investors except for an insignificant amount of insurance, which is often expensive to acquire. This difference further tilts the composition of capital flows and makes banks more willing than direct investors to do business with corrupt countries.

Both reasons suggest the possibility that corruption may affect the composition of capital inflows in such a way that the country is more likely to experience a currency crisis. Of course, the composition of capital flows affects economic development in ways that go beyond its effect on the propensity for a currency crisis. Indeed, many would argue that attracting FDI as opposed to international bank loans or portfolio investment is a more useful way to transfer technology and managerial know-how.

As some concrete examples, table 10.2 shows the total amount of inward FDI, foreign bank loans, portfolio capital inflows, and their ratios for New Zealand, Singapore, Uruguay, and Thailand. Figure 10.2 summarizes the comparison by pie charts. On the one hand, New Zealand and Singapore (are perceived to) have relatively low corruption (the exact source is explained in the next section) and relatively low loan-FDI and portfolio investment-FDI ratios. On the other hand, Uruguay and Thailand (are perceived to) have relatively high corruption and relatively high loan-FDI and portfolio investment to FDI ratios. These examples, then, are consistent with the notion that local corruption correlates to patterns of capital inflows. Of course, these four countries are merely examples. Consequently, there are two questions that must be addressed more formally. First, does the association between corruption and composition of capital flows generalize beyond these four countries? Second, after we control for a number of other characteristics that affect the composition of capital inflows, will we still find the positive association between corruption and the loan-FDI ratio?

---

7. McKinnon and Pill (1996, 1999) argue that the government guarantee generates moral hazard, which in turn leads the developing countries to overborrow from the international credit market.

Table 10.2   Quality of Public Governance and the Composition of Capital Inflows

	New Zealand	Singapore	Uruguay	Thailand
Corruption	0.6	0.9	5.7	7.0
(TI index)	(less corrupt)			(more corrupt)
Ratios (averaged over 1994–96)				
Loan-FDI	0.11	0.44	1.77	5.77
Portfolio-FDI	0.07	0.09	1.40	1.76
Absolute amount (averaged over 1994–96)				
Loan	920	10,500	794	2,500
Portfolio	610	2,200	627	761
FDI	8,400	23,600	448	432

Source: Total inward loans, portfolio investment, and FDI are from the IMF's Balance of Payments Statistics CD-ROM.

Notes: To minimize the impact of the year-to-year fluctuation, the reported numbers are averaged over 1994–96. The corruption index is explained in appendix B. "Absolute amount" is the amount the three inflows in millions of U.S. dollars.

Aside from measuring composition of capital inflows in terms of the relative share of the FDI versus non-FDI, two other compositions of capital flows have been suggested to be relevant in discussing currency crises. The first is the term structure of foreign borrowing. It has been suggested that the higher the share of short-term borrowing in a country's total borrowing, the more likely the country may run into a future crisis (Rodrik and Velasco 1999). The second is the currency denomination of the foreign borrowing. It has been hypothesized that the greater the share of international borrowing that is denominated in a hard currency (most often the U.S. dollar), the more likely a country may run into a future crisis. In this connection, the inability of a country to borrow internationally in its own currency (which would have reduced the probability of a crisis) has been termed "original sin" (Hausmann and Fernandez-Arias 2000). The limitation of the data places a more severe constraint on measuring well these two compositions of international borrowing. Nonetheless, in the later part of the paper, we will also report some preliminary findings regarding possible links between corruption and these measures of the composition of foreign borrowing.

We organize the rest of the paper in the following way. Section 10.2 describes the data. Section 10.3 presents the methodology and the statistical results of the analyses, and Section 10.4 concludes.

10.2   Data

The key components of international capital flows in the empirical investigation are bilateral direct investment and bilateral bank loans. To our

New Zealand (Corruption level 0.6, less corrupt)

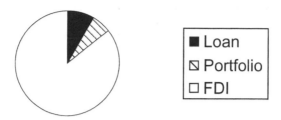

Singapore (Corruption level: 0.9)

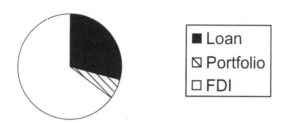

Uruguay (Corruption level: 5.7)

Thailand (Corruption level: 7.0)

Fig. 10.2   Quality of public governance and the composition of capital inflows
Source: Authors' calculations

Table 10.3   List of Countries in the Sample

	Countries
	Bilateral Foreign Direct Investment
Source countries	Australia, Austria, Canada, Finland, France, Germany, Iceland, Italy, Japan, Korea, the Netherlands, New Zealand, Norway, Poland, Sweden, Switzerland, United Kingdom, United States
Host countries	Algeria, Argentina, Australia, Austria, Belgium-Luxembourg, Brazil, Bulgaria, Canada, Chile, China, Colombia, Costa Rica, Czech Republic, Denmark, Egypt, Finland, France, Germany, Greece, Hong Kong, Hungary, Iceland, India, Indonesia, Iran, Ireland, Israel, Italy, Japan, Korea, Kuwait, Libya, Malaysia, Mexico, Morocco, the Netherlands, New Zealand, Norway, Panama, the Philippines, Poland, Portugal, Romania, Russia, Saudi Arabia, Singapore, Slovak Republic, Slovenia, South Africa, Spain, Sweden, Switzerland, Taiwan, Thailand, Turkey, Ukraine, United Arab Emirates, United Kingdom, United States, Venezuela
	Bilateral International Bank Loans
Lending countries	Austria, Belgium, Canada, Finland, France, Germany, Italy, Japan, Luxembourg, the Netherlands, Spain, United Kingdom, United States
Borrowing countries	Albania, Argentina, Armenia, Australia, Azerbaijan, Belarus, Benin, Bolivia, Brazil, Bulgaria, Cameroon, Chad, Chile, China, Colombia, Congo (Republic of the), Costa Rica, Côte d'Ivoire, Czech Republic, Ecuador, Egypt, El Salvador, Estonia, Fiji, Georgia, Ghana, Greece, Guatemala, Guinea, Guinea-Bissau, Honduras, Hungary, Iceland, India, Indonesia, Israel, Jamaica, Jordan, Kazakhstan, Kenya, Korea, Kyrgyzstan, Latvia, Lithuania, Madagascar, Malawi, Malaysia, Mali, Mauritius, Mexico, Moldova, Morocco, Mozambique, Namibia, New Zealand, Nicaragua, Niger, Nigeria, Pakistan, Paraguay, Peru, the Philippines, Poland, Portugal, Romania, Russia, Senegal, Slovakia, South Africa, Taiwan, Tanzania, Thailand, Tonga, Tunisia, Turkey, Uganda, Ukraine, Uruguay, Uzbekistan, Venezuela, Vietnam, Zambia, Zimbabwe

knowledge, other forms of capital flows are not available on a bilateral basis for a broad set of capital-exporting countries examined in this paper.

The *bilateral FDI* data are an average over three years (1994–96) of the stock of FDI from eighteen source countries to fifty-nine host countries. Table 10.3 presents a list of all source and host countries in our sample. The data come from the OECD's *International Direct Investment 1998*. To reduce year-to-year fluctuation in the data due to measurement error, the simple average over 1994–96 (year-end stocks) is used.

The *bilateral bank lending* data are an average over three years of the outstanding loans from thirteen lending countries to eighty-three borrowing countries. After we exclude missing observations, there are altogether 793 country pairs. The data come from the Bank for International Settlement's (BIS's) *Consolidated International Claims of BIS Reporting Banks on Individual Countries* and are given in millions of dollars. To reduce measurement errors in a given year, we use the simple average over three years (1994–96, year-end outstanding amounts).

Next we consider *term structure of bank lending*. The BIS data identify loans with "maturity up to and including one year," "maturity over one year up to two years," "maturity over two years," and "unallocated maturity." These data are disaggregated by borrowing countries but not by the lender-borrower pairs. Consequently, we construct a measure of the term structure of borrowing at the borrowing country level as the ratio of all outstanding bank loans with maturity up to and including one year to total loans. We also construct an alternative of the importance of short-term borrowing as the ratio of the short-term borrowing (loans up to and including one year) to the sum of total loans and inward FDI.

The *corruption* level, by its very nature (secrecy and illegality), is difficult to measure. Three types of measures of corruption are available, and all are perception-based subjective indexes. The first is a rating given by consulting firms' in-house consultants or experts. Representative indexes are produced by the Business International (BI, now part of the Economist's Economic Intelligence Unit), and by Political Risk Services (which calls its product an International Country Risk Group [ICRG] rating). The second type is based on surveys of business executives (or other people in the country in question). The rating for a country is typically the average of the respondents' ratings. Examples of this include indexes in the *Global Competitiveness Report* (*GCR*) and *World Development Report* (*WDR*), which will be explained in more detail shortly. The third type is based on an average of existing indexes. The best-known example is the index produced by Transparency International (TI), a Germany-based nongovernmental organization devoted to fighting corruption. A drawback of this type of index is that mixing indexes with different country coverage and methodologies could potentially introduce more noise to the measure.

Overall, corruption ratings based on surveys of firms are preferable to those based on the intuition of in-house experts, for two main reasons. First, the executives who respond to the *GCR* or *WDR* surveys presumably have more direct experience with the corruption problem than do the consultants who typically have to rate many countries each. Second, to the extent that each individual respondent has idiosyncratic errors in judgment, the averaging process in the *GCR* or *WDR* indexes can minimize the influence of such errors. In this paper, we use the indexes from the *GCR* and *WDR* surveys as our basic measure of corruption.

The *GCR* index is derived from the *Global Competitiveness Report 1997*, produced jointly by the Geneva-based World Economic Forum and Harvard Institute for International Development. The survey for the report was conducted in late 1996 on 2,827 firms in fifty-eight countries. The *GCR* survey asked respondents (in question 8.03) to rate the level of corruption in their country on a scale of 1 to 7, based on the extent of "irregular, additional payments connected with imports and exports permits, business licenses, exchange controls, tax assessments, police protection or loan applications." The *GCR* corruption index is based on the country average of the individual ratings.

The *WDR* index is derived from a World Bank survey in 1996 of 3,866 firms in seventy-three countries in preparation for its *World Development Report 1997*. Question 14 of that survey asks: "Is it common for firms in my line of business to have to pay some irregular, 'additional' payments to get things done?" The respondents were asked to rate the level of corruption on a scale of 1 to 6. The *WDR* corruption index is based on the country average of the individual answers. For both corruption indexes, the original sources are such that a higher number implies lower corruption. To avoid awkwardness in interpretation, they are rescaled in this paper so that a high number now implies high corruption.

Since each index covers only a (different) subset of countries for which we have data on FDI or other forms of capital flows, it may be desirable to form a composite corruption index that combines the two indexes. The two indexes are derived from surveys with similar methodologies and similar questions. The correlation between the two is 0.83. We follow a simple three-step procedure to construct the composite index: (a) use *GCR* as the benchmark; (b) compute the average of the individual ratios of *GCR* to *WDR* for all countries that are available in both *GCR* and the *WDR;* and (c) for those countries that are covered by *WDR* but not *GCR* (which are relatively rare), convert the *WDR* rating into the *GCR* scale by using the average ratio in (b).

For *government policies toward FDI,* we rely on detailed descriptions compiled by the PricewaterhouseCoopers (PwC) in a series of country reports entitled "Doing Business and Investing in China" (or in whatever country may be the subject of the report). This series is written for multinational firms intending to do business in a particular country and is collected in one CD-ROM entitled "Doing Business and Investing Worldwide" (PwC 2000). For each potential host country, the relevant PwC country report covers a variety of legal and regulatory issues of interest to foreign investors, including "Restrictions on Foreign Investment and Investors" (typically chap. 5), "Investment Incentives" (typically chap. 4), and "Taxation of Foreign Corporations" (typically chap. 16).

With a desire to convert textual information into numerical codes, we read through the relevant chapters for all countries that the PwC covers. For "restrictions on FDI," we create a variable taking a value from zero to 4, based on the presence or absence of restrictions in the following four areas:

1. Existence of foreign exchange control (may interfere with foreign firms' ability to import intermediate inputs or repatriate profits abroad)

2. Exclusion of foreign firms from certain strategic sectors (particularly national defense and mass media)

3. Exclusion of foreign firms from additional sectors that would otherwise be considered harmless in most developed countries

4. Restrictions on foreign ownership (e.g., prohibition of 100 percent ownership)

Each of the four dimensions can be represented by a dummy that takes the value 1 (in the presence of the specific restriction) or zero (in the absence of the restriction). We create an overall FDI restriction variable that is equal to the sum of these four dummies. FDI restriction is zero if there is no restriction in any of the four categories and 4 if there is restriction in each category.

Similarly, we create an FDI incentives index based on information in the following areas:

1. Existence of special incentives to invest in certain industries or geographic areas

2. Tax concessions specific to foreign firms (including tax holidays and tax rebates, but excluding tax concessions specifically designed for export promotion, which is in a separate category)

3. Cash grants, subsidized loans, reduced rent for land use, or other nontax concessions specific to foreign firms

4. Special promotion for exports (including the presence of export processing zones, special economic zones, etc.)

An overall FDI incentives variable is created as the sum of the above four dummies, so it can take a value of zero if there is no incentive in any of the four categories and 4 if there are incentives in all of them.

Our coding of the incentives/restrictions measures is still coarse and may not capture the true variations of the government policies. Nonetheless, it is important to have a way to control for these types of government policies in a statistical analysis of international capital flows. Our contribution is to create a first-of-its-kind index. We let the data speak to the usefulness of such an index.

Table 10.3 lists all the countries in our sample. Table 10.4 presents the summary statistics for some key variables and the coefficients of the pairwise correlation among the three measures of corruption and GDP per capita.

10.3   Statistical Analyses

Studying the effect of corruption on the composition of capital inflows is equivalent to asking whether corruption may have a differential impact on

Table 10.4   **Summary Statistics**

Variable	N	Mean	Standard Deviation	Minimum	Maximum
Corruption					
GCR/WDR combined	99	3.62	1.19	1.3	5.5
Transparency International	85	5.12	2.40	0	8.6
Tax rate (highest corporate					
income tax rate)	56	32.39	6.86	0	42
FDI incentives	49	1.65	0.69	0	3
FDI restrictions	49	1.69	1.18	0	4
Per capita GDP, 1994–96	154	5,792	9,222	104	43,602
ln(loan-FDI), bilateral					
1994–96	288	1.53	2.21	−8.06	8.75
ln(loan-FDI), balance of					
payments, 1994–96	125	0.31	2.00	−4.84	6.18
ln(portfolio-FDI), balance					
of payments, 1994–96	89	−0.66	1.98	−5.28	5.77

Correlation Matrix

	GDP Per Capita	Corruption TI	Corruption GCR	Corruption WDR
GDP per capita	1			
Corruption (TI)	−0.82	1		
Corruption (GCR)	−0.78	0.87	1	
Corruption (WDR)	−0.72	0.86	0.83	1

Source: See appendix B.

different forms of capital flows. In this section, we proceed by sequentially examining FDI, international bank lending, and the ratio between the two.

10.3.1   Corruption and Foreign Direct Investment

We first examine the effect of local corruption on the volume of inward FDI. Our specification can be motivated by a simple optimization problem solved by a multinational firm. Let K_j be the stock of investment the multinational firm intends to allocate to host country j. Let t_j be the rate of corporate income tax in host country j, b_j be the rate of bribery the firm must pay per unit of output, and r be the rental rate of capital. Let $f(K_j)$ be the output of the firm in host country j. There are N possible host countries in which the firm can invest. The firm chooses the level of K_j for $j = 1, 2, \ldots$ N, in order to maximize its total after-tax and after-bribery profit:

$$\pi = \sum_{j=1}^{N} [(1 - t_j - b_j)f(K_j) - rK_j]$$

Note that as a simple way to indicate that tax and corruption are distortionary, we let $(1 - t_j - b_j)$ premultiply output rather than profit. The optimal stock of FDI in country j, K_j, would of course be related to both the rate of tax and that of corruption in the host country: $K = K(t_j, b_j)$, where $\partial K/\partial t <$ and $\partial K/\partial b < 0$.[8]

Let FDI_{kj} be the bilateral stock of FDI from source country k to host country j. In our empirical work, we begin with the following benchmark specification:

$$\log[FDI_{kj}] = \sum_i \alpha_i D_i + \beta_1 \text{tax}_j + \beta_2 \text{corruption}_j + X_j \delta + Z_{kj} \gamma + e_{kj},$$

where D_i is a source country dummy that takes the value of 1 if the source country is i (i.e., if $k = i$), and zero otherwise; X_j is a vector of characteristics of host country j other than its tax and corruption levels; Z_{kj} is a vector of characteristics specific to the source-host country pairs; e_{kj} is an independently and identically distributed (i.i.d.) error that follows a normal distribution; and α_i, β_1, β_2, δ, and γ are parameters to be estimated.

This is a quasi–fixed effects regression in that source country dummies are included. They are meant to capture all characteristics of the source countries that may affect the size of their outward FDI, including their size and level of development. In addition, possible differences in the source countries' definition of FDI are controlled for by these fixed effects under the assumption that the FDI values for a particular country pair under these definitions are proportional to each other except for an additive error that is not correlated with other regressors in the regression. We do not impose host country fixed effects, as doing so would eliminate the possibility of estimating all the interesting parameters, including the effect of corruption.

Using the combined *GCR/WDR* rating as the measure of corruption, the regression is run and reported in column (1) of table 10.5. Most variables have the expected signs and are statistically significant. A rise in host country tax rate is associated with less inward FDI. Government incentives and the restrictions on FDI have a positive and a negative coefficient, respectively, consistent with our intuition. Most importantly, corruption has a negative and statistically significant effect on FDI. Note that in the regressions, we have standardized the corruption measure (by subtracting the mean and dividing it by the sample standard deviation) so that the point estimate can be interpreted as the response of the left-hand side variable with respect to a 1–standard deviation increase in corruption. Therefore, using the *GCR/WDR* measure of corruption (columns [1]–[2] of table 10.5), a 1–standard deviation increase in corruption is associated with a 40 percent decline in FDI. In other words, the negative effect of corruption is not just

---

8. More sophisticated generalization includes endogenizing the level of corruption (and tax) such as in Shleifer and Vishny (1993) or Kaufmann and Wei (1999). These generalizations are outside the scope of the current paper.

Table 10.5   **Corruption and Foreign Direct Investment**

Measure of Corruption	GCR/WDR		Transparency International	
	Fixed Effects (1)	Random Effects (2)	Fixed Effects (3)	Random Effects (4)
Corruption	−0.427**	−0.407**	−0.502**	−0.508**
	(0.103)	(0.168)	(0.111)	(0.183)
Tax rate	−0.031**	−0.034*	−0.030**	−0.034*
	(0.011)	(0.019)	(0.011)	(0.019)
FDI incentives	0.403**	0.324**	0.400**	0.345**
	(0.095)	(0.162)	(0.095)	(0.157)
FDI restrictions	−0.335**	−0.323**	−0.324**	−0.308**
	(0.058)	(0.098)	(0.058)	(0.096)
Log(GDP)	0.857**	0.942**	0.909**	0.994**
	(0.053)	(0.091)	(0.055)	(0.091)
Log(per capita GDP)	−0.039	−0.121	−0.125	−0.218
	(0.086)	(0.143)	(0.096)	(0.158)
Log distance	−0.555**	−0.856**	−0.557**	−0.844**
	(0.060)	(0.067)	(0.060)	(0.067)
Linguistic tie	1.426**	1.041**	1.409**	1.049**
	(0.211)	(0.194)	(0.210)	(0.195)
Exchange rate volatility	0.053	−2.752	0.210	−2.354
	(1.968)	(3.033)	(1.960)	(2.954)
Adjusted R^2/overall R^2	0.74	0.74	0.74	0.74
N	628	628	628	628

Source: Authors' calculations.

Notes: Standard errors are in parentheses. Fixed effects regression: log FDI_{kj} = source country dummies + $bX_{kj} + e_{kj}$, where FDI_{kj} is FDI from source country k to host country j. All regressions include source country dummies whose coefficients are not reported to save space. Random-effects specification: Y_{kj} = source country dummies + $bX_{kj} + u_j + e_{kj}$, where u_j is the host-country random effect. Log(FDI), log(GDP), and log(per capita GDP) are averaged over 1994–96. Exchange rate volatility = standard deviation of the first difference in log monthly exchange rate (per US$) from January 1994 through December 1996. The corruption measure is standardized (i.e., corruption in the regressions = [original corruption − sample mean]/[sample standard deviation]). Hence, the coefficient on corruption can be read as the response of the left-hand-side variable with respect to a 1 standard deviation increase in corruption.
**Significant at the 5 percent level.
*Significant at the 10 percent level.

statistically significant, but also quantitatively large. This finding is qualitatively in line with Wei (2000a), which employed a different econometric specification.

We perform several robustness checks. First, we add host country random effects to the specification. The regression result is reported in column (2) of table 10.5. The point estimate on corruption declines slightly, but remains negative and significant. We also adopt an alternative measure of corruption from the TI and repeated the regressions (columns [3]–[4]). The qualitative results are unchanged. The estimated elasticity of FDI with re-

Table 10.6   **Corruption and Bank Lending**

| | GCR/WDR | | Transparency International | |
| | Fixed Effects | Random Effects | Fixed Effects | Random Effects |
Measure of Corruption	(1)	(2)	(3)	(4)
Corruption	0.376**	0.390**	0.197†	0.135
	(0.092)	(0.120)	(0.127)	(0.166)
East of investing in securities	0.219**	0.262**	0.110	0.161
and bonds market	(0.088)	(0.115)	(0.089)	(0.116)
Log(GDP)	1.004**	1.054**	0.984**	1.052**
	(0.054)	(0.068)	(0.060)	(0.076)
Log(per capita GDP)	0.366**	0.356**	0.388**	0.337**
	(0.063)	(0.081)	(0.096)	(0.125)
Log distance	−0.244**	−0.428**	−0.224**	−0.432**
	(0.072)	(0.082)	(0.076)	(0.085)
Linguistic tie	0.633**	0.818**	0.556**	0.776**
	(0.207)	(0.198)	(0.210)	(0.200)
Exchange rate volatility	−5.917**	−7.253**	−5.359**	−6.598**
	(1.564)	(1.966)	(1.618)	(2.060)
Adjusted R^2/overall R^2	0.72	0.73	0.71	0.72
N	396	396	396	396

Source: Authors' calculations.
Notes: See notes to table 10.5
**Significant at the 5 percent level.
†Significant at the 15 percent level.

spect to corruption is somewhat larger: a 1–standard deviation increase in corruption in the host country is associated with a 50 percent drop in inward FDI.

10.3.2   Corruption and Composition of Capital Inflows

We now move to the central empirical question in the paper: does corruption affect the composition of capital inflows? This is equivalent to asking whether corruption affects FDI and international bank loans differently. We start by examining the relationship between corruption and bilateral bank loans, in a manner analogous to our previous studies of bilateral FDI (except that government policies toward FDI and tax rate on foreign-invested firms are omitted).[9]

Table 10.6 reports four regressions, with different specifications (only source country fixed effects, or additional host country random effects), or with difference sources of corruption measures (*GCR/WDR* and TI). The results are basically consistent (and somewhat surprising). When corrup-

9. We have not found a consistent data source on government policies toward international bank borrowing across countries, nor are we able to construct such a series from the PwC country reports.

tion is measured by the *GCR/WDR* index, it has a positive and statistically significant coefficient. In other words, in contrast with the previous results on FDI, corruption in borrowing countries seems to be associated with a higher level of borrowing from international banks. In appendix D, we also restrict the sample to a single lending country (such as France, Japan, or the United States). Generally speaking, the coefficient on corruption in the loan regression continues to be positive (although not always significant).

The earlier part of the paper suggests two stories in which international direct investors are more discouraged by local corruption than international banks. The first is that greater sunk costs or greater *ex post* vulnerability of the direct investment would make direct investors more cautious *ex ante* than international banks in doing business in a corrupt host country. The second is the greater probability of an implicit or explicit bailout provided by the current international financial system to international loans than international direct investment. These stories explain only a compositional shift away from FDI toward bank loans in corrupt recipient countries. Are they also consistent with an absolute increase in the borrowing from international banks by corrupt countries? One possibility is that FDI and international bank loans are imperfect substitutes. In a corrupt recipient country, precisely because of the lost FDI due to corruption, there are relatively more activities that must be financed by borrowing from international banks.[10]

In columns (3) and (4) of table 10.6, an alternative measure of corruption by the TI index is used. This time, corruption still has a positive coefficient, although the estimate is not statistically different from zero when host country random effects are added.

When we combine the results on FDI and bank loans, it would seem natural to expect that corruption would raise the ratio of bank loans to FDI. To verify that this is indeed the case, we also check directly the connection between the ratio of bank loans to FDI and host country corruption. We perform a fixed-effects regression of the following sort:

$$\log\left(\frac{\text{loan}_{kj}}{\text{FDI}_{kj}}\right) = \frac{\text{source country}}{\text{fixed effects}} + \beta \text{corruption}_j + X_{kj}\Gamma + e_{kj}$$

β is a scalar parameter and Γ is a vector of parameters with an appropriate dimension. The regression results are reported in columns (1–4) in table 10.7. As expected, the coefficient on corruption is positive and statistically

---

10. Following a suggestion from Martin Feldstein, we have added other determinants of FDI, specifically tax, government restrictions on inward FDI, and government incentives for FDI into the loan regression. Our objective is to determine whether other factors that discourage (or encourage) FDI would show up as encouraging (or discouraging) international bank loans. Unfortunately, these variables are statistically not different from zero. An example of this is reported as column (2) of appendix D.

Table 10.7   Composition of Capital Flows

Measure of Corruption	GCR/WDR		Transparency International		GCR/WDR	
					IV,	IV,
	Fixe d	Random	Fixed	Random	Fixed	Fixed
	Effects	Effects	Effects	Effects	Effects	Effects
	(1)	(2)	(3)	(4)	(5)	(6)
Corruption	0.662**	0.680**	0.707**	0.720**	0.296†	0.285†
	(0.128)	(0.225)	(0.176)	(0.290)	(0.181)	(0.182)
Tax rate	0.021	0.021	0.021	0.020		
	(0.017)	(0.031)	(0.018)	(0.029)		
FDI incentives	0.194	0.244	−0.056	−0.019	0.111	0.095
	(0.152)	(0.260)	(0.160)	(0.254)	(0.156)	(0.157)
FDI restrictions	0.440**	0.446**	0.458**	0.446**	0.336**	0.333**
	(0.086)	(0.157)	(0.088)	(0.145)	(0.093)	(0.093)
Log(GDP)	−0.569**	−0.651**	−0.597**	−0.655**	−0.274**	−0.254**
	(0.107)	(0.186)	(0.110)	(0.174)	(0.115)	(0.118)
Log(per capita GDP)	0.172*	0.205	0.272**	0.302	0.034	0.033
	(0.098)	(0.181)	(0.125)	(0.210)	(0.103)	(0.103)
Log distance	0.350**	0.543**	0.357**	0.525**	0.123	0.111
	(0.094)	(0.114)	(0.096)	(0.114)	(0.132)	(0.132)
Linguistic tie	−0.699**	−0.680**	−0.722**	−0.700**	−0.753**	−0.803**
	(0.305)	(0.287)	(0.313)	(0.292)	(0.289)	(0.296)
Exchange rate volatility	−0.661	−0.007	−1.351	−0.755		−1.793
	(2.060)	(3.505)	(2.216)	(3.488)		(2.226)
Overidentifying restriction (*p*-value of the test)					0.43	0.40
Adjusted R^2/overall R^2	0.49	0.52	0.46	0.50	a	a
N	225	225	225	225	180	180

Source: Authors' calculations.

Notes: Dependent variable: log(loan) − log(FDI), averaged over 1994–96. IV = instrumental variables. See also notes to table 10.5.

[a]R^2 for IV regressions are not reported, as they do not have the standard interpretation.

**Significant at the 5 percent level.

*Significant at thc 10 percent level.

†Significant at the 15 percent level.

significant at the 5 percent level. Using the point estimate in the first regression, we see that a 1–standard deviation increase in corruption is associated with roughly a 66 percent increase in the loan-FDI ratio (e.g., roughly from 100 to 166 percent).

Based on the first regression in table 10.7, figure 10.3 presents a partial scatter plot of loan-FDI ratio against corruption, controlling for several characteristics of the host countries as described in the regression. A visual inspection of the plot suggests that positive association between corruption and capital composition is unlikely to go away if we omit any one or two observations. Hence, the evidence suggests that a corrupt country tends to

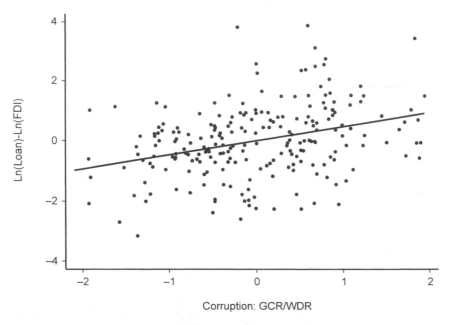

Fig. 10.3   Composition of capital inflows and corruption (partial correlation based on table 10.7, column [1])
Source: Authors' calculations.

have a composition of capital inflows that is relatively light in FDI and relatively heavy in bank loans.

Also note that because FDI is more relationship-intensive (as proxied by physical and linguistic distances) than bank loans, the coefficients on geographic distance and the linguistic tie dummy are positive and negative, respectively.

One might be concerned with possible endogeneity of the corruption measure. For example, survey respondents may perceive a country to be corrupt in part because they observe very little FDI going there. In this case, the positive association between the loan-FDI ratio and corruption can be due to a reverse causality.

We perform instrumental variable (IV) regressions on our key regressions. Mauro (1995) argued that ethnolinguistic fragmentation is a good IV for corruption. His ethnolinguistic indicator measures the probability that two persons from a country are from two distinct ethnic groups. The greater the indicator, the more fragmented the country. In addition, La Porta et al. (1998) argued that legal origin or colonial history has an important impact on the quality of government bureaucracy. These variables are used as instruments for the corruption measure. A first-stage regression suggests that ethnically more fragmented countries are more corrupt. In addition, it suggests that countries with a French legal origin (including colonies of Spain and Portugal) are more corrupt than former British colonies.

The IV regressions are reported in the last two columns of table 10.7. A test of overidentifying restrictions does not reject the null hypothesis that the instruments are uncorrelated with the error term. The results from these two IV regressions are still consistent with the notion that corruption deters FDI more than bank loans. Therefore, countries that are more corrupt tend to have a capital inflow structure that relies relatively more on bank borrowing than FDI.

Our sample is potentially censored. A source country may choose not to invest at all in a particular host country precisely because of the corruption level and other characteristics of that country. In that case, either FDI or bank lending or both may be zero. The regression procedure used so far would drop these observations. However, our left-hand side variable, the ratio of bank loans to FDI, does not lend itself naturally to a Tobit specification. For this reason, the following transformation of the ratio is constructed as the left-hand side variable: log(bank lending+0.1) − log(FDI + 0.1). The results are presented in table 10.8. With this new variable, there is a small increase in the number of observations (from 225 to 231). The most important message from table 10.8 is that the earlier conclusion remains true: Corruption tilts the composition of capital inflows away from FDI and toward international bank loans.

10.3.3   Portfolio and Direct Investments from the United States

Although bilateral data on portfolio investment other than bank credits are not available for the whole set of capital-exporting countries examined in the previous sections, we can obtain data on portfolio investment originating from the United States (to a set of developing countries). In this section, the data on U.S. outward capital flows are used to examine whether the ratio of portfolio to direct investment in a capital-receiving country is affected by its corruption level. We must caution at the outset that the number of observations is small (between 35 to 39, depending on the regression specification). Thus, the power of the statistical tests is likely to be low.

Six fixed effects regressions are performed and reported in table 10.9. In the first three columns, we use the *GCR/WDR* indicator of corruption. We see again that, at least for this subsample, the ratio of portfolio investment to FDI is also positively related to the capital-importing country's corruption level. The more corrupt a country, the less FDI it receives (relative to portfolio capital). However, when we use the TI corruption index (in the last three columns), the coefficients on corruption are no longer statistically

Table 10.8   Transformed Ratio of Loans to Foreign Direct Investment

Measure of Corruption	GCR/WDR		Transparency International		GCR/WDR	
	Fixed Effects (1)	Random Effects (2)	Fixed Effects (3)	Random Effects (4)	IV, Fixed Effects (5)	IV, Fixed Effects (6)
Corruption	0.675**	0.674**	0.701**	0.681**	0.382*	0.374*
	(0.151)	(0.226)	(0.210)	(0.320)	(0.199)	(0.196)
Tax rate	0.011	0.013	0.012	0.012		
	(0.020)	(0.031)	(0.021)	(0.032)		
FDI incentives	0.040	0.072	−0.196	−0.166	−0.014	−0.023
	(0.178)	(0.262)	(0.187)	(0.280)	(0.171)	(0.169)
FDI restrictions	0.546**	0.550**	0.558**	0.547**	0.427**	0.425**
	(0.101)	(0.156)	(0.103)	(0.159)	(0.103)	(0.102)
Log(GDP)	−0.591**	−0.645**	−0.615**	−0.657**	−0.323**	−0.309**
	(0.128)	(0.189)	(0.131)	(0.194)	(0.128)	(0.129)
Log(per capita GDP)	0.227**	0.239	0.314***	0.318	0.114	0.113
	(0.117)	(0.182)	(0.149)	(0.232)	(0.114)	(0.112)
Log distance	0.391**	0.477**	0.396**	0.479**	0.159	0.151
	(0.112)	(0.133)	(0.115)	(0.135)	(0.147)	(0.146)
Linguistic tie	−0.490	−0.504	−0.513	−0.522†	−0.752**	−0.787**
	(0.365)	(0.356)	(0.373)	(0.360)	(0.325)	(0.326)
Exchange rate volatility	0.563	1.091	−0.279	0.442		−1.257
	(2.368)	(3.490)	(2.553)	(3.798)		(2.451)
Overidentifying restriction (p-value of the test)					0.28	0.28
Adjusted R^2/overall R^2	0.48	0.51	0.45	0.50	——	——
N	231	231	231	231	183	183

Source: Authors' calculations.

Notes: Dependent variable: log(loan + 0.1) – log(FDI + 0.1), averaged over 1994–96. IV = instrumental variables. See also notes to table 10.5.

**Significant at the 5 percent level.

*Significant at the 10 percent level.

†Significant at the 15 percent level.

significant, although they are always positive. The insignificance can be consistent with a genuinely zero coefficient or can result from a low power of the test due to the small sample size.

10.3.4   Evidence from the Balance-of-Payments Data

If we are willing to forgo bilateral data and employ data from the balance-of-payments (BOP) statistics, we may be able to include more capital-importing countries in our analysis.[11] In particular, we continue to use the ratio of portfolio inflow to FDI, or the loan–FDI ratio, as the dependent

11. Note, however, that the number of observations with the BOP data may not be greater than that with the bilateral loan-FDI data.

Table 10.9   **U.S.-bilateral Portfolio Data**

Measure of Corruption	GCR/WDR			Transparency International		
	(1)	(2)	(3)	(4)	(5)	(6)
Corruption	0.321*	0.319*	0.341†	0.283	0.324	0.307
	(0.173)	(0.171)	(0.208)	(0.247)	(0.270)	(0.275)
Tax rate			−0.023		−0.033	
			(0.036)		(0.033)	
FDI incentives			−0.218		−0.215	
			(0.255)		(0.249)	
FDI restrictions			0.214		0.167	
			(0.156)		(0.165)	
Ease of investing in securities and bonds market			0.364*		0.280	
			(0.203)		(0.199)	
Log(GDP)	0.304**	0.311**	0.371**	0.289**	0.287**	0.344**
	(0.138)	(0.152)	(0.161)	(0.124)	(0.137)	(0.155)
Log(per capita GDP)	0.506**	0.517**	0.441**	0.512**	0.557**	0.461**
	(0.100)	(0.100)	(0.152)	(0.163)	(0.177)	(0.202)
Log distance	−0.200*	−0.187†	−0.194†	−0.198**	−0.180†	−0.203†
	(0.101)	(0.113)	(0.129)	(0.085)	(0.107)	(0.127)
Linguistic tie	0.870**	0.814**	1.004**	0.853**	0.797**	0.984**
	(0.238)	(0.251)	(0.287)	(0.269)	(0.278)	(0.294)
Exchange rate volatility		3.515**	3.990†		2.436	3.281
		(1.649)	(2.367)		(2.254)	(2.739)
Government deficit		0.009	0.023		0.006	0.005
		(0.034)	(0.047)		(0.039)	(0.049)
Adjusted R^2	0.52	0.56	0.60	0.51	0.54	0.58
N	39	36	35	39	36	35

Source. Authors' calculations.

Notes: Dependent variable: log(portfolio investment) − log(FDI), averaged over 1994–96. The portfolio and FDI values are the sum of the flows over 1994–96. Also see the notes to table 10.5.

**Significant at the 5 percent level.

*Significant at the 10 percent level.

†Significant at the 15 percent level.

variable. To minimize the effect of year-to-year fluctuation, we again average the ratios over a three-year period (1994–96).

The results are reported in the upper half of table 10.10. In column (1), where the dependent variable is the ratio of portfolio and FDI, we can see that corruption (as measured by a hybrid of *GCR* and *WDR*) is positive and statistically significant: More corrupt countries on average attract more portfolio inflows than FDI. In column (2), we examine the loan-FDI ratio as the dependent variable. The corruption variable is not significant. However, we observe that many other regressors are not significant either. If we drop two of the insignificant regressors (FDI incentives and restrictions), then the coefficient on corruption becomes positive and significant. If we further drop two additional insignificant variables (tax rate and exchange rate volatility), corruption remains positive and significant. Thus, even with the BOP data,

Table 10.10   Corruption and Composition of Capital Inflows Based on
                     Balance-of-Payments Data

Measure of Corruption	Dependent Variable					
	GCR/WDR				Transparency International	
	Portfolio Flow-FDI (1)	Loan-FDI (2)	Loan-FDI (3)	Loan-FDI (4)	Portfolio Flow-FDI (5)	Loan-FDI (6)
Corruption	1.296**	0.356	0.702**	0.669**	1.046**	0.832*
	(0.319)	(0.417)	(0.347)	(0.269)	(0.382)	(0.428)
Tax rate	0.069	0.010	0.041		0.045	0.001
	(0.050)	(0.053)	(0.051)		(0.052)	(0.051)
FDI incentives	−0.260	−0.562		−0.263	−0.572	
	(0.484)	(0.582)		(0.442)	(0.506)	
FDI restrictions	0.197	0.281		0.023	0.245	
	(0.280)	(0.249)		(0.326)	(0.252)	
Ease of portfolio investment	0.288			−0.056		
	(0.471)			(0.554)		
Log (GDP)	0.559**	0.414	0.022	−0.256†	0.548**	0.332
	(0.252)	(0.349)	(0.293)	(0.165)	(0.239)	(0.313)
Log (per capita GDP)	0.861**	0.314	0.560*	0.316†	0.851**	0.641*
	(0.304)	(0.360)	(0.283)	(0.198)	(0.390)	(0.367)
Exchange rate volatility	−7.148†	−10.322	−6.070		−5.067	−11.410
	(4.406)	(12.181)	(11.489)		(5.838)	(11.525)
Adjusted R^2	0.51	0.24	0.13	0.16	0.46	0.31
N	41	39	44	73	41	39

Source: Authors' calculations.

Notes: Standard errors are in parentheses. The left-hand-side variables are in logarithm form and are averaged over 1994–96. Exchange rate volatility = standard deviation of the first difference in log monthly exchange rate (per US$) from January 1994 through December 1996. The corruption variable is standardized (i.e., corruption in the regressions = [original corruption – sample mean]/[sample standard deviation]). Hence, the coefficient on corruption can be read as the response of the left-hand-side variable with respect to a one standard deviation increase in corruption.

**Significant at the 5 percent level.

*Significant at the 10 percent level.

†Significant at the 15 percent level.

there is evidence that corrupt countries would have greater difficulties in attracting FDI relative to bank loans. In columns (5)–(6) of table 10.10, we use a different measure of corruption (TI index). The results remain the same: Corruption discourages FDI more than bank loans or portfolio inflows.

We repeat the exercise with the left-hand side variables over a different time period (1997–98), which is the period that Hausmann and Fernandez-Arias (2000) examined. The regression results are reported in the lower half of table 10.11. Contrary to their inference, we find exactly the same pattern as in our previous tables: corrupt countries on average have relatively more difficulties in attracting FDI than the other forms of capital inflows.

Table 10.11 Corruption and Composition of Capital Inflows Based on Balance-of-Payments Data (1997–98)

	Dependent Variable							
	GCR/WDR			Transparency International			GCR/WDR	Transparency International
Measure of Corruption	Portfolio Flows-FDI (1)	Loan-FDI (2)	Loan-FDI (3)	Portfolio Flow-FDI (4)	Portfolio Flow-FDI (5)	Loan-FDI (6)	FDI/(FDI + loan + portfolio) (7)	FDI/(FDI + loan + portfolio) (8)
Corruption	0.570*	0.579†	0.600*	0.398	0.657*	0.725*	−0.374*	−0.481**
	(0.330)	(0.385)	(0.348)	(0.319)	(0.330)	(0.412)	(0.193)	(0.198)
Tax rate	0.102**	0.041	0.040	0.090**	0.089**	0.034	−0.045*	−0.041*
	(0.043)	(0.045)	(0.044)	(0.038)	(0.041)	(0.045)	(0.024)	(0.023)
FDI incentives	−0.733**	−0.449	−0.461	−0.601*	−0.679*	−0.465	0.030	0.048
	(0.340)	(0.366)	(0.350)	(0.312)	(0.339)	(0.362)	(0.188)	(0.183)
FDI restrictions	0.222	−0.072	−0.066	0.006	0.150	−0.109	0.010	0.024
	(0.215)	(0.230)	(0.224)	(0.201)	(0.210)	(0.229)	(0.117)	(0.114)
Ease of investing in securities and bonds market	0.394			0.652†	0.222			
	(0.407)			(0.405)	(0.402)			
Log(GDP)	0.071	0.158	0.152	0.187	0.059	0.093	−0.272**	−0.228**
	(0.191)	(0.214)	(0.207)	(0.180)	(0.188)	(0.218)	(0.100)	(0.100)
Log(per capita GDP)	0.713**	0.473†	0.479†	0.492	0.849**	0.610*	−0.350**	−0.458**
	(0.305)	(0.316)	(0.308)	(0.335)	(0.332)	(0.347)	(0.163)	(0.176)
Exchange rate volatility		0.763		19.980**		1.916	−3.058	−3.770
		(5.571)		(7.796)		(5.201)	(2.856)	(2.647)
Adjusted R^2	0.39	0.07	0.09	0.50	0.41	0.09	0.31	0.34
N	37	41	41	37	37	41	45	45

Source: Authors' calculations.

Notes: Standard errors are in parentheses. The left-hand-side variables, log(FDI), log(GDP), and log(per capita GDP) are averaged over 1994–96. Exchange rate volatility = standard deviation of the first difference in log monthly exchange rate (per US$) from January 1997 through December 1998. The corruption measure is standardized.

**Significant at the 5 percent level.

*Significant at the 10 percent level.

†Significant at the 15 percent level.

Table 10.12   **Maturity of Debt**

	(Short-term bank loan)/ (total loan + FDI)		(Short-term bank loan)/ (total loan)	
	GCR/WDR	TI	*GCR/WDR*	TI
Corruption	0.040	0.155†	−0.108	0.027
	(0.082)	(0.102)	(0.083)	(0.089)
Log(GDP)	0.097*	0.067	−0.013	−0.009
	(0.049)	(0.048)	(0.036)	(0.032)
Log(per capita GDP)	0.032	0.101	−0.032	0.007
	(0.063)	(0.080)	(0.058)	(0.060)
Adjusted R^2	0.04	0.09	0.03	0.003
N	32	33	77	64

Source: Authors' calculations.

Notes: Standard errors are in parentheses. Short-term loans are loans with maturity of less than and up to one year. Bank loans for a particular recipient country are its borrowing from all BIS-reporting countries (mostly OECD countries). To maximize comparability, the value of FDI for a host country is the sum of inward FDI from OECD countries (rather than total inward FDI from the balance-of-payments source).

*Significant at the 10 percent level.

†Significant at the 15 percent level.

10.3.5   Maturity Structure of the Foreign Borrowing

A different dimension of the capital flow composition, namely, the relative share of the short-term borrowing, has been stressed in the literature as also being related to the likelihood of a currency crisis (see Rodrik and Velasco 1999).

We look into the possible connection between this measure of composition of capital inflows and corruption. The results are reported in table 10.12. It turns out that there is no robust evidence for a systematic relationship between the two. Thus, contrary to the share of FDI in total capital flows, higher corruption *per se* may not be associated with a greater reliance on short-term borrowing.

10.3.6   Currency Structure of Foreign Borrowing

Countries that experience a BOP crisis are often criticized for having either too much short-term borrowing or too much borrowing in a hard currency. Of course, both the tendency to borrow in the short term and the tendency to borrow in a hard currency are linked to a country's inability to borrow internationally in its own currency.

Using the ratio of international bonds issued in a country's currency to all international bonds issued by that country as a measure of a country's ability to borrow in its own currency, we can examine possible connections between a country's extent of corruption and this ability to borrow in its own currency. The results are reported in table 10.13. When we use the

Table 10.13   Ability to Borrow Internationally in Own Currency

Measure of Corruption	GCR/WDR				Transparency International			
	OLS (1)	OLS (2)	Tobit (3)	Tobit (4)	OLS (5)	OLS (6)	Tobit (7)	Tobit (8)
Corruption	-0.252**	-0.115**	-0.767**	0.008	-0.252**	-0.074	-0.689**	-0.067
	(0.059)	(0.052)	(0.132)	(0.185)	(0.062)	(0.077)	(0.130)	(0.187)
Log (per capita GDP)		0.109**		0.653**		0.139**		1.584**
		(0.031)		(0.167)		(0.052)		(0.403)
Adjusted R^2/pseudo-R^2	0.28	0.34	0.30	0.46	0.24	0.29	0.24	0.37
N	99	98	99	98	85	84	85	84

Source: The data were kindly provided by Ernesto Stein and Ugo Panizza.

Notes: Standard errors are in parentheses. The dependent variable is the ability of a country to borrow internationally in its own currency. Log(per capita GDP) are averaged over 1994–96. Ability to borrow internationally is measured by proportion of international securities issued in a country's own currency relative to the amount issued by that country's residents in 1998.

**Significant at the 5 percent level.

GCR/WDR measure of corruption, there is a negative and statistically significant association between corruption and the ability to borrow in the country's own currency. This negative association remains when we add income level as a control. On the other hand, when we use an alternative measure of corruption (the TI index) and when income level is controlled for, the coefficient on corruption is no longer significant (although still negative). We have also tried a tobit specification in which zero percent issuance of international debt in a country's own currency is assumed to be censored from below. The coefficient on corruption is negative if there is no per capita income in the regression but insignificantly different from zero if there is per capita income. Overall, there is some (weak) support for the notion that higher corruption is associated with a lower ability to borrow internationally in one's own currency. This may be considered corroborative evidence that corruption may have raised a country's likelihood to slide into a currency crisis.

10.4   Conclusion

Corruption affects the composition of capital inflows in a way that is unfavorable to the country. A corrupt country receives substantially less FDI; however, it may not be disadvantaged as much in obtaining bank loans. As a result, corruption in a capital-importing country tends to tilt the composition of its capital inflows away from FDI and toward foreign bank loans. The data support this hypothesis. This result is robust across different measures of corruption and different econometric specifications.

There are two possible reasons for this effect. First, FDI is more likely to be exploited by local corrupt officials *ex post* than foreign loans. As a result, less FDI would go to corrupt countries *ex ante*. Second, the current international financial architecture is such that there is more insurance or protection from the IMF and the G7 governments for bank lenders from developed countries than for direct investors.

Previous research (starting with Frankel and Rose 1996) has shown that a capital inflow structure that is relatively low in FDI is associated with a greater propensity for a future currency crisis. It may be that international bank loans (or other portfolio flows) swing more than direct investment in the event of bad news (whether genuine or self-generated by international investors) about economic or policy fundamentals. If so, this paper has provided evidence for one possible channel through which corruption in a developing country may increase its chances of running into a future crisis.

In the literature on the causes of currency crises, crony capitalism and self-fulfilling expectations by international creditors are often proposed as two *rival* hypotheses. Indeed, authors who subscribe to one view often do not accept the other. The evidence in this paper suggests a natural linkage between the two. Crony capitalism, through its effect on the composition of a country's capital inflows, makes it more vulnerable to the self-fulfilling-expectations type of currency crisis.

Corruption could also lead to a financial crisis by weakening domestic financial supervision and damaging the quality of banks' and firms' balance sheets. This possibility itself can be a topic for a useful research project.

Appendix A
Justification for the Econometric Specification That Links the Composition of Capital Inflows and Corruption

In the main empirical part of the paper, we have performed several regressions that examine the connection between corruption and the ratio of FDI and non-FDI capital flows. In this section, a simple model is used to demonstrate how such a reduced-form specification can be justified. For simplicity, let us consider that there are two types of international capital flows: direct investment and bank credit.

Let us suppose that the government in the capital-importing country k maximizes the two-period objective function

$$U(G_{k1}) + \delta U(G_{k2}),$$

where G_{k1} and G_{k2} are expenditures by the government in country k in period 1 and period 2, respectively, and δ is the subjective discount factor. For simplicity, we assume that the tax revenues in the two periods, T_{k1} and T_{k2}, are exogenously given. Let B_k and D_k are first-period borrowing by country k from international banks and first-period direct investment in country k, respectively. To abstract from unnecessary complications, we assume that bank credit and FDI are merely two forms of additional funding sources. No production is explicitly modeled. In this case, the gap between the first-period expenditure and tax revenue must be met by the inflow of international capital:

$$G_{k1} = T_{k1} + B_k + D_k$$

In the second period, the international credit must be repaid. Moreover, international direct investors are assumed to recoup both the investment and the gross profit.

$$G_{k2} = T_{k2} - R(B_k)B_k - R(D_k)D_k,$$

where $R(B_k)$ and $R(D_k)$ are the gross returns that international creditors and international director investors would demand from country k. Suppose R^* is the gross return on the risk-free bond (say, the U.S. government bond as an approximation), then, we assume that

$$R(B_k) = R^* + \theta B_k$$

and

$$R(D_k) = R^* + \theta D_k + \rho_k D_k.$$

Both θ and ρ_k are positive. Think of ρ_k as proportional to country k's perceived level of corruption. The positive θ reflects the assumption that the warranted returns on either bank credit or direct investment increase with the size of the capital inflow. Note that ρ_k appears in the return on the direct investment but not in that on bank credit because corruption represents a greater risk to direct investment than to bank loans (for the two reasons described in the previous section; relative to bank lending, FDI faces greater sunk costs and less protection from the international financial system).

A few points are worth noting here. First, we assume that the bank credit is obtained and later paid back by the government. In reality, either the private or the public sector can borrow from the international credit market. Many researchers have observed that the distinction between private and public borrowing is very thin because private borrowing from the international credit market often carries an implicit, and sometimes an explicit, guarantee from the government of the borrowing country. Second, while direct investment is supposed to be for the long term, investors eventually would want to recoup both the initial investment and the cumulative profits along the way.

The government's maximization problem yields the following two first-order conditions:

$$U'(G_{k1}) - \delta U'(G_{k2})(R^* + 2\theta B_k) = 0$$

and

$$U'(G_{k1}) - \delta U'(G_{k2})(R^* + 2\theta B_k + 2\rho_k D_k) = 0$$

This implies a particular relationship between the composition of capital inflow for country k and its corruption level:

$$\frac{B_k}{D_k} = \frac{\theta + \rho_k}{\theta}.$$

Hence, the higher the corruption level in country k, the less FDI it would receive relative to its bank borrowing. The ratio of non-FDI forms of capital flow to FDI can be linked to the recipient country's level of corruption.

Appendix B

Source and Construction of the Variables

Bilateral Bank Loans

Source: BIS website [http://www.bis.org/publ/index.htm]. Data are at the end of December in US$ millions. Loans to offshore banking centers are omitted.

Bilateral Foreign Direct Investment

Source: OECD, *International Direct Investment Statistics Yearbook 1998* diskettes. Unit: US$ millions (converted into US$ using the yearly average exchange rates from annex III of the book).

Total Inward FDI, Portfolio, and Other Investment

Source: IMF, Balance of Payments Statistics CD-ROM, lines 78bed, 78bgd, and 78bid, respectively.

Distance

Source for latitude and longitude: Rudloff (1981), updated from Pearce and Smith (1984). Greater circle distance (in kilometers) between economic centers (usually capital cities) in a pair of countries based on the latitude and longitude data.

Argentina. Used the average latitude and longitude of Buenos Aires, Cordoba, and Rosario.

Australia. Used the average latitude and longitude of Canberra, Sydney, and Melbourne.

Bahrain. Used the latitude and longitude data from the city of Muharraq.

Bermuda. Used the latitude and longitude data from Kindley Air Force Base.

Bhutan. Used the latitude and longitude data from [http://www.kingdom ofbhutan.com/kingdom.html].

Canada. Used the average latitude and longitude of Toronto, Vancouver, and Montreal.

Equatorial Guinea. Used the latitude and longitude data from the city of Santa Isabel.

Greenland. Used the latitude and longitude data from the city of Peary Land.

India. Used the average latitude and longitude of New Delhi, Bombay, and Calcutta.

Israel. Used the latitude and longitude data from Lod Airport (near Java and Tel Aviv).

Mauritius. Used the latitude and longitude data from the city of Diego Gracia.

The Netherlands. Used the latitude and longitude data from the city of De Bilt.

Slovak. Used the latitude and longitude data from the city of Poprad.

Sudan. Used the average latitude and longitude of Atbara Khartoum and El Fasher.

Switzerland. Used the latitude and longitude data from the city of Zurich.

Brazil. Used the average latitude and longitude of Brasilia, Rio de Janeiro, and Sao Paulo.

Panama. Used the latitude and longitude data from Panama City.

Russia. Used the average latitude and longitude of Moscow, St. Petersburg, and Nizhni.

Nizhny Novogorod. Used the data from [http://www.unn.runnet.ru/nn/whereis.htm].

Kazakhstan. Used the average latitude and longitude of Almaty, Chimkent, and Karaganda.

United States. Used the latitude and longitude data from Kansas City, Missouri.

Linguistic Tie

Source of major languages: CIA (1999).

Dummy = 1 if the two countries share a common language or have a former colonial relation.

Corruption

GCR Index

Source: World Economic Forum (1997).

Transformation: Values in this paper = 8 – original values.

WDR Index

Original source: World Bank (1997). Data are from Kaufmann and Wei (1999).

Transformation: Values in this paper = 8 – original values.

TI Index

Source: Transparency International 1998 index [http://www.gwdg.de/~uwvw/icr.htm].

Transformation: Values in this paper = 10 – original values. Thus, a larger number means more corruption.

Gross Domestic Product and GDP per Capita

Source: World Bank, *SIMA/GDF* and *WDR* central database. GDP data are GDP at market prices (constant 1995 US$); GDP per capita data are calculated using GDP divided by population.

Monthly Exchange Rate (end of period)

Source: IMF, International Financial Statistics, via the World Bank *SIMA* database.

Government Deficit to GDP Ratio

Source: World Bank, *SIMA/GDF* and *WDI* central database.

U.S. Bilateral Data

Source. U.S. Department of the Treasury website [http://www.ustreas.gov/tic/ticsec.htm]. Sum of the U.S. portfolio investments in other countries (gross sale by foreigners to U.S. residents, foreign bonds and foreign stocks), 1994–96. All amounts in US$ millions.

Legal Origins

Source: La Porta et al. (1998).

Accounting Standard

Source: La Porta et al. (1998).

Corporate Tax Rates

Source: PwC (2000), updated from World Economic Forum (1997).

Appendix C

Table 10A.1   Standard Deviation and Coefficient of Variation of FDI-GDP, Loan-GDP, and Portfolio-GDP, by Country

Country	FDI/GDP			Loan/GDP			Portfolio/GDP		
	Standard Deviation	Mean	Coefficient of Variation	Standard Deviation	Mean	Coefficient of Variation	Standard Deviation	Mean	Coefficient of Variation
Albania	0.017	0.013	1.372	0.024	0.020	1.222			
Algeria	0.002	0.001	3.518	0.013	0.001	16.046	0.000	0.000	-3.464
Angola	0.030	0.035	0.870	0.085	-0.017	-4.876			
Argentina	0.006	0.010	0.614	0.032	0.020	1.623	0.034	0.021	1.618
Australia	0.009	0.018	0.469	0.016	0.016	0.971	0.015	0.028	0.513
Austria	0.004	0.005	0.830	0.019	0.011	1.672	0.012	0.027	0.426
Bangladesh	0.000	0.000	1.319	0.009	0.025	0.346	0.001	0.000	97.667
Benin	0.020	0.013	1.551	0.060	0.013	4.570	0.000	0.000	-4.650
Bolivia	0.021	0.020	1.063	0.057	0.037	1.519	0.001	0.000	-2.925
Botswana	0.036	0.024	1.494	0.023	0.023	1.002	0.001	0.000	3.396
Brazil	0.003	0.006	0.557	0.028	0.004	7.771	0.026	0.013	2.042
Bulgaria	0.004	0.002	1.576	0.058	-0.003	-17.827	0.003	-0.001	-2.771
Burkina Faso	0.001	0.001	1.304	0.038	0.033	1.155	0.000	0.000	3.742
Burundi	0.001	0.001	0.726	0.036	0.053	0.675			
Cameroon	0.014	0.007	1.926	0.021	0.026	0.830			
Canada	0.006	0.011	0.573	0.005	0.004	1.234	0.014	0.035	0.400
Central African Republic	0.006	0.003	2.000	0.021	0.051	0.417			
Chad	0.015	0.010	1.484	0.042	0.035	1.187			
Chile	0.019	0.027	0.696	0.064	0.033	1.960	0.008	0.005	1.632
China	0.023	0.022	1.051	0.007	0.007	1.047	0.003	0.003	1.039

Colombia	0.008	0.015	0.550	0.020	0.019	1.039	0.008	0.005	1.702
Congo, Republic of the	0.010	0.008	1.163	0.245	0.106	2.309	0.007	0.000	−203.494
Costa Rica	0.010	0.025	0.417	0.107	0.028	3.821	0.001	0.000	4.386
Côte d'Ivoire	0.009	0.006	1.507	0.060	0.052	1.145	0.001	0.000	1.753
Denmark	0.009	0.008	1.172	0.036	0.016	2.202	0.035	0.020	1.753
Dominican Republic	0.008	0.014	0.576	0.036	0.023	1.580	0.013	0.004	3.742
Ecuador	0.010	0.014	0.737	0.046	0.016	2.910			
Egypt	0.010	0.021	0.473	0.046	0.002	29.621	0.002	0.001	3.880
El Salvador	0.003	0.003	0.947	0.031	0.026	1.181	0.004	0.001	3.227
Finland	0.004	0.005	0.938	0.013	0.007	1.682	0.027	0.032	0.857
France	0.005	0.009	0.545	0.022	0.023	0.921	0.015	0.014	1.066
Gabon	0.022	0.009	2.539	0.105	0.042	2.521			
Gambia	0.016	0.013	1.172	0.044	0.047	0.933			
Ghana	0.011	0.007	1.510	0.022	0.043	0.515			
Greece	0.002	0.011	0.139	0.015	0.032	0.485			
Guatemala	0.009	0.011	0.833	0.013	0.008	1.648	0.009	0.000	40.526
Guinea	0.004	0.005	0.743	0.038	0.062	0.610			
Haiti	0.003	0.003	1.090	0.024	0.020	1.174			
Honduras	0.006	0.010	0.578	0.042	0.044	0.960			
Hungary	0.031	0.021	1.465	0.035	0.025	1.374	0.032	0.013	2.494
India	0.002	0.001	1.896	0.004	0.008	0.533	0.005	0.002	2.119
Indonesia	0.007	0.009	0.820	0.017	0.024	0.717	0.009	0.005	1.722
Iran	0.000	0.000	3.106	0.017	−0.008	−2.264			
Ireland	0.011	0.014	0.778	0.033	0.008	3.885	0.031	0.025	1.282
Italy	0.002	0.003	0.617	0.008	0.010	0.814	0.022	0.016	1.348
Jamaica	0.019	0.016	1.188	0.079	0.058	1.359			
Japan	0.000	0.000	1.301	0.007	0.000	−48.772	0.011	0.011	0.941
Jordan	0.008	0.006	1.355	0.038	0.049	0.771			
Kenya	0.003	0.003	0.857	0.032	0.016	2.078	0.000	0.000	2.631
Korea	0.002	0.003	0.591	0.037	0.018	2.039	0.014	0.011	1.338

(*continued*)

Table 10A.1 (continued)

Country	FDI/GDP			Loan/GDP			Portfolio/GDP		
	Standard Deviation	Mean	Coefficient of Variation	Standard Deviation	Mean	Coefficient of Variation	Standard Deviation	Mean	Coefficient of Variation
Laos	0.026	0.018	1.493	0.028	0.053	0.528	0.000	0.000	2.441
Lesotho	0.104	0.053	1.975	0.033	0.074	0.444			
Libya	0.012	−0.008	−1.577	0.008	0.003	2.439			
Madagascar	0.003	0.002	1.250	0.055	0.031	1.740			
Malawi	0.002	0.001	2.674	0.045	0.061	0.734	0.001	0.001	1.186
Malaysia	0.023	0.046	0.490	0.034	0.008	4.397	0.023	0.007	3.544
Mali	0.013	0.006	2.258	0.020	0.072	0.278			
Mauritania	0.010	0.009	1.082	0.089	0.126	0.703	0.000	0.000	−2.197
Mauritius	0.005	0.006	0.725	0.036	0.026	1.392	0.011	0.003	3.437
Mexico	0.007	0.016	0.452	0.033	0.016	2.048	0.026	0.012	2.088
Morocco	0.006	0.007	0.753	0.036	0.029	1.245	0.002	0.001	2.606
Mozambique	0.008	0.006	1.301	0.163	0.179	0.908			
Nepal	0.001	0.000	4.123	0.015	0.039	0.374			
The Netherlands	0.011	0.021	0.490	0.012	0.008	1.428	0.014	0.018	0.809
New Zealand	0.018	0.037	0.477	0.036	0.012	2.937	0.011	0.003	3.189
Nicaragua	0.016	0.008	1.878	0.195	0.070	2.794	0.002	0.001	3.241
Niger	0.011	0.004	2.672	0.034	0.034	0.979			
Nigeria	0.026	0.028	0.936	0.061	−0.066	−0.931	0.020	0.009	2.211
Norway	0.009	0.007	1.298	0.011	0.006	1.686	0.023	0.011	2.061
Oman	0.006	0.013	0.459	0.029	0.016	1.815			
Pakistan	0.004	0.006	0.638	0.011	0.027	0.409	0.007	0.004	1.779
Panama	0.050	0.018	2.833	0.187	0.017	10.755	0.094	0.022	4.273
Papua New Guinea	0.019	0.037	0.506	0.077	0.008	9.981	0.102	0.069	1.480
Paraguay	0.008	0.009	0.920	0.025	0.012	2.023	0.001	0.000	30.180
Peru	0.020	0.011	1.843	0.060	0.018	3.308	0.004	0.002	1.648
The Philippines	0.009	0.010	0.921	0.026	0.027	0.956	0.017	0.008	1.979

Country									
Poland	0.011	0.007	1.625	0.060	0.012	5.186	0.002	0.001	4.062
Portugal	0.010	0.015	0.688	0.034	0.014	2.407	0.019	0.016	1.199
Romania	0.005	0.004	1.234	0.051	0.003	19.273	0.012	0.004	3.023
Rwanda	0.005	0.007	0.719	0.015	0.025	0.627	0.000	0.000	2.677
Saudi Arabia	0.029	0.012	2.398						
Senegal	0.008	0.004	2.026	0.043	0.073	0.583	0.001	0.000	1.520
Sierra Leone	0.044	-0.007	-6.311	0.041	0.031	1.330	0.000	0.000	-4.000
Somalia	0.007	-0.003	-2.045	0.077	0.116	0.667			
South Africa	0.004	0.001	3.185	0.015	0.003	5.954	0.013	0.006	2.272
Spain	0.006	0.016	0.397	0.012	0.007	1.632	0.032	0.015	2.133
Sri Lanka	0.004	0.008	0.515	0.019	0.085	0.227	0.006	-0.003	-2.190
Sudan	0.000	0.000	3.858	0.020	0.025	0.811			
Sweden	0.016	0.013	1.261	0.023	0.039	0.598	0.029	0.000	132.630
Switzerland	0.006	0.011	0.483	0.007	0.004	1.835	0.021	0.024	0.889
Syria	0.005	0.002	2.139	0.046	0.036	1.277			
Thailand	0.007	0.013	0.571	0.028	0.044	0.629	0.012	0.011	1.137
Togo	0.012	0.008	1.417	0.048	0.026	1.857	0.001	0.001	1.056
Trinidad and Tobago	0.029	0.033	0.865	0.026	0.002	12.877	0.001	0.000	6.616
Tunisia	0.012	0.019	0.644	0.017	0.024	0.710	0.003	0.004	0.895
Turkey	0.002	0.003	0.637	0.025	0.005	4.623	0.008	0.007	1.056
Uganda	0.009	0.005	1.830	0.035	0.033	1.080			
United Kingdom	0.009	0.017	0.518	0.063	0.047	1.343	0.028	0.032	0.875
United States	0.003	0.008	0.425	0.000	0.000	-2.828	0.012	0.015	0.769
Uruguay	0.007	0.005	1.420	0.033	0.017	1.984	0.012	0.013	0.914
Venezuela	0.011	0.008	1.335	0.080	-0.017	-4.814	0.089	0.026	3.417
Zambia	0.019	0.020	0.926	0.089	0.075	1.186			
Zimbabwe	0.002	0.000	8.913	0.036	0.035	1.035	0.004	-0.004	-0.853
Mean	0.012	0.011	1.135	0.039	0.028	0.932	0.011	0.008	-0.579
Median	0.008	0.009	1.063	0.033	0.023	1.174	0.008	0.003	1.632

Note: Empty cells indicate missing data or zero mean.

Appendix D

Table 10A.2   Corruption and Bank Lending

	Lending Country				
	All	All	France	Japan	United States
Methodology	Fixed Effects	Fixed Effects	OLS	OLS	OLS
Measure of corruption	GCR/WDR	GCR/WDR	GCR/WDR	GCR/WDR	GCR/WDR
Corruption	0.376**	0.286**	0.419*	0.427	0.747**
	(0.092)	(0.107)	(0.221)	(0.363)	(0.344)
Ease of investing in securities	0.219**	0.257*	0.253	0.402	0.591*
and bonds market	(0.088)	(0.134)	(0.211)	(0.433)	(0.311)
Tax rate		−0.009			
		(0.015)			
FDI incentives		−0.081			
		(0.121)			
FDI restrictions		−0.001			
		(0.078)			
Log (GDP)	1.004**	1.065**	0.860**	1.081**	1.229**
	(0.054)	(0.109)	(0.131)	(0.222)	(0.187)

Log (per capita GDP)	0.366**	0.281**	0.078	0.492*	0.340*
	(0.063)	(0.088)	(0.156)	(0.273)	(0.220)
Log distance	−0.244**	−0.235**	0.245	−1.451**	−1.392**
	(0.072)	(0.080)	(0.179)	(0.655)	(0.624)
Linguistic tie	0.633**	0.542**	−0.528	−1.585	0.689
	(0.207)	(0.236)	(0.914)	(1.872)	(0.607)
Exchange rate volatility	−5.917**	−5.781**	−9.459**	−1.298	−15.111**
	(1.564)	(1.781)	(3.473)	(8.374)	(5.250)
Adjusted R^2	0.72	0.69	0.75	0.57	0.65
N	396	317	32	30	30

Source: Authors' calculations.

Notes: Source-country fixed effects are included in the first two regressions. Standard errors are in parentheses.

**Significant at the 5 percent level.

*Significant at the 10 percent level.

References

Bai, Chong-En, and Shang-Jin Wei. 2000. Quality of bureaucracy and open-economy macro policies. NBER Working Paper no. 7766. Cambridge, Mass.: National Bureau of Economic Research, June.

Bank for International Settlements (BIS). Various years. Consolidated international claims of BIS reporting banks on individual countries. Available at [http://www.bis.org/publ.index.htm].

Bardhan, Pranab. 1997. Corruption and development: A review of issues. *Journal of Economic Literature* 35 (Sept.): 1320–46.

Central Intelligence Agency (CIA). 1999. *The world factbook 1999.* Available at [http://www.cia.gov/cia/publications/factbook/].

Dooley, Michael P., Stijn Claessens, and Andrew Warner. 1995. Portfolio capital flows: Hot or cool? *World Bank Economic Review* 9 (1): 153–74.

Frankel, Jeffrey A., and Andrew Rose. 1996. Currency crashes in emerging markets: An empirical treatment. *Journal of International Economics* 41 (3–4): 351–66.

Hausmann, Ricardo, and Eduardo Fernandez-Arias. 2000. Foreign direct investment: Good cholesterol? IADB Working Paper no. 417. Washington, D.C.: Inter-American Development Bank.

Hausmann, Ricardo, Ugo Panizza, and Ernesto Stein. 2000. Why do countries float the way they float? IADB Working Paper. Washington, D.C.: Inter-American Development Bank.

Hines, James. 1995. Forbidden payment: Foreign bribery and American business after 1977. NBER Working Paper no. 5266. Cambridge, Mass.: National Bureau of Economic Research, September.

International Monetary Fund (IMF). Balance of Payments Statistics [database on CD-ROM].

———. International Financial Statistics. World Bank *SIMA* electronic database.

Johnson, Simon, Peter Boone, Alasdair Breach, and Eric Friedman. 2000. Corporate governance in the Asian financial crisis. *Journal of Financial Economics* 58 (1–2): 141–86.

Kaufmann, Daniel. 1997. Corruption: Some myths and facts. *Foreign Policy* 107: 114–31.

Kaufmann, Daniel, and Shang-Jin Wei. 1999. Does "grease payment" speed up the wheels of commerce? National Bureau of Economic Research Working Paper no. 7093. Cambridge, Mass.: National Bureau of Economic Research, April.

La Porta, Rafael, Florencio Lopez-de-Silanes, Andrei Shleifer, and Robert Vishny. 1998. Law and finance. *Journal of Political Economy* 106:1113–55.

Mauro, Paulo. 1995. Corruption and growth. *Quarterly Journal of Economics* 110: 681–712.

McKinnon, Ronald, and Huw Pill. 1996. Credible liberalization and international capital flows: The overborrowing syndrome. In *Financial deregulation and integration in East Asia,* ed. Takatoshi Ito and Anne O. Krueger, 7–45. Chicago: University of Chicago Press.

———. 1999. Exchange rate regimes for emerging markets: Moral hazard and international overborrowing. *Oxford Review of Economic Policy* 15 (3): 19–38.

Organization for Economic Cooperation and Development (OECD). 1999. *International direct investment statistics yearbook.* Paris: OECD.

Pearce, E. A., and Charles Gordon Smith. 1984. *The world weather guide.* London: Hutchinson.

PricewaterhouseCoopers (PwC). 2000. Doing business and investing worldwide. [CD-ROM]. Washington, D.C.: PricewaterhouseCoopers.

Radelet, Steven, and Jeffrey Sachs. 1998. The East Asian financial crisis: Diagnosis, remedies, and prospects. *Brookings Papers on Economic Activity,* Issue no. 1:1–74.

Razin, Assaf, Efraim Sadka, and Chi-Wa Yuen. 1998. A pecking order of capital inflows and international tax principles. *Journal of International Economics* 44:45–68.

Reisen, Helmut. 1999. The great Asian slump. Paris, France, OECD Development Center, Working Paper.

Rodrik, Dani, and Andres Velasco. 1999. Short-term capital flows. Paper presented at the 1999 World Bank Annual Bank Conference on Development Economics. Harvard University and New York University, Washington, D.C.

Rudloff, Willy. 1981. *World climates, with tables of climatic data and practical suggestions.* Stuttgart, Germany: Wissenschaftliche Verlagsgessellschaft.

Shleifer, Andrei, and Robert Vishny. 1993. Corruption. *Quarterly Journal of Economics* 108:599–617.

Smarzynska, Beata, and Shang-Jin Wei. 2000. Corruption and the composition of foreign direct investment: Firm-level evidence. NBER Working Paper no. 7969. Cambridge, Mass.: National Bureau of Economic Research, June.

Transparency International (TI). 1998. Transparency International Corruption Perceptions Index. Available at [http://www.gwdg.de/~icr.htm].

Tornell, Aaron. 1990. Real vs. financial investment: Can Tobin taxes eliminate the irreversibility distortion? *Journal of Development Economics* 32:419–44.

Wei, Shang-Jin. 1999. Corruption in economic development: Beneficial grease, minor annoyance, or major obstacle? World Bank Policy Research Working Paper no. 2048. Washington, D.C.: World Bank, February.

———. 2000a. How taxing is corruption on international investors? *Review of Economics and Statistics* 82 (1): 1–11.

———. 2000b. Local corruption and global capital flows. *Brookings Papers on Economic Activity,* Issue no. 2:303–46.

———. 2000c. Natural openness and good government. NBER Working Paper no. 7765. Cambridge, Mass.: National Bureau of Economic Research, June.

———. 2000d. Why does China attract so little foreign direct investment? In *The role of foreign direct investment in East Asian economic development,* ed. Takatoshi Ito and Anne O. Krueger, 239–61. Chicago: University of Chicago Press.

Wheeler, David, and Ashoka Mody. 1992. International investment location decisions: The case of U.S. firms. *Journal of International Economics* 33:57–76.

World Bank. 1997. *World development report.* Washington, D.C.: World Bank.

———. *SIMA/GDF* and *WDR* central database. Washington, D.C.: World Bank.

World Economic Forum. 1997. *Global competitiveness report.* Geneva: World Economic Forum.

Comment   Martin Feldstein

This is a very good paper. It is innovative and convincing. It deals with a significant problem and brings new data to bear on this issue. Its starting point

Martin Feldstein is the George F. Baker Professor of Economics at Harvard University and the president of the National Bureau of Economic Research.

is the general agreement that an excessive dependence on foreign loans increases the risk of currency crises because foreign banks can decide not to renew maturing loans when they suspect potential repayment problems. In contrast, foreign direct investment (FDI) is a much less volatile source of external financing. The mix of external financing and, in particular, the extent of dependence on foreign loans is therefore important to a country that is looking for strategies to reduce its vulnerability.

The central point of the paper by Wei and Wu is that domestic corruption can increase the risk of a currency crisis by shifting the availability of foreign funds from direct investment to bank loans. If corruption does reduce the inflow of FDI and if the unexploited investment opportunities that result from reduced FDI are financed instead by foreign loans, it follows that corruption indirectly increases the risk of crisis.

The Wei-Wu paper therefore focuses on whether corruption (as measured by the survey data that the authors describe) reduces FDI. The results of the regression analysis are very clear in showing that corruption does appear to reduce the inflow of FDI. An obvious question is whether the corruption variable is really capturing the effect of corruption per se or is simply a proxy for something else that is responsible for depressing FDI. For example, are countries that are more corrupt than average and that practice more than the usual amount of cronyism also countries that want to keep out foreign investment in order to save the investment opportunities for local investors?

To deal with this potential problem, Wei and Wu construct two clever indexes: One measures the attraction that the country's current policy provides to FDI, and the other measures the extent to which the country's policies discourage FDI. When the authors add these two variables to their regression, the coefficients imply that the measures of things that would attract FDI are positively associated with higher levels of FDI, and the variable measuring things that would repel FDI is negatively associated with FDI. Both of these variables are statistically significant. Most important, adding them to the regression does not change the basic result that the corruption variable discourages FDI.

There may of course be other variables that are omitted and that are correlated with corruption. One candidate for that would be the legal system itself. The work that Andrei Shleifer (and his co-authors LaPorta, Lopez-de-Silanes, and Vishney) and others have done suggests that foreign investors (especially those from the United States and Britain) would be attracted to countries that had Anglo-Saxon–type legal systems that provide greater protection for investors. Those legal safeguards might tilt the balance in favor of more FDI in such countries.

Wei and Wu do not include a measure of the legal system among the regressions but note that they use such a variable as an instrument for the corruption variable when doing instrumental variable estimation. They also report that they performed an explicit test of whether the variable ought to be in the equation in its own right and concluded (rather surprisingly to me) that although the legal system variable is a good instrument, it does not belong in the equation as an explicit variable in its own right. I would be a little more comfortable if the authors performed a sensitivity analysis by including it in the regression and gave us an ordinary least squares regression estimate of the equation with corruption and legal variables both included.

However, demonstrating that corruption reduces FDI is not the same as demonstrating that corruption leads to an increased dependence on loans, and it is the dependence on loans that is the key link to the risk of international crises. Wei and Wu do show that corruption leads to an increase in the ratio of loans to FDI. However, the risk comes from the volume of foreign loans and not from the ratio of loans to FDI. The effect of corruption on the ratio of loans to FDI may simply be driven by its effect on the denominator.

What matters for the risk of crises is not the ratio of foreign loans to FDI but the level of foreign loans relative to gross domestic product (GDP) or export earnings. The ratio of foreign loans to FDI could be high with very little foreign loan exposure relative to GDP or to exports if FDI is very low. Fortunately, the paper does give us direct evidence on the effect of corruption on the ratio of loans to GDP (in table 10.6.) The positive effect of the corruption variable on the volume of foreign loans supports the idea that corruption increases foreign loans.

What remains to establish is that the positive effect of corruption on loans is the result of a shift from the discouraged FDI to the use of loans to finance the same investment. That is, the key question is this: If there are some investment opportunities and if FDI is reduced, is foreign borrowing the alternative route through which foreign capital can be tapped?

This line of reasoning would be more convincing if it could be shown that the other factors that encourage FDI reduce foreign loans whereas those factors that discourage FDI cause an increase in foreign loans. I suggested this at the conference, and Wei and Wu now provide explicit evidence in the postconference version of their paper. Because the coefficients of these additional regressions are not significantly different from zero, this test does not strengthen the conviction in the Wei-Wu mechanism.

It is nevertheless hard to think of an alternative theory that explains the other features of the Wei-Wu regressions. Although there may in principle be other explanations and other variables that ought to be considered, I do not have any specific suggestions. I believe that this paper has provided a very useful framework for thinking about the potential impact of corruption on FDI and foreign loans. The burden of proof is now on anybody who would argue that corruption does not discourage FDI and encourage the inflow of foreign loans.

I have two final thoughts about the implications of this paper. First, it implies that the link between corruption and financial crises provides a reason to reduce corruption. That reason seems to be a valid one, but of course a country should not need that as a reason to reduce corruption. Reducing corruption is something that countries should do for many other reasons.

Second, the key to greater financial stability emphasized in this paper is not corruption per se but foreign loans and other short-term capital. A country that wants to reduce the risk of crisis can do so even if it cannot attract FDI (either because of corruption of because of other qualities of the country) by avoiding such large inflows of short-term loans and other financial liabilities.

Discussion Summary

Roberto Rigobon proposed a different view of the findings of the paper—the corporate finance view on the composition of financing. According to the corporate finance view, he said, there are two additional channels through which corruption may affect the choice of financing. That is, when asset returns or the ability of managers is highly uncertain, investors tend to choose loan financing rather than FDI. If corruption increases the variability of the ability of managers or the assets' returns, he said, then more corrupt countries will have a greater share of loan financing, as the paper finds.

On the empirical part of the paper, *Linda S. Goldberg* made two comments. The first is related to the cross-sectional approach of the paper. The authors regressed the average ratio of the different types of foreign financing between 1994 and 1996 on a country-specific corruption index plus a number of other control variables. Goldberg said that the regressions show the correlation between these variables, but they do not necessarily mean that the causality is from the corruption to the choice of foreign financing. For example, the correlation could be due to the fact that some other country-specific institutions affect the foreign financing and these institutions are highly correlated with the corruption index used in the paper.

Moreover, Goldberg said that in order to answer a more interesting question—that is, how a change of the corruption level in a country would affect its FDI relative to other forms of capital inflow—one needs to regress the changes in the share of FDI on the changes of corruption. This kind of time-series panel regression would net out other country-specific effects that could not be controlled for. *Kristin J. Forbes* raised a similar suggestion on running panel regressions and controlling for country-fixed effects.

Federico Sturzenegger shared a similar concern. He used a story to illustrate that Argentina's government and its regulatory bodies care little about the protection of minority shareholders. As a result, he said, many foreign companies choose to invest in a private way and avoid putting money in the stock market when they invest in Argentina. The lack of protection of minority shareholders may have led to an increase in FDI relative to portfolio investment. He concluded that if corruption is correlated with weak financial institutions, then the corruption variable in the regression could capture this effect.

Simon Johnson said that many studies have shown that it is very difficult to distinguish different measures of institutions. The corruption effects found in the paper could be interpreted as the effects of institutions in general, which interpretation would also make the paper more appealing. Moreover, he said, the instruments for corruption used in the paper are measures of institutions and could be correlated with financing for many different reasons. He suggested that the authors try alternative measures of corruption, such as measures of how institutions have developed historically.

Rigobon proposed the addition of "financial development" as a control variable to account for the fact that at different stages of banking sector development there are different instruments in the banking sector. *Charles W. Calomiris* suggested that the authors look deeper into the relationship between the dependency on bank lending and the special protection that bank lending enjoys. Johnson questioned the inclusion of GDP per capita as an explanatory variable because GDP per capita itself is affected by the institutional variables, and this could lead to biased estimates of the effects of corruption. On the interpretation of the results, Forbes asked about the magnitude of the effects of corruption on capital flows.

Sebastian Edwards suggested that the authors present more details on the corruption index to show the distribution and dynamics of this variable because its definition is not very clear. For example, he said, the transparency index used in the paper is a ranking of countries from the least to the most corrupt ones. Over time, as more countries were added to the sample, their rankings changed for reasons not related to corruption.

A few people raised concerns on the hypothesis of the paper that in a more corrupt country foreign capital inflows tend to take the form of loan financing. Intuitively, the paper argues that foreign banking lending requires less contact with the local bureaucrats and thus is less subject to the local corruption. *Carlos A. Végh* suggested that the authors lay out a more solid analytical framework, because the current model basically assumes the hypothesis rather than providing a rationale for it. Moreover, Végh said that to make a portfolio investment, foreign investors also need to interact with the locals, so it is not clear which financing—FDI or portfolio investment—is subject to more corruption. The model could also incorporate the fact that bank portfolio investment is more likely to be bailed out than FDI by either the government or international institutions, such as the IMF. *Michael P. Dooley* raised a similar concern and said that FDI could be used as a way to bypass the local credit markets and to maintain a direct control of the investment. Thus, it could potentially be a choice of foreign financing in a very corrupt system.

Nouriel Roubini commented that "corruption" and "crony capitalism" were used interchangeably in the paper, but these two terms do not always mean the same thing and should be distinguished. The findings of the paper—highly corrupt countries have higher share of loan financing—could be due to the dominance of the banking sector in emerging markets, which leads to a high ratio of loan financing. Roubini also suggested that the authors study the outliers in the sample. China, he said, could be an outlier with a high level of corruption and a high ratio of FDI. This may happen because foreign direct investors also get advantages, such as monopoly power, tax deduction, and the like, by bribing the local government.

On the meaning of the corruption variable, *Shang-Jin Wei* agreed with the general discussion. He said that he used "corruption" as shorthand to refer to weak public institutions and that it has many dimensions to it. He also said that there are attempts to give separate scores to corruption and other dimensions of institutions, but these scores are always highly correlated with each other.

On the suggestions to conduct panel regressions, Wei said that they are desirable, but not feasible at this time. The reason is that there is not much variation in the corruption index over time, and the time series data on corruption are not reliable. He puts more trust in the cross-country variation of this index. For example, he said, the corruption index of Indonesia worsened substantially after the fall of Suharto.

On the magnitude of the effect of corruption, Wei cited one of his earlier papers. He found that an increase of the corruption from the level of Singapore (very low) to that of Mexico (very high) has the same magnitude effect on FDI as an increase of the marginal corporate tax rate by about 50 percentage points.

Regarding Roubini's remark on outliers, Wei showed the partial correlation of the corruption index and the share of FDI where there is no obvious outlier. Moreover, Wei cited one of his papers to show that China is not an exception to the rule, and that Chinese FDI could have been much higher had China managed to reduce its corruption.

Domestic Bank Regulation and Financial Crises
Theory and Empirical Evidence from East Asia

Robert Dekle and Kenneth Kletzer

11.1 Introduction

The financial crises in East Asia followed several years of large foreign financial capital inflows intermediated by the domestic banking system. The crisis countries suffered tandem banking and currency crises that produced sharp reductions in economic growth and subsequent ongoing domestic financial distress. In some cases, it was clear beforehand that the domestic financial system was becoming increasingly fragile and crisis-prone—for example, in Thailand. The currency crisis made matters worse due to the uncovered foreign currency exposure of the banking system. A number of authors have also argued that implicit government guarantees of foreign currency liabilities of the domestic banks contributed to the financial crisis in Asia. More generally, Calvo (1998a) observes that emerging-market financial crises evolve through complicated interactions between domestic financial sectors, international lenders, and national monetary and fiscal authorities. Our paper considers the dynamic consequences of interactions between the microeconomics of private financial intermediation and public-sector financial and macroeconomic policies in a currency crisis model. We focus on the relationship between foreign capital inflows, eco-

Robert Dekle is associate professor of economics at the University of Southern California. Kenneth Kletzer is professor of economics at the University of California, Santa Cruz.

The authors are grateful to Peter Clark, Vikram Haksar, Kalpana Kochhar, Kanitta Meesook, Reza Moghadam, Paolo Pesenti, Charles W. Calomiris, Sebastian Edwards, Jeffrey A. Frankel, and other conference participants for many useful and insightful comments and suggestions. Kletzer is grateful to the research department of the International Monetary Fund (IMF) for supporting his research on this paper. The views expressed herein are solely those of the authors and do not represent those of the IMF, IMF policy, or other organizations with which the authors are affiliated.

nomic growth, and subsequent banking crises under a fixed exchange rate. Most importantly, we relate the assumptions and implications of our model to the East Asian currency crisis. We use the theoretical framework as a basis for comparing the experience of five East Asian economies in the 1990s. This sample includes two economies that experienced currency crises, Korea and Thailand; one that almost experienced a crisis, Malaysia; and two economies that did not experience crises, Taiwan and Singapore.

In an insightful paper, Carlos Diaz-Alejandro (1985) uses the Chilean financial crisis of 1981–83 to illustrate the dangers of financial reforms under fixed exchange rates, free international capital flows, and implicit guarantees of bank deposits but weak domestic financial supervisory systems. The financial crisis in Chile followed several years of steady liberalization and privatization of domestic banking under explicit and repeated claims by the authorities that deposits would not be insured by the government. When tested in the late 1970s, the government intervened and rescued all depositors. When capital inflow restrictions were relaxed in 1981, capital inflows surged under the anticipation of public bailouts as the domestic financial sector continued to deteriorate until their sudden reversal in the currency crisis.

Diaz-Alejandro (1985) is impressively prescient of the East Asian crisis. In this paper, we propose a theoretical model that formalizes his interpretation by concentrating on the interactions between domestic financial institutions, the regulation and subsidization of domestic financial intermediation by the government, and foreign capital inflows leading up to a financial crisis. The model generates a path for domestic bank lending, capital accumulation, and the growth of the foreign currency debt of domestic banks that ultimately leads to a financial crisis with the collapse of the fixed exchange rate regime. The underlying disturbances in the model are simply idiosyncratic productivity shocks across firms that occur when there are a large number of firms; there are no exogenous aggregate shocks. However, a problem of agency in domestic financial intermediation leads banks to accumulate increasingly risky assets in equilibrium until the financial system is vulnerable to collapse with a reversal of foreign capital flows. A key element of our model is that the government provides implicit guarantees of the foreign currency liabilities incurred by domestic banks following Diaz-Alejandro (1985) and recent "third-generation" models of currency crises.

The theoretical model introduces an agency model of banking in the spirit of Bernanke and Gertler (1989, 1990) and Bernanke, Gertler, and Gilchrist (1999), in which domestic banks have an informational advantage in lending to domestic firms, into a simple endogenous growth model. Adverse selection in the choice of risky projects by firms leads to the cofinancing of investments by firm owners and banks. Individual firms become insolvent with positive probability in finite time, in which event banks have incentives to renegotiate the firm's debt in this model. With time, the proportion of firms that have been unable to repay their gross debt and re-negotiated their loans in the past increases stochastically.

Foreign capital inflows allow lending and aggregate output to grow without being constrained by domestic savings. The implicit insurance provided to foreign creditors in the event that the government abandons the fixed exchange rate sustains capital inflows to the banking system until the crisis occurs. Over time, the domestic financial sector becomes increasingly fragile in this model. Prior to the crisis, capital inflows rise in proportion to domestic production under constant returns to accumulable factors of production. Investment may or may not rise as a ratio of output. The model also predicts that the total equity value of the banking sector will be decreasing in absolute value and in proportion to the equity value of the borrowing firms. The banking system becomes progressively more indebted through foreign borrowing until it is ultimately insolvent. Capital inflows cease in a sudden stop, investment reverses, and output drops sharply. The postcrisis rate of growth will depend upon the new incentives for foreign capital inflows after the crisis.

Other papers adopt the financial accelerator model of Bernanke and Gertler or its underlying agency model of financial intermediation to analyze the link between foreign capital inflows and currency crises. Velasco (1987) introduces banking into a version of the Krugman (1979) model of speculative attacks on a fixed exchange rate regime, and Aghion, Bacchetta, and Banerjee (1999a, 2000) study the amplification of aggregate shocks in credit-constrained economies. Our analysis is quite different in that we detail the microeconomics of intermediation and focus on the path dependence of financial fragility in the open economy leading up to a crisis with only firm-specific idiosyncratic shocks. The role of the implicit government guarantees follows the observations made by Diaz-Alejandro (1985) and Calvo (1998a) that a sovereign government has an incentive to subsidize foreign capital inflows to overcome the problem of its own moral hazard in setting trade, fiscal, and monetary policies. Mishkin (1996) and Obstfeld (1998) among others have observed that government guarantees of foreign currency deposits in the event of devaluation appear to be an implicit companion to a pegged exchange rate regime. The currency crisis in our model is generated by contingent public-sector insurance in the same way as in the "third-generation" models proposed by Calvo (1998a, b) and Dooley (2000). The emphasis on the fragility of the banking sector bears much in common with the description and analysis of the East Asian crisis in Corsetti, Pesenti, and Roubini (1998a). Other models that elaborate on the role of public-sector guarantees of foreign currency debt and domestic banking include Burnside, Eichenbaum, and Rebelo (1999) and Chinn and Kletzer (2000).

A number of theoretical and empirical papers have been written on the possible causes of the East Asian crisis and its consequences. These include fundamentals-based models, following Krugman (1979) and Flood and Garber (1984), such as this one, and others based on liquidity crises, as exemplified by Chang and Velasco (1999).[1] An alternative approach for modeling domestic intermediation would be to adopt a model in which collateral plays a central role in enforcing repayment. Caballero and Krishnamurthy (1998) and Edison, Luangarum, and Miller (2000) both adopt the Kiyotaki and Moore (1997) model of credit cycles to study financial crises in emerging markets. The Kiyotaki and Moore model precludes the renegotiation of bank loans, although it can portray the collapse of the value of fixed assets and bank insolvencies during a systemic crisis. Christiano, Gust, and Roldos (2000) develop a different version of the Kiyotaki and Moore model in a financial crisis model that endogenizes asset values more richly. Although collateral does not enter contract enforcement in our model of financial intermediation, the model could be extended to endogenize the value of physical assets.

Section 11.2 presents the theoretical model and its empirical implications. Sections 11.3 and 11.4 compare the assumptions of the model and its predictions to the data for the five Asian economies in our sample with broad success. We first discuss how Korea, Thailand, Malaysia, Taiwan, and Singapore differ with respect to the institutional characteristics of banking and corporate borrowing underlying our assumptions. We argue that the necessary assumptions for the endogenous banking and currency crisis to arise in the theoretical model fit Korea and Thailand, the crisis cases, very well and Malaysia reasonably well, but do not fit the cases of Taiwan and Singapore. Section 11.5 shows how the paths for aggregate measures of economic and banking system performance differ across the economies in a manner predicted by the model.

11.2   A Theoretical Model of Financial Crises

We model international capital flows and domestic financial intermediation in an infinitely lived small open economy with capital accumulation in discrete time. Firms are established by entrepreneurs each of whom has access to a set of projects that can be undertaken. Investment by firms is financed by domestic household saving or by foreign financial capital inflows. These financial flows are intermediated by banks. In our model, banks operate a monitoring technology, and some of the potential entrepreneurs have access to this technology.

The model's economic environment is described first and followed by an

1. In addition to the papers already cited, related papers include Aghion, Bacchetta, and Banerjee (1999b), Caballero and Krishnamurthy (1998), Corsetti, Pesenti, and Roubini (1998a-c), Edison, Luangarum, and Miller (2000), Eichengreen and Rose (1998), Furman and Stiglitz (1998), Goldfajn and Valdés (1997), Kumhof (1998), Krugman (1999), McKinnon and Pill (1999), Radelet and Sachs (1998), and Sachs, Tornell, and Velasco (1996).

analysis of the dynamics of bank lending. The role of foreign capital inflows and the dynamics of a financial crisis are then discussed.

11.2.1 Economic Environment

There is a single good that can be consumed, invested, or traded internationally. It can be produced using entrepreneurial labor and capital. The model allows investment to be reversible, although we will consider the consequences of a costly dismantling of a firm's capital stock. For simplicity, there is no depreciation. Production takes one period, and the gross output produced in any period is stochastic.

All residents have identical preferences over infinite-horizon consumption plans and are endowed with a single unit of labor each period. Each person is a potential entrepreneur, who can select and invest in a new project every period. The investment opportunities available to different people do not need to be identical, so that entrepreneurs may be heterogeneous with respect to skills or knowledge. However, the set of techniques of production available to each entrepreneur does not change over time, and a subset of entrepreneurs know how to operate banks.

Households are risk averse and seek to smooth consumption over time. They receive entrepreneurial income and interest earnings from financial savings. The utility function for a household is given by

$$(1) \qquad U_t = E_t \sum_{s=t}^{\infty} \beta^{s-t} u(c_s),$$

where $u(c)$ is strictly concave and $0 < \beta < 1$. This is maximized with respect to a consumption plan subject to the intertemporal budget identity.

$$(2) \qquad a_{s+1} - a_s = (r_s^d w_s + r^* f_s) + \pi_s - c_s - \varphi(w_s),$$

and the solvency condition,

$$(3) \qquad \lim_{s \to \infty} a_s \prod_{v=t}^{s-1} \left(\frac{1}{1 + r_v^*} \right) \geq 0,$$

given initial financial wealth, $a_t = w_t + f_t$. Here, w equals deposits held in domestic banks, which earn a deposit rate of interest r^d, and f equals holdings of foreign deposits, which earn interest r^*. Domestic transactions are denominated in units of domestic currency, and the nominal exchange rate is fixed. Money is held (in the form of interest-bearing deposits) to economize on transactions costs, $\varphi(w_t)$, where $\varphi'(w_t) < 0$. If domestic residents hold foreign assets in equilibrium, then the opportunity return to domestic bank deposits, $r^d - \varphi'(w_t)$, will be equal to the foreign currency rate of interest, r^*, less any currency risk premium. If foreign residents hold domestic deposits (as we will assume they do in equilibrium), then r^d will equal r^* corrected for currency risk and all domestic financial saving will be held in

domestic banks. Entrepreneurial income from production is represented by
π. The model has been written under the assumption that each entrepreneur owns the equity in his or her firm. Tradable equity complicates the
presentation without much gain, but we will be interested in the value of
firm equity later. The inclusion of a demand for money is later used to justify invoking a conventional monetary model of the nominal exchange rate.[2]
Demand deposits pay a positive rate of return so that money is held only as
deposits in equilibrium for the model economy.

Each firm is established by a particular entrepreneur. Production uses
capital and one unit of entrepreneurial labor to produce output each period. Production displays constant returns to capital and increasing returns
to entrepreneurial effort. The quantity of output produced by any given input bundle is stochastic. Each entrepreneur has access to a particular collection of possible projects to undertake. Projects differ with respect to the
distribution of output produced across states of nature for any given capital input. For example, the distribution of output for one project might be
a mean-preserving spread of another. The set of projects available to each
nonbank entrepreneur can either be the same or different. In either case, entrepreneurs can choose to undertake different projects.

The production function for a firm j is given by

$$(4) \qquad\qquad y_t^j = \alpha_t^j k_t^j,$$

where k_t^j is the capital stock of firm j predetermined by investment undertaken in period $t - 1$. Output gross of the capital stock is y_t^j, so that α_t^j is the
stochastic (marginal and average) gross productivity of capital. For each
possible project, α_t^j is nonnegative and distributed identically and independently across time. A project is uniquely determined by its distribution over
the productivity of capital.

Firms can finance capital accumulation by borrowing from banks or by
investing their own saving. All entrepreneurs will seek to diversify their income risk by allocating their wealth between bank deposits and equity in
their own firms. Their choices are limited to these two by imperfect information. Bankers have an absolute advantage at monitoring firm choices of
projects and realized output each period. Households reduce their exposure to risk by lending to banks, which in turn lend to many firms, thereby
diversifying individual firm project risk for their depositors. Firms can use
current profits to finance investment (retained earnings) or pay dividends to
the owner-household. To make the connection to corporate borrowing
from this model of entrepreneurship, we add the restriction that the house-

---

2. Our innovation concerns the dynamics of a banking crisis. We do not write out the model
of the shadow exchange rate because we simply use the model of Krugman (1979) and Flood
and Garber (1984).

hold cannot be forced to draw against its other assets (bank deposits) to supply additional capital to the firm it owns. That is, we separate the entrepreneurial role of the owner from the saving and consumption role of the household in Robinson Crusoe fashion.

The well-known model of banking as delegated monitoring (Diamond 1984; Freixas and Rochet 1997) works to rule out direct equity investment by households in the projects of other entrepreneurs and implies that banks use conventional debt contracts. The model assumes that output realizations by a firm in any period are costlessly observed only by the entrepreneur of that firm and that bankers have access to a technology that allows them to observe project outcomes at a lower cost than households. To make things simple, assume that households are unable to observe the actual output of any firm other than their own at any cost; below we discuss weakening this assumption and allowing equity trade. We also assume that the costs of monitoring a firm are indivisible, so that economies of scale are realized when firms borrow from a single bank in equilibrium.[3]

Whereas costly observability can be used to rationalize bank lending via standard debt contracts, the primary informational asymmetry here concerns the choice of project by the firm. This choice involves adverse selection as in a variety of credit market models that follow Stiglitz and Weiss (1981). The bank lends an amount ℓ_t to a typical firm in period $t-1$ to finance a capital stock equal to k_t, which will produce output in period t. The firm selects its project for period t in period $t-1$ to maximize its value. The firm's capital stock evolves according to

$$(5) \qquad k_{t+1} = \alpha k_t - R_t \ell_t + \ell_{t+1} - \pi_t,$$

where R_t is the gross interest charged to the period t loan. Consider the simple case a single round of lending with no ongoing capital accumulation and production. In this case the return to the firm under limited liability is given by

$$(6) \qquad \text{firm's return} = \max\{\alpha_t k_t - R_t \ell_t, 0\},$$

whereas the return to the bank is given by

$$(7) \qquad \text{bank's return} = \min\{R_t \ell_t, \alpha_t k_t - \gamma\} - (1 + r_t^d)\ell_t,$$

where γ represents observation costs. The borrower will choose a riskier project from among those with a common mean than is in the best interests of the lender. Although informational imperfections restrict an entrepreneur's capacity to diversify income risk, limited liability and the conven-

---

3. In the literature on financial intermediation as delegated monitoring, increasing returns to scale in banking are a common assumption. See Freixas and Rochet (1997) and Holmstrom and Tirole (1997). This assumption is essential to our conclusions about loan renegotiation because it precludes complex arguments involving game models.

tional debt contract provide a degree of risk sharing between households that is constrained by the disincentives for borrower risk avoidance.

Cofinancing given by the difference $x_t = k_t - \ell_t$ reduces the incentives for the firm to choose a riskier project and raises the expected return to the lender. This is immediately true for the repeated lending case in our capital accumulation model. The bank chooses a combination of loan size, ℓ_t, rate of interest, $r_t = R_t - 1$, and cofinancing requirement,

$$z_t = \frac{k_t - \ell_t}{k_t},$$

to maximize its expected return. This is demonstrated by Bernanke and Gertler (1989, 1990) in a moral hazard model. They explain the importance of cofinancing as a solution to the agency problem in banking and for generating financial fragility. Another way to motivate bank lending in our model is to assume that banks have a cost advantage setting z_t by monitoring the investment level of the firm.

Limited liability plays a key role in this economy. Firms can go bankrupt, which means here that current assets, $\alpha_t k_t$, accrue to the bank, and the firm ceases to exist. A firm would only choose bankruptcy if its value as an ongoing enterprise was nonpositive. When the firm cannot service its debts in full, the bank faces a choice of declaring the firm bankrupt or renegotiating the terms of its loan. Equivalently, a bank can go bankrupt if it cannot meet its deposit liabilities as demanded by depositors. With reversible investment, all the assets of the client firms of a bank can be used to meet depositors' claims, so that a bank will only be unable to repay its deposit liabilities on demand if the sum of the capital stocks of each of its client firms fails to exceed the gross interest it has promised depositors. When investment is nonreversible, at least in the short run, then the bank can be illiquid without being insolvent. The production function could be rewritten to incorporate time to build to allow for the possibility of self-fulfilling bank runs, as demonstrated by Diamond and Dybvig (1983) and used in the Chang and Velasco (1999) model of financial crises. This extension is not explored in this paper. The renegotiation of bank loans, option value of the firm, and the role of deposit insurance are discussed in the next subsection.

The economy will be open to international financial capital inflows and outflows. Net capital inflows are equal to the current account deficit plus any increase in central bank reserves through the balance-of-payments identity. Private foreign borrowing is intermediated by domestic banks. The current account surplus is given by

$$(8) \qquad b_{t+1} - b_t = r_t^* b_t + [y_t - \varphi(w_t)] - c_t - k_{t+1},$$

where b_t is the current stock of foreign debt for the country denominated in units of foreign currency, and other variables are expressed as economy-wide aggregates. Because quantities are expressed in nominal terms, we assume that nominal prices are perfectly flexible and that purchasing power parity and uncovered interest parity hold. All debt in the model is short-term debt.

Fiscal policy plays a key role for generating a currency crisis under the fixed exchange rate regime. There are no public expenditures, but the government can provide deposit insurance for domestic residents and debt repayment guarantees to foreign lenders. These contingent liabilities could be financed through taxes (including premia charged to banks or depositors) or through monetization. For simplicity, deposit guarantees will be financed by current or future monetization in the model.

11.2.2   Capital Accumulation and Bank Lending

In this section, we consider the dynamics of domestic bank lending and economic growth in the closed economy. The capital account will be opened later. The economy starts in a state in which all firms have the same capital stock, and, for expositional simplicity, we allow all projects to be chosen from a common set.

First, consider the case of a firm that realizes a high output in period t. The net income for the firm is given by

$$(9) \qquad\qquad (\alpha - 1)k_t - r_t \ell_t > 0,$$

so that the entrepreneur can consume a dividend or increase his or her equity in the firm ($r \equiv R - 1$). This firm's bank made its loan offer in period $t - 1$, ℓ_t, optimally given the collection of projects available and the entrepreneur's contribution to the firm's investment. In general, the equilibrium loan will lead to a positive value of z less than 1.[4] The banker is then willing to lend an additional amount,

$$(10) \qquad\qquad \ell_{t+1} - \ell_t = \frac{1}{z}[(\alpha - 1)k_t - r_t\ell_t],$$

leading to an increase in the firm's capital stock of

$$(11) \qquad\qquad k_{t+1} - k_t = \frac{1 + z}{z}[(\alpha - 1)k_t - r_t\ell_t],$$

if the interest rate r_t^d remains unchanged. This equation of motion incorporates the financial accelerator that plays a central role in Bernanke and Gertler (1989, 1990). Furthermore, this firm is able to repay its entire debt at time t. Therefore, it could pay off its debt to its current bank and take a

---

4. For an interior solution with respect to cofinancing and loan supply, the bank's return (eq. [7]) needs to be increasing in z given the firm's optimal choice of project from maximization of equation (6). The very simple version of Stiglitz and Weiss (1981) in Mankiw (1986) can be used to demonstrate an interior solution.

new loan (of size ℓ_{t+1} above) from another bank. That is, it can roll over its short-term debt on the market. Competition among banks ensures that the interest rate charged on the loan, ℓ_{t+1}, is independent of the rest of the bank's particular portfolio.[5]

Instead, suppose that the firm realizes a low level of output. In this case, we have

$$(12) \qquad\qquad (\alpha - 1)k_t - r_t\ell_t < 0$$

but either

$$(13) \qquad\qquad \alpha k_t - R_t\ell_t \geq 0 \qquad \text{or} \qquad \alpha k_t - R_t\ell_t < 0.$$

In the first instance, the firm contracts according to equation (11). In the second, the firm is unable to meet its debt obligations even if it liquidates its entire stock of capital. In this case, the firm can be declared bankrupt by its creditor. However, the bank can possibly do better than to liquidate the firm and use the proceeds to repay its depositors or pay its owner dividends. This is because the bank now has market power vis-à-vis the firm in a debt rollover or renegotiation under a simple seniority rule. Another bank could possibly offer a new loan to the firm, allowing it to pay off its debt and invest for the next period. Under such a loan, investment is given by

$$(14) \qquad\qquad k_{t+1} - \ell_{t+1} = \alpha k_t - R_t\ell_t < 0.$$

That is, the firm's investment is less than the loan principal. The new bank must charge an interest premium to recover the opportunity cost of the portion of the loan used by the firm to pay off its period t debt. This kind of loan may not even be offered, because the entrepreneur now owns none of the capital stock of the firm (z is zero), which situation, along with the higher interest rate, encourages greater risk taking by the entrepreneur.

The current bank, however, may gain by offering a new loan when other lenders will not. This is the case if

$$(15) \qquad\qquad \max_{R, \ell} E_t [\min(R\ell, \alpha\ell - \gamma) - (1 + r_{t+1}^d)\ell] > 0,$$

given the optimal choice of project by the borrower conditional on R and ℓ. The implied interest rate premium is constrained by the premium that a new lender would charge. When such a premium does not exist, as a consequence of the agency problem, the firm's current banker faces no potential competition in the rollover market. The excess returns on such a new loan are applied against the opportunity cost of the unpaid period t debt, $R_t\ell_t$. Therefore, the firm's bank can choose to roll over the unpaid debt and offer new capital in exchange for a deeper claim, $R_{t+1}(\ell_t + k_{t+1})$, against the earn-

---

5. This is stated in this way because bankers are risk averse in this model. With risk-neutral banks, the expected profit from this loan would be zero in equilibrium.

ings of the firm, αk_{t+1}, in favorable states of nature. The supernormal profits on these rollovers encourage the renegotiation of short-term bank debt
and discourage the formal bankruptcy of insolvent firms when equations
(14) and (15) hold. For equation (15) to hold, we need to impose the condition that the optimal project choice of the entrepreneur when $z = 0$ yields
at least positive expected total surplus; that is, $E_t\alpha > 1 + r_t^d$. The level of new
capital provided to the firm is chosen by the banker along with the interest
rate to maximize utility from the profits realized on the banker's entire portfolio. These incentives will rise if liquidating a debtor is costly for banks.

We note that the equilibrium loan renegotiation can simply be written
as a rollover of the unpaid gross interest at the new rate of interest. Write-
downs are unnecessary, because any unpaid gross interest in the future can
continue to be rolled over in renegotiations. Through repeated loan rollovers, the bank may acquire a permanent monopoly franchise on lending
to the firm, but it will only enforce repayment terms in equilibrium that maximize the banker's expected utility from her portfolio.[6]

The projects undertaken by insolvent firms in a rollover will be riskier
than those the same firm chose when its net worth was positive. Suppose
that the set of projects includes a continuum of mean-preserving spreads of
the project chosen by the firm at the initial equilibrium cofinancing requirement, z. When the firm becomes insolvent (eq. [14] holds) and the loan
is renegotiated, the entrepreneur will choose a mean-preserving spread of
the original project because z is zero. The interest premium provides an additional reason for the debtor to make a riskier choice of project. The probability that the bank's borrowing cost of the new capital, $(1 + r_{t+1}^d)k_{t+1}$, exceeds the gross project returns, αk_{t+1}, is greater for the renegotiated loans of
insolvent firms than for loans to solvent firms.

Once a bank has rolled over the debt of one of its clients, it faces a higher
probability of loan rollovers for this firm in the future. The probability that
the firm will need to renegotiate its debts again,

$$\Pr(\alpha k_t \le R_t\ell_t),$$

rises with $\ell_t - k_t$. Further, for the new capital provided to the firm, the probability that its cost to the bank will not be covered,

$$\Pr[\alpha k_t \le (1 + r_t^d)k_t],$$

rises as the project choice becomes riskier. These rollovers are negotiated in
a forward-looking fashion, but their probability and terms are path dependent. Renegotiating bank debt through rollovers and providing new

---

6. In the adverse selection model, increasing the rate of interest induces riskier project choice
by the entrepreneur and eventually lowers the lender's expected return (Stiglitz and Weiss
1981). This implies that the bank may not claim all of the entrepreneur's potential future profits in every event in the equilibrium following renegotiation, no matter how large the firm's debt
on the bank's books grows. This depends on the set of projects available to the firm.

capital is superior for the bank to cutting its losses. While the bank is rolling over loans, it must also be rolling over deposit liabilities. A firm's debt will continue to be rolled over in equilibrium as low output states of nature are realized until the claim of the bank exhausts all the possible payments that it can extract from the firm in every future event. This occurs with positive probability and means that the opportunity cost (deposit liability incurred) of the ultimate loan exceeds its expected return.

Banks face competition from each other for loans to firms that have been able to repay their debts in full in the previous period (for example, growing firms). The interest premium charged on loans to these customers covers the expected present value loss if revenues fall short of the opportunity cost of the funds lent. This present value is calculated taking into account the equilibrium renegotiation of loans that fall into default. However, a bank cannot successfully charge a premium on loans to cover the losses on other, renegotiated, loans in its portfolio. As loans are renegotiated (an event that occurs with positive probability), the portfolio of the bank changes. In this model, banks will not hold perfectly diversified loan portfolios even if they can because their aversion to risk and their liability are both limited.

Consider an individual bank with a constant level of deposits. Eventually, in this model, one of its client firms will be unable to repay and will renegotiate its loans with the bank because productivity shocks are independently and identically distributed (i.i.d.) for any given project. The bank will begin shifting its loan portfolio toward this firm, and the probability of a subsequent rollover rises with each renegotiation as the positive probability that $\alpha k_t \leq R_t \ell_t$ rises as $\ell_t - k_t$ rises with each realization of productivity less than $R_t \ell_t / k_t$. The probability of a reallocation away from other firms toward those clients that have suffered low output realizations is path dependent and increases with each poor outcome, when the loan terms offered by other banks are taken as given. The bank's portfolio becomes riskier over time. The probability that the bank will be unable to meet a withdrawal of its deposits as contracted,

$$(16) \qquad \Pr\left[\sum_j \min(\alpha^j k_t^j - \gamma, R_t^j \ell_t^j) < (1 + r_t^d) \sum_j \ell_t^j \right] > 0,$$

rises stochastically. That is, its expectation must be nondecreasing. The sum in equation (16) is taken with respect to the client firms of the individual bank.

With capital accumulation, banks can grow because household savings is positive. In this endogenous growth model, we let the average net productivity of capital exceed the discount rate of households, or, alternatively, the world real rate of interest for the open economy. Starting out with positive initial firm assets (uniform across all firms) and a large number of firms, the growth rate of the capital stock rises with $E\alpha - (1 + r^d)$. For example, if we ignore the residual risk faced by households and let utility be logarithmic, we conclude that the capital stock grows in expectation as

$$E\alpha - (1 + \rho),$$

where ρ is the pure subjective discount rate of households and $E\alpha$ is average gross return to capital across the economy. Eventually, however, some firms do become insolvent, as implied by equation (11). As they do so, banks renegotiate these loans and lend more capital to these firms. In a closed economy equilibrium, saving constrains the growth of the aggregate capital stock, so that loan rollovers necessarily reduce the growth rates of other firms. This implies that the cofinancing share for solvent firms rises as other firms are unable to repay their current debts. This provides a partially offsetting effect in the closed economy—solvent firms will expand more slowly but make less risky project selections.

In this economy, the probability that a bank becomes insolvent rises over time as renegotiation of individual client loans takes place. Path dependence of the riskiness of bank portfolios and the probability of eventual bank insolvencies arise from the renegotiation of loans in the presence of the agency problem. This shift in the riskiness of the aggregate portfolio of the banking system would not occur if banks simply closed firms that were insolvent. The riskiness of each bank's portfolio in that case would remain the same over time. Forcing banks to write-down debts by marking loans to market under capitalization requirements may be a way of reducing this type of increasing vulnerability to idiosyncratic shocks.

In the standard banking model adopted here, depositors face a moral hazard problem when lending to banks. Each saver cannot monitor the bank's portfolio choices. The solution for this problem is the conventional deposit contract, which allows a depositor to reclaim the gross deposit with interest at any time and prevents the bank from renegotiating with individual depositors. It is possible to model bank runs in this economy as the probability that some banks cannot service their deposit claims rises over time, but depositors do not know which banks these will be. Such a run is not self-fulfilling, as demonstrated by Diamond and Dybvig (1983), and we do not add the assumptions needed to generate such possibilities. The introduction of deposit insurance could be justified in this manner or by its effect of lowering the deposit rate of interest in this economy. Without perfect information about the loan portfolio of each bank at all times, deposit insurance can exacerbate the tendency of banks to choose riskier portfolios and raise the transition probabilities of bank insolvencies. Deposit insurance should be associated with greater fragility of the financial sector in the absence of enforced regulations that restrict loan renegotiation.

The problem of loan renegotiation may realistically extend to the case of a firm that cannot meet its net interest obligation. This is the event in which

(17) $(\alpha - 1)k_t - r_t\ell_t < 0$ but $\alpha k_t - R_t\ell_t > 0.$

If capital is not costlessly reversible, then the firm is illiquid but not insolvent. In this case, loan rollovers can also be optimal. Under this type of rollover, the firm's capital stock in period $t + 1$ is higher than otherwise, and its choice of project is riskier. The probability of bank collapses rises with costly disinvestment.

Another possible extension of the model is to introduce differential costs of monitoring firm behavior between savers and banks. In the model by Holmstrom and Tirole (1997), firms begin to borrow directly as their capital increases. Such access to direct borrowing could be introduced into this framework (and associated with the equity of entrepreneurs in their firms) to provide another reason for competitive pressure to keep down interest rates for successful borrowers as bank portfolios become heavier in rolled-over firm debt.

11.2.3   Foreign Capital Inflows to Domestic Banks

We now consider this banking sector in the open economy. Again, domestic banks have a cost advantage over foreign lenders in observing the output realizations of domestic entrepreneurs. This advantage can be assumed to be large enough to preclude any direct foreign portfolio lending to domestic entrepreneurs. Alternatively, following Holmstrom and Tirole (1997), foreign creditors might have a cost disadvantage in monitoring firm behavior that leads to direct lending only after a threshold in firm equity is passed. In that case, the increase in monitoring costs is offset by the incentive effect of a larger share of the firm's capital that is owned by the entrepreneur.

When deposit insurance guarantees discriminate between foreign and domestic depositors, foreigners accumulate risky deposit claims against domestic banks. In the event that a bank is unable to meet its entire deposit liabilities, the total current assets of the bank,

$$\sum_j \min\{\alpha^j k_t^j - \gamma, R_t^j \ell_t^j\},$$

are divided between foreign depositors and the deposit insurer. The inflow of foreign capital to the banking sector will be sensitive to the anticipated ex post seniority rights of foreign creditors vis-à-vis the insurer (typically, the government).

The government can encourage capital inflows in the presence of moral hazard and adverse selection in domestic banking and investment by guaranteeing the real value of the gross exposure of foreign lenders. In the short run, the government can do this by fixing the exchange rate, which removes the incentives for banks to hedge foreign currency risk (as demonstrated by Burnside, Eichenbaum, and Rebelo 1999). If banks borrow in foreign currency denominated loans under a floating rate, they face the risk of insolvency (balance sheet risk) in the event of a depreciation that raises the deposit insurance obligation of the government ceteris paribus. We are interested in the consequences of a fixed exchange rate regime with an explicit or implicit government guarantee of the foreign liabilities of the banking sector in the event of a switch to a float, and not the welfare economics of this policy. Therefore, we make the assumption that the government implicitly guarantees foreign liabilities denominated in foreign currency in the event that it abandons the exchange rate peg. In this event, there can be a broad financial crisis, because banks do not hedge foreign currency risk (in anticipation of this type of bailout) and devaluation reduces foreign currency values on the asset side of the balance sheets for all banks. We impose an upper bound to the amount that the government will guarantee, given by $\bar{d}$. Up to this limit, foreign loans to the domestic banking sector are riskless. That is, there is no currency risk until $\bar{d}$ is reached. For simplicity, we assume that $\bar{d}$ is known with certainty. A limit on the indemnity liability of the government comes from the requirement that the government satisfy its intertemporal budget constraint. Foreign lenders are not protected by the deposit insurance scheme offered to domestic savers.

Foreign capital inflows can raise the aggregate growth rate of the model economy. Banks will borrow at the constant world rate of interest to lend either to firms that have not yet renegotiated their debts or to firms that have. As rollovers accumulate, foreign inflows allow banks to expand their lending to firms that are liquid according to the solution to the agency problem,

$$(18) \qquad k_{t+1} - k_t = \frac{1+z}{z}[(\alpha - 1)k_t - r_t \ell_t],$$

where $(\alpha - 1)k_t - r_t \ell_t > 0$. Similarly, they are able to continue lending to firms that are either illiquid (in the case of irreversible investment) or insolvent (in the case of either irreversible or reversible investment) with rollovers. In the open economy, foreign capital inflows allow banks to continue lending to solvent firms at the ex ante optimal choice of cofinancing, z, while providing capital to insolvent firms under renegotiated loans. In contrast with the closed-economy case, the growth of solvent firms is not reduced by renegotiation, so that the financial accelerator is larger for the open economy. However, z also does not rise for these firms as banks lend more capital to renegotiating firms. The offsetting reduction in the riskiness of project choices for solvent firms experienced in the closed economy disappears, and the riskiness of bank portfolios rises with the opening of the capital account.

Consider the instance of an economy with reversible investment and no firms that have renegotiated debts. The capital stock and gross output grow according to the AK model at the difference between equilibrium net productivity, $E(\alpha - 1)$, and the foreign rate of interest (lower than the appropriate risk-adjusted rate-of-time preference so that capital inflows are positive). However, once there is a rollover, the capital stock will grow faster for the small open economy that faces a perfectly elastic supply of deposits at the foreign rate of interest. This is because bank loan renegotiation prevents firms from contracting on one end of the spectrum while firms continue to grow (stochastically) under constant returns to capital at the other end.

Foreign lenders, however, face different incentives under the implicit guarantee associated only with a broad crisis in the event of a collapsing exchange rate regime. They lose if a single bank is forced into bankruptcy idiosyncratically while domestic deposits are insured. However, as the portfolios of individual banks become ever riskier with infusions of foreign deposits, more and more banks reach potential crisis. This follows from the result that renegotiation leads to increasingly risky bank portfolios and rising contingent liabilities for the banks' creditor (the deposit insurer). Banks enter insolvency with positive probability. The probability of leaving insolvency decreases as more of the bank's firms renegotiate loans with positive probability and choose ever riskier projects in the absence of cofinancing. Foreign inflows that sustain these banks allow more and more banks to become insolvent. The contingent liability of government, d_t, is a random variable that also follows a submartingale. It must reach its upper bound in finite time.

This process is driven by the ultimate prospect of a bailout of foreign lenders. Such a bailout could happen immediately if foreign lenders realized a larger rate of return from the government bailout than the world rate of interest. We think that it is unrealistic to assume they do. Therefore, a bailout happens progressively and with stochastic timing because there are positive real net returns to domestic investment.

In the equilibrium path for the economy with foreign capital inflows, this process implies that we should observe increasing financial capital inflows as the crisis draws nearer. Each rollover raises the ratio of bank deposit liabilities to physical capital, ℓ/k, in this model. As rollovers become more probable, this ratio rises faster. In the model, output is proportional to capital, $y = \alpha k$, so that the debt to gross domestic product ratio is rising, as is its foreign component. We also note that the capital stock will be growing at a faster rate with an open capital account and implicit guarantees of foreign currency bank debts, in contrast to the case for the closed economy. However, gross domestic product may not be rising with the capital stock as more and more firms no longer cofinance investment and choose riskier projects.

11.2.4   Foreign Capital Inflows and Twin Crises

The link to currency crises comes about by the same mechanism proposed by Dooley (2000), Burnside, Eichenbaum, and Rebelo (1999), Chinn and Kletzer (2000), and others. These "third-generation" models of financial crises are based on first-generation models of a speculative attack but add the twist that domestic credit creation follows the attack and is contingent on the collapse. It is assumed that the cost of the bailout is ultimately monetized and that the implied ex post growth rate of domestic credit is inconsistent with the exchange rate peg.

The mechanics of a crisis need to be described a bit more. There is an upper bound on the credit that will be extended by foreign lenders to the domestic banks when the ultimate bailout is bounded from above by $\bar{d}$. This is the sum of the government's implicit guarantee, central bank reserves, and the residual capital of the banking system in the event of a financial crisis. This upper bound is reached in finite time with probability 1 as a consequence of the bank debt rollover dynamics for the agency model as explained above. Eventually, the foreign debt of the banking sector exceeds the value of the banking sector plus central bank reserves minus domestic deposits.[7] This excess claim at time T is d_T.

Suppose a run occurs in period T, so that the debt of the government rises by the amount d_T, which will be paid through domestic credit creation. The expected rate of depreciation after the abandonment of the fixed exchange rate is increasing in d_T. A rise in the rate of depreciation lowers domestic money demand at the instant of the speculative attack. This reduction is also increasing in d_T. Therefore, a portion of central bank reserves is taken by parties other than holders of foreign bank deposits in the currency crisis. This amount is given by $R_T^d = \psi(d_T)$, where $\psi'(d_T) > 0$. The reserves taken by foreign holders of short-term foreign currency bank debt, R_T^f exhaust the remaining reserves used in defense of the peg, $\bar{R}_T$. These equal the difference between total foreign claims against the domestic banking sector, denoted b_T, and the government's guarantee, so that $R_T^f - b_T - d_T$.

At the time of the twin banking and currency crises, we have the equilibrium condition,

$$(19) \qquad \bar{R}_T = R_T^d + R_T^f = b_T - d_T + \psi(d_T),$$

where d_t is a stochastic function of b_t. That is, both depend on the history of lending, investment, and production in the domestic economy leading up to the crisis. The timing of the crisis is stochastic and path dependent.

Whether a crisis can occur in this economy depends upon the size of the maximal government guarantee, $\bar{d}$, relative to reserves. This is because an increase in government debt equal to $\bar{d}$ leads to a particular rate of domestic credit creation if it is entirely monetized. This rate of domestic credit creation may or may not lead to a first-generation currency crisis at the moment it is incurred. It can be too small, implying a collapse of the fixed

---

7. We do not preclude banks' lending to each other. Since they can do so, what matters is the aggregate solvency of the banking sector and not the solvency of individual banks.

exchange rate regime at some later date. If this is the case, foreign creditors will not be bailed out until the collapse and incur the net opportunity cost of lending $\bar{d}$, $r^*\bar{d}$. Thus, if $\bar{d}$ is too small, the eventual bailout will not be sufficient in present value to keep foreign lenders in the market.

Does this mean that foreign capital inflows are zero if $\bar{d}$ is small? The answer is no as long as banks hold deposit liabilities to domestic savers covered by deposit insurance. Foreign deposits can be serviced in full as a bank's portfolio deteriorates up to the point that the current value of the bank's net assets,

$$(20) \qquad \sum_j \min\{\alpha^j k_t^j, R_t^j \ell_t^j\},$$

just equals the foreign deposit liability. Domestic savers are fully covered by deposit insurance, and the withdrawal of foreign deposits busts the bank. This type of foreign exit from the banks occurs idiosyncratically across banks in this model because the only productivity risk is idiosyncratic across firms.

A currency crisis occurs when the rate of domestic credit creation necessary to finance the government's liability at time T, d_T, is exactly consistent with a collapse of the fixed rate at time T. The timing depends on the stochastic processes for b_t and d_t (which depend on the entire structure of the economy), as well as the level of reserves. Thus, if $\bar{d}$ is sufficient to allow a currency crisis soon enough that foreign lenders realize their opportunity rate of return on loans with bailout, then there is a widespread financial crisis as all foreign loans are pulled from the banking system. Put differently, if the government guarantee is sufficient to encourage any foreign capital inflows, then it leads to an inevitable currency and banking crisis. If $\bar{d}$ is too small to generate an eventual currency crisis, then it also has no impact on capital inflows. The possibility of equilibria in which lending never begins can be ruled out by the condition that

$$(21) \qquad E(\min\{r, \tilde{\alpha} - 1\}) \geq r^*,$$

where $\tilde{\alpha} - 1$ is the net rate of return to bank loan portfolios inclusive of the returns from rollovers.

We could delink this crisis from the exchange rate peg by changing the assumptions about government guarantees. If there can be a bailout of the banks in the event of a systemic banking crisis that insures foreign creditors, then a banking crisis can occur under a floating exchange rate regime. If the subsequent liabilities of the government are monetized, the rate of exchange rate depreciation naturally rises. If the bailout is financed by taxes on domestic residents, then consumption growth is depressed (because the timing is stochastic, Ricardian consumers will not fully smooth consumption against the tax increase).

11.2.5   Postcrisis Contraction

At the moment of the financial crisis, there is a sudden reversal of capital inflows as foreign lending stops and households reduce their demand for domestic currency deposits. The contraction in domestic deposits causes a contraction in the capital stock given by

$$(22) \qquad k_{t+1} - k_t = \ell_{t+1} - \ell_t + [(\alpha - 1)k_t - r_t\ell_t - \pi_t]$$

for a solvent firm where $\ell_{t+1} - \ell_t < 0$. This increases the ratio of self-financing to capital sharply,

$$(23) \qquad z_{t+1} = \frac{[(\alpha - 1)k_t - r_t\ell_t - \pi_t]}{k_{t+1}},$$

implying that new bank lending will be forthcoming if the banks can borrow. Insolvent firms may also be able to borrow if their debt is restructured with write-downs that leave them at least solvent. However, with the guarantees of the government exhausted, new foreign deposits to the banks are not supported. Domestic household income and consumption drop along with the capital stock. If the banks remain in business for intermediating loans, then domestic saving deposits will flow to domestic firms, allowing growth from the new low aggregate capital stock. These deposits are smaller, in proportion with domestic income, and are only made if there is deposit insurance as before. As noted, foreign inflows will be lower than before the crisis, so that the growth rate of the economy is also lower than before the crisis.

If the government does not restructure the domestic financial sector, the growth rate of output could fall even more after the crisis because the intermediation benefits of banks are lost, as argued by Calvo (1998a). The loss of domestic banking would force the use of alternative, higher cost, means of intermediation.

11.2.6   Empirical Implications

In the model economy, domestic financial and currency crises occur simultaneously and are inevitable under the policies assumed. These include the absence of effective prudential regulation of the banks. The foreign indebtedness of the banking sector rises in proportion to gross domestic output and the capital stock before the financial crisis. The production and banking model also implies a rise in the growth rate of the capital stock as the crisis becomes more likely. This will coincide with an increase in the aggregate riskiness of the banking sector's loan portfolio.

The model also has implications for the market value of firm and bank equities. Because loans can be renegotiated, the value of a firm is not zero when

$$\alpha_t k_t - R_t \ell_t \leq 0.$$

The firm is an ongoing enterprise that could potentially pay off its debts, allowing the entrepreneur to accumulate capital in the firm once more. Therefore, the stock market value of the firm includes the option value of "redemption" and will remain positive.

The equity value of the firm is given by the expected present value of the dividends that it can pay subject to the imposition of the transversality condition. For firms that have positive net income, the capital stock is rising, and so is firm equity. This increase is larger than the rise in productivity for a positive shock. This can be seen simply by ignoring dividends and calculating the discounted expected equity of the entrepreneur's ownership (how the stock market value of a firm that does not pay a dividend changes). This evolves according to

$$x_{t+1} = (\alpha - R_t)k_t + R_t x_t,$$

which equals

(24)
$$x_{t+1} = \left[(\alpha - R_t)\frac{1}{z} + \alpha\right]x_t$$

with lending in the agency model. The present value of the owner's equity is given by

(25)
$$E_t\left(\frac{x_t + 1}{R_t}\right) = E_t\left[\left(\frac{\alpha}{R_t} - 1\right)\frac{1}{z} + \frac{\alpha}{R_t}\right]x_t > x_t.$$

Differentiating with respect to α shows that the equity value of the firm rises more than proportionately with the discounted productivity of capital. For firms that remain solvent but realize negative net incomes, $(\alpha - 1)k_t - r_t\ell_t < 0$, the value of equity falls along with the capital stock.

The average value of all producers' equity evolves over time as capital accumulates and some firms renegotiate bank loans. Beginning with all firms cofinancing investment, the total stock market value of firms rises as the average capital stock rises. It also rises to the extent that the equity value of firms that have low outputs and downsize (but remain solvent) reflects an increase in the likelihood that they will become insolvent in the future and renegotiate their loans. For such firms, the option value of redemption rises. Once firms do become insolvent and renegotiate their bank debts, the value of these firms remains nonnegative, while the average equity value of firms that have been successful continues to rise with the capital stock. Ignoring the expectation that there will be a collapse in the capital stock at date T, the total stock market value of producers would be rising over time (in the case of large numbers with uncorrelated firm-specific shocks) under foreign capital inflows as long as the net expected return to capital exceeds the rate of interest. However, these dynamics imply a rise followed by a decline in the total value of firm equity prior to crisis under rational expectations.

The equity value of banks also evolves dynamically as loan rollovers take place. However, banks face an upper bound on the share of the returns to successful projects they can claim in proportion to the firms' capital stocks in the face of competition from other banks. The banks are accumulating losses over time, and their equity value must decline in expectation once one bank has had to roll over the loan of a firm that cannot repay its short-term debt. Clearly, the average equity value of banks is lower when some client firm has to renegotiate. In the model set up here, the probability of more renegotiations and of increasing liability for the deposit insurer means that the expected equity of the bank is decreasing thereafter. It decreases as

$$\Pr\left\{ \sum_j \min\{\alpha^j k_t^j,\, R_t^j \ell_t^j\} < (1 + r_t^d) j \ell_t^j \right\}$$

rises.

Therefore, the model of an evolving banking crisis driven by loan rollovers fueled by foreign capital inflows implies that the ratio of the equity value of banks to the equity value of corporations should be declining in trend before the crisis. Foreign capital inflows should be rising in proportion to gross domestic product if the assumptions of constant returns to capital and unchanging investment opportunities hold. Output should collapse sharply after the crisis.

The Bernanke and Gertler model of financial fragility shows how aggregate productivity cycles are exacerbated through the financial accelerator. This implies that the capital stock falls but that the growth rate could recover in a simple closed-economy Ak model. In our model, foreign capital inflows would need to return to avoid a reduction in the growth rate of the postcrisis economy.

11.3   The Assumptions of the Theoretical Model and the Precrisis Financial Systems of East Asia

The theoretical model generates endogenous accumulations of foreign debt by a domestic banking sector that is progressively less stable, leading to an eventual crisis. Three of the model's assumptions are crucial in this process. First is the predominance of corporate borrowing from domestic banks, arising from the informational advantage of banks over other lenders. Second is the prospect of government deposit insurance, or government bailouts of the domestic banking sector, and government guarantees of foreign loans to the domestic banking sector. Third is supervisory forbearance and the absence of effective prudential regulation of the banking sector. In this section, we briefly examine the precrisis financial systems of Korea, Taiwan, Thailand, Malaysia, and Singapore in relation to these assumptions. Table 11.1 briefly summarizes this section's findings. The economies with financial systems that fit the model's assumptions most closely are assigned the highest negative ratings. We find that the model's assumptions characterize the financial systems of Korea and Thailand very well (negative ratings: 9) and the financial system of Malaysia reasonably well (negative ratings: 6). The model's assumptions fail to fit the financial systems of Taiwan and Singapore (negative ratings: 5).

11.3.1   Corporate Reliance on Domestic Bank Borrowing

With regard to the predominance of bank lending, only Korean firms were highly reliant on domestic bank borrowing. In Thailand, domestic banks were not always the dominant lender, because corporations borrowed directly from foreign banks in the offshore market. In Thailand, however, the importance of finance companies increased in the 1990s, as licensing requirements were eased. Malaysian, Taiwanese, and Singaporean firms were not as reliant on domestic banks, because they actively tapped bond and equity markets.

Just prior to the crisis, the reliance of Korean corporations on domestic commercial and merchant bank financing was large and increasing. In 1997, borrowing from banks accounted for close to 50 percent of total corporate financing; this was up from about 35 percent in the mid-1990s (Pomerleano 1998). Moreover, most of the remaining corporate financing—corporate bonds, commercial paper, and foreign borrowing—was explicitly guaranteed by banks. For example, in 1996, 87 percent of the bonds issued by corporations had bank guarantees. The default risk on these bonds was borne by the banks, because if the corporation failed, the bondholder would have recourse to the guaranteeing bank (Dekle and Ubide 1998). Equity financing was small; in early 1997, equity financing accounted for only 7 percent of total corporate financing, down from about 20 percent in the early 1990s. Thus, by early 1997, the debt-equity ratio of manufacturing corporations was over 300 percent, and most of this debt was explicitly or implicitly owed to domestic banks (Pomerleano 1998).

Compared to Korea, the reliance of Taiwanese corporations on domestic bank financing was markedly lower. In 1996, borrowing from banks accounted for less than 22 percent of total corporate financing, down from about 50 percent in the early 1990s (Chu 1999). By the late 1980s, large corporations could raise most of their funds from the equity market (Chu 1999). Moreover, Taiwan developed a successful venture capital industry and industry and initial public offering market. In 1997, small and medium-sized firms raised $2 billion and $27 billion from venture capital and initial public offerings respectively. Thus, by early 1997, the debt-equity ratio of corporations was down to about 85 percent, lower than even the debt-equity ratios in many industrialized countries.

The reliance of Thai corporations on bank and finance company

Table 11.1   The Assumptions of the Theoretical Model: Do They Fit?

	Korea	Taiwan	Thailand	Malaysia	Singapore
Predominance of corporate borrowing from domestic banks	3 Corporate bank borrowing ratio: Over 50%. 87% of corporate bonds bank-guaranteed.	1 Corporate bank borrowing ratio: About 22%. High equity financing.	3 Corporate bank borrowing ratio: About 75%. Of which 20% from foreign banks (in FX).	2 Corporate bank borrowing ratio: About 40%. Good corporate bond and equity markets.	2 Corporate bank borrowing ratio: About 40%. Strong corporate bond and equity markets.
Government explicit and implicit guarantees of domestic and foreign loans to the domestic banking sector	3 Limited explicit deposit insurance system. Depositors always bailed-out. Blanket-guarantees of foreign loans (during Crisis).	3 Limited explicit deposit insurance system. Depositors always bailed-out.	3 No explicit deposit insurance system. Depositors always bailed-out. Blanket-guarantees of deposits in banks, finance companies, and foreign loans (during Crisis).	2 No explicit deposit insurance system. Depositors always bailed-out. Blanket-guarantees of domestic resident deposits in banks (during Crisis). Foreigners faced losses on ringgit deposits	2 No explicit deposit insurance system. Implicit guarantees to depositors in domestic banks.
Absence of effective prudential regulation of and supervisory forbearance of the domestic banking sector	3 Supervision fragmented between MOF and BOK. Prudential regulations relaxed in mid-1990s. Limits on loan exposure to specific corporate groups disregarded.	1 Supervision consolidated at CBC. CBC applied prudential standards stricter than law.	3 Supervision fragmented between MOF and BOT. Loan classification rules too lenient or ignored. No limits on loan exposure to specific sectors (e.g., real estate).	2 Supervision consolidated at BNM. Strict limits on connected lending and lending to corporate groups.	1 Supervision consolidated at MAS. Prudential regulations comparable to those in U.K. Required capital-asset ratios (at 12 percent) higher than in other Asian countries.
Total rating	9	5	9	6	5

financing was among the highest of the crisis-inflicted Asian countries, although some of this reliance was to foreign banks. Between 1992 and 1996, borrowing from banks and finance companies accounted for 74 percent of total corporate financing (Pomerleano 1998), and the average debt-equity ratio was about 180 percent (Pomerleano and Zhang 1999). In 1995 and 1996, borrowing from finance companies accounted for about 27 percent of this corporate borrowing. Finance companies tended to focus more on consumer and real estate financing, whereas banks loaned more to the manufacturing sector. A significant fraction of this corporate borrowing was from foreign, particularly Japanese, banks. Most of the borrowing from foreign banks was through the Bangkok International Banking Facility (BIBF), whose "out-in" lending is entirely foreign currency–denominated. In 1996, BIBF borrowing accounted for about 18 percent of all bank borrowing by Thai corporations (IMF 2000b).

Between 1992 and 1996, Malaysian corporations raised about 40 percent of their funds from domestic banks, finance companies, and merchant banks, all deposit-taking institutions (Pomerleano 1998). This ratio of private corporate borrowing may understate the dependence of the Malaysian economy on the banking sector. Consumers and nonincorporated businesses were also large bank borrowers. Finance companies accounted for about 20 percent of domestic borrowing and loaned mostly to consumers and nonincorporated businesses. Foreign-owned banks accounted for about 15 percent of all domestic borrowing, although the main source of funds for foreign banks was domestic deposits. Compared to corporations elsewhere in Asia, Malaysian corporations have relied somewhat more on bond, and significantly more on equity, financing; the debt-equity ratio was relatively low, at under 100 percent (Pomerleano and Zhang 1999).

Between 1992 and 1996, Singapore corporations raised about 40 percent of their funds from banks (Pomerleano 1998). Only four banks, all of them domestic, accounted for 80 percent of these loans. The remaining loans were from smaller banks, foreign banks, and finance companies. Although Singapore has a large offshore market, regulations have kept the domestic currency and foreign currency markets separate. Borrowing from offshore in domestic currency by domestic corporations was restricted, although foreign currency borrowing was not. As in Malaysia, Singapore corporations have tended to rely more on bond and equity financing, thus keeping the debt-equity ratio to under 90 percent.

11.3.2   Government Explicit and Implicit Guarantees
of Domestic Bank Liabilities

With regard to government guarantees, in Korea, Taiwan, Thailand, and Malaysia, bank deposits were implicitly guaranteed by the government, given that no domestic bank was ever allowed to fail and close. Failing banks were usually taken over by the government and forced to restructure or merge with another bank. Singapore also did not provide explicit bank deposit guarantees, but in the absence of domestic bank failures or take-overs, it is difficult to assess the extent of implicit guarantees to depositors. Foreign loans to the domestic banking sector were implicitly guaranteed in each instance. However, such loans were important only for Korea and, to a lesser extent, Thailand. Banks in Taiwan, Malaysia, and Singapore borrowed little from abroad.

Prior to the crisis, the Korean deposit insurance system was segmented; different deposit insurance systems covered different financial institutions. Moreover, given the relative newness of the various systems (which started in the mid-1990s) and the low deposit insurance rates, the accumulated deposit insurance premiums were negligibly small. Thus, for all practical purposes, Korea did not have an explicit deposit insurance system. However, depositors probably viewed their deposits as implicitly insured, because the Korean government had never allowed a bank to fail (Park 1994). Between 1960 and the mid-1980s, the idea of deposit insurance was moot: Banks were publicly owned, and monetary authorities controlled every aspect of bank management. Although banks were privatized in the early 1980s and financial markets were deregulated, the government continued to exercise control over banks by appointing bank management and by the system of government policy loans (Dekle and Ubide 1998). Policy loans were used by the government to direct bank lending to preferred sectors, with the provision that, should the firms receiving the loans default, the lending bank would be bailed out. Although policy loans were largely phased out by the mid-1990s, the historical involvement of the government meant that banks developed few skills in credit analysis. Lending decisions were still based on the availability of collateral, normally real estate (45 percent of all loans), and government moral suasion.

Domestic banks have intermediated virtually all foreign borrowing by Korean corporations, in won or in foreign currency. Of the loans borrowed directly from foreign banks, almost all carried guarantees by domestic banks (Collins and Park 1989). In the mid-1990s, some companies were able to directly borrow in overseas bond markets, but this borrowing had to be bank guaranteed. These various types of bank-intermediated foreign loans were not explicitly government guaranteed, but given that no domestic bank had failed, the government was in effect implicitly guaranteeing these loans. In fact, in August 1997, in the midst of the crisis, the authorities made explicit their commitment by guaranteeing all foreign liabilities of Korean banks.

As in Korea, for all practical purposes, Taiwan did not have an explicit deposit insurance system. Participation in the Taiwanese deposit insurance system was voluntary, and as a result the accumulated insurance premiums were very small (Yang 1994). However, as in Korea, depositors viewed their deposits as implicitly insured, because most deposits were with banks owned by various branches of the government. Although the banking system was partially privatized in the early 1990s, government-owned banks still accounted for about 60 percent of total bank loans in 1996 (Chen 2000). Customers of the government-owned banks were mainly public enterprises and large private manufacturing firms (Shea 1994). Private banks were numerous, but all were very small. When insolvent, these private banks were bailed out by the government (Yang 1994). Most of the bank lending (66 percent) was collateralized, with real estate or, more often, with equity.

Of the Taiwanese foreign borrowing, only 5 percent was explicitly guaranteed by the government (Haggard 2000, 134). In any event, the total amount of foreign borrowing remained small (gross foreign debt: 10.6 percent of GDP). Banks intermediated only about half of this foreign borrowing.

Thailand has never had an official, explicit deposit insurance system. However, the Thai government has always bailed out depositors. Insolvent banks were usually recapitalized and allowed to operate as normal. During the crisis, six of fifteen commercial banks were taken over by the government. In addition, the government issued a blanket guarantee of all bank deposits. Finance companies were allowed to fail, but the government has always guaranteed their deposits ex post. During the crisis, fifty-six out of ninety-one finance companies failed, but all deposits were guaranteed, although credits held by the directors and management of failed institutions were not covered (IMF 2000b).

There were two main sources of foreign borrowing by Thai corporations. First, corporations borrowed in baht from nonresident deposits in Thai banks. Nonresident bank deposits have historically received the same guarantees as resident deposits. Second, corporations borrowed in foreign currency from Thai and foreign banks through the BIBF. None of this foreign currency borrowing was explicitly guaranteed by the government. However, the foreign currency borrowing intermediated through Thai banks (one-third of total BIBF borrowing) was, like all domestic bank liabilities, implicitly guaranteed, because these domestic banks could not fail. The government did not implicitly guarantee the borrowing through foreign banks, because most of this borrowing went to joint ventures—for example, in the case of Thai-Mitsubishi Motors, the responsibility for paying back this borrowing was viewed as belonging to the parent firm, Mitsubishi Motors of Japan.

There was no explicit deposit insurance system in Malaysia. However, Malaysia has never allowed a bank or finance company to fail, although finance companies have been merged. Thus, all deposits at domestic financial institutions were implicitly guaranteed, at least for residents. In fact, ex post, the government has guaranteed even the deposits at foreign banks; during the crisis, the government issued a blanket guarantee of all deposits.

Borrowing by domestic banks from foreign banks in foreign currency has never been sizable in Malaysia, given very strict foreign borrowing regulations. The small amount of borrowing that took place was never explicitly guaranteed. Historically, Malaysia has often imposed controls on portfolio outflows. For example, in 1994, controls on short-term portfolio inflows were imposed, and in 1998, minimum holding periods (twelve months) and exit levies (30 percent) on the repatriation of bank deposits held by nonresidents were imposed (IMF 1999a). In the case of repatriation restrictions, the subsequent depreciation of the ringgit has meant that nonresidents experienced capital losses on their ringgit deposits. Thus, for certain types of foreign borrowing, such as nonresident ringgit deposits, there were no implicit guarantees either.

Singapore never had an official, explicit deposit insurance system. However, as elsewhere in Asia, no domestic bank or finance company has ever been allowed to fail, although the government has not always bailed out depositors with deposits at failed foreign banks. Thus, it may be the case that the implicit guarantee of deposits was selective, limited to deposits at domestic financial institutions.

Regulations have prevented Singapore corporations from borrowing offshore in domestic currency. Given Singapore's ample saving and low interest rates, offshore foreign currency borrowing by corporations remained very small; this borrowing was not guaranteed, either explicitly or implicitly.

11.3.3 Government Prudential Regulations and Enforcement

With regard to weak prudential supervision, in Korea and Thailand prudential regulations were lax and poorly enforced because of fragmented supervisory systems and supervisory forbearance. Supervisory systems were strict and well enforced in Malaysia, Taiwan, and Singapore.

Lax prudential standards and supervisory forbearance were major deficiencies in the Korean banking system (Dekle and Ubide 1998). Supervision of financial institutions was fragmented; the Bank of Korea supervised commercial banks, but the ministry of finance supervised merchant banks. Defects in the soundness of banks were not immediately remedied once detected by the bank supervisors, and changes to prudential regulations were made to allow banks to report profits and capital positions that were misleading. For example, provisioning requirements for nonperforming loans were relaxed over 1995–96; those for "doubtful" loans were decreased to 75 percent from 100 percent. Although there were regulations on bank loan exposure to large corporate groups, these regulations were rarely enforced. For example, the Hanbo group, which collapsed in early 1997, had outstanding loans from the Korea First Bank that were five times larger than what was considered prudent. Knowledge of such supervisory forbearance, together with less than fully transparent accounting, meant that Korean banks were not encouraged to take speedy action to improve their solvency.

Although on paper Taiwan's prudential standards were no stronger than Korea's, its supervisory authorities exercised much less forbearance (Chu 1999). The Central Bank of China (CBC) was Taiwan's main supervisory authority, rather than the Ministry of Finance. In contrast to most finance ministries, the CBC was unusually independent from political influence. The CBC governor appointed the senior officers of all government-owned banks and forced these banks to observe stricter prudential standards than those mandated by law. For example, most government-owned banks were forced to maintain capital-asset ratios above 12 percent (greater than the law's 8 percent), and a liquid asset–reserve ratio of 9.5 percent (above the law's 7 percent). The CBC also kept government policy loans under tight limits.

Lax prudential standards were major deficiencies of the Thai banking system (Lindgren et al. 2000). The rules for loan classification and accounting were too lenient and were often ignored. For example, loans had to be in a nonaccrual state for twelve months before being classified as nonperforming. Banks and finance companies built up large portfolios of questionable loans that were often simply rolled over, rather than being classified as nonperforming. There were no limits on loan exposures to specific sectors, such as real estate, although there were limits to individual borrowers. Bank supervision was fragmented between the Ministry of Finance and the Bank of Thailand. The Ministry of Finance was entrusted with the overall authority for supervision, but the day-to-day responsibility for supervision was delegated to the Bank of Thailand. All decisions by the Bank of Thailand had to be ratified by the Ministry of Finance.

Malaysia's prudential regulations were drawn from British sources and were, on paper, more stringent than those of other Asian economies (Scott 1999). Moreover, these regulations were strengthened in the late 1980s and in the mid-1990s. In particular, broad regulatory and intervention powers were consolidated at Bank Negara Malaysia (Lindgren et al. 2000). There were strict limits on connected lending and loan exposure limits (30 percent of a bank's capital) to corporate groups. A two-tiered regulatory system, which provided extra privileges to banks that increased their capital, was introduced. As a consequence, capital-asset ratios of deposit-taking institutions approached 10 percent.

Singapore's prudential regulations were also drawn from foreign sources, primarily Britain and the United States, and were far more conservative than elsewhere in Asia. By law, banks were required to maintain capital-asset ratios above 12 percent. Broad regulatory and intervention powers were consolidated at the Monetary Authority of Singapore. In addition, foreign banks were allowed to operate only on the strength of their home regulations. Comfort letters were required that stated that home offices would meet liquidity or capital shortfalls of their offshore affiliates (IMF

2000a). However, bank disclosure was weak; bank assets were recorded on accounting statements at historical cost rather than at market value, and contingent liabilities, such as derivatives positions, were not disclosed (IMF 1999b). Nevertheless, these problems with bank disclosure were worse in other Asian economies and led to the adoption of more rigorous requirements in recent years.

11.3.4 Earlier Studies

Recent studies have examined more systematically the relationship between banking and regulatory structure, and banking crisis. Demirgüç-Kunt and Detragiache (2000) create an index that represents the extent of explicit deposit insurance for sixty-one countries. Using cross-section probit econometric techniques, the authors find that countries with explicit deposit insurance systems are more likely to incur a crisis in their banking systems. The authors find that proxies for bank regulation such as rule of law, quality of bureaucracy, and degree of corruption perform an important role in curbing the negative effect of deposit insurance on bank stability. Finally, the authors find that in more concentrated banking systems, the probability of a banking crisis is smaller. This finding is somewhat surprising, because in more concentrated systems banks are "too big to fail" and may be implicitly insured, thus worsening moral hazard.

Rossi (1999) creates a "bank safety net" index for a sample of fifteen countries. The index captures the presence of explicit deposit insurance, of lender of last resort facilities, and of a history of bank bailouts. The index is noteworthy in that it partially captures the implicit insurance assumptions of our model. The author finds that the index is significantly positively correlated with bank fragility.

In a cross-section study of sixty countries, Barth, Caprio, and Levine (2000) find that the probability of a banking crisis is decreased by securities market development (especially equity market liquidity), the issuance of primary-market equity as a share of GDP, and the issuance of long-term bonds (in the primary market) as a share of GDP. This is consistent with the assumption of our model that higher corporate security financing and lower bank dependence decrease the probability of crisis.

11.4 Empirical Implications of the Model

Our theoretical model implies that banking and currency crises coincide and inevitably occur in the absence of effective prudential regulation. Before the crisis, private foreign debt rises as a ratio of gross domestic production. Foreign financial capital inflows will be a constant fraction of trend output in the case in which consumption growth equals income growth. Otherwise, the ratio of inflows to output can rise or fall in trend. The investment-output ratio is constant before the crisis. The shadow value of domestic banks should decline before the crisis. This can be measured by comparing the stock market value of domestic banks to the stock market value of the domestic sector.

After a financial crisis, the model implies that output contracts and that the growth rate of output is lower in recovery than it was before the crisis. This is the case because contingent government bailout has been exercised, so that the resources that previously subsidized foreign capital inflows are no longer available to subsidize new inflows at the same level. The currency crisis should also lead to a contraction in money demand and an increase in the rate of monetary growth. The latter is consistent with the monetization of the sudden increase in government liabilities.

The riskiness of the loan portfolio of domestic intermediaries is rising in this model. An increasing share of bank loans goes to firms that have realized low capital productivities in the past, whereas a decreasing share goes to firms that have realized high productivities of capital. In the endogenous growth model used, the productivity of capital is an i.i.d. random variable. If we allow for a small degree of serial correlation in the productivity of inputs for individual firms, then the marginal productivity of capital will be decreasing in trend.

11.4.1   Empirical Evidence for the Model

The model can be examined along a number of dimensions using indirect measures of the factors of interest. The model predicts several relationships. The key relationship is that increases in capital inflows are intermediated through the banking system and result in increases in lending to the private sector. This is the case to the extent that capital inflows to the domestic sector are not sterilized, resulting in reserve accumulations rather than financing debits on the current account.

The model predicts an increasing ratio of foreign capital inflows and domestic lending as a ratio of output prior to crisis. It also implies that domestic investment will become increasingly risky. This may be reflected by falling capital productivity in the data. Bank portfolios are predicted to be deteriorating before the crisis, with the banking system carrying a rising share of nonperforming assets. The market value of total bank equity shares should be falling absolutely and in ratio to the total value of outstanding equity in domestic corporations.

The model also makes postcrisis predictions. There should be an immediate contraction in output and investment. The currency crisis in this model results from the anticipated postcrisis monetization of government bailouts of lenders. Consistency with this hypothesis requires that we observe an increase in the rate of domestic credit creation and growth rate of the monetary base after the crisis.

The predictions should hold most strongly for the two economies that fit the assumptions of the model most closely—that is, for Korea and Thailand. The predictions should hold less strongly for Malaysia, and the predictions should fail for Taiwan and Singapore. In this section, we examine whether these predictions hold, using pre- and postcrisis data. The data sources for all charts are described in the appendix.

11.4.2   Precrisis Capital Inflows and Domestic Lending

An important implication of the model is that capital inflows are manifested in lending by banks and nonbank financial intermediaries. We measure capital inflows using the balance-of-payments data reported by the IMF, and deposit bank lending to the domestic private sector is measured by domestic credit. Capital inflows are net-gross inflows minus gross outflows. Figure 11.1 depicts the ratios of lending and capital inflows to GDP for Korea, Taiwan, Malaysia, Thailand, and Singapore. In Korea, the capital inflow-GDP ratio began to rise sharply in 1993, while the lending-GDP started to rise in 1995. In Taiwan, the lending-GDP and the capital inflow-GDP ratios were constant precrisis, whereas the capital inflow ratio rose sharply postcrisis. In Malaysia, the lending-GDP ratio increased moderately from 1990 to 1994 and more strongly from 1994. The growth in the capital inflow ratio was very strong between 1990 and 1993, but the capital inflow ratio plummeted in 1994, when the government imposed capital controls; subsequently, strong capital inflow growth resumed. In Thailand, the lending-GDP ratio grew strongly from 1990 to 1997; correspondingly, the capital inflow ratio grew strongly after 1994. In Singapore, although the lending-GDP ratio grew moderately after 1990, the capital inflow ratio declined sharply from 1990 to 1994. Subsequently, the capital inflow ratio resumed its growth. As our model predicts, the physical investment-GDP ratios were relatively constant in each case.

As is well known, capital inflows can be sterilized by central banks; this sterilization can break the link between capital inflows and lending. We do not present a detailed discussion of how effectively capital inflows were sterilized in the five cases; accounts are provided by Spiegel (1995) and Moreno (1996). There is a strong link between capital inflows and lending for Korea, Malaysia and Thailand, especially since 1994, suggesting that these countries have not been successful in sterilizing capital inflows. Figure 11.2 depicts the levels of official foreign exchange reserves and the ratio of foreign exchange reserves to short-term (of maturity less than one year) external debt. Central banks that engage heavily in sterilized intervention should have high and rising foreign exchange reserves. Reported official Korean reserves are net of Bank of Korea foreign currency deposits at overseas branches. As is well known, the Bank of Thailand had outstanding net forward contracts totaling $7 billion in 1997 and $4 billion in 1996; the resources available to the Bank of Thailand for intervention may be overstated by the level of official reserves. Compared to Taiwan and Singapore, between 1996 and 1997 Korea, Malaysia, and Thailand all had low and

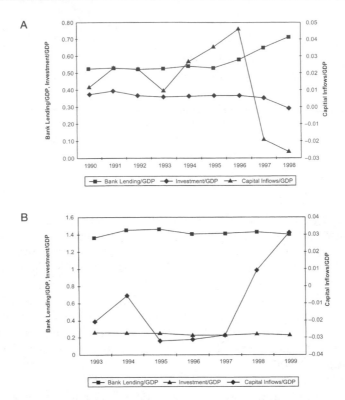

Figure 11.1   Bank lending, capital inflows, and investment for *A*, Korea; *B*, Taiwan; *C*, Malaysia; *D*, Thailand; and *E*, Singapore
Source: See appendix.

constant or declining foreign exchange reserves in dollar terms or as a ratio of short-term external debt, suggesting that these countries have not been successful in sterilizing capital inflows. Taiwan and especially Singapore had high and rising foreign exchange reserves.

Thus, the evidence on capital flows and lending is consistent with our model. Korea and Thailand had the strongest association between capital flows and lending, whereas capital controls broke the strong association in Malaysia in 1994.

Riskiness of Domestic Investment and
Falling Marginal Productivity of Capital

In our model, adverse selection under limited liability in financial intermediation implies bank portfolios that become progressively riskier. In the aggregate, lending and investment are increasingly allocated to firms that have experienced low productivities in the past, rather than to firms that have had high productivity experiences. If productivity has a small serial correlation, then the productivity of capital for firms will be decreasing over time.

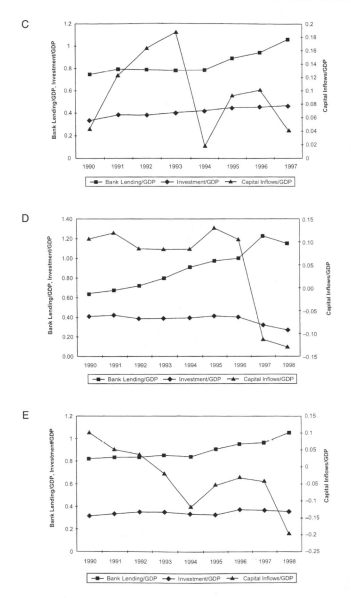

Figure 11.1   (cont.)

Between 1992 and 1996, the productivity of capital for firms in Korea, Taiwan, and Singapore all declined, with the sharpest decline for firms in Thailand. The productivity of capital for firms in Malaysia rose slightly. (The data are all from Pomerleano and Zhang 1999.) For Korean firms, the average return on assets (ROA) declined from 4.5 percent in 1992 to 4.2 percent in 1996, and their average return on investment (ROI) declined from 6.4 percent in 1992 to 5.6 percent in 1996. For Taiwanese firms, the average ROA

A

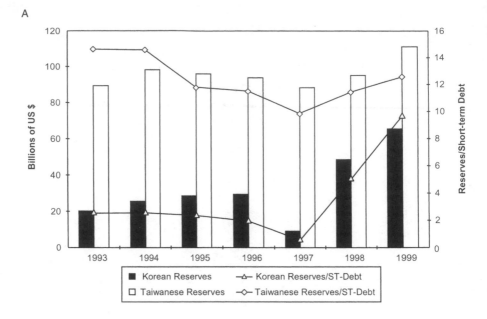

B

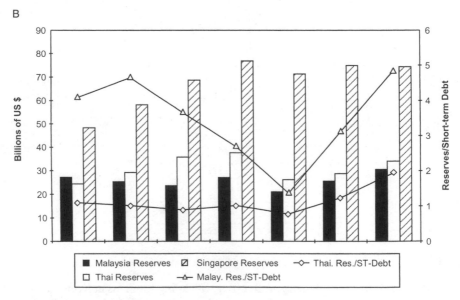

Figure 11.2   Foreign exchange reserves for *A,* Korea and Taiwan; and *B,* Malaysia, Thailand, and Singapore

Source: See appendix.

declined from 7.6 percent in 1992 to 7.3 percent in 1996, but their average ROI was constant at 8.6 percent between 1992 and 1996. For Thai firms, the average ROA sharply declined, from 9.5 percent in 1992 to 6.0 percent in 1996, and the average ROI sharply declined from 11.6 percent to 7.0 percent. For Singapore firms, the average ROA declined from 6.7 percent in 1992 to 6.4 percent in 1996, and the average ROI declined from 9.0 percent in 1992 to 8.6 percent in 1996. For Malaysian firms, the average ROA actually rose slightly from 15.5 percent in 1992 to 16.1 percent in 1996, and the average ROI also rose slightly from 11.7 percent in 1992 to 12.1 percent in 1996.

In the case of Korea, the ROA declined only 1 percentage point over the 1990s. However, Korea was unique in that its ROA was uniformly low between 1992 and 1996. If we compare Korea to Taiwan, we find that the gap in ROA was over 3.0 percent in the 1990s.

Deterioration of Bank Portfolios

The model predicts that in the presence of government guarantees the ratio of lending to GDP will rise and that the quality of bank portfolios will decline. The trend in the share of nonperforming loans (NPLs) gives a measure of the quality of bank portfolios. Panel A of figure 11.3 compares the share of NPLs for Korean and Taiwanese commercial banks. In the early 1990s, Korean banks had a much higher NPL share than Taiwanese banks, owing to the Korean government's rationalization plans for the chemical and heavy industries in the mid-1980s, in which Korean banks were forced to assume the losses of their corporate borrowers. Subsequently, as the problems of the mid-1980s waned, Korea's NPLs declined and Taiwan's rose; by 1996, the share of NPLs in Taiwan approached that in Korea. Panel B of figure 11.3 compares the share of NPLs for Malaysian and Thai deposit-taking institutions. In the early 1990s, Malaysia's NPLs were higher than Thailand's. Subsequently, Malaysia's NPLs declined and Thailand's rose sharply, so that by 1996 Thailand's NPLs were double those of Malaysia.

Given differences in accounting standards and regulatory definitions, however, cross-border comparisons of NPLs must be viewed with great caution. Even within-country time series patterns may not be very informative, because in the 1990s many countries changed their NPL classification standards. For example, in the mid-1990s Korean loan classification standards were made more lenient, accounting in part for the decline in NPLs from the early to the middle 1990s.

An implication of our theoretical model is that the stock market value of the domestic banks should be declining much more in the crisis cases before the crisis than in the noncrisis cases. This decline should be evidenced by a significant decline in the ratio of the value of domestic bank equities to the stock market value of the entire domestic sector. This comparison allows us to compensate for overall stock market fluctuations and trends. Panel A of figure 11.4 compares these ratios for Korea and Taiwan. In Korea, the ratio sharply declined between 1992 and 1996, while

A

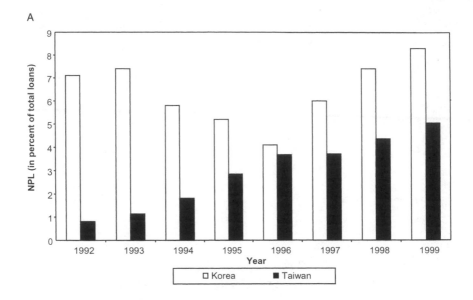

B

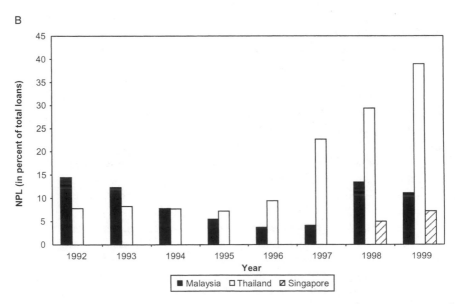

Figure 11.3   Nonperforming loans for *A*, Korea and Taiwan; and *B*, Malaysia, Thailand, and Singapore

Source: See appendix.

A

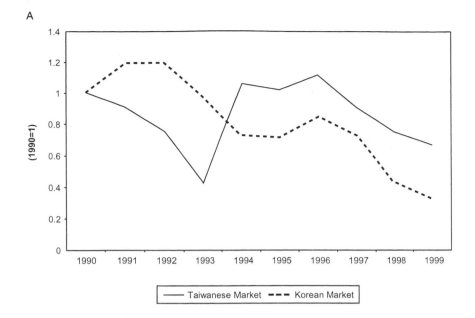

B

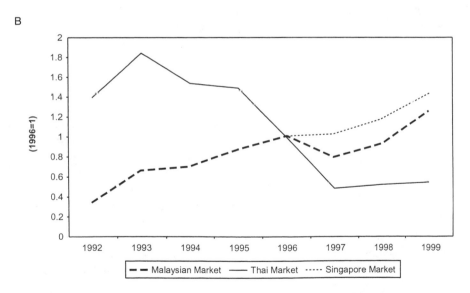

Figure 11.4   Ratio of bank stocks to total stock market value for *A*, Korea and Taiwan; and *B*, Malaysia, Thailand, and Singapore

Source: See appendix.

in Taiwan, the ratio increased. Panel B of figure 11.4 compares these ratios for Malaysia and Thailand. In Thailand, the ratio sharply declined between 1992 and 1996, whereas in Malaysia the ratio increased. Thus, the comparison of the ratios indicates that the values of domestic banks were deteriorating in Korea and Thailand, whereas in Taiwan and Malaysia the values of domestic banks were improving. As with cross-border comparisons of NPLs, the cross-border comparisons of bank equity values should also be viewed with caution. Capital markets in many of these economies were still developing, whereas in Singapore they were much more mature, making comparisons across economies somewhat dubious. In addition, standards of loan classification, provisioning, and accounting varied widely, and it is not clear that market valuations of bank stocks took adequate account of these differences.

Postcrisis Increases in Money Supply Growth Rates

Currency crises in our model's equilibrium arise because the sudden increase in the public-sector budget deficit is monetized in the wake of a financial crisis. This should result in sharp postcrisis growth in money supply. Figure 11.5 depicts the ratio of narrow money to GDP. In Korea, there was sharp growth in the narrow money–GDP ratio in 1998. In Thailand, the growth in the ratio of narrow money to GDP was more muted, owing to the sterilization of government liquidity support to the banks. In Taiwan, Malaysia, and Singapore, the ratio of narrow money to GDP declined in 1998. The results are similar if we use the ratio of broad money to GDP.

The Decline in Loan Collateral Values and Crisis

Some models, but not ours, follow Kiyotaki and Moore (1997) and emphasize the role of credit constraints based on the value of collateral in precipitating a crisis under aggregate shocks. These models typically have multiple equilibria, and the decline in loan collateral values, especially real estate values, plays a key role in shifting the economy from a "good" equilibrium to a "bad" equilibrium, in which the crisis is self-fulfilling. Figure 11.6 plots the trend in real estate values. Only in Thailand have real estate prices begun to decline before the crisis. In Korea and in Malaysia, real estate values were constant or rising before the crisis; the real estate values in these two countries fell only after the crisis.[8] The decline in real estate prices after the crisis is consistent with any number of models of financial crises.

11.5 Conclusions

The case study comparisons support rather well the hypotheses and implied dynamics of the model of intermediation of foreign capital inflows by

---

8. Aghion, Bacchetta, and Banerjee (1999b) also introduce real estate prices in a crisis model with credit constraints. In their model, a collapse of the aggregate value of real estate plays an equilibrating role in the aftermath of crisis.

A

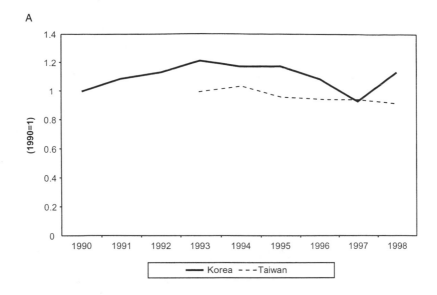

B

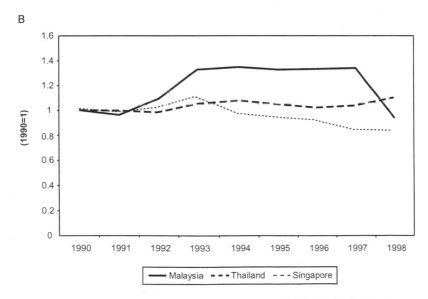

Figure 11.5   M1/GDP of *A*, Korea and Taiwan; and *B*, Malaysia, Thailand, and Singapore

Source: See appendix.

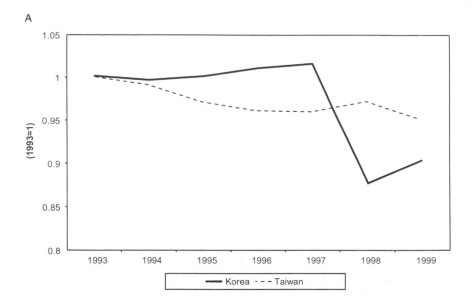

A

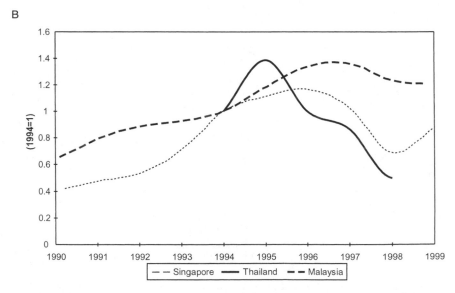

B

Figure 11.6   Real estate prices for *A*, Korea and Taiwan; and *B*, Malaysia, Thailand, and Singapore

Source: See appendix.

the domestic banking system under imperfect information. The pattern of prudential regulation, deposit insurance, foreign currency debt guarantees, and corporate reliance on bank credit in Korea and Thailand—two countries that suffered crisis most severely—matches the assumptions of the theory well. These institutional features of the economies of Taiwan and Singapore do not match the maintained hypotheses of the banking model and did not suffer either crisis or display many of the implied dynamics of the model. We also find significant differences in the time series for the ratios of nonperforming loans in bank portfolios and the relative stock market value of the banking sector between Korea and Thailand on the one side and Taiwan and Singapore on the other that are consistent with the theory.

The dynamic relationship between foreign capital inflows and bank lending from the model corresponds roughly to the differences across the crisis and noncrisis economies. The comparisons of the rate of return to assets for the cases studied do not clearly fit the model. However, the production side of the model economy is very simple and does not allow endogenous or exogenous changes in the technologies available to investors over time. It also does not determine how the average rate of return to capital changes with choices of investment projects; this is ambiguous in the absence of specific parameterization.

The empirical picture for Malaysia falls between that for Taiwan and Singapore and that for Korea and Thailand. The relationship between foreign capital inflows and bank lending fits Malaysia except under the imposition of capital controls; this supports the model's implications. The ratio of nonperforming loans rises, perhaps as the result of directed lending, whereas the value of bank shares rises in proportion to the market in the case of Malaysia. With respect to the institutional hypotheses, Malaysia is also an intermediate case. We might argue that this result is consistent with our hypotheses, although it may also support the alternative hypothesis that Malaysia suffered a loss of investor confidence, which led by association to a liquidity crisis.

Appendix
Data Sources for Figures
Figure 11.1

Bank lending: All countries except for Taiwan, "Claims on Private Sector by Private Money Banks" (from IMF *International Financial Statistics*). For Taiwan, "Claims on Private Sector by Private Money Banks" (from Central Bank of China web page). Capital inflows: All countries except for Taiwan, "Financial Account of Balance of Payments" (from IMF *Interna-*

tional Financial Statistics). For Taiwan, "Financial Account of Balance of Payments" (from Central Bank of China web page). Investment: All countries except for Taiwan, "Investment in the National Accounts" (from IMF *International Financial Statistics*). For Taiwan, "Investment in the National Accounts" (from Central Bank of China web page). GDP: All countries except for Taiwan, "GDP in the National Accounts" (from IMF *International Financial Statistics*). For Taiwan, "GDP in the National Accounts" (from Central Bank of China web page).

Figure 11.2

Reserves: All countries except for Taiwan, "Reserves" (from IMF *International Financial Statistics*). For Taiwan, "Reserves" (from Central Bank of China web page).

Short-term debt: All countries and provinces (from country central bank web pages).

Figure 11.3

Non-performing loan ratios of the banking sector: For Korea, "NPLs of Deposit Money Banks" (from Bank of Korea web page). For Taiwan, "NPLs of Deposit Money Banks" (from Central Bank of China, personal correspondence). For Thailand, "NPLs of Financial Institutions, Including Finance Companies" (from Bank of Thailand web page). For Malaysia, "NPLs of Financial Institutions, Including Finance Companies" (from Bank Negara Malaysia, personal correspondence). For Singapore, "NPLs of Financial Institutions" (from Monetary Authority of Singapore web page).

Figure 11.4

Stock market values of domestic banks and stock market values of entire domestic sector: For all countries and provinces (from Bloomburg Financial Services).

Figure 11.5

Money supplies: All countries except for Taiwan, "Narrow Money" (from IMF *International Financial Statistics*). For Taiwan, "Narrow Money" (from Central Bank of China web page).

Figure 11.6

Real estate values: For Korea (from *Social Indicators of Korea*). For Taiwan (from Government of Taiwan, private correspondence). For Thailand, Malaysia, and Singapore (from Bloomberg Financial Services).

References

Aghion, Philippe, Philippe Bacchetta, and Abhijit Banerjee. 1999a. Capital markets and the instability of open economies. CEPR Discussion Paper no. 2083. London: Center for Economic Policy Research, March.

————. 1999b. Financial liberalization and volatility in emerging market economies. In *The Asian financial crisis: Causes, contagion and consequences,* ed. P. R. Agenor, M. Miller, D. Vines, and A. Weber, 167–90. Cambridge: Cambridge University Press.

————. 2000. Currency crises and monetary policy in an economy with credit-constraints. CEPR Discussion Paper no. 2529. London: Centre for Economic Policy Research, August.

Barth, James R., Gerard Caprio, and Ross Levine. 2000. Banking systems around the globe. World Bank Development Research Group Working Paper no. 2325. Washington, D.C.: World Bank, April.

Bernanke, Benjamin, and Mark Gertler. 1989. Agency costs, net worth and business fluctuations. *American Economic Review* 79 (March): 14–31.

————. 1990. Financial fragility and economic performance. *Quarterly Journal of Economics* 105 (February): 87–114.

Bernanke, Benjamin, Mark Gertler, and Simon Gilchrist. 1999. The financial accelerator in a quantitative business cycle framework. In *Handbook of macroeconomics,* Vol. 1c, ed. John Taylor and Michael Woodford, 1341–93. Amsterdam: North-Holland.

Burnside, Craig, Martin Eichenbaum, and Sergio Rebelo. 1999. Hedging and financial fragility in fixed exchange rate regimes. NBER Working Paper no. 7143. Cambridge, Mass.: National Bureau of Economic Research, May.

Caballero, Ricardo, and Arvind Krishnamurthy. 1998. Emerging markets crises: An assets markets perspective. MIT, Department of Economics, Working Paper.

Calvo, Guillermo. 1998a. Balance-of-payments crises in emerging markets: Large capital inflows and sovereign governments. In *Currency crises,* ed. Paul Krugman, 71–104. Chicago: University of Chicago Press.

————. 1998b. Varieties of capital-market crises. In *The debt burden and its consequences for monetary policy,* ed. Guillermo Calvo and Mervyn King, 181–202. London: Macmillan.

Chang, Roberto, and Andres Velasco. 1999. Illiquidity and crises in emerging markets: Theory and policy. New York University, Department of Economics, Working Paper.

Chen, Tsaubin. 2000. The Taiwanese financial system at the time of the Asian crisis. University of Southern California, Department of Economics. Mimeograph.

Chinn, Menzie, and Kenneth Kletzer. 2000. International capital inflows, domestic financial intermediation, and financial crises under imperfect information. In *Emerging market crises,* ed. Reuven Glick, Ramon Moreno, and Mark Spiegel, 196–237. New York: Cambridge University Press.

Christiano, Lawrence, Chris Gust, and Jorge Roldos. 2000. Monetary policy in an international financial crisis. Paper presented at first annual International Monetary Fund research conference. 8 November, Washington, D.C.

Chu, Yun-Han. 1999. Surviving the East Asian financial storm: The political foundation of Taiwan's economic resilience. In *The politics of the Asian economic crisis,* ed. T. J. Pempel, 184–202. Ithaca: Cornell University Press.

Collins, Susan, and Won-Am Park. 1989. External debt and macroeconomic performance in South Korea. In *Developing country debt and economic performance,* ed. Susan Collins and Jeffrey Sachs, 151–369. Chicago: University of Chicago Press.

Corsetti, Giancarlo, Paolo Pesenti, and Nouriel Roubini, 1998a. Paper tigers? A preliminary assessment of the Asian crisis. NBER Working Paper no. 6783. Cambridge, Mass.: National Bureau of Economic Research, November.

———. 1998b. What caused the Asian currency and financial crisis? Part I: A macroeconomic overview. NBER Working Paper no. 6833. Cambridge, Mass.: National Bureau of Economic Research, December.

———. 1998c. What caused the Asian currency and financial crisis? Part II: Theory and policy responses. NBER Working Paper no. 6834, Cambridge, Mass.: National Bureau of Economic Research, December.

Dekle, Robert, and Angel Ubide. 1998. Korea: Financial sector development and reform. International Monetary Fund. Mimeograph.

Demirgüç-Kunt, Asli, and Enrica Detragiache. 2000. Does deposit insurance increase banking system stability? An empirical investigation. Paper presented at World Bank Development Research Group Deposit Insurance Conference. 16 April, Washington, D.C.

Diamond, Douglas. 1984. Financial intermediation and delegated monitoring. *Review of Economic Studies* 51:393–414.

Diamond, Douglas, and Phillip Dybvig. 1983. Bank runs, deposit insurance, and liquidity. *Journal of Political Economy* 91 (June): 401–19.

Diaz-Alejandro, Carlos. 1985. Good-bye financial repression, hello financial crash. *Journal of Development Economics* 19:1–24.

Dooley, Michael P. 2000. A model of crises in emerging markets. *Economic Journal* 110 (January): 256–72.

Edison, Hali, P. Luangarum, and Marcus Miller. 2000. Asset bubbles, "leverage and lifeboats." Elements of the East Asian crisis. *Economic Journal* 110:309–34.

Eichengreen, Barry, and Andrew K. Rose. 1998. Staying afloat when the wind shifts: External factors and emerging-market banking crises. NBER Working Paper no. 6370. Cambridge, Mass.: National Bureau of Economic Research, January.

Flood, Robert, and Peter Garber. 1984. Collapsing exchange rate regimes: Some linear examples. *Journal of International Economics* 17 (August): 1–13.

Freixas, Xavier, and Jean-Charles Rochet. 1997. *Microeconomics of banking.* Cambridge: MIT Press.

Furman, Jason, and Joseph Stiglitz. 1998. Economic crises: Evidence and insights from East Asia. *Brookings Papers on Economic Activity,* issue no. 2:1–115.

Goldfajn, Ilan, and Rodrigo Valdés. 1997. Capital flows and the twin crises: The role of liquidity. IMF Working Paper no. WP/97/87. Washington, D.C.: International Monetary Fund.

Haggard, Steven. 2000. *The political economy of the Asian Financial crisis.* Washington, D.C.: Institute for International Economics.

Holmstrom, Bengt, and Jean Tirole. 1997. Financial intermediation, loanable funds, and the real sector. *Quarterly Journal of Economics* 112 (August): 663–91.

International Monetary Fund (IMF). 1999a. Malaysia: Selected economic issues. International Monetary Fund. Mimeograph.

———. 1999b. Singapore: Selected economic issues. International Monetary Fund. Mimeograph.

———. 2000a. Singapore: Selected economic issues. International Monetary Fund. Mimeograph.

———. 2000b. Thailand: Selected economic issues. International Monetary Fund. Mimeograph.

Kiyotaki, Nobuhiro, and John Moore. 1997. Credit cycles. *Journal of Political Economy* 105:211–48.

Krugman, Paul. 1979. A model of balance-of-payments crises. *Journal of Money, Credit and Banking* 11 (August): 311–25.

———. 1999. Balance sheets, the transfer problem, and financial crises. In *International finance and financial crises: Essays in honor of Robert P. Flood,* ed. Peter Isard, Assaf Razin, and Andrew Rose, 459–72. Dordrecht, the Netherlands: Kluwer.

Kumhof, Michael. 1998. Balance of payments crises: The role of short-term debt. Stanford University, Department of Economics. Unpublished Manuscript.

Lindgren, Carl-Johan, Thomas Balino, Charles Enoch, and Anne-Marie Gulde. 2000. *Financial sector crisis and restructuring: Lessons from Asia.* Washington, D.C.: International Monetary Fund.

Mankiw, N. Gregory. 1986. The allocation of credit and financial collapse. *Quarterly Journal of Economics* 101:455–70.

McKinnon, Ronald, and Huw Pill. 1999. Credible liberalizations and international capital flows: The overborrowing syndrome. In *Financial deregulation and integration in East Asia,* ed. Takatoshi Ito and Anne O. Krueger, 7–50. Chicago: University of Chicago Press.

Mishkin, Frederic. 1996. Understanding financial crises: A developing country perspective. In *Annual World Bank Conference on Development Economics 1996,* ed. Michael Bruno and Boris Pleskovic, 29–62. Washington, D.C.: World Bank.

Moreno, Ramon. 1996. Intervention, sterilization, and monetary control in Korea and Taiwan. *Federal Reserve Bank of San Francisco Economic Review* 1996 (3): 23–33.

Obstfeld, Maurice. 1998. The global capital market: Benefactor or menace? *Journal of Economic Perspectives* 12:9–30.

Park, Yung Chul. 1994. Korea: Development and structural change of the financial system. In *The Financial Development of Japan, Korea, and Taiwan,* ed. Yung Chul Park and Hugh Patrick, 129–87. Oxford: Oxford University Press.

Pomerleano, Michael. 1998. The East Asian crisis and corporate finances: The untold micro story. World Bank Policy Research Working Paper no. 1990. Washington, D.C.: World Bank.

Pomerleano, Michael, and Xin Zhang. 1999. Corporate fundamentals and the behavior of capital markets in Asia. In *Financial markets and development,* ed. Alison Harwood, Robert Litan, and Michael Pomerleano, 117–57. Washington, D.C.: Brookings Institution.

Radelet, Stephen, and Jeffrey Sachs. 1998. The East Asian financial crisis: Diagnosis, remedies, prospects. *Brookings Papers on Economic Activity,* issue no. 1:1–90.

Rossi, Marco. 1999. Financial fragility and economic performance in developing countries: Do capital controls, prudential regulation, and supervision matter? IMF Working Paper no. WP/99/66. Washington, D.C.: International Monetary Fund.

Sachs, Jeffrey, Aaron Tornell, and Andres Velasco. 1996. Financial crises in emerging markets: The lessons from 1995. *Brookings Papers on Economic Activity,* Issue no. 1:147–215.

Scott, Kenneth. 1999. Corporate governance and East Asia: Korea, Indonesia, Malaysia, and Thailand. In *Financial markets and development,* ed. Alison Harwood, Robert Litan, and Michael Pomerleano, 172–98. Washington, D.C.: Brookings Institution.

Shea, Jia-Dong. 1994. Taiwan: Development and structural change of the financial system. In *The financial development of Japan, Korea, and Taiwan,* ed. Yung Chul Park and Hugh Patrick, 222–87. Oxford: Oxford University Press.

Spiegel, Mark M. 1995. Sterilization of capital inflows through the banking sector: Evidence from Asia. Federal Reserve Bank of San Francisco. Unpublished Manuscript.

Stiglitz, Joseph, and Andrew Weiss. 1981. Credit rationing in markets with imperfect information. *American Economic Review* 71:393–410.

Velasco, Andrés. 1987. Financial crises and balance of payments crises: A simple model of the Southern Cone experience. *Journal of Development Economics* 27: 263–83.

Yang, Ya-Hwei. 1994. Taiwan: Development and structural change of the banking system. In *The financial development of Japan, Korea, and Taiwan,* ed. Yung Chul Park and Hugh Patrick, 228–324. Oxford: Oxford University Press.

Comment   Paolo Pesenti

In contrast to many other branches of international economics, the literature on currency attacks and financial meltdown cannot quite rely, at least not for the time being, on a "neoclassical" theoretical core—that is, on a widely accepted, formally elegant paradigm linking pervasive normative implications to rigorous behavioral microfoundations. However, in the absence of a neoclassical synthesis, the model of currency and financial crises that is rapidly emerging as the focal point in the recent body of research on causes and implications of market turbulence can be appropriately labeled "neo-Alexandrian," or, better, "neo-Alejandrian." The "Alejandro" here is, of course, Carlos Diaz-Alejandro, author of, among many other things, the classic article "Good-Bye Financial Repression, Hello Financial Crash." That article may well represent the mother of all papers on twin crises, judging from the number of "third-generation" models that continue to build directly or indirectly on its insights fifteen years (and counting) since its publication. The chapter by Dekle and Kletzer in this volume is a highly enjoyable contribution to such "neo-Alejandrian" paradigm, and a very fine one.

Substantially, the "neo-Alejandrian" paradigm relies on three building blocks. The first is the overborrowing/overlending/overinvestment syndrome—that is, the role of lending booms in the buildup of a financial turmoil. The idea is that, to the extent that domestic and foreign creditors are willing to lend against future bailout revenue, unprofitable projects, excessively risky investments, and cash shortfalls continue to be refinanced and rolled over. In the case of foreign borrowing and evergreening, this translates into an unsustainable path of current account deficits.

Underlying the previous syndrome is the second key ingredient of the "neo-Alejandrian" construction, namely public guarantees (explicit, implicit, or simply presumed) and expected bailouts. Agents act under the pre-

Paolo Pesenti is research officer at the Federal Reserve Bank of New York and a faculty research fellow of the National Bureau of Economic Research.

The views expressed here are those of the author and do not necessarily reflect those of the Federal Reserve Bank of New York, the Federal Reserve System, or any other institution with which the author is affiliated.

sumption that corporate and financial investment is guaranteed, so that the return on assets is implicitly insured against bad shocks. To quote Diaz-Alejandro directly, "whether or not depositors are explicitly insured, the public expects governments to intervene to save most depositors from losses when financial intermediaries run into trouble. Warnings that intervention will not be forthcoming appear to be simply not believable" (Diaz-Alejandro 1985, 13). In other words, a time consistency problem is at work here, as the government cannot commit credibly to a laissez-faire stance.

The third element is contingent liabilities. Public deficits may not be high before a crisis, but when the government steps in and guarantees the stock of private liabilities, it must undertake the appropriate fiscal reforms. If these involve recourse to seigniorage revenue and money creation, expectations of inflationary financing may lead to speculation in the currency market. If the central bank intervenes to stabilize the domestic currency, it loses reserves that could otherwise be used to bail out insolvent private institutions, and vice versa. Thus results the parallel phenomenon of currency and banking crises.

Many authors, several of whom are represented in this volume or quoted in the Dekle and Kletzer chapter, have contributed to the elaboration and refinement of the "neo-Alejandrian" framework for policy analysis and evaluation, especially in relation to the Asian crisis. Of course, recent interpretations of crisis episodes have highlighted the role of several factors, ranging from self-validating panics to magnification effects related to "financial accelerator" mechanisms and liquidity constraints, to institutional characteristics, to the strategies of large players and highly leveraged institutions, and so on. Still, it remains true that the building blocks of the "neo-Alejandrian" approach are recurrent themes in the vast majority of recent contributions and analyses of turmoil episodes, perhaps providing the minimum common denominator that underlies the formation of a consensus view of emerging-market crises.

With this in mind, what is new in the chapter by Dekle and Kletzer? Arguably, the value of the paper is the abundance of detail rather than the originality of vision. Thanks to a clever modeling strategy in which only idiosyncratic shocks matter, the role of macroeconomic shocks is deemphasized, and corporate governance, institutional characteristics, and prudential regulations and enforcement are brought center stage, the authors are able to articulate a set of close comparisons between theoretical assumptions and predictions and the empirical evidence for the Asian countries. For most scholars and analysts, this exemplary overview will represent the most appealing aspect of the chapter.

On the theoretical side, especially convincing is the way the authors model the links between financial intermediaries and the corporate sector, providing the foundations for an analysis of twin crises whose occurrence can be foretold (and therefore prevented). Briefly, the authors set up their analysis by focusing on households (and firm owners) whose only form of financial diversification is through bank deposits. Banks are able to monitor firms' performance and diversify risk by lending to many firms. A firm finances capital with bank loans. Profitability is stochastic. When things go badly, the entire capital of the firm goes to the bank. The bank can declare the firm bankrupt, but this would not be the best course of action. Rather, the bank that now has monopoly power can renegotiate the loan, at a premium.

If the bank rolls over the existing loan, the firm has an incentive to undertake riskier projects (it has no capital, has limited liability, and pays an interest premium). Ultimately, the bank's portfolio becomes riskier over time, raising the contingent liabilities of the deposit insurer. If banks can borrow from foreign intermediaries and there are limited government guarantees on their foreign exposure (including schemes of fixed exchange rate) but prudential regulation is not in place, the rollover/evergreening game can continue until the government reaches its limit on the indemnity liability. The rest of the story is well known: A twin currency and banking crisis occurs when foreign loans are pulled from the banking system, forcing the government to step in and finance its bailouts through taxes, inflation, and depreciation.

One aspect of the model that may warrant deeper investigation in the future is the welfare analysis of a twin crisis and its determinants. Indeed, similar remarks may apply to virtually the entire spectrum of "third-generation" theories, which are much more focused on the dynamics and the mechanism of a crisis than on its costs and benefits. We understand quite well what guarantees do and what role they play in the buildup of an unsustainable lending boom. What we still do not quite understand is why guarantees, implicit or explicit, are extended in the first place (even when there is a good story to explain their presence, the literature has been agnostic on why they work in some cases but not in others). It remains rather unclear why exchange rates are pegged in this type of model, given that nobody gains anything by limiting exchange rate flexibility. The typical answer is that fixed rates are a form of implicit guarantee, but this does not solve the problem. It simply reintroduces the previous question of why there are guarantees in the first place. The authors are well aware of the limits of their interpretive framework and openly admit they are "interested in the consequences of a fixed exchange rate regime with an explicit or implicit government guarantee of the foreign liabilities of the banking sector in the event of a switch to a float, and not the welfare economics of this policy." It is easy to predict that, for the next generation of contributions to the "neo-Alejandrian" paradigm, the latter will be a natural starting point.

References

Diaz-Alejandro, Carlos F. 1985. Good-bye financial repression, hello financial crash. *Journal of Development Economics* 19 (1–2): 1–24.

Discussion Summary

Sebastian Edwards made two comments. First, he said that it was appropriate to bring to the discussion Carlos Diaz-Alejandro's work "Goodbye Financial Repression, Hello Financial Crash," published in the *Journal of Development Economics* in 1985. That paper was a reflection of the Southern corn debt crises of 1982, but it had been completely ignored until now except for one follow-up by a graduate student at Columbia University, Andrés Velasco. Velasco did the mathematics of the Diaz-Alejandro paper and also published in the *Journal of Development Economics,* and his work was also ignored. Edwards also said that a similar narrative on the Southern corn crises appeared in the special issue of the *Economic Development and Culture Change* in 1985 following a meeting on the crisis. It discussed the devastation of the crises in Latin American countries. Those crises, especially the Chilean crisis, were really the first crises of the twenty-first century, because there were no fiscal deficits or speculative crises in the Krugman style, but the banking system was involved and devastated, and there were government guarantees. Edwards concluded by emphasizing our remarkable ability to ignore and repeat history. He said that it is important to emphasize this point in this crisis prevention conference and remind everyone that we bear the responsibility of preventing newly discovered things—which may not even be mistaken for new if one looks at history carefully—from being ignored again.

Second, Edwards pointed out that a similar exercise of counting how many "negative" marks countries get as a way to predict crises was performed by Goldman and Sachs before the Asian crises. Goldman and Sachs computed the so-called Short-Term Indicator of Monetary Pressure (STIMP) of twenty-eight emerging markets, in which the maximum number of negatives a country could receive was eighteen and the cutoff number for crises was thirteen. Before the Asian crises, Korea received fourteen negatives, but in their report Goldman and Sachs predicted no crisis for Korea. When challenged to provide an explanation for violating the rule, Goldman and Sachs referred to the capital controls in place in Korea, but they did not realize that the controls were not of the right type and that they might not be working.

Jeffrey A. Frankel said that Michael Dooley's early work needs to be mentioned in the literature review of the third-generation crisis models (models in which implicit bailout creates moral hazard).

Martin Feldstein commented on the implementation issue. He said that we all agree with the conclusion that financial supervision and prudential regulation play an important role in enhancing financial stability. However, the question for developing countries is how to carry out these suggestions without having experts in these fields. In these developing countries, bank lending was not true bank lending for a long time; it was a government activity channeled through something called "banks" on behalf of the Ministry of Finance. For example, Korea has not figured out what to do next after nationalizing all the banks, and Thailand, with no tradition in banking, is still wondering how to make the system work.

Jorge Braga de Macedo suggested making direct comparisons between countries when discussing the roles of structural reforms. For example, the effect of financial supervision could be seen clearly by comparing Korea (where there was no enforcement) and Taiwan (where there was enforcement). Braga de Macedo also suggested comparing countries in good times in addition to crisis periods. Second, Braga de Macedo remarked that there are also differences in corporate structure behind differences in financial supervision. For example, he said, the laws are far more protective of small and medium-sized enterprises in Taiwan than in Korea, where small business were discouraged until very recently.

Linda S. Goldberg made the comment that the issue is probably not whether there should be capital account openness, but whether there should be financial-sector openness. For countries with small financial systems, she said that the debate is whether they should have their own banking sector and to what degree or give up their own banking supervision entirely (as New Zealand did) and have another country run their systems.

Giancarlo Corsetti commended the paper for solving a model with both time inconsistency and a macro shock. He suggested that the author emphasize that the exogenous timing of crises in the paper is a simplification and could be endogenized with an endogenous credit constraint. (This problem is discussed by Corsetti and his co-authors in several papers.)

Liliana Rojas-Suarez said that she disagreed with the pessimistic view about improvements in regulation and supervision in Asia. She said that the world experience shows that most serious reforms of banking regulation and supervision have occurred as a response to severe crises. Indeed, one can say that there are very limited exceptions to the observation that crises have preceded the implementation of good supervision. The reason is that crises bring about the necessary political will to undertake reforms. This was certainly true in Chile, Mexico, Argentina, the United States, the Nordic countries, and now Asia. In all these cases, crisis resolution implied not only a significant reduction in the number of financial institutions but also the implementation of effective entry and exit rules from the banking system. She therefore holds an optimistic view of the reform process in Asia.

Charles W. Calomiris said that there is a large and growing literature related to the paper. For example, the World Bank has a micro-level data set in which countries' regulatory systems are characterized in the same way as in the paper, simply with more dimensions and better standards for characterization. He said that many papers have used this data set and have found strong evidence on whether designed features of governmental protection produced risk-taking and in turn affected macroeconomic stability. Calomiris also said that there was a literature studying what banking systems were like prior to the creation of safety nets using micro data, which found that during the second period of renegotiation there was a contraction in lending—even in the United States, during its early developing stage. Calomiris suggested that the authors include these findings as supportive evidence to their theory.

Another comment by Calomiris concerned the nonperforming loan data, which, he said, are not uniform across countries and are subject to flaws. Lastly, Calomiris made the remark that people who had paid attention to the financial sector knew in advance that the Asian crisis was coming.

Simon Johnson suggested including the ownership of banks—in particular, the linkage between banks and firms—in the analysis. He said that the corporate set of issues was not addressed in the paper, and it was worth thinking about how to incorporate it.

Robert Dekle said that it is endogenous that Taiwan has good supervision. Taiwan is not a member of an international financial institution; therefore, it has strong incentives to develop a good bank supervisory system. For example, its central bank could resist the pressure from the Ministry of Finance and politicians to extend loans given their overarching national security type of protection. Dekle also said that he and Kletzer did not study the Indonesian case because their model was motivated by the Korean example.

Kenneth Kletzer appreciated the suggestion that the timing of the crisis could be endogenized and was treated as exogenous in the model only for simplicity's sake.

The authors noted that they were pleased that Sebastian Edwards appreciated that their paper was motivated by Carlos Diaz-Alejandro's paper, and in response to Jeffrey A. Frankel noted that they did refer to Michael P. Dooley's papers on financial crises.

Dollarization of Liabilities, Net Worth Effects, and Optimal Monetary Policy

Luis Felipe Céspedes, Roberto Chang, and
Andrés Velasco

12.1 Introduction

Recent crises in emerging markets have caused the profession to reevaluate received wisdom about exchange rate regimes. In particular, analysis of the connection between imperfections in the financial sector and exchange rate policy has risen to the top of the research agenda.[1] There are strong reasons for this focus. Both casual observation and formal econometric analysis[2] suggest the existence of an empirical link between financial turmoil and currency crashes. Moreover, the question of whether central banks should defend their currencies against a speculative attack has emerged as a key and controversial aspect of the policy response, and this choice is increasingly governed by possible effects on the financial sector. Some analysts, such as Furman and Stiglitz (1998) and Radelet and Sachs (2000), have called for monetary expansion and depreciation in response to adverse shocks, reaffirming the validity of prescriptions derived from the conventional Mundell-Fleming analysis. Others, such as Calvo (2000), Dornbusch (1999), and Hausmann et al. (1999), have argued that in the presence of sizable dollar debts a sudden depreciation may do more harm than good.

In a previous paper (Céspedes, Chang, and Velasco 2000, henceforth

Luis Felipe Céspedes is an economist in the research department of the International Monetary Fund. Roberto Chang is associate professor of economics at Rutgers University. Andrés Velasco is Sumitomo Professor of International Finance and Development at the Kennedy School of Government, Harvard University.

The authors are grateful to Nouriel Roubini and conference participants for useful comments and discussion and to Paul Söderlind and Lars Svensson for Gauss programs. Of course, any errors or shortcomings are the authors' alone.

1. See Chang and Velasco (2000) for a detailed discussion of recent developments on this front.
2. The standard reference is Kaminsky and Reinhart (1999).

CCV) we made an attempt to identify the role of financial imperfections in the design of exchange rate policy within a dynamic stochastic model with explicit microfoundations. CCV's model focuses on a small open economy that borrows in the world market to finance investment. Crucially, information frictions imply that the economy's borrowing, and hence aggregate demand, is constrained by its net worth, as emphasized by Bernanke and Gertler (1989). Exchange rate behavior may then exacerbate net worth effects because domestic residents borrow in foreign currency, whereas domestic income depends on the value of domestic money; or, in Calvo's (1999) parlance, the economy's liabilities are dollarized. In such a scenario a devaluation exerts, in addition to its conventional effects, a contractionary effect hitherto ignored in conventional literature. By weakening the economy's balance sheet, a devaluation exacerbates the effect of financial frictions, pushing down aggregate demand, output, and employment.

CCV's analysis yields at least two suggestions for the theory of exchange rate regimes. First, under reasonable parameter values, the coexistence of a net worth channel and liability dollarization may well imply a potentially contractionary channel of devaluation. Second, and somewhat surprisingly, the existence of such a channel does not justify defending the exchange rate against exogenous shocks, particularly real shocks from abroad. The reason is that adjustment to an exogenous shock requires a *real* devaluation, which will take place regardless of nominal exchange rate behavior; and it is real, not nominal, devaluation that determines the net worth effect. Hence, the unwanted effect of real devaluation on balance sheets will take place one way or the other, and exchange rate policy can only affect the manner and timing of the adjustment. In fact, under CCV's assumptions, fixed exchange rates emerge as being more contractionary than flexible rates, since the former imply that a real devaluation can only take place via price deflation, which, if nominal wages are rigid, exacerbates the contraction in employment and output.

To obtain analytically tractable closed-form solutions, in CCV we imposed very strong and simple assumptions about monetary policy. We compared a completely fixed exchange rate regime against a flexible rate regime that kept the price level fixed. Such a focus left unanswered the question of what is the optimal exchange rate regime in the presence of balance sheet effects and liability dollarization. That question can only be answered by specifying a social loss function and computing the optimal policy function under alternative shocks.

A related issue is that of credibility of policy—that is, ensuring that the monetary authority will not want to renege on an ongoing date- and state-contingent plan for the setting of its instruments. Optimal policy is meaningless unless it is also credible; this means that, in the absence of commitment devices, the relevant optimal policy is that computed under discretion. On the other hand, it is often argued that fixed exchange rates enjoy the advantage of serving as a commitment device. This is relevant insofar as our result in CCV—that price-targeting rules are superior in welfare terms to exchange rate–targeting rules—could be meaningless if the latter are for some reason more credible than the former. The appropriate comparison then would be that of a fixed exchange rate regime against a credible (discretionary) policy of flexible rates.

The purpose of the present paper is to shed light on these questions. We study the determination of the optimal monetary and exchange rate policy with and without commitment and compare its implications (including welfare implications) to those of fixed exchange rates. Since it is key to confront these questions in the presence of financial imperfections, our framework is a version of the CCV model, extended to introduce money demand explicitly and to allow for staggered nominal wage-setting in the style of Calvo (1983).

To characterize optimal policy we assume that the central bank minimizes social loss, which is taken to be a function of income, inflation, and possibly real exchange rates. We compute the optimal policy with commitment, so that the monetary authority decides at the start of all time on the optimal policy path. More importantly, we also compute optimal policy under discretion, allowing the central bank to reoptimize and choose current policy at every point along the way. Under discretion and assuming rational expectations, market behavior must be consistent with future central bank strategy, which itself responds to market behavior. The outcomes of this interaction are given by the time-consistent equilibrium of the model, defined as in Oudiz and Sachs (1985) and Svensson (2000).

Under discretion, we consider three possibilities: the benchmark *flexible inflation targeting,* in which inflation and output fluctuations matter for social loss; *strict inflation targeting,* in which social loss depends only on inflation; and *flexible inflation–cum–real exchange rate targeting,* in which real exchange rate fluctuations are also present in the social loss function. We study the dynamic outcomes under the three discretionary regimes as well as under fixed exchange rates. Finally, we compare the social loss under commitment to the social loss under each discretionary regime and against the loss under fixed rates.

A main finding is that when the policy maker engages in flexible inflation targeting, whether under commitment or discretion, monetary policy relies on large changes in nominal and real exchange rates to deal with foreign shocks, a result that is similar to that obtained by Svensson (2000) in a very different model. Exchange rate flexibility is effective in stabilizing output fluctuations in our model, in spite of the presence of balance sheet effects and liability dollarization, and optimal policy exploits that effectiveness.

A second result is that fixed rates imply a loss not only larger than that of optimal policy under commitment, but also larger than each of the three discretionary regimes. The gains in output stabilization outweigh the losses from higher wage inflation. Hence, our model simulations provide no support for those who argue that, although an idealized floating regime might be desirable, real-life floating under discretion (and the attendant higher inflation) renders a simple fix superior in terms of welfare.

The quantitative results of the paper are also useful in assessing the validity of some commonly made claims about why emerging market countries "float the way they do," raising nominal interest rates in response to adverse shocks and apparently engaging in procyclical monetary policy (see Calvo 2000; Calvo and Reinhart 2002; and Hausmann et al. 1999). We find below that in a policy of pure fixing, the required nominal rate increase is smaller when responding to adverse export and foreign interest rate shock than under discretion and flexible inflation targeting. A short-sighted analysis would interpret this as evidence of fear of floating. However, that interpretation is wrong for two reasons. First, inflation is higher under floating, and hence the nominal rate is an uninformative indicator of the policy stance. Indeed, correcting for expected inflation reveals an expansionary, not deflationary, interest rate policy under flexible inflation targeting. Second, the optimal policy rule[3] also adjusts the home interest rate down whenever investment is below its steady-state level. Since investment falls persistently after a bad shock from abroad, the initial rise in the nominal rate is typically very short-lived and often does not extend beyond an initial impact period. In short, highly variable nominal interest rates, or nominal rates that rise when adverse shocks hit, are not an indication of fear of floating.

The paper is organized as follows. Section 12.2 describes the economic environment. Section 12.3 computes benchmark optimal policy under discretion. Perfect commitment and fixed exchange rates are discussed and compared with the discretionary, flexible rate cases in section 12.4. Section 12.5 studies alternative specifications of the central bank objective function, and section 12.6 concludes.

12.2 The Model

As already mentioned, our basic environment is taken from CCV, extended to explicitly include money demand and to allow for overlapping wage contracts of the Calvo (1983) type. For the sake of brevity, here we only sketch the main aspects of the model and describe the two extensions just mentioned. For a more detailed exposition, the interested reader is referred to CCV.

We focus on a small open economy that produces a single good using domestic labor and domestic capital. These two factors of production are owned by distinct agents called workers and capitalists. Workers consume

---

3. Again under discretion and flexible inflation targeting.

and capitalists invest an aggregate of the home good and a single imported good. For simplicity, capitalists are assumed to consume only imports.

A crucial aspect of the model is that capitalists can invest in excess of their own net worth by borrowing abroad, but, because of informational asymmetries, the cost of borrowing exceeds the world interest rate and depends on the ratio of net worth to investment. Hence, the model features balance sheet effects of the kind stressed by Bernanke and Gertler (1989) that may be quantitatively important.

12.2.1   Domestic Production

The home good is produced by competitive firms with a common Cobb-Douglas technology that, in the neighborhood of the steady state, can be written as

$$(1) \qquad\qquad y_t = \alpha k_t + (1-\alpha)l_t, \qquad 0 < \alpha < 1.$$

Here and in the rest of the paper, lowercase letters (except when noted) denote percentage deviations of the corresponding uppercase variables from their nonstochastic steady-state levels;[4] for instance, if Y_t denotes the level of output in period t and Y its steady state level, $y_t = (Y_t - Y)/Y$. Hence equation (1) is simply a log-linear version of the production function $Y_t = AK_t^\alpha L_t^{1-\alpha}$, where K_t and L_t denote capital and labor inputs in period t.

As in Obstfeld and Rogoff (2000), workers are heterogeneous. Correspondingly, L_t is assumed to be a constant elasticity of substitution (CES) aggregate of the services of the different home workers, and the market for labor exhibits monopolistic competition as in Dixit and Stiglitz (1977). The representative firm, however, takes all prices as given and chooses output and factor demands to maximize profits in every period. The main implication is that, in equilibrium, factor prices must equal marginal productivities, which (in percentage deviations from steady state) can be expressed as

$$(2) \qquad\qquad r_t - p_t = y_t - k_t,$$

$$(3) \qquad\qquad w_t - p_t = y_t - l_t,$$

where p_t denotes the price of the home good, r_t the rental rate of capital, and w_t the aggregate wage (that is, W_t is the minimum cost of obtaining a unit of L_t), all expressed in terms of the domestic currency (the peso).

The solution to the representative firm's problem also implies a downward-sloping demand curve for each worker's labor. Such a demand schedule is described later, when we discuss workers and the maximization problem they face. Finally, firm profits are zero in equilibrium.

---

4. See CCV for a proof of the existence and uniqueness of the steady state.

12.2.2   Capitalists

Capitalists finance investment with their own net worth and with foreign loans. However, because of informational asymmetries, foreign borrowing is subject to agency costs of the kind emphasized by Bernanke and Gertler (1989). This is the key ingredient for the model to feature balance sheet effects.

In every period, capitalists must invest for next period's capital, which is assumed to be a Cobb Douglas aggregate of home goods and imports. Imports have a fixed price in terms of a world currency, called the dollar. The law of one price holds and implies that the peso price of imports is equal to the nominal exchange rate. The implication is that the peso price of capital satisfies

$$(4) \qquad\qquad q_t = \gamma p_t + (1 - \gamma)s_t,$$

where γ is the share of home goods in the Cobb Douglas aggregator and s_t is the nominal exchange rate.

To finance investment, capitalists use their net worth and also borrow from a world capital market in which the safe interest rate for dollars between t and $t + 1$ is random but known at t. However, the cost of borrowing abroad will be higher than the world interest rate because of informational problems. We follow Bernanke, Gertler, and Gilchrist (1999) and assume that the yield on investment is subject to idiosyncratic shocks that can be monitored by lenders only at a positive cost. This results in a costly state verification problem as in Townsend (1979) and Williamson (1987). The optimal contract to deal with this problem implies that there will be a divergence between the expected return on investment and the world interest rate, which can be written as

$$(5) \qquad \eta_{t+1} = [_t(r_{t+1} + k_{t+1} - s_{t+1}) - (q_t + k_{t+1} - s_t)] - \rho_t.$$

For any variable z_{t+j}, the expression $_t z_{t+j}$ will denote the expectation of z_{t+j} conditional on period t information. Hence, in the right-hand side of equation (5), the term in square brackets is the expected dollar return on capital, given by the (log) difference between the dollar revenue from capital investment and the dollar cost of the investment. On the other hand, ρ_t is the world interest rate on dollar loans between t and $(t + 1)$, expressed as a difference from its steady state value. Thus, η_{t+1} represents the agency costs associated with external finance or, for short, a risk premium.

In turn, the optimal contract implies that

$$(6) \qquad \eta_{t+1} = \mu(q_t + k_{t+1} - p_t - n_t),$$

where (close to the steady state) μ is a positive constant, and n_t is the capitalist's net worth, expressed in terms of home goods. In words, equation (6) says that the risk premium is higher the larger the value of investment relative to net worth.

That investment is financed via foreign loans and net worth implies that

$$(7) \qquad q_t + k_{t+1} = \omega(s_t + d_{t+1}) + (1 - \omega)(p_t + n_t),$$

where d_{t+1} is the amount borrowed at t and due for repayment at $(t + 1)$, and ω is the steady-state ratio of foreign borrowing to the dollar value of investment.

Next we describe the evolution of net worth. At the beginning of each period, capitalists collect the income from capital and settle their foreign debts. Then, a fraction $(1 - \delta)$ of the capitalist population dies and is replaced by new capitalists. The dying capitalists consume their wealth; to simplify, we assume that they only consume imports. Consequently, n_t is the aggregate net worth of the surviving capitalists, and its evolution is given by

$$(8) \qquad n_t = \chi(r_t + k_t - p_t) - (1 - \chi)(\rho_{t-1} + s_t - p_t + d_t) - \zeta\eta_t$$
$$= \chi y_t - (1 - \chi)(\rho_{t-1} + s_t - p_t + d_t) - \zeta\eta_t,$$

where χ and ζ are positive constants that depend on the steady state. Intuitively, net worth increases with capital income and falls with debt repayments due at t. In addition, the term $\zeta\eta_t$ captures the fact that agency costs, which are directly related to the risk premium, raise the cost of servicing the debt due at t, and hence reduce net worth.

The second line of equation (8) implies that, ceteris paribus, a *real* devaluation of the peso (an increase in $s_t - p_t$) reduces net worth by increasing the relative burden of debt due at t. This is the crucial aspect of the model in CCV and implies that, in contrast with conventional analysis, a devaluation may have contractionary effects.

12.2.3   Workers

As mentioned earlier, labor services provided by individual workers are imperfect substitutes of each other. Consequently, each worker enjoys some monopoly power over the services he provides and, as in CCV, the labor market is monopolistically competitive, as in Dixit and Stiglitz (1977). We depart from CCV here by assuming that, as in Calvo (1983), only a random subset of the workers can set a new nominal wage each period. Moreover, we model money demand explicitly, which is useful to allow for different specifications of monetary policy. Because of these changes, we will be more detailed in our discussion of workers than in the rest of the model.

Workers are indexed by $i \in [0, 1]$, and worker i's preferences are given by the expectation of

$$(9) \qquad \sum_{t=0}^{\infty} \beta^t \left[\log C_{it} - \left(\frac{\sigma - 1}{\sigma} \right) \left(\frac{1}{\nu} \right) L_{it}^\nu + \left(\frac{1}{1 - \phi} \right) \left(\frac{M_{it}}{Q_t} \right)^{1-\phi} \right].$$

In this expression C_{it} is an aggregate of home goods and imports; note that for simplicity we assume the same Cobb Douglas aggregator as the one relevant for investment, which implies that the peso price of consumption is Q_t. The variable L_{it} denotes i's supply of labor and M_{it} his peso holdings at the end of period t. Hence equation (9) simply says that worker i enjoys consumption and money holdings, and dislikes working.

Worker i's choices include what to consume, how much to charge for the labor he supplies, and how many pesos to hold. In addition, each worker will hold a portfolio of securities, as will be described shortly. His constraints are of three types. First, he faces a downward demand curve for his labor services:

$$(10) \qquad L_{it} = \left(\frac{W_{it}}{W_t}\right)^{-\sigma} L_t,$$

where W_{it} is the peso price of i's labor services, that is, i's wage rate. As in Dixit and Stiglitz (1977), the worker is small enough so that he takes the evolution of W_t and L_t as given.

The second constraint is that, as in Calvo (1983), worker i sets wages in pesos, and he can change his wage in period t only with some probability $(1 - \theta)$. Hence, with probability θ, his nominal wage must be the same as in the previous period, and it is assumed that he must satisfy any demand forthcoming (as given by eq. [10])[5] at that wage.

Third, worker i is restricted by his budget constraint. Note that, because different workers change wages at different times, workers are subject to idiosyncratic uncertainty. We assume that workers cannot borrow from abroad to smooth such uncertainty. However, and following Woodford (1996), we assume that workers can trade enough contingent securities among themselves to, in effect, insure completely against idiosyncratic shocks. This implies that the flow budget constraint of worker i can be written as

$$(11) \qquad Q_t C_{it} + M_{it} + {}_t(\Delta_{t,t+1} H_{i,t+1}) = W_{it} L_{it} + M_{i,t-1} + H_{it} + T_t,$$

where T_t is a peso transfer from the government; H_{it} is the peso value, at t, of the portfolio of contingent securities chosen at $(t-1)$; and $\Delta_{t,s}$ is the *pricing kernel,* such that the value at t of a portfolio delivering the random payoff H_s in period $s > t$ is ${}_t(\Delta_{t,s} H_s)$.

As discussed by Woodford (1996), under our assumptions (together with a technical assumption to rule out Ponzi games), the budget constraint can be written in present value form. Assuming, in addition, that workers have identical initial wealth, it follows that they will completely

5. More precisely, the worker will provide labor elastically as long as the real wage is no smaller than the marginal disutility of working; beyond that, labor would be rationed. In what follows we assume that we are always in the nonrationing range. This can be ensured by considering exogenous shocks that are not "too large."

pool their idiosyncratic risk and choose identical consumption plans and peso holdings.

One consequence is that the pricing kernel is given by the marginal rate of substitution between consumption at different dates and states

$$\Delta_{t,s} = \beta^{s-t} \frac{Q_t C_t}{Q_s C_s},$$

where C_t denotes the consumption level common to all workers in period t. This implies, in particular, that the nominal interest rate at t, which we denote by i'_t, must satisfy

(12) $$\frac{1}{1 + i'_t} = {}_t\Delta_{t,t+1} = \beta_t \left(\frac{Q_t C_t}{Q_{t+1} C_{t+1}} \right),$$

as the inverse of $(1 + i'_t)$ is the price at t of a sure peso at $t + 1$.

Another consequence is that peso demand is given by

(13) $$\left(\frac{M_t}{Q_t} \right)^{-\phi} = \left(\frac{1}{C_t} \right) \frac{i'_t}{1 + i'_t},$$

which has the familiar interpretation that the marginal rate of substitution between money balances and consumption must equal its relative cost.

We assume that pesos are held only by workers and that the lump-sum transfer T_t is the only way in which pesos are introduced in the economy. Hence, the supply of pesos satisfies $M_t = M_{t-1} + T_t$. Then, adding up equation (11) over i, and recognizing the fact that the net supply of contingent securities is zero, implies that

(14) $$Q_t C_t - W_t L_t.$$

In other words, the value of workers' consumption in every period must equal the aggregate wage bill.

Note that, log-linearizing equations (12) and (14) around the steady state, and using equation (3), the deviation of i'_t from its steady-state level can be written as

(15) $$i_t = {}_t y_{t+1} - y_t + ({}_t p_{t+1} - p_t),$$

which is an equation of the Fischer type.

Finally, worker i must decide what wage to set in period t, assuming he is allowed to. This is a tedious problem and is discussed at length by Woodford (1996). The upshot is that the evolution of the aggregate wage is given by

(16) $$w_t - w_{t-1} = \left[\frac{1 - \beta\theta}{1 + \sigma(\nu - 1)} \right] \left[\frac{\nu(1 - \theta)}{\theta} \right] l_t + \beta ({}_t w_{t+1} - w_t).$$

This is a wage Phillips curve: wage inflation increases with expected future wage inflation as well as with labor employment. Intuitively, the reaction of the current aggregate wage to labor demand pressure is faster if nominal wages are less rigid, as given by a smaller θ.

12.2.4 Competitive Equilibrium

To define equilibrium it remains to impose market clearing for home goods. Under our assumptions, domestic expenditure in home goods is a fixed fraction of final home expenditures. In addition, the home good can be sold to foreigners. As in Krugman (1999) and CCV, we assume that the value of home exports in dollars is exogenous. Clearing of the market for home goods then implies

$$(17) \qquad p_t + y_t = \lambda(q_t + k_{t+1}) + (1 - \lambda)(s_t + x_t).$$

We must finally specify the stochastic processes driving the exogenous variables. Dollar exports are given by a first-order autoregression process

$$(18) \qquad x_t = a_x x_{t-1} + \varepsilon_t^x,$$

where a_x is between zero and 1, and ε_t^x is white noise. Assume also that the world interest rate follows an AR(1) process

$$(19) \qquad \rho_t = a_\rho \rho_{t-1} + \varepsilon_t^\rho,$$

where again a_ρ is between zero and 1, and ε_t^ρ is white noise.

This completes the description of the economic environment. Once monetary policy is specified, the system of equations (1) through (8) and (15) through (19) suffices to determine the dynamic behavior of y, k, l, r, p, w, s, q, η, n, d, x, i, and ρ. We can, therefore, turn to the study of monetary policy.

12.3   Computing Optimal Policy

In this section we analyze the policy choices of a monetary authority whose objective is to minimize expected social loss. Social loss is, in turn, assumed to depend on the deviations of output and inflation from their steady-state values and possibly on other variables. Our assumptions about the preferences of the policy maker are, we believe, realistic and may in particular reflect the existence of an inflation-targeting regime (as in Svensson 2000). Alternatively, our assumptions on social loss may be seen as an approximation to (some aggregate of) the welfare of workers and capitalists.[6]

As in much of the recent literature, we shall assume that the instrument of the monetary authority is the short nominal interest rate i_t. This implies

---

6. However, such an interpretation may require some additional assumptions to be accurate. See Kim and Kim (2002) and Benigno and Benigno (2000).

that the behavior of monetary aggregates plays no essential role in the analysis: The money, in particular, adjusts passively as given by equation (14) and can be ignored.

As in Svensson (2000), the monetary authority's loss function is the unconditional expectation of a period loss function[7] of the form

$$\psi_\pi \pi_t^2 + \psi_y y_t^2 + \psi_e e_t^2,$$

where e_t corresponds to the real exchange rate, or $s_t - p_t$. Hence, after taking expectations, the loss function becomes

$$(20) \qquad \psi_\pi \text{Var}(\pi_t) + \psi_y \text{Var}(y_t) + \psi_e \text{Var}(e_t).$$

In the previous expressions, π_t denotes the deviation of a measure of inflation from its steady-state value. In our benchmark computations, such a measure is given by wage inflation. The fact that we attribute social costs to wage inflation can easily be justified in the context of the Calvo (1983) staggering context. As Woodford (1996, 2000) shows in detail, with staggering inflation causes the dispersion of relative prices (or wages), and this is in turn costly for output and welfare. Because in our model it is wages that are sticky and staggered, it is ongoing wage inflation that causes such relative price distortions.

Notice that under this specification, the policy maker attempts to minimize the deviations of output from its steady-state or "natural rate" level, not from some higher threshold, as in some of the literature. This means that the "inflation bias" problem familiar from Barro and Gordon (1983) and related work is absent here. However, this does not mean that there is no time consistency problem: optimal policy computed under discretion and under commitment will in general not coincide. This is because, to the extent that wage setting depends on future economic conditions, a monetary policy that can commit to future actions may face an improved inflation-output trade-off in the short run (see Clarida, Galí, and Gertler 1999).

We begin with a benchmark regime corresponding to what Svensson (2000) terms *flexible inflation targeting*: $\psi_\pi = 1$, $\psi_y = 0.5$, and $\psi_e = 0$. Social loss depends on inflation but also on domestic output. Later we analyze other regimes.[8]

12.3.1 Parametrization

We set the model parameters to ensure that the steady state is empirically plausible. Thus, the steady-state world real interest rate is 4 percent in annual terms. The share of the home good in the production of capital and in

---

7. It is well known that such an objective is the limit, as the discount factor goes to zero, of a scaled discounted sum of expected losses in all periods.

8. Notice that we follow Svensson's (1999) somewhat special terminology, which defines a regime not by the actions it involves, but by the loss function it minimizes.

the consumption index, γ, is set at 0.75, which is consistent with observed shares of imported goods in total output. The capital share in the production of the home good, α, is assumed to be 0.35.

We set θ, the probability of nonadjustment in wages, to 0.75, which implies that (on average) wages are adjusted every four quarters. The elasticity of demand for worker services, σ, and the elasticity of labor supply, v, are both set to be 2.0.

We choose the rest of the parameters in the model to generate a steady-state risk premium of 600 basis points, a ratio of investment expenditures to debt that equals to 1.8, and an annualized business failure rate of 8.8 percent. The monitoring costs are assumed to be 15 percent of the total assets of the firm in case of bankruptcy. Additionally, the fraction of capitalists surviving to the next period, δ, is set to 0.9615, while the idiosyncratic shock to the return of capital is assumed to be distributed log-normally with a standard deviation equal to 0.28. Finally, the persistence parameter of the world interest rate and the export demand shocks is assumed to be 0.9.

12.3.2   Discretionary Policy

In analyzing the policy problem, we find that it is crucial to specify when the monetary authority can commit to a particular choice. Begin with the case of *discretion:* the monetary authority sets i_t in period t, after observing shocks in that period. The discretionary case is arguably the most relevant in practice. However, perhaps more importantly in our context, much of the recent debate on fixed versus flexible rates is based on the view that fixed rates may improve upon discretion by serving as an imperfect commitment device. Hence, evaluating such a view requires comparing outcomes under fixed rates against discretionary outcomes.

The policy maker's problem is to minimize social loss by choosing a strategy for setting i_t in every period t after observing the state of the economy and all shocks up to period t. To formalize this problem, it is useful to note that the dynamic system that determines the economy's equilibrium has a convenient state space representation. Letting $b_t = d_t + \rho_t$ denote aggregate debt repayment in period t, and letting $\pi_t = w_t - w_{t-1}$ denote wage inflation, one can write the model in the form

(21)
$$\begin{pmatrix} \mathbf{Z}_{t+1} \\ {}_t\mathbf{J}_{t+1} \end{pmatrix} = A_1 \begin{pmatrix} \mathbf{Z}_t \\ \mathbf{J}_t \end{pmatrix} + A_2 i_t + \varepsilon_{t+1},$$

where $\mathbf{Z}_t = (\rho_t, x_t, k_t, \eta_t, b_t, w_{t-1})'$ is a vector of predetermined variables at t, $\mathbf{J}_t = (s_t, p_t, \pi_t)'$ is a vector of jumping variables, $\varepsilon_t = (\varepsilon_t^\rho, \varepsilon_t^x, 0, 0,..,0)'$ is a vector of exogenous shocks, and A_1 and A_2 are matrices whose coefficients are determined by the equilibrium system.

Given the state space equation (21), the techniques of Oudiz and Sachs (1985) and Backus and Driffill (1986) can be used to compute a discretionary outcome summarized by two linear maps. First, market behavior is given by a map

$$(22) \qquad\qquad \mathbf{J}_t = \mathbf{JZ}_t,$$

where $\mathbf{J}$ is a matrix defining values for the jumping variables at t as a linear function of the predetermined ones.

Second, policy choices are given by

$$(23) \qquad\qquad i_t = \mathbf{fZ}_t,$$

where $\mathbf{f}$ is a row vector defining the interest rate at t as a linear combination of the predetermined variables.

The two linear maps thus defined have the property that (a) given the policy map in equation (23), the market behavior defined by equation (22) defines a rational expectations equilibrium of the economy given by equation (21), and (b) given the system in equation (21) and the market behavior in equation (22), the policy given by equation (23) in fact minimizes social loss subject to equations (21) and (22).

Once the maps in equations (22) and (23) are obtained, they can be used in equation (21) to arrive at the law of motion for the vector $\mathbf{Z}_t$. Then it is straightforward to obtain variances and covariances for all the variables in the model and therefore to compute the value of the social loss function.

The solution for the optimal policy rule turns out to be

$$(24) \qquad i_t = 0.79\rho_t - 0.20x_t + 0.53k_t + 0.02\eta_t + 0.07b_t - 0.0w_{t-1}.$$

Several aspects of this rule warrant attention. The first is that the exchange rate floats, and considerably. The nominal interest rate adjusts to exogenous shocks, but not to the extent that would be necessary to stabilize the nominal and real exchange rates. Indeed, it is possible to solve for the exchange rate as a function of predetermined variables; the discretionary solution implies that the coefficients are nonzero. Equivalently, it is apparent from the impulse responses below that optimal policy requires flexible exchange rates.

In response to an increase of 100 basis points in the world interest rate ρ_t, the monetary authority *increases* the nominal interest rate by almost 80 basis points. At first glance, one may conjecture that this reflects that the monetary authority is partially defending the exchange rate. However, such an interpretation would be misleading for two reasons. First, i_t is a *nominal* rate, and hence an increase in i_t may merely be compensating for an increase in expected domestic inflation (see eq. [15]). Indeed, we shall see that domestic inflation increases after a rise in ρ_t. Second, the response of i_t cannot be understood independently of the full dynamics of the model. This is because, when policy is given by equation (24), interest rates increase by more than 55 basis points if domestic capital is 1 percent above its steady-state

Table 12.1   Unconditional Standard Deviations

	Variables		
	π_t	y_t	e_t
Flexible inflation targeting			
Discretion	0.44	0.04	2.77
Commitment	0.24	0.07	2.68
Fixed exchange rate	0.27	2.07	1.33

value. Because an unexpected increase in the world interest rate will cause a fall in domestic investment and capital in subsequent periods, i_t will increase very little, except for the very first period.

In response to an unexpected 1 percent increase in the demand for exports, the discretionary policy implies that the interest rate must fall on impact. Again, this is only the very short-run response and should not be taken as an indication of a procyclical monetary policy. In particular, a rise in x_t will increase capital accumulation, which then will push interest rates up under the discretionary policy.

Table 12.1 shows the standard deviations of the variables of ultimate relevance for welfare. Under the discretionary policy in equation (24), the standard deviation of the real exchange rate is 2.77, and the standard deviations of the nominal exchange rate and the price of the home goods are much higher. Hence, the optimal discretionary policy actively takes advantage of the ability to change the exchange rate, a finding similar to that of Svensson (2000). The main payoff is that output is stabilized almost completely. The standard deviation of (wage) inflation is also low (0.44 percent) but certainly not negligible, and is consistent with the high variability of the exchange rate.

Some further intuition can be obtained by studying the impulse response functions associated with equation (24), the discretionary solution. Figure 12.1 displays the responses to a 1 percent increase in the world interest rate. As we saw above, on impact the interest rate increases by 0.79 basis points over its steady-state value, but this increase is only temporary: after one period, the interest rate has fallen to only 2.5 basis points over its steady-state value, and from then on it converges slowly to the steady state.

Because capital depreciation is complete, the dynamic behavior of i_t mirrors the adjustment of capital, which in turn responds to the real interest rate on loans. On impact, investment and capital fall more than one for one with the increase in the world interest rate. Investment then recovers gradually, as the real cost of loans falls.[9] The latter reflects not only the return of the world interest rate to its steady state, but also a gradual fall in the risk

9. The real cost of loans corresponds to the world interest rate plus the risk premium and the expected real devaluation.

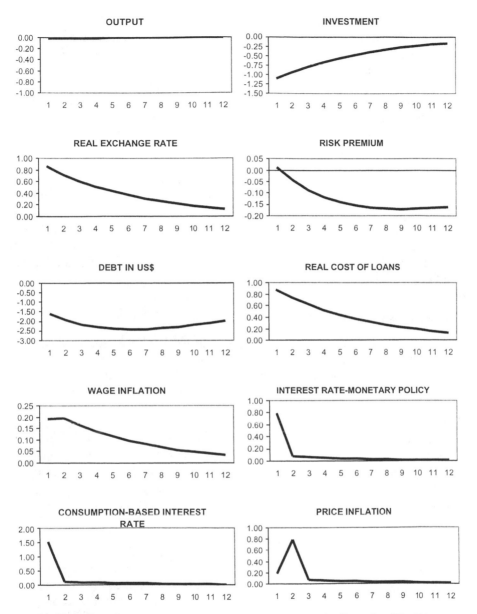

Fig. 12.1   Impulse responses to a world interest rate shock, discretion: Flexible inflation targeting

premium below its steady-state level after an initial increase. The risk premium falls, in turn, because the interest rate increase reduces investment and foreign borrowing, which is apparent from figure 12.1. In fact, the reaction of foreign debt is quite strong, falling by almost 2.5 percent in the first six periods and then recovering slowly.

Finally, note that because capital adjusts toward the steady state only gradually, the discretionary rule in equation (24) limits the deviation of the home interest rate from its steady state. This confirms our previous observation that the optimal policy can only be interpreted in the context of the model's dynamic properties.

The impulse responses to a 1 percent *decrease* in export demand are given in figure 12.2. The shape of the response is the same as in the case of a world interest rate shock, although the magnitudes are smaller. The shock leads to a depreciation of the real exchange rate and to a fall in investment of 0.25 percentage points. Monetary policy almost perfectly stabilizes output. The shock and the associated monetary policy also lead to an increase in wage inflation.

12.4   How Costly Is the Inability to Precommit?

We now turn to the issue of quantifying the welfare loss associated with the absence of commitment. We start with a case of full commitment, in which the monetary authority can implement a date- and state-contingent policy specified at the start of time. We treat that case briefly, because it is unlikely to be of much relevance in practice. It is helpful, however, in providing a benchmark of how costly lack of commitment can be. We then turn to fixed exchange rates, considered as an imperfect but feasible commitment device. This is of interest because one may believe that some simple rules, including fixed exchange rate regimes, may be implementable even if they are time inconsistent. In such a case, fixed exchange rates may in principle be superior to the optimal policy under discretion, reflecting the stronger commitment associated with fixing.

12.4.1   Optimal Policy under Full Commitment[10]

Under full commitment, the optimal rule is generally not simply a map from period t's exogenous or predetermined variables to the policy or control variable i_t. That is because the monetary authority takes into account the whole future expected path of the economy. However, in period 0 it is indeed possible to write down such a representation, which turns out to be[11]

---

10. The calculations in this section follow Söderlind (1999).

11. The difference is that actions at period zero are by definition unexpected, and hence the central bank does not have to worry about the effect of such actions on expectations along the equilibrium path. The same is not true of actions to be taken in some future period T, which affect expectations in all periods $t \leq T$. Technically, the difference is that for periods after $t = 0$ the policy rule also contains a number of Lagrange multipliers, which are set to zero at time $t = 0$.

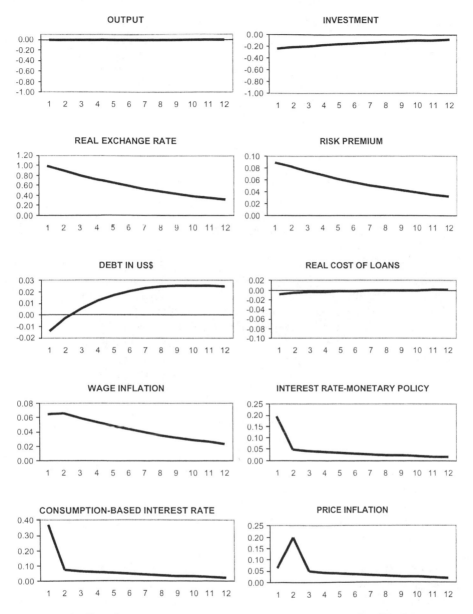

Fig. 12.2   Impulse responses to an export demand shock, discretion: Flexible inflation targeting

(25) $i_t = 0.69\rho_t - 0.16x_t + 0.54k_t + 0.02\eta_t + 0.06b_t - 0.0w_{t-1}.$

This rule is remarkably similar to the one under discretion. In particular, the exchange rate is again floating, in the sense that the domestic interest rate does not eliminate exchange rate fluctuations in response to shocks in external borrowing costs.

The main difference is that now the initial reactions of the nominal interest rate to foreign interest rate and export shocks are significantly smaller. Under commitment, less "toughness" is required from the central bank when it faces adverse circumstances. This is because a precommitting central bank can promise to engineer less inflation in the future; because price setting is forward looking, less expected inflation in the future means less actual inflation today, which in turn allows the central bank to choose a less restrictive level for domestic interest rate today.

Table 12.1 reveals that under commitment the standard deviation of output is slightly higher than under discretion, whereas that of inflation is much lower: 0.24 versus 0.44 percent. Interestingly, the policy maker who can commit also takes full advantage of the flexibility in relative prices implied by floating: now the standard deviation of the real exchange rate is 2.68 percent, only slightly below the 2.77 percent obtained under discretion. Moreover, the standard deviations of the nominal exchange rate and the price of the home good are significantly smaller compared to the discretionary case.

This general analysis can be enriched by examining the impulse response functions in figures 12.3 and 12.4. For concreteness, focus on the latter figure, which contains the case of a 1 percent adverse export shock. The main difference with discretion is in the behavior of wage inflation, which now peaks at half the value of the discretionary case. The lower inflation allows the monetary authority initially to raise nominal interest rates by less: 158 basis points, compared to 197 under discretion. As suggested by the standard deviation calculations, output falls by more and stays below the steady state longer under commitment. However, the size of these deviations is fairly small, and under commitment the output fall is more gradual and occurs later than under discretion.

Notably, the response of the risk premium is identical to that in the discretionary case. This may seem surprising, although not unexpected given our previous work. In the context of CCV we showed that, in equilibrium, the response of the risk premium was the same under fixed exchange rates and under a flexible rate, price-targeting policy. Our finding here is similar, although it refers to the response of the risk premium to different monetary rules. Indeed, we will see below that the change in the risk premium is the same across regimes, contrary to the conjectures in much of the recent policy literature.

The explanation for this result is straightforward: it can be shown with a bit of algebra (the details are in CCV) that movements in the risk premium

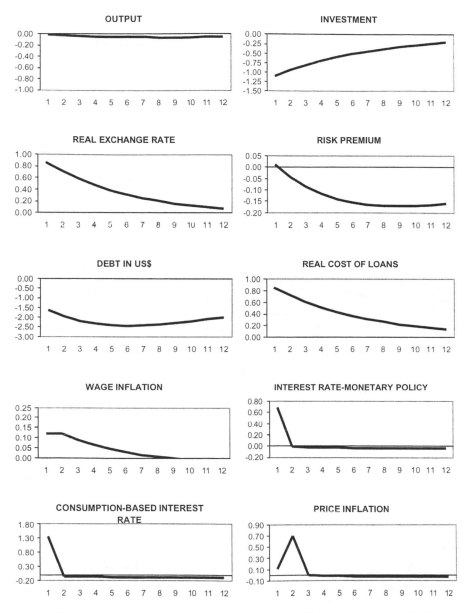

Fig. 12.3   Impulse responses to a world interest rate shock, commitment: Flexible inflation targeting

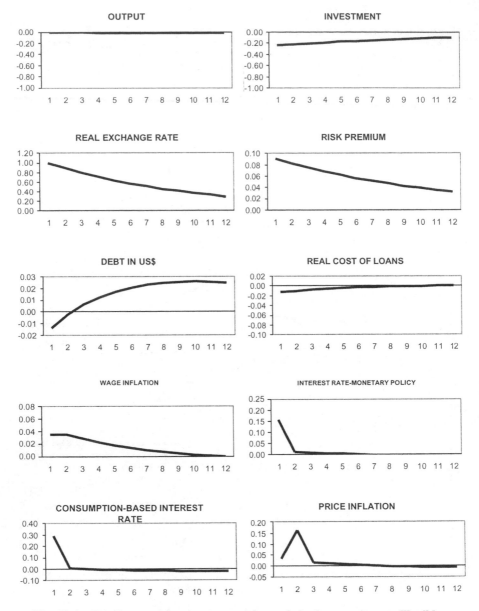

Fig. 12.4 Impulse responses to an export demand shock, commitment: Flexible inflation targeting

depend on the response of overall dollar output. This is natural, as the risk premium depends on net worth relative to the value of investment, both of which depend on dollar output. Ultimately we find that in response to shocks, dollar output changes by the same amount independently of interest and exchange rate policy. Policy determines the split between movements in real output and movements in the real exchange rate.

12.4.2   Fixed Exchange Rates

Next we analyze the outcomes of the model under a fixed exchange rate regime. This is achieved by setting $s_t = 0$, all t, as an equilibrium condition. Note that the nominal interest rate then responds passively to the resulting dynamic equilibrium and follows equation (15).

Under this policy the standard deviation of wage inflation falls to 0.27 percent, which reduces social loss relative to the discretionary solution. However, this is achieved at the price of an increase in the standard deviation of output from virtually zero in the flexible inflation targeting case to 2.07 percent.

Figure 12.5 shows the responses of the fixed rate regime to a 1 percent increase in the world interest rate. The nominal interest rate increases, on impact, by less than 15 basis points. It is interesting to note here that this increase is much less than the discretionary impact response, but this observation says little about the stance of monetary policy. With fixed rates the interest rate is endogenous, and the fact that the increase in the interest rate is relatively mild reflects the fact that, following the shock, there is strong price deflation and a fall in output.

Indeed, output falls by almost 0.5 percent on impact and by more than 0.85 percent in the second period, relative to its steady-state value. The response of investment and capital is even stronger: the short-run contraction is about 1.5 percent, and the recovery is relatively slow. In this case, inflation is negative for the first few periods and slightly positive in the medium run.

Finally, figure 12.6 presents the impulse responses of the economy to a 1 percent decrease in export demand. Again, output and investment reactions are stronger and more persistent than in the full commitment and discretionary policy cases.

These impulse responses suggest that, once the analysis goes beyond impact effects, fixed exchange rates exacerbate rather than ameliorating the adverse effects of financial frictions. This conjecture clearly warrants more research, if only because it contradicts the current conventional wisdom based on the existence of liability dollarization.

12.4.3   Welfare Comparisons

Table 12.2 compares the social loss associated with commitment, the discretionary case, and fixed exchange rates. By construction, welfare is highest under commitment. The main result is that welfare is lowest under fixed

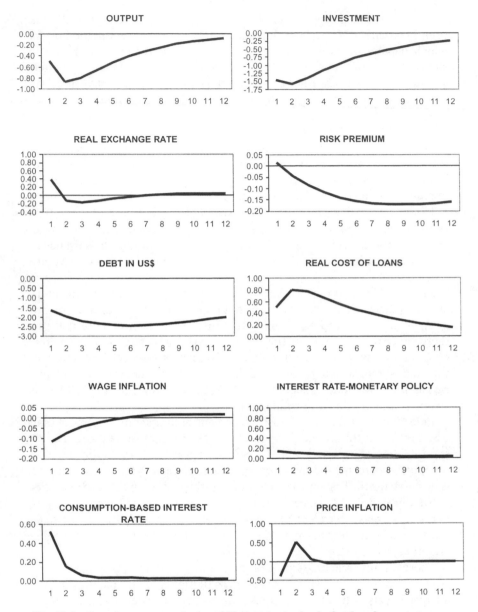

Fig. 12.5 Impulse responses to a world interest rate shock, fixed exchange rate

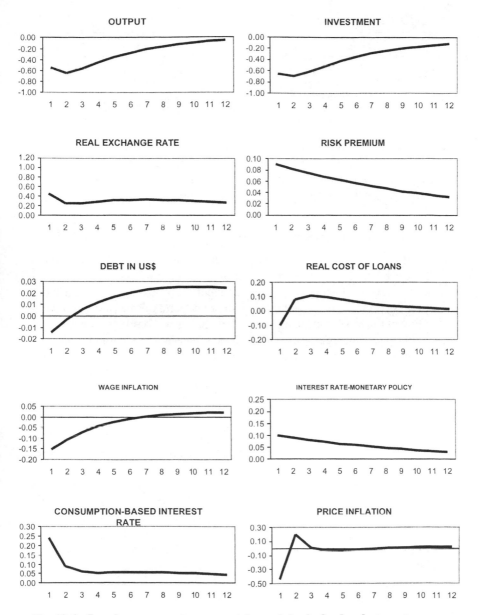

Fig. 12.6   Impulse responses to an export demand shock, fixed exchange rate

Table 12.2   Loss Function

	Loss Function Value
Flexible inflation targeting	
Discretion	0.20
Commitment	0.06
Fixed exchange rate	2.21

exchange rates, and the difference is large: social loss is eleven times larger than under discretion and flexible inflation targeting. That is, the commitment gain associated with fixing does not even come close to offsetting the benefits of greater output stabilization under floating.

12.5   Alternative Objective Functions

What we have termed *flexible inflation targeting* is a plausible and practically relevant policy stance, but certainly not the only one. To make sure that our results—particularly the conclusion that flexible rates under discretion are preferable to fixed rates—do not depend on the particular specification of the loss function minimized by the central bank, we now analyze two alternative formulations: one with no concern for output stabilization and one in which the central bank attempts to stabilize the real exchange as well as the other two more conventional targets. For the sake of brevity, in what follows we omit the full commitment case.

12.5.1   Strict Inflation Targeting

Under a stance of *strict inflation targeting* the parameters of the loss function are $\psi_\pi = 1$, $\psi_y = 0$, and $\psi_e = 0$. In other words, the monetary authority's sole objective is to stabilize wage inflation.

We discover that under strict inflation targeting the monetary authority finds it optimal to keep the interest rate unchanged in response to shocks. The intuition is that, given the wage Phillips curve in equation (16), wages and wage inflation can be held to their steady-state values if labor demand can also be held at its steady-state value. The latter can be achieved, by equation (3), if home nominal output is constant. However, equation (15) implies that home nominal output must be constant if the domestic short interest rate is constant.[12]

Table 12.3 confirms that, if inflation targeting is strict, the discretionary solution indeed manages to keep wage inflation constant. The change with respect to the flexible inflation targeting case is that output becomes more variable: the standard deviation of the output is almost 1 percent. However,

---

12. Note that, in this sense, a policy of keeping i_t at its steady-state value is equivalent to a policy of "nominal GDP targeting," as studied by Frankel and Chinn (1995).

Table 12.3   **Unconditional Standard Deviations**

	Variables		
	π_t	y_t	e_t
Flexible inflation targeting	0.44	0.04	2.77
Strict inflation targeting	0.00	0.96	2.29
Flexible inflation-RER targeting	0.49	1.39	1.42
Fixed exchange rate	0.27	2.07	1.33

Note: RER = real exchange rate.

this is intuitive, as output variability implies no loss under strict inflation targeting. The standard deviation of the real exchange rate turns out to be 2.29 percent, somewhat lower than under flexible inflation targeting.

Figure 12.7 shows the response of the economy to a 1 percent increase in the world interest rate for the case of strict inflation targeting. As one might expect, output and investment exhibit stronger and more persistent falls under strict inflation targeting than in the flexible targeting case. Interestingly, output has a hump-shaped response, which replicates some existing vector autoregression evidence without relying on assumptions about the timing of investment. Even though the increase on impact of the real exchange rate under strict inflation targeting is similar to that in the flexible case, its persistence is lower.

The response of the economy to a 1 percent fall in export demand appears in figure 12.8. Again, monetary policy completely stabilizes inflation. Compared to flexible inflation targeting, strict inflation targeting results in a deeper contraction in output and investment. Whereas the reaction of the real exchange rate is rather similar in shape and magnitude, the depreciation (increase) of the nominal exchange rate (price of the home goods) is smaller under strict inflation targeting.

12.5.2   Flexible Inflation and Real Exchange Rate Targeting

In a third and last case under discretion, we allow the variance of the real exchange rate to affect the monetary authority's loss function. This can be termed flexible inflation–cum–real exchange rate targeting. Assuming that the exchange rate objective is as important to the central bank as the output objective, we chose $\psi_\pi = 1$, $\psi_y = 0.5$, and $\psi_e = 0.5$ to represent this case. Under dollarization of liabilities there are especially powerful reasons that the monetary authority may want to stabilize the real exchange rate, because we have seen that sharp sudden devaluations typically have nasty effects on balance sheets.

The solution for the policy rule is

$$(28) \qquad i_t = 0.93\rho_t - 0.22x_t + 0.53k_t + 0.02\eta_t + 0.08b_t - 0.0w_{t-1}.$$

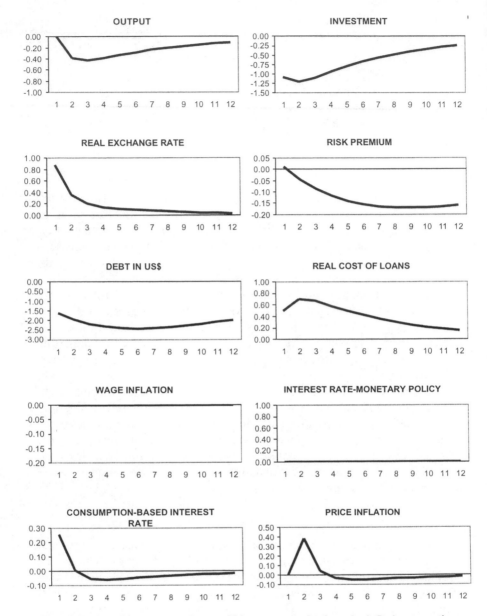

Fig. 12.7   Impulse responses to a world interest rate shock, strict inflation targeting

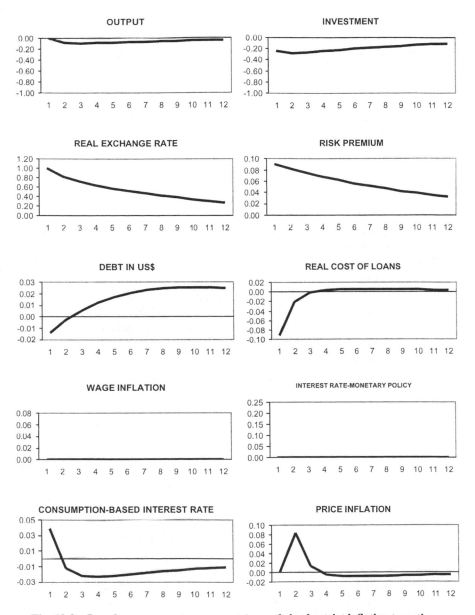

Fig. 12.8   Impulse responses to an export demand shock, strict inflation targeting

Now, in response to an increase of 100 basis points in the world interest rate the monetary authority increases the nominal domestic interest rate by more than 90 basis points. Naturally, this reaction is stronger than in the flexible inflation targeting case. The rest of the coefficients are quite similar to the ones in that case.

As can be seen from table 12.3, flexible inflation–exchange rate targeting implies that inflation and output are more variable and the real exchange rate less variable than in the two previous cases. This is not surprising, because the monetary authority now prefers to reduce exchange rate volatility at the cost of more variable inflation and output. In fact, the standard deviation of output in this regime is almost 50 percent higher than strict inflation targeting and more than thirty-five times higher than under flexible inflation targeting. The standard deviation of the real exchange rate is half the standard deviation under flexible inflation targeting and 40 percent lower than under strict inflation targeting.

Figure 12.9 presents the impulse responses to a 1 percent increase in the world interest rate. The initial fall of output is stronger compared to both flexible and strict inflation targeting. Investment is also lower. However, the initial response of the real exchange rate is reduced by almost one-half. Wage inflation is lower than in the flexible inflation targeting but higher than in the strict inflation targeting. The response of the risk premium is identical to that in the two previous cases.

Finally, figure 12.10 displays the response of the economy to a 1 percent decrease in export demand. Notice that in the first period the interest rate increases, but thereafter monetary policy turns clearly expansionary. Moreover, output and investment exhibit a stronger fall compared to the previous cases under discretion. The real exchange rate reaction is less pronounced and inflation is in fact negative under this particular specification of the central bank objectives.

12.5.3   Welfare Comparisons

Table 12.4 compares the social loss associated with both these discretionary cases with the loss under fixed exchange rates. For each discretionary alternative, the loss under fixed rates is evaluated using the weights in the welfare function associated with that alternative.

Again, social loss is larger under fixed rates than under either discretionary solution. The disadvantages of fixed rates appear to be larger if output enters the social loss function. Conversely, fixed rates seem almost as good as flexible rates if in the latter case there is strict inflation targeting.

12.6   Final Remarks

We have found that, even if fixed exchange rates enjoy a credibility advantage, they do not yield higher welfare than does optimal floating under

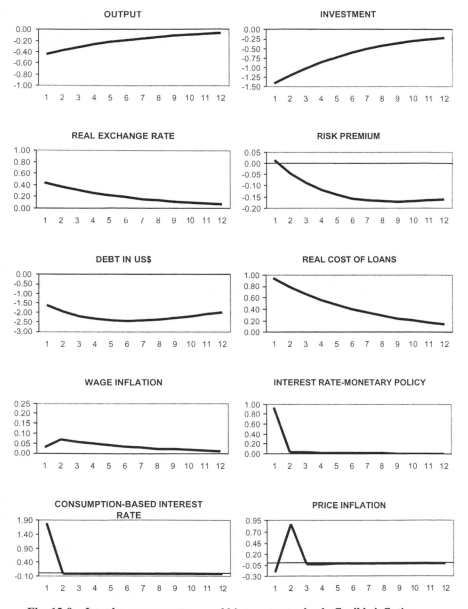

Fig. 12.9   Impulse responses to a world interest rate shock, flexible inflation—real exchange rate targeting

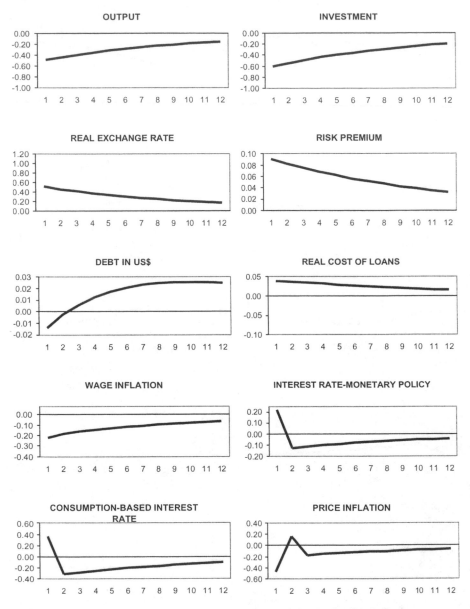

Fig. 12.10 **Impulse responses to an export demand shock, flexible inflation—real exchange rate targeting**

Table 12.4   Loss Function

	Loss Function Value	
	(Col. 1)	(Col. 2)
Flexible inflation targeting vs. fixed exchange rate	0.20	2.21
Strict inflation targeting vs. fixed exchange rate	0.00	0.07
Flexible inflation-RER targeting vs. fixed exchange rate	2.21	3.10

Note: RER = real exchange rate.

discretion. Fixing turns out to have adverse consequences for aggregate real variability, particularly of output. This outweighs the inflation gains associated with fixed rates. This conclusion does not depend on—instead, it seems to be reinforced by—the existence of financial imperfections that interact with net worth effects. Naturally, these findings must be checked further for robustness, under alternative parameters and model specifications. However, it is notable that they are consistent with our previous theoretical analysis in CCV.

Of the many extensions suggested by the analysis, perhaps the most obvious one is to drop the ad hoc specification of the monetary authority's loss function in favor of a true social welfare function derived from microfoundations, as in Woodford (1996, 2000) and Rotemberg and Woodford (1997). This involves not only aggregating the interests of agents in the home population, but also finding a tractable way to do so. This task is not trivial, because here there are a number of distortions (financial frictions in addition to sticky prices and monopoly power) and therefore Taylor approximations to the social objective function may not always yield the quadratic forms we have relied on. On the other hand, the recent work of Chang (1998), Phelan and Stachetti (2002), and Sleet (2001) suggests that there may be computationally feasible ways to tackle directly the nonlinear discretionary policy problem without relying on linear-quadratic approximations.

References

Backus, D., and J. Driffill. 1986. The consistency of optimal policy in stochastic rational expectations models. CEPR Discussion Paper no. 124. London: Center for Economic Policy Research.

Barro, R., and D. Gordon. 1983. A positive theory of monetary policy in a natural rate model. *Journal of Political Economy* 91:589–610.

Benigno, G., and P. Benigno. 2000. Price stability as a nash equilibrium in monetary open-economy models. New York University. Unpublished Manuscript, October.

Bernanke, B., and M. Gertler. 1989. Agency costs, net worth, and business fluctuations. *American Economic Review* 79:14–31.

Bernanke, B., M. Gertler, and S. Gilchrist. 1999. The financial accelerator in a quantitative business cycle framework. In *Handbook of macroeconomics,* ed. J. Taylor and M. Woodford, 1341–93. Amsterdam: North-Holland.

Calvo, G. 1983. Staggered prices in a utility maximizing framework. *Journal of Monetary Economics* 12:383–98.

———. 1999. Fixed vs. flexible exchange rates: Preliminaries of a turn-of-millennium rematch. May. Available at [http://www.bsos.umd.edu.econ/ciecalvo.htm].

———. 2000. Capital market and the exchange rate with special reference to the dollarization debate in Latin America. April. Available at [http://www.bsos.umd.edu/econ/ciecalvo.htm].

Calvo, G., and C. Reinhart. 2002. Fear of floating. *Quarterly Journal of Economics,* forthcoming.

Céspedes, L., R. Chang, and A. Velasco. 2000. Balance sheets and exchange rate policy. NBER Working Paper no. 7840. Cambridge, Mass.: National Bureau of Economic Research, August.

Chang, R. 1998. Credible monetary policy in an infinite horizon model: Recursive approaches. *Journal of Economic Theory* 81:431–61.

Chang, R., and A. Velasco. 2000. Exchange rate regimes for developing countries. *American Economic Review* 90 (2): 71–75.

Clarida, R., J. Galí and M. Gertler. 1999. The science of monetary policy: A new Keynesian perspective. *Journal of Economic Literature* 37 (December): 1661–707.

Dixit, A., and J. Stiglitz. Monopolistic competition and optimum product diversity. *American Economic Review* 67:297–308.

Dornbusch, R. 1999. After Asia: New directions for the international financial system. MIT, Department of Economics. Mimeograph. Available at [http://web.mit.edu/rudi/www/].

Frankel, J., and M. Chinn. 1995. The stabilizing properties of a nominal GDP rule. *Journal of Money, Credit, and Banking* 27 (May): 318–34.

Furman, J., and J. Stiglitz. 1998. Economic crises: Evidence and insights from East Asia. *Brookings Papers on Economic Activity,* Issue no. 2:1–135.

Hausmann, R., M. Gavin, C. Pagés-Serra, and E. H. Stein. 1999. Financial turmoil and choice of exchange rate regime. IADB Working Paper no. WP-400. Washington, D.C.: Inter-American Development Bank, January.

Kaminsky, G., and C. Reinhart. 1999. The twin crises: The causes of banking and balance of payments problems. *American Economic Review* 89 (June): 473–500.

Kim, J., and S. Kim. 2002. Spurious welfare reversal in international business cycle models. *Journal of International Economics,* forthcoming.

Krugman, P. 1999. Balance sheets, the transfer problem and financial crises. In *International finance and financial crises,* ed. P. Isard, A. Razin, and A. Rose, 31–44. Boston: Kluwer Academic Publishers.

Obstfeld, M., and K. Rogoff. 2000. New directions for stochastic open economy models. *Journal of International Economics* 50:117–54.

Oudiz, G., and J. Sachs. 1985. International policy coordination in dynamic macroeconomic models. In *International policy coordination,* ed. W. Buiter and R. Marston, 274–319. Cambridge: Cambridge University Press.

Phelan, C., and E. Stachetti. 2002. Subgame perfect equilibria in a Ramsey taxes model. *Econometrica,* forthcoming.

Radelet, S., and J. Sachs. 2000. The onset of the Asian financial crisis. In *Currency crises,* ed. P. Krugman, 105–53. Chicago: University of Chicago Press.

Rotemberg, J., and M. Woodford. 1997. An optimization-based framework for the conduct of monetary policy. In *NBER macroeconomics annual,* ed. B. Bernanke and J. Rotemberg, 297–346. Cambridge: MIT Press.

Sleet, C. 2001. On credible monetary policy and private government information. *Journal of Economic Theory* 99 (July): 338–76.

Söderlind, P. 1999. Solution and estimation of RE macromodels with optimal policy. *European Economic Review* 43:813–23.

Svensson, L. 1999. Inflation targeting as a monetary policy rule. *Journal of Monetary Economics* 43:607–54.

———. 2000. Open economy inflation targeting. *Journal of international economics* 50:155–84.

Townsend, R. 1979. Optimal contracts and competitive markets with costly state verification. *Journal of Economic Theory* 21:265–93.

Williamson, S. 1987. Costly monitoring, loan contracts, and equilibrium credit rationing. *Quarterly Journal of Economics* 102:135–45.

Woodford, M. 1996. Control of the public debt: A requirement for price stability? NBER Working Paper no. 5684. Cambridge, Mass.: National Bureau of Economic Research, July.

———. 2000. *Interest and prices.* Princeton University, Department of Economics. Unpublished Manuscript.

Comment   Nouriel Roubini

This is an interesting and important contribution to the literature on exchange rates and balance sheet effects. In a previous paper (Cespedes, Chang, and Velasco 2000, hereafter CCV), the authors showed that flexible rate regimes dominate fixed rate regimes even when one considers the balance sheet effects deriving from liability dollarization (large stock of foreign currency debt).

The intuition for such a result was simple: If an external shock—such as an increase in the world interest rate or a fall in the demand for exports—requires a real devaluation, such devaluation can occur in two ways: via a nominal depreciation under flexible exchange rates, or via a domestic deflation under fixed exchange rates.

Thus, under both regimes there are going to be negative balance sheet effects when shock hits the economy; these effects imply contractions in output in both regimes. However, under fixed rates the output effects of the shock will be larger because, if nominal wages are rigid, deflation exacerbates the contraction in output and employment.

The question addressed in this new paper by the authors is whether this result holds when monetary policy is time inconsistent under the discre-

Nouriel Roubini is associate professor of economics at the Stern School of Business, New York University, and a research associate of the National Bureau of Economic Research.

tionary flexible rate regime. Fixed exchange rates may thus be superior to flexible rates as they are a commitment device that may provide lower inflation levels and variability.

The main result of the paper is that, under three alternative discretionary flexible exchange rate regimes, the welfare losses are lower than under fixed rate regimes.

Note that the role of balance sheet effects in currency crises has been considered by recent theoretical literature on this subject. Contributions include Chang and Velasco (1999); CCV; Krugman (1999); Gertler, Gilchrist, and Natalucci (2000); Aghion, Bacchetta, and Banerjee (2000); Christiano, Gust, and Roldós (2000); Caballero and Krishnamurthy (2000); Kiyotaki and Moore (1997).

On the empirical side, a number of studies have looked at the implications of balance sheet effect; studies include Gelos and Werner (1999); Broda (2000); Frankel (2000); Schaechter, Stone, and Zelmer (2000); Blejer et al. (2000); and Dornbusch (chap. 16 in this volume).

Although part of the analytical literature has addressed the question of the relative performance of fixed versus flexible exchange rates, other researchers have analyzed the actual performance of emerging markets under alternative exchange rate regimes. Such studies include Borensztein, Zettelmeyer, and Philippon (2000); Calvo and Reinhart (1999, 2000); and Hausman (1999). The latter authors have stressed that flexible exchange rates lead to a fear of floating hypothesis and that flexible rates are not desirable in an environment in which liabilities are dollarized (the "original sin" that does not allow an emerging market long-term borrowing in its own currency).

One of the limitations of the CCV paper is that it does not present a survey of this literature on balance sheet effects and thus explain its contribution relative to the rest of the literature. Since there are many related analytical contributions with a similar analytical approach (open-economy variants of the Bernanke-Gertler "financial accelerator" model) and similar results, presenting this contribution in the context of the literature would have been useful.

I will discuss first the arguments against flexible exchange rates, because this paper presents the argument that flexible rates dominate fixed rates. Calvo and Reinhart (1999, 2000) and Hausman's (1999) "fear of floating" hypothesis can be summarized as follows:

1. Emerging-market (EM) economies often have a history of high inflation or hyperinflation and lack of fiscal discipline. Thus, they need policy credibility and something to anchor inflation expectations. Fixed rates anchor expectations, whereas flexible rates leave too much room for discretion, and this means high nominal and real interest rates when credibility is imperfect. Also, sensitivity to U.S. Fed tightening is stronger under flexible

rates. Finally, given that exchange rates are often not driven by fundamentals, especially when credibility is limited, there is excessive exchange rate volatility, which is harmful to trade and economic performance.

2. Because of a history of high inflation, debt restructurings and defaults, and limited policy credibility, emerging markets suffer from "original sin": they are unable to borrow long term in their own currency. Thus, their external debt is mostly short-term and in foreign currency. Worse, most of these countries are effectively liability dollarized—that is, most of their domestic debt, bank deposits, and other liabilities are also in dollars.

3. Because of imperfect policy credibility and effective dollarization, these emerging markets with alleged flexible rate regimes *do not have monetary independence and autonomy.* Their monetary policy is procyclical, not countercyclical. When a negative shock hits them, such as a terms-of-trade shock or a cutoff from international capital markets because of contagion, they are forced to increase interest rates while their currency is falling. Thus, they do not receive the benefits of a falling currency (they effectively peg) and they still pay the real costs of high nominal and real interest rates.

4. Being subject to original sin and liability dollarization means that devaluations and flexible exchange rates are not effective tools to deal with external imbalances. Devaluations lead to recessions (they are contractionary rather than expansionary) because they have strong balance sheet effects: firms, banks, and private agents as well as the government suffer financial distress when the currency moves.

5. Since they are dollarized, they cannot use the exchange rate tool to *absorb external shocks* such as a terms-of-trade shock, a reduction in world demand for domestic goods, or similar shocks. The exchange rate does not work as a shock absorber for these external shocks.

6. Given all of the above, some argue that it is better to *fully dollarize.*

Is this "fear of floating" justified? Only partially: flexible exchange rates have provided some monetary autonomy and ability to respond to external shocks and thus successfully minimize the real effects of such disturbances even when economies are partially dollarized. Indeed, evidence and experience with flexible exchange rates in recent years, as well as some recent academic research, suggest that the arguments against flexible exchange rates are exaggerated, for reasons that include the following:

1. Policy credibility is gained with sound policies, not with the choice of the exchange rate regime. Fixed rates do not necessarily provide monetary or fiscal discipline, as the collapse of many pegs proves.

2. There is only partial liability dollarization in EMs (little in Asia, South Africa, and other EMs), and sound policies may lead over time to a reduction in the degree of dollarization. Brazil has more financial indexation than liability dollarization.

3. There is some degree of monetary autonomy under flexible rates.

Borensztein and Zettelmeyer find that floaters are less sensitive to Fed tightening than fixers. In 1997–99, it was appropriate for floaters to increase interest rates in the face of external shocks. Even fixers were forced to tighten a great deal due to the financial turmoil. (However, see some different evidence by Frankel 2000).

4. Devaluations are contractionary under fixed rates because this regime leads to a buildup of foreign currency liabilities. Depreciations are less likely to be contractionary under flexible exchange rates. Moreover, negative balance sheet effects also occur in fixed rate regimes when there are shocks that require a real depreciation (CCV).

5. Flexible exchange rates provide some shock-absorbing functions when there are terms-of-trade shocks (Broda 2000): the real exchange rate depreciates, and output falls less, under flexible rates. This is also consistent with the experience of recent years (Taiwan and Singapore versus Hong Kong; Chile, Brazil, Peru, and Mexico versus Argentina).

Now, let us go back and consider the argument in favor of flexible exchange rates in the CCV paper and the related analytical literature. In my view, the main problems with current work on balance sheet effects and the choice of exchange rate regime are as follows.

Such studies compare a regime of flexible exchange rates with a regime of fixed exchange rates that is maintained in the face of pressures deriving from external shocks. They do not compare fixed exchange rates with a move to flexible exchange rates that derives from a currency crisis (a collapse in a pegged regime).

This issue is important because evidence from all recent currency crises shows that, once a peg is broken, there is a significant overshooting of the nominal and real exchange rates. That is, while current models assume that nominal and real exchange rates change only as much as is warranted by economic fundamentals (the size of the shock), evidence shows that once a peg is broken and an economy moves to float there is significant overshooting beyond what is warranted by traditional economic fundamentals.

This implies that balance sheet effects are very severe when the move to floating exchange rates is a result of a currency collapse. When the exchange rate overshoots following a collapse, the balance sheet effects are extremely severe and are a source of widespread financial distress in the corporate and banking system. This distress is the source of the excessively contractionary effects of a move to a float when a peg breaks.

There are many examples of this overshooting phenomenon. For example, in Korea the won/dollar exchange rate depreciated from about 900 won to the U.S. dollar to 1,800 (at the peak of the crisis in 1998) and then appreciated back to 1,200 by the end of 1998. In Indonesia, the rupiah/dollar exchange rate depreciated from about 2,200 to 16,000 (at the peak of the crisis in 1998) and then appreciated back to 7,000–8,000 by 1999–2000.

Note that, while the competitive benefits of a weaker yen for Korean firms were sizeable at 1,200 won, at 1,800 won most of these firms were effectively bankrupt or in financial distress, given the large amount of foreign currency–denominated debt. This phenomenon was even more pronounced in the case of Indonesia, where the very sharp and extreme depreciation of the rupiah bankrupted a large part of the corporate and financial system.

Similar overshooting of nominal and real exchange rates occurred in Mexico, Thailand, Brazil, and, partly, Russia during their currency crises. The reversal of real exchange rates after the initial overshooting occurred both through a nominal appreciation and an increase in the price level via inflation. Evidence shows that the long-term real depreciation is much smaller than peak real depreciation.

Given net foreign currency liabilities of these economies, these collapses of fixed pegs resulted in a sharp fall in economic activity in all these countries. The extent of the fall is related to the magnitude of these balance sheet effects.

Most recently, serious concerns about the balance sheet effects of a devaluation played an important role in the official sector's decision to rescue countries such as Turkey. The effects of a depreciation following a break in the peg were estimated to be severe on the balance sheets of these countries.

CCV and the other contributions to this literature are unable to capture these disruptive effects of a sharp fall of currency value after a currency crisis, because in all of these models the exchange rates are driven only by fundamentals, and no overshooting occurs. Indeed, to capture these empirically relevant balance sheet effects, one needs a model in which such overshooting does occur. Indeed, in a recent work in progress, Perri, Kisselev, Cavallo, and I (Perri, Roubini, Kisselev, and Cavallo 2001) develop such a model of overshooting and balance sheet effects in which lack of currency hedging before a currency crisis and heavy exposure to foreign currency debt lead to short-run overshooting of exchange rates. The implications of such a model are tested for a sample of twenty-three currency crises in the last decade. We estimate a simultaneous equations model to evaluate quantitatively the determinants of overshooting and output contraction.

First, we find that the amount of exchange rate overshooting is related to the heaviness of a country's debt burden and to the degree to which the currency composition of external assets and liabilities is mismatched. In particular, we find that a 1 percent increase in the ratio of net foreign debt to gross (GDP) causes on average an overshooting of the exchange rate of 0.9 percent, therefore confirming that insufficient hedging is related to overshooting.

Second, we find that the main predictor of the degree of output contraction is the product of the net debt term and the total amount of devaluation (fundamental plus overshooting) term. In particular, we find that countries with small or negative net foreign debt experience small or negative contractions following a devaluation (regardless of the size of the devaluation). This finding confirms the balance sheet hypothesis that relates the contractionary effect of devaluations to the amount of liabilities denominated in foreign currency.

We conclude by decomposing the output consequence of devaluations in two effects: the direct effect that depends on the size of net debt and on the size of the fundamental devaluation, and the indirect effect that depends on the amount of overshooting. In countries with large net foreign debt, both these effects are large, and so currency crises can be severely contractionary.

I have a few other comments on the CCV paper. CCV find that flexible rates dominate fixed rates even in a model in which discretionary monetary policy (flexible rates) suffers from a time-inconsistency problem. CCV find that these results do not depend on their parameter specification. How robust are these results? The following may be some open issues.

In the CCV model, monetary policy is time inconsistent but does not suffer from the Barro-Gordon "inflation-bias" problem. If an "inflation bias" were present in the model, fixed rates would dominate flexible rates for some specification of preferences: In fact, if the inflation bias of the monetary authorities is large enough, equilibrium inflation would be large enough under discretionary flexible rates that fixed rate regimes would end up dominating flexible rate regimes. Thus, the traditional results in the literature that fixed rates (a device for commitment to low inflation) may be superior to flexible rate discretion would still hold.

In the CCV welfare function, the measure of inflation is given by wage inflation rather than the more traditional consumer price index (CPI) inflation. This specification choice may bias the results in favor of flexible rate regimes. In fact, note that under both strict and flexible inflation targeting the volatility of nominal and real exchange rates is very high. Thus, CPI inflation that depends on the price of imported goods would also be highly volatile (because purchasing power parity holds for tradeables) when the nominal exchange rate is highly volatile. Instead, wage inflation is more sluggish given the Calvo adjustment assumption in the paper. Thus, the specification of inflation in the welfare function may bias the results in favor of fixed rates. Consequently, it may be worth conducting the same welfare analysis using the traditional definition of inflation.

CCV use, for welfare analysis, the one-period loss function of the monetary authority rather than the more traditional discounted sum of losses in all periods. Although the former function is the limit, for the discount factor going to zero, of the latter, it may be worthwhile to perform the analysis using the latter to test whether the results are sensitive to this specification.

Moreover, in the model the real responses to international capital market shocks are small, but in the real world they are much sharper. In the CCV model, shocks to international capital markets are modeled as increases in the world interest rate. Such shocks have very modest effects on output as investment falls, but the risk premium falls too. Also, the increase in interest rates is sharp but only very temporary.

This does not square with the reality faced by EM economies, where the most important shocks are not the usually modest increases in international interest rates but the much sharper reductions in international capital market access that take two forms: sharp exogenous increases in the risk premium for emerging markets, as captured by large increases in Emerging Markets Bond Index (EMBI) spreads; and sudden cutoffs in the ability of EMs to borrow in international capital markets ("sudden stops").

To consider in a more realistic setting the relative performance of fixed and flexible exchange rates, one would have to consider the response of the model economy to exogenous large shocks to the risk premium faced by an emerging market. In that setup, it is not clear whether flexible rates would be superior to fixed.

Of course, in both regimes, authorities will be faced with unpleasant tradeoffs: under a fixed rate regime, nominal and real interest rates sharply increase to prevent a devaluation, and recessionary effects are the outcome. Additionally, under flexible rates, if the authorities decide not to increase interest rates, the exchange rate will sharply depreciate (even beyond what is warranted by fundamentals if there is excessive volatility of asset prices); in that case, the balance sheet effects may be large, and the loss of inflation credibility may also be large if policy makers already suffer a lack of policy credibility.

Alternatively, policy makers under flexible rates may respond to the shock by sharply tightening interest rates to minimize devaluation effects and the ensuing balance sheet and inflation-confidence effects. However, in this case, the contractionary effects on output may be similar to those under fixed exchange rates.

Thus, we do not know a priori which regime would be superior when an EM suddenly experiences a "sudden stop" or a sharp exogenous increase in the international investors' risk aversion.

In conclusion, this is an interesting and valuable contribution. However, there are a number of issues in the comparison between fixed and flexible exchange rates that this paper has not fully addressed. In particular, although in the long run a regime of flexible exchange rates may dominate one of fixed rates, in the short run the relevant comparison is between the costs of maintaining fixed rates versus moving to flexible rates through a currency crisis; such a move to flexible rates via a currency collapse and exchange rate overshooting may lead to balance sheet effects that may be severely contractionary. This is an empirical phenomenon that current models of balance sheet effects and exchange rates have not addressed.

References

Aghion, Philippe, Philippe Bacchetta, and Abhijit Banerjee. 2000. Currency crises and monetary policy with credit constraints. Harvard University. Mimeograph.

Blejer, Mario, Alain Ize, Alfredo Leone, and Sergio Werlang. 2000. Inflation targeting in practice: Strategic and operational issues and application to emerging market economies. Washington, D.C.: International Monetary Fund, August.

Borensztein, Eduardo R., Jeromin Zettelmeyer, and Thomas Philippon. 2000. Monetary independence in emerging markets: Does the exchange rate regime make a difference? IMF Working Paper no. WP/01/1. Washington, D.C.: International Monetary Fund, January. Available at [http://www.imf.org/external/pubs/ft/wp/2001/wp0101.pdf].

Broda, Christian. 2000. Coping with terms of trade shocks: Pegs vs. floats. *American Economic Review* 91 (2): 376–80.

Caballero, Ricardo, and Arvind Krishnamurthy. 2000. Emerging market crises: An asset market perspective. Massachusetts Institute of Technology, Sloan School of Business. Unpublished Manuscript.

Calvo, Guillermo A., and Carmen M. Reinhart. 1999. Fixing for your life. NBER Working Paper no. 8006. Cambridge, Mass.: National Bureau of Economic Research, November.

———. 2000. Fear of floating. NBER Working Paper no. 7993. Cambridge, Mass.: National Bureau of Economic Research, November.

Céspedes, Luis, Roberto Chang, and Andres Velasco. 2000. Balance sheets and exchange rate policy. NBER Working Paper no. 7840. Cambridge, Mass.: National Bureau of Economic Research, August.

Chang, Roberto, and Andres Velasco. 1999. Liquidity crises in emerging markets: Theory and policy. NBER Working Paper no. 7272. Cambridge, Mass.: National Bureau of Economic Research, July.

Christiano, Lawrence J., Christopher Gust, and Jorge Roldós. 2000. Monetary policy in an international financial crisis. International Monetary Fund, research department. Mimeograph.

Frankel, Jeffrey. 2000. No single currency is right for all countries at all times. Graham Lecture presented at Princeton University, May.

Gelos, Gaston, and Alejandro Werner. 1999. Financial liberalization, credit constraints, and collateral-investment in the Mexican manufacturing sector. IMF Working Paper no. WP/99/25. Washington, D.C.: International Monetary Fund, March.

Gertler, Mark, Simon Gilchrist, and Fabio Natalucci. 2000. External constraints on monetary policy and the financial accelerator. New York University. Mimeograph.

Hausmann, Ricardo. 1999. Should there be five currencies or one hundred and five? *Foreign Policy* 116:65–79.

Kiyotaki, Nobuhiro, and John Moore. 1997. Credit cycles. *Journal of Political Economy* 105:211–48.

Krugman, Paul. 1999. Balance sheets, the transfer problem, and financial crises. Massachusetts Institute of Technology. Mimeograph. January. Available at [http://web.mit.edu/krugman/www/FLOOD.pdf].

Perri, Fabrizio, Nouriel Roubini, Kate Kisselev, and Michele Cavallo. 2001. Exchange rates overshooting and the costs of floating. New York University, Stern School of Business. Unpublished Manuscript.

Schaechter, Andrea, Mark Stone, and Mark Zelmer. 2000. Adopting inflation targeting: Practical issues for emerging market countries. Washington, D.C.: International Monetary Fund, December.

Discussion Summary

On the related literature, *Sebastian Edwards* commented that the discussion of contractionary devaluation and balance sheet effects is preceded by the work of Guillermo Calvo (and others). The most memorable episode of this kind was in the 1970s and 1980s and related to the whole discussion of the Southern Cone liberalization. The reason that Chile did not devalue at that time was that every single large bank had a very large dollarized liability. This was also the reason that the Chilean banking system had to be nationalized and taken over by the government at the cost of 60 percent of the GDP.

Edwards agreed with the discussant, Nouriel Roubini, that the paper should be clearer on what the relevant comparison is, that is, what system flexible rates should be compared with. However, he did not agree with the discussant's suggestion that the two exchange rate systems should be compared during an exchange rate overshooting, that is, starting from a currency crisis. The question of whether to float from a period of tranquility is very important because many countries are facing this problem right now. One example is Chile's dilemma: whether to follow Argentina and fix its exchange rate to the dollar or follow Mexico to float. Also, Guatemala—located between El Salvador, which will dollarize, and Mexico, which is floating—should make a decision in a tranquil economic situation.

Edwards expressed his surprise regarding the last comparison of the discretional policy to the policy of flexible inflation with real exchange rate targeting. He had expected to see that the flexible inflation with real exchange rate targeting would come last. He speculated that this is not the case because in the model the real exchange rate targeting does not generate huge inflationary inertia due to the way the Calvo-style staggered contracts work. In another framework (which Carlos A. Végh used in his work), real exchange rate targeting will be very costly due to inflationary inertia.

Jorge Braga de Macedo remarked that, in his view, it is too simple to focus on corner solutions, especially if one wants to draw policy implications from the analysis. For example, in the fixed corner, there is a vast difference between dollarization and monetary union.

Roberto Rigobon commented that the paper seems to treat what he thought were the means of monetary policy as the objectives of the policy. For example, pure inflation targeting and imperfect inflation targeting appear as the objectives of the policy in the paper, whereas Rigobon thought inflation targeting referred to the way monetary policy was conducted independent of the objective of the central bank. His related point was that if different targets are treated as objectives, one can't compare welfare losses: it is like comparing two models with different utility functions, he said.

Paolo Pesenti commented on the choice of welfare metric. He observed that the loss function is ad hoc and unrelated to the positive model of the paper. He suggested that the Rotemberg-Woodford quadratic approximation could provide a more appropriate welfare metric. Secondly, he said that the model is skewed a priori against fixed exchange rates. The parameters are chosen so that there is no Barro-Gordon–style inflationary bias, thus ruling out the possibility that a fixed exchange rate rule may be preferred to discretion in monetary policy. Instead, in a setup in which the pass-through is not 100 percent, the economy is highly open, and there is monopolistic competition, optimization under discretion would entail a large inflation bias that would make the fixed rate regime more appealing than what appears in the framework of the paper.

Carlos A. Végh said that he liked what the paper was trying to do, but not how it did it. He was wondering why the authors did not study the optimal policy simply by looking at the policy that maximizes the household's welfare or the combination of the households and workers' welfare.

Rudi Dornbusch pointed out that the bias against fixed rates in the paper could be due to equation (9), which contains the real balances (M/P) in the households' and workers' preferences. The specification with real balances in the preferences implies a preference towards volatility.

Roberto Chang agreed with the discussant that the choice of exchange rate regime starting from a crisis period is very important, but, as pointed out by Edwards, it is also an important question during a tranquil period. It is not obvious whether these two issues can be studied in one setting, and the paper focuses on the second question.

On the technical issues, first, he said the paper is well specified. The model is solved by taking log-linear approximation around the nonstochastic steady state. If one takes uncertainty seriously and looks at correctly specified dynamic stationary equilibrium of an economy, then risk premium will be a true random variable and will have different expectation and variance. This paper did not address this point, but it is important. The approach of the paper is justified by concerns of tractability, which approach also explains why the loss function is ad hoc in the model.

He also commented on Végh's question of specifying the welfare function as the welfare of the inhabitants of the economy, given that the paper has fully specified a general equilibrium problem. He said that the paper wanted to postpone this question because the authors are not sure about the objectives of the central bank (i.e., whether it is benevolent). There is also a complication when dealing with this question, that is, how to approximate the welfare function of the agents of an open economy with a quadratic function. The paper chose the most tractable method, although in recent work he and others have been developing approaches that are more general.

Regarding Rigobon's comments, he noted that the paper followed Svensson's (2000) usage of the term *targeting*.

13

Chaebol Capitalism and the Currency-Financial Crisis in Korea

Anne O. Krueger and Jungho Yoo

In the aftermath of the Asian "financial crises," a number of factors have been identified as the culprits in leading to the crises and intensifying their severity. Among them, so-called "crony capitalism," the weakness of the banking system precrisis, financial liberalization and opening of the capital account, and the nominal exchange rate regime have all been singled out.

However, although all these factors obviously contributed, their relative quantitative importance and the interactions between them are little understood. It is the purpose of this paper to delve, insofar as is feasible, into the contributions of exchange rate depreciation, the weak financial system, financial and capital account liberalization, and crony capitalism in leading up to the crisis and intensifying its severity. For that purpose, we focus on the Korean experience and trace the roles of the *chaebol,* the history of credit rationing and buildup of domestic credit and foreign indebtedness prior to the crisis, the opening of the capital account, and the impact of exchange rate depreciation on the crisis.

It is important to understand the role and relative importance of each of the key variables. If, for example, exchange rate depreciation was forced as the consequence of maintaining an unsustainable nominal exchange rate for a long period of time prior to the crisis and was quantitatively the largest factor in leading to the deterioration of the banks' portfolios, resort in the future to a genuinely floating exchange rate or preventing uncovered liabil-

Anne O. Krueger is the first deputy managing director of the International Monetary Fund and a research associate of the National Bureau of Economic Research. Jungho Yoo is a senior fellow of the Korea Development Institute, currently serving as the director of the KDI Center for Economic Information.

The authors are indebted to Mu Yang for valuable research assistance and to conference participants for helpful comments on the paper.

ities denominated in foreign exchange should greatly reduce the likelihood of future crises. Likewise, if bank lending practices had resulted in a rapidly increasing proportion of nonperforming loans (NPLs) in the banking system even had the exchange rate not been a significant factor, the relative importance of improving bank lending practices as a preventive measure for future crises looms much larger.[1] Moreover, if rigidities in the banking and financial system resulting from failure to liberalize or regulate sufficiently were a major contributing factor, the policy lessons would focus on the urgent need to liberalize and strengthen banking and financial systems in emerging markets.

In our first section, we briefly sketch the roles that each of these factors can play in theory in financial crises. In section 13.2 we then provide background on the Korean economy and the evolution of the banking and financial systems, the *chaebol,* and linkages to the international economy, which are essential building blocks for our later analysis. Section 13.3 then examines the history of financing of the *chaebol* and their role in the Korean economy. The fourth section then examines the financial structure and performance of the *chaebol* and the banking system. The fifth section then considers the role of foreign currency–denominated debt in intensifying the crisis. The final section then provides our best judgment as to the relative importance of the variables widely pointed to as contributing to crisis.

13.1   Domestic Credit Expansion, Lending to *Chaebol* or Cronies, Exchange Rate Depreciation, Capital Account Opening, and Crises

As the title of this section suggests, the problem for analysis of the Asian crises is not the lack of explanations: it is that there are too many. In those crises, and in the Mexican crisis of 1994, a foreign exchange crisis and a financial crisis occurred almost simultaneously and have come to be termed *twin crises.* As will be seen, there are a number of reasons to anticipate that these twin crises are likely to have a far more severe impact on a domestic economy than either a financial or a currency crisis alone, and it is not coincidental that their onset is virtually simultaneous.

In this section, we briefly review the role of each of the possible causal factors in precipitating and intensifying twin crises. Once that is done, focus turns to interactions between them. Thereafter, we attempt to assess how important these factors were and the quantitative magnitude of the interactions.

---

1. In some countries, NPLs increase because of lending to the politically well connected, who apparently do not expect, and are not expected, to repay. In Korea, however, the "cronyism" concerns surrounding bank lending focus on the lending by the banks to the large *chaebol.* Earlier lending to them had been sound, as will be seen, although as will also be seen, government officials supported lending to the *chaebol* by the banks when their profitability was falling sharply in the precrisis period.

13.1.1   Exchange Rate Pegging

Although any nominal exchange rate could, in theory, be associated with the appropriate real exchange rate,[2] empirical evidence shows that governmental policies with respect to nominal exchange rates over periods of three to five years, if not longer, significantly affect real exchange rates. Whether this is because of long lags in adjustment or the unwillingness of the domestic authorities to adopt the monetary and fiscal policies consistent with their choice of nominal exchange rate is not relevant for present purposes. Empirically, if the authorities intervene in the foreign exchange market for purposes other than smoothing short-term fluctuations (such as maintaining a fixed nominal exchange rate), the real exchange rate appreciates relative to major trading partners when domestic inflation exceeds the inflation rate in the partner countries. Likewise, if for any reason (such as changes in the terms of trade or rapid growth of domestic demand for imports) the real exchange rate would adjust in a well-functioning free market but is prevented from doing so, there can be imbalances between the demand for and supply of foreign exchange. As long as the authorities can meet this demand, buying or selling foreign exchange as demanded, they can maintain their exchange rate policy.

All of the countries afflicted with twin crises in the 1990s had intervened heavily in their foreign exchange market in one way or another to achieve target nominal exchange rates. In the cases of Mexico and Thailand, the nominal exchange rate had been either fixed, or adjusted according to a formula that resulted in significant appreciation of the real exchange rate. In Indonesia and Korea, terms-of-trade shocks probably called for a significant real exchange rate depreciation at a time when there was some degree of real appreciation—as will be seen below for Korea.

When government officials implicitly or explicitly indicate that they will maintain an exchange rate policy that results in an appreciating currency in real terms, they provide individuals and firms with a strong incentive to access the international capital market, because the real interest rate is typically lower than in the domestic market.[3] When domestic residents have access to the foreign capital market, or when domestic banks can borrow abroad, the result is an increase in the nation's liabilities, and exchange rate policy means that the government is increasing its contingent liabilities. The

2. This would require that the domestic authorities refrain from using monetary and fiscal policies in pursuit of domestic economic objectives and instead allow inflation or deflation to occur as the "equilibrium" real exchange rate changed. Thus, if from an initial position of balance the terms of trade deteriorated and warranted a real depreciation of the currency, the domestic price level would have to be allowed to decline to achieve that real depreciation.

3. Lowering the domestic nominal interest rate would result in more domestic inflation and is thus eschewed by the authorities. See Krueger (1997) for the calculation of Mexican real interest rates during the precrisis period when a nominal anchor exchange rate policy was followed.

unsustainability of the nominal exchange rate policy results in a buildup of domestic credit and foreign liabilities until the time when either domestic residents and foreigners anticipate that the exchange rate will alter and attempt to get out of domestic money and into foreign currency or the public or private debt-servicing obligations denominated in foreign exchange are not voluntarily met. At that point, either the run on the currency results in a currency crisis, or the prospective inability to continue voluntary debt-servicing forces the same outcome. Resolving the crisis almost always involves an alteration in the exchange rate, and usually in exchange rate policy.[4]

It should be noted here that there can be a "pure" currency crisis, one that exists without a financial crisis. The normal precondition for this outcome is a reasonably sound banking and financial system at the time of the onset of the currency crisis, or a preexisting highly restrictive set of capital controls that prevented the buildup of significant foreign indebtedness. Brazil's devaluation in 1999 is one good example of a currency crisis in which there was no serious domestic financial spillover.

13.1.2   Crony Capitalism and Crisis

If there is a continuing buildup of NPLs in the banking system, a financial crisis will result unless effective measures are taken to reverse the buildup. NPLs can come about for several reasons: (a) there can be an unforeseen macroeconomic disturbance (originating abroad or domestically) that leads to unfavorable outcomes for borrowers; (b) domestic credit expansion may be so rapid that banks are unwilling or unable to exercise normal prudence in lending, and a disproportionate number of borrowers are unable to service their debts (often after a macroeconomic downturn); (c) banks may be directed or induced to lend to politically well-connected cronies, who do not service their outstanding loans; and, finally, (d) banks may lend to favored (economically important) enterprises that do not or cannot service their debt obligations. This last case includes the circumstance in which banks provide "evergreen" accounts for large businesses that are indebted to them, rolling over existing debt and extending credit to finance interest payments on it.

For Indonesia, it is thought that the third explanation—obligatory lending to politically well-connected friends and relatives of the president—was a significant factor in the NPLs of the banking system. In Thailand (and to a degree in Korea, as will be seen below), rapid expansion of domestic credit, certainly at least somewhat associated with the fixed nominal exchange rate, was a major culprit. In Japan in the late 1980s, where currency

---

4. It should be noted that not all exchange rate changes will immediately quell the crisis. In the Mexican case, there was already a significant capital outflow when the authorities announced a nominal devaluation. In the view of most market participants, the magnitude of the announced devaluation was too small, and the run on the currency intensified. It was not until the exchange rate was permitted to float that the immediate crisis subsided.

crisis was not a factor, a large negative macroeconomic shock when the rapid inflation of asset prices was reversed was the trigger for difficulties in the banking system. Probably the best example of the last explanation, lending to favored enterprises and evergreening their accounts, is the Korean case, to be discussed below.

Here, the important point is that once NPLs become significant in a bank's portfolios, serious difficulties are likely to result in the absence of sufficient provisioning or capital. A bank with sizable NPLs must charge higher interest rates on its lending in order to cover its costs over a smaller proportion of its business. Consequently, if it has more NPLs than its competitors, only those unable to obtain cheaper credit at banks with healthier balance sheets will borrow from it, thus increasing the riskiness of its portfolio. At the same time, as depositors learn of the bank's difficulties, they are likely to attempt to withdraw their deposits.

When many domestic banks have these difficulties at the same time, domestic credit can contract sharply. If there are foreign competitors (or if creditworthy borrowers can borrow abroad), the entire domestic banking system can be threatened.

13.1.3 Domestic Credit Expansion

Domestic credit can expand unduly rapidly because of government direction of credit to cronies or to favored enterprises. However, it can also expand rapidly because of the incentives provided by the exchange rate regime or simply because government monetary and fiscal policy is very loose for whatever reason. Rapid expansion of credit is dangerous. On one hand, it is inflationary, which means that for a while a permissive environment will enable borrowers to service their debts until tighter monetary policy is adopted to curb the resulting inflation. On the other hand, accelerated lending is associated with a deteriorating quality of borrower, both because there are simply not enough sound borrowers to finance such a rapid expansion and because banks do not have the capacity to evaluate lending at such an increasing rate.

Rapid expansion of domestic credit was a feature of the precrisis period in Mexico, Indonesia, Thailand, Malaysia, and Korea. In the Indonesian case, the expansion of domestic credit exceeded 20 percent of gross domestic product (GDP) in the precrisis years.

13.1.4 Capital Account Liberalization

Many observers have blamed the opening of the capital account for the twin crises of the 1990s. The simple argument goes that without an open capital account, indebtedness could not have built up. However, there have been many experiences with foreign exchange crises in countries where the capital account was relatively closed. The degree to which cross-border financial flows must be regulated to prevent speculative flows when exchange rates are greatly misaligned is more restrictive than is compatible with a relatively open trading regime.

Moreover, many countries with open capital accounts have not experienced the difficulties that the Asian countries did. Economies such as those of Taiwan and Singapore, where there were current account surpluses and high levels of foreign exchange reserves relative to trade volumes, did not experience difficulties.

To the extent that the opening of the capital account results in difficulties, there are more complex avenues than those associated with real appreciation of the currency. First, when the capital account is open and the nominal exchange rate is fixed without appropriate supportive monetary and fiscal policies, as discussed above, there are strong incentives for banks or private entities to incur foreign exchange–denominated liabilities (capital inflow) because of lower borrowing costs. When they view the government as having guaranteed the exchange rate, they may not match their future foreign exchange liabilities with foreign exchange assets. Second, banks may not have sufficient incentives for appropriate prudence in their lending policies, due either to a lack of capital adequacy (and existing NPLs) or to an absence of appropriate supervision.

In the first case, it would appear that the exchange rate regime is the real culprit; in the second, it is weaknesses in the domestic financial system, which become exacerbated with the opening of the capital account.

13.2   The Korean Economy, the *Chaebol,* Credit Rationing, and Growth

13.2.1   Korean Economic Growth After 1960

As is well known, Korea was one of the poorest countries in the world in the late 1950s and was then widely regarded as a country without serious growth prospects. After economic policy reforms began in the early 1960s, Korea began growing at sustained rates previously unheard of in world history.[5] Real GDP grew at an average annual rate of 10 percent per annum in the decade starting in 1963. High growth rates continued into the 1990s, and Korea's real per capita income in the mid-1990s was nearly nine times what it had been in the early 1960s (see fig. 13.1).

---

5. Taiwan's rate of economic growth was equally rapid. Prior to the crisis of the late 1990s, most observers would have claimed that the major difference between the Taiwanese and Korean economies was the relatively small scale of Taiwanese enterprises contrasted with the large share of the Korean *chaebol* in the Korean economy. However, there were other differences: perhaps because of greater strategic insecurity, the Taiwanese held very large foreign exchange reserves in relation to the size of their trade or their economy; the Taiwanese dollar showed no tendency for real appreciation; and Taiwan's current account had been consistently in surplus. The Taiwanese financial system appears to have been considerably sounder than that of Korea in the late 1990s, and the rate of expansion of domestic credit at that time was much lower than that in Korea.

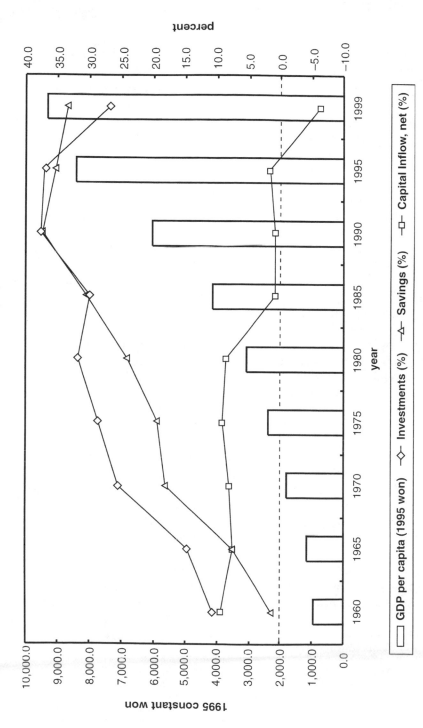

Fig. 13.1 GDP per capita, investments, savings, capital flows
Source: Appendix table 13A.1.

Economic liberalization took place throughout the first thirty-five years of Korea's rapid growth. In 1960, the country had had the usual developing-country mix of an overvalued exchange rate supported by quantitative restrictions on imports (and a black market in foreign exchange), consequent high walls of protection for domestic manufacturers, price controls on many key commodities, credit rationing, a large fiscal deficit, one of the highest rates of inflation in the world, and a huge (averaging around 9 percent of GDP over the period 1953–58) current account deficit, financed largely by foreign aid inflows.[6]

First steps in reform included a move to a more realistic (and constant real) exchange rate for exports and the relaxation of restrictions on importing by exporters. Imports were liberalized further in the late 1960s, and the exchange regime was unified by that time. Other major reforms also took place, including a major fiscal and tax reform in 1964, gradual removal of price controls, a shift from a regime discriminating against agriculture to a protective one, and further liberalization of the trade regime. In the later 1960s, quantitative restrictions on imports were greatly eased and tariffs were lowered in several steps, and further trade liberalization took place in the 1990s.

In the early years of rapid growth, however, the banking system remained tightly controlled. Even after a reform in 1965 (which resulted in a positive real rate of interest for borrowers), credit was rationed and the curb market rate was well above the controlled interest rate (see Hong 1981). Only in the late 1980s did deregulation of interest rates begin, although the apparent gap between demand and supply of loanable funds was declining over time (see section 13.3).

When economic policy reform began, Korea's exports were only about 3 percent of GDP, whereas imports were about 13 percent. Policy makers therefore began to focus on measures to increase exports. They did so by encouraging all exports uniformly,[7] but nonetheless they held something that might be regarded as approaching an "export theory of value." Any firm that could export was rewarded in proportion to the foreign exchange receipts from exporting. Moreover, many of the firms that were initially successful were *chaebol* (although they were very small at the time, and some Korean analysts today do not regard the Hyundais, Samsungs, and the like of the 1960s as *chaebol* at all). Because they were successful, they grew rap-

---

6. See Krueger (1979) and Frank, Kim, and Westphal (1975) for an account of the early period of Korea's rapid development.

7. All exporters were given an "export subsidy," an "interest subsidy," and a tax subsidy, each of a specified number of won per dollar of exports (the number being altered from time to time as conditions were deemed to warrant). In addition, exporters were permitted to import goods for their use in generous quantities, which undoubtedly permitted some profits through use of the excess for domestic sales. To a significant degree, these "incentives" offset the duties and other charges on imports and resulted in reasonably uniform incentives for import competing and exportable production.

idly. They received new loans as their exports grew and as they expanded into new exporting activities.[8] Given the underdeveloped state of the Korean financial markets at that time (and in the absence of measures to strengthen them), access to credit was vital for expansion.

The *chaebol* were successful exporters and, for the first decade or more of Korean growth, were regarded almost as the heroes of Korean development. They were rewarded for export performance and were highly profitable. Hong (1981) estimates the real rate of return on capital to have been about 35 percent or more in the first decade following the start of reforms. Although the *chaebol* were highly profitable and generally encouraged to enter whatever export markets they could, when the authorities wanted a venture undertaken, the *chaebol* were asked to do so. They undertook these ventures with the implicit guarantee of the government that credit, tax exemptions, and other support would be available to make the venture profitable.[9] However, the *chaebol* were on the whole remarkably profitable and had little difficulty in servicing their (subsidized) debt.

The extent to which the Korean economy changed structure is remarkable (see fig. 13.2). Exports and export earnings (the dollar price index of traded goods being stable in the 1960s) grew at over 41 percent annually for the period 1959–69 and continued growing almost that rapidly thereafter. Exports of goods and services as a percentage of GDP rose from 3 percent in 1960 to 14 percent in 1970 and to 33 percent in 1980; imports also rose, from their 10 percent level in 1960 to 41 percent of GDP in 1980. Hence, the Korean economy was becoming much more open.[10]

At the start of reforms, rationed credit financed a large fraction of new investment, especially in the manufacturing sector. The subsidies implicit in

8. Some of these activities were chosen by the *chaebol*. On occasion, however, the authorities suggested to *chaebol* owners that they should move into certain lines of production. This attempt to "pick winners" was not always successful; when it reached its height in the heavy and chemical industry (HCI) drive of the mid-1970s, the rate of economic growth and of export expansion slowed substantially, and policies were reversed by the late 1970s. When *chaebol* incurred losses while undertaking these mandated activities, the banks were directed to extend additional credit to the *chaebol,* thus setting a precedent for later difficulties.

9. It is important to underscore that these government "rewards" existed in the context of the export drive. When *chaebol* could not produce competitive exports, there was little support. Even in the HCI drive—the most industry-specific interventionist phase of Korean policy—the output from HCI industries was to be exported within a specified period. When it became clear that that performance test was not being passed, the entire thrust of policy was reevaluated.

10. Some of the increase in imports was of course intermediate goods used in the production of exportables. However, the percentage import content of exports remained fairly stable at around 35 percent of the value of exports over the period of rapid growth. From 1960 onward, exporters were entitled to import with little paperwork virtually anything that they might use in producing exportables; in addition, they were permitted to import a "wastage" allowance, which they were free to sell on the domestic market. Thus, the de facto liberalization exceeded that which took place because of the removal of quantitative restrictions and lowering of tariffs. With an average tariff rate in the tariff schedule of around 15 percent in 1970, average tariff collections as a percent of imports were about 6 percent.

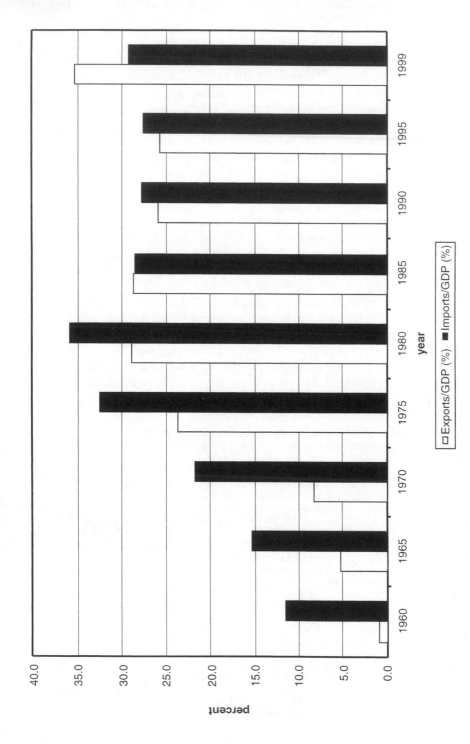

Fig. 13.2 Dependency on trade
Source: Appendix table 13A.2.

this credit served as a stimulus to industry and permitted much more rapid expansion than would have been possible had companies been forced to rely on reinvesting their own profits.[11] Exporters were allocated preferential credit based upon their export performance. The real rate of return was so high that all the *chaebol* would happily have borrowed more had they been able to; most of them, as reported by Hong (1981), borrowed additional funds at the much higher curb market rates. Thus, lending at controlled interest rates was, at least in the early years, equivalent to an intramarginal subsidy to the *chaebol.*

Estimates of rates of return suggest that the *chaebol* were highly profitable at that time even without subsidies. Indeed, given the huge distortions in the economy that prevailed in the late 1950s, it is likely that, at least in the 1960s, almost any reasonably sensible venture into unskilled labor–intensive exportable production had a high real rate of return.

As already mentioned, by the mid-1960s the borrowing rate from the banks was positive in real terms although below a market-clearing rate. Over the following three decades, the banking system was further liberalized as the real interest rate charged for loans rose and the gap between the controlled rate and what might have cleared the market diminished (see section 13.3). At the same time, the real rate of return on investments naturally fell, because the very high initial returns obviously could not be sustained. We trace the decline in real returns and the increase in the real cost of credit in the next section.

When policy reforms began in the early 1960s, the Korean saving rate was very low, even negative by some estimates. As growth accelerated and per capita incomes rose, domestic saving began to increase rapidly, rising from around zero percent of GDP[12] in 1960 to 18 percent by 1970 and to 24 percent by 1980 (see fig. 13.1). However, at least until the late 1970s, profitable investment opportunities greatly exceeded domestic saving. As a result, domestic saving was supplemented by borrowing from abroad, equaling as much as 13 percent of GDP in years in the late 1960s.[13] Despite the large capital inflows, however, the ratios of debt service to exports and debt to

11. In much of the public discussion about the reliance of firms in crisis countries on borrowing, what seems to be forgotten is that, starting from very low levels of income and development, there is very little equity, and a large fraction of investment must therefore be financed through other channels.

12. In 1960, it is estimated that private saving was a positive 3.2 percent of GDP, whereas government saving was a negative 2 percent of GDP. Foreign sources financed 78 percent of investment, which was 10 percent of GDP. See Krueger (1979, 206–07). In 1960, most foreign resources were foreign aid.

13. Most of the capital inflow was from the private sector—largely commercial bank lending—by the late 1960s. Foreign aid had peaked in 1958 and was less than 2 percent of GDP by the mid-1960s. The current account deficit was sustainable because of the profitability of investment and the declining debt-service ratio that resulted from such rapid growth of exports and of real GDP.

GDP did not increase because of the rapid rate of growth of export earnings and real GDP.

The Korean government guaranteed these credits and determined the maximum that could be borrowed, allocating borrowing rights among exporting firms. Because the foreign interest rate was well below the domestic interest rate (especially in the curb market) and the real exchange rate was fairly stable for exporters, there was intense competition for foreign loans.

As domestic saving rose, the proportionate reliance on foreign resources to supplement domestic saving in financing investment fell. By the 1980s, the domestic saving rate was in excess of 30 percent, and the current account went into surplus for several years in the mid-1980s.[14] Beginning at this time, the American government in bilateral trade negotiations began to pressure the Koreans to allow the won to appreciate in order to reduce the bilateral trade surplus with the United States.[15] By the mid-1990s most Korean economists believed that some real depreciation of the won would be in Korea's best interest but the pressures against such a move prevented it. Although the won exchange rate was not fixed, the range within which it fluctuated was relatively narrow: it appreciated from 890 won per dollar at the end of 1985 to 679 won per dollar in 1989, and thereafter it gradually depreciated to 808 won per dollar in 1993, appreciating again to 788 won per dollar in 1995. At the end of 1996 it stood at 844 won per dollar, and of course it depreciated almost 50 percent in 1997.[16] For the decade prior to the 1997 crisis, however, there had been little change in the real exchange rate.

Thus, by the mid-1990s, Korea had sustained three and a half decades of rapid growth. Although there had been periods of difficulty—both slowdowns and overheating—Korean policy makers had met their challenges successfully. As noted by the Organization for Economic Cooperation and Development (OECD), the country had progressed from being one of the poorest developing countries in 1960 to having a per capita income equal to that of some OECD countries and a higher rate of economic growth.[17]

The late 1980s had witnessed the introduction of a democratic process

14. Korean policy makers viewed the emergence of the current account surplus as a transitory phenomenon explicable by "three lows": the fall in oil prices in the mid-1980s, the drop in world interest rates (so that debt-servicing costs declined), and the low dollar (or high yen). The current account turned positive in 1986, rose to a peak of 8.5 percent of GDP in 1988, fell to 2.4 percent of GDP in 1989, turned negative (-0.5 percent) in 1990, and remained negative in the 1–2 percent range until 1997, when the deficit increased to 4.7 percent of GDP.

15. Korea was running a bilateral surplus with the United States and a bilateral deficit with Japan, and policy makers resisted as far as they could these pressures. One response was to ask the American authorities whether they should devalue with respect to the yen while they appreciated with respect to the U.S. dollar!

16. Exchange rates, saving rates, and current account deficit data are all taken from various issues of the IMF's *International Financial Statistics* unless otherwise noted.

17. For an account of the Korean economy in the mid-1990s reflecting this consensus view, see OECD (1994).

into Korea. The elected governments chose to liberalize further, especially in the financial sector and international capital flows.[18] In 1992–93 there was a "growth recession," as the growth rate slowed to just over 5 percent (in contrast with rates over 9 percent in the preceding two years and an average rate above 8 percent in the preceding decade). One response was to ease monetary policy: domestic credit expanded by over 18 percent in 1994, 14 percent in 1995, and 21 percent in 1996.[19] Real GDP growth responded, exceeding 8 percent in 1994 and 1995. However, as will be argued in section 13.3, underlying weaknesses were not addressed, and the stimulus to the economy, through expansion of domestic credit and other measures, increased the vulnerability of the financial system later on.

13.2.2 The Crisis

Export earnings failed to maintain their growth rate in 1996, increasing only 3 percent in dollar terms, as falling prices for semiconductors and a number of other factors resulted in the slowdown. Then, early in 1997, a number of events took place that surely eroded confidence. One of the large *chaebol,* Hanbo, went bankrupt early in the year. Given that the large *chaebol* were widely believed to be "too big to fail," this in and of itself must have resulted in some loss of confidence and a reexamination of Korea's creditworthiness. Moreover, 1997 was an election year, with the presidential elections scheduled for early in December. That the market anticipated difficulties is reflected in the fact that the Korean stock exchange index fell from 981 in April 1996 to 677 by the end of March 1997 and to 471 at the end of October, even before the outbreak of the currency crisis.

However, although the net and gross foreign (and especially short-term) liabilities of the banking and financial systems were continuing to increase, there was no visible evidence of crisis until the final quarter of the year. The Thai crisis had exploded in June, and the Indonesian crisis had begun during the summer of 1997, but most foreign observers were confident, given Korea's past history, that Korea would not be affected.[20] Korea's offshore banks were holding paper from Indonesia, Russia, and other countries with dollar liabilities, which would further deteriorate the net foreign asset position, but that was not widely known at the time.

However, capital flight began early in the fourth quarter of the year. In many instances, it was simply due to a refusal to roll over short-term debt,

---

18. See the OECD (1994) description of the five-year financial liberalization plan.

19. This rate was not markedly faster, however, than it had been over the entire preceding decade. Hahm and Mishkin (2000, 91) reject the notion that liberalization of the capital account was responsible for the increase in domestic credit, but note that it did play a role in permitting the banks to take on greater exposures to foreign exchange risk.

20. However, many Korean economists and policy analysts were very concerned. Krueger was at a conference of Korean economic policy makers in August 1997, and the mood was one of deep gloom. Many of the participants were extremely pessimistic about the *chaebol,* the state of the financial system, and the potential for reforms of economic policy.

but other factors contributed: Korea's sovereign risk status was downgraded by Standard & Poor's in October; reported NPLs in the banking system doubled between the end of 1996 and the fourth quarter of 1998, reaching 7.5 percent of total loans by that time, owing largely to the bankruptcy of six *chaebol* and the sharp drop in the Korean stock exchange. However, once it became known that reserves were decreasing, others sought to get out of won, and the capital outflow intensified rapidly.[21] Total reserves less overseas branch deposits and other unusable foreign exchange were $22.3 billion at the end of October and fell to $7.3 billion by the end of November.[22] It is reported that, by the time the International Monetary Fund (IMF) was approached, gross reserves were being depleted at a rate so rapid that they would have approached zero within forty-eight hours. In the program presented to the IMF board, it was reported that usable reserves had dropped from $22.5 billion on 31 October to $13 billion on 21 November and to $6 billion on 2 December.[23]

13.2.3   The IMF Program[24]

All three presidential candidates had declared repeatedly that under no circumstances would they approach the IMF. When the government did approach the IMF, the IMF's problem was complicated by several things: (a) it was not known who the new president would be, and hence with whom the IMF would have to deal on the economics team; (b) there was very little time to put together a program, and both because Korea had been viewed as "sound" until recently and because the candidates had all said they would not approach the Fund, there had been less preliminary work done than was usually the case;[25] (c) the exchange rate was depreciating sharply after the end of October, and when the band was widened to 10 percent on 19 November, the rate of depreciation began to accelerate rapidly; and (d) as has already been mentioned, the government was rapidly running out of foreign exchange reserves, and would soon be forced to default on its obligations (see Boughton 2000). The high short-term indebtedness meant that

21. However, even in November, the Finance Ministry was issuing reassuring statements, and private forecasters were minimizing the likelihood that Korea would approach the IMF. For a representative account, see John Burton's "Korean Currency Slide Shakes Economy" in the *Financial Times,* 12 November 1997, 5.

22. Data are from Hahm and Mishkin (2000, table 11).

23. Other factors also contributed. A financial reform bill, proposed by a blue ribbon committee, had been turned down by parliament, and it was not clear whether the government had legally guaranteed the foreign exchange liabilities of the financial institutions. Although interest rates had risen by about 200 basis points, the Bank of Korea was nonetheless injecting liquidity into the system, which reversed the increase.

24. The IMF documents cited in this section may be found at [http://www.imf.org/external/country/KOR/index.htm].

25. The fact that the Thai and Indonesian crises had already occurred no doubt diverted some of the attention that Korea otherwise might have received. At that time, too, it must have been anticipated that there would be Malaysian and Philippine programs.

foreigners could get out of won simply by refusing to roll over outstanding debt.[26]

The first (hastily assembled) program set forth the following as its objectives: "building the conditions for an early return of confidence so as to limit the deceleration of real GDP growth to about 3 percent of GDP in 1998, followed by a recovery towards potential in 1999; containing inflation at or below 5 percent; and building international reserves to more than two months of imports by end-1998."[27] The staff memorandum stated that there were three pillars in the government's program: the macroeconomic framework,[28] the restructuring and recapitalizing of the financial sector, and a reduction in the reliance of corporations and financial institutions on short-term debt.

For present purposes, the specifics of the IMF program are not relevant. However, understanding those aspects of the program that were important in affecting the severity of the downturn is necessary if an assessment of the role of the various factors leading in the downturn is to be made. In attempting to stem the speculative pressures, the exchange rate was allowed to float, and the won depreciated from the mid-800s level per dollar to almost 1,800 per U.S. dollar.[29] The liquidity that had been introduced into the financial system in prior weeks (in an effort to support the *chaebol*) was removed, and money market rates were raised sharply. In the words of the IMF staff, these rates would "be maintained at as high a level as needed to stabilize markets" (5). Day-to-day monetary policy was to be geared to exchange rate and short-term interest rate movements, whereas exchange rate policy was to be flexible, with intervention "limited to smoothing operations."

The 1998 budget as passed by the government had projected a surplus of about 0.25 percent of GDP. However, the IMF staff estimated that lower growth and the altered exchange rate would reduce the balance by 0.8 percent of GDP and that it would require 5.5 percent of GDP to recapitalize the banks to meet the Basel minimum capital standards. It was assumed

---

26. Hahm and Mishkin (2000) point out that "the speculative attack was not in the usual form of direct currency attack to exploit expected depreciation. Due to the tight regulation on currency forwards which should be backed by corresponding current account transactions and the absence of currency futures markets inside Korea at the time, opportunities for direct speculative attack had been much limited. Rather, the drastic depreciation of Korean won was driven by foreign creditors' run on Korean financial institutions and chaebols to collect their loans, and by foreign investors to exit from the Korean stock market" (25).

27. IMF, Korea, "Request for Standby," 3 December 1997, 5.

28. Much of the controversy surrounding the Korean program centers on whether the program tightened fiscal policy too much. This is discussed below. It should be noted that the Fund staff's introduction of the macroeconomic program indicated that the program would involve "a tighter monetary stance and significant fiscal adjustment" (5).

29. As stated in the "Request for Standby," "The inflation target reflects a very limited pass-through of the recent depreciation of the won to the aggregate price level.... In order to achieve the inflation objective, the government will aim to reduce broad money growth (M3) from an estimated 16.4 percent at end-September to 15.4 percent at end-December 1997, and to a rate consistent with the inflation objective in 1998" (5–6).

that these funds would have to be borrowed, and interest costs (0.8 percent of GDP) were therefore also included in the altered budget estimates. According to fund estimates, these factors would have shifted the fiscal account into deficit of about 1.5 percent of GDP in 1998. As stated by staff, "In order to prevent such a deficit and alleviate the burden on monetary policy in the overall macroeconomic adjustment, fiscal policy will be tightened to achieve at least balance and, preferably, a small surplus." The program therefore called for fiscal changes approximately offsetting the negative anticipated changes and thus for maintenance of the fiscal stance as anticipated prior to the crisis, with the 1.5 percent of GDP cuts equally distributed between government expenditures and revenues. The government initially raised some taxes to yield about 0.5 percent of GDP.

The second leg of the program was financial restructuring. As already indicated, NPLs were large and increasing prior to the crisis. The depreciation of the exchange rate increased debt-servicing obligations for *chaebol* and financial institutions, as did the increase in interest rates that came about with monetary tightening. An exit policy was to be adopted to close down weak financial institutions, and the remaining banks were to be recapitalized (through mergers or other means). A deposit guarantee was to be phased out at the end of December 2000 and replaced with deposit insurance for small depositors only.[30]

Bank restructuring required a prior, or at least concurrent, restructuring of the *chaebol* finances. Given their very high debt-equity ratios (for one *chaebol* at the height of the crisis, the debt-equity ratio reached 12:1),[31] financial viability, where feasible at all, would surely require swaps of debt by the *chaebol* to the banks, giving the banks equity in return. For this reason, it was predictable that the restructuring would require time. Data on the finances of the *chaebol* are given in section 13.3. The standby also addressed corporate governance and corporate financial structure issues, focusing on improving incentives and supervision for banking operations and reforming bankruptcy laws. The government also agreed to refrain from providing financial support, providing tax privileges, or forcing mergers for individual companies.

30. There were a number of other significant measures, which are less important for present purposes. For example, transparency was to be increased in a variety of ways. Large firms were to be audited by international accounting houses. Supervisory functions were to be reorganized, and the Bank of Korea was given much greater independence. Importantly, the government undertook to refrain from attempting to influence lending decisions, leaving those to the financial institutions. However, these actions had little impact on the short-run downturn.

31. These high debt-equity ratios were public knowledge. The *Financial Times* published data on debt-equity ratios for twenty *chaebol* on 8 August 1997. The highest was Sammi, with 33.3 times as much debt as equity; Jinro had 85.0 times as much debt as equity and Halla 20.0 times; Hyundai's debt was 4.4 times its equity, and so on. Profits were relatively small as a percentage of assets or sales. In Samsung's case, for example, net profits were 179.5 billion won on sales of 60 trillion won and total assets of 51 trillion won. Nine of the twenty *chaebol* listed in the *Financial Times* on that day had taken losses.

A final issue of concern here is the projected magnitude of the financial support for the Korean program. The current account deficit was expected to decline markedly in 1997 to about 3 percent of GDP, and then—with export growth and won depreciation—to about 0.5 percent of GDP in 1998. However, the very high level of short-term debt was considered worrisome. As stated in the "Request for Standby":

> It is difficult to estimate with any certainty the likely developments in capital flows . . . , given the uncertainty surrounding the rolling over of private sector short-term debt and the recent collapse in market confidence. . . . The working assumption is that, on the basis of the beneficial effects on market confidence of the announced program and the large financing package, the bulk of the short-term debt will be rolled over. Under this scenario, the purpose of the exceptional financing would be largely to reconstitute reserves. For this outcome to materialize, it is critical that the financing package provided is adequately large and the program is perceived to be strong. It is anticipated that a comprehensive financing package of about $55 billion will be provided on a multilateral and bilateral basis. (12)

13.2.4   The Severity of the Crisis

For at least two weeks after the announcement of the IMF program, questions remained as to whether the downward slide had been halted.[32] By late December, however, the exchange rate had stabilized, and by mid-January, foreign banks announced a $24 billion package of rollovers and new money.[33]

Domestic economic activity slowed markedly in 1998. For the year as a whole, real GDP fell by 6.7 percent, contrasted with the IMF's fund's projected 3 percent. The unemployment rate, which had been 2.2 percent at the end of the third quarter of 1997, rose throughout 1998 and peaked in the first quarter of 1999 at 8.4 percent. The seasonally adjusted industrial production index fell by 15 percent from the end of 1997 to the second quarter of 1998. Thereafter it rose, reaching its precrisis level by the end of 1998 and 144.9 at the end of 1999.

The external accounts improved markedly. There was a sharp drop in imports in immediate response to the crisis and a much-increased current account balance: Although exports were slightly lower in dollar terms in 1998 than in 1997, imports fell 22.4 percent, and the current account balance was equal to an astonishing 12.5 percent of GDP for the year. Foreign exchange reserves rose in response, reaching $74 billion by the end of 1999 and $83.6 billion by the end of the first quarter of 2000. The decline in real GDP ended

---

32. Because of this, it is very difficult to accept the argument that the Fund program was "too stringent." Indeed, given those uncertainties, it is more plausible to argue that the program might have been even more restrictive initially.

33. Financial Times, 30 January 1998, ll.

in mid-1998, and by the end of the year real GDP had exceeded its precrisis level. For 1999, real GDP growth exceeded 9 percent and was projected to attain the same rate for 2000.

After early 1998, the nominal exchange rate appreciated in dollar terms, entering the year 2000 at around 1,100 won to the dollar, contrasted with 1,800 to the dollar at the peak of the crisis. Moreover, prices at the end of 1998 were about 7 percent higher than at the end of 1997; in 1999 the rate of inflation was just 0.8 percent, as measured by the consumer price index.

Progress in restructuring the financial sector was necessarily considerably slower. Although interest rates had fallen below their precrisis levels by the end of 1999, restructuring of *chaebol* and financial institutions met with considerable resistance.[34] Government policy pronouncements and actions have continued to push for reforms, but the pace of reform has been much slower than that of the balance of payments and external finances.

However, by any measure, the negative impact of the crisis and the measures addressing it was felt most heavily in 1998. By early 2000, the Korean recovery was more rapid and more pronounced than had been anticipated by any.[35]

13.3   Estimating the Role of Financial and Other Variables in Leading to Crisis

Financial restructuring was absolutely essential—first to make the reforms credible (or capital outflows would have continued) and second as a prerequisite for economic recovery. Additionally, because the devaluation and higher interest rates would both weaken the financial sector in the short run (and this was understood by the markets), failure to address the issue of financial restructuring would clearly have increased the severity of the recession and delayed, if not aborted, the recovery. Moreover, financial restructuring could not be satisfactorily undertaken without addressing the very high debt-equity ratios of the *chaebol.* How much this intensified the downturn, however, cannot be addressed until consideration of the finances of the *chaebol* and the financial system are considered.

Either a financial crisis or a currency crisis must be addressed with measures that will cause economic pain in the short run. However, when the two interact, the resulting costs are much higher. To see how this scenario played out in Korea, we begin with an examination of the finances of the *chaebol*

---

34. See, for example, John Burton's "Boxed into a Corner" in the *Financial Times,* 23 November 1998, 17, whose first sentence read, "South Korea's *chaebol* are fighting a stiff rearguard action against government reforms but the conglomerates are being forced to change their ways."

35. This is not to say that corporate and financial restructuring had been completed. At the time of this writing (late 2000), unprofitable *chaebol* activities, including some large entities, are still being closed down, with attendant concerns about a slowing of the rate of growth in 2001.

prior to late 1997. An overview of their evolution and the problems that developed will be useful before we turn to details. As mentioned earlier, the *chaebol* had earlier contributed enormously to Korea's rapid economic growth. By the early 1990s, the largest thirty *chaebol* accounted for 49 percent of assets and 42 percent of sales in the manufacturing sector. Although they had received subsidized credit, this implicit subsidy was probably mostly intramarginal in the 1960s and 1970s and probably simply increased overall profitability and reinvestment rates. However, over time, the profitability of the *chaebol* necessarily diminished, while the real interest rate at which they borrowed was increasing.

Table 13.1 gives data on lending rates of deposit money banks from 1961 to 1987, the period during which interest rates were controlled. In 1987, the quantity of regulated loans was sharply reduced, and the Bank of Korea stopped reporting the interest rates by those loan categories separately. To estimate how much of a subsidy was involved in deposit money banks (DMBs) lending, it is necessary to contrast that rate with an estimate of what a market-clearing real interest rate might have been.[36] To that end, table 13.2 gives the curb market interest rates, the inflation rates, and the growth rates over the years from 1961 to 1998. We then construct an estimate of what a realistic real borrowing rate might have been by adding the inflation rate to the growth rate and calculating a three-year moving average.

Table 13.3 then gives the DMB loans enjoying preferential interest rates by type of loan. The last column gives these loans as a percentage of the total. As can be seen, they peaked in the late 1970s (which coincided with the so-called heavy chemical and industry [HCI] drive), but were sizable during the 1980s as well. Only in the 1990s after interest rate liberalization did their share drop to less than 5 percent of outstanding loans.

We then derive estimates of the subsidy through DMB loans in the first column of table 13.4. The estimates are made by multiplying the volume of DMB loans by the difference between the reference interest rate and the actual borrowing rate. Also shown in table 13.4 are similarly derived estimates of the subsidy through loans to the manufacturing sector from the Korea Development Bank, a nonbank financial institution that lent for investment in public utilities, infrastructure, equipment for manufacturing, and other purchases deemed desirable for developmental purposes. The sum of these estimates should be compared with the final column of table 13.4, which gives the estimates of all manufacturing firms' ordinary incomes (that re-

---

36. The curb market rate, given in column (1) of table 13.4, provides an alternate "reference interest rate." As can be seen, the estimated subsidy to borrowers would be considerably higher if the difference between the borrowing rates and the curb market rate were used. The two move together, however, and it seems reasonable that some part of the curb market rate would have been to adjust for additional risk. Our estimates of the implicit subsidy must, however, probably be taken as a lower bound on the value of loans to their recipients.

Table 13.1   **Interest Rates on Loans and Discounts, Deposit Money Banks**

Year	Discounts on Commercial Bills	Loan for Trade	Loans for Machine Industry Promotion	Loans for Equipment of Export Industry	Loans with NIF	"Lending Rate"
1961	13.9	13.9	n.a.	n.a.	n.a.	n.a.
1962	13.9	12.7	n.a.	n.a.	n.a.	n.a.
1963	13.9	9.1	n.a.	n.a.	n.a.	n.a.
1964	14.0	6.8	n.a.	n.a.	n.a.	n.a.
1965	16.5	6.5	n.a.	n.a.	n.a.	n.a.
1966	24.0	6.5	n.a.	n.a.	n.a.	n.a.
1967	24.0	6.3	n.a.	n.a.	n.a.	n.a.
1968	24.3	6.0	12.0	n.a.	n.a.	n.a.
1969	25.2	6.0	12.0	n.a.	n.a.	n.a.
1970	24.3	6.0	12.0	n.a.	n.a.	n.a.
1971	22.9	6.0	12.0	n.a.	n.a.	n.a.
1972	17.7	6.0	10.1	n.a.	n.a.	n.a.
1973	15.5	6.6	10.0	12.0	n.a.	n.a.
1974	15.5	8.9	11.1	12.0	9.2	n.a.
1975	15.3	7.6	12.0	12.0	12.0	n.a.
1976	16.3	7.4	12.4	12.8	12.8	n.a.
1977	16.7	8.0	13.0	14.0	14.0	n.a.
1978	17.8	8.5	14.1	15.1	15.1	n.a.
1979	18.8	9.0	15.0	16.0	14.7	n.a.
1980	24.1	14.8	20.2	21.2	18.2	18.0
1981	19.4	15.0	17.9	18.8	16.4	17.4
1982	12.3	10.8	12.1	n.a.	12.2	11.8

Year						Lending rate
1983	10.0	10.0	10.0	n.a.	10.0	10.0
1984	10.3	10.0	10.0	n.a.	10.7	10.0
1985	10.8	10.0	n.a.	n.a.	10.8	10.0
1986	10.8	10.0	n.a.	n.a.	10.5	10.0
1987	10.8	10.0	n.a.	n.a.	n.a.	10.0
1988	n.a.	n.a.	n.a.	n.a.	n.a.	10.1
1989	n.a.	n.a.	n.a.	n.a.	n.a.	11.3
1990	n.a.	n.a.	n.a.	n.a.	n.a.	10.0
1991	n.a.	n.a.	n.a.	n.a.	n.a.	10.0
1992	n.a.	n.a.	n.a.	n.a.	n.a.	10.0
1993	n.a.	n.a.	n.a.	n.a.	n.a.	8.6
1994	n.a.	n.a.	n.a.	n.a.	n.a.	8.5
1995	n.a.	n.a.	n.a.	n.a.	n.a.	9.0
1996	n.a.	n.a.	n.a.	n.a.	n.a.	8.8
1997	n.a.	n.a.	n.a.	n.a.	n.a.	11.9
1998	n.a.	n.a.	n.a.	n.a.	n.a.	15.3

Sources: The first five columns are from Bank of Korea, *Monthly Statistical Bulletin* (various issues). "Lending rate" is obtained from *International Financial Statistics* (various issues).

Notes: Bank of Korea stopped reporting DMB interest rates in this format in 1988. "Lending rate" is the minimum rate charged to general enterprises by DMBs on loans of general funds for up to one year. From 1977 it is a weighted average, weighted by loans by nationwide commercial banks. National Investment Fund (NIF) was created in 1973 to help finance policy-favored investment projects. n.a. = not available.

Table 13.2   **Reference Interest Rates (percent per annum)**

Year	Curb Market Interest Rate (1)	Inflation, CPI (2)	GDP Growth Rate (3)	Reference Interest Rate (4) = (2) + (3)
1961	n.a.	6.5	3.5	10.1
1962	n.a.	7.7	3.3	11.0
1963	n.a.	11.5	5.7	17.2
1964	61.8	18.1	7.3	25.3
1965	58.9	20.4	8.2	28.6
1966	58.7	17.6	9.4	26.9
1967	56.7	11.9	8.4	20.3
1968	56.0	11.0	10.2	21.2
1969	51.4	11.3	10.6	21.9
1970	50.2	13.0	10.9	23.9
1971	46.4	13.9	10.0	23.9
1972	39.0	13.7	7.0	20.7
1973	33.2	9.4	8.6	18.0
1974	40.6	13.0	8.2	21.2
1975	47.6	17.6	8.8	26.3
1976	40.5	21.6	8.4	30.0
1977	38.1	16.9	9.2	26.1
1978	41.7	13.3	10.1	23.3
1979	42.4	14.3	8.7	23.0
1980	44.9	20.5	4.7	25.1
1981	35.3	22.8	3.8	26.6
1982	33.1	19.1	3.9	22.9
1983	25.8	10.6	8.1	18.8
1984	24.8	4.3	8.7	13.0
1985	24.0	2.7	8.5	11.2
1986	23.1	2.5	8.6	11.1
1987	23.0	2.8	9.5	12.2
1988	22.7	4.3	10.8	15.1
1989	19.1	5.3	9.2	14.4
1990	18.7	7.1	8.5	15.6
1991	21.4	7.9	8.1	16.0
1992	20.2	8.0	7.9	15.9
1993	16.2	6.8	6.7	13.5
1994	16.0	5.8	6.4	12.2
1995	15.3	5.2	7.6	12.8
1996	13.7	5.2	8.0	13.2
1997	14.6	4.6	6.9	11.5
1998	n.a.	5.6	1.7	7.3

Source: Bank of Korea, *Economic Statistics Yearbook* (various issues).

Notes: Inflation and GDP growth rates shown are three-year moving averages. n.a. = not available.

ported on their balance sheets). As can be seen, the estimated subsidy component of loans exceeded ordinary income in some years and represented a substantial portion of it in others.

There was almost certainly an element of subsidy in bank lending after 1988 and even in lending at nonpreferential rates prior to that date. Esti-

Table 13.3   **Deposit Money Bank Preferential Loans (billions of won)**

Year	Loans for Trade (1)	Loans for Machine Industry Promotion (2)	Loans Equipment of Export Industry (3)	Loans with NIF (4)	Sum of Preferential Loans [(1) – (4)] (5)	Total Loans (6)	Preferential Loans (% of total) (7)
1963	2.7	n.a.	n.a.	n.a.	2.7	49.0	5.5
1964	2.5	n.a.	n.a.	n.a.	2.5	53.0	4.6
1965	4.6	n.a.	n.a.	n.a.	4.6	72.1	6.4
1966	4.9	n.a.	n.a.	n.a.	4.9	102.7	4.7
1967	16.7	n.a.	n.a.	n.a.	15.7	178.0	9.4
1968	24.5	n.a.	n.a.	n.a.	24.5	331.2	7.4
1969	35.1	10.0	n.a.	n.a.	45.1	563.0	8.0
1970	55.9	15.9	n.a.	n.a.	71.7	722.4	9.9
1971	80.1	15.8	n.a.	n.a.	96.0	919.5	10.4
1972	108.4	20.2	n.a.	n.a.	128.6	1,198.0	10.7
1973	224.1	26.1	35.0	n.a.	285.3	1,587.5	18.0
1974	359.5	25.0	56.0	20.4	460.9	2,427.8	19.0
1975	338.9	23.2	61.2	53.4	476.7	2,905.5	16.4
1976	461.8	31.5	76.9	121.0	691.1	3,724.9	18.6
1977	567.4	28.2	70.9	196.7	863.2	4,709.0	18.3
1978	883.2	26.1	57.0	287.7	1,254.0	6,609.0	19.0
1979	1,227.2	15.1	42.7	362.7	1,647.7	8,977.8	18.4
1980	1,720.8	10.2	26.2	405.3	2,162.4	12,204.4	17.7
1981	2,197.2	6.1	179.9	487.2	2,870.4	16,481.7	17.4
1982	2,278.4	n.a.	192.1	626.7	3,097.2	20,225.8	15.3
1983	2,620.0	n.a.	185.7	831.1	3,636.8	24,150.3	15.1
1984	2,765.4	n.a.	176.3	909.2	3,850.9	27,978.9	13.8

(*continued*)

Table 13.3 (continued)

Year	Loans for Trade (1)	Loans for Machine Industry Promotion (2)	Loans Equipment of Export Industry (3)	Loans with NIF (4)	Sum of Preferential Loans [(1) – (4)] (5)	Total Loans (6)	Preferential Loans (% of total) (7)
1985	3,129.9	n.a.	595.2	965.6	4,690.7	33,810.7	13.9
1986	3,444.5	n.a.	1,866.9	1,055.0	6,366.4	39,098.6	16.3
1987	2,420.4	n.a.	2,416.5	1,067.1	5,904.0	43,095.8	13.7
1988	1,201.6	n.a.	2,725.8	1,076.1	5,003.5	48,805.4	10.3
1989	1,382.2	n.a.	2,905.0	1,053.3	5,340.5	62,547.1	8.5
1990	1,947.3	n.a.	3,015.0	1,023.8	5,986.1	74,028.6	8.1
1991	2,254.3	n.a.	3,201.1	983.9	6,439.3	89,415.6	7.2
1992	2,542.2	n.a.	3,043.9	803.3	6,389.4	102,797.0	6.2
1993	2,473.4	n.a.	2,838.0	609.2	5,920.6	115,137.4	5.1
1994	2,711.3	n.a.	2,492.2	445.2	5,648.7	135,850.3	4.2
1995	2,846.9	n.a.	1,841.4	316.7	5,005.0	152,477.7	3.3
1996	2,679.3	n.a.	1,214.5	197.1	4,090.9	177,184.2	2.3
1997	2,698.2	n.a.	711.2	119.5	3,528.9	200,401.0	1.8
1998	3,395.8	n.a.	355.7	73.6	3,825.1	200,289.1	1.9

Source: Bank of Korea, *Economic Statistics Yearbook* (various issues).
Note: n.a. = not available.

Table 13.4   **Estimates of Implicit Subsidy through Deposit Money Bank and Korea Development Bank Loans (billions of won)**

Year	Through DMB Loans	Through KDB Loans	Sum of Subsidy Estimates	Ordinary Income, Manufacturing Total
1963	0.2	1.1	1.2	4.5
1964	0.5	2.2	2.7	5.6
1965	0.8	3.1	3.9	6.6
1966	1.0	2.9	3.9	11.4
1967	1.5	1.8	3.3	13.4
1968	3.1	2.3	5.5	20.6
1969	5.2	2.7	7.9	24.3
1970	9.7	4.8	14.5	22.9
1971	14.1	6.2	20.3	11.8
1972	15.8	5.7	21.5	56.5
1973	21.9	4.2	26.0	62.3
1974	44.1	10.1	54.2	176.1
1975	82.6	25.0	107.6	169.7
1976	122.1	43.6	165.7	313.6
1977	125.6	47.3	172.9	390.0
1978	135.0	52.2	187.3	615.1
1979	179.4	77.3	256.7	573.9
1980	185.0	86.8	271.8	−55.7
1981	286.4	167.7	454.1	5.6
1982	331.5	215.1	546.6	403.6

Source: The last column is from Bank of Korea, *Financial Statements Analysis* (various issues).
Note: Estimates of subsidy are made in tables 13A.10 and 13A.11.

mating its magnitude is considerably more difficult, because there are no records of the interest rates at which loans were extended. An estimate was made using the "lending rate" reported by the IMF in *International Financial Statistics,* and taking the difference between the reference rate and that rate times the volume of loans outstanding. The results of those estimates are reported in appendix table 13A.3. Unlike the estimates used here, those estimates probably represent the upper bounds of the magnitude of the subsidy implicit in bank loans, both because some loans may have been extended at higher interest rates and because the reference rate may overstate the "true" interest rate, especially during periods of falling inflation. Nonetheless, even by our most conservative measure, the subsidy component of lending was large and constituted an important element of reported profits for the *chaebol.*

Figure 13.3 shows the rates of return on assets and on equity in manufacturing from 1962 to 1997. For the 1962–82 period for which we have estimates of the subsidy component of loans, estimates are given as to the rates of return that would have prevailed, all else being equal, had there been no subsidy implicit in borrowing. Three things should be noted. First, rates of return declined over time. Second, in earlier periods the returns to

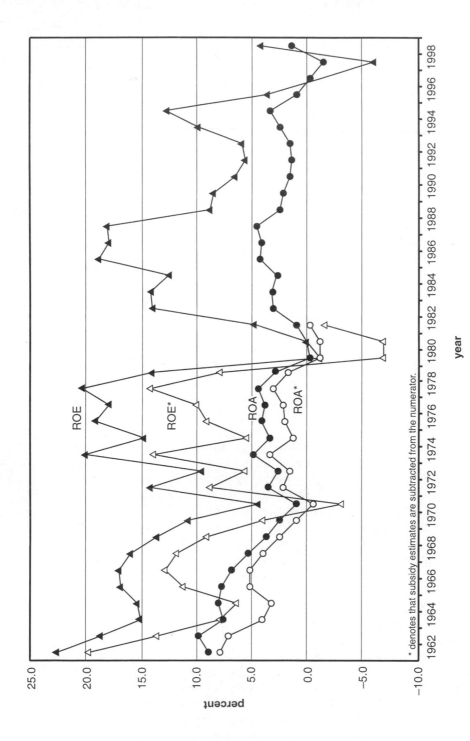

* denotes that subsidy estimates are subtracted from the numerator.

Fig. 13.3   Rates of return, manufacturing sector total
Source: Appendix table 13A.4.

firms would have been negative had it not been for the subsidized credit. Third, it is small wonder that *chaebol* were highly leveraged: given the incentive to use debt financing entailed in the loans, they were more profitable for doing so, and their founders could retain a stronger controlling interest.

13.4 The Status of the Banking System and the *Chaebol* Finances at the Time of the Crisis

There is little doubt that the *chaebol* had strong incentives to rely on credit rather than equity as much as they could for many years. The next step in the analysis is to consider the *chaebol* and their profitability in the years leading up to the crisis. Figure 13.4 shows the debt-equity ratios for the "Big 5," the largest five *chaebol,* and for all manufacturing firms.[37] The debt-equity ratios are given for Japan and the United States as well, for purposes of comparison. The ratios for all firms included in the largest thirty *chaebol* are provided in appendix table 13A.5 in the column labeled "Korea Big 30, All Firms."

As can be seen, and as is consistent with the incentives with which they were confronted, the financial structures of the Korean firms were in general highly leveraged. The manufacturing firms had a debt equivalent to three and a half times their equity in the mid-1980s. Although this ratio declined somewhat in the 1990s, it was usually two or three times higher than those in the United States. *Chaebol* firms were even more highly leveraged than Korean manufacturing as a whole.[38]

Obviously, highly leveraged firms are vulnerable to shocks, such as increases in the cost of capital, sharp changes in macroeconomic conditions, and sudden drops in foreign demand. The vulnerability of the *chaebol* was especially dangerous, given their importance to the Korean economy. The situation was even worse because the *chaebol* firms were closely linked to each other financially. Firms belonging to the same *chaebol* tended to invest in each other and guarantee the repayment of bank loans for each other. Although this may make sense for the individual *chaebol,* from the economy-wide viewpoint, there were risks. On one hand, *chaebol* activities that should have been closed down could continue operating, given financial support from their *chaebol* affiliates. When difficulties were short-run, this support was evidently warranted. However, problems arose because there was little way to determine when difficulties were short-run, and compo-

37. Each year, the Fair Trade Commission (FTC) of the Korean government designates the thirty largest *chaebol* in terms of assets and lists the firms belonging to them. The list changes over time. The list used in this paper is the same for each year as that which the FTC designates, and therefore changes over time. The Big 5 are Hyundai, Samsung, Daewoo, LG, and SK.

38. The debt-equity ratios, rates of return, and asset growth rates were estimated on the basis of the financial statements of firms subject to the requirement of external audit, compiled by the National Information and Credit Evaluation agency (NICE). This source is used throughout this paper, unless otherwise noted.

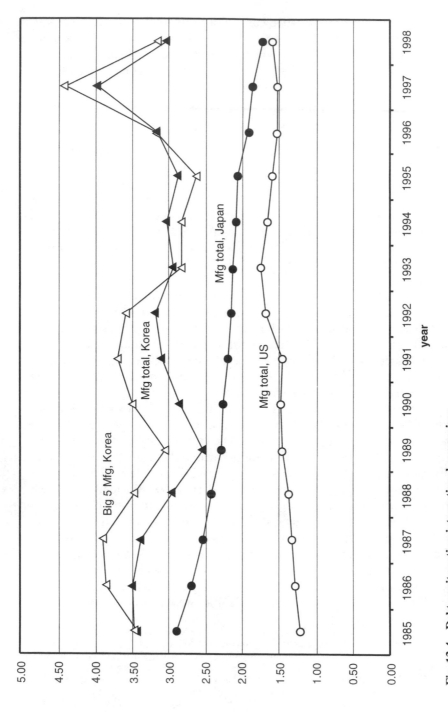

Fig. 13.4 Debt-equity ratios, international comparison
Source: Appendix table 13A.5.

nents of the *chaebol* remained in business regardless of their own situation, reducing the profitability of the *chaebol* as a whole. Because of this, the high leverage combined with subsidized lending resulted in declining rates of return for *chaebol* over time.[39]

We turn, then, to the estimated rates of return on assets in figure 13.5 and those on equity (appendix table 13A.7), for the same comparison groups. The rates of return were also falling during the 1990s except for the cyclical boom years of 1994 and 1995. For all Korean manufacturing, the rate of return on assets fell from an average above 4 percent in the late 1980s to under 2 percent in the early 1990s, and becoming negative in 1997. This contrasts sharply with rates of return in the United States, which were both higher and more sustained (with the exception of the recession years 1991 and 1992), and Japan, where returns fell but were still about 2.3 percent in 1998, after the impact of the Asian financial crisis. Returns on equity show the same pattern, with more pronounced fluctuations. The pattern for the Big 5 was much the same, except that the rates of return for the *chaebol* tended to be lower than for all Korean manufacturing firms over the same period, excluding the boom years of 1994 and 1995.

Table 13.5 gives estimates of the growth rates of assets of the Korean firms. What is striking, given the high debt-equity ratios and low rates of return of the *chaebol,* is the fact that the growth of their assets has been incomparably more rapid than that of the non-*chaebol* firms. As can be seen in columns (2) to (4) the Big 30 and Big 5 have been growing at 20 to 30 percent annually since the mid 1980s. As a result, their assets in 1997 at the time of the financial crisis were 14.0 and 19.0 times, respectively, as large as in 1985.[40] The same holds true within the manufacturing sector. Whereas manufacturing as a whole saw its total assets increase 8.5 times, the Big 5's assets rose 20.0 times, and the assets of the firms other than the Big 5 rose 6.5 times.

As a result, *chaebol* assets accounted for an increasing proportion of the corporate sector's total. In 1985, the Big 5 *chaebol* firms in the data used here held 16 percent of the assets in the manufacturing sector; the proportion rose to 40 percent in 1997.

The disproportionate increase in lending to *chaebol* by the banks, despite their lower returns, seems to reflect the banks' preference for lending to the *chaebol* in the later period. From the banks' viewpoint, the *chaebol* were relatively safer borrowers, as they were likely to have better collateral, and repayments were often guaranteed by other member firms of the same

---

39. It should be noted that the practice not only increased vulnerability and lowered the rates of return for the *chaebol* but also doubtless resulted in the banks' turning down loan applications from small firms that might have had very high rates of return.

40. Although Korean inflation was double-digit for some earlier years, it was relatively low during the late 1980s and early 1990s: most of the increase in assets reflects changes in real variables.

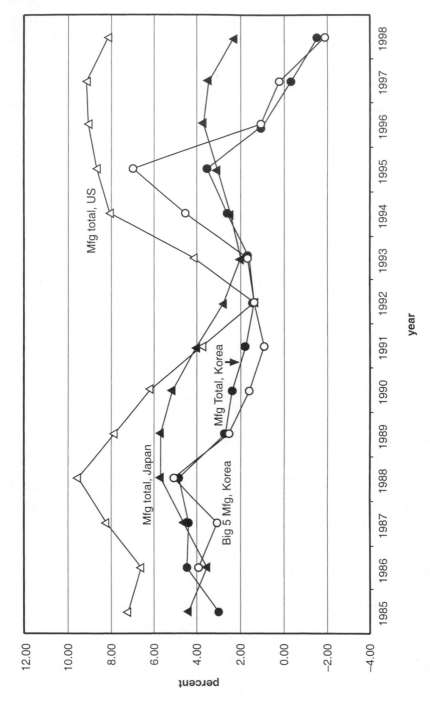

Fig. 13.5   Return on assets, international comparison
Source: Appendix table 13A.6.

Table 13.5   **Asset Growth Rates (percentage change per annum)**

Year	Big 30 Total	Big 5		Manufacturing Total
		Total	Manufacturing	
1986	51.84	45.96	60.90	14.1
1987	20.03	26.44	29.15	23.4
1988	20.03	26.44	29.15	16.4
1989	31.19	27.04	31.59	22.7
1990	29.07	33.03	33.81	36.2
1991	24.17	22.09	25.20	23.0
1992	11.91	10.94	6.26	10.5
1993	12.03	10.84	11.03	15.0
1994	23.45	25.92	28.73	21.6
1995	25.57	30.20	27.81	15.5
1996	19.48	21.29	20.72	13.6
1997	34.97	40.63	42.23	24.9
1998	3.91	13.12	11.35	1.9
1999	n.a.	n.a.	n.a.	10.6
1997/1985 (ratio)	14.4	18.7	19.7	8.5

Source: See table 13A.5.

Notes: The growth rates for Big 5 and Big 30 shown for 1987 and 1988 are averages for the two years. Big 5 held 16 percent of all assets in manufacturing sector in 1985 and 40 percent in 1997. n.a. = not available.

chaebol. Indeed, the government intervened and set a minimum quota of bank lending that should go to small and medium-sized firms so that their access to bank credits might not be unduly restricted.

However, government policy was not repressive toward the *chaebol.* They had come into being supported by policy favors, especially during the (HCI) drive of the 1970s. As they grew in assets, sales, employment, exports, and the like and increased their relative importance in the economy, they became indispensable and appeared "too big to fail."

In this regard, an episode of interest rate cuts in the early 1990s provides an interesting case. In January 1993 and again in March 1993, interest rates were cut. The cuts were the policy response to sharply deteriorating economic conditions, especially falling investment (in part in response to the American recession of 1990–91). However, it is noteworthy that these cuts coincided with a period of financial difficulty for the *chaebol.* The return on assets (ROA) of the Big 5 was barely 1 percent in 1991 (see fig. 13.5 and appendix table 13A.6), and there was a sharp drop in the growth rate of assets in 1992 (table 13.5).

In two steps, the Bank of Korea lowered the rediscount rates under its control by 2 percentage points "to counter the slowdown of economic growth and contraction of firms' equipment investment." In line with the slowing growth, the Bank "encouraged" the deposit money banks to lower their loan rates twice, by 1 percentage point each time. Each time, their loan and deposit rates were reduced (Bank of Korea, 1993a,b).

This is significant because the 1993 action was similar to those of earlier years when the ROA had fallen (in 1971 and in 1980–82). If all manufacturing firms, including the *chaebol,* had had to pay interest on all their debts, their income would have dropped almost 3.6 trillion won, more than wiping out their incomes for that year (see appendix table 13A.3). The interest rate cuts preceded the cyclical boom of 1994 and 1995, when credit expansion in their aftermath resulted in rapid economic growth.

We conclude that, by 1997, the *chaebol* were highly vulnerable to negative shocks. Their profitability had been falling and was low, so that there was little margin for a reduction in cash flow or an increase in debt-servicing costs. However, debt-servicing obligations were mounting, and cash flow does not appear to have been increasing commensurately. The large increase in lending by the commercial banks would appear to have had a significant element of "evergreening" to it. Had the interest rate risen in 1994 or 1995 because of macroeconomic conditions, it seems reasonable to conjecture that NPLs would have increased substantially (or evergreening would have increased significantly) at that time. The *chaebol* were overleveraged and vulnerable to interest rate increases.[41]

We turn now to the banking side of the picture. Figure 13.6 shows the rates of return for the commercial banks during the 1990s. As can be seen, total assets of the banks rose dramatically during the 1992–97 period, more than tripling. Net income, however, peaked in 1994 and turned negative by 1997 (appendix table 13A.8). The rate of return on assets was falling continuously during the period, as was the rate of return on equity.

Table 13.6 provides more detail. By 1998 the combined net loss of the banks was 46 percent of their equity. The changes up to and including the crisis year reflect three things. The loss provision for NPLs peaked in 1994 and was declining until it rose sharply in 1997 and 1998. Provision for valuation loss on securities was steadily increasing. And non-operating income dropped by more than 2.4 trillion won in 1997.[42]

There was little prior indication of the deterioration in the banks' assets. Interest had been paid, although it is difficult to estimate how much of this may have been "evergreening" accounts by lending to enable *chaebol* to service their debts. The sudden jump in NPLs in 1997 would seem to suggest that evergreening had been taking place in earlier years (as shown in table 13.7).

Not all banks collapsed in 1997, and some had, for all practical purposes,

41. Most of the chaebol sold large proportions of their products overseas. For that reason, they were almost surely less vulnerable to exchange rate changes, as their won sales would have increased significantly in response to a currency depreciation.

42. This loss reflects the losses banks suffered when they had to sell their NPLs to Korea Asset Management Company (KAMCO), a public enterprise charged with clearing the financial institutions' balance sheets of their bad loans.

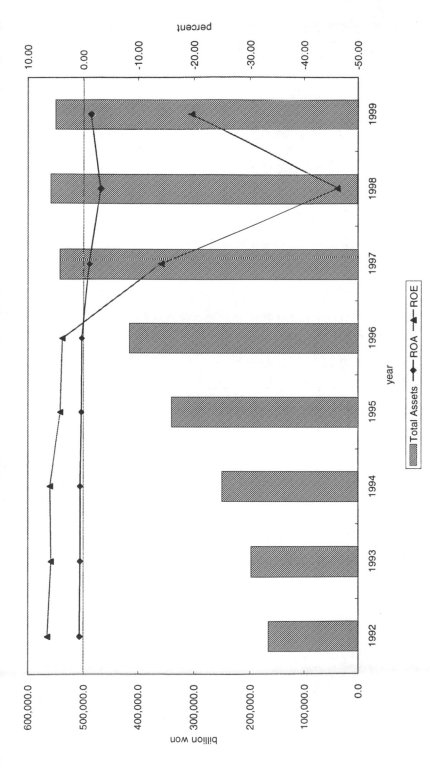

Fig. 13.6 Assets and rates of returns, commercial banks total

Source: Appendix table 13A.8.

Table 13.6   Changes in Income, Commercial Banks Total (billions of won)

	1992	1993	1994	1995	1996	1997	1998	1999
Gross Income	5,336.0	5,995.8	8,332.7	9,339.7	10,418.0	10,505.9	2,909.4	8,367.1
Interest income, net	3,088.1	3,127.0	3,426.7	4,920.2	6,059.5	7,817.2	6,777.2	9,046.8
Interests received	10,471.3	10,109.9	12,308.6	18,321.7	21,755.8	31,892.0	37,943.0	35,017.4
Interests paid (less)	7,383.2	6,983.0	8,882.0	13,401.6	15,696.3	24,074.8	31,165.9	25,970.7
Non-interest income	2,247.9	2,868.9	4,906.1	4,419.5	4,358.6	2,688.7	-3,867.8	-679.6
Fees received	1,250.5	1,551.8	2,480.8	2,249.4	2,281.0	10,299.2	13,266.4	8,210.3
Fees paid (less)	184.1	175.9	237.9	372.8	650.1	8,039.4	11,849.0	5,292.1
Other non-interest income	1,139.7	1,453.1	2,407.9	2,353.9	2,569.1	2,696.9	614.7	444.1
Non-operating incomes	41.8	39.9	255.3	189.1	158.6	-2,268.1	-5,899.9	-4,041.9
Operating expenses (less)	3,176.5	3,649.8	4,362.6	6,033.0	6,982.0	8,093.9	7,587.3	6,445.6
Of which, personnel expenses	2,221.3	2,595.4	3,187.4	4,228.8	4,964.4	5,609.0	5,596.0	2,885.9
Ordinary income	2,159.5	2,346.0	3,970.1	3,306.7	3,436.0	2,412.0	-4,677.8	1,921.5
Increase in loss provision (less)	942.5	1,023.4	2,371.8	2,319.7	2,342.0	6,192.7	7,780.4	7,487.3
Loans	787.6	995.5	2,127.3	1,758.0	1,547.7	3,511.3	8,066.7	7,487.3
Security valuation	95.7	-33.1	183.6	543.5	895.0	2,759.4	-125.8	0.0
Others	59.2	61.0	60.9	18.2	-100.7	-78.0	-160.5	0.0
Income before income tax	1,217.0	1,322.6	1,598.3	987.0	1,094.1	-3,780.7	-12,458.2	-5,565.8
Income tax (less)	285.5	433.6	550.1	119.2	247.2	139.2	52.4	430.2
Net income	931.5	889.0	1,048.2	867.8	846.9	-3,919.9	-12,510.6	-5,996.0

Source: Financial Supervisory Commission, online service

Table 13.7   **NPLs of the Commercial Banks**

	1991	1992	1993	1994	1995	1996	1997	1998
Billion won	8.27	10.16	11.93	11.39	12.48	11.87	22.85	21.22
Percent of loans	7.0	7.1	7.4	5.8	5.2	4.1	6.2	7.4

Source: Financial Supervisory Commission, online service.

been in difficulty earlier. Table 13.8 shows the changes in net income in 1993–98 for the six largest nationwide commercial banks. It also gives data on the three factors that contributed most to the income changes. The last column gives the reported NPLs on their balance sheets. As can be seen, Seoul Bank reported virtually zero net income in 1995, as did Korea First in 1996, before other banks experienced income losses in 1997. Their plight seems unrelated to the currency crisis in the region or to the sudden and sharp depreciation of the won that occurred in the last month of 1997.

There is thus considerable evidence of a weakening of the quality of the banks' portfolios prior to the crisis, in the sense that the financial health of the borrowers was deteriorating. Nonetheless, the proportion of NPLs in their portfolios was generally stationary or falling until the crisis, although this may in part have reflected the evergreening of accounts. After the crisis, the proportion of NPLs rose sharply, and they were then assumed by the asset management company, whereupon the banks booked their losses. The key question is whether those losses were already there and being evergreened, or whether the events associated with the exchange rate crisis itself precipitated the financial crisis. Certainly, the *chaebol* were highly leveraged, and a small change either in their profitability or interest charges would have been enough to tip them into nonperforming status.

13.5   The Foreign Currency Vulnerability of the Banks

Table 13.9 gives data on foreign currency–denominated assets and liabilities of the commercial banks, and appendix table 13A.9 gives the same data for deposit money banks. As can be seen, foreign currency–denominated assets were slightly below liabilities throughout the 1990s for both the commercial banks and the deposit money banks. At their peak in February 1998, postcrisis, commercial banks' liabilities denominated in foreign currency were 25.1 percent of total liabilities, whereas assets were 21.8 percent. The same general pattern held for deposit money banks, although the imbalance between foreign currency assets and liabilities was smaller. Interestingly, both the assets and liabilities had risen by about the same percentage during the crisis months, although the gap between them was about 2 percent wider in early 1998 than it had been in mid-1997.

A question that these data do not answer is the extent to which the

Table 13.8   **Factors behind the Sudden Changes in Income, Individual Banks (billions of won)**

	Net Income	Provision for NPLs	Provision for Valuation Loss	Non-Operating Income	NPLs, Reported
Choheung					
1993	975	1,520	−72	68	n.a.
1994	1,363	2,967	44	125	14,465
1995	1,066	1,867	860	181	15,476
1996	1,102	1,484	873	214	14,137
1997	−2,896	3,891	3,094	−1,136	26,232
1998	−19,708	5,840	n.a.	−10,071	15,155
Korea Commercial Bank					
1993	87	1,376	−32	50	n.a.
1994	545	3,622	423	2,205	20,260
1995	916	1,860	776	999	19,193
1996	1,055	893	686	442	10,340
1997	−1,639	1,775	1,982	-1,206	14,512
1998	−16,438	3,721	n.a.	−9,918	9,686
Han II					
1993	1,195	660	22	56	n.a.
1994	1,292	1,490	342	117	12,131
1995	805	828	875	120	11,569
1996	590	688	974	142	6,756
1997	−2,809	2,989	3,634	−313	13,244
1998	−17,166	5,696	n.a.	−3,795	17,495
Korea Exchange Bank					
1993	834	1,224	−107	16	n.a.
1994	1,003	2,996	−109	90	17,886
1995	1,053	1,700	501	125	17,433
1996	1,041	1,283	757	58	12,943
1997	−684	2,859	2,072	−1,543	25,176
1998	−8,435	2,056	n.a.	−8,927	15,084
Korea First					
1993	1,541	913	−36	7	n.a.
1994	1,313	3,168	354	50	14,186
1995	174	2,667	112	188	15,913
1996	62	2,732	871	393	18,697
1997	−16,151	4,514	3,518	−9,064	30,559
1998	−26,149	2,581	n.a.	−6,769	38,323
Seoul					
1993	103	1,712	−19	107	n.a.
1994	531	2,694	33	103	16,958
1995	50	2,216	341	204	16,639
1996	−1,668	2,735	977	208	20,353
1997	−9,166	1,731	3,047	−3,996	24,040
1998	−22,424	3,530	n.a.	−2,266	29,872

Source: Financial Supervisory Commission, online service.

Note: n.a. = not available.

Table 13.9 **Foreign Currency–Denominated Assets and Liabilities, Commercial Banks (billions of won)**

	Assets			Liabilities		
	Total	Foreign Currency–Denominated	Share (%)	Total	Foreign Currency–Denominated	Share (%)
1991	161,516.6	18,511.7	11.5	147,736.0	19,169.8	13.0
1992	180,615.6	20,809.4	11.5	165,724.4	20,963.7	12.6
1993	194,988.6	23,787.2	12.2	178,766.0	24,672.2	13.8
1994	228,961.5	30,165.5	13.2	210,044.8	31,313.1	14.9
1995	288,687.8	39,621.3	13.7	267,308.2	40,466.9	15.1
1996	341,558.7	51,861.5	15.2	318,321.7	52,802.2	16.6
1997						
J	354,654.9	55,596.3	15.7	325,827.7	55,608.7	17.1
A	360,179.4	56,504.4	15.7	331,075.6	57,767.2	17.4
S	402,529.2	58,197.9	14.5	370,370.1	59,758.2	16.1
O	414,296.5	61,738.5	14.9	381,377.5	64,719.6	17.0
N	435,322.1	72,772.1	16.7	402,357.5	74,440.5	18.5
D	483,498.6	96,448.7	19.9	461,208.8	102,828.2	22.3
1998						
J	498,298.8	101,167.1	20.3	467,189.8	113,532.7	24.3
F	504,682.4	110,024.8	21.8	472,441.0	118,551.5	25.1
M	479,636.4	96,407.9	20.1	445,908.6	99,483.8	22.3
A	469,613.1	93,215.7	19.8	435,165.8	96,635.3	22.2
M	471,013.8	97,461.6	20.7	435,140.6	101,132.7	23.2
J	467,583.0	92,560.0	19.8	433,414.5	96,257.4	22.2
J	459,565.3	81,936.0	17.8	425,298.6	85,374.6	20.1
1998						
D	469,280.5	72,676.7	15.5	448,765.9	70,633.9	15.7
1999	519,748.6	58,092.9	11.2	493,261.7	55,028.4	11.2

Source: Bank of Korea, *Monthly Statistical Bulletin* (various issues).

quality of the assets and the liabilities were similar. At the time of the crisis, there were reports that many of the loans denominated in foreign currency were to Indonesia, Thailand, and Russia, and that one of the factors precipitating the Korean crisis was the nonperformance of those loans. The data may therefore understate the differential between foreign currency assets and liabilities when risk-adjusted. Even so, it is not evident that the differential was so large that exchange rate changes should have triggered a major decline in the banks' balance sheets. To the extent that there was deterioration caused by the exchange-rate change, it would have had to be either in the ability of the *chaebol* to service their outstanding debts or in the failure of foreign debtors to continue servicing their loans to Korean banks.

13.6 Conclusions

The *chaebol* were in weak financial condition long before the crisis. Although the data do not indicate an increase in NPLs, the rapid increase in assets, combined with their deteriorating profitability, certainly seems to indicate that the banks were evergreening the outstanding *chaebol* debt. If even a quarter of the net increase in *chaebol* borrowing from the banks was evergreened, the banks were in very bad shape prior to the Korean crisis in 1997.

In an important sense, the vulnerability of the system was extreme. While very favorable conditions—increased semiconductor prices on world markets, falling world interest rates, a pickup in economic activity in the rest of the world—might have prevented the crisis and enabled the *chaebol* to regain profitability and reduce the degree to which they were leveraged, their behavior during the boom of 1994 and 1995 does not suggest that they were inclined to do so. Instead, in the boom years, they continued to borrow and to increase their assets, while the rate of return remained low with only a slight cyclical upturn.

The conclusion must be that the Korean crisis was a disaster waiting to happen: When very favorable circumstances did not materialize, the needed increase in evergreening was more rapid than the system could tolerate. The foreign exchange crisis itself probably did not trigger the financial crisis: rather, the increase in interest rates did.

The *chaebol* debts to the banks are the chief culprit, and because the *chaebol* were major exporters, the change in the exchange rate per se probably did not harm their ability to service their debts. However, the increased interest rate clearly did.

In the short run, therefore, more exchange rate depreciation and less interest rate increase—as was in fact the chosen stabilization path—was probably appropriate. Failure to raise the interest rate at all would surely have resulted in larger capital outflows and perpetuated the foreign exchange crisis. Indeed, as was seen, there were doubts over the several weeks after the first IMF program that the package as undertaken was enough. However, further increases in the interest rate (which probably would have reduced the magnitude of exchange rate depreciation) would surely have intensified the financial crisis.

At an analytical level, the impact of the exchange rate depreciation on the banks' balance sheets either directly or indirectly through the ability of the *chaebol* to service their debts must be deemed to have been relatively small in the Korean case. The fundamental problem was the magnitude of the *chaebol* precrisis leveraging. That, in turn, made the postcrisis workout of the banking system extremely difficult because of the necessity of restructuring the finances of the *chaebol* first.

Appendix
Chronology of Selected Events

1945	Liberation from Japanese colonial rule
1948	Establishment of Republic of Korea
1950–53	Korean war
1957–58	IMF stabilization program
1960–65	Announcement of first major step in trade policy reform and continuous expansion of export incentives
1961	Nationalization of commercial banks
1964	Major devaluation of won, the domestic currency
1965	Unification of exchange rates; move to positive real interest rate for commercial banks
1967	Korea joins the General Agreement on Tariffs and Trade (GATT); import regime is liberalized by switching from positive list to negative list system
1972	First domestic debt crisis; presidential emergency decree places a three-year moratorium on the payment of corporate debts to curb-market lenders
1973	Government launches a heavy and chemical industry (HCI) drive
1979	Government announces "comprehensive stabilization program," which ends the HCI drive
1980	Major devaluation of the won; further trade liberalization, including multi-year tariff reduction plan
1980s	"Rationalization" of industries in financial troubles
1983	Privatization of commercial banks
1988	Interest rate deregulation begins
1989	Piecemeal liberalization of international financial transactions begins, including a more market-determined exchange rate
1993	Government announces "new economy 100 days plan"; Bank of Korea lowers its rediscount rates from 7 to 5 percent
1996	Korea joins OECD; commitments to financial liberalization are made
1997	December: Korea and IMF agree on a rescue package; free floating exchange rate system
1998	Sweeping reform and liberalization of financial sector

Table 13A.1   **Korea's GDP, GDP Per Capita, Investment, Capital Inflows, and Saving (1960–2000)**

Year	Real GDP (billions of 1995 won)	GDP per capita (1995 won)	Investments (%)	Saving (%)	Capital Inflow, Net (%)
1960	24,524.5	981.4	10.8	1.4	9.3
1965	33,207.5	1,158.3	14.8	7.5	7.4
1970	56,209.0	1,788.1	25.4	18.2	8.1
1975	82,257.5	2,372.0	28.7	19.4	9.0
1980	114,977.7	3,073.7	31.9	24.2	8.5
1985	167,501.9	4,142.8	30.0	30.6	0.8
1990	263,430.4	6,068.3	37.7	37.6	0.8
1995	377,349.8	8,459.1	37.2	35.4	1.8
1999	436,798.5	9,321.4	26.8	33.5	−6.1

Source: Bank of Korea, *Economic Statistics Yearbook* (various issues) and online service.

Table 13A.2   **Foreign Trade in the Korean Economy (1960–2000)**

Year	Exports ($millions)	Imports ($millions)	Exports/ GDP (%)	Imports/ GDP (%)
For Goods and Services on the Balance-of-Payments Basis				
1960	116.9	379.2	3.4	12.7
1965	289.8	488.4	8.6	16.2
1970	1,379.0	2,181.7	13.8	23.9
1975	5,883.6	7,997.2	27.2	35.7
1980	19,815.3	25,151.5	32.7	40.6
1985	30,455.4	30,017.0	32.9	32.1
1990	73,295.4	76,360.5	29.1	30.3
1995	147,459.5	154,882.5	30.2	31.7
1999	171,692.4	143,972.5	42.1	35.3
For Goods Only on the Custom Clearance Basis				
1960	32.8	343.5	1.0	11.5
1965	175.1	463.4	5.2	15.3
1970	835.2	1,984.0	8.3	21.8
1975	5,081.0	7,274.4	23.5	32.5
1980	17,504.9	22,291.7	28.9	36.0
1985	26,632.6	26,652.8	28.8	28.5
1990	65,015.7	69,843.7	25.8	27.7
1995	125,058.0	135,118.9	25.6	27.6
1999	143,685.5	119,752.3	35.2	29.3

Source: Bank of Korea, *Economic Statistics Yearbook* (various issues).

Table 13A.3   **Estimates of Upper Bounds of Subsidy through DMB Loans (billions of won)**

Year	Estimate I	Estimate II	Ordinary Income, Manufacturing Total
1963	1.5	n.a.	4.5
1964	5.5	n.a.	5.6
1965	7.1	n.a.	6.6
1966	2.4	n.a.	11.4
1967	−4.8	n.a.	13.4
1968	−7.4	n.a.	20.6
1969	−13.5	n.a.	24.3
1970	−2.2	n.a.	22.9
1971	7.2	n.a.	11.8
1972	28.7	n.a.	56.5
1973	30.0	n.a.	62.3
1974	93.8	n.a.	176.1
1975	243.0	n.a.	169.7
1976	373.5	n.a.	313.6
1977	326.1	n.a.	390.0
1978	253.6	n.a.	615.1
1979	267.0	n.a.	573.9
1980	91.6	754.8	−55.7
1981	847.4	1,316.5	5.6
1982	1,628.3	2,044.8	403.6
1983	n.a.	1,946.1	1,454.3
1984	n.a.	790.2	1,619.1
1985	n.a.	372.8	1,666.5
1986	n.a.	399.4	2,839.4
1987	n.a.	921.1	3,413.5
1988	n.a.	2,299.1	4,433.1
1989	n.a.	1,749.7	2,950.7
1990	n.a.	3,851.9	3,575.7
1991	n.a.	4,873.3	3,199.2
1992	n.a.	5,678.1	2,948.4
1993	n.a.	5,348.9	3,855.8
1994	n.a.	4,586.5	7,623.0
1995	n.a.	5,410.5	11,842.4
1996	n.a.	7,213.1	3,551.7
1997	n.a.	−721.0	−1,408.7
1998	n.a.	16,004.9	−7,754.1

Notes: This estimation recognizes that DMBs' general purpose loans other than the loans enjoying preferential rates also had an element of subsidy, since the loan rates were lower than a market-clearing rate might have been. However, Estimate II, since it must make use of the *IFS*'s "lending rate," is an estimate of the upper bounds of subsidy rather than that of actual subsidy.

Estimate I is made by multiplying the total loans less sum of preferential loans (table 13.3) by the difference between the reference interest rate (table 13.2) and the loan rate applied to "discounts on commercial bills" (table 13.1).

Estimate II is made by multiplying the total loans (table 13.3) by the difference between the reference interest rates and the lending rates (table 13.1). n.a. = not available.

Table 13A.4 **Rates of Return, Manufacturing Sector (percent per annum)**

Year	ROA	ROA[a]	ROE	ROE[a]
1962	8.9	7.8	22.6	19.8
1963	9.7	7.1	18.8	13.7
1964	7.5	3.9	15.1	7.8
1965	7.9	3.3	15.3	6.3
1966	7.8	5.1	16.9	11.1
1967	6.8	5.1	17.0	12.8
1968	5.3	3.9	16.1	11.8
1969	3.7	2.5	13.5	9.1
1970	2.5	0.9	10.7	3.9
1971	0.9	−0.6	4.4	−3.2
1972	3.4	2.1	14.2	8.8
1973	2.6	1.5	9.6	5.6
1974	4.8	3.3	20.0	13.9
1975	3.4	1.2	14.7	5.4
1976	4.1	1.9	19.1	9.0
1977	3.8	2.1	18.0	10.0
1978	4.4	3.0	20.3	14.2
1979	3.0	1.6	14.1	7.8
1980	−0.2	−1.2	−1.2	−6.8
1981	0.0	−1.2	0.1	−6.8
1982	0.9	−0.3	4.6	−1.6
1983	3.1	n.a.	14.1	n.a.
1984	3.2	n.a.	14.1	n.a.
1985	2.8	n.a.	12.5	n.a.
1986	4.2	n.a.	18.8	n.a.
1987	4.1	n.a	17.9	n.a
1988	4.6	n.a.	18.2	n.a.
1989	2.5	n.a.	8.7	n.a.
1990	2.2	n.a.	8.5	n.a.
1991	1.6	n.a.	6.5	n.a.
1992	1.3	n.a.	5.6	n.a.
1993	1.5	n.a.	6.0	n.a.
1994	2.5	n.a.	9.9	n.a.
1995	3.3	n.a.	12.8	n.a.
1996	0.9	n.a.	3.6	n.a.
1997	−0.3	n.a.	−1.4	n.a.
1998	−1.5	n.a.	−6.0	n.a.
1999	1.4	n.a.	4.3	n.a.

Source: ROA and ROE are estimates based on Bank of Korea, *Financial Statements Analysis* (various issues).

Note: n.a. = not available.

[a]Indicates that numerator is ordinary income less subsidy estimates reported in table 13.6.

Table 13A.5   Debt-Equity Ratios

Year	Korea Big 30, All Firms	Korea Big 5		Korea, Manufacturing Total	United States, Manufacturing Total	Japan, Manufacturing Total	Taiwan, Manufacturing Total
		All Firms	Manufacturing Firms				
1985	4.62	4.40	3.44	3.49	1.21	2.89	1.37
1986	4.93	4.42	3.87	3.51	1.27	2.69	1.26
1987	4.62	4.45	3.90	3.40	1.33	2.55	1.11
1988	3.32	3.64	3.48	2.96	1.38	2.44	1.08
1989	3.31	3.14	3.06	2.54	1.47	2.30	0.91
1990	3.70	3.61	3.51	2.86	1.49	2.27	0.83
1991	3.89	3.77	3.71	3.09	1.47	2.21	0.98
1992	4.00	3.75	3.60	3.20	1.68	2.16	0.93
1993	3.51	3.17	2.83	2.95	1.75	2.13	0.88
1994	3.59	3.18	2.82	3.02	1.67	2.10	n.a.
1995	3.53	3.07	2.64	2.87	1.60	2.07	n.a.
1996	3.90	3.54	3.18	3.17	1.54	1.93	n.a.
1997	5.24	4.67	4.41	3.96	1.54	1.87	n.a.
1998	3.62	3.31	3.16	3.03	1.59	1.73	n.a.
1999	n.a.	n.a.	n.a.	2.15	n.a.	n.a.	n.a.

Sources: The first three columns are estimated from the firm-level data by National Information and Credit Evaluation in its magnetic tapes *Financial Statements of Non-Financial Firms* (various years). The rest are from Bank of Korea, *Financial Statement Analysis for 1999* and *Explanation of Financial Statement Analysis* (1985).

Notes: The estimates for 1987 are not directly comparable with those for other years. n.a. = not available.

Table 13A.6 Return on Assets (percent per annum)

Year	Korea Big 30, All Firms	Korea Big 5		Korea, Manufacturing Total	United States, Manufacturing Total	Japan, Manufacturing Total	Taiwan, Manufacturing Total
		All Firms	Manufacturing Firms				
1985	n.a.	n.a.	n.a.	3.00	7.23	4.40	3.12
1986	1.95	3.03	3.93	4.50	6.67	3.60	6.84
1987	2.11	2.54	3.09	4.40	8.29	4.60	6.89
1988	3.96	4.23	5.07	4.90	9.57	5.70	5.72
1989	2.30	2.72	2.55	2.70	7.87	5.70	3.84
1990	1.57	1.71	1.61	2.40	6.22	5.20	4.27
1991	1.22	1.20	0.97	1.80	3.79	4.00	3.99
1992	1.09	1.49	1.38	1.40	1.40	2.80	2.89
1993	1.24	1.78	1.75	1.60	4.19	2.00	2.50
1994	2.50	3.82	4.55	2.60	8.12	2.50	n.a.
1995	3.35	5.41	7.03	3.59	8.72	3.10	n.a.
1996	0.61	1.18	1.07	0.93	9.10	3.70	n.a.
1997	-0.87	0.37	0.27	-0.30	9.16	3.50	n.a.
1998	-1.82	-1.33	-1.82	-1.52	8.20	2.30	n.a.
1999	n.a.	n.a.	n.a.	1.38	n.a.	n.a.	n.a.

Source: See table 13A.5.

Notes: The estimates in the first three columns for 1987 and 1988 are not directly comparable with those for other years. n.a. = not available.

Table 13A.7   Return on Equity (percent per annum)

| Year | Korea Big 30, All Firms | Korea Big 5 | | Korea, Manufacturing Total | United States, Manufacturing Total | Japan, Manufacturing Total | Taiwan, Manufacturing Total |
		All Firms	Manufacturing Firms				
1985	n.a.	n.a.	n.a.	13.20	15.98	17.70	7.57
1986	11.33	16.37	18.42	20.10	15.16	13.30	15.89
1987	12.20	13.80	15.08	19.90	19.33	16.60	15.00
1988	18.76	20.76	23.38	20.60	22.80	20.10	12.14
1989	9.94	11.84	10.77	10.10	19.42	19.10	7.51
1990	7.11	7.51	6.93	9.10	15.47	16.90	7.94
1991	5.86	5.62	4.47	7.00	9.37	13.10	7.87
1992	5.40	7.09	6.41	5.80	3.75	9.00	5.54
1993	5.87	7.86	7.30	6.40	11.50	6.50	4.76
1994	11.38	15.95	17.40	10.50	21.64	7.70	n.a.
1995	15.26	22.28	26.12	14.00	22.65	9.60	n.a.
1996	2.89	5.08	4.18	3.74	23.07	10.80	n.a.
1997	−4.83	1.92	1.28	−1.38	23.26	10.20	n.a.
1998	−9.61	−6.47	−8.51	−6.72	21.23	6.40	n.a.
1999	n.a.	n.a.	n.a.	4.96	n.a.	n.a.	n.a.

Source: See table 13A.5.
Notes: The estimates in the first three columns for 1987 and 1988 are not directly comparable with those for other years. n.a. = not available.

Table 13A.8   **Rates of Return, Commercial Banks Total**

Year	Total Assets (billions of won)	Net Income (billions of won)	ROA (%)	ROE (%)
1992	167,425.1	931.5	0.71	6.56
1993	198,481.3	889.0	0.62	5.90
1994	250,081.2	1,048.2	0.62	6.09
1995	340,543.0	867.8	0.38	4.19
1996	415,437.8	846.9	0.31	3.80
1997	542,552.8	–3,919.9	–1.06	–14.19
1998	560,059.7	–12,510.6	–3.15	–46.15
1999	550,345.3	–5,996.0	–1.42	–19.62

Source: Financial Supervisory Commission, online service, available at [http://www.fsc.go.kr].

Table 13A.9   **Foreign Currency–Denominated Assets and Liabilities, Deposit Money Banks (billions of won)**

	Assets			Liabilities		
	Total	Foreign Currency–Denominated	Share (%)	Total	Foreign Currency–Denominated	Share (%)
1991	220,388.9	19,468.4	8.8	205,736.3	19,890.5	9.7
1992	251,321.4	21,936.1	8.7	235,470.7	21,802.8	9.3
1993	275,689.9	25,339.1	9.2	258,353.5	26,035.6	10.1
1994	322,956.2	32,294.4	10.0	302,300.1	32,856.3	10.9
1995	379,517.1	41,872.6	11.0	356,754.7	42,157.2	11.8
1996	451,180.2	55,390.7	12.3	426,074.9	55,445.4	13.0
1997						
J	467,317.3	59,759.7	12.8	433,348.2	58,823.7	13.6
A	474,123.4	60,605.0	12.8	439,853.5	60,720.3	13.8
S	486,928.8	61,079.6	12.5	452,840.5	61,870.5	13.7
O	499,979.2	64,830.9	13.0	464,928.4	66,957.9	14.4
N	523,516.3	76,362.1	14.6	488,161.1	76,587.6	15.7
D	573,695.5	100,370.8	17.5	550,809.0	105,597.1	19.2
1998						
J	587,023.5	105,081.9	17.9	554,035.1	116,204.9	21.0
F	593,032.3	114,330.5	19.3	558,806.3	121,549.8	21.8
M	568,554.5	100,139.0	17.6	532,861.5	101,892.1	19.1
A	557,955.0	96,606.7	17.3	521,434.1	98,887.7	19.0
M	559,347.1	101,118.8	18.1	521,442.7	103,574.4	19.9
J	558,430.3	96,174.0	17.2	522,543.7	98,821.8	18.9
J	552,177.6	84,909.6	15.4	516,205.7	87,797.6	17.0
1998						
D	576,919.5	75,757.1	13.1	554,868.3	72,683.9	13.1
1999	640,011.2	61,181.4	9.6	611,824.4	57,534.5	9.4

Source: Bank of Korea, *Monthly Statistical Bulletin* (various issues).

Table 13A.10　　　**Estimates of Subsidy through DMB Loans (billions of won)**

Year	Loan for Trade	Loans for Machine Industry Promotion	Loans for Equipment of Export Industry	Loans NIF	Subsidy Estimates
1963	0.2	n.a.	n.a.	n.a.	0.2
1964	0.5	n.a.	n.a.	n.a.	0.5
1965	0.8	n.a.	n.a.	n.a.	0.8
1966	1.0	n.a.	n.a.	n.a.	1.0
1967	1.5	n.a.	n.a.	n.a.	1.5
1968	3.1	n.a.	n.a.	n.a.	3.1
1969	4.7	0.5	n.a.	n.a.	5.2
1970	8.1	1.5	n.a.	n.a.	9.7
1971	12.2	1.9	n.a.	n.a.	14.1
1972	13.9	1.9	n.a.	n.a.	15.8
1973	19.0	1.9	1.1	n.a.	21.9
1974	36.1	2.6	4.2	1.2	44.1
1975	65.4	3.4	8.4	5.3	82.6
1976	90.4	4.8	11.9	15.0	122.1
1977	93.4	3.9	9.0	19.3	125.6
1978	107.3	2.5	5.3	20.0	135.0
1979	147.3	1.6	3.5	27.0	179.4
1980	151.9	0.6	1.3	31.1	185.0
1981	226.8	0.7	8.0	50.9	286.4
1982	271.0	0.3	n.a.	60.2	331.5

Notes: Estimates are based on tables 13.1–13.3. For the purpose of estimation the amount of a loan for a given year is taken to be the same as the average of the outstanding loan amounts at the end of the year and of the previous year. n.a. = not available.

Table 13A.11　　　**KDB Loans and Interest Rate**

Year	KDB Loans to Manufacturing Sector (billions of won)	KDB Interest Rate (%)
1962	11.0	8.4
1963	11.9	8.3
1964	13.2	8.4
1965	16.4	9.6
1966	21.2	13.0
1967	24.6	13.1
1968	29.0	13.1
1969	37.3	14.7
1970	51.7	14.5
1971	65.4	14.4
1972	75.4	13.1
1973	79.0	12.8
1974	118.6	12.7
1975	186.7	12.9
1976	258.0	13.1
1977	377.4	13.6
1978	550.7	13.9
1979	856.8	13.9
1980	1348.9	18.7
1981	1771.2	17.1
1982	2097.6	12.7

Source: Bank of Korea, *Monthly Statistical Bulletin* (various issues).

Note: One representative interest rate was estimated for each year.

Table 13A.12   **Won/Dollar Exchange Rate**

	End of Period	Period Average
1980	659.9	607.9
1981	700.5	681.3
1982	748.8	731.5
1983	795.5	776.2
1984	827.4	806.0
1985	890.2	870.5
1986	861.4	881.3
1987	792.3	822.4
1988	684.1	730.5
1989	679.6	671.4
1990	716.4	708.0
1991	760.8	733.6
1992	788.4	780.8
1993	808.1	802.7
1994	788.7	803.6
1995	774.7	771.0
1996	844.2	804.8
1997		
J	892.0	890.5
A	902.0	895.9
S	914.8	909.5
O	965.1	921.9
N	1,163.8	1,025.6
D	1,415.2	1,484.1
1998		
J	1,572.9	1,706.8
F	1,640.1	1,623.1
M	1,378.8	1,505.3
A	1,338.2	1,392.0
M	1,410.8	1,394.6
J	1,385.2	1,397.2
J	1,236.0	1,300.8
1998		
D	1,207.8	1,213.7
1999	1,145.4	1,189.5

Source: Bank of Korea, online service, available at [http://www.bok.or.kr].

References

Bank of Korea. 1985. *Explanation of financial statement analysis.* Seoul: Bank of Korea.
———. 1993a. *Quarterly Economic Review* (March).
———. 1993b. *Quarterly Economic Review* (June).
———. Various years. *Economic statistics yearbook.* Seoul: Bank of Korea. Available at [http://bok.or.kr].
———. Various years. *Financial statement analysis.* Seoul: Bank of Korea.

————. Various issues. *Monthly Statistical Bulletin.* Seoul: Bank of Korea.

Boughton, James M. 2000. From Suez to Tequila: The IMF as crisis manager. *Economic Journal* 110 (460): 273–91.

Frank, Charles R., Jr., Kwang Suk Kim, and Larry Westphal. 1975. *Foreign trade regimes and economic development: South Korea.* New York: Columbia University Press.

Hahm, Joon-Ho, and Frederic S. Mishkin. 2000. Causes of the Korean financial crisis: Lessons for policy. In *The Korean crisis: Before and after,* ed. Inseok Shin, 55–144. Seoul: Korea Development Institute Press.

Hong, Wontack. 1981. Export promotion and employment growth in South Korea. In *Trade and employment in developing countries,* ed. Anne O. Krueger, Hal B. Lary, Terry Monson, and Narongchai Akrasanee, 341–91. Chicago: University of Chicago Press.

International Monetary Fund (IMF). 1995. *International capital markets: Developments, prospects, and policy issues.* Washington, D.C.: IMF.

————. Various issues. *International Financial Statistics.* Washington, D.C.: IMF.

Krueger, Anne O. 1979. *The developmental role of the foreign sector and aid: Studies in the modernization of the Republic of Korea, 1948–1975.* Cambridge, Mass.: Harvard University Press.

————. 1997. Lessons for policy reform in light of the Mexican experience. In *International trade and labour markets,* ed. Jitendralal Borkakoti and Chris Milner, 44–61. London: Macmillan.

Organization for Economic Cooperation and Development (OECD). 1994. *OECD economic surveys: Korea 1994.* Paris: OECD.

Comment   Jorge Braga de Macedo

Anne O. Krueger, one of the world's experts on Korea, has joined forces with Jungho Yoo to understand the factors leading to the Korean financial crisis of late 1997. The authors suggest a chain of causation going from *chaebol* capitalism to the collapse of the won, via weak banks and excessive foreign borrowing. As stated in the conclusion, the "*chaebol* were in weak financial condition long before the crisis," the extreme vulnerability of the system being due to the fact that "banks were 'evergreening' the outstanding *chaebol* debt." In short, "the Korean crisis was a disaster waiting to happen."

In terms of diagnostics, Krueger and Yoo conclude that there was no currency trigger for crisis but rather that the increase in interest rates made *chaebol* debt to banks more difficult to service. Since exports helped recovery, they surmise that the path of stabilization was probably appropriate.

Jorge Braga de Macedo is president of the Organization for Economic Cooperation and Development Development Center, and a research associate of the National Bureau of Economic Research.

The views expressed here are personal and do not reflect positions of the OECD Development Center or its member counties. The author is grateful to Jose Oliveira Martins and Soogil Young for help, and to Randall Jones for detailed comments on an earlier draft (with the usual caveat).

The paper ends with the argument that "the necessity of restructuring the finances of the *chaebol* first" made "the postcrisis workout of the banking system extremely difficult." Depending on whether the difficulty is overcome, then, future prospects will be better or worse.

While Krueger and Yoo do not attempt to measure the relative importance of each one of the four factors they mention, Dekle and Kletzer (chap. 11 in this volume) show a fairly consistent pairing of Korea and Thailand on the one hand and Singapore and Taiwan on the other in terms of rising financial reputation. Malaysia is somewhere in between, and the debate continues on whether its response to the crisis was special. In chapter 9 in this volume, Rudi Dornbusch shows convincingly that this is not so, while Kaplan and Rodrik (chap. 8) present evidence in defense of the Malaysian way.

According to the latest country survey by the Organization for Economic Cooperation and Development (OECD; 2001) the sustained recovery of the Korean economy is threatened by the possibility that reforms may stall. Since then, of course, the rise in the price of oil and the slowdown of world growth have each taken a toll as output fell in the fourth quarter of 2000. In this comment I plan to elaborate on this point and to assess whether the crisis helped bring about structural reforms that could prevent future crises. In so doing I will go back in time, following the historical and institutional approach of Krueger and Yoo but perhaps giving greater weight to the ambiguity of domestic liberalization in Korea, following the common description of the country as a "permit kingdom."

With respect to the currency-financial crisis itself, it is generally acknowledged that a financial crisis with severe real consequences on the economy typically involves a combination of exchange rate devaluation, debt service difficulties, and banking failures (Dornbusch, chap. 16, in this volume; Macedo 1999), and that the three elements were undoubtedly present in Korea. Moreover, recalling earlier National Bureau of Economic Research (NBER) work on the Korean financial crisis, summarized in McHale (2000), it is evident that noted Korean economists tend to see this crisis as a good example of contagion through herd behavior, rather than as a "disaster waiting to happen."

It is to be hoped that taking the analysis back in time and giving greater weight to domestic distortions will help promote consensus on the Korean pattern of development, which was once described as a miracle but has recently come under closer scrutiny, notably through the regular OECD peer reviews.

Korean Miracle?

Korea can certainly be seen as one of the best examples of what was called the Asian miracle. Not only was its 1960 gross domestic product (GDP) per capita about the same as Sudan's, but growth expectations at the time were also higher for Africa than for Southeast Asia. Krueger and Yoo coin the elegant phrase an "export theory of value" held by Korean policy makers over the last four decades, illustrating the power of export-led growth over import-substituting industrialization.

This power has been recognized at least since the work of Ian Little, Tibor Scitovsky, and Maurice Scott at the OECD Development Center in the late 1960s. Anne's former colleague at Stanford Ron McKinnon (1973) pointed out, however, that financial development was often neglected in the assessment of experiences of export-led growth, which tended to focus on trade in goods and services rather than trade in assets. International trade theory shows that value comes from imports, not exports, so that the export theory of value is bound to tolerate or even to create domestic distortions. The distortions may pertain to domestic factor mobility between sectors, as captured by the traditional Fei-Ranis two-sector model of domestic labor mobility from agriculture to manufacturing. This model was taught for many years at the Yale Economic Growth Center as a rationalization of the Asian miracle. There are many other sources of distortion, however, from imperfect competition in goods markets to financial repression.

At the Growth Center's twenty-fifth anniversary conference, McKinnon introduced macroeconomic instability as an additional distortion and showed how this distortion exacerbated the Stiglitz-Weiss equilibrium credit rationing brought about by the inability of banks to monitor project returns perfectly. Indeed, McKinnon (1988, 390) noted that, compared to Japan, Taiwan, and Singapore, Korea in 1980 "had a much lower ratio of M2 to GDP (0.34) and had to make up for this shortage of domestic loanable funds by borrowing heavily abroad." Again, the Singapore-Taiwan pair is close to the Japanese benchmark.

The interaction between macro-instability and the covariance of returns is bad enough. In Korea, however, the determining factor of the crisis may have been the interaction between industrial and financial structures associated with the export theory of value thought to be behind the Korean miracle.

Industrial and Financial Structure

The latest OECD survey (2001) summarizes Korea's industrial structure as follows:

> One dilemma for Korean policymakers, both before and after the crisis, has been setting appropriate policies to deal with the chaebols, which have played a key role in the country's economic development. Chaebols are large conglomerates linking many individual companies—an average of 27 in 1997—that are diversified across a wide range of industries. The companies are linked by centralized family control and management, ownership links and mutual debt guarantees that facilitate high levels of leverage. At the beginning of the 1980s, the authorities were faced with

two possible methods of dealing with the chaebols, a transition to a free-market economy in which the pressure of stakeholders, competition, both domestic and international, and the threat of bankruptcy would discipline chaebol behavior; or the use of various regulations on financing, investment and loan guarantees to control the chaebols.

The authorities relied primarily on the latter approach to limit the role of the conglomerates. This choice, however, has had several negative consequences. First, it implied considerable government intervention in the private-sector's economic decision-making, thus limiting the role of market forces. The negative impact was compounded by the lack of an effective corporate governance framework to guide management decision-making. Second, it created considerable moral hazard for chaebols, which were essentially protected from bankruptcy. Policies to limit the role of the conglomerates were accompanied by measures to assist small and medium sized enterprises (SMEs), which, nevertheless, remained a relatively backward part of the Korean economy.

Korea's industrialization was led by large firms affiliated with the chaebols. During the 1960s and 1970s, SMEs accounted for only a third of growth in value-added and less than half of the rise in employment. Since the end of the Heavy and Chemical Industry drive of the 1970s, government policy has gradually shifted to place more emphasis on assisting SMEs in ways that have not always been market-conforming.

As the literature on financial structure in Japan and Germany quoted by McKinnon (1973, 1988) emphasizes, the preference for conglomerates, including financial institutions (called *grupos* in Latin America), has disadvantages that become apparent during the process of economic development. The effects of linking a financial structure too closely with the industrial structure go beyond the efficiency with which saving is transformed into productive investment. Under the *grupos* system, no domestic constituency for financial freedom arises, and that bailout guarantees become part of corporate culture. As illustrated by Macedo (1996) regarding the Portuguese change in economic regime toward stability in convertibility that preceded the creation of the euro, all of this makes the combination of political and financial freedom appear less relevant, and thus threatens the growth of civil society.

Other examples can be gathered from Latin America and Europe. Perhaps the most celebrated case is the bailout of Banco Osorno in 1997 by Chilean authorities, to which Carlos Diaz-Alejandro attributed the banking crash of a few years later. Some work along these lines has been carried out for European countries in the process of development (Macedo 1988), and the role of the curb market in Korea and Turkey was investigated in Sweder van Winjbergen's Ph.D. dissertation at MIT in the late 1970s. Recently, Bradley (2001) contrasted the Korean to the Irish model, with the latter encouraging "export-oriented foreign investment inflows," in contrast to the former's exclusive objective of "capturing greater export market share."

In other words, to understand *chaebol* capitalism it is essential to go back to the heavy and chemical industry period in the mid-1970s, which not coincidentally was used as a model for the Portuguese nationalization of banks and insurance companies in 1975 by the industry minister João Cravinho.[1] Note that *chaebol* are not allowed to own banks—the 4 percent limit on bank ownership is designed specifically to exclude them. However, they have been allowed to own nonbank financial institutions and have used them as cash cows, with the result of a falling market share for banks. In sum, when the Korean administration embraced globalization in the early 1990s, it did not put in place the appropriate governance structures, and the question is whether this contradiction remained after the crisis.

Crisis and Recovery

In spite of the distortions in the industrial and financial structures, there was no sense of vulnerability—instead, complacency was widespread in policy circles as the 1997 Korean presidential election neared. No one thought of calling the International Monetary Fund (IMF) in the summer of 1997 (despite the gloom Krueger observed at that time). Indeed, during the NBER meeting on Korea's crisis, Jeff Shafer made it clear that banks were not being asked to coordinate a response in November. Dooley and Shin (2000) note that central bank deposits in foreign currency rose from zero to US$5 billion in the week of 17 November and to US$10 billion in the week of 24 November; this rate would have exhausted reserves by the time the IMF program was announced. Dooley and Shin (2000) also report that the rollover of credits falls to 24 percent in the first week of December, from a 50 percent average in October. As they note, the lack of reliable figures on useable foreign exchange reserves, foreign debt, nonperforming loans, and so on was astonishing. Whatever the initial complacency, once the debt/banking crisis hit, combining the end of the passive dollar peg with tight money may have been the only viable alternative, even though a huge controversy remains in Korea about the appropriateness of the IMF's monetary conditions.

It is widely recognized that the Korean recovery was faster than that of other OECD economies—namely, Mexico, Turkey, Sweden, and Finland—that had been hit by financial crises. The main reason noted in the OECD survey (2001) is that import compression was greater in Korea than in the other countries, to the point that the current account balance moved

---

1. Cravinho does not mention the Korean model in his written remarks at the 1976 international conference on the Portuguese economy, but he did make the point while presenting his paper.

into a surplus that reached 13 percent of GDP. The increase in reserves was sterilized, so that there was no increase in inflation. Wage flexibility is another reason for the subdued response of inflation to the sharp fall in the currency. The decline in nominal wages in 1998 prevented a wage-price spiral.

The central bank was given independence in matters of monetary policy, with a regime that may be characterized as "quasi–inflation targeting" at a rate set around 2.5 percent per annum. The monetary regime remains ambiguous, however, because there is the objective of seeking a current account surplus, which may confuse the market.

In addition, an activist fiscal policy toward SMEs is being implemented, and the past tradition of government handouts to enterprises may not yet have been fully overcome, even though the stated objective is to promote the new economy. This explains part of the debt buildup (with debt reaching 40 percent of GDP), even though much of it is government-guaranteed debt related to financial-sector restructuring.

The danger of expenditure rises due to the social safety net, North Korea, and tax reform may be less now than it was in 2000; but, on the other hand, Korea is set to experience the most rapid aging process of any OECD country.

The structural reforms brought about by the crisis thus pertain to the macroeconomic regime, including the independence of the central bank, more effective financial supervision, the beginning of public-debt management, and more transparent budgetary procedures. Because a new government framework cannot change the industrial and financial structure, more progress is to be expected in areas related to the issue of how the government is dealing with the *chaebol,* such as competition policy, regulatory reform, and corporate governance. Until then, the signals are conflicting. On the one hand, the government limits and controls the *chaebol* through the Fair Trade Commission, which has enforced rules on intragroup dealing, cross-ownership, and debt guarantees since the late 1980s. On the other hand, the government is involved in guiding companies' decisions.

Competition

One measure of competition, the degree of mark-up of price over cost for manufactured goods, suggests that—before the crisis—competition was relatively weak in Korea compared to other OECD countries (it was found to be 36 percent in Korea, compared with 25 percent in Japan, 20 percent in Germany, and 15 percent in the United States).

After recent initiatives to promote competition through reforming government regulations, strengthening competition policy, reducing trade barriers, encouraging inflows of direct foreign investment, and privatizing state-owned enterprise, it can be said with the OECD (2000) regulatory review:

[T]he competition law and competition authority are well designed, consistent with good international practices. The most serious kinds of horizontal agreements are now treated more harshly and the Fair Trade Commission is moving away from a purely structural approach to abuse of dominance. Most statutory exemptions have now been eliminated. Enforcement processes are adequate, although more power to collect evidence would be welcome, and criminal sanctions may not be effective. Consumer protection is also the responsibility of the competition agency, helping ensure that consumers see the benefits of market-based reforms. Competition authorities have also been responsible for chaebol policy, though many chaebol policies deal with corporate governance and financial prudence rather than with competition policy. Chaebol reforms may also involve conventional competition policy issues such as market domination, exclusion, and discrimination, that can be dealt with using consistent economy-wide principles.

After the crisis, the Korea Asset Management Corporation was created to buy bad loans, and it has been very successful in selling those loans to private investors. However, there have been no sales of the government shares in recapitalized banks held by the Korean Deposit Insurance Corporation. There also remains considerable ambiguity about the extent of government involvement in enterprises. This is especially worrying in view of likely political paralysis toward the end of the year, with both presidential and local elections scheduled in 2002.

Since the crisis, the *chaebol* have restructured by reducing debt-equity ratios and cutting the number of affiliates. Hyundai, in particular, will soon become three separate *chaebol,* as shareholding ties are cut. This is a positive development because it limits the risk of chain insolvencies. Nevertheless, the *chaebol* as a group remain highly indebted (they increased equity more than they cut debt during the sharp 1998–2000 upturn).

Regulatory Reform

Quoting the survey, "the conglomerates' measures to reduce the number of affiliates and sell assets created competitive opportunities for SMEs. In addition, the requirement that chaebols lower their debt to equity ratios to 200 per cent reduced their borrowing from banks, improving loan availability for smaller firms. Indeed, SMEs accounted for 46 per cent of the increase in bank lending in 1999."

According to the review, new disciplines of transparency and market principles are needed throughout the entire policy apparatus, at all levels of government. Massive deregulation was accomplished in 1998–99, when the number of government regulations was cut by nearly 50 percent. Reforms are now shifting toward more proactive and comprehensive attention to regulatory quality and institution building. Institutions have been established to promote regulatory reform at political and administrative levels.

Korea has taken steps to improve regulatory transparency, although stakeholder representation in decision making should be broadened. Korea's program of regulatory impact analysis (RIA) is well conceived, although implementation by the ministries remains weak and new legislation proposed by the members of parliament is not subject to RIA. Transparency and accountability would be boosted by establishing independent sectoral regulators. Implementation is now a high priority to embed new practices throughout the public administration, since, as President Kim Dae-Jung said, "Reform must begin with the government."

Corporate Governance

In spite of the reforms induced by the crisis, the survey argues that the creation of a strong corporate governance framework will require significant changes in Korea's corporate culture. To hasten such changes, detailed, prescriptive legal measures that in some cases go beyond those found in other countries are needed to achieve fundamental change. For example, although outside directors are required to make up at least 50 percent of the boards of directors at listed companies, the actual independence of these "independent" directors is in doubt.

To promote further improvements in this area, the Ministry of Finance and Economy established the Committee on Improving Corporate Governance in March 1999. The committee, which consisted entirely of private-sector experts, issued a "Code of Best Practices" in September 1999. The recommendations of this committee, in line with OECD principles for corporate governance, are voluntary. However, the Korea Stock Exchange has required listed companies to provide information to their shareholders about the extent to which they conform with the code. Moreover, the efforts of Jang Hasung, who participated in the OECD Development Center's workshop on corporate governance in the spring of 2000, have been well publicized (as can be seen, e.g., in Hamlin, 2000, Larkin 2000, Lee 1999, Scott 1998, *The Economist* 1999).

An example of improved corporate governance is the refusal of other *chaebol* to assist Hyundai Engineering and Construction in spite of the government's encouragement, when the company teetered on the edge of bankruptcy. The other *chaebol* were afraid of being sued by minority shareholders.

Conclusion

The Korean case suggests four possible lessons for crisis prevention:

1. Even in a crisis, you can't import credibility; you have to earn it in domestic market institutions.

2. There are many exchange rate/convertibility options besides the two-corner solutions of a currency board and pure float. The exact solution should recognize that financial freedom interacts with political freedom,

and therefore that a constituency for capital account openness cannot arise unless financial supervision is operative. This is developed in Macedo, Cohen, and Reisen (2001).

3. Peer-pressure mechanisms are useful to intermediate the process of earning credibility; this can be facilitated by regional surveillance. In addition to the worldwide surveillance provided by the IMF and the peer pressure derived from OECD membership, the mechanism adopted by the European Union can be helpful. This is evident in the Association of Southeast Asian Nations (ASEAN+3) swaps (also called the Chiang Mai initiative). The alternative chosen by Taiwan, stressing bilateral rather than multilateral surveillance mechanisms, implies a high standard (as pointed out earlier). The caveat about peer pressure suggested by the European experience, as reviewed in Macedo (2000) and in Macedo, Cohen, and Reisen (2001), is that entry conditions may not be as effective in earning credibility as accepted norms would be. This is the difference between the so-called Maastricht criteria and the stability pact approved in 1996. In Korea, the liberalization brought about to qualify for OECD membership was defensive rather than cooperative, so that additional measures must be agreed upon domestically.

4. A myth concerning "Asian values" has often been contrasted with supposed Latin American values, when in fact policies and institutions that are appropriate for one stage of development may not be appropriate for another. This is similar to the comparison made at the outset between Korea and Sudan at a time when Africa was seen as having greater potential than Asia. The importance of making comparisons is, of course, that it is an essential prerequisite of peer pressure. The comparison between the Korean and the Irish model, for example, suggests that domestic taxation and foreign investment policies can go a long way toward differentiating the two experiences of export promotion, with a clear advantage for Ireland's model.

References

Bradley, John. 2001. Cohesion and transition: Comparing the Irish experience with the prospects of the Central and Eastern European countries. Paper presented at UFSIA-RUCA Faculty of Applied Economics conference, An Expanding Europe. 26 January, University of Antwerp, Belgium.

Dooley, Michael P., and Inseok Shin. 2000. Private inflows when crises are anticipated: A case study of Korea. NBER Working Paper no. 7992. Cambridge, Mass.: National Bureau of Economic Research, November.

The Economist. 1999. Scourge of the *chaebol.* 23 March, p. 78.

Hamlin, Kevin. 2000. Is corporate Asia getting the message? *Institutional Investor* 25 (March): 68.

Larkin, John. 2000. Korea's winter of discontent. *Far Eastern Economic Review,* 17 December, p. 16.

Lee, Charles S. 1999. Fairer shares. *Far Eastern Economic Review,* 1 April, p. 56.

Macedo, Jorge Braga de. 1988. Comment on "Financial liberalization and economic development: Interest rate policies in LDCs." In *The state of development economics,* ed. Gustav Ranis and T. Paul Schultz, 411–15. Oxford, U.K.: Basil Blackwell.

———. 1996. Portugal and European Monetary Union: Selling stability at home, earning credibility abroad. In *Monetary reform in Europe,* ed. Francisco Torres, 23–58. Lisbon, Spain: Universidade Católica.

———. 1999. Comment on "Part VII: Financial markets." In *Global financial turmoil and reform: A United Nations perspective,* ed. Barry Herman, 438–47. Tokyo: United Nations University Press.

———. 2000. Financial crises and international architecture: A Eurocentric perspective. OECD Development Center Technical Paper no. 162. Paris: Organization for Economic Cooperation and Development, August.

Macedo, Jorge Braga de, Daniel Cohen, and Helmut Reisen. 2001. Monetary integration for sustained convergence: Earning rather than importing credibility. In *Don't fix, don't float,* ed. Jorge Braga de Macedo, Daniel Cohen, and Helmut Reisen, 11–54. Paris: Organization for Economic Cooperation and Development.

McHale, John. 2000. The Korean currency crisis: A report on the third country meeting of the NBER project on exchange rate crisis in emerging market countries. Cambridge, Mass.: National Bureau of Economic Research. Available online at [http://www.nber.org/crisis/korea_report.htm].

McKinnon, Ronald. 1973. *Money and finance in economic development.* Washington, D.C.: Brookings Institution.

———. 1988. Financial liberalization and economic development: Interest rate polities in LDC. In *The state of development economics,* ed. Gustav Ranis and T. Paul Schultz, 380–410. Oxford, U.K.: Basil Blackwell.

Organization for Economic Cooperation and Research (OECD). 2000. *OECD reviews of regulatory reform: Regulatory reform in Korea.* Paris: OECD.

———. 2001. *Economic surveys: Korea 2000/2001.* Paris: OECD.

Scott, Kenneth. 1998. The role of corporate governance in South Korean economic reform. *Journal of Applied Corporate Finance* 10 (4): 8–15.

Discussion Summary

Sebastian Edwards made two comments. First, he expressed his sympathy with the view that the discussion of crises should focus on economic arguments rather than cultural differences. He said that, unfortunately, this is not the trend in the current public debate. The most popular book of the year 2000 on public policy (according to the *New York Times*), *Culture Matters,* edited by Harrison and Huntington, argues the exact opposite—that perhaps the only thing that matters is values. Second, he praised the paper for discussing the historical events that affected the Korea's present situation and suggested that the authors add a timetable. He emphasized that the fact that the United States labeled Korea an exchange manipulator (the only country ever given that title by the United States) and pushed Korea to open up its capital account in the late 1980s had a great deal to do with the currency crisis in 1997. *Martin Feldstein* later shared this view.

Joshua Aizenman asked about the welfare effects of opening capital markets. He said that the effect is ambiguous, because opening up the capital markets in Korea might have advanced the occurrence of the crisis, but it also helped to prevent Korea from running into a later crisis with more serious internal problems (like those that occurred in Japan).

Dani Rodrik commented that the paper seemed to support the idea that Korea had structural problems and therefore it also seemed to support the IMF program, which emphasized structural reforms and cleaning up the financial sector. However, he said that this was contradicted somewhat by the fact that Korea had recovered very nicely since the crisis and had been doing very well long before any of these policies were implemented. The question is how to reconcile the high speed of recovery and argument in favor of structural reform; one possibility could be that the current growth is a short-term leap. Rodrik also said that one could have made the same argument regarding the earlier Korean crisis in the 1980s, which was also preceded by severe structural problems in the heavy and chemical industries and a very large current account deficit. Yet Korea not only turned around in one year, but also had very nice growth rates for another seventeen years before it was hit by the Asian crisis.

Robert Dekle also commented on the structural problems of Korea and said that a paper by Yung-Chul Park (1991) found that the heavy and chemical industry policies led to many problems for the commercial banks, and the Bank of Korea was forced to use policy lending to maintain them.

Charles W. Calomiris said that a recent McKinsey report on Korean manufacturing argued that the heavy protection through trade policy, rather than corporate governance, was the cause of the Korean crisis. He personally disagrees with this view, which, however, seems to be influential. He suggested that the author refer to and contradict the viewpoint of the report.

John McHale remarked that this paper complemented the paper by Dekle and Keltzer (presented earlier in the conference) and described a march toward disaster through domestic credit expansion. He asked if the authors could discuss the time inconsistency problem in the context of Korea and provide some explanation why the Korean government could not make a commitment not to provide guarantees and stop the domestic expansion.

Simon Johnson pointed out that the paper rightly put corporate structures and corporate financial relationships at the center of the cause of the Korean crisis. Second, he commented that the paper was convincing on the issue of vulnerability, but there was still a question why and how the crisis happened in 1997. As shown in the paper, the debt-equity ratio was high and asset returns were negative for a long period of time. He stressed that domestic investors believed that if individual *chaebol* did badly, the group as a whole would bail out that individual company, and that was why investors trusted their money to *chaebol.* What triggered the crisis in 1997 was the collapse of Hanbo and, later, that of the heavily leveraged Daewoo, which underscored the vulnerability of the system. Once people stopped believing that individual companies could be bailed out, the whole *chaebol* system collapsed, resulting in a crisis.

Alejandro M. Werner commented on the data on the currency composition of assets and liabilities of Korean banks. He said that before the Mexican crisis in 1994, the official balance sheet of banks showed very good currency composition of registered assets and liabilities (because of obligations imposed by bank regulations), but the off–balance sheet items were actually in a much more vulnerable position. His question was to what extent the official balance sheet data could be confirmed by other evidence, and whether one could be sure that Korean banks really did not have problems in this respect. Later in the discussion *Michael P. Dooley* cited his joint paper with Shin in which they found that Korean regulators did watch the exposure of the banking system carefully and there was no anecdotal evidence of unbalanced exposure.

Feldstein remarked on the paper's finding that the damage to the Korean economy through the interest rates was greater than that through the exchange rate. He said these findings were important in light of the argument put forward by the IMF, namely that high interest rates would support the won and the currency would be adversely affected by the depreciation of the exchange rate without a corresponding increase in the interest rates. Feldstein also talked about the issue of exit strategy, that is, how to get out of the government protection of *chaebol* and individual firms. He said that the problem of not having an exit strategy was that once it became clear that the economy had become too big and complex for the government to apply first aid, there would be a change of expectation, and consequently a crisis would unravel.

On the comment that the structural problem in Korea may not have been very severe, given its rapid recovery, *Jungho Yoo* said that the rapid recovery should be thought of as a "technical rebound." He said that the huge cut in investments and drop in consumption after the crisis could not continue forever. In addition, the large depreciation of the currency had helped exports to grow, which provided the impetus for the rapid recovery in Korea. The question is whether the recovery could be sustained for a few years, and this does not seem to be the case. *Anne O. Krueger* said that she also found the conclusion that Korea had successfully recovered to be premature. She added that the *chaebol* issue was critical in understanding the cause of the crisis. For example, she said, *chaebol* accounted for 17 percent of the Korean manufacturing output in 1985, a share that increased to 40 percent in 1995 with expanded and diverted credit. This was not only a problem of corporate governance, but also a political problem: these large *chaebol* were so powerful that politicians themselves did not know how to handle them.

In response to the question why the crisis happened in 1997, Yoo said the following. Up to the mid-1980s, Korean firms were competitive, especially in the labor-intensive products, but they were beginning to face tough competition from Southeast Asian countries and China. The weakening international competitiveness did not immediately give rise to noticeable difficulties for the firms, however. In the second half of the 1980s, because of such external factors as substantial realignment of major international currencies, which depreciated the effective exchange rate of Korean won, and the huge increase in U.S. imports, Korean firms experienced a surge in foreign demand, and the current account registered large surpluses. The favorable external conditions could not continue to improve, and the firms began to have serious difficulties in the early 1990s. Following the past practice of helping the corporate sector out of financial trouble, the Bank of Korea lowered the rediscount rate and the commercial banks their lending rates. This expansionary monetary policy, together with the semiconductor boom in the international market, postponed the crisis to the second half of the 1990s.

On capital account liberalization, Krueger confirmed that there was a strong fear in Korea of opening up the capital account ahead of time, but she disagreed with the view that the capital account liberalization had much to do with either the timing or the magnitude of the crisis. She said that having capital controls might have postponed the crisis, but it would not have led to a very different result. On the welfare effect of opening the capital account, Krueger said that one had to answer two other questions first: that is, whether the liberalization delayed or had anything to do with the crisis, and whether crises are good because they imply earlier structural reforms or bad because they bring huge short-term losses. Because we do not know much about either of these questions, she said it would not be easy to address the welfare effects.

Krueger also discussed issues related to the heavy and chemical industries in Korea. She said that the promotion of these industries in Korea was not economically desirable by all measures, and it was the only time that the Korean government systematically handpicked the industry and told the investors what to do. Fortunately, Korea spotted the problem quickly and stopped many projects within a few years.

On the role of excessive government protection, Krueger stressed that the effect came through the implicit guarantee to *chaebol,* rather than from the trade channel. She also said that she and Yoo had checked the Korean data on banks' currency exposure and did not find any inconsistency similar to the Mexican case.

Living with the Fear of Floating
An Optimal Policy Perspective

Amartya Lahiri and Carlos A. Végh

14.1 Introduction

It has long been recognized that "pure" floating exchange rate regimes (defined as regimes in which the monetary authority does not intervene at all in foreign exchange markets) have rarely—if ever—existed in practice. More surprising, however, is the extent to which developing countries (which claim to be floaters) are reluctant to let the nominal exchange rate fluctuate in response to shocks, as convincingly documented by Calvo and Reinhart (2000a).[1] To assess this phenomenon, consider, as a benchmark for a relatively pure floater, the cases of the United States and Japan. As indicated in table 14.1, the probability that the monthly variation in the nominal exchange rate falls within a ±2.5 percent band is 58.7 percent for the United States and 61.2 percent for Japan. In contrast, for developing countries classified by the International Monetary Fund (IMF) as *free floaters* (FL) or *managed floaters* (MF), the average probability is 77.4 percent. This is even more remarkable considering that one would conjecture that developing countries are subject to larger and more frequent shocks.[2] Thus, the

Amartya Lahiri is assistant professor of economics at the University of California, Los Angeles. Carlos A. Végh is professor of economics at the University of California, Los Angeles, and a research associate of the National Bureau of Economic Research.

The authors would like to thank Joshua Aizenman, Eduardo Borensztein, Jaewoo Lee, Eduardo Moron, and participants at the 2001 AEA meetings in New Orleans and the NBER conference in Florida for helpful comments and suggestions. Both authors gratefully acknowledge research support provided by grants from the UCLA Academic Senate and thank Rajesh Singh for superb research assistance.

1. See also Levy and Sturzenegger (2000). On Peru's experience, see Moron and Castro (2000).

2. As evidenced, for instance, by the fact that real output is between two and two and a half times more volatile in developing countries than in the Group of Seven countries, whereas real

Table 14.1   Exchange Rate, Reserves, Interest Rates, and Money Fluctuations

Country	Regime	Period	Probability That Monthly Variation Falls Within a Given Range			
			E (±2.5% band)	R (±2.5% band)	I (±25 basis-point band)	M (±2% band)
Bolivia	FL	September 1985–December 1997	93.9	19.6	16.3	33.8
India	FL	March 1993–April 1999	93.4	50.0	6.4	53.4
Kenya	FL	October 1993–December 1997	72.2	27.4	19.6	31.4
Mexico	FL	December 1994–April 1999	63.5	28.3	5.7	22.7
Nigeria	FL	October 1986–March 1993	74.5	12.8	89.7	18.0
Peru	FL	August 1990–April 1999	71.4	48.1	24.8	34.3
The Philippines	FL	January 1988–April 1999	74.9	26.1	22.1	27.9
South Africa	FL	January 1983–April 1999	66.2	17.4	35.6	75.0
Uganda	FL	January 1992–April 1999	77.9	32.9	11.6	25.9
Venezuela	FL	March 1989–June 1994	n.a.	35.9	0.0	25.0
Indonesia	FL	July 1997–April 1999	14.3	29.9	13.3	9.5
Korea	FL	November 1997–April 1999	17.7	5.6	4.6	12.5
Thailand	FL	July 1997–April 1999	38.1	40.9	62.5	45.4
Bolivia	MF	January 1998–April 1999	100.0	12.5	31.1	0.0
Brazil	MF	July 1994–December 1998	94.3	51.8	11.1	27.8
Chile	MF	October 1982–April 1999	83.8	48.2	5.0	53.8
Colombia	MF	January 1979–April 1999	86.8	54.2	50.6	40.5

Egypt	MF	February 1991–December 1998	98.9	69.4	78.9	52.6
India	MF	February 1979–February 1993	84.5	36.7	49.7	46.8
Indonesia	MF	November 1978–June 1997	99.1	41.5	30.6	33.9
Israel	MF	December 1991–April 1999	90.9	43.8	26.4	39.8
Kenya	MF	January 1988–April 1999	70.6	14.3	28.6	71.4
Korea	MF	March 1980–October 1997	97.6	37.7	31.1	24.1
Malaysia	MF	December 1992–September 1998	81.2	55.7	66.7	47.2
Mexico	MF	January 1989–November 1994	95.7	31.9	8.3	27.8
Pakistan	MF	January 1982–April 1999	92.8	12.1	34.8	40.2
Singapore	MF	January 1988–April 1999	88.9	74.8	51.9	51.5
Turkey	MF	January 1980–April 1999	36.8	23.3	3.4	21.7
Uruguay	MF	January 1993–April 1999	92.0	36.5	2.7	39.5
Venezuela	MF	April 1996–April 1999	93.9	29.4	n.a.	23.5
United States	FL	February 1973–April 1999	58.7	62.2	59.7	67.2
Japan	FL	February 1973–April 1999	61.2	74.3	67.9	41.9
Average (excluding United States and Japan)			77.4	35.0	28.4	35.2

Source: Calvo and Reinhart (2000a).

Notes: E = nominal exchange rate; R = international reserves; I = nominal interest rate; M = nominal money base; FL = floating exchange rate regime; MF = managed float regime; n.a. = not available.

revealed preference for smoothing out exchange rate fluctuations—or "fear of floating"—is nothing short of remarkable.

How do emerging countries smooth out exchange rate fluctuations in practice? Not surprisingly, they do so by actively intervening in foreign exchange markets and engaging in an active interest rate defense of the currency. Again, for the United States and Japan, the probability that the monthly variation in international reserves falls within a ±2.5 percent band is 62.2 percent and 74.3 percent, respectively. The corresponding average for developing countries is 35.0 percent, indicating a much larger variability in international reserves. Similarly, the probability that the monthly variation in nominal interest rates falls in a ±25 basis point band is 59.7 percent for the United States and 67.9 percent for Japan. The corresponding figure for emerging countries is 28.4 percent, suggesting a much more active interest rate defense of the currency.

In addition, based on contemporaneous correlations among residuals from a vector autoregression analysis for individual episodes, Calvo and Reinhart (2000a) conclude that, in most instances, (a) the correlation between the exchange rate and interest rates is positive, (b) the correlation between reserves and the exchange rate is negative, and (c) the correlation between interest rates and reserves is negative. All three correlations seem to be consistent with the overall story told by table 14.1.

This paper starts from the presumption that the policies just described reflect an optimal policy response to underlying shocks.[3] In this light, this extreme fear of floating is puzzling because, even if nominal exchange rate fluctuations were costly, one would expect a monotonic relationship between nominal exchange rate variability and the size of the underlying shock (i.e., the larger the shocks, the larger the nominal exchange rate variability). At best, costly exchange rate fluctuations would explain a departure from a pure floating but would not explain the fact that countries subject to larger shocks have less volatile exchange rates, as suggested by the data.

The theoretical challenge is thus to build a simple model that allows for an explicit welfare evaluation of alternative policies and analyze whether the optimal policy in the model roughly replicates the observed policies. This paper represents a first effort on our part to tackle this important question.[4] We

---

private consumption is between three and four times more volatile (as shown by Talvi and Végh 2000, based on Hodrick-Prescott filtered data for 1970–94).

3. We consider the main alternative hypothesis (irrational policy makers) to be, by and large, factually wrong, and theoretically uninteresting (as we do not have good theories of irrationality).

4. Naturally, the choice of how much to intervene or raise interest rates in response to a negative shock that tends to weaken the domestic currency is related to the optimal choice of exchange rate regimes. An important literature in the 1980s emphasized the fact that the choice was not limited to the alternatives of fixed versus fully flexible exchange rates, but entailed a decision on the optimal degree of foreign exchange market intervention (with fixed and flexible rates merely being the extreme cases), as captured by the classic contribution of Aizenman and Frenkel (1985).

develop a simple theoretical model in which, in response to monetary shocks, the optimal policy response replicates most of the key policy facts just described.[5] In particular, the model predicts that the nominal exchange rate is a nonmonotonic function of the underlying shock (i.e., for small shocks, the nominal exchange rate is an increasing function of the shock, but for large shocks the nominal exchange rate is fully stabilized).

What are the main ingredients of our model? In the model, the fear of floating stems from the fact that exchange rate variability leads to output costs. In the presence of nominal wage rigidities, changes in the exchange rate lead to changes in the actual real wage, which in turn lead to "voluntary unemployment" (to use Barro and Grossman's 1971 terminology) if the real wage falls below its equilibrium value, or to "involuntary unemployment" if the real wage rises above its equilibrium level. (Notice that exchange rate variability is costly regardless of whether the domestic currency depreciates or appreciates.[6] We model active interest rate defense of the currency along the lines of Calvo and Végh (1995) by assuming that it basically entails paying interest on some interest-bearing liquid asset.[7] As in Lahiri and Végh (2000b), we incorporate into the model an output cost of raising interest rates. Hence, in our model, higher interest rates raise the demand for domestic liquid assets, but at the cost of a fall in output. Finally, we assume that there is a fixed (social) cost of intervening in foreign exchange markets.[8]

In the context of such a model, consider a negative shock to real money demand. If the shock is small, the output costs entailed by the resulting currency depreciation will also be small. It is thus optimal for policy makers not to intervene and to let the currency depreciate. Because exchange rate fluctuations are costly, however, it is optimal for policy makers to partially offset the shock to money demand by raising domestic interest rates. Hence, for small shocks to money demand, the exchange rate and domestic interest rates move in the same direction, whereas reserves do not change.

If the shock is large (i.e., above a well-defined threshold), the output costs resulting from exchange rate fluctuations would be too large relative to the cost of intervening. It thus becomes optimal to intervene and stabilize the ex-

5. For analytical simplicity, we focus only on monetary shocks. As indicated in table 14.1, monetary aggregates are much more volatile in developing countries, which is consistent with the idea that monetary shocks are larger.

6. We should stress that this is just a convenient analytical way of capturing costs of exchange rate fluctuations. In practice, there may be other (and possibly more important) sources of costly exchange rate fluctuations (see Calvo and Reinhart 2000b). Our focus is on analyzing the resulting optimal policy mix and *not* on providing sophisticated microfoundations for the cost of exchange rate fluctuations.

7. This paper is therefore related to an incipient theoretical literature that analyzes the active use of interest rates to defend an exchange rate peg (see Drazen 1999a,b; Flood and Jeanne 2000; Lahiri and Végh 2000a,b).

8. Although it is not explicitly modeled, we view this cost as capturing a fixed cost of portfolio adjustment for the private sector when it has to deal with the central bank (in the spirit of asset market segmentation stories in the tradition of Alvarez, Atkeson, and Kehoe [1999]).

change rate completely. Consequently, there is no need to raise interest rates to prop up the currency. Hence, for large negative shocks, international reserves fall, but the exchange rate and domestic interest rates do not change.

If we think of the real world as involving a sequence of monetary shocks (with developed countries facing mostly small shocks and emerging countries facing mostly large shocks), the model would predict the following.[9] First, from a cross-sectional point of view, (a) developing countries should exhibit low exchange rate variability and high reserve variability, and (b) conversely, developed countries should exhibit high exchange rate variability and low reserve variability. Moreover, from a time-series point of view (i.e., in individual countries), (c) the correlation between exchange rates and interest rates should be positive, (d) the correlation between the exchange rate and reserves should be negative, and (e) the correlation between interest rates and reserves should be negative. The model thus captures some of the main features of the data described above and should therefore provide a useful conceptual framework for thinking about policy responses in a world in which policy makers live with the fear of floating (i.e., in which nominal exchange rate fluctuations are costly).

The paper proceeds as follows. Section 14.2 develops the model under flexible wages. Section 14.3 introduces sticky wages into the picture. Section 14.4 analyzes the optimal policy mix under costless intervention. Section 14.5 derives the main results of the paper. Section 14.6 concludes.

14.2   The Model

Consider a small open economy inhabited by an infinitely lived representative household. The economy consumes and produces two goods, x and y, both of which are freely traded. The economy takes the world price of the two goods as given, and the law of one price is assumed to hold for both goods. The foreign currency price of good y is assumed to be constant and, for convenience, normalized to unity. The world relative price of good x in terms of good y is p, which is also assumed to be constant over time. The economy has access to perfectly competitive world capital markets where it can borrow and lend freely in terms of good y at the constant world interest rate r. Interest parity then implies that $i = r + \varepsilon$, where i is the nominal interest rate and ε is the rate of devaluation or depreciation.

14.2.1   Households

The representative household derives utility from consuming the two goods and disutility from supplying labor. The household's lifetime welfare (W) is given by

---

9. Our model is nonstochastic, so this characterization of the predictions is based on the comovement of variables in response to a monetary shock. A stochastic simulation of the model is left for future research.

(1)
$$W \equiv \int_0^\infty \frac{1}{1 - 1/\sigma} \{[c_t - \zeta\,(l_t^s)^\nu]^{1-(1/\sigma)} - 1\}e^{-\beta t}dt,$$

$$\sigma > 0, \quad \zeta > 0, \quad \nu > 1,$$

where

(2)
$$c = (c^y)^\rho(c^x)^{1-\rho}$$

is a consumption composite index (with c^y and c^x denoting consumption of goods y and x, respectively), l^s denotes labor supplied by the household, σ is the intertemporal elasticity of substitution, $\nu - 1$ is the inverse of the elasticity of labor supply with respect to the real wage (as will become evident below), and $\beta(> 0)$ is the exogenous and constant rate of time preference.[10] In order to rule out secular consumption dynamics, we make the standard assumption that $\beta = r$. Throughout the paper we maintain a notational distinction between labor supply and labor demand because, in the presence of nominal wage rigidities, labor supply will not necessarily equal labor demand at all times.

The household's flow budget constraint in terms of good y (or foreign currency) is given by

(3) $\quad \dot{a}_t = ra_t + w_t l_t^s + \Omega_t^y + \Omega_t^x + \Omega_t^b + \tau_t - c_t^y - pc_t^x - I_t^d h_t - \upsilon(\hat{h}_t; \alpha),$

where w denotes the wage rate in terms of foreign currency (henceforth referred to as the real wage), $I^d (\equiv i - i^d)$ is the deposit spread (with i^d denoting the interest rate paid on deposits), Ω^y and Ω^x are dividends received from firms in sectors y and x, respectively, Ω^b are dividends from commercial banks, τ denotes lump-sum transfers from the government to households, and $a(= b + h)$ represents net household assets in terms of foreign currency (where b and h denote net foreign bonds and demand deposits, respectively, both in terms of the foreign currency).

Real demand deposits held by the household are denoted by $\hat{h} = H/P$, where II denotes nominal demand deposits and P is the domestic currency price index of the composite consumption good, c. Transaction costs incurred by the household are denoted by $\upsilon(\hat{h}; \alpha)$, where $\alpha > 0$ is a positive constant. As is standard, we assume that the function $\upsilon(\hat{h}; \alpha)$ is strictly convex in $\hat{h}$ so that $\upsilon_{\hat{h}} \leq 0$ and $\upsilon_{\hat{h}\hat{h}} > 0$. Thus, the household can reduce transaction costs by holding additional demand deposits in terms of the composite consumption good. The parameter $\alpha(> 0)$ is a shift parameter for money demand. In particular, we assume that $\upsilon_\alpha < 0$ and $\upsilon_{\hat{h}\alpha} < 0$. As will be clear below, this implies that money demand, $\hat{h}$, is an increasing function of the parameter α.

---

10. We adopt these preferences for analytical convenience, because they imply that the labor supply decision becomes independent of wealth. Moreover, Correia, Neves, and Rebelo (1995) have shown that these preferences provide a better description of current account dynamics for small open economies than standard constant elasticity of substitution preferences.

Given equation (2), it is easy to establish that the domestic currency price index is given by

$$(4) \qquad P = \frac{p^{1-\rho}}{\rho^\rho (1-\rho)^{1-\rho}} E \equiv \frac{E}{B},$$

where E denotes the nominal exchange rate (domestic currency price of the foreign currency), while $B = [\rho^\rho (1-\rho)^{1-\rho}]/[p^{1-\rho}]$ is a positive constant.[11] Since $h = H/E$, equation (4) implies that $\hat{h} = Bh$. Hence, transaction costs are given by $\upsilon(\hat{h}; \alpha) = \upsilon(Bh; \alpha)$. Since the relative price p is constant over time, it is also easy to see from equation (4) that the rate of inflation must equal the rate of currency depreciation (ε) at all points in time. Hence, we must have $\dot{P}/P = \dot{E}/E = \varepsilon$.

Integrating the household's flow constraint subject to the transversality condition on a gives

$$(5) \quad a_0 + \int_0^\infty (w_t l_t^s + \Omega_t^y + \Omega_t^x + \Omega_t^b + \tau_t) e^{-rt} dt$$

$$= \int_0^\infty [c_t^y + p c_t^x + I_t^d h_t + \upsilon(\hat{h}_t; \alpha)] e^{-rt} dt.$$

To simplify the analysis, it will be assumed that the transaction costs technology is quadratic. Formally,

$$(6) \qquad \upsilon(\hat{h}, \alpha) = \hat{h}^2 - \alpha \hat{h} + \kappa, \qquad \hat{h} \in \left[0, \frac{\alpha}{2} \right],$$

where α and κ are positive constants.

The household chooses time paths for c^y, c^x, l^s and h to maximize equation (1) subject to equations (5) and (6), where $\hat{h} = Bh$, and taking as given a_0 and the paths for w, τ, r, p, I^d, Ω^y, Ω^x and Ω^b. The first-order conditions for utility maximization imply that

$$(7) \qquad \rho c_t [c_t - \zeta(l_t^s)^\nu]^{-1/\sigma} = \lambda c_t^y,$$

$$(8) \qquad (1-\rho) c_t [c_t - \zeta(l_t^s)^\nu]^{-1/\sigma} = p \lambda c_t^x,$$

$$(9) \qquad \nu \zeta (l_t^s)^{\nu-1} = B w_t,$$

$$(10) \qquad \alpha - 2\hat{h}_t = \frac{I_t^d}{B}.$$

Equations (7)–(10) can be used to derive the following relationships:

$$(11) \qquad \frac{1-\rho}{\rho} \frac{c_t^y}{c_t^x} = p,$$

---

11. P is the consumption-based price index, which is defined as the minimum expenditure required to purchase one unit of the composite consumption index, $(c^y)^\rho (c^x)^{1-\rho}$.

(12)
$$l_t^s = \left(\frac{Bw_t}{v\zeta}\right)^{1/(v-1)},$$

(13)
$$Bh_t = \hat{h}_t = \frac{\alpha}{2} - \frac{I_t^d}{2B}.$$

Equation (11) says that the marginal rate of consumption substitution between the two goods must equal their relative price. Equation (12) shows that households' labor supply is an increasing function of the real wage. Finally, equation (13) says that real money demand in terms of good y must be falling in the opportunity cost of holding deposits, I^d. Also, for a given I^d, a higher α implies that h must go up. Hence, the parameter α can be thought of as a shock to money demand.

14.2.2 Firms

Since there are two distinct sectors in this economy, there are two types of firms: those that produce good y and those that produce good x. Both sectors are assumed to be perfectly competitive.[12]

Sector y Firms

The industry producing good y is characterized by perfectly competitive firms that hire labor to produce the good using the technology

(14)
$$y_t = (l_t^d)^\eta, \qquad \eta \in (0, 1],$$

where l^d denotes labor demand. Firms may hold foreign bonds, b^y. Thus, the flow constraint faced by the firm is

(15)
$$\dot{b}_t^y = rb_t^y + (l_t^d)^\eta - w_t l_t^d - \Omega_t^y.$$

Integrating forward equation (15), imposing the standard transversality condition, and using equation (14) yields

(16)
$$\int_0^\infty e^{-rt} \Omega_t^y dt = b_0^y + \int_0^\infty [(l_t^d)^\eta - w_t l_t^d] e^{-rt} dt.$$

The firm chooses a path of l^d to maximize the present discounted value of dividends, which is given by the right-hand side (RHS) of equation (16), taking as given the paths for w_t, I_t^l, r, and the initial stock of financial assets b_0^f. The first-order condition for this problem is given by

(17)
$$\eta(l_t^d)^{\eta-1} = w_t.$$

Equation (17) yields the firm's demand for labor:

---

12. In case of decreasing returns, we implicitly assume—as is standard—that there is some fixed factor in the background (owned by households), which makes the technology (inclusive of this fixed factor) constant returns to scale.

(18)
$$l_t^d = \left(\frac{w_t}{\eta}\right)^{1/(\eta-1)},$$

which shows that, for $0 < \eta < 1$, labor demand by firms is decreasing in the real wage.

One should note that in the case of a linear production function (i.e., $\eta = 1$), the first-order condition for profit maximization (eq. [17]) reduces to

$$w_t = 1.$$

The labor demand schedule in this case is zero for any real wage above 1 and infinitely elastic for $w_t = 1$.

Sector x Firms

Sector x is also characterized by perfectly competitive firms that produce good x. Firms in this sector use an imported input q to produce good x, according to the technology given by

(19)
$$x_t = q_t^\theta, \qquad \theta \in (0, 1),$$

where q denotes the imported input. The world relative price of q in terms of good y is p_q, which is assumed to be constant. To economize on notation and with no loss of generality, we assume $p_q = 1$. Sector-x firms are, however, dependent on bank loans for their working capital needs. In particular, we assume that firms face a credit-in-advance constraint to pay for the imported input:

(20)
$$n_t \geq \psi q_t, \qquad \psi > 0,$$

where n denotes loans from commercial banks. This constraint introduces a demand for bank loans, and hence a credit channel, into the model. As is well known, this constraint will hold as an equality along all paths where the cost of loans, I^l, is positive. (In addition, we will assume that it holds as an equality if $I^l = 0$.)

Firms may hold foreign bonds, b^x. Hence, the real financial wealth of the representative firm at time t is given by $a_t^x = b_t^x - n_t$. Using i^l to denote the lending rate charged by banks and letting $I^l \equiv i^l - i$ denote the lending spread, we can write the flow constraint faced by the firm as

(21)
$$\dot{a}_t^x = r a_t^x + p x_t - q_t - I_t^l n_t - \Omega_t^x.$$

Integrating forward equation (21), imposing the standard transversality condition, and using equations (19) and (20) yields

(22)
$$\int_0^\infty e^{-rt} \Omega_t^x dt = a_0^x + \int_0^\infty [p q_t^\theta - q_t(1 + \psi I_t^l)] e^{-rt} dt.$$

Note that the credit-in-advance constraint introduces an extra cost of inputs to the firm, given by ψI^l (per unit of input).

The firm chooses a path of q to maximize the present discounted value of dividends, given by the RHS of equation (22), taking as given the paths for I_t^l, r, and the initial stock of financial assets, a_0^x. The first-order condition for profit maximization is given by

(23) $$p\theta q_t^{\theta-1} = 1 + \psi I_t^l.$$

Equation (23) implies that the demand for the imported input is given by

(24) $$q_t = \left(\frac{p\theta}{1 + \psi I_t^l}\right)^{1/(1-\theta)}.$$

Hence, the firm's demand for the imported input is decreasing in the lending spread. This captures the credit channel in our model. Finally, the loan demand by sector-x firms can be determined from equation (24) as

(25) $$n_t = \psi\left(\frac{p\theta}{1 + \psi I_t^l}\right)^{1/(1-\theta)}.$$

For later reference, it is useful to note $\partial n/\partial I^l < 0$ and $\partial^2 n/\partial(I^l)^2 > 0$. Hence, the input demand for q is also a decreasing and convex function of I^l.

14.2.3   Banks

The economy is assumed to have a perfectly competitive banking sector. We formalize the banking sector along the lines of Lahiri and Végh (2000b). The representative bank takes deposits from consumers, lends to sector-x firms (n), and holds domestic government bonds (z^b).[13] The bank charges an interest rate of i^l to firms and earns i^g on government bonds. It also holds required cash reserves, m (high-powered money). The bank pays depositors an interest rate of i^d. Thus, the balance sheet identity of the bank implies that $m_t + n_t + z_t^b = h_t$.[14]

Letting $I^g = i^g - i$ denote the interest rate spread from lending to the government, the flow constraint of the representative bank is

(26) $$\Omega_t^b = I_t^l n_t + I_t^d h_t + I_t^g z_t^b - i_t m_t.$$

Let $\delta(> 0)$ denote the reserve-requirement ratio imposed by the central bank. Note that, because required reserves are non–interest bearing, the

13. Commercial bank lending to governments is particularly common in developing countries. Government debt is held not only as a compulsory (and remunerated) reverse requirement but also voluntarily, due to the lack of profitable investment opportunities in crisis-prone countries. This phenomenon was so pervasive in some Latin American countries during the 1980s that Rodriguez (1991) aptly refers to such governments as "borrowers of first resort." For additional evidence, see Druck and Garibaldi (2000).

14. Similar results would go through if we allowed banks to hold foreign bonds in world capital markets as long as banks face a cost of managing domestic assets (along the lines of Edwards and Végh 1997, Burnside, Eichenbaum, and Rebelo 1999, or Agenor and Aizenman 1999). Put differently—and as is well known—some friction needs to exist at the banking level in order for banks to play a nontrivial role in the credit-transmission mechanism. We chose the specification with no foreign borrowing because it is analytically simpler.

opportunity cost of holding required reserves for banks is the forgone nominal interest rate, i. Hence, at an optimum, the bank will not hold any excess reserves. Formally,

$$(27) \qquad\qquad m_t = \delta h_t.$$

The representative commercial bank's balance sheet identity can thus be written as

$$(28) \qquad\qquad (1 - \delta)h_t = n_t + z_t^b.$$

The bank maximizes profits by choosing sequences of n_t, z_t^b, h_t, and m_t subject to equations (27) and (28), taking as given the paths of I^l, I^d, I^g, δ, and i. The first-order conditions for the banks' optimization problem are (assuming an interior solution)

$$(29) \qquad\qquad (1 - \delta)\, I_t^l + I_t^d = \delta i_t,$$

$$(30) \qquad\qquad (1 - \delta)\, I_t^g + I_t^d = \delta i_t.$$

Conditions (29) and (30) simply say that, at an optimum, the representative bank equates the marginal cost of deposits (RHS) to the marginal revenue from an extra unit of deposits (left-hand side). Note that the marginal revenue from an additional unit of deposits has two components. The first, given by I_t^d, is due to the fact that borrowing from consumers is cheaper for banks (whenever $I_t^d > 0$) than borrowing in the open market. The second, given by either $(1 - \delta)\, I_t^l$ or $(1 - \delta)\, I_t^g$, captures the fact that banks can lend a fraction $1 - \delta$ of each additional unit of deposits to either firms or the government.

Equations (29) and (30) imply that we must have

$$(31) \qquad\qquad I_t^g = I_t^l.$$

This also implies that $i^l = i^g$: that is, the lending rate to firms must equal the interest rate on government bonds. Intuitively, loans and government bonds are perfect substitutes in the bank's asset portfolio. Because the bank can get i^g by lending to the government, it must receive at least as much from firms in order to extend loans to them.

From equation (30), it is also easy to see that the deposit spread, I^d, is given by

$$(32) \qquad\qquad I_t^d = i_t - (1 - \delta)i_t^g.$$

Because $I^d = i - i^d$, it follows immediately that we must have $i_t^d = (1 - \delta)i_t^g$ for all t. Thus, a rise in the domestic interest rate, i^g, must result in a higher deposit rate for consumers and, hence, an increase in demand deposits. Because i^g may be controlled by policy makers, the preceding shows that interest rate policy in this model effectively amounts to the government being able to pay interest on money.

Finally, we will restrict attention to parameter ranges for which I^d and I^l

are nonnegative. Thus, we will confine attention to environments where $i^d \leq i \leq i^g$. This restriction is needed to ensure a determinate demand for both loans and demand deposits. Note that this amounts to restricting the relevant interest rates to the range $0 \leq i^g - i \leq \delta i^g$.

14.2.4 Government

The government is composed of the fiscal authority and the monetary authority (i.e., the central bank). The fiscal authority makes lump-sum transfers (τ) to the public and issues domestic bonds (Z), which are held either by the monetary authority or commercial banks. Domestic bonds are interest bearing and pay i^g per unit. The monetary authority issues high-powered money (M), holds government bonds (Z^g), and sets the reserve requirement ratio (δ) on deposits. The central bank also holds foreign exchange reserves (R), which bear the world rate of interest, r. Thus, the *consolidated* government's flow budget constraint is given by

$$(33) \qquad \dot{R}_t = rR_t + \dot{m}_t + \dot{z}_t^b + \varepsilon_t m_t + (\varepsilon_t - i_t^g)z_t^b - \tau_t,$$

where we have used the fact that the government's net liability to the private sector (in terms of domestic bonds) is $z^b = z - z^g$ (where z denotes the real stock of domestic bonds and z^g is the real stock of domestic bonds held by the central bank).

The central bank's balance sheet identity (in terms of foreign currency) is given by

$$(34) \qquad R_t + z_t - z_t^b = m_t.$$

Note that $z^g (= z - z^b)$ is the monetary authority's real domestic credit to the public sector. We assume that the fiscal authority keeps the *nominal* stock of outstanding government debt fixed at $\overline{Z}$.[15] Hence,

$$(35) \qquad \frac{\dot{Z}_t}{Z_t} \equiv \mu_t = 0, \qquad Z_0 = \overline{Z}.$$

Using equations (34) and (35), equation (33) can be rewritten as:

$$(36) \qquad \tau_t = rR_t + \varepsilon_t(m_t - z_t) + (\varepsilon_t - i_t^g)z_t^b.$$

In this model, policy makers may choose to use i^g as a policy instrument. In that case, and for analytical convenience, we will think of I^g as the policy instrument (recall that, by definition, $I^g = i^g - i$). Given that, as shown below, $i_t = r$ for all t, the central bank can always set an i^g to implement the desired value of I^g.[16] We shall also assume that the government lets fiscal transfers τ adjust endogenously so that equation (36) is satisfied.

---

15. This is the natural assumption to make, given that we will abstract from fiscal considerations and focus only on stationary equilibria involving constant nominal variables.

16. For expositional purposes, we will often refer to I^g as the domestic interest rate.

It is useful at this stage to restate the two key effects of interest rate policy in the model. First, because government bonds and bank credit to firms are perfect substitutes in the banks' portfolios, a higher interest rate on government bonds leads to an increase in the lending rate. This reduces bank credit and causes an output contraction (see eq. [24] and [31]). This effect will be referred to as the *output effect* of interest rate policy. Second, the higher interest rate on government bonds induces banks to also pay a higher rate on bank deposits (recall that $i^d = (1 - \delta)i^g$) and, as a result, increases the demand for bank deposits. We will refer to this as the *money demand effect*.

14.2.5   Resource Constraint

By combining the flow constraints for the consumer, the firms in sector x and sector y, the bank and the government (eq. [3], [15], [21], [26], and [33]) we get the economy's flow resource constraint:

$$(37) \qquad \dot{k}_t = rk_t + y_t + px_t - c_t^y - pc_t^x - q_t - \upsilon(Bh_t; \alpha),$$

where $k = R + b + b^y + b^x$. Note that the RHS of equation (37) is simply the economy's current account. Integrating forward subject to the no-Ponzi-game condition gives

$$(38) \qquad k_0 + \int_0^\infty [y_t + px_t - c_t^y - pc_t^x - q_t - \upsilon(Bh_t; \alpha)]e^{-rt}dt = 0.$$

14.2.6   Policy Regimes

Before proceeding to define the different policy regimes in this economy, notice that the rate of devaluation or depreciation (ε) will always be zero in this stationary economy. Under a fixed exchange rate, this is trivially true. Under a floating regime, this follows from the fact that (as shown below), the real stock of domestic bonds will be constant along a perfect foresight equilibrium path.

In this economy, policy makers have, in principle, four different policy instruments: the exchange rate (E), international reserves (R), the domestic interest rate (I^g), and nominal domestic credit (Z^g). Only two of these four instruments, however, can be chosen independently. For any two instruments controlled by the central bank, the other two will adjust endogenously. To see this, consider the following equations, which are the relevant ones for monetary policy purposes:

$$(39) \qquad\qquad\qquad R + \frac{Z^g}{E} = \delta h,$$

$$(40) \qquad\qquad\qquad \overline{Z} = Ez^b + Z^g,$$

$$(41) \qquad\qquad\qquad n + z^b = (1 - \delta)h,$$

where n is a function of I^g through the loan demand equation (25) (recall that $I^g = I^l$), h is a function of I^d through the money demand equation (13), and I^g and I^d are linked through equation (30) (recall that, as will be shown below, $\varepsilon = 0$). Equation (39) is the central bank's balance sheet, equation (40) is the equilibrium condition in the government bond market, and equation (41) is the commercial bank's balance sheet. Equations (39)–(41) thus define a system of three equations in five unknowns (E, R, z^b, Z^g, and I^g). This implies that there are two policy variables that can be set by policy makers.

For the purposes of the subsequent analysis, we can therefore define the following policy regimes:

1. *Fixed exchange rate.* Policy makers fix E at a certain level and set Z^g. Both international reserves and I^g adjust endogenously.[17] This regime is intended to capture a hard peg (in the style of Argentina or Hong Kong) in which the monetary authority maintains a constant backing (in terms of international reserves) of the monetary base and thus completely forgoes active monetary policy (i.e., the monetary authority allows I^g to be determined by market forces).

2. *Pure floating.* Policy makers fix R at a certain level and set I^g. Both the exchange rate and Z^g adjust endogenously. This regime is intended to capture a floating regime in which policy makers actively engage in monetary policy by setting domestic interest rates.

3. *Dirty floating.* Policy makers set R (and may change it in response to shocks) as well as I^g, whereas E and Z^g adjust endogenously.

4. *Fully sterilized intervention.* Policy makers target a constant level of h (real demand deposits)—and hence of the real monetary base—and set the level of z^g (real domestic credit). In this case, both reserves and the exchange rate adjust endogenously.

14.2.7 Flexible Wages Equilibrium

We now characterize the perfect foresight equilibrium path (PFEP) for this economy under flexible wages and floating exchange rates (either the pure floating or the dirty floating regimes, as defined above) under the assumption that α is expected to remain constant over time. In both cases (pure and dirty floating), policy makers keep the stock of international reserves constant along a PFEP.[18] Along this PFEP, policy makers set i^g at a

---

17. We will also refer to this case below as the full intervention case, because the central bank keeps the exchange rate fixed by intervening in the foreign exchange market.

18. Under dirty floating, and in response to unanticipated shocks to money demand (as analyzed below), the central bank will be allowed to undertake a discrete intervention when the shock hits. Notice that if the path of α were not constant over time (a case we do not address here), dirty floating could also be characterized by discrete interventions along a PFEP.

constant level. Because, as shown above, $i^d = (1 - \delta)i^g$, this implies that i^d is also constant along a PFEP.

The labor market clearing condition dictates that labor demand equal labor supply, that is, $l_t^s = l_t^d$. Imposing this condition on equations (12), (17), and (25) yields the equilibrium labor and real wage for this economy (equilibrium values of labor and real wage are denoted with a bar):

$$(42) \qquad\qquad \bar{l} \equiv \left(\frac{B\eta}{\zeta v}\right)^{1/(v-\eta)},$$

$$(43) \qquad\qquad \overline{w} = \eta\left(\frac{B\eta}{\zeta v}\right)^{(\eta-1)/(v-\eta)}.$$

In other words, along a PFEP, both employment and the real wage are constant.

Next, notice that the evolution of the stock of real domestic bonds is given by $\dot{z}/z = -\varepsilon$ (because, by definition, $z = Z/E$ and Z is constant from eq. [35]). By combining equations (39) and (41), we obtain $z = h - n - R_0$. Recall from equations (13) and (25) that h is a decreasing function of $r + \varepsilon - i^d$, whereas n is a decreasing function of $i^g - r - \varepsilon$. Because i^g and i^d are constant along a PFEP, it follows that z is solely a function of ε along such a path. Furthermore, we can implicitly solve for ε as a function of z and write $\varepsilon = \widetilde{\varepsilon}(z)$, where, as can be easily verified, $\widetilde{\varepsilon}'(z) < 0$. Hence, it follows that

$$(44) \qquad\qquad \dot{z}_t = -\widetilde{\varepsilon}(z_t)z_t.$$

By linearizing equation (44) around a steady state (where $\widetilde{\varepsilon}[z_t] = 0$), it follows that this is an unstable differential equation. Hence, z must always be equal to its steady-state level. This implies, in turn, that $\varepsilon = 0$ along a PFEP. Hence, h and n are also constant along a PFEP. This determines, through equation (41), the level of z^b. For this level of z^b and a given R_0, equations (39) and (40) determine the constant level of the exchange rate:

$$(45) \qquad\qquad \overline{E} = \frac{\overline{Z}}{\overline{m} - R_0 + \overline{z}^b},$$

where $\overline{m}(= \delta\overline{h})$ and $\overline{z}^b$ denote the constant values of real money balances and loans. Equation (45) shows that policy makers have two avenues for influencing the exchange rate. First, for a given R_0, they can use interest rate policy to affect I^d and I^l. This will influence $\overline{m}$ and $\overline{z}^b$ directly and, hence, change E. Second, for a given $\overline{m}$ and $\overline{z}^b$, they can intervene in the foreign exchange market and alter the level of R_0 and, hence, E. The determination of the optimal mix of these two policies is an issue that we will return to later.

In order to determine steady-state consumption, notice that equation (11) implies that the ratio c^x/c^y is a constant. Hence, c/c^y must also be constant. This, combined with the first-order condition for consumption and the fact that the equilibrium level of employment $\bar{l}$ is constant, implies that

c^y, c^x, and c must all be constant. The country resource constraint then implies that the constant levels of consumption of the two goods are given by

$$\bar{c}^y = \rho\left[rk_0 + \bar{l}^n + p\left(\frac{p\theta}{1 + \psi I^l}\right)^{\theta/(1-\theta)} - \left(\frac{p\theta}{1 + \psi I^l}\right)^{1/(1-\theta)} - \upsilon(Bh_t; \alpha) \right],$$

$$p\bar{c}^x = (1 - \rho)\left[rk_0 + \bar{l}^n + p\left(\frac{p\theta}{1 + \psi I^l}\right)^{\theta/(1-\theta)} - \left(\frac{p\theta}{1 + \psi I^l}\right)^{1/(1-\theta)} - \upsilon(Bh_t; \alpha) \right].$$

14.2.8 Money Demand Shocks under Flexible Wages

As a benchmark case, consider an unanticipated and permanent fall in α (i.e., a negative money demand shock) under a pure floating rate and flexible wages. Because real money demand decreases, the nominal exchange rate rises instantaneously (i.e., the currency depreciates) to accommodate the lower real money demand (see eq. [45]). Furthermore, the nominal wage rises by the same proportion as the exchange rate. Thus, with an unchanged interest rate policy, the real side of the economy remains completely insulated. Consumption of both goods falls because the equilibrium level of transactions cost rises. Note that under a fixed exchange rate (i.e., full intervention), the economy would also adjust instantaneously as the central bank intervenes in the foreign exchange market (by selling international reserves), thus accommodating the fall in real money demand.

14.3 Nominal Wage Rigidities

14.3.1 Perfect Foresight Equilibrium Path
under Flexible Exchange Rates

We now depart from the flexible wages paradigm by introducing a nominal wage rigidity into the model. We will examine first the case of flexible exchange rates.[19] We assume that nominal wages cannot jump at any point in time. Hence, the labor market clearing condition $l^d = l^s = \bar{l}$ does not necessarily hold at all points in time. In particular, it is assumed that nominal wages, W, adjust according to the following dynamic equation:

$$(46) \qquad \dot{W}_t = \gamma\left(\bar{w} - \frac{W_t}{E_t}\right), \qquad W_0 \text{ given,}$$

where $\gamma \in (0, \infty)$ captures the speed of adjustment toward the equilibrium real wage, $\bar{w}$. Recall that $\bar{w}$ is given by equation (43). The implication of introducing sticky nominal wages (as shown below) is that a depreciation of the currency will now lead to a fall in the real wage and cause a temporary labor market disequilibrium and concomitant output losses in sector y.

---

19. As will become clear below, in the fixed exchange rate case, the real sector remains insulated from monetary shocks.

Using the previously shown result that, along any PFEP with flexible exchange rates, E must already be at its steady state value $\bar{E}$ at time $t = 0$, one can solve equation (46) to get

$$(47) \qquad w_t = \bar{w} + e^{-(\gamma/\bar{E})t} (w_0 - \bar{w}),$$

where $w_t = W_t/\bar{E}$ and $w_0 = W_0/\bar{E}$. Notice that $\lim_{t \to \infty} w_t = \bar{w}$. Moreover, $\dot{w}_t \gtreqless 0$ for $w_t \lesseqgtr \bar{w}$. Finally, the equilibrium nominal wage is given by $\bar{W} = \bar{w}\bar{E}$.

As in standard disequilibrium models, it will be assumed that actual employment is given by the short end of the market. In other words, when the real wage is below (above) its equilibrium value, actual labor is determined by labor supply (demand). Notice that this disequilibrium model implies that only one of the two labor optimality conditions will hold. If the real wage is below its equilibrium value, the household's labor condition (eq. [9]) will hold, but the firm's (eq. [18]) will not. Conversely, if the real wage is above its equilibrium value, the firm's first order condition will hold, but the household's will not.

There are two potential cases of disequilibrium. For $w_0 < w_t < \bar{w}$, we have $l_t^a = l_t^s = (Bw_t/\nu\zeta)^{1/(\nu-1)}$. Substituting in for w_t from equation (47) and simplifying the result yields the path for actual employment:

$$(48) \qquad l_t^a = \bar{l} \left[1 + \left(\frac{w_0}{\bar{w}} - 1 \right) e^{-(\gamma/\bar{E})t} \right]^{1/(\nu-1)},$$

with $l_0^a = (Bw_0/\nu\zeta)^{1/(\nu-1)}$. Analogously, for the case $w_0 > w_t > \bar{w}$, we have $l_t^a = l_t^d = (w_t/\eta)^{1/(\eta-1)}$. The path for actual employment is now given by

$$(49) \qquad l_t^a = \bar{l} \left[1 + \left(\frac{w_0}{\bar{w}} - 1 \right) e^{-(\gamma/\bar{E})t} \right]^{-1/(1-\eta)},$$

with $l_0^a = (w_0/\eta)^{1/(\eta-1)}$. Substituting these relations into equation (14) yields the time path of output of good y for each case.

It is useful to note that, in both cases, $l^a < \bar{l}$ throughout the transition. Intuitively, any deviation of the real wage from its equilibrium value implies that the short end of the labor market determines actual employment. In the case of an unanticipated increase in the real wage, labor demand falls while labor supply goes up (relative to the equilibrium). Because labor demand is the short side of the market, actual employment equals labor demand. Hence, output of sector y falls. Conversely, when the real wage is below the equilibrium, labor supply is smaller, whereas labor demand is greater relative to the equilibrium. In this event, actual employment is supply-determined. Hence, employment falls and output of sector y declines.[20]

This result is key to understanding the real effects of exchange rate fluctuations within this model. It implies that currency appreciation and depreciation are *both* contractionary. This result stands in stark contrast to

---

20. This case is exactly what Barro and Grossman (1971) called "voluntary unemployment" in their analysis of disequilibrium models.

Table 14.2   **Response to a Negative Money Demand Shock**

Policy Regime	R	E	I^g	z^g	h
Fixed exchange rate	↓	→	↑	→	↓
Floating exchange rate	→	↑	→	↓	↓
Dirty floating	↓	↑	→	→	↓
Full sterilization	↓	↓	↑	↑	→
Optimal policy (small shock)	→	↑	↑	↓	↓
Optimal policy (large shock)	↓	→	→	↑	↓

Note: Under dirty floating, the increase in E is smaller than under pure floating.

the standard Mundell-Fleming model with rigid prices in which deprecia-tions are expansionary whereas appreciations are contractionary. The difference arises because the standard models in the Mundell-Fleming tra-dition postulate output to be demand-determined, with demand being a function of the real exchange rate. As this model shows, introduction of an explicit supply side alters the implications quite dramatically.

The consumption dynamics along the adjustment path can be deter-mined directly from the employment dynamics. Noting that λ is constant along a PFEP and c^x/c^y and c/c^y are both constants at all times, one can di-fferentiate the first-order condition (eq. [7]) with respect to time to get

$$(50) \qquad \dot{c}_t = \zeta v (l_t^a)^{v-1}\, \dot{l}_t^a > 0,$$

which says that consumption rises along with employment during the tran-sition. There is a unique time path of consumption that satisfies equation (50) and the intertemporal resource constraint. Given the paths for c and l^a, the values of c_0 and l_0^a would then determine the value of the multiplier through the first-order condition given by equation (7). Clearly, welfare will be lower than it would be under flexible wages (and floating rates), because either firms in sector y are forced to accept a path for labor that does not sat-isfy their first-order condition given by equation (17), or the first-order con-dition for households, equation (9), is violated.[21]

14.3.2 The Menu of Policy Options

We can now describe the economy's response to a negative money de-mand shock (i.e., an unanticipated and permanent fall in α) in the presence of sticky wages under the four policy regimes defined above. (Table 14.2 summarizes the outcome under these four different options.) Notice that, on the monetary side, the economy will always adjust instantaneously to this shock. On the real side, sector-x output will always adjust instanta-neously as well. On the other hand, sector-y output will adjust gradually over time if the exchange rate deviates from its initial steady state along the lines described above.

21. Notice that an important advantage of this framework over a model with demand-determined output is that welfare analysis in our model is well defined.

1. *Fixed exchange rate.* Under a fixed exchange rate, policy makers respond to the shock by keeping E and Z^g unchanged. Hence, real domestic credit, z^g, also remains unchanged. From equation (40), it follows that z^b will not change either. Because the negative money demand shock reduces real demand for deposits, the commercial bank's balance sheet (eq. [41]) implies that loans, n, must fall. However, this can only occur through a rise in I^g. In the new equilibrium, the fall in real money demand is smaller than the initial shock because the rise in the domestic interest rate partially offsets the money demand shock. International reserves decline endogenously to accommodate the lower level of base money.

Intuitively, the initial fall in real demand deposits induces a fall in the demand for government bonds by commercial banks. At unchanged levels of central bank holdings of government bonds, z^g, and the nominal exchange rate, E, this implies an excess supply of government bonds. The central bank responds to this by raising domestic interest rates, because this makes domestic bonds and demand deposits more attractive to the private sector.

On the real side, sector-y output remains unchanged at its equilibrium level. Since the exchange rate is fixed, the actual wage will not deviate from the equilibrium real wage, and there will be no disequilibrium in the labor market. In contrast, higher domestic interest rates extract an output cost in sector x as banking credit becomes more expensive and banking lending falls. In addition, the fall in real money balances implies an increase in transaction costs.

2. *Pure floating.* Under pure floating, policy makers respond to the negative money demand shock by keeping international reserves, R, and the domestic interest rate, I^g, unchanged, while allowing the exchange rate and domestic credit to adjust endogenously. An unchanged domestic interest rate implies that base money falls by the full amount of the shock. Because R is unchanged, real domestic credit, z^g, must fall to accommodate the shock. The fall in demand deposits along with an unchanged lending rate (and hence loan demand) implies that the demand for government bonds by commercial banks, z^b, falls. The excess supply of government bonds implies that its price, $1/E$, falls: that is, the currency depreciates.

In the pure floating case, sector x remains completely insulated from the shock, because the domestic interest rate remains unchanged. However, the depreciation of the currency implies a fall in the real wage. Hence, the labor market goes into disequilibrium on impact and returns to the steady state asymptotically, as shown by equations (47) and (48). Hence, the output of sector y remains below the steady-state level throughout the adjustment period. Moreover, the policy also implies a contraction in real deposits and, hence, higher transaction costs and lower consumption.

3. *Dirty floating.* Under dirty floating, policy makers intervene in the foreign exchange market (by selling international reserves) to achieve a smaller increase in the exchange rate (i.e., a smaller depreciation) than under the pure floating case. Specifically, suppose that policy makers reduce R so as to main-

tain the stock of real domestic credit unchanged. Then, because I^g does not change, it follows from equation (41) that z^b will fall. This, in turn, implies from equation (40) that E rises. Notice that this rise in E will be less than in the pure floating case described above. The reason is that z^b falls by the same amount in either case, whereas z^g falls under a pure float but does not change under dirty floating. From equation (40), it follows that E will rise by less.

Intuitively, starting from the pure floating case described above, policy makers intervene in foreign exchange markets by selling international reserves. Because the domestic interest rate is kept unchanged, the lower stock of international reserves will be reflected in a higher stock of real domestic credit. This implies that, at the level of the exchange rate that prevails under pure floating, there is an excess demand for government bonds. Hence, their price ($1/E$) must increase, which implies that E must fall (relative to the pure floating case). The outcome is that the currency depreciates by less than it does in the pure floating case, while international reserves fall.

Because the currency depreciates by less under dirty floating, the output losses in sector y will be lower than under pure floating. There are no output costs in sector x.

4. *Fully sterilized intervention.* In our definition, the case of a fully sterilized intervention means keeping the level of real money demand unchanged and targeting a higher level of real domestic credit.[22] In this case, the domestic interest rate, the level of international reserves, and the exchange rate will adjust endogenously. In order for real demand deposits to remain unchanged, equation (13) implies that $(\alpha/2) - (I^d/2B)$ must remain unchanged. Hence, in response to a fall in α, I^d must fall. From equation (30), a fall in I^d implies a rise in I^g. Hence, loans (n) must fall, while commercial bank holdings of government debt (z^b) rise by an offsetting amount. Because, by construction, z^g has gone up, the nominal exchange rate must fall (i.e., the currency appreciates). International reserves fall one-to-one with the increase in real domestic credit.

Intuitively, under a fully sterilized intervention, the central bank reacts to a negative money demand shock by increasing domestic credit through a purchase of government bonds while raising the domestic interest rate in order to keep money demand unchanged. The resulting increase in the lending rate causes sector-x firms to reduce their loan demand. Commercial banks react to the lower demand for loans by increasing their demand for government bonds. Hence, the total demand for government bonds rises. Because the nominal supply of these bonds is fixed, their price, $1/E$, must rise. Hence, E must fall (i.e., the currency appreciates). The final outcome is a change in the composition of central bank assets (lower international reserves and higher real domestic credit) with no change in the level.

---

22. Naturally, this scenario assumes that the initial level of $\hat{h}$ is still technologically feasible after the shock. (Recall from eq. [6] that the transaction technology imposes the restriction that $\hat{h} \leq \alpha/2$.)

While this policy succeeds in insulating domestic money demand from the negative shock (which implies that transaction costs fall by less than they would otherwise), this insulation comes at the expense of higher domestic interest rates and an appreciation of the currency. The higher interest rate causes an output contraction in sector x. The appreciation, on the other hand, induces a rise in the real wage (recall that nominal wages are rigid) and a fall in labor demand and sector-y output.

In the next section we will show that the optimal policy mix (when intervention is costless) implies that none of these extreme cases is optimal. Instead, the optimum falls somewhere in the "interior" of these pure cases.

14.3.3   Real versus Monetary Shocks

We conclude this section by noting that this model reproduces the standard Mundell-Fleming results regarding the optimal exchange rate regime under fixed and flexible rates. Under fixed exchange rates, sticky wages make no difference in the adjustment path of the economy. Put differently, the economy adjusts instantaneously under fixed rates and sticky wages, as the central bank buys and sells reserves to keep E unchanged. Thus, relative to flexible exchange rates, fixed exchange rates are better for insulating the real side of the economy from monetary shocks.

To think about real shocks in this model, consider a shock to p, the relative price of good x. This shock changes the equilibrium real wage and, hence, requires a change in the market real wage. Under flexible rates, this would happen instantaneously through a change in the nominal exchange rate. Under fixed exchange rates and rigid nominal wages, the economy cannot adjust instantaneously, because neither the nominal wage nor the nominal exchange rate can jump. The economy returns to the long-run equilibrium only through a slow adjustment of the nominal wage accompanied by an output contraction in sector y (unless, of course, there is a policy change in the exchange rate). Thus, for the purposes of insulating the real side of the economy from real shocks, flexible exchange rates are better than fixed exchange rates.

14.4   Optimal Stabilization Policy

Having described the adjustment of the economy to money demand shocks under different policy regimes, we now turn to the issue of the optimal policy response to such shocks.[23] For the purposes of solving for the optimal policy response to a monetary shock, we will view policy makers as optimally choosing the domestic interest rate, I^g, and the level of international reserves (which, if different from the preshock level, implies a discrete

---

23. For analytical convenience, this section solves for the optimal policy in the absence of a fixed cost of intervention (a key feature of the model to be introduced in the next section). The next section solves for the optimal policy problem in the complete model.

one-shot intervention in the foreign exchange market). It is clear from equations (39)–(41) that an optimal choice of I^g and R will imply a unique choice of E, Z^g, and z^b.

To study the optimal policy response, start from a steady state with $\alpha = 1$, $E = \overline{E}$, $m = \overline{m}$, and $R = \overline{R}$, and consider an unanticipated and permanent fall in α at time $t = 0$. The policy maker's goal is to choose I_0^g and R_0 to maximize the welfare of the representative agent. Solving the optimal policy problem becomes greatly simplified due to the following proposition.

PROPOSITION 1. *Given any choice of I_0^g by the policy maker in response to a money demand shock (i.e., an α shock), it can never be optimal for the central bank to choose an R_0 such that $E_0 \neq \overline{E}$.*

PROOF. Recall that any $E_0 \neq \overline{E}$ implies that the market real wage $W_0/E_0 \neq \overline{w} = W_0/\overline{E}$, where $\overline{w}$ is the equilibrium real wage. Hence, output and employment must fall on impact and then rise gradually back toward the long-run steady state. The central bank can always choose R_0 such that $\overline{m} - \overline{R} + \overline{z}^b = m_0 - R_0 + z_0^b$. Such a choice of R_0 would imply that $E_0 = \overline{E}$, which would leave the labor market completely unaffected and, hence, the output of sector y unchanged. Moreover, output of sector x is independent of the size of the intervention. Because intervention is costless from the perspective of the country as a whole, country wealth is unaffected by the size of intervention (a larger R merely corresponds to lower private foreign bond holdings, b, leaving k unchanged). Hence, this particular choice of R_0 dominates any other postshock choice of reserves.

Proposition 1 implies that the policy maker will respond to a monetary shock by always keeping the nominal exchange rate unchanged so as to insulate the economy from any labor market frictions. Hence, at the time of the shock, the economy adjusts immediately to a new stationary equilibrium. The problem is thus reduced to a choice of optimal real money balances in a stationary economy through an appropriate choice of I^g. Once m (and hence z^b) is chosen, the optimal intervention involves choosing an R_0 such that $E_0 = \overline{E}$.

Note that proposition 1 immediately eliminates from the set of optimal policies the option of allowing the adjustment (in part or in its entirety) to occur through an adjustment of the nominal exchange rate. Hence, it is already clear that neither the pure floating nor the dirty floating regimes considered above will prove to be the optimal policy response.

The stationarity of the economy implies that the representative household's lifetime welfare is given by

$$W = \frac{1}{r\left(1 - \frac{1}{\sigma}\right)} [(c - \zeta \bar{l}^v)^{1-(1/\sigma)} - 1],$$

which takes into account the fact that the policy maker will ensure that the labor market is always in equilibrium. Hence, $l^a = \bar{l}$. For a stationary economy, the country resource constraint given by equation (38) implies that

$$c^y + pc^x = rk_0 + \bar{l}^\eta + pq^\theta - q - (\hat{h}^2 - \alpha\hat{h} + \kappa).$$

Moreover, the first-order conditions for consumption imply that $c^y + pc^x = c^y/\rho$ and $c/B = c^y/\rho$. Hence, the economy's resource constraint reduces to

$$c = B[rk_0 + \bar{l}^\eta + pq^\theta - q - (\hat{h}^2 - \alpha\hat{h} + \kappa)].$$

Because $c - \zeta\bar{l}^\nu$ is constant along any perfect foresight equilibrium path while W is monotonically rising in $c - \zeta\bar{l}^\nu$, the policy maker's problem reduces to choosing I^g, $I^g \in \{0, [\delta/(1-\delta)]r\}$, to maximize $c - \zeta\bar{l}^\nu (\equiv \hat{W}^{peg})$ subject to equations (13), (24), and (30), for a given α, k_0, and $\bar{l}$. Note that welfare in this case corresponds to welfare under a fixed exchange rate.

The country resource constraint implies that

(51) $\hat{W}^{peg} = Brk_0 + B\bar{l}^\eta - \zeta\bar{l}^\nu + B(pq^\theta - q) - B(\hat{h}^2 - \alpha\hat{h} + \kappa).$

Differentiating $\hat{W}^{peg}$ with respect to I^g gives

(52) $$\frac{d\hat{W}^{peg}}{dI^g} \equiv \Gamma = -\frac{B\psi^2 (p\theta)^{1/(1-\theta)}I^g}{(1-\theta)}\left(\frac{1}{1+\psi I^g}\right)^{(2-\theta)/(1-\theta)} + \frac{(1-\delta)}{2B}I^d.$$

In the following we shall use I^g_{peg} to denote the optimal value of I^g in the case where the policy maker keeps the exchange rate pegged at all times. I^g_{peg} is defined by the relation $\Gamma|_{I^g_{peg}} = 0$. It is easy to determine from equation (52) that $\Gamma|_{I^g=0} > 0$ and $\Gamma|_{I^g=[\delta/(1-\delta)]r} < 0$. Hence, $I^g_{peg} \in \{0, [\delta/(1-\delta)]r\}$. In other words, the optimal domestic interest rate lies strictly in the interior of the permissible range. Note that $I^g = [\delta/(1-\delta)]r$ corresponds to $I^d = 0$, which is equivalent to implementing the Friedman rule.

Equation (52) clearly shows the two key margins over which the policy maker chooses the optimal I^g. First, a higher I^g implies that I^l goes up. Hence, the cost of funds for sector-x firms goes up, which implies that output (net of the import bill) and, consequently, consumption falls. This effect is captured by the first term on the RHS of equation (52). However, a higher I^g also implies a higher deposit rate for depositors and hence a lower opportunity cost of holding deposits, I^d. This causes money demand to go up, which, in turn, reduces transaction costs and thereby increases consumption. This is the positive money demand effect of higher domestic interest rates that is captured by the second term in the RHS of equation (52). Note that the Friedman rule ($I^d = 0$) emerges as the optimum when $\psi = 0$. When $\psi = 0$, higher lending rates do not have any output effect, because firms do not rely on bank credit at all. Thus, it is optimal to raise the domestic interest rate all the way to $I^g = [\delta/(1 - \delta)]r$, which implies that $I^d = 0$, thereby achieving the lowest possible level of transaction costs.

For I^g_{peg} to be an optimum, we must also ensure that the second-order condition for a maximum is satisfied. The condition $\psi r[\delta/(1-\delta)] < 1 - \theta$ is sufficient (but not necessary) to satisfy the second-order condition for the government's welfare maximization problem. Moreover, this condition implies that $\hat{W}^{peg}$ is globally concave in I^g; hence, the optimal solution, I^g_{peg}, is unique. We omit a detailed statement of the proof because it follows simply from differentiating Γ with respect to I^g. In what follows we shall restrict attention to parameter ranges for which the second-order condition is satisfied.

Of key interest to us is the behavior of the optimal domestic interest rate as a function of α. In particular,

$$\frac{dI^g_{peg}}{d\alpha} = -\frac{\partial\Gamma/\partial\alpha}{\partial\Gamma/\partial I^g} = 0,$$

since $\partial\Gamma/\partial I^g < 0$ (from the second-order condition for welfare maximization) and $\partial\Gamma/\partial\alpha = 0$. We state this result in the following proposition.

PROPOSITION 2. *The optimal domestic interest rate, I^g_{peg}, is independent of the money demand parameter α. Hence, a negative money demand shock (a fall in α) or a positive money demand shock (a rise in α) leaves I^g_{peg} unchanged.*

This proposition says that a social welfare–maximizing policy-maker, who keeps the exchange rate fixed by fully intervening in the foreign exchange market, should not alter the domestic interest rate in response to money demand shocks. Intuitively, at an optimum, the marginal benefit in terms of reducing transaction costs, given by the last term on the RHS of equation (52), is independent of α. There is therefore no reason for the optimal domestic interest rate to change. Because $\hat{h} = (\alpha/2) - (I^d/2B)$, a change in α merely induces a corresponding parallel shift up or down in money demand but leaves unchanged the marginal benefit of changing the domestic interest rate. Hence, both $\hat{h}$ and h fall in response to a negative money demand shock.

The preceding analysis allows us to tie down the behavior of all the endogenous variables in the model in response to a money demand shock. We summarize them in the following proposition.

PROPOSITION 3. *An unexpected fall (rise) in α causes real money balances to fall (rise). The central bank responds to the shock by intervening in the foreign exchange market by selling (buying) international reserves in order to keep the nominal exchange rate unchanged at the preshock level. The domestic interest rate, I^g, is kept unchanged. Because neither the domestic interest rate nor the exchange rate changes, output of both sectors remains unaffected. Furthermore, real domestic credit increases (falls) whereas international reserves fall (increase).*

Notice how, in response to a negative money demand shock, the optimal policy response involves elements of the four regimes described above. Specifically, the fall in real money demand is accommodated fully through foreign exchange market intervention (i.e., selling reserves), without any change in the exchange rate, as would happen under a fixed exchange rate. In addition, the domestic interest rate is kept unchanged (i.e., monetary policy is not tightened in response to the shock), as would occur under either a pure or dirty float. Finally, the optimal response also involves an increase in real domestic credit, as would occur if policy makers were attempting to (partially) sterilize the fall in real money demand.

It is worth stressing that the existence of nominal wage rigidities is key in generating the result that the nominal exchange rate should be kept fixed. In the absence of nominal wage rigidities, exchange rate fluctuations are costless. In that event, the central bank has no incentive to intervene, which implies that a pure float is optimal.[24,25]

14.5 Costly Intervention

This section completes the specification of the general model by incorporating costly intervention and derives the optimal policy response in such a case. We proceed in two steps. We first study the optimal policy contingent on no intervention and then contingent on intervention; we then confront the question of when it will be optimal for policy makers to intervene.

14.5.1 Optimal Policy under Intervention

As before, we analyze the effects of a negative money demand shock. In particular, starting from a steady state with $\alpha = 1$, we study the effects of an unanticipated and permanent fall in α. To simplify notation, and without loss of generality, we also choose initial conditions such that $\overline{E} = 1$ and $\overline{R} = 0$. For $\overline{R} = 0$, this corresponds to an initial situation in which $\overline{Z} = h - n$. To see this, one can rewrite the central bank balance sheet as $E = \overline{Z}/(z^b + m - R)$. However, the commercial bank balance sheet implies that $z^b = h - m - n$. Hence, for $R = 0$, the expression for E reduces to

$$(53) \qquad\qquad E = \frac{\overline{Z}}{h - n}.$$

---

24. In the absence of nominal wage rigidities, the policy maker is essentially indifferent between intervening and not intervening, because allocations are independent of the level of the exchange rate. However, even an infinitesimal cost of intervening would imply that the optimal policy is a pure float.

25. We should note that the strict independence of the optimal interest rate from the money demand shock is due to the quadratic transaction costs technology. In a more general setup for transaction costs, say $\alpha\upsilon(\hat{h})$, it is easy to show that the optimal response to a negative money demand shock is to raise the domestic interest rate to partially offset the effect of the shock on money demand. Hence, optimal policy, in general, would entail a combination of higher interest rates and foreign exchange market intervention.

Finally, we also assume that in the initial steady state the domestic interest rate is given by the solution to the optimal policy problem under costless intervention. Hence, $\bar{I}^g = I^g_{peg}$, while n and h are given by their corresponding levels under I^g_{peg}.

For simplicity, we assume that the central bank incurs a fixed cost $\phi > 0$ in the event that it intervenes in the foreign exchange market. Moreover, this fixed cost is symmetric: it applies to either an increase or a decrease in the stock of reserves.[26] Clearly, if $\phi = 0$, the model reduces to the one analyzed earlier in which the optimal response is to fully insulate the exchange rate from all money shocks. Under this general specification, the resource constraint for the economy now becomes

$$(54) \quad k_0 - \phi + \int_0^\infty [(l_t^a)^\eta + pq_t^\theta - c_t^y - pc_t^x - q_t - (\hat{h}^2 - \alpha\hat{h} + \kappa)] e^{-rt} dt = 0.$$

It is useful to begin by noting that, because the intervention cost is fixed and independent of the size of the intervention, there can only be two potential outcomes to the policy maker's problem. Either the monetary authority pays the fixed cost of intervention and intervenes by the full amount necessary to keep the nominal exchange rate unchanged, or it does not intervene at all.[27]

In the event that the policy maker intervenes, optimal policy will coincide with that under costless intervention (which was derived above). This follows from the fact that the cost of intervention is independent of the size of intervention. Consequently, none of the marginal conditions for optimal policy are affected. The policy maker would thus respond to a negative money demand shock by keeping the domestic interest rate and the nominal exchange rate unchanged. Money demand would therefore fall by the full amount of the shock. Hence, under full intervention, output of both sectors remains completely invariant to changes in α.

In this case, the representative household's welfare is increasing in $c - \zeta \bar{l}^v$ ($\equiv \hat{W}^I$), which is given by

$$(55) \quad \hat{W}^I = Brk_0 + B\bar{l}^\eta - \zeta\bar{l}^v + B(pq^\theta - q) - B(\hat{h}^2 - \alpha\hat{h} + \kappa) - Br\phi,$$

where we have used the resource constraint (eq. [54]) to substitute out for c. The only difference between this expression and the RHS of equation (51)

26. We take this fixed cost to be a highly heuristic representation of a world with asset market segmentation in which agents must pay a fixed cost to transfer money between the goods market and the asset market, along the lines of Alvarez, Atkeson, and Kehoe (1999). Formalizing this channel is far from trivial (because the main exercise involves performing comparative statics for the optimal policy) and is left for future research. See also Cadenillas and Zapatero (1999), who derive the optimal intervention policy for the central bank in a stochastic model with a fixed cost of intervention.

27. Note that partial intervention would imply that the exchange rate must change, which, in turn, would imply output losses in sector y. Because these losses are costless to avoid through an appropriate intervention (the fixed cost implies that the marginal intervention is costless), partial intervention can never be an optimal policy choice.

is the cost of intervention term, $Br\phi$, which is independent of all endogenous variables. This establishes our assertion that, if it is optimal to intervene, optimal policy in this instance must coincide with optimal policy under the costless intervention case. For future reference, it is also useful to note that

$$(56) \qquad \frac{dW^I}{d\alpha} = \frac{B\alpha}{2} > 0,$$

where we have used the first-order condition given by equation (10), the money demand equation (13), and the fact that the optimal domestic interest rate is independent of α. Thus, the smaller the money demand parameter α (i.e., the bigger the shock), the lower the welfare.

14.5.2   Optimal Policy under No Intervention

If the policy maker chooses not to pay the cost of intervention, then there will be no intervention at all. Hence, reserves will remain unchanged in response to the money demand shock. In this event, there emerges a role for interest rate policy for domestic macroeconomic management. To see this, consider the case in which the central bank reacts to the negative money demand shock not only by not intervening but also by keeping domestic interest rates unchanged. Money demand falls by the full amount of the shock, whereas domestic loans (and, hence, sector-x output) remain unchanged. With an unchanged nominal stock of government bonds, $\overline{Z}$, equation (53) implies that the nominal exchange rate must increase (because h falls and n does not change). The nominal depreciation along with the nominal wage rigidity implies a fall in the real wage. This causes a contraction of labor supply and output of sector y, which returns to the steady-state level only asymptotically.

Now suppose that the central bank raised the domestic interest rate marginally in response to the shock. This would lower loans while reducing the fall in money demand. From equation (53) it is easy to see that, relative to the previous case of unchanged interest rates, the nominal depreciation induced by the shock must be smaller. Accordingly, the fall in the real wage must also be smaller, which in turn implies a smaller contraction of sector y. Of course, this benefit comes at the cost of an output contraction in sector x, because the credit cost of the imported input is greater. It is clear, however, that in choosing the optimal domestic interest rate policy makers should be trading off these two margins.

To formalize the government's problem, notice again that welfare is strictly increasing in $c - \zeta(l^s)^\nu (\equiv \hat{W}^{NI})$, which takes into account that, for negative money demand shocks, actual employment equals labor supply; that is, $l^a = l^s$. In the event of no intervention, the economy's resource constraint implies that

(57) $\hat{W}^{NI} = Brk_0 + B(pq^\theta - q) - B(\hat{h}^2 - \alpha\hat{h} + \kappa) + rY,$

where $Y = \int_0^\infty [B(l_t^s)^\eta - \zeta(l_t^s)^\nu]e^{-rt}dt$ is the present discounted value of sector-y output net of the disutility from labor supply.

At this stage, it is easy to see that the optimal policy problem under intervention becomes more complicated than in the costless intervention case. The reason is that, in response to a depreciation of the currency, the nominal wage rigidity implies that the economy displays intrinsic output dynamics because the labor market goes into disequilibrium. In order to make analytical progress, we simplify the model by setting $\eta = 1$ and $\nu = 2$. These parameter values make both the production function of sector y and the marginal disutility from labor supply linear in labor. This simplification allows us to compute the change in optimal policies even in the presence of intrinsic output dynamics.

From equation (43), notice that, under linear production in sector y, the equilibrium real wage is unity (i.e., $\overline{w} = 1$), which implies that the nominal wage in the initial steady state must be unity as well. Hence, on impact, the real wage is given by $w_0 = 1/E_0 < 1$. Moreover, under negative money demand shocks we are restricting attention to $w_0 \in [0, 1]$. From equation (53) it follows that

(58) $w_0 = \dfrac{h - n}{\overline{Z}}.$

Because $h - n$ is increasing in I^g, it is obvious that the initial real wage is an increasing function of the domestic interest rate. In particular, $\partial w_0/\partial I^g = (1/\overline{Z})[(1 - \delta)/2B^2 - (\partial n/\partial I^g)] > 0$, whereas $\partial^2 w_0/\partial(I^g)^2 = -(1/\overline{Z})[\partial^2 n/\partial(I^g)^2] < 0$. Hence, the initial real wage is an increasing and concave function of the domestic interest rate.

As shown above, an unexpected currency depreciation implies that labor supply is the short end of the labor market. Hence, actual employment is given by labor supply. Under our assumptions on η and ν, the actual path of employment, given by equation (48), reduces to

(59) $l_t^a = \overline{l}[1 + (w_0 - 1)e^{-\gamma w_0 t}].$

Because employment and labor supply are linear in the initial real wage while $Y = \int_0^\infty [Bl_t^a - \zeta(l_t^a)^2]e^{-rt}dt$, one can differentiate Y with respect to w_0 to get

(60) $Y_w = \dfrac{B\overline{l}(1 - w_0)}{(r + 2\gamma w_0)^2}[r + \gamma(1 + w_0)] \geq 0,$

where we have used equations (9) and (59) to integrate out over t. For later reference, it is useful to note that $Y_w|_{w_0=0} = (B\overline{l}/r^2)(r + \gamma) > 0$ and $Y_w|_{w_0=1} = 0$. It is straightforward to check that $Y_{ww} < 0$ for $w_0 \in [0, 1]$.

The policy choices at time zero are w_0 $(= 1/E_0)$ and I^g. However, equation (58) makes clear that only one of these two variables can be freely chosen. We shall assume that the policy maker chooses I^g. Because $\bar{Z}$ is given exogenously and $R_0 = \bar{R} = 0$, a given choice of I^g determines h and n. These two variables allow us to uniquely determine w_0 from equation (58). Moreover, all private-sector behavior can be expressed as functions solely of E_0 and I^g. Thus, the government's problem can be formalized as choosing I_0^g to maximize the RHS of equation (57) subject to equations (13), (24), (31), (32), (58), and (59). The first-order condition for this problem is[28]

$$(61) \quad \frac{d\hat{W}^{NI}}{dI^g} \equiv \Gamma^{NI} = -\frac{B\psi^2(p\theta)^{1/(1-\theta)}I^g}{(1-\theta)}\left(\frac{1}{1+\psi I^g}\right)^{(2-\theta)/(1-\theta)}$$

$$+ \frac{(1-\delta)}{2B}I^d + rY_w\frac{\partial w_0}{\partial I^g}.$$

In the following we shall denote the optimal interest rate for the no-intervention case by I_{NI}^g. Specifically, $\Gamma^{NI}\big|_{I^g = I_{NI}^g} = 0$. Three results follow directly from the first-order condition. First, for $\alpha = 1$ the optimal domestic interest rate continues to be I_{peg}^g. This can be seen from the fact that $\Gamma^{NI} = 0$ for $I^g = I_{peg}^g$ and $\alpha = 1$. Note that for $I^g = I_{peg}^g$ and $\alpha = 1$ we must have $w_0 = 1$. Because $Y_w\big|_{w_0=1} = 0$, the last term on the RHS of equation (61) drops out. The result then follows from the fact that the first two terms on the RHS are merely $d\hat{W}^{peg}/dI^g$, which is zero for $I^g = I_{peg}^g$ (see eq. [52]). Hence, absent a money demand shock, $I_{NI}^g = I_{peg}^g$.[29]

Second, for $\alpha < 1$ and $I^g = I_{peg}^g$, it is easy to check that $\Gamma^{NI} > 0$. Thus, it is optimal for the policy maker to respond to a negative money demand shock by raising the domestic interest rate—that is, $I_{NI}^g > I_{peg}^g$. Third, in the case of $\alpha < 1$, it is never optimal for the policy maker to raise the domestic interest rate all the way to the point that $w_0 = E_0 = 1$. Because $Y_w\big|_{w_0=1} = 0$, this follows from equation (52), which says that the sum of the first two terms on the RHS of equation (61) is negative for $I^g > I_{peg}^g$.

Let us now turn to the relationship between the optimal domestic interest rate and the size of the money demand shock. To determine this, we start by noting that, from the implicit function theorem, $dI_{NI}^g/d\alpha = -(\Gamma_\alpha^{NI}/\Gamma_{I^g}^{NI})$.

---

28. It is important to note that we will only focus on values of ψ for which there are interior solutions when $\alpha < 1$. In general, however, there will be corner solutions. In fact, it is easy to show that, for $\psi = 0$ and $\alpha < 1$, there will be a corner solution at the I^g corresponding to the Friedman rule (i.e., $I^d = 0$). The intuition is clear: If $\psi = 0$ and $\alpha < 1$, "increasing" I^g (if it were possible) above the Friedman rule would have no first-order effects on transactions costs but would have a first-order positive effect on sector-y output as the currency appreciates (i.e., $\Gamma^{NI} > 0$, when evaluated at $I^d = 0$ for $\psi = 0$ and $\alpha < 1$). By continuity, therefore, there will also be corner solutions for very small values of ψ. For larger values of ψ, interior solutions exist (as we have established using numerical examples).

29. As in the case of costless intervention studied earlier, it can be shown that the condition $\psi r[\delta/(1-\delta)] < 1 - \theta$ continues to be sufficient (but not necessary) to satisfy the second-order condition.

Because $-\Gamma_{I^g}^{NI} > 0$ from the second-order condition, it follows that the signs of $dI_{NI}^g/d\alpha$ and Γ_α^{NI} are the same. Partially differentiating equation (61) with respect to α gives $\Gamma_\alpha^{NI} = (r/2B\overline{Z})(\partial w_0/\partial I^g)\, Y_{ww} < 0$. Hence,

$$(62) \qquad \frac{dI_{NI}^g}{d\alpha} = \frac{(r/2B\overline{Z})(\partial w_0/\partial I^g)\, Y_{ww}}{-\Gamma_{I^g}^{NI}} < 0,$$

which says that the optimal domestic interest rate increases with the size of the shock (i.e., the smaller the value of α, and hence the larger the shock, the higher the value of I_{NI}^g).

The next issue of interest is the behavior of the nominal exchange rate as a function of the money demand shock. This is not immediately obvious, because there are two potentially offsetting effects. A fall in α directly reduces money demand and thus, all else being equal, reduces the real wage by increasing E. (Recall that $w_0 = 1/E_0 = (h-n)/\overline{Z}$). However, the fact that the central bank raises interest rates in response to a bigger money demand shock implies that, for a given α, money demand rises, which appreciates the currency and raises w_0. If the latter effect is strong enough, then the nominal exchange rate will fall (i.e., the currency would appreciate) in response to larger shocks.

To shed light on this issue, we totally differentiate equation (58) to get, after some rearrangement,

$$\frac{dw_0}{d\alpha} = \frac{1}{2\overline{Z}B\Gamma_{I^g}^{NI}}\left[\Gamma_{I^g}^{NI} - r\,Y_{ww}\left(\frac{\partial w_0}{\partial I^g}\right)^2\right],$$

where $\Gamma_{I^g}^{NI}$ is the partial derivative of equation (61) with respect to I^g. As noted above, $\psi r[\delta/(1-\delta)] < 1 - \theta$ is a *sufficient* condition to satisfy the second-order condition for welfare maximization (i.e., $\Gamma_{I^g}^{NI} < 0$). It is straightforward to check that this sufficiency condition is also a sufficient condition for $\Gamma_{I^g}^{NI} < r\,Y_{ww}\,(\partial w_0/\partial I^g)^2$.[30] Hence, $\psi r[\delta/(1-\delta)] < 1 - \theta$ is a *sufficient* condition for $dw_0/d\alpha > 0$, which implies that as α becomes smaller (i.e., the money demand shock gets larger), the initial real wage, w_0, becomes progressively smaller. Because $E_0 = 1/w_0$, this implies that, with no intervention, the nominal exchange rate is a decreasing function of α; that is, the larger the negative money demand shock, the larger the currency depreciation.

Finally, it is useful to characterize the welfare effect of a negative money demand shock under the no-intervention regime. Totally differentiating equation (57) with respect to α gives

$$(63) \qquad \frac{d\hat{W}^{NI}}{d\alpha} = \frac{B\alpha}{2} + \frac{r}{2B\overline{Z}}\,Y_w > 0,$$

---

30. To see this, define $N = pq^\theta - q$. Hence, $\Gamma^{NI} = B(\partial N/\partial I^g) + [(1-\delta)/2B]I^d + r\,Y_w(\partial w_0/\partial I^g)$ and $\Gamma_{I^g}^{NI} = B[\partial^2 N/\partial(I^g)^2] - (1-\delta)^2/2B + r\,Y_{ww}(\partial w_0/\partial I^g)^2 + r\,Y_w[\partial^2 w_0/\partial(I^g)^2]$. Moreover, $\Gamma_{I^g}^{NI} - r\,Y_{ww}(\partial w_0/\partial I^g)^2 = B[\partial^2 N/\partial(I^g)^2] - (1-\delta)^2/2B + r\,Y_w[\partial^2 w_0/\partial(I^g)^2]$. Because Y_{ww} and $\partial^2 w_0/\partial(I^g)^2$ are both negative, a sufficient condition for both $\Gamma_{I^g}^{NI} < 0$ and $\Gamma_{I^g}^{NI} < r\,Y_{ww}(\partial w_0/\partial I^g)^2$ is $\partial^2 N/\partial(I^g)^2 < 0$. It is easy to check that $\partial^2 N/\partial(I^g)^2 < 0$ for $\psi r[\delta/(1-\delta)] < 1 - \theta$.

where we have used the fact that, at an optimum, the first-order condition for welfare maximization (eq. [61]) says that $(\partial \hat{W}^{NI}/\partial I^g)(\partial I^g_{NI}/\partial \alpha) = 0$. We collect these results in the following proposition.

PROPOSITION 4. *Under no foreign exchange market intervention, the central bank responds to a negative money demand shock by raising the domestic interest rate while allowing some currency depreciation to occur. Moreover, the larger the negative money demand shock, the larger the increase in the optimal domestic interest rate, the larger the currency depreciation, and the larger the fall in welfare.*

14.5.3   To Intervene or Not To Intervene

Having described the behavior of optimal interest rate policy contingent on the intervention regime (i.e., intervention or no intervention), we now turn to the determination of the optimal intervention regime itself. For a given α, it is straightforward to see that the optimal intervention strategy is determined by

$$\text{Do not intervene if} \quad \hat{W}^{NI}\big|_{I^g=I^g_{NI}} > \hat{W}^I\big|_{I^g=I^g_{peg}},$$

$$\text{Intervene if} \quad \hat{W}^{NI}\big|_{I^g=I^g_{NI}} \le \hat{W}^I\big|_{I^g=I^g_{peg}}.$$

Notice first that around $\alpha = 1$, $\hat{W}^{NI} - \hat{W}^I = Br\phi$. This follows from the facts that for $\alpha = 1$, $I^g_{NI} = I^g_I = I^g_{peg}$ and $w_0 = 1$, whereas $l^s = l^a = \bar{l}$. Intuitively, around $\alpha = 1$, the only difference between the two regimes is the cost of intervention, whereas the nominal exchange rate and the domestic interest rates are identical. Consequently, welfare under intervention is lower.

From equations (56) and (63), it is also easy to see that $(d\hat{W}^{NI}/d\alpha) - (d\hat{W}^I/d\alpha) = (r/2B\bar{Z})Y_w > 0$. This indicates that although bigger money demand shocks (or lower α's) cause welfare to decline under both regimes (as indicated by eq. [56] and [63]), welfare under the no-intervention regime falls faster than under the full intervention regime. Intuitively, the direct effect of the money demand shock on transaction costs is the same under the two regimes. However, under the no-intervention regime, a smaller α leads to a lower real wage due to the nominal wage rigidity, which extracts an output cost from sector y.

The preceding implies that the relative welfare comparison between the two regimes reduces to a trade-off between the fixed cost of intervention and the output cost associated with not intervening. Crucially, the output costs under the no-intervention regime increase as the shock grows bigger, but the corresponding cost of intervention is independent of the size of the shock. Hence, the welfare differential between the two regimes shifts in favor of intervention as the shock grows larger. Because $\hat{W}^{NI} - \hat{W}^I = Br\phi > 0$ around $\alpha = 1$, this implies that for a given ϕ there must exist a threshold value of α, $\hat{\alpha} < 1$, such that $\hat{W}^{NI}\big|_{\alpha=\hat{\alpha}} = \hat{W}^I\big|_{\alpha=\hat{\alpha}}$. Further, for all $\alpha < \hat{\alpha}$ we

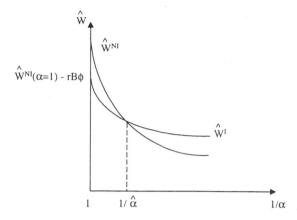

Fig. 14.1   Welfare comparison

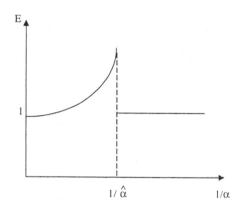

Fig. 14.2   Optimal exchange rate

must have $\hat{W}^{NI} < \hat{W}^{I}$. These features of the optimal policy problem are captured in figure 14.1, which depicts welfare under the two regimes as a function of $1/\alpha$, so that moving to the right along the horizontal axis implies a larger shock (i.e., a smaller value of α).

Using the above results, one can now completely characterize the optimal policy response to money demand shocks (see table 14.2). For small money demand shocks—that is, $\alpha \in (\hat{\alpha}, 1)$—it is optimal for the policy maker not to intervene but rather let the currency float and raise the domestic interest rate to fight the currency depreciation in order to reduce the resulting output cost. As we saw earlier, this also implies that in this range, the larger the money demand shock, the bigger the currency depreciation. However, for large money demand shocks, (i.e., $\alpha < \hat{\alpha}$), it is optimal for the policy maker to keep domestic interest rates unchanged and intervene fully in order to prevent the nominal exchange rate from fluctuating at all. Figure 14.2 depicts the behavior of the nominal exchange rate as a function of $1/\alpha$. For small shocks (i.e., $1/\alpha < 1/\hat{\alpha}$) the exchange rate is an increasing function of the shock, whereas for large shocks (i.e., $1/\alpha > 1/\hat{\alpha}$) the exchange rate remains fixed (relative to the preshock equilibrium).

The last result worth noting is that the threshold value of the shock parameter, $\hat{\alpha}$, is a decreasing function of the fixed cost of intervention, ϕ. This result follows from noting that $(d\hat{W}^{NI}/d\alpha) - (d\hat{W}^{I}/d\alpha) = (r/2B\overline{Z})) Y_w$ is independent of ϕ. However, a smaller ϕ implies that $\hat{W}^{NI} - \hat{W}^{I} = Br\phi$ is smaller. In terms of figure 14.1, a smaller ϕ causes a parallel shift upward of the $\hat{W}^{I}$ schedule, leaving its slope with respect to α unaffected. Hence, the threshold $\hat{\alpha}$ must be larger (i.e., it must be closer to unity). When $\phi = 0$, the two schedules coincide for $\alpha = 1$, with $\hat{W}^{I}$ exceeding $\hat{W}^{NI}$ for all $\alpha < 1$.

We summarize the preceding results in the following proposition.

PROPOSITION 5. *The optimal policy response to a negative money demand shock is a function of the size of the shock. For small shocks, it is optimal for the policy maker not to intervene in the foreign exchange market but instead to raise the domestic interest rate and let the currency depreciate. Moreover, in this range, the larger the shock, the higher both the nominal exchange rate and the domestic interest rate. For large shocks, however, it is optimal for the central bank to intervene by the full amount necessary to keep the exchange rate and domestic interest rates unchanged. Furthermore, the smaller the fixed cost of intervention, the smaller the threshold size of the shock for which the full intervention policy becomes optimal.*

To assess how well the model might explain the key stylized facts outlined in the introduction, let us perform the following conceptual experiment. Suppose that this economy were subject to a sequence of (stochastic) monetary shocks. Assume, further, that developing countries were hit, on average, by larger shocks than industrial countries. The outcome would be a series of changes in the endogenous policy variables, as captured by the last two rows in table 14.2. From a cross-sectional point of view, the model would predict that developing countries (which face mostly large shocks) would exhibit low exchange rate variability and high reserve variability, whereas developed countries (which face mostly small shocks) would exhibit high exchange rate variability and low reserve variability. From a time-series perspective, we would observe an average response (because countries are hit by both small and large shocks) that would consist (for, say, negative monetary shocks) of falling reserves, a more depreciated currency, and higher interest rates. Hence, the correlation between changes in the exchange rate and interest rates would be positive, but the correlation between (a) reserves and the exchange rate and (b) reserves and interest rates would be negative. All these predictions match the stylized policy facts described in the introduction.

14.6   Conclusions

The starting point for this paper has been the observation that, in spite of suffering larger shocks, developing countries (classified as floaters or managed floaters) exhibit lower exchange rate variability and higher reserve variability than developed countries which float. This extreme "fear of floating" is puzzling because, even if nominal exchange rate fluctuations were costly, one would still expect that larger shocks would lead to larger changes in the nominal exchange rate.

This paper has developed a simple and highly stylized theoretical model that is capable of explaining this puzzle. In particular, the model predicts that for small negative money shocks, policy makers find it optimal to let the exchange rate adjust while partly offsetting the shock by raising domestic interest rates. For large shocks, however, policy makers find it optimal to completely stabilize the exchange rate by intervening in the foreign exchange market. The model thus predicts a nonmonotonic relationship between the nominal exchange rate and the size of the shock. If we identify small shocks with developed countries and large shocks with developing countries, the model predicts that developing countries should exhibit low exchange rate variability and high reserve variability, whereas the converse is true for developed countries.

While we view this as a useful first step toward an understanding of the "fear of floating" puzzle, there are at least two directions in which this line of research should be taken. To begin with, we would like to endogenize the fixed cost of intervention, which is of course key to our results. A natural avenue for doing this would be to consider a setup with asset market segmentation along the lines of Alvarez, Atkeson, and Kehoe (1999). Although this would be a major undertaking (given that our focus is on optimal policies, which makes the problem already much more complicated from a formal point of view), it would certainly be worthwhile to pursue. Second, it would be useful to develop a stochastic version of this model, calibrate it for some representative developing country, and try to match the observed correlations. Developing richer models along these lines should prove extremely useful both for understanding the actual responses observed in the data and for devising implementable and usable policy rules for central bankers.

References

Agenor, P. R., and J. Aizenman. 1999. Financial sector inefficiencies and coordination failures: Implications for crisis management. NBER Working Paper no. 7446. Cambridge, Mass.: National Bureau of Economic Research.

Aizenman, J., and J. Frenkel. 1985. Optimal wage indexation, foreign exchange intervention, and monetary policy. *American Economic Review* 75:402–23.

Alvarez, F., A. Atkeson, and P. Kehoe. 1999. Volatile exchange rates and the forward premium anomaly: A segmented asset market view. Federal Reserve Bank of Minneapolis. Mimeograph.

Barro, R., and H. Grossman. 1971. A general disequilibrium model of income and unemployment. *American Economic Review* 61:82–93.

Burnside, C., M. Eichenbaum, and S. Rebelo. 1999. Hedging and financial fragility in fixed exchange rate regimes. NBER Working Paper no. 7143. Cambridge, Mass.: National Bureau of Economic Research.

Cadenillas, A., and F. Zapatero. 1999. Optimal central bank intervention in the foreign exchange market. *Journal of Economic Theory* 87:218–42.

Calvo, G., and C. Reinhart. 2000a. Fear of floating. NBER Working Paper no. 7993. Cambridge, Mass.: National Bureau of Economic Research, November.

———. 2000b. Fixing for your life. NBER Working Paper no. 8006. Cambridge, Mass.: National Bureau of Economic Research, November.

Calvo, G., and C. Végh. 1995. Fighting inflation with high interest rates: The small open economy case under flexible prices. *Journal of Money, Credit, and Banking* 27:49–66.

Correia, I., J. Neves, and S. Rebelo. 1995. Business cycles in a small open economy. *European Economic Review* 39:1089–113.

Drazen, A. 1999a. Interest rate defense against speculative attack under asymmetric information. University of Maryland, Department of Economics. Mimeograph.

———. 1999b. Interest rate and borrowing defense against speculative attack. University of Maryland, Department of Economics. Mimeograph.

Druck, P., and P. Garibaldi. 2000. Inflation risk and portfolio allocation in the banking system. University of California, Los Angeles, Department of Economics, and International Monetary Fund. Mimeograph.

Edwards, S. and C. Végh. 1997. Banks and macroeconomic disturbances under predetermined exchange rates. *Journal of Monetary Economics* 40:239–78.

Flood, R., and O. Jeanne. 2000. An interest rate defense of a fixed exchange rate? International Monetary Fund. Mimeograph.

Lahiri, A., and C. Végh. 2000a. Delaying the inevitable: Optimal interest rate policy and BOP crises. NBER Working Paper no. 7734. Cambridge, Mass.: National Bureau of Economic Research, June.

———. 2000b. Output costs, BOP crises, and optimal interest rate defense of a peg. University of California, Los Angeles, Department of Economics. Mimeograph.

Levy, E., and F. Sturzenegger. 1999. Classifying exchange rate regimes: Deeds vs. words. Universidad Di Tella, Buenos Aires, Argentina. Mimeograph.

Moron, E., and J. F. Castro. 2000. Uncovering central bank's monetary policy objective: Going beyond fear of floating. Universidad del Pacifico, Lima, Peru. Mimeograph.

Rodriguez, C. A. 1991. Financial reform and macroeconomic developments in Argentina, Chile, and Uruguay during the decade of the 1980s. Universidad del CEMA, Buenos Aires, Argentina. Mimeograph.

Talvi, E., and C. Végh. 2000. Tax base variability and procyclical fiscal policy. NBER Working Paper no. 7499. Cambridge, Mass.: National Bureau of Economic Research, January.

Comment   Eduardo Borensztein

This paper by Lahiri and Végh (LV) takes an interesting first step in addressing a very important question, one frequently met when designing monetary or exchange rate policies in emerging markets today. The question is how to respond to a capital outflow, or "exchange market pressure," in an economy with a managed floating exchange rate and an active interest in what happens to the exchange rate. The model is nicely done and clearly presented, but there are some modeling strategy decisions in the monetary and financial area that I do not entirely like.

I like to represent the policy options in a triangle, as in the figure. In the diagram, as we move down, the central bank is intervening more in the foreign exchange market and dampening any adjustment in the exchange rate, perhaps preventing a large depreciation when the country suffers a cutback in external financing or an outflow of capital.

At the top vertex of the triangle, we are in a clean float, with no central bank intervention at any time. Along the bottom of the triangle, the exchange rate is completely fixed, and the adjustment to a negative external shock comes fully through a loss in international reserves. However, here there is another dimension of policies, namely the extent to which the central bank sterilizes the monetary effect of a loss in reserves by creating domestic credit. At one extreme there is no attempt to sterilize, and the fall in reserves is fully reflected in the monetary base (and in domestic interest rates). In this vertex, the central bank would be operating as a (textbook) currency board. At the other extreme, the central bank completely sterilizes the monetary impact of its intervention in the foreign exchange market, allowing domestic monetary conditions to remain undisturbed.

Suppose there is a shock to external financing, say because of contagion. Which point in this triangle is it optimal to choose? Intuition would suggest some interior point in the triangle, avoiding the financial-sector distress that can come from excessive depreciation or too high interest rates and the fiscal implications of, and perhaps also market constraints on, sterilized intervention on a large scale.[1] LV, while not intentionally attempting to represent the above story, find that countries *should* choose an interior point in the triangle, at least for large shocks.

The results in LV can be easily summarized. In what concerns the extent of exchange rate flexibility (the choice along the vertical direction in the diagram) in the basic framework with wage rigidity but no cost of foreign exchange intervention, traditional results apply: for monetary shocks, a con-

Eduardo Borensztein is chief of the developing countries studies division of the International Monetary Fund research department.

1. This implicitly ignores arguments about the institutional strength or credibility of a legally established regime such as a currency board.

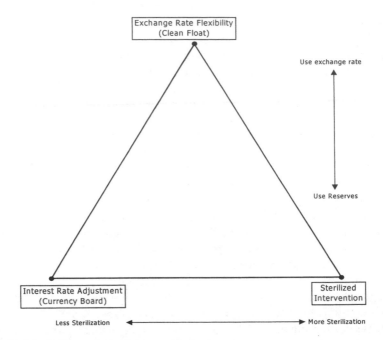

Fig. 14C.1   Response to exchange market pressure

stant exchange rate is superior, and for real shocks the opposite holds—namely, a full adjustment in the exchange rate is preferable. The basic reason is that, in each case, those are the regimes that will allow real wages to stay at or near their equilibrium levels. LV then introduce a fixed cost to foreign exchange market intervention by the central bank. With this cost, the optimal response to a shock to a somewhat idiosyncratic money demand (more on this later) depends on the size of the shock. For small changes, the cost of intervention is too high, and it is preferable to let the exchange rate adjust fully. For sufficiently large shocks to money demand, however, it is optimal to intervene, and we return to the standard result of keeping the exchange rate fixed and using reserves to the full extent necessary.

The main weakness that I find in the LV framework is that all the relevant domestic interest rates (on bank deposits and loans and on government bonds) are not related to the international interest rate, the expected depreciation of the exchange rate, or the country risk premium because they correspond to assets that are "nontraded" by assumption. That is, the kind of transactions that individuals, firms, and the government can perform preclude any competition between domestic and foreign financial assets. Although I understand that the model would become too complicated if these assets were "traded," I would happily give up the careful, first-principles, infinite-horizon detail in the consumer and real sectors in exchange for a less crude financial-sector framework. Particularly when considering the apparent puzzle of limited exchange rate variability in emerging-market economies, as this paper sets out to do, it seems important to try to incorporate the reaction of the central bank to changes in country risk, credibility, and the like.

Money demand is also special. It is the demand for an interest-bearing demand deposit used for transactions, and thus it depends *positively* on the interest rate. It is somewhat difficult to interpret money demand shocks in this framework. Do they approximate a "capital outflow" that is reversed when domestic interest rates increase? The framework also does not permit differentiation between money demand and "bond demand," that is, between liquidity conditions and the demand for government and private liabilities that reflects considerations of risk premium and so on. Once again, in view of the exchange rate variability puzzle that motivates the paper, it is not clear how relevant these LV money demand shocks are in explaining the contrast between emerging markets and advanced economies in their management of exchange rates.

As concerns the extent of sterilization of the monetary impact of changes in international reserves (the choice along the horizontal direction of the triangle), the results are less easy to interpret. It is not entirely clear what sterilization of a money demand shock should mean. Central banks sterilize to avoid the monetary impact of a change in reserves generated by some current account or capital account shock. However, the shock considered in the paper originates in domestic monetary and financial markets themselves. In any event, when the optimal policy involves foreign exchange market intervention by the central bank, it also involves expanding domestic credit so that domestic interest rates remain constant. LV define a "fully sterilized intervention" policy as one that always keeps the real quantity of money constant, which seems appropriate in general. For this particular shock, however, the optimal policy comes close to what one could think of as full sterilization, keeping interest rates and the level of bank loans constant, although the level of deposits (money demand) declines.

Discussion Summary

Sebastian Edwards commented on the policy options that a country may choose from when facing external shocks. The optimal policy is probably some combination of the three instruments—higher interest rates, sterilized intervention, and exchange rate flexibility—inside the "triangle" that Eduardo Borensztein showed. Roberto Chang and Andrés Velasco's paper derives formally a similar result, but Edwards was concerned with how useful this type of result is to policy makers. Drawing on the recent experience of Mexico, he proposed to analyze the trigger strategy for interest rate intervention. The Mexican authorities selected the upper corner of the triangle and are floating the exchange rate without using any other policy most of the time. However, when shocks surpass some threshold, that triggers the use of another policy, namely, interest rate intervention. This policy arrangement is highly asymmetrical, but it has worked. For example, when peso intraday trading against the dollar reached 11 in September 1998, the authorities increased the interest rate to about 55 percent and suspended the CETES auction. When things calmed down, however, they stopped using interest rate policy and returned to the corner of floating the exchange rate. The question to those at the table was what the likelihood is of generating this kind of model and evaluating this kind of policy. This is what policy makers are looking for.

Federico Sturzenegger made the remark that in the model any change of interest rates will lead to a loss of output, which leads to a bias toward fixed exchange rates. To circumvent this effect, the model then imposes the unnatural cost of intervention. An alternative method would be to allow for the benefits from a flexible exchange rate, which is a much more plausible specification.

Jaume Ventura commented on the way the model generates a fear-of-floating exchange rate through nominal wage rigidity. The standard Friedman argument is that when there is nominal wage rigidity, there is a fear of fixed rates, and the exchange rate must equate the labor market. Thus, if one thinks that most shocks to an economy affect labor demand and labor supply, then the floating exchange rate is really better, because it can be used to keep the real wage at the level where it should be. This is true in the model, but the paper focuses on discussing the effects of a shock to money demand, which is why things are reversed. Because real wage should never change, one should avoid as much as possible a change in the exchange rate. There are two problems. First, one has to make an assessment of the kinds of shocks an economy goes through: are most shocks hitting the labor market or money demand? Depending on the answer, one can choose one policy or another. Second, even if the shocks to money demand are very important, one wants to fix the interest rate, as most standard results suggest. This is not the case here because the paper does not allow for sterilization. However, if sterilization is not very costly, then nominal wage rigidity cannot be a convincing channel to create the fear of floating.

Alejandro M. Werner said that central bankers who float their currencies and use interest rate policy are not concerned with money demand shocks—they can always adjust money supply at a given interest rate. Thus, the important shocks to the monetary authorities are real shocks and portfolio shocks.

Enrique G. Mendoza raised this question: how strong is the assumption that domestically issued bonds cannot be traded? He also commented on the assumption that firms use credit from the banking system to buy imports, and asked whether similar results would hold if firms could use foreign loans instead.

Amartya Lahiri agreed that the paper took an extreme stand on the validity of interest rate policy; however, he said, other approaches (for example, Flood and Ventura's portfolio model approach) lead to similar results. The key feature is how the risk premium between the domestic and foreign interest rates changes with policies. He said that other modeling strategies are feasible and can handle the sterilization interventions, which they are working on.

Lahiri also agreed with Ventura that in the case of a real shock, one should allow the exchange rate to float. The authors plan to calibrate both monetary and real shocks and determine whether the model can produce the moments that they find in the data on exchange rate and interest rate fluctuations.

He also said that the paper focused on money demand shocks because this was the easiest way to create an environment with a capital outflow and a depreciation pressure on the currency. He asked the audience not to take this aspect of the model very seriously.

Carlos A. Végh agreed with discussant Borensztein that the optimal policy choice should lie inside the triangle. He said that the model could be easily generalized (by introducing imperfect substitutability between domestic and foreign assets) to have this result. On the issue of monetary shocks, he pointed out that in this model shocks to money demand should be interpreted as portfolio shocks because the monetary aggregate in the model is in the spirit of saving accounts.

15

Policy in an Economy with Balance Sheet Effects

Aaron Tornell

15.1 Introduction

The 1990s have witnessed several balance-of-payments crises. In contrast to the crises of previous decades, in which government deficits took center stage, these new crises have been twin currency and banking crises, in which bank lending has taken center stage.

The blame for these new crises has been laid at the feet of the policies that have been implemented in emerging markets during the last decade. Frequently, financial liberalization and banks' privatization have led to lending booms and asset price inflation episodes that have resulted in crises. It has been argued in some policy quarters that this has occurred because financial liberalization has been inevitably associated with bailout guarantees, which have encouraged overinvestment and excessive risk taking.[1] Furthermore, it has been suggested that fixed exchange rates have exacerbated the problem by inducing agents to borrow in foreign currency on an unhedged basis. This paper will question these views.

Even if we accept that bailout guarantees are the inevitable consequence of financial liberalization and banks' privatization, it does not follow that the liberalization policies of the early 1990s were doomed to fail.[2] I will argue that neither financial liberalization, the exchange rate regime, nor bailout guarantees were the main villains; rather, the culprit was the lack of an appropriate regulatory framework in the financial sector.

Aaron Tornell is professor of economics at the University of California, Los Angeles, and a faculty research fellow of the National Bureau of Economic Research.

1. Bailout guarantees are deemed necessary either because many firms face a severely credit-constrained environment or because of political pressures.
2. I would like to emphasize that I am not defending policy measures enacted simply to mask corruption.

In the course of my argument I will make a distinction between "systemic" and "unconditional" bailout guarantees. The former are granted only if a critical mass of agents defaults. The latter are granted on an idiosyncratic basis whenever there is an individual default. I will argue that if authorities can commit to granting only systemic guarantees, and if the other parts of the regulatory framework work efficiently, then financial liberalization policies will induce higher long-run growth in a credit-constrained economy. In this environment, crises are thus not the inevitable consequence of bad policy, but simply bad draws that need not happen. The risk of bad draws is the price that must be paid in order to attain faster growth in a credit-constrained environment. In contrast, if guarantees are granted on an unconditional basis or if the regulatory framework is inefficient, the monitoring and disciplinary role of banks will be nonexistent. Therefore, financial liberalization will simply lead to overinvestment and corruption. Liberalization in such an economy will surely end in crisis.

This paper makes five main points. First, systemic bailout guarantees are a second-best instrument to promote investment in emerging economies. Severe enforceability problems make bank credit practically the only source of external finance for firms in the nontradables sector. In this environment, many profitable investment projects cannot be undertaken because agents are credit-constrained. Guarantees promote investment because they ease borrowing constraints and provide an implicit subsidy. In contrast to deposit insurance schemes, systemic bailout guarantees are only granted if a critical mass of agents goes bust. Thus, they do not eliminate the monitoring role of banks.

Second, risky debt plays a useful role in promoting investment. The subsidy implicit in systemic bailout guarantees can be cashed in only if there exist some states of the world in which there is a systemic crisis. In the absence of exogenous shocks that bankrupt many agents, there must be endogenous expected volatility. Lending booms and risky dollar debt can generate this endogenous volatility by making the economy vulnerable to self-fulfilling crises. Clearly, an economy might evolve along the transition path without experiencing any crisis. In fact, the likelihood of crisis must be small. Otherwise, systemic bailout guarantees might have the unintended effect of drastically reducing productive investment.

Third, a consequence of the previous point is that if prudential regulation tries to eliminate all risk in the banking system, it might block the investment-enhancing effect of systemic bailout guarantees. In contrast, a very important role of prudential regulation is prevention of fraudulent activities. If not accompanied by a concurrent improvement in prudential regulation, bank privatization and other reforms that improve the contracting environment among private agents might not improve social welfare. This raises the issue of why many emerging countries have failed to improve their regulatory frameworks; I suggest that in some cases it has been due to political causes.

Fourth, the forces that generate boom-bust cycles are independent of the exchange rate regime. In particular, systemic bailout guarantees can induce the adoption of risky debt structures in fixed as well as in flexible exchange rate regimes. Guarantees may appear under different guises and need not be explicit. The precise form the bailout takes will depend on the regime. For instance, under fixed rates the bailout rate is mostly determined by the amount of reserves authorities are willing to use in order to defend the currency. In contrast, in a pure floating regime the bailout may take the form of direct transfers to agents.

Fifth, in the event of a crisis the amount of nonperforming loans increases dramatically. If they are recognized, the most likely outcome is that the government will have to take over the banking system, make a once-and-for-all bailout payment, and incur a huge fiscal cost up front. This will increase government debt and, probably, interest rates. On the other hand, if only a small share of nonperforming loans is recognized, the up-front bailout and fiscal cost will be low. However, this strategy might lead to evergreening and generate perverse incentives. Over time the problem might grow and the credit crunch might last longer, as the experiences of Japan and Mexico have shown.

The structure of the paper is as follows. The next section presents some stylized facts. Section 15.3 presents the conceptual framework. Section 15.4, which is the main part of the paper, analyzes the issues raised above. Finally, section 15.5 concludes.

15.2 Stylized Facts

Typically, during the 1990s crises were preceded by real exchange rate appreciation and by lending booms, during which bank lending grew unusually rapidly.[3] During these lending booms, emerging economies became fragile because a significant amount of banks' short-term liabilities were denominated in foreign currency on an unhedged basis. Meanwhile, banks lent mainly to firms in the nontradables sector. Much of this lending was guaranteed by governments—at least implicitly.

Twin banking and currency crises often occurred in the absence of any major external shock and came as a surprise to financial markets. In these episodes, a small incipient reduction in capital inflows was followed by a significant real exchange rate depreciation. Because debt was largely denominated in foreign currency, the depreciation has induced widespread bankruptcies and a collapse of new lending. In most countries, rescue packages were designed to support the banking system and to bail out foreign lenders. Nevertheless, these countries still experienced sharp and long-lasting credit crunches.

3. Real appreciation has been particularly severe in Latin America. See Corsetti, Pesenti, and Roubini (1999). Eichengreen, Rose, and Wyplosz (1995); Gourinchas, Landerretche, and Valdés (2001). Kaminsky and Reinhart (1999); Sachs, Tornell, and Velasco (1996); and Tornell (1999).

A puzzling pattern is that the contraction in the growth rate of bank credit that typically develops in the aftermath of crises is quite pronounced and persistent. In contrast, although growth in aggregate GDP and in deposits declines initially, it recuperates rather quickly. This puzzle can be explained by two additional stylized facts, which we will emphasize throughout this paper. First, the milder decline and faster recovery of aggregate activity in the aftermath of a crisis masks an asymmetric performance between different sectors of the economy. Whereas tradables (T) sectors suffer a very mild decline, nontradables (N) sectors suffer a very deep and persistent recession.

Second, the banking system is typically strongly exposed to the N sector. Because the real depreciation had a "balance sheet" effect mainly in the N sector, entrepreneurial wealth in the N sector is drastically reduced. This, in turn, keeps the growth rate of bank credit depressed, despite the fast resumption of growth in aggregate gross domestic product (GDP) and deposits—that is, a credit crunch.

These stylized facts are illustrated in figures 15.1 through 15.3. These figures depict the evolution of the real exchange rate, bank credit and deposits, GDP, and the ratio of nontradables to tradables production for six emerging economies: Argentina and Mexico, which suffered a crisis in 1995; Korea, Malaysia, the Philippines, and Thailand, which experienced a crisis in 1997; and Chile, which experienced a severe crisis in the early 1980s but not during the 1990s, and so can be considered as a benchmark.

15.3 Conceptual Framework

In order to address the policy issues we have raised, it is necessary to understand the context in which policy rules were designed and the underlying imperfections they were supposed to counteract. In order to do this, one needs a conceptual framework that can explain the basic features of the boom-bust cycles experienced by emerging economies during the 1990s. This paper will use the model developed by Schneider and Tornell (2000) to make such an evaluation.

To explain some of the stylized facts that we have described, "third-generation" crises models have looked to financial market imperfections as key fundamentals. The models are typically based on *one of two* distortions: either bad policy, in the form of bailout guarantees, or bad markets, in the form of an imperfection that induces balance sheet effects, such as asymmetric information, or the imperfect enforceability of contracts.[4] Schneider and Tornell (2000) consider an economy that is *simultaneously* subject to

---

4. See Aghion, Bachetta, and Banerjee (2000); Bernanke, Gertler, and Gilchrist (1999); Burnside, Eichenbaum, and Rebelo (2000); Caballero and Krishnamurthy (1999); Calvo (1998); Corsetti, Pesenti, and Roubini (1999); Krugman (1998); and McKinnon and Pill (1998).

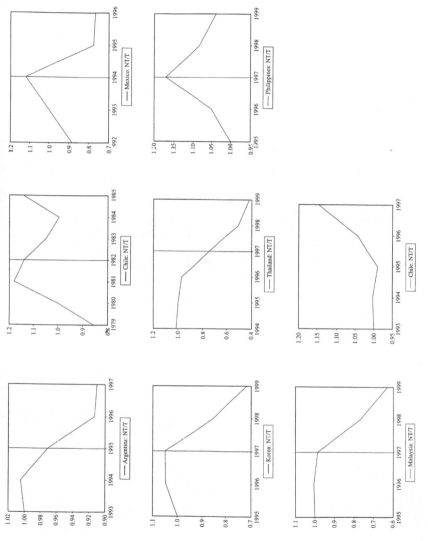

Fig. 15.1 Ratio of nontradables to tradables

Sources: Central Banks

Note: The tradables and nontradables sectors are proxied by manufacturing and construction, respectively.

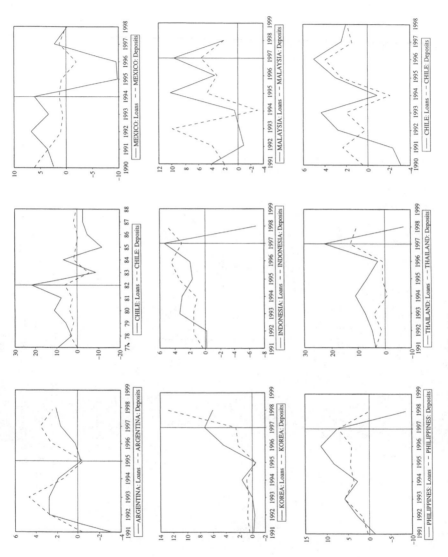

Fig. 15.2 Changes in banks' loans and deposits

Source: International Financial Statistics of the International Monetary Fund, line 22d, 24 and 25.

Note: Loans and deposits are measured as percentages of GDP.

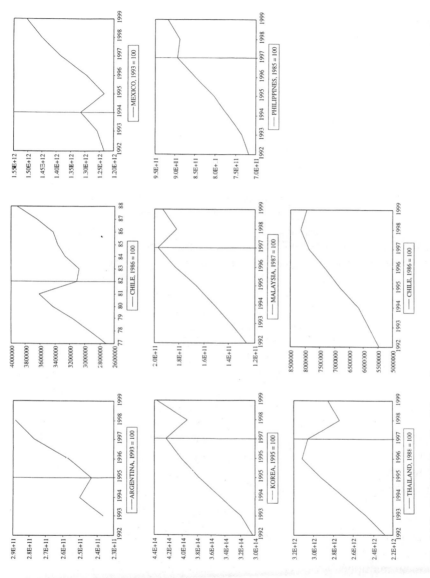

Fig. 15.3   Real GDP, units of domestic currency

Source: International Financial Statistics of the International Monetary Fund

these two distortions: systemic bailout guarantees and the imperfect enforceability of contracts. They show that the *interaction* of the two distortions generates a coherent account of a *complete* boom-bust episode and explains the stylized facts described in the previous section. Thus, this framework will prove useful in addressing the policy issues the paper has raised.

This section presents some elements of the Schneider-Tornell model that will be useful in addressing the policy issues raised in the introduction. The model considers an economy with enforceability problems in financial markets that exhibits underinvestment, especially in the N sector. The introduction of systemic bailout guarantees can increase investment and growth by relaxing borrowing constraints. However, this comes at the cost of making the economy vulnerable to self-fulfilling meltdowns. Systemic bailout guarantees induce agents to switch from safe debt to risky foreign currency–denominated debt, generating aggregate real exchange rate risk.

Consider an economy with a T sector and an N sector. Agents in the T sector can be financed in international capital markets. In contrast, bank credit is the only source of external finance for agents in the N sector. Agents in the N sector demand T goods for consumption and produce non-tradables using only nontradables as inputs according to a linear production technology: $q_t = \theta I_t$. Agents in the T sector are endowed with T goods and consume both T and N goods.

In order to model the debt-denomination decision, allow N-sector agents to issue either "risky debt" or "safe debt." Risky debt is denominated in T goods (foreign currency) on an unhedged basis, whereas safe debt is denominated in N goods. Thus, it has no real exchange rate risk.

N-sector financing is subject to two distortions: enforceability problems and bailout guarantees. Consider first an economy in which only enforceability problems are present, as in standard financial accelerator models. High enforceability problems imply that lenders will limit the amount they lend regardless of what the interest rate is. As a result, the amount of credit available to a firm will be determined by the level of its internal funds. If investment has a sufficiently high rate of return, an N-sector firm will borrow as much as it can. As a result, the credit multiplier becomes an investment multiplier. One can show that

(1) $$p_t I_t^s = m^s(h) \cdot w_t,$$

where w_t is internal funds (denominated in T goods) of a representative N-sector firm; $p_t = p_t^N / p_t^T$ is the inverse of the real exchange rate; $m^s(h)$ is the investment multiplier, which is decreasing in the degree of the enforceability problem (indexed by $1/h$); and I_t is physical investment by the N sector. Although safe debt is more expensive than risky debt, in the presence of bankruptcy costs, issuing safe debt is individually optimal. Thus, in the absence of exogenous shocks, the economy will not exhibit fragility to meltdowns. Under no circumstances will firms go bust.

Let us introduce the second distortion: bailout guarantees. As mentioned in the introduction, one should distinguish two types of bailout guarantees: unconditional and systemic. The former are granted whenever there is a default by an individual borrower (e.g., deposit insurance), whereas the latter are granted only if a critical mass of borrowers goes bust. Clearly, if all debt were covered by unconditional bailout guarantees, then the enforceability problem would become irrelevant and borrowing constraints would not arise in equilibrium. Because a lender would be bailed out in the case of an idiosyncratic default, he does not have incentives to limit the amount of credit he extends to an individual borrower. Hence, in order for bailout guarantees not to neutralize the effects of enforceability problems, and for borrowing constraints to arise in equilibrium, it is necessary that some part of banks' liabilities be covered only by systemic bailout guarantees.

As we shall see, systemic bailout guarantees provide an implicit subsidy that eases borrowing constraints. However, this subsidy can be cashed in only if there are some states of nature in which a critical mass of borrowers goes bust. In the absence of exogenous shocks that bankrupt a critical mass of borrowers, the introduction of systemic bailout guarantees will have an effect only if there is aggregate endogenous risk.

15.3.1 Bailout Guarantees and Risky Debt Denomination

The first main result is that the *interaction* of systemic bailout guarantees and enforceability problems might generate aggregate endogenous risk. This is because there is a self-reinforcing mechanism at work. On the one hand, if there is sufficient real exchange rate risk, it is individually optimal for an N-sector agent to issue risky T debt (i.e., borrow in foreign currency on a short-term and unhedged basis). On the other hand, if *many* N-sector agents gamble by denominating their debt in T goods, exchange rate risk might be endogenously created, as the economy becomes vulnerable to *self-fulfilling meltdowns* of the banking system. If the amount of T-denominated debt is high, a real depreciation can severely squeeze cash flow or even bankrupt banks altogether. Because they face binding borrowing constraints, they then must curtail lending to the N sector. Weak investment demand from the N sector for its own products in turn validates the real depreciation. The systemic credit risk created by the banking system thus induces endogenous exchange rate risk.[5]

Real exchange rate variability can make risky T debt cheaper than safe N debt. As an illustration, suppose that tomorrow's real exchange rate can take on two values: an appreciated one that leaves every firm solvent ($\bar{p}_{t+1}$),

---

5. There are several ways in which agents can adopt risky projects. However, risky debt denomination (borrowing in dollars to finance nontradables activities) is a wonderful "coordinating device." Because debt denomination is easily observed, agents can implicitly collude to cash in the subsidy implicit in the bailout guarantee.

and a depreciated one that makes a majority of N-sector firms go bust
($\underline{p}_{t+1}$). Because lenders constrain credit to ensure that borrowers will repay
in the no-crisis state, it follows that in the no-crisis state debt is repaid in full
and there is no bailout. Meanwhile, in the crisis state there is bankruptcy,
and each lender receives a proportion F of what he or she was promised. Because the probability of crisis is $1 - \alpha$, interest rates on T goods–and N-
good–denominated debt (ρ_t and ρ_t^n, respectively) satisfy

(2)
$$(1 + \rho_t)[\alpha + (1 - \alpha)F] = 1 + r,$$

$$(1 + \rho_t^n)[\alpha \bar{p}_{t+1} + (1 - \alpha)\underline{p}_{t+1}F] = 1 + r,$$

where r is the world interest rate. If we set $F = 1$, interest rates are given by

(3)
$$1 + \rho_t = 1 + r,$$

$$1 + \rho_t^n = \frac{1 + r}{\alpha \bar{p}_{t+1} + (1 - \alpha)\underline{p}_{t+1}}.$$

Because $\bar{p}_{t+1} > \underline{p}_{t+1}$, we can see that T debt is cheaper than N debt for all positive bailout rates ($F > 0$): the interest rate as well as the expected repay-
ments per unit debt is lower for T debt. We can see directly from equation
(2) that $\rho_t < \rho_t^n$. Because debt is repaid with probability α, expected repayment per unit debt is $\alpha(1 + r)/[\alpha + (1 - \alpha)F]$ for T debt and $\alpha(1 + r)/[\alpha +
(1 - \alpha)F_{\bar{p}}^p]$ for N debt.

The fact that T debt is cheaper than N debt does not imply that agents
will always be willing to issue T debt: T debt in the books might lead a borrower to go bust. One can show that when there are no guarantees ($F = 0$)
it is optimal for an agent to choose a safe plan that never leads to bankruptcy. However, if crises are rare events (α is large), bailouts are generous
(F is large), and there is enough real exchange rate variability

(4)
$$\frac{\theta \bar{p}_{t+1}}{p_t} > 1 + r > h > \frac{\theta \underline{p}_{t+1}}{p_t},$$

then it is individually optimal to choose a risky plan that leads to bankruptcy in the crisis state. Because the bailout agency will pay part of the
promise in the bad state, it is desirable for an agent to shift as much of the
payment as possible into the bad state. This is achieved precisely by denominating all debt in tradables. Because lenders must break even, switching from N to T debt always shifts some of the debt burden from the good
to the bad state, making the borrower better off.

An important implication of the preceding results is that systemic bailout
guarantees may alleviate the "underinvestment" problem usually associated with borrowing-constrained economies. They permit high leverage
with debt denominated in T goods and faster credit growth. As we have
seen, the presence of guarantees induces N-sector agents to issue T debt.
Because the real exchange rate is expected to appreciate in the no-crisis state

(i.e., eq. [4] holds), this allows agents to reduce the expected value of debt repayments, measured in terms of nontradables.[6] This reduction, in turn, permits agents to borrow more at each level of internal funds. Therefore, at a given point in time, the investment multiplier is greater than that of an economy that features only enforceability problems (m^s). In fact, one can show that in the presence of bailout guarantees ($F > 0$) the value of investment by the N sector is

(5) $$ p_t I_t = m^r(h, F) \cdot w_t, \qquad m^s(h) < m^r(h, F) \ if \ F > 0. $$

Thus, the N sector grows faster than it would if guarantees were absent.

15.3.2 Endogenous Real Exchange Rate Risk

When is it that the existence of T debt generates real exchange rate risk? To answer this question, consider the determination of the equilibrium real exchange rate ($1/p_t$). This price equalizes aggregate demand and the (predetermined) supply of nontradables (θI_{t-1}). The aggregate demand for N goods has two components: the demand by the T sector, $d^T(p_t)$, and the investment demand by the N sector for its own goods (I_t). Thus, p_t is determined by

(6) $$ \theta I_{t-1} = d^T(p_t) + I_t(p_t, b_{t-1}, b^N_{t-1}), $$

where b_{t-1} and b^N_{t-1} are the amounts of T debt and N debt carried over from the last period. Because at a given point in time supply is given, the key to having multiple equilibria is a backward-bending aggregate demand curve. This is impossible if N-sector firms have only N debt. In this case, price changes lead to variations in both firms' revenues and their debt payments. In fact, profits (measured in nontradables) are completely insulated against price movements. The upshot is that as long as firms are solvent, demand slopes downward and there is a *unique* equilibrium real exchange rate.

Multiple equilibria are possible only if N-sector agents have T debt. In this case, real exchange rate movements affect revenues but not the debt burden. Thus, it becomes important to distinguish between insolvent and solvent firms. For real exchange rates more depreciated than a cutoff level $1/p^c_t$, all N firms go bankrupt because revenues do not cover the debt burden. As a result, internal funds collapse. Total demand in this range is downward sloping. In contrast, for real exchange rates more appreciated than $1/p^c_t$, a further real appreciation is accompanied by a *more than proportional* increase in internal funds. The reason is that revenues increase the debt burden remains the same. Equivalently, part of the debt burden measured in terms of nontradables is inflated away. Consequently, investment demand *increases*.

It is apparent that if the balance sheet effect is strong enough to make

---

6. Below I discuss the conditions under which equation (4) holds along the equilibrium path.

aggregate demand "bend backward," as in figure 15.4, multiple market-clearing real exchange rates, and hence self-fulfilling twin crises, can exist. With identical fundamentals, in terms of supply and debt, the market may clear in one of two equilibria. In a solvent equilibrium (point B in fig. 15.4), the price (the reciprocal of the real exchange) is high, inflating away enough of firms' debt (measured in nontradables) to allow them to bid away a large share of output from the T sector. In contrast, in the crisis equilibrium of point A, the price is low to allow the T-sector and bankrupt N-sector agents with little internal funds to absorb the supply of nontradables. Expectations determine which of these two points is reached. Fundamentals determine only whether the environment is fragile enough to allow two equilibria.

15.3.3   Equilibrium Dynamics

We have seen that, in the absence of bailout guarantees, managers will not be inclined to issue T debt. In the model, the only source of uncertainty is the sunspot. Furthermore, multiple market-clearing prices, which are crucial for a sunspot to matter, exist only if debt is denominated in trad-ables. It follows that, in the absence of bailout guarantees, there cannot be an equilibrium in which prices depend on the sunspot. Instead, in economies without bailout guarantees, equilibria must be "safe," and firms are always solvent.

Consider now an economy in which systemic bailout guarantees are present. Will the economy exhibit risky lending booms, which allow for faster growth (financed by cheap T debt) but may end in self-fulfilling twin crises? To address this question we need to establish the existence of *sunspot equilibria* along which crises can actually occur with positive probability (i.e., $1 - \alpha > 0$).[7] That is, we need to construct an equilibrium price process by making the sunspot select among market-clearing prices, such that the resulting return distribution encourages firms to issue enough T debt to validate the price process.

Recall that there are two mechanisms at work. On the one hand, if there is enough T debt, there are two possible market-clearing prices, of which the lower price bankrupts firms and hence triggers a bailout. On the other hand, agents will choose T debt if there is enough real exchange rate variability. The question is whether these two mechanisms can be elements of one consistent dynamic story.

Suppose that the future demand for N goods is high enough that agents will be able to repay their debts. Then one can prove that if bailouts are generous enough, initial funds of the representative agent are large enough, and the horizon is long enough, then there exists a certain time interval in which

---

7. It is technically simpler to focus on unanticipated crises, but this is conceptually unsatisfactory for several reasons. First, only if crises are anticipated can one rationalize this fragility as a result of risky debt denomination. Second, only if crises are anticipated can one make the point that growth is faster with bailout guarantees.

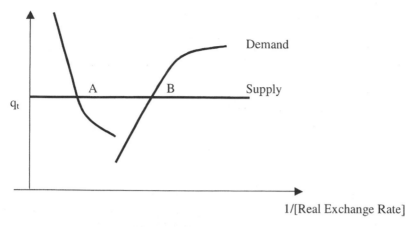

Fig. 15.4   Equilibrium in the nontradables' market

the sunspot can matter and self-fulfilling crises can be anticipated. During this time interval a crisis must be a rare event in order for an equilibrium to exist.

Along the equilibrium path, as long as no crisis has occurred, there is a self-reinforcing feedback between lending and real exchange rate appreciation, which explains the other stylized facts described in the previous section. Because N goods are demanded for investment by the N sector itself, both output and the relative price of nontradables increase during the boom. Furthermore, because debt is denominated in T goods, a real appreciation (a relative price increase) reduces the debt burden measured in terms of nontradables. This increases N-sector agents' cash flow. For constrained agents, this translates into more lending through a balance sheet effect. More lending, in turn, permits more investment in N goods. In order to close the circle, note that if the investment increase is greater than the higher output, the real exchange rate must appreciate in order to eliminate the excess demand for nontradables.

A crisis occurs when the bad state of the sunspot is realized. The result is a real depreciation and widespread bankruptcies in the N sector. This depletes the internal funds of the N sector. Thus, its investment drops and can only gradually recover (due to the financial adjustment costs mentioned above). At the same time, demand by the T sector jumps up. Again, this highlights the asymmetric patterns followed by the N sector and the T sector.

To highlight the fact that, although systemic bailout guarantees might induce faster economic growth by easing borrowing constraints, they increase the likelihood of a crisis, consider two economies, A and B. The only difference between these economies is that A has systemic bailout guarantees.

Then there is a sunspot equilibrium in which A and B behave identically up to a certain time, after which the N sector in economy A grows faster and exhibits higher leverage along the lucky path, as long as a crisis does not occur. However, A experiences a crisis and subsequent recession with positive probability, whereas B does not.

15.3.4   Necessary Ingredients for Boom-Bust Cycles

A key point of Schneider and Tornell (2000) is that the *interaction* of contract enforceability problems and bailout guarantees creates the fragility required for self-fulfilling crises. If there were no guarantees, firms would not be willing to take on price risk to claim a subsidy. Costly enforceability of contracts would still imply that the N sector could grow only gradually, and balance sheet effects would play a role during the lending boom. However, there would be no force that makes a boom end in a crisis. Alternatively, if there were only guarantees but no enforceability problems, then there would not be any balance sheet effects that make demand backward-bending, a necessary condition for a sunspot to matter.

Lending booms that feature fragility cannot occur in just any economy with bailout guarantees and enforceability problems. It is also necessary to have a future increase in the demand of the T sector for nontradables. Otherwise, the N sector would not be able to repay the accumulated deficits it runs during the lending boom. Backward induction then indicates that the sequence of returns that supports the lending boom would collapse. This suggests that the boom-bust episodes are more likely to occur during a transition period (for instance, following a far-reaching reform or a natural resource discovery).

Even during a transitional period, *the likelihood of a self-fulling crisis is not a free parameter.* If crises were not rare events, either borrowing constraints would not arise, or they would not be binding in equilibrium if they did arise. In either case, credit would not be constrained by internal funds, and balance sheet effects would not exist in equilibrium. Clearly, if this were the case, crises could not occur. If the probability of crises is not small enough, enforceability problems do not generate borrowing constraints.

15.4   Policy Evaluation

An emerging economy is an economy in which the future is much brighter than the present but profitable investment projects cannot be undertaken because the private sector is small (i.e., entrepreneurial wealth is low) and the amount of external financing is severely limited. The reforms of the late 1980s liberalized trade and financial markets in many emerging markets. These reforms also significantly reduced the role of the state in the economy. Suddenly, the future looked much brighter than before, and the private sector much smaller than was desirable. Unfortunately, legal and judicial reform could not be implemented as easily as the other reforms. As a result, many of the institutions that support the provision of external finance in developed economies did not flourish in emerging markets.

The policy problem then became one of better promoting the fast development of the private sector in an environment in which external finance to the domestic sector is constrained by internal funds of firms, and credit and investment are too low relative to investment opportunities. One is tempted to say that if a government had had the appropriate information and correct incentives, the optimal policy would have been to transfer resources to those in the population with better entrepreneurial skills and to let them make the investing decisions. Of course, we now know that this is wishful thinking. After many failed experiments of this sort during the last century, we now know that either governments do not posses the appropriate information, or crony capitalism and rampant corruption take over.

Since direct made-to-measure government transfers are not feasible, during the 1990s governments had to design second-best policies to foster the development of the private sector. Many countries made the decision to privatize the banks and allow them to be the means through which resources would be channeled to the nascent private sector. The issues described in the introduction should be analyzed from this perspective.

If financial liberalization and bank privatization are implemented in a context of unconditional bailout guarantees and a lax regulatory framework, then they will clearly lead to corruption and crisis. However, if appropriate regulation is put in place and authorities are committed to grant bailouts only in a systemic fashion, then one might argue that, when taking into consideration the distortions that exist in emerging markets there is a sense in which these policies are second-best instruments for fostering the private sector's growth. We would like to emphasize that we are not defending some policy measures that simply mask corruption. Those are clearly indefensible.

Consider the two-sector economy described in section 15.3. Firms in the T sector can easily obtain financing in international capital markets, either because they can pledge their export receivables as collateral or because they are closely linked to firms that can secure their debt. In contrast, firms in the N sector must rely more heavily on domestic bank credit. Furthermore, because emerging markets face acute enforceability problems, firms in the N sector face severe borrowing constraints that limit their ability to undertake profitable projects. As a result, the growth rate of the economy is kept below its potential. It follows that a policy maker whose objective is to maximize social welfare must design second-best policies that will ease borrowing constraints and increase investment in the N sector. Because the N sector and the T sector compete for productive resources, and because any policies to support the N sector have implicit fiscal costs, the optimal support level for the N sector cannot be arbitrarily large.[8]

15.4.1   Policies During a Boom

Systemic versus Unconditional Bailout Guarantees

We have seen that in the presence of severe enforceability problems in financial markets, credit is constrained by internal funds. As a result, profitable investment projects will not be undertaken, especially in the N sector. Thus, over the medium run, growth will be significantly lower than its potential. This indicates that systemic bailout guarantees might actually play a socially beneficial role. Systemic bailout guarantees provide an implicit subsidy that reduces the cost at which firms can fund themselves and increases the credit multiplier. This increases investment and growth at each level of internal funds. In the absence of better instruments to promote investment and growth of the N sector, systemic bailout guarantees are a second-best instrument for making transfers to this sector. We would like to emphasize that this mechanism uses the information and monitoring capacity of banks.

Consider the generosity of bailout guarantees (F) as the policy instrument.[9] An increase in F induces an increase in the investment multiplier in equation (5), which in turn leads to a higher growth rate of the N sector. Therefore, in an emerging economy it is optimal to set F higher than zero in order to reduce the underinvestment problem. However, there are tradeoffs. First, the greater F is, the greater the contingent fiscal cost; second, the greater F is, the greater the share of resources allocated to the N sector at the expense of the T sector. Therefore, the level of F should not be set too high. There is an interior optimum.

Three points should be emphasized. First, if banks in a given country play no monitoring role and are prone to fraud, systemic bailout guarantees will not be socially beneficial. Second, systemic bailout guarantees do not curtail the discipline faced by either individual banks or firms, because they are granted only if a critical mass of agents defaults. At the same time, systemic bailout guarantees generate an investment subsidy only if the banks' portfolios are risky, that is, only if there exist states of nature in which there is systemic crisis. In the absence of large exogenous shocks, this means that some risk must be endogenously generated by the banking system in order for guarantees to be effective in promoting investment (the paper addresses this issue below). Third, systemic bailout guarantees imply that the govern-

8. The fiscal costs associated with bailout guarantees are typically paid by domestic taxpayers, not by international organizations. Jeanne and Zettelmeyer (2000) show that in most cases the IMF has been repaid the loans it made to crisis countries in order to bail out lenders.

9. As shall be discussed below, there are several ways in which systemic bailout guarantees can be implemented.

ment can credibly commit not to bail out individual agents in the case of idiosyncratic default.

The experience of Mexico during the 1990s illustrates, in a rather sharp manner, the policy dilemma faced by reformers. Several critics have pointed to the "false rosy expectations" generated by the government in the early 1990s and the promises of bailout guarantees as the culprits in the Tequila crisis. Certainly, in hindsight this is true, a policy maker would say. However, at that time the policy seemed a sensible one. It was a way to avoid low growth and bottlenecks in the N sector that would otherwise have limited the overall future growth of the economy. Moreover, from a political standpoint the development of the private sector encouraged by the policy had the added virtue of creating new power bases that would block attempts by statist groups to return to the old ways. It was a way to ensure the continuity of the reforms.

An important issue has not yet been discussed is unconditional bailout guarantees, which are granted whenever an individual debtor defaults. Deposit insurance is a prime example. If all guarantees were unconditional, the discipline in the banking system would disappear and guarantees would not play the investment-promoting role described above. However, if unconditional bailout guarantees are granted to small bank depositors, they may play a socially beneficial role. This policy avoids bank-runs generated by burgeoning rumors but does not impinge negatively on the market discipline faced by an individual bank because small depositors typically have very little information regarding the bank's portfolio. As is the case in the United States, market discipline should be imposed by noninsured bank debt, the interest rate of which should serve as an indicator of a bank's health.

The Role of Risky Dollar Debt

As mentioned above, systemic bailout guarantees have only investment-enhancing effects in the presence of risk. In the absence of large exogenous shocks, some endogenous volatility must be present if the policy is to be effective. Therefore, outlawing risky dollar debt could undo the investment-enhancing effects of systemic bailout guarantees. Thus, if the conditions of a country call for bailouts as a second-best policy to promote the growth of the private sector, then risky debt (or another way to generate endogenous volatility) must also be allowed. Of course, this does not mean that banks should be allowed to have outrageously risky portfolios. It merely means that a naive policy of outlawing risky dollar debt is not correct from a normative perspective.

Because systemic bailout guarantees can only be cashed in states of the world in which a critical mass of borrowers goes bust, they are effective in increasing investment only if an important sector of the economy is vulnerable to a meltdown. It is only during such a meltdown that the bailout agency makes payments to lenders. Thus, the expected value of the subsidy is determined by the likelihood of the crisis and the generosity of the bailout. The greater the expected value of the subsidy, the lower the interest rates that lenders are willing to accept. Clearly, bank portfolios cannot be outrageously risky, because the likelihood of crisis must be quite small in order for the mechanism identified in this paper to be operative. Otherwise, firms would not find it profitable to borrow and invest in the first place! Note, however, that small is not the same as zero. In the absence of major exogenous shocks, fragility must come from within the system. This is precisely the role of risky debt denomination. As explained above, if a majority of borrowers has unhedged debt, the economy as a whole can become vulnerable to self-fulfilling crises. Furthermore, dollar debt is a wonderful coordinating device, because it can be observed by others. It plays the same role as the real-estate buildup on an uninsured basis in catastrophe-prone areas. The principle that "if everyone else does it, then I am safe" reigns.

From a positive perspective, it is also impossible to outlaw dollar short-term debt. Many firms need such debt in order to carry out their international transactions. Because it is impossible to distinguish what part of dollar debt is used by a given firm to finance international transactions, it is not feasible to enforce a law that forbids dollar debt for uses other than international trade. This lesson has been painfully learned by many countries that have tried to implement dual exchange rates and then were faced with rampant misinvoicing of imports and exports.

In conclusion, the degree of banks' and firms' portfolio riskiness should be strictly regulated. However, risky debt should not be outlawed altogether. It is neither socially optimal nor practically implementable.

The Role of Lending Booms and Asset Price Inflation

During a lending boom credit grows unusually fast, and, as many observers have pointed out, monitoring effectiveness declines. Thus, it is less likely that unprofitable and white elephant projects will be detected and stopped. At the same time, firms in emerging markets have a very low level of external finance, especially in the N sector. Thus, a lending boom is a mechanism by which faster growth can be attained. In fact, the lending boom is a transitional phase ignited by deep economic reforms that make the future much brighter than the present.

Stopping a lending boom, as for example by increasing reserve requirements, would interrupt the policy of promoting the growth of the private sector. However, allowing the lending boom to continue unchecked increases the debt burden of the economy, which makes it more vulnerable to crises. Hence, it is not clear ex ante at which point a lending boom should be stopped.

It is interesting to note that although crises typically are preceded by lending booms (Tornell 1999), the converse is not true. Gourinchas, Landerretche, and Valdes (2001) find that for a large panel of countries the probability that a lending boom will end in a crisis is quite small. That is, in the majority of cases, lending booms end with soft landings. Furthermore, theoretically lending booms can only develop if the probability of crisis is small, and they are expected to end with a soft landing if they last long enough (see Schneider and Tornell 1999, 2000).

Clearly, India has not experienced lending booms of the magnitude as the ones experienced by Korea. Moreover, India has not suffered currency crises as deep as those endured by Korea. Certainly, this does not mean that over the last half century the Indian economy has performed better than Korea's. Of course, in hindsight, Korean performance could have been improved on the margin. However, we should beware of fine-tuning policies designed to look great ex post.

Prior to several crises it has been observed that some assets, such as real estate, experience a steep price inflation, which is followed by a price collapse at the time of crisis. Because real estate is used as collateral, there is a close link between lending and asset price inflation during a boom. Thus, implementing policies that would stop asset price inflation will also reduce the growth of credit. Clearly, it might be dangerous to leave asset price inflation unchecked. However, some degree of inflation might be desirable as a tool to ease borrowing constraints.[10]

What Are the Effects of Reforms That Improve the
Contracting Technology in Financial Markets?

During the last decade several countries privatized their banks, liberalized their financial markets, and implemented legal reforms that facilitated contracts between private agents. Unfortunately, in several cases these reforms have led to an increase in fraud instead of economic growth (see Tornell 2000). The lack of a concurrent improvement in prudential regulation is often cited as being responsible for this lackluster outcome. Given that the regulatory framework cannot be improved by decree, the question arises as to whether such reforms should be implemented regardless of the regulatory framework.

To address this issue it is important to note than there is a *nonlinearity* in the relationship between the degree of contract enforceability and the desirability of financial-sector reforms. This paper will argue that such reforms are socially beneficial only if contract enforceability is very low or if the reforms are radical enough to eliminate balance sheet effects.

An improvement in the financial markets' contracting technology has the effect of increasing credit at each level of internal funds. In terms of equations (1) and (5), it means a reduction in the parameter h and an increase in

10. Schneider and Tornell (1999) study the interplay between asset prices and lending along a boom.

the investment multipliers m^s and m^r. In the extreme case, if contracts are not enforceable and the legal system is nonfunctional, it will be almost impossible for creditors and lenders to establish a bilateral debt agreement. With certainty, borrowers would divert funds and default. As a result, credit to the N sector will be almost nil, and the economy will not be fragile to crises. In this environment the introduction of systemic bailout guarantees would obviously not induce greater investment, as suggested in the previous section. Thus, in these extreme circumstances, privatization of the banking system and reforms that improve the contractual environment are clearly socially beneficial.

Consider now the other extreme, in which it is possible to implement legal reforms that reduce the enforceability problem to such a level that even small firms in the N sector may enter into bilateral agreements with foreign lenders. Clearly, in this extreme case, borrowing constraints will not be an issue. As a result, firms could borrow up to the level determined by profitability and technological conditions. Therefore, it is socially beneficial to bring the enforceability of contracts to a level where the majority of domestic firms and banks do not face borrowing constraints. Moreover, if this were the case, there would be no role for systemic bailout guarantees. Even if they were put in place, they would be irrelevant!

However, what if contract enforceability (h) is at an intermediate level? Would privatization and financial reforms that improve private contracting unambiguously be socially beneficial? The answer is no. A concurrent improvement in prudential regulation is essential. Recall that it is not socially optimal to increase credit to the N sector indefinitely at the expense of the T sector. There is an interior optimum. Taking as given the generosity of bailouts (F), an improvement in contract enforceability ($1/h$) eases borrowing constraints and increases the credit multiplier. However, it does not eliminate borrowing constraints and balance sheet effects altogether. As a result, such an improvement in private contracting might induce more fragility than is socially desirable. Clearly, if one could fine-tune the generosity of bailout guarantees, one could envision some tradeoff. Unfortunately, systemic bailout guarantees are more often than not determined by political forces. Either they exist or they do not.

Another way of stating this argument is that, after some point, a further improvement in contract enforcement will only serve to permit borrowers and lenders to better collude in ripping off the bailout agency and tax payers. Instead of enhancing the rate of growth of the economy, it will simply facilitate the adoption of white elephant investment projects that mask theft, or it might make it easier to design fraudulent lending schemes. If not accompanied by improvements in the regulatory framework, reforms that simply improve contractual arrangements marginally might have the unintended effect of fostering crony capitalism.

The Role of Prudential Regulation

The previous discussion highlights the need to improve prudential regulation concurrently with privatization and financial reforms. There are two levels at which the regulatory body should act. First, it should ensure that the banking system does not undertake more risk than is socially desirable. As discussed in the previous section, a risky debt profile might be necessary in order for the subsidy implicit in systemic bailout guarantees to have the desired effect of increasing credit and investment. However, this does not mean that anything goes. Appropriate regulation must determine the financial ratios in accordance with the situation of a given country. Blindly applying the Basel accord requirements does not make sense, because the level of riskiness induced might be greater than is appropriate for the country in question.

The second level at which the regulatory body should act is in minimizing the extent of fraudulent schemes and the adoption of white elephants. The more efficient the regulatory agency is in blocking these manifestations of crony capitalism, the more likely it is that systemic bailout guarantees will induce fast and sustainable economic growth, and the greater the social payoff associated with reforms that improve contractual enforceability. In the absence of a strong and independent regulatory agency, it becomes important to consider whether the ownership of banks should be strictly separated from ownership of industrial corporations. We will discuss this below.

Reforms that permit better bilateral private contracting should go hand in hand with improvements in regulatory capacity. However, it seems that here lies one of the greatest bottlenecks faced by emerging markets. More often than not, regulatory agencies fall prey to those they regulate. We now know that this is a political distortion that cannot be eliminated by decree.

In the case of banks, at the time of privatization a significant part of de facto nonperforming loans are passed on to the new owners. These invisible nonperforming loans typically reflect past hidden fiscal deficits or political payoffs. At the time of privatization, it is politically expedient not to recognize them and to pass them on to the new owners. This has two implications. First, the true capitalization of the newly privatized banks is lower than what the standard ratios indicate. Second, if the privatizers are also the regulators, there is a strong reason for regulators to oversee some future malpractices of the banks: bankers help regulators hide some nonperforming loans to begin with. Both implications make it more likely that the recently privatized banking system will engage in excessively risky lending and even in fraudulent activities.

Even if the capture of regulatory agencies is not a issue, one must still worry about regulatory forbearance and evergreening. Regulators have incentives to consider the negative shocks that hit banks' balance sheets as being more transitory than they actually are. Doing so avoids forcing banks either to recapitalize or else seek fiscal resources to cover the gap. Because such actions are politically costly, it is always better to ignore the problem at least for the time being. Thus, with the acquiescence of regulators, banks capitalize the past-due interest of de facto nonperforming loans. These loans now become evergreen accounts. Obviously, this is an explosive situation: the capitalization of banks will have to be confronted at some point in the future. In more perverse situations, evergreen accounts reflect political favors to specific powerful groups.

The Federal Deposit Insurance Corporation Improvement Act (FDI-CIA) implemented in the United States in 1991 has several elements that might be effective ways to improve the regulatory framework in emerging markets. This law makes sanctions to banks mandatory and thus lessens political pressure on regulators. It also includes a prompt corrective action clause, according to which a bank's problems must be solved before effective capital becomes negative. Sanctions are applied in stages that depend on the level of effective capital. These sanctions include restrictions on dividends payouts, limits on assets' growth, and the revocation of management rights. Furthermore, new capital must be injected by owners before effective capital becomes negative. With this law, the resolution of a bank does not imply fiscal costs. International organizations could focus attention on this area.

The Role of Foreign Banks

During the last decade, the share of the domestic banking system owned by foreigners has increased spectacularly. The accepted wisdom is that foreign ownership of banks brings three main benefits to an emerging market. First, foreign banks improve the banking practice and increase know-how. Second, since the size of the private sector in emerging markets is too small to permit such a separation, the existence of foreign banks makes it easier to separate ownership of banks from ownership of industrial corporations. As we discussed earlier, in the presence of a weak regulatory framework this separation might reduce the likelihood of fraudulent schemes between lenders and borrowers.

Third, in case of a systemic crisis, parents of foreign subsidiaries will inject the resources necessary to withstand a run. Note, however, that in general foreign subsidiaries are legally separate entities from the parents. Thus, subsidiaries can declare themselves bankrupt during a crisis without affecting the parent company. Reputation considerations are frequently invoked to defend the notion that resources would be transferred by the parent in case of a crisis. This argument is far from obvious, because in case of a systemic crisis all parent banks can refuse to support their subsidiaries (by invoking some sort of force majeure clause) without losing reputational capital vis-à-vis the other major international banks.

Bailout Guarantees and the Exchange Rate Regime

Systemic bailout guarantees can be implemented in several ways. The particulars will, of course, depend on the exchange rate regime. A nice feature of Schneider and Tornell's framework is that the effects of guarantees and the forces that generate boom-bust cycles are independent of the exchange rate regime or monetary policy rule. This feature permits us to study how guarantees affect the economy under different regimes.

With fully flexible exchange rates, the mechanism is literally the same as the one considered in section 15.3. If agents are highly leveraged and have risky dollar debt, the economy is vulnerable to self-fulfilling crises in which there is a severe real depreciation, and several agents in the N sector, suffering from balance sheet effects, are unable to repay their debts. As a result, creditors are paid a proportion F of the contracted payment. This bailout payment can be financed by an international organization or by an increase in future taxes to the rest of the economy. The real depreciation can arise by either a nominal depreciation, a change in nominal prices, or a combination of both.

Consider the other extreme of a fixed exchange rate regime. In the case of an attack the central bank can defend the currency by either running down reserves or increasing the interest rate. If the attack is successful, the reduction in reserves constitutes a bailout payment to bank creditors that withdraw their funds and convert them into foreign currency. Thus, any defense policy has associated with it a bailout rate F. Clearly, the bailout rate need not be 100 percent, because reserves might not suffice to cover all the liabilities of the banking system. We should add that the bailout can be complemented by an explicit transfer, as in Mexico during the Tequila crisis. Again, the real depreciation can come about through a combination of a nominal depreciation and a change in nominal prices.

In the real world we observe a mixture of both regimes. However, it should be clear that the forces at work are essentially the same in both regimes.

15.4.2   Policy in the Aftermath of Crisis

Bailing Out Borrowers versus Bailing Out Lenders

Once a crisis has erupted and a severe real depreciation has taken place, the main objective should be to contain the meltdown and to minimize the number of bankruptcies, because inefficient bankruptcy procedures generate deadweight losses. Productive assets are inefficiently liquidated, and human capital networks are destroyed. Furthermore, reputational capital in credit markets, which takes a long time to build, is destroyed (Wyne 2000).

Typically, bailouts are granted to lenders, not to borrowers. However, bailing out lenders does not save borrowers from being decapitalized and suffering bankruptcy. Therefore, despite the occurrence of generous bailouts, credit crunches have developed in the aftermath of crises during the 1990s. This has been reflected in three regularities. First, depositors' bank runs have seldom been observed in the crises of the 1990s. Second, in the aftermath of crises the growth rate of bank loans has typically remained below the growth rate of deposits. Because the value of collateral collapses, banks shift their portfolios toward others assets, such as government securities. Third, the interest rate spread has typically remained above its pre-crisis level after GDP growth has returned to its trend.

Ex post, extending some type of bailout to borrowers might avoid bankruptcies and ameliorate the credit crunch. This policy, however, might not be possible to implement because the fiscal cost might be enormous. Furthermore, it has perverse incentives effects. First, many borrowers that have the ability to pay might simply refuse to do so. Because it is extremely difficult to distinguish liquid and illiquid borrowers during a generalized crisis, it is basically impossible to implement a borrowers' bailout policy that discriminates among different types of borrowers. Second, market mechanisms might be blocked, as borrowers and lenders might delay the resolution of certain loans.

Piecemeal versus All-at-Once Bailouts

In the aftermath of a crisis the share of nonperforming loans increases spectacularly. Both regulators and banks have incentives to underreport the true share of nonperforming loans. This way, bank owners need to inject less capital, and the government needs to spend less fiscal resources up front. In contrast, reporting the true nonperforming loans might force a takeover of several banks by either the government or other banks. As a result, bank owners will lose their franchises, and government officials will face political criticism for their failure to regulate the banking system appropriately.

Thus, bankers and regulators have incentives to believe that negative news is more transitory than it actually is and to make predictions about the banks' portfolios that are more optimistic than is warranted by the facts. The effect of this misperception is an evergreening of banks' balance sheets. That is, there is a tendency for banks to classify as performing those loans that are actually never going to be repaid and for regulators to turn a blind eye to this mistake. The problem with evergreening is that it generally leads to an increase in the share of nonperforming loans over time. This is because interest is not repaid and because banks have incentives to undertake very risky projects that might have negative expected net present value. Banks might even have incentives to extend outright fraudulent loans.

Evergreening has two negative effects on the economy as a whole. First, the fiscal cost of the bailout grows over time, and it might even grow faster than GDP. Second, the credit crunch suffered by small nontradables firms will be deeper and more persistent, because banks will have more incentives to engage in risky activities than to lend to firms with low internal funds (Krueger and Tornell 2000 analyze the Mexican case).

The alternative policy is to recognize at once all nonperforming loans. Because it is unlikely that bank shareholders will be able to come up with the necessary capital, the government will have to take over all the liabilities of the banking system. This policy implies that government debt must increase by several percentage points of GDP in a single year. This is politically very costly. However, the evergreening alternative is likely to be more costly socially, as the experience of Japan and Mexico has shown.

Interest Rate and Exchange Rate Responses to Crises

In the standard Mundell-Fleming model, when there is a capital outflow the needed improvement in the current account can be attained with a real depreciation and with no output costs. According to this view, a depreciation induces a shift of resources from the N sector to the T sector and makes the economy more competitive in world markets. As a result, growth resumes quite rapidly after the depreciation.

The Mundell-Fleming framework and traditional balance-of-payments crisis models are not appropriate for explaining these new boom-bust episodes because the banking system plays no essential role in these models. Once we move into a world in which bank lending is essential and debt is denominated in foreign currency, the traditional policy recommendation becomes invalid. As we have seen, allowing the real exchange rate to depreciate in order to close the external gap has perverse effects. Because domestic firms have dollar-denominated debt but revenues denominated in domestic currency, a real depreciation will make some domestic firms unable to repay their debts and bankrupt them. This, in turn, will make the problem even worse. Capital flight will increase, the real exchange rate will depreciate even further, and more firms will go bust. This vicious circle will generate a meltdown of the domestic sector of the economy.

In this situation an increase in interest rates might not be such a bad idea, but does it actually work? It is unclear from both an empirical and a conceptual perspective. In a sample of seventy-five countries over the period 1960–97, Kraay (2000) finds no evidence that interest rates systematically increase during failed speculative attacks, nor that raising interest rates increases the probability that an attack will fail. Basurto and Gosh (2000) find that, for the case of Indonesia, Korea, and Thailand in the aftermath of the 1997 crisis, there is little evidence of a perverse effect of a monetary tightening on the exchange rate.

From a conceptual perspective, an interest rate hike is effective in stemming a crisis only if such an increase does not bankrupt a critical mass of firms. If a critical mass of firms goes bust because the firms are unable to meet their debt service, then the investment demand will collapse and the real exchange rate will have to depreciate in order to clear the market for nontradables. The end result will be the same as that described above.

In contrast, if an interest rate hike simply induces a reduction in absorption but does not induce generalized bankruptcies, then an immediate crisis might be avoided. The question then arises as to whether the time of reckoning will not simply be pushed forward. Will higher domestic interest rates simply induce foreign investors to exploit arbitrage opportunities during a short period until central bank reserves are depleted? Will higher domestic interest rates make several firms insolvent and lead them to bankruptcy in the near future? It is necessary that the answers to these questions be in the negative in order for an interest rate increase to avoid a crisis. Clearly, the specific situation of a country will determine the correct mix of exchange rate depreciation and interest rate increase.

15.5   Conclusions

This paper has argued that even if bailout guarantees are an inevitable consequence of financial liberalization and bank privatization, it does not follow that the liberalization policies of the late 1980s and early 1990s were doomed to fail. We argue that financial liberalization policies can induce higher long-run growth if they are accompanied by an appropriate regulatory framework.

The reforms of the late 1980s liberalized trade and financial markets in many emerging markets. These reforms also significantly reduced the role of the state in the economy. Suddenly, the future looked much brighter than before, and the private sector much smaller than was desirable. Unfortunately, legal and judicial reform could not be implemented as easily as the other reforms; as a result, many of the institutions that support the provision of external finance have not yet developed in emerging markets. Therefore, most firms in these economies have been severely credit constrained.

The introduction of systemic bailout guarantees into such credit-constrained economies eases borrowing constraints and permits higher investment and higher growth. However, this comes at the cost of higher vulnerability to crises, because systemic bailout guarantees induce agents to adopt risky debt profiles. In fact, systemic bailout guarantees lead to higher growth only if the economy becomes vulnerable to crises, so that there exist some states of the world in which the implicit subsidy can be cashed in. It is important to note that the likelihood of a crisis must be small in order for investment and growth to increase.

Clearly, not every bailout-guarantee scheme will lead to higher growth. It is essential that authorities can commit to refrain from granting bailouts on an idiosyncratic basis. Furthermore, an efficient regulatory framework must be in place to ensure that banks perform their monitoring and screening role efficiently and to avoid corrupt banking practices.

References

Aghion, Philippe, Philippe Bachetta, and Abhijit Banerjee. 2000. Capital markets and the instability of open economies. Study Center Gerzensee. Mimeograph.

Basurto, Gabriela, and Atish Gosh. 2000. The interest rate-exchange rate nexus in currency crises. IMF. Mimeograph. Washington, D.C.: International Monetary Fund.

Bernanke, Ben, Mark Gertler, and Simon Gilchrist. 1999. The financial accelerator in a quantitative business cycle framework. In *Handbook of macroeconomics,* ed. John Taylor and Michael Woodford. Amsterdam: Elsevier.

Burnside, Craig, Martin Eichenbaum, and Sergio Rebelo. 2000. On the fundamentals of self-fulfilling speculative attacks. NBER Working Paper no. 7554. Cambridge, Mass.: National Bureau of Economic Research.

Caballero, Ricardo, and Arvind Krishnamurthy. 1999. Emerging markets crises: An asset markets perspective. MIT, Sloan School of Business. Mimeograph.

Calvo, Guillermo. 1998. Capital flows and capital market crises: The simple economics of sudden stops. *Journal of Applied Economics* 1 (1): 35–54.

Corsetti, Giancarlo, Paolo Pesenti, and Nouriel Roubini. 1999. Paper tigers. *European Economic Review* 43 (7): 1211–36.

Eichengreen, Barry, Andrew Rose, and Charles Wyplosz. 1995. Exchange market mayhem: The antecedents and aftermath of speculative attacks. *Economic Policy* 21:249–312.

Gourinchas, Pierre Olivier, Oscar Landerretche, and Rodrigo Valdés. 2001. Lending booms: Some stylized facts. NBER Working Paper no. 8249. Cambridge, Mass.: National Bureau of Economic Research.

Jeanne, Olivier, and Jeromin Zettelmeyer. 2000. International bailouts, financial transparency and moral hazard. IMF. Mimeograph. Washington, D.C.: International Monetary Fund.

Kaminsky, Graciela, and Carmen M. Reinhart. 1999. The twin crises: The causes of banking and balance-of-payments problems. *American Economic Review* 89 (3): 473–500.

Kraay, Aart. 2000. Do high interest rates defend currencies during speculative attacks? The World Bank. Mimeograph.

Krueger, Anne O., and Aaron Tornell. 2000. The role of bank lending in recovering from crises: Mexico 1995–1998. NBER Working Paper no. 7042. Cambridge, Mass.: National Bureau of Economic Research.

Krugman, Paul. 1998. Bubble, boom, crash: Theoretical notes on Asia's crisis. MIT. Working Paper.

McKinnon, Ronald, and Huw Pill. 1998. International overborrowing: A decomposition of credit and currency risks. *World Development* 26 (7): 1267–82.

Sachs, Jeffrey, Aaron Tornell, and Andres Velasco. 1996. Financial crises in emerging markets: The lessons from 1995. *Brookings Papers on Economic Activity,* Issue no. 1:147–98. Washington, D.C.: Brookings Institution.

Schneider, Martin, and Aaron Tornell. 1999. Lending booms and asset price inflation. University of California, Los Angeles. Working Paper.

———. 2000. Balance sheet effects, bailout guarantees and financial crises. NBER

Working Paper no. 8060. Cambridge, Mass.: National Bureau of Economic Research.

Tornell, Aaron. 1999. Common fundamentals in the Tequila and Asian crises. NBER Working Paper no. 7193. Cambridge, Mass.: National Bureau of Economic Research.

———. 2000. Privatizing the privatized. In *Economic policy reform: The second stage,* ed. Anne O. Krueger, 157–82. Chicago: University of Chicago Press.

Wyne, Jose. 2000. Business cycles and firm dynamics in small emerging economies. University of California, Los Angeles. Mimeograph.

Comment   Charles W. Calomiris

Aaron Tornell's paper might be retitled "Learning to Love Twin Crises." In essence, Tornell derives conditions under which government policies that promote anticipated bailouts, moral hazard in lending, and credit-driven boom and bust cycles might be better than a laissez-faire policy of benign neglect. The essential idea of the paper—that imperfect capital markets can provide a rationale for bailouts—is not entirely new. Economists and politicians frequently defend bailouts on the static, ex post grounds that in the presence of imperfect capital markets, bank failures and a collapse of corporate balance sheets make it very hard for efficient capital allocation to occur. The logic of this static approach runs as follows: Firms with positive net present value projects may be in scarce supply. If those firms are not creditworthy (because of their high postcrisis debt burdens or because the insolvent or weakened banks on which those firms must rely for credit cannot themselves raise funds), then efficient financing of positive net present value projects may not occur. Bailouts that relax credit constraints on borrowers or their banks thus have a positive side: they keep funds flowing to efficient users that otherwise would not receive funding (in the absence of government interventions).[1]

Tornell's analysis, which is founded on Schneider and Tornell (2000), however, is more interesting than the standard ex post, static argument for bailouts, for several reasons. First, he makes explicit the role of hard currency borrowing and nontradable goods in connecting intrinsic macroeconomic risk and financial fragility in developing countries. Second, Tornell's focus is on ex ante bailout policy. He argues that a policy of anticipated bailouts may be desirable because it promotes greater lending *before* the cri-

Charles W. Calomiris is Paul M. Montrone Professor of Finance and Economics at the Graduate School of Business, Columbia University, and a research associate of the National Bureau of Economic Research.

1. This line of static reasoning can be supported by models of imperfect capital markets (e.g., Leland and Pyle 1977; Stiglitz and Weiss 1981; Calomiris and Hubbard 1990) and by empirical evidence, much of which pertains to the U.S. experience during the Depression (Fisher 1933; Bernanke 1983; Calomiris and Mason 2001).

sis. Third, while many advocates of bailouts neglect or underestimate the role that bailouts play in causing crises, Tornell, in contrast, assumes that bailouts will be anticipated and that bailout policies themselves will *cause* twin crises to occur. The novelty of Tornell's paper is that it shows that, notwithstanding the fact that bailouts cause and are known to cause costly twin crises, anticipated bailouts may still be worthwhile as a "second-best" means of addressing capital market imperfections.

Let me begin by commenting on the proposition that bailout policies cause twin crises to occur in developing economies. The primary mechanism linking banking collapse and currency collapse (the two elements of twin crises) operates through the effect of bailouts on government debt burdens and the resulting pressure to increase the supply of money. Government payments to failed financial institutions can so weaken government finances that the only viable currency policy in the wake of a bank bailout is depreciation. A secondary linkage (which I will return to below) is also important: currency markets are a convenient means for desperate banks to take on risk as a resurrection strategy. As the economy weakens, insolvent or weak banks increase their exposure to exchange rate risk intentionally on the off chance that depreciation can be avoided (an outcome that would deliver substantial profit to them). Protected banks' and firms' decisions to increase their exchange rate risk exposure in the presence of bailouts also increase the potential fiscal costs of twin crises.

Historical evidence clearly supports the view that foreseeable bailouts, and the fiscal links that connect bank risk and exchange risk, cause severe twin crises. In the past two decades, government protection of failed banks has been nearly ubiquitous. At the same time, there have been scores of twin crises throughout the world. That experience has been unprecedented. For example, in the three decades prior to World War I, anticipated bailout policies were very rare, as were twin crises, and the countries that experienced a simultaneous collapse of banks and exchange rates during the pre-World War I era were precisely those that had established bailout policies.[2]

Argentina in 1890 is the clearest historical case in which a twin crisis was caused by an anticipated bailout in the wake of an adverse terms-of-trade shock. State-guaranteed, bank-issued mortgages (cedulas) were traded in the London capital market in the years before the crisis and enjoyed essentially the same yield as Argentine government debt. Banks profited by borrowing at the government rate and lending at higher interest rates (thus pocketing the difference). The spread earned by the lender increased with the riskiness of the mortgage and thus encouraged lenders to originate risky mortgages. The exchange rate collapse during the Argentine crisis of 1890 reflected the magnitude of increased government debt as the holders of government guarantees sought relief from the government.

2. See Calomiris (2001) for a review of the pre–World War I experience.

In Italy in 1893, the simultaneous failure of banks and depreciation of the currency similarly reflected the fiscal costs the government bore from protecting the banking sector. The extent of promised protection in Italy was less than in Argentina, and the extent of banking and exchange rate collapse was also less. In other countries (e.g., Australia in 1893 and Russia and Norway in 1900–91), substantial banking collapse occurred with few or no government bailouts of banks, and exchange rates remained fixed.

An interesting feature of the Tornell paper is the distinction it draws, in theory, between conditional bailout policies (state-contingent policies that address credit-market imperfections) and unconditional bailouts. Tornell shows that the economic benefit of bailouts is to reduce the contractionary effect of *system-wide risk* on the supply of credit in developing economies. There is little ex ante gain from providing bailouts for individual firms during normal times, and therefore firms and banks that fail during normal times should not be protected.

How could Tornell's state-contingent rule be implemented? In theory, one could come close with a two-part policy that (a) insures bank deposits (and perhaps even some of bank stock value, by putting in place a policy of state-contingent government recapitalization of failed banks, as described in Calomiris 1999) and (b) requires protected banks to hold sufficient capital, so that government insurance of deposits and capital would only be drawn upon if aggregate bank losses are large.

It is tempting to conclude from this theoretical discussion that confining protection to a narrowly defined set of macroeconomic states by establishing an appropriate mix of bank or borrower protection and capital standards would enable one to expand the supply of credit but limit the moral-hazard costs of protection, and thus provide a useful subsidy for lending to productive activities at little social cost. In fact, however, I am extremely skeptical of the practicality of that conclusion for several reasons.

First, it is very difficult to construct a capital standard for banks that ensures that banks do not abuse the government safety net by holding insufficient amounts of capital (relative to the amount the regulator would want them to hold, and reflecting the risk position of the bank). Capital is difficult to measure because the value of nonmarketable assets held by banks is hard for regulators to gauge in real time, and risk is also difficult to measure. Furthermore, the incentives of regulators to measure capital and risk and to punish violations of capital standards can be weak or perverse, which also serves to undermine the effectiveness of these rules. That is not to say that the problem is hopeless, but in the vast majority of countries (largely for political reasons) there is little immediate prospect of establishing a credit capital standard (for a review, see Calomiris 1999; Shadow Financial Regulatory Committee 2000).

Second, Tornell's model imagines that the extent of the systematic risk is exogenous and that increased risk corresponds to increased productive lending. In reality, however, decisions about the *extent, timing,* and *type* of systematic risk are *endogenous* to protected banks' and firms' choices (e.g., choices about foreign exchange risk exposure) in ways that can make the benefits of protection lower and the costs higher than those imagined in the model.

With regard to the type of systematic risk firms choose, it is possible that much of the protection offered by the government will be used to subsidize useless or negative present-value activities. Some firms, for example, will take on exchange rate risk, not because they must borrow in foreign currency, but because it is the easiest way to increase risk quickly when one is engaging in a "resurrection" strategy. Furthermore, the creation of protection for banks entails the creation of rents, and those rents typically will be distributed through political competition. Thus, protection will be captured by cronies and used to support the risks of the powerful, who in general are not necessarily the most productive.

With regard to the extent of systematic risk, state-contingent protection will itself substantially increase the endogenous choice of "factor loadings" on systematic risks by individual firms, and those loadings can suddenly *increase* in the wake of adverse shocks that firms face. As noted above, weak or insolvent firms often undertake to increase their risk in response to a recessionary shock. The reason is that the "put option" value of protection increases as the firm's capital shrinks (in the wake of an adverse shock), which encourages firms to adopt resurrection strategies. If risk is a choice variable that can be increased very quickly (via exchange rate swaps, for example), then the frequency and social costs of state-contingent protection can be much larger than the model contemplates, even though in the years prior to the crisis the expected subsidies were relatively small (as were the social benefits from increased lending as the result of the expected subsidies). In other words, in order to be more realistic, the Tornell model needs to add a middle period to its dynamics—a period in which firms may choose to add risk after adverse shocks have occurred and in pursuit of objectives that are not necessarily socially desirable.

In practice, therefore, it is unlikely that protection will result in a net social benefit because of endogenous choices by firms and banks to undertake very risky and very wasteful projects and to substantially increase unproductive risks in the midst of a recession. These choices have been visible in the major crises observed recently. Mexican banks' speculative swap transactions in 1994–95 are one example; wasteful transfers to Korean *chaebol* or to unproductive Russian banks or crony capitalists in Indonesia are other examples. The devastating twin crises in these and scores of other countries over the past twenty years (Chile in 1982–83 was arguably the first major case) typically were preceded by years (sometimes decades) of wasteful capital allocation by protected banks.

Studies of the effects of financial protection on economic growth, macroeconomic stability, and financial depth have uniformly concluded that increases in ex ante protection are associated with lower economic growth, less financial depth, and greater financial and economic instability (for a review, see Beim and Calomiris 2001, chap. 7). These adverse effects of protection on growth and financial depth are clearly at odds with the predictions of the Tornell model.

What kinds of alternatives to bailout policies should be considered in light of the practical problems with implementing such protection? One possibility (call it the "mercantilist" approach) is to grant monopoly rights to certain merchants to overcome capital scarcity. This can be a way to create "capital" in the form of charter value, which can help mitigate financial constraints. This was a popular and successful means for promoting conquest and development used by European sovereigns in the seventeenth and eighteenth centuries. Like bailout policies, this approach entails large social costs (inefficient monopolistic pricing and the concentration of political power) that may outweigh any gains from capital market improvements.

A second option would be to go in the opposite direction—to encourage, and perhaps even subsidize, foreign entry by banks and other firms into the domestic economy on a competitive basis. Global firms are better diversified and have greater access to capital markets. Tornell is right to object that subsidiaries of international banks may still be subject to local risks (because they are chartered as independent entities), but their costs of capital are much lower than those of domestic banks because they can raise capital in international equity markets. This advantage is substantial and important, even if foreign subsidiaries remain legally independent. Furthermore, I do not believe that large global banks would abandon their subsidiaries lightly, even if they became insolvent. Finally, given that foreign subsidiaries are unlikely to be protected by local governments, they maintain sufficient capital and risk controls so that they are much less likely to fail. For these reasons, I think the potential gains from the relaxation of capital-market constraints resulting from free foreign entry are very large.

A third alternative approach would be to develop a means to hedge national risk (e.g., via the gross domestic product derivatives contracts imagined by Shiller 1993), and to rely on these new hedges to insulate domestic firms and domestic banks in developing countries from country-specific macroeconomic risks that produce severe exogenous shocks. In essence, these prospective innovations would provide the means for countries to undo the consequences of borrowing in hard currency. In fact, if such hedges were costlessly available, it would be possible for all lending to occur in local currency and for lenders to use derivatives to insulate themselves from local macroeconomic shocks.

Of the possible alternative approaches, I think the second option (encouraging foreign entry) has the most immediate promise. It is, of course, not politically viable in many countries, where protection of rent-seeking cronies or nationalistic sentiment would not permit such an approach.

To the extent to which we are stuck with bailouts as a policy option because of political constraints on international diversification, our efforts should focus on ways to limit the adverse incentives that magnify the social costs of bailouts. In particular, I have argued elsewhere that creating effective, clear, and credible rules to guide bailout policies would make bailouts less frequent and less costly and protection of banks more incentive-compatible. These rules would include credible loss-sharing arrangements for recapitalizing banks and reforms to bank capital standards that encourage greater use of market signals in the regulatory process (Calomiris 1999; Shadow Financial Regulatory Committee 2000).

To the extent that these improvements are feasible, it may someday be possible to rcap some of the social gains from anticipated bailouts that the Tornell model envisions. However, we should consider alternative policies (especially free foreign entry) that solve capital-market imperfections in a simpler and more robust way. Moreover, before we can even contemplate the potential benefits of limited, state-contingent bailouts, we must put in place the institutional infrastructure, which is currently lacking, that would make such benefits possible. It would be unfortunate if a reader of the Tornell paper saw it as a justification for existing bailout policies (which operate without necessary and elusive complementary institutional reforms), which it is not; it is important to emphasize that in the real world bailout policies do much more harm than good.

References

Beim, David O., and Charles W. Calomiris. 2001. *Emerging financial markets.* New York: McGraw-Hill.

Bernanke, Ben S. 1983. Non-monetary effects of the financial crisis in the propagation of the Great Depression. *American Economic Review* 73 (June): 29–51.

Calomiris, Charles W. 1999. Building an incentive-compatible safety net. *Journal of Banking and Finance* 23 (October): 1499–520.

———. 2001. *Victorian perspectives on the banking crises of the 1980s and 1990s.* Columbia Business School. Unpublished manuscript.

Calomiris, Charles W., and R. Glenn Hubbard. 1990. Firm heterogeneity, internal finance, and credit rationing. *Economic Journal* 100 (March): 90–104.

Calomiris, Charles W., and Joseph R. Mason. 2001. Consequences of bank distress during the Great Depression. Columbia Business School, Working Paper.

Fisher, Irving. 1933. The debt-deflation theory of the Great Depression. *Econometrica* 1 (October): 337–57.

Leland, Hayne, and David Pyle. 1977. Informational asymmetries, financial structure, and financial intermediation. *Journal of Finance* 32 (May): 371–87.

Schneider, Martin, and Aaron Tornell. 2000. Balance sheet effects, bailout guarantees and financial crises. University of California, Los Angeles, Working Paper.

Shadow Financial Regulatory Committee. 2000. *Reforming bank capital regulation.* Washington, D.C.: American Enterprise Institute.

Shiller, Robert. 1993. *Macro markets: Creating institutions for managing society's largest economic risks.* Oxford: Oxford University Press.
Stiglitz, Joseph E., and Andrew Weiss. 1981. Credit rationing in markets with imperfect information. *American Economic Review* 71 (June): 393–410.

Discussion Summary

Anne O. Krueger said that the intuitive argument of the paper was that there was some distortion in the economy that would lead to a lower investment level and result in a lower growth rate unless we do something to correct it, such as instituting government bailout guarantees. However, she said, the right question is how to correct the distortion and achieve the "first-best" situation rather than focusing on choices of second-best policies. She pointed out that this is different from the strategy that first accepts the existence of the bailout guarantee policy, then tries to mitigate its consequences and make it a better bailout. Krueger conjectured that the first-best policies are the ones that reduce the bailout and achieve the growth rate, as by giving an across-the-board subsidy to investment through tax policy or giving investment tax credits directly. She suggested that the lessons of the Asian crisis are that governments must find a structure or a set of incentives to prevent nonhedged foreign exchange exposure, which tends to intensify crises. Indeed, she said, it is possible to find a way that borrowing could only be conducted in domestic currency throughout the world, which would remove the interaction between the domestic and international crises.

Paolo Pesenti praised the paper for providing a welfare analysis for the presence of government bailout policy. In the paper, bailout guarantee stems from a need to partially offset the borrowing constraints, and the government ends up with a "Goldilocks" bailout policy: not too much, nor too little, but just right! It may sometimes lead to crises, but ex ante it maximizes over the trade-off between higher growth and potential crisis outcomes. However, he said, if it was really possible to commit to such an instrument, why couldn't the government think of other ways to lift the borrowing constraints by designing policies that are less "dangerous" and more efficient in addressing the original distortion problem, such as, for instance, free entry of foreign banks, as suggested by Charles W. Calomiris? *Jaume Ventura* also expressed the similar view that the bailout guarantee policy is second best, not the first-best policy.

Ventura pointed out that the bailout policy was perceived as a solution to the underinvestment problem in the paper, but that the paper did not adequately address the reasons for the underinvestment, that is, whether it was relative to the perfect information case or due to some kind of external problems. He said that if the underinvestment problem is a result of the lack of perfect information but there is no externality, then we cannot do anything about it. He suggested that the author devote more discussion to the source of underinvestment, especially the externality of it.

Ventura also commented on a common assumption that the nontradables sector cannot borrow from and sell to foreigners in the paper. He gave an example—Spanish utility companies' buying from Latin America—to show that this assumption seems to be empirically faulty. He inquired about the exact role this assumption plays in the model and the alternative assumptions, asking, if it is a shortcut for other assumptions, what they are. *Enrique G. Mendoza* followed up on this issue. It is important to look at the real exchange rate facts to think of them as a disciplining device and to determine how to model them. The experiences of the emerging market are striking and differ from those of the developed countries. First, the fluctuation in real exchange rate is not the same as the fluctuation in the tradables-sector price vis-à-vis the nontradables-sector price. Second, one would have thought, from the standard theory, the nontradables-sector prices meant the prices of haircuts and services, but this, he said, turns out not to be the case. In Mexico, there is a large bias toward one particular sector, that is, the cost of housing. One of the capital-market reports from the IMF that examines the Asian countries also discussed this phenomenon. Thus, the change of real exchange rate in these countries has a lot to do with the change of housing as an asset market.

Michael P. Dooley commented on whether the government can credibly commit to whom to bail out ex ante. He said that the government chooses whom to bailout and whom not to, and that the investors who are bailed out in cases of crisis are the ones that pose the biggest threat to the government. Investors, knowing that, will only lend to people who would be bailed out in crises. This implies that the government cannot credibly commit to whom to bail out ex ante: the market will make its own judgment.

Sebastian Edwards agreed with this view and gave the Chilean case as an example. According to him, after the massive bailout following the Chilean banking crisis in 1977, the authorities (Pinochet) made a public announcement that there would be "no more bailouts." However, when the debt crisis of 1982 erupted in Chile, the government could keep its promise only with respect to domestic investors: the American bank creditors threatened the government with the cutting off of all trade credits to Chile, and they eventually were bailed out by the government.

Aaron Tornell said that in the 1970s researchers had worked on the first-best policy questions, such as how better to transfer resources to the right agents in the economy. However, consider a country such as Mexico that had the objective to grow rapidly but could not raise enough financing from abroad. Moreover, the government did not know to which investors to give transfers, and the investment subsidies were not well implemented. It was against such a background that the government chose to use banks as a means to make (implicit) transfers to entrepreneurs and implemented the guarantees through the fixed exchange rate regime, hoping this might boost the economy. Tornell said that he was not defending the bailout policies, agreeing with the opinion of Dooley and others that one cannot fine-tune these policies. The paper focused only on the welfare implication of policies that provide implicit bailout guarantees. The paper shows that these policies can increase investment at the cost of a higher risk of currency crises.

On the implementation of the bailout guarantee policies, Tornell said that there is a systemic problem, and the challenge is how to design a mechanism that will advance the rule-based resolution of crises. He said that the specific ways to implement these policies proposed by Charles W. Calomiris would probably achieve this goal.

On the welfare aspects, Tornell said that it is very important that regulators be able to exclude, at the outset, white elephant and connected projects. The outright corruption is an obviously concern, and one should make sure that it does not happen.

Finally, Tornell answered the question regarding the role played by the nontradables sector. He said that in Mexico, firms in tradables sectors could borrow quite easily on foreign markets via commercial papers and equities. However, small and medium-sized firms in nontradables sectors are the main clients of banks, and they have suffered a credit crunch greater than the GDP growth. Thus, there is a large asymmetry between the tradables and nontradables sectors, and policy makers are wondering how to improve the productivity in nontradables sectors.

Overview

16

A Primer on
Emerging-Market Crises

Rudi Dornbusch

Over the past twenty years there has been an explosion of emerging-market crises and a vast accumulation of commentary—descriptive, theoretical, and applied—highlighting the origins and mechanics of each crisis and of crises in general. There is plenty of analysis on how to deal with crises both in terms of prevention and of cures. Is it possible now to distill from all this analysis a simple set of propositions that summarize the experience and capture the chief lessons?

This paper attempts to set out a few propositions that summarize what is known and accepted. The purpose in doing so is to promote a set of presumptions that define unsound practice with a presumption that it cannot fail to engender, in time, a crisis. Moreover, crises are not merely financial experiences; rather, they involve large and lasting social costs and important redistribution of income and wealth. These consequences make it especially important to secure agreement on what constitutes bad practice and to identify areas of continuing controversy.

16.1 Slow versus Fast and Bad Regimes versus Big Collapses

A useful distinction can be drawn between old-style (slow-motion) crises, which focus on the financing of the current account in a financially repressed economy, and the new-style balance sheet crises of a financially opened economy. The distinction is useful not only to highlight what is new

Rudi Dornbusch is Ford Professor of Economics and International Management at the Massachusetts Institute of Technology and a research associate of the National Bureau of Economic Research.

but also to help policy makers understand the great speed of new-style crises and their devastating cost compared to earlier experiences.

Old-style crises involve a cycle of overspending and real appreciation that increasingly worsens the current account; while resources are ample, and before real appreciation bites into growth, the process is politically popular. In time, resources become more limited, and unpleasant options such as demand restraint and trade restrictions must be mounted, but they cannot last. Ultimately devaluation comes, and the process begins all over again. The "stabilization" may last if there is little accommodation, but if money is passive and the increased external room is used for quick expansion, the process is more nearly a *regime* of an inflation-devaluation spiral.

Exchange rate adjustments in an old-style setting have very few qualities of a crisis. Richard Cooper has noted that these events normally or invariably involve the fall of the finance minister, but little more. The central issue, as Diaz-Alejandro (1966) noted, is the fall of the real wage and the politics surrounding it.[1] Because finance is repressed, the buildup of sensitive balance sheets is ruled out. One example of the few old-style situations still in play is Egypt, where occasionally a widely anticipated moderate devaluation happens to relieve trickling reserve losses from current account imbalances and suitcase capital flight.

An important part of the story, obscuring its simplicity, is the occasional arrival of external resources (new access to the world capital market, the World Bank, etc.), which provides room for better growth without the early arrival of the external constraint. However, these resources more often than not are debt and hence have an adverse effect on the current account. Accordingly, unless there is significant productivity growth, trend real wages will have to decline in order to generate debt service. Alternatively, new resources or debt reduction must make room to keep up real wages.

A *new-style crisis* involves doubt about creditworthiness of the *balance sheet* of a significant part of the economy—private or public—and the exchange rate. It may originate with questions about either the balance sheet or the exchange rate, but when there is a question about one, the implied capital flight makes it immediately a question about both. In no time, capital flight wipes out reserves and precipitates a currency collapse. That process is only brought to an end by a resolution of the credit issues *and* the commitment of monetary policy. External intervention has high leverage in resolving credit and credibility issues.

The capital account plays a key role in the run-up to the crisis and in its unfolding. There is too much credit on the way in, and far too little once the

---

1. Diaz-Alejandro (1984), writing about the debt crisis of the early 1980s, keenly appreciated that finance had now become the key actor and aptly signaled this with the catchy title "We Are Not in Kansas Anymore." He would have needed yet another title to characterize the extraordinary increase in size and speed of the finance factor in recent crises.

crisis hits. The bankers' adage is "it's not speed that kills, but the sudden stop." Taussig (1927) captured the point when he wrote,

> The loans from creditor countries . . . begin with modest amounts, then increase and proceed crescendo. They are likely to be made in exceptionally larger amounts toward the culminating stage of a period of activity and speculative upswing, and during that stage become larger from month to month so long as the upswing continues. With the advent of crises, they are at once cut down sharply, even cease entirely. (130)

The central part of the new-style crisis is the focus on balance sheets and capital flight. Balance sheet issues are, of course, fundamentally linked to mismatches; even if there were solvency, they still create vulnerability related to liquidity problems. Exchange rate depreciation, in a mismatch situation, works in an unstable fashion to increase the prospect of insolvency and hence the urgency of capital flight.

Because new-style crises involve the national balance sheet, they involve a far more dramatic impact on economic activity than mere current account disturbances; this larger impact arises in terms of both the magnitude of the financial shock and the *disorganization effects* stemming from illiquidity or bankruptcy.[2]

16.2 Vulnerabilities

Sources of vulnerability include a substantially misaligned exchange rate and balance sheet problems. Trouble in the balance sheet can come in one of two ways: exposure, or existing holes in the form of nonperforming loans. Nonperforming loans or vulnerable loans speak for themselves, although one should note that they limit the room for higher interest rates and hence are a major problem for an interest rate defense. The other problem is exposure in the form of mismatches. In a national balance sheet there can be two kinds of mismatches: *maturity* mismatches, which lead to liquidity issues, and *currency* mismatches. In a situation in which the willingness to hold assets on current terms is impaired, these misalignments or mismatches become explosive. The willingness to hold assets can be impaired because there is a question either about the exchange rate or about the willingness and ability of debtors to meet their liabilities.

The exchange rate can be the starting point of a crisis when it is patently out of line. This is typically the case in exchange rate–based disinflation programs, which succeed in bringing down inflation but do so at the cost of a significant real appreciation. The resulting widening of the current account

---

2. *Disorganization effects* are developed in Blanchard and Kremer (1997) to aid understanding of the output collapse in transition economies but have not been applied in the setting of emerging-markets crises, where they are as useful a guide to grasping dramatic output adjustments.

deficit and the disappearance of growth from appreciation, and as a result of increased interest rates required to attract continued financing, make it obvious that the program cannot last because it is not self-correcting. At some point (see below for details) a speculative attack occurs that cannot be met by high rates or reserve depletion. At that point, currency depreciation interacts with balance sheet issues. The worse the balance sheets, the bigger the collapse.

The initial large real appreciation of an exchange rate is often justified by the argument that it reflects restructuring-induced dramatic rates of productivity growth, generating inflation of the Balassa-Samuelson kind. The argument is invariably suspect because this appreciation should not affect manufacturing price-based competitiveness measures and is less likely to be the case in an environment where unemployment is high and rising and the current account is deteriorating.

What are sustainable rates of real appreciation or of current account deficits, and what invites a crisis? Because of such issues as lasting improvements in capital market access, persistent terms-of-trade improvements, and productivity growth, emerging economies can experience trend real appreciation; they certainly can expect to finance some deficit-GDP ratio on an ongoing basis. It is safe to say, however, that a rapid real appreciation (say, over two or three years) amounting to 25 percent or more and an increase in the current account deficit to exceed 4 percent of GDP, without prospect of correction, take a country into the red zone.

Mexico with its recurrent end of sexennio currency collapses is an example of an economy in which the exchange rate and the current account are in the foreground and concern about the possibility of a devaluation (or the fact of a small devaluation) triggers massive capital flight. Because devaluation is postponed by shortening and dollarizing debt (the Tesobonos issue; see below) the balance sheet issues triggered by the currency depreciation are huge.

Consider next a balance sheet with substantial nonperforming loans. If interest rates are lowered, the currency comes under attack. If interest rates are raised, the loan portfolio goes even further under water. This is commonly a situation that leads to a crisis.

Consider as examples Thailand and Malaysia, which in 1997 had substantial nonperforming loans. In Thailand these were in real estate and consumer finance, whereas in Malaysia they included stock market loans that had financed a market boom. Protracted unwillingness to raise mandated lending rates brought about a "carry trade," and the pressure on the currency created an offshore market and ultimately led to crisis.

A large budget deficit and large short-term public debt are factors of vulnerability. A change in the growth prospects undermines the sustainability of debt, as does an increase in world interest rates, and thus undermines the willingness to hold and add to lenders' portfolios. The same is true of the perception that the willingness to service the debt is impaired. The result is a flight from public debt, and the direction of that flight is invariably foreign assets. The resulting funding crisis translates into increased interest rates, which further worsen the fiscal situation and thus act in a destabilizing fashion.

For example, Brazil's crisis was centered on a large short-term debt, part of which was dollar-linked; depreciation prospects put debt service into the express lane, and actual depreciation completed the picture.

Argentina in late 2000 is a case in point. A deteriorated growth outlook put into question the financing of budget deficits and the rollover of the public debt by external creditors. Interest rates shot up, and the prospect of a massive capital flight was in the air. A massive International Monetary Fund (IMF) loan postponed the fiscal crisis until further notice.

If the exchange rate is fixed, reserves are being depleted, and that process increasingly adds currency risk to the equation. If the rate is flexible, depreciation ensues and increasing depreciation is projected. That in turn may spread risks to foreign exchange–denominated parts of the balance sheet and aggravate capital flight.

Banking problems are a frequent part, and possibly the initiating factor, of a currency crisis. When creditors of short-term interbank lines, or depositors, withdraw from suspect banks, the resulting flows tend to go offshore and hence translate into reserve losses or depreciation. The situation is likely to become a banking and foreign exchange crisis: the worse the nonperforming loan situation, the larger the maturity mismatching in the balance sheet, and the more significant the mismatching of denominations on the asset and liability side.

It is invariably important to look behind the balance sheet of the banking system at the underlying exposure generated by the banks' loan customers. Although the banks' balance sheets may look proper, the loan customers may have mismatching on their books and hence may shift it to the banking system if and when they run into trouble.

It is also important to recognize that a banking system's situation can change dramatically in a very short time. This easily happens when a concentration of liabilities (say, real estate loans) becomes bad, or a spell of high interest rates causes a general deterioration of a loan portfolio that had been only slightly above marginal. If the banking system's funding is short-term, the makings of a crisis emerge very quickly.

The Turkish crisis of December 2000 is a great example. In a situation of a large number of bad banks (not the major part of the banking system though), a withdrawal of credit lines triggered a banking crisis; the central bank financed the run on the banks by pumping in credit only to repurchase the liquidity in selling foreign exchange. Reserve depletion within days threatened the maintenance of an IMF-supported, exchange rate–based stabilization program.

The corporate sector, like the banking system, has balance sheets that are vulnerable to mismatch issues of maturity and denomination. The larger the corporate sector's short-term debt in the national balance sheet, the more vulnerable the country is to a funding crisis, which can then become a currency crisis. Once again, when credit to a particular sector is withdrawn, in emerging markets that means a capital outflow and not a substitution into other assets. For that reason, balance sheet problems become currency crisis issues.

Indonesia and Korea are examples of countries where formidably bad balance sheets—huge debt-equity ratios and large foreign exchange exposure—were a major part of the crisis situation. Typically, it takes weeks to determine just how large the external exposure is. Creditors will be reluctant to take haircuts, and debtors are under no pressure to yield. The protracted debt problem overshadows postcrisis credit normalization.

Whenever capital flight emerges, the question of the exchange rate regime is immediate. Under fixed rates, that means the amount of reserves the central bank has and is willing to commit; under managed or flexible rates, it means the extent and speed at which the rate will depreciate. Either way, the question is how urgent it is to bring money out. Once that question emerges, the answer is already *very urgent*. Reserves are almost never sufficient to withstand a balance sheet attack, and often they are less than reported.

Vulnerability can, at least conceptually, be expressed in terms of a value-at-risk exercise: what are the relevant shocks, what are the exposure areas, and how large a deterioration of the balance sheet would result? Mismatches are the key triggers of extreme vulnerability, and the worse the risk in part of the balance sheet, the more likely that it will spread to all of it—if only because, in case of doubt, creditors want recovery and asset holders refrain from lending.

An example of this phenomenon is provided by the Asian economies, which experienced crises due to bad corporate financial structures (high debt, high foreign exchange debt) relative to equity and a high ratio of short-term external liabilities to reserves. The combination made for fireworks.

Table 16.1   Critical Indicators: 1996 (%)

Country	Corporate Debt/Equity	Short-Term External Debt/Reserves
Indonesia	310	177
Korea	518	193
Malaysia	150	41
The Philippines	160	80
Thailand	250	100

Source: World Bank

16.3   Timing

There is no hard and fast rule about the timing of crises. It is surprising how long basically unsustainable situations can endure, notably if an election is in sight. With an election on the horizon, creditors are willing to believe that action be taken to hold off a crisis or a corrective devaluation. At such a time, they believe, governments will do anything, including instituting high interest rates and (preferably) shortening maturities and redenominating claims into foreign exchange. As a result, crises happen after elections, not before. This phenomenon is akin to the myopic political business cycle but is no less real. It is clear that the more the crisis is postponed, the worse the balance sheet, and the larger the fallout, once it does happen. Mexico, for example, always postpones crises until after the election. So did Brazil, Korea, and Russia. The post-election discovery of a Taiwan banking problem, and crisis, is another instance.

Bad balance sheets—as opposed to significant overvaluation, escalating current account deficits, or vanishing growth—in principle can last almost forever provided net inflows cover up the hole and transparency is absent ("clear water, no fish," as the Chinese saying goes). As a result, the proverbial straw that broke the camel's back can easily be the trigger. A relatively minor event might break a precarious refinancing scheme, or a suspicion arising anywhere else in the world might cause creditors to kick the tires somewhere else. Importantly, changes in the relative attractiveness of domestic and foreign assets or a change in the growth scenario can suddenly bring the test of the balance sheet and, with it, the move to crisis. If the balance sheet is bad enough, as a rule, quite small events are sufficient to undermine the funding scenario and precipitate the crisis.

For example, Turkey had forever been on the short list for a crisis but somehow got by. The failure of a Rumanian subsidiary of a bad Turkish bank, in an environment of political agitation about a sleazy banking system, started the stone rolling, and within days Turkey reached the prospect of immediate currency collapse.

Contamination easily fits the pattern of balance sheets that are bad enough to invite an accident. When that is the case, in time the right circumstances for a crisis will materialize. This takes longer than one would expect, but then it happens faster than one would have thought. A shift in the external environment—Group of Three exchange rates, federal interest rates, a slump in new commodity exports—can work as a trigger. The spread of crisis in Asia fits this pattern.

16.4   Good Balance Sheets, No Crisis

Do countries with good balance sheets and a currency that is not vastly misaligned face crisis risks? Of course, there is the trivial answer that for any exchange rate or any balance sheet there can exist a shock large enough to render it unviable. However, the striking fact of the past twenty years of crises is surely this: well-managed emerging-market economies have suffered slowdowns in growth, high interest rates, and currency depreciation, but they have not suffered crises. Moreover, the better the balance sheets, the better the ability to absorb shocks to capital flows and trade without outsized adjustments in exchange rates or interest rates. The proposition "good balance sheets, no crisis" risks circularity, but, pending a good counter example, I will let it strand. The good balance sheets of banks in Singapore, Hong Kong, and Argentina are a large part of why these countries, while surely affected, were not pushed under by the crises of Mexico or Russia and Brazil.

16.5   Why Are Collapses so Large?

Currency collapses are large for two reasons: the interaction of mismatch factors and the difficulty governments face, once a meltdown is underway, in establishing their willingness and ability to engage in an uncompromising stabilization effort. In this environment, the IMF's role is to restore credibility and hence credit.[3]

The interaction of mismatch factors produces an instability in the response of asset holders: the more the exchange rate goes, the more bankrupt the balance sheet, and hence the more reason to deny credit and get out. The higher the maturity mismatch, the more liquid the creditors, and the more easily the debtor is moved into the gray zone between illiquidity and insolvency. The interaction of depreciation and illiquidity causes markets to cease functioning, and thus record interest rates and (initially) a vast overshooting of exchange rates are the rule.

The crisis itself weakens the government politically and makes doubtful its willingness to stick with a policy that dries up credit and hence starves off capital flight. The absence of effective property rights and of transparency renders the possibility of bottom-fishing very hazardous. Hence, there are no capital inflows and no stabilizing speculation, and only a one-way downward pressure on asset prices, the currency, and the balance sheets. Indonesia, with a political collapse and an ongoing struggle about who will pay the debts and who will gain, offers a clear case of an unresolved crisis.

Disorganization in the Blanchard-Kremer sense becomes a dramatic issue when creditworthiness collapses and bankruptcy spreads to attack the real economy. The real economy is a complex layer of relationships in two

---

3. For the Asian economies, the initial level is January 1999; for Mexico, January 1994; for Brazil and Russia, January 1998. The most recent data are for December 2000.

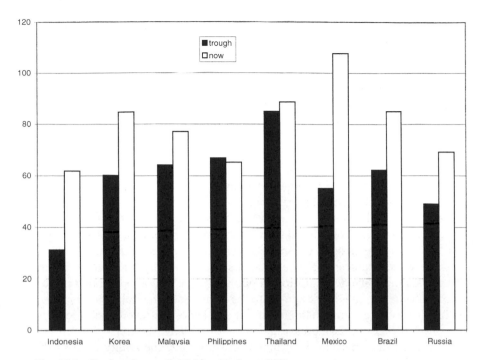

Fig. 16.1   Real exchange (initial level index = 100)
Source: JPMorgan data

ways. First, there are input-output relationships that can be disrupted at any point in the chain because a critical supply or demand link disappears and hence impairs or destroys the whole chain. Second, there is often a credit relationship, rather than cash and carry, and this is sensitive to creditworthiness suspicions and can become the disruptive factor. Disorganization is an important part of the output collapse.

The IMF's role in reversing the dramatic immediate events is twofold. First, it offers a commitment device for governments to underwrite a stabilization strategy that is known to work. Second, it offers temporary credits and debt reorganization, including lock-up of short-term credits and commercial bank credits, and thus helps stem the outflows.

High interest rates may hurt growth and the balance sheets, but they definitely stem the depreciation of the currency. Ultimately that is the single most important beachhead of the stabilization program. As long as the currency melts, there is no prospect of stabilization. (Below I discuss an alternative to controls.) In the collapse phase, currencies depreciate formidably relative to any current account-based view of what is necessary for adjustment. They are driven by the capital account. When a credible program is put in place, there is a rapid normalization, as in Korea or Brazil.

The adoption of an IMF strategy and demonstrated adherence soon shut off the hemorrhage and turn an economy around into currency recovery and a decline in interest rates. The combination of postcollapse, over-depreciated exchange rates and a credible credit program provides for ap-preciating exchange, and declining interest, rates. A virtuous circle begins. Wavering commitment, by contrast, remains reflected in volatile currency and high interest rates.

16.6   Costs

Currency crises are formidably expensive; even more so is a history of re-current crises. The costs arise in three ways: a substantial increase in public debt associated with the crisis, a loss of output and disruption, and the pos-sibility of socially controversial redistribution of income and wealth.

In a currency crisis, because the government will bail out banks and (of-ten) even companies, public debt increases substantially, and, with it, future tax liabilities. The deterioration in public finance also arises from a period of high interest rates in the run-up to the crisis and in the stabilization phase. It will also arise from the fall in output and hence tax revenues in the crisis period. Moreover, the increase in debt may itself bear the seeds of future cri-sis if it occurs when the government dos not have the ability to meet the higher debt service burden by taxation or reduction in spending.

The numbers can be staggeringly large. The government burden from a bank bailout can easily be 20 or 30 percent and more of GDP. In addition, there is easily a 10 or 15 percent increase in debt from high interest rates ap-plied to a large debt and from recession-induced tax losses.

Also, there is always a large loss of reserves, which are sacrificed during the defense part of the crisis. To some extent these may be captured by the private sector and hence merely amount to a transfer, but often they are the counterpart of a bet the government makes with the rest of the world and loses. To the extent that a crisis experience weakens a country's credit rating, there is also a lasting cost in terms of a higher international cost of capital.

A currency crisis redistributes wealth and income. It is said that more money was made in the few years of collapse of the Holy Roman Empire than in the long years of its existence. The same is true of crises that enrich those who can be in time in foreign exchange or can induce the government to assume their debt while keeping their assets. That is routine. The striking regularity, of course, is the dramatic fall in real wages and employment, as well as the bankruptcy of small debtors.

Periods of recurrent currency crises translate into poor growth perfor-mance, short horizons, slow increases in the standard of living, and a dete-riorating social and economic infrastructure. Major asset sales along the way, increases in external debt, or spurts of reform can obscure the degra-

Table 16.2   **Latin American Growth Per Capita**

Year	Growth Rate
1980–90	−0.3
1990–99	1.7

dation of the productive economy at any one time. However, ultimately medium-term growth rates, far from reflecting catch-up, reflect the costs of persistently poor finance.

16.7   The Alternative Medicine Controversy

There are two areas of controversy. The first involves capital controls, and the second surrounds the appropriateness of IMF programs. On both issues the controversy is alive and conducted with great vehemence.

The appropriateness of IMF programs is quite obviously questioned because they seem, at least on the surface, to make a bad situation worse. Raising interest rates at a time when balance sheets are already under water makes a bad debt situation worse. Raising interest rates and tightening fiscal policy at a time when the economy is already in steep decline seems to be outright counterproductive.

What are the alternatives? Capital flight will certainly continue as long as the central bank pumps in credit at unchanged interest rates: obviously, the immediate gains from borrowing in a depreciating currency far outweigh the cost of borrowing. Hence, borrowing and capital flight remain active, depreciation deepens, balance sheet problems increase—there is no obvious end to the process.

There are, of course, two ways of trying to reconcile unchanging interest rates—rather than extraordinary short-run levels of 100 or 1,000 percent per annum—with an end to capital outflows. One possibility is credit allocation controls, and the other is capital control; the best possibility is a combination of the two. There are obvious questions regarding the effectiveness of controls, but even if these are settled, there is also the issue of efficiency. If controls were temporary, this might not be an issue, but if they are lasting, suspending the capital market is much more of an issue. For the system at large, the presumption that controls are the response to outflows will reduce the perception of liquidity and hence translate into a higher cost of capital and more trigger-happy investors.

Surely there is agreement that the better strategy is to reduce the risk of a crisis situation, including means such as predetermined limits on liquidity and profitability, but that leaves open the question of what to choose in the midst of a crisis: IMF or controls. The debate continues.

References

Blanchard, O., and M. Kremer. 1997. Disorganization. *Quarterly Journal of Economics* 112 (4): 1091–126.

Diaz-Alejandro, C. 1966. *Exchange devaluation in a semi-industrial country: The experience of Argentina, 1955–1961.* Cambridge: MIT Press.

———. 1984. Latin American debt: I don't think we are in Kansas anymore. *Brookings Papers on Economic Activity,* Issue no. 2:335–89. Washington, D.C.: Brookings Institution.

Taussig, F. 1927. *International trade.* New York: Macmillan.

Contributors

Joshua Aizenman
Department of Economics
Social Sciences I
University of California, Santa Cruz
Santa Cruz, CA 95064

Eduardo Borensztein
Room 9-700
International Monetary Fund
700 19th Street NW
Washington, DC 20431

Charles W. Calomiris
Graduate School of Business
Columbia University
3022 Broadway Street, Uris Hall
New York, NY 10027

Luis Felipe Céspedes
Research Department
International Monetary Fund
700 19th Street
Washington, DC 20431

Roberto Chang
Department of Economics
Rutgers University
75 Hamilton Street
New Brunswick, NJ 08901-1248

Giancarlo Corsetti
Department of Economics
University of Rome, III
Via Ostiense, 139
00154, Rome Italy

Robert Dekle
Department of Economics
University of Southern California
Los Angeles, CA 90089

Michael P. Dooley
Deutsche Bank
31 West 52nd Street
NYC01-1204
New York, NY 10019

Rudi Dornbusch
Department of Economics, E52-357
Massachusetts Institute of Technology
50 Memorial Drive
Cambridge, MA 02139

Sebastian Edwards
Anderson Graduate School of Business
University of California, Los Angeles
110 Westwood Plaza, Suite C508
Box 951481
Los Angeles, CA 90095-1481

Martin Feldstein
National Bureau of Economic
    Research
1050 Massachusetts Avenue
Cambridge, MA 02138

Kristin J. Forbes
Sloan School of Management,
    E52-446
Massachusetts Institute of
    Technology
50 Memorial Drive
Cambridge, MA 02142-1347

Jeffrey A. Frankel
Kennedy School of Government
Harvard University
79 JFK Street
Cambridge, MA 02138

Linda S. Goldberg
Research Department, 3rd Floor
Federal Reserve Bank of New York
33 Liberty Street
New York, NY 10045

Simon Johnson
Sloan School of Management,
    E52-562
Massachusetts Institute of
    Technology
50 Memorial Drive
Cambridge, MA 02142-1347

Ethan Kaplan
Department of Economics
University of California at Berkeley
549 Evans Hall
Berkeley, CA 94720

Kenneth Kletzer
Department of Economics
Social Sciences I
University of California, Santa Cruz
Santa Cruz, CA 95064

Anne O. Krueger
Suite 12-300F
International Monetary Fund
700 19th Street NW
Washington, DC 20431

Amartya Lahiri
Department of Economics
University of California, Los Angeles
Bunche Hall 8357
Box 951447
Los Angeles, CA 90095-1477

Jorge Braga de Macedo
Development Centre
Organization for Economic
    Cooperation and Development
94, rue Chardon-Lagache
75016 Paris France

Enrique G. Mendoza
Department of Economics
Room 305, Social Science Building
Duke University, Box 90097
Durham, NC 27708-0097

Paolo Pesenti
International Research Function
Federal Reserve Bank of New York
33 Liberty Street
New York, NY 10045

Carmen M. Reinhart
Research Department, Room 10-700H
International Monetary Fund
700 19th Street NW
Washington, DC 20431

Vincent Raymond Reinhart
Division of International Finance
Board of Governors of the Federal
    Reserve System
20th Street and Constitution Avenue
    NW
Washington, DC 20551

Roberto Rigobon
Sloan School of Management, E52-447
Massachusetts Institute of Technology
50 Memorial Drive
Cambridge, MA 02142-1347

Dani Rodrik
Kennedy School of Government
Harvard University
79 JFK Street
Cambridge, MA 02138

Liliana Rojas-Suarez
Institute for International Economics
1750 Massachusetts Avenue NW
Washington, DC 20036-1903

Nouriel Roubini
Department of Economics, KMC 7-83
Stern School of Business
New York University
44 West 4th Street
New York, NY 10012-1126

Federico Sturzenegger
Universidad Torcuato Di Tella
Minones 2177
1428 Buenos Aires
Argentina

Aaron Tornell
Department of Economics
University of California, Los Angeles
Bunche Hall 8387
Box 951477
Los Angeles, CA 90095-1477

Carlos A. Végh
Department of Economics
University of California, Los Angeles
Bunche Hall 8349
Box 951477
Los Angeles, CA 90095-1477

Andrés Velasco
Kennedy School of Government
Harvard University
79 JFK Street
Cambridge, MA 02138

Jaume Ventura
Department of Economics
Massachusetts Institute of
    Technology
Cambridge, MA 02139

Shang-Jin Wei
Room 10-700
International Monetary Fund
700 19th Street NW
Washington, DC 20433

Alejandro M. Werner
Bank of Mexico
Av. 5 de Mayo No 18, Piso 4,
    Seccion D
Col. Centro, Deleg. Cuauhtemoc,
    06059
Mexico DF
Mexico

Yi Wu
Department of Economics
Georgetown University
Washington, DC 20057-1036

Jungho Yoo
Center for Economic Information
Korea Development Institute
207-41 Cheongnyangni-dong,
    Dongdaemun-ku
Seoul, Korea

Author Index

Subject Index